D0787310

DISCARDED

Contemporary
Literary Criticism

Guide to Thomson Gale Literary Criticism Series

For criticism on	Consult these Thomson Gale series
Authors now living or who died after December 31, 1999	*CONTEMPORARY LITERARY CRITICISM (CLC)*
Authors who died between 1900 and 1999	*TWENTIETH-CENTURY LITERARY CRITICISM (TCLC)*
Authors who died between 1800 and 1899	*NINETEENTH-CENTURY LITERATURE CRITICISM (NCLC)*
Authors who died between 1400 and 1799	*LITERATURE CRITICISM FROM 1400 TO 1800 (LC)* *SHAKESPEAREAN CRITICISM (SC)*
Authors who died before 1400	*CLASSICAL AND MEDIEVAL LITERATURE CRITICISM (CMLC)*
Authors of books for children and young adults	*CHILDREN'S LITERATURE REVIEW (CLR)*
Dramatists	*DRAMA CRITICISM (DC)*
Poets	*POETRY CRITICISM (PC)*
Short story writers	*SHORT STORY CRITICISM (SSC)*
Literary topics and movements	*HARLEM RENAISSANCE: A GALE CRITICAL COMPANION (HR)* *THE BEAT GENERATION: A GALE CRITICAL COMPANION (BG)* *FEMINISM IN LITERATURE: A GALE CRITICAL COMPANION (FL)* *GOTHIC LITERATURE: A GALE CRITICAL COMPANION (GL)*
Asian American writers of the last two hundred years	*ASIAN AMERICAN LITERATURE (AAL)*
Black writers of the past two hundred years	*BLACK LITERATURE CRITICISM (BLC)* *BLACK LITERATURE CRITICISM SUPPLEMENT (BLCS)*
Hispanic writers of the late nineteenth and twentieth centuries	*HISPANIC LITERATURE CRITICISM (HLC)* *HISPANIC LITERATURE CRITICISM SUPPLEMENT (HLCS)*
Native North American writers and orators of the eighteenth, nineteenth, and twentieth centuries	*NATIVE NORTH AMERICAN LITERATURE (NNAL)*
Major authors from the Renaissance to the present	*WORLD LITERATURE CRITICISM, 1500 TO THE PRESENT (WLC)* *WORLD LITERATURE CRITICISM SUPPLEMENT (WLCS)*

ISSN 0091-3421

Volume 230

Contemporary Literary Criticism

Criticism of the Works
of Today's Novelists, Poets, Playwrights,
Short Story Writers, Scriptwriters, and
Other Creative Writers

Jeffrey W. Hunter
PROJECT EDITOR

R
809.04
C761

THOMSON
GALE

Detroit • New York • San Francisco • New Haven, Conn. • Waterville, Maine • London

COLLEGE OF THE SEQUOIAS
LIBRARY

Contemporary Literary Criticism, Vol. 230

Project Editor
Jeffrey W. Hunter

Editorial
Kathy D. Darrow, Jelena O. Krstović, Michelle Lee, Thomas J. Schoenberg, Noah Schusterbauer, Lawrence J. Trudeau, Russel Whitaker

Data Capture
Frances Monroe, Gwen Tucker

Indexing Services
Laurie Andriot

Rights and Acquisitions
Lisa Kincade, Timothy Sisler, Andrew Specht

Imaging and Multimedia
Randy Bassett, Lezlie Light, Mike Logusz, Dan Newell, Christine O'Bryan

Composition and Electronic Prepress
Gary Oudersluys

Manufacturing
Rhonda Dover

Associate Product Manager
Marc Cormier

© 2007 Thomson Gale, a part of The Thomson Corporation. Thomson and Star Logo are trademarks and Gale is a registered trademark used herein under license.

For more information, contact
Thomson Gale
27500 Drake Rd.
Farmington Hills, MI 48331-3535
Or you can visit our internet site at
http://www.gale.com

ALL RIGHTS RESERVED
No part of this work covered by the copyright herein may be reproduced or used in any form or by any means—graphic, electronic, or mechanical, including photocopying, recording, taping, Web distribution, or information storage retrieval systems—without the written permission of the publisher.

This publication is a creative work fully protected by all applicable copyright laws, as well as by misappropriation, trade secret, unfair competition, and other applicable laws. The authors and editors of this work have added value to the underlying factual material herein through one or more of the following: unique and original selection, coordination, expression, arrangement, and classification of the information.

For permission to use material from the product, submit your request via the Web at http://www.gale-edit.com/permissions, or you may download our Permissions Request form and submit your request by fax or mail to:

Permisssions Department
Thomson Gale
27500 Drake Rd.
Farmington Hills, MI 48331-3535
Permissions Hotline:
248-699-8006 or 800-877-4253, ext. 8006
Fax 248-699-8074 or 800-762-4058

Since this page cannot legibly accommodate all copyright notices, the acknowledgments constitute an extension of the copyright notice.

While every effort has been made to secure permission to reprint material and to ensure the reliability of the information presented in this publication, Thomson Gale neither guarantees the accuracy of the data contained herein nor assumes any responsibility for errors, omissions or discrepancies. Thomson Gale accepts no payment for listing; and inclusion in the publication of any organization, agency, institution, publication, service, or individual does not imply endorsement of the editors or publisher. Errors brought to the attention of the publisher and verified to the satisfaction of the publisher will be corrected in future editions.

LIBRARY OF CONGRESS CATALOG CARD NUMBER 76-46132

ISBN-13: 978-0-7876-8000-8

ISBN-10: 0-7876-8000-1
ISSN 0091-3421

Printed in the United States of America
10 9 8 7 6 5 4 3 2 1

Contents

Preface

Named "one of the twenty-five most distinguished reference titles published during the past twenty-five years" by *Reference Quarterly,* the *Contemporary Literary Criticism* (*CLC*) series provides readers with critical commentary and general information on more than 2,000 authors now living or who died after December 31, 1999. Volumes published from 1973 through 1999 include authors who died after December 31, 1959. Previous to the publication of the first volume of *CLC* in 1973, there was no ongoing digest monitoring scholarly and popular sources of critical opinion and explication of modern literature. *CLC,* therefore, has fulfilled an essential need, particularly since the complexity and variety of contemporary literature makes the function of criticism especially important to today's reader.

Scope of the Series

CLC provides significant passages from published criticism of works by creative writers. Since many of the authors covered in *CLC* inspire continual critical commentary, writers are often represented in more than one volume. There is, of course, no duplication of reprinted criticism.

Authors are selected for inclusion for a variety of reasons, among them the publication or dramatic production of a critically acclaimed new work, the reception of a major literary award, revival of interest in past writings, or the adaptation of a literary work to film or television.

Attention is also given to several other groups of writers—authors of considerable public interest—about whose work criticism is often difficult to locate. These include mystery and science fiction writers, literary and social critics, foreign authors, and authors who represent particular ethnic groups.

Each *CLC* volume contains individual essays and reviews taken from hundreds of book review periodicals, general magazines, scholarly journals, monographs, and books. Entries include critical evaluations spanning from the beginning of an author's career to the most current commentary. Interviews, feature articles, and other published writings that offer insight into the author's works are also presented. Students, teachers, librarians, and researchers will find that the general critical and biographical material in *CLC* provides them with vital information required to write a term paper, analyze a poem, or lead a book discussion group. In addition, complete bibliographical citations note the original source and all of the information necessary for a term paper footnote or bibliography.

Organization of the Book

A *CLC* entry consists of the following elements:

- The **Author Heading** cites the name under which the author most commonly wrote, followed by birth and death dates. Also located here are any name variations under which an author wrote, including transliterated forms for authors whose native languages use nonroman alphabets. If the author wrote consistently under a pseudonym, the pseudonym will be listed in the author heading and the author's actual name given in parenthesis on the first line of the biographical and critical information. Uncertain birth or death dates are indicated by question marks. Single-work entries are preceded by a heading that consists of the most common form of the title in English translation (if applicable) and the original date of composition.

- A **Portrait of the Author** is included when available.

- The **Introduction** contains background information that introduces the reader to the author, work, or topic that is the subject of the entry.

- The list of **Principal Works** is ordered chronologically by date of first publication and lists the most important works by the author. The genre and publication date of each work is given. In the case of foreign authors whose works have been translated into English, the English-language version of the title follows in brackets. Unless otherwise indicated, dramas are dated by first performance, not first publication.

- Reprinted **Criticism** is arranged chronologically in each entry to provide a useful perspective on changes in critical evaluation over time. The critic's name and the date of composition or publication of the critical work are given at the beginning of each piece of criticism. Unsigned criticism is preceded by the title of the source in which it appeared. All titles by the author featured in the text are printed in boldface type. Footnotes are reprinted at the end of each essay or excerpt. In the case of excerpted criticism, only those footnotes that pertain to the excerpted texts are included.

- A complete **Bibliographical Citation** of the original essay or book precedes each piece of criticism. Source citations in the Literary Criticism Series follow University of Chicago Press style, as outlined in *The Chicago Manual of Style,* 15th ed. (Chicago: The University of Chicago Press, 2003).

- Critical essays are prefaced by brief **Annotations** explicating each piece.

- Whenever possible, a recent **Author Interview** accompanies each entry.

- An annotated bibliography of **Further Reading** appears at the end of each entry and suggests resources for additional study. In some cases, significant essays for which the editors could not obtain reprint rights are included here. Boxed material following the further reading list provides references to other biographical and critical sources on the author in series published by Thomson Gale.

Indexes

A **Cumulative Author Index** lists all of the authors that appear in a wide variety of reference sources published by Thomson Gale, including *CLC*. A complete list of these sources is found facing the first page of the Author Index. The index also includes birth and death dates and cross references between pseudonyms and actual names.

A **Cumulative Nationality Index** lists all authors featured in *CLC* by nationality, followed by the number of the *CLC* volume in which their entry appears.

A **Cumulative Topic Index** lists the literary themes and topics treated in the series as well as in other Literature Criticism series.

An alphabetical **Title Index** accompanies each volume of *CLC*. Listings of titles by authors covered in the given volume are followed by the author's name and the corresponding page numbers where the titles are discussed. English translations of foreign titles and variations of titles are cross-referenced to the title under which a work was originally published. Titles of novels, dramas, films, nonfiction books, and poetry, short story, or essay collections are printed in italics, while individual poems, short stories, and essays are printed in roman type within quotation marks.

In response to numerous suggestions from librarians, Thomson Gale also produces an annual cumulative title index that alphabetically lists all titles reviewed in *CLC* and is available to all customers. Additional copies of this index are available upon request. Librarians and patrons will welcome this separate index; it saves shelf space, is easy to use, and is recyclable upon receipt of the next edition.

Citing *Contemporary Literary Criticism*

When citing criticism reprinted in the Literary Criticism Series, students should provide complete bibliographic information so that the cited essay can be located in the original print or electronic source. Students who quote directly from reprinted criticism may use any accepted bibliographic format, such as University of Chicago Press style or Modern Language Association (MLA) style. Both the MLA and the University of Chicago formats are acceptable and recognized as being the current standards for citations. It is important, however, to choose one format for all citations; do not mix the two formats within a list of citations.

The examples below follow recommendations for preparing a bibliography set forth in *The Chicago Manual of Style,* 15th ed. (Chicago: The University of Chicago Press, 2003); the first example pertains to material drawn from periodicals, the second to material reprinted from books:

Miller, Mae. "Patterns of Nature and Confluence in Eudora Welty's *The Optimist's Daughter." Southern Quarterly: A Journal of the Arts in the South* 35, no. 1 (fall 1996): 55-61. Reprinted in *Contemporary Literary Criticism.* Vol. 220, edited by Jeffrey W. Hunter, 304-09. Detroit: Thomson Gale, 2006.

Aronoff, Myron J. "Learning to Live with Ambiguity: Balancing Ethical and Political Imperatives." In *The Spy Novels of John le Carré: Balancing Ethics and Politics,* 201-14. New York: St. Martin's Press, 1999. Reprinted in *Contemporary Literary Criticism.* Vol. 220, edited by Jeffrey W. Hunter, 84-92. Detroit: Thomson Gale, 2006.

The examples below follow recommendations for preparing a works cited list set forth in the *MLA Handbook for Writers of Research Papers,* 5th ed. (New York: The Modern Language Association of America, 1999); the first example pertains to material drawn from periodicals, the second to material reprinted from books:

Miller, Mae. "Patterns of Nature and Confluence in Eudora Welty's *The Optimist's Daughter." Southern Quarterly: A Journal of the Arts in the South* 35.1 (fall 1996): 55-61. Reprinted in *Contemporary Literary Criticism.* Ed. Jeffrey W. Hunter. Vol. 220. Detroit: Thomson Gale, 2006. 304-09.

Aronoff, Myron J. "Learning to Live with Ambiguity: Balancing Ethical and Political Imperatives." *The Spy Novels of John le Carré: Balancing Ethics and Politics,* New York: St. Martin's Press, 1999. 201-14. Reprinted in *Contemporary Literary Criticism.* Ed. Jeffrey W. Hunter. Vol. 220. Detroit: Thomson Gale, 2006. 84-92.

Suggestions are Welcome

Readers who wish to suggest new features, topics, or authors to appear in future volumes, or who have other suggestions or comments are cordially invited to call, write, or fax the Associate Product Manager:

Associate Product Manager, Literary Criticism Series
Thomson Gale
27500 Drake Road
Farmington Hills, MI 48331-3535
1-800-347-4253 (GALE)
Fax: 248-699-8983

Acknowledgments

The editors wish to thank the copyright holders of the criticism included in this volume and the permissions managers of many book and magazine publishing companies for assisting us in securing reproduction rights. Following is a list of the copyright holders who have granted us permission to reproduce material in this volume of *CLC*. Every effort has been made to trace copyright, but if omissions have been made, please let us know.

COPYRIGHTED MATERIAL IN *CLC*, VOLUME 230, WAS REPRODUCED FROM THE FOLLOWING PERIODICALS:

African American Review, v. 33, spring, 1999. © 1999, Scott MacPhail. Reproduced by permission.—*Artforum,* v. 42, February, 2004 for "Twin Bills" by Theresa Duncan. Copyright © 2004 by *Artforum*. Reproduced by permission of the publisher and the author.—*Black Issues Book Review,* v. 2, September-October, 2000; v. 4, September-October, 2002. Both reproduced by permission.—*Callaloo,* winter, 1986; v. 25, 2002. Copyright © 1986, 2002 The Johns Hopkins University Press. Both reproduced by permission.—*Children's Literature,* 2002. Copyright © 2002 The Johns Hopkins University Press. Reproduced by permission.—*CLA Journal,* v. 47, 2003. Copyright, 2003 by The College Language Association. Used by permission of The College Language Association.—*College English,* v. 55, February, 1993. Copyright © 1993 by the National Council of Teachers of English. Reproduced by permission of the publisher.—*Cross Currents,* v. 54, spring, 2004. Copyright 2004 by Cross Currents Inc. Reproduced by permission.—*English Education,* v. 37, 2005. Reproduced by permission.—*English Journal,* v. 92, July, 2003. Copyright © 2003 by the National Council of Teachers of English. Reproduced by permission of the publisher.—*Extrapolation,* v. 39, fall, 1998; v. 43, spring, 2002; v. 46, spring, 2005; v. 46, fall, 2005. Copyright © 1998, 2002, 2005 by The Kent State University Press. All reproduced by permission.—*FEMSPEC,* v. 3, 2002. Reproduced by permission.—*Foundation,* v. 48, spring, 1990. © 1990 by the Science Fiction Foundation. Reproduced by permission.—*Image & Narrative: Online Magazine of the Visual Narrative,* January, 2003. Reproduced by permission.—*ImageText,* v. 1, fall, 2004 for "Alan Moore and the Graphic Novel: Confronting the Fourth Dimension" by Mark Bernard and James Bucky Carter. Copyright © 2004 Mark Bernard and James Bucky Carter. All rights reserved. Reproduced by permission of the respective authors.—*International Journal of Comic Art,* v. 6, spring, 2004; v. 7, spring-summer, 2005. Both reproduced by permission of John A. Lent—*Journal of Popular Culture,* v. 33, spring, 2000. Copyright © 2000 Basil Blackwell Ltd. Reproduced by permission of Blackwell Publishers.—*Journal of the American Academy of Psychoanalysis,* v. 30, fall, 2002. © 2002 The American Academy of Psychoanalysis. Reprinted with permission of The Guilford Press.—*Literary Review,* v. 38, spring, 1995 for "Genre to the Rear, Race and Gender to the Fore: The Novels of Octavia E. Butler" by Burton Raffel. Reproduced by permission of the author.—*Literature Film Quarterly,* v. 32, 2004. Copyright © 2004 Salisbury State College. Reproduced by permission.—*Locus,* v. 51, July, 2003. Reproduced by permission.—*MELUS,* vol. 13, spring-summer, 1986. Copyright *MELUS: The Society for the Study of Multi-Ethnic Literature of the United States*, 1986. Reproduced by permission.—*Metro Magazine,* v. 148, 2006. Copyright 2006 Australian Teachers of Media. Reproduced by permission.—*Michigan Feminist Studies,* 2004. Reproduced by permission.—*Ninth Art,* March 31, 2003; April 7, 2003. Both reproduced by permission.—*Novel,* v. 35, spring, 2002. Copyright © NOVEL Corp., 2002. Reproduced with permission.—*Post Script,* v. 20, summer, 2000. Copyright © 2000 by POST SCRIPT, INC. Reproduced by permission.—*Salon,* October 26, 1999; October 18, 2000. Copyright 1999, 2000 Salon.com. These articles first appeared in Salon.com, at http://www.salon.com. Online versions remain in the Salon archives. Both reprinted with permission.—*Science-Fiction Studies,* v. 22, March, 1995. Copyright © 1995 by SFS Publications. Reproduced by permission.—*Sight and Sound,* v. 13, October, 2003. Copyright © 2003 by The British Film Institute. Reproduced by permission.—*Slate,* December 17, 2003. Copyright © 2003 United Feature Syndicate, Inc. All rights reserved. Distributed by United Feature Syndicate, Inc.—*Studies in American Fiction,* v. 27, spring, 1999. Copyright © 1999 Northeastern University. Reproduced by permission.—*Transition,* 1994 for "After Identity" by Peter Erickson. Reproduced by permission of the author.

COPYRIGHTED MATERIAL IN *CLC*, VOLUME 230, WAS REPRODUCED FROM THE FOLLOWING BOOKS:

Accomando, Christina. From "Exposing the Lie of Neutrality: June Jordan's Affirmative Acts," in *Still Seeking an Attitude: Critical Reflections on the Work of June Jordan.* Edited by Valerie Kinloch and Margaret Grebowicz. Lexington

Books, 2004. Copyright © 2004 by Rowman & Littlefield Publishers, Inc. Reproduced by permission.—Bartholomew Ortega, Kirsten. From "June Jordan's Radical Pedagogy: Activist Poetry in Public Education," in *Still Seeking an Attitude: Critical Reflections on the Work of June Jordan.* Edited by Valerie Kinloch and Margaret Grebowicz. Lexington Books, 2004. Copyright © 2004 by Rowman & Littlefield Publishers, Inc. Reproduced by permission.—Brogan, Jacqueline Vaught. From "From Warrior to Womanist: The Development of June Jordan's Poetry," in *Speaking the Other Self: American Women Writers.* Edited by Jeanne Campbell Reesman. University of Georgia Press, 1997. © 1997 by the University of Georgia Press. All rights reserved. Reproduced by permission.—Coleman, Ramona. From "Narrating Nation: Exploring the Space of Americanness and the Place of African American Women through the Works of June Jordan," in *Still Seeking an Attitude: Critical Reflections on the Work of June Jordan.* Edited by Valerie Kinloch and Margaret Grebowicz. Lexington Books, 2004. Copyright © 2004 by Rowman & Littlefield Publishers, Inc. Reproduced by permission.—Creeber, Glen. From "TV Ruined the Movies: Television, Tarantino, and the Intimate World of 'The Sopranos,'" in *This Thing of Ours: Investigating The Sopranos.* Edited by David Lavery. Columbia University Press, 2002. Copyright © 2002 Columbia University Press, New York. All rights reserved. Republished in North America with permission of the Columbia University Press, 61 W. 62nd St., New York, NY 10023. In the U. K. by permission of Wallflower Press.—Creighton, Jane. From "Writing War, Writing Memory," in *Still Seeking an Attitude: Critical Reflections on the Work of June Jordan.* Edited by Valerie Kinloch and Margaret Grebowicz. Lexington Books, 2004. Copyright © 2004 by Rowman & Littlefield Publishers, Inc. Reproduced by permission.—Eagleton, Mary. From "Working Across Difference: Examples from Minnie Bruce Pratt and June Jordan," in *Caught Between Cultures: Women, Writing & Subjectivities.* Edited by Elizabeth Russell. Rodopi, 2002. Copyright © 2002 Editions Rodopi B. V. Reproduced by permission.—Fausty, Joshua, and Edvige Giunta. From "Quentin Tarantino: An Ethnic Enigma," in *Screening Ethnicity: Cinematographic Representations of Italian Americans in the United States.* Edited by Anna Camaiti Hostert and Anthony Julian Tamburri. Bordighera Press, 2002. Copyright © 2002 by Anna Camaiti Hostert, Anthony Julian Tamburri, Joshua Fausty and Edvige Giunta. Reproduced by permission.—Garner, Ken. From "'Would You Like to Hear Some Music?' Music In and Out of Control in the Films of Quentin Tarantino," in *Film Music: Critical Approaches.* Edited by K. J. Donnelly. Continuum International Publishing, 2001. Copyright © K. J. Donnelly 2001. All rights reserved. Republished with permission of Continuum International Publishing, conveyed through Copyright Clearance Center, Inc.—Green, Michelle Erica. From "'There Goes the Neighborhood": Octavia Butler's Demand for Diversity in Utopias," in *Utopian and Science Fiction by Women: Worlds of Difference.* Edited by Jane Donawerth and Carol Kolmerten. Syracuse, NY: Syracuse University Press, 1994. Copyright © 1994 by Syracuse University Press. All rights reserved. Reproduced by permission.—Keating, AnaLouise. From "The Intimate Distance of Desire: June Jordan's Bisexual Inflections," in *Romancing the Margins? Lesbian Writing in the 1990's.* Edited by Gabriele Grifin. Harrington Park Press, 2000. Copyright © 2000 by The Haworth Press, Inc. Binghamton, New York. All rights reserved. Reproduced by permission.—Pfeiffer, John R. From "Octavia Butler Writes the Bible," in *Shaw and Other Matters.* Edited by Susan Rusinko. Cranbury, NJ: Susquehanna University Press, 1998. Copyright © 1998 by Associated University Presses, Inc. All rights reserved. Reproduced by permission.—Walsh, Rebecca. From "Where Metaphor Meets Materiality: The Spatialized Subject and the Limits of Locational Feminism," in *Exclusions in Feminist Thought: Challenging the Boundaries of Womanhood.* Edited by Mary Brewer. Sussex Academic Press, 2002. Copyright © Academic Press 2002. Reproduced by permission.—Willis, Sharon. From "Style, Posture and Idiom: Tarantino's Figures of Masculinity," in *Reinventing Film Studies.* Edited by Christine Gledhill and Linda Williams. Arnold, 2000. Copyright © 2000 by Arnold. Used by permission of Hodder & Stoughton Educational.

Thomson Gale Literature Product Advisory Board

The members of the Thomson Gale Literature Product Advisory Board—reference librarians from public and academic library systems—represent a cross-section of our customer base and offer a variety of informed perspectives on both the presentation and content of our literature products. Advisory board members assess and define such quality issues as the relevance, currency, and usefulness of the author coverage, critical content, and literary topics included in our series; evaluate the layout, presentation, and general quality of our printed volumes; provide feedback on the criteria used for selecting authors and topics covered in our series; provide suggestions for potential enhancements to our series; identify any gaps in our coverage of authors or literary topics, recommending authors or topics for inclusion; analyze the appropriateness of our content and presentation for various user audiences, such as high school students, undergraduates, graduate students, librarians, and educators; and offer feedback on any proposed changes/enhancements to our series. We wish to thank the following advisors for their advice throughout the year.

Barbara M. Bibel
Librarian
Oakland Public Library
Oakland, California

Dr. Toby Burrows
Principal Librarian
The Scholars' Centre
University of Western Australia Library
Nedlands, Western Australia

Celia C. Daniel
Associate Reference Librarian
Howard University Libraries
Washington, D.C.

David M. Durant
Reference Librarian
Joyner Library
East Carolina University
Greenville, North Carolina

Nancy T. Guidry
Librarian
Bakersfield Community College
Bakersfield, California

Heather Martin
Arts & Humanities Librarian
University of Alabama at Birmingham, Sterne Library
Birmingham, Alabama

Susan Mikula
Librarian
Indiana Free Library
Indiana, Pennsylvania

Thomas Nixon
Humanities Reference Librarian
University of North Carolina at Chapel Hill, Davis
 Library
Chapel Hill, North Carolina

Mark Schumacher
Jackson Library
University of North Carolina at Greensboro
Greensboro, North Carolina

Gwen Scott-Miller
Assistant Director
Sno-Isle Regional Library System
Marysville, Washington

Octavia E. Butler
1947-2006

(Full name Octavia Estelle Butler) American novelist, short story writer, and essayist.

The following entry provides an overview of Butler's career through 2005. For additional information on her life and work, see *CLC*, Volumes 38 and 121.

INTRODUCTION

Butler is best known for her "Patternist" series of science fiction novels which portrays a society whose inhabitants have developed telepathic powers over several centuries. Butler's writing explores themes that have generally received cursory treatments in the sci-fi genre, including sexual identity, racial conflict, and contemporary politics. Butler's heroines typically are powerful black women who possess large measures of both mental and physical acumen. While they exemplify the traditional female gender roles of nurturer, healer, and conciliator, these women also display courage, independence, and ambition and embody the belief that hierarchical systems are flawed. They enhance their influence through alliances with or opposition to powerful males. Butler, whose works have been compared to those of Toni Morrison and Margaret Atwood, has received many top honors within the field of science fiction and has earned recognition as a pioneer amongst women writers.

BIOGRAPHICAL INFORMATION

Born in 1947, Butler grew up in a racially mixed neighborhood in Pasadena, California. Her father died during her childhood and her mother worked as a maid to support their family. Butler has written memoirs of her mother's sacrifices, which included buying Butler a typewriter at age ten, and paying a large fee to an unscrupulous agent. Butler entered student writing contests as a teenager and attended such workshops as the Screenwriters' Guild of America's Open Door Program and the Clarion Science Fiction Writer's Workshop. This early training led to contacts with a range of well-known science fiction writers, including Joanna Russ and Harlan Ellison; Ellison became one of Butler's most significant mentors. Butler went on to earn an Associate of Arts degree at Pasadena City College in 1968. She also attended California State

University and the University of California, Los Angeles. After several years of working low-wage jobs in restaurants and factories, Butler sold her first work of fiction. With the encouragement of Ellison, Butler published her short story "Crossover" in *Clarion* in 1971. Butler has won several prizes for her science fiction works, including the Locus Award in 1985 for her novella "Bloodchild," the Nebula Award for "Bloodchild" and for the novel *Parable of the Talents* (1998), and the Hugo Award in 1984 for the short story "Speech Sounds" and again for "Bloodchild." She also received the prestigious MacArthur Foundation "Genius" Grant in 1995, a PEN Lifetime Achievement award in 2000, and a Langston Hughes Medal from The City College of New York. On February 24, 2006 Butler died from a head injury that she sustained after a fall outside of her home near Seattle, Washington.

MAJOR WORKS

Five of Butler's novels—*Patternmaster* (1976), *Mind of My Mind* (1977), *Survivor* (1978), *Wild Seed* (1980), and *Clay's Ark* (1984)—revolve around the Patternists, a group of mentally superior beings connected to one another telepathically. These beings descend from Doro, a four thousand-year-old Nubian man who has selectively bred with humans throughout time with the intention of establishing a race of superhumans. He prolongs his life by killing others, including his family members, and inhabiting their bodies. *Wild Seed,* which begins in seventeenth-century Africa and spans more than two centuries, outlines the origin of the Patternists. The novel recounts Doro's uneasy alliance with Anyanwu, an earth mother figure with extraordinary powers. Their relationship progresses from power struggles and tests of will to mutual need and dependency. Doro's tyranny ends when one of his children, the heroine of *Mind of My Mind,* destroys him and unites the Patternists with care and compassion. The rest of the "Patternist" novels take place in the future. In *Patternmaster,* two brothers fight for the role of Patternmaster, the one who controls the telepathic network that unites the Patternists. Meanwhile, a group of humans genetically mutated by a mysterious disease attacks the Patternist community and threatens its destruction. *Clay's Ark* explains the origin of the disease and how it came to Earth. This novel reflects Butler's interest in the psychological traits of men and women. Set on an alien planet, *Survivor* examines human attitudes toward racial and ethnic differences and their effects on two alien creatures. Alanna, the human protagonist, triumphs over racial prejudice and enslavement by teaching her alien captors tolerance and respect for individuality. *Kindred* (1979) departs from the "Patternist" series yet shares its focus on male/female relationships and racial matters. The novel focuses on Dana, a contemporary African American writer who is transported to a pre-Civil War plantation several times over the course of the work. She suffers as a victim of both her slave-owning ancestor who summons her to the past when he is in danger, and of the slaveholding age in which she finds herself trapped for increasingly lengthy periods of time.

Known collectively as the *Xenogenesis* trilogy, the novels *Dawn* (1987), *Adulthood Rites* (1988), and *Imago* (1989) take place in an apocalyptic future. The trilogy begins following a nuclear war that has destroyed Earth. A group of aliens called the Oankali has begun to mate with the surviving humans. Critics have interpreted these three novels, published together in 2000 as *Lilith's Brood*, as reflecting a positive analysis of society as evolutionary and dynamic. In Butler's story "Speech Sounds," violence and anarchy erupt after a disease robs humans of their ability to communicate; while some lose the ability to speak, others can no longer read or write. Butler's acclaimed novella "Bloodchild," anthologized in the collection *Bloodchild and Other Stories* (1995), explores patriarchal society. This story presents a world inhabited by human-like beings called Terrans who live on "Preserves" provided for them by a government run by a monstrous race of creatures known as Tlics. The Tlics employ the Terrans for breeding, requiring each Terran family to sacrifice at least one of its sons to function as a "host" for Tlic eggs; the process produces highly desirable offspring but sometimes results in the death of the host. The novella centers on the relationship between T'Gatoi, a government official who manages the Preserves, and Gan, the Terran boy who serves as the host for her eggs. *Parable of the Sower* (1993), the first novel in Butler's "Earthseed" series, is presented in the form of a journal written by a young black woman named Lauren Olamina. This work takes place in California of the 2020s. Society has descended into chaos: food, gasoline, and electricity are in short supply, and crime and drug use have overwhelmed Los Angeles. While Laura witnesses the destruction of her neighborhood and the death of her family, she creates a new religion called Earthseed based on the idea that "God is change." Eventually Laura flees southern California and heads north, where she establishes an Earthseed community named Acorn. In *Parable of the Talents*, a Christian fundamentalist organization founded by a newly elected president of the United States threatens to destroy the thriving Acorn community. *Fledgling* (2005) concerns a race of vampires called Ina who maintain symbiotic relationships with humans—they rely on human blood to

survive, and they also give pleasure and health benefits to the people they bite. The novel follows Shori, a 53-year-old Ina with the appearance of a 10-year-old black girl, who must flee for her life after the murder of her family.

CRITICAL RECEPTION

Critics applaud Butler's lack of sentimentality in her work, and respond favorably to her direct treatment of subjects that science fiction writers have not traditionally addressed. As Patricia Melzer has written, "Butler emphasizes that the embracing of difference does not only enhance the quality of human interactions, but that it is an act of survival and of necessity if humankind wants to end conditions of hate and violence." Several reviewers have asserted that Butler's fiction contains an underlying theme of slavery, but Butler herself has disputed this. In an interview with Stephen W. Potts, she has stated, "The only places I am writing about slavery is where I actually say so." Critics have noted Butler's ambiguous endings that leave open possibilities and limitations for mankind, with Jim Miller having observed that "Whether she is dealing with the role of medical science, biological determinism, the politics of disease, or the complex interrelations of race, class, and gender, Butler's dystopian imagination challenges us to think the worst in complex ways while simultaneously planting utopian seeds of hope." As the most prominent female science fiction writer in a field dominated by men, Butler has garnered praise for the feminist themes in her writing. She has also earned recognition for her role as a trailblazer for African-American authors in the genre of science fiction. According to Sandra Y. Govan, Butler "is a writer very conscious of the power of art to affect social perceptions and behavior and a writer unafraid to admit that, when appropriate, she borrows from tradition, that she takes and reshapes African and Afro-American cultural values, that she has heuristic and didactic impulses which she transforms into art."

PRINCIPAL WORKS

Patternmaster (novel) 1976
Mind of My Mind (novel) 1977
Survivor (novel) 1978
Kindred (novel) 1979
Wild Seed (novel) 1980
Clay's Ark (novel) 1984
†*Dawn* (novel) 1987
†*Adulthood Rites* (novel) 1988
†*Imago* (novel) 1989

The Evening and the Morning and the Night (novella)
  1991
‡*Parable of the Sower* (novel) 1993
Bloodchild and Other Stories (novella, short stories,
  and essays) 1995
‡*Parable of the Talents* (novel) 1998
§*Lilith's Brood* (novels) 2000
Fledgling: A Novel (novel) 2005
‖*Seed to Harvest* (novels) 2007

*These works comprise the "Patternist" series.

†These works comprise the *Xenogenesis* trilogy.

‡These works comprise the "Earthseed" series.

§This work contains the complete *Xenogenesis* series: *Dawn, Adulthood Rites,* and *Imago.*

‖This work contains the novels *Wild Seed, Mind of My Mind, Clay's Ark,* and *Patternmaster.*

CRITICISM

Sandra Y. Govan (essay date spring-summer 1986)

SOURCE: Govan, Sandra Y. "Homage to Tradition: Octavia Butler Renovates the Historical Novel." *ME-LUS* 13, nos. 1-2 (spring-summer 1986): 79-96.

[*In the following essay, Govan places Butler's novels in the tradition of slave narratives and historical novels.*]

Despite the fact that her novels are sometimes difficult to find, Octavia Butler has nonetheless firmly established herself as a major new voice in science fiction. The five published novels of her "Patternist" saga, depicting over a vast time span both the genesis and evolution of Homo Superior (psionically enhanced human beings) and his mutated bestial counterpart; the one novel, ***Kindred,*** outside the serial story; and the short stories, all speak exceptionally well for Butler's artistry and growth.[1]

Through the interviews she has given, the articles she's written, the pieces published about her, and of course, her novels, Octavia Butler emerges as a forthright and honest author. She is a writer very conscious of the power of art to affect social perceptions and behavior and a writer unafraid to admit that, when appropriate, she borrows from tradition, that she takes and reshapes African and Afro-American cultural values, that she has heuristic and didactic impulses which she transforms into art. With ***Wild Seed*** and ***Kindred,*** for instance, Butler seizes the possibilities inherent in the historical novel and the Black tradition in autobiography. She adapts these forms to produce extrapolative fiction

which, for its impetus, looks to an historically grounded African-American past rather than to a completely speculative future. On the surface, this seems indeed a curious connection, this linkage of future fiction to the past. Regardless of the surface appearance, the format itself, extrapolating or projecting from social structures of the past to those possible in the future, is not new (Isaac Asimov's *Foundation* series is a model precursor). What *is* new and distinctive is Butler's handling of the format or frame, her particular choice of past cultures to extrapolate from. She has chosen to link science fiction not only to anthropology and history, via the historical novel, but directly to the Black American slavery experiences via the slave narrative. This is a fundamental departure for science fiction as genre. ***Wild Seed*** and ***Kindred*** demonstrate this new configuration aptly. However, before engaging in an immediate discussion of these two novels, it seems appropriate to delay the discussion momentarily in order to better frame it with some critical definitions.

Most of us probably have seen the historical novel as a continuation of the realistic social novel; we associate it with Sir Walter Scott or Charles Dickens, or perhaps with Margaret Mitchell or Margaret Walker. We know that its setting and characters are established in a particular historic context—the age of chivalry or the French Revolution or the antebellum American South. Casual readers of the European or Western historical novel are usually content to forgo the kind of rigorous economic, philosophic, political analysis that Georg Lukács, in *The Historical Novel,* brings to his discussion of the form's origins. Lukács argues, for instance, that of prime importance to the historical novel's development "is the increasing historical awareness of the decisive role played in human progress by the struggle of classes in history." In his analysis, knowledge of "the rise of modern bourgeois society" from "the class struggles between nobility and bourgeoisie, . . . class struggles which raged throughout the entire 'idyllic Middle Ages' and whose last decisive stage was the great French Revolution," is crucial to the historical novel (27-28).

Using Sir Walter Scott as his archetypal model, Lukács outlines Scott's principal contributions to the form: "the broad delineation of manners and circumstances attendant upon events, the dramatic character of action and, in close connection with this, the new and important role of dialog in the novel" (31). For my immediate purposes however, Lukács' remarks are most germane when he says the authentic historical novel is "specifically historical," that its history is not "mere costumery," and that it presents an "artistically faithful image of a concrete historical epoch" (19).

Slave narratives, the first Black autobiographies, have a great deal in common with our understanding of the attributes of the historical novel. Each narrative is "specifically historical" (Marion Starling has traced narratives as far back as 1703 and followed them forward to 1944; their peak period was 1836-1860).² The historical circumstances of each text are so far removed from "mere costumery" that extensive, often intrusive, documentation of the ex-slave's veracity is quite frequently an established feature of the text, part of what Robert Stepto refers to as the "authenticating" strategy of the narrative voice (35). And without question, slave narrators strove to produce a powerful yet "faithful image of a concrete historical epoch." Perhaps only a handful of the six thousand extant narratives became artistic successes, works with the strength and quality of Frederick Douglass' *The Narrative of the Life of Frederick Douglass* or Harriet Jacobs' *Incidents in the Life of a Slave Girl* or the dramatic tale of William and Ellen Craft's *Running a Thousand Miles for Freedom*.³ But successful literary works or not, most slave narratives depicted faithfully and graphically the brutal reality of slave life and each showed the direct impact of slavery, that peculiar institution, not only on the narrator's own life and that of his/her family but also the debilitating and corrupting effects of such an institution on those who held power within it, slaveholders.

Because the slave narrative and the historical novel, especially the historical novel which concerns itself with life in the antebellum South, share some common characteristics, a clear relationship between them may be easily established. For instance, Harriet Beecher Stowe's *Uncle Tom's Cabin* is unquestionably indebted to the life story of Josiah Henson, fugitive slave. But, of more importance than demonstrating a relationship between the historical novel and the slave narrative is our understanding of the specific function slave narratives served. Unlike the novel, whose primary purpose was entertainment, the primary function of the slave narrative was to educate and politicize in no uncertain terms. At the height of their popularity, slave narratives, called "those literary nigritudes—little tadpoles of the press which run to editions of hundreds of thousands,"⁴ were highly influential tools used by abolitionist societies here and abroad to mold public opinion, to bend the public mind toward the task of eliminating slavery. As a group, slave narratives exhibited these characteristics traits: they focused on the special experience of racial oppression; they were intended to be records of resistance; they employed a variety of literary/rhetorical devices including concrete imagery and diction, understatement, polemical voice, and satire to describe vividly the actual conditions of slavery; they looked at the self outside the typical western perspective of the individual and chose instead to recognize or represent the self in relationship to the oppressed group with ties and responsibilities to group members.⁵ Slave narrators were conscious of their own cultural schizophrenia, their burden of blackness in white America, or, as W. E.

B. DuBois said in his seminal *The Souls of Black Folk*, their "double consciousness," their two "warring selves in one dark skin."

Slave narrators were conscious, too, that they were presenting objective fact through the filter of their own subjective experience. Taken collectively, their narratives frequently show recurrent patterns. There is a loss of innocence wherein the slave, usually as a child, recollects his or her first awareness of the personal impact of slavery. There are detailed descriptions of various phases of bondage as the slave witnesses them and then experiences them. There is the punishment factor, the resistance motif, the glimpse of life-in-the-quarters. There is also the slave's quest for education, the slave's encounter with abusive sexual misconduct and immoral behavior, the slave's recognition of religious hypocrisy and the adulterated Christianity practiced by "Christian" slave holders, the slave's escape attempts, and, finally, the slave's successful escape. Of course, this pattern varied from narrative to narrative and oftentimes, what was stressed depended upon the discretion and sensibilities of the narrator or, sometimes, on the concerns or dictates of an editor or an amanuensis.

Butler's *Wild Seed* and *Kindred* are rich texts which neatly define the junction where the historical novel, the slave narrative, and science fiction meet. The two novels build upon tenets clearly identified with the expected conventions or norms of the genres she employs. Then, because Butler's forte is extrapolative fiction, we can easily see the melding as each novel moves us through the recreated, historically plausible, viable, yet totally speculative alternative reality which is the realm of science fiction—as distinct from the codified expectations we have of fiction which operates from the realistic or naturalistic realm. To phrase it succinctly, Octavia Butler's work stands on the foundation of traditional form and proceeds to renovate that form.

Wild Seed is not about Arthurian England or the French Revolution. Instead, it is about alienation and loneliness; about needs, dreams, ambitions, and power. It is also about love. Africa provides the cultural backdrop for the initial interaction between plot and character. Although the opening setting of *Wild Seed* is 17th-century west Africa, specifically the Niger river region of eastern Nigeria, the setting shifts through the course of the novel and we follow the lives of Butler's two immortal central characters, Doro, a four thousand year old Nubian, and Anyanwu, a three hundred year old Onitsha priestess, through the Middle Passage voyage to life in a colonial New England village, to life on an antebellum Louisiana plantation, to California just after the Civil War. In the course of two hundred years of movement we are privy to a broad and vivid historical canvas. Again, however, Butler's use of history and cultural anthropology do more than simply illuminate the text or serve as mere coloration. Both disciplines are intrinsic to our understanding of character, theme, and action. Their use also permits Butler to employ a more original approach to the old theme of the trials of immortality, the theme of the spiritual disintegration of the man who cannot die.

The specifically African segment of **Wild Seed** only occupies four chapters of the text but an African ethos dominates the whole book. The novel opens in 1690. Doro has returned to Africa to look for one of his "seed villages," one of several communities he has carefully nurtured, composed of people with nascent or lateral mutant abilities. They know things or hear things or see things others cannot and so in their home communities, they are misfits or outcasts or "witches" because of their abilities. In his autonomous villages wherein he collects and breeds these people, Doro is their protector; his motives, however, are far from altruistic for he needs his people in a very real way. He "enjoys their company and sadly, they provide his most satisfying kills."[6] Doro's mutant power is the ability to transfer his psychic essence to any human host; thus, he kills to live. And, as he kills, he literally "feeds" off the spirit of the host body. But whenever Doro kills or "takes" his own kind, he gains more sustenance from their heightened psychic energy than he derives from the "taking" of ordinary non-mutant human beings.

The village Doro returns to has been destroyed by slave hunters and as he contemplates the carnage and thinks about tracking and regrouping the captured survivors, his gift of attraction to other mutants, an innate tracking sense or "telescent" subtly makes him conscious of the distant Anyanwu. He finds himself pulled toward her. Butler's narration here adeptly conveys both character and place.

> He wandered southwest toward the forest, leaving as he had arrived—alone, unarmed, without supplies, accepting the savanna and later the forest as easily as he accepted any terrain. He was killed several times—by disease, by animals, by hostile people. This was a harsh land. Yet he continued to move southwest, unthinkingly veering away from the section of the coast where his ship awaited him. After a while, he realized it was no longer his anger at the loss of his seed village that drove him. It was something new—an impulse, a feeling, a kind of mental undertow pulling at him.
>
> (9)

It is a subtle awareness of Anyanwu which attracts Doro and pulls him to a country he has not visited in three hundred years. When he finally meets and talks with her, Doro suspects immediately that they are distant kin, that she is "wild seed," the fruit of [his] peoples' passing by [hers] during one of Africa's many periods of flux. Ironically, Anyanwu herself supports this idea when she recalls a half remembered and whispered rumor that she was not father's child but had been begotten by a passing stranger. Originally, Doro's people were the Kush, an ancient people part of the vast Ethiopian Empire (Williams, 92). Anyanwu's people are the Igbo or Onitsha Ibo people of eastern Nigeria. Traditional Onitsha society, explains ethnologist Richard Henderson, was a "community strongly concerned with maintaining oral accounts of the past." Henderson tells us that "Onitsha lacked an elaborate mythology as its cultural charter, and instead emphasized a quasi-historical 'ideology' based on stories tracing the founding of its villages to prehistoric migrations and political fusions" (31). We see an example of this quasi-history when Doro questions Anyanwu, trying to place her in his long personal history. "'Your people have crossed the Niger'—he hesitated, frowning, then gave the river its proper name—'the Orumili. When I saw them last, they lived on the other side in Benin'" (14). At this point Butler deliberately employs the omniscient narrative voice in conjunction with Doro's to signal the embedded signs of heritage and culture she wants her audience to note. Anyanwu's near poetic reply compresses years of African history, years of tribal warfare and tribal development, years of gradual adaptation to change. "We crossed long ago. . . . Children born in that time have grown old and died. We were Ado and Idu, subject to Benin before the crossing. Then we fought Benin and crossed the river to Onitsha to become free people, our own masters" (14).

Butler's Anyanwu is partly based on a legendary Ibo heroine, Atagbusi, a village protector and a magical "shape shifter." Henderson, whom Butler acknowledges as a source,[7] says that Atagbusi "is said to have been a daughter of the tiny clan called Okposi-eke, a descent group renowned for its native doctors and responsible for magical protection of the northwestern bush outskirts of the town. She was believed capable, as are other persons of Okposi-eke, of transforming herself into various large and dangerous animals, and it is believed that she concocted the medicine that protects the community on its western front" (311).

Like the legendary Atagbusi, Butler's Anyanwu is also a shape-shifter, a woman capable of physical metamorphosis. She can become a leopard, a python, an eagle, a dolphin, a dog, or a man. For self-protection, most of Anyanwu's powers are hidden from the villagers. And to reduce fear of the inexplicable, Anyanwu alters her body gradually so that she seemingly ages at the same rate as the various husbands she has married over the years, the same rate as the people around her. But whenever she chooses Anyanwu can regain her natural body, that of a sturdy, beautiful, twenty-year-old woman. Anyanwu is the village healer, a doctor for her people. She grows traditional herbs to make the customary medicines even though her power to heal does not always require the use of herbs. A respected and powerful person in the village hierarchy, Anyanwu's place is well defined.

> She served her people by giving them relief from pain and sickness. Also, she enriched them by allowing them to spread word of her abilities to neighboring people. She was an oracle. A woman through whom a god spoke. Strangers paid heavily for her services. They paid her people, then they paid her. That was as it should have been. Her people could see that they benefited from her presence, and that they had reason to fear her abilities. Thus she was protected from them—and they from her—most of the time.
>
> (10)

Anyanwu's sense of protection, her maternal instinct of care and concern for her people, is part of the African ethos which pervades the text. Of paramount importance to Anyanwu is the well being and safety of her kin— her children and her grandchildren. This is entirely in keeping with African tradition which holds "children are worth." Henderson affirms this with the observation that the Onitsha are "rooted firmly in notions of filiation and descent. When Onitsha people assess the career of a person, their primary criterion is the number of children he has raised to support and survive him. Children are extolled in proverbs above any other good, even above the accumulation of wealth; 'children first, wealth follows' is a proverb affirming the route to success" (106).

After three hundred years, ten husbands and forty-seven children, Anyanwu's descendants people the land. Their security is the lever Doro uses to pry Anyanwu away from her homeland. He appeals first to her innate sense of isolation and loneliness, proclaiming her place is among her own kind, then he appeals to her maternal spirit, promising children with genetic traits like their mother. "A mother," he tells her, "should not have to watch her children grow old and die. If you live, they should live. It is the fault of their fathers that they die. Let me give you children who will live!" (26) Reluctantly and somewhat apprehensively, Anyanwu agrees to leave the village with Doro. But, when Doro speculates that her children, although they manifest no sign of her mutant ability, are also his peoples' children and that perhaps they should accompany them to the new world, Anyanwu becomes adamant—"you will not touch my children"—and remains so until Doro pledges he will not harm her children.

Unwittingly, Anyanwu's resolute stand in protection of her children gives Doro yet another lever to use against her. Totally devoid of scruples, and possessing a keen insight into her psychological makeup, quite early in their journey to the coast Doro plots the strategy he will use to bind Anyanwu to him. It is a time-encrusted masculine ploy. He will get her pregnant; then, with a new child,

> her independence would vanish without a struggle. She would do whatever he asked then to keep the child safe. She was too valuable to kill, and if he abducted any of her descendants, she would no doubt goad him into killing her. But once she was isolated in America with an infant to care for, she would learn submissiveness.
>
> (30)

Doro's power play, his perception of the most immediate method he can use to control Anyanwu reflects his understanding of cultural ties, of the "appropriate manners and customs" which are part of Anyanwu's historical legacy. Though a powerful woman on her own turf, essentially Anyanwu leaves her tribal homeland to protect her kin.

Of course, Anyanwu never does learn submissiveness. Although she and Doro share a link forged in a bygone age, his name means "the east—the direction from which the sun comes" and hers means "the sun," they are not alike. Anyanwu is distinct from any woman Doro has encountered in thirty-seven hundred years. She is his female counterpart with one important distinction—she is not a predator. Her powers have long made her independent not withstanding her emergence from a culture where wives are considered the property of husbands. In one sense, however, Doro assesses Anyanwu correctly; she remains in his compound for years, she even marries as he directs (primarily out of fear and a strong survival instinct); but, she remains, too, for the sake of the children she bears and out of her concern for the strange, sometimes pitiable, sometimes warped or dangerous children who are the products of Doro's mutant communities. Much of *Wild Seed*'s tension is controlled by Doro's efforts to break Anyanwu, to use and then destroy her. She resists and fights back with the resources she has—her own strength of will. Again, however, the struggle is not solely for her sake but also for the safety of the children, the kin she forever shields.

African kinship networks seem to be the major structural device Butler uses to build dramatic complexity in this novel. When the principal characters first meet, the question of identity is crucial. Following the customary "who are you?" comes the equally important "who are your people?" The latter question springs from the African sense of connectedness to a specific place, a specific people, or a specific heritage. As indicated above, Doro traces his origins to the ancient Kush, one of the three great sub-Saharan societies. Anyanwu ties the history of her people, through wars and unification, to the powerful kingdom of Benin.

The importance of kinship is demonstrated repeatedly. When Anyanwu embarks on an attenuated version of the slaves trade's Middle Passage, she happens upon two captured slaves she can actually help. Fortunately, they have been sold to Doro. It is their good fortune in this sense: Okoye is the son of Anyanwu's youngest daughter. Udenkwo, a young mother stolen from her village and separated from her five-year-old son, is a more distant relative. Anyanwu tells Udenkwo to trace her lineage through her clan and her male ancestry, a process which suggests subtly the value Africans attached to collective identity, familial bonding, and communal history. It happens that one of Udenkwo's ancestors was Anyanwu's eighth son, another, Anyanwu's third husband. (Here Butler slips in a quick feminist thrust: although Udenkwo traces her patrilineage, it is her matrilineal descent, her connection to Anyanwu, literally an earth mother, which saves her.) Because both Okoye and Udenkwo are Anyanwu's descendants, they will be spared the more brutal aspects of slavery. They will not be separated or sold again to some terrifying white plantation master. They will not be assaulted or beaten by Doro or his people. And although they are kinsmen, they will be permitted to marry despite the idea of "abomination" such an act connotes for Anyanwu. The marriage will permit them to offer each other comfort in their new and strange surroundings for as Doro says of his seed people, "our kind have a special need to be either with our kinsmen or others who are like us" (61).

The initial contact with the new world is not quite as traumatic for Anyanwu as it was for true slaves but still, she must cope with complete change. She must reckon with strange and restrictive western clothing, with a new diet (animal milk—another "abomination"), with learning a new language and new customs among a new and foreign people. And she must make all these adjustments in a land where color automatically determines status. The New England village Doro brings Anyanwu to is Wheatley, ostensibly named for an English family Doro supports and a principal cash crop. Butler slips in another quick thrust here for "Wheatley" is an allusion to young Phillis Wheatley, the child stolen from Africa who became known as the "Sable Muse" and was recognized as a significant contributor to 18th-century American poetry. Wheatley, however, is significant for another reason: life in the village cushions the impact of Anyanwu's contact with America's hardening race and color caste system. Doro's villagers are a racial amalgam—Blacks, Indians, mixed bloods, and whites, a mixture not uncommon in the northeastern states before the increase in the slave trade. Anyanwu finds most of the villagers are friendly and also that village society is tight-knit, functioning roughly in a manner that approximates the familiar rhythms of clan life she had known. Relatives within the compound live with or near other relatives. People who share a common language are allowed to group together. Where no blood or tribal ties previously exist, newly formed families function as extended family and

the weak, insecure, or unstable are placed with those who will care for them. The villagers see Doro as a guardian spirit who protects them from Indian raids and like disasters even as he controls their lives. They even make blood sacrifices to him for he takes from among them when he needs a new body. Yet despite the death he inevitably brings, whenever Doro is present in his compound he receives all the homage due a titled tribal elder with many children. And in fact, he has several children within the village.

The most serious clash of wills between Doro and Anyanwu is about the value assigned kinship. Doro's genetics program respects no tradition or socially sanctioned belief. He breeds people, related or not, to improve the pedigree of his stock. When in Wheatley he commands Anyanwu to marry and bear children by his son, and suggests that later she will also bear *his* children, Anyanwu withdraws in total revulsion—a greater abomination she cannot imagine. A century will pass, Anyanwu will have escaped Doro and formed her own special protected community (composed of mutants linked by blood and heightened psychic sensitivity) on a Louisiana plantation where she is the master, before she and Doro can come to civil terms again. They forge a new alliance based on respect and compromise. She recognizes he must kill to live but he learns genuine respect for her feelings and abilities and he also realizes that he must cease killing those of his own who serve him best or any of her close relatives. For Doro to regain Anyanwu's companionship, he must salvage what humanity remains to him.

If kinship is an underlying motif contributing to the dramatic tension in *Wild Seed,* it is clearly the focal point of *Kindred,* the motif underscoring the theme. *Kindred* is outside the "Patternist" saga, yet it shares with *Wild Seed* three common denominators: Black and white characters who move through an historically viable setting, one which explores the tangled complexities of interracial mixing during slavery and beyond; linkage through phenomenal psychic energy; an emphasis on blood ties and the responsibilities that result. The bonds of blood in *Kindred* however are not created by exotic mutation nor genetic engineering. They are the result of plain undisguised lust and the raw exertion of power.

Kindred is a neatly packaged historical novel which uses scenes of plantation life and the techniques of the slave narrative to frame the plot. Dana Franklin, the heroine, is a Black woman, a writer who lives in Los Angeles, California, a woman very much of the present. Her family's roots are in Maryland; a fact made all the more pertinent when Dana finds herself traversing time and geography to move between twentieth-century California and nineteenth-century Maryland. The reason she moves is simple—Rufus Weylin "calls" her to him whenever he gets into trouble he cannot resolve alone, be it drowning, or arson, a bad fall, or a beating. Rufus is a child when he and Dana first meet. He is also white and destined to become her great grandfather, several times removed. The agency which moves Dana is never clear. She never understands *how* it happens. The "why" is easier. Whenever Rufus fears for his life, his subconscious mind somehow reaches out to Dana and transfers her to his setting and his time to meet his need. The only way she can return to her era is if she believes a corresponding threat to her own life exists. Time is totally disjointed for Dana during these transferences. There is no correlation between the time she spends in the past, her own history, and the time which passes while she is absent from her present. Dana's only clue to the mystery surrounding these transfers is the blood tie linking her to Rufus; but even the blood relationship is not, for her, a satisfactory explanation for an inexplicable process.

Once Dana knows Rufus' identity and comprehends what his relationship to her will become, she understands her role more precisely. She is to assure the child's survival until he can father the first branch of her family tree. She must serve as his mentor and be his teacher. The task of trying to mold a humane slave holder, in an era where all the accepted social norms mitigate against the possibility, falls to her. And an awesome responsibility it is considering her circumstances: a modern Black woman periodically surfaces in antebellum Maryland over approximately a twenty-year span, with no free papers, no owner to vouch for her, no way to explain her dress, her speech, or her behavior. Her role is to protect a boy/man who is alternately and erratically "generous and vicious." Immediately, Dana recognizes that she is "the worst possible guardian" for Rufus—"a black woman to watch over him in a society that considered Blacks sub-human, and a woman to watch over him in a society that considered women perennial children" (77). In that age and in that place, Dana is simply a "strange nigger," a fact the child Rufus promptly explains. But because she saves his life and because he realizes they are linked, even though he does not know the extent of their relationship, Rufus, the child, is Dana's unexpected, if unstable, ally.

Quite apart from her role as mentor to Rufus stands Dana's other function. *Kindred,* far more than *Wild Seed,* is an overtly didactic novel, although its artistry is such that one does not realize how much antebellum history gets absorbed. Dana is Butler's tool for sketching a far less romanticized portrait of plantation life from 1815 through the 1830s. She is both a reporter and a corespondent for she witnesses and participates in the slave experience. In fact, *Kindred,* is so closely

related to the experience disclosed in slave narratives that its plot structure follows the classic patterns with only the requisite changes to flesh out character, story, and action.

Dana's loss of innocence, her discovery that she has slave status is as abrupt and brutal as the same discoveries recorded by Frederick Douglass or Harriet Jacobs in their respective narratives. Tom Weylin is a harsh disciplinarian; he beats his slaves, his horses, and his son with the same whip. On her first visit, he almost shoots the "strange nigger" caught with his son and wife. On her second visit, having seen Rufus' scars, Dana acquires some of her own. Seeking safety away from the big house, she leaves the Weylins' to seek help from the black family destined to become her forbears. Patrollers (and Butler carefully identifies them as young whites charged with policing or "maintaining order" among the slave population) arrive at the cabin first. Ostensibly, they have come to see whether a slave husband is meeting illegally with his free wife. The man is. He has no pass permitting his absence from his owner's plantation. For the crime of visiting his family the slave is beaten, then tied to a tree and whipped savagely while his wife and child watch helplessly. Dana is our hidden mute witness. Yet in order to bring her readers closer to the immediacy of the horror we have just seen, Butler moves Dana rapidly from witnessing slavery to experiencing it, from watching, to feeling, to testifying what life was like for a Black woman, even if she were nominally free. After the slave is dragged away, Dana goes to the assistance of his wife. They talk guardedly for Dana cannot explain who she is or where she comes from; nevertheless, the woman grants her permission to stay. Shortly thereafter, Dana steps outside of the cabin and is captured and attacked by one of the patrollers who had returned alone to rape the slave's wife. He realizes instantly that he has not captured the wife but determines almost as quickly that Dana will satisfy his lust. Degradation, brutality, powerlessness, the commonplace violence directed against Black men and women could be no more sharply delineated. Dana's violent struggle to escape the patroller returns her to her own time.

The third time Dana is called into her own history we are privy to a much broader look at life on the plantation from the master's big house to the slave's quarters. She learns that even "favored" house slaves are given a meager diet of table scraps and corn meal mush, occasionally supplemented by what can be stolen from the plantation's larders. Field hands are supposed to work even harder yet are expected to subsist off even less. Just as almost every slave narrative dramatizes the theme of family separation, Butler also brings this theme to life. Dana is sent to the kitchen to learn from Sarah, the plantation's cook. She learns quickly that Sarah has had three children sold away from her; a fourth she was allowed to keep because the child was born mute, therefore "defective," therefore "not worth much" on the slave market. Both in and out of the kitchen Dana discovers what the typical slave's work day is like, first in the big house and later in the fields. She also discovers how slavery can effect a plantation mistress if the woman has no viable authority. Margaret Weylin is described as temperamental, flighty, beautiful, bored, useless. Her husband controls all of the plantation's business affairs and Margaret is left with nothing to do but lavish unreturned affection on her son because "slaves kept her house clean, did much of her sewing, all of her cooking and washing" (109). Margaret cannot even dress or undress without a slave attendant. During her extended third journey into the past, Dana is called to witness another brutal whipping, this time administered for the offense of "answering back." Shortly thereafter, she is the recipient of the same treatment but her offense is far more serious. She has been caught reading to a slave and almost caught teaching slaves thirsty for knowledge how to read and write. An education was, of course, legally denied slaves. Dana's infraction of this rule was both a courageous and dangerous act. The same hostility which fell on Frederick Douglass' attempts to teach his fellow slaves fell on Dana; Tom Weylin seizes her and whips her viciously. He fears a slave who can read and write will escape by forging a pass; for their part, slaves knew being armed with knowledge was freedom and many took great risks in order to learn.

The large, panoramic slice-of-plantation-life we see in this segment of the novel is deftly handled "faction," that blend of authentic verifiable historical fact and well-rendered fiction. Butler treats the recurring themes of casual brutality, forceable separation of families, the quest for knowledge, the desire to escape, the tremendous work loads expected of slaves as effectively as any of the narratives or documentary histories discussing the slavery experience. Her use of these details is more than mere costumery, it is part of the "broad delineation of manners and circumstances" inherent in the historical record and essential for developing plot and character.

Kindred incorporates other devices and themes associated with the slave narrative. These narratives repeatedly demonstrate that slavery as a system displayed little regard for marital status among slaves and no respect for the sanctity of the family unit unless a master chose to recognize a family bond. *Kindred* illustrates this. The narratives record ad infinitum the harsh punishment meted out to any slave who dared evince a sense of self-respect, pride, manhood; but if a slave's spirit would not be broken, it could be sorely tried and his body could be broken.[8] *Kindred* illustrates this extreme as well. Although Butler does not belabor the Christian hypocrisy theme, a popular and effective tactic used in

many narrative accounts to arouse moral indignation, she does make the novel's climatic denouement turn on the other principal axis of the formulaic narrative, careful attention to socially sanctioned yet unacknowledged miscegenation, illicit sex and lust behind the facade of law and respectability.

Tom Weylin has sired at least three children by slave mothers who are still on his plantation. On Dana's second trip to the past the patroller who attacks her was actually returning to the cabin to molest a free Black woman; when he found himself with Dana instead, the difference between the two Black women never disturbed him. On her third journey back, Dana's husband Kevin is transported with her. Because Kevin is white, he affords her some measure of protection by posing as her master. Ironically, in 1976, while their marriage must withstand some subtle societal disapproval, it is at least legally recognized. In 1819 Maryland, Dana and Kevin dare not admit their marital bond because such a relationship is illegal, unimaginable, and dangerous. Casual sexual liaisons between white men and Black women were permissible but intermarriage was not. White men were expected to be rakes, or at least their licentiousness was tacitly condoned; white women were expected to be chaste (certainly they dare not openly consort with Black men the way their husbands, fathers, sons took liberties with Black women); and Black women, of course, were often treated as mere sexual vessels. A brief glance at an actual narrative describing the entanglements produced by an absence of moral integrity is pertinent and may make Butler's account of events at the Weylin plantation even more credible. *Incidents in the Life of a Slave Girl* bluntly discusses the moral "corruption produced by slavery." Jacobs records how "the slave girl is reared in an atmosphere of licentiousness and fear." She is "bribed" . . . or "whipped or starved into submission" to the will of her master and/or his sons. "The slaveholder's sons, are, of course, vitiated, even while boys, by the unclean influences everywhere around them. Nor do the master's daughters always escape." At this point the Jacobs narrative discloses the forbidden activities of some white women in response to the moral degeneracy surrounding them. Jacobs' testimony is explicit:

> They know that the women slaves are subject to their father's authority in all things; and in some cases they exercise the same authority over the men slaves. I have myself seen the master of such a household. . . . It was known in the neighborhood that his daughter had selected one of the meanest slaves on his plantation to be the father of his first grandchild. She did not make her advances to her equals, nor even to her father's more intelligent servants. In such cases the infant is smothered, or sent where it is never seen by any who knows its history. But if the white parent is the father, instead of the mother, the offspring are unblushingly reared for market.

(51-52)

The sexual tension existing at the Weylin home poses both the customary morality/hypocrisy questions and also allows Butler the opportunity to explore another dimension of this tension, sexuality-and-the-white-woman with a little gallows humor. Margaret Weylin discovers that Dana has been sleeping in Kevin's room on a pallet rather than in the attic where other house slaves are expected to sleep. She turns livid with rage. As the Jacobs narrative shows, white men may not be denied their concubines yet they certainly are not supposed to conduct their liaisons in the big house; just down in the slave quarters, out of sight. Margaret slaps Dana, screams at her that she is "a filthy black whore!" and protests loudly that hers is a "Christian house." (108) Of course, Dana cannot retaliate but she does think, rather charitably, that for all her flaws, Margaret Weylin must be a moral woman. However, Dana is soon made privy to an irony she had not anticipated. Margaret, although long married, is smitten by a strong attraction to Kevin; she chases him with a barely concealed ardor and is, therefore, extremely jealous of the near connubial relationship Kevin and Dana attempt to maintain. Jealousy based on the unacknowledged sexual tension between white mistresses and Black slave women linked to white men surfaces frequently in slavery annals.

The most critical sexual relationship in the text however remains the relationship an adult Rufus Weylin forces on Alice Greenwood, a free Black woman on the Weylin plantation. Rufus' feelings for Alice are a mixture of love and lust. He loves her, and he wants her to love him, but he also feels he has a "right" to her and that he is entitled to win her or take her any way he can. Unfortunately, Alice loves a Black man, a slave. Since neither man can openly compete for Alice's affections, this triangle degenerates into an extraordinarily painful relationship, one compounded by rivalry, passion, guilt, love, lust, punishment, pride, power, and implacable hatred. But there are two Black women in young Rufus' life and this adds another level to the sexual tension. Dana and Alice are virtual doubles of each other. Physically, they look alike; intellectually and emotionally, they function as two halves of the same woman, flawed duplicates separated by the dictates of their respective historical time and the resultant sexual-political consciousness each maintains by virtue of their particular social circumstances. In other words, although she is unaccountably displaced in time, Dana retains the attributes of a late twentieth-century woman—knowledgeable, assertive, independent. In contrast, Alice is a nineteenth-century Black woman forced into chattel slavery—by definition her assumed posture is that of ignorance, passiveness, dependence on the will or whim of her owner. Yet even as Butler draws these distinctions they become superficial and the space between Dana and Alice shrinks. For Dana, looking at Alice is like looking at herself, to use Alice Walker's

term, "suspended" by historical circumstance.[9] It is as if the folk wisdom of "there but for the grace of God go I" had suddenly been made manifest.

From Dana, Rufus draws a controlled, limited, camaraderie and intellectual stimulation. From Alice he demands sexual attention and actually expects emotional attachment. Although he cannot make her love him, Rufus can and does force Alice to share his bed. And despite the obvious pain that being a witness to (almost a participant in) this crude liaison causes her, Dana abets it until Alice gives birth to Hagar, the woman who is the founder of her family tree. (Distasteful as the situation is, Dana must assist Rufus in his conquest of Alice or her personal history, her present, will be irrevocably altered. This is a variant of science fiction's time travel paradox, the problem of the time-space continuum theme.) Eventually, unable to endure the vicious games of Rufus (he pretends to sell her children), her powerlessness, or her concubinage any longer, Alice commits suicide. Almost immediately, a chastened and tortured Rufus then transfers his entire emotional attention to Dana, seeing her as a replicate of Alice, virtually the same woman, this time whole and complete. Because the insidious institution of slavery has given him virtual carte blanche power over Black lives, Rufus has no misgivings, feels no remorse about attempting to seduce or possess Dana in the same manner he won Alice—that is, by cajolery if possible, force or violence if necessary. It does not matter that Dana has saved his life repeatedly, that she has been, in common parlance, a "good" slave for Rufus. Nor does it matter that the "love" he bears for her borders on incestuousness; after all, Dana has been his protector, his confidant, his mentor, and in some respects, his mother and his sister. Since selfish, childish and unstable Rufus can think only of his own immediate needs and wants, and since the system gives him the power to take what he wants—he decides that Dana shall replace Alice and he will not hear her refusal.

Without turning to an actual slave narrative, there probably is no more vivid depiction of life on an Eastern Shore plantation than that found in **Kindred.** The composite rendering is as exact as detailed research could make it. Butler admits to having tempered some of the harshness of the real experience because the slave narratives proved such "grim reading" that she realized she would have to present a "cleaned-up, somewhat gentler version of slavery for there was no entertainment in the real thing."[10] **Kindred,** however, is entertaining and compelling; yet for all the history it enlivens, the average reader absorbs the information without any awareness of an inherently didactic purpose framing an exciting, action filled story. Far from impeding the story line, the didacticism informs it.

Kindred and **Wild Seed** break new ground in science fiction. They are both novels which feature Black characters in major significant roles; they both feature Black women as heroic characters, protagonists who either share power with men or who maintain their right to wield power on an equal basis." Neither of the two women principals yields her basic integrity or submits to male dominance. In each novel we look at a speculative past firmly grounded in an African and African-American social and cultural history. Both **Wild Seed** and **Kindred** mirror Lukács' "broad delineation of manners and circumstances attendant upon events," his insistence upon "dramatic character of action," and his large role for voice and dialog within the narrative. Each text is "specifically historical," indeed history is integral to plot, and each effectively welds function to form giving us precise yet "artistically faithful" images of "concrete historical epochs," whole chapters of African-American history, keeping us spellbound all the while.

Butler's works do something else not generally asked of good historical fiction. They reach an entirely different audience, an established science fiction readership which, taken as a whole, is more accustomed to future histories and alien spaces than it is to authentic African and African-American landscapes. That is, I suppose, one of the benefits of renovation: more people are attracted to the old, the historically significant, recreated and redressed in a new light.

Notes

1. The five novels are *Wild Seed* (New York: Pocket Books—Timescape, 1981), *Mind of My Mind* (New York: Avon, 1978), *Survivor* (New York: Signet, 1979), *Patternmaster* (New York: Avon, 1979), and *Clay's Ark* (New York: St. Martin's P, 1984). Butler's "Speech Sounds" appeared in the Mid-December 1983 issue of *Isaac Asimov's Science Fiction Magazine.* "Bloodchild" is scheduled for a June 1984 appearance in the same journal, and "Near of Kin" was published in *Chrysalis* 4, an anthology edited by Roy Torgeson in 1979. Her first published short story, "Crossover," was published in *Clarion,* an anthology edited by Robin S. Wilson in 1971. Butler calls this one and "Childfinder," a story sold to Harlan Ellison's as yet unpublished *The Last Dangerous Visions,* "student writing." Octavia E. Butler, letter to Sandra Y. Govan, 16 April, 1984.

2. For a full discussion of slave narratives as historical documents see Marion Wilson Starling, *The Slave Narrative: Its Place in American History* (Boston: G. K. Hall, 1981) xviii.

3. The narratives cited are nineteenth century narratives which have been republished and are available in a variety of editions. The texts used here are Frederick Douglass, *Narrative of the Life of Frederick Douglass, An American Slave* (1845; New York: Anchor Books, 1973), William and Ellen Craft's *Running a*

Thousand Miles for Freedom, or the Escape of William and Ellen Craft from Slavery (1860; collected in *Great Slave Narratives,* ed. Arna Bontemps [Boston: Beacon P, 1969]), and Harriet Jacobs, *Incidents in the Life of a Slave Girl* (1861; New York: Harcourt Brace, Jovanovich, 1973).

4. Starling, p. 2. The original citation is to "Black Letters," *Graham's Magazine* 42 (January 1853): 215.

5. Several scholars have enlarged upon the principal characteristics of and patterns within the slave narrative. See Richard K. Barksdale, "Black Autobiography and the Comic Vision," *Black American Literature Forum* 15 (Spring 1981): 22-27; John Blassingame, "Black Autobiographies as History and Literature," *The Black Scholar* (Dec. 1973-Jan. 1974): 2-9; and Steven T. Butterfield, "The Use of Language in the Slave Narrative," *Negro American Literature Forum* 6 (Fall, 1972): 72-78. The introduction and comments from various chapters in Butterfield's *Black Autobiography in America* (Amherst: U of Massachusetts P, 1974) also proved useful.

6. Octavia E. Butler, Letter to Sandra Y. Govan, 16 January, 1984.

7. *Ibid.,* Henderson, p. 311

8. Frederick Douglass' *Narrative* provides a graphic depiction of "slave breaking." See chapter ten of the *Narrative,* 63-68.

9. In an interview Alice Walker has argued that Black women in the eighteenth, nineteenth, and early twentieth centuries were "suspended" women. These women "were suspended in a time in history where [their] options were severely limited. And they either kill themselves or they are used up by the men or by the children or by. . . . whatever the pressures against them. And they cannot go anywhere." See Mary Helen Washington, "An Essay on Alice Walker," *Sturdy Black Bridges: Visions of Black Women in Literature.* Eds., Roseann Bell et al. (New York: Anchor Books, 1979) 137-43.

10. Butler to Govan, 16 January, 1984.

11. Butler is fascinated by the question of power. In an interview she said, "I began writing about power because I had so little." Cited in Carolyn S. Davidson's review, "The Science Fiction of Octavia Butler," *Sagala* II, No. 1 (A Howard U Magazine, n.d.). Janice Bogstad devoted an essay to examining this theme called "Octavia E. Butler and Power Relationships," *Janus* 14 (Winter, 1978-79). My own previous essay on Butler, "Connections, Links, and Extended Networks: Patterns in Octavia Butler's Science Fiction," *Black American Literature Forum* 18, (Summer, 1984) also examines this theme.

Works Cited

Butler, Octavia E. *Wild Seed.* New York: Pocket Books—Timescape, 1981.

———. *Kindred.* New York: Doubleday, 1979.

Craft, William & Ellen. *Running a Thousand Miles for Freedom, or The Escape of William & Ellen Craft. Great Slave Narratives.* ed. Arna Bontemps. Boston: Beacon P, 1969.

Douglass, Frederick. *Narrative of the Life of Frederick Douglass, An American Slave.* New York: Anchor, 1973.

Henderson, Richard N. *The King in Every Man: Evolutionary Trends in Onitsha Ibo Society & Culture.* New Haven: Yale U P, 1972.

Jacobs, Harriet. *Incidents in the Life of a Slave Girl.* New York: Harcourt Brace, Jovanovich, 1973.

Lukács, Georg. *The Historical Novel.* New York: Humanities P, 1965.

Starling, Marion. *The Slave Narrative: Its Place in American History.* Boston: G. K. Hall, 1981.

Stepto, Robert. *From Behind the Veil.* Urbana, Illinois: U of Illinois P, 1979.

Williams, Chancellor. *The Destruction of Black Civilization: Great Issues of a Race from 4500 BC to 2000 AD.* Chicago: Third World P, 1974.

Frances Bonner (essay date spring 1990)

SOURCE: Bonner, Frances. "Difference and Desire, Slavery and Seduction: Octavia Butler's *Xenogenesis.*" *Foundation* 48 (spring 1990): 50-62.

[*In the following essay, Bonner chronicles issues of slavery, rape, and power in science fiction works by Butler and others.*]

Octavia E. Butler's recently completed *Xenogenesis* trilogy (*Dawn, Adulthood Rites* and *Imago*) is a striking addition not just to her already fascinating body of work, but also to the field of sf trilogies generally. Too often it seems, especially when the first volume is published as "Book 1 of the whatever trilogy", the reader is prepared for the second-rate and the too heavy-handedly formulaic. The sf reader is often told that trilogies (and even longer sequences) are preferred by publishers because they enhance the predictability of sales, rather than being the result of authors desiring a particular format to enhance the exploration of specific themes or situations. Fortunately, with *Xenogenesis,* the lowering feeling is unnecessary, and indeed, given her predilection for connected novels evidenced in the "Patternist" books, perhaps should not have been felt at all. Yet reception of the second volume was characteristic of responses to the second in the less rewarding trilogies—disappointment and let-down, as if the pleasures of the first could not be sustained. My own first reading of *Adulthood Rites* was no exception, and it is part of

my intention in this essay to explore why this may have been so (re-reading dispelled it) and where the pleasure in so downbeat a sequence lies, within a more general exploration of Butler's concerns.

Xenogenesis tells of the activities of an alien race of gene-traders, the Oankali, and the remnants of humanity they salvage after a global nuclear war for use in their incessant quest for incorporable genetic diversity. The first volume, *Dawn,* is from the point-of-view of Lilith, an Afro-American survivor of the war, who is chosen to train the first group of humans to be returned, with their Oankali mates, to the restored but mutated Earth. *Adulthood Rites,* the second, recounts the early life of Lilith's first son, the human-Oankali construct Akin, as he comes to realize, and then to convince others of, the need for the humans who resisted breeding with the Oankali to be given a chance to continue the (unhybridized) human race, despite the Oankali certainty that humanity is doomed. The last, *Imago,* is the story of another of Lilith's children, Jodahs, the first construct ooloi—the third Oankali sex, whose members are the actual gene manipulators. His acceptance by the polity signals the absorption of humanity into the Oankali (there is no question of equal partnership) and the eventual complete destruction of the Earth. The Oankali rescue neither humanity nor their/our planet, they merely delay our demise.

One of the more unusual aspects of the trilogy is that it has no triumphal conclusion. Humanity has lost before the story begins, has still lost and is disappearing as it ends, and their/our short (and we are assured, temporary) victory occurs, as it were offstage, between *Adulthood Rites* and *Imago.* Even more disturbing from a feminist writer is, as Rachel Pollack's review of *Dawn* points out, the centrality and apparent acceptance of rape.[1] This is no easy read; or to put it more precisely, it is quite an easy read, since stylistically it is even less challenging than the "Patternist" books (the point-of-view only changes between volumes), but it is no easy ingestion. The pleasures are not just fugitive, they are thorny as well, but, to continue the metaphor, once they have hooked in, you cannot readily stop worrying away at them.

Despite a quite ludicrous review in *Publishers Weekly* which claimed that in *Adulthood Rites* "the author gives us a brief ecstatic experience of this utopian alternative to human society,"[2] there is nothing utopian about the societies in *Xenogenesis,* even for the alien Oankali driven by their need to "trade" for genetic diversity. Butler has herself quite explicitly denied utopian intentions. In an interview given at the time she was finishing writing *Dawn,* she claimed "I don't write utopian science fiction because I don't believe that imperfect humans can form a perfect society."[3] And it is the imperfections that interest, even obsess, her. A recurrent concern, especially of the "Patternist" books, is with child abuse and child murder (generally explained there as resulting from the pressures of uncontrolled telepathy) and in the interview just quoted she says that the Oanka-li's diagnosis of what is wrong with humanity is hers too—intelligence and hierarchical behaviour (which latter she believes inborn) is a potentially lethal combination.[4] Not only would it be impossible reasonably to consider Butler's work without reference to her race, it would be improper to do so given her foregrounding of it. The specificity of the Afro-American experience is basic to the "Patternist" books and the one-off *Kindred,* and central to *Xenogenesis.* The general absence of black sf writers (and readers) has not infrequently been a matter for comment. Kathleen L. Spencer's aside in her review of a combined Starmont guide to the work of Butler, Suzy McKee Charnas and Joan D. Vinge, that Butler was "one of only three Black sf writers to date and the only Black woman"[5] led both to protesting letters about the possible existence of "unknown" black sf writers and readers and Spencer's admission that she should have written "three recognized Black SF writers", but to no new names (the other two given were Samuel R. Delany and Steven Barnes) and not even a comment on Butler's being the only black woman.[6]

Butler has explained the absence of black sf writers as derived from the way the lack of black characters in the literature limits its appeal to black readers (and writers of sf, arguably even more than other genres, come from devoted sf readers). Compounding this has been the tendency of editors and publishers to regard the inclusion of black characters as a distraction, acceptable only if the focus of the story is on racism.[7] Even so, there has been the belief that aliens can substitute as all-purpose Others. One big blue extra-terrestrial whose humanity is revealed and accepted can be metaphorically substituted for an examination of any number of actual social divisions, as witness many past discussions on the absence of women/non-Caucasians/homosexuals/disabled people from sf. This very point was at the centre of Butler's response in 1980 to a question addressed by *Future Life* to a number of writers: "What role can and should science fiction writers play in working with America's major corporations in planning for the future of society?"[8]

Adele S. Newson has said that the myth that blacks are uninvolved in sf is "fed by the notion that they cannot afford to indulge in fantasy"[9] which may help explain why it is that Delany has to keep defending himself against charges by whites that he is not "black enough".[10] It is not, however, a suggestion he advances in his exposition which, no doubt not fortuitously, chimes very well with Butler's exasperation with expectations that the traces of blackness in black writing will be stereotypical and deal unrelievedly with racism.

Concerned as she is with the specificity of the Afro-American experience, it is unsurprising that Butler again and again explores the phenomenon of slavery, in particular the initial stage in which the self—body, soul and subjectivity—is stolen and declared an item of exchange. While most obvious in *Wild Seed* and *Kindred,* people are appropriated by others in virtually all her writings. Furthermore after the appropriation there are usually the issues both of forced reproduction and of love for the captor—the former of these at least, characteristic of the Afro-American slave experience.

It is worth recalling that part of the point of Delany's famous discovery late in his reading of Heinlein's *Starship Troopers* that one of the characters was Filipino was that it had been possible even for a black reader to assume that the character was white. It is unlikely that any reader could get far into Butler's novels in ignorance of the race or ethnicity of any but the most incidental character. To some extent this is a function of the times and the abjuring of the integrationist model. If only in her assertion of the importance and value of difference, Butler is as postmodern as sf writers come. In stylistic concerns it is another matter altogether. She is a traditionalist. She is the absent case in Maria Minchin Brewer's suggestion that male writers of what she terms "surviving fictions" are postmodern only in their experimental style, but not in their attitudes and concerns. (Brewer, who I suspect has not read Geoff Ryman, to name just one male writer who should escape her accusation, cites various canonical feminist sf works as escaping into thorough-going post-modernity.[11] I am not entirely convinced here either, except, of course, for Joanna Russ.) As well as her insistence on difference, her concern with survival in a (post-)nuclear world and, as I intend to demonstrate later, her attitude to the Oedipal conflict, are characteristically (female) postmodern.

A comparison of Butler's and Delany's treatments of slavery is instructive, for both of them explore the intermingling of slavery and desire in the sexual relationships between slave and owner. The complex meditations on pleasure in perversity, the sado-masochistic game-playing and role reversals of the "Nevèryöna" series is not for Butler—she is neither that kind of adult writer, nor that kind of postmodern. She is also constrained by different literary allegiances, especially ones which hold her in some ways closer to the mundane world. Not only does she locate her settings geographically closer to home (and usually on Earth), but temporally they are closer too. The far future is not her domain. Nor does she perceive what she writes as fantasy. Indeed the only one of her books she refers to as fantasy is *Kindred*—the one marketed as mainstream, the one most readily perceived as subject to requirements of historical accuracy.

It may be that it is her gender which is of greater importance to the question of desire, if it is this that results in the various investigations of forced reproduction. In both *Wild Seed* and *Mind of My Mind,* Doro breeds "his" people, without regard for their own wishes; in *Kindred,* the time-travelling twentieth-century heroine, Dana, fears her existence depends on her keeping the nineteenth-century white slave owner Rufus alive to father her grandmother on the black servant/slave Alice; in *Survivor* the alien Garkohn steal humans to breed hybrids; and in *Xenogenesis* the sole purpose of the Oankali's salvaging of humanity is for breeding, to incorporate some of their genes into the next manifestation of the Oankali. But these are not stories of undiluted outrage. As pleasure and fetishism mut(at)e the power relations in Delany's novels, so love enters Butler's. But love rarely effects her power relations. The moral difficulties such unequal love creates are solved to some extent in *Xenogenesis* by the announcement that love is chemical. The element of choice has disappeared. Where the slave or captive may have had no choice about bearing the captor's child (or little, if male, in impregnating the designated woman), loving him had been another matter. The Oankali ooloi however create a chemical bond between human and alien. There is still a degree of equivocation however, for while breeders may blame the bond, not all humans succumb. The resisters reject chemical entrapment, even at the cost of infertility and avoidable ill-health.

It is probably fatuous to ask whether gender is less important than race in Butler's work. Possibly it is, and given the comparative scarcities of black and female sf writers, who would want to suggest it should be otherwise? The conjunction however is what matters; gender articulates race in a most illuminating way. The point is perhaps best made by Adele S. Newson who says that in Lilith's struggle to remain on terms with the Oankali and her fellow humans, the plot of *Dawn* parallels "the historical, albeit self-imposed, function of the Afro-American woman".[12] As mediator, Lilith must bear the odium of her fellows as well as her own guilt over the collaboration, tempered only by her belief that without her, things would be worse. That this too is nothing new for a Butler heroine is revealed by Ruth Salvaggio's comment about the heroines of *Wild Seed* and *Survivor*: "Anyanwu closely resembles Alanna, accepting the constraints of her world and trying to make something decent and productive out of the indecent situation in which she finds herself."[13] The particular articulation can also be seen in the importance of food and the domestic—not just a sign of the female, but, with for example the emphasis on yams, cassava and African agricultural practices, a sign of the black female of African origin.

That we should privilege the viewpoints of the subjugated, and specifically those of women of colour, has

long been the argument of the primatologist and historian of science, Donna Haraway.[14] This is not because they are immune from criticism, but because they are more likely to be aware of the various tricks of the dominant in asserting the adequacy, indeed sufficiency, of its knowledge. Haraway argues most persuasively for situated knowledge, for the acknowledged partial perspective rather than for implicit assertions of universalism. In the specificity of the acknowledged position from which Butler writes, she provides just such an example, and Haraway implicitly accepts this in her most recent work which includes an analysis of *Dawn.*

I have already indicated that Butler's works repeatedly assert the value of difference. Haraway too sees this as one of Butler's main themes, saying that *Dawn,* like many of Butler's other fictions "is about resistance to the imperative to recreate the sacred image of the same",[15] and adding that "from the perspective of an ontology based on mutation, metamorphosis and diaspora, restoring the sacred image can be a bad joke".[16] The explicit raison d'être of the Missionaries of *Survivor* is to maintain the sacred (human) image of the Creator. Likewise, Lilith's name, that of Eve's uppity predecessor, while linking her to the Oankali whose tentacles are often referred to as snakes, emphasises her repudiation of the (human) Creator. The transitions of the mutant Doro's people and their descendants, the Patternists, during which they reveal their psychic powers, foreshadow the metamorphoses of the Oankali and their genetic constructs during which their gender is revealed. Both groups are diasporic. Difference is not just a given that is accepted, it is something which is intensified, enhanced and valued, even if not unequivocally—it is, after all, most desired by Doro and the Oankali whose viewpoints the narratives, but not necessarily the narrative intentions, endorse. The shifting points-of-view themselves also present difference.

Haraway notes one point on which difference is not explored, saying that heterosexuality is not questioned.

> "The different social subjects, the different genders that
> could emerge from another embodiment of resistance
> to compulsory heterosexuality and reproductive politics
> do not inhabit this *Dawn*."[17]

Yet perhaps she is being too harsh. A concentration on forced reproduction leaves limited space for the non-heterosexual, but the unease of Tino, the human male with his male Oankali mate (the mixed families of *Xenogenesis* have five members: one male and one female human and a male, female and ooloi Oankali) raises, even if it does not explore, the issue. It may also be that readers find it explored in the relationship between the part-human ooloi, Jodahs, and his male human mate, Tomas. Although the pronoun "it" is used throughout to refer to an ooloi, and this linguistic choice foregrounded by reference to the impossibility of doing so in languages lacking neuter pronouns,[18] the tendency to read as male a character unmarked by specific gender may result in a perception of Jodahs as a male and hence of Tomas's eagerness for sex with it, as homosexual. Certainly with this mating the question of rape does not occur.

Butler's dealing with homosexuality is characteristically oblique. In **Wild Seed,** the shape-shifting Anyanwu spends many years married to a white woman, who is however aware that her husband is really a black woman. Although Denice, the wife, appears only as a photograph, Anyanwu explains to Doro that they married not only to save Denice (who saw ghosts) from an asylum, but also "because after a while, we started to want each other".[19] Earlier, however, Amber in **Patternmaster** quite cheerfully announces her bisexuality. Haraway's comment about **Dawn** does however retain its force for women, not just in that book but in the trilogy as a whole. Women are not there allowed to opt out of heterosexuality and they escape forced reproduction only by accepting no reproduction at all.

Difference is not however Butler's dominant theme. That is power. Slavery is after all the most dramatic manifestation of unequal power. Butler has commented on the effect of her fascination with power. "I began writing about power because I had so little."[20] Writing before the publication of **Clay's Ark** or **Xenogenesis,** Sandra Y. Govan remarked how in each of the novels to that point "the implicit struggle for power revolves around explicit conflicts of will and the contests of survival a heroine endures."[21] Certainly this is Lilith's story too and, and if it is modulated a little when the heroine is replaced by her male and ooloi children, then that serves to emphasise how central the gender articulation is.

I referred above to Butler's endorsement of her Oankali creations' perception of hierarchical behaviour as at the root of humanity's problems. Yet, just because the Oankali claim to have avoided hierarchies, it does not mean they have eschewed power. As Haraway says "hierarchy is not power's only shape."[22] They deny humans choice as a matter of course. The exceptions are moments to remark, or are freighted with such negative consequences that they verge on the suicidal. The Oankali know best. As Rachel Pollack notes "this recalls that favorite White American fantasy, the benefits of slavery for the happy Blacks."[23] Yet as Pollack also emphasises, Butler is not pointing an easy ethical lesson, she is examining a "terrible conundrum": at times the Oankali seem right, for the humans have destroyed their planet by their foolishness. The core of the conundrum, and one suspects the crunch for Pollack, is the question of rape.

Other writers on Butler do not foreground the issue; indeed until **Xenogenesis** (with the notable exception of **Kindred**) neither did Butler—it is subsumed under forced reproduction. In **Dawn,** however, the practice is named, but in circumstances that echo oddly. Lilith, using her Oankali-improved strength, saves one of the women she is preparing to return to Earth from rape by a newly awoken man. The woman questions whether the enhanced Lilith is really human after all. Lilith dismisses the question "If I weren't human, why the hell would I care whether you got raped?"[24] Yet one of the things for which she is preparing her charges is enforced mating with the Oankali. Pollack's paralleling of the ooloi Nikanj's knowing that Lilith's lover Joseph "really" wants to have sex with it, despite his inability to say "yes", with the typical male defense to rape charges,[25] is telling. The unimportance of human verbal consent to Oankali behaviour (and their privileging of what they read the body desiring) recurs when Nikanj makes Lilith pregnant. In a central moment, when asked if she had really wanted a child, Lilith replies "Oh, yes. But if I had the strength not to ask, it should have had the strength to let me alone."[26] The Oankali may have power over the choices of the humans, but over their own mating urge, they are powerless (or choose to declare themselves so). Butler has them revealed as driven by their need to "trade" for genetic diversity as humans are by their hierarchical behaviour.

Yet it remains unclear whether Butler is engaging in her characteristic equivocating, or does not herself regard Oankali sexual behaviour as rape. She certainly calls it by other names. "Rape" is used only of humans—not just on the occasion just quoted, but also intermittently in **Imago** where it serves as part of the revelation of the degeneration of humanity in the absence of Oankali. As far as the aliens are concerned, it seems to me quite reasonable to apply it to the early instances of interspecies sexual activity, when they drug the humans into insensitivity, even insensibility, and submission (the very figures of "white" slavery). Yet the language used would not be all that inappropriate at a getting-to-know-you party. A quite disquieting moment occurs in **Dawn** just after that to which Pollack refers. Nikanj has once again drugged Joseph because it "knows" he really wants to repeat the experience (on the first occasion he did not even get the opportunity to refuse, being anaesthetized at the moment consent could have been asked) and Lilith, instead of joining in the experience which is supposedly better with three, sits back and watches. "She was patient and interested. This might be her only chance ever to watch up close as an ooloi seduced someone."[27] Throughout the trilogy much is made of Nikanj's powers of seduction (in **Adulthood Rites** a human male even makes a friendly joke about it), but this is also our first opportunity to observe an ooloi "seduction" and I for one certainly find the scene, in which a drugged man is subjected not just to casuistry but to a "poor little me" turn from a misunderstood alien, a little hard to take. I wish in some ways that I could say I found it utterly repellent; it would be so much easier. There are points of identification with Nikanj available; the idea that any human would be preferable to the lovable sensitive alien is touching. If only there were not the drugged removal of volition!

It is I think particularly notable that Butler presents this scene with the male rather than the female human and indeed does not show us the scene in which Nikanj first rapes/seduces Lilith at all. It occurs between the first and second sections of *Dawn* and is not even recalled in memory. It is however a most telling absence. With Lilith there to assure the reader that the sexual experience is pleasurable and something she is all too willing to engage in herself, rape more easily masquerades as seduction. Her own first encounter, devoid of any such commentary, would be difficult to present convincingly as a desirable experience.

The problem of Oankali rape/seduction echoes that in the "Patternist" books of the sexual activity of Doro and his daughters. The incest is muted not only by Doro's endorsement of it as part of his breeding plans, but by his "wearing" different bodies—the body which sleeps with the daughter is not the one which engendered her. The paedophilic aspect is blurred by the imprecision about the age at which it occurs. The only one of which we are certain is late teenage, but there is a suggestion that this may have been unusual restraint on Doro's part. That the children are not averse, having been brought up to expect it and having a semi-mystical regard for their father, removes accusations of rape. Certainly Butler presents Doro as a monster and yet there are oddities about the general presentation of sexual relationships between beings of unequal power bubbling away beneath the surface of Butler's fictions. One of the problems I have is in determining the extent to which they are in the books' unconscious or hers.

One obvious seat of power is the family, yet, in common with other feminist writers, Butler is concerned with examining alternatives to the nuclear family, at least in part to relocate power. In the "Patternist" books, children are often adopted to remove them from actual or potential child abuse, and domestic groupings tend to be larger than currently regarded as normal. In *Xenogenesis,* Butler goes into considerable detail about the human-Oankali families and their operation. Because the Oankali extend life-spans, particularly the reproductive portion of them, the number of children is great, especially as there are two females both giving birth. (In *Imago,* late in Lilith's life, an aside informs us that in view of her and her mates' age, they are now having "only" a pair of children a decade. Since she is at least 100 and quite possibly 200 or so at this time, the size of her family can only be conjectured.) In any case,

Butler avoids Oedipal constructions, with their power determinations, by all the means at her disposal. The incest taboo is rejected both by Doro and by the Oankali, who customarily mate brother and sister through unrelated ooloi. The acceptance of the wandering male, refusing monogamy and family involvement, in both "Patternist" books and *Xenogenesis,* not only makes Oedipal passages problematic, but reflects the characteristic asserted to be typical of Afro-American males and in fact increasingly common of males in Anglo-Celtic dominant cultures generally. As a third blow to Freudian normality, in *Xenogenesis* gender is physically determined by affinity with the same-sex parent, not psychically through rivalry and thwarted desire, or the establishing of Otherness. Although Butler is not one of the female writers of "surviving fictions" that Maria Minich Brewer considers, her comment that they

> "link the nuclear narrative to a politics of gender that thoroughly displaces the Oedipal narrative-of-conflict with the system by inventing new forms of non-hierarchical mediation and community."[28]

certainly applies, (The term "nuclear narrative" here should not be read in a limiting way; Butler's postnuclear stories are indisputably such narratives.)

My comments so far have been concerned to demonstrate Butler's common concerns in the "Patternist" and *Xenogenesis* books. Yet there are discontinuities too. The webs of connectedness that Govan identified as central to the "Patternist" books, and evident in *Kindred* too, are not so important. Controlled creation has overtaken the mix of attempted control and the operation of chance; mutation in *Xenogenesis* ceases to be accidental. Because, as Haraway points out, the Oankali differ from humans by engaging in self-formation not through non-living technologies, but on life itself,[29] there is an absence of Oankali art. This is not characteristic of Butler—Anyanwu's Igbo pots and Jan's learning blocks and paintings (in *Mind of My Mind*) testify to this—but it is not an accidental omission. A sustained passage in *Adulthood Rites* details Akin's Oankali-derived distaste for myths and any stories not based on fact; we are repeatedly told how bare the Oankali living spaces are and how only the humans (indeed only women, though this may not be a meaningful exclusion) paint and draw; for quite some time the Oankali deny Lilith even writing materials. In case readers could get to the end of the trilogy still deluded that Butler was depicting an utopia, they should be warned that the society depicted would have no use for the depiction: sf along with all the other "lies" (Akin's term for fiction) would disappear.

I said at the beginning that I would attempt to explore my initial disappointment with *Adulthood Rites* and where the pleasure in so downbeat a trilogy lies. I trust

I have done the second already; the pleasures in teasing out the patterns and preoccupations of Butler's work are considerable, as is the hard work of reconciliation. I suspect that one of the reasons for my initial personal disappointment with *Adulthood Rites* was something which is not uncommon in Butler's novels, which I think of as the disappearing heroine. Readers of the Gollancz paperback edition graced with John Varley's comment that *Dawn* "Gives us the best heroine I've met in a long time", are likely to be particularly disappointed, for *Adulthood Rites* gives us little of her. I agree with Varley; Lilith is a wonderful heroine—strong, competent, flawed, moody, fighting to make the best of a situation over which she has virtually no control. Childlike, I wanted to read more about her in the second book and watch her win out, but Butler is not concerned with satisfying childish longings in adults. *Adulthood Rites* is from her son's point-of-view and Lilith becomes a comparatively minor character. With *Imago* the shift in point-of-view to the ooloi, Jodahs, and the continuation of Lilith in a minor role is not unexpected. The change is not as startling however as that from *Wild Seed* to *Mind of My Mind* where Anyanwu/Emma not merely becomes a minor character, but also alters in moral evaluation (from heroine-saviour to minor nuisance). Relevant here however are the disjunctions in chronologies—of narration, writing and publication—that do not apply to *Xenogenesis,* In narrative chronology *Wild Seed* precedes *Mind of My Mind* and is followed by *Clay's Ark, Patternmaster* and *Survivor,* yet the publication order is *Patternmaster* (1976), *Mind of My Mind* (1977), *Survivor* (1978), *Wild Seed* (1980) and *Clay's Ark* (1984), while *Survivor,* although revised extensively in the light of *Patternmaster* and *Mind of My Mind,* was initially written considerably before.[30]

The problems of disjunctive chronologies have been referred to (though not under that name) by Delany in a complaint about publishers' impositions of narrative chronology on collections of works in a series in a way which obscures if not obliterates the writer's self-critical dialogue with her- or himself.[31] This may give an extra clue as to why series, which may lack pre-determined structures, are often more satisfying intellectually than the more predictably-structured trilogies. Nonetheless a comparison of the reappearance of, for example, Lessa in Anne McCaffrey's "Pern" series with the reappearance of Lilith in the two later *Xenogenesis* volumes is an indication that trilogies are not always less surprising. (It is, incidentally, hard to imagine anything more heretical than an authorial re-evaluation of Lessa, who even when not the main focus of a novel can never be other than the dominant character in any scene in which she appears.)

I cannot resist concluding with another quotation from Donna Haraway. No reader, one trusts, could leave Oc-

tavia E. Butler's work believing she valued the fixity of the Natural. Whether by mutation, transmutation or direct manipulation, in her fictions nature changes. The most negatively valued groups of humans are those who, like the Missionaries in *Survivor,* attempt to stop variation. Even *Xenogenesis*'s resister humans are only allowed to start breeding again on a transformed Mars. As in so many other instances, I concur with Haraway when she says "I am not interested in policing the boundaries between nature and culture—quite the opposite, I am edified by the traffic."[32] Reading Butler is part of such an edification.

Notes

1. Rachel Pollack, review of *Dawn: Xenogenesis 1, Foundation* 44, Winter 1988/9, pp. 68-71, pp. 69-70.

2. Review of *Adulthood Rites, Publishers Weekly,* 233 (18), 6 May 1988, p. 98.

3. Frances M. Beal, "Black Women and the Science Fiction Genre", (Interview with Octavia Butler), *Black Scholar,* 17(2), 1986, pp. 14-18, p. 14.

4. Ibid., p. 17.

5. Kathleen L. Spencer, "One Out of Three", *Science-Fiction Studies* 43, 14(3), November 1987, pp. 407-410, p. 407.

6. Letters from Frederick Lerner and Graham Stone and responses from Kathleen L. Spencer in *Science-Fiction Studies* 44, 15(1), March 1988, pp. 118-9 and 48, 16(2), July 1989, pp. 246-8.

7. Beal: op. cit., pp. 16, 18.

8. Jeffrey Elliot, "Future Forum", *Future Life,* 17, March 1980, pp. 59-62, p. 60. As a devotee of this particular kind of prognostication, may I recommend this example as a humdinger of a piece of ephemera.

9. Adele S. Newson, review of *Dawn* and *Adulthood Rites, Black American Literature Forum,* 23(2), Summer 1989, pp. 389-396, p. 389.

10. Samuel R. Delany, "The Semiology of Silence", *Science-Fiction Studies* 42, 14(2), July 1987, pp. 134-164, p. 158.

11. Maria Minchin Brewer, "Surviving Fictions: Gender and Difference in Postmodern and Postnuclear Narrative", *Discourse,* 9, Spring-Summer 1987, pp. 37-52, p. 46.

12. Newson: op. cit., p. 391.

13. Ruth Salvaggio, "Octavia Butler and the Black Science Fiction Heroine", *Black American Literature Forum,* 18(2), Summer 1984, pp. 78-81, p. 81. This issue of the journal is entirely devoted to black sf, with articles and bibliographies on Butler and Delany and an interview with the black heroic fantasy writer Charles R. Saunders.

14. Donna Haraway, "A Manifesto for Cyborgs: Science, Technology, and Socialist Feminism in the 1980s", *Socialist Review* 80, 1985, pp. 65-107; and "Situated Knowledges: The Science Question in Feminism and the Privilege of Partial Perspective", *Feminist Studies* 14(3), Fall 1988, pp. 575-599.

15. Donna Haraway, "Monkeys, Aliens and Women: Love, Science, and Politics at the intersection of Feminist Theory and Colonial Discourse", *Women's Studies International Forum* 12(3), pp. 295-312, p. 307.

16. loc. cit.

17. Ibid., p. 309.

18. Butler's decision on this is in contrast to Ursula Le Guin's well-known earlier (in-)decision over a similar situation in *The Left Hand of Darkness.* (Ursula Le Guin, "Is Gender Necessary?", in *The Language of the Night,* New York, Berkeley, 1982, but also see the story "Winter's King" and in particular the introduction to it in *The Wind's Twelve Quarters,* and Le Guin's most recent comments on the problem added in the new edition of *The Language of the Night,* London, Women's Press, 1989, p. 145.)

19. Octavia E. Butler, *Wild Seed,* New York, Popular Books, 1988, p. 218.

20. Carolyn S. Davidson, "The Science Fiction of Octavia Butler", *Sagala,* 2(1), 1981, quoted in Sandra Y. Govan, "Connections, Links and Extended Networks: Patterns in Octavia Butler's Science Fiction", *Black American Literature Forum* 18(2), 1984, pp. 82-87.

21. Ibid., p. 82.

22. Haraway (1989), op. cit., p. 308.

23. Pollack, op. cit., p. 70.

24. Octavia E. Butler, *Dawn,* London, VGSF, 1988, p. 190.

25. Pollack, op. cit., p. 69.

26. Octavia E. Butler, *Adulthood Rites,* London, VGSF, 1989, p. 25.

27. Butler (1988), op. cit., p. 199.

28. Brewer: op. cit., p. 47.

29. Haraway (1989): op. cit., p. 308.

30. Beal: op. cit., p. 18.

31. Delany: op. cit., p. 156.

32. Haraway (1989): op. cit., p. 307.

Ashraf H. A. Rushdy (essay date February 1993)

SOURCE: Rushdy, Ashraf H. A. "Families of Orphans: Relation and Disrelation in Octavia Butler's *Kindred.*" *College English* 55, no. 2 (February 1993): 135-57.

[*In the essay below, Rushdy analyzes the concepts of history, memory, and family in Butler's* Kindred.]

i am accused of tending to the past
as if i made it,
as if i sculpted it
with my own hands. i did not.
the past was waiting for me
when i came,
a monstrous unnamed baby,
and i with my mother's itch
took it to breast
and named it
History.
she is more human now . . .

lucille clifton

Probably no contemporary African-American novelist has so successfully exercised the imagination of her readers with acute representations of familial and historical relations as has Octavia Butler, and nowhere more so than in her 1979 novel ***Kindred. Kindred*** is a novel which challenges our usual generic categories. It seems to be both science fiction, because it apparently employs time travel, and historical novel, because it is predominantly set in antebellum Maryland. In the novel, Dana, a black woman celebrating her twenty-sixth birthday in America's bicentennial year, discovers that her familial past has a unique claim on her: her white, slaveholding great-grandfather Rufus Weylin is able to "call" her back to antebellum Maryland whenever his life is endangered; she is able to return to contemporary Los Angeles only when *her* life is endangered. Her encounters with the past complicate her relationship to "home" and "kin," forcing her to reconcile her Los Angeles home in 1976 with her nineteenth-century Maryland home and to see the differences and similarities between her relationship to her white husband, Kevin Franklin, who is described as a "kindred spirit" (57), and her relationship to her white ancestor, who is literally her "kindred."

Critics have reached various conclusions about the genre of ***Kindred*** (see Crossley; Willis; Shinn; Johnson; Salvaggio). Butler herself denies that it is science fiction (Beal 14). The point of generic classification is rendered moot if we accept the connection Fredric Jameson finds between science fiction and historical fiction: what both science fiction and historical fiction do, he argues, is create a "violent formal and narrative dislocation" in their modes of representing the future or the past in order to restore "life and feeling to the only intermittently functioning organ that is our capacity to organize and live time historically" (284). ***Kindred*** is most fruitfully seen as part of a movement in recent African-American fiction to produce the conditions of historicity by reconstructing the past to endow the present with new meaning—especially by implementing what Mary Frances Berry and John Blassingame call "long memory." "Much of black writing in the last decade or so," writes Charles Johnson in 1988, has been a concerted "meditation on remembrance" (74).

As Robert Crossley notes, **Kindred** belongs to this "literature of memory" (xiv). Karla Holloway calls **Kindred** a novel of "ancestry" and "translucence" in which there is a "hefty historical revisioning of black women's experiences" through the agency of memory (113, 133), and Missy Dehn Kubitschek says it offers an almost perfect paradigm of the strategies of contemporary African-American women novelists in depicting an encounter with history as the liminal act of assuming a developed identity (22). **Kindred,** like other such novels, notes Kubitschek, transforms the concept of "history" by enlarging its definition to include "memory" (149).

Octavia Butler, however, goes one step further. Like other novels in this tradition of rewriting history by incorporating a familial and racial past into the received historiographical tradition, **Kindred** is a novel of memory (in much the same way as Gayl Jones's *Corregidora*). Unlike those other novels, **Kindred** is *also* a historical novel set in the antebellum South (in much the same way as Sherley Anne Williams's *Dessa Rose*). Butler, that is, writes one novel which represents both primary forms of the narrative of slavery. Her achievement is to make memory transformative to the degree of literally translating the remembering subject into the past. The difference between Butler's novel and, say, David Bradley's *The Chaneysville Incident,* in which the past is narrated and effectively transforms the present, is that Butler treats time as a more flexible structure and takes more seriously than most the theory of a mind-body continuum. I am not denying that Dana travels back in time to antebellum Maryland; she does— and that is part of the magic of Butler's novel. What I am saying is that her time travel is less important to the way she defines herself and her place in history than her narrative version of that time travel, a narrative version in which memory is the most important means of transportation.

Kindred begins with a "Prologue" about loss and ends with an "Epilogue" about partial recovery. In the first words of the novel, Dana tells us that she has "lost an arm," "lost about a year" of her life, and lost "much of the comfort and security" she had "not valued until it was gone" (9). The only thing she apparently has not lost is Kevin, although it is only after he is released by the police that she realizes she "hadn't lost him too." The rest of the novel is about recovery—more precisely, the rest of the novel *is* the recovery of a coherent story explaining Dana's various losses. When she talks with Kevin about the loss of her arm, she notes that she "didn't know" what happened. Kevin, too, apparently doesn't know (11). For them to understand their recent experience of loss and their present condition as historicized beings, both Kevin and Dana require a return to the past in the form of a narrative. "The existential question of self-identity," writes Anthony Giddens, "is bound up with the fragile nature of the biography which

the individual 'supplies' about herself. A person's identity is not to be found in behaviour, nor—important though this is—in the reactions of others, but in the capacity *to keep a particular narrative going*" (54). Dana provides the possibility for that narrative—which would give her a sense of selfhood by returning her to and re-engaging her with the past—when she employs her memory: "I closed my eyes again remembering the way I had been hurt—remembering the pain" (10). Within the parameters of her recollection, as presented in the novel's seven chapters, we receive the story of Dana's unique relationship to her slaveholding great-grandfather Rufus Weylin. Dana's memory, then, acts as a framing device for constructing the story of her relationship with her ancestor. The first sentence of the first narrative chapter reminds us that we are remembering along with Dana: "The trouble began long before June 9, 1976, when I became aware of it, but June 9 is the day I remember" (12).

Remembering for Dana involves different kinds of intensity. After her first trip back, she considers remembering to be like reading—"like something I got secondhand" (17). But by the time she nears the end of her relation with the past, she finds that there is "no distance at all" between "myself and this alien time" (221). Dana's act of memory, however, is more than a framing device for narrating her story. Her memory is a performance of history, a performance of such potency that it incorporates her into the past, leaving "no distance at all" between her and the remembered events. These performances of what Ellison calls "unwritten history" are necessary for African-American subjects precisely because the history is unwritten. At the end of Butler's novel, Dana and Kevin drive to modern Maryland and look in the Maryland Historical Society for historical records of the events they had lived through. All they find, however, are scattered newspaper reports of the death of Mr. Rufus Weylin in a fire and the consequent sale of his slaves (262-63). All the written documentation available attests to, then, is that the master of the plantation, Mr. Rufus Weylin, died under mysterious conditions. Nobody else in the newspaper reports matters. They are known merely as the "slaves from Mr. Rufus Weylin's estate" and "listed by their first names with their approximate ages and their skills given" (262-63). Dana discovers what Ellison had discovered: that "our unwritten history looms" as the "obscure alter ego" of "our recorded history" (124). That "unwritten history" is revived at a cost, however, just as it is repressed at a cost. For Dana, the retrieving of the past in an act of what Ellison calls "historical memory" costs her an arm, amongst other things.

Working within one interpretive framework, we might be tempted to agree with Karla Holloway that "Dana's loss of her left arm figuratively expresses her loss of the symbol-making intuitive side of the feminine" (117).

Dana, however, loses more than her arm; she also loses two teeth from a punch in the mouth (174) and is viciously scarred from a brutal whipping (113). Moreover, given the tension between memory and historical records as it is represented in this novel, we might suggest that Dana's losses and scars figure the way that the past exacts a cost which is not just psychic. We recall that Dana began the story by recounting both her physical and her psychic losses (her arm and her sense of well-being). As with other novels in which there is an implicit play between "remembering" and "dismembering"—novels such as Sherley Anne Williams's *Dessa Rose* or Toni Morrison's *Beloved*—the slave's body with its scarifications becomes a site of historical interpretation.

Like Morrison's Sethe, whose back is marked as a sign of her mental scarring, or Dessa, whose genitalia are scarred as a sign of the sexual commodification of black women (or as a symbol of how slave women are made to signify the "vestibular," as Hortense Spillers cogently argues [76]), Dana loses part of her body to history, part of her fundamental integrity to the past. The difference, obviously, is that Dana loses her arm to an era in which she does not live, at least not in the same way and to the same degree as Dessa and Sethe live in the antebellum South. Unlike Dessa or Sethe, who lose parts of their body *in* the past, Dana loses parts of her body *to* the past. Dana's lost arm, then, is less a sign of how the peculiar institution brutalized her body—although her body certainly suffers from its exposure to slavery—than a symptom of how recovering the past involves losing a grip on the present. The task of "genealogy," notes Foucault, is "to expose a body totally imprinted by history and the process of history's destruction of the body" (148). Butler, who is writing a kind of genealogy in *Kindred,* literally represents history (or remembrance of the past) in the process of destroying a body. What Dana's physical losses signify is that to flesh out the past means to leave part of one's being there.

Most commentators who write on the role of memory for contemporary African-American subjects maintain that the act of remembering is curative and leads to a sense of wholeness which would not be possible for the cultural amnesiac. To "bear the burden of memory," bell hooks concludes, means first and foremost to search out the "debris of history for traces of the unforgettable" ("Representing Whiteness" 342) and to emerge from the past with a sense of integrity: "It is the telling of that history that makes possible political self-recovery" (345). Memory, as Barbara Christian also writes, is a way of countering the tendency of history to become abstract and of historical subjects to remain fragmented. If "we want to be whole," she notes, "we must recall the past, those parts that we want to remember, those parts that we want to forget" (341). An apt example of how physical integrity is a result of focused memory comes to us in Toni Morrison's *Song of Solomon.* In order to distinguish himself from his capitalist and soulless father, the hero Milkman Dead affects a limp (62); once he learns about his ancestral history and his African forebears and learns to see the contingencies of history that made his father as he is, Milkman gives up the limp and becomes able-bodied again (284).

Clearly, Butler agrees with these assessments of the necessity of remembering the past as a way of comprehending the present and developing a coherent sense of a historically-defined self. In *Kindred,* however, Butler also demonstrates the genuine physical danger involved in remembering the past. Remembering can lead to wholeness, but it also carries a risk of loss. The path toward integrity, ironically, requires as a toll exposing one's self (and body) to possible mutilation. And even more than the body is at stake in recalling the past. What can also be lost, as bell hooks notes, is a sense of place. "For black folks," she writes, "reconstructing an archaeology of memory makes return possible, the journey to a place we can never call home even as we reinhabit it to make sense of present locations" (343). *Kindred* opens with the words, "I lost an arm on my last trip home" (9). This declaration is, at best, ambiguous. Where is the "home" Dana mentions? Did she lose her arm in antebellum Maryland or in contemporary Los Angeles, or in between? The only unambiguous thing we can say is that there is an intimate connection between the body (her arm) and the question of "home."

Dana's fullest description of losing her arm occurs at the end of the seventh chapter. She has just killed Rufus after his attempt to rape her, when she finds herself transported to Los Angeles. Although he is dead, Rufus still has her arm in his death grip. "Something harder and stronger than Rufus's hand clamped down on my arm. . . . Something cold and nonliving. . . . The wall of my living room. I was back at home—in my own house, in my own time. But I was still caught somehow, joined to the wall as though my arm were growing out of it—or growing into it. From the elbow to the ends of the fingers, my left arm had become a part of the wall. I looked at the spot where flesh joined with plaster, stared at it uncomprehending. It was the exact spot Rufus's fingers had grasped" (260-61). She loses her arm, apparently, between "homes"—between a past that has a claim on her and a present on which she has a claim. "Home," in *Kindred,* is more than a place; it signifies the liminal site where one can lose or reclaim a historically-defined modern self. As John Washington says, in David Bradley's *The Chaneysville Incident,* home "is a place to which you belong and which belongs to you even if you do not particularly like it or want it, a place you cannot escape, no matter how far you go or how furiously you run" (13). Both

Dana's and Kevin's meditations on their travels involve a concept of home as the place they must seek and escape, must construct and avoid. When Dana returns to Los Angeles, she defines the term for herself: "Home. It didn't have to do with where I had been. It was real. It was where I belonged" (115). However, shortly after she is transported back to Maryland, she is "startled to catch [herself] saying wearily, 'Home at last'" at the sight of the Weylin plantation (127). Even more ominous, though, is Rufus's insistence that Dana is "home" (143). "Home" becomes a variously significant term and concept. For Dana, it marks the place between present relations with Kevin and past relations with Rufus. For Rufus, it marks ownership—of property as different as the house and Dana. For Kevin, it marks the places where he and Dana can communicate.

When she is transported to the Weylin plantation the second time, Dana refers to the place as "this house." What she wants is to be "transported home" to Los Angeles (30). Just before her penultimate trip to Maryland, Dana considers how her sense of place has changed. She recalls "feeling relief at seeing the [Weylin] house, feeling that [she] had come home." She has to correct herself and remind herself that the Weylin plantation is an "alien and dangerous place." "I could recall being surprised that I would come to think of such a place as home" (190). Now she thinks of her Los Angeles house with the same suspicion: "I had been home to 1976, to this house, and it hadn't felt that homelike. It didn't now" (191). Likewise, Kevin feels an ambivalence about both Maryland and Los Angeles. He tells Dana that the "only time [he] ever felt relieved and eager to be going to a place" when he was left behind in 1819 was when he approached the Weylin plantation. Dana acknowledges their mutual feeling: "it was so much like coming home that it scared me" (192). So, too, Kevin loses his feeling for 1976 and Los Angeles. After wandering around the Los Angeles house for a few hours, he finds himself restless: "'Christ,' he muttered. 'If I'm not home yet, maybe I don't have a home'" (190). Both Kevin and Dana feel as though they are historical anomalies whether they are in 1819 or 1976. Their excursions to the past leave them alienated from the present and their returns to the present leave them discomforted by the unfamiliarity and the relative ease of life in 1976. Even though it creates a limbo for them, the antebellum South had at least provided them with a "sharper, stronger reality" than the urban, modern West (191). What they need, apparently, is a contemporary medium which provides them with an opportunity to record the astringency of the past at the same time as it provides them with a way of maintaining themselves in the present.

At first, both Dana and Kevin feel that writing is going to provide them with a means of reconstructing a sense of place and home. For some writers—and both Dana and Kevin are published professional authors—writing is the only way to construct a home. As Ellison puts it, "I had to become a writer . . . to feel at home in the world" (74). Writing, like certain forms of music, he notes, is a way of "seeking the homeness of home" (143). At first glance, Dana and Kevin seem to be suffering their modern malaise of not having a sense of home because they are both currently disabled from writing. Dana returns to Los Angeles, sits down at her typewriter, and "tried to write about what had happened." She makes six attempts before she gives up and throws them all away. "Someday when this was over," she thinks, "if it was ever over, maybe [she] would be able to write about it" (116). Likewise, Kevin finds it impossible to write about his experiences in the past (196). Apparently writing cannot provide Dana or Kevin with the necessary medium for self-recovery or recovery of home. Writing, as Dana notes, is an isolating activity: "Sometimes I wrote things because I couldn't say them, couldn't sort out my feelings about them, couldn't keep them bottled up inside me. It was a kind of writing I always destroyed afterward. It was for no one else. Not even Kevin" (252). Dana must learn to appreciate and employ a form of communication which is more dialogic, more capable of communing with her partner at the same time as it communicates with the past. That medium is *memory*.

The particular form of memory in which Dana is engaged—a form Robert Hayden calls "this nostalgia" for things "we / have never known and yet recall" (183)—provides her with a way of constructing, or perhaps reconstructing, a sense of home. In her poem "Momma," Paulette Childress White says that her mother "gifted us with memory / and created home" (97). Having no living mother, Dana is forced to employ a transporting memory which takes her back to her familial history and reinforces for her a sense of home and a sense of family. And these two senses are interdependent. After she is transported to the Maryland plantation, Dana notes that she could feel safe amongst her family and on this place that she will later call "home." "These people were my relatives, my ancestors. And this place could be my refuge" (37). More important than Dana's making a connection between family and home, between kindred and place, is what Dana will learn over the course of her adventures—that is, that neither term (*home* or *family*) is a given in a world where history is contingent. Like the concept of home, the concept of family is something we generate out of shared histories and collective memories.

Family, we can say, is a construct as much of shared narratives of memory as it is of common blood. As Mary Helen Washington says in her superb introduction to her anthology *Memory of Kin,* "much of what we call family is constructed through memory" (7). In Marita Golden's latest novel, the family members who descend from Naomi Johnson realize that their sense of family comes from hearing "stories they had known since before they were born" (59). At the end of the novel Logan sits at his grandmother's side as she "unearthed and recalled family history, private pain." Logan listens to her narratives of memory, her "griot-like rendering of all that had made them a family," and feels reaffirmed as "inheritor and link in a family he did not know how to deny" (320-21). Like "home," "family" is a place we have to find and define. It is worth noting that both concepts rely on a past which is beyond immediate physical experience. As Hayden says, we remember what we have never known; as Golden notes, we begin hearing the stories that will form our sense of home before birth. Or, as John Edgar Wideman says to his brother, "Down Home" is "everywhere we've never been, the rural South, the old days, slavery, Africa" (*Damballah* 5). Home and family are more than what we are born into; they are what our ancestors have made for us and what we come to occupy in an almost existential sense.

No matter how much narratives of memory help construct a sense of family, we cannot escape the obvious fact that family, as the saying goes, is not something you choose. Generally, we believe that a family is something we inherit, affirm, or even escape, but it is not something whose history we can remake according to our desires. A family is a family, after all, by virtue of its blood ties and through its legal records. When Dana first discovers that she has been transported to the past and then discovers that she and Rufus have a "blood relationship" (29), her initial response is to think of the written records which attest to the relationship. "Maybe [Rufus] was my several times great grandfather," Dana muses. She also realizes that Rufus has been "kept alive in the memory of my family because his daughter had bought a large Bible in an ornately carved, wooden chest and had begun keeping family records in it" (28). This daughter, Hagar, died in 1880, and most of the information about her life "had died with her"—or, as Dana more significantly puts it, "at least it had died before it filtered down to me. There was only the Bible left" (28). Dana's most important discovery, and something which the Bible apparently did not record, is that one of her great-grandparents was white: "why hadn't someone in my family mentioned that Rufus Weylin was white?" (28). It is tempting, given this scenario, to argue, as Holloway does about Corregidora's relationship to Ursa, that "white slaveowners have compromised her cultural history" (130), and to suggest, therefore, that Dana's lost arm is either a symptom of that compromise or a sacrifice necessary to remedy it. That is, one could argue that Dana loses part of her body to history because, like Dorothy Spruill Redford in *Somerset Homecoming,* she had to "trace [her] line into slavery . . . to find the white connections" (61); but, in Dana's case, she had to find them

and then exorcise them. That argument has some validity once we add to it the most significant fact about *Kindred*—which is that this is a story about how we can make our own sense of family if we are willing to alter the past.

Dana does not lose her arm because her family line has been corrupted by white slaveholding ancestors (although the fact that she loses her arm while her dead white slaveholding ancestor Rufus holds on to it is highly significant). Rather, her physical and her psychic losses are sacrifices made in her successful attempt to alter the past. It is, finally, not the mysterious time travel that is Butler's most spectacular gesture in *Kindred*; it is the fact that Dana is able to change history, albeit at a cost. At one point in the story, when both Dana and Kevin are in antebellum Maryland, he says to her: "It already happened. We're in the middle of history. We surely can't change it" (100). Dana does change it, however. She kills Rufus—after he has fathered her grandmother Hagar—and thereby ends the demands of the past on her present. She also profoundly affects the lives of the surviving slaves on the Weylin plantation, who are sold at the auction because of her act. It is worth noting that Kevin tells Dana that she cannot change history just after she is horrified to learn that the slave children play a game in which they act as if they were at a slave auction (a game which was popular amongst children in slave communities, as Eugene Genovese has shown [506]). Dana's act, ironically, changes the children's game into reality. After she kills Rufus, the slaves on the Weylin plantation are sold.

Seeing the children's game gives Dana her first insight into the workings of the ideology of a slaveholding society. She had accepted the odd phenomenon that translated her physically into the past because, as she says, she felt that she and Kevin were not at risk:

> We weren't really in. We were observers watching a show. We were watching history happen around us. And we were actors. While we waited to go home, we humored the people around us by pretending to be like them. But we were poor actors. We never really got into our roles. We never forgot that we were acting. This was something I tried to explain to Kevin on the day the children broke through my act.
>
> (98)

That is the day she sees the children playing at slave auction. When she overhears the children fighting about their relative values—"'I'm worth more than two hundred dollars, Sammy!' she protested. 'You sold Martha for five hundred dollars!'" (99)—Dana feels disgusted and begins thinking that "this place is diseased." Even the games children play, Dana remarks to Kevin when he suggests that the children are merely playing at something they do not understand, "are preparing them for their future—and that future will come whether they understand it or not" (99). The children's game "broke through" Dana's act because she now learns how easily and fluidly ideology works: "The ease. Us, the children . . . I never realized how easily people could be trained to accept slavery" (101; Butler's ellipsis). It is a startling realization because it marks Dana's immersion into history. She is no longer treating the past with any sort of nostalgia. She is no longer able to fool herself into believing that she can return to the past equipped with present-day sensibilities which protect her or make her immune to the forces of that past. After seeing the children play, after realizing how potent are the forces of socialization in any institution, even the most clearly offensive and brutal ones, Dana is disabused of her sense that she has "nineteen seventy-six shielding and cushioning eighteen nineteen" for her (101). It is at this moment of profound insight that "history" for Dana takes on a new form. History no longer consists of data or records of events which happened and have causes and effects. History is what she feels when she "can't maintain the distance" between her present self and her ancestral past. History is what she feels when she is "drawn all the way into eighteen nineteen"—to the extent that she becomes physically and psychically involved. History, finally, is what we are not immune to because we are immersed in it. The past, as Faulkner was fond of saying, is not over yet; it is not even past. The past, as Dana also discovers, precisely because it is not over yet, is also capable of being made over.

First, Dana has to discover that history is not a disembodied text that is either analogous to or coincidental with the values held by present citizens. History is not a scene on which actors tread without consequence. As Sonia Sanchez says in an interview with Zala Chandler, "You must always be responsible" to history (360). So, too, in the same interview, Toni Cade Bambara claims a "responsibility to self and to history"—and to the connections between them (348). Her calling as an instructor, she says, requires her to "teach about the necessity of being connected, and about the necessity of resurrecting the truth about our experiences (and revising the texts) in this place called America" (351). When Dana confronts the rawness of slave history, as Karla Holloway points out, she "is faced with an immediate need to subjectify the experiences she had known only academically" (114). After poignantly coming into contact with the past, Dana can certainly agree with Sanchez's claim: "I can truly *feel* history" (356). One way of feeling history enables us to see how present social relations are effects of the past. Like Cudjoe in John Edgar Wideman's *Philadelphia Fire,* who comes to realize that the fire of 1985 is intimately connected to Philadelphia's Independence Square riot of 1805, Dana, too, observes present social relations in terms of what she now knows of the slave history of America. She sees the connections between slavery and present street violence (33), rape (42), labor relations (52), sexual relations (97), wife beating (151), and apartheid (196).

In ***Kindred,*** though, there is also a more profound way of feeling history. In remembering the past, Dana also transforms it. When Kevin discovers her plan to change the thinking of the young Rufus, he tells her that she is "gambling against history" (83). By becoming an agent capable of transforming history, Dana becomes to the same degree *subject to history*—one who is liable to be transformed by seemingly dead historical forces. When she gambles against history, in other words, she can also lose to history; moreover, she endangers not only her own future, but also those who will not live to experience that future.

Dana's first plan is to make her ancestors' future more tolerable by educating the young Rufus to treat slaves with more respect: "I would try to keep friendship with him, maybe plant a few ideas in his mind that would help both me and the people who would be his slaves in the years to come" (68). She finds this an almost impossible task, however, and concludes that the social forces of the environment are overwhelming; she cannot counter the institutionally-granted power that accrues to one who holds the power of life and death over other human beings.

Later we see that, although Dana knows full well that her grandmother Hagar is born to Rufus Weylin and Alice Greenwood, she is willing to change history in ways that will endanger the possibility of that union. During her third venture into the past, Kevin was transported with her, but did not manage to grasp her when she was transported back to Los Angeles, and so was left behind in Maryland for five years. Dana returns the fourth time to discover the enslaved Isaac Jackson, who is married to Alice, beating Rufus because Rufus had apparently attempted to rape Alice. As she looks on, Dana realizes that Isaac is killing Rufus: "Then it occurred to me that he might be . . . killing the only person who might be able to help me find Kevin. Killing my ancestor" (117). The order of her realizations is significant. Dana is concerned with Kevin first and her ancestry second. As she sums up, she reinforces that order of priorities: "I needed [Rufus] alive—for Kevin's sake and for my own" (118). Unlike Marty McFly in the film *Back to the Future,* who returns to the past and must ensure that his parents form a union to create the conditions for his own birth, Dana is unconcerned about maintaining the integrity of her family tree as a way of ensuring her own birth. When she finally does remove Isaac from the battered Rufus, she advises the couple to flee north and offers to write them a pass (120). By doing so, Dana might be endangering her own future existence— that is, if we believe that Hagar can be born only of the union of Alice and Rufus, Dana's mother born only of Hagar, and Dana born only of her own mother. On the other hand, she might not be endangering her family line, but trying to reconstruct it.

Shortly after this, Dana becomes aware of a new possibility. She has brought a modern history book to Maryland with her, and Rufus starts to read it. Dana is worried, not so much about his response to the historical tone of the 1960s—he calls it "the biggest lot of abolitionist trash I ever saw" (140)—but about what would happen if he were to read about future events whose outcome he might alter. He might read about Sojourner Truth or Frederick Douglass, both still slaves at the time, and affect their future careers. He might discover Harriet Ross and prevent her development into the rebel Harriet Tubman; he might read about Nat Turner and reveal his future insurrection before it happened. What Dana comes to realize once she introduces records of the future into the past is that history is contingent: "I had said I couldn't do anything to change history. Yet, if history could be changed, this book in the hands of a white man—even a sympathetic white man—might be the thing to change it" (141). With this discovery, Dana begins her career of reconstructing her past and that of her family.

From the start, she has questioned the nature of her relationship to Rufus. When she realizes that they share a "blood relationship," her first thought is that her return in time is to save Rufus from his various accidents and therefore to keep alive her "mother's family." "Was that why I was here?" she asks herself. "Not only to insure the survival of one accident-prone small boy, but to insure my family's survival, my own birth" (29). Dana is not certain, however, that her life depends on her saving Rufus's. She finds it odd to think that his "life could depend on the actions of his unconceived descendent" and equally odd, therefore, to think that her life depends on the survival of a preconceived ancestor. "Somehow," she says, "it didn't make enough sense to give me any comfort." She concludes that her relationship with Rufus is unique: "We had something new, something that didn't even have a name. Some matching strangeness in us that may or may not have come from our being related" (29). She discounts the importance of their blood relationship, then; there are, she intimates, more significant ways of being connected to and of becoming disconnected from our putative ancestors. Eventually Dana will move towards what we might call *disrelating* herself from Rufus and the Weylin clan. It all begins because Rufus is intensely possessive of Dana; when he tells her that she is "home," he means that she is safe in his possession (143). After he discovers one of his field slaves, Sam, talking to Dana, Rufus sells him to an itinerant coffle driver. Dana sees Sam "being chained into line" and "people a few feet away from him crying loudly. Two women, a boy and a

girl. His family" (238). She pleads with Rufus not to sell Sam: "I caught Rufus by the hand and spoke low to him. 'Please, Rufe. If you do this, you'll destroy what you mean to preserve. Please don't . . .'" As Dana tapers off, Rufus hits her. As Dana notes, "it was a mistake. It was the breaking of an unspoken agreement between us—a very basic agreement—and he knew it" (239). She goes into the house, warms some water, washes her knife in antiseptic, and slits her wrists. She wakes up in Los Angeles, but the act symbolizes more than her desire to return home. As she rouses herself from sleep, she wonders where she is: "For a moment, I thought Rufus was pulling me back to him before I could even see home" (240). By spilling her own blood, Dana manages to escape her "blood relationship" with Rufus. This happens just a few weeks after Hagar is born, an event Dana had responded to by feeling herself "almost free, half-free if such a thing was possible, half-way home" (234).

Because Dana says that Rufus has broken an unspoken agreement between them right after he hits her, it seems that the agreement was that he would not molest her. That is partially the case. But Rufus also broke a tacit agreement when he sold Sam away from his family. The only time they talk about this subject, which they had always "talked around" before, Dana establishes the importance of that event to her sense of family. "'I'm black,' I said. 'And when you sell a black man away from his family just because he talked to me, you can't expect me to have any good feelings toward you'" (256). At the beginning of her adventures, Dana says that her connection to Rufus "may or may not have come from [their] being related" (29). Now, though, she has realigned her connections. Her sympathies do not follow the contours of blood relations; they flow towards the community to which she belongs. Her "family" is in the quarters and not in the big house; her sense of family is wrought from a common experience, and is not simply a matter of blood. She has, effectively, rewritten the family Bible so that her relations are with a different set of ancestors—those she loves and not those she has learned to hate. She would rather salvage her relationship with Kevin—her "kindred spirit"—than her "blood relationship" with Rufus, her "kindred." To do so, she discovers, requires her to assume a certain stance towards her family history—to generate a certain amount of sheer hatred.

History, as Benjamin said, is an account of "enslaved ancestors" which nourishes us, as contemporary subjects, with a revolutionary "hatred" and spirit of sacrifice (260). Bradley's 1981 novel *The Chaneysville Incident* provides us with a sophisticated treatment of this *topos* in the character of John Washington, a black historian who reconstructs the history of a dozen fugitive slaves (including his great-grandfather) in searching out an antebellum story with which to explicate his present love affair with his white lover, Judith Powell. "I'm a historian," John says, and history "means hating for things that still mean something. And trying to understand what it is they mean, so you hate the right things for the right reasons" (274). When he tries to prevent Judith from assuming that he is talking about racial relations—"You're thinking . . . that I'm talking about black people and white people"—she corrects his own assumption: "No. . . . I'm thinking you're talking about you and me." Unlike Lula in Amiri Baraka's *Dutchman*, who attempts to seduce Clay by fatally suggesting that he should be "free of [his] own history" and she "free of [her] history" (88), Judith comes to understand that "talking about us" means "talking about history." More importantly, she learns to understand his emotional response to the history of American slavery: "'You don't have to hate, John,' she said. 'I'll do it for you.'" "For us," he replies, showing that he has begun the process of allowing himself to trust her by sharing with her both his past and his emotional attitude towards that past (285).

Dialogue, Bradley suggests, is the only way towards shared narratives—dialogue with ancestors and dialogue with present partners. As John tells the final story of his escaped slave great-grandparents, C. K. Washington and Harriette Brewer, it is difficult for the reader to distinguish between the scene of narration (John and Judith sitting around a campfire) and the narrated scene (C. K. and Harriette sitting around a fire in the cabin). As Harriette reaches for C. K.'s hand, we find Judith holding John's; as John discovers some aspect of Judith's personality, it becomes part of Harriette's character. This blurring of episodes occurring in quite different historical epochs is part of Bradley's achievement in showing the connections between the past and the present. And John is not able to accede to this historical insight until he acquires a form of orally transmitted memory which permits him to share his ancestral past with his future spouse.

Kindred, like *The Chaneysville Incident,* is about an interracial marriage in which the African-American partner learns to share an ancestral past with a white spouse. And in *Kindred,* too, we have what Holloway terms the representation of "voice as reconstructed memory" (15), or what John Callahan calls the "fiction of voice" in which "memories fuse the past with the present moment of identity" (14). We recall that writing does not offer Dana an opportunity to make sense of her experiences because it is a solitary act. Confronted and confounded by the most troubling event in her life, she finds that writing does not help her to formulate her feelings and salve her soul. This peculiar experience requires her to share herself in a new way and within a different form of communication. She must employ something like a collective memory. Remembering, as Dana realizes, takes on a different valency when it is a

collaborative effort. When she returns from her first trip back to Maryland, the sound of Kevin's talking is disruptive: "The sound of his voice seemed to put distance between me and the memory." Engaging in dialogue with Kevin—in a sort of call-and-response historiography—Dana finds that as she "remembered it all for him" she also and simultaneously "relived it all in detail" (15). After returning from her second trip back, she again "remembered it for him in detail" (46). This form of collective, shared memory gives their life that sense of connection to the past which writing had not provided. We recall that they responded to the present with disgust because contemporary life lacked the immediacy and danger of the past. Memory gives them a forum for making the present exciting in a way writing could not. After two acts of memory of such potency that she finds herself "reliving" the events she recalls, Dana inadvertently and unwillingly transports Kevin into her ancestral past.

When Dana is called back to Maryland the third time, Kevin rushes to her side and holds her. She tries to push him away because she "was afraid for him without knowing why" (58). After they arrive together in Maryland, she is more aware of her fears and more honest about why she wished Kevin not to live in the antebellum South: "I didn't want him here. I didn't want this place to touch him except through me" (59). Later she realizes more precisely why she wishes Kevin to receive his knowledge about the past only through her telling of it. "A place like this," she thinks, "would endanger him in a way [she] didn't want to talk to him about. If he was stranded here for years, some part of this place would rub off on him" (77). At first, she finds her fears realized. When Kevin negotiates with Thomas Weylin about assuming the duties of Rufus's tutor, he forgets to mention anything about Dana (79). She is disturbed by Kevin's easy acceptance of this "particular segment of history"—especially the accommodations they have to make to live in the house of a slaveholder (97). After spending five years in the past, Kevin returns to the present scarred and aged. Seeing him, Dana wonders what effect living in the nineteenth century might have on his outlook: "What might he be willing to do now that he would not have done before?" (184). Kevin has acquired a slight accent while he was gone: "Nothing really noticeable, but he did sound a little like Rufus and Tom Weylin. Just a little" (190). Finding himself frustrated at not being able to make sense of his return to the present, Kevin becomes cold and brusque with Dana. As he pulls away from her, his face takes on a ferocious aspect—"like something I'd seen," notes Dana, "something I was used to seeing on Tom Weylin. Something closed and ugly" (194). When she is transported for the penultimate time, Dana wakes up in a field and finds herself confused by Rufus's voice and face, thinking that she is looking at Kevin and hearing him (213-14).

Even though he acquires the voice and facial expressions of the Weylin men by being exposed to the antebellum South, Kevin is not made into a monster once he realizes some of the freedoms granted white men in nineteenth-century Maryland. He does exhibit a more pronounced tendency to demean Dana and to ignore certain features of the risks she is perpetually under on the plantation. But this tendency is not something he acquires by living in the past; his actions in the past are expanded versions of gestures he was prone to making in the present also. After all, he is not exactly a model of male sympathy in 1976 when he suggests that Dana throw away some of her books so that they can both fit into his apartment (108). When Dana turns the tables on him and suggests that he throw some of his books out, he just sighs. Likewise, he insists on having Dana type his manuscripts for him, thinking it natural that a woman wouldn't mind typing (109) or writing his correspondence for him (136). Again, when Dana objects, he responds with some bewilderment and resentment. What Kevin's transportation to the past does is accentuate those residual aspects of his patriarchal thinking. When he first meets Rufus, the boy asks Kevin whether Dana "belongs" to him. His response is frightening: "'In a way,' said Kevin. 'She's my wife'" (60). When Rufus commands Dana to write his correspondence for him, he is only following Kevin's lead (136). Kevin's return to the past, then, offers him some enlightenment about the extremity of a patriarchal form of thinking in which he is still mildly engaged. What Dana tells Kevin about the slave experience helps him change some of his ways of thinking.

Of course there are limits to Kevin's understanding of Dana's ancestral past—if she could make him fully aware of what it was like to be a black slave woman this novel would indeed have been science fiction, or fantasy. There is no way for Dana to communicate fully to Kevin what is crucial to her—the kinds of physical abuse a slave woman is likely to suffer, the anxiety about connections of a deracinated being, the persistent fear for her life and her ancestors' lives as she alters her familial past. She tries to tell him, but there are limits to communicative norms. The point at which Kevin's understanding and Dana's capacity to communicate her experiences to him falter most is when they discuss rape. When she returns after Hagar is born, Kevin intimates that Dana should now kill Rufus: "it doesn't seem to me that you have such a difficult decision ahead of you" (242). Because she knows that the slaves on the Weylin plantation would be sold if Rufus were dead, Dana realizes that her decision is not so simple. Kevin then broaches the topic he had been unwilling to mention before. "He drew a deep breath. 'All right. You've said he was a man of his time, and you've told me what he's done to Alice. What's he done to you?'" (245). It is a poignant moment, because Dana knows that Kevin will never be able to experience what she has experienced. As Harriet Jacobs addresses her reader, Dana can address her spouse and say: "You never knew what it is to be a slave; to be entirely unprotected by law or custom; to have the laws reduce you to the condition of a chattel, entirely subject to the will of another" (55). And although "slavery is terrible for men," as Dana might echo Jacobs, "it is far more terrible for women. Superadded to the burden common to all, *they* have wrongs, sufferings, and mortifications peculiarly their own" (77). Dana responds in her own fashion: "Sent me to the field, had me beaten, made me spend nearly eight months sleeping on the floor of his mother's room, sold people . . . He's done plenty, but the worst of it was to other people. He hasn't raped me, Kevin. He understands, though you don't seem to, that for him that would be a form of suicide." Kevin responds sarcastically, "You mean there's something he could do to make you kill him, after all?" (245; Butler's ellipsis). Even after she assures him that Rufus has not raped her, Kevin shows little understanding of her life as a slave woman. He says that he could understand if "anything did happen." Dana asks ferociously: "You mean you could forgive me for having been raped?" Kevin apparently still thinks after his return, as he did at the beginning of his journey, that Dana "belongs" to him and that a crime committed on her body and being is a crime committed against his property.

Dana's anger at Kevin is short-lived, however. Although she might never be able to make him understand fully what she went through or the forces to which she was subject, she still feels that he is the only person she wants to understand her suffering. Despite his inability to appreciate the fullness of her pain, he is, as she says, the "only person who had any idea" what she was going through (246). She considers carefully how to tell Kevin that although she loves him, there is "another reason" she refuses Rufus, and it is, she adds "the most important reason." "I thought for a moment, tried to find the right words. If I could make him understand, then surely he would believe me. He had to believe. He was my anchor here in my own time" (246). She starts to tell him about her feelings as she watched a coffle being driven away: "I thought, that could be me—standing there with a rope around my neck waiting to be led away like someone's dog." She tells Kevin that she accepts certain limitations on her freedom because of the conditions in antebellum Maryland but she also sets certain limits on Rufus's behavior toward her. "He has to leave me enough control of my own life to make living look better to me than killing and dying," she concludes. To Kevin's suggestion that she would not be here if her "black ancestors had felt that way," Dana responds by asserting that she lacks their endurance; they "go on struggling to survive, no matter what," but she is "not like that." When Kevin states that he suspects she is, she demurs. His final words are that he "had to know"—but we are not entirely clear as to what he had to know, whether it was that Dana had not been raped or that her greatest suffering was caused by watching her community suffer. Dana's final thoughts on the conversation are equally ambivalent: "That felt like truth. It felt enough like truth for me not to mind that he had only half understood me" (246).

Despite her disagreement with Kevin—which she assures us is not false modesty—Dana does exhibit a remarkable will to survive enslavement. Her conversation with Sam centers on this issue. When he hints that "some folks" look askance at the special relationship Dana evidently has with Rufus, she speaks of field hands who work "like mules": "They do it to keep the skin on their backs and breath in their bodies. Well, they're not the only ones who have to do things they don't like to stay alive and whole. Now you tell me why that should be so hard for 'some folks' to understand?" (238). It is the first and only time Dana articulates to a slave—to someone living in the institution—what the ideology of enslavement is all about.

Hitherto, only to Kevin had she mentioned her realization of the "ease" with which people could be trained to accept slavery (101). When she meets slaves who seem too easily to accept their situation, she judges them harshly. When the otherwise courageous Sarah refuses to listen to Dana's talk about slaves escaping to freedom, Dana thinks to herself that Sarah "had accepted a life of slavery because she was afraid." She feels a moral superiority to Sarah—whom she thinks of as the "house-nigger, the handkerchief-head, the female Uncle Tom"—because Sarah had "done the safe thing" (145). Ironically, when Alice recovers from the horrific beating she received, she considers Dana to be precisely the same thing. Not knowing that she has lost her own freedom because she ran away with Isaac, she asks Dana what it feels like to be a slave (156) and then calls her a "mammy" (167). When Alice says that she would rather be dead than a slave, Dana says it is "Better to stay alive . . . while there's a chance to get free" (157). She has learned now, effectively and not just academically, what she tells Sam in conversation—that slavery is a condition of compromising everything in order to stay alive and whole. By finally learning to talk to the past (as she does with Sam) instead of judging it (as she judges Sarah), Dana begins her revolutionary dialogue with history. Here, Dana gives up the pretense of maintaining a distance between herself and the past and becomes an agent of history by revealing to historically-immersed subjects the ideological forces at work in the peculiar institution.

At the crux of the novel, Dana is confronted with the reality of what had been merely speculation on ideology. As Rufus is about to rape her, she "realized how easy it would be for [her] to continue to be still and forgive him even this. So easy, in spite of all [her] talk.

But it would be so hard to raise the knife, drive it into the flesh [she] had saved so many times. So hard to kill . . ." (259-60). Here, for the final time, Dana has to make herself a historical subject—not just an actor but an agency in the unfolding of her ancestors' lives. Like Barbara Omolade, Dana realizes that the "story of slavery is in her blood, not just in the books" (294). For Dana, history is what makes her aware of her blood connections and what finally makes her capable of killing. In discovering through historical memory a collective experience capable of transforming her pacifist tendencies, Dana is much like Alice Walker's Meridian. Meridian's meditations on the past begin after she states that she is willing to die for the cause of freedom but not to kill for it. She believes her pacifism comes from a feeling of indebtedness to the past: "she felt herself to be, not only holding on to something from the past, but *held* by something in the past" (27). Soon, however, she sees that being held by that particular version of the past endangers her future and the future of black America. As she regards the father of a brutally murdered black boy, she decides that she has to "weave" the father's story and the son's life and death into the fabric of "what we already know" and construct a strategy of survival for the collective group (199). She comes to realize that "she *would* kill, before she allowed anyone to murder his son again." She comes to terms with the idea of "retaliatory murder" after she negotiates the connections between a "historical background and [a] present setting" (200). History, that is, teaches Meridian that we are still in the middle of a struggle for freedom; the past can teach her to accept and struggle peacefully or to rebel and retaliate. She does not find any easy solution; for the rest of her life, apparently, she will remain ambivalent about what action constitutes a responsible attitude towards the past. But she has seen that the past which had held her enthralled and unable to rebel in a situation clearly calling for violent reaction is only one version of a manifold and complex past.

Dana, too, realizes that it is so "hard to kill" because the past holds her enthralled and could entirely consume her. Like Meridian, Dana has to appreciate the contingencies of history and to see that no version of the past which would rape her is a version she should accept. As she turns to Rufus, she defines herself in terms of Alice's question—"What's it like to be a slave?" (156): "A slave was a slave. Anything could be done to her." She then looks at her great-grandfather and defines him and the limits of his relationship to her and her life: "And Rufus was Rufus—erratic, alternatively generous and vicious. I could accept him as my ancestor, my younger brother, my friend, but not as my master, and not as my lover. He had understood that once" (260). Dana kills Rufus, and, like her own attempted suicide, it is an act by which she disrelates him. Ironically, in order for Dana "to stay alive and whole," as she says to

Sam, she has to attempt suicide once—"in the warm water I cut my wrists" (239)—and lose an arm to escape the hold of the past (261). But, at the end, Dana is restored to her contemporary home and reunited with her husband—with what appears to be a more solid foundation.

At the end of the story, notes Missy Dehn Kubitschek, Dana escapes the constraints on her writing—represented by white males like Rufus, who commands her to write his letters—and learns to use the historical material of slavery to deal with the past and then define herself in her own writing (47, 50-51). Under these terms, the story offers us a fairly clear resolution. Under other terms, and in another critic's estimation, *Kindred* offers no such clarity. Butler, says Dorothy Allison, "offers no resolutions at the end of *Kindred*" (476). We do not "know what will become of her marriage to Kevin," or what "has become of Hagar." It is true that Hagar's ultimate fate is a mystery, but that is entirely fit for a novel about how history is a contingent entity. When Kevin and Dana go to modern Maryland in order to search out the records of what happened to the Weylin plantation slaves, they discover no mention of Hagar or Joe (Alice and Rufus's other child). What Dana has to do, then, is consider their potential histories and, in the same gesture, reconstruct their familial ties. "Margaret might have taken both children. Perhaps with Alice dead she had accepted them. They were her grandchildren, after all, the son and daughter of her only child. She might have cared for them. She might also have held them as slaves" (263). Margaret, who is Dana's great-great-grandmother (Rufus's mother), might be claimed as kindred if she did raise and care for Hagar, or she, like Rufus, might be disrelated if she chose to enslave her. It is another story, but equally a story about how to reconstruct a family according to the history she relives. It is significant, of course, that Hagar is the one who wrote the family records in the family Bible—and yet her own story requires her granddaughter's reconstructive touch.

As for Kevin and Dana's relationship, everything we are told suggests that it will grow stronger because of this experience. Kevin, as I mentioned above, felt the need to know whether Dana was raped or not. It was for him the one piece of information he required to put his mind at ease. Dana, too, feels the need to know something about what happened to Kevin when he was immersed in the past. She tells Kevin that she needs to know "One more thing. Just one." She asks him if he was "helping slaves to escape" (193). Upon finding out that he was, Dana smiles and says nothing. What is important for her is to know that Kevin also "gambled against history," that he acted upon his beliefs and tried to alter the past. He obviously still has much to learn about how rape is not the crime of the victim, but he seems capable, more capable after his historical sojourn,

of learning that lesson in time. In the end, Kevin and Dana learn to share their present lives more fully because she has shared her past with him. Even though they are both alienated from the present when they return, they do not "have to grow back into each other." They find it "easy to be together, knowing [they] shared experiences no one else would believe" (243). As Dana kills one set of relations, she also aligns herself with another. Her past and her future have met, and her future has been salvaged at the cost of her past.

What finally provides Kevin and Dana with a shared communion is the experience of altering the past so that their sympathies can be recognized as historical agencies. Each returns to the time of American chattel slavery and gambles against its history. They both lose something, and they both gain something. Ironically, what they most lose—a sense of "home"—is also what they most stand to regain in a newer, stronger form. When Dana returns to the past, she reconstructs her family ties so that her blood ancestors become less important to her sense of home and family than those people who are spiritual kindred—the slave community on the Weylin plantation, people like Sam and his family, and, ultimately, Kevin. "Natal alienation" is Orlando Patterson's term to describe the deracinated slave (7). Using Patterson's idea as her guide, Barbara Chase-Riboud provides us with an interesting metaphor for African-Americans looking at their slave past: "We are orphans, standing on the blank page of America, waiting to be acknowledged" (367). In *Kindred,* both Kevin and Dana, we learn, are orphans (55), and both return to history to claim and reclaim a reconstructed family which is based not on biological but on social ties.

At one point in the novel, just after they have tried to get their marriage plans blessed by their respective families (her uncle and aunt, his sister), Kevin suggests to Dana: "let's pretend we haven't got any relatives" (112). It is a pleasant dream for these two orphans whose plans to marry provoke a racist response from each of their families—but it is not something they can do. Butler's story does not propose that those who would alter their familial alignments can simply transcend them, because those alignments belong to a past which must be confronted if it is to be altered. Rather than pretend to lose their relatives, Kevin and Dana must remember the past and reconstruct from its debris a new sense of kindred. Some kindred come to you by blood, but others come to you by love and common experience. After recounting the utter importance of his family to his sense of identity, Ralph Ellison concludes: "even while I affirm our common bloodline, I recognize that we are bound less by blood than by our cultural and political circumstances" (303). At the end of *Kindred,* after she has lived in history and seen the dislocations slave families suffered and the adaptations they made, Dana recalls the loss of her "father who had died before [she] was old enough to know him" (252) and "remember[s] the pain of [her] own mother's death" (258). As she does at the beginning of the novel, Dana remembers the loss in order to reform its ramifications. Her recollection of becoming an orphan is part of her act of remembering and defining new kinship ties. Butler's orphan heroine shows us how an excavation of history can provide the orphan with a family—partially by relation and partially by disrelation. The past, as lucille clifton suggests, is there to be adopted one way or the other. Home and kindred, as Dana learns, are what you make with your own performance of history.

Works Cited

Allison, Dorothy, "The Future of Female: Octavia Butler's Mother Lode." Gates 471-78.

Baraka, Amiri. *Dutchman. The LeRoi Jones/Amiri Baraka Reader.* Ed. William J. Harris. New York: Thunder's Mouth P, 1991. 76-99.

Beal, Frances M. "Black Women and the Science Fiction Genre: Interview with Octavia Butler," *Black Scholar* 17 (March-April 1986): 14-18.

Benjamin, Walter. "Theses on the Philosophy of History." *Illuminations: Essays and Reflections.* Ed. Hannah Arendt. Trans. Harry Zohn. 1968. New York: Schocken, 1969. 253-64.

Berry, Mary Frances, and John W. Blassingame. *Long Memory: The Black Experience in America.* New York: Oxford UP, 1982.

Bradley, David. *The Chaneysville Incident.* New York: Harper & Row, 1981.

Braxton, Joanne, and Andrée McLaughlin, eds. *Wild Women in the Whirlwind: Afra-American Culture and the Contemporary Literary Renaissance.* New Brunswick: Rutgers UP, 1990.

Butler, Octavia E. *Kindred.* 1979. Boston: Beacon, 1988.

Callahan, John F. *In the African-American Grain: Call-and-Response in Twentieth-Century Black Fiction.* 1988. Middletown, CT.: Wesleyan UP, 1989.

Chandler, Zala. "Voices Beyond the Veil: An Interview with Toni Cade Bambara and Sonia Sanchez." Braxton and McLaughlin 342-62.

Chase-Riboud, Barbara. *Echo of Lions.* New York: William Morrow, 1989.

Christian, Barbara. "'Somebody Forgot to Tell Somebody Something': African-American Women's Historical Novels." Braxton and McLaughlin 326-41.

clifton, lucille. "i am accused of tending to the past . . ." *quilting: poems 1987-1990.* Brockport, NY: BOA Editions, 1991.

Crossley, Robert. Introduction. *Kindred.* By Octavia Butler. ix-xxvii.

Ellison, Ralph. *Going to the Territory.* New York: Random, 1986.

Foucault, Michel. "Nietzsche, Genealogy, History." *Language, Counter-Memory, Practice: Selected Essays and Interviews.* Ed. Donald F. Bouchard. Trans. Donald F. Bouchard and Sherry Simon. Oxford: Basil Blackwell, 1977. 139-64.

Gates, Henry Louis, Jr., ed. *Reading Black, Reading Feminist: A Critical Anthology.* New York: Meridian, 1990.

Genovese, Eugene D. *Roll, Jordan, Roll: The World the Slaves Made.* 1974. New York: Random, 1976.

Giddens, Anthony. *Modernity and Self-Identity: Self and Society in the Late Modern Age.* Stanford: Stanford UP, 1991.

Golden, Marita. *Long Distance Life.* 1989. New York: Ballantine, 1992.

Hayden, Robert. *Robert Hayden: Collected Poems.* Ed. Frederick Glaysher. New York: Liveright, 1985.

Holloway, Karla F. C. *Moorings and Metaphors: Figures of Culture and Gender in Black Women's Literature.* New Brunswick: Rutgers UP, 1992.

hooks, bell. "Representing Whiteness in the Black Imagination." *Cultural Studies.* Ed. Lawrence Grossberg, Cary Nelson, and Paula Treichler. New York: Routledge, 1992. 338-46.

———. *Yearning: Race, Gender, and Cultural Politics.* Boston: South End, 1990.

Jacobs, Harriet. *Incidents in the Life of a Slave Girl Written by Herself.* Ed. Jean Fagan Yellin. Cambridge: Harvard UP, 1987.

Jameson, Fredric. *Postmodernism, or, The Cultural Logic of Late Capitalism.* Durham: Duke UP, 1991.

Johnson, Charles. *Being and Race: Black Writing Since 1970.* Bloomington: Indiana UP, 1988.

Jones, Gayl. *Corregidora.* 1975. Boston: Beacon, 1986.

Kubitschek, Missy Dehn. *Claiming the Heritage: African-American Women Novelists and History.* Jackson: UP of Mississippi, 1991.

Morrison, Toni. *Beloved.* 1987. New York: NAL, 1988.

———. *Song of Solomon.* 1977. New York: NAL, 1978.

Omolade, Barbara. "The Silence and the Song: Toward a Black Woman's History through a Language of Her Own." Braxton and McLaughlin 282-95.

Patterson, Orlando. *Slavery and Social Death: A Comparative Study.* Cambridge: Harvard UP, 1982.

Redford, Dorothy Spruill, with Michael D'Orso. *Somerset Homecoming: Recovering a Lost Heritage.* New York: Doubleday, 1988.

Salvaggio, Ruth. "Octavia Butler." *Suzy McKee Charnas, Octavia Butler, Joan D. Vinge.* By Marleen S. Barr et al. Mercer Island, WA: Starmont, 1986.

Shinn, Thelma J. "The Wise Witches: Black Women Mentors in the Fiction of Octavia E. Butler." *Conjuring: Black Women, Fiction, and Literary Tradition.* Ed. Marjorie Pryse and Hortense J. Spillers. Bloomington: Indiana UP, 1985. 203-15.

Spillers, Hortense. "Interstices: A Small Drama of Words." *Pleasure and Danger: Exploring Female Sexuality.* Ed. Carole S. Vance. 1984. London: Pandora, 1989. 73-100.

Walker, Alice. *Meridian.* 1976. New York: Pocket, 1986.

Washington, Mary Helen, ed. *Memory of Kin: Stories About Family by Black Writers.* New York: Anchor, 1991.

White, Paulette Childress. "Momma." Washington 97.

Wideman, John Edgar. *Damballah.* 1981. New York: Random, 1988.

———. *Philadelphia Fire.* New York: Henry Holt, 1990.

Williams, Sherley Anne. *Dessa Rose.* 1986. New York: Berkley, 1987.

Willis, Susan. *Specifying: Black Women Writing the American Experience.* Madison: U of Wisconsin P, 1987.

Michelle Erica Green (essay date 1994)

SOURCE: Green, Michelle Erica. "'There Goes the Neighborhood': Octavia Butler's Demand for Diversity in Utopias." In *Utopian and Science Fiction by Women: Worlds of Difference,* edited by Jane L. Donawerth and Carol A. Kolmerten, pp. 166-89. Syracuse, N.Y.: Syracuse University Press, 1994.

[*In the following essay, Green uncovers the role of difference in Butler's version of utopia.*]

Octavia E. Butler's **Dawn,** the first novel in the trilogy **Xenogenesis,** is an angry utopian novel, a scathing condemnation of the tendency of human beings to hate, repress, and attack differences they do not understand. It pleads for an end to fear and prejudice, insisting that aggressive social intervention must counteract the ancient hierarchical structures of thought that humans share with their closest animal relatives. The illustration on the jacket sleeve of **Dawn** ironically emphasizes

Butler's cause for anger. Though the novel clearly identifies its heroine, Lilith Iyapo, as a muscular black woman in her late twenties (*Xenogenesis* 11, 13), the cover depicts a slender white girl apprehensively unwrapping what looks like a blanket from the body of a naked white woman. The girl is Lilith, here young, fair-skinned and delicate, peering shyly at the first potential friend she has had in years because she cannot look with eagerness at naked woman. Following Audre Lorde's description of the role of difference within a capitalist economy, the mass-market paperback industry thus puts its desire to reap profits from off-the-shelf sales of **Dawn** over the demands of the novel itself. In redrawing Lilith as a modest white girl rather than the powerful black heroine her creator described, the publishing industry allows forms of sexism, racism, ageism, and homophobia to be perpetuated on the cover of a novel that demands an end to prejudices and acceptance of differences.

I want to look closely at Butler's fiction and the criticism it directs at popular discourse, particularly at science fiction utopias created by recent feminist writers. I also want to consider the transformation of the utopian form when a writer such as Butler, who challenges various forms of cultural hegemony, adapts it for the purposes of social critique. Several of Butler's critics label her work "essentialist"—a term often used pejoratively by poststructuralist feminists to attack biologically based models of human behavior—because of her insistence that humans will behave inhumanely without a series of checks upon them.[1] But Butler's "essentialism" is tricky; her novels focus on the exceptions to the rules she posits as human norms rather than on those who exemplify them.

Many recent women's utopias deal with contemporary problems by defusing the differences that cause conflicts to develop among people. Joanna Russ and Ursula Le Guin experiment with biological androgyny as a means for ending the battle of the sexes. Marge Piercy and Melissa Scott explore futures in which skin color and racial identity are unrelated. Sheri Tepper unites all people under one religion, while Suzy McKee Charnas erases political struggles under a classless anarchy. Feminist utopias of the past twenty years have launched a powerful attack on the ideologies, practices, and textual strategies of the patriarchy, which their authors posit as the principal source of the rejection of differences. Some texts, like Le Guin's *Left Hand of Darkness* and Scott's *Kindly Ones,* have done so by rejecting the binary construction of sexuality, insisting that the gender-defining characteristics of males and females are socially rather than biologically based. Others, like Cynthia Felice's *Double Nocturne* and Pamela Sargent's *Shore of Women,* have rescripted gender relations with the assumption that, even if men and women are fundamentally different, those differences need not lead to the oppression of women under patriarchy. By refusing to allow women to be posited as Other in a binary social and conceptual system, these and many additional novels defamiliarize patriarchy, calling for a world in which men and women can benefit rather than suffer from one another's differences.[2]

Yet many of the texts that challenge the gender status quo ignore, erase, and repress other differences among people. Though Mattapoisett—the utopia in Piercy's *Woman on the Edge of Time*—nurtures people of many different ages, races, ethnic groups, sexual orientations, and interests, the differences among them seem only skin-deep. Some people have Southeast Asian features without any sense of Southeast Asian heritage, while others participate in Jewish religious services without any connection to the thousands of years of Jewish culture that preceded the founding of Mattapoisett. Again, in Charnas's *Motherlines*, because of the emphasis on the vast gulf between the genders, little attention is paid to the material differences between the women protagonists, who at times seem interchangeable. In *The Left Hand of Darkness*, neither race nor sexual preference operate as conceptual categories; if they exist at all, they pass unnoticed. Thus, despite their insistence that patriarchy can be overcome, relatively few utopian feminists seem able or willing to tackle even their own tendency to ignore, erase, and oppress human difference.

This tendency is the focus of Butler's critique of both human society and recent utopian fiction. Difference, disagreement, and diversity provide the life force of her utopias. Though the need to rethink women's roles in human society is a central concern, it is by no means the only problem attacked by Butler. Racism, class oppression, nationalism, religious intolerance, homophobia, and mistreatment of animals and handicapped people are all touched upon in Butler's critique of humanism—itself a form of prejudice here, for "humanism" accepts that human beings should be at the center of their own universes. Butler refuses to categorize people through biology, behavior or even species, demanding new solutions cultivated through a community based on differences. And just as Butler insists upon differences among people, she insists upon differences among utopias. Her work implicitly criticizes utopias by women that avoid conflicts stemming from difference and reject challenges and change from within. Her social critique resembles that of another feminist African-American, Audre Lorde, who writes, "In a society where good is defined in terms of profit rather than in terms of human need, there must always be some group of people who, through systematized oppression, can be made to feel surplus, to occupy the place of the dehumanized inferior. . . . Institutionalized rejection of difference is an absolute necessity in a profit economy which needs outsiders as surplus people.

As members of such an economy, we have *all* been programmed to respond to the human differences between us with fear and loathing. The future of our earth may depend upon the ability . . . to identify and develop new definitions of power and new patterns of relating across difference. The old definitions have not served us, nor the earth that supports us. The old patterns, no matter how cleverly rearranged to imitate progress, still condemn us to cosmetically altered repetitions of the same old exchanges, the same old guilt, hatred, recrimination, lamentation, and suspicion" (*Sister Outsider* 115, 123). Expanding on Lorde's critique of capitalist society, Butler blames not only human greed for the creation of prejudice, but also the deep-rooted human compulsion to structure societies and thoughts hierarchically. Butler's fictions contain an oft-repeating warning that the human race has long been in the process of destroying itself—a warning that leads several critics to label her work dystopian rather than utopian. Butler's characters often do seem to be living in a nightmare rather than an ideal society; they find themselves trapped among aliens, powerless, angry, and frightened. All of them face the same dilemma: they must force themselves to evolve, accepting differences and rejecting a world view that centers upon their lives and values, or become extinct. In the "Patternist" books, the **Xenogenesis** trilogy, and **"Bloodchild,"** such evolution requires pan-human acceptance of alien ideas and values, leading to a merger with the aliens to create a new form of life. In **Kindred**, **"Speech Sounds"** and **"The Evening and the Morning and the Night,"** evolution involves one group of humans accepting "alien" ideas and values from another group of humans, taking personal responsibility for transforming themselves and the species.

MISCEGENATION: "BLOODCHILD" AND "PATTERNIST" SERIES

Octavia Butler once told an interviewer that she did not write utopian fiction: "I don't believe that imperfect humans can form a perfect society" (Beal 14). But, as any number of texts from Thomas More's prototype onward have indicated, a utopia does not have to be a "perfect" society. "Utopia" is a Greek pun that can be read as "nowhere" *(utopia)* or "good place" *(eutopia)*; literary utopias engage the paradox between these two meanings, straddling issues of locality, textuality, and ideology in an attempt to bridge the gap between fictional discourse and everyday life. Thus the utopian form is already a miscegenation of sorts, a blending of pragmatic local concerns with transcendent idealism. For women, utopian fiction permits reimaginings of worlds without patriarchy, without biology-based notions of gender, even without men—all within the context of a critique of contemporary politics. As critic

Jean Pfaelzer notes, the question "What if the world were perfect?" is not the same as "What if the world were feminist?" ("The Changing" 291).

The latter question seems to interest Butler more than the former, for her utopias are certainly far from perfect. **"The Evening and the Morning and the Night"** relates the events that follow a "cure" for cancer that turns lethal; *Clay's Ark,* the last of the "Patternist" books, tells of the catastrophic spread of an extraterrestrial virus that transforms human genetics; *Dawn,* the first book of *Xenogenesis,* begins shortly after the earth has been rendered uninhabitable by a nuclear war. Butler's worlds often seem far from feminist as well: few possess egalitarian social structures or communities of women; none has eradicated rape, incest, or compulsory heterosexuality; and the females who inhabit those worlds often rely on threats, coercion, and violence to achieve their own ends. As Dorothy Allison observes, Butler's female characters must "heroically adjust to family life and through example, largeness of spirit, and resistance to domination make the lives of their children better—even though this means sacrificing personal freedom" (472).

Both the utopianism and the feminism of Butler's work are slippery because neither emerges in isolation from a variety of other interests. Butler is not interested in creating a utopia of human beings who seem too gentle to be believed, like those who inhabit Piercy's Mattapoisett and never get into fistfights; nor is she interested in glorifying either women or some abstract notion of the feminine. In fact, despite her insistence that human beings can transform themselves and their world, Butler often seems not to like people—men or women—at all. Her works border on the dystopian because she insists on confronting problems that have occurred so often in human communities that they seem almost an unavoidable part of human nature, such as greed, prejudices based on appearances, oppression of women, and might-makes-right ideologies. Rather than create utopias in which these problems have simply ceased to exist, Butler demonstrates time and again in her fiction that they must be worked through—even if that process involves the use of dangerous human tendencies like aggression and coercion to counter similar dangerous human tendencies like violence.

Both **"Bloodchild"** and the *Xenogenesis* books have one explicitly feminist project: to make male characters experience sex and reproduction from the position of females in male-dominated culture. **"Bloodchild,"** which offers a very short glimpse at a fascinating world, reflects on the extent to which patriarchal cultures find it necessary to use ideology, violence, and oppression to force women to participate in "natural" reproduction.[3] In **"Bloodchild,"** men get pregnant, an ironic twist on a slogan made popular by supporters of abortion rights:

"If men could get pregnant, abortion would be a sacrament." In **"Bloodchild,"** an alien race called Tlic require the bodies of healthy young men in which to incubate their eggs. When the eggs hatch inside the men's bodies, the aliens cut the men open to remove the alien grubs.

Although the Tlic attempt to make the process bearable for the men by incorporating them into nuclear families and creating an ideology of spousal love to persuade the men that their participation is voluntary and beneficial, the human male narrator stresses that the men—or, as in his own case, boys—may be "raped," impregnated against their wills, and forced to carry to term fetuses that have never been a part of themselves if they do not submit.

Tlic society is hierarchical, with fertile females possessing the most power—which they use to compete, sometimes violently, for human males. The Tlic who will mate with the narrator is particularly important; she is in charge of the Preserve, the human dwelling on the Tlic planet (an animal farm, ghetto, Native American resettlement, and Nazi concentration camp all at once). As such, she is both protector and pimp. "Only she and her political faction stood between us and the horded who did not understand why there was a Preserve— why any Terran could not be courted, paid, drafted, in some way made available to them. She parceled us out to the desperate and sold us to the rich and powerful for their political support" (195). Despite the fact that they are all female, the adult Tlic employ many of the ideologies and practices of patriarchalism: compulsory heterosexuality, reproductive colonization, marital rape, and oppression of the childbearing sex, to name the most deadly. For, like childbirth, Tlic deliveries can be lethal to humans; if the grubs are not removed at the right moment, by the right Tlic, the infants devour their hosts from the inside out.

Though the interference of the aliens has brought about an end to the struggle between the sexes, human women are as subject to Tlic oppression as men; they are not used as Tlic breeders only because bearing Tlic young leaves them too weak to bear the next generation of humans to carry a subsequent generation of Tlic. Familial relationships are quasi-incestuous. The narrator, Gan, and the Tlic whose children he will carry, T'Gatoi, are both children of the same father, whose sperm produced Gan and whose belly carried T'Gatoi. Gan's mother, who is many years younger than his father, grew up with T'Gatoi as a sort of sister; T'Gatoi has thus served as sister and aunt to her future spouse, and has been a second mother to him as well. Gan's relationship to her is laden with Oedipal conflict—he is grateful that he can stroke her as he cannot caress his mother, but feels revulsion and horror at the thought of their eventual mating—and T'Gatoi's desire for him, expressed alternately through parental and romantic cli-chés, smacks of pederasty. Under Tlic ideology, biology is destiny; none of the beings involved in a human-Tlic mating perceives an alternative.

"Bloodchild" hardly seems a feminist fantasy. It is impossible to perceive the planet of the Tlic as a radical utopia that empowers women, like Joanna Russ's Whileaway in *The Female Man*; Butler's human women are as oppressed as her men, and her female Tlic begin to act like human male oppressors. But **"Bloodchild"** is neither dystopian nor essentialistic.[4] The circumstances that oppress the narrator do not stem from any meta-physical imperative; they are not historically inevitable, and therefore can be altered. The "biology" that complicates human-Tlic relationships is neither transpar-ent nor predictable. The traits of human and Tlic nature that have placed Gan and T'Gatoi in the perverse relationship they negotiate are not "essential"; they are constructed out of social and material conditions that result in the appalling crisis at the start of the story—the Tlic have changed themselves and the humans before, and can do so again.

More important, Gan's human agency begins a process of reform that may lead to Tlic recognition of the subjectivity of all humans. Gan does not believe or expect that an ideal space of perfect equality can be created, given the material difficulties of life on the Tlic world for humans and Tlic; he does, however, insist on new social structures with the potential for ongoing evolution. Butler's insistence on maintaining a closed family structure, which Haraway and Zaki criticize as a sign of her "conservatism" in sexual matters (Haraway 378; Zaki 244), serves as her means of emphasizing the vital need for collaboration underlying both the Tlic-human and the male-female relationships of the story; the future of both depends on a joint solution, with mutual extinction the only alternative.

Butler might have chosen to transform reader expecta-tions about "normal" gender behavior by demonstrating how natural giving birth seems to human men, rather than how unnatural. Yet if Butler truly believed that hu-man biology makes rape, compulsory heterosexuality, and enforced childbirth inevitable, she would have no motivation for writing **"Bloodchild"** in the first place. Like the circumstances of Gan's oppression, the produc-tion of the story must be situated within a historical framework. Butler published **"Bloodchild"** during a year when controversies over abortion, in-vitro fertiliza-tion, and the prevalence of unnecessary caesarean sec-tions—topics cloaked in the metaphors of the story—reached a peak. 1984 also witnessed a political campaign characterized by the polarization of complex constitutional issues into monolithic positions: school prayer versus religious freedom, welfare abuse versus urban poverty, "pro-life" versus "pro-choice," apartheid

versus sanctions. Rather than accepting such binaries, which lead neither to productive debate nor to a synthesized answer, Butler insists that individuals consider what is left out of such formulations. The social problems of **"Bloodchild"** cannot be broken down into anything so simple as "Tlic versus humans" or "female versus male." The fundamental problem stems from the need for cooperation rather than binar-ism—and accompanying hierarchialism—to structure an imperfect but just society.[5]

This problem creates the crux of the "Patternmaster" novels as well. The last book of the series, *Clay's Ark*, constitutes the beginning of a history played out in the earlier volumes. A man returns to earth from a distant galaxy, inadvertently carrying a disease organism that begins the transformation of the human race. "The organisms were not intelligent. They could not tell him how to keep himself alive, free, and able to find new hosts. But they became intensely uncomfortable if he did not, and their discomfort was his discomfort" (*Clay's Ark* 29). The organisms invade and recode human DNA, threatening the lives of their hosts if they are not transmitted to other humans. Because transmission requires the breaking of the skin of the uninfected person, the organisms trigger violent behavior and overwhelming lust. The children of the inevitable sexual couplings between infected individuals are not human; they look like catlike, graceful "animals" (60) and mature rapidly into highly intelligent quadrupeds with superhuman senses of smell and hearing. Resistance to the organism's need to spread, which is impossible except in the case of isolated individuals, ensures physi-cal and mental anguish culminating in death.

Clay's Ark—the least utopian of the "Patternist" books—presents three recently infected individuals at-tempting to maintain their "humanity," which in this context signifies their control over biological drives. Blake Maslin, a doctor, believes physical strength and medical technology can prevent the disease's spread; his beautiful and brilliant daughter Rane relies instead on mental willpower and morality. Both try to escape the consequences of the disease, refusing to adapt to the physical and psychological changes it demands, and both ultimately lose their lives in the struggle. Only the younger daughter, Keira, who was wasting away with leukemia before surrendering to the new disease, survives. In progressing toward death, she has already begun to transform into something "ethereal not quite of this world," with a vastly different physiology and psychology from her father and sister. Keira survives because she takes the step neither her father nor sister is willing to take: she bonds with the disease and its carriers, willingly accepting the inevitability of the changes necessitated by the organism. Such evolution represents the only possibility for saving Keira's life, for the recently invented epigenetic therapy, a process that has all but eradicated leukemia by reprogramming faulty genes, has failed to correct her cells. Keira may have less of a stake in "protecting" human biology because her own biology has never been normatively human; she has less of a stake in protecting human morality because, unlike her sister Rane, she understands it as a utilitarian construct that can be discarded when its social value ceases to function.[6]

The humans "lose" to the organism and to another group of humans carrying a different mutation. The species divides into three competing groups. The self-destructive, telepathic "Patternists," bred by the ancient patriarch Doro for their psychic skills, develop from victims to oppressors in their struggle against nontelepathic humans and "Clayarks" (the descendants of the characters in *Clay's Ark*). Telepaths treat the nonpsychic humans as an inferior race, referring to them by the denigrating label "mute."[7] The nomadic Clayarks, considered nonhuman by the others, are despised and shunned as carriers of the terrifying disease. The "Patternist" novels share the interest in **"Bloodchild"** in the prevalence of patriarchy, tyranny, and slavery across many different human cultures. None offers a universal utopia, though several characters create utopian spaces within a primarily hostile world. In *Survivor,* Alanna resists deep prejudices to join an alien tribe; in *Mind of My Mind,* Mary becomes a tyrant with the hopes of singlehandedly achieving the peace and group survival her father Doro made impossible. In these books human nature again proves more flexible than some of the characters would like to admit. They cannot preserve an "essential humanity" in the face of mutation and disease; instead, they learn to recognize the extent to which human morality and even human biology are constructed through careful breeding and teaching, and can be changed a good deal.

EX-COMMUNICATION: "SPEECH SOUNDS" AND "THE EVENING AND THE MORNING AND THE NIGHT"

Donna Haraway writes: "[Competing stories of human evolution] have been bound together in a contentious discourse on technology, often staged in the high-technology media that embody the dream of communication promised by international science and global organization" (186). Having argued against claims for Butler's essentialism, I would like to turn to her two most "essentialistic" worlds, found in the acclaimed short stories **"Speech Sounds"** and **"The Evening and the Morning and the Night."** Both involve the destruction of "the dream of perfect communication promised by international science," to quote Haraway (186). Each of these fictions is set on earth and begins with a devastating disease that challenges human myths of control over their physical selves and destroys the capacity for traditional verbal expression among

victims. Though the diseases are very different—the illness in **"Speech Sounds"** affects all people, while that in **"The Evening and the Morning and the Night"** afflicts only children of drug-damaged parents—both trigger acts of violence capable of destroying entire societies. Butler never explains whether the violence stems from the diseases themselves, or from the rage and terror felt by the diseased individuals whose bodies no longer respond to their commands, although the latter seems more likely. The stories thus concern methods for interpersonal contact when verbal communication fails, and when the possibility of life-threatening violence is just under the surface of all relationships. Although grounded in the biology of individual bodies, the problems that arise are primarily social in nature.

"Speech Sounds," set in California, follows a devastating worldwide epidemic that, though initially blamed on the Soviets, has no traceable cause or cure. The illness is "highly specific . . . language was always lost or severely impaired. . . . Often there was also paralysis, intellectual impairment, death" (203-4). Some victims abruptly lose the capacity to read and write; others can still read, but no longer speak; some can do neither, while others can do both but cannot remember what words mean. Of course, one immediate result is the breakdown of late capitalist civilization. The mass communications gone, the vast social apparatus rendered useless, people become like children cut off from parental discipline and love. They are forced instead to struggle for survival against armed criminals, suicidal thoughts, and jealous individuals who will kill for spite those who can speak, read, or write. The protagonist, Valerie Rye, has lost her husband and children to the disease; she can no longer read, write, or remember many things, and her ability to speak can put her life in danger if she demonstrates it in public. Maddened with illness, loneliness, and envy, she is overwhelmed at times with the desire to murder those who can still read; at other times she is overcome by the need for any nonviolent contact with any human being, willing to make love with a man she can never converse with.

Set in Los Angeles—a city where in the 1990s rival gangs fight territorial battles over who has the right to speak which language in which section—**"Speech Sounds"** reflects and explores the relationship between modes of communication and social structures. Like the biblical story of the Tower of Babel, Butler indicates that, deprived of the ability to share a primary language, individuals will leave off building their cities and wander into isolation. Certainly everyone in the story leaves off constructing skyscrapers and focuses on basic survival issues: scavenging for and growing food, finding shelter, establishing defenses against the robbers and rapists who patrol the streets. Although a large series of gestures to represent curses have sprung up, no real sign system has been developed. Violence is a universal language: people take what they can, keep what they defend, and destroy what they resent, without the need for debate or defensiveness.

The loss of speech is less the cause of social breakdown than the loss of literacy. The necessities for remaining alive have continued—food and fuels still circulate, transportation still runs between cities, and apparently firearms are still manufactured—but without the electronic media, capitalist society cannot function. It is in the process of reverting to feudalism when the story begins. **"Speech Sounds"** thus tells the tale of an extremely public society forced to "go private" without any warning. Without the printing press and descendant machines, the public sphere falls apart. Everything from government and law enforcement to scientific research and social aid ceases to function, leaving people to an anarchistic state where, although some of the machinery still functions, the superstructure that controls it does not. Society is at best vestigial. Soon the gas will run out, the cars will break down, groups sharing food and protection will begin to disintegrate, men will forget that rape was ever a crime.

Rye, the protagonist, thinks she is lonely because she is not a "private" person; she tells herself she needs people out of a biological need for communication, nurturing, and sex. But she is not a "private" person in a far more important sense: she depends upon a public sphere to satisfy her as a consumer. Not coincidentally, the man she links up with still wears the uniform of the Los Angeles Police Department. Rye finds this anachronism amusing because it reminds her of a little boy playing cop. But it also reminds her of the public life she had before the disease, and she longs for her lover—whom she calls Obsidian, having no way to ask his real name—to protect her, to take her places, to help her get to Pasadena where she may have relatives.

But Rye and Obsidian cannot go back; the world of instantaneous communication, across a room or across the globe, has been destroyed. Obsidian is shot for attempting to interfere in what would once have been called a "domestic disturbance." The police have minimal power because "domestic violence" is still considered a private matter in some areas, but Obsidian is still trapped in a code of ethics from the world before. Rye is as well. Despite her longing for her own lost nuclear family, she feels little sense of social obligation to the two children orphaned in the fight that killed Obsidian, as though she expects a social welfare agency to step in. "She did not need a stranger's children who would grow up to be hairless chimps" (210). But finally the desperateness of their situation reaches her; she realizes that if she does not take them with her, they will die, and she wants no more death on her hands. Then comes the greatest shock: the children can speak

normally. Whether the disease has run its course or these two have a rare immunity, they can talk to her.

"Speech Sounds" are not the same thing as "speech"; they are less determinate. To those accustomed to a delimited sign system, speech sounds are crude and incoherent; in eighteenth- and nineteenth-century books on American slave and subaltern cultures, for example, the dialects spoken by the oppressed were assumed to be "speech sounds," not language. Butler's **"Speech Sounds"** ends with Rye contemplating what it will mean to be a teacher to the children—to educate them in the use of a skill that may no longer be of any use, that others will envy enough to murder them. What will she teach them? The value of the old language, or the need for a new mode of communication? The hierarchical difference between "speech" and "speech sounds," or the need for a common language between the verbal and the mute? The story ends before such questions can be resolved, but it ends on a hopeful note. Rye knows that, speech or no speech, the next generation will never bring back the world as it was. They will have to create instead a new public order, more diffuse in form and more accepting of difference than the old. They will have to be different.

The disease in **"The Evening and the Morning and the Night"** also leaves different children as the hope of the future. A late twentieth-century "wonder drug," which cures cancer and most viral diseases, causes a genetic disorder in all the descendants of every individual who uses it. The disorder, called DGD (Duryea-Gode disease), initially causes an inability to concentrate, then a psychotic retreat into fantasy; finally, it spurs horrific self-destructive and species-destructive behavior. The father of Lynn, the narrator, killed and skinned her mother completely before dying in an attempt to skin himself alive. This rending of the flesh—"digging out"—is common to all end-stage DGD victims; when they reach this point, they are locked away in exploitative DGD wards, usually chained up, but sometimes allowed to kill themselves if they prove too inventive in attacking their jailers. Although maintaining a medically supervised diet can put off the worst symptoms for several years, eventually the "digging" becomes inevitable. The only alternative to a horrible death in a DGD ward is an innovative private hospital called Dilg, which has a long waiting list. Dilg—named for the Dilg family, which made capital profits from the drug that caused DGD, and then funded research to cure it—also funds scholarships for DGD victims. Lynn is the recipient of such a scholarship. When she visits Dilg, she discovers that the reason has more to do with her biology than her scholarly ability: Lynn is the daughter of two parents with DGD, and as such carries pheromones that enable her to control violent DGD victims.

The Dilg retreat is Butler's strangest utopia, though in some ways her most successful. Under the guidance of "double-DGD" females, patients who would otherwise destroy themselves invent life-saving technology, produce brilliant artwork, and lead otherwise productive lives. Although most of the patients work in isolation because the illness makes collaboration impossible—particularly among members of the same sex—the Dilg community provides a space for education, productivity, and care while protecting DGD victims and their families from exploitation at the hands of high-priced private wards or mismanaged government institutions. The pheremones are both a blessing and a curse. Two females of double-DGD parentage cannot abide contact with one another; Lynn has to fight overpowering urges to inflict violence on Beatrice, the woman who explains Lynn's rare privilege to her. As Lynn acknowledges, she has little choice but to join Dilg, although the thought of spending the rest of her life "in something that was basically a refined DGD ward" does not appeal to her (301). She shares her lover's suspicion that Dilg's complete control over its patients could lead to exploitation, even though the supervisors are DGDs, too—people who have not yet developed end-stage symptoms. However, she sees little alternative for herself or for the violent victims men like her lover will inevitably become. "If the pheremone were something only men had, you would do it," she tells him.

Like the patients aboard *Clay's Ark,* the DGD sufferers subtly resemble AIDS victims. Butler portrays them as heroic, attempting to commit suicide or quarantine themselves to avoid injuring the healthy. As in the case of AIDS, some people angrily blame irresponsible sexuality for the spread of DGD: "The damned disease could be wiped out in one generation, but people are still animals when it comes to breeding. Still following mindless urges, like dogs and cats" (286). Although this sounds like essentialist rhetoric—"People are at the mercy of their biological urges"—it is important to note that the speaker has undergone voluntary sterilization, proving that biology does not have to be destiny. Lynn's response to his urging that she do the same is to insist on maintaining control of the one part of her biology functioning normally. "I don't want kids, but I don't want someone else telling me I can't have any. . . . [Would] you want someone else telling you what to do with your body?" she asks (285). The DGD victims also share some parallels with babies born addicted to crack. They suffer from specific motor and speech dysfunctions; some have never met their fathers for their own safety, while others have met only the brain-damaged ruin of their mothers; the "crimes" that cause prejudice against them are not their own.

Butler's appeal for victims' rights, however, shifts dramatically in light of her insistence that the disease may actually benefit society in the long run. Just as

AIDS research has led to new discoveries about the immune system and provided valuable information in treating cancer, leukemia, and chronic viral infections, DGD produces highly intelligent individuals who devote their lives to improving life for others; the special value of double-DGD females was discovered by DGD victims, and their own laboratories represent the best hope for a cure. **"The Evening and the Morning and the Night"** would thus seem to offer the most essentialistic position yet in a Butler story, dividing humanity into the haves and the have-nots. But even here Butler demands diversity. The first half of the story focuses on the prejudice still-healthy DGD carriers suffer; although many of them have spectacular careers as scientists (ironically, DGD victims cure many forms of cancer), they are ignored or abused by uninformed and frightened associates. Lynn rooms at college with a DGD victim who becomes a special education major, hoping "the handicapped would accept her more readily than the able-bodied." They share a house with other DGD victims because they have "all had enough of being lepers twenty-four hours a day" (283).

As always, Butler subtly points out the multiethnicism of her character—Lynn is the child of two American fundamentalist Christians, while her lover Alan is half-American Catholic, half-Nigerian polytheistic. Butler also indicates that many of the scientists and doctors are female, black, or another minority. The disease itself trivializes most other forms of prejudice in a transformation similar to that caused by the presence of aliens in the *Xenogenesis* books.

Dilg is feminist by necessity; females simply handle certain aspects of the disease better than males. But never does Butler consider the possibility of having the females shun male society to protect their assets. In what appears to be a calculated attack on Russ's *The Female Man* and Charnas's *Motherlines,* Butler insists that sexual cooperation is absolutely vital; the segregation of the genders would be deadly for both. Women take on the roles of leader and nurturer not because they are innately more equipped to do so than men, but because the DGD pheremone coincidentally attaches itself to double-DGD females; as Lynn says, if men had the pheremone, they would take on the guidance positions. Women are certainly no less prone to violence than men. Next to Lynn's father, Alan's mother is the most violent character in **"The Evening and the Morning and the Night."**

Similar ideas about gender permeate **"Speech Sounds,"** though the roles are reversed. Left-handed men suffer less brain damage than any other group. Rye kills people more easily than Obsidian. Biology thus is never destiny, even when it seems to be so. Even without the ability to read, Rye has a choice: she can work with people, attempting to create a new society, or become destructive like some of the people she witnesses. And Lynn has a similar choice: she can commit suicide, or live for the moment until the illness takes her, or she can work with Dilg to develop a haven and a cure. The characters in these two stories share some basic similarities, but their best chances for survival come from putting their differences to work.

RE-CREATION: *KINDRED*

In an essay on fiction set in the antebellum South, Deborah E. McDowell writes: "Contemporary novels of slavery [witness] slavery after freedom in order to engrave that past on the memory of the present but, more importantly, on future generations that might otherwise succumb to the cultural amnesia that has begun to re-enslave us all in social and literary texts that impoverish our imaginations" (160-61).

Kindred, Butler's fantasy of time-travel into the past of her race and gender, engraves that past into the flesh of her heroine as well as her memory. *Kindred* is Butler's most troubling novel—yet also, in many ways, her most optimistic. The mechanism for the temporal shifts is never explained; this novel is not interested in alien sciences, and can scarcely be described as "science fiction." Rather, the "aliens" in *Kindred* are all too human. They are white Americans from the antebellum South, and they are more frightening than the Tlic. Dana, the black contemporary protagonist, unexpectedly finds herself transported to Maryland before the Civil War. Her great-great-grandfather Rufus calls her there to save his life, which she does several times. Rufus, much to Dana's shock, is not black; her grandmother never told her that not all of her ancestors were slaves.

Dana finds herself faced with a dilemma similar to those of Butler's other heroines: she must decide whether to collaborate with an oppressive agent that threatens her identity as a human being, or whether to cause her own extinction. *Kindred*'s particular situation requires that Dana cooperate with her white ancestors as they beat, rape, and murder her black ancestors; if she does not, her great-grandmother may never be born, and she may cease to exist. Rufus, who fathered this great-grandmother, closely resembles Dana's white husband. As he grows from a confused child to a murderous patriarch, Dana finds herself forced to suppress every moral, value, and desire she has ever held dear.

Dorothy Allison's criticism of Butler stems from what Allison perceives as Butler's assumption that children and family always come first. Though Butler's black female characters are aggressive, independent, and in control, they often sacrifice personal freedom and autonomy in order to make the lives of their children better—a tendency that makes Allison "want to scream with frustration" (471). Since utopian thought is

optimistic, holding out hope for a better future, Butler does insist time and again on the need for people—especially for women—to make sacrifices for their children. But she indicates that such a demand compromises the present, forcing characters to submit to situations they find unbearable. Women make such sacrifices more often than men not because they are genetically more prone to do so, but because they have been socially driven to do so. They refuse the consequences of *not* being the ones to take action: the deaths of their children and their future.

If **"Speech Sounds"** and **"The Evening and the Morning and the Night"** may be interpreted as theorizing a biological view of human nature to a greater degree than Butler's other texts, then *Kindred* is their opposite; it insists absolutely that personality and behavior are constructed within a social frame. Rufus beats, rapes, and kills not because white men are inherently more prone to do so than black men or white women, but because white men happen to hold the power in his society and he has been taught from a young age that he *can* beat, rape, and kill. Even Dana insists that the differences between herself and Rufus stem from culture rather than birth.

> Could I make him see why I thought his blackmail was worse than my own? It was. He threatened to keep me from my husband if I did not submit to his whim. . . . I acted out of desperation. He acted out of whimsy or anger. Or so it seemed. "Rufe, there are things we just can't bargain on. This is one of them."
>
> "You're going to tell me what we can't bargain on?" He sounded more surprised than indignant.
>
> "You're damn right I am. . . . I won't bargain away my husband or my freedom!"
>
> "You don't have either to bargain."
>
> "Neither do you."
>
> (142)

Rufus is both more reasonable and more impossible than Dana expects: more reasonable because he will listen to her debate, more impossible because he refuses to change even when he understands her. But Rufus shares this flaw with the other men in the novel—including the sympathetic men. On one of her journeys back through time, Dana's husband accompanies her, and she is horrified to discover the extent to which Kevin acts like a patriarchal white man when people treat him as one. In his own time, he is another person. Kevin becomes horrified as well, although he strongly resists acknowledging that the new conditions have altered his behavior; he wants to believe that his personality cannot be changed by circumstance.

Dana is even more horrified to learn that, treated as an enslaved black woman, she will act like one. Her personality, which she always thought of as her fundamental self, modifies in response to Rufus's and Kevin's betrayals until she is no longer sure who she is in her own time or in the past. Dana helps Rufus against her every instinct, not because her nurturing instincts prove stronger than her need for autonomy, freedom, and self-pride, but because she recognizes the strategic importance of doing so. When she does not assist Rufus, she risks not merely her biological ancestry, but the lives of other slaves. Only when he threatens her autonomy by trying to seduce her—only when she realizes "how easy it would be for me to continue to be still and forgive him even this"—does she strike at him: "I could accept him as my ancestor, my younger brother, my friend, but not as my master" (260).

People in **Kindred** do not change because of humanist impulses or moral imperatives. They respond to the agency of others, either immediately or over time. Readers are meant to feel real horror at Dana's periods of complacency as a slave; like her, we respond with a kind of gratitude to the worst excesses of Rufus's behavior because they remind us of the need for action and challenge, no matter how painful. **Kindred** offers a challenge to utopian fictions that value ideals over survival—like *Women on the Edge of Time,* in which the protagonist sacrifices herself (and kills several other people) in order to defend her values, or like the cultures described in **Dawn,** which decide en masse to commit suicide once it becomes clear they will never achieve perfect stasis. Butler instead acknowledges all that has been and remains unbearable in human society, but insists that human agency can change even the most dystopian world over time. It demands patience; Dana must be willing to work, but she must also be willing to wait for substantial change, not to force it in the past at the expense of the future. The work and the waiting pays off. Although Dana is dispossessed of her era, her nation, her family, her belongings, her values, and her beliefs, she gains the understanding that she can make a difference in history. The novel is unfailingly optimistic in this regard. At the conclusion, Dana and her husband return to Maryland in 1976, to mourn those who suffered and to reassure themselves that they have escaped. Utopia in **Kindred** is thus in Dana's own era, when diversity is celebrated in marriage rather than conquered through rape and domination. Not that the scars go away: Dana loses an arm to Rufus's grip, and her knees and skin are marked by the tortures of slavery—just as all descendants of slaves are scarred from America's racist past. But she is still alive and capable of further change. Butler literally engraves the past onto the present by engraving Dana's body as a readable text.[8] As Deborah McDowell predicts, she also engraves the past onto the memory of the future through the act of writing. The text warns people like Dana and like us of the dangers of complacency; it demands utopian thinking.

CONTRADICTION: XENOGENESIS

Donna Haraway tells us: "Conventions within the narrative field of SF seem to require readers radically to rewrite stories in the act of reading them. . . . I want the readers to find an 'elsewhere' from which to envision a different and less hostile order or relationships among people, animals, technologies, and land" (15). This statement could easily describe the project of "Xenogenesis." "Xenogenesis" mobilizes human adaptability to reform a species that arrives on earth to reform humanity. The Oankali, whose name means "gene traders," arrive in the Terran system at the end of a nuclear holocaust that has decimated the planet. They bring the remaining humans onto their world-ship with a plan to return them to earth equipped to survive there; the "equipment" will consist of Oankali genes, provided by forcing humans to mate with Oankali partners and evolve into a new species. This crossbreeding is necessary for two reasons. The main one, according to the Oankali, stems from a flaw in human biology: ancient hierarchical tendencies drive humans to violence and self-destruction, and human intelligence only exacerbates the dangers.

But the Oankali have another purpose. They desperately desire to mate with the humans not only to trade genes, but because they find humans extremely attractive. Like the humans with the disease of **Clay's Ark,** the Oankali are driven to spread their organelles or become extinct. Humans particularly attract them because they are susceptible to cancers. If they can understand the cancers and adapt the renegade cells to their purposes, the Oankali feel certain they can make themselves attractive as mates to many new species.

Genetic exchanges occur with the help of ooloi, an Oankali third sex who "mix" the DNA of parents to form genetically desirable children. The ooloi also give enormous sexual pleasure to human and Oankali partners—so much pleasure, in fact, that humans shun all physical contact with humans of the opposite sex without ooloi intervention once they have participated in mating with an ooloi. The ooloi discover what they label the "Human Contradiction":

> You are hierarchical. That's the older and more entrenched characteristic. We saw it in your closest animal relatives and in your most distant ones. It's a terrestrial characteristic. When human intelligence served it instead of guiding it, when human intelligence did not even acknowledge it as a problem, but took pride in it or did not notice it at all . . . that was like ignoring cancer. I think your people did not realize what a dangerous thing they were doing. . . . Your denial doesn't matter. A cancer growing in someone's body will go on growing despite denial. And a complex combination of genes that work together to make you intelligent as well as hierarchical will still handicap you whether you acknowledge it or not.

(42)

This incompatible "conflict in their genes—the new intelligence put at the service of ancient hierarchical tendencies" (371), according to many of the Oankali, doom the human race to eventual destruction. Because of the Contradiction, the Oankali never feel remorse about their complete colonization of an independent species; it is for the salvation of the human race as well as for their own purposes that they interfere. The Oankali, who can communicate empathically and work communally, are certain of their superiority. It is never clear that they want anything from the humans other than their cancers and their cooperation, for there is little the Oankali seem to value in human beings except the potential for making them adaptable.

But even the Oankali cannot predict everything. Their "test" group of humans, experimented on while the majority of survivors remain in suspended animation, reveal several surprises: for example, that humans can perform a variety of different identities, that they become uncooperative when information is withheld, that making one human more powerful than others may lead to that person's persecution rather than domination. They also discover that the Contradiction is not equally strong in all people; women, for example, seem to display less of it than men, a fact that the Oankali attribute to male biology, but that the women attribute to conditioning that trains women to demonstrate their skills through nurture rather than force. Most of the Oankali expect Lilith, the strong black heroine of *Dawn,* to choose for a human mate "one of the big dark ones because they're like you" (161); only her best Oankali friend, Nikanj, is not surprised when she chooses instead a short, soft-spoken Chinese-Canadian man. But the humans shock the Oankali most with the force of their drive to survive. When the humans learn of the plan to breed them, they kill the ooloi who have become their mentors and sexual partners to escape.

For relatively few humans, anti-Oankali feelings arise from racial or sexual prejudices—the Oankali have "ugly" tentacles (383), and "take men as though they were women" (581)—but for the majority, the desire to survive as a species is the tantamount issue in the conflict with the Oankali takeover of earth. After bonding chemically with humans—only to have the humans flee—several ooloi are forced to admit that their understanding of genetics cannot prevent them from making errors. Many Oankali agree that intelligence might eventually allow humans to conquer their hierarchical tendencies, particularly if they have a new world to conquer, a distraction that would require cooperation and ingenuity. Eventually, after "resister" humans attempt to kidnap and alter "construct" children (half-human, half-ooloi) in order to maintain their species identity, the Oankali are convinced by a construct child that not all humans should be forced to mate with the Oankali. Those who choose not to can be sent to Mars, made habitable by Oankali technology, to continue as an independent race. Of course the Oankali—and some humans—hope that most of the humans stay. But the Oankali, who have always planned to retain a group of "pure" Oankali in case the Human Contradiction destroys them as well, finally recognize the need for "Humans who don't change or die— Humans to go on if the . . . unions fail" (371).

It is a mistake to interpret *Xenogenesis* as a serious discussion of essential flaws in human genetics. The novels scarcely seem interested in proving whether or not humans actually suffer from the Contradiction; rather, they illustrate how human agency can triumph over prejudice, violence, and essentialism. The humans in *Xenogenesis* express absolutely no racial prejudice; the only subset of individuals other than the Oankali who receive any real group hostility are "faggots," for in the postwar world compulsory heterosexuality becomes an important component of the dream of reproducing the species. In *Dawn,* the group of humans who have been dominant—white Christian men—act exactly as the Oankali expect all humans to behave; having lost the most power and prestige, they fight the most strongly against the dominant alien presence. There is also a large, highly xenophobic German resister village. Among the "non-Aryan" groups of humans, there is less violence; Hispanic and Chinese people may choose to go to Mars, but rarely become gun-toting resisters. It is not surprising that a black woman first joins an Oankali family; after years of oppression by other humans, Lilith has less prejudice toward the aliens and a stronger appreciation of the need for change. While she resents the unequal power relationships between Oankali and humans, she resents as well the unequal relationships among the humans she supervises.

Lilith is willing to work with the Oankali to create change. Her son Akin, the hero of *Adulthood Rites* and the first male human-Oankali construct child, is expected by his elders to be nomadic and prone to violence; instead, he bonds strongly with two separate communities and devotes his life to finding a workable solution to the increasing human-Oankali conflict. Jodahs, the human-Oankali construct ooloi protagonist of *Imago,* proves to the Oankali that the aspects of humanity they most fear can be used fruitfully for the benefit of both humans and Oankali. There may be a biological flaw—or there may not—but Butler implies time and again that culture has the power either to reassert the old hierarchies or to triumph over them.

Hoda Zaki has argued that in the *Xenogenesis* books Butler demonstrates "a pervasive human need to alienate from oneself those who appear to be different—i.e., to create Others" (241). Zaki cites the way humans of different races band together only to oppress the Oankali in the series as proof of this assertion. In fact, I would like to argue that Butler indicates exactly the opposite. The *humans* have been constituted as the colonized Other *by* the Oankali; as Donna Haraway points out, their reeducation on the Oankali ship resembles the Middle Passage of slaves on their way to America (379). At this point, the humans are like animals to the Oankali, more interesting for their cancers than their thoughts; their identities have been stripped away, and they are "reduced to flesh" (Spillers 68)—texts to be inscribed by their oppressors, who identify them as nothing but a package of genes. The human resistance to the Oankali parallels the resistance of a slave to rape by a master who will later claim her child as his property. The agency required to transform this situation into a relationship of equality and trust is staggering, but the transformation occurs. By the end of ***Imago,*** a group of fertile humans enter an Oankali community of their own free will, after a consensus formed through argument and communication. They can do so because, for the first time, they are not an oppressed minority victimized by the Oankali.

It is interesting that Butler's sympathy for the oppressor leads so many readers to interpret *Xenogenesis* as a condemnation of humanity. Although she points out that in many ways the Oankali are superior to human beings, Butler insists—through the mouths of many different characters, human and Oankali—that the enforced crossbreeding of an unwilling species is a terrible crime. The Oankali (like the Tlic) commit miscegenation not in their attempt to create a new species, but in an attempt to dominate the old—the humans, who have value in and of themselves. *Xenogenesis* represents a breakthrough in Butler's fiction in that, for the first time, the protagonists do not have to work alone to achieve their ends. Although Lilith initially resembles Dana, Mary, and other Butler female heroes who take on entire worlds isolated from community support or input, she becomes a member of a large "family" that includes not only humans and Oankali, but animals, plants, and sentient spaceships as well. The world at the end of ***Imago*** is truly utopian, a society in which all have an equal chance to work together on the construction of a new world. It fulfills Donna Haraway's dream of "an 'elsewhere' from which to envision a different and less hostile order of relationships among people, animals, technologies, and land," and Butler's dream of a world in which differences can be recognized without prejudice and celebrated.[9] "'Human beings fear difference,' Lilith had told him once. 'Oankali crave difference. Humans persecute their different ones, yet they need them to give themselves definition and status. Oankali seek difference and collect it. They need it to keep themselves from stagnation and overspecialization. . . . When you feel a conflict, try to go the Oankali way. Embrace difference'" (*Xenogenesis* 321).

Notes

1. Some of the recent texts that have particularly influenced my thinking about trends in women's utopian writing are Le Guin, *The Left Hand of Darkness, The Dispossessed,* and *Always Coming Home*; Russ, *The Female Man*; Wittig, *Les Guérillères*; Piercy, *Woman on the Edge of Time*; Gearhart, *The Wanderground*; Charnas, *Walk to the End of the World* and *Motherlines*; Tepper, *The Gate to Women's Country*; Elgin, *Native Tongue* and *The Judas Rose*; Slonczewski, *A Door Into Ocean*; Moffett, *Penterra*; Pamela Sargent, *The Shore of Women*; Felice, *Double Nocturne*; and Melissa Scott, *The Kindly Ones* and *Mighty Good Road.*

2. Zaki argues that "Butler believes that human nature is fundamentally violent and therefore flawed. The origin of violence, she suggests, lies in the human genetic structure, which is responsible for the contradictory impulses towards intelligence and hierarchy. These two conflicting impulses inevitably propel humans to wage war. . . . Connected to this trait is an inability to tolerate differences, usually physical differences of race and gender" (241), an argument Zaki takes nearly word for word from Butler's Oankali characters in *Xenogenesis.* I find it unconvincing in light of the adaptability of humans portrayed throughout Butler's work; but more important, the Oankali themselves prove to be wrong about many aspects of "human nature" through the course of the series. Dorothy Allison attempts to characterize Butler's views of men and women as essentialistic; again, I find the overall argument unconvincing, though she indicates points of contradiction in Butler's texts. Haraway's discussions of essentialism in Butler's work are much more complex. Haraway is troubled by what she perceives as the heterosexism of Butler's assumptions about human sexual behavior—a concern I share. But I would like to note that Butler's eradication of intercourse in *Xenogenesis* does not necessarily stem from her conservatism, as Zaki claims. Rather, Butler brings into question another "essential" component of humanity in bringing the "naturalness" of genital reproduction into question.

3. Sarah Lefanu, who notes that Butler is one of a number of women writing science fiction who uses "a traditional science fiction narrative framework . . . to undermine sexual and racial stereotypes," finds violence an essential component of Butler's feminist approach (88). "There is an element of violence . . . which is traditionally not a quality of 'feminine' writing," she writes. "[The violence] is transgressive; the construction of the inviolable body is a corollary of the construction of the coherent self" (99). Lefanu thus argues against the conception of Butler as having an essentialistic view of human nature.

4. Zaki's assertion that Butler's writing constitutes "dystopian pessimism, [which] assumes that dystopia

is inevitable because its origins are ontological or otherwise metaphysical" and is therefore "anti-utopian and conservative," seems to me a misreading of Butler's project, particularly when Zaki states that "Butler's unmediated connections between biology and behavior have an implicit corollary: that abandoning the human body is a necessary prerequisite for real human alteration" (242). Butler's fiction insists on the possibilities for transforming a biological "human nature," which is fluid and unpredictable, responding to specific material forces as well as to biology. The characters in *Xenogenesis* who claim to have genetic "proof" of humanity's innate destructive tendencies are themselves perpetually surprised by human behavior, which a genetic map alone often does not help them to predict.

5. In regard to Butler's insistence on re-creating the human biological conditions of reproduction, it seems important to point out that many feminist critics target the social contract, which excludes women from participation in citizenship by positing them as objects rather than subjects of the political sphere, not the biological conditions of reproduction, as the juncture that renders patriarchy inevitable (and seemingly natural). See Pateman for a more thorough discussion of this argument. Three feminist utopias that follow a similar theme, removing women from the nuclear family structure and allowing them full interaction in the public sphere, are Shuler, *She Who Remembers*; Thomas, *Reindeer Moon*; and Holland, *Pillar of the Sky*. Since Zaki questions whether Butler's "conservative" family structures may arise from her sensitivity to "the increasing conservatism of the contemporary social and political order, which has made substantial inroads upon Afro-American communities" (245), it may be helpful to note three other recent novels by African-American women— Alice Walker, *The Temple of My Familiar* (1989); Toni Morrison, *Beloved* (1987); and Sherley Anne Williams, *Dessa Rose* (1986); the first two of which fit into the fantasy genre—develop utopian themes based on radical restructurings of public and private spaces within the family and community.

6. Although the condition that afflicts the characters in *Clay's Ark* is described in earlier novels, I find it interesting that Butler chose to concentrate on the spread of the disease itself in the only "Patternist" novel published after the start of the AIDS epidemic. Like AIDS, the Clayark organism is spread through bodily fluids shared during physical contact, particularly during sex; when Keira chooses to lose her virginity with an infected man, she is fully aware that the consequence may be death. Yet rather than suggesting abstinence for affected individuals (as have some groups working to prevent the spread of AIDS), Butler insists that sexual activity is necessary for health: the disease exacerbates desire, and the individuals who shun physical contact die. She also insists that quarantine is an untenable solution, for a single individual who escapes can infect people "all over the world." Although the characters in *Clay's Ark* heroically attempt to isolate themselves, when the inevitable happens and the disease is spread beyond their community, they agree that "we knew it would happen sooner or later" (183).

7. "Mute" is a racial label as well as the name for a "handicap" in the "Patternist" books. In one of the contradictions of the dominant group, the mutes are alternately called "latents," implying the capacity to become telepathic, or treated as another species entirely with nothing to offer the dominant group but their bodies. When one character in *Mind of My Mind* hears the term "mute," she exclaims, "I know what it means . . . it means nigger!"

8. Hortense Spillers's "Mama's Baby, Papa's Maybe" discusses the physical inscription of the body by torture as a discursive signifier. The black body is "interpreted" by the white master discourse to mean "slave"; it is then reinscribed, by whippings or brandings, as the property of a particular owner, available alone for his interpretation. The relationship between this bodily "text" and the written text of slave narratives is extremely complicated, but Spillers links the two as spaces of resistance to a hegemonic interpretation. As such, the slave narrative text may be seen as utopian because it necessarily posits a place outside the site of the master discourse that made its writing necessary.

9. I want to thank Jane Donawerth for helping to shape my ideas about Butler's writing and for editing this essay through several different drafts. I also want to thank my husband, Paul Anderson, for proofreading and fact-checking.

Works Cited

Butler, Octavia E. "Bloodchild." In *The 1985 Annual World's Best SF*, edited by Donald A. Wollheim, 193-212. New York: DAW, 1985. (Originally published in *Isaac Asimov's Science Fiction Magazine* [June 1984]).

———. *Clay's Ark.* New York: St. Martin's. 1984.

———. "The Evening and the Morning and the Night." In *The Year's Best Science Fiction Fifth Annual Collection,* edited by Gardner Dozois, 280-302. New York: St. Martin's, 1988.

———. *Kindred.* Boston: Beacon, 1988.

———. *Mind of My Mind.* New York: Doubleday, 1977.

———. "Speech Sounds." In *The New Hugo Winners,* edited by Isaac Asimov, 199-216. New York: Wynwood, 1989. (Originally published in *Isaac Asimov's Science Fiction Magazine* [Dec. 1983]).

———. *Survivor.* New York: Doubleday, 1978.

———. *Wild Seed.* New York: Doubleday, 1980.

————. *Xenogenesis: Dawn, Adulthood Rites, Imago.* New York: Warner, 1987, 1988, 1989. Reprint. New York: Guild America, 1989.

Charnas, Suzy McKee. *Motherlines.* New York: Berkley, 1978.

————. *Walk to the End of the World.* New York: Ballantine, 1974.

Elgin, Suzette Haden. *The Judas Rose.* New York: DAW, 1986.

————. *Native Tongue.* New York: DAW, 1984.

Felice, Cynthia. *Double Nocturne.* New York: DAW, 1987.

Gearhart, Sally Miller. *The Wanderground: Stories of the Hill Women.* Watertown, Mass.: Persephone, 1979.

Haraway, Donna Jeanne. *Primate Visions: Gender, Race, and Nature in the World of Modern Science.* New York: Routledge, 1989.

Holland, Cecelia. *Pillar of the Sky.* New York: Knopf, 1985.

Le Guin, Ursula K. *Always Coming Home.* New York: Harper and Row, 1985.

————. *The Dispossessed.* New York: Harper and Row, 1974.

————. *The Left Hand of Darkness.* 1969. New York: Ace, 1976.

Lefanu, Sarah. *In the Chinks of the World Machine.* London: Women's Press, 1988. Reprinted as *Feminism and Science Fiction.* Bloomington: Indiana Univ. Press, 1989.

Lorde, Audre. *Sister Outsider.* Trumansburg: Crossing, 1984.

Moffett, Judith. *Penterra.* New York: Worldwide, 1988.

Morrison, Toni. *Beloved.* New York: Knopf, 1987.

Pateman, Carole. *The Sexual Contract.* Stanford: Stanford Univ. Press, 1988.

Pfaelzer, Jean. "The Changing of the Avant-Garde: The Feminist Utopia." *Science Fiction Studies* 15 (Nov. 1988): 282-94.

Piercy, Marge. *Woman on the Edge of Time.* New York: Knopf: Reprint. New York: Fawcett, 1976.

Russ, Joanna. *The Female Man.* New York: Bantam, 1975.

Sargent, Pamela. *The Shore of Women.* New York: Crown, 1986.

Scott, Melissa. *The Kindly Ones.* New York: Baen, 1987.

————. *Mighty Good Road.* New York: Baen, 1990.

Shuler, Linda Lay. *She Who Remembers.* New York: Arbor House, 1988.

Spillers, Hortense J. "Mama's Baby, Papa's Maybe: An American Grammar Book." *Diacritics* (Summer 1987): 64-81.

Tepper, Sheri S. *The Gate to Women's Country.* New York: Doubleday, 1988.

Thomas, Elizabeth Marshall. *Reindeer Moon.* Boston: Houghton Mifflin, 1987.

Walker, Alice. *The Temple of My Familiar.* New York: Harcourt Brace Jovanovich, 1989.

Williams, Sherley Anne. *Dessa Rose.* New York: William Morrow, 1986.

Wittig, Monique. *Les Guérillères.* Boston: Beacon, 1985.

Zaki, Hoda. "Utopia, Dystopia, and Ideology in the Science Fiction of Octavia Butler." *Science Fiction Studies* 17 (1990): 239-51.

Cathy Peppers (essay date March 1995)

SOURCE: Peppers, Cathy. "Dialogic Origins and Alien Identities in Butler's *Xenogenesis*." *Science-Fiction Studies* 22, no. 1 (March 1995): 47-62.

[*In the following essay, Peppers explores the multiple theories of origins in Butler's* Xenogenesis *trilogy.*]

Octavia E. Butler's post-apocalyptic trilogy **Xenogenesis** is about a new beginning for the remnants of humanity, those few humans who are still alive after a nuclear apocalypse to be "rescued" by the alien Oankali. In order to continue to survive, the humans are offered the "choice" of reproduction only if they engage in a species-order version of miscegenation with the Oankali. As the title of the trilogy suggests, **Xenogenesis** is an origin story, a story about the origins of human identity, but it is a story with a difference. "Xenogenesis" means "the production of offspring different from either of its parents"; this is reproduction with a difference, the (re)production of difference. And the "Xeno" of this genesis comes from the Greek *xenos*, which in its original bivalence meant both guest/friend and alien/stranger. As an origin story, this trilogy tells about the genesis of an alien humanity, of a humanity which will survive not, as Donna Haraway puts it, by "recreat[ing] the sacred image of the same" (*Primate Visions* 378), but because Lilith, the African-American heroine of the first novel, will become the progenitrix of the new race of "constructs" (children born of Oankali and human parents). She will give birth to herself as other. As she asks the Oankali, "What will our children be?" Their answer: "Different. . . . Not quite like you. A little like us" (***Dawn*** §1.5:44).[1]

The focus of my reading is to see how Butler's trilogy enacts what Donna Haraway calls a "cyborg" origin story. While Haraway claims in "A Cyborg Manifesto" that "the cyborg has no origin story in the Western sense," it is important to note that she does not say that cyborgs have no origin stories. She makes a distinction between traditional Western origin stories, which are based on "salvation history," and are "about the Fall, the imagination of a once-upon-a-time wholeness before language, before writing," and cyborg origin stories, which "subvert the central myths of origin of Western culture" by focusing on "the power to survive, not on the basis of original innocence, but on the basis of seizing the tools to mark the world that has marked them as other" ("A Cyborg Manifesto" 175).[2] This distinction is important because it offers a way out of the double-bind "feminism" often finds itself in when it encounters the "postmodern."

In general, postmodern critics/theorists exhibit an allergy to origin stories, seeing them, as Lyotard sees "master narratives" in general, as outmoded reifications of humanist, essentialist notions of identity. The various versions of the postmodern "anti-aesthetic, anti-essentialism" offered by such critics as Brian McHale and Larry McCaffery tend to construct an image of postmodern fiction as dismantling master narratives wherever it finds them, eschewing the "individual" as a sentimental attachment, and replacing the nostalgic search for origins with a sometimes grim, sometimes gleeful insistence on Baudrillard's simulacrum (which tells us that we live in a world of copies with no originals). In the postmodern/sf critical tradition (which has its own origin stories[3]), this has led to a privileging of cyberpunk as "apotheosis of the postmodern" (Csicsery-Ronay, Jr. 193). It has also led to claiming a "post-gender," origin-less cyborg as the new ideal for our posthumanist bodies and identities. In the process, as postmodern sf's other, feminist sf is characterized as being mired in essentialist humanism, nostalgically longing for maternal origins.[4]

For a feminist, for this feminist, the anti-essentialist, anti-origins attitude taken up by mainstream postmodernism needs to be challenged, in order to recognize that those whose stories have been written out of the dominant accounts have different stakes in the desire to re-write origin stories. As a way out of the dichotomy set up between the postmodern allergy to origins and the (supposed) feminist recuperation of essentialist origins, one might merely out-Foucault Foucault. It is, after all, to Michel Foucault's 1971 article, "Nietzsche, Genealogy, and History," that we might look to establish the "origin" of contemporary postmodern attitudes about origin stories.

In that article, Foucault claims that we should "challenge the pursuit of the origin" because "it is an attempt to capture the exact essence of things, their purest possibilities, and their carefully protected identities; because this search assumes the existence of immobile forms that precede the external world of accident and succession" (78). To challenge this discourse about origins, and the lack of value in origin stories it implies, one need only turn to Foucault's *History of Sexuality,* in which he notes that "discourse can be both an instrument . . . of power, but also a hindrance, a stumbling block, a point of resistance and a starting point for an opposing strategy" (101).

There's an ambivalence in Foucault here, one I'd like to exploit in order to open up the discourse on origin stories to questions of gender and race. As a feminist, I can recognize the problems in how traditional origin stories are used to reproduce the logics of domination by positing "natural, original" gender and race differences. At the same time, it's important to read how alternative/rewritten feminist origin stories destabilize, contradict, and contest the traditional discourses of origin on their own turf. These origin stories are powerful precisely because they not only denaturalize the dominant accounts, but also because they partake of the enabling power that marks all discourse about origins.

Xenogenesis, as a "cyborg" origin story, partakes of these qualities. It "seizes as tools" our culture's most powerful origin stories, those stories which are at the origin of what it means to be human in the Western order: the Biblical story of our genesis as "Male and Female, created He them"; the sociobiological story, which situates our identities in our genes; and the paleoanthropological story of our evolution from our Stone Age ancestors. To these dominant discourses, the trilogy adds what Foucault might call a "subjugated knowledge," a genealogy often written out of the dominant accounts, and therefore a powerful tool for resistance: the narrative of the African diaspora and slavery (a/the origin story of African-American identity). ***Xenogenesis*** as an origin story and as sf, is not about denying the discourses of science (biology, anthropology), nor the discourse of Biblical genesis; rather, it's about changing them from within, using the very power of these discourses to help us imagine the origins of human identity in other ways.

Xenogenesis resists "recreating the sacred image of the same," not by merely re-telling one origin story with a difference, but by putting the four originary discourses I mentioned above into a dialogic relation with each other. As Mikhail Bakhtin sees it, while monologic discourse, or a traditional Western origin story, might pretend to the illusion that there is one Truth to tell, "any living discourse" cannot escape its existence in a "dialogically agitated environment . . . entangled with alien" contexts (276). Just as the surviving humans in *Xenogenesis* cannot escape being entangled with the alien Oankali, the origin stories retold in the text exist only in dialogic relation to each other, and it is in this excess of genealogies that oppressive ideologies are exposed and resisted, and simple essential identities are contested.

So here I want to map the four originary discourses/origin stories which Butler makes use of in *Xenogenesis*: the Biblical, the sociobiological, the paleoanthropological, and the slave narrative. My point will not be simply to see how each traditional narrative is changed, but also to consider the changed meanings made from their dialogic interaction with each other. As I hope to show, the kinds of identities we can imagine are dependent on the kinds of origin stories we can tell. Ultimately, Butler's trilogy exposes the relationships between gender/race and genealogy, showing us how to acknowledge difference without necessarily resorting to "essentialist," traditional humanist, bounded-self identities.

1. ADAM'S OTHERS: BIBLICAL GENESIS AND
SLAVERY.

A quotation from Bakhtin on the (almost) inevitably dialogic nature of any living discourse:

> Every discourse . . . cannot fail to be oriented toward the "already uttered," the "already known". . . . Only the mythic Adam, who approached a virginal and as yet verbally unqualified world with the first word, could really have escaped . . . this dialogic inter-orientation with the alien [word, self, language].
>
> (279)

In place of this "mythic Adam," *Xenogenesis* begins with one of Adam's others, Lilith, which reminds us that even "our originary ancestor" in Biblical discourse did not stand alone at the start of the human story.

Adam himself is "created" in two slightly different versions of Genesis: in 1:27, "God created man in his own image; male and female created He them"; in 2:7-25, God creates Adam from dust, Adam gives names to the animals, and then Woman (Eve) is created from Adam's rib. Lilith's genesis story, however, happens off-stage between these two chapters. Originally a Sumero-Babylonian goddess, she was assimilated into the Biblical genesis by Hebraic tradition as Adam's first wife; however, because she refused to submit to his rule (in particular, would not lie beneath him in sex), she was repudiated and cast out of Eden. Her "fate" was to couple with "demons" and give birth to a monstrous brood of children.[5] Clearly, in a genesis story that begins with Lilith as first ancestor, we have a text which does not pretend to have the privilege of escaping a dialogic relation with the "alien" or with the "already known" stories of the origins of gender and race.

But this re-telling of genesis from Lilith's point of view is not a simple utopian re-valuing of maternal origins. This "reconstruction" of Lilith is not innocent of the power dynamics of the history of race and gender. While some feminist revisions of Lilith's story insist on her heroic agency,[6] Butler's African-American Lilith is forced to live the "choice" enforced during slavery. Lilith is "awakened" by the Oankali in order to "parent" the first group of humans who will be returned to the reconstructed post-apocalyptic Earth. Once there, they will only be allowed to reproduce and survive if they engage in "miscegenation" with the "demons"/the Oankali. Lilith sees her role as being a "Judas goat" leading humanity to an undesired mutation, and her hope throughout the first novel is to prepare the humans for escape once they reach Earth. In short, she is anything but eager to embrace the power of being the progenitrix of the new human race. In a conversation with the first Oankali who tells her what will be, she says, "It is crossbreeding, whatever you call it. . . . Then she thought of grotesque, Medusa children. . . . Snakes for hair. Nests of nightcrawlers for eyes and ears" (*Dawn* §1.5:44-5). Lilith's use of Medusa imagery here is not only a reference to what the Oankali look like—their sensory organs are tentacles—but also an echo of the serpent-like demon children of the Biblical Lilith.

This re-creation of the black woman's "choice" under slavery—that is, the non-choice of being permanently "available" to the sexual desires of the slave owners—reminds us not only that any historically accurate genealogy of African-Americans must acknowledge the spectre of coerced miscegenation at its origins.[7] It also reminds us to take racial history into account in any recreation of Lilith. As Sondra O'Neale notes, while earlier religious iconography included "the black woman . . . as a glorious archetype . . . these images of black women as equally acceptable cultural standards of beauty" began to change, until, by the 16th century, "art created to accommodate the emerging slave trade" presented black women "as icons of evil rather than . . . divine beauty." For example, "the black woman was introduced as Lilith . . . made responsible for [Adam's] sin" (142).

Here, because the text puts the origin story of African diaspora and slavery into dialogue with Biblical discourse, we are led to see how a recovery of black women's identity must also take into account the fact that a potentially empowering goddess like Lilith was "racialized," "became black" as part of aesthetic representation in the service of slavery. Thus, while Lilith in *Xenogenesis* does eventually "concede" to mating with the Oankali,[8] and while she does gain power from this "choice" (physically—the Oankali enhance her strength and memory; and narratively—she becomes the "mother" of the new race of "construct" children whose lives are chronicled in the second and third novels), Lilith is still a "slave" to the negative connotations of her name. Throughout the rest of the trilogy, she continues small resistances to her life with the Oankali: her construct children note that she clings to writing things down, even though she's been given an eidetic memory; she continues to touch her human husband's hair, even though mating with the Oankali leaves the other partners unable to stand physical contact without mediation by the ooloi (the third sex of the Oankali). And she repeatedly "escapes" temporarily to be alone as much as she can, even though mating with the Oankali makes one physically dependent on being near the ooloi.

Further, in **Adulthood Rites,** she tacitly approves of the desire of the Resisters—those humans who, on Earth, have escaped mating with the Oankali even though it means their continued sterility and eventual extinction—to be allowed to settle a human-only colony on Mars. This, despite the fact that the Resisters have, in their legends, recreated Lilith as the traditional Biblical icon of the evil mother. As one of the Resisters tells her:

> You should change [your name]. It isn't very popular.
>
> I know . . . I'm the one who made it unpopular. . . . I awakened the first three groups of Humans to be sent back to Earth. I told them what their situation was, what their options were, and they decided I was responsible for it all. . . . Some of the younger ones have been taught to blame me for everything—as though I were a second Satan or Satan's wife.

> (*Rites* [*Adulthood Rites* §1.6:289-90])

They further accuse her of having "sold out" humanity like Judas, and even speculate that she did so because she's lesbian (*Rites* §1.6:291).

The second novel's narrative shows how, in the struggle to remain "pure, essential humans," the Resisters retell the traditional Biblical story to narrate their new "origins." The third novel, **Imago,** includes a group of Peruvians who escaped being found by the Oankali, and they also use the Biblical story of Mary to narrate their origins and to remain "pure." In both cases, putting the origin story of African-American diaspora and slavery into dialogue with traditional Biblical accounts does not deny the enabling power of the genesis origin story, but rather asks "enabling for whom?" by resisting it on its own turf, opening it up to accounts of the origin of gender and race.

2. (Eu)Gen(et)ic Engineering: Sociobiology and Slavery.

From the beginning of **Dawn,** Lilith's perception of her situation echoes the discourses of both the slave narrative and sociobiology. Her "awakening" to discover that she has been taken from Earth to be kept captive on an alien ship orbiting beyond the moon reconstructs the African slave's Middle Passage. Like the African slaves in America, she is (at first) denied access to reading or writing materials, those things "humans need . . . to help us remember" (§2.4:65). Hence, while the Oankali can tell Lilith the "stories of the long, multispecies Oankali history," the most Lilith can do is scratch Nikanj's name in the dirt with her finger (§2.4:64-65). And, like Harriet Jacobs describing the moral contradictions fundamental to life under slavery—"There may be sophistry in all this; but the condition of a slave confuses all principles of morality, and, in fact, renders the practice of them impossible" (55)—Lilith, too, realizes that "She was a captive. What courtesy did a captive owe beyond what was necessary for self-preservation?" (§2.4:67). She perceives the morality of "her job . . . to prepare [the other humans] to be the Oankali's new [reproductive] trading partners" as "impossible" (§3.1:117).

At the same time, the slave master Oankali are also figured as the ultimate sociobiologists. One of the meanings of "Oankali" is "gene traders," or, as one Oankali puts it, "We do what you would call genetic engineering . . . naturally" (§1.5:43). Because the very essence of the Oankali compels them to "acquire new life," to mate with and thereby use and manipulate other species' genes, Lilith perceives herself as a "genetic experiment." While the "genetic engineers" insist that their gene trading is not about "slavery" (§1.5:26), the narrative of **Xenogenesis** relentlessly keeps the discourses of slavery and sociobiology in continuous dialogue.

But this dialogue is not about using the story of slavery to flatly deny the explanatory power of biology to construct our human identity; it is about changing the sociobiological story from within, using its very real explanatory power to help us imagine the origins of humanity in alien ways, ways more open to including our "imperfections," our differences within. In this way, **Xenogenesis** is a "cyborg" origin story in two senses: discursively, it's not a monologic "salvation history," but a dialogic hybrid, creating an other human identity by "seizing the tools to mark the world that has marked" everyone except white men "as other"; and it's also a story of our origins as cyborgs. As Donna Haraway claims, "we are cyborgs. The cyborg is our ontology" ("Cyborg Manifesto" 150). Though the cyborg generally indicates a hybrid of machine and (usually human) organism (e.g., Robocop or Terminator), Haraway expands it to encompass a broader notion of boundary-crossing identity, an ontology within which, in general, the boundaries which have separated "organic/natural" from "technological" have grown porous. In this sense, we are reminded that what we know of the "natural body" is the product of the culturally powerful discourse of biology. And biology is a "logos," a discursive technology, and such "technologies [are] instruments for enforcing meanings" about the individual ("A Cyborg Manifesto" 164).

Where the African-American narrative of slavery finds its origin in miscegenation, rather than in the "purity" of the races, the cyborg narrative of human identity might find its origin in a sociobiological determinism. But rather than reinforcing the story of the "pure, bounded individual" who "evolves" through a competitive "survival of the fittest," it finds our origins in genetic "miscegenations"—mutations, symbiosis. Perhaps we are "biologically determined" ("our fate is in our genes"), but not in the ways we usually think.

Butler's use of sociobiological explanations for human identity in her sf tends to focus on "imperfections," (Bonner 52) and she continues this focus with a vengeance in *Xenogenesis*. For example, the Oankali are particularly attracted to Lilith's "talent" for cancer, which they are able to genetically engineer to enable the regrowth of lost limbs, and eventually to create construct children who are shapeshifters. Seeing cancer in this way not only puts a positive spin on something we normally find hideous (and fatal), it also disrupts the usual sociobiological story of human evolution, which assumes that every biological characteristic has a clear purpose either favouring or disfavouring survival. And, as I've had reason to come to understand, cancer is a particularly frightening disease because it doesn't allow for the usual medicalized use of military language to describe it. We cannot "battle" cancer as a "foreign enemy" which has "invaded" us and must be "expelled"; cancer cells are not wholly other, but exist precisely on the border of me/not me. In revaluing cancer, the text is also therefore valuing "mutation" and "boundary-crossing" identity.

Beyond the use of cancer, the Oankali themselves are represented as completely symbiotic beings: originating from a single-celled organelle ancestor which proved itself capable of mutating enough to mate with virtually any other organism (even ones which "were unable to perceive one another as alive" [*Imago* §1.4:530]), the Oankali have gone on to grow and change in interbreeding with species across the galaxy. Some of the new "species" of Oankali which have resulted are embodiments of Oankali technologies (e.g., their ships and transport vehicles)—they do not make non-living technologies—and all the Oankali, including these, are able to link up in a sort of embodied version of the internet and communicate together in "the closest thing to telepathy" Lilith has ever seen (*Dawn* §2.11:107). But it's not just the Oankali who are symbionts; enforced contact with them makes humans see how we, too, are already symbiotic beings. As Nikanj (an ooloi) explains:

> Examine [a human]. Inside him, so many different things are working together to keep him alive. Inside his cells, mitochondria, a previously independent form of life, have found a haven and trade their ability to synthesize proteins and metabolize fats for room to live and reproduce. We're in his cells too now, and the cells have accepted us. . . . Even before we arrived, they had bacteria living in their intestines and protecting them from other bacteria that would hurt or kill them. They could not exist without symbiotic relationships with other creatures. Yet such relationships frighten them. . . . I think we're as much symbionts as their mitochondria were originally. They could not have evolved into what they are without mitochondria.
>
> (*Rites* §3.1:418)

Here we see Butler making use of sociobiology to tell a story not only of Oankali origins, but of ours, as well. And yet, it is not quite the usual sociobiological story, nor is there a simple, unquestioned acceptance of this idea of symbiotic identity. Despite the fact that the humans' relations with the Oankali are marked by a powerful erotic desire, "such relationships [still] frighten them," and with good historical reason.

As an African-American writer of sf, Butler's use of the discourse of sociobiology is similar to that of the minority writers examined by Nancy Stepan and Sander Gilman in "Appropriating the Idioms of Science." As the discourse of science in the late 19th century rose to become "an especially weighty discourse of identity," and in particular, as science was (and still is) marked by the ideology of racism as a reinforcement of slavery, many minority writers, who were constructed as raced objects of study by this very science, "reacted by actively seeking . . . to seize and control . . . the idioms" of science, "to use its tools and techniques to define and defend themselves" (171-72).[9]

Butler's appropriation and redeployment of the idioms of sociobiology involves recasting the usual origin story of the evolutionary rise to dominance of the heroic individual (that first organelle floating in the primeval soup) through ruthless competition and survival of the fittest, by privileging instead the "marginally acceptable" story of Lynn Margulis, the microbiologist who collaborated with James Lovelock on the Gaia hypothesis. Her "symbiotic theory of the origin" of the species remains "controversial" (McDermott 49). Margulis' theory that many of the microbiotic components of our cells, like the mitochondria, evolved from free-living species which later entered into symbiotic relationships, posits a human identity which suggests that "All of us are walking communities." As Jeanne McDermott describes the implication of this alternative origin story: "Margulis challenges the . . . myth of the rugged individual—alone, self-contained, and able to survive" (50). If, as Margulis suggests, "our concept of the individual is totally warped," and "we . . . are [really] composites," or symbionts, "living together in intimate association of different kinds of organisms," then our usual notions of "individuality" and "independence" are really "illusions." In addition, "the traditional view of a cutthroat Darwinian world," in which the mechanics of evolution justified "exploitation, since it was natural, [as therefore] morally acceptable," is also an illusion. It becomes "a fallacy" to think that "evolution works at all times for the 'good of the individual'"; instead, there is a "thin line between evolutionary competition and cooperation . . . guests and prisoners can be the same thing, and the deadliest enemies can be indispensable to survival" (Margulis and Sagan 57-66).[10]

It's hard to think of a better representation of the relationship between the Oankali and the humans in *Xenogenesis.* As Lilith and the other humans are forced into an intimate alliance with the Oankali, these "deadliest enemies" become "indispensable to human survival." In choosing to privilege Margulis' symbiotic story of origins over the traditional Darwinian one, Butler is able to expose and contest the eugenic aspirations driving the latter. The eugenics movement, born at the turn of the century, xenophobically reacting to immigration and nostalgically carrying forward the logic of slavery, dreams of a recreation of the (imagined) racially "pure" origin of the species. Eugenic dreams were both supported by the Darwinian logic that "exploitation" of "inferior races" by "superior" ones is "natural" and therefore "morally acceptable," and in turn supported the scientific use of biological discourse to construct "race." And they still function in this way. Currently, eugenic dreams of creating a "pure and perfect humanity" continue to supply the logic for our contemporary uses of the prime technology of sociobiology, genetic engineering.

Butler's representation of genetic engineering in *Xenogenesis* is complex because she insists on restoring the originary history of this science to its contemporary manifestations. Thus, the Oankali genetic engineers are neither simply "indispensable" aids to human evolution nor "deadliest enemies"; the dialogue between these two versions is never neatly resolved. Early in *Dawn,* here is Lilith's reaction to the Oankali plan:

> In a very real sense, she was an experimental animal. Experimental animal, parent to domestic animals? Or . . . nearly extinct animal, part of a captive breeding program? Human biologists had done that before . . . used a few captive members of an endangered animal species to breed more for the wild population. Was that what she was headed for? Forced artificial insemination. Surrogate motherhood? Fertility drugs and forced "donations" of eggs? Implantation of unrelated fertilized eggs. Removal of children from mothers at birth. . . . Humans had done these things to captive breeders—all for a higher good, of course.
>
> (§2.4:63)

Notice how this paragraph traces a genealogy of genetic engineering back to its origins in slavery. From the apparently laudable goal of saving species from extinction, to the contested use of reproductive technologies on women, to the use of slave women as captive breeders is indeed a slippery slope.

And yet, we are reminded, the Oankali genetic engineers don't trade on the basis of slavery (§1.3:26). What humans have done historically in the interest of eugenic control (mired in what the Oankali call our "Human Contradiction," which puts intelligence at the service of hierarchical behavior), the Oankali do "naturally." And in contrast to Lilith's negative description above, when we later see examples of Oankali use of genetic engineering, we clearly see the intense, usually erotic, pleasure involved in their manipulations, and, on the whole, the Oankali seem to be engaged in biophilic, not eugenic, uses of technology.

The unresolved dialogic relation between the discourses of slavery and sociobiology in *Xenogenesis* exposes the racist and sexist genealogy of the traditional biological origin story, but, by including Lynn Margulis' alternative story of our symbiotic microbiological origins, Bulter's text also shows us the possibility of imagining less reductive notions of individual identity. In this, Butler's narrative functions like the other narratives of women scientists described by Haraway: "In dispersing single meanings and subverting stable narratives of sex [and race], they . . . open degrees of freedom in their culture's constructions" of identities (*Primate Visions* 342). But this dispersion of meanings of "the biological individual" does not lead to what Susan Bordo calls deconstructionist postmodernism's "imagination of disembodiment: a dream of being everywhere" (143). Butler's sf contestation of sociobiology's story of the individual does not argue that biology is irrelevant and human identity only the reflection of a disembodied culture. What is being argued instead is that our choice of biological stories makes a difference; as "cyborgs" whose "organic" identities are produced in part through an "interface" with the "technology" of meaning which is biology, we (or some of us) might have good reason to choose the alternative story offered by the Oankali.

However, as for other feminists trying to imagine the nature of identity in the face of a relentless ideology of "anatomy is destiny," for Butler, too, the problem of "essence" will not simply go away with the advent of an alternative story for microbiological anatomy. If the essence of human nature resides only in our genes, then the Oankali have already taken this essence before the trilogy begins; they have already read and copied all the genetic codes of the humans before awakening them to set up human-Oankali settlements. Taking E. O. Wilson's (frightening) promise that sociobiology can "monitor the genetic basis of social behavior" as a caution (575), the text also raises the question of how far our biological nature determines our cultural structures and human behaviors. As even the Oankali genetic engineers know, there's more to human evolution than genes; as they say, "we need cultural as well as genetic diversity for a good trade" (*Rites* 283).

3. RESISTING A PALEOANTHROPOLOGICAL RECREATION OF THE SAME.

As a post-apocalyptic story, *Xenogenesis* has wiped the cultural slate clean in order to retell the story of human evolution. This enables Butler to question just how biologically determined the most "interesting" aspects of "human nature" are. As Stephen Gould notes, debates about biological determinism engender no controversy when it comes to such biological constraints as our inability to photosynthesize, but the social and political stakes involved in the paleoanthropological story are exposed when we come to the "interesting" "specific behaviors that distress us and that we struggle to change (or enjoy and fear to abandon): aggression, xenophobia, and male dominance, for example" (*The Mismeasure of Man* 328). The traditional story of human evolution from the trees to the development of technology and civilization has tended, as Misia Landau notes, to tell the same story over and over again: these "interesting" cultural structures and human behaviors find their origins in the logic of a Darwinian teleology, where natural selection determines them as most fit for survival (178).[11] Thus we are told, especially by the likes of Desmond Morris and Robert Ardrey, that "territoriality" (read: aggression, violence), "xenophobia" (read: racism), and "gross sexual dimorphism" (read: sexism) are "innate" features of human nature, and therefore biologically inevitable, both in the past and into the future.[12]

That Butler chose to title the ultimate volume of her trilogy *Imago*—which means the "perfect stage" of an animal at the end of its evolution—suggests that she is indeed telling a story of evolution in which the "most fit" will survive. But there is an irony to this title, and to its teleological implications as well. This evolutionary use of the term "imago" was coined in Linnaeus' taxonomy for insects to name the final and perfect form after metamorphosis. In terms of the trilogy as a whole, what metamorphosis will humanity, and the paleoanthropological origin story, undergo before reaching "perfection"? And what will happen to those "innate" and "interesting" qualities of human nature, aggression, xenophobia, male dominance?

Hoda Zaki reads *Xenogenesis* as reflecting Butler's belief that "human nature is a biologically-determined entity"; the trilogy's representation of "unmediated connections between biology and behavior" mean "Butler believes that human nature is fundamentally violent," that xenophobia is "innate," and that "men are intrinsically more violent than women." For Zaki, the trilogy posits "a human incapacity to change in response to

radically altered conditions" (241-42). To be sure, we do see characters recapitulate those behaviors which traditional paleoanthropology tells us are the naturally-selected-for products of our evolution. The first human male Lilith meets after being awakened tries to rape her; in the Resister colonies it is not long before some humans create weapons and begin raiding and killing each other; and some of the Resister colonies divide themselves by race and react xenophobically to others.

But I don't think the text rests this easily with the traditional story. As with the other origin stories it retells, *Xenogenesis* puts this "already known" story into dialogue with an "alien" story of another evolution, redeploying the idioms of paleoanthropology in order to contest the "innateness" of a human nature based on violence, xenophobia and male dominance.

This dialogue begins in *Dawn*, staged as a "debate" between first Lilith and Paul Titus (the first awakened human she's allowed to meet), and then between Lilith and Tate Marah (the first human Lilith awakens to prepare for resettlement with the Oankali). In the largest sense, it's a debate about whether or not humans can rewrite the "Stone Age" origin story/script. Lilith, by virtue of her personal history as an African-American woman who has studied anthropology as a means of knowing cultural difference, and as one who has already lived with the Oankali, represents a version of the paleoanthropological story Haraway calls "Woman the Gatherer," as opposed to characters like Paul Titus and some Resisters who recapitulate the "Man the Hunter" story.

In the Man-the-Hunter story, human culture is built on innate aggression, dominance structures, and xenophobia, reflected in hunting, weapon-making, and traffic in women. As Haraway notes, in this story, "the crucial evolutionary adaptations making possible a human way of life" were those associated with "male ways of life as the motors of the human past and future. . . . Hunting was a male innovation . . . the principle of change" ("The Contest for Primate Nature" 82). In contrast, Woman the Gatherer (a contestatory story told by such scientists as Adrienne Zihlman, Sarah Hrdy, and others) is about "female mobility [as gatherers and] the transformative power of . . . mother-young relationships"; in this version, instead of meat-eating produced by hunting, the crucial evolutionary change was about becoming better gatherers—"the shift was not from plants to meat, but from fruits to tubers"—where "a sharp sexual division of labor was not" crucial. Altogether, the Woman-the-Gatherer story is about "the deconstruction of staples in the narrative of . . . technological determinism, masculinism, and war: e.g., male-female sexual bonding, male-male agonism, home bases as hearths for nuclear families, and the trope of the tool-weapon" (*Primate Visions* 345, 337).

We see several of these competing story elements being debated in the scene between Lilith and Paul Titus. Paul Titus, embodying the Man-the-Hunter story, dreams of hamburgers, and assumes that human life back on Earth will be like the (Desmond Morris version of the) "Stone Age," where giving birth in the jungle will be brutish and likely lead to death (and keep women in their place), and Lilith will end up living "like a cave-woman"; men will "drag [her] around, put [her] in a harem, beat the shit out of [her]." In contrast, Lilith claims, "we don't have to go back to the Stone Age," or at least not that version. Lilith does not miss eating meat (the Oankali don't eat it, nor do they encourage hunting) and sees the value of subsisting primarily on cassava and other roots/vegetables. And for her, "natural childbirth" (which she has already undergone in her pre-apocalypse life) may not be "fun," but it is preferable to pregnant women "being treated as though they were sick" (*Dawn* §2.8:90-93).

Lilith sees the possibility of living an alternative story of human evolution with the Oankali, and, when we see her and others living this story in *Adulthood Rites,* it is indeed a life which "deconstructs the staples in the narrative" of Man the Hunter. Hunting has been replaced by agriculture and gathering, which in turn obviates the sexual division of labor, weapons production, aggression and hierarchy, and leads to the displacement of the nuclear family.[13] In short, the behaviors and social structures which traditional paleoanthropology tells us are innate and therefore ineluctable can be changed, not only by changing the story of our biological identity, but also by the processes of cultural evolution.

Still, as Lilith knows, there will always be those who choose to re-live the same old story. There is Paul Titus, whose "caveman" logic leads him to attempt to rape Lilith.[14] There are the men Lilith awakens who attempt to reinstate male violence, dominance, and harem building. And there is Tate Marah, a white woman, who at first believes that "human beings are more alike than different" and are therefore doomed to keep repeating the mistakes of the past (§3.3:131). In *Adulthood Rites,* this is essentially what the Resisters do. In their desire to remain "pure, essential humans," they recreate the traditional story of Man the Hunter, with various villages divided along racial lines, the (re)manufacture of guns and Bibles, raiding between villages, and social structures built around nuclear (albeit sterile) families and the traffic in women. As one Resister puts it: "That's the way human beings are now [again]. Shoot the men. Steal the women" (§4.5:485). But the narrative makes clear that humans are not biologically determined to restore the sacred image of the same.

While a xenophobic reaction to the alien Oankali is figured in the text as a biological revulsion, so is attraction to them, and Lilith and others learn to overcome

their revulsion. While human males, in particular, seem most invested in maintaining a Man the Hunter way of life (and, indeed, according to the Oankali, "human males bear more of the [tendency to hierarchical behavior] than any other people" [*Rites* §3.4:432]), we see various male characters resist this presumably biological imperative. And Tate, who becomes a leader of the Resisters, is finally shown to be both adaptable and dedicated to changing the "Stone Age" script of violence and male dominance. Thus the narrative implies that it is not necessarily biology that determines these behaviors and cultural structures, but social and political vested interests. Perhaps this is why it is characters in the middle of the sexual/racial (and species?) hierarchy of privilege—Tate, a woman but white; and Akin, Lilith's construct son, who is male but bears the mark of race and species otherness—who convince the Oankali that the Resister humans should be given a chance to begin their evolution again on Mars. Perhaps because these characters gain some privilege from their places in the traditional evolutionary story, they are also in a position to question it most effectively. In any case, the Oankali do relent, although the "fitness" of this colony to survive on Mars is left ambiguous. Akin cannot decide whether the Oankali represent a necessary symbiosis ensuring human survival or predatory enemies blocking human evolution (§3.4:433), and while he is convinced, as are the Oankali, that human evolution is biologically determined, at the same time, "chance exists. Mutation. Unexpected effects of the new environment" (§4.5:488), so that perhaps the new genesis of humanity on Mars may not replicate the same old nuclear apocalyptic future.

While Butler questions the biological innateness of the Man-the-Hunter paleoanthropological story, she also turns the trope of evolutionary inevitability against itself by showing how the cultural structures and human behaviors produced by this story may themselves be evolutionary "dead ends," making humans unfit for survival. By the end of *Adulthood Rites,* several of the Resister villages have committed mass suicide, and the escalating weapons production and raiding have killed many more. In a particularly ironic and funny scene, the Resisters' archaeological salvage operation of a Catholic church turns up a plastic icon of Christ which Akin determines to be poisonous and nonbiodegradeable. While Tate suggests that humans need these icons as reflections of their identity, it is also clear that as long as humans cling to this recreation of the same, this is how "people poison each other. . . . In a way, that's how the war started" (§2.16:380-81). And, while the Oankali do relent and allow the Resisters to begin again on Mars, this part of the story happens off-stage, between *Adulthood Rites* and *Imago,* and is therefore a "dead end" in the trilogy's narrative of evolution. Apparently, *Xenogenesis* is not very interested in yet another story of origins which will probably only replicate a logic of purity and produce human identities which are (willfully?) "innocent" of the possibilities inherent in the "pollution" of symbiotic, cyborg identities.

Overall, as a story of origins, *Xenogenesis* contests our culture's most powerful originary discourses (Biblical, biological, anthropological), which are also therefore our most weighty discourses of identity, by insistently keeping each one in dialogue with the others, and with the African-American origin story of slavery as well. In this way, the text offers a reading lesson for keeping feminism in dialogue with postmodernism in the context of origin stories. If the Oankali are figures for postmodern anti-origins ("going back . . . is the one direction that's closed to us" [*Dawn* §1.5:39]), and the Resisters are figures for an insistence on an essential notion of identity, neither comes away unchanged from the encounter. The text offers a third choice between: 1) a postmodern call to "forsake the pursuit of the origin" (as Foucault recommends) or to reveal science as yet one more meaningless master narrative (in the Lyotardian sense), and 2) an essentialist desire to claim some gender/race identity based in a "biology" outside history or cultural construction (as feminists are accused of doing). We can, as cyborgs, choose among alternative stories of our biological inheritance (themselves technologies of meanings) with which to interface.

The trilogy itself privileges this third choice, represented by Lilith's origin of a new "race" of "constructs": her children with the Oankali are the hero(ine)s of the second and third novels, and these constructs, being constructed out of the complex discursive dialogue I've described above, carry with them both the desire to reclaim potentially powerful origin stories which marks "feminism," and the recognition, which marks "postmodernism," that traditional origin stories have historically been oppressively reductive in their creation of identity. By the time we get to the third novel, the text fully embodies in its construct ooloi hero(ine) Jodahs a cyborg identity which breaks down the boundaries between human/nonhuman, male/female, and natural/technological. This "genetic engineer" is both the scientist and the laboratory (it is the ooloi who manipulate the genetic exchanges of reproduction within their own bodies [*Imago* §1.4:530]); both (and neither) male and female (Jodahs is a shapeshifter, and we see it become both genders in different scenes). While Lilith's presence doesn't allow us to forget the erotic violence of forced reproduction at the hands (tentacles?) of the Oankali, the text still seduces us into a reading dialogue with the alien, partly by "romancing" Jodahs (note the use of romance discourse in a scene where it seduces a human mate [§2.7:614]), but more importantly by showing how, with the creation of Jodahs, the trilogy has come to the "perfection" of a new species which, while

it may not be entirely "safe," seems preferable to the notions of identity we hold now.

It is this desire for the alien, the other, for difference within ourselves which, more powerfully than forsaking origin stories altogether, can allow us to recognize the value of origin stories while resisting and changing them from within. As Lilith says, "Human beings fear difference. . . . Oankali crave difference" (*Rites* §2.4:321); by putting readers in intimate association with the Oankali, *Xenogenesis* generates xenophilia in place of xenophobia.

Notes

1. The three novels which comprise the *Xenogenesis* trilogy are *Dawn* (1987), *Adulthood Rites* (1988), and *Imago* (1989). I am quoting from the Science Fiction Book Club edition, which contains all three novels bound together with continuous pagination. Page and chapter references will be given in the text.

2. Haraway's claim here, and in general her idea that women of colour provide the best models for a "cyborg" ontology, might be seen as a "postmodern turn" to Audre Lorde's famous dictum that "the master's tools will never dismantle the master's house."

3. In these stories of the origins of cyberpunk, written by the likes of Bruce Sterling and Larry McCaffery, William Gibson is cited as its male progenitor. If the origin story looks for earlier ancestors, as does, for example, Kadrey and McCaffery's "Cyberpunk 101," writers like Alfred Bester, Thomas Pynchon, and William Burroughs are cited as sorts of sympathetic uncles; in any case, the lineage remains primarily male. The Kadrey and McCaffery story makes an obligatory nod to Mary Shelley's *Frankenstein* (the "prehistory" of sf is apparently a safe enough place to acknowledge women in the family tree), and mentions James Tiptree Jr (Alice Sheldon) as the only other woman sf writer (though she is not included in the actual anthology). While Joanna Russ's *The Female Man* often gets an honorable mention as a precursor to postmodern sf, feminist sf is generally characterized as merely nostalgically utopian and in need of cyberpunk's tough edge (see, for example, Gordon's "Yin and Yang Duke It Out"). This amnesia about the women sf writers between Mary Shelley and Pat Cadigan reveals the feminist stakes involved in continuing to contest origin stories.

4. See Gordon, "Yin and Yang Duke It Out."

5. See Barbara Walker, *The Women's Encyclopedia of Myths and Secrets,* 541-2; Marta Weigle, *Spiders and Spinsters,* 252-5.

6. For example, Weigle mentions the version written by writer-journalist Lilly Rivlin. See also Judith Plaskow, "The Coming of Lilith: Toward a Feminist Theology," *Womanspirit Rising,* ed. Carol Christ and Judith Plaskow (San Francisco: Harper & Row, 1979), 198-209.

7. Octavia Butter's *Kindred* (1979), in particular, focuses on the heroine's time travel back to American slavery in order to ensure that her slave ancestress has sex with the slave owner and originates the heroine's family genealogy. As Sandra Y. Govan puts it in "Homage to Tradition: Octavia Butter Renovates the Historical Novel," *Kindred* "explores the tangled complexities of interracial mixing during slavery and beyond . . . the bonds of blood in *Kindred* . . . are the result of plain undisguised lust and the raw exertion of power" (88).

8. Though, as Frances Bonner points out in "Difference and Desire, Slavery and Seduction," Lilith's first sexual encounter with the Oankali happens outside the representation of the narrative. And, indeed, Bonner's reading traces the troubling "equivocating" in the novel's representation of seduction/rape.

9. Stepan and Gilman also note that science's discursive rise to prominence involved becoming more of what Bakhtin would call a monologic discourse, one which sharply distinguished itself from other literary and Biblical discourses. Early minority writers intent on challenging the hegemony of science's ability to construct raced identities used the alternative Biblical discourse of "monogenism," but this was soon not a very effective contestatory choice.

10. See also Chapter 32 in Gould's *Ever Since Darwin*.

11. Landau's reading of the way a Proppian "hero narrative" provides the logic for traditional Western scientific accounts of the origin of the species is interesting. It is nonetheless a shame that considerations of "women, children, and those human groups who have been largely left out of Western accounts" is relegated to an admission of her text's "limitations" and a footnote (184).

12. See, for example, Desmond Morris' *The Naked Ape* (1967), *The Human Zoo* (1969), or my personal favorite, the movie *Quest for Fire,* for which Morris was a consultant; Robert Ardrey, *African Genesis* (1961), *The Territorial Imperative* (1966), *The Social Contract* (1970), and *The Hunting Hypothesis* (1976).

13. See Bonner's "Difference and Desire" for a more extended discussion of how *Xenogenesis* deconstructs Oedipal imperatives and the nuclear family.

14. It is also interesting to note that one way Lilith fights off this rape attempt, in addition to physical resistance, is by playing Paul Titus' own "caveman" logic against itself by conjuring up fear of violating the incest taboo.

14. I would like to thank the SFRA for the opportunity to run a portion of this paper by an interested and helpful audience at its July 1994 conference. Thanks also to Octavia Butler, whose assessment of Wilson and Margulis in a quick hallway conversation encouraged me to keep questioning the "big guns" of Big Science. All misjudgments, misreadings, and uppity polemics are, of course, my own responsibility.

Works Cited

Bakhtin, Mikhail. "Discourse in the Novel." In *The Dialogic Imagination.* Ed. Caryl Emerson and Michael Holquist. Austin: U Texas P, 1981. 259-422.

Barlow, Connie. *From Gaia to Selfish Genes.* Cambridge, MA: MIT Press, 1991.

Bonner, Frances. "Difference and Desire, Slavery and Seduction: Octavia Butler's *Xenogenesis.*" *Foundation* 48:50-62, Spring 1990.

Bordo, Susan. "Feminism, Postmodernism, and Gender-Scepticism." *Feminism/Postmodernism.* Ed. Linda Nicholson. NY: Routledge, 1990. 133-56.

Butler, Octavia. *Xenogenesis.* NY: Guild America, n.d.

Csicsery-Ronay Jr, Istvan. "Cyberpunk and Neuromanticism." McCaffery, q.v. 182-193.

Foucault, Michel. *The History of Sexuality.* NY: Random House, 1978.

———. "Nietzsche, Genealogy, and History." *The Foucault Reader,* Ed. Paul Rabinow. NY: Pantheon, 1984. 76-100.

Gordon, Joan. "Yin and Yang Duke It Out." McCaffery, q.v. 196-202.

Gould, Stephen Jay. *Ever Since Darwin.* NY: Norton, 1979.

———. *The Mismeasure of Man.* NY: Norton, 1983.

Govan, Sandra Y. "Homage to Tradition: Octavia Butler Renovates the Historical Novel." *Melus* 13:79-96, Spring-Summer 1986.

Haraway, Donna. "The Contest for Primate Nature." *Simians, Cyborgs, and Women.* By Haraway. NY: Routledge, 1991. 81-108.

———. "A Cyborg Manifesto: Science, Technology, and Socialist-Feminism in the Late Twentieth Century." *Simians, Cyborgs, and Women.* 49-81.

———. *Primate Visions: Gender, Race, and Nature in the World of Modern Science.* NY: Routledge, 1989.

Jacobs, Harriet. *Incidents in the Life of a Slave Girl.* 1861. Ed. and with an Introduction by Jean Fagan Yellin. Cambridge, MA: Harvard UP, 1987.

Kadrey, Richard, and Larry McCaffery. "Cyberpunk 101: A Schematic Guide to *Storming the Reality Studio.*" McCaffery, q.v. 17-29.

Landau, Misia. *Narratives of Human Evolution.* New Haven: Yale UP, 1991.

McCaffery, Larry, ed. *Storming the Reality Studio: A Casebook of Cyberpunk and Postmodern Fiction.* Durham, NC: Duke UP, 1991.

Margulis, Lynn, and Dorion Sagan. "Microcosmos." Barlow, q.v. 57-66.

McDermott, Jeanne. "Lynn Margulis: Vindicated Heretic." Barlow, q.v. 47-56.

O'Neale, Sondra. "Inhibiting Midwives, Usurping Creators: The Struggling Emergence of Black Women in American Fiction." *Feminist Studies/Critical Studies.* Ed. Teresa de Lauretis. Bloomington: Indiana UP, 1986, 139-56.

Stepan, Nancy Leys, and Sander L. Gilman. "Appropriating the Idioms of Science." *The "Racial" Economy of Science.* Ed. Sandra Harding. Bloomington: Indiana UP, 1993. 170-93.

Walker, Barbara. *The Women's Encyclopedia of Myths and Secrets.* San Francisco: Harper & Row, 1983.

Weigle, Marta. *Spiders and Spinsters: Women and Mythology.* Albuquerque: U New Mexico P, 1982.

Wilson, E. O. *Sociobiology: The New Synthesis.* Cambridge, MA: Harvard UP, 1975.

Zaki, Hoda M. "Utopia, Dystopia, and Ideology in the Science Fiction of Octavia Butler." *SFS* 17:239-51, #51, July 1990.

Burton Raffel (essay date spring 1995)

SOURCE: Raffel, Burton. "Genre to the Rear, Race and Gender to the Fore: The Novels of Octavia E. Butler." *Literary Review* 38, no. 3 (spring 1995): 454-61.

[*In the following essay, Raffel posits that Butler's novels transcend the science fiction genre.*]

Just as you cannot always tell a book by its cover, so too you cannot always know a novel by its apparent or even by its declared genre. Is *Crime and Punishment* merely a detective (or mystery) novel? *Huck Finn* simply (as Mark Twain once said of it) "another boy's book," *War and Peace* merely historical, *The Trial* only a *Mittel Europa* Perry Mason drama? Is *Middlemarch* (as its title page proclaims) nothing more than "a study of provincial life"?

A book's transcendence of straightforward genre distinctions can be in part thematic, but is mostly a matter of execution: far more importantly than its intention, what a novel *does* with its chosen materials stands directly at the heart of its achievement, as it also defines its very nature. Whatever his own artistic imbalances, no one knew this better than Henry James: "There are bad novels and good novels, as there are bad pictures and good pictures, but that is the only distinction in which I see any meaning . . . It goes without saying that you will not write a good novel unless you possess the sense of reality; but it will be difficult to give you a recipe for calling that sense into being. Humanity is immense, and reality has a myriad forms . . . and when the mind is imaginative . . . it takes to itself the faintest hints of life, it converts the very pulses of the air into revelations." In this 1884 essay, "The Art of Fiction," James therefore lays down one standard: "The only obligation to which in advance we may hold a novel, without incurring the accusation of being arbitrary, is that it be interesting." Or, as the equally but on the face of it oppositely dedicated D. H. Lawrence put it, in a pair of essays published in 1925, "The novel is the highest example of subtle inter-relatedness that man has discovered. Everything is true in its own time, place, circumstance, and untrue outside of its own place, time, circumstance. If you try to nail anything down, in the novel, either it kills the novel, or the novel gets up and walks away with the nail. . . . The novel is a perfect medium for revealing to us the changing rainbow of our living relationships . . . the one bright book of life."

Operating as I try to do, more or less according to the standards set out by James and Lawrence, I have just finished reading, seriatim, eight of the ten published novels of Octavia E. Butler, initially drawn on by the utterly unexpected power and subtly complex intelligence of her extraordinary trilogy, *Xenogenesis*,[1] but sustained and even compelled by the rich dramatic textures, the profound psychological insights, the strong, challenging ideational matrices of virtually all her books. And in my seventh decade of reading fiction, there are not many novelists, neither those so bubbly light as Wodehouse nor even so broadly and diversely rewarding as Dickens or Balzac, Proust or Thomas Mann, who could have held me so long or so closely. Every one of these eight novels (and I stopped at eight only because I could not easily find her second and third books, some fifteen years out of print) was published under the explicit rubric of "science fiction," but four completely transcend the genre and only one is, though neither weak nor bad, less than absolutely first-rate. Perhaps just as significantly, I do not think any of these eight books could have been written by a man, as they most emphatically were not, nor, with the single exception of her first book, *Patternmaster* (1976), are likely to have been written, as they most emphatically were, by anyone but an African-American. Butler's work, in short, is both fascinating and highly unusual, representing—not only in my mind, but to the growing number of critics and scholars being drawn to it—a richly rewarding and relatively rare fusion of sensibility, perception, and a driven, insightful intelligence.

That this is serious literature I have no doubt. But I must stress from the start that Butler is not, like some science fiction practitioners, overtly (and is never, like more than a few, overbearingly) "literary." Her prose is crystalline, at its best, sensuous, sensitive, exact, but not in the least directed at calling attention to itself.[2] The moving final paragraph of the *Xenogenesis* trilogy—the title signifying "the fancied projection of an organism altogether and permanently unlike the parent"—is thus a model of quietly passionate writing:

> I chose a spot near the river. There I prepared the seed to go into the ground. I gave it a thick, nutritious coating, then brought it out of my body through my right sensory hand. I planted it deep in the rich soil of the riverbank. Seconds after I had expelled it, I felt it begin the tiny positioning movements of independent life.

Carefully, expertly crafted, deeply satisfying as it is to the reader of more than seven hundred preceding pages, and tautly, firmly resolving as it does the major plotline question, this is nevertheless determinedly functional, essentially unobtrusive prose—unlike, say, the highly literary writing of Samuel R. Delany (the only other black s.f. writer of major status): "It was foggy that morning, and the sun across the water moiled the mists like a brass ladle. I lurched to the top of the rocks, looked down through the tall grasses into the frothing inlet where she lay, and blinked." Delany makes it work; as Henry James noted, the very good are very good. But more typically, "literary" s.f. prose reads like the early work of a writer who has since learned better, Walter Jon Williams, whose *Ambassador of Progress* opens, with a self-conscious flourish, "In a storm of rain, its brightness a steadier glow among lightning flashes, the shuttle dropped into the high pasture, scattering alarmed cattle who ran in a clatter of bells for the sheltering trees." One can go a good deal farther down the literary ladder; this is for my purposes quite far enough. Plainly, Octavia Butler does not thus tongue a golden-mouthed trumpet, summoning the word-drunk flocks to drink from her overflowing flagons of sweet-scented nectar.

The passionate, abiding importance of the nurturing of new life, which clearly informs the *Xenogenesis* passage I have quoted, equally deeply informs the entire trilogy, as in every book of hers I have read. It seems to me feminist writing at its very best, writing which, like the poetry of Sheryl St. Germain I have discussed in these pages (see *TLR,* Fall 1993), proudly and utterly comfortably accepts itself as female. That strong, self-assured stance toward the fact of femaleness has been in Butler's work from the very first. The protagonist of *Patternmaster* is, unlike the central figures in her other work, male. But he is quickly made to realize that the major female figure in the book, the woman "healer" with whom he binds himself, though clearly female and just as clearly both attractive and attracted to him, is "harder than she felt." Soon thereafter, he learns that her sexual interests are not limited to men. And some pages still further, when another female character makes

the mistake of assuming that the healer is "his" woman, she is quickly, forcefully corrected. "I'm my own woman, Lady Darah. Now as before." (The two women have had prior contact, professional rather than sexual.) Finally, the protagonist asks the healer, bluntly, "Which do you prefer," men or women? She replies, "I'll tell you . . . But you won't like it. . . . When I meet a woman who attracts me, I prefer women . . . And when I meet a man who attracts me, I prefer men." The protagonist then effectively closes the discussion by announcing: "If that's the way you are, I don't mind." Nor does he, even though, when he asks her to marry him, she refuses, once again for reasons of independence. "As my lead wife," he argues, "you'd have authority, freedom," but she swiftly responds, "How interested would you be in becoming my lead husband?"

For all its excellences, however, *Patternmaster* is a smaller, less complex, less far-reaching fiction; in many ways it suggests the sweep and depth of *Xenogenesis* without quite achieving the trilogy's impact. Another striking precursor is *Wild Seed* (1980), which mythologizes Butler's black African heritage in an extraordinary fusion of both pre-slavery African and post-slavery American strands with what seems clearly the most urgent impulse behind all her writing, the drive to define, achieve, and nurture new life. "You steal, you kill," says the witch-like female protagonist, Anyanwu, to the even more wraith-like male protagonist, Doro. "What else do you do?" And he answers, speaking speech-words framed in Butler's beautifully calm prose, "'I build,' he said quietly. 'I search the land for people who are a little different—or very different. I search them out, I bring them together in groups, I begin to build them into a strong new people.'"

But Butler does not deal, as writers with lesser gifts so often do, with *themes*. Her novels teem with fully realized characters, male and female alike, who fascinatingly embody rather than merely represent ideas. Her fertile imagination throws up such intensely functioning, intricately enmeshed human beings that even minor personages take on vivid life—for yet another quality of a major fictive talent is a profound, virtually universal sympathy that permits imagined beings to be exactly what they in fact are, not idea-driven puppets who do only what their creators think the plot requires. The best writers are regularly, even easily, able to inhabit many skins, and to move and speak inside those superficially alien persons as if they were inside themselves. When a wondrously uncontrolled witch-like young woman leaps away from Doro, in terror, and falls heavily on a half-unconscious son of Doro, a man endowed with a propulsive power to move objects outside of his own body, the result is brilliantly, dramatically, tragically in character:

> He gripped Nweke, threw her upward away from his pain-racked body—threw her upward with all the power

he had used so many times to propel great ships out of storms[3] He did not know what he was doing any more than she did. He never saw her hit the ceiling, never saw her body flatten into it, distorted, crushed, never saw her head slam into one of the great beams and break and send down a grisly rain of blood and bits of bone and brain.

Again, this is not fancy writing; it is simply precise and tautly cadenced prose, forceful because it is focused, fictively superbly effective because it is in each and every detail true to the characters' lives. It is the furthest thing from accidental that the high point of such wonderfully accurate truthfulness, in the final pages, deals head-on with, and satisfyingly resolves, the novel's emotional and intellectual core. Anyanwu has fought, all along, to humanize Doro. She has sometimes seemed about to succeed, only again and again to fail. She therefore decides to commit suicide—and just when she is about to die, produces in Doro the reversion to human feeling for which she has so long struggled. But we are not told this in so many words, not at least right away. The novel's final words show us, first Doro's humanization, and then the success of what was not a strategy but Anyanwu's deep, thoroughly comprehensible decision:

> His voice caught and broke. He wept. He choked out great sobs that shook his already shaking body almost beyond bearing. He wept as though for all the past times when no tears would come, when there was no relief. He could not stop. He did not know when she pulled off his boots and pulled the blanket up over him, when she bathed his face in cool water. He did know the comfort of her arms, the warmth of her body next to him. He slept, finally, exhausted, his head on her breast, and at sunrise when he awoke, that breast was still warm, still rising and falling gently with her breathing.

Butler does not need to resort to artificial icons or frantic adjectives. There is symbolism here, to be sure. But it is fully organic, neither laid on like icing nor, heavily, as with a trowel.

Butler's one comparative failure, *Kindred* (1979), is a much more predictable, far too consciously wrought attempt at a twentieth-century slave narrative. Even in this novel, the stale, overly conscious plot is in good part redeemed by some fine (if not universally three-dimensional) characterization and, hardly surprisingly, by much strongly evocative writing. But *Kindred* is about as close to an unsuccessful book as Butler is capable of producing, just as *Clay's Ark* (1984), though a fine, suspenseful novel, is about as standard a s.f. story as she is likely ever to tell, strongly imbued with her trademark concerns, nurturing and the survival of that most endangered of all species, homo sapiens.

I do not think, Butler being the kind of quietly powerful writer she is, that anything short of an attentive reading of *Xenogenesis* can convey anything like the book's

multiple strengths. Not that it is deficient in either technical or substantive accomplishments. Each of the three component novels has a different though connected narrative point of view, the first using as its protagonist a black woman, Lilith Iyapo, the second using a part-human, Akin, and the third, told in the first person, experienced through the persona of Jodahs, also but markedly a part-human. Butler starts with the premise that humans have come very close to killing off one another, as well as destroying the earth humans have inhabited. An extra-terrestrial race, the Oankali, who speak of themselves, cryptically and rather oddly, as "traders," finds and preserves the few survivors. The how and why of that almost miraculous preservation, as also the full flowering of what it means that the Oankalis thus describe themselves, is what the three novels expose for us. The trilogy constitutes a remarkable exposition of eminently plausible emotional and genetic possibilities—imagined, from start to finish, in splendid detail, with a great range of characters both human and alien, and a fascinating unfolding of passionately felt, profoundly experienced events. More than all but a very small handful of "genre" books, *Xenogenesis* deals in basic wisdoms of a totally unparochial nature.[4]

Absolutely nothing is predictable, here. Indeed, it is I think utterly impossible for even the most ingenious reader ever to catch up to, much less overtake, the author's comprehensive, delicately modulated unfolding of her story. Lilith Iyapo, the first novel's protagonist (she appears in all three of the novels), is by the end of that first book still deeply unsure, on almost all levels, of what she ought to be doing and of what the Oankali truly intend.

> Perhaps they could find an answer to what the Oankali had done . . . And perhaps the Oankali were not perfect. A few fertile people might slip through and find one another. Perhaps. *Learn and run!* If she were lost, others did not have to be. Humanity did not have to be.
>
> She let Nikanj [an Oankali] lead her into the dark forest and to one of the concealed dry exits.

The narrative weight of every one of these sparse sentences is, in context, enormous. Indeed, the small excision I have made in the first sentence is designed to avoid discussing, here, perhaps the most pregnant and yet certainly the hardest to encapsulate in a brief essay of all the trilogy's concerns. We are to learn, in painful detail, that the Oankali are, in effect, no more "perfect" than are humans. Fertile people do slip through, and they do find each other. Lilith is in a sense "lost," but others, as she foresees, are not. At least, not necessarily. And the fascinating ambiguity of "Humanity did not have to be" will only be apparent hundreds of pages into the reading, just as the significance of that "dark forest" (a construct, not located anywhere on earth) and of the "dry exits," or why they are "concealed," cannot be dealt with here. An "answer" is given, by the trilogy's end: it rests, though not visible to someone who has not read the trilogy, in *Xenogenesis*'s final paragraph, quoted near the start of this essay.

Not that Butler, unlike such handy-andy novelists as Robertson Davies, ever plays unfair with the reader, ever conceals or manipulates fictional truth for mere novelistic effect. On the contrary: she is completely forthcoming, absolutely open. Like all her books, *Xenogenesis* provides us with a great deal of straightforward, old-fashioned storytelling, nor is there the slightest attempt at artful trickery. Butler's art is a substantive, not a merely technical one: she plainly cares about her material, cares about her characters, and is too deeply responsible to both to betray them in any way. The intensity of that caring is obvious throughout: here, for example, is a passage from the second of the trilogy's novels, dealing with Akin, a child and partly human, and Tino, an adult and wholly human. The human adult has just remarked on how "everything goes into" Akin's mouth, and how surprised he is that the only partly human child has not poisoned himself, ten times over:

> Akin ignored this and began investigating the bark on the sapling and looking to see what insects or fungi might be eating it and what might be eating them. Tino had been told why Akin put things in his mouth. He did not understand, but he never tried to keep things out of Akin's mouth the way other visitors did. He could accept without understanding. Once he had seen that a strange thing did no harm, he no longer feared it. He said Akin's tongue looked like a big gray slug, but somehow this did not seem to bother him. He allowed himself to be probed and studied when he carried Akin about. Lilith worried that he was concealing disgust or resentment, but he could not have concealed such strong emotions even from Akin. He certainly could not have concealed them from Nikanj.

There is what I can only call a very special tenderness in such writing. (What may seem hard to understand, here, has been in context long since fully explained.) The writer sees herself, in a sense, as a kind of filter through which the fictive experience is transmitted to her readers. But she makes no claims for herself, assumes no privileges not absolutely required by the careful, orderly telling of her story. Just as her prose, sharp, clear, determinedly explicative, asserts no extraordinary claims for itself, so too her narration is made to appear simply "there," eminently apprehendable but in no way forcing itself on the reader. Just as we do not read *Xenogenesis* on account of stylistic pyrotechnics, so too we do not read it for anything but substantive reasons. The people are real, their doings are both believable and continuously interesting, and the stakes, though not fussed over, are obviously very high—I would myself say, with the author, that they could not be higher, involving as they do the present state of humanity and perhaps its future as well.

The following paragraph, which concludes the second section of the trilogy's third book, can perhaps most effectively summarize *Xenogenesis*'s complex effect (showing more clearly than the other passages I have chosen something, too, of the book's scientific alertness). I will not annotate or indeed comment on this quotation, but simply set it forth and hope that, as it should, it leads you to seek out the rest for yourself:

> Tomás [human, male] lifted my unconscious body, Jesusa [human, female] helping him with me now that I was deadweight. I have a clear, treasured memory of the two of them carrying me into the small room. They did not know then that my memory went on recording everything my senses perceived even when I was unconscious. Yet they handled me with great gentleness and care, as they had from the beginning of my change [maturing Oankali experience, a kind of metamorphosis]. They did not know that this was exactly what Oankali mates did at these times. And they did not see Aaor [like the narrator, part-human, part-Oankali] watching them with a hunger that was so intense that its face was distorted and its head and body tentacles elongated toward us.

Notes

1. Originally published, in 1987, 1988, and 1989, as *Dawn, Adulthood Rites,* and *Imago.*

2. I have argued, in *The Art of Translating Prose* (1994) and elsewhere, that perhaps the most fundamental difference between poetry and prose is that the former stresses non-linear and thus stylistic elements, while the latter necessarily stresses that which is linear and thus less narrowly stylistic. Poetry in a sense always calls attention to how it is written. But prose not only need not, but indeed cannot, have anything like the same emphasis: there is inevitably more mind in prose, more sheer emotionality in poetry.

3. The sort of thing we have previously seen him do, more than once.

4. I can report that not only do its various "messages" stay with the reader, but they so continuously and deeply involve him/her that, while reading and for some while thereafter, one finds oneself living partly in the "real" world and partly in Butler's. I do not think it is possible to more basically transcend a genre limitation: this sort of holistic absorption of the reader is, indeed, almost a definition of literary power.

John R. Pfeiffer (essay date 1998)

SOURCE: Pfeiffer, John R. "Octavia Butler Writes the Bible." In *Shaw and Other Matters,* edited by Susan Rusinko, pp. 140-54. Selinsgrove, Pa.: Susquehanna University Press, 1998.

[*In the following essay, Pfeiffer addresses references to the Judeo-Christian Bible in Butler's writing.*]

The author of ten novels and five short stories, Octavia Butler has received critical commentary as a writer of science fiction, a feminist writer, and an African-American storyteller. Yet, largely ignored in that commentary, the single most pervasive reference in her writing has been the Judeo-Christian Bible.

In fact, the protagonist (possibly Butler's fictional persona) Lauren Oya Olamina in Butler's *Parable of the Sower* (1993) explains the nature of the influence of the Bible on *Earthseed,* a religious book she is writing:

> "A lot of it isn't very poetical. . . . But it's what I believe, and I've written it as well as I could." I showed him four verses in all—gentle, brief verses that might take hold of him without his realizing it and live in his memory without his intending that they should. Bits of the Bible had done that to me, staying with me even after I stopped believing.[1]

The sentiments of Olamina are directly repeated by Butler in the "Afterword" of her short story, **"Near of Kin"** (1979), collected in *Bloodchild and Other Stories* (1995). Here Butler comments not only on the significance of her debt to the Bible and to her Baptist upbringing but also on the paradoxical nature of the debt:

> As a good Baptist kid, I read the Bible first as a series of instructions as to how I should believe and behave, then as bits of verse that I was required to memorize, then as a series of interesting interconnected stories.
>
> The stories got me: stories of conflict, betrayal, torture, murder, exile, and incest. I read them avidly. This was, of course, not exactly what my mother had in mind when she encouraged me to read the Bible. Nevertheless, I found these things fascinating, and when I began writing, I explored these themes in my own stories.[2]

In her fiction Butler has transformed religious training and belief into literary myth. Remarkably her novels successively exhibit an increasing incidence of biblical references, even though, like her fictional counterpart, Olamina, Butler "stopped believing." Meanwhile, she is predictably hostile where she might be expected to be, considering that traditional interpretations of the Bible have rationalized male chauvinism, justified slavery, and supported fraudulent secular and religious institutional agendas. Although she asserts that she has set belief in Judeo-Christian theology aside and is keenly aware of the terrible suffering the Bible has been made to sponsor in the world, she uses it in her stories as a touchstone. She says she was weaned on the Bible and loved its stories, especially their violence. Her reference to the Bible is therefore not surprising. It is clear, too, that she is taken with the epic conception of time and human personality, as well as the evangelical voice, of the Bible. Her stories exhibit these elements. Ultimately Butler's appropriation of the Bible is meant to subvert it where it is perverse, embrace it where it is cogent,

and finally to substitute for it a personal scripture, indeed, a theology, of her own. Beyond this her agenda must be the gnomic one of storyteller.

Biblical influence is present in Butler's first novel *Patternmaster* (1976)—one of five "Patternist" novels that also include *Mind of My Mind* (1977), *Survivor* (1978), *Wild Seed* (1980), and *Clay's Ark* (1984)—even though the novel presents no explicit reference to the Bible.[3] In *Patternmaster,* the biblical elements consist of references to fertility and genealogy, even as the story of the emergence of a successor-leader of the superhuman patternists progresses. The Southern California climate and terrain of the story are not unlike the Middle East where Old Testament Hebrews struggled and longed for a messiah to lead them to a land where they could settle in security. The familial houses in *Patternmaster* are patriarchal, and characters have biblical names such as Joachim, Michael, and Jason. Still, this biblical tone might be accidental or subconscious were it not corroborated by the increasing explicitness in all of Butler's later novels. Furthermore, her imagination is provoked by history, and her stories are in search of epic meanings. The epic multiplicity of "books" of the Bible seems to be the inspiration moving Butler to write groups of novels, the extraordinary *Kindred* (1979) being the only book she has written that is not part of a series.

An explicit allusion to the Bible appears for the first time in Butler's second novel, *Mind of My Mind,* in the characterization of Rachel Davidson, one of the parapsychological superperson protagonists of the novel. Her parents were ministers, and Rachel has assumed the identity of a Christian preacher faith-healer as a way to use her psychokinetic healing powers. More than merely healing cancer and psychological illnesses, she could regrow limbs for her flock. However, she stops short because "she would have had to show herself to be more than a faith healer. She was afraid of what people might decide she was. Whether or not she accepted the story of Christ as fact, she realized that anyone with abilities like his—and hers—could get into trouble if he really put them to work" (71). Set in a late twentieth-century America, *Mind* [*Mind of My Mind*] makes this reference to the Bible as if its importance in culture were vestigial and marginal.

Like *Patternmaster, Mind* is also preoccupied with fertility and genealogy. *Mind* includes the death of the demonic parapsychological patriarch Doro, whose four thousand-year life is a calendric analogue for the age of Hebrew culture, with its concomitant emphasis on preserving a special race/species of people who mate within the tribe, often within the family, incestuously. Doro is like an Old Testament patriarch with his fabulous longevity, autocratic personality, and power. He is displaced and killed by Mary, who is more powerful than he and who represents a new parapsychological dispensation, the beginning of the Patternist web. In *Mind,* the killing of Doro by Mary replays the Judeo/Christian biblical tension in the advent of Christianity as a threat to end the Jewish history that fostered it.

In *Survivor,* Butler's debt to the Bible is more explicit and extensive. Jules Verrick is a Christian minister who has adopted an Asian-African woman child and called her Alanna, saving her from summary extermination by members of his congregation, as was the usual fate of feral children on the unhappy future earth of Butler's story. Alanna's salvation recalls the escape of the child Jesus from Herod's decree that all infant male children under two years of age be killed. Verrick takes Alanna with his wife and congregation to a colony on the planet of the Kohns. Alanna's identity is symbolically messianic, while Verrick's community of Christians seems Hebraic in the tyranny imposed by the Kohn planet's indigenous Garkohn. The Garkohn force the humans to use meklah, a drug to which they have been addicted for generations. Alanna's role is to be captured by another Kohn people, the Tehkohn, who force her to withdraw from her addiction to meklah, the first human to do so. Eventually she leads the Tehkohn to defeat the Garkohn, enabling Verrick's people to begin a migration, Hebrew-like, to find their own land on the new planet. Alanna remains behind with the Tehkohn to breed with their leader in an interspecies miscegenation, an analogue to Jesus' eventual embrace of gentiles.

Butler's incorporation of other explicit biblical references in *Survivor* is not facilely allegorical. Verrick's community is unequivocally a Christian splinter sect. The biblical references are a means to present Alanna's character. Pregnant with a Tehkohn-fathered child, Alanna is fearful, and "for the first time in her life, she longed to be the wife of some ordinary Bible-quoting Missionary man" (164). Earlier, Verrick and Alanna discuss whether Alanna could bring herself to kill an enemy in battle (she can) and refer to the Bible for support: "'Thou shalt not kill,' quoted Jules. 'Not that,' she said. '. . . He that smiteth a man, so that he die, shall surely be put to death'" (30). Earlier still, in considering her preference for practical clothing, usually men's styles, Alanna remembers that her foster mother Neila Verrick quoted Deut, 22:5, "The woman shall not wear that which pertaineth unto a man, . . . for all that do so are abominations unto the Lord thy God" (19). Alanna disregards her mother's admonition without qualm. In these references the Bible is a nuisance or irrelevant to a self-respecting person.

Butler removes any doubt of the importance of the Bible in her stories in *Wild Seed,* the genesis myth of her "Patternist" saga. A chronicle of the Patternist people, the novel consists of three books with biblically extracted titles: "Book I, Covenant, 1690" (six chapters);

"Book II, Lot's Children, 1741" (chapters 7 to 10); and "Book III, Canaan, 1840" (chapters 11 to 14, plus Epilogue). Beyond the biblical section titles, there are no direct references to the Bible in the stories themselves. Even so, the story in each section is a combination of biblical tale analogues. "Covenant" clearly substitutes the Doro/Anyanwu relationship for the God/Abraham relationship of Genesis. The female Anyanwu replaces the spurious patriarchal maleness of the Hebraic Abraham in Butler's reinvention of the biblical fable. *Seed* [*Wild Seed*] sets up a matriarchal genealogy, and Anyanwu is assigned the fabulous longevity and fertility of a biblical patriarch. Moreover, the capricious treatment of Anyanwu by Doro as he tries to bend her to his will by threatening her children is a transmutation of the Old Testament God's cruel test of Abraham, ordering him to sacrifice his son Isaac. That Doro and God are cruel because the inexorable events of nature are cruel, Anyanwu must accept. Butler invites the reader to contemplate such implacable forces.

Butler's conversion of the Genesis myth in *Seed* continues in the marriage of Anyanwu, at first the consort of Doro, to one of Doro's sons, Isaac. With Isaac she has children. Her marriage to Isaac also insinuates incest between mother and son. The tincture of blasphemy and moral abomination of this is very likely Butler's intent. Aware that the Bible itself acquiesces in the confounding of tradition and morality, she has deliberately written her own violation of tradition. Such is Butler's alteration of the Old Testament story of Lot. Thus *Seed*'s second section, "Lot's Children," recalls the daughters of Lot, Abraham's nephew, who had children in incest with their father. These children founded the tribes of Moab and Ammon. The incest notwithstanding, God intervened to preserve lands so that the Moabites and Ammonites would prosper. At worst the Old Testament God did not punish the incest. In fact God clearly blessed its issue. Butler uses the suggestion of incest in *Seed* to depict the conflict between Doro and Anyanwu that arises when he wants to breed her with her children, or her children with her children. Optimistically considering the possibility of offspring with new and different parapsychological powers from his eugenic program, Doro reflects, "They were a pleasant mystery that careful inbreeding would solve" (146).

In *Seed*'s final chapter, "Canaan," Butler has the shape-shifting Anyanwu transform herself into a male plantation owner, Edward Warrick. Hermaphroditic, she can bear children as a woman and sire them as a man, but as a man she can sire only female children. Her longevity and parapsychological power enable her to secure the plantation and make it an oasis of safety in a history of slavery. It is not Canaan, a "promised land," but it encourages the hope of one. More like an actual land of milk and honey in *Seed,* California is named in the

Epilogue as the place to which Anyanwu will eventually migrate to help establish the Patternists there, where they will establish a thriving culture.

The latest written of the "Patternist" novels, *Clay's Ark,* is set in the southwestern United States desert country of the early twenty-first century. Biblical allusions pervade it. The "Ark" of the title invokes Noah's Ark of Genesis, as it names the spaceship that brings back to earth from a Proxima Centauri planet the colonizing microorganism that will extinguish homo sapiens and repopulate Earth with a new species. The "Clay" of the title is for Clay Dana, the instigator of the star expedition, who had feared that the expedition would be stopped by "turn-of-the-century irrationality—religious overzealousness on one side, destructive hedonism on the other, with both heated by ideological intolerance and corporate greed. The Dana faction feared humanity would extinguish itself on Earth, the only world in the solar system that could support human life" (154). In the overview of the "Patternist" novels, original humanity is, if not extinguished, at best a zoological antique. Three of *Ark*'s [*Clay's Ark*] five chapters bear biblically associated titles: "Part 1: Physician," "Part 3: Manna," and "Part 5: Jacob." The black, principal protagonist of *Ark* is Asa Elias Doyle ("Eli"). Asa is the biblical name for physician. Though Eli was the expedition geologist, he assimilates a physician's identity because his wife, Disa, was a doctor. He had also been "a minister for a while, . . . [a] boy minister at the turn of the century when the country was full of ministers" (36). Eli follows in the footsteps of his maternal grandfather, Jacob Moore (Jake), "a good man, an old-style shouting Baptist preacher who had stepped in and taken the place of his father when his father died" (29). More biblical reference appears when Blake Maslin's daughter Keira asks Eli if he is part of a religious cult:

> "Cultists?" Eli said smiling a real smile. "No, we didn't come up here to worship anybody, girl. There were some religious people up here once, though. Not cultists, just . . . What do you call them? People who never saw sweet reason around the turn of the century, and who decided to make a decent, moral, God-fearing place of their own to raise their kids and wait for the Second Coming."
>
> (21)

The events of the novel and the Second Coming are again connected when the perverted "family" of "car rats" that has kidnapped Blake and his daughters are observed

> . . . watching a movie from the ranch family's library—a 1998 classic about the Second Coming of Christ. There had been a whole genre of such films just before the turn of the century. Some were religious, some antireligious, some merely exploitive—Sodom-

and-Gomorrah films, Some were cause oriented—God arrived as a woman or a dolphin or a throwaway kid. And some were science fiction. God arrives from Eighty-two Eridani Seven.

> Well, maybe God had arrived a few years late from Proxima Centauri Two. God in the form of a deadly little microbe that for its own procreation made a father try to rape his dying daughter—and made the daughter not mind.
>
> (168)

In these passages *Ark* explicitly associates the biblical apocalypse of the Second Coming with its own story of pestilence, catastrophe, and apocalypse. The degraded late twentieth-century humanity of Butler's earth is in a process of self-annihilation. The Proxima Centauri Two organism is one of the means by which a staggering humanity will be transformed into a new species— "converted" (39, 50, 85, 92, 125, 145, 196) is the term Butler uses. Conversion causes biologically invaded humans literally to be "born again," that is, be genetically altered, and thereafter not human any longer. Their muscles and senses are stronger and keener than human. Significantly, their morality is prospectively more noble. The children of the converted are even stranger than their once-human parents. Genetic transformation through breeding as well as parapsychologically manipulated DNA are processes under way in the other "Patternist" novels as well as in the *Xenogenesis* Trilogy novels discussed below.

The narrative report of the disposition of the microorganism to "survive and multiply" (30) echoes the Genesis "increase and multiply." Biblical personality appears in the person of Gabriel Boyd, the "white-haired patriarch of the household—a stern man who believed in an outdated, angry God and who knew how to use a shotgun" (41). He thinks "heaven is only for God and his chosen" (56). He is the puritanically protective father of the caucasian Meda with whom Eli would have twin boy "clayarks" named Jacob and Joseph— only a minor liberty by Butler with the biblical twin-son issue of Isaac in Esau and Jacob. Eli gets along with Gabriel because Eli

> . . . knew his Bible. This in particular impressed both the old man and his wife. Few people read the Bible now, except as literature. Religion was about as far out of fashion as it had ever been in the United States—a reaction against the intense religious feeling at the turn of the century. But Eli had been a boy preacher during that strange, not entirely sane time. He had been precocious and sincere, had read the Bible from Genesis to Revelation, and could still talk about it knowledgeably.
>
> (55)

Eventually infected by the organism and experiencing the compulsion to "multiply," Gabriel ". . . felt he had gone from Patriarch and man of God to criminally depraved pervert unable to keep his hands off his own daughter. Nor could he accept these feelings as his own. They must be signs of either demonic possession or God's punishment for some terrible sin" (69). Gabriel, however, rises about his puritanical delusion before he dies, and blesses the Eli/Meda union, which has produced Joseph and Jacob. Jacob in particular is the vanguard "clayark" offspring, a herald of the arrival of one of the new species (the other species is of evolved humans with parapsychological powers) of the Patternist earth.

Butler's persistent theme in the "Patternist" novels is that humanity as it is is not sufficient. She replaces mankind in her stories with species that are potentially morally superior. The overarching biblical themes of migration and aspiration to moral transcendence are epic enough and popular enough to be a founding metaphor for *Clay's Ark.*

In *Kindred* (1979), published one year after *Survivor,* Dana, the protagonist, has been brought up by an aunt and an uncle, the latter a minister.[4] Her ancestors go back to slavery times, and their names are written in a family Bible. Thereafter, plunged by time travel into the maelstrom of slavery in the antebellum South, Dana/Butler make only a few explicit references to the Bible and Christianity. The Methodist minister quotes the Bible to rationalize the keeping of slaves: He "dispensed candy and 'safe' Bible verses ('Servants, be obedient to them that are your masters'). The kids got candy for repeating the verses" (183). The same minister also pronounces that education is bad for slaves (237). When Hagar, Dana's great-grandmother, whose birth and survival Dana must assure, is born, Alice reflects, "If Hagar had been a boy, I would have called her Ishmael. In the Bible, people might be slaves for awhile, but they didn't have to stay slaves" (234). This remark transforms the biblical story of the concubine Hagar and her son Ishmael who are banished from Abraham's household. Subsequently God blessed Ishmael and his children by allowing them to have destinies as free people. In response Dana thinks, "I . . . congratulated myself that the Bible wasn't the only place where slaves broke free. Her names were only symbolic, but I had more than symbols to remind me that freedom was possible—probably—and for me, very near" (234). After Hagar is safely born, Alice dies and is buried by a "coal-black deep-voiced freedman" minister who reads from Job and Ecclesiastes until Dana "could hardly stand to listen. I had shrugged off my aunt and uncle's strict Baptist teachings years before. But even now, especially now, the bitter melancholy words of Job could still reach me. 'Man that is born of a woman is of few days, and full of trouble. He cometh forth like a flower, and is cut down: he fleeth also as a shadow, and continueth not'" (252).

With just six explicit references to the Bible, *Kindred* also contains numerous implicit references. The novel re-creates the historic slavery of Africans, like that of the Old Testament Hebrews, a subjugated nation/people/ race that somehow kept its integrity. Dana, thrust from the 1970s into antebellum American history, resembles a would-be messiah transported from New Testament to Old Testament times. In *Kindred,* as in her other novels, the biblical reference is mostly to the Old Testament. It is often a history and an anthropology of people who, despite their lives of helplessness and pain, chose to live them.

The Old Testament describes slavery in Hebrew families as if it were moral, even natural, with slaves instructed to keep their places and accept their condition. As a people, African-Americans felt a powerful kinship with Old Testament Hebrews who were enslaved in Egypt before wandering landless and homeless. Permitted opportunities to worship, even to have their own ministers, they used biblical materials in their work songs but were allowed to profess openly only themes of resignation, patience, grieving, and hope for rest in a "promised land." These elements are all easy to find in the African-American slave narratives, the primary models and sources for *Kindred.*

In 1987, Butler published the first novel of her *Xenogenesis* Trilogy. The invitation to read the trilogy as a biblical analogue is immediate. *Dawn,* subtitled *Xenogenesis,* immediately elicits an association with Genesis.[5] The protagonist of all three novels is pre-biblical Lilith, the name in rabbinical literature of Adam's first wife, not mentioned in Genesis. Her dispensation is primordial, wilder than Eve's and wonderfully maverick in possibility of offspring, and Butler revels in the latitude that she allows Lilith. Galactic traders in genes, the alien Oankali arrive on earth after mankind's nuclear war. Their spaceship is a Noah's ark of new genetic material that they will barter in exchange for human material, and in the process they will vitalize and improve surviving human DNA. They rescue Lilith, nursing her to health and changing her genetically so that she, now alien in DNA, can become the instrument of a repopulation of earth. Like Anyanwu in *Seed,* she, as healer, can alter genetic codes. *Xenogenesis* is literally an "alien beginning." The Oankali use genetic material just as the Old Testament God made Eve from Adam's rib. "If they've got one of you, they can use it to make another you even if you've been dead for a hundred years and they haven't got anything at all left of your body. And that's just the start. They can make people in ways I don't even know how to talk about" (93). There are other Genesis echoes as well. Lilith is told that she has been made pregnant, and will bear a daughter: "I mixed a girl to be a companion for you. You've been very lonely" (246). Later the reader learns the Oankali plan to "reseed Earth with human communities" (143). The pervasive concern with seminal seed in the Old Testament so passionately inspires Butler that she uses as titles *Wild Seed, Parable of the Sower,* and *Earthseed: The Books of the Living.* The God analogue, the Oankali, recreate Lilith genetically to give her great strength and longevity.

In *Adulthood Rites* (1988), the second novel of the *Xenogenesis* series, the "genesis" enterprise proceeds.[6] The process of putting genetically improved humans back in communities on earth is ongoing. On the very first page, there is another Genesis echo: "There was light!" (3). Later the reader learns that "the books most likely to be desired by other villages" are "Bibles— using the memories of every village they could reach, Phoenix researchers had put together the most complete Bible available" (124). The only other major biblical reference in *Adulthood* is a symbolically complex passage describing the artifacts in a museum at the first of the new villages planted on the postholocaust earth:

> There were crosses like the one on Gabe's coin— crosses of metal, each with a metal man hanging from them. Christ on the cross, Akin remembered. There were also a picture of Christ rapping his knuckles on a wooden door and another of him pulling open his clothing to reveal a red shape that contained a torch. There was a picture of Christ sitting at a table with a lot of other men. Some of the pictures seemed to move as Akin viewed them from different angles.
>
> Tate, who had reached the house before him, took one of the moving pictures—a small one of Christ standing on a hill and talking to people—and handed it to Akin. He moved it slightly in his hand, watching the apparent movement of Christ, whose mouth opened and closed and whose arm moved up and down. The picture, though scratched, was hard and flat—made of a material Akin did not understand. He tasted it—then threw it away from him, disgusted, nauseated.
>
> (142)

With Butler's relegation of artifacts of the Christian myth to a museum in the new land, she begins her regeneration of the human race. Her description of the museum's contents evokes the Sermon on the Mount, the Last Supper, Christ's crucifixion, and a perverse communion rite in the form of Akin's tasting of the plastic picture. Cast in the role of matriarch-as-the-new-messiah, Lilith, in her bearing of new DNA to humanity, is equivalent to Jesus' bringing in a new moral order to mankind.

In *Imago* (1989), the third *Xenogenesis* novel, two remarkable references stand out.[7] In the first, the woman Jesusa and her man Tomás are troubled about their physical and emotional dependence on the mutant human Jodahs. Jesusa is obviously a female substitute for the biblical Jesus. Tomás's role, in imitation of the biblical doubting Thomas, is to question Jesusa's doubt

about the new order. Ultimately they will accept this symbiosis but not without profound fear. Jesusa remarks: "This is an alien thing Jodahs wants of us. Certainly it's an un-Christian thing, an un-Human thing. *It's the thing we've been taught against all our lives.* How can we be accepting it or even considering it so easily?" (124). The two eventually accept the ménage à trois analogic relationship with Jodahs. In so doing, they consecrate a new dispensation. For Butler the new era represents a healing of the diseased human genetic code, despite its being a permutation of bestiality and sodomy. The healed humans must now adopt new behavior that will fulfill their destiny as altered beings. The analogy with Jesus as a transformer of the rigidly genetic Hebraic law is apparent. At one point, the narrative of the genetic reconstruction of humanity, a "First Mother," story is retold. She is reported to have had a number of daughters and a son, all of whom were human and properly formed. The details of this account are vintage Genesis analogues. They illustrate Butler's title, *Imago,* in their suggestion of the Genesis pronouncement that man is made in the image of God, even though Butler ironically asserts that the Old Testament image is flawed and that the transhuman new species is, perhaps, a healed image of God.

Parable of the Sower (1993) as a novel is baldly proselytizing and explicit in its definition of the human condition and what to do about it. Written entirely as a personal journal, it is captioned with excerpts from a book of spiritual guidance that the protagonist journal writer published sometime after the journal's events had transpired. It is titled *Earthseed: The Books of the Living* by Lauren Oya Olamina. It is carefully dated, beginning on Lauren's fifteenth birthday, 20 July 2024, and includes entries for seventy-three days before ending on 10 October 2027.

Biblical reference in *Parable* [*Parable of the Sower*] is especially important to this novel's meaning, Lauren's favorite book of the Bible is Job (14). She is challenged by the inscrutability of human experience, where justice and happiness are chimeras more often than reality. Later Lauren remembers words from Ecclesiastes, "To everything there is a season" from which she draws the center of the belief system that she is forming: "Change is part of life" (25). The quotation from Ecclesiastes is very near the verse that includes the words "earth abides," which are used as a title for George R. Stewart's celebrated postcatastrophe novel of 1949. The setting of *Parable* is fittingly postcatastrophic. Lauren later quotes a long passage from Genesis:

> Today, Dad preached from Genesis six, Noah and the ark: "And God saw that the wickedness of man was great in the earth, and that every imagination of the thoughts and of his heart was only evil continually. And it repented the Lord that he had made man on the earth, and it grieved him at his heart. And the Lord

said, I will destroy man whom I have created from the face of the earth; both man, and beast, and the creeping thing and the fowls of the air; for it repenteth me that I have made them. But Noah found grace in the eyes of the Lord."

And then, of course, later God says to Noah, "make thee an ark of gopher wood; rooms shalt thou make in the ark, and shalt pitch it within and without with pitch."

Dad focused on the two-part nature of this situation, God decides to destroy everything except Noah, his family, and some animals. *But* if Noah is going to be saved, he has plenty of hard work to do.

(63)

Butler uses this Old Testament excerpt to define the conditions of humanity as self-mutilating, self-destructive, and self-defeating for the most part. But there is a hope to which Lauren clings.

Later when her minister father is murdered outside the Robledo enclave, Lauren takes his place as preacher, an identity she adopts with increasing deliberateness as she writes and expounds more of her *Earthseed* scripture. On one occasion she preaches from Luke 18:1-8:

The parable of the importunate widow. It's one I've always liked. A widow is so persistent, [*sic*] in her demands for justice that she overcomes the resistance of a judge who fears neither God nor man. She wears him down.

Moral: The weak can overcome the strong if the weak persist. Persisting isn't always safe, but it's often necessary. . . .

"We have God and we have each other. We have our island community, fragile, and yet a fortress. Sometimes it seems too small and too weak to survive. And like the widow in Christ's parable, its enemies fear neither God nor man. But also like the widow, it persists. *We persist.* This is our place, no matter what."

(124-25)

Lauren's family will be driven from their home in Robledo and killed, but Lauren does not give up her resolve to survive. Meanwhile, as conditions in Robledo deteriorate and drug-driven pyromaniacs begin burning the homes in the enclave, Cory Olimina, Lauren's foster mother, declares, "'My God,' . . . in a small whispery voice, . . . from the Book of Revelation: 'Babylon the great is fallen, is fallen, and is become the habitation of devils'" (133). Deep into the narrative, the reader learns that Lauren has heard the commandments "Honor thy father and mother" and "Thou shalt not kill" (169), but she must violate the one against killing to survive. Other references occur as fifty-seven-year-old Taylor Franklin Bankole, whom eighteen-year-old Lauren will eventually marry, remembers, "When my wife was alive, we went to a Methodist church. Her religion was important to her, so I went along. I saw how it comforted her, and

I wanted to believe, but I never could." Lauren answers, "We were Baptists. . . . I couldn't make myself believe either" (239). Still, Lauren does believe in the religion that she is creating in Earthseed, about the future of which Bankole is doubtful:

"It sounds too simple. . . . If you get people to accept it they'll make it more complicated, more open to interpretation, more mystical, and more comforting." . . . "With you or without you, they will. All religions change. Think about the big ones. What do you think Christ would be these days? A Baptist? A Methodist? A Catholic? And the Buddha—do you think he'd be a Buddhist now? What kind of Buddhism would he practice?"

(240)

The book ends with the excerpt from Luke 8:5-8 that has inspired the novel:

A sower went out to sow his seed; and as he sowed, some fell by the way side; and it was trodden down, and the fowls of the air devoured it. And some fell upon a rock; and as soon as it was sprung up, it withered away because it lacked moisture. And some fell among thorns; and the thorns sprang up with it and choked it. And other fell on good ground, and sprang up, and bare fruit an hundredfold.

(299)

In this context of biblical reference, Butler builds the story of Lauren's creation of Earthseed. People are Earthseed. Some will live and prosper. The mood and content of Earthseed are biblical without embarrassment: "Bits of the Bible had done that to me, staying with me even after I stopped believing" (183). Although Lauren insists that she does not believe in the *Bible* or in "that kind of God" (72), her actual personal beliefs are catechetical and biblical in procedure, if not in substance. She concludes, *"Why is the universe? / To shape God. Why is God? / To shape the universe. . . . God / is Change"* (72-73). Out of her biblical rehearsal, Lauren (and Butler herself perhaps) seems to evolve a dynamic pantheism and a Bible of her own.

The importance of biblical reference to Butler's inspiration continues. In a 1995 interview reporting details of a $295,000 MacArthur grant she was awarded, Butler announced that she was at work on a new novel tentatively entitled ***Parable of the Talents.***[8]

Notes

1. Octavia Butler, *Parable of the Sower* (New York and London: Four Walls Eight Windows, 1993), 183. Further page references to this and the other Butler works mentioned in this article are expressed parenthetically in the text.

2. Octavia Butler, *Bloodchild and Other Stories* (New York and London: Four Walls Eight Windows, 1995), 85.

3. Octavia Butler, *Patternmaster* (New York: Avon Books, 1979); *Survivor* (Garden City, N.Y.: Doubleday & Company, Inc., 1978); *Mind of My Mind* (New York: Warner Books, 1994); *Wild Seed* (New York: Warner Books, 1988); and *Clay's Ark* (New York: St. Martin's Press, 1984).

4. Octavia Butler, *Kindred* (Boston: Beacon Press, 1988).

5. Octavia Butler, *Dawn* (New York: Warner Books, 1987).

6. Octavia Butler, *Adulthood Rites* (New York: Warner Books, 1988).

7. Octavia Butler, *Imago* (New York: Warner Books, 1989).

8. "Octavia E. Butler Gets $295,000 MacArthur Grant," *Locus* (July 1995), 8.

Madhu Dubey (essay date spring 1999)

SOURCE: Dubey, Madhu. "Folk and Urban Communities in African-American Women's Fiction: Octavia Butler's *Parable of the Sower.*" *Studies in American Fiction* 27, no. 1 (spring 1999): 103-28.

[*In the following essay, Dubey examines* Parable of the Sower *within the context of a "Southern folk aesthetic."*]

In "The Politics of Fiction, Anthropology, and the Folk: Zora Neale Hurston," first published in 1991, Hazel Carby seeks to account for the recent academic revival of Zora Neale Hurston's southern folk aesthetic. Carby argues that Hurston's writing, locating authentic black community in the rural south, displaced the difficulties of representing the complex and contested black culture that was taking shape in the cities and that the current academic reclamation of Hurston's work illustrates a parallel logic of displacement. Carby concludes with the suggestion that present-day critics of African-American literature and culture "begin to acknowledge the complexity of [their] own discursive displacement of contemporary conflict and cultural transformation in the search for black cultural authenticity. The privileging of Hurston . . . at a moment of intense urban crisis and conflict is perhaps a sign of that displacement."[1]

Carby's provocative argument can be extended beyond its specific reference to the academic recovery of Zora Neale Hurston, and applied to the turn toward southern folk culture taken in so much of the criticism surrounding novels by Toni Morrison, Alice Walker, Gloria Naylor, Ntozake Shange, and others. Although most of these writers have published city novels, criticism on these novelists has tended to privilege those selected texts and textual elements that help consolidate a black

feminine literary tradition derived from southern folk culture.[2] Following Carby's logic, we might argue that these critical texts are executing a "discursive displacement" of problems of urban literary representation, but this displacement is itself an oblique form of response to the widely prevalent rhetoric of contemporary urban crisis. This rhetoric, magnetized around the notorious term "underclass," tends to frame the issue of urban crisis essentially as a crisis in black culture and community. In popular media and academic discourses, the underclass is commonly represented as a recalcitrant urban mass polarized against an expanding black middle class and caught in an illicit culture of poverty.[3] Given the public sway of these discourses, it is not surprising that so much recent African-American literature is framing urban crisis as a problem of representation, and grappling with the questions of whether and how the writer can bridge class divides and speak for, as well as to, a wider black urban community. This problem of representation is exacerbated by the fact that contemporary literary readerships are highly specialized and restricted as well as racially and culturally diverse, and are certainly not coextensive with "the black community."

The southern folk aesthetic exemplifies a "discursive displacement" of this crisis in literary representation in the sense that, if black community is perceived to be irreparably fractured in the contemporary city, the folk domain of the rural south operates as a site where integral black communities can be imaginatively restored. These face-to-face models of community are typically bound together by ties of place, distinctive cultural modes of knowing (clustered around the term "conjuring") and styles of communication (oral tradition). The turn toward southern folk culture works essentially to guarantee the writer's ability to identify, address, and speak for a wider black community. For example, Alice Walker declares, in a much-quoted passage from her essay "The Black Writer and the Southern Experience," that "what the black Southern writer inherits as a natural right is a sense of *community*. Something simple but surprisingly hard, especially these days, to come by."[4] If we accredit current discourses of urban crisis, black community *does* appear surprisingly hard to come by these days, requiring as it does difficult acts of mediation across intraracial class, regional, and cultural distinctions. The literary turn toward a rural southern past helps short-circuit this labor of mediation, furnishing community as the writer's "natural right." Alice Walker's remembered image of wholesome southern community hinges on a "cooperative ethos"[5] that mitigates intraracial class divisions, precisely the ethos that is often said to have dissolved in the contemporary city.

Houston Baker, in his study of black women novelists, specifies the type of community implicit in the southern folk aesthetic, as he opposes the "mulattoization"—or racial dilution—of black urban culture to "a field of 'particular' or vernacular imagery unique to the Afro-American imagination," a field Baker situates in the rural south.[6] Even Addison Gayle, a prominent advocate of the city-based Black Aesthetic of the 1960s, has more recently argued that black southern folklore gives us "the genesis of a racial literature"; despite "the fact that modernization, urbanization, and all the concomitant evils have come to the South," the African-American writer who taps into southern folklore can be "one with his community, and his works . . . validated and legitimized by the community itself."[7] As these passages suggest, the southern folk aesthetic stakes a claim to crisis-free literary representation, and strives to recover, in Toni Morrison's words, "a time when an artist could be genuinely representative *of* the tribe and *in* it."[8] Morrison's use of the word "tribe" (and, elsewhere, "village")[9] invokes a metaphor of organic community that serves to secure the contemporary writer's claims to literary representation, and that bespeaks the difficulty of affirming the writer's social function within the more complex and conflicted conditions of contemporary urban community.

The critical currency of the southern folk aesthetic has obscured those African-American novelists who explicitly engage the difficulties of writing an urban fiction that cannot configure its reading audience as an organic racial community. In this essay, I shall focus on one such novelist, Octavia Butler, whose recent novel, *Parable of the Sower* (1993), addresses several concerns feeding into a contemporary crisis of urban literary representation. Octavia Butler is a prolific writer whose novels have usually been targeted at a restricted science-fiction readership and, with the exception of *Kindred,* have therefore remained outside the critical purview of the African-American women's fictional tradition. Butler's latest novel merits attention because its unusual approach to questions of community broadens and complicates influential current accounts of black women's literary tradition. If, as Hazel Carby contends, southern folk aesthetics exemplify a discursive displacement of urban crisis, *Parable of the Sower* attempts squarely to confront this crisis through its starkly dystopian urban setting. The novel self-reflexively deploys scientific modes of knowing and textual forms of communication (rather than the magical epistemology of "conjuring" or oral tradition) in order to assess the writer's role in mediating urban crisis. The novel forcefully rejects localist and organic notions of community, reaching instead for more complex ways of representing communities that are not coextensive with places or with discrete cultural traditions. In what follows, I treat *Parable of the Sower* as a lens that clarifies the dangers of advancing folk resolutions to current urban problems. I then go on to examine Butler's resolution to dilemmas of urban literary representation,

which depends on the very same model of organic community that her novel struggles to discredit as an unrealistic and undesirable ideal. As I shall argue, the contradictory terms of this resolution reveal not only the difficulty of investing literature with broad-based social value within contemporary urban conditions, but also the constraints placed by current discourses of urban crisis on the African-American literary imagination.

If the urban migrations of the first half of the twentieth century constituted a mass movement of African-Americans from "medieval America to modern" as well as a collective effort to seize "the larger and more democratic chance,"[10] the reverse literary turn toward the rural south in the last decades of this century may be read as a form of "desperate pastoralism" born out of acute disenchantment with the failed promise of urban modernity for African-Americans.[11] As so many urban historians have observed, the American city at the end of the twentieth century is typified by two contradictory but interdependent trends—hardening racial and economic divisions on the one hand, and on the other a promiscuous intercourse between cultural signs of racial difference that maintains the mirage of a "consumer democracy."[12] Locating authentic black community in a segregated folk domain, the southern aesthetic enables writers to divest from the illusory pluralism promised by the contemporary city.

Parable of the Sower similarly exposes the hollowness and duplicity of recent American ideologies of urban development. The novel takes as its point of departure an uncannily credible future in which ideals of the American city as a "consumption artifact"[13] have devolved into a precarious urban order founded on economic and racial inequality. Octavia Butler has said in an interview that in this novel she "made an effort to talk about what could actually happen or is in the process of happening."[14] The dystopia presented in *Parable of the Sower* is so closely extrapolated from current trends, as Stephen Potts observes,[15] that it produces a shock of familiarity rather than estrangement. Butler identifies the walling of communities as one process that is actually and already occurring in contemporary urban America.[16] And, in fact, the novel's depiction of walled neighborhoods as spatial manifestations of a segregated urban order based on unequal distribution of economic resources uncannily resembles both John Edgar Wideman's journalistic description of contemporary Los Angeles as a city structured by "invisible walls" and Mike Davis's grim account of "Fortress L.A."[17]

Set in Robledo, a "little city" near Los Angeles,[18] during the years 2024-27, the first half of *Parable of the Sower* presents a walled neighborhood whose residents have armed themselves to protect their property against threats of looting and arson. The streets outside this enclave are occupied by an urban underclass made up of "the street poor—squatters, winos, junkies, homeless people in general" who are "desperate or crazy or both" (9). Inhabitants of the walled neighborhood are too fearful of street violence to send their children to the few schools that still exist; few jobs are available even for the educated. Past patterns of production and consumption have so thoroughly stripped the earth of its natural resources that even water has become an expensive commodity. Vegetable gardens, fruit trees, and livestock provide the means of subsistence for the relatively well-to-do, such as the residents of Robledo, whose struggle to preserve their property, their families, and their community ends when their neighborhood is destroyed by pyromaniacs, users of a popular drug that stimulates arson.

Projecting widespread scarcity and heightened class and racial antagonisms as the probable results of current patterns of production and consumption, the novel thoroughly discredits the enduring image (revived in recent times) of the city as a marketplace of abundant and diverse consumer options.[19] It is the gated community rather than the vibrant and heterogeneous marketplace that Butler presents as the epitome of contemporary urbanism. Lauren Olamina, the eighteen-year old protagonist and narrator of the novel, describes Robledo as "a tiny, walled, fish-bowl cul-de-sac community" (11). The novel's only other extended image of urban order is equally, if not more, dystopian. Olivar, a city bought out and controlled by a multinational company, offers its citizens employment, a "guaranteed food-supply," and security from the "spreading chaos of the rest of Los Angeles County" (106). But the safety of a company town like Olivar is based on a system of labor exploitation that seems "half antebellum revival and half science fiction" (109). Corporations pay their workers wages that barely meet living expenses, forcing them into a cycle of debt slavery that perpetuates their dependence on the company. The order of this privatized city is maintained by the suspension of "'overly restrictive' minimum wage, environmental, and worker protection laws," so that corporations can do away with money wages altogether and hire labor in exchange for room and board (24).

The gated communities of Olivar and Robledo sketch a future scenario in which American cities can no longer continue to function as systems supporting an equitable organization of production and consumption. In response, the novel's protagonist urges other characters to seek more viable economic and ecological alternatives, such as living off the land (52). This turn to a simple agricultural economy is certainly a logical consequence of the novel's refusal to equate current directions of urban development with the promise of progress. Lauren's mother remembers a past when this urban promise seemed tangible, when cities were "a blaze of light." In the novel's present, however, "lights, progress, growth" are discredited as the thwarted goals of urban development (5). In its critique of an urban order rationalized by ideologies of conspicuous consumption and in its turn to a modest agricultural order, *Parable of the Sower* decidedly recalls novels such as Toni Morrison's *Song of Solomon* and Gloria Naylor's *Mama Day,* which affirm primitive social orders situated in an imaginary rural south as alternatives to contemporary capitalist cities organized as artifacts of consumption. As Susan Willis has argued, seemingly nostalgic images of the rural south in black women's fiction often serve as Archimedean levers for criticizing urban capitalism.[20]

Parable of the Sower shares this critique but refuses the polarization of rural and urban spheres that bolsters the southern folk aesthetic. Raymond Williams warns, in *The Country and the City,* that "we need not, at any stage, accept the town and country contrast at face value,"[21] because literary constructions of this contrast so often repress the realities of agricultural labor and thereby blind us to the functional interdependence of country and city in advanced capitalist economies. Butler is careful not to disguise the harsh facts of agricultural labor or to represent the rural sphere as an elsewhere to the urban capitalist economy. Emery, the only farm worker in the novel, has worked for an agri-business conglomerate that paid wages in company scrip and practiced a form of exploitation through debt as pernicious as the debt slavery common in privatized cities such as Olivar. By means of such exact parallels between conditions of labor in rural and urban areas, the novel resists constructing an idealized fiction of the countryside to ground its opposition to urban capitalism.

Butler even more emphatically refuses the retrospective stance that typically characterizes rural-based critiques of urban conditions. Commenting on the literary method of using a fabricated rural past as a "stick to beat the present," Raymond Williams remarks on its tendency to turn "protest into retrospect," a tendency that curtails the radical reach of rurally grounded critiques of urban capitalism.[22] In *Parable of the Sower,* Butler clarifies the strongly conservative (and conservationist) ideologies that tend to accompany a retrospective critical stance toward the present. The adults in Robledo are "still anchored in the past, waiting for the good old days to come back" (50); as Lauren frequently points out, this backward vision prevents them from reckoning with the many changes that have already occurred and from imagining future social transformation.

In explicit opposition to the "dying, denying, backward-looking" posture of her community (22), Lauren searches for a belief system that can "pry them loose from the rotting past" (70) and push them into building a different and better future. To this end, Lauren establishes her own religion, which she names Earthseed. This name comes to her as she is working in her garden and thinking of the way "plants seed themselves, away from their parent plants" (68). Based on her observation that "A tree cannot grow in its parents' shadows" (73), Lauren envisions members of the Earthseed community (which, at this point in the novel, exists only in her imagination) as "Earthlife . . . preparing to fall away from the parent world" (135), as "earthseed cast on new ground" (160), far from the familiar spaces of home, family, and neighborhood.

Butler's seed metaphor carries both a critical and a constructive response to conditions of urban crisis that strikingly diverges from the southern folk resolution to urban problems, crystallized around the metaphors of roots and ancestry. Taking their cue from Toni Morrison's essays, "Rootedness: The Ancestor as Foundation" and "City Limits, Village Values," critics including Karla Holloway, Joanne Braxton, and Farah Jasmine Griffin configure the ancestor as a repository of southern folk tradition and a means of combating the presumed fracture of black urban community.[23] The ancestor, as a bearer of collective folk memory, helps displaced city-dwellers to preserve their roots in the rural south; these roots support the foundation of "village" models of home, family, and community that alone can withstand urban alienation and dislocation.[24] In this conception of the ancestor as the root or foundation of urban community, a remembered and imagined rural past grounds a critique of the capitalist city as well as an alternative vision of social order.

In contrast, Butler's critique of the capitalist city does not take its bearings from the past (whether real or imagined). If the metaphor of roots points toward consolidation of past values as a positive response to present urban problems, in *Parable of the Sower,* attachment to the "apparent stability" (91) of home, family, and neighborhood obstructs action directed at change. Like the gated community, home, too, in this novel is figured as "a cul-de-sac with a wall around it" (73). This is not to suggest that Lauren does not draw emotional solace from her home, family, and neighborhood. Butler has said in an interview that family seems to her to make up "our most important set of relationships" and, in fact, other novels by Butler have been criticized for the heavy redemptive weight they place on family.[25] *Parable of the Sower* fully grants the sustaining value of home and family, but the novel sketches an emergency scenario of such wholesale urban devastation that these constructs cannot offer refuge from or guide a viable critique of dystopian urban conditions. As exemplified by the reactions of the adults in Robledo, people often react to perceived crisis by conserving familiar structures and values in an attempt

to fend off the inevitability of change. This defense of traditional values associated with an idealized past often serves dubious political ends, as is obvious from contemporary discussions of the urban "underclass" that promote familial stability (associated either with rural southern life or with a "golden age of the ghetto"[26]) as a resolution to structural economic and political problems. The seed metaphor in *Parable of the Sower* suggests a valuable corrective to such approaches, urging as it does the necessity of discarding ideas and ideologies rooted in the past that aim only to stabilize, not to transform, present social conditions. Home and family in Butler's novel cannot escape or counter the systemic logic of urban poverty and unemployment. The novel delineates the broad national and international economic processes that impinge on every home and every neighborhood, clarifying the futility (and impossibility) of constructing urban communities on "village" foundations. Lauren's aspiration to seed herself away from the shadow of home and family signals her readiness to relinquish available mirages of stability and to embrace drastic change and rupture if these are the only means to future survival and growth. This readiness is expressed in the central principle of Lauren's Earthseed religion: "When apparent stability disintegrates, as it must—God is Change" (91).

Both the name of Lauren's religion, Earthseed, and its governing metaphor of seeding suggest notions of place and community other than those inhering in the roots metaphor, which consolidates cultural and ancestral traditions as bulwarks against modern urban forces of displacement. Lauren's religion assumes mobility across space as its necessary and enabling condition. Recognizing that all visionary schemes of social transformation require an imagined elsewhere to inspire and focus action, Lauren writes that the "heaven" or "destiny" of Earthseed is "to take root among the stars" (74). By this Lauren literally means that the future of the human race lies in extrasolar space. The importance of this image of heaven is its orientation toward a future space that can only be reached by means of modern technology. The extraterrestrial direction of Earthseed, a common enough science fiction device, hyperbolically conveys the expansive globalism of the novel's vision, a vision far removed from the localism of folk models of place-bound community.

I do not mean to suggest here that mobility is in itself a forward-looking urban value or that localism is necessarily aligned with nostalgic folk models of community.[27] In fact, urban community movements have often sought to conserve the use values attached to specific neighborhoods as the only available means of resisting the instability of an urban space that is repeatedly deformed and reformed by the dictates of capitalist exchange value. As Logan and Molotch have persuasively argued, contradictions between use and exchange values, between place as the site of lived community and place as commodity, are at the root of "truly urban conflict."[28] Poor neighborhoods inhabited by racial minorities have been especially vulnerable to the rapid conversions of urban space over the last two or three decades; the forcible dislocation of these residents has been the invariable byproduct of urban renewal and gentrification projects intended to raise property values.[29] In this kind of urban context, mobility can hardly be affirmed as a more progressive stance than efforts to defend the use values of places and communities against the disembedding forces of capitalist spatial turnover.

This conflict between urban use and exchange values is dramatized in a recent novel, *Tumbling,* by Diane McKinney-Whetstone, which depicts a low-income black residential neighborhood in Philadelphia that forms the site of a closely knit community modeled on the southern "village." Residents band together to protest and obstruct an urban renewal project undertaken by real-estate developers and subsidized by the city administration, which threatens to raze the neighborhood. Despite the residents' efforts, their neighborhood church is bulldozed to clear the space for highway construction. *Tumbling* ends with the lines, "They would not be moved. No way, no way."[30] In the novel's closing scene, residents form a makeshift community on the debris of the church in a last-ditch and ultimately futile effort to defend the use value of their neighborhood—futile because the community lacks the political and economic power to overcome the urban "growth machine" jointly run by "place entrepreneurs," city officials, and political leaders.[31]

It is because neighborhoods and communities are imbricated in wider and unequally structured grids of exchange value and political power that struggles to preserve local value and communal integrity are almost always unsuccessful. For this reason, *Parable of the Sower* insists that readiness to move—to outer space, if need be—is crucial to survival in modern capitalist cities. Like *Tumbling,* the first part of *Parable* [*Parable of the Sower*] laments the inevitable defeat of movements to maintain local and communal self-sufficiency. The Robledo neighborhood cannot be sustained because its relative financial and social stability is structurally interconnected to the extreme instability of the poor and the pyromaniacs who throng outside the walls of Robledo and who eventually raid and burn down the neighborhood.

Just before the destruction of Robledo, Lauren Olamina preaches a funeral sermon for her father (who has disappeared and is presumed dead) and for the ideal of self-contained, stable, place-bound community that Lauren associates with an older way of life. Lauren's sermon commemorates her father's attempts to preserve the integrity and durability of locale and community: "We

have our island community, fragile, and yet a fortress. Sometimes it seems too small and too weak to survive. . . . But . . . it persists. . . . This is our place, no matter what" (120). This is, however, a funeral sermon and Lauren is mourning the death of traditional conceptions of community rooted in a fixed and impermeable sense of place. At the end of her sermon, a member of the community begins to sing the spiritual, "We Shall Not Be Moved," to which Lauren mentally responds, "We'll be moved, all right. It's just a matter of when, by whom, and in how many pieces" (121). Appropriately enough, then, the first half of the novel traces the literal destruction of Lauren's home, neighborhood, and community in Robledo, and the second half describes her journey north (with a band of fellow travelers she picks up on the way) toward a new home and community. The novel ends soon after the group reaches its destination. The entire action of the novel reveals the impossibility of maintaining "village" ideals of bounded community rooted in a stable locale. In this sense, even as it presents the complete collapse of actual cities, the novel insists on an urban understanding of place as the inescapable basis for constructing alternative images of social order.

In contrast to the Robledo community, based on the principle of self-contained localism, the journey section that constitutes the bulk of the novel presents community as process rather than settlement. This section traces the contingent formation of a community on the move—"born right here on Highway 101," as Lauren puts it (200)—unified not by its attachment to past or place but by a common set of practical objectives that must be continually adjusted to meet changing circumstances. When Robledo burns down, halfway through the novel, Lauren runs into two survivors of the neighborhood, Harry and Zahra, who share her will to move toward a better life. The other fourteen people who join the group in the course of the journey north are distinguished primarily by the fact that most of them are racially mixed, and therefore "natural allies" (186) in a society that frowns on miscegenation. Most members of the group have suffered some form of injustice, whether caused by poverty, forced prostitution, child abuse, or debt slavery. The sole purpose that unifies this group of diverse people is their shared resolve to move toward a better future.

Even though the itinerary of this "crew of a modern underground railroad" (262) is explicitly calculated to bypass cities, which are sites of danger, their operation as a community is emphatically urban in most crucial respects. Despite the natural reference of its name, Earthseed is definitely not an organic community unified by collective memory, ethnicity, shared cultural heritage, or attachment to place. If, in order to resist the "mulattoization" of urban community, the southern folk aesthetic strives to recuperate cohesive racial communities consisting of cultural insiders,[32] the Earthseed community, in contrast, is racially and culturally mixed and thus demands constant efforts of mediation and translation. The boundaries of this community, the porous lines between insiders and outsiders, friends and enemies, must be continually redrawn; they must "embrace diversity or be destroyed" (176). The process of finding unity in diversity is necessarily risky and difficult, requiring the ability to interpret unfamiliar cultural codes and the alert balancing of suspicion and trust typical of urban social interactions. This group makes collective decisions by way of rational argument and persuasion rather than by appeals to past precedent or tradition.

Given the novel's insistence on this thoroughly urban conception of community, the settlement established by Lauren and her Earthseed community at the end of the novel surely appears puzzling. The journey that takes up most of the second half of the novel ends in Humboldt County in northern California, on a piece of property owned by Bankole, one of the group of travelers who journey north with Lauren. Bankole offers the group (which by the end of the novel consists of four men, five women, and four children) rent-free use of his land. Several geographical features of Bankole's property make it a suitable (though not ideal) place for establishing an Earthseed community. Most importantly, arable land and a dependable water supply make the property amenable to gardening and farming. The economy projected at the end of the novel is small-scale, primitive, and self-sufficient[33] in the sense that farming, breeding livestock, and building shelters are expected to take care of basic production and consumption needs. It is clear that jobs paying money are scarce in neighboring towns and, given that several members of the community are former debt slaves or throwaway laborers, working Bankole's land seems preferable to selling labor to "strangers" who "shouldn't be trusted" (289). One of the more valuable characteristics of Bankole's land is its isolation; because it is "far removed from any city" (281) and "miles from everywhere with no decent road" (287), it is relatively immune to attack from outsiders. That the area's distance from cities constitutes a strongly emphasized advantage is not surprising considering that cities, as centers of asymmetrical accumulation, have been shown throughout the novel to be the most vulnerable to criminal violence targeting the scarce commodity. The Earthseed community plans to guard its settlement by assigning members to keep watch at night and later by training dogs to protect the property.

How is this settlement different from the walled and heavily guarded neighborhood of the beginning of the novel? We have seen that the Robledo community was destroyed because its goal of local self-sufficiency was inviable given its dependence on a wider, starkly inequitable economic order. The community at the end of the novel does acknowledge, though it does not adequately reckon with, the inevitability of such connections. Despite some affinities with arcadian rural communities such as the island of Willow Springs in Gloria Naylor's *Mama Day,* the Earthseed community cannot be regarded as arcadian, in that it does not assume the essential moderacy, simplicity, or stability of human needs.[34] The potentially destabilizing desire to accumulate surplus, on the part of individuals and the group, is expressed in Harry's remark that he wants a job outside the community that will pay money as well as in the community's plan to sell surplus produce in nearby towns. The members of the Earthseed community insist on the provisional nature of their settlement; as Lauren points out, there are "no guarantees" (288), and should their experimental community fail (as most members of the group expect it to do), they will have to be prepared to move on.

Yet the Earthseed community also aims impossibly to maintain local self-containment and stability. The novel's concluding image of community does not suggest a more workable balancing between use and exchange value, between localism and mobility, than does its opening image of the walled cul-de-sac neighborhood. As we have seen, Butler's representation of Robledo forcefully repudiates notions of place-bound community, and the journey section of the novel reaches for a more complex way of imagining community that is not coextensive with place, and place that is conceived as a "concrete abstraction" rather than as a self-enclosed site of social meaning.[35] Butler wrestles with the difficulties of writing a fiction adequate to this understanding of place and community, yet the Earthseed settlement at the end of the novel ends up establishing an insulated, agrarian, face-to-face model of community that is not so different, after all, from the organic communities associated with southern folk aesthetics. In this respect, the Earthseed community is symptomatic of the difficulty that limits the contemporary literary imagination seeking utopian urban alternatives.[36] Its small-scale, self-sufficient, agrarian ideal is rife with contradictions: even if we know that any truly alternative social vision requires wholesale transformation of global economic order, we end up thinking small because the abstraction of this order makes it difficult to grasp and imagine large-scale change. Or, in Manuel Castells' succinct expression, "When people find themselves unable to control the world, they simply shrink the world to the size of their community."[37]

A similar contradiction marks Butler's effort to constitute a belief-system that might spur an effective practical response to urban crisis. Lauren Olamina's Earthseed religion suggests that such a response does not have to hinge on the creation of pure epistemological alternatives to modern urbanism. In this respect, *Par-*

able of the Sower disengages itself from the project of defining a distinctive black women's epistemology derived from southern folk culture, a project common to novels such as *Song of Solomon, Mama Day,* Toni Cade Bambara's *The Salt Eaters,* and Ntozake Shange's *Sassafras, Cypress, and Indigo,* as well as to several critical texts on black women's fiction that might be clustered together around the term "conjuring." Works including Marjorie Pryse's "Zora Neale Hurston, Alice Walker, and the 'Ancient Power' of Black Women," Karla Holloway's *Moorings and Metaphors,* and Houston Baker's *Workings of the Spirit* all seek to specify and recover what Baker describes as "a revered site of culturally specific interests and values."[38] These forms of "discredited knowledge," in Toni Morrison's phrase,[39] constitute an alternative epistemology intended to clarify the limitations of modern science and rationality (aligned with urbanity), and to reinstate suprarational, supernatural, and magical modes of knowing as distinctive of southern folk communities. *Parable of the Sower* certainly shares the disenchantment with urban modernity that fuels the "conjuring" paradigm, in that the Earthseed community resembles a religious cult seeking refuge from the nightmarish effects of the supposedly rational order of the city.

But, contrary to "conjuring," the epistemology of Earthseed unreservedly espouses scientific and rational methods of arriving at truth. The guiding tenet of Earthseed—"God is change"—is compatible with scientific principles such as the second law of thermodynamics (195).[40] The possibility of attaining the ultimate "destiny" of this religion—the heaven located in outer space—is also dependent on the future development of "science and space projects" (75). In this sense, Earthseed is a belief-system enabled more by science than by the magical or mystical epistemologies affirmed in "conjuring" criticism. Lauren insists that Earthseed is not "mythology or mysticism or magic" (195) and that the measure of its legitimacy is "ongoing reality" rather than "supernatural authority" (197).

In Lauren's view, Earthseed reflects a "reality" that is immediately accessible to empirical observation:

> I've never felt that I was making any of this up . . . I mean, I've never felt that it was anything other than real: discovery rather than invention, exploration rather than creation. I wish I could believe it was all supernatural, and that I'm getting messages from God. But then, I don't believe in that kind of God. All I do is observe and take notes.
>
> (69)

It is Lauren's observation of natural phenomena that gives rise to the principle of god as change—"Seed to tree, / tree to forest; / Rain to river, / river to sea" (283). Early in the novel, Lauren feels some uncertainty about

the truth value of her religion, wondering, "Is any of this real? Dangerous question. Sometimes I don't know the answer. I doubt myself. I doubt what I think I know" (23). But as the novel progresses, Lauren becomes increasingly confident that her religion reveals a "literal truth" (22) directly available to the senses. The pragmatic purpose of Earthseed, which is to impel people to respond to conditions of extreme social disorder by taking decisive action directed at change, suspends epistemological doubt and speculation. Like the "conjuring" practices of Pilate in *Song of Solomon* or Gloria Naylor's *Mama Day* or Minnie Ransom of *The Salt Eaters,* the Earthseed credo arises as a reaction against an urban disorder exemplifying the discontents of modern rationality, but *Parable of the Sower* unequivocally promotes modern science, technology, and reason as the necessary instruments for opposing and constructing alternatives to urban dystopia.

However, the significant distinction between the conjuring and Earthseed epistemologies paradoxically ends up serving similar ends—both offer the writer a smooth imaginary resolution to crises of urban literary representation. A brief glance at conjuring criticism should help to clarify this point. Both Houston Baker and Marjorie Pryse have described conjuring as a literary device drawn from southern folk culture that can help invest black women's novels with unique "literary authority."[41] Given that folk-based claims to cultural authority usually privilege orality, it is not surprising that conjuring, aided by oral tradition, installs a type of literary community that is explicitly opposed to the readerly or textual. Karla Holloway, Joyce Ann Joyce, and Jocelyn Donlon all deploy conjuring and orality to mitigate the indeterminacies, mediations, and distanciations involved in the act of reading a book. Holloway argues that the oral mode fuses storyteller and listener, and reorganizes the subjects and objects of knowledge into metaphorical community; in the oralized magical text, the "reader's voice is invited to join its community of tellers." According to Joyce, the conjurer-critic takes a collaborative approach to the literary text—an approach that "mystically merges" author, critic, and community. In a similar vein, Donlon claims that oral storytelling communities elicit interpretive assent and operate through collective authentication of shared cultural modes of knowledge and communication.[42] Conjuring and orality thus combine to consolidate an emphatically anti-urban and anti-textual model of community. The appeal of this model lies in its elimination of the complexities and risks of mediation, and in its discursive construction of a unified community engaged in harmonious, crisis-free acts of knowing, speaking, and listening.

If the southern folk aesthetic draws on magical epistemologies and oral modes of communication to resolve dilemmas of urban authorship and to institute a clearly knowable and integral cultural community, *Par-*

able employs the reflective truth claims of science as well as the trope of the book-within-a-book to affirm the writer's distinctive capacity to know, represent, and, indeed, redeem urban community. The book within Butler's book is a sacred text, authored by Lauren Olamina and titled *Earthseed: The Books of the Living*, which consists of a collection of verses encapsulating the precepts of the Earthseed religion. This book is written by hand in one of Lauren's school exercise books and passed around and read aloud among the members of the traveling Earthseed community. That *Earthseed* is not a printed text or a commodity to be bought and sold is crucial to the novel's redemptive vision of urban writing. Unlike a commodity, the manuscript of *Earthseed* can circulate freely among a select group of readers and can thus manage to address the immediately present and knowable community that is typically associated with oral modes of communication. The polarization of book and oral tradition, city and village that prevails in the southern folk aesthetic simply does not figure in **Parable of the Sower,** because the novel's fictional situation closes the gap between reading and listening, author and audience. *Earthseed* is a written text that is orally disseminated. Its author, Lauren, is physically present to oversee the text's reception by her audience, which is the clearly delimited community of her fellow travelers. If the commodity object of the printed book often arouses authorial anxieties about the highly mediated and dispersed nature of urban community,[43] in Butler's novel the processes of reading and discussing the text of *Earthseed* bind the community together into a purposive whole.

The author of *Earthseed* is there in person to defend and explain the book's contents, which are often contested by its audience of listeners and readers. Moreover, *Earthseed* is very much a context-bound text, a process rather than a finished product, in that Lauren is engaged in writing the text throughout the course of the journey. Her writing bears a dialectical relation to the ongoing life of the group, both drawing its content from the group's experience and in turn shaping the group's understanding of this experience. In this sense, the book, as suggested by its subtitle, is literally a book of and for the living. In another sense, however, the content of this book remains fixed and unrevised by its readers' contestations. Despite the group's vigorous arguments over the meaning of the book, the dissemination and interpretation of *Earthseed* are never subject to crisis. Lauren dismisses Bankole's suggestion that readers of the text will transform it beyond recognition with the assertion, "Not around me they won't!" (234). Although Lauren explicitly disavows claims to authorial originality (111), she certainly wishes to exercise an impossible authorial power to control and fix the meaning of her text—ironic, considering that this text takes change to be its governing principle.

The authoritative status of *Earthseed* is further reinforced by the fact that, although excerpts from it are occasionally included as quoted passages within the text of the novel, they most often appear in the form of epigraphs to the novel's chapters. As clearly demarcated passages that are typographically set off from the body of the text, these epigraphs visually signal the transcendent authority of disembedded discourse and, indeed, function as sacred discourse. Lauren observes that sacred books like the Bible, the Talmud, or the Koran help people in times of trouble to "remember a truth or a comfort or a reminder to action" (198). This is exactly how the text of *Earthseed* works, inspiring and guiding the novel's characters as well as framing and illuminating the action presented in the novel.

The book, *Earthseed,* exercises this sacred power even in its oral dissemination. When Lauren preaches from the book, one member of her audience mockingly responds with an "Amen" (197), but Lauren quite literally refers to her readers as converts (200). The only text other than *Earthseed* that appears in the novel as decontextualized, framing discourse is a passage from another sacred book, the Bible. The parable of the sower, quoted from the Book of St. Luke, provides both the title and the epilogue for the novel. Figuring Jesus Christ as the sower, the seed as the sacred word, and varieties of soil as different types of listeners, the parable of the sower essentially addresses the problems of creating a responsive spiritual community. The parallels between the appearance of this parable and of excerpts from *Earthseed* as typographically distinct forms of textual discourse, as well as obvious parallels between the seed metaphor employed by the two sacred texts, encourage us to equate the written text of *Earthseed* with divine oral utterance. This equation appears truly remarkable in light of the fact that, in so much criticism on African-American women's fiction, writing is presented as a technology that desacralizes and disrupts the organic community unified around oral utterance. Synthesizing the spoken and written word, text and interpretation, author and community, Butler's novel invests the writer with sacred, redemptive powers.

And, in fact, what is truly unique about **Parable of the Sower** is that the figure of the writer (rather than the oral storyteller) is central to the novel's vision of social transformation and improvement. **Parable of the Sower** emphasizes the continuing and crucial importance of print literacy to any credible vision of an equitable democratic society. Widespread adult illiteracy is one of the emphasized features of the urban dystopia presented in the novel. In contrast to novels like *Song of Solomon* or *Mama Day* that voice strong reservations about the liberating powers of print literacy, Butler reaches back to a seemingly distant moment in African-American literary tradition to press the case for literacy. Indeed, the novel's frequent echoing of the classic slave narrative scenario, in which the slave learns to read and write despite the master's prohibition,[44] suggests that the historical moment of slavery is not so distant from ours, that unequal access to literacy and education remain serious obstacles to the achievement of a democratic society. The Earthseed ideal of an equitable, democratic society depends on education in literacy. One of the major goals of the Earthseed community is to provide instruction in reading and writing to illiterate adults. Lauren's profession of choice is to be a teacher and, in fact, while the group is on the road, Lauren uses the *Earthseed* text to teach the many illiterate members of the group how to read and write.

Literacy is a highly marketable skill in *Parable of the Sower,* as becomes clear when Lauren's brother Keith is generously paid for reading instruction manuals to help illiterate adults operate their stolen, high-tech equipment. Through this and other instances, the novel underscores the urgent and continuing importance of print literacy in a future era dominated by electronic communications technologies.[45] Lauren hopes that in the future she can get paid for her reading and writing skills, which are crucial to the very struggle for physical survival. Early in the novel, when Lauren first begins to realize that the future of the Robledo neighborhood is in jeopardy, she prepares herself for the impending catastrophe by reading her father's old books. From these books, Lauren gains practical information about handling medical emergencies, using plants for medicinal and nutritional purposes, building log cabins, raising livestock, making soap, and so on. The skills Lauren learns from her reading pay off when Earthseed is on the road, in an area where water is scarce and exorbitantly costly, and Lauren is able to draw drinking water out of sand: "According to a couple of books I read, water is supposed to seep through the sand with most of the salt filtered out of it. . . . It might save our lives someday" (184). In this instance, as in many others (such as Lauren's father drawing on a book about Native American uses of California plants to make acorn bread, which is the only grain their family can afford), books possess an immediate, pragmatic use value that literally saves lives.

"Even some fiction might be useful," says Lauren Olamina as she tries to persuade a friend about the importance of books to physical survival (56). But *Parable of the Sower* does not invest any special redemptive power in the literary or fictional imagination as such. If the southern folk aesthetic draws on oral vernacular culture in an effort to allay anxieties about the restricted social sway of literary culture, we know that Octavia Butler is not immune to these anxieties. In a recent interview, Butler says that she wants to preach to her audience but, knowing that her writing must compete with a mass electronic culture (of television and video games), she makes an effort to hook her read-

ers with a compelling story that will help them swallow the didactic social messages of her fiction.[46] But in the social context created in *Parable of the Sower,* such concerns are obviated by the fact that, on the move for sheer physical survival, the characters have no other entertainment options that might compete with the activity of reading and listening to Lauren's book. In addition, Lauren insists that *Earthseed* is more akin to scientific "discovery" than to imaginative "invention," and given the novel's unqualified affirmation of scientific epistemologies, the writer of the *Earthseed* book can lay claim to "literal" truths that are easily verifiable and directly applicable to life. Its recourse to the putatively transparent truth value and instrumentality of science helps the novel to bracket all doubts about the more tricky question of literary representation.

Parable of the Sower is able to attribute socially transformative power to writing and to present books as essential tools "of the living" only by effacing its modality as literary invention. Lauren Olamina is not the only author in this book to insist that her writing is based on "discovery" rather than "invention." Octavia Butler, too, in interviews, underplays the inventive and fantastic elements of her novel, emphasizing instead its close reflection of actual social trends that she has observed or read about. For example, in an interview with Jerome Jackson, Butler says that as a writer, she has "to say what I feel is true. Obviously, I mean verisimilitude as well as the literal truth,"[47] exactly echoing Lauren Olamina's claim that the Earthseed text reflects the "literal truth" (22). It is surely telling that the rare recent novel by an African-American woman to elevate urban writing (rather than southern oral tradition) to a position of unquestionable communal authority and social centrality can do so only through a repression of its own literary medium.

The novel's unqualified affirmation of the writer's effectivity in conditions of urban crisis depends on a number of contradictions that become apparent through a close analysis of Butler's use of the trope of the book. Representing the book (the Earthseed text) as a noncommodity object that circulates among a select group of readers including the author, the novel manages to circumvent the crises of knowability and communication generated by the urban writer's inability to assume a well-defined community of readers. The *Earthseed* book addresses and fully represents a community which, although it is not settled in a specific locale, is nevertheless visible to its author and cemented by an urgent social purpose defined by this author. The fact that some Earthseed members are educated and literate and others are not never seems to generate conflict within the group. Even the teacher-student relation between Lauren and the illiterate members of the group such as Zahra is free of the power imbalance built into this relation. The kinds of hierarchical specialization of roles that inevitably accompany reading and writing are simply not issues in this novel, for the Earthseed community will erase all social distinctions deriving from literacy by ensuring all its members equal access to education.

Although **Parable of the Sower** struggles against the option of displacing urban crisis to a rural southern elsewhere, the novel's resolution to problems of urban authorship ultimately suspends urban conditions of community-building, in a move quite similar to the displacement effected by the southern folk aesthetic. Both resolutions—Butler's and the southern folk turn—hinge on an affirmation of immediately knowable and bounded communities that alone can authenticate (and, indeed, sacralize) the writer's social function. As I argue earlier in this essay, **Parable of the Sower** insists on a thoroughly urban understanding of place and community as concrete abstractions, yet the novel appears abruptly to retreat from the consequences of this urban vision for the writer. Although it makes a strong case against models of community that ground cultural value in a fixed locale, the novel does not reckon with the complex implications that contingently formed and makeshift urban communities might bear for the writer. The readership of the *Earthseed* text is culturally and racially heterogeneous, but the author's negotiation of these differences is not raised as a substantive issue in **Parable of the Sower.** The novel's construction of a state of social emergency ensures that all communal concerns are geared toward the goal of physical survival, thereby bracketing all kinds of problems that any settled community would have to work through. Epistemological uncertainties as well as conflicts in communication arising from class, educational, racial, and gender divisions are credibly suppressed by the acutely dystopian urban setting of **Parable of the Sower.** Such bracketing of social conflicts and mediations enables the literary constitution of an organic community that legitimizes the writer as teacher, preacher, prophet, and literal savior of life.

The contradictory terms of Butler's resolution to crises of urban literary representation are instructive. **Parable of the Sower** frontally encounters contemporary urban crises and struggles against the impulse to project organic models of community as viable forms of refuge or resolution to the social and economic problems plaguing American cities. But when it comes to affirming a crucial and transformative social role for the writer, the novel relapses into precisely the sort of displacement of urban realities that it has so strenuously sought to resist. Although it systematically exposes the dangers and limitations of organic notions of community, the novel, in common with southern folk aesthetics, ultimately resorts to such notions in order to achieve a smooth resolution to problems of urban literary representation. The significantly different cases of

Parable of the Sower and the southern folk aesthetic commonly indicate that, when urban crisis is staged essentially as a problem of representation, literary displacements of contemporary urban realities become likely consequences. The resolutions projected in Butler's novel as well as in southern folk aesthetics, hinging on an affirmation of the writer's ability to represent unified and clearly knowable cultural communities, are overdetermined by the terms set by current discourses on urban problems in the popular media as well as the academy, which themselves displace political and economic problems on to the sphere of black culture. This displacement exerts severe pressure on black culture; literary claims to broad social representation are bound to become fraught in a contemporary scene in which alarmist rhetorics proclaim an unprecedented state of emergency in urban America that is widely understood as a crisis in black cultural community.

Notes

1. Hazel Carby, "The Politics of Fiction, Anthropology, and the Folk: Zora Neale Hurston," in *History and Memory in African-American Culture,* ed. Genevieve Fabre and Robert O'Mealy (New York: Oxford Univ. Press, 1994), 41.

2. Some key texts that have contributed to the formation of folk vernacular theories of black women's fiction are: Susan Willis, *Specifying: Black Women Writing the American Experience* (Madison: Univ. of Wisconsin Press, 1987); Houston Baker, *Workings of the Spirit: The Poetics of Afro-American Women's Writing* (Chicago: Univ. of Chicago Press, 1991); Marjorie Pryse, "Zora Neale Hurston, Alice Walker, and the 'Ancient Power' of Black Women," in *Conjuring: Black Women, Fiction, and Literary Tradition,* ed. Marjorie Pryse and Hortense Spillers (Bloomington: Indiana Univ. Press, 1985), 1-24; Joanne M. Braxton, "Afra-American Culture and the Contemporary Literary Renaissance," in *Wild Women in the Whirlwind: Afra-American Culture and the Contemporary Literary Renaissance,* ed. Joanne Braxton and Andree Nicola McLaughlin (New Brunswick: Rutgers Univ. Press, 1990), xxi-xxx; Toni Morrison, "Rootedness: The Ancestor as Foundation," in *Black Women Writers (1950-1980),* ed. Mari Evans (New York: Doubleday, 1984), 339-45; Toni Morrison, "City Limits, Village Values," in *Literature and the Urban Experience,* ed. Michael C. Jaye and Ann Chalmers Watts (New Brunswick: Rutgers Univ. Press, 1981), 35-43; and Alice Walker, "The Black Writer and the Southern Experience" and "In Search of Our Mothers' Gardens," repr. in *In Search of Our Mothers' Gardens,* by Alice Walker (New York: Harcourt, 1984), 15-21, 231-43.

3. The most widely known examples of journalistic and academic works that take such an approach to urban poverty are: Nicholas Lemann, "The Origins of the

Underclass," Parts I and II, *Atlantic Monthly* 257 (June 1986): 31-61, and 258 (July 1986): 54-68; Ken Auletta, *The Underclass* (New York: Random House, 1982); William Julius Wilson, *The Truly Disadvantaged: The Inner City, the Underclass, and Public Policy* (Chicago: Univ. of Chicago Press, 1987); and Douglas Massey and Nancy Denton, *American Apartheid: Segregation and the Making of the Underclass* (Cambridge: Harvard Univ. Press, 1993). For strong critiques of these culturalist approaches, see Adolph Reed, "The Underclass as Myth and Symbol," *Radical America* 24, no. 1 (1990): 21-40, and the essays collected in Michael Katz, ed., *The 'Underclass' Debate: Views from History* (Princeton: Princeton Univ. Press, 1993).

4. Alice Walker, "The Black Writer and the Southern Experience," 17.

5. Jacqueline Jones uses the phrase "cooperative ethos" to describe southern black communities as well as an earlier era of northern urban life characterized by strong ties between middle-class and poor blacks. See Jones, *The Dispossessed: America's Underclasses from the Civil War to the Present* (New York: Harper Collins, 1992), 277.

6. Houston Baker, *Workings of the Spirit,* 35, 61.

7. Addison Gayle, Jr., "Reclaiming the Southern Experience: The Black Aesthetic 10 Years Later," in *Black Southern Voices,* ed. John Oliver Killens and Jerry W. Ward, Jr. (New York: Meridian, 1992), 559, 563, 560.

8. Toni Morrison, "Rootedness: The Ancestor as Foundation," 339.

9. Morrison claims to write "village literature, fiction that is really for the village, for the tribe. Peasant literature for my people," in Thomas LeClair, "'The Language Must Not Sweat': A Conversation with Toni Morrison," 1981, repr. in *Conversations with Toni Morrison,* ed. Danille Taylor-Guthrie (Jackson: Univ. Press of Mississippi, 1994), 370.

10. I am quoting Alain Locke, "The New Negro," in *The New Negro,* ed. Alain Locke (1925; repr. New York: Macmillan, 1992), 6.

11. I take the phrase "desperate pastoralism" from Jerry Phillips. My reading of *Parable of the Sower* has benefitted greatly from Phillips's discussion of the novel in "Looking Forward Through a Glass Darkly: The Geography of the Future in Octavia Butler's *Parable of the Sower,*" paper presented at the Marxist Literary Group's Summer Institute on Culture and Society, University of Illinois at Chicago, June 1998.

12. Stuart Ewen, *All-Consuming Images: The Politics of Style in Contemporary Culture* (New York: Basic Books, 1988), 32.

13. The phrase is David Harvey's, *The Urban Experience* (Baltimore: Johns Hopkins Univ. Press, 1985), 43.

14. Stephen W. Potts, "'We Keep Playing the Same Record': A Conversation with Octavia E. Butler," *Science-Fiction Studies* 23 (1996): 336.

15. Potts, 334.

16. Potts, 336.

17. When Wideman writes, "The South Central ghettos, brutally cordoned and policed, and the barred, burglar-alarmed, security-patrolled enclaves of Hollywood Hills mirror one another obscenely, grotesquely. Who's locked in? Who's locked out? Who's free?", he might well be describing any of the Californian cities we encounter in Butler's novel. See John Edgar Wideman, "Dead Black Men and Other Fallout from the American Dream," *Esquire* 118, no. 3 (1992): 156. Also see Mike Davis, *City of Quartz* (New York: Vintage, 1992), Chapter 4.

18. Octavia Butler, *Parable of the Sower* (New York: Warner, 1993), 9. Hereafter cited parenthetically.

19. In "Four Images of Organized Diversity: Bazaar, Jungle, Organism, and Machine," in *Cities of the Mind,* ed. Lloyd Rodwin and Robert M. Hollister (New York: Plenum, 1984), Peter Langer writes that the marketplace metaphor configures the city "as a place of astonishing richness of activity and diversity unparalleled in rural areas . . . , a place of almost infinite exploration and opportunity, a center of exchange" (100). Also see Michael A. Hindery and Thomas A. Reiner on the "life, stimulation, creativity, and openness" conveyed by the market image of the city "City Planning: Image of the Ideal and Existing City." in *Cities of the Mind,* 138.

20. Susan Willis, *Specifying,* 10.

21. Raymond Williams, *The Country and the City* (London: Oxford Univ. Press, 1973), 54.

22. Raymond Williams, 12, 83.

23. Joanne Braxton, "Afra-American Culture and the Contemporary Literary Renaissance," xxv-xxvi; Farah Jasmine Griffin, *"Who Set You Flowin'?": The African-American Migration Narrative* (New York: Oxford Univ. Press, 1995), 5-6: Karla F. C. Holloway, *Moorings and Metaphors: Figures of Culture and Gender in Black Women's Literature* (New Brunswick: Rutgers Univ. Press, 1992), 115.

24. Morrison, "Rootedness," 339-45, and "City Limits, Village Values," 35-43. By "village" models of community, I refer not only to the kind of community, based in an imagined and preindustrial rural south, that Toni Morrison evokes in these two essays, but also to Hindery and Reiner's discussion of the village ideal of community, which, "with its connotations of stability, integration and solidarity, self-sufficiency, [and] maintenance of traditional ways," represents "a challenging reaction . . . to the excesses of the industrial city" ("City Planning," 136).

25. Butler, in Stephen Potts, 333. For an example of such a critique, see Dorothy Allison, "The Future of Female: Octavia Butler's Mother Lode," in *Reading Black, Reading Feminist,* ed. Henry Louis Gates, Jr. (New York: Meridian, 1990), 471-80.

26. The "golden age of the ghetto" is described by Robin D. G. Kelley as "a dominant trope in the popular social science literature on the so-called underclass," a trope that presumes "the existence (until recently) of a tight-knit, harmonious black community—an age when any elder could beat a misbehaving child, when the black middle class mingled with the poor and offered themselves as 'role models,' when black professionals cared more about their downtrodden race than about their bank accounts." See Kelley, "'We Are Not What We Seem': Rethinking Black Working-Class Opposition in the Jim Crow South," in *The New African American Urban History,* ed. Kenneth W. Goings and Raymond A. Mohl (Thousand Oaks: Sage, 1996), 193.

27. If many urban community movements over the last few decades have sought to preserve local stability, it is important to remember, conversely, that the life of the rural poor is often characterized by enforced mobility. See Jacqueline Jones's discussion of the movement and migration of poor black agricultural workers in the south, dictated by employment conditions, "Southern Diaspora," in Katz, ed., *The 'Underclass' Debate,* 39-46.

28. John R. Logan and Harvey L. Molotch, *Urban Fortunes: The Political Economy of Place* (Berkeley: Univ, of California Press, 1987), 35. I am also drawing here on David Harvey, *The Urban Experience,* 250-55; J. Nicholas Entrikin, *The Betweenness of Place: Towards a Geography of Modernity* (Baltimore: Johns Hopkins Univ. Press, 1991), 31, 41, 57-58, 77-80; Sharon Zukin, *Landscapes of Power* (Berkeley: Univ. of California Press, 1991), 12-14; and Manuel Castells, *The City and the Grassroots* (Berkeley: Univ. of California Press, 1983), 308.

29. For discussions of the dislocating effects of urban redevelopment projects on the poor and racial minorities, see Logan and Molotch, *Urban Fortunes,* Chapter 4; Gregory Squires, *Capital and Communities in Black and White* (Albany: State Univ. of New York Press, 1994), Chapter 5; Massey and Denton, *American Apartheid,* 56-57; and David Bartelt, "Housing the 'Underclass'," in *The 'Underclass' Debate,* ed. Michael Katz, 18-57.

30. Diane McKinney-Whetstone, *Tumbling* (New York: Simon and Schuster, 1996), 340.

31. The quoted phrases are from Logan and Molotch, *Urban Fortunes,* 32.

32. Houston Baker, *Workings of the Spirit,* 35. Two obvious fictional instances of such communities are Shalimar in *Song of Solomon* (a community so insular as to verge on the incestuous) and Willow Springs in *Mama Day.*

33. In each of these respects, the Earthseed community resembles the "ecotopias" that Krishan Kumar characterizes in *Utopia and Anti-Utopia in Modern Times* (New York: Blackwell, 1987). Kumar writes that the literary ecotopias that burgeoned during and after the 1960s present small, self-governing, cooperative communities which, out of their ecological concern for diminishing natural resources, advocate modest levels of economic growth and consumption. These ecotopias, like the Earthseed settlement, can be characterized as postindustrial, in the sense that they are not opposed to technology per se or nostalgic for a preindustrial past (406-9).

34. I am drawing here on Ruth Levitas's discussion of arcadian resolutions to the problem of human needs: in arcadian images of ideal society, "wants do not outstrip satisfactions, not because satisfactions are limitless, but because wants are reduced to a 'natural' level, Arcadia implicitly involves a distinction between true and false needs and abolishes the scarcity gap by limiting true needs to believable available satisfactions." See Levitas, *The Concept of Utopia* (Syracuse: Syracuse Univ. Press, 1990), 162. The Earthseed community in Butler's novel refuses to predetermine true and false needs, in keeping with its dynamic conception of human nature as fundamentally unstable and changeable.

35. Place grasped as a "concrete abstraction" entails "concrete representations" of local experience that is fully explicable only through analyses of "abstract and non-observable" global structural processes (Harvey, *The Urban Experience,* 9).

36. I am echoing Fredric Jameson here: "It is . . . the limits, the systemic restrictions and repressions, or empty places, in the Utopian blueprint that are the most interesting, for these alone testify to the ways a culture or system marks the most visionary mind and contains its movement toward transcendence." *Postmodernism, or, The Cultural Logic of Late Capitalism* (Durham: Duke Univ. Press, 1991), 208.

37. Manuel Castells, *The City and the Grassroots,* 331.

38. Houston Baker, 99.

39. Morrison, "Rootedness," 342.

40. In this respect, *Parable of the Sower* is akin to Toni Cade Bambara's *The Salt Eaters* (New York: Vintage, 1980), which, although it participates in the quest to recover and affirm a unique black feminine epistemology centered around magic and mysticism, does not share the strong suspicion of scientific epistemologies that drives the conjuring paradigm. In fact, *The Salt Eaters* seeks a universal and holistic system of knowledge in which scientific, religious, and magical claims might be equalized and synthesized—a system

in which "Damballah is the first law of thermodynamics and is the Biblical wisdom and is the law of time" (249).

41. Houston Baker, *Workings of the Spirit,* 93; Marjorie Pryse, "Zora Neale Hurston, Alice Walker, and the 'Ancient Power' of Black Women," 8.

42. Holloway, *Moorings and Metaphors,* 126; Joyce Ann Joyce, *Warriors, Conjurers and Priests: Defining African-Centered Literary Criticism* (Chicago: Third World Press, 1994), 42; Jocelyn Hazelwood Donlon, "Hearing is Believing: Southern Racial Communities and Strategies of Story-Listening in Gloria Naylor and Lee Smith," *Twentieth Century Literature* 41, no. 4 (1995): 25-27.

43. For example, Toni Morrison's novel *Jazz* represents the printed book as a commodity object that mutely mourns the urban writer's difficulty in imagining a clearly demarcated and immediately knowable community, in contrast to oral tradition, which draws its listeners into a circle of intimate community. Similarly, the prologue of Naylor's *Mama Day* strives to override the temporal and spatial distancing entailed in commodity consumption by refiguring the act of reading a book as an act of vernacular listening.

44. For example, Travis's story of how his mother, a domestic servant, taught him to read and write despite her employer's prohibition ends with an explicit allusion to slave narratives (196).

45. In this respect, the novel bears out Walter Ong's argument that the electronic media depend heavily on print literacy [in *Orality and Literacy: The Technologizing of the Word* (New York: Methuen, 1982), 2, 135], contrary to widespread modernist fears, as expressed, for example, in Sven Birkerts' *The Gutenberg Elegies: The Fate of Reading in an Electronic Age* (New York: Fawcett Columbine, 1994), that the new technology is fast displacing and eroding print culture.

46. H. Jerome Jackson, "Sci-Fi Tales from Octavia Butler," *Crisis* (April 1994): 4.

47. Jerome Jackson, 5.

Nancy Jesser (essay date spring 2002)

SOURCE: Jesser, Nancy. "Blood, Genes and Gender in Octavia Butler's *Kindred* and *Dawn*." *Extrapolation* 43, no. 1 (spring 2002): 36-61.

[In the following essay, Jesser examines themes of race and gender in Butler's writing along with her treatment of the female body.]

For feminist critics eager to claim the most prominent African-American woman writer of science fiction as one of their own, Octavia Butler is both a heroine and a problem child. Butler herself has proclaimed herself a feminist. So what could be the problem? Donna Haraway points to her as an exemplar of cyborg writing whose heroines are pioneer cyborgs. In addition, both African-American and feminist literary critics have long seen her novels as crucial in opening up spaces for African American heroines as well as revising science fiction's boundaries with regard to history and the experience of African Diaspora.[1] Usually, they disagree on exactly how Butler's female protagonists are feminist. For instance, is it because they reject the binary fracturing and myths of innocence and organicism, as Haraway claims? Or are her heroines, like Anyanwu "Black Eves" and "archetypal earthmothers" as Sandra Govan describes them (83)? Or are they feminist heroines because they are "healers, teachers, artists, mothers" who use their powers and exercise their authority "directly," killing "when necessary," "brutally, efficiently, and even joyfully?" as in Frances Smith Foster's assessment (41)? Finally, do they epitomize Ruth Salvaggio's vision of proper female heroines for exercising "brute feminist force"?[2]

In this article, I analyze two of Butler's most frequently discussed heroines, Lilith and Dana from the novels ***Dawn*** and ***Kindred,*** respectively. I focus on the question of Butler's biological essentialism as it relates to the genetic body, articulating key differences in her biologism with regard to race and sex.[3] Then, I examine the implications of her "gene theory" on her feminism. What kind of feminist is Butler if in her fictions she holds to a biologically informed notion of lived female experience and behavior? And perhaps more importantly, what kind of feminism does a biologically informed notion make possible?

Most feminist critics of Butler who discuss race and gender conflate the two forms of biological essentialism. Elyce Rae Helford in "'Would You Really Rather Die than Bear My Young?': The Construction of Gender, Race and Species" concedes Butler's "tendency to fall back on biological determinants in her representations of gender," but this does not stop her from arguing for a correspondence between race and gender constructions in Butler (268). She modifies Alice Jardine's concept of *gynesis* (a process of troubling masculinist master narratives) to create a corresponding process regarding race and species (*ethnesis* and *zoomorphesis,* respectively). She suggests that Butler "deconstructs" categories of race and gender and destabilizes them all. She argues that Butler's narrative resistance to "simple categorization and identification" shows us "the degree to which species, like gender and race, is primarily a matter of who has the power to construct and label whom" (264). The "emotional" and "intellectual" state of "disturbing awareness" that the story **"Bloodchild"** leaves the reader in is Helford's most powerful argument for seeing gender and race/

species in the same light, as "entirely relative to the position from which we are permitted to understand these categories" (265). However, by her own admission, the sexual biology in Butler's story is remarkably fixed even for the most other "otherworldly" and hybrid categories that Butler creates. For instance, in **Dawn,** among the alien species while there are three sexual forms required for reproduction, two are male and female. I believe this is because Helford's (following Jardine's) mastering narrative of gender is drawn from "humanistic philosophies" and Western political thought, not twentieth-century evolutionary biology. The gendered stereotypes on which such narratives rely are quite different from the ones promulgated by post-Darwinian sociobiologists. For instance, female passivity and deference is not always part of the story of maternal caring described in many biology texts and nature documentaries.[4] One common nature-show narrative includes invoking caution when approaching females *with* young. The story goes that the scientific observers must always be aware of how potentially dangerously aggressive a female animal is . . . if only when protecting her young. In this case, she is more aggressive then even a male protecting his territory. Therefore, the behavioral "norms" presented by this evolutionary sociobiology are often quite different from those cultural norms informed by Biblical and cultural sources,[5] though they constantly interact and interface.

The associative chain linking gender to race is powerful. The argument for the analogy between race and sex was used to justify, in the 19th century, sex inequality before the law and European imperialism.[6] Recently, it has had a different political orientation. But the same kind of logic is used to solidify and justify political and social alliances between feminism and anti-racism. Solidarity between anti-racism and anti-sexism is certainly in my opinion a positive thing; however, I would argue that race and gender have been linked with little thought given to this construction and its implications. Considering then metaphorical equivalents with corresponding modes of action and origins may not be the best way to change the material and social conditions of raced and sexed bodies. While the "interlocking" oppressions have some similarities in their modes of action and reproduction, we ought to pay close attention to the differences. The raced body and the sexed body have and have had different relationships to biology. I am not arguing that the "recognizable" is always simple and uncomplicated, somehow outside the social. Judith Butler's *Gender Trouble* has pointed to the lengths and depths of "normalization" that the sexed body undergoes. Though its boundaries and signs are produced socially, it is useful to recognize that the effects of the social on the sexed body are distinct. In contemporary biological accounts race is no longer described as a biological/scientific category as are species and sex.

Like the plots of many of Butler's novels, biologists' determinations are based on the reproductive possibilities of individuals. I want to emphasize here that in both cases, the *social* meanings of these "different" bodies are imaginary and discursive. But differently so. Butler's fictions offer us a good place to tease apart these relationships and explore her relationship to biological narratives of gender difference even as her plots contest the socially constituted boundaries of racial difference. Difference matters in Butler, but racial difference matters differently than sexual difference, which makes possible future generations.

Therefore, it is fair to say that Butler is "constructivist," when relating to racial identities;[7] however, when relating to sex/gender her female characters are often, biologically coded as female—that is devoted to self-sacrifice in the name of nurturing at one's own expense and the urging of maternal instincts. The terms of gender in Butler are drawn from the discourses of sociobiology and population biology. Her female heroines' biological position as mothers/potential mothers affects their actions, predisposing them to a kind of altruism notably lacking in most of her male characters. There is a strong correlation between "other-directed thinking" and the female body. The correlation in Butler is not always traceable to social circumstances.[8] In some characters, as in **Kindred**'s 19th c. Black heroine, Alice, it goes against the immediate circumstances of culture, though always at a cost. Butler manages to be at once committed to the accountable influence of the X chromosome on behavior, emotions, reactions of her female characters, a position rooted in sociobiology's reliance on genetics as determining factors in behavior and personality.

The implications of these commitments are varied. She is, in ways unaccounted for in Haraway's and others readings, deeply committed to a scientific worldview based on enlightenment individualism that produced today's prevailing scientific perspectives on genetics. However, what genes and sex allow her to do philosophically is use so-called blood connections to assert a metaphoric and physical connection between the past and future. At the same time, her rather biologized notions of female behavior (with regard to "offspring" and others) rescue her communities and characters from both the "hierarchical" nature of human beings, as well as a radical and self-isolating individualism usually associated with genetic explanations for human behavior (selfish gene theories and the like).

Butler's essentialism should be read within a context of a gene theory that undermines racial categories and constructs, but that does not abandon genetic input in other human aspects, most importantly sex/gender. Her turn to a sexed body may not be read as solely disappointing as Dorothy Allison's reading of it. In "The

Future of Female: Octavia Butler's Mother Lode," Allison mourns that Butler's protagonists act like heroines, counter-stereotypically, only in the name of others, confirming and implying that a biologically maternal and nurturing body plays a role in directing their power. While she professes to enjoy Butler's "powerful" females, she expressed disappointment that they act so in the name of an essentially heterosexually coded reproductive code. Rather than succumbing to an Allison-like disappointment about Butler's females, I read Butler's historical and biological female body as a way to return us to de Beauvoir's concept of the "situated body."[9] This is refreshing after the persistent impasse between pure constructivists and what I would call female body feminists. Butler proposes a world of interaction between the female body and the culture it is situated within, while condemning formulations of racial purity and cultural identities based on genes rather than history and experience.

Butler, while she undermines racial essentialism as corrupt and unscientific, retains a commitment to a qualified essentialist stance toward the biologically sexed body. We need not establish correspondences between gender and race when reading Butler's texts. Furthermore, we ought to recognize that her reliance on biological determinants is more than a lapse in an otherwise thoroughly postmodern position.

Cathy Peppers, in her article "Dialogic Origins and Alien Identities in Butler's *Xenogenesis*," positions Butler's plot as a dialogic text with opposing "master narratives" of origins—she asserts that Butler's entire **Xenogenesis** trilogy offers "alternative/rewritten feminist origin stories [which] destabilize, contradict, and contest the traditional discourses of origin on their own turf (48)." The accounts of human origins found in the novels, of which **Dawn** is the first, are in dialogue with the powerful and mastering narratives of western civilization and science. She argues that these counter-narratives produce alternate kinds of identities and relations to gender/race, "showing us how to acknowledge difference without necessarily resorting to 'essentialist,' traditional humanist bounded-self identities." Peppers analyzes four of these narratives and Butler's counter-narratives. The two that I am most interested in are those that partake in scientific stories about the human. The primary trope Peppers uses in her article is that of "miscegenation," which comes to stand for a postmodern, Haraway-echoing reproduction story that transgresses established boundaries. Peppers' analysis itself works most successfully when she is showing how Butler destabilizes racial/species boundaries "on their own turf" (48).

However, her argument for Butler's destabilizing gender boundaries or the prevailing scientific/cultural narratives about sex and the human behaviors associated with it is far less extensive and less convincing. This is because in Butler, I think, race and sex bear two completely different relationships to the body, so it is hard to make an equivalent argument. Race, as has been noted by critical race scholars and biologists alike, is a historical category written onto the body. It is not a biological, scientific category that can be described in any real sense outside of historical conditions. Race scientists of the late 19th and early 20th c. tried, by going through extraordinary and suspect data collection, toward sketchy conclusions. Peppers effectively demonstrates that Butler's narratives of identity challenge 'essentialist' arguments about difference and the reproduction of sameness with regard to race through the metaphoric genesis of an alien humanity. However, as I hope to show, Butler does little to destabilize the scientific reifications of sex/gender and little to dismantle a normative heterosexuality that demands stable sex/gender positions. In short, Peppers argues that the consequence of the dialogues among competing narratives leaves the reader uncertain and in a place to theoretically re-write the narratives of both race and gender. I would argue that Butler, through her heroines and plots points to a way out of radical humanist self. The way out is through a narrative of biological extra-individual drives; the ability/need to see beyond individual survival to survival of one's kin. While there are competing "narrative" drives, the one story that dominates is an evolutionary one. It is, however, left up to readers to decide whether to take the story literally or metaphorically—as a description of the way things really are or as a parable.[10]

According to Peppers, Butler's novels dialogue with competing narratives of sociobiology and paleo-anthropology. Both of these "stories" of human biological and cultural origins have been popularized and promulgated through the educative practices of schools and educational television. And they interact to form a network of tales that code human behaviors genetically and transhistorically. These "tendencies" are out of time, though not always emergent. Donna Haraway and Ruth Hubbard discuss how sociobiology and paleo-anthropology have teamed up to offer different but mutually affirming accounts of human behavior and development that naturalize female subservience, passivity and dependence and reinforce the already powerful trope of maternal instinct.[11]

Through her discussion of sociobiology and slavery, Peppers shows how Butler appropriates the "myths of science" to write a parable about racialized slavery. Pepper describes Butler's parallel narrative of human capture and coercive control of reproduction as "not about using the story of slavery to flatly deny the explanatory of biology to construct our human identity; it is about changing the sociobiological story from within, using its very real explanatory power to help us imagine the origins of humanity in alien ways" (52). For Peppers, Butler does not deny the "very real explanatory power of sociobiology," but rather re-deploys it under the rubric of a positive, progressive mixing of genetic potentials for the good of the human race.[12] (When one reads this redeployment against Martin Barker's "Biology and the New Racism," it feels more like the recuperated post-War eugenics, but that is the subject of another essay.) Using an alternative story of evolution and genetic/environmental interactions, a different technototem,[13] Butler can substitute a new organic myth, one that has at its center organic coopera-tions and a kind of evolution that eschews "selfish gene" theories and the privileged position of the Master Molecule, DNA. According to Peppers, Butler privileges an "alternative" reading of microbiology and its evolutionary implications and this puts both selfish gene and Master molecule narratives into crisis.[14] She uses them within the context of a discussion of "miscegena-tion," thereby enacting a linkage between narratives of race and narratives of gender. For Peppers, a narrative that undermines the biologized reasoning for racism also undermines a sexual biologism and vice versa.[15] It is entirely possible to recast sociobiological narratives in such a way that they undermine retrograde, out-dated theories and insert in their place more modern, better narratives with "real explanatory power." That is the scientific process. Rather than seeing these narratives as in competition, it is possible that Butler is enacting the scientific process, supplanting old stories with a new more empirically accurate story. Watson and Crick's master molecule theory gets deposed by Lynn Margulis, "marginal" theories. The process is momentarily destabilizing, but it does not lay out a new road. For Butler, biology still has tremendous (narrative) power, and scientific process is progress.

In so far as Butler is plotting "miscegenation," Peppers' reading is right on. However, the final claim that Pep-pers makes for Butler, that she "exposes" the sexist genealogy of the biological origin story is far less convincing. In fact, what is in itself interesting is the desire Peppers has to equate critiques of race biology and gender biology. The critique is nearly always grounded on the same turf, race, and then argued to ap-ply to sex, by analogy. She makes few arguments about Butler's heroines' specific mentions of sex/gender, of genetic differences between men and women and their consequent behaviors. While Butler's heroine, Lilith, maintains what could be *generously* read as an agnostic understanding of the role of biology in women's behaviors and choices, the plot relentlessly reinforces certain sociobiological notions of essential and "natural" male and female through the concept of biological "tendency." Butler's biological essentialism with refer-ence to sex and sexuality is by no means ham-fisted. She does not show a woman uninterested in child rear-ing suddenly transformed into a yearning breeder under

the influence of the biological clock. However, over and over again specific female and male behavior differ-ences are displayed through probabilities and tenden-cies. The explanatory power of genetic materials, while very weak for racial categories, are strong for sex-based ones; they persist cross-time, cross-species, across the universe.

In *Dawn,*[16] the Oankali, who are "biophilic," not "eugenic," according to Peppers, manipulate human behaviors by adjusting human genetic material (55). The changes disturb the human heroine, Lilith. She argues with them when they propose or describe manipulating her physically and genetically. She feels attached to her purely human (and damaged) nature/ genes, though at times ambivalently, to the end. She understand that it has been human nature that got her into this predicament and a non-human nature that will get her out.

Butler's heroine certainly displays characteristics that often fall into the "masculine" code of behaviors, such as greed, aggression and a desire to dominate. For Butler, unlike many die-hard sociobiologists gone conservative political theorists, simply because a genetic tendency exists does not mean it *will be* phenotypically expressed. But Butler makes explicit comparisons to human behaviors and cancer. Like a cancer treatment where the cells that are malignant must be removed, watched, or changed, so must malignant human social behavior. And perhaps most importantly, this is possible in Butler's novel, not only through alien genetic manipulations but also through human interventions.

In a sense, Butler takes on a pragmatic view that it seems that men are aggressive and violent disproportion-ately; therefore, social treatments and conditions demand that they be watched, controlled and modified, much as a genetic predisposition to cancer would be. So while Butler offers some counter narratives to the most retrograde of evolutionary biology, she continues to be very much bound to the explanatory and predic-tive power of genetic sexual difference. Xenophilia comes into being under evolutionary pressure. Xenopho-bia is no longer a functional way to pass on one's genes to the future. While her xenogenesis is marked by boundary crossings, impurities, and transgressive pleasures with regard to race/species, the stories of male-female interactions and behaviors are largely organized according to categories that naturalize and give gender to aggression, nurturing, hierarchy and heterosexuality.

When critics want to read Butler's perspective as post structural, they are forced to make her counter-essentialist and counter-eugenic. Her counter-racialized accounts stand as analogies to her attitudes about sex or see her production of women capable of violence and power as marks of her disavowal of naturalized female stereotypes. A closer look at her characters reveals that these heroines, as Allison asserts, while they counter some stereotypes of female behavior, actually reinforce sociobiological accounts of sex differences and human reproductive behaviors.[17]

Michelle Erica Green, in "'There Goes the Neighborhood': Octavia Butler's Demand for Diversity in Utopias," focuses on Butler's introduction of race into the spate of recent feminist science fiction (Marge Piercy, Joanna Russ, Sheri Tepper among others). She argues that in the "Patternist" books (***Wild Seed, Survivor, Mind of My Mind*** and ***Clay's Ark*** as well as their seed story **"Bloodchild"**) Butler's essentialism is "tricky; her novels focus on the exceptions to the rules she posits as human norms rather than on those who exemplify them" (167). Again racial and gender essentialism are considered within the same rubric. Furthermore, she does not distinguish between the cultural "norms" for female behavior and biological "norms." She says, "Butler might have chosen to transform reader expectations about those 'normal' gender behavior by demonstrating how natural giving birth seems to human men, rather than how unnatural. Yet, if Butler truly believed that human biology makes rape, compulsory heterosexuality, and enforced child-birth inevitable, she would have no motivation for writing **'Bloodchild'** in the first place." I would argue that because Butler sees these things as biologically encoded does not follow, however, that they are "inevitable" or occur in all circumstances. But it is the fact of this tendency that makes her "cautionary tales" all the more important to tell. She is working under the rubric of recent gene theory where the codes interact with cytoplasmic and bodily environments. The genes are not simply translated into a fixed reality, even in the case of the sex chromosomes. Green later argues that for Butler "careful breeding" and "teaching" can change human biology "a good deal:"

> In these books [***Survivor*** and ***Mind of My Mind***] human nature proves more flexible than some of the characters would like to admit. They cannot preserve an "essential" humanity. . . . instead, they learn to recognize the extent to which human morality and even human biology are constructed through careful breeding and teaching.
>
> (175)

A biological humanity is not, it seems Butler is saying, a "fixed" humanity. Butler acknowledges the force of biology and environment/history/learning. She could certainly believe that enforced birth was "natural." Indeed rape and heterosexuality may well be both natural and avoidable. In **Dawn,** human nature proves flexible, but only with serious forms of social and biological intervention. As Green points out, humans can intervene in their own "nature" through both breeding and learning. The essentialism, or more accurately, biologism, is not as tricky as it might first appear. It follows a fairly widespread understanding of the interaction between environmental "factors" and genetic "factors."

Cathy Peppers looks more completely at Butler's biology of gender roles and behaviors when she analyzes Butler's rearticulation of prevailing and popular paleo-anthropological accounts of the origins of human culture. She sees Lilith re-writing the Man the Hunter premise of stories of early human social development. In its place, she articulates an idea of human social development more closely akin to feminist re-interpretations of paleolithic society that place more emphasis on women's roles in food procurement (Woman the Gatherer postulates).[18] Peppers is right in that the narrative does "make it clear that humans are not biologically determined to restore the sacred image of the same" (58). While Lilith refuses to replay the earlier unfoldings of civilization from the raping cave man onwards, the story she directs in its place does little to counter what Hoda Zaki has called Butler's belief in a "human nature biologically determined" (241). The story "recapitulates" past histories of human violence and it is a sexed violence. It is not just Paul Titus (another human kept in suspended animation after the nuclear holocaust) who is kept in a sustained adolescent male state by the Oankali whose mode of interaction with the first woman he sees is to rape her. One human male literally comes out of the pod and tries to rape one of the women standing by. In a turn almost worthy of *Gone with the Wind,* this woman ends up "consensually" pairing with this same man, who when disoriented and barely conscious, in that liminal stage before the social, acts aggressively and violently sexual. This sexual story is coupled with disjunctions between "will" and "body" displayed when the men and women engage sexually with the assistance of their ooloi.[19] Taken together these two stories of sexuality, one "hetero" and the other vaguely voyeuristic, point to some very fundamental recapitulations of standard sociobiological descriptions and justifications for a violent (masculine) sexuality in the name of the gene-trade.

In the coercive nature of gene exchanges in **Dawn,** human and Oankali, Butler echoes "she said no, but her body said yes rape defenses," making them *morally* reprehensible. However, they appear as part and portion of the human tendency that lead them to destroy the earth. Humans are served up to the aliens because of their own self-destructive will to dominate and hier-archize—a will that once served an evolutionary purpose, but no longer. Lilith tries a cultural solution. She teaches lessons aimed at instilling in the humans a learned communal behavior. She is not very successful. In Butler's plot, it is the Oankali's modification of the human genome that will accomplish what centuries of civilization, getting burnt in the hot fire of human stupidity, failed to do. Peppers points out that the human's desire for blood is manifested in the story by their rejection of the meatless diet as their first act of free human will. And the driving force behind the recapitulation—the fact that "males have more of the hierarchical tendency" than do females—never relents (58). Male resistance to female authority, while idiotic, is natural.

Peppers is right that Butler offers the reader the possibility that humans as cyborgs can "choose among alternative stories of our biological inheritance (themselves technologies of meanings) with which to interface" (59). The conditions of "choices" are themselves constantly and darkly investigated by Butler's characters. Even so, if we grant that Butler offers an alternative mode of civilizing to the "Man the Hunter" story by offering a counter "Woman the Gatherer," it is not clear what difference this choice makes, if any, to the prevailing arguments for biological roots of human behaviors, especially with regard to sex. With race it is clearer that the categories of difference and sameness are constructs whose origins are suspect and which function as body technologies. With regard to sex/gender and biology, the story Butler offers is one that demands deep surgery of the sort engaged by the aliens to mitigate the powerfully inscribed male/female behaviors that shaped the stories of gatherer/hunter. While it may be feminist to revise paleo-anthropology with women's roles as central if just as mastering, it is certainly not a story that takes the essential facts of biology out of the equation. And it makes Butler a difficult fit as a female science fiction author through whose body and text the claims for a constructivist feminism can be reconciled.

Donna Haraway initiated the cyborg writer role for Octavia Butler, but Peppers, and other poststructurally minded critics, take it up as the standard under which they march forward into battle with 'liberal' feminism. However, to do so they must overlook huge tracts of Butler's straightforwardly liberal ideas about human nature, science and the role of society in mitigating human tendencies. If Butler's stories are analyzed using Ruth Hubbard's critique offered in her book *The Politics of Women's Biology* and other essays, then it is possible to discern the politics of Butler's human nature. In such an undertaking one must distinguish carefully between essentialisms of race and gender. What emerges from such a dis-articulation is slightly less the cyborgian 90s model of impurities, transgressions, than a vision of bodies that are often bad for us. At least as far as sex and sexuality go. Butler's bodies have a will of their own, and it is to be found most often lodged in genetic "tendencies" if not fixities. Or their socialized will is in conflict with their biological imperatives. Butler's reli-

ance on these "tendencies" is remarkably conservative in relation to women's behavior and heterosexuality. Her bodies say women are more or less likely to be altruistic and cooperative and men selfish, domineering and driven to rape. The question for Butler is not if this is so, but rather, what then must be done?

Let me now turn to the heroines and plots of two important novels in order to make clear the uses Butler makes of gene theories of human behavior and theories of the interactions between genes and environment.[20] In both *Kindred* and *Dawn*, the physical body relentlessly asserts its presence, demands, and vulnerabilities. Even as both novels take place under opposite temporal conditions—one an imaginative leap into the past and the other into the future—the characters in both are negotiating between sometimes-conflicting needs and experiences of self. It is precisely how the main characters, heroines Dana and Lilith, react to these conflicts that sets them in some ways apart from other characters and make them heroic. Through these characters Butler stages contemporary debates over the physical, biological mechanisms of human emotions and behaviors as well as the relationship between genes (genotype) and manifested, lived experiences (phenotype). Butler's plots stage a debate between competing "technototems" of reproduction.

According to David Hess, Barbara McClintock's studies of DNA replication and reproduction contest the DNA replication theories that name DNA as masterful and in control of the process. In McClintock's theory, crucial interactions between genetic material and cellular environments produce the specific organic outcome of reproduction. In powerfully similar ways, the plots of Butler's novels contest the Master cell theories of Watson and Crick, as noted by Peppers. Both novels and their heroines use the plot line of interaction between cell/environment in its stead to undermine any overly deterministic readings of genetic material. Some examples of Butler's appropriation of this particular genetic theory are visible in the development of parallel characters. In *Kindred*, Kevin and Rufus are paralleled as European American males, whose characteristics of whiteness and maleness are tested in different environments. Likewise, the experiences of an African American woman are tested "empirically" by contrasting and paralleling the experiences of "twins" under different conditions. Obviously, the experiments are not "double-blind." The characters themselves are at some moments unaware of their parallel natures (though the reader is cued to it) and at other moments resist or embrace this identification.[21]

In *Dawn*, the discussion of genetics is much more explicit. Because the Oankali are expert readers of the human genome as well as its manipulators, Butler uses them to explore the mechanisms and limits of the effects of genotype manipulations and the experiences of lived bodies. In addition, because they can accomplish deep cellular manipulations, they put into crisis the seamless experience of pain and pleasure, will and self. Before the Oankali "press" their emotional buttons, they were less keenly aware, although they had an inkling, that their emotional experiences had a biochemical component. The Oankali show them just how physical their psychology is. This produces the acute sense of dissociation of self, felt by the humans as they are programmed to find pleasure in an alternative/perverse sexuality. Most experience this as a terrible loss of self and will. But from the reader's perspective, and from Lilith's reluctant acknowledgement of the realities of the body and the primacy of its desires, it is as though we are peering from behind the one-way glass, seeing the experimental animals react either to the Oankali drugs or to their own genetically determined behaviors (xenophobia, tendency to hierarchize, men's desire to dominate). In addition, the new triadic sexuality is counterposed to a natural heterosexuality assumed by Lilith and all others, including perhaps Butler. It is striking that in the Oankali's 250-year study of human behavior and human culture, they never came across a reference to "faggot" and need to ask Lilith what it means.

Both books represent explorations in human "tendencies" and the role of environments in the fulfillment or adjustment of these "tendencies." What's important here is to tease apart Butler's exposition of contemporary beliefs on the interactions between genes and environment, and an agnostic stand on the exact relationship between the two, then to see how she distinguishes between racial difference and sexual difference. One is seen as a massively orchestrated deployment of a human tendency to xenophobia, but which represents race and racism as socially constructed and historically contingent. The other, sexual difference is seen as transhistorical and while influenced historically and environmentally, largely "natural" and outside the bounds of human and alien manipulations. Sexual difference is even a universal concept, the Oankali, though they have three genders (one "neuter") understand and live the male/female split. However, having a third term does not disrupt the binary as completely as it might in the most hopeful imaginings. That Lilith can "know" the sex of her captor/interrogator gives her great comfort in the face of the utterly alien and disgusting presence of the sea slug. This is the first "comforting" news she gets upon being "awakened" fully by the Oankali. Part of the creature's initial horror is that its sex is not discernible to Lilith. It does not seem categorical in human terms. But to her immense relief it is. Her first contact with the wholly other turns out to be familiar on at least this one point.

In addition, the Oankali learn about human responses to difference/race through years of behavioral observation. And given their "empirical" study most assume that Lilith will choose for her mate someone with similar complexion but different genitalia. The Oankali who knows Lilith best witnesses "deeper" similarities that drive her to choose someone "like" her on the "inside" rather than superficially. But not so alike as to have the same sex organs. So early on in the novel, racial and sex difference are plotted with different trajectories. Genital likeness is deemed as somehow "undesirable," relegating a homosexual "choice" as virtually unimaginable to both Lilith and the Oankali. "Likeness" resides below the surface of skin, but not so far as to not follow a heteronormative pattern. Lilith's choice makes her different from most humans who are trapped in their acculturated understandings of race and culture or who tend to hate racial difference. And it demonstrates the learned nature of racial difference recognition. And even though distinguishing sex is also, obviously learned, Butler's view on the origins of this knowledge is quite different.

Xenophobia, while manifested in new situations, dissipates, even in the face of the extreme alien-ness of the Oankali. Some residue of human history remains in the memories of those raised on earth in English speaking places before the nuclear war, but racial differences lose their power in the face of the differences between humans and Oankali. In addition, this xenophobia quickly becomes a maladaptive behavior that will not be passed on. The behavior is controlled through drugs, coercion, and 'brain washing'.

Genetic sexual identity manifests itself without the same authorial scrutiny. The female characters demonstrate a tendency to "not want to lead" for the sake of leadership, but who will lead in the name of helping others (altruism). The males crave power, are consistently violent, wish to lead at any cost, seem (irrationally) driven to be alpha and threatened by all other males. When Lilith, with Oankali backing, leads the group intended to re-colonize Earth, it is not so much Lilith's leading them that sets the males off in rebellion. Rather, they are rankled by the power of her mate Joseph. First, Peter, then Curt, then Gabriel, and all the other males fall into the pattern of hierarchical violence, despite the fact that it goes against their personal survival, and probably group survival as well. In addition, the men consistently use rape (which is naturalized and located in the male body in both Susan Brownmiller's sense[22] and a 70s sociobiological one as described in Fausto-Sterling) to assert male dominance. While Lilith describes this as "cave man" style human behavior, it is there and abiding always under the surface ready to be revealed when social constraints and powerful regulations of law are taken away. They are in the Oankali-made forest the group inhabits as it prepares to recolonize Earth.

Following on her genetically informed theory of human behaviors, Butler provides therapeutic models for the potentially dangerous genetic condition of human life. One of these models involves the deep surgery done by the Oankali. This alternative meets resistance from Lilith because it modifies the essence of what it means to be human. However, this is not the only therapeutic model offered in the story. Lilith's body's "talent" for cancer gives Butler a way to discuss interventions into genetic predispositions. The cancer she is disposed to is a model for genetic alterations on both individual and species levels. The presence of cancer and its mechanism shows that genetic changes/alterations in human cells is not "un-natural". When this talent is taken and used it can provide ways to transform the body and the species without the intervention of a fantastic alien species. Another therapeutic alternative outlined in the book is the contemporary treatment for cancer. First, invasive and in a sense "radical" surgery, followed by continuous "watching."

In essence, this is the strategy Lilith employs when faced with male predispositions to violence and aggression. When men enter the community, she is willing and compelled to use coercion to control them. In addition, she takes an ever-watchful stance. Of course, like early therapies for cancer, the success rate is not total; recurrence happens, as does the occasional disease that is undetected until too late. This doesn't mean therapeutically that one gives up on interventions because they are not totally effective; rather it is a call for increased interventions and watchfulness. Lilith as the one charged with Waking and raising a community of humans offers cures for the human tendency to hierarchize. She approaches the biological condition both epidemiologically by setting up Public Health rules that supersede individual pleasures and rights as well as intervening in individual cases, bodies, and exercising both attempts to cure bad behaviors as well as, with the help of the Oankali, isolating the incurables who by initiating violent behavior set off a cascade of the "disease" throughout the community (an epidemic of misogyny). In addition, through changes of "diet," "environment" and community interaction, Lilith hopes to make the conditions sufficiently different than earlier environmental conditions. In these new conditions, the body, situated as it is with certain "tendencies" and potentials can therefore be lived differently. Just as a person with a family history of cancer lives in their body differently with this historical knowledge, so can human species with their differing 'tendencies' to hierarchization change.

Of course, the danger here is that, within the community, one's biological situation could be taken as a script for one's future. Such a deterministic model would demand that humans, unmodified, would all remain in their pods. But Butler's hope for the human body and species is a therapy based on a theory of genetic and environmental interaction and the validation of human cultural interventions in the human body. So, even as her character mourns her bodily integrity, and purity, she accepts surgical interventions to save her body from cancer. She touches the scar as a reminder that she has been modified. Only in this way can what has been a curse and a disease passed on be transformed into a talent, a potential for modification and new bodies in which surgeries would be less and less necessary. The scope of time and evolution, however, proves to be a long journey, in part because of human resistance to surrendering their idea of their body as inviolable. In this way, Butler does manage to embrace the cyborg impurities Haraway anoints her with. But it is through a fairly conservative view based on common tenets of evolutionary and medical biology. This 'tricky' essentialism could be construed as 'realism' or as a way to infect the future with the same stereotypical knowledge of gender contained in the sociobiological tales told by biologists and anthropologists about human behavior. And while conceding a role for the environment and culture, the bottom line is still the reduction of complex human interactions and behaviors into easy gendered categories. Lost is the true complexity of sex, genetically, and sex, phenotypically. Lost are the role of potentials and manifestations. Hubbard's critique still applies. She asserts that we can never adequately separate and understand the relations between genes and environments. The Oankali's knowledge of genes and environments sway Lilith. She believes they know what they are doing, and that gene therapy works, though only in a limited way for gendered genetic flaws. In *Dawn,* while the modifications may not be sufficient, the process itself never fails to change the human being at his/her core.

So while Butler messes with racial categories and understandings of difference, the one difference that is important and operative in human behavior is sex and sexual reproduction. Yet if we read the stories as parables, the biological difference between men and women is the way out. If women did not tend toward being less aggressive, less hierachizing, and therefore able to escape their own "selfish" desire for social position motivated by a desire for the good of their community and kin, then the species would be totally doomed. She takes theories of "kin altruism" and rescues them from their racism, by asserting that human kinship overrides superficial, and socially constructed, differences (though perhaps only in the face of enormous extra-human threats). Whether this gender difference is real, and I think for Butler it is, or "metaphoric," acting on it may be the way to save humanity from itself, by asserting the female self-sacrifice over the self-interested power-hungry male. The therapy depends on one's understanding of the disease. It is radical, invasive, and requires violation of the body and the self in the name of others. If women have a "talent" for this then it should be exploited, that is the only morally tenable position. Butler is a lot less postmodern than she appears. The transgressions are postmodern, but they are grounded in liberal understandings of social orders, ethics and genetics.

The fantastic tales Butler weaves refuse an easy resolution of Butler's ambivalence about and attachment to biology in general, and genetics in particular. Nevertheless, she is not a thorough going postmodern, anti-essentialist, hip to the latest theory produced by Judith Butler. Her female heroines consistently act as women driven by their need to over-ride self-interest and act for the good of their children and kin (a popular sociobiological theory). They look out for and nurture others unlike the characters who inhabit male bodies. They act solely on the basis of a more powerfully genetically determined tendency—which though human is clearly lodged disproportionately in males—the compulsion to "hierarchize." Butler's women, *because* of their gender, have a way out of that tendency because of another genetically and biologically determined tendency. Causation is exactly the point of contention for Hubbard, who argues that it is often the product of analysis as much as empirically constituted. Butler herself consistently undermines racially based biological determinism and promotes "miscegenation" as a solution to dangerous or cherished genetic "purities," even to the extent of interbreeding with non-humans. Communities across time and across generations are established because of quasi-genetic, blood connections to offspring and ancestors. At the same time that Butler forces an examination of the human tendency to note and fear "difference," a social position that is dangerous and bad for family and species, she codes biological sex differences, and the genders they produce, as *a way out* of that other human tendency, to "hierarchize" differences. A tendency in males is largely unmitigated by the female "urge" to care for and mind offspring and relations. These blood and species connections motivate individual women's desires and actions,[23] sometimes against their better judgment. Self-sacrifice goes against rational self-interest, the cornerstone of enlightenment citizenship.

Butler writes about the costs of damaging ideological fantasies such as slavery and an unwillingness to change fetishized notions of genetic purity. Butler's often biologized understanding of survival and survival strategies encodes racial purity and ideologies of racial purity as both mistaken identifications of kinship and bad for the future of the species. On the other hand, she continues to hold onto biological gender differences in order to provide a mechanism out of an equally biologi-

cal human situation—the desire for dominance even to the extent of self and species destruction. Whether this belief is a rhetorical trope or a scientific conviction is almost impossible to determine. What is variously called compromise, collaboration, or trade, sexual and reproductive acts produce situations that are morally questionable, but biologically on target. As Lilith says to one of her companions, "we're all a little bit co-opted" (240). Co-optation, in *Kindred* and *Dawn*, almost always means a woman crossing racial or species boundaries emotionally, sexually and reproductively in the name of the future. It does not mean a woman performing her way out of a discursively constructed female body. These "co-optations" are powerfully counter stereotyped gendered behavior with women taking on powerful systems and institutions to manipulate them into ceding the future. Butler's heroines act, however, according to biologically coded imperatives and in line with recent evolutionary biological theories of gender.

Another mode through which Donna Haraway invokes Butler's writing as a source for theorizing is the cyborg. Haraway's call to break down the machine/organism split, and her dismissal of organic holism are the prelude to her discussion of SF to stand as models for the monstrous cyborg logic that could release feminists from received doctrine of a radical and necessary separation of the technical and the organic. In her compendium and admittedly "very partial reading" of Butler's text, Haraway presents Butler's plots and heroines who trouble the "statuses of man or woman, human, artifact, member of a race, individual entity, or body" (171). Specifically, Butler offers us a series of alternatives to natural, innocent (white) goddesses. These maternal figures are motivated by maternal connections, "blood mothers" and "Community othermothers."[24]

Haraway credits Butler with writing in *Wild Seed* of "an African sorceress pitting her powers of transformation against the genetic manipulations of her rival." Of Butler's *Kindred,* she describes a tale "of time warps that bring a modern U.S. black woman into slavery where her actions in relation to her white master-ancestor determine the possibility of her own birth." And finally, in *Dawn,* Haraway's assessment is that it is "a novel that interrogates reproductive, linguistic, and nuclear politics in a mythic field structured by late twentieth-century race and gender." Haraway sees Butler largely as the creator of cyborg heroines, heroines who are neither wholly innocent nor innocently whole. Damaging and damaged, they constantly negotiate with power and with their own "humanity." In order to transform their position in the world and their communities position in the world, they parlay with their oppressors, always mindful of their limits. These limits are demarcated by two competing ties—individual integrity (of the body and mind) and the survival of kin—present and future.

Butler, for Haraway, is an exemplar of cyborg writing because of her willingness to sacrifice the notion of organic and moral purity as well as the radical separation of humans from the world of species. I agree that while Butler's heroines refuse innocence, refuse organic holism (but not an organic/originary Eden-Africa), and interrogate the boundaries of individuality, humanity, history, time, they do so with a constant eye towards a pragmatic survival and generation—generation not of raceless, historyless, people but of communities tied together through affinity and blood. In this way, Butler does "stand for" cyborg writing when it "is about the power to survive, not on the basis of original innocence, but on the basis of seizing the tools to mark the world that marked them as other" (Haraway, "A Cyborg Manifesto: Science, Technology, and Socialist-Feminism in the Late Twentieth-century" in *Simians . . .* 175).

However, as I have shown, the iconic Butler Haraway presents is "very partial" and for feminists seeking cyborg heroines, in an important way. While Butler disrupts body/identity equations, undoes myths of original innocence, and their "longing of their fulfillment in apocalypse," she does so in very particular ways, ways which make her ill suited to the cyborg fantasy. Her tracing of ancestorship, her depiction of Africa as a generative Edenic site, and her focus on "blood" as productive of and guarantor for ancestral bonds and genetic connections show a Butler more fixed in determinative organicism. This organicism is one not bound to racial categories, but to connections produced through the reproductive body, and in particular the female body. Butler lives up to Haraway's assessment in the sense that she is keen on genetic coding as a major trope of the new (postmodern) order.

Genetics is the science of Butler's science fiction. The translation of genotype to phenotype is the plot. The network among humans is determined and actualized by the genetic pattern passed on, though not always acted on. The plots of her novels, especially the ones I focus on, turn on coercive intercourse with its resultant offspring. Importantly, the link established by genes is never diluted to the point of inconsequence—ancestry and shared DNA force and establish contacts generations down the line. At the same moment that the fixity of identity of an individual human is challenged, both in a physical and a cultural sense, the individual is fixed into kinship, and shared genes represent a powerful determinative of destiny, affinity, and connection. For feminists who are seeking to disrupt the sex/gender connection, the naturalized causal connections between genotype and phenotype, Butler's "naturalized" hierarchies and the inevitable workings out of biological destinies force a reconsideration of the terms of debate—nature and nurture.

Her reworking of the family into an extended network of kinship with concomitant links and responsibilities represents a utopian vision of feminist generation, but it is also one that is bound to a troubling foundation of biological difference and sociobiological notions of human behavior. Communities are built upon extended notions of kin. Female characters are "gifted" with the desire to escape their own "selfish" condition and selfish propagations in order to construct a larger social world where hierarchies of difference are not the only operative sociobiological behaviors. As in the novel *Kindred,* it is only when they have no chance to help secure a better future for their offspring that they consider "selfish" acts like suicide. And in a parallel, it is when Lilith bears the mixed species child, she gives up her own (irrational) dreams of escaping into a completely human world.

In ways that make anti-essentialist feminists uncomfortable, Butler finds disparities in power engendered by genetic dispositions to be real and determinative. Butler presents us with several alternative "biologies." For Butler's humans and aliens, there are the choices to survive or to die as individuals and as species. Left to its own, human nature will work to weed out in humans the inborn (though to differing degrees) tendency to "hierarchize." Evolution will help the cause. One of the only and best weapons in our genetic arsenal is the almost as compelling tendency of women to be self-sacrificing in the name of their children or species. Difference and its concomitant inequality will constantly emerge. Struggles for power happen just as "naturally."

For Butler, this is a sad fact, one that tends toward apocalypse, given humans' intellectual abilities. It is countered only by the impulse to generation, toward using power to protect kin. This parallels, though not as pessimistically, de Beauvoir's sad facts of female biological "enslavement" to reproduction. The consolation is that this commitment to the future, to the community, and to children is what drives community and survival. It leads to both accommodation to power and resistance to it. It is no coincidence that the beings in Dawn and *Kindred,* who most often act this way, have female or neuter bodies (though not always human). Butler has stated that she believes that "hierarchies are inborn" but that does not mean they must be "lethal." (**"Interview"** [**"An Interview with Octavia E. Butler"**]). Often they manage to not be "lethal" because of heroic female acts of self-sacrifice and nurturing across socially maintained hierarchies of difference whose origins are biological. In *Dawn,* the "lethal gene" is genetically and physiologically mitigated. In any case, amidst her fantastic narratives the given world which includes both the social circumstances and the biological is always a place where we work out less lethal consequences, find our homes amidst oppressive structures, and most importantly survive. The offspring of "indecent" situations—Dana, (Alice her great-great grandmother is forced into a sexual relationship with Rufus) and Lilith's child, an alien human hybrid—are not only survivors and products, but they are powerful and promising alterations of a bad past. One case demonstrates the species' need to be genetically altered if they hope to undo the pattern of hierarchization and violence, the other demonstrating the historical construction of categories of race, which have social but not physical meanings.

In *Dawn,* sexual intercourse with the aliens and the deep penetration of Lilith's genes rule out the replication of sameness—disconnects her profoundly from the offspring—and yet she comes to see that the fetishizing of purity, genetic purity—is the source of the replication of violent, hierarchical, human traits into the future—that will guarantee the repetition of the history as a one way journey to apocalypse. Indecent situations are indeed productive, thus their consequences are never purely decent, always a "little bit co-opted." But the crucial difference between the two situations is that one brings into being a socially constructed human hybrid and the other a hybrid whose human-ness is qualified. The nostalgic fantasy Dana feels for her slave "home," the plantation which comes to be a welcoming light in a dark and unwelcoming past and Lilith's desire to produce a wholly human child for a wholly human earth must be acknowledged as lost (though it may never actually have existed in that pure form), and then put aside for the sake of the future.

In *Kindred* and *Dawn,* respectively, Dana and Lilith's compliance with indecent sexual/genetic exchanges to gain their ends—survival of themselves and their kin—is the central question of the plot. Their very purposefulness and power is in negotiations with and allied to the powerful men who force them to engage in indecent actions. It is precisely because they are connected to the future and future generations that they do have to "rely upon eroticism to gain their ends." The sexual exchanges are not always quid pro quo—they are more often about instigating the least painful or least tragic outcome.

In the case of *Kindred,* Dana acts as a procurer to the slave master Rufus in order to spare Alice the violence of forcible rape (the sexual violation is written by Rufus as inevitable and read by Dana as inevitable because she is the product of the violation. And it is clear that Alice would never have "consented" to intercourse). She herself refuses the erotic exchange offered to her by Rufus, but she is nonetheless part of the economy. She is its broker.

In *Dawn,* Lilith is never violently "forced" against her will into genetic exchange or penetration by an alien "tentacle." This allows Peppers to describe the Oankali

as the more positive "biophilic." However, she comes to tolerate the exchange when she realizes there is no other way for humans to survive and when she feels a genetic bond with the Oankali through her child. The logic parallels Alice's "acceptance" of Rufus's brutal sexuality, though methods of coercion are far less brutal. Lilith's acceptance of "trade" with the aliens is the only way she has of ever returning to earth and building a human community. In addition, the aliens intervene in her lovemaking to her chosen human mate—producing a child only after he is dead. Her consent to these "unnatural" acts is indeed driven by her purposefulness, and she is chosen for them because of her power—and yet her power and her knowledge are manipulated if not controlled by the aliens. Without resorting to violence or "lying," they manage her; her assent to their suggestions and manipulations cannot be seen as consent in any real sense of the word.

And yet, Butler argues compellingly for recognizing the actualities and demands of the powerful as survival and future generation compel us to act indecently with regard to racial and species purities. Her heroines, however, always act as mothers and caretakers against their own self-interest. The drive to secure a future for one's offspring is the only uncompromised female desire. This trait has earned Butler the criticism that her heroines act heroic in the name of others, confirming that their nurturing body plays a role in directing their power. The powerful females and the powerful males resemble each other in all other ways.

Critics get caught up in either/or notions of "essentialism" in Butler, seeing her as either wedded to an overly scientist biologism or a feminist revising traditionally held notions of women. Butler is in some aspects "constructivist" and when relating to race she is almost completely so, though she writes into her plots bloodlines and recognition of kinships, though not always directly parent-offspring. When relating, however, to sex/gender her female characters are devoted to self-sacrifice in the name of the future, embodied by offspring or the young of the species. Their biological position as mothers/potential mothers affects their actions, predisposing them to a kind of "altruism"[25] notably lacking in most of her male characters.

Butler authors plots committed to the accountable influence of the X chromosome on behavior. The emotions and reactions of her female characters rely on genetics to explain otherwise irrational behaviors and personalities. Her characters make sense because we know the stories of a biological nurturance deeply written into the female body. In ways totally unaccounted for in Haraway, Butler is also deeply committed to individualism and social progress (both wedded distinctly non-postmodern metanarratives). What genes and sex allow her to do is use genetic connections across time to assert a metaphoric connection between the past and future. At the same time, her rather "essentialized" notions of female behavior (with regard to "offspring" and others) rescue her communities and characters from both the "hierarchical" nature of human beings as well as a radical and self-isolating individualism usually associated with genetic explanations for human behavior (selfish gene theories, "kin altruism," and the like.)

Butler's essentialism should be read within a context of a gene theory that undermines racial categories and constructs, but does not abandon genetic determinants of other human aspects, most importantly sex/gender. But this turn to a sexed body may not be solely reactionary.[26] Such a turn allows us to leave behind the hopelessly Manichean positions of essentialism and constructivism. Beauvoir's concept of the situated body, which is recently receiving renewed critical attention, may offer a way out of the impasse of the body in feminism. And it may also offer a way to understand some of Butler's choices about a biologically informed female body. She could be read to propose a world of interaction among the human genome, the female body and the culture it is shaped by, while condemning outright any scientized formulations of racial purity and cultural identities. For racial aspects of difference, for Butler, history and culture offer the proper explanatory referents of human behaviors and actions.

De Beauvoir begins *The Second Sex* with the "Destiny: The Data of Biology." She describes reproduction as an "enslavement" of the body by biological demands. This assertion coexists with her insistence that the body's "resistance" to dismissal is not tantamount to destiny. Women, like men, she insists are bodies. But the body is insufficient to describe the social position of women as well as the organization of society. Butler's science fiction plottings of the female heroine seem also to insist on the bodies' refusal to be dismissed. De Beauvoir says:

> The enslavement of the female of the species and the limitations of her various powers are extremely important facts; the body of woman is one of the essential elements in her situation in the world. But that body is not enough to define her as woman; there is no true living reality except as manifested by the conscious individual through activities and in the bosom of society.
>
> (36-37)

Butler's female heroines in **Kindred** and **Dawn** confront the "data" of biology, but not as an "enslavement" or "limitation." Instead, their connections to their bodies are more than a form of bondage. Rather these constitute the possibility of connection, joining together in common and transcending the limits of self. Butler mirrors de Beauvoir's materialist existentialism, mending the monstrous Cartesian self/body split.[27] In place of the

enslaved female body, Butler imagines a powerful, emancipating intersubjective body in which the social bosom and the maternal bosom are newly coherent.

Notes

1. Among these are Frances Smith Foster, Sandra Govan, Ruth Salvaggio, Michelle Erica Green and Beverly Friend. See bibliography for citations.

2. Elizabeth Gant-Britton in her dissertation "Women of Color Constructing Subjectivity Towards the Future: Toni Morrison, Octavia Butler and Cynthia Kadohata," Univ. of California-Los Angeles, 1997, argues that Butler imagines a future in which female and African American agency is greater. She discusses Butler's narrative and temporal strategies in *Kindred* and *Parable of the Sower,* among others.

3. The argument in my essay has been informed by several articles that discuss this issue only indirectly. Following Haraway, Robin Roberts in "'No Woman Born': Immortality and Gender in Science Fiction" suggests that Butler offers a female vision of immortality via regeneration and biology to counter male science fiction writers accessing immortality through technologies that abandon the body. She describes the regenerations contained in Butler's novel *Wild Seed* as an "altruistic hope based on biology" (141). Brett Cooke in *"Biopoetics of Immortality: A Darwinist Perspective on Science Fiction"* was valuable for formulating Butler's use of Darwinist evolutionary biology theories, especially Dawkin's selfish gene theory. He discusses Pamela Sargent's *Earthseed,* but not Butler. Stacy Alaimo in "'Skin Dreaming': The Bodily Transgressions of Fielding Burke, Octavia Butler and Linda Hogan." Judith Lee describes the *Xenogenesis* series (of which *Dawn* is the first novel) as an exploration of the concepts "human" and "immortality." She argues Butler replaces religious immortality and scientific theories of longevity popular in much speculative fiction. The replacement concept is "relatedness," which Lee claims Butler "represents as biological interdependence" that is acutely felt because of "unstable corporealities" (176-7). Jim Miller does an excellent and thorough reading of Butler and Butler scholarship. He sees Butler as confronting not only race and gender in the context of science fiction, but also class. He argues that Butler offers a cyborg and postmodern view on the body, social and individual, both of which are "constructs." He does not give much credit to any of those who read Butler as in any way essentialist, even while he acknowledges that Butler essentializes human and Oankali behaviors toward difference. His discussion has a lot of merit, but I believe it also conflates race and sex essentialisms.

4. Examples of re-assessments of female passivity in evolutionary biology/anthropology range from descriptions of female chimps actively seeking out sex from non-dominant males, on the sly, to the "ac-

tive" role of the egg in its meeting with and reaction to sperm. Ehrenreich has a summary of most of the counter-70s sociobiology data emerging in the 80s and 90s.

5. The conflict between these two "norms" of female behavior is highlighted when a woman kills her children. The anxiety about Susan Smith's "maternal" condition took on two forms. One that her normal instincts had been interfered with by her sexual abuse, confirming a biological foundation for maternal instincts and the other that her desire for a new mate had superseded her protection of her offspring. Her actions could be read as confirmation of the role of the social in over-riding the biological, as well as its reverse.

6. See Nancy Leys Stepan "Race and Gender: The Role of Analogy in Science" in *Anatomy of Racism,* Ed. David Theo Goldberg. Stepan describes how the metaphoric associations of race, gender and class played a role in producing data supporting the analogy and with it a science of racial and sexual inferiorities located in the body. In the same collection, Sander Gilman describes the power of the "associative chain" in producing a logic that connected race (Jewishness), gender and disease. The chain worked its way through various historical moments from the 18th c. through the 20th. In Stephen Jay Gould's *Mismeasure of Man,* revised edition, he laments the recursive power of racist modes of assessing intelligences within evolutionary biology and psychology.

7. This is not to say that Butler does not regard race as a central "matter." Many have written about her commitment to "kinship" and Africa as a more than symbolic ancestral place. I am not arguing that Butler doesn't think race matters. Rather that it is that race is the sign and symbol, culturally and socially constructed to stand for bloodlines and genetic links. What is operative is the genetic link, not the physical racial characteristics that might link any two people of a racial group. This is, in Butler, extremely complex. She by no means abandons the importance of racial categories, even as she suggests that they are social. It is actual genetic links (often across racial categories) that link her characters across time and in kinship. Racial characteristics point not only to a potential genetic kinship, but also to shared histories and experiences. They do not represent for Butler a stable transhistorical category as does sex.

8. The slippery boundaries here can also be teased out in Carol Gilligan's psychological theories of women's thinking and their popularized versions found in such books as *Men are from Mars, Women are from Venus.* De Beauvoir, and even Mary Wollstonecraft have all admitted that women "act" differently. The question has always been why?

9. Indeed, it is the heterosexist components that are for me most disappointing in Butler, rather than the es-

sentializing of female "nurturance" and "altruism." Butler's evolutionary biologism sidesteps non-heterosexualities as invisible or inconsequential. Since reproduction does not necessarily require a full-time commitment to heterosexual intercourse, one has to wonder if this is not the more dangerously "naturalized" discourse in Butler. And one given surprisingly scant attention by critics who see her as a "cyborg" author-heroine.

10. Butler's more recent novel *Parable of the Sower* suggests that she sees her novels as "speaking" in parables. In an interview she describe her books to Elizabeth Gant-Britton as "cautionary tales" (October 1995, cited in Gant-Britton.)

11. See Haraway in *Simians, Cyborgs and Women* and Hubbard in her essay "The Political Nature of Human Nature" in *Feminists Theorize the Political,* ed. Judith Butler and Joan W. Scott.

12. Peppers goes on to specify: "Butler's appropriation and redeployment of the idioms of sociobiology involves recasting the usual origin story of the evolutionary rise to dominance of the heroic individual (that first organelle floating in the primeval soup) through ruthless competition and survival of the fittest, by privileging instead the "marginally acceptable" story of Lynn Margulis" (54)

13. Technototem, David Hess's term refers to the "co-production of technical and social difference" (21 and following).

14. If this were the case, then I would argue that Butler also invokes Barbara McClintock's alternative to Crick and Watson.

15. Anne Fausto-Sterling discusses the "gendered" readings of cell biology in Women's Bodies. In *Science and Technology in a Multicultural World,* David Hess discusses the implications of race and gender in "technototems" of cell biology. He discusses Barbara McClintock and Ernest Everett Just's "alternative" conceptions of the interactions of genes and cytoplasm on pages 27-32.

16. *Dawn* is a projection into the future of the present trajectory of history. This trajectory leads to an apocalypse, a spasm of nuclear war that would have ended history, if it were not for alien intervention. The alien intervention is the miracle that saves the earth and humanity from total annihilation. The Oankali keep humans in suspended animation while the earth heals. They wake them slowly and delicately in order to gain their trust. Lilith is the first of the humans who manages to overcome her disgust with the Oankali's alien-ness in order to interact with them and learn their ways. Within the conventions of the post-apocalyptic novel in which a few human survivors "begin again," Butler plays out Lilith's desire to escape and re-build a (human) community and the Oankali plan to repopulate earth with a new

(nonhuman) species. Lilith has been recruited as leader of the first settlement because they feel she is the most promising individual human. Throughout the novel, Lilith sees the humans' chance of escape as a matter of playing along, playing for time, with the Oankali. She must learns survival skills as well as understand "the enemy." Things become more complicated when she becomes incorporated or absorbed into the Oankali kinship structure and experiences love for them. With and without her consent, she is modified both biochemically and intellectually. Through her interactions with them, she learns about this alternative family (two sexes and a gene manipulator) and alternative species plan (gene trading). She begins to love her captors/rescuers even as she learns that she is a pawn in their acquisitive project. The Oankali are "gene traders."

17. Jim Miller has an excellent discussion of this debate over essentialism using Butler. He cites Zaki and Allison's arguments and attempts to unravel them. He says that Zaki reads Butler as essentialist because she "confuses Butler's position with the biologistic Oankali" (432). Instead he suggests that Butler "favors" social construction as just as important as biology. He dismisses Allison's critique out of hand and concurs with Michelle Erica Green. That is, the heroine's very actions define them as counter to "traditional notions." The debate contained in this argument suggests how very important it is that we separate out "traditional" cultural notions of female behavior from contemporary biological notions of female behavior. Anne Fausto-Sterling in *Myths of Gender* describes sociobiology as a "theory of essences" (195). But as the content of her book shows, the exact nature of the essences in the biological story are changeable and change. New assessments of female athletes (Fausto-Sterling, 213 and following) as well as new theories about female sexual appetites, and chimpanzee "cheating" appear almost as frequently as re-assertion of old sociobiological stereotypes of female monogamy and male propensities to rape. That Butler's female heroines go against traditional, [i.e.] E. O. White's and Dawkins' sociobiologized norms, do not mean that they do not conform to other biological theories of gendered behavior.

18. Discussion of these can be found in Haraway's "A Cyborg Manifesto" in *Simians, Cyborgs and Women.* 149-181.

19. The Oankali accomplish their genetic and physiological manipulations through the ooloi, the "non-gendered" beings. Through a snaking arm-like protuberance the ooloi both controls the gene exchange and delivers pleasure through brain chemicals to both the men and women in a whole body orgasm that eclipses "regular" orgasms. Most

of the humans become addicted to this pleasure, even as they resent their dependence on the ooloi. They rebel, with disastrous results, to the ooloi and the human colony.

20. Note here Anne Fausto-Sterling's discussion of recent biological theories of reproduction and gender in "Sex and the Brain: Addendum to the Second Edition," pages 223 and following.

21. Dana and other characters recognize her physical and psychological similarities to her ancestor. Kevin resents Dana's implied comparisons of him to Rufus. Maternal connections are inscribed as more powerfully written into the body-mind, while paternal ones exercise other more fabular forms of power.

22. In *Against Our Will,* Brownmiller states that men rape because they can: "In terms of human anatomy the possibility of forcible intercourse incontrovertibly exists. . . . When men discovered that they could rape, they proceeded to do it" (4).

23. This kind of community across generations can be seen in the *Xenogenesis* series as well as the "Paternist" group of novels. It is also evident in *Kindred* as I have discussed in my manuscript "Troubled Worlds: feminist theory, practice and fantasy in the US anti-rape movement."

24. For a description of these two models of Black motherhood see Patricia Hill Collins in "Black Women and Motherhood" *Black Feminist Thought,* 115 and following.

25. See Martin Baker's discussion of the cloaked racial content of "kin altruism" and new sociobiological understandings of "difference" and "aggression" in "Biology and the New Racism," in *Anatomy of Racism,* especially pages 30-33.

26. Here I think it is important to distinguish the claims for female bodies made in fiction and those made as Truth with a capital "T." In her March 1999 article for *Time,* Barbara Ehrenreich recuperates science and the narratives of biological truths about female bodies in a way that seems only to prove that science often discovers emergent social truths. Her's is a kind of "I told you so" narrative that, ironically, confirms science as the best arbiter of the natural and the potential of female bodies; the cover proudly offers science's backing to feminist "opinions," "The latest research into the secrets of biology and evolution reveals that women are tougher, stronger and lustier than anyone ever thought." In the article, Ehrenreich uses biological data to underscore her vision of the female body liberated from social norms into a wild, natural and powerful state. In a sense Butler tells a similar story; however, Butler writes science fiction, parable and cautionary tales, not popularized versions of scientific truths, which, as has been amply pointed out by even Ehrenreich herself, often are fantasies cloaked as biology "the

prostitution theory of human evolution." By couching new data as more "advanced" and more "real," she reinvigorates science's disciplining of the female body. Today's "truth" becomes tomorrow's enslavement, as history has shown. Her account of the "new science" would have been well-served to contain some of Ruth Hubbard's agnosticism and Donna Haraway's skepticism about our ability to discover "sacred tenets" of evolutionary theory, psychology and physiology.

27. See Alaimo for a discussion of "bodily transgressions" and "monstrous Cartesian portraits" in Butler's *Wild Seed* and *Mind of My Mind.* She argues that Butler "casts off the body as a mere vestment or investment and transforms it into a liminal space that blurs divisions between humans and animals, subjects and objects, nature and culture" (130). The boundary not blurred by the bodies in these books, however, is gender. The male Doro represents the monstrous Cartesian portrait while Anyanwu the "embodied" knowledges. She is an "alternative" not only because she shapeshifts instead of stealing bodies, but also because those beings that are bred live with her as family and kin, not slaves. (127-130).

Works Cited

Allison, Dorothy. "The Future of Female: Octavia Butler's Mother Lode." In *Reading Black, Reading Feminist,* ed. Henry Louis Gates, Jr. NY: Meridian, 1990. 471-478.

Butler, Octavia. *Dawn.* New York: Warner, 1987.

———. *Kindred.* Boston: Beacon, 1989.

Collins, Patricia Hill. *Black Feminist Thought: Knowledge, Consciousness and the Politics of Empowerment.* New York: Routledge, 1991.

De Beauvoir, Simone. *The Second Sex.* Trans. H. M. Parshley. 1953. New York: Vintage, 1974.

Ehrenreich, Barbara. "The Real Truth about the Female" *Time* 8 Mar. 1999: 56-66.

Fausto-Sterling, Anne. *Myths of Gender: Biological Theories about Women and Men,* rev. ed. New York: Basic Books, 1985.

Foster, Frances Smith. "Octavia Butler's Black Female Future Fiction." *Extrapolation* 23.1 (1982): 37-49.

Friend, Beverly. "Time Travel as a Feminist Didactic in works by Phyllis Eisenstein, Marlys Milhiser and Octavia Butler" *Extrapolation* 23.1 (1982): 50-55.

Goldberg, David Theo, ed. *Anatomy of Racism.* Minneapolis: U. of Minnesota Press, 1990.

Govan, Sandra. "Connections, Links, and Extended Networks: Patterns in Octavia Butler's Science Fiction." *Black American Literature Forum* 18.2 (1984): 82-87.

Helford, Elyce Rae. "'Would You Really Rather Die than Bear My Young?:' The Construction of Gender, Race, and Species in Octavia E. Butler's 'Bloodchild.'" *African American Review,* 28.2 (1994): 259-271.

Hess, David *Science and Technology in a Multicultural World.* New York: Columbia UP, 1995.

Haraway, Donna J. *Simians, Cyborgs and Women: The Reinvention of Nature.* London: Free Association Books, 1991.

Hubbard, Ruth. "The Political Nature of Human Nature." in *Feminists Theorize the Political.* Ed. Judith Butler and Joan W. Scott. New York: Routledge, 1992. 175-191.

Kenan, Randalt "An Interview with Octavia E. Butler" *Callaloo* (14) 2: 1991. 495-504.

Peppers, Cathy, "Dialogic Origins and Alien Identities in Butler's *Xenogenesis.*" *Science-Fiction Studies* 22.1 (1995): 47-62.

Salvaggio, Ruth "Octavia Butler and the Black Science-Fiction Heroine," *Black American Literature Forum.* 18.2 (1984): 78-81.

Zaki, Hoda. "Utopia, Dystopia and Ideology in the Science Fiction of Octavia Butler." *SFS* 17 (1990): 239-51.

Jerry Phillips (essay date spring 2002)

SOURCE: Phillips, Jerry. "The Intuition of the Future: Utopia and Catastrophe in Octavia Butler's *Parable of the Sower.*" *Novel* 35, nos. 2/3 (spring 2002): 299-311.

[*In this essay, Phillips explores Butler's notions of utopia in her novel* Parable of the Sower.]

In *Modernity and the Holocaust,* Zygmunt Bauman argues that one strain in "the historical tendency of modernity" was horribly dramatized at Auschwitz (2). Auschwitz showed what "the rationalizing, designing, controlling dreams and efforts of modern civilization are able to accomplish if not mitigated, curbed or counteracted" (93). Bauman points out that the Holocaust was at bottom "a means to an end," a pathway to utopia (91). The National Socialist state employed genocide as "an element of social engineering" with the aim of bringing about "a social order conforming to the design of the perfect society"—a society purged of the unfit and the racially inferior (91). The bloody utopianism of Nazism has thrown into relief the dystopic aspect of modernity: not simply the advance of rationalism and enlightened civility, modernity is also the advance of rationalized barbarism and naked terror. In the aftermath of Auschwitz, the modern writer was faced with the immense problem of how to recuperate modern utopia. The writer was obliged to consider whether it was still possible to hold faith in, and to make art in the name of, the perfectionist claims of modernity.

It was in this context that Lewis Mumford counseled, "[i]f our civilization is not to produce greater holocausts, our writers will have to become something more than merely mirrors of its violence and disintegration; they, through their own efforts, will have to regain the initiative for the human person and the forces of life. . . . For the writer is still a maker, a creator, not merely a recorder of fact, but above all an interpreter of possibilities. His intuitions of the future may still give body to a better world and help start our civilization on a fresh cycle of adventure and effort" (Mumford 109-10). As Mumford sees it, the highest office of the writer is to wrest from a barbarous world, in which catastrophe looms large, the positive sense of a "better world," even an ideal world, that is somehow immanent in the deadly facts of our social condition. The writer has the responsibility to restore dynamic possibility to social processes that seem static, permanent, and untranscendable. By exploring "possible worlds," "intuitions of the future" that critique the present as we know it, the writer recovers purposive human time, the sense that history is not something that simply happens to us, irrespective of our will and desires, but is, indeed, ours to make. In short, the responsible writer defends human agency as a necessary existential value, or what William James called a "living option," a hypothesis which "appeals as a real possibility to him to whom it is proposed" (199).

Mumford's definition of the writer as an "interpreter of possibilities" and his claim that utopia is modernity's most urgent question provide useful points of departure for understanding Octavia Butler's *Parable of the Sower* (1993), a futuristic novel that explores latent and manifest tendencies (with regard to both utopia and dystopia) in the postmodern condition. Insofar as one accepts Bauman's assertion that "the history of modernity in general" (77-78) remains unfinished, then one has to regard postmodernity as the extension, or perhaps the intensification, of certain contradictory tendencies within modernity itself.[1]

Butler's futurism similarly intensifies the contradictions of modern society. In particular, *Parable of the Sower* reflects on two classic pathways to modern utopia or, as Bauman puts it, "the design of the perfect society" (91): first, the application of bureaucratic rationality to socioeconomic problems through the agency of the state; and second, the constitution of communities of "them" and "us" through the politics of race. Butler's main concern is to incite her readers to "consider alternative ways of thinking and doing" (Butler, **"The Birth"** [*The Birth of a Writer*] 134). *Parable of the Sower* seeks to reinvent the utopian vision at a time when utopia allegedly has been rendered impossible, not least by the two pathways mentioned above, which have Auschwitz as their ultimate possibility. In this regard, the novel adumbrates that paradoxical aestheticism which Fredric Jameson identifies as characteristically postmodern: the project of "Utopianism after the end of utopia" (154).

Parable of the Sower is set in California in the year 2024. Butler depicts the golden state in the imagined near future as representative of all the sickness of our present world. In 2024, Los Angeles has become an "oozing sore" (96), a "carcass covered with too many maggots" (8); "there are fewer and fewer jobs"—children are "growing up with nothing to look forward to" (13); "debt slavery" is rampant—in general, "workers are more throwaway than slaves" (291); "there are too many poor people" (47)—"living skeletons" (79) are everywhere visible; "thieves, rapists and cannibals" haunt the streets and freeways (259); "crazies" have banded together with no other purpose in mind than to "burn-the-rich" (145); "private armies of security guards" (104) protect "estates, enclaves, and businesses" (35); "there are at least two guns in every household" (34)—gunfire is so common people no longer attend to it. Those who have eyes to see are sharply conscious of the fact that "things are unraveling, disintegrating, bit by bit" (110), that, fundamentally, "the world is falling apart" (247).

Butler's portrait of twenty-first-century California combines empiricism with speculation, extant facts, and facts that are (possibly) in the making. Madhu Dubey writes that "[t]he dystopia presented in *Parable of the Sower* is so closely extrapolated from current trends, as Stephen Potts observes, that it produces a shock of familiarity rather than estrangement" (106). But (and this is the crucial point) the future *in toto* is not yet with us and might still be avoided if we take the requisite actions. As the novel puts it, "We haven't hit bottom yet" (*Parable* [*Parable of the Sower*]294) in our descent into the abyss. Butler's perspective on historical time is authentically prophetic. "[T]he task of the genuine prophet," notes Martin Buber, "was not to predict but to confront man with the alternatives of decision" (197). The true prophet does not foretell an inevitable future, but warns of likely consequences should a present course of action continue. Butler's apocalyptic vision of the American future is nothing so much as a "weapon for averting catastrophe," to quote R. W. B. Lewis (235). By dramatizing historical time as moving in the direction of the disastrous end of the world, the apocalyptic narrative throws into relief its dialectical opposite, historical time as the renewal of life, the journey towards utopia. As Eric Rabkin notes, such narratives display both "the consequences of our social values" and "the meanings of our wishes" (xv).

The prophetic perspective and postmodernity seem to cut in different directions. Jean-François Lyotard has argued that "incredulity toward metanarratives" (i.e., foundational values) is the defining characteristic of the postmodern sensibility (xxiv). Where prophecy intuits a likely future on the basis of tendencies within the present (thus assuming the unfolding of a sufficient course of events), postmodernity emphasizes that all is uncertainty, contingency, and unpredictability. As an exercise in utopianism after the end of utopia, *Parable of the Sower* aligns itself with both prophetic and post-modern values. On the one hand, the novel rejects the idea that metanarratives can be sensibly dispensed with: metanarratives lend psychological force and ethical direction to human agency. In their absence, the individual too readily lends herself to barbarous social practices which appear as timeless Necessity. On the other hand, the novel rejects the telos of what Lewis calls "the secular apocalyptic tradition" (191), which posits social revolution as the key transformative force in human history.[2]

And thus the sense of the redemptive or salvific potential of human agency is radically diminished in scale. Indeed, one can pose the question of the extent to which *Parable of the Sower* regains the "initiative for the human person" (Lewis 109). For, in denying the possibility of revolutionary transformation, the novel perhaps succeeds in doing the opposite of what its author intended: consolidating the crushing facticity of our present world, in which the ideal of the whole human person has all but vanished. In other words, at one level, *Parable of the Sower* transcends postmodern "incredulity"; but, at another level, it bolsters the fatalism implicit in diminished utopianism. The latter tendency leads to a narrowing of moral vision that I shall argue has ominous significance for how we might imagine a transformative politics to set against the deepening barbarism of our time.

Parable of the Sower is written in the form of a diary as kept by a fifteen-year-old African American girl. Lauren Olamina, the diarist, lives behind walls in a besieged "cul-de-sac community" (10), an "island surrounded by sharks" (44). In order to keep at bay the hordes of "street poor" who live without the walls, Lauren's community establishes "a regular neighborhood watch" (63) of armed residents. A communitarian ethos binds the community together. "We all know each other here," says Lauren's father, "we depend on each other" (31). Thus, Butler presents militarized "privatopia" as one version of an ideal society (notwithstanding the degradation of utopian imaginings).[3]

Although Lauren finds it impossible to conceive of life "without walls" (51), she recognizes that the apocalyptic world beyond the walls makes plain "illusions of security" (118). Privatopia, the walled or gated com-munity, is, at bottom, a fantasy of escape, that one can be in the world without having to live through the sharp contradictions that the world presents. Lauren sees that a community based on such bad faith has little hope of averting eventual catastrophe.

The notion that one can be in the world without being really of it implies a providential rather than existential sense of the human condition. The former expresses faith in the progressive unfolding of a necessary order decreed by God, while the latter accepts contingent possibility as shaped by concrete human action. The "horrible shape" of the world, its definite tendency towards catastrophe, makes it well-nigh impossible for Lauren to accept the metanarrative of Providence, that God is a "kind of super-person" (13) who will "look after us" (23). Nor will she accept the idea that God is "nature" or an "ultimate reality" (13) that we cannot know.

For Lauren, "God is change" (15). The proposition that "God is change" brings to the fore Butler's concern with immanence in historical process, the way that time speaks to the unfolding of latent possibilities in the world. In Lauren's view, change or God has no necessary direction and is devoid of anthropomorphic qualities like good and evil. As she puts it, "I'm not some kind of potential Job, long-suffering, stiff-necked, then, at last, either humble before an all-knowing Almighty, or destroyed. My God doesn't love me or hate me or watch over me or know me at all, and I feel no love for or loyalty to my God. My God just is" (22). Change has constructive and destructive aspects; it is the most "pervasive power" in the universe (242). "Everyone knows that change is inevitable," reflects Lauren (23).

Conceived as the force of the world, the concept of change leads to a dialectical view of reality. According to David Harvey, "dialectical thinking emphasizes the understanding of processes, flows, fluxes, and relations over the analysis of elements, things, structures, and organized systems" (49). Clearly, a dialectical sensibility underpins Lauren's belief that "[e]verything changes in some way, size, position, composition, frequency, velocity, thinking, whatever. Every living thing, every bit of matter, all the energy in the universe changes in some way" (*Parable* 195). To grasp the world in perpetual motion is to confront the problem of future possible worlds. Which is to say, one is obliged to consider the conditions under which an intuition of the future is concretely realized as social reality. Lauren rejects simple determinism: she holds that we shape change and change shapes us. Lauren's insights lead her to develop a new religion, a new ethics of Being: Earthseed.

Throughout the novel, Lauren explores the implications of Earthseed in her *Books of the Living*. She avers that, if "God is change," and change shapes us, then human beings should assert their will and shape change in accordance with their needs and desires. In brief, human beings should aspire to shape God. Lauren's concept of God gives her a basis on which to build "a future that makes sense," in a present moment that seems all but determined by a "rotting past" (70). Her God does not permit her to escape the fundamental burden imposed upon us by existential time (a time without necessary direction): that "the self must create its own reasons for being" (231) and cannot hope to find them in a non-human, transcendental realm.[4]

When an army of the street poor attacks and destroys Lauren's community, she understands that her exploration of Earthseed, as a philosophy of life, will now proceed on the terms of open-ended practical activity as opposed to pure contemplation. She has no choice but to test out the pragmatic proposition that "[b]elief initiates and guides action—Or it does nothing" (41). With the violent deaths of her brother and father, Lauren is left alone in the world, and all the walls between her and the feral barbarism of Southern California have at last come down. She realizes that she is "one of the street poor now" (140). In order to escape the fate of being "some kind of twenty-first-century slave," Lauren resolves to make her way to one of the "northern edens," either Washington State, Oregon, or Canada, where things are allegedly better (151, 190).[5]

In her capacity for adventure and self renewal, Lauren is presented to the reader as a moral exemplum.[6] She is "life that perceives itself changing" (112)—and thus she possesses what her society can no longer give her, even as it is existentially necessary for the human way of being, namely, a definite sense of direction and purpose. "A victim of God may, through learning adaptation, become a partner of God," contends Lauren, and "[a] victim of God may, through forethought and planning, become a shaper of God" (27). In contrast to the residents of Privatopia, who seek to avoid the realities of the world, Lauren genuinely transcends the "chaos" without, because she understands that only by working through the contradictions of the world does one move beyond them.

"I am earthseed," writes Lauren in her diary, "Anyone can be. Someday, I think there will be a lot of us. And I think we'll have to seed ourselves farther and farther from this dying place" (69). In Lauren's formulation of a future possible society—an Earthseed community—that arises out of, and yet negates, the world as we know it, the utopian aspect of space stands in dialectical contrast to the dystopian character of place. What, then, are the objective forces that transform vital space into deadly place, that arrest "processes, flows, and fluxes" and make of them the "structures and organized systems" that now threaten catastrophe? *Parable of the Sower* identifies two principal agents of destruction: the business corporation and the militarized state.

Lauren notes that the new president, elected in 2024, "has a plan for putting people back to work. He hopes to get laws changed, suspend 'overly restrictive' minimum wage, environmental, and worker protection laws for those employers willing to take on homeless employees" (24). This explicit allusion to contemporary neoliberal economic policy, which promotes the demands of capital over the needs of labor, reveals one aspect of Butler's understanding of modern dystopia: the reduction of community to market economy.[7]

Parable of the Sower depicts a harrowing world in which market exchanges and private property are the exclusive means of organizing social life. On the one hand, Butler portrays certain aspects of late capitalism—its atomistic culture, its elevation of profits over people, its volatile race relations, and its ecological destructiveness—as dystopia achieved. On the other hand, she intimates that the present has not yet exhausted its barbaric potentialities; cannibalism, widespread terrorism, and brutal social repression are the defining characteristics of the terrible future that possibly awaits us—a dystopia imagined. Lauren notes that, for those who can afford it, security can be purchased. However, the real price of security is political freedom: "safety and comfort" (109) are available only in company towns or "privatized cities" (114), social forms that degrade the meaning of citizenship. Lauren sees that the reduction of community to the terms of a corporate order is bound to culminate in tyranny, or what she calls twenty-first-century slavery (151).

According to Lauren, the moral destiny of earthseed is "to take root among the stars" (75)—in plainer terms, to create "some kind of community where people look out for each other" (200). But this spiritual and political ideal is rendered impossible by a social order based on stark economic polarities, namely, "walled enclaves of the rich" (221) and grim ghettos of the poor. *Parable of the Sower* contends that human purpose has been lost at not merely the individual level, but also at the widest social level. By bending the future back into the present, the novel shows us that late capitalist society cannot generate a future worth believing in. Indeed, insofar as an alternative society is deemed impossible, insofar as history is considered at an end, the only authentic image of the future must be the present, with all its manifest shortcomings. In this regard, the postmodern claim that "the grand narrative has lost its credibility" and that this is particularly true of "narrative[s] of emancipation" (Lyotard 37), severely restricts what we can imagine as political possibility. Such claims render us impotent in a world of our own making. This scenario Butler finds intolerable: her novel repeatedly states the argument that "without positive obsession, there is nothing at all" (1).

The social disintegration brought on by a market system, based squarely on the competitive drive for profits, with all else going to the wall, leads to the erosion of moral community. The result is an atavistic, nihilistic world in which people are either predator or prey. Butler was surely influenced by Thomas Hobbes's description of the state of nature in her imagining of the American future. According to Hobbes, people in the state of nature have "no account of Time; no Arts; no Letters; no Society; and which is worst of all, continuall feare, and danger of violent death; And the life of man, solitary, poore, nasty, brutish, and short" (186). Butler follows in the footsteps of Hobbes by linking the breakdown of social order to the advent of "leviathan," the all-powerful state.

With social control rather than justice as its primary goal, the state establishes quasi-permanent "structures and organized systems" which secure the interests of the few at the expense of the many. Butler suggests that, caught in the vise between corporate tyranny and state authoritarianism, the individual suffers a crushing loss of self-identity: neurosis and psychosis become normal states of being; murderous impulses are given release; the death-wish takes hold.[8] The end-result is a people well prepared to accept something like fascism. As Lauren puts it in a key passage:

> *When apparent stability disintegrates, as it must—God is change—people tend to give in to fear and depression, to need and greed. When no influence is strong enough to unify people they divide, they struggle, one against one, group against group, for survival, position, power. They remember old hates and generate new ones, they create chaos and nùrture it. They kill and kill and kill. . . . [U]ntil one of them becomes a leader most will follow, or a tyrant most fear.*

(91)

Throughout her oeuvre, Butler has always been interested in the fascistic aspects of modern society, the sense in which power systems generate "patternmasters" who seek dominance over others through one means or another.[9] As the militarized police state replaces the welfare state as the measure of social control in our time, Butler implies that fascism looms over the future as catastrophic possibility. In 2024, patterns of race and class dominance have hardened to the point where they have genocidal implications—others are those I must kill.

Butler conceives Lauren as a symbolic negation of the psychopathology of atomized, corporate society. Lauren suffers from "hyperempathy syndrome" (102), the capacity to feel what others feel, be it pleasure or pain. Lauren is a "sharer," a person whose sense of self is phenomenologically bound up with the humanity of the other. Unsurprisingly, the doctors of the corporate order view hyperempathy as a psycho-physical malady, "an

organic delusional syndrome" (10). But Lauren would have us understand it as a utopian political value. She poses the question: "If everyone could feel everyone else's pain who would torture?" (102). If men and women realized their potential as social beings, if they lived by the axiom that "from one, many; from many, one" (283), then how much more difficult it would be to starve, rape, exploit, terrorize, and murder the other? Indeed, in a hyperempathetic world, the other would cease to exist as the ontological antithesis of the self, but would instead become a real aspect of oneself, insofar as one accepts oneself as a social being. Earthseed is the practical ethics of this heightened consciousness of what it means to experience being as, irreducibly, being-with-others.

In the modern era, the master pattern of race thinking has largely determined the meaning of human diversity, with deadly consequences. As Lauren traverses the "crazy," "desperate," and "dangerous" world of the future, the novel foregrounds an old American fantasy: the coming war between the races. In Butler's novel, that fantasy plays out "[o]n the street," where "people were expected to fear and hate everyone but their own kind" (31). And Lauren observes that "[m]ixed couples are rare out here," because "mixed couples catch hell" (186, 153).

Few elements of the present are more charged with apocalyptic potential than the current racial formation of American society. Inner city ghettos of the poor are increasingly isolated. Incarceration rates and chronic levels of unemployment for young persons of color ominously point to what Sidney Willhelm called the fact of "black obsolescence" in North America. In *Who Needs the Negro?* (1970), Willhelm argues that the growing superfluousness of the poorest African Americans could lead to their eventual extermination. Holocaust scholar Richard Rubenstein contends that Willhelm's analysis "deserves more attention than it has received" (112n). Rubenstein notes that the precondition for genocide is the political transformation of a people into the "living dead," and this is done by imagining them as superfluous to the social order. As Rubenstein puts it, "[t]here could come a time when bureaucrats might attempt to eliminate all of the ills associated with urban blight, such as crime, drugs, and unsafe streets, by eliminating those segments of the population that are regarded as most prone to social pathology" (86). Bauman concurs with Rubenstein's assessment that the possibility of genocide resides within "the house of modernity" (Bauman 17). Bauman observes that "none of the societal conditions that made Auschwitz possible has truly disappeared and no effective measures have been undertaken to prevent such possibilities and principles from generating Auschwitz-like catastrophes" (11). To the extent that it speaks to immanence within the social realities of the present,

Parable of the Sower suggests that genocide—the ultimate human catastrophe—is a latent tendency within our socioeconomic order. Fascism may well come about on the politics of "hate" and "fear," and its ultimate logic, as we well know, is the bloody sacrifice of scapegoats to right the world.

If one compares *Parable of the Sower* to *The Turner Diaries,* an overtly fascistic novel, one sees in the latter the same apocalyptic imagining of the American future. However, Butler's novel employs a race-transcendent communalist ethics to frame a sense of hope, whereas *The Turner Diaries* portrays white supremacist solidarity as the ultimate (utopian) value. *The Turner Diaries* frames hope in the triumphalist terms of a ruthless race war, in which strong white warriors regain their lost birthright in North America by murdering all the "inferior" races, especially blacks and Jews. To imagine genocide as a worthy moral project is to give it a possible existence in the world; it is to make of it a "living option." In this regard, as a work of the moral imagination, *Parable of the Sower* has to be read in concert with precisely the most fascistic versions of the future; for it is only in this light that one can fully comprehend its prophetic message—we can still avert the worst by taking purposeful concrete action.

Lauren's *Books of the Living* strongly assert the value of a transcendent consciousness, which sees hopeful possibility in the deadliest of seemingly arrested states. Butler has stressed that "I don't write utopian science fiction because I don't believe that imperfect humans can form a perfect society" (qtd. in Beal 14). Nonetheless, in its indictment of existing barbarism, *Parable of the Sower* does offer a vague blueprint of what, ideally, ought to be. It is precisely this sense of the ideal political imperative that has come under attack in postmodern thought. Lyotard counsels against utopianism on the grounds that "we all know" that "a pure alternative to the system . . . would end up resembling the system it was meant to replace" (89). But if alternatives are ruled out of the realm of political possibility, then no other system but the present one is truly imaginable. Butler's novel advances a thesis with which few would disagree: "human beings are good at creating hells for themselves" (234). But without the concept of "heaven," hell loses its significance as a measure of human failing; it simply becomes the reflection of what we are and what we must be, because we know no other way.

Parable of the Sower rejects fatalism in favor of emancipatory human agency. Butler would most likely agree with David Harvey that "it is not change per se that has to be explained, but the forces that hold down change and/or give it a certain directionality. There is no single moment within the social process devoid of the capacity for transformative activity" (105). In the wilderness of the apocalyptic world, Lauren manages to create an earthseed community, a "harvest of survivors" (93). She gives the commune the fitting name of "Acorn," for to see a forest of oak trees as latent in a handful of acorns is to see the world as radical possibility. One sows as one reaps, which is to say, conscious human activity is the key force in determining social evolution.

The Acorn commune is not socialist in the manner of, say, Robert Owen's *New Lanark*; nor is Acorn an anarchist community like the Annares society described in Ursula Le Guin's *The Dispossessed* (1974). Acorn does not represent a pure alternative to the dystopian world without. In many ways, it is caught up in the very contradictions it seeks to transcend. For instance, the commune is unable to escape the rule of the market and the violence that attends a private property order. "I think that any serious money we make here will come from the land," says Bankole, the proprietor of the land where Acorn is situated. "Food is gold these days, and we can grow food here. We have guns to protect ourselves, so we can sell our crops in nearby towns or on the highway" (288). I suggest that Acorn is best viewed as a kind of left-wing communitarian survivalism. Lauren voices its fundamental ethos: "The world is full of crazy, dangerous people. We see signs of that every day. If we don't watch out for ourselves, they will rob us, kill us, and maybe eat us. It's a world gone to hell and we've only got each other to keep it off us" (257). As opposed to the fascistic, wider world where people seek only their "kind," Acorn is a community that embraces diversity, in terms of race, class, and sexual identity: its members are black, white, Asian, and Latino, rich and poor, gay and straight. However, Butler makes clear that Acorn is not so much "heaven on earth" as the modest attempt to realize that ideal.

Heaven beyond the world does not exist, so if we would occupy heaven, we have no choice but to fashion it in the here and now. However, Lauren realizes that in a world become hell, her harvest of survivors might well have to dominate, rob, terrorize, and even kill outsiders. "[I]f people threaten us or our crops," says Lauren, "we kill them. . . . We kill them, or they kill us. If we work together, we can defend ourselves" (288). The absence of a social revolutionary force in the imagined American future makes a politics of survival the only means of averting the coming catastrophe.[10] In the last analysis, it is arguable that survivalism, in any form, is a positive transcendence of the barbarous "power struggles" of our time. Survivalism represents "adaptation" to a violent world, and in this respect it severely compromises the fundamental premise of existential time—that authentic free acts are always possible, and the dawning of each new day is the demonstration of this truth.

I have argued that *Parable of the Sower* must be read in the light of the central problematic of modernity (only intensified by the postmodern turn): how to discover a pathway to utopia, when all pathways thrown up by modernity itself—in particular, the dystopias of fascism and Stalinism—have collapsed utopia into catastrophe. Utopianism after the end of utopia names the project that Butler explores. However, a utopianism that has shrunk to the dimensions of survivalism is perhaps part of the problem rather than its solution. Notwithstanding its implication in the money economy, Acorn's distinct agrarian character—the fact that its relation to the land is "more like gardening than farming" (288)—would seem to make it an anti-modern undertaking, not unlike a type of the utopian commune that sprang up in the nineteenth century as part of the revolt against industrialism. But the supposition that Acorn is an anti-modern project misses a crucial point about its distinctive human elements.

Butler's presentation of Acorn as a hopeful experiment in enlightened communalism (a communalism that transcends differences in race, class, gender, and sexuality) is itself a statement of faith in one (utopian) tendency of modernity: its existential undoing of all forms of chauvinistic particularism, the way it obliges the subject to come to terms with ever-widening possibilities of human identity. Acorn proposes nothing new in the realm of political economy; however, as an ethics of culture, it promotes the essential superiority of human diversity to the taxonomic systems imposed by sinister patternmasters. Bauman argues that "the modern drive to a fully designed, fully controlled world" is typically negated by "the pluralism of the human world" (93). From this perspective, the pluralism of Acorn affirms the hope that what is the best in the house of modernity will win out over what is worst.

An unwillingness to go beyond the vaguest blueprint of the good society marks utopianism after the end of utopia. One has only to compare **Parable of the Sower** with, say, Edward Bellamy's *Looking Backward* (1888), which depicts a totally reconstructed world, to see how confidence in utopian projects has drastically declined. Or, perhaps, the chief value of literary utopias does not reside in their depictions of particular ideal societies, but rather in the fact that such depictions, to quote David Ketterer, cause *"a metaphorical destruction of that 'real' world in the reader's head"* (13). In other words, literary utopias foreground the ideologies that affirm the natural aspect or timelessness of a given social order. By juxtaposing ideology with compelling moral ideals, the literary utopia, however diminished in its ambitions, still makes it possible to derive an ought from what is. On the one hand, Butler's reduction of utopianism to survivalism is based on the pragmatic axiom that vital truth is a consequence of action and does not lie beyond the subject in a realm of grim necessity as Marxists and others have supposed. On the other hand, the removal of social revolution as at least one possibility for the future has the effect of making us

feel that disastrous times are destined, that we are merely reeds borne along by the river of time. Butler would have us swim against the current. She extends a hand to the desperate swimmer who struggles to make the shore. But she is all too aware, as only prophets can be, that "drowning people sometimes die fighting their rescuers" (54).

Notes

1. This is the argument advanced by Jameson and Eagleton.

2. Lewis observes: "the secular apocalyptic tradition which, descending through the imaginative responses to the American and French Revolutions and catching fire again with the Russian upheaval, has focused less upon the grand conflict than upon the millennium it will usher in" (191). The secularization of apocalyptic temporality into Enlightenment historicity reaches its apotheosis in the revolutionary project of Marxism. It is this project, above all, that postmodern thinkers like Lyotard are apt to critique. However, they perhaps throw out the baby with the bathwater: for in rejecting Marxism they lose sight of revolution as a force within human history.

3. Davis has produced the most comprehensive analyses to date of the militarization of California's urban culture. Like Butler, Davis perceives a sinister social order taking shape in this development. I borrow the term "privatopia" from McKenzie, whose study of homeowner associations and residential private communities illuminates the real historical context of Butler's treatment of the city. See also work by Dubey, who keenly delineates this trend.

4. One is strongly reminded of the humanistic existentialism of Sartre—and with good reason. When Lauren describes the philosophy of Earthseed to Bankole, he replies, "it sounds like a combination of Buddhism, existentialism, Sufism and I don't know what else" (234).

5. The south-north trajectory of the action of *Parable of the Sower* calls to mind the fundamental narrative pattern of that early utopian form in African American letters, the slave narrative.

6. Butler's heroines are typically concerned to explore human potentiality in a world of definite limits. For discussions of this theme in Butler's work, see Foster, Salvaggio, and Govan.

7. This process is insightfully analyzed in Herman.

8. Like other works in the utopia/catastrophe school of speculative fiction (say, Ignatius Donnelly's *Caesar's Column* [1890]), *Parable of the Sower* is essentially a critique of "civilization and its discontents." Freud's analysis of the link between class society and the psychic disintegration of the individual is directly relevant to the world depicted in *Parable of*

the Sower. "If . . . a culture has not got beyond a point at which the satisfaction of one portion of its participants depends upon the suppression of another, and perhaps larger, portion . . . it is understandable that the suppressed people should develop an intense hostility towards a culture whose existence they make possible by their work, but in whose wealth they have too small a share. . . . It goes without saying that a civilization which leaves so large a number of its participants unsatisfied and drives them into revolt neither has nor deserves the prospect of a lasting experience" (Freud 15).

9. Butler's analysis of the philosophy of power systems has taken varied forms in her books. However, such forms are united by a controlling vision of human potentiality, which Butler describes in the following terms: "My characters are told that human beings have two characteristics that are fine and conducive to the species survival individually, but are a lethal combination. The first of those characteristics is intelligence and the other is something that can be projected through history—something that keeps showing up in us that has been doing a great deal of harm: It's hierarchical structure/behavior. The combination, because intelligence tends to serve the hierarchical behavior, is what may eventually wipe us out" (qtd. in Beal 17). Here, Butler makes explicit her interest in the real possibility of universal disaster.

10. Consider in this regard Jack London's apocalyptic novel, *The Iron Heel* (1907). Like *Parable of the Sower, The Iron Heel* portrays a barbaric world in which fascism looms on the horizon. However, London places at the center of his novel a revolutionary movement, that labors mightily to send history in another direction. *The Iron Heel* is not necessarily more aesthetically satisfying than *Parable of the Sower,* but, in terms of the moral imagination, the former moves the reader to value subjective freedom over objective necessity in a way that the latter perhaps does not.

Works Cited

Bauman, Zygmunt. *Modernity and the Holocaust.* Ithaca: Cornell UP, 1989.

Beal, Frances M. "*Black Scholar* Interview with Octavia Butler: Black Women and Science Fiction Genre." *Black Scholar* 17 (1986): 14-18.

Buber, Martin. "Prophecy, Apocalyptic, and the Historical Hour." *Pointing the Way: Collected Essays by Martin Buber.* Ed. Maurice S. Friedman. New York: Harper & Row, 1957, 192-207.

Butler, Octavia. "The Birth of a Writer." *Essence* 20 (1989): 74-79, 132-34.

———. *Parable of the Sower.* New York: Warner, 1995.

Davis, Mike. *City of Quartz: Excavating the Future in Los Angeles.* New York: Vintage, 1990.

———. *Ecology of Fear: Los Angeles and The Imagination of Disaster.* New York: Vintage, 1998.

Dubey, Madhu. "Folk and Urban Communities In African-American Women's Fiction: Octavia Butler's *Parable of the Sower.*" *Studies in American Fiction* 27 (1999): 103-28.

Eagleton, Terry. *The Illusions of Postmodernism.* Oxford: Blackwell, 1996.

Foster, Frances Smith. "Octavia Butler's Black Female Future Fiction." *Extrapolation* 23 (1982): 37-55.

Freud, Sigmund. *The Future of An Illusion.* Trans. & Ed. James Strachey. New York: Norton, 1961.

Govan, Sandra Y. "Connections, Links, And Extended Networks: Patterns in Octavia Butler's Science Fiction." *Black American Literature Forum* 18 (1984): 82-87.

Harvey, David. *Justice, Nature, and the Geography of Difference.* Cambridge: Blackwell, 1996.

Herman, Edward S. *Triumph of the Market: Essays on Economics, Politics and the Media.* Boston: South End, 1995.

Hobbes, Thomas. 1651. *Leviathan.* Harmondsworth: Penguin, 1968.

James, William. "The Will To Believe." *Pragmatism and Other Writings.* Harmondsworth: Penguin, 2000. 198-218.

Jameson, Fredric. *Postmodernism: Or the Cultural Logic of Late Capitalism.* Durham: Duke UP, 1991.

Ketterer, David. *New Worlds For Old: The Apocalyptic Imagination, Science Fiction, and American Literature.* Bloomington: Indiana UP, 1974.

Lewis, R. W. B. "Days of Wrath and Laughter." *Trials of the Word: Essays In American Literature and the Humanistic Tradition.* New Haven: Yale UP, 1965. 184-235.

Lyotard, Jean-François. *The Postmodern Condition: A Report On Knowledge.* Trans. Geoff Bennington and Brian Massumi. Minneapolis: U of Minnesota P, 1984.

McDonald, Andrew. *The Turner Diaries.* Hillsboro, WV: National Vanguard Books, 1978.

McKenzie, Evan. *Privatopia: Homeowner Associations and the Rise of Residential Private Government.* New Haven: Yale UP, 1994.

Mumford, Lewis. *In The Name of Sanity.* New York: Harcourt, Brace & Co., 1954.

Rabkin, Eric S. "Introduction: Why Destroy the World?" *The End of the World.* Ed. Rabkin, Martin H. Greenberg, and Joseph D. Olander. Carbondale: Southern Illinois UP, 1983. vii-xv.

Rubenstein, Richard. *The Cunning of History: The Holocaust and the American Future.* New York: Harper, 1975.

Salvaggio, Ruth. "Octavia Butler and the Black Science Fiction Heroine." *Black American Literature Forum* 18 (1984): 78-81.

Willhelm, Sidney. *Who Needs the Negro?* Hampton, VA: UB & US Communications Systems Inc., 1993.

Patricia Melzer (essay date 2002)

SOURCE: Melzer, Patricia. "'All That You Touch You Change': Utopian Desire and the Concept of Change in Octavia Butler's *Parable of the Sower* and *Parable of the Talents.*" *FEMSPEC* 3, no. 2 (2002): 31-52.

[*In the following essay, Melzer examines Butler's treatment of feminist notions of utopia, politics, and science fiction in* Parable of the Sower *and* Parable of the Talents.]

This analysis examines two literary narratives by Octavia Butler, **Parable of the Sower** and **Parable of the Talents,** that elucidate the intersection of three fields in Western thought: the notion of utopia, feminist politics and theory, and feminist science fiction. This intersection is crucial for feminists in that it provides tools for negotiating difference within feminist politics. I lay out the dynamics within Octavia Butler's feminist utopian/dystopian writing that define her concept of "utopia" as both a utopian desire and a longing to transform. These allow her to theorize about future social relations and inform the strategies for feminist politics that she develops.

Feminist debates on difference address the complex ways in which women are positioned in relation to power based on race, class, and sexual difference. Within these debates, many postmodern feminist theories reject the essentialist notion of "woman" as an identity and instead emphasize the interrelated construction of gender and other social categories, such as race and class.[1] Butler's utopian writing contributes to the deconstruction of difference as the "other" to a stable identity. Here difference is not the opposite component of identity, but becomes a part of the self. While others have discussed Butler's treatment of difference mainly in terms of her "miscegenation" between species (an approach Donna Haraway introduced in *Primate Visions*), I explore how difference in her narratives relates to notions of utopia. At the center of Butler's utopian desire lies the concept of change that adds an element of *process* to the feminist discourse on difference. It not only places categories of difference into a historical context, but also connects them with time.

This temporal aspect that complicates absolute concepts of identity/subjectivity based on race, class, and gender, I believe, is a valuable contribution to the feminist debate on how to negotiate difference politically and theoretically.

UTOPIA, FEMINIST POLITICS, AND SCIENCE
FICTION

The concept of the ideal community—nation, city, and/or village—is central to Western thought, and finds its most direct expression in fiction. Defined by Ernst Bloch as the principle of hope,[2] the human urge to transform and re-create living environments is the foundation of most politics, including feminist. It constitutes also the most challenging component in feminist theories, in which the discourse on difference has proven U.S. feminist politics to be at times exclusionary in their formulation of women's interests, goals, and visions.

The construction of utopian societies is primarily an articulation of power relations, with the interests of various groups in the foreground. When approached from this perspective, utopian formulations convey theoretical developments outside the norms of what we define as "theory," and create a window into the realm of the utopian imagination's relationship to politics. They remind us of the importance in feminist theories to develop utopian impulses. bell hooks' concept of yearning is one example of utopian desires articulated in feminist theory:

> "[D]epths of longing, [. . .] a displacement for the longed-for liberation—the freedom to control one's destiny" found in "folks across race, class, gender, and sexual practice. [. . .] The shared space and feeling of 'yearning' opens up the possibility of common ground where all these differences might meet and engage one another."
>
> (12-3)

Similarly, so is Audre Lorde's feminist re-definition of difference in *Sister Outsider*: "The future of our earth may depend upon the ability of all women to identify and develop new definitions of power and new patterns of relating across difference" (123). Iris Young's "unoppressive city" of difference, a model that she develops in "The Ideal Community and the Politics of Difference" and that refutes the humanist ideal of sameness that characterizes traditional utopias, serves as an example of a utopian construction within theoretical discourse, and as a strategy for a feminist politics of difference. Its basic element is diversity, with new cultures, potential interests, and social experiences constantly transforming the environment in which people live. The ultimate goal is not to create unity through assimilation, but "openness to unassimilated otherness" (Young 319).

Young criticizes the Western, male "ideal of community" as inherently non-progressive, even if formulated within a "left" political claim expressed in utopian novels and social theory alike. These communities emphasize the notion of a unitary group of transparent selves, with a common identity. Young identifies the structures of the ideal community as based on metaphysics of presence, a desire to "formulate a representation of a whole, a totality" (302), that is unable to tolerate fragmentation and uncertainty. She also pinpoints an inherent opposition of individualism and community that denies difference by defining the individual as a self-sufficient and solid unity. This "ideal of community" is also non-progressive because it denies difference within and between subjects by demanding recognition of, and identification with, all members, "making it difficult for people to respect those with whom they don't identify" (311). These "ideal communities," says Young, are politically problematic, racist and class chauvinistic, rendering them contrary to inclusive feminist politics. Butler's fiction mirrors these theories' concern with feminist politics in that her utopian communities problematize the possibility of an "ideal community" and its vulnerabilities and problems.

As a literary genre, utopian writings reflect and participate in the critical discourse on ideal communities, often reproducing the inherently dystopian concept of a homogenous enclosed community. The theoretical object of these utopian writings is what Bulent Somay terms the "utopian locus" in "Towards an Open-Ended Utopia" (25). Here the utopian desire (*i.e.* the principle of hope), is projected into, and is conserved within the boundaries of the imagined ideal:

> What the utographer did was to verbalize and enclose the *utopian horizon* of an age, which was in itself non-discursive, infinite, and open-ended. [. . .] The utopian horizon was "stabilized" or finalized, and the final product was presented to the audience. [. . .] The main characteristic of this structure is the imprisonment of the utopian horizon within a closed and ordered utopian locus, whose description is the central narrative element of traditional utopian fiction.
>
> (25, 26)

Contemporary utopian fiction expands the utopian horizon and explodes the closed and limited space in which the narrative takes place. The implicit, not explicit, elements constitute the utopian moment of an open-ended utopia, the *potential* of the expressed utopian desire. It points to the opportunities, without the claim of authority inherent in the one-dimensional utopian ideal that strives for a closed and controlled way of being—similar to the ideal communities Young criticizes. Butler's narratives reflect the notion of utopia as a potential that needs to be negotiated in its complexity, the people affected by it discuss and sometimes reject it. Butler develops the utopian term dialectically,

not absolutely, and always in relation to the dystopian term, or its possibility. The existing tension between the actual narrative and its utopian spaces, and the potential of the utopian horizon (Somay 33) is what is in the center of the narrative, not the perfected ideal itself.

Generally, past feminist utopian writings in the U.S. have been inspirational to, and interactive with, feminist politics in their conceptualization of possible feminist futures. They defy the notion that "Utopia—the vision of the radically better world that our world could potentially be—was declared dead along with the movements for change [of the New Left] that had inscribed it on their banners" (Bammer 1). Instead, they redefine the term, and make the desire for a more just world part of feminist conceptualizations, understanding "'the utopian' as an *approach toward,* a movement beyond set limits into the realm of the not-yet-set" (Bammer 7). Similar to traditional utopian narratives that conceptualize the "ideal of community," in feminist utopias, the discussion of alternative social models is in the foreground of the texts. At the same time, however, they undermine the artistic and theoretical limitations of traditional utopian novels, thereby problematizing issues like the "ideal nation" and "social equality" (Bartkowski 12).

In the 1970s, feminist utopias were extremely popular and their audience extended beyond the science fiction community. They created a space for what Jean Pfaelzer defined as a feminist "political epistemology," serving as a "metaphor for potential histories" (283). Their relation to feminist social and political theories is evident: as Frances Bartkowski observes, the peak of feminist literary production and political activity coincided in the mid-1970s (5).[3] In feminist utopias from the 1970s, authors such as Marge Piercy, Sally Miller Gearheart, and Ursula Le Guin created imaginative societies where feminist politics were set to work. Their stories reveal that the concept of a utopian community continued to be the most prevalent narrative drive within feminist writing and that the utopian desire remained a vital component of feminist politics: "[T]he act of fantasizing a feminist future—i.e., the genre itself—relocates the source of women's identity within a women's community" (Pfaelzer 292). In doing so, these stories depict the problematic elements of alternative (supposedly ideal) social institutions, the development of which is one main aspect in traditional utopian novels.

At the same time, as feminist utopian writing increased in the 1970s, these authors' visions projected more and more into a science fiction narrative framework. Because science fiction is a particular fantastic narrative mode that is rooted in contemporary phenomena, it lends itself to social criticism as do few other genres and is therefore interesting to feminists. As Scott Bukatman points out, "Given a thematics profoundly engaged with social structures and sexual difference, and potentially heterotopic discursive practices, the relevance of SF to a feminist politics should not be mysterious" (5). This connection between science fiction and feminist inquiries, what Sarah Lefanu describes as the "marriage between feminist politics and science fiction" (5), is what makes utopian writing situated within science fiction narratives so important to a discourse concerned with feminist issues and social power relations. Donna Haraway identifies in "A Cyborg Manifesto" feminist science fiction writers as "our storytellers exploring what it means to be embodied in high-tech worlds." As "theorists for cyborgs" (1990, 216), these authors problematize the formula for identity and the norms for politics that Western discourse prescribes—including traditional utopian discourse.

In *Partial Visions,* Angelika Bammer examines the relationship of feminist utopias to feminist social politics in the 1970s, with the underlying thesis that it was in literary utopias that the women's movement explored implications of its political agendas. Today the feminist movement manifests itself differently than from the 1970s; differences between social groups dominate discussions, and the visibility of the movement has declined. Butler's feminist science fiction narratives of the 1990s express and develop utopianism in the context of changing feminist politics. This speculative fiction further critically examines the "we" problematized in writings by women of color challenging U.S. "hegemonic feminism" (Sandoval). Following the feminist debate that has grown out of milestone publications like Gloria Anzaldúa and Cherríe Moraga's *This Bridge Called My Back,* bell hooks' *Ain't I a Woman: Black Women and Feminism,* and Barbara Smith, Patricia Bell Scott, and Gloria Tull's *All the Women Are White, All the Blacks Are Men, But Some of Us Are Brave* in the 1980s,[4] and feminist postcolonial writings in the 1990s, "our" world needs to be revisited and redefined. Difference hereby is the main concern.

Feminist utopias and dystopias provide conceptual tools for expressing utopian desire. In their narratives, the utopian impulse stands in relation to criticisms of monolithic models of ideal communities. They create a realm for optimistic speculation in which the acceptance of difference, not the striving for sameness, is the basis for a utopian society. It is from these utopian imaginations that feminist theories can draw the visions and hope necessary for developing models of feminist interaction. At the same time that difference is a dividing factor in many feminist theories and makes the imagining of a shared future difficult, these narratives of hope reclaim the utopian moment. They redefine a feminist political vision of the future. One of Butler's contributions to this discourse is her concept of change that lies at the basis of every political interaction. Instead of "freezing" the manifestations of difference

within their theoretical conceptualizations (*i.e.* "gender," "race," "class"), she emphasizes the fluid and transforming aspect behind the term. At the same time, she makes these manifestations concrete and turns them into a moment of agency by claiming that they can be "shaped." Change and its implications inject a transformative element into the conceptualizations of difference that enables not only a new perception of difference, such as Audre Lorde calls for in *Sister Outsider,* but that demands a constant redefinition of its categories. It is especially in this respect that Butler's utopian desire contributes to the feminist discourse on difference.

The feminist debate on Butler's work as utopian in its radical dealings with difference mainly concentrates on her *Xenogenesis* trilogy.[5] My analysis will focus on her two latest novels, *Parable of the Sower* and *Parable of the Talents.* In these novels, Butler's conception of feminist politics, including grassroots activism, and her theorizing about utopian communities in general is less developed in the metaphorical mode of the *Xenogenesis* trilogy and its conceptualizations of the "other order of difference" (Haraway, 1989, 379). Instead, Butler's latest fiction represents a concrete discussion of political strategies combined with the intense desire for change itself. My analysis examines issues within Butler's imagined futures that are of concern within the feminist debate on feminist utopias.[6] Therefore, the question here is how Butler critically re-visits concepts of political strategizing and organizing, community, family, economics, racial and sexual diversity, religion and spirituality (as developed within feminist utopias in the 1970s) within the context of feminist politics.

UTOPIAN DESIRE IN BUTLER'S NARRATIVES

In her work, Butler visualizes inclusive utopian societies that struggle with, and at times celebrate, difference. As Michelle Green states: "Her work implicitly criticizes utopias by women that avoid conflicts stemming from difference and reject challenges and changes from within" (168). The setting is always a problematic one. Often a dystopian framework dominates the narratives, and lays out feminist concerns and critiques of contemporary political and social trends. The connection to feminist politics is less obvious than in the utopian novels of the 1970s; it is more complex and mirrors changing feminist politics.[7] The utopian impulse in Butler's narratives stands in dialectic relation to the dystopian; they are not merely contrasted but constitute each other. This insistence that both terms are relative, not absolute, points to the significance of negotiating difference. The agent of utopia is the individual, but always in the context of a community; the defining factor of that agency is the utopian desire underlying the events in Butler's stories. The struggle of power relations is at the center of her writing and informs the manifestations of the utopian desire that run through her narratives. Survival and resistance define this struggle and the identities involved in it. In these narratives, Butler returns to the feminist articulation of social critique through speculative literature that has its tradition in literary utopias and that was so strong in the 1970s. She problematizes social and political issues of feminist concern, and conceptualizes ways to incorporate difference into a utopian future.

In *Parable of the Sower* (henceforth: *Sower*) and *Parable of the Talents* (henceforth: *Talents*),[8] Butler weaves complex stories of survival, power, and vision in a future time frame between 2024 to 2090. At the center of the narratives is the figure of Lauren Oya Olamina, the founder of the religion Earthseed, and how she strives to realize her vision. The spiritual component is central in Butler's conceptualizations. In *Sower,* Lauren develops or "receives" Earthseed, in contrast to the increasingly weakened and powerless Christian faith her father preaches. In *Talents,* Butler juxtaposes this new faith as a spiritual alternative to a frenzied and destructive Christian fundamentalism modeled after the contemporary Religious Right in the U.S. *Sower* is structured around the motif of the journey, an important stylistic feature that Butler, significantly, picks up in the last third of *Talents.* With this, she revives the theme of the journey as the vehicle for utopian desire in Lauren's travels through an apocalyptic future.[9] While *Sower* develops Earthseed and the concept of an ideal community, *Talents* revisits this concept critically, examining and revising it.

The world Butler describes is disconcertingly constructed after tendencies present in contemporary U.S. society. The connection of a present society and an imagined future that becomes a central theme within her narratives conveys the self-reflexivity of what Tom Moylan termed 'critical utopias': "The critical utopias, then, suggest [. . .] a shift from simple negation to a negation with alternatives. These narratives feature utopian societies related to and in conflict with nonutopian, parent societies" (237). The conditions from which Lauren constructs her vision are dystopian in every sense of the word, representing Butler's insistence that utopian desire grows dialectically from despair and chaos: based on change, on constant transformation, the relationship between utopian and dystopian elements is of mutual interdependency. Dystopia precedes transformation; it does not exclude utopia, but challenges it into existence.

There are two major differences between *Sower* and *Talents* that point to Butler's inherent ambivalence toward a utopian community. One is a stylistic device: the voice that narrates the story. Both texts use journal entries as their narrative form. Yet, in *Sower,* Lauren's journal is the only reference for the reader, while in *Talents* the voices are multiple. Lauren's reflections are

the most frequent, but her daughter's entries comment upon them decades later; and her brother's and husband's voices challenge her presentation of events in the course of the novel. Even though in *Sower* Lauren develops her vision in constant exchange with people around her and Earthseed is a discursive (i.e. open) belief system, Lauren's perspective is the only narrative voice. By multiplying the perspectives on events in *Talents,* Butler problematizes the concept of a utopian vision that a single individual formulates. Her notion of difference and its inherent changing nature that is part of Butler's utopian desire becomes apparent in her narrative technique when the estranged daughter's doubts of the validity of her mother's vision critique the utopian dream. The second difference is the changing political strategies that Butler discusses in the novels: in *Sower,* the utopian idea spreads through the words of one person; the concept is to gather and protect a following within a chaotic environment without the tools of political campaigning. In *Talents,* her failings to enlarge and strengthen her community during the time of a fascist regime haunt Lauren after Christian fundamentalists capture Earthseed followers and destroy their homes. Once freed, she changes her political tactics. Instead of only trying to win the disempowered for Earthseed, Lauren begins to utilize the power and influence of richer people in spreading her message and gathering people. This narrative exploration of what form of activism has the most potential to achieve social change is crucial when looking at Butler in terms of feminist politics.

The basis for the utopian community that Butler constructs in *Sower* and further develops in *Talents* is Earthseed. The young Lauren in *Sower,* who later in *Talents* becomes the mature and powerful leader of her influential sect, develops this religion and life-philosophy. Earthseed transcends the definition of religion as well as philosophy by combining elements of spirituality with political and social issues, echoing religious principles in "Buddhism, existentialism, Sufism" (*Sower* 239), where it is not the divine presence (God) himself that is the aim of actions. Butler conceptualizes the utopian impulse in her futuristic vision as a religious spirituality that rejects both the patriarchal concept of "God" and the essentialist notion of an "earth mother goddess" (Pearson 58) based in cultural feminism that is often an element within feminist utopias of the 1970s.[10] The centrality of religion in Butler's writings is crucial in the context of feminist utopias: feminist concepts of the future reject most organized religion.[11] Earthseed, with its rituals and "shapers" especially in *Talents,* seems at times contradictory to feminist notions of an anti-hierarchical spirituality situated in the individual, not in the representative of a religion. Unlike other organized religions, though, Earthseed's long-term goal is not Paradise, but the migration of humankind into outer space: *"The Destiny of Earthseed / Is to take root among the stars"* (*Sower* 78). The main message of Earthseed is that God is Change, and that change is constant. Humans, through their actions, shape God.

> All that you touch
> You Change.
>
> All that you Change
> Changes you.
>
> The only lasting truth
> Is Change.
>
> God
> Is Change.

(*Sower* 3)

In *Sower,* Lauren writes of Earthseed from 2024 to 2027, and relates it to the apocalyptic world around her. She travels from Southern California up North, where whole states have been spared the destructive effects of pollution and violence. Destruction, violence, and chaos induced by capitalism dominate the futuristic world that Lauren travels; a state she later refers to in *Talents* as the "Pox," which lasts from 2015 through 2030 (*Talents* 13-4). The chaotic make-up of the Pox develops into a power vacuum that the fascist fundamentalist Christian Right seize under the name "Christian Americans" with Andrew Steele Jarret as their leader. In *Talents,* results of the fascist regime are concentration camps, and war with Canada and Alaska. Out of this nightmare—chaos in *Sower* on the one hand, and organized terror in *Talents* on the other—Butler creates the vision of a better and just world, based on the belief that each individual has the power to manipulate and change existing conditions. Change is inherent to the world and needs to be seized as a tool of empowerment.

> God exists to be shaped, and will be shaped, with or without our forethought, with or without our intent. [. . .] There's hope in understanding the nature of God—not punishing or jealous, but infinitely malleable. [. . .] there's power in knowing that God can be focused, diverted, shaped by anyone at all.

(*Sower* 24, 202)

UTOPIAN COMMUNITIES AND NARRATIVE DISRUPTION

Butler's depiction of Earthseed's political organization is reminiscent of what Russ calls *"communal even quasi-tribal"* (Russ 73), typical for feminist utopias' attempts to conceptualize communities where "Order is kept [. . .] not by use of force, but by persuasion" (Pearson 54). In order to be active in shaping inevitable change, the community members meet on a regular basis to exchange ideas, worries and strategies, and to discuss Earthseed verses collected in *The Book of the Living.* These weekly Gatherings, "discussions," create

a sense of belonging and solidarity and at the same time function as democratic, political decision-making processes.[12]

Butler emphasizes that the embracing of difference does not only enhance the quality of human interactions, but that it is an act of survival and of necessity if humankind wants to end conditions of hate and violence. This concept is present in Audre Lorde's writing as well as in other feminist theories on difference. As Butler writes:

> Embrace diversity.
> Unite—
> Or be divided
> robbed,
> ruled,
> killed
> By those who see you as prey.
> Embrace diversity
> Or be destroyed.

(*Sower* 181)

Earthseed, its religion as well as its community, is a moment of resistance and an opportunity for its followers to gain control over their lives. The community with its growing number of members with diverse personal narratives and backgrounds develops a complexity on various levels. It is, from the beginning, an assembly of refugees who are fleeing destruction and oppression, and later, with Acorn as its first settlement, represents shelter for disoriented and abused people that are on the receiving end of patriarchal capitalism's oppressions. These include girls forced into prostitution by their fathers, a young woman whose homeless mother sold her to a man with several wives, a couple that worked as domestics and had to leave after the woman had been sexually approached by their employer, a physician whose wife had been killed by a group of looting madmen, and corporate slaves that ran away—families and individuals uprooted by the violence erupting from an out-of-control capitalist system. Earthseed defines itself concretely as an active element of political resistance when Lauren relates it to a crucial aspect in U.S. history: "'So we become the crew of a modern underground railroad,' I said. Slavery again—even worse than my father thought, or at least sooner" (*Sower* 268). Butler's critique of power based in contemporary economic relations in *Sower* becomes more complex when she portrays slavery in *Talents* in the context of concentration work camps where political dissidents and other "anti-social" people are kept prisoners.[13]

Earthseed's emphasis on economic self-sufficiency through subsistence farming and bartering apparently represents a yearning for a pastoral, pre-technological past. Yet Butler complicates utopian vision: the rejection of exploitative capitalist values and the promotion of ecologically safe production is not a return to an "ideal community," but a strategy of survival that in *Talents* goes horribly wrong when fascists destroy the isolated settlement. As Madhu Dubey discusses in "Folk and Urban Communities in African-American Women's Fiction: Octavia Butler's *Parable of the Sower,*" Earthseed is not an arcadian utopia. Butler understands human nature's needs to be complex and changing, opposing the predetermined simplicity of "natural" human needs in arcadian utopias.

One main difference between the actual and imagined utopian communities of 19th century America and the 1960s Hippie communes that Acorn resembles and Earthseed is their relationship to technology. In this, Earthseed resembles postindustrial literary ecotopias in that they do not reject technology or yearn for a mythical past, but imagine an ecologically sustainable economic system (Dubey 6). Instead of rejecting any high technology, Lauren actively seeks access to it—it is the key to Earthseed's Destiny.

Butler weaves controversial notions on technology into her narratives that address crucial elements within feminist utopian writing, such as reproductive technology. Lauren in *Talents* reflects on the possible effects on society's perception of reproductive issues when a child is incubated in an artificial womb. Her initial repulsion gives way to a contemplation of existing structures based on economic classes where poor women function as surrogate mothers for affluent couples. Instead of viewing the process as an inevitable threat to women, Butler points to the potential technology holds. She rejects any sentimental notion of a pre-technological world as more desirable: "And, of course, women will be free to do without men completely, since women can provide their own ova. I wonder what this will mean for humanity in the future. Radical change or just one more option among the many?" (*Talents* 83). Earthseed promotes the radical notion of artificial incubation and transcends biological differences by making them irrelevant: the shuttles heading for the starship carry "frozen human and animal embryos, plant seeds, tools, equipment, memories, dreams, and hopes" (*Talents,* 363). With this, Butler takes a radical stance in the feminist debate over reproductive technology.[14] Above all, though, Earthseed is "not an organic community unified by collective memory, ethnicity, shared cultural heritage, or attachment to place" (Dubey 6). Its principle is change and its members are from diverse backgrounds. The separate racial and ethnic origins that translate into different cultural and historical memories demand constant negotiation and mediation. As Dubey points out: "The process of finding unity in diversity is necessarily risky and difficult" (6) and is incompatible with the notion of an "ideal community" that rests on homogenous patterns of identity.[15]

The importance of literacy for individual agency runs through both novels. Education, i.e. research in the sci-ences, is essential for Earthseed's long-term goal. The apocalyptic setting in *Sower* and *Talents* does not only lend Earthseed a distinct character of a New Beginning. It also points to the disintegrating power system within the "technoscience"[16] apparatus that is (mis)guided by political interests. The failure of the U.S. Space Program mirrors the power apparatus' incompetence. Lauren comments on the relationship of technological development and politics: "Secretaries of Astronautics don't have to know much about science. They have to know about politics" (*Sower* 19-20). Lauren recognizes that a return to a mythic past is paralyzing, not liberating. She insists on technology as a part of any new social order. The re-definition of technology's role from capitalist investment to a tool of resistance becomes concrete in *Talents* when in the last part of the book the movement has developed into a powerful sect with the economic and political resources to prepare space flight. Earthseed uses science and knowledge solely for the purpose of Destiny; there is no research in the name of science itself. Here science and technology, both elements of science fiction, become the basis for survival. Butler re-appropriates the empowering potential of knowledge from the capitalist agenda, and turns technoscience into a symbol of resistance.

In terms of sexual politics, Butler's fiction redefines gender roles and relations in interactions between men and women. There are no inherent duties or rights based on gender, nor are sexist notions carried over from traditional understandings. In *Sower,* the most prominent form of gender specific experiences is violence against women, especially rape. In a disconcerting fashion, Butler depicts violence against women to be a form of violence that unleashes itself whenever social control fails. Rape is a common encounter for the people traveling North. Only as a group can the women prevent attacks. Lauren cross-dresses as a man on her journey, and resorts to that tactic when she takes up her travels later in *Talents.* This narrative device critically points out the social constructions of gender roles in U.S. society, where being recognized as a woman can be life threatening. Lauren is spared the experience in *Sower,* whereas in *Talents* fundamentalists who run the concentration camp rape her as part of organized control. Here Butler depicts the sexual violence against women as a weapon of social control by terror regimes. She echoes recent manifestations of the institutionalization and broad application of violence against women as part of political control, such as the systematic rapes in Bosnia during the war and in Argentina during the military regime. Earthseed, in stark contrast to both forms of sexual violence (as a result of social disorder or as a form of social control) does not tolerate any form of oppression of children or any adult. Therefore, the community would not tolerate gendered violence.[17]

Heterosexuality is normative in both *Sower* and *Talents,* but Butler does not treat this particular form of sexuality as prescriptive. For example, she is critical of Lauren's brother Marcus in *Talents,* who betrays his sister by keeping her daughter Larkin/Asha without telling her about her origin. He struggles with his homosexuality that his Christian faith forbids him, and Larkin/Asha becomes the only child he can ever have. Butler's emphasis on the restricting effects of Christianity on its members that seems to construct homosexuality as an acceptable form of sexuality is supported by the betrayal of two lesbian lovers by non-Earthseed people in the concentration camp. The moment in which Lauren feels sexual desire for a woman at the end of *Talents* similarly disrupts the rather conservative element of normative heterosexuality that runs through most of Butler's narratives,[18] introducing what Russ calls sexual "permissiveness" (Russ 77).

Most feminist utopias, as Green points out, "deal with contemporary problems by defusing the differences that cause conflicts to develop among people" (167). Yet, Butler insists on the acknowledgment of socially constructed difference, such as gender and race difference, on which she bases the strength of her utopian community. Rather than envisioning an "overcoming" of difference (as it is present in liberal discourse of "multiculturalism"), she creates a less-than-perfect world where the potential of negotiating difference in non-oppressive ways constitutes the utopian desire.

Indeed, Butler perceives difference as a primary element of survival. Yet, as progressively as Butler treats the acceptance of difference as a crucial strategy for feminist political movements, and as directly as she problematizes sexism, she does not explicitly address problems of violence based on race in American society. Butler extensively problematizes oppressions based on class and gender differences, as well as on religious/ideological beliefs, such as in the form of rape and forced prostitution and economic slavery. Indirectly, it becomes clear that the winners in this chaos are wealthy white people. In contrast, the inhabitants of Earthseed communities have multiracial backgrounds. Also, Lauren's personal identity and family history is affirmatively African American. She openly discusses Jarret's past career in the Ku Klux Klan, and compares the behavior of his Crusaders with Hitler's SS and the Christian reeducation camps with Nazi concentration camps. Yet, neither the fact that her daughter is placed in a black upper middle-class Christian family, nor that her brother becomes an influential man in the Church, are put critically into the context of the racist background of the Christian Americans. While women and the poor become victims of mob violence, the lynching of people of color is not mentioned even though the history in American race relations and current racial violence would project such incidents in a chaotic

uncontrolled state of society.[19] Butler discusses race relations mainly in the diversity-affirming structure of Earthseed that opposes both a white racist, as well as an exclusive African American folk community, and in Lauren's strong African American identity.[20]

The imagery of plants and seeds that dominates Earthseed echoes Lauren's identity. This imagery emphasizes Earthseed's anti-capitalist and agricultural identity, and suggests the affirmative recognition of black women's experiences in Alice Walker's "In Search of Our Mothers' Gardens" that celebrates African American woman's unwritten history and creativity. In accordance with this, the central metaphor of Earthseed and its relation to feminist political activism is the seed. It grows from destruction, represents the life-affirming component, and evokes ideas of multiplying. At the core of the metaphor stands, of course, change. The seed symbolizes the success of the vision, the concept of sowing ideas and growing communities not modeled after a remote, idealized past, but focus on the future. Its main device is writing, the gathering and preserving of knowledge. The gender politics developed within an Earthseed context echo Walker's concept of "womanist," "committed to survival and wholeness of entire people, male *and* female" *(xi),* which evokes gender relations distinct from radical or cultural feminist notions of separatism. With Lauren's status as a spiritual leader with an essentially political vision, Butler speaks to a historical pattern of strong spiritual leaders in the African American community—most of whom were/are men, and offers an alternative to contemporary U.S. society.[21]

Butler's approach to race issues that at first appear to be in the background of her social critique can be understood as a (narrative) strategy that undermines the binary of white/black that dominates U.S. discourse on race relations. She explicitly rejects what Tucker Farley names the "white fantasy about earning unity" (243) often present in feminist science fiction, at the same time as Butler resists representation of the black folk community, exclusively defined as African American, as the only empowering form of community.[22] Instead, Butler places racial oppression into the complexity of social power relations, such as in terms of economic and ideological oppression. She does not foreground racial oppression in her analysis of social injustice, but undermines the juxtapositions and binaries of racial discourse of self/other by portraying racial diversity as a main component of her utopian vision. The "other" (people of color) is not included within the story of the "self," but constitutes the perspective of narration. As Robert Crossley explains: "All her fiction stands in quiet resistance to the notion that a black character in a science fiction novel is there *for a reason*" (xviii). Butler firmly roots her protagonist within an African-American context, yet at the same time she refuses to ideologically ghettoize her characters. Her fiction is too complex to be reduced to a single, exclusive political position. "How a feminist science-fiction character responds to a male-dominated world is one thing; how Butler's black heroines respond to racist and sexist worlds is quite another" (Salvaggio, 1984, 78).[23] By insisting on the presence of people of color in her narratives as normal, not exceptional, Butler also implicitly rejects the tokenism that categorizes her work primarily in terms of her identity as African American.[24]

In both novels, children represent the survival of the community. In *Sower,* the group welcomes and protects them on their travels North. They embody the future that the adults are trying to create. The interactions of adults and children transcend the definition of the nuclear family, typical of feminist utopias: "The dissolution of the nuclear family and the de-emphasis on the biological link between mother and child leads to a redefinition of the parent-child relationship" (Pearson, 1997, 56). In *Sower,* parenting is not related to shared blood (several individual members in the group "adopt" children and every adult is responsible for every child's well being). Lauren, herself a rather "un-motherly" figure in the conventional sense in that she rejects the passivity regarding public/political life associated with that role throughout both novels, early on recognizes the growing solidarity between adults that the children's dependency triggers. She realizes how responsibility for others, children or adults, can give meaning to life and can heal internal wounds: "taking care of other people can be a good cure for nightmares" (*Sower* 235). Butler's use of metaphors and structures that are reminiscent of tribal organization comments on the increasing tendency of contemporary society to alienate its members from each other. In the Earthseed community, the ordering principles are not hierarchies and a division of labor, but mutual respect, responsibility, and, formed by their current surrounding, the security of others. Thus, the sense of belonging, of being taken care of, extends from the children to every member of the community. In *Sower,* after a woman dies of a gun-wound during an attack, the group embraces her sister in a feeling of protection and solidarity: "*In spite of your loss and pain, you aren't alone. You still have people who care about you and want you to be all right. You still have family*" (*Sower* 277). "Mothering" (i.e. behavior based on qualities associated in the West with women), becomes a fundamental characteristic of an Earthseed community. Butler's concept of mothering rejects the white stereotypical ideal of the nurturing, self-sacrificing mother within patriarchal society. Instead, it embodies involvement and commitment to the community at large that in principle is independent of gender. Unlike creators of separatist utopias, and more similar to writers like Marge Piercy, Butler extends the principle of mothering to men and draws them into the responsibility of parenting.

In *Talents,* Butler further explores the question of origin—regarding physical birth as well as ideological belonging—when Lauren loses her daughter to the fascist government who gives away children of dissidents to regime-friendly couples. Larkin/Asha ends up living with her uncle Marcus, who keeps Lauren's identity as her mother from her. The girl's removal from her mother and her origin problematizes issues of identity and biological origin. Larkin/Asha's alienation from everything her mother stands for, including her rejection of the name she gave her, becomes a symbol for Lauren's lost chance to pass on her belief to her descendants, and conveys a sense of loneliness that her status as "Mother of All" entails.

The kidnapping of Acorn's children and the loss this poses for the whole community, not just for their immediate families, is critical in understanding the subversive function of Earthseed communities and the threat their principles pose to the system. Here Butler touches on contemporary feminist concerns with families separated through totalitarian regimes in order to undermine the identity and self confidence of groups that disrupt dominant ideologies, such as in Argentina under the fascist regime.[25] The undermining of communities by removing their children also takes place under the "protection" of a "democratic" system, such as the placing of Native American children with white families that took place in the U.S. until the 1970s and that still affects tribes today; and the removal of children from their "unfit" mothers by the state today that especially affects women of color who face racism and poverty.[26]

In Butler's narratives, children represent the treasure of the community, the foundation of any future and shared identity as a group passed down from generation to generation. They are symbolic for the resistance against assimilation by a dominant group and secure the survival of values and beliefs. Their systematic removal from the community by the system undermines the basis of resistance, and is a tool for raising a regime-friendly generation.

> Now we are told that our children have been saved from our wickedness. They've been given "good Christian homes." [. . .] The Crusaders deliberately divided siblings because if they were together, they might support one another in secret heathen practices or beliefs. But if each child was isolated and dropped into a family of good Christian Americans, then each would be changed. Parent pressure, peer pressure, and time would remake them as good Christian Americans.
>
> (*Talents,* 189, 237)[27]

Butler builds the narrative structure in *Talents* around two conflicting concepts of leadership: one that encourages hate and homogenous cultural conventions on the one hand, and that which seeks diversity and justice on the other. With Lauren, Butler introduces the concept of a strong, spiritual leader to her feminist future vision. This strongly contrasts with the political leader of the Christian fundamentalists, Jarret, who later disappears from the political scene—a broken and insane man. Lauren's function as spiritual leader reflects the discursive and changing nature of Earthseed communities. At the end of *Talents,* her position has developed into almost mythical status, that of a High Priestess or a Mother to All. Yet evaluating Lauren's role and decisions, a critical disruption takes place that complicates the binary construction of "good" and "bad" leader as well as the authority of utopian imagination. Her daughter, watching from afar, challengingly questions Lauren's position as leader. Larkin/Asha defines her mother's strength as controlling and manipulative, and reflects after her mother's death on her "damned Earthseed" (*Talents* 9), accusing Lauren of a hidden hunger for personal power. Larkin/Asha not only doubts the vision of Earthseed itself, but also her mother's motives for pursuing it.

> They'll make a god of her. I think that would please her, if she could know about it. In spite of all her protests and denials, she's always needed devoted, obedient followers—disciples—who would listen to her and believe everything she told them. And she needed large events to manipulate. All gods seem to need these things.
>
> (*Talents* 7)

Larkin/Asha's critical perspective that opens the narrative in *Talents* interrupts the representation of Lauren as impartial leader of a movement at the end of *Sower,* and negates the utopian vision within the narrative by declaring it empty and artificial. She depicts her mother as a person driven by personal desires who works "hard to seduce people" (*Talents* 62), adding a ring of falsehood to Lauren's visionary ambitions. Her daughter accuses Lauren of taking advantage of people's vulnerability, physically and emotionally, when she "collects" them on her travels or when they come to seek refuge at Acorn by giving them an illusion, born by her mistaking her "fantasy for reality" (*Talents* 44). The daughter's voice reflects Butler's critical discussion of the limits of her own concept of leadership as well as the conflicting loyalties tied to it.

> I have wanted to love her and to believe that what happened between her and me wasn't her fault. I've wanted that. But instead, I've hated her, feared her, needed her. I've never trusted her though, never understood how she could be the way she was—focused, and yet so misguided, there for all the world, but never there for me. I still don't understand.
>
> (*Talents* 7-8)

The narrative significance of Larkin/Asha's estrangement from her mother surfaces in its contrast to the central role children inhabit in Butler's writing. As the lost daughter, the ideal foundation of her mother's vision, Larkin/Asha's voice disrupts the narrative voice that is intact in *Sower.* There Lauren's journal entries become the movement's history, and constitute a powerful, authentic narration. Lauren's ability to read and write enables her to formulate her goals and to make them available to her "followers," most of whom are illiterate at the time they join the community. Her skills place her in a position of mastery, as she metaphorically and actually "shapes" the voices of Earthseed's people. Yet, as Dubey points out, this does not result in social hierarchies since "the Earthseed community will erase all social distinctions deriving from literacy by ensuring all its members equal access to education" (10). Accordingly, the title of spiritual educators in Earthseed is not priest or preacher, but shaper. In *Sower,* the context of an individual's spiritual journey and endurance that resists chaos and destruction frames the concepts of Earthseed. In *Talents,* a fragmented and split narration process critically reevaluates these concepts. This disruption takes place not just in regard to the persons speaking. The positions and beliefs they hold point to the complexity of utopian imagination when Larkin/Asha criticizes her mother's authoritarian position as shaper and charges her with manipulating her role to her advantage in the service of Earthseed.

At the end of *Talents,* Earthseed, now a powerful and influential sect, launches the first shuttles to assemble a starship partly on the Moon and partly in orbit. Unable to go, Lauren is dead at 81 before the shuttle is ready to take on its journey to the stars. Lauren's final prophetic entries into her journal stand in stark contrast to Larkin/Asha's dismissal of her "long, narrow story" (*Talents* 362) as fantastic and irrelevant: "I know what I've done. I have not given them heaven, but I've helped them to give themselves the heavens. I can't give them individual immortality, but I've helped them to give our species its only chance at immortality" (*Talents* 362-3).

UTOPIAN DESIRE AND POLITICAL STRATEGIES: CONCEPTS OF AGENCY

Earthseed becomes a metaphor for a political conviction that grows into a movement. Its Destiny (space flight) is the future goal that focuses the desire, while the Earthseed principles create utopian communities in the here and now. Without creating exclusive structures that define normative behavior, morality, and self-perception that theorists like Young criticize in the concept of the traditional "ideal community," Earthseed provides a shared identity and life experience that are not based in a particular unified racial or cultural background. Above all, it provides for the survival of the human species—a crucial element throughout the two novels where Earthseed develops amidst a dystopian environment. The most powerful aspect from a feminist analysis is the concept of agency that Butler develops: the agent of change—of the utopian desire—is human, the individual in mutual relationship with a nurturing community, a partnership that allows resistance to oppressive structures. The possibility to redefine fate is not determined by a prayer to an outside power, "God" (i.e. the appeal to a higher authority, may it be the state or other social institutions or a historical determinism), but by the community themselves.

Change is the liberating element in Butler's concept of utopian desire. Change defines Earthseed and becomes its major component, as encapsulated in the phrase "God is Change." Change elevated in this manner declares "utopia" itself as a process, as something never completed. This is what makes this concept so valuable to the feminist discourse on utopian writing. The utopian locus, the world it conceptualizes, is automatically open and discursive; there is no *one* perfect community. The changing visions of people with diverse backgrounds and different experiences that need constant adapting and negotiating that constitute Butler's utopia, echo Young's unoppressive city. The binding element within this inconsistent utopian space that Butler creates is the shared notion that there *is* a better world—in what shape and in what form depends on the action of the people involved, and as a concept remains undefined. Butler constructs change not as a frightening, but as a life-affirming principle, as a hope for a self-destructive, materialistic society immobilized by static social categories. This active force of transformation in Butler's narratives defines them as open-ended utopias. Here it is the potential and its implications (and its relation to the dystopian environment that generates it) that constitutes the utopian moment and that allows for difference within a community.

In addition to the concept of change, Butler creates metaphors of boundary transgression that implicate new ways of conceptualizing difference as part of a feminist subjectivity. Lauren suffers from "hyperempathy syndrome" (*Sower* 10) that Butler's characters refer to as "sharing." This new psycho-physiological disease is caused by the abuse of either parent of the drug Paracetco, a "smart pill," before the birth of a child, and runs through both novels. A sharer experiences the physical sensations (pain as well as pleasure) of other people. Their visual and acoustic expressions, such as the sight of a person shot, and cries of pain, transmit the other's sensations onto the sharer. On their travels, Butler depicts sharing as a vulnerability, and in *Talents,* within the confines of the concentration camp, sharing is another instrument for torture since it transfers pain from other prisoners as well as pleasure from torturers onto their victims, such as during rape. Since it is next to impossible for a sharer to inflict pain on others without suffering, violence becomes only viable in self-defense. Though Butler introduces the affliction to the reader via the intimate channel of Lauren's journal

entries, the phenomenon develops from a single case into a social disease that increasingly informs personal as well as social interactions. As a physical mechanism that prohibits the disconnection and alienation from others, sharing represents the painful and pleasurable process of crossing differences and of actually *experiencing* the other's world beyond a mere willingness to *understand* it. Sharing blurs and shifts boundaries and discloses a stable, autonomous identity to be a myth—sharing becomes a symbol against the binary construction of self and other and thus constitutes a crucial metaphor for re-defining social relations in Butler's narratives, as Lauren's thoughts convey:

> But if everyone could feel everyone else's pain, who would torture? Who would cause anyone unnecessary pain? I've never thought of my problem as something that might do some good before, but the way things are, I think it would help. I wish I could give it to people. Failing that, I wish I could find other people who have it, and live among them.
>
> (*Sower* 105-6)

Earthseed's emphasis on change, the boundary crossings of sharing, and the value of diversity throughout the novels that reject the nostalgic notion of an original perfect past that the Christian fundamentalists are trying to revive (see *Talents* 23) is reminiscent of a Harawayan cyborg politics. Here the concept of change intersects with that of difference: as an inevitable principle, change can be shaped, thereby releasing difference from static identity/social politics. The metaphor of change as the center of feminist politics and theories adds a temporal aspect to what Trinh Minh-ha in *Woman, Native, Other* calls the "politics of differentiation" (82). Thus, difference is not understood as an absolute, a given, that needs to be re-positioned in relation to identity; nor is it understood to be simply an historical moment that economic and social relations create. Instead, Butler acknowledges that just as identity is not stable, so difference is a shifting constituent. The metaphor of change re-conceptualizes identity so that it "refers no more to a consistent 'pattern of sameness' than to an inconsequential patterns of otherness" (Trinh 95). Otherness, difference, becomes not an element to define oneself against, but an integral aspect of any concept of self, such as with Butler's metaphor of sharing. This position allows a debate on difference that moves beyond the immobilizing "multiculturalism" that locks difference into an exotic and safely contained other, as well as beyond the static categories of identity politics that do not allow for difference to be articulated outside a defined political agenda. Butler contributes to feminist debates on how to negotiate difference by insisting on its transforming ability and on the inability to define categories of difference and their respective roles in social relations.

The power of Butler's narratives lies, without question, in the utopian desire and the resulting visions she describes. Yet, at the same time she is critical of the implicit politics of these visions, and the element of faith involved. Through the different political strategies Lauren employs in her attempts to create Earthseed communities, Butler addresses problems feminist grass-roots movements encounter. They give complex insight into the dynamics of the issues involved: In *Sower,* there is at first no system behind Lauren's mission. She speaks about Earthseed to the people she meets, and wins over believers in the course of their journey. "She meant to make Earthseed a nationwide movement, but she had no idea how to do this" (*Talents* 141). Resistance in *Sower* manifests as pure survival, and oppression emanates from capitalism gone mad. There is no system from which the group needs to protect itself. Instead, random violence and destruction of individuals terrorize through lack of social structure.

Butler constructs Earthseed as a political metaphor in contrast to the violent rhetoric and actions of the Christian Americans in *Talents* that echo the contemporary Religious Right's ideological warfare on unassimilated others. Once the fascist regime takes over in *Talents,* the form of resistance must change. Oppression becomes systematic, and collaborators with the regime are political/ideological as well as capitalist. Reactionary fundamentalists, "Crusaders," whose excesses of violence the fascist Right government tolerates,[28] destroy and transform Acorn into a Christian re-education camp in *Talents* and turn Lauren and her people into slaves and prisoners. After the destruction of Acorn and the systematic oppression of Earthseed as a dissident sect, Lauren changes her political strategies. The vision of many small individual communities as the decentralized, flexible parts of her organization that convert their surroundings in the course of the years, "[she imagined] a Hazelnut, a Pine, a Manzanita, a Sunflower, an Almond . . ." (*Talents* 156), makes room for an organized political movement. Earthseed utilizes traditional liberal forms of political strategies including outreach projects, door to door campaigning, city hall events, and speeches at schools and universities, and the publication of *Earthseed—the Book of the Living.* Lauren initially resists the notion of winning people for her cause by impressing them through rhetoric and tactical reasoning. Later she realizes the strategic necessity to give up her insistence that religious faith precedes membership within the Earthseed community. Her contemplation echoes the concerns of political activists in how to turn their cause into a mass movement:

> I must create not a dedicated little group of followers, not only a collection of communities as I had once imagined, but a movement. I must create a new fashion in faith—a fashion that can evolve into a new religion, a new guiding force, that can help humanity to put its great energy, competitiveness, and creativity to work doing the truly vast job of fulfilling the Destiny.
>
> (*Talents* 267)

With this comes the realization that a movement needs financial resources and influence in political matters in order to achieve social change. By emphasizing issues they might find interesting, Lauren involves wealthy people who have enough political influence to protect the sect from further harassment from the Christian Americans before the Church eventually loses its power. Through these "supporters" (*Talents* 348), the movement gains in power and financial strength and eventually is in the position to actively pursue the Destiny.

Butler describes the shift from individual grassroots activism to an organized and strategic movement that includes forming alliances based on certain issues addressed in Earthseed, an important feminist tactic, also as problematic. In *Sower,* and in the beginning of *Talents,* Earthseed is a refuge for those the system oppresses. It constitutes a major site of resistance. In the final part of *Talents,* affluent new members of the movement "rescue" the disempowered, such as when Lauren is able to relocate some members of Acorn and gets them settled in safe environments provided by the supporters. On the one hand, this represents a concept of agency that empowers the disenfranchised through their negotiations with representatives of power, such as the anthropologist Anna Lowenhaupt Tsing argues in *In the Realm of the Diamond Queen.* A study on Indonesian forest tribes and their means of negotiating with colonial and postcolonial powers, this text similarly examines "the ways in which people actively engage their marginality by protesting, reinterpreting, and embellishing their exclusion" (Tsing 5). Lauren's utilization of resources of people in power, and her persuasion of them to believe in Earthseed in order to empower those at the margin, echoes this concept of a displaced agency.

On the other hand, the reader can understand the shift from small to large as a critique of feminist alliances with groups in power that compromise feminist political integrity. What began as a seemingly limitless potential to shape the world surrounding them becomes useless utilized within the context of already established power. This introduces the danger of defining and "naming" difference from privileged positions. The Earthseed community builds itself around notions of equality and fairness, yet the true element of the utopian desire, change, seems limited to those already in power. This raises the question of the "utopian form [that] is already a miscegenation of sorts, a blending of pragmatic local concerns with transcendent idealism" (Green 169). Butler in the end opts for the pragmatic solution within her utopian vision, and with that speaks to concerns within feminist grassroots movements: With whom to ally? What compromises are acceptable, what is not open for negotiation? And above all, she addresses issues of agency and the potential to seize the moment and change the world around us, the promise of "All that you touch, you change."

Notes

1. Examples of works that conceptualize the interrelation of gender identity with race and class, as well as nationality, include Higgenbotham, Nicholson, Butler and Scott, Spivak, and Trinh.

2. See Bloch.

3. The activity of both feminist activists and theorists as *writers* of feminist utopias, one example being the cultural feminist Sally Miller Gearheart, also reflects the close connection of feminist politics and literary imagination.

4. For further discussion see Bammer (160).

5. *Dawn* (1987), *Adulthood Rites* (1988), and *Imago* (1989). See, for example, Green and Haraway (1989). Articles that examine utopian aspects in *Parable of the Sower* include Dubey, Gant-Britton, and Miller.

6. For a discussion of social and political issues as they are conceptualized within feminist utopias, see: Bartkowski, Gearheart (1984), Pearson (1984, 1988), and Russ.

7. For more information see Bartkowski (6).

8. Both novels are part of a series of which the third book, *Parable of the Trickster,* is in progress.

9. The metaphor of the journey inhabits a special role in the discourse on utopia. Bartkowski claims that the realization of the utopian desire in a literary utopia is an inner journey (Bartkowski 4, 10). Butler works with this by sending her protagonist, the "carrier" of the utopian desire, on a journey, where she develops and pursues this desire.

10. One example is Gearheart (1979).

11. The most prominent and oppressive account of a patriarchal totalitarian regime in feminist science fiction is Atwood's *The Handmaid's Tale,* where Christian fundamentalists also restructure society. Atwood's narrative is one example for feminists' rejection of any society based on organized religion.

12. "They're problem-solving sessions, they're times of planning, healing, learning, creating, times of focusing, and reshaping ourselves" (*Talents* 65). The goal is to celebrate people's own agency (*Sower* 197). This organizing element of Earthseed as religion becomes, unlike in the Christian tradition that is contrasted with Earthseed especially in *Talents,* not a legitimizing tool for power structures and exclusion, but a means to discursively construct a shared future.

13. As a symbol of complete and absolute oppression Butler introduces electronic collars used on the prisoners by their tormentors, "also known as slave collars, dog collars, and choke chains" (*Talents* 80). With her devastating account of the effects of the collar on people, Butler directly comments on contemporary tendencies of using electronically controlled devices in prisons on inmates, such as the electronic belt. It is the escape from the collars that becomes Butler's most powerful metaphor in *Talents.*

14. Butler's perspective on reproductive technology of course echoes the theories Shulamith Firestone formulated over 30 years ago in *The Dialectic of Sex* (1970). Her radical envisioning of a reproduction "not of woman born" and rejection of motherhood as a liberating institution, also reflected in the utopia in Marge Piercy's *Woman on the Edge of Time* (1976), caused controversial reactions within feminist communities.

15. Dubey discusses Butler's novel in the context of African-American writing and the urban crisis, and the resulting representation of the rural folk community as "a site where integral black communities can be imaginatively restored" (1). She points out how Butler's writing on community "complicates influential current accounts of black women's literary tradition" (2) by employing scientific modes of knowing and textual forms of communication instead of the magical epistemology of "conjuring" or oral tradition that occur in the writing of influential authors like Toni Morrison and Gloria Naylor.

16. Haraway coined the term that indicates the commercially-used and socially and ideologically structured practice of science culturally manifested in semiotic systems of representation. Haraway argues that we need to resist technoscience, a complex net of economic, ideological, and political relationships defined by global capitalism, by appropriating its tools as well as its products, which both are embedded within cultural meaning.

17. In opposition to Earthseed's structures of gender equality and opposition to sexual violence, the Christian Americans are propagating gender relations based in traditional roles of strictly patriarchal Christian societies where women are considered inferior in all respects to men, and are subject to violence and punishment. Above all, a woman is never allowed to hold a position of spiritual authority, where she might influence and guide a man's fate. Lauren's role as the spiritual leader of Earthseed directly challenges the Christian values promoted by fundamentalists not only in the novels, but also in U.S. society today.

18. For example, the reproductive units in the *Xenogenesis* series consist of two males, two females, and one androgynous gender—the terms of heterosexual pleasure define sexuality, never those between the same-sexed parents, despite the "mediating" role of the neutral gender, and reproduction. In *Survivor* (1978), Butler's depiction of an alien species and cross-species reproduction do not incorporate any sexual relations outside the heterosexual matrix, either.

19. See Davis (1981) for an historical analysis of violence against African Americans in times of economic/political unrest in the U.S.

20. Lauren's name already reflects her affirmative identity as African American: Lauren Oya Olamina Bankole, the last two surnames being African names adopted by her father and her husband, respectively, in the 1970s during the Black Power movement. Her African middle name is that of a Nigerian Goddess, and her status of matriarch, as well as Earthseed's concept of growth and change, defies the notion of a white male God.

21. In Chapter 6 of *Black Atlantic,* Paul Gilroy speaks of African-American leaders drawing on the first testament for inspiration in their attempt to gain freedom for their people, from Marcus Garvey to Martin Luther King. Biblical images of the enslaved and chosen people who will be led to a promised land construct analogies between African-American leaders and Moses leading his people out of Egypt. Butler's two novels refer to this tradition with their titles (both are taken from the bible), with the importance spirituality has in Lauren's future vision, and with the Destiny in Earthseed that pronounces distant planets as the promised land.

22. See Dubey for an extensive discussion of this issue.

23. For further discussion on Butler's black female characters, see Foster, Salvaggio (1986), Shinn, and Govan.

24. One aspect that does contradict Earthseed's commitment to accepting and promoting diversity as its norm is the prohibition of expressing or following other religious systems within the community. What in *Sower* appears like a quest to persuade others of Earthseed, in *Talents* is supported by an institutionalized exclusion of other beliefs, i.e. opinions (see *Talents* 145). In her attempt to protect her utopian vision, Lauren, as the founder of Earthseed, sanctions the silencing of other believers within the community. Even though Earthseed does not aggressively and never with violence impress their belief system onto others, its politics of protection to remain a united whole gives it an exclusive frame, which stand in ironic contrast to the core of its definition: Change.

25. This issue that Butler addresses is the object of Rita Arditti's impressive book (1999) that traces the attempts of women in Argentina to locate the children of their daughters and daughters-in-law that "disappeared;" i.e. were murdered, under the military regime in the 1980s.

26. For a critical view on social and state sanctions that punish and control "bad" mothers, especially in relation to poverty and racism in the U.S., see the essay compilation *"Bad" Mother: The Politics of Blame in Twentieth-Century America.* Eds. Molly Ladd-Taylor and Lauri Umansky, and Angela Davis, Chapter 12: "Racism, Birth Control, and Reproductive Rights" in *Women, Race, and Class.*

27. Larkin/Asha's alienation partly derives from the realization that her mother is a mother to all believers in Earthseed, that she would have to share her status as Lauren's priority with the community. "I wonder what my life would have been like if my mother had found me. [. . .] How long would it have been before she put me aside for Earthseed, her other kid? [. . .] I was her weakness, Earthseed was her strength. No wonder it was her favorite" (*Talents* 265).

28. These self-organized groups that act in the name of Jarret, who denies all connection with them, are reminiscent of Hitler's SS (storm troops) in fascist Germany and of the Serbian terror troops in the Bosnian and Kosovo war.

Works Cited

Arditti, Rita. *Searching for Life: The Grandmothers of the Plaza de Mayo and the Disappeared Children of Argentina.* Berkeley: U of California P, 1999.

Atwood, Margaret. *The Handmaid's Tale.* New York: Fawcett Crest, Ballantine Books, 1986.

Bammer, Angelika. *Partial Visions: Feminism and Utopianism in the 1970s.* New York: Routledge, 1991.

Bartkowski, Frances. *Feminist Utopias.* Lincoln: U of Nebraska P, 1989.

Barr, Marleen S., ed. *Future Females: A Critical Anthology.* Bowling Green, OH: Bowling Green U Popular P, 1981.

———, Ruth Salvaggio and Richard Law. *Suzy McKee Charnas: Octavia Butler: Joan D. Vinge.* Mercer Island, WA: Starmont, 1986.

Bloch, Ernst. *The Principle of Hope.* Cambridge: MIT Press, 1986.

Bukatman, Scott. *Terminal Identity: The Virtual Subject in Postmodern Science Fiction.* Durham: Duke UP, 1993.

Butler, Judith, and Joan W. Scott, eds. *Feminists Theorize the Political.* New York: Routledge, 1992.

Butler, Octavia. *Adulthood Rites.* New York: Warner Books, 1989.

———. *Dawn.* New York: Warner Books, 1988.

———. *Imago.* New York: Warner Books, 1990.

———. *Survivor.* London: Sidgwick & Jackson (Special Edition), 1981.

Crossley, Robert. "Introduction." *Kindred.* Octavia E. Butler. Boston: Beacon, 1988. ix-xxvii.

Davis, Angela. *Women, Race, and Class.* New York: Vintage Books, 1981.

Donawerth, Jane L. and Carola A. Kolmerten. *Utopian and Science Fiction by Women: Worlds of Difference.* Liverpool: Liverpool UP, 1994.

Dubey, Madhu. "Folk and Urban Communities in African-American Women's Fiction: Octavia Butler's *Parable of the Sower.*" *Studies in American Fiction* 27 (Spring 1999): 103. (Internet print out: Expanded Academic ASAP).

Farley, Tucker. "Realities and Fictions: Lesbian Visions of Utopia." *Women in Search of Utopia: Mavericks and Mythmakers.* Ed. Ruby Rohrlich and Elaine Hoffman. New York: Schocken, 1984. 233-46.

Foster, Frances S. "Octavia Butler's Black Female Future Fiction." *Extrapolation* 23 (1982): 37-49.

Freibert, Lucy M. "World Views in Utopian Novels by Women." *Journal of Popular Culture* 17 (1983): 49-60.

Gant-Britton, Lisbeth. "Octavia Butler's *Parable of the Sower* [sic]: One Alternative to a Futureless Future." *Women of Other Worlds: Excursions through Science Fiction and Feminism.* Ed. Helen Merrick and Tess Williams. Melbourne: U of Australia P, 1999. 278-94.

Gearheart, Sally. "Future Visions: Today's Politics: Feminist Utopias in Review." *Women in Search of Utopia.* Ed. Ruby Rohrlich and Elaine Hoffman Baruch. New York: Schocken, 1984. 296-309.

———. *The Wanderground: Stories of the Hill Women.* Waterfront, MA: Persephone, 1979.

Gilroy, Paul. *Black Atlantic.* Cambridge, MA: Harvard UP, 1993.

Gomez, Jewelle. "Black Women Heroes: Here's Reality, Where's the Fiction?" *The Black Scholar* 17 (1986): 8-13.

Govan, Sandra Y. "Connections, Links, and Extended Networks: Patterns in Octavia Butler's Science Fiction." *Black American Literature Forum* 18 (1984): 82-7.

Green, Michelle. "There Goes the Neighborhood. Octavia Butler's Demand for Diversity in Utopias." *Utopian and Science Fiction by Women: Worlds of Difference.* Ed. Jane L. Donawerth and Carola A. Kolmerten. Liverpool: Liverpool UP, 1994.

Haraway, Donna. "A Manifesto for Cyborgs: Science, Technology, and Socialist Feminism in the 1980s." *Feminism/Postmodernism.* Ed. Linda Nicholson. London: Routledge, 1990. 190-233.

———. *Primate Visions: Gender, Race and Nature in the World of Modern Science.* New York: Routledge, 1989.

Higgenbotham, Evelyn Brooks. "African-American Women's History and the Metalanguage of Race." *Signs* 17 (1992): 91-114.

hooks, bell. *Yearning: Race, Gender, and Cultural Politics.* Boston: South End, 1990.

Ladd-Taylor, Molly and Lauri Umansky, eds. *"Bad" Mothers: The Politics of Blame in Twentieth-Century America.* New York: New York UP, 1998.

Lefanu, Sarah. *In the Chinks of the World Machine: Feminism and Science Fiction.* London: The Women's Press, 1988.

Lorde, Audre. *Sister Outsider.* Freedom, CA: The Crossing Press, 1984.

Merrick, Helen and Tess Williams, eds. *Women of Other Worlds: Excursions through Science Fiction and Feminism.* Melbourne: U of Australia P, 1999.

Miller, Jim. "Post-Apocalyptic Hoping: Octavia Butler's Dystopian/Utopian Vision." *Science Fiction Studies* 25 (1998): 336-60.

Moylan, Tom. "Beyond Negation: The Critical Utopias of Ursula K. Le Guin and Samuel R. Delany." *Extrapolation* 21 (1980): 236-53.

Nicholson, Linda, ed. *Feminism/Postmodernism.* London: Routledge, 1990.

Pearson, Carol. "Of Time and Revolution: Theories of Social Change in Contemporary Feminist Science Fiction." *Women in Search of Utopia: Mavericks and Mythmakers.* Ed. Ruby Rohrlich and Elaine Hoffman Baruch. New York: Schocken, 1984.

———. "Women's Fantasies and Feminist Utopias." *Frontiers* 2 (1977): 55-61.

Pfaelzer, Jean. "The Changing of the Avant Garde: The Feminist Utopia." *Science Fiction Studies* 15 (1988): 282-94.

Pryse, Marjorie and Hortense J. Spillers. *Conjuring: Black Women, Fiction, and Literary Tradition.* Bloomington: Indiana UP, 1985.

Rohrlich, Ruby and Elaine Hoffman, eds. *Women in Search of Utopia: Mavericks and Mythmakers.* New York: Schocken, 1984.

Russ, Joanna. "Recent Feminist Utopias." *Future Females: A Critical Anthology.* Ed. Marleen S. Barr. Bowling Green, OH: Bowling Green U Popular P, 1981. 71-85.

Salvaggio, Ruth "Octavia Butler and the Black Science-Fiction Heroine." *Black American Literature Forum* 8 (1984). 78-81.

———. "Octavia Butler." *Suzy McKee Charnas: Octavia Butler: Joan D. Vinge.* Ed. Marleen S. Barr, Ruth Salvaggio and Richard Law. Mercer Island, WA: Starmont, 1986.

Sandoval, Chela. "U.S. Third World Feminism: The Theory and Method of Oppositional Consciousness," *Genders* 10 (1991): 1-24.

Shinn, Thelma J. "The Wise Witches: Black Women Mentors in the Fiction of Octavia E. Butler." *Conjuring: Black Women, Fiction, and Literary Tradition.* Ed. Marjorie Pryse and Hortense J. Spillers, Bloomington: Indiana UP, 1985. 203-15.

Somay, Bulent. "Towards an Open-Ended Utopia." *Science Fiction Studies* 11 (1984): 25-38.

Spivak, Gayatri Chakravorty. *A Critique of Postcolonial Reason: Toward a History of the Vanishing Present.* Cambridge, MA: Harvard UP, 1999.

Trinh T. Minh-ha. *Woman, Native, Other.* Bloomington: Indiana UP, 1989.

Tsing, Anna Lowenhaupt. *In the Realm of the Diamond Queen.* New Jersey: Princeton, 1993.

Walker, Alice. *In Search of Our Mothers' Gardens: Womanist Prose.* San Diego: Harcourt, 1983.

Young, Iris Marion. "The Ideal of Community and the Politics of Difference." *Feminism/Postmodernism.* Ed. Linda J. Nicholson. New York: Routledge, 1990. 300-23.

Gregory Jerome Hampton and Wanda M. Brooks (essay date July 2003)

SOURCE: Hampton, Gregory Jerome and Wanda M. Brooks. "Octavia Butler and Virginia Hamilton: Black Women Writers and Science Fiction." *English Journal* 92, no. 6 (July 2003): 70-4.

[*In the essay below, Hampton and Brooks explore themes of alienation, marginalization, and African-American identity in the works of Butler and Virginia Hamilton.*]

African American literature has always had elements of what many would refer to as science fiction. As is common in a significant number of books written by and about African Americans, science fiction has historically been focused on narratives of the alienated and/or marginalized "other." In African American literature for children and adults, many authors approach the themes of alienation and "otherness" through the genres of historical and realistic fiction as well as biography. The genre of science fiction, acting as a voice that reminds humanity of the depth of alienation experienced by countless people of color, is less often chosen. In the minds of many, it appears that science fiction is equated with robots and distant planets inhabited by aliens. Despite the lack of black characters in books of this sort, the association is a straightforward one; where there is a discussion of alienation, the unknown and "otherness," there is an analogous link to the African American experience. This link, however, has not proven to be a strong impetus for the publication of science fiction novels written about and/or by African Americans. There is a scarcity of published works in books traditionally classified for adult readers, and there are even fewer made available yearly for teenagers and children.

Among the small but growing number of African American writers of science fiction, Octavia Butler and Virginia Hamilton are two worthy of mention. These authors are unique because their books examine the connections between the stories of a culture and the genre of science fiction. Butler, typically classified as a writer for teenagers and adults, and Hamilton, well known as a children's author, are both individuals who masterfully locate and translate cultural experiences through science fiction stories.

THE WRITERS

Over the past three decades Octavia Butler has written eleven novels appropriate for high school and/or college readers: ***Patternmaster, Mind of My Mind, Survivor, Kindred, Wild Seed, Clay's Ark, Dawn, Adulthood Rites, Imago, Parable of the Sower*** and ***Parable of the Talents***; and a collection of short stories, ***Bloodchild and Other Stories.*** She has received both the Hugo Award and the Nebula Award, the highest honors in the genre of science fiction, in addition to establishing herself as a permanent fixture in the libraries of sci-fi fanatics all over the world. Butler was a young girl when she decided to try her hand at becoming a writer. She grew up in a segregated America and was fortunate to overcome the myth that the profession of writing was reserved for white men. After being exposed to science fiction that did not include images of African Americans or particularly well-written storylines, Butler decided to produce her own version of literature. About her writing, she says, "I write about people who do extraordinary things. It just turned out that it was called science fiction" (***Bloodchild*** 145). Her prose is fluid and inviting, devoid of convoluted, esoteric techno-gibberish found in some of the more "traditional" examples of sci-fi.

Butler's fiction has transcended its way far beyond juvenile literature into what might be referred to as mature African American literature. As a fifty-three-year-old black woman who has overcome dyslexia, elements of racist America, and the myriad obstacles in the publication process, Butler has become a person who does extraordinary things. In no uncertain terms, she has opened the door to the genre of science fiction for the African American novelist and theorist via the fundamental questions of the alienated and marginalized "other."

About the same time that Butler published her first novel, Virginia Hamilton entered the world of science fiction writers for children. Interestingly enough, prior to and after publishing her science fiction works, Hamilton wrote in varied genres. Part of her success as a writer derives from her ability to constantly cross genre and subject matter boundaries. Her genres of choice were often those infrequently selected by African American authors who write for young people. In addition to realistic and historical fiction, Hamilton has written magical realism, mysteries, folktales, myths, and science fiction. Her three science fiction novels, commonly read in the upper elementary or middle school grades, include *Justice and Her Brothers, Dustland,* and *The Gathering.*

In her books Hamilton frequently creates plots that are infused with historical content, and she brings to life characters who are dually situated in multiple time periods. Hamilton explains, "The time motif goes through many of my books. I have been trying to find ways to say that we carry our past with us wherever we go, even though we are not aware of it" (Apseloff 209). Hamilton's reverence for writing about the past and future simultaneously allows her to reveal the ways in which cultural traditions are transmitted intergenerationally. Keeping cultural traditions alive through her writing is one of the underlying focal points of Hamilton's craft.

In 1974 Hamilton was the first African American awarded a John Newbery Medal. From there, she was subsequently honored with a collection of significant literary awards in the field of children's literature. In fact, in 1992 she accepted the Hans Christian Andersen Medal, a prize given to her in recognition of her entire body of written work (Mikkelsen 67). Throughout her illustrious career, Hamilton wrote over thirty books for children and young adults. She is extremely rare as a children's author because many of her works challenge the norms and standards of books typically created for young readers. Indeed, her genres are often blurred; her writing style is sophisticated, and her subject matter complex. Nonetheless, the literary world and youth continue to gravitate toward her books.

Writers of science fiction like Octavia Butler and Virginia Hamilton entered a genre that is still being defined by contemporary history and the imagination of its contributors. It is this dynamic generic structure that allowed Butler and Hamilton to write science fiction stories that challenge commonly accepted mainstream characteristics. Robots, time travel, life in the future, and the lives of extraterrestrial beings (a figure of the "other" in general) are usually understood to connote science fiction. Butler's and Hamilton's books are somewhat different because they present unique ways to imagine and ultimately to understand the body and its plethora of identities. Their work allows alienation to be imagined outside of the traditional definitions of the term. These authors present the concepts of time travel

and life in the past or future by creating characters who live in worlds where evolution is not robotically or technologically influenced. As the following analysis of excerpts from Butler's and Hamilton's stories demonstrates, the worlds created by these authors are ones where the issue of alienation exists, more profoundly, in the hearts and minds of individual characters. In addition, these characters possess the innate ability to evolve into beings who celebrate and explore, rather than distance, the "Other."

BUTLER'S SCIENCE FICTION

Butler's "Patternmaster" Series takes the reader on a journey of genesis filled with shape-shifters and non-material entities who manipulate their material and spiritual worlds in order to create a new race of people or an "other." The book of genesis for the "Patternmaster" Series is *Wild Seed.* Very much like the biblical Book of Genesis, *Wild Seed* is the beginning of a creation story and the introduction of a patriarch and matriarch, Doro and Anyanwu.

Anyanwu is a black woman who possesses the ability to take the shape of any animal (human or beast) whom she understands genetically or intuitively. Such understanding is obtained by visual assessment or by ingesting the flesh of an animal and simply reproducing its genetic structure and physical form. In explaining her ability to Doro, Anyanwu says:

> . . . I could see what the leopard was like. I could mold myself into what I saw. I was not a true leopard, though, until I killed one and ate a little of it. At first, I was a woman pretending to be a leopard—clay molded into leopard shape. Now when I change, I am a leopard.
>
> (80)

A more accurate assessment of what Anyanwu becomes after tasting the flesh of an animal and imitating its form externally and internally is something very similar to Doro: an essence of an individual in the shell of a temporary body. Thus, it is this act of incorporation of another body and becoming that body that is at the foundation of the questions that act as primary engines for the entire series. Is the body dependent or independent of the notion of essence or self? Does the identity and existence of a person necessarily begin and end with a material body? In Butler's fiction the body matters because it extends far beyond flesh and bone; the body becomes a boundless edifice for the articulation of "otherness."

Butler places Doro in the role of a complicated patriarch. Doro's character is not formulated from simplistic binary perspectives. He is never portrayed in the narrative as being completely evil or good. Doro is presented as a complicated and ambiguous persona focused on accomplishing his goals with the least amount of resistance and interference from his charges.

The reader does, however, learn by the third paragraph of chapter one that Doro cannot be completely or simply human. Wandering from the village, being pulled by an unexplained awareness, Doro "was killed several times—by disease, by animals, and by hostile people . . . Yet he continued to move southwest . . ." (80). Thus, Doro's existence is independent of the birth or death of body, but is dependent upon the inhabitation of body for life. This phenomenon raises the question of who or what Doro is and how his identity is constructed.

Doro's identity is independent of flesh and bone. The body for Doro can act as a disposable mobile home to be used primarily for reproduction and transportation, not completely dissimilar to that of a "normal" person. His physical identity changes depending on the body he inhabits, but his "essence" remains constant:

> He was like an *ogbanje,* an evil child spirit born to one woman again and again, only to die and give the mother pain. A woman tormented by an *ogbanje* could give birth many times and still have no living child. But Doro was an adult. He did not enter and re-enter his mother's womb. He did not want the bodies of children. He preferred to steal the bodies of men.
>
> (12)

In the above passage Anyanwu identifies Doro as something from the spirit world that manifests only as body, in or among the world of bodies, without being only one body. Anyanwu questions her hypothesis because Doro is an adult and does not live in the womb of mothers. But as the narrative unfolds we learn that Doro does indeed operate largely through and from the reproductive systems of women and men.

Butler's *Xenogenesis* Series (*Dawn, Adulthood Rites, Imago*) goes one step further by introducing the post-apocalyptic humanity to gene traders who rewrite gender and sexuality with a third gender. The second and third books in the *Xenogenesis* Series suggest the argument that ambiguity in regard to identity can be both empowering and necessary for survival. Through a close examination of Butler's characters Akin (one of the first human/Oankali constructs) and Jodahs (the first third sex human/Oankali construct), the importance of ambiguity in regard to race, gender, and human identity is shown to be immeasurable. The ability of both characters, human-Oankali constructs, to act as go-betweens and bridges between human and nonhuman difference suggests a new way of thinking about the figure of a multiple-referenced identity. Akin's ability to understand humanity's need to survive independently and Jodahs's ability to shape and color its body to please its partners all suggest that being in a state of ambiguity is a positive attribute that should be sought after instead of avoided.

As introduced in the above analysis, Octavia Butler's fiction presents methods of imagining the body that allow us to question how and why we must be categorized as male, female, black, white, or "other." From this window readers of her work are better able to explore the meaning of various concepts such as alienation and marginalization and various identities such as race and gender. These terms are seen for what they are, arbitrary markers designed to give stability to that which is unstable and ambiguous. Science fiction is the window Butler uses to open the imagination of readers to the construction of "otherness" by painting the fantastic as the realistic.

In an interview with Rosalie G. Harrison, Butler says that in the standard science fiction novel the "universe is either green or all white" (Harrison 30-34). In such literature the "extraterrestrial being" or "alien" is used as metaphor and literal embodiment of the other. Butler, on the other hand, locates highly visual (race, sex, or species) and non-visual (gender and sexuality) identities at the center of her text and forces the reader to grapple with the notion of "otherness" as more than a metaphor of allusion.

HAMILTON'S SCIENCE FICTION

Hamilton's "Justice" Trilogy—*Justice and Her Brothers, Dustland,* and *The Gathering*—is an intriguing collection of African American children's literature because it writes black children into a future that does not seem to be concerned with the racial differences of the twentieth century. Justice Douglass and her twin brothers, Thomas and Levi, along with a neighbor named Dorian, form what is referred to as the "unit." Relying on an understanding of their own "otherness" and feeling somewhat alienated from their friends and family, the three adolescents travel beyond their physical bodies to an apocalyptic Earth on a mission to save humanity with their special collective abilities.

The East African proverb "I am because we are; We are because I am" plays a significant role in the thematic structure of the Justice series. Eleven-year-old Justice is the "watcher" and leader of the unit. As the watcher, she holds the ability to initiate the transportation of the unit from the present to the future. Her character might be interpreted as the village griot or an individual with the role of observing and recording historical events. Justice's ability to observe the present and predict the past enables her to manifest the future. As the unit gathers around an old buckeye tree (firmly rooted in the past), the individuals are transported mentally beyond their bodies into a forward (re)memory navigated by Justice.

Justice's older brothers, Thomas and Levi, at thirteen, further the communal metaphor of the series in that they are psychically bonded twins. Thomas is an aggressive clairvoyant with powerful telepathic ability and a speech impediment, while Levi is a sickly hypersympathetic victim who bears the pain for the entire unit. More importantly, Levi is bullied and used as a tool to weaken the unit by Thomas, who is filled with an irrational sibling jealousy toward his younger sister, Justice.

Dorian, the healer for the unit and not a biological family member, serves as a seemingly older and rational sibling. When there is injury in the unit, he manages to provide the appropriate bandage or cure. Dorian completes a family unit that is not traditionally Western in its structure. As Justice is the leader and consequently the most powerful member of the unit, the family takes the form of a matriarchy.

Like Butler's Doro and Anyanwu, Justice and her brother Thomas act as obstacles to one another throughout the series. In *Justice and Her Brothers,* Thomas is an embittered soul who is incomplete without his brother Levi and his sister Justice, but he has not yet come to understand their connection as a family and a unit. The immature and jealous Thomas takes every opportunity to use his abilities to gain all the power a little black boy can handle in his neighborhood, even to the point of terrorizing his brother Levi through mental manipulation:

> I'll take away the bars [in your mind] and everything and we'll continue this talk later. But you'll say what I want to Mom. Because I know who has to be keeping me from Justice.
>
> (166)

Because he can enter and control the mind of anyone he chooses, Thomas suffers from the same sort of god-complex as Doro. Levi becomes a trickstermask that Thomas wears to veil his speech impediment and any other insecurity that might limit his power. Justice ultimately establishes herself as the most powerful and clever of the two by winning "The Great Snake Race," utilizing a tool that Thomas did not consider (196). The snake that Justice captures for the race is pregnant and consequently gives birth to the largest number of snakes in the contest. Levi admits, "There's no rule I know of against having lots of babies . . . Tice [Justice], I guess you win The Great Snake Race!" (246). Through motherhood and mother-wit, Justice outwits her would-be enslaver and misguided older brother.

The rivalry between Justice and Thomas continues throughout the series until their encounter with the machines and "Slakers" of the Dustlands of the future. In both *Dustland* and *The Gathering* Hamilton's references to the African American experience and issues of alienation and "otherness" are subtle yet apparent. The unit is constructed of talented but marginalized characters who are dependent on the survival of their family. Each member plays an integral role in the success or failure of their mission to ensure the existence of extended family (humanity) in the speculative future.

For Hamilton the highest goal for humanity is survival by any means necessary, but mainly by accepting difference and acknowledging the inevitability and omnipotence of change. The synchronization of humanity is an impossibility not worthy of pursuit in the "Justice" Trilogy, primarily because sameness is not in Hamilton's definition of a better world. As the three books seem to suggest, sameness, or conformity, does not ensure the survival of a species in a hostile environment. In fact, the ability to change and adapt to nonconformity is often essential if a character wishes to survive. Notwithstanding this fact, Hamilton constructs communities dependent upon individuals and individuals dependent upon communities.

CONCLUSION

Whether written for adults or children, African American literature has sought to express the humanity of black people through narratives of struggle, adaptation, and survival. Many African American authors, like Butler and Hamilton, share in their desire to translate the lasting effects of one of the most fundamental motifs at the root of much, if not all, African American literature: the alienation and marginalization of a people through the possession and transportation of their bodies for free or cheap labor.

Through their reinterpretation of the issues of alienation and marginalization, Octavia Butler and Virginia Hamilton have forged a path in a genre that is prime for African American exploration. "Otherness" is posited in Butler and Hamilton's science fiction narratives as functions of difference and likeness that demonstrate both the flaws and strengths in human behavior. The genre of science fiction is the new frontier for African American literature that might lead to a more critical view of the past and a future that dismantles the concepts of alienation and marginalization, while it reinterprets the meaning of "otherness."

Works Cited

Apseloff, Marilyn. "A Conversation with Virginia Hamilton." *Children's Literature* 14 (1983): 204-13.

Butler, Octavia. *Adulthood Rites.* New York: Warner, 1988.

———. *Bloodchild and Other Stories.* New York: Four Walls Eight Windows, 1995.

———. *Clay's Ark.* New York: Warner, 1984.

———. *Dawn.* New York: Warner, 1987.

———. *Imago.* New York: Warner, 1989.

———. *Kindred.* Boston: Beacon, 1979.

———. *Mind of My Mind.* Garden City, NY: Doubleday, 1977.

———. *Parable of the Sower.* New York: Four Walls Eight Windows, 1993.

———. *Parable of the Talents.* New York: Seven Stories Press, 1998.

———. *Patternmaster.* New York: Warner, 1976.

———. *Survivor.* New York: Doubleday, 1978.

———. *Wild Seed.* New York: Warner, 1980.

Hamilton, Virginia. *Dustland.* San Diego: Harcourt Brace Jovanovich, 1980.

———. *The Gathering.* New York: Scholastic, 1981.

———. *Justice and Her Brothers.* New York: Scholastic, 1978.

Harrison, Rosalie G. "Sci-Fi Visions: An Interview with Octavia Butler." *Equal Forum.* Nov. 1980: 30-34.

Mikkelsen, Nina. "Virginia Hamilton: Continuing the Conversation." *The New Advocate* 8.2 (1995): 67-81.

Brian K. Reed (essay date 2003)

SOURCE: Reed, Brian K. "Behold the Woman: The Imaginary Wife in Octavia Butler's *Kindred.*" *CLA Journal* 47, no. 1 (2003): 66-74.

[*In the following essay, Reed focuses on the portrayal of Dana Franklin, the main character in Butler's* Kindred.]

In Ralph Ellison's novel *Invisible Man,* when the narrator descends into his marijuana-induced dreamworld, he meets a former slave who tells him that she both loved and hated her master. The narrator replies, "I too have become acquainted with ambivalence. . . . That's why I'm here."[1] Dana Franklin, the time traveler in Octavia Butler's novel ***Kindred,*** could have explained her presence in the antebellum South in the same way. More than her need to save the life of her great grandfather Rufus Weylin, is her need to resolve the contradictory feelings about her marriage that brings her to this troubled era in American history. Rufus Weylin and Alice Greenwood allow Dana to participate in a drama which is distant enough from her own life to be nonthreatening and yet close enough to be relevant, a drama in which she works out a conflict in her feelings toward her husband, a conflict which she has previously evaded because it was too sensitive for her to face directly.

Dana's relationship with Rufus is a journey from evasion to decision. When she has her first conversation with him, it is easy to ignore the conflict between her feelings for the child and her concern for the slaves on his father's plantation. The abuse he describes having suffered at the hands of his father helps her to associate him less with this cruel man than with his slaves. The welts on Rufus' back, marks from his father's most recent lashing, suggest this connection, especially when Rufus mentions that the stripes were administered with the same whip his father uses on "niggers and horses."[2] Having watched his father sell a horse he loved, he may have some sympathy for people who have had family members or loved ones sold away from them.

However, as Rufus grows older, it becomes increasingly difficult to ignore the conflict her feelings for him create:

> I thought of Rufus and his father, of Rufus becoming his father. It would happen someday in at least one way. Someday Rufus would own the plantation. Someday he would be the slaveholder, responsible in his own right for what happened to the people who lived in those half-hidden cabins. The boy was literally growing up as I watched—growing up because I watched and because I helped keep him safe.
>
> (77)

Though she is not ready to give up this friendship, now she must do more to justify taking care of this child who would some day own her ancestors:

> And I would try to keep friendship with him, maybe plant a few ideas in his mind that would help both me and the people who would be his slaves in the years to come. I might even be making things easier for Alice.
>
> (77)

When Dana tells Kevin about her plan to help the slaves by shaping Rufus' ideas, Kevin warns, "You're gambling. Hell, you're gambling against history" (95). Ashraf H. A. Rushdy notes:

> By becoming an agent capable of transforming history, Dana becomes to the same degree subject to history—one who is liable to be transformed by seemingly dead historical forces. When she gambles against history, in other words, she can also lose to history.[3]

When she unintentionally brings Kevin with her on her third trip to the plantation, Dana wonders about the transforming effect history might have on him. While she is trying to teach Rufus to think like Kevin, Kevin might be learning to think like Rufus' father. When Kevin assures her that he "wouldn't be in the danger [she] would be in" (88), Dana worries, "But he'd be in another kind of danger. . . . If he was stranded here for years, some part of this place would rub off on him" (88). Even more threatening is the effect history might have on her. It is not only the children she is concerned about when she sees them playing "slave auction." She observes, "The ease. Us, the children . . . I never realized how easily people could be trained to accept slavery" (119).

In this psychological battle Dana is more vulnerable than the other blacks on the property, for her enemy is not fear but complacency, a more subtle villain whose weapons are not the chain and the lash but privilege and favor. Whether or not her friendship with Rufus succeeds in making the lives of the slaves easier, it undoubtedly does so for her own. The breakfasts he shares with her are the clearest example of this special treatment. As she and Rufus talk genially over the morning meal, much more sumptuous fare than slaves commonly enjoy, Rufus remarks, "Daddy'd do some cussin' if he came in here and found us eating together" (160), words which indicate that he knows that with Dana he has strayed far from the traditional master-slave relationship.

Unfortunately, a smooth relationship with Rufus means a troubled one with Alice. Seeing Dana getting along so well with Alice's tormentor drives Alice into occasional outbursts of disgust. It is as if Rufus forces Dana to be the "white nigger" (193) that Alice calls her when he manipulates Dana into serving as emissary for his sexual tyranny by threatening to have Alice beaten if Dana does not persuade her to come to him without compulsion. Though Dana is merely trying to save Alice from another lashing, a part of her understands only that she is sending Alice to Rufus as an unwilling object of his lust. The awful message Dana carries in her heart, unable to find the words to express, makes her deeply sensitive to Alice's hostility as Alice derides her for grieving over her missing white husband. When Alice again calls her a "white nigger" (199), Dana cannot bring herself to respond. After Dana finally manages to tell Alice about Rufus' heartless demand, Alice spits, "I ought to take a knife in there with me and cut his damn throat" (202). Something inside Dana tells her that this is what she should be doing instead of helping Rufus exploit her friend. As Alice storms at Dana with the fury she longs to unleash on Rufus, Dana's silence is so startling that Alice is compelled to ask, "What's the matter with you? . . . Why you let me run you down like that? . . . Why you let me talk about you so bad?" (202-03). Somewhere inside herself Dana knows that her tongue is bound with cords not of forbearance but of shame.

Perhaps even more than Rufus's perfidy in not mailing Dana's letters to Kevin after promising to do so, is this shame that makes Dana decide to try to escape. When she is caught and mercilessly whipped, she senses that her defeat has more meaning than she wants to face. Tasting the true barbarity of slavery for the first time, she does not know whether she has the strength to endure the brutality the other slaves face. Though she tells herself that she will try again to escape, the thoughts she tries to bar from her mind tell her she is losing her gamble with history. *"See how easily slaves are made?* they said" (215). In this defeat she feels she

has failed not only herself but Alice and the other slaves as well. As she resumes the relatively easy life which friendship with Rufus brings her, she finds it difficult to look her fellow blacks in the eye. Regarding one occasion when she quietly left the cookhouse rather than endure their hostile glances and disdainful silence, she reflects, "I wondered why I crept away like that. Why hadn't I fought back?" (269). As when Alice asked a similar question, deep inside she knows the answer.

The contrast in Rufus's treatment of these two women suggests that they serve two distinct yet equally important roles in his life. He gives a clue to these roles when, a little drunk after visiting friends, he sees Alice and Dana sitting together and remarks, "Behold the woman. . . . You really are only one woman. Did you know that?" (277). With these words Rufus reveals that he has found a way to have Alice as he truly wants her. Not content with her body, Rufus wants a part of her that slavery cannot claim—her heart. He dreams of possessing her not through concubinage but through marriage, a dream that is unrealizable not only because it would be illegal in the antebellum South, but also because Alice despises him. Yet if he cannot be married to her in reality, he is determined to be married to her in his mind. He uses Dana's friendship and the similarity in appearance between the two women to make this fantasy seem real. Alice nearly solves this mystery as she observes, "He likes me in bed, and you out of bed, and you and I look alike if you can believe what people say. . . . Anyway, all that means we're two halves of the same woman—at least in his crazy head" (279-80). These two halves become Rufus's perfect whole. By pretending that Alice and Dana are one woman, a woman he makes love to at night and chats with pleasantly over breakfast the next morning, he tricks himself into believing that this woman is his wife.

Rufus's imaginary marriage parallels Dana and Kevin's real one, suggesting Dana's secret resentment toward her husband. Though she knows Kevin is a compassionate, fair-minded man, a part of her cannot see beyond his whiteness. This irrational part of her holds him responsible for every injustice committed by a white person against a black. Unable to see him as a loving husband, this person inside her transforms him instead into an evil, raping slaveholder. Thus the narrator is both Dana, the contented wife, and Alice, the unwilling concubine. Like the real Alice, this inner Alice represents to Dana every black person who has ever been abused by a white, thus accusing Dana of betraying her race by getting too close to a white man.

Dana's mounting self-contempt is reflected in the increasing sharpness of Alice's contumely. The more pressure Rufus puts on Alice to be like Dana, the more bitterly Alice reviles Dana. When Rufus talks of freeing Alice's children, Alice surmises what he wants in return and finds in it an opportunity to take another verbal slap at her fellow captive. She seethes, "He wants me to like him. . . . Or maybe even love him. I think he wants me to be more like you!" (284). Explaining to Dana why she must run away, Alice snaps, "I got to go before I turn into what you are!" (287). Hearing no response to this venom, Sarah becomes the third character to wonder at Dana's passivity in the face of such hostility. The question she asks is essentially the same question Alice once asked Dana, the question Dana once asked herself: "What you let her talk to you like that for? She can't get away with nobody else" (287). Dana's introspection brings her close to the answer: "I didn't know. Guilt, maybe. In spite of everything, my life was easier than hers. Maybe I tried to make up for that by taking her abuse" (288).

Yet it is not only the contrast between Alice's suffering and Dana's privilege that causes Dana to look inward with a scornful eye; it is also Alice's refusal to be vanquished by her suffering. Missy Dehn Kubitschek writes, "To a certain extent, each woman feels the other's choices as a critique of her own; each sees, in the distorting mirror of the other, her own potential face."[4] Just as Alice sees in Dana the person she is afraid she might become, Dana sees in Alice the person she flagellates herself for failing to be. When she hears of Alice's plans to run away again, Dana feels the same self-reproach she felt when Alice spoke of using a knife on Rufus. Though Dana is at first reluctant to help Alice escape, protesting that the children are too young to face such hardship, Alice perceives enough of Dana's secret torment to be confident of her assistance. When Dana threatens to stop caring about what happens to her, Alice sneers, "You'll care. And you'll help me. Else, you'd have to see yourself for the white nigger you are, and you couldn't stand that" (288).

However, the true test of Dana's blackness is not whether or not she will help Alice gain freedom, but whether or not she can embrace Alice's passion for freedom. While the horrors of the plantation have taught Dana how easily slaves are made, perhaps Alice's willfulness has reminded her of Frederick Douglass' famous chiasmus: "You have seen how a man was made a slave; now you shall see how a slave was made a man,"[5] words with which he introduces his narration of the moment he chooses to fight rather than endure a beating. When Dana thinks of these two defiant spirits, perhaps she wonders how much dehumanization it would take to make her use her concealed weapon. The sale of Sam triggers an incident that tells Dana she will soon learn the answer to this question. When Rufus strikes her for interfering with the transaction, he releases a side of himself he has previously shown to Alice but never to Dana. Dana knows that this physical brutality is a mere harbinger of the sexual brutality that has also been part of Alice's misery. Slashing her wrists

is Dana's way of gaining respite in which to examine herself in preparation for this other, more sinister Rufus.

Dana is relieved to find herself transported back to her own century with her husband. This time, Kevin's absence from the stress of the plantation allows her to clarify her thoughts. At one point she hopes Kevin will relieve her of the responsibility of the dreadful decision she must make; however, their exchange only emphasizes what a terrible thing killing would be:

> "Kevin, tell me what you want me to do."
>
> He looked away, saying nothing. I gave him several seconds, but he kept silent.
>
> ". . . Kevin, if you can't even say it, how can you expect me to do it?"
>
> (298)

The full weight of this responsibility presses heavily on Dana's shoulders when she discovers the body hanging in the barn upon her return to antebellum Maryland. Her bones ache not only with the agony of confronting the appalling consequence of her complicity with cruelty, but also with the realization that without Alice, Rufus is even more certain to come to her with his sexual demands. Alice's death helps Dana to clarify her inescapable decision. Now she begins to sort out her confused feelings toward the two men in her life, for now in her mind the slaveholder begins to disentangle himself from the husband. Though she is still distressed by the thought of killing another human being, this new clarity of thought makes the alternative seem more revolting than ever. To surrender her body to the man who made Alice's life so miserable and brief would be a betrayal more vile than anything she has done since her time travels began. She feels she owes it to Alice to do for her what Alice once wished aloud she could do for herself. By killing herself, Alice has found new life in Dana's soul.

Though possessed by the will of her fallen friend, Dana also fears her soul's fierce new inmate, whose fingers lust for the feel of the knife handle. She dreads more than ever the agonizing choice she must make, for she is afraid to release this wrathful energy inside her. When she observes Rufus fondling a pistol as if contemplating suicide, once again she hopes to be relieved of the terrible responsibility she bears. When Rufus fails to pull the trigger, like Kevin he leaves the burden with her.

This responsibility is manifest the moment Rufus grabs her with lust in his eyes. His words have more meaning than he intends when he says, "It's up to you" (318). Dana tries to deny what is ineluctably hers. "No, God-dammit, it isn't! Keeping you alive has been up to me for too long! Why didn't you shoot yourself when you started to? I wouldn't have stopped you!" (318). Even now the debate rages in her mind. "I realized how easy it would be for me to continue to be still and forgive him even this. So easy, in spite of all my talk. But it would be so hard to raise the knife, drive it into the flesh I had saved so many times. So hard to kill . . ." (319).

As Dana finally forces herself to use the knife, she is more aware than ever of how much a part of her Rufus has become. When she is transported back to her own time, she has paid a monstrous price, a price that goes deeper than the part of her arm that is left joined to the wall, a price that includes the part of her heart that is lost with it.

Yet for this price she has begun to heal the wound in her marriage. In David Bradley's novel *The Chaneysville Incident,* John Washington, who struggles with conflicting feelings in his own interracial relationship, says it is important to understand history "so you hate the right things for the right reasons."[6] In her journey into history, Dana has learned to redirect her hatred from her husband, whose only crime is being white, to the slaveholder, who represents the true oppressors of her race. In killing Rufus she has satisfied the secret rage she has harbored against Kevin, for she has slain the monster who has inhabited his form.

Notes

1. Ralph Ellison, *Invisible Man* (New York: Random, 1992) 10.

2. Octavia Butler, *Kindred* (New York: Simon, 1979) 23. Hereafter cited parenthetically in the text by page number(s) only.

3. Ashraf H. A. Rushdy, "Families of Orphans: Relation and Disrelation in Octavia Butler's *Kindred,*" *College English* 55 (1993): 145.

4. Missy Dehn Kubitschek, *Claiming the Heritage: African-American Women Novelists and History* (Jackson: UP of Mississippi, 1991) 39.

5. Frederick Douglass, *The Oxford Frederick Douglass Reader,* ed. William L. Andrews (New York: Oxford UP, 1996) 65.

6. David Bradley, *The Chaneysville Incident* (New York: Harper, 1981) 274.

Alison Tara Walker (essay date spring 2005)

SOURCE: Walker, Alison Tara. "Destabilizing Order, Challenging History: Octavia Butler, Deleuze and Guattari, and Affective Beginnings." *Extrapolation* 46, no. 1 (spring 2005): 103-19.

[In this essay, Walker explores hierarchy's role in two sets of theories: within the theory of evolution as presented in Butler's novels, and within the ideas of Gilles Deleuze and Pierre-Félix Guattari.]

The world is full of origin stories—tales of the world's genesis. Whether in the form of myths passed down through generations or as scientific theories that order the world, the desire to understand the origins of life on Earth remains constant. In her science fiction trilogy, *Xenogenesis [Dawn, Adulthood Rites, Imago]* Octavia Butler posits an alternate origin chronicle for Earth. Written in the mid-nineteen-eighties, *Xenogenesis* draws on traditions of post-apocalyptic and origin narratives as humans cross-breed with an alien species in order to repopulate Earth. Butler challenges and revises other foundational stories by framing hers within the format of a slave narrative—making a marginalized textual format the heart of her book and the impetus for Earth's new population. At the same time, *Xenogenesis* questions and reevaluates contemporary scientific principles of evolution and natural history by presenting alternate forms of generation and descent. By placing a black woman as the origin for the new species on Earth, and creating alien forms of filiation, Butler questions evolutionary models and highlights natural history's racist and sexist underpinnings.

Like Butler, theorists Gilles Deleuze and Felix Guattari emphasize alternate theories of species' development and generation in their essay, "Becoming-Intense, Becoming-Animal, Becoming-Imperceptible." Deleuze and Guattari question natural history's reliance on "the sum and value of differences," and instead propose a rupture within natural history that makes room for a jump from "A to x" not just "A to B" (234). In their essay, Deleuze and Guattari also counter filial and descent-based evolution's long, straight line and instead propose a theory of 'involution' and 'becoming,' focusing on a more affective, rhizomatic theory of generation. The emergence of alternate theories of species formation and development that Butler and Deleuze and Guattari propose leave the hierarchy of evolution and natural history behind to initiate and become something completely dissimilar than Darwin and Linnaeus could imagine; the recontextualization of evolutionary and origin narratives provide a space whereby alternate—oftentimes subversive—origins can be imagined.

In this paper, I examine Deleuze and Guattari's, and Butler's interrogation and reconsideration of evolutionary structures; I trace the ways that both Butler, and Deleuze and Guattari reposition such a discussion from the realm of strict scientific hierarchy into one devoid of rigid categories and hierarchical groupings. More specifically, both authors place species fruition in the realm of affect—one of metaphor and feeling—creating "spaces of affect" in which these new evolutionary processes take place (Stivale 160). Charles J. Stivale defines "spaces of affect" as places that take on the "forms" and "feelings" associated with affect (164). These spaces arise through intensive communicatory practices and interactions. Both Butler, and Deleuze and

Guattari create such affective spaces within their stories and through the constructions of their narratives. In the case of *Xenogenesis,* the alien Oankali generate such spaces through which genetic transfers and exchanges between groups can be made, fashioning new species that are neither human nor alien, all spawning from Lilith, a black woman. Genetic exchange and scientific practice, from healing to informational trading, take place within a space governed not by scientific models, but instead by pleasure and desire—all occurring within an affective, metaphorical space. Thus, evolution and natural history move to a space not already mapped out and categorized, but one that becomes generative of new possibilities.

A History of Natural History and Evolution

The beginnings of natural history can be traced to the Renaissance concept of the great chain of being, which saw all life on earth involved in a linear procession from a God-head at its highest point to the simplest of organisms at the bottom. In the 18th Century scientists like Linneaus begin to classify plants and place them within systematic groupings. Far from being merely a scientific catalogue, providing a composite list of flora and fauna, such a system orders the world—specifically in terms of what should be considered "natural" and "abnormal." Theorists from Mary Louise Pratt to Michel Foucault interrogate the foundation of such systems by highlighting the ways in which natural history came about.[1] Mary Louise Pratt traces the conception of natural history: beginning with Linnaeus' catalogues of various plants and people, and examines natural history's colonialist underpinnings. In addition to providing a litmus test as to the normality of the world, natural history, as Mary Louise Pratt argues, is inherently a colonialist project. Linnaeus' system, as Pratt defines it, is:

> designed to classify all the plants on the earth, known and unknown, according to the characteristics of their reproductive parts [. . .] all the plants on earth, Linnaeus claimed, could be incorporated into this single system of distinctions, including any yet unknown to Europeans.

> (Pratt 24-25)

I want to underscore one concept from Pratt's critique: Linnaeus' system does not only categorize that which is already present, but anticipates all other plants will be the same as those in Europe, thus cataloguing, and making sense of any future discoveries as well within an European model. Such a system relies on the 18th Century's colonialist voyages, and attempts to "'naturalize' the myth of European superiority" by centralizing masculine, European authority and knowledge (32). This leads to what Foucault calls natural history's reduction of "the whole area of the visible to a

system of variables all of whose values can be designated, if not by a quantity, at least by a perfectly clear and always finite description" (28). Natural history then, codifies distinctions between various species, but also—especially as Linnaeus moves on to classify people as well as plants—designates which plants, and beings, are superior, creating a linear imagining of the chain of human and plant existence.[2]

Linnaeus' distinctions between plants and animals affect racial divisions in Darwinian evolution and color the ways natural science currently categorizes both old and newly found species. Darwin's voyages on the *Beagle* as a naturalist, owe a great debt to Linnaeus' and other naturalists' classifications, as Darwin takes part in the naturalism that Linnaeus began in the 18th Century. Indeed, the evolutionary tree, which traces the simplest of organisms upward, relies heavily on Linnaeus' system of organization. In *Origin of the Species* Darwin takes scientific codices and refines them through his theory of natural selection.[3] In *The Descent of Man,* Darwin traces human evolution from animals to the most civilized of European men, creating a linear progression from what Darwin deems "savage" to the educated European ideal. Such a vertical linkage creates a metaphorical space from high to low upon which natural history and Darwinian evolution figure themselves. Not only do both these concepts create such a space in their use of high-low language and models like the evolutionary ladder and tree, but they also create a temporal space, tracing the passage of time between species, always assuming a mode of progression and hierarchical superiority as species ascend the ladder in the great chain. Not only do Darwin and Linnaeus trace linkages between species and subspecies, both place each plant and animal within a greater ordering that privileges the European, colonialist project. Such Darwinian language makes its way into contemporary discourse in Murray and Herrnstein's book *The Bell Curve,* and other nationalist projects, which attempt to classify Anglo superiority through an evolutionary model.[4] The scientific stability of evolutionary language slips as the words lose their classificatory emphasis and gain new popularity as cultural capital in Murray and Herrnstein's book.

Anti-Order, Deleuze and Guattari

In *A Thousand Plateau*'s, Deleuze and Guattari attempt to destabilize the binarisms and hierarchical systems that produce Western society. Deleuze and Guattari propose a new way of understanding the world through the concept of deterritorialization. Deleuze and Guattari suggest that the rhizome is the ultimate example of a deterritorialized state, rather than the image of the "root-tree," which disciplines such as computer science and evolution take up as an organizational and hierarchical model: "even a discipline as 'advanced' as linguistics retains the root-tree as its fundamental image, and thus remains wedded to classical reflection" (5). For example, in genealogical narratives, the image of the tree traces both time and history and serves as a visualization of familial lines. It is the "binary logic" of the tree—"endlessly develop[ing] the law one that becomes two, then of two that becomes four"—which Deleuze and Guattari refuse to embrace within *A Thousand Plateaus* (7). Within such a binary system, "nature is conceived as an enormous *mimesis* [. . .] they all imitate by graduated resemblance, as the model for and principle behind the series . . ." (235). In the "root-tree" system, everything branches from a single, central taproot, thus everything can only exist as derivative and hierarchically distributed.

Deleuze and Guattari's alternate model to the ordered pairing of the tree is the fascicular model, or rhizome—constantly multiplying, shifting, and unable to produce only binarisms. In fascicular roots, "the principal root has been aborted, or its tip has been destroyed; an immediate, indefinite multiplicity of secondary roots grafts onto it and it undergoes a flourishing development" (5). The primary difference between the ordering of a tree and a rhizomatic structure is that "any point of a rhizome can be connected to anything other, and must be. This is very different from the tree or root, which plots a point, fixes an order" (7). Ultimately, the rhizomatic model destabilizes the tree's binarisms; in light of evolution and natural history, a rhizome disallows the linear progression of the natural historical record and the evolutionary tree from existing because a rhizome can never continue in a straight line with a beginning and ending.

In their essay, "Becoming-Intense, Becoming-Animal, Becoming-Imperceptible" Deleuze and Guattari illustrate a rhizomatic reassessment of evolution. Natural history and evolution are realized through "a chain of beings perpetually imitating one another, progressively and regressively, and tending toward the divine higher term" (235). This structured form of beings—one *evolving* to the next—points at a trajectory whose main objective lies in progressing and finally in perfection. Within such a linear chain, only imitation remains possible, while within a rhizome, the possibilities for different associations and links become endless. With their reconsideration of the linear nature of natural history and evolution, Deleuze and Guattari challenge linear-reliant models as well. Ideas are inseparable from the linear narrative that stems them simply because:

> ideas do not die. Not that they survive simply as archaisms. At a given moment they may reach a scientific stage, and then lose that status or emigrate to other sciences. Their application and status, even their form and content, may change; yet they retain something essential throughout the process, across the displacement, in the distribution of a new domain. Ideas are always reusable, because they have been usable before [. . .]
>
> (235)

Here, Deleuze and Guattari compare the history of ideas with evolution, as over time, the evolutionary ladder changes slightly, but at the same time, there is always a distinguishable path backwards. Even the idea of evolution itself evolves, migrating not only to other sciences, but also to books such as *The Bell Curve* that foster popular culture to utilize models like evolution to explain away social problems. It is the linear passage and progression through time of such ideas that Deleuze and Guattari hope to shatter. "The history of ideas should never be continuous" argue Deleuze and Guattari, "it should be wary of resemblances, but also of descents or filiations" (235). The destabilization of the idea-tree by which so many Western models structure themselves, furthers with Deleuze and Guattari's notion of "becoming."

Specifically, becoming occurs between two beings that are not necessarily closely linked in the evolutionary chain or any hierarchical model. "Becoming" marks a shift away from the hierarchy of evolution and processes and a move towards what Deleuze and Guattari call "involution." Becoming differs from evolution even further because Deleuze and Guattari anticipate that becomings can "contribut[e] to the creation of a nonorganic life that is not captured by natural selection and its values of adaptation and survival (of the fittest)" (Pearson 162). Within a rhizomatic structure, becomings and involution epitomize the connections that occur—twisting and gesturing—between seemingly disparate ideas and beings. Deleuze and Guattari suggest that examples of becoming can be found in propagation by epidemic and contagion. Specifically, they give the vampire as a perfect example of becoming because each new vampire is produced through infection instead of filiation—becoming heterogeneous instead of propagating through a tree-model (241-2). Like becomings, Deleuze and Guattari attest that involution occurs in *symbioses*: where animals and plants form relationships with each other without any potential filiation. "To involve," argue Deleuze and Guattari, "is to form a block that runs its own line 'between' the terms in play and beneath assignable relations" (239). Rather than following evolution's long, straight line, the lines of involution and becoming playfully stretch along with the rhizome, tracing paths through the incongruent and dissimilar.

As Deleuze and Guattari differentiate between taproot/rhizome and evolution/involution, they do so through the notion of affect. If evolution takes place along the taproot of scientific thought, then the rhizome of involution occurs through more affective channels. Affect, more than emotional response, inhabits and engenders the space of becoming. "For affect is not a personal feeling," claim Deleuze and Guattari:

> nor is it a characteristic; it is the effectuation of a power of the pack that throws the self into upheaval and makes it reel. Who has not known the violence of these animal sequences, which uproot one from humanity, if only for an instant, making one scrape at one's bread like a rodent or giving one the yellow eyes of a feline? A fearsome involution calling us toward unheard-of becomings.
>
> (240)

Affect is the stored potential, rising up to the action. It is the unknowable intensity that causes becomings and compels becomings to diverge from the taproot and to instead follow fascicles. This intensity comes-and-goes without a trace because, as Brian Massumi notes, affect "is a prepersonal intensity corresponding to the passage from one experiential state of the body to another" (xvi). In this way, affect creates dynamic formations such as spaces of becoming and involution. Deleuze and Guattari define affect's chaotic potential through the term *haecceities,* or the "thisness" of events (260-2). *Haecceities* and affect go hand-in-hand, as Guattari notes: "As soon as one decides to quantify and affect, one loses its qualitative dimensions and its power of singularization, of heterogenesis, in other words, its eventful compositions, the 'haecceities' that it promulgates" (67). For Deleuze and Guattari, the reason why affect cannot be explained so easily stems from its "thisness" in events and also because of its difference from simple, quantifiable emotion—affect is not the result, but the causal agent.

Octavia Butler and Becoming Oankali

Such affective, frenetic lines of becomings and involutions run throughout Octavia Butler's trilogy, *Xenogenesis.* In *Xenogenesis,* Butler de-centers traditional origin narratives, which form the basis for many catalogues of human culture; she provides a new "involution" of an origin story by presenting hers as a slave narrative. A tentacle-covered, alien species called the Oankali attempts to save a dying Earth and takes Lilith Iyapo, the primary character in the series' first book, and uses her to begin rehabitating a new Earth and help propagate the next generation of the Oankali. At the beginning of the book, Lilith finds herself in a room without doors and windows, with no knowledge of where she has been taken, the identity of her captors, or control of her own body. As Lilith tells her story, her story mirrors the "form of autobiography that blend[s] personal memory and a rhetorical attack" that Henry Louis Gates Jr. highlights as one of the features of a mid-nineteenth-century slave's narrative (3). Gates goes on to cite that some slave narratives "portray slavery as a condition of extreme physical, intellectual, emotional, and spiritual

deprivation, a kind of hell on earth" (7). The series' first book echoes such emotive intensity and dispossession, as Lilith finds herself a captive away from any recognizable home, and retells her internment and subsequent return to a new Earth, to the reader.

If, as Deleuze and Guattari posit, "becoming is a rhizome, not a classificatory or genealogical tree," then *Xenogenesis*'s becoming as a tale of origins, diverges from classificatory structures that would position a black woman at the bottom rungs of the human evolutionary ladder, and arrives at a narrative of becoming through its repositioning and emphasis on involution (239). Butler further complicates her origin story by naming the woman who comes to lead a new population on Earth, Lilith. According to legend, Lilith is the first wife of Adam, made from the same dust as he. Lilith is not obedient to Adam and refuses to lie with him in the missionary position because she sees herself as his equal. She bears demons instead of children and is finally cast out of paradise.[5] Butler adjusts her narrative to spotlight Lilith, who always inhabits the periphery of the Hebrew and Christian origin story. Not only does Butler amend her origin story to include a slave narrative, she also names the first woman of the new Earth after the original woman who was cast out of the previous one. Like Lilith, Butler's protagonist finds herself cast out of Earth (albeit for different reasons) and forced to make a new earth for herself. Butler alters the Lilith myth in order to reenvision positive, most importantly generative, possibilities for such a negative narrative.

Even the title of the series' first book, *Xenogenesis,* emphasizes a move away from descent-based filiation. *Xenogenesis* can be defined as the production of offspring that are distinctly different from either parent; such a title hints at the new population that will come to inhabit earth after the Oankali recolonize it. Section One of the first book of the *Xenogenesis* trilogy is titled: "The Womb." Not only does this subtitle signify an ironic move on Butler's to pair a space of captivity with a place of growth and generation, it also highlights the trilogy's emphasis on new ways of life. The first lines of the book illustrate that although Lilith may be in a womb, it does not appear to be an ordinary one:

> "Alive!
>
> Still Alive.
>
> Alive . . . again."
>
> (5)

There is no "In the beginning, God created the heavens and the earth," during this origin story: it begins with an exclamation, soon followed by what seems like resignation, as the exclamation point adjusts to a period. The second and third line give way to acceptance, as the reader finds that the narrator has been alive before, and that awakening into a new life has turned into the "ultimate disappointment" (5). The story changes completely when the reader is made aware that Lilith Iyapo has not only awakened many times, but that "she was confined [. . .] kept helpless, alone, and ignorant" and could be "insane or drugged, physically ill or injured" because she has no recollection of what has happened to her other than she remembers constantly awaking in this prison-like space (5). The heavens and the earth of the Hebrew and Christian origin story are drastically reduced, as the reader slowly finds out that Lilith has been trapped in a single room for an indeterminable amount of time.

Butler's move, to withhold all pertinent information as to Lilith's whereabouts and captivity, positions the reader along the same lines as Lilith—another move away from the typical origin story, and towards a retelling of a slave's life, where many accounts are written in first person and detail the slave's internment and subsequent quest for freedom (Gates 5). The reader's place within the telling of the narrative is not next to God, looking down on the finished Earth, but as a captive awaking in a new, and very frightening, place. Parallels with a slave narrative continue, as both the reader and Lilith acclimate to Lilith's new surroundings and learn about her previous awakenings. Not only does Lilith's chamber always have no doors or windows, twice, Lilith has been without a bathroom (5-6). Lilith goes on to exclaim, "clothes!" as she finds a pile of clothes; "she had not been allowed clothing from her first Awakening until now" even though she has repeatedly asked for something in which to cover herself (6). Lilith illustrates her captivity further by examining herself for new scars:

> her hand touched the long scar across her abdomen [. . .] what had she lost or gained, and why? And what else might be done? She did not own herself any longer. Even her flesh could be cut and stitched without her consent.
>
> (7)

Lilith has no control over what her captors take and remove from inside her body. This moment illustrates the complete lack of control that Lilith exerts over both her environment and subjugators. Even as she remains "sealed [. . .] in a large box, like a rat in a cage," she no longer maintains control over her body because her captors can even make her sleep when they wish (7). Ultimately, Lilith's only recourse is to "beg[i]n the most futile of her activities:" to search for any kind of exit, even though, because of her earlier Awakenings, she knows there will not find a means to escape (7).

If Butler's origin story opens in a shocking way, then what Lilith encounters next shatters anything that was left of the reader's previous experiences with origin

myths. Lilith soon finds out that her captors are members of an alien species called the Oankali, who trade genes as a part of their evolutionary processes. The Oankali have been alive for several million years, although exactly what makes up an Oankali differs with each generation. There are four different types of Oankali and three different genders, two that correspond to the Earth's male and female genders, and one called the Ooloi, who can genetically modify Oankali through two sensory tentacles. The Oankali whom Lilith first encounters is named Jdahya; it becomes his job to tell Lilith about what happened to the Earth she knows and about the new species that she encounters.

The reader soon learns that humans have all but destroyed the Earth in a series of wars and environmental disasters and the Oankali step in and save what is left of Earth, taking many people aboard a plant-like, almost-sentient ship to trade with them and repopulate Earth with a new breed of human/Oankali. As Jdahya tells Lilith, it has been "several million years since we dared to interfere in another people's act of self-destruction," but humans' genetic make-up was incredibly complex and interesting to the Oankali (16). Humans are attractive to the Oankali because they have a "mismatched pair of genetic characteristics:" intelligence and hierarchical behavior (38). Lilith does not understand how hierarchical behavior can be defined as a problem since even the ways that humans understand the world form themselves upon such hierarchies. "You are hierarchical," Jdahya tells Lilith of humanity:

> That's the older and more entrenched characteristic. We saw it in your closest animal relatives and in your most distant ones [. . .] When human intelligence served it instead of guiding it, when human intelligence did not even acknowledge it as a problem, but took pride in it or did not notice it at all [. . .] that was like ignoring cancer. I think your people did not realize what a dangerous thing they were doing.
>
> (39)

As natural selection progresses on the Earth, hierarchy becomes a trait that humans seek from even their most distant relatives. As another Ooloi puts it, humans' "intelligence is relatively new to life on Earth, but your hierarchical tendencies are ancient. The new was too often put at the service of the old" (530). Hierarchy becomes much more than a way to organize a chaotic world for humanity, combined with human intelligence, it becomes insidious, as it signals humans' eventual demise because hierarchy overtakes any new developments in human culture.

The Oankali do not rely on the same hierarchical structures for evolution as humans do; they are gene traders whose evolutionary process differs from Earth's substantially. The Oankali can only progress as a species if they trade their genetic material with other species' genetics—each generation creating a new species by incorporating different genetic material into their genome. As Jdahya puts it: "We *must* do it. It renews us, enables us to survive as an evolving species instead of specializing ourselves into extinction or stagnation" (40, emphasis in original). Specifically, the Oankali have traveled millions of miles in search of genes to help develop their species. Like Deleuze and Guattari suggest, Oankali species progression does not follow a tree-like pattern from A to B, but can skip from A to X by integrating new traits with each generation. "We're not hierarchical, you see," Jdahya explains to Lilith:

> We never were. But we are powerfully acquisitive. We acquire new life—seek it, investigate it, manipulate it, sort it, use it. We carry the drive to do this in a minuscule cell within a cell—a tiny organelle within every cell of our bodies [. . .] One of the meanings of Oankali is gene trader. Another is that organelle—the essence of ourselves, the origin of ourselves. Because of that organelle, the Ooloi can perceive DNA and manipulate it precisely.
>
> (41)

Just as the human drive to develop and maintain hierarchies stems from their earliest relations, Oankali are biologically driven to seek out new life and blend it with their own genes. Even the human definition of *species* falls short when attempting to describe the Oankali since they are not descended from an evolutionary chain, but instead evolve by blending various species together, like fascicular roots bursting forth and multiplying.

Humans' need for hierarchy remains in stark contrast to Oankali species formation, but humans' ability to form cancer cells and cancerous growths baffles and intrigues the Oankali. In humans, the Oankali see both the "talent" to spawn growths, such as cancer, that defy hierarchy, and the ability to squelch out anything that does not fit within a tree-like structure (22). The Oankali see Lilith's ability to grow cancerous cells not only as a "talent," but also as "beautiful"; in fact, the Oankali's primary interest in trading with humans stems from the possible positive uses for cancer (22). Just as human's entrenched hierarchy combined with their intelligence can have only negative outcomes, cancer—something with profoundly dire connotations within human culture—becomes generative of "possibilities" for the Oankali. Deleuze and Guattari also speak of a becoming that is removed from heredity; cancer becomes in just such a manner: breaking off from the hierarchy of cells and growing and spreading through a rhizomatic "anti-genealogy" (240, 11). When utilized correctly, cancer can give the Oankali the possibility of redeveloping lost limbs, the ability to control and change their appearance, and longevity beyond any stretch of the human imagination (41). Cancer, an agent of death within humans, is a becoming—a key element in Oankali involution.

The ability of the Oankali to evolve is not evolution at all, but something much more analogous to Deleuze and Guattari's notion of involution. Each time the Oankali trade genes, they participate in "evolution between two heterogeneous terms"—what Deleuze and Guattari deem as involution—by taking two distinct species and blending them together, forming something completely different each time they "trade" with a new species (239). "A given species," states De Landa, "(or more accurately, the gene pool of a species) can be seen as the historical outcome of a sorting process" (136). In the case of Oankali genetics, the historical outcome that De Landa speaks of, whereby genes map-out a historical path, differs greatly from the human gene pool. The selection pressures of the Oankali create a gene-map that runs frenetic lines around the slowly evolving process of human evolution as well as changes the historical outcome of humanity's genes altogether, as the Oankali remove and redefine human genes. Oankali are able to manipulate genes in Lilith, making her stronger and removing her body's "talent" for cancer, thus amending her reliance on inherited traits to form her genetic structure; such a transition—from descent-based attributes to genetic manipulation—removes heredity's hold on Lilith, as the Oankali change her genetic make-up. As Deleuze and Guattari aver when they speak of involution and becoming: "this is a far cry from the filiative production or hereditary reproduction, in which the only differences retained are a simple duality between the sexes within the same species, and small modifications across generations" (243). Indeed, through their gene trade and genetic manipulation, the Oankali are constantly becoming. Since becoming is never a fixed state but rather a constant process, the Oankali themselves are ephemeral, insofar as what defines them as a species relies on constant change.

The Oankali perform involution not through filial reproduction, but through the Ooloi, the third gender of Oankali. Ooloi are integral for the Oankali gene trade because they have the ability to observe and manipulate genes. "They have special organs for their kind of observation," Jdahya explains to Lilith:

> [. . .] maybe perceiving would be a better word [. . .] there's much more involved than sight. It knows everything that can be learned about you from your genes. And by now, it knows your medical history and a great deal about the way you think.
>
> (22)

The organ that Jdahya speaks of is the Ooloi' *yashi*, which manipulates DNA, stores cells and information of unfamiliar species, and imprints of various species' DNA. Ooloi do not just perceive medical history, they also can recognize what lies in one's genes for the future, from cancers to other genetic anomalies. When Oankali explore, they bring back bits of cellular matter so that the Ooloi can have more information with which to implement their genetic changes. Within its *yashi*, Ooloi "manipulate DNA more deftly than Human women manipulate the bits of thread they use to sew their cloth" (543). The yashi becomes a veritable hard-drive, or "a mental blue-print" the Ooloi fill it with any bits of information that it needs throughout its life (99).

The Ooloi are instrumental in more than just maneuvering genes, they are also indelible in Oankali reproduction. Ooloi control procreation by manipulating reproductive cells and managing conception through their sensory tentacles and *yashi*, guiding how each generation looks, acts, and comes to be. The Ooloi represent the biggest possibility for change for the human gender binary, and are the most frightening possibility for Lilith and her partner. It is not just the change from dual genders that frightens Lilith; the new form of procreation is possibly the most difficult aspect of Oankali culture for Lilith and the other humans to grasp. By procreating and trading genes with the Oankali, humanity will never be what it once was:

> your people will change. Your young will be more like us and ours more like you. Your hierarchical tendencies will be modified and if we learn to regenerate limbs and reshape our bodies, we'll share those abilities with you.
>
> (42)

When Lilith asks Jdahya "what" their children will be like, he replies: "different [. . .] not quite like you. A little like us" (42). To the Oankali, such a blending would become, as Jdahya tells Lilith: "the rebirth of your people and mine" (43). To Jdahya and other Oankali, this rebirth and reimagining of his species has always been a normal part of Oankali reproduction; to Lilith, such a concept remains deeply frightening.

Sexual relations with an Ooloi are altogether different than human sexual practice. Once a set of human partners include an Ooloi in their sexual relations, the Ooloi becomes an indispensable part of the sex act. Human partners begin to think of the Ooloi as part of their relationship and the human partners do not want to pursue sexual relations without it. During intercourse, the Ooloi use two sensory tentacles, resembling arms, to penetrate the base of each partner's skull. This allows the Ooloi to "hook into [one's] nervous systems" and "bond" with a male and female (169). During the sex-act, the male and female only touch each other through a "neurosensory illusion" provided by the Ooloi (168). In short, sex becomes an entirely virtual experience that the Ooloi control by "pushing the right electrochemical buttons" (169). Specifically, the Ooloi generate such gratification by creating an imagined space within the minds of those it brings together sexually where they imagine the sexual experience to be whatever they wish without any kind of physical contact.

Completely dissimilar from human sexual intercourse, the Ooloi's place within this new set of sexual relations makes both Lilith and her partner Joseph uneasy. As one Ooloi explains to Lilith's partner, Joseph: "what happened was real. Your body knows how real it was. Your interpretations were illusion. The sensations were entirely real" (188). Even though the illusion that Joseph and Lilith were sexually intimate remains powerfully real, the Ooloi constructs the images and sensations for each human within their respective minds, creating an affective space that humans cannot understand through any kind of interpretation. The mind may attempt to construe meanings onto the bonding experience, but it remains only recognizable for a brief moment in the "thisness" of the event, or as Deleuze and Guattari suggest, the *haecceities* of affect. These experiences mirror the pleasure that Ooloi neurologically give to their sexual partners. By directly stimulating the brain, Ooloi simulate and deliver touch, pleasure, and pain, all within a space each partner virtually inhabits. Since the Ooloi have the ability to directly stimulate nerves and senses, they give "perfect hallucinations," synthesizing feeling, both emotive and physical—joining affective and virtual experience together (162). As Lilith describes, after she bonds with Joseph and an Ooloi, Nikanj: "She never knew whether she was receiving Nikanj's approximation of Joseph, a true transmission of what Joseph was feeling, some combination of truth and approximation, or just a pleasant fiction" (162). As Nikanj builds Joseph and Lilith's experience, it explores genes, pleasure, and the melding of molecules.

Time breaks down in the world that Nikanj creates for Lilith and Joseph: the only thing that remains is affect's line of flight, as Lilith and Joseph lose sense of time and the oneness of their own bodies: "he had always been part of her, essential [. . .] it seemed, itself, to vanish. She sensed only Joseph [. . .] Noon, evening, dusk, darkness" (162). Nikanj—"it" as Lilith describes—vanishes, serving as the conduit, by creating this space of intense feeling. Indeed, Lilith's experience with Nikanj and Joseph resonate with Brian Massumi's definition of affect and virtual space, as one where:

> past and future brush shoulders with no mediating present, and as having a different, recursive causality; the virtual as cresting in a liminal realm of emergence, where half-actualized actions and expressions arise like waves on a sea to which most no sooner return.
>
> (31)

When Lilith asks Nikanj how he invents the experiences that she and Joseph have, Nikanj answers: "I've never made up an experience for you [. . .] You both have memories filled with experiences" (163). Nikanj embodies the virtual, as he strips away both time and relative actions, and instead combines past experiences and memories with present feelings to construct their affective space. As Lilith and Joseph participate within this virtual, affective space, the temporal is completely erased, as Butler emphasizes by listing the parts of the day that Lilith and Joseph miss while they are with Nikanj. Just as Oankali involution breaks down the chain of evolution, the space that Nikanj creates also eclipses the temporal as experiences and memories become active—removed from the past, reshaped, and inserted into the present moment.

Butler's *Xenogenesis* trilogy concludes with the book *Imago,* a word that denotes the final or adult stage in most insects. While Lilith begins the trilogy as a human, attempting to resurrect humanity, the end of the trilogy focuses on her various children, part Oankali and part human. Specifically, the final book of the trilogy centers around two of the first human/Ooloi children who, more than any of the Ooloi before them, can truly utilize human genes in order to foster their development as a species:

> You'll be able to change yourself. What we can do from one generation to the next—changing our form, reverting to earlier forms or combinations of forms— you'll be able to do within yourself. Superficially you may even be able to create new forms, new shells for camouflage. That's what we intended.
>
> (547)

Oankali involution takes place within a single Ooloi because of human DNA. This reflects the ultimate form of becoming: the ability to change at will, without reliance on filiation or familial traits. Before human DNA Ooloi had their *yashi* to find compatible genes for what they need, now all that an Ooloi needs is the need for change itself: the Ooloi can invent new forms and figures for both Oankali and humans. Human cancer cells provide the missing link for the Oankali to truly step away from the evolutionary record. Jodahs, the first human/Oankali Ooloi realizes his new place within the changing human/Oankali species and comments: "I would be the most extreme version of a construct—not just a mix of Human and Oankali characteristics, but able to use my body in ways that neither Human or Oankali could. Synergy" (549). With the next generation of Constructs (Oankali/Human hybrids), evolution no longer centers itself on the concept of mimesis that Deleuze and Guattari argue against, but on something new and creative, just as Deleuze and Guattari suggest when they speak about involution (235).

It is at this point in *Xenogenesis* when the evolutionary chain finally breaks, and with it, all its political foundations as well. Jodahs and Aaor (both Construct Ooloi) are in a constant state of becoming. Depending on their moods, habitat, or lovers, they can transform their bodies dramatically—"like the sky, constantly changing, clouded, clear, clouded clear"—their appearance even

fooling Lilith and other Oankali (598). Lilith asks Jodahs, when she realizes that its appearance changes constantly: "What are you doing? [. . .] Letting your body do whatever it wants to?" (591). Jodahs has the unconscious ability to constantly become something else, to constantly involve. "A line of becoming is not defined by points that it connects," suggests Deleuze and Guattari:

> or by points that compose it; on the contrary, it passes *between* points, it comes up through the middle, it runs perpendicular to the points first perceived, transversally to the localizable relation to distant or contiguous points. A point is always a point of origin. But a line of becoming has neither beginning nor end, departure nor arrival, origin nor destination. [. . .] a line of becoming has only a middle; one can only get it by the middle.
>
> (293)

The Constructs' line of becoming strikes directly through the middle of what it means to be Human and Oankali, arriving at a perfect synergy that runs between both species. Since the Constructs are always becoming, like Deleuze and Guattari suggest, there is no beginning or end in their line, but only a path of endless possibilities. There can be no destination in the Construct Ooloi's becomings because there is not a stable identity from which to start or a concept of a pinnacle to reach—its self is becoming.

TOWARD BECOMINGS AND CONCLUSIONS

Linneaus's and Darwin's systems of classifications are not natural or the only method of organization, they are only the most recognizable. So familiar in fact, that hierarchical trees span disparate disciplines, bringing these dissimilar entities together, and causing ideas, like evolution, to migrate outward, and foster hybrid-theories such as social Darwinism. It is such a discernable path backwards that Deleuze and Guattari attempt to dissect in *A Thousand Plateaus.* Through the model of a rhizome and specifically through their concept of involution, Deleuze and Guattari begin to decenter the concept of evolution, and more importantly, suggests a way, through affective becomings, to understand a new manner of species' fruition.

Octavia Butler also puts forward an alternative imagining of hierarchical trees through *Xenogenesis.* Within her trilogy, she not only questions the foundations of evolutions—from a scientific evolution, to the evolution and propagation of origin stories—but, through framing her story within a slave narrative, imagines the rebirth of Earth through a subjugated black woman's eyes. Butler's trilogy traces an earth subsumed by its own hierarchical structures to one that begins profoundly differently, and through its difference disables such hierarchical underpinnings altogether. Butler removes hierarchy's hold on evolution by moving science into the affective, virtual space of the Oolois' imaginings.

Though through different means, Octavia Butler and Deleuze and Guattari interrogate the same structures within both of their works. Most importantly, they imagine new possibilities for species fruition and development that flourish apart from the seemingly intrinsic hierarchy of the root-tree. Through fascicular becomings, Butler, Deleuze and Guattari all propose that it is not through scientific descent and filiation where species' growth occurs, but such amplification can also take place within areas of involution and becoming. These affective spaces encourage growth that the root-tree model ignores and leaves behind. Such spaces encourage growth that hierarchical systems deny, making it possible to engender imaginative possibilities for race, gender, evolution, and formations of completely new species as well.

Notes

1. Foucault's preface to *The Order of Things: An Archeology of the Human Sciences,* highlights the "strange categories" in which Western knowledge, natural history included, has been ordered (xv).

2. Linnaeus arranges quadrupeds within a single category of *homo* and divides them between *homo sapiens* and *homo monstrosus,* and then by 1758 divides *homo sapien* into 6 categories: Wild man, American, European, Asiatic, African, and monstrous. Linnaeus also mentions what governs each of the categories; for example, Europeans are governed by laws, while Africans are governed by caprice (Pratt 32).

3. From the introduction to *Origin of the Species,* Darwin gives this definition of natural selection: "As many more individuals of each species are born than can possibly survive; and as, consequently, there is a frequently recurring struggle for existence, it follows that any being, if it vary however slightly in any manner profitable to itself, under the complex and sometimes varying conditions of life, will have a better chance of surviving, and thus be NATURALLY SELECTED. From the strong principle of inheritance, any selected variety will tend to propagate its new and modified form" (Introduction, emphasis in original).

4. Specifically, *The Bell Curve* purports that low intelligence is the root cause of many social problems.

5. The tradition of Lilith is a rich and amazing one. I provide the barest of essentials about the Lilith legend here. I have found the archives of "altmyth" very helpful in describing the rich tradition surrounding the figure of Lilith. The website/archive can be found here: *http://www.lilitu.com/lilith/lil_altmyth.html*

Works Cited

Butler, Octavia. *Lilith's Brood.* (*Xenogenesis Trilogy*). New York: Warner Books, 1989.

Darwin, Charles. *On The Origin of the Species.* Classic Literature Library. 26, Nove. 2004 <http://charles-darwin.classic-literature.co.uk/on-the-origin-of-species/.

Darwin, Charles. *The Descent of Man.* Classic Literature Library. 26, Nov. 2004 <http://charles-darwin.classic-literature.co.uk/the-descent-of-man/.

De Landa, Manuel. *A Thousand Years of Nonlinear History.* New York: Zone Books, 1997.

Deleuze, Gilles, and Guattari, Felix. *A Thousand Plateaus: Capitalism and Schizophrenia.* Tr. Brian Massumi. Minneapolis: University of Minnesota Press, 1987.

———. *Kafka: Toward a Minor Literature.* Trans. Dana Polan. Minneapolis: University of Minnesota Press, 1986.

Gates, Henry Louis Jr. "Introduction" *The Civitas Anthology of African American Slave Narratives.* Eds. Gates and Andrews. Washington DC: Civitas, 1999.

Herrnstein, Richard and Charles Murray. *The Bell Curve.* New York: Free Press, 1994.

Massumi, Brian. *Movement, Affect, Sensation: Parables for the Virtual.* Durham: Duke University Press, 2002.

Pearson, Keith Ansell. *Germinal Life: The Difference and Repetition of Deleuze.* New York: Routledge, 1999.

Pratt, Mary Louise. *Imperial Eyes: Travel Writing and Transculturation.* New York: Routledge, 1992.

Stivale, Charles J. *The Two-Fold Thought of Deleuze and Guattari.* New York: The Guilford Press, 1998.

Clara Escoda Agustí (essay date fall 2005)

SOURCE: Agustí, Clara Escoda. "The Relationship Between Community and Subjectivity in Octavia E. Butler's *Parable of the Sower.*" *Extrapolation* 46, no. 3 (fall 2005): 351-59.

[*In the essay below, Agustí examines the ways in which Butler's female protagonists overcome exploitation.*]

Butler's future world of 2024 shares many of the characteristics Immanuel Wallerstein attributes to our contemporary society. In our contemporary world of economic globalization, says Wallerstein in his book *Utopistics,* "transnational corporations are so truly global that they can circumvent the states" (47). In her fictive world of 2024, Butler projects the political fantasies of the anti-government right into the future, a powerful segment of American society which would resolve the current capitalist crisis by accentuating economic inequality and by annulling the power of the state to protect and organize its subjects. In this context, as Tom Moylan argues in *Scraps of the Untainted Sky,* competing corporate values, "without the safety nets of regulation, support, and service . . . have completed the destruction of the social matrix and as the basic requirements of existence are being sold back to people who have been just deprived of them" (224). This leads Butler's female protagonist to assert that debt-slavery, something "old and nasty" (105), has revived.

This essay focuses on how Butler dramatizes and overcomes the exploitation of the female that ensues from such a form of capitalism. In her novel, sexual slavery and prostitution are inherent tendencies of a system that favors profit at the expense of human well-being. Lauren Olamina, the female protagonist, slowly unfolds in her diary how society allows for the sexual exploitation of, particularly, black women. When her house is burnt down by thieves, she flees to the North in order to forge her own utopian community. On her way North, Olamina meets a series of black and Hispanic women who have suffered sexual abuse, like Allison and Jillian, two young girls whose "pimp was their father" (212). So she will tell Bankole, her future husband, after listening to their stories: "You realize that women and children were sold like cattle—and no doubt sold into prostitution" (263). Olamina will begin to observe the close link between economic exploitation and sexual exploitation: "I wondered how much difference there was between Natividad's former employer, who treated her as though he owned her, and Richard Moss who purchased young girls to be part of his harem" (200). By inquiring into their personal lives, Olamina recognizes what Adam McKible terms in his article "'These are the Facts of the Darky's History:' Thinking History and Reading Names in Four African American Texts," "the gendering and racializing of reproduction; the exploitation of women as the producers of surplus value—children—and the exploitation of 'free' black women as low-wage producers and surplus reproducers" (232). In her double marginality, being both female and black, Olamina is exposed to the contradictions of a society which supposedly characterizes itself by "the 'equality' of 'free' wage-labor" (225). This subject position at the crossroads of society's contradictions that the African American woman occupies may become a site of awareness and, therefore, of powerful self-assertion.

This article focuses on how Olamina counteracts the oppression that the system wields over her as a black woman and how she is able to re-write her own utopian community's approach to gender and racial difference, thus creating a community of equals. The essay will trace the strategies by which Olamina acquires a subjectivity that allows her to modify the pattern of relationships in the group. Olamina will redefine the concepts of femaleness and masculinity in her community, in order to undermine sexual exploitation based

on gender and race discrimination. Peter Stillman comments on the nature of Lauren's utopia, affirming that "Earthseed is definitely concerned with welfare and education on this earth, but by creating enclaves within the political system, not by changing that system" (32). Indeed, as Hoda Zaki specifies, as a black female writer who was influenced by the greater gender and racial equality that was achieved through the Civil Rights movements, as well as by the feminist movements of the 70s, Butler "demonstrates a conflation of the public and private spheres: she will attain her utopia by foregrounding personal relationships" (245). Olamina will achieve a more democratic society not by proposing a specific economic system, that is, by defining a society's infrastructure, but by modifying its cultural relationships, and this will lead us to observe how, from her interior utopia of relationships, a more rational organization of work and wealth can ensue.

"YOU REALIZE THAT WOMEN AND CHILDREN WERE SOLD LIKE CATTLE" —OCTAVIA E. BUTLER

The inherent exploitation of human beings that the capitalist system allows for informs the relationships between male and female on a daily basis, and it indeed penetrates into Olamina's household. "The economic foundations, the way in which men earn their living," states W. E. B. DuBois, "are the determining factors in the development of civilization . . . and the pattern of culture" (303). The interactions between the members of Olamina's family reveal what McKible calls "the actuality of two separate spheres—one public, male, valuable and productive; the other private, female, worthless, and somehow 'outside' capitalist production" (230). "The exploitation of gender and race," he continues, "is integral to the machinations of capitalism, and it extorts profit from the womb as surely as it does from the field or factory" (230).

Olamina's brother Keith repeatedly reduces Olamina's capacity for an extraordinary empathy to a female weakness, a pathology from the point of view of the male world, which justifies her exclusion from it: "[it] would bring you down even if nobody touched you. [. . .] You better marry Curtis and have babies. Out there you wouldn't last a day" (97). In "Dystopian Critiques, Utopian Possibilities, and Human Purposes in Octavia Butler's *Parables,* [*Parable of the Sower* and *Parable of the Talents*]" Peter Stillman finds that "dream" of domesticity "especially for the woman—only a dead-end of greater responsibility and fewer possibilities" (20).

Keith is imbued by the culture's binary oppositions, and his male identity is shown to depend upon the exclusion of the "female" in him. On his eighteenth birthday, he asks his parents for a gun, so that he may become a "man:" "I am a man! I shouldn't be hiding in the house" (82), he says. "He wanted to show he was a man, not a scared girl" (82). So Olamina records her disagreement with her parents' acquiescence to satisfy Keith's wish: "My parents' good judgment failed them this week on my brother Keith's birthday. They gave him his own BB gun" (83). Diana Fuss argues, in *Essentially Speaking,* that white patriarchy, traditionally based upon an understanding of the white, male subject as stable and unitary, is constructed upon an exclusion of difference: "to the extent that identity always contains the specter of non-identity, or otherness, within it, identity is always purchased at the price of the exclusion of the Other, the repression or repudiation of non-identity" (103). This way, woman is produced in social signification as the "other" on which the very existence of man depends, as much as other asymmetrical relations: that of exploitation, privilege, and patriarchy (Davies, 70). If manhood is defined in terms of privilege and the ability to rule over others, it should not surprise us that Olamina's brother has a strong power rivalry with his father in relation to the female: "Dad was home so he wouldn't come in. I thanked him for the money and told him I would give it to Cory" (99).

Indeed, Cory, Olamina's stepmother, is a crucial character who will allow us to trace the beginnings of Olamina's model of an empowered subjectivity. Cory functions as Olamina's mirror image; she is the woman in her family who does not survive the system, who cannot create a female subjectivity under oppression. Even though Cory is a PhD, she cannot project her identity and preparation into her job, as her husband does. This lack of freedom in the social world parallels her growing disadvantage and loss of authority inside the home, as opposed to her husband's growing influence on their children, and in the larger neighborhood community. Cory finally collapses when her husband forbids her to take a new job in Olivar, arguing that the town has been sold by a corporation and it enslaves workers through debt: "Freedom is dangerous Cory . . . but it is precious" (119), he argues. She finally gives up her voice and enters a state of "walking coma" (119).

In her double marginality, being both female and black, Olamina is exposed to the contradictions of a society which, in Angela Davis' words, supposedly characterizes itself by "the 'equality' of a 'free' wage-labor" (qtd. in McKible 225). Whereas other women, like Cory, cannot survive, Olamina is aware of the potential for subversion that her position allows her, the powerful site of self-assertion her position can be. Lisbeth Gant-Britton quotes precisely such an affirmation from the words of D. Soyini Madison, in *The Woman that I Am*: "Being the woman that I am I will make a way out of no way . . . [these] are the words of all women of color who assert who they are, who create sound out of

silence, and who build worlds out of remnants" (282). At the crossroads between the liberal discourses of her society and her actual marginalization, Olamina envisions personal and communal change. In her diary, she painstakingly records Cory's incapacity for change and adaptation and, between the lines of Cory's disempowerment, she rewrites social relations.

AN INTERIOR UTOPIAN MODEL

This complex subject position in which Olamina, as an African American woman, finds herself—one of race, gender and class oppression—"experiences gender from a 'racialized' position and race from a gendered position; so that any notion of the unified self is challenged both from without and from within" (McKible 226). As such, this new subject can relate to difference in terms of identification and interpellation. Butler demonstrates how Olamina is able to blur the differences between subject and Other, manhood and femaleness in herself, in a way that difference is incorporated into the self, and it can be taught to the community in the process of relating, in order to downplay the legal fictions of gender and race which distort the growth of a community and its individuals. Her utopia is interior because, contrary to traditional male utopias, change takes place within the individual and, in her process of relating, at the juncture between subject and object.

Lauren achieves this blurring and fragmentation of previously unitary and unconnected gender categories particularly through cross-dressing. Indeed, in order to protect herself from rape and violence inflicted on women, in her escape to the North Olamina decides she will dress as a man. By doing this she does not surrender to the invisibility or vulnerability of her sex, but she demonstrates her ability to understand gender not as essential, but as performative, and her eagerness to play with gender categories as well as with her own body. She understands her body as a site of political discourses and as a fluid space where gender categories are not mutually exclusive. Michael M. Levy, in his essay "The Survival of Adolescent Girls," calls this strategy of unfixing gender categories "androgyny." He argues that Olamina's survival is linked to her ability to be androgynous, "adapting actively in any situation regardless of gender constraints" (37). Olamina does not regard the body as an immutable biological given, but rather, as a field of inscription of socio-symbolic codes: it stands for the radical materiality of the subject. As Catherine S. Ramirez argues in "Cyborg Feminism," "the body is simultaneously material and discursive. Our conceptions and experiences of it as material are always socially mediated" (386).

Androgyny was a very influential concept during the 70s, mainly as a reaction to feminism as it was conceived in the 60s, where the centrality of motherhood still championed other alternatives. Androgyny is based on a definition of human characteristics as particular to one sex or another, with the androgynous individual exhibiting characteristics of both sex roles. Yet from the 1990s onward, some have questioned whether human characteristics need to be dichotomized and defined by gender at all. Even if it has been questioned, androgyny implies a sharing of tasks and emotions between genders that is subversive and challenges the traditional approach to difference. Butler will insist on the importance of this concept to the point of making it explicit in the novel's sequel, *Parable of the Talents,* where Olamina claims: "I usually travel as a man, by the way. I am big enough and androgynous-looking enough to get away with it" (370). Like Levy, Butler relates androgyny to adaptation and survival.

Olamina does not regard the body as an immutable biological given. Rather, it is a "field of inscription of socio-symbolic codes: it stands for the radical materiality of the subject. The body is simultaneously material and discursive. Our conceptions and experiences of it as material are always socially mediated" (Ramirez 386). She understands her body as a site where gender categories are not mutually exclusive.

Another strategy is dialogue: by engaging in active dialogue with the members of the group, Olamina gives a power message to the reader on how to de-legitimize the dominant ideology and introduce her subjectivity. She does this through discursive techniques which rewrite the dominant story; in this case, the construct of masculinity. In McKible's words, the privilege of Olamina's marginalization is a "consciousness that defies the purported truthfulness of History" (224). Indeed, feminine initiative is, at the beginning, still not well-regarded by the male members of the group, and Olamina rewrites the threats she experiences, responding to them in dialogic contestation: "Travis grunted, still non-commital. Well, I had helped him twice, and now I was a woman. It might take him a while to forgive me for that" (191). Her response both signals and de-legitimizes the construct of masculinity. She produces and activates her subjectivity by causing a rupture with the dominant story "resulting in a de-legitimating of the prior story or a displacement which shifts attention to the other side of the story" (McKible 226).

"BUT IT WAS UNUSUAL THAT HE HAD TAKEN CARE OF THIS CHILD" —OCTAVIA E. BUTLER

Out of her transformation, Olamina influences the members of the community into perceiving themselves as well as a site of dialogic differences, working against the perception of the subject as unitary and closed, and towards androgyny. In her contact with the male members of the group, she teaches about accepting gender and racial difference through empathy and mothering.

Olamina's "hyperempathy," which she got due to a pill her mother abused while she was pregnant with her, causes her to feel the suffering of others. As she explains: "Thanks to Paracecto [. . .] the particular pill my mother chose to abuse before my birth killed her, I get a lot of grief that doesn't belong to me" (Butler 11). As a result, the Earthseed community will only use violence to defend itself, not to dominate. An apparent "disability," hyperempathy helps her re-define manhood and its approach to arms. If violence is allowed exclusively for self-defense, manhood will cease to define itself in relation to domination. According to Ramirez, "Lauren's hyperempathy defies the notion of the stable and closed subject as it assumes and/or is catapulted into various social and subject positions, blurring the boundaries of consciousness" (Ramirez 385). Patricia Melzer adds, in her article "'All That You Touch You Change:' Utopian Desire and the Concept of Change in Octavia Butler's *Parables*:"

> [Hyperempathy] represents the painful and pleasurable process of crossing differences and of actually *experiencing* the other's world beyond a mere willingness to *understand* it. Sharing blurs and shifts boundaries and discloses a stable, autonomous identity to be a myth—sharing becomes a symbol against the binary construction of self and other and thus constitutes a crucial metaphor for re-defining social relations.
>
> (45)

Olamina, therefore, creates a blank space where male domination was hegemonic. Now she will insert the female characteristic of mothering, or nurturing, in its core. Both mothering and "hyperempathy" have subversive qualities because they embrace difference without interposing society's symbolic codes, such as racist and sexist legal fictions. It is a source of stability and equality that can be used politically to counteract discourses of oppression.

The members of the group, as much the males as the females, take care of the children of others. This incorporation of difference can only make the community stronger. In Melzer's words, "children embody the future the adults are trying to create" (41), and she continues: "Olamina realizes how responsibility for others, children or adults, can give meaning to life and can heal internal wounds: 'taking care of other people can be a good cure for nightmares'" (41).

Olamina's redefinition of manhood is now complete. Males as well as females can embrace androgynous aspects into the self. According to Mary Pipher in *Reviving Ophelia: Saving the Selves of Adolescent Girls,* androgyny is a survival strategy whereby adults adapt to their reality, males as well as females: "An androgynous person can comfort a baby or change a tire, cook a meal or chair a meeting. . . . They are free to act without worrying if their behavior is feminine or masculine; androgynous adults are the most well adjusted" (qtd. in Levy 37). Olamina observes this change in Grayson Mora, a male who took care of his daughter just as a female member of the group did: "the man had become a father almost as young as the woman had become a mother. That wasn't unusual, but it was unusual that he had taken care of the child" (261). Butler, therefore, subversively extends traditional motherhood to males, dissociating it from female biology. In including and arguing in favor of non-biological parenting she can extend the activity of care-taking to men, and separate it from her society's idea that it is a woman's enforced biological "destiny." Butler emphasizes the aspects of otherness in motherhood, not those of sameness, by extending the ability to care and support others beyond biological ties. Again, both mothering and "hyperempathy," therefore, have subversive qualities, embracing difference without interposing racist and sexist legal fictions.

An example of this is embodied by Natividad, who breast feeds both her baby and another woman's baby when she is found dead, incorporating the Other:

> A lone, dark figure came away from the truck and took several steps towards us. At that moment, Natividad took the new child, and in spite of his age, gave him one breast and Dominic [her son] the other. . . . It worked. Both children were comforted almost at once. They made a few more small sounds, then settled down to nursing.

(226)

And indeed, an ironic, final comment, demonstrates that the dominant ideology still informs the community members, but that they have learnt to undermine it. Once the group has found the land that will be a home to the Earthseed community, they talk about the social roles each might now perform. Harry, the white male, is assigned the role of overseer, but he immediately achieves distance from such a power position, as it corresponds to previous definitions of masculinity with which he does not identify: "Are you telling me you believe I'd like a job pushing slaves around and taking away their children?" (290). The dominant ideology is now counteracted and re-thought, and a powerful alternative has taken its place.

CONCLUSION

The novel's aim is to map a subjectivity, or a series of viable strategies, as they take place within the consciousness of a black female, through which she is able to externalize a political voice and actively effect social change. Olamina's utopia is then an interior utopia, an interior model that, in the process of her actively relating to the group, is able to achieve change amongst its members, to actually shape society. It is from modifying gender and actively relating to the diversity of the

group that change occurs. Whereas Olamina's proposal limits traditional individualism, the novel does affirm the individuality of the members of the group, in that change must first occur within the individuals in order to modify society in any lasting manner.

Interestingly, the group's search for the North as a site of freedom and possibilities echoes slave narratives' quest for the North as the site of utopian desire. The slave narratives perceived the North as a land where the possibilities of work generated freedom, and where the racist and gendered exploitation of human beings that had taken place in the South would be overcome. Olamina tells us the process whereby this goal of opportunity and equality could be successfully sustained.

As a result of Olamina's reconfiguration of the subject as a site of dialogic differences, her utopia remains open to conflict. It is based on difference, and difference needs to be continually acknowledged and renegotiated. Her utopia is imperfect in the sense of being unfinished. As a Critical Utopia, it differs from traditional utopias in the sense that it is no longer defined in absolute terms, it does not seek to "emphasize the notion of a unitary group of transparent selves, with a common identity," and thus stabilize the utopian horizon (Melzer 32).

Also, Olamina's leadership differs from that of former black and white historical leaders. In having little resource to authority because she is a woman, she does not base her leadership on charisma or on the retention of power. Instead, she builds a group of equally powerful and self-conscious individuals, seeking to uncover leadership potential in others. As Peter Stillman argues: "She does not try to force a connection, but lets it develop" (24), or "they arrive at decisions by open and unfettered discussions free from domination or imposed claims of authority" (21).

Indeed, in Butler's utopia no woman can be silenced like Cory, or be sexually exploited like Zahra or Natividad due to skin color, if an appropriate redefinition of manhood and femaleness takes place. From here, an equal distribution of goods and work can ensue; one which is not based on an essentialist perception of the sexes and races, but on a perception of any subject as a site of creative differences that enriches the group. In Olamina's utopia, "life commemorates life" (293) because the black, female body and agency are not distorted.

Works Cited

Butler, Octavia E. *Parable of the Sower,* New York: Warner Books, 1993.

———. *Parable of the Talents,* New York: Warner Books, 1998.

Davies, Carole Boyce. *Black Women, Writing and Identity. Migrations of the Subject,* London and New York: Routledge, 1994.

DuBois, W. E. B. *Dusk of Dawn. An Essay Toward an Autobiography of a Race Concept.* New Brunswick and London: Transaction, 2002.

Fuss, Diana. *Essentially Speaking. Feminism, Nature and Difference,* New York and London: Routledge, 1989.

Levy, Michael M. "The Survival of Adolescent Girls in Recent Fiction by Butler and Womack," *Foundation,* no. 72 (1998): 34-41.

McKible, Adam. "'These Are the Facts of the Darky's History:' Thinking History and Reading Names in Four African American Texts," *African American Review,* vol. 28, no. 2 (Summer 1994): 223-235.

Melzer, Patricia. "'All That You Touch You Change:' Utopian Desire and the Concept of Change in Octavia Butler's *Parable of the Sower* and *Parable of the Talents,*" *Femspec,* vol. 3, no. 2 (2002): 31-52.

Moylan, Tom. *Scraps of the Untainted Sky. Science Fiction, Utopia, Dystopia.* Boulder, CO: Westview, 2000.

Ramirez, Catherine S. "Cyborg Feminism: The Science Fiction of Octavia E. Butler and Gloria Anzaldua," *Reload. Rethinking Women + Cyberculture.* Eds. Mary Flanagan and Austin Booth. Cambridge and London: M.I.T., 2002: 374-402.

Stillman, Peter G. "Dystopian Critiques, Utopian Possibilities and Human Purposes in Octavia Butler's *Parables,*" *Utopian Studies,* vol. 14, no. 1 (2003): 15-35.

Wallerstein, Immanuel. *Utopistics. Or, Historical Choices of the Twenty-First Century.* New York: The New Press, 1998.

Zaki, Hoda. "Utopia, Dystopia and Ideology in the Science Fiction of Octavia E. Butler," *Science Fiction Studies,* vol. 17, no. 2 (1990): 239-51.

FURTHER READING

Criticism

Anderson, Crystal S. "'The Girl Isn't White': New Racial Dimensions in Octavia Butler's *Survivor.*" *Extrapolation* 47, no. 1 (spring 2006): 35-50.

Addresses Butler's exploration of racial identity in her novel *Survivor.*

Antczak, Janice. "Octavia E. Butler: New Designs for a Challenging Future." In *African-American Voices in Young Adult Literature,* pp. 311-36. Metuchen, N.J.: Scarecrow, 1994.

Presents an overview of Butler's writings geared towards adolescents.

Bedore, Pamela. "Slavery and Symbiosis in Octavia Butler's *Kindred.*" *Foundation* 31, no. 84 (spring 2002): 73-81.

Provides an exploration of how Butler deals with issues of power in her fiction.

Boulter, Amanda. "Polymorphous Futures: Octavia E. Butler's *Xenogenesis* Trilogy." In *American Bodies: Cultural Histories of the Physique,* edited by Tim Armstrong, pp. 170-85. New York: New York University Press, 1996.

Provides an examination of Butler's treatment of the female body in her writings.

Foster, Frances Smith. "Octavia Butler's Black Female Future Fiction." *Extrapolation* 23, no. 1 (spring 1982): 37-49.

Provides an analysis of Butler's treatment of black women in her works.

Gant-Britton, Lisbeth. "Octavia Butler's *Parable of the Sower*: One Alternative to a Futureless Future." In *Women of Other Worlds,* edited by Helen Merrick and Tess Williams, pp. 277-308. Nedlands, Western Australia: University of Western Australia Press, 1999.

Gant-Britton probes how Butler reconciles an optimistic vision of the future with "still-open" wounds from the past.

Govan, Sandra Y. "Connections, Links, and Extended Networks: Patterns in Octavia Butler's Science Fiction." *Black American Literature Forum* 18, no. 2 (summer 1984): 82-87.

Provides an examination of "power relationships" in Butler's fiction.

Holden, Rebecca J. "The High Costs of Cyborg Survival: Octavia Butler's *Xenogenesis* Trilogy." *Foundation,* no. 72 (spring 1998): 49-56.

Examines issues of survival as portrayed in Butler's *Xenogenesis* trilogy.

Mehaffy, Marilyn, and AnaLouise Keating. "'Radio Imagination': Octavia Butler on the Poetics of Narrative Embodiment: Interviews." *MELUS* 26, no. 1 (spring 2001): 45-76.

Presents a series of interviews with Butler.

Miller, Jim. "Post-Apocalyptic Hoping: Octavia Butler's Dystopian/Utopian Vision." *Science-Fiction Studies* 25, no. 2 (July 1998): 336-60.

Places Butler's fiction firmly within the tradition of "feminist utopian writing."

Porter, Evette. "Having Her Say: Octavia Butler Talks with Evette Porter about *Fledgling,* the Author's Latest Novel." *Essence* 35, no. 6 (October 2005): 96.

Discusses the genesis of Butler's vampire tale *Fledgling.*

Potts, Stephen W. "'We Keep Playing the Same Record': A Conversation with Octavia Butler." *Science-Fiction Studies* 23, no. 3 (November 1996): 331-38.

Presents a brief interview with Butler.

Salvaggio, Ruth. "Octavia Butler and the Black Science-Fiction Heroine." *Black American Literature Forum* 18, no. 2 (summer 1984): 78-81.

Explores the notion of an African American female writer working within the male-dominated field of science fiction.

Shinn, Thelma J. "The Wise Witches: Black Women Mentors in the Fiction of Octavia Butler." In *Conjuring: Black Women, Fiction, and Literary Tradition,* pp. 203-15. Bloomington, Ind.: Indiana University Press, 1985.

Shinn examines "archetypes" of strong black women in literature, specifically focusing on characters in Butler's fiction.

Steinberg, Marc. "Inverting History in Octavia Butler's Postmodern Slave Narrative." *African American Review* 38, no. 3 (fall 2004): 467-76.

Provides a reading of Butler's novel *Kindred* as slave narrative.

Sturgis, Amy H. "The Parables of Octavia Butler: A Science-Fiction Writer's Rich Libertarian Legacy." *Reason* 38, no. 2 (June 2006): 72-3.

Lauds Butler's treatment of power dynamics and the human condition.

Sturgis, Susanna J. "Living the Undead Life." *Women's Review of Books* 23, no. 1 (January-February 2006): 11-12.

Praises Butler's novel *Fledgling* for its innovative reinterpretation of the vampire myth.

Zaki, Hoda M. "Utopia, Dystopia, and Ideology in the Science Fiction of Octavia Butler." *Science-Fiction Studies* 17, no. 2 (July 1990): 239-51.

Provides a discussion of Butler's treatments of utopia in her fiction.

Additional coverage of Butler's life and career is contained in the following sources published by Thomson Gale: *African American Writers,* **Ed. 2;** *American Writers Supplement,* **Vol. 13;** *Authors and Artists for Young Adults,* **Vols. 18, 48;** *Beacham's Encyclopedia of Popular Fiction: Biography & Resources,* **Vol. 1;** *Black Literature Criticism Supplement; Black Writers,* **Eds. 2, 3;** *Children's Literature Review,* **Vol. 65;** *Contemporary Authors,* **Vols. 73-76, 248;** *Contemporary Authors New Revision Series,* **Vols. 12, 24, 38, 73, 145;** *Contemporary Literary Criticism,* **Vols. 38, 121;** *Contemporary Novelists,* **Ed. 7;** *Contemporary Popular Writers; Dictionary of Literary Biography,* **Vol. 33;** *Discovering Authors Modules: Multicultural Authors* **and** *Popular Fiction and Genre Authors; Discovering Authors 3.0; Literature and Its Times Supplement,* **Ed. 1:2;** *Literature Resource Center; Major 20th-Century Writers,* **Eds. 1, 2;** *Major 21st-Century Writers,* **(eBook) 2005;** *Novels for Students,* **Vols. 8, 21;** *Science Fiction Writers,* **Ed. 2;** *Short Stories for Students,* **Vol. 6;** *Something About the Author,* **Vol. 84;** *St. James Guide to Science Fiction Writers,* **Ed. 4;** *St. James Guide to Young Adult Writers;* **and** *Twayne Companion to Contemporary Literature in English,* **Ed. 1:1.**

June Jordan
1936-2002

(Full name June Meyer Jordan) American poet, essayist, novelist, editor, journalist, and dramatist.

The following entry provides an overview of Jordan's career through 2005. For additional information about her life and work, see *CLC,* Volumes 5, 11, 23, and 114.

INTRODUCTION

Best known as a poet, Jordan has also written a substantial number of essays, plays, and children's books. Her works typically focus on African American experiences in the U.S. and explore a wide range of political and social topics including sexual identity, violence, terrorism, the conflicts in Nicaragua, the Middle East, and Africa. Jordan has also addressed personal issues such as love and self-awareness in her writing, infusing many of her poems and essays with details of her turbulent childhood. Critics have praised Jordan for uniting concepts of personal, everyday struggles with the wider political oppression experienced by African Americans in her writing.

BIOGRAPHICAL INFORMATION

Born in Harlem in 1936, the only child of Jamaican-born parents, Jordan grew up in the Bedford-Stuyvesant neighborhood of Brooklyn, moving there with her parents at age five. Her father, a post-office clerk, introduced her to such poetry as Biblical Scripture and the verses of African American Paul Laurence Dunbar, and her mother, a nurse, served as a role model who provided community service. Yet Jordan's parents hampered their daughter's developing sense of identity with harsh treatment—her father beat her and her mother failed to intervene—and they opposed Jordan's ambition to become a poet. Confronting such issues from her childhood in her writing is a major theme in Jordan's work. Jordan spent her high school years immersed in an entirely white world—first as the only African American student at a Brooklyn high school one hour's commute from her home, and later, as a student at the Northfield School for Girls in Massachusetts. Jordan studied poetry extensively, and has remarked that her formal education exposed her almost exclusively to the work of white male writers. In 1953 she enrolled at Barnard College, where she met Michael Meyer, a white student at Columbia University. Jordan attended the University of Chicago for one year, then later returned to Barnard, although she did not earn a degree from either institution. In 1955 she married Meyer; the marriage ended in divorce ten years later. Jordan's son, Christopher David Meyer, has provided another theme for her writing—that of motherhood—a theme which extends into a broader focus of nurturing for the overall African American community. She dedicated her first book, *Who Look at Me* (1969), and her 1981 essay collection *Civil Wars* to her son. In 1970 Jordan served as editor for *Soulscript,* a collection of poetry penned by various African American writers. Jordan enjoyed a distinguished teaching career, holding positions as a full-time professor at the State University of New York at Stony Brook, the University of California-Berkeley, and Sarah Lawrence College, and has also serving as visiting professor at several colleges and universities across the United States. In addition to teaching, Jordan demonstrated a strong concern for education by holding writing workshops for students—particularly black and Hispanic youths—and writing several children's books. In 1970 she collaborated with Terri Bush to edit *The Voice of the Children,* a collection of poetry written by children. She also founded Poetry for the People, a program that instructs undergraduate students how to teach poetry and encourages community involvement. Jordan's first novel, *His Own Where* (1971), received a National Book Award nomination and earned an ALA Best Book for Young Adults award. Jordan received a Rockefeller grant for creative writing in the years 1969-1970, a Yaddo fellowship in 1979, a 1982 National Endowment for the Arts fellowship, and the Achievement Award for International Reporting from the National Association of Black Journalists in 1984. From February 1989 through November 2001 Jordan wrote a column called "Just Inside the Door" for *The Progressive,* a monthly journal. In 1991 she received the PEN Center USA West Freedom to Write Award. In 1994 The Woman's Foundation honored her with a Ground Breakers-Dream Makers award. Jordan also garnered the Lila Wallace Reader's Digest Writers Award from 1995 to 1998 and received the Chancellor's Distinguished Lectureship from the University of California at Berkeley. Her collection *Directed by Desire: The Collected Poems of*

June Jordan (2005), earned a 2006 Lambda Literary Award for Lesbian Poetry. On June 14, 2002 Jordan died of breast cancer in Berkeley, California.

MAJOR WORKS

Who Look at Me builds upon a recurring image of eye contact between two races to examine the history of African Americans in a prejudiced white America. Twenty-seven paintings of African Americans, spanning from the colonial period to the present, complement the book-length poem and underscore the theme of viewing others as individuals rather than as stereotypes. Poet Langston Hughes originally worked on this book; after his death in 1967, a publisher requested that Jordan complete the project. In her collection *Some Changes* (1971), Jordan explores her efforts to find her poetic voice despite a troubled relationship with her parents. While continuing to address the African American experience in general, she elucidated her artistic ideals, writing about social consciousness and appealing for a revision of the literary canon that would incorporate African American writers. Certain poems in this volume demonstrate the influence of Emily Dickinson, T. S. Eliot, and Shakespeare. A novel for teens, *His Own Where* follows a young man and woman as they create a home for themselves in the midst of urban ruin. This work attracted significant critical attention due to Jordan's use of Black English, a style she fervently espouses and promoted in her writing. Jordan employs Black English in several of her poems and addresses this type of speech in several essays, including "White English/Black English: The Politics of Translation" (published in *Civil Wars*), and "Nobody Mean More to Me Than You and the Future Life of Willie Jordan," which appeared in *On Call: Political Essays* (1985). *Dry Victories* (1972) features a conversation between two boys, focusing on the Reconstruction following the American Civil War and the 1960s civil rights movement. Jordan's poetry collection *New Days: Poems of Exile and Return* (1974) also deals with the civil rights movement and returns to her evolving perception of her mother. This volume contains a poem addressed to civil rights activist Fannie Lou Hamer, whom Jordan met during trips to Mississippi, and who became a surrogate mother-figure to the poet. In 1972 Jordan published a biography on Hamer. *Things That I Do in the Dark* (1977) includes poems from earlier collections as well as new pieces. *Passion: New Poems* (1980) explores themes of violence, particularly violence against women. This volume contains "Poem about My Rights," an expression of power and self-confidence that has become one of Jordan's most well-known works. In *Civil Wars*—a compilation of essays, speeches, and letters—Jordan forges a connection between the personal and political, relating her own experiences to such subjects as violence, racism, and feminism. *Naming*

Our Destiny (1989) was critically lauded for finding synergy between the lyrical and the political, utilizing a variety of voices and personas to convey Jordan's investigation of the "we/us" versus "they/them" rhetoric which she sees as central to the divisiveness of American culture. *Living Room: New Poems* and *On Call: Political Essays,* both published in 1985, feature writing centering on political and social issues relating to Palestine, Lebanon, Nicaragua, and South Africa. In *Technical Difficulties: African-American Notes on the State of the Union* (1992) and *Affirmative Acts: Political Essays* (1998) Jordan tackles domestic social and political topics, including education and her belief in the necessity for affirmative action. In response to her memoir *Soldier: A Poet's Childhood* (2000), critics appreciated Jordan's ability to tell a believable story from the perspective of a child. Scholars also commented on her refusal to portray her young narrator as simply the victim of a brutal father. While depictions of abuse are present in the text, they are tempered by Jordan's recollections of her father's encouragement and love which helped her to grow into a strong, educated individual. *Some of Us Did Not Die: New and Selected Essays* (2002) features essays spanning the length of Jordan's career. The book's title originates from an essay written on the topic of the September 11, 2001 terrorist attacks in New York. In 2005 Jan Heller Levi and Sara Miles collected Jordan's poetry into one volume and published it as *Directed by Desire: The Collected Works of June Jordan.*

CRITICAL RECEPTION

Critic Brian Norman observed that "Jordan rigorously seeks out voices of displaced peoples" in her writing; she has focused in particular on the rights of African Americans, women, and children. The combination of her commitment to urgent political issues and her concern for the quotidian is reflected in an "oratorical" style that critic David Baker has likened to that of Carl Sandburg and the blues. Jordan's propagation of Black English, however, has sparked debate, most notably when African American parents attempted to ban *His Own Where,* believing that the book would prevent students from learning standard English and impede success in school and the workplace. Jordan has also encountered opposition for what some have judged as a radical stance on certain political and social issues. Within the literary community and intellectual circles, P. Jane Splawn has placed Jordan's writing in the category of a "New World consciousness," an aesthetic and sensibility traceable to Walt Whitman and postcolonial thinker and activist Frantz Fanon, characterized by a heterogeneous, pluralistic, and democratic spirit. In addition, many reviewers have cited Jordan's avoidance of scholarly and academic veins of discourse as one of her strengths. Though she deals with weighty subjects such as race, gender, and social justice, she does so with imagery and language taken from a world that readers recognize, using situations with which readers are familiar. As Kirsten Bartholomew Ortega remarked, "For June Jordan, writing poetry that is accessible to children and general readers was essential to her vision of herself as both a poet and an educator." Commenting on Jordan for the dustjacket of *Soulscript,* novelist and Nobel Laureate Toni Morrison wrote, "[I]n political journalism that cuts like razors, in essays that blast the darkness of confusion with relentless light; in poetry that looks as closely into lilac buds as into death's mouth . . . she has comforted, explained, described, wrestled with, taught and made us laugh out loud before we wept."

PRINCIPAL WORKS

Who Look at Me (poetry) 1969

Soulscript: Afro-American Poetry [editor] (poetry) 1970

The Voice of the Children [co-editor] (poetry) 1970

His Own Where (novel) 1971

Some Changes (poetry) 1971

Dry Victories (juvenilia) 1972

Fannie Lou Hamer (biography) 1972

New Days: Poems of Exile and Return (poetry) 1974

New Life: New Room (juvenilia) 1975

Things That I Do in the Dark: Selected Poetry (poetry) 1977

In the Spirit of Sojourner Truth (play) 1979

Passion: New Poems 1977-1980 (poetry) 1980

Civil Wars (essays) 1981

For the Arrow that Flies by Day (staged reading) 1981

Kimako's Story (juvenilia) 1981

Living Room: New Poems, 1980-1984 (poetry) 1985

On Call: Political Essays (essays) 1985

Bang Bang Uber Alles (play) 1986

Lyrical Campaigns: Selected Poems (poetry) 1989

Moving Towards Home: Political Essays (essays) 1989

Naming Our Destiny: New and Selected Poems (poetry) 1989

Technical Difficulties: African-American Notes on the State of the Union (essays) 1992

Haruko/Love Poems (poetry) 1994

I Was Looking at the Ceiling and Then I Saw the Sky (libretto) 1995

Kissing God Goodbye: New Poems, 1991-1997 (poetry) 1997

Affirmative Acts: Political Essays (essays) 1998

Soldier: A Poet's Childhood (autobiography) 2000

Some of Us Did Not Die: New and Selected Essays (essays) 2002

Directed by Desire: The Collected Poems of June Jordan (poetry) 2005

CRITICISM

Peter Erickson (essay date winter 1986)

SOURCE: Erickson, Peter. "The Love Poetry of June Jordan." *Callaloo,* no. 26 (winter 1986): 221-34.

[*In the following essay, Erickson surveys Jordan's poetry in* Passion, *along with some of her other writings as well.*]

In an earlier article I undertook a comprehensive survey of June Jordan's work, including fiction, children's stories, drama, and essays as well as poetry.[1] The present study focuses more specifically on the poetry.[2] Two poems from *Passion*—**"A Short Note to My Very Critical and Well-Beloved Friends and Comrades"** and **"Poem about My Rights"**—may be taken as coordinates or lightning rods for the deeper motives of the poetry as a whole. Placing the two poems next to each other, we are struck first by their differences. The latter presents a strenuous drive toward self-definition, while the former flaunts a facetious, capricious resistance to self-definition. This contrast is reinforced by the respective tones of the two poems: the one serious, urgent, menacing; the other flippant, elusive. Yet earnestness and insouciance converge as two sides of the same coin. Both poems testify to the connection between naming and identity, to the power of language to deform the self. For all its positive insistence on "self-determination," **"Poem about My Rights"** spends most of its energy fending and sloughing off false terms: *"I am not wrong: Wrong is not my name."* This denial, this rejection of destructive labels, gives the two poems a common denominator, despite their different tactics. Because **"Poem about My Rights"** makes its appeal so directly and emphatically, we are apt to see it as the more impressive poem, leading us to underestimate its apparently slighter counterpart. But **"A Short Note"** makes an equal claim on us.

The impact of the poem lies in its last line. Jordan builds a linear momentum, whose predictable, repetitive structure frustrates and mocks the need to find a label. Impervious, the "I" bides its time until, leaping the gap to the final line, it becomes subject and takes action. The tables are turned, the problem summarily dropped in the laps of "my very critical and well-beloved friends and comrades":

> First they said I was too light
> Then they said I was too dark
> Then they said I was too different
> Then they said I was too much the same
> Then they said I was too young
> Then they said I was too old
> Then they said I was too interracial

Then they said I was too much a nationalist
Then they said I was too silly
Then they said I was too angry
. . . .
Then they said I was too confusing altogether:
Make up your mind! They said. Are you militant
or sweet? Are you vegetarian or meat? Are you straight
or are you gay?

And I said, Hey! It's not about *my* mind.

We as readers can enjoy this game until we realize that we have been put in the same position as the friends. We are placed on the defensive, our minds placed in question. Our first reaction might be to feel cheated by a trick poem, to accuse the author of evasiveness, of hiding behind the mirror she holds up to our mental habits. Having aroused our irritation, the poem dares us to examine it, to probe our discomfort at being unable to pin down the poet's identity.

The larger issue **"A Short Note"** raises in its teasing way is the relation between classificatory schemes and actual experience. Behind Jordan's sheer delight in mischievously outwitting inadequate categories and remaining unclassifiable is her dedication to freedom of self-exploration, regardless of ideological proprieties. In the satirical poem **"Letter to the Local Police,"** Jordan projects this human freedom on "certain unidentified roses, growing to no discernible purpose, and according to no perceptible control." Aligning herself with the roses, Jordan celebrates their "near riot of wild behavior"; they defy control because they "do not demonstrate the least inclination toward categorization." Social and linguistic images of order thus overlap. Though the poem is kept resolutely humorous, the latent implication is that, since the roses do not display any intrinsic principle of order, order can be achieved only by the imposition of legal fictions ("appropriate legal response") enforced by political power ("the Local Police"). The distance in *Passion* between the playful **"Letter to the Local Police"** and the angry, explosive **"Poem about Police Violence"** is perhaps not so great.

Returning to **"A Short Note,"** we may ask: Is there any word which Jordan's "friends and comrades" could pronounce to stop the endless chase of the Protean escape-artist? Is there any word to which the poet would answer? "I would call myself an anarchist," comments Jordan in a 1981 interview.[3] In the final essay of *Civil Wars* which gives the book its title, Jordan uses the term "anarchy" to characterize the black response to the murder of Arthur MacDuffie in Miami, 1980: "Miami was a peoples' uprising, and not an organized demonstration. It was extraordinary; an authentic spontaneous combustion. . . . It was anarchy in the best sense: it was pure" (*Civil Wars*, p. 184). Jordan's particular concern with leadership in this essay can be grounded in the root meaning of anarchy (an-archos—rulerless):

It came to me that self-determination has to mean that the leader is your individual gut, and heart, and mind. . . .

The only leadership I can respect is one that enables every man and woman to be his or her own leader. . . .

Neither race nor gender provides the final definitions of jeopardy or refuge. The final risk or final safety lies within each one of us attuned to the messy and intricate and unending challenge of self-determination. . . .

And what should we fear? No movement, not the Republican, nor the Black nor the women's nor the environmental movement can exist without you and me.

(pp. 186-87)

If this passage takes us to the heart of Jordan's vision, the question becomes: can we trace the process by which she arrived at this point? I think we can do so by using the idea of anarchy, provided that we see it as a clue rather than an all-encompassing term. "Anarchy" can turn into another misleading or reductive label, especially if we restrict its reference to classical political theory and attempt to place Jordan within a systematic philosophical tradition. I propose a different route.

The significance of the term anarchy in Jordan's work comes as much from its internal focus on the self as from its external focus on the state. The image of the anarchist as a promoter of social dislocation is extended and modified by the figure of the poet who attends to the anarchy within herself. What distinguishes Jordan's political sensibility is its inwardness, as when she gravitates backward to "bed," "heart," and "skull":

My life seems to be an increasing revelation of the intimate face of universal struggle. You begin with your family and the kids on the block, and next you open your eyes to what you call your people and that leads you into land reform into Black English into Angola leads you back to your own bed where you lie by yourself, wondering if you deserve to be peaceful, or trusted or desired or left to the freedom of your own unfaltering heart. And the scale shrinks to the size of a skull: your own interior cage.

(*Civil Wars*, p. xi)[4]

As the term "cage" suggests, anarchic freedom is harder to attain than it might seem.

In order to expand the range of anarchy as a concept, I shall examine Jordan's love poetry, seeing in love an experience of anarchy described by **"Poem about My Rights"** as "each and every desire / that I know from my personal and idiosyncratic / and indisputably single and singular heart." Witness Jordan's definition of the "wildness" of "New World" poetry: "It means *wild* in the sense that a tree growing away from the earth enacts a wild event."[5] In the presence of a poet who can see the anarchic possibilities of a tree, we know our understanding of the term anarchy needs revision. We must try to learn how each of Jordan's love poems "enacts a wild event"—"wild event" referring both to love and to the poetic process.

I. "THE PRECIPICE NOBODY DARES TO FORGET"

Those who come to June Jordan's poetry because of her reputation as a strictly political poet will be surprised at the large number of love poems and of her constant recourse to this genre. Setting aside political concerns, the poet indulges her erotic longing: "I can use no historic no national no family bliss / I need an absolutely one to one a seven-day kiss" (**"Alla Tha's All Right, but,"** *Passion*). What is here a raucous assertion and celebration of sexual need has earlier—more often than not—been an expression of intense vulnerability in love. Jordan's first collection of poetry, *Some Changes* (1971), is divided into four untitled sections, the implicit rationale for section two being love. This second section, arguably the richest in the volume, has an important long-term effect on Jordan's overall poetic development, thus providing a key to that development.

An atmosphere of deep malaise—interrupted by occasional, though still muted, bursts of erotic release or self-affirmation—dominates section two of *Some Changes.* The last poem of section one, **"I Live in Subtraction,"** makes the transition to the next section by firmly setting a dejected tone. Though "I" is the first word and subject of every line, the action of the poem is to reduce rather than enlarge this self, the continual subtracting effect culminating in the contemplation of a suicidal gesture: "I can end a dream with death." We are not told how this psychological state came about, though we might guess the poet has been hurt by love when she says that she has forgotten or directs herself to "forget your name." Her demoralization is presented as a given, its origin and cause left a mystery.

Nor are we told the reason for the sadness in **"My Sadness Sits Around Me."** This title is reiterated in the poem's first and last lines, creating a literal enclosure which represents the emotional isolation that envelops the poet. We are forced simply to note and to accept this sadness which the poems gingerly explore without explaining more precisely. The same image of being cut and sealed off is reproduced in **"Nobody Riding the Roads Today,"** where the last stanza can only repeat the first: "Nobody riding the roads today / But I hear the living rush / far away from my heart." The formal circularity mimics and heightens the poet's desolation.[6]

The troubled mood of these poems can be usefully associated with the general background of Jordan's life during this period, so long as we do not insist on a one-

to-one correspondence by which the life is supposed to explain the poetry. The two crucial events of which the reader needs to be aware are, in successive years, Jordan's divorce from her husband (1965) and her mother's suicide (1966). Both events have evidently proven difficult for Jordan to talk about. It is not until fifteen years after the fact that Jordan explicitly refers to the suicide: first with a brief mention in *Civil Wars* (p. xvii), then at length in her second address at Barnard College.[7] In the latter, Jordan presents her recollection of the suicide with such vivid immediacy that it is almost as if it were occurring in the present rather than fifteen years ago, as if Jordan must relive her confused feelings in order finally to attain expiation.

Though there are allusions to her husband in *Civil Wars,* it is also only in the 1981 Barnard talk that Jordan decisively breaks the silence surrounding her divorce. She gives for the first time specific details, so that it now becomes possible to begin to gauge the effect of her role as wife on the poetry (in my previous essay on Jordan's work, the discussion of the family motif in the poems was by necessity limited to her roles as daughter and mother). When interviewed by Alexis DeVeaux for the April 1981 issue of *Essence,* Jordan defended her marriage in 1955 to a white student at Columbia University: "'When I married Michael, that was defiant,' she tells me with agitation. 'In the fifties the central thrust against racism in this country was to integrate, whether it was the schools or getting married. I didn't feel that marrying interracially was any kind of copout'" (p. 143). But she is unable to explain the separation (1963) and divorce (1965): "When pressed, it is difficult for her to articulate a reason. She absolutely refuses to call it racial, or to give it any name at all" (p. 145). In the 1981 Barnard address, Jordan begins to tell the story of the divorce. It is a protofeminist moment, for the husband makes the decision to end the marriage: "I could see how my husband would proceed more or less naturally from graduate school to a professional occupation of his choice, just as he had shifted rather easily from me, his wife, to another man's wife—another woman."[8]

This new information about the husband resonates with the testimony of **"Fibrous Ruin"** (section one) to: "a bruise new broken / from new pain inside / the feeling of let go." The last line carries the double meaning of being let go by someone else, followed by the painful process of letting go the rejecting other. In retrospect, we can see that two titles in *Some Changes* tacitly acknowledge the two changes associated with the husband and the mother: **"Let Me Live with Marriage"** and **"Not a Suicide Poem."** In both relationships the central fact is abandonment. Yet the two figures do not simply vanish, but have an afterlife, a ghostly presence in Jordan's imagination. In **"Not Looking,"** for example, the poet perhaps faces, and needs to communicate with, a person not actually there, though present in spirit:

> Not looking now and then I find you here
> not knowing where you are.
> Talk to me. Tell me the things I see
> fill the table between us or surround
> the precipice nobody dares to forget.

It is impossible to specify what this "precipice" is, but it is consonant with an experience of absolute separation. While biographical information about Jordan's husband and mother can help to account for the haunted, pained quality of the love relationships evoked in the poetry of *Some Changes,* this knowledge does not dispel the fundamental obscurity which is part of our experience as readers of these poems.

The obscurity is of two kinds: circumstantial and linguistic. First, we never know the exact situation. In **"What Declaration"** for instance, basic questions—who is the "you" the poet is addressing? what has happened? what is the "fear" which separates them?—remain unanswerable:

> You look at me not knowing
> I must guess what question I can ask
> to open every mouth (and mine)
> to free the throat (and yours) from fear.

Nor can we assume that the "you" is the same person from poem to poem. Consequently the reader is faced with a paradoxical combination of intimacy and inaccessibility. The poetry swiftly draws us in because of the intensity of the poet's distress, yet at the same time keeps us at a distance by withholding specific details. This mixture of confession and insistence on privacy is codified in a recent poem where Jordan interrupts the erotic flow with a direct plea to the lover: "I will never tell you the meaning of this poem: / Just say, 'She wrote it and I recognize / the reference.' Please / let it go at that" (**"Toward a City That Sings,"** *Passion*).

Second, the poems possess a verbal compression and density that resist our efforts to decipher. Words are jammed against one another, squeezing out connectives and leaving syntactical gaps impossible to fill. In part this elliptical writing can be ascribed to the "quasi-automatic process" of composition Jordan herself has noted in her early work (*Civil Wars,* p. 123). However, the poem entitled **"Toward a Personal Semantics"** suggests a more profound reason for the difficulty of Jordan's language. One source of the power of her love poems is their ability to communicate how emotional anguish is compounded by the imperfect fit between words and things, words and experience. Here the implications of the adjective "personal" must be stressed. Routine semantics, the standard set of verbal signs will not do: the poet begins as if from scratch, determined to forge a language answering to her own sense of pain. Even though she may only reach the poignant conclusion—"I sing of stillborn lyrics almost sung"—she has nevertheless successfully named her situation.

The overall formal effect is that, against an inchoate, disorienting background, a fragment emerges that strikes us as utterly convincing, apt, and precious. The form of Jordan's love poem corresponds to the psychological situation hinted in **"All the World Moved"** (from section one). Jordan outgrows the philosophical framework supplied by her religious upbringing: "but later / life began and strangely / I survived his innocence / without my own." But this triumph is revealed to be problematic as the love poems trace in distilled, guarded fashion the dilemmas to which loss of innocence can lead. The poems in section two of *Some Changes* struggle to survive (to work through and come to terms with) guilt. Their ultimate strength comes from Jordan's refusal to represent herself simply as a victim. In the poems preoccupied with fidelity, the poet scrutinizes her own contribution to the failure of love.

"When I or Else" begins with the poet's image of herself as "loser" in the conflict with her lover, but ends with a defiant final line affirming what the relationship seems to require be restricted or denied: "and / yes directed by desire." In **"Let Me Live with Marriage,"** confronted by the apparent incompatibility of marital love with a desire that directs her to be both "unruly" and "alive," the poet presents an ultimatum:

> Let me live with marriage
> as unruly as alive
> or else alone and longing
> not too long alone.

In order to reject a love "unduly held by guilt," she is forced sarcastically to take upon herself the stereotypical rhetorical meaning of black as evil—"Oh yes! / I am black within / as is this skin / without one pore / to bleed a pale defense"—and to sever the bond—"With word with silence / I have flung myself from you." Sacrificing the marriage rather than her vital "unruliness," the poet ruefully terminates both poem and relationship: "If this be baffling then the error's proved / To love so long and leave my love unmoved."[9]

"Toward a Personal Semantics" begins with the issue of fidelity: "if I do take somebody's word on / it means I don't know and you have to / believe if you just don't know." But the outcome of this agonizing effort to trust is an imagery of unrelieved bleakness, including perhaps an admission of the poet's own deficient faith: "after all the plunging / myself is no sanctuary." In a mood of resignation and pathos, the poet sees herself left to the mercy of the elements (and to her own complicity in the specifically human element of deteriorated love): "to twist and sting / the tree of my remaining / like the wind." Yet the final self-image of the poet as a tree conveys not only tragic desolation or an Ovidian punishment of stasis, but also a staying power. The tree implies a latent capacity for further growth, a potential strength which might be realized when a new, transformative perspective gave access to it: ". . . a tree growing away from the earth enacts a wild event."

Anticipating the resolve underlying the dismay at the conclusion of **"Toward a Personal Semantics,"** the last poem in section two—**"In Love"**—points forward to Jordan's subsequent explorations in love poetry. After an extended mimetic celebration of sexuality as a quasi-cosmic force, this poem precipitates a simple testimony to love in its final line: "particular and chronic." Incorporating the tribulations of loving, the word "chronic" remains open to the whole range of connotations from disease (love sickness) and habitual routine to its root evocation of time and the periodic cycle of falling in and out of love. Cupid, the classic embodiment of the love force, can be tyrannical and predictable as well as anarchic and liberating—a recognition perhaps contained in the line from **"Toward a Personal Semantics"**: "arrows create me." What saves Jordan's love poetry from conformity to a compulsively repeated pattern in which eros dictates and dominates the self is its particularity. The two adjectives "particular and chronic" are carefully counterpointed so that the first pulls back against the weight of the second.

II. "Let me more than words"

The importance of section two in *Some Changes* is indicated by the way Jordan uses it to structure *Things That I Do in the Dark* (1977), her selected poems. Two of the four divisions in *Things* [*Things That I Do in the Dark*] have titles drawn from poems in section two—"Directed by Desire" (the last line of **"When I or Else"**) and "Toward a Personal Semantics" (after the poem of that name)—all the poems from section two being dispersed between these two categories in *Things*.[10] This reorganization separates into two distinct issues—love and language (semantics)—what had been merged in section two of *Some Changes*. The chief result is to isolate and heighten the theme of language.

Jordan reinforces this division by placing at the beginning of each of the two parts a previously unpublished poem from 1954. Using the dates provided by *Things*, we can determine that the earliest poem in section two of *Some Changes* is **"Then It Was,"** dated 1955. Since it is the one poem in the sequence which portrays unqualified erotic fulfillment, it is tempting to regard **"Then It Was,"** with its decisively inflected title, as the original pristine moment of first love. But the two 1954 poems cancel its claim to chronological priority: the sexual harmony recorded in **"Then It Was"** has been preceded by the complicating features of love—sadness, guilt, and pain—already familiar to us from the other poems in *Some Changes*. In **"The Round of Grief,"** which introduces the "Directed by Desire" section in *Things*, love is enmeshed by an imagery of "clean thorn tongue" and "suckled fearful," and the poem is entwined by reiterated lines that pronounce love inevitably doomed to "grief": "Your hand is bone and mine is skin / Like lonely fools our limbs do not combine."

The lead poem for "Towards a Personal Semantics," the final part of *Things*, is called **"I Am Untrue Yet I,"** a title which suggests the prospect of a defense for the poet's infidelity. But the impulse behind **"Yet I"** is never completed, conveying an effect of speechlessness, as if the poet has no language for self-defense. The title, its promise unfulfilled, remains the most resonant element in the poem. As such, it draws attention to the search for a true language as well as a true love. Is there a language which will faithfully render the poet's experience and to which she can plight her artistic troth? Or do all words betray just as love does?

"Fragments from a Parable (of the 1950's)" is Jordan's most stubborn effort to pursue the motif of linguistic fidelity. This work consists of a revised version of the short poem **"Toward a Personal Semantics,"** with the addition of a lengthy mythological rumination. The significance Jordan attaches to the project is implied by her carrying it through three volumes of poetry: from its initial appearance in *Some Changes* to its elaboration in *New Days* and finally to Jordan's making the expanded piece serve as the conclusion of *Things*. This position among "the last things" suggests that **"Fragments of a Parable"** represents the farthest reach of her metaphysical inquiry, that it might have the status of revelation (as hinted by the headnote on Saul's conversion to Paul).

The prose myth Jordan spins out of her poem suggests a potentially feminist critique of the triumph of a rigid patriarchal principle over a life-giving matriarchal principle. Using the poem's first line—"if I do take somebody's word on"—as her cue, Jordan focuses on the role of language as the source of the father's power over the mother: "He came to name my mother, His. He came to tame my mother and to shelter her." Paternal language is employed to coerce and repress. "The Wall" and "The House," like the language which confers on them "a holy name," are man-made constructs whose function is to imprison the female. The daughter is equally condemned by the father's linguistic authority: ". . . I asked my father to tell me a word for my first dream. / He held me on his lap as he gave me the word for my dream / *Cemetery* was what he whispered in my ear."

The new context supplied by the parable redefines the phrase, "take somebody's word on." The neutral meaning, to accept another's word in order to engage in human relationship, is under these conditions no longer a possibility. The choice is now between two stark options: either passively take on the word as a crushing burden, or take on the word in the sense of fighting back. The poet attempts here the latter course. She identifies with the mother in resistance against the father: "She is who I am." But the mother lacks language. Her song has turned to babble, finally to silence: "For almost a year she wandered with a great song of hatred troubling her lips. She became deranged, an idiot. . . ." How can the poet, entrapped in paternal language, release the maternal song?

The poet strives to cleanse herself of the father's contaminated language, her screaming capitals a measure of the acuteness of her dilemma:

> I AM SEEKING
> THE CAPITAL INTRODUCTION TO THE VERY
> FIRST WORD OF
> MY MIND. I WANT TO DESTROY IT. I KNOW
> THAT THE VERY
> LAST WORD IS NOT ME.

Since all language belongs to the father, it seems impossible for the poet to discover her own words. Her opening statement has conceded to the father an apparently insurmountable power that tinges rebellion with a futile, self-defeating quality: "And this is my story of Her. The story is properly yours to tell. You have created her. . . ." An analogue for the father's creation here is Jordan's description elsewhere of poetic composition as enthrallment: "At first, say roughly from the age of seven through my mid-twenties, poetry was the inside dictator to whom I more or less simply submitted myself. . . ."

Jordan tries to end her submission to the "inside dictator" in **"Fragments from a Parable"** by fashioning a poetry of desire. The effort to revolt in prose is intrinsically limited because prose is the father's medium. To conduct the revolt in his terms is to play into his hands: the poet becomes entangled by her own labored, tortured, turgid prose. In a last, desperate struggle to free herself, she endeavors to shake loose from the dead linguistic weight through poetic flight. Harking back to the imagery of "birds" and "wings" in the original poem **"Toward a Personal Semantics"** that has been her starting-point, she offers an even briefer love lyric:

> gulls fly along a shoulder
> I am baffled by
> your neck concealing
> flight

This poem leads to the one word the father cannot completely control, the word which might serve as the

basis for a new (or renewed) language: "But there is that word. Desire. . . ."

Trying to keep desire free of linguistic degradation, Jordan sharply opposes word and physical act:

> Touch my tongue with yours.
> I would swallow the limbs of your body and refuse
> to Write Down and disturb the magic of my
> engorgement.
> Let me more than words. . . .

We can of course be quick to point out the paradox that this escape from words is represented in words: she can only render nonverbal erotic experience in language or what will subsequently be called "Metarhetoric." "Touch my tongue with yours" finds its equivalent in the finely tuned impatience of **"Meta-Rhetoric,"** the final poem in the section "Directed by Desire" in ***Things***:

> Can you give me the statistical dimensions
> of your mouth on my mouth
> your breasts resting on my own?

This poem is a breakthrough not only because of its treatment of lesbian sexuality but also because of its emotional and aesthetic composure. As the poem shows, there is a crucial difference between ordinary rhetoric and the metarhetoric of poetic desire. No matter how important or subtle the political terminology with which Jordan begins—*"Homophobia / racism / self-definition / revolution struggle"*—the poem runs the danger of performing a premature closure. Against this, Jordan insists on language and bodies that remain open to "coincidence":

> My hope is that our lives will declare
> this meeting
> open

"Fragments from a Parable" fails to enact a comparable declaration of open-endedness. Instead, the poet finally succumbs to the father's dictum: "You will not let me more than words." In the end, he is the speaker, she the receiver of his words. The actual content of his fiat does not matter: it could be "anything." It matters only that he has spoken:

> I have heard the rope in your throat ready to squeeze
> me into the syntax of stone
> The sound of my life is a name you may not remember
> I am losing the touch of the world to a word
> *You must have said anything to me*

In the long term, **"Fragments from a Parable"** should be seen as a transitional work, a work of purgation that clears the way for the confidence of a poem like **"Meta-Rhetoric."**

III. "AS SUDDENLY AS LOVE"

"Meta-Rhetoric" is the final poem in a series of new love poems in ***Things*** beginning with **"On a New**

Year's Eve." This group of poems exhibits a fluency and freshness that contrast with the more obscure, burdened love poetry we have examined in *Some Changes.* The new poems seem freer, as if Jordan has found both a felicitous vocabulary and a psychological peace with regard to the vagaries of erotic love. Jordan as love poet rededicates herself to the unpredictable:

> Some would rather know the rules
> be miserable but safe
> a well-dressed certainty
> that runs from rain
> and other
> unbid
> possibilities

> **("Minutes from the Meeting")**

We have no trouble recognizing the continuity between this statement and the voice that asked to "live with marriage / as unruly as alive." What is new is the greater assurance and complexity of Jordan's treatment of "unbid / possibilities": sexual and linguistic abandon are more finely calibrated, and both are more subtly held by poetic form.

To conclude **"For Dave: 1976,"** an anecdotal poem about a sexual encounter, the poet stands back to make a "simple," "forthright" generalization:

> And I accept again
> that there are simple ways of being joined
> to someone
> absolutely different from myself
> And I admire the forthright
> crocus first to mitigate the winter
> with its thrust voluptuous/
> on time

This final touch—the shift to "admiration" of the crocus, the translation of "voluptuous" occasion into poetic image—enables the poem to transcend immediate circumstance, to give it a wider, potent range of reference. The crystallizing image of the flower also occurs in **"Queen Anne's Lace"** where, "Unseemly as a marvelous as astral renegade," it symbolized "unbid / possibilities":

> You (where are you really?) never leave me
> to my boredom: numb as I might like to be.
> Repeatedly
> you do revive
> arouse alive
> a suffering.

The "renegade" or anarchic possibilities of the flower exceed expectation, stimulating not only aliveness but also—in the surprising last line—"a suffering." This term anticipates the root meaning of *Passion,* which it glances back to the connection of love with pain in her earlier poems.

The potential for suffering in love is deftly acknowledged and mediated in the pair of "Sunflower Sonnets" [**"Sunflower Sonnet Number One"** and **"Sunflower Sonnet Number Two"**]. **"Let Me Live with Marriage"** provides a useful reference point:

> Love if unduly held by guilt
> is guilty with fear
> wronging that fixed impulse
> to seek and ever more
> to bind with love.

The **"Sunflower Sonnets"** deal once again with the "fixed impulse" and with its distortion by "guilt." But where the mood of the earlier poem is plaintive and floundering, these poems are spirited and poised. This poise derives in large measure from formal structure. The flow and overflow of the conversational line strains against the rhyme scheme which makes each poetic line end-stopped: this built-in formal tension vividly dramatizes the thematic conflict between fidelity and instability, permanence and transience, in love. The self-conscious artistry displayed in the sonnets carries over to the poems in "free form."

"On a New Year's Eve," a sustained philosophical meditation on the impermanence of love, ultimately suggests a distinction between poetic and amorous activity. Jordan opposes "infinity" with "the temporary," and makes her resolution to choose the latter: "the temporary is the sacred." Her verbs signify humble devotion, the transient and finite requiring performance of their own exacting rites:

> I crawl and kneel and grub about
> I beg and listen for
>
> what can go away
>
>   (as easily as love)

But as Jordan celebrates the momentary, the time-bound against the timeless, her term "history" introduces a double perspective of present and past:

> it is this time
> that matters
>
> it is this history
> I care about
>
> the one we make together
> awkward
> inconsistent

Love's gestures are unique and fleeting, but even after love is ended, the "history" can be preserved as "an uncontrolled / heartbeating memory."

She speaks here as a poet as much as a lover. The two roles are interdependent, but nonetheless distinct. Jordan's earlier poetry is often based on a fusion of the roles; finding love an engulfing contingency, she tends to produce a poetic experience of pure contingency. In

"On a New Year's Eve" however, the differentiation between the actual love and its poetic recapitulation permits a saving grace. The end of love no longer means total loss, since it can be redeemed by poetic recollection. As the coda insists, "all things are dear / that disappear." What disappears in life can be recovered in art. Jordan does not simply resign herself to the evanescence of things, but more actively commits herself to finding the "dearness" in "things that disappear." Conferring such value is the poet's task. Nor does Jordan deny contingency:

> do not amount to much
> unless these things submit to some disturbance
> some derangement such
> as when I yield myself/belonging
> to your unmistaken
> body

Instead, the openness to poetic "derangement" is no longer seen as incompatible with poetic control.

If **"Fragments from a Parable"** is the dividing line between Jordan's early and later poetry, the crucible through which she had to pass to go from one to the other, then the outcome of this process can be briefly summarized by **"Poem toward the Bottom Line."** The title itself proudly and punningly announces the poem's artifice—the interest in formal delight and structural control. The poem is a tightly-knit verbal web in which linguistic difficulty is counterpoised by artistic command. The poem as a whole is shaped by a movement from chaos ("we began here / where no road existed"), then "unpredictable around the corner / of this sweet occasion" to the climactic final line: "tenderly enough." The poem "enacts a wild event," while keeping the wildness firmly under artistic control and while reconciling erotic "disturbance" and "derangement" with "tenderness." In the context of *Passion* as a whole, **"Poem toward the Bottom Line"** helps to provide an important contrast with the poems concerned with rape (**"Case in Point," "Rape Is Not a Poem,"** and **"Poem about My Rights"**). The theme of rape is not new; it goes back to the mother's rape in **"Fragments of a Parable"**: "They made their rabid inquiry and left her." In *Passion,* Jordan needs a distinction between erotic force and rape. She must be able artfully to enter the sexual labyrinth and find that the bottom line is tenderness: "the body of your trusting me."

The achievement of trust is particularly powerful when seen from the perspective of the early love poetry where much trust, though ardently sought, was unobtainable. The overall shift in Jordan's poetic development from a negative image of love as desolation to a positive version of love as affirmation thus provides an indispensable context in which to read individual poems. The exploration of love is not an end in itself since it becomes a resource for a larger political vision. But the

political rhetoric is the stronger for being grounded in Jordan's sustained, intimate engagement with love's anarchy. To use the final phrase of the poem **"From Sea to Shining Sea"** in Jordan's most recent volume *Living Room,* the energy to overcome despair and to imagine political change, which turns the poem around, issues from the celebration of love as "a natural disorder."

Notes

1. This article appears in *Afro-American Writers After 1955: Prose Writers and Dramatists,* ed. Thadious M. Davis and Trudier Harris, *Dictionary of Literary Biography,* 38 (Detroit: Gale Research, 1985) 146-62.

2. Jordan's books of poetry are: *Who Look at Me* (1969), *Some Changes* (1971), *New Days: Poems of Exile and Return* (1974), *Things That I Do in the Dark: Selected Poems* (1977), *Passion: New Poems 1977-1980* (1980), and *Living Room* (1985). For a discussion of *Who Look at Me,* which consists of a single, long poem, readers are referred to my previous essay. *Things That I Do in the Dark* includes almost all poems from the two earlier collections, *Some Changes* and *New Days.* The poems are dated for the first time in *Things That I Do in the Dark,* but appear neither in their original nor in their chronological order. Since in *Things That I Do in the Dark* Jordan has dispersed and rearranged these poems, they have two contexts: their position in the original volume and their position in the new sequence in *Things.* Of particular interest are the twenty-eight new poems (dated 1973-1976) in *Things* and the ways they suggest a transition to *Passion.*

3. Sharon Bray, "A Poet of the People: An Interview with June Jordan," *WIN* magazine (March 1, 1981), p. 22.

4. Jordan's commentary on the "political poetry" of the sixties and its tendency to adopt "postures of self-righteousness" is apposite here: see "The Black Poet Speaks of Poetry: Towards a Differing Sense of Things," *American Poetry Review* (July/August 1976), pp. 15-16.

5. From "For the Sake of People's Poetry: Walt Whitman and the Rest of Us," Preface to *Passion* (Boston: Beacon, 1980) xix.

6. Jordan leaves this poem undated in *Things That I Do in the Dark*; it is tempting to speculate that the "Today" of the title refers to an ultimate separation from the beloved ("Nobody sleeping in my bed") that is too momentous to be limited to a single point in time.

7. Jordan's mother is the primary theme of Jordan's first address at Barnard College in 1975, reprinted as Chapter 12 in *Civil Wars* (Boston: Beacon, 1981). The second address, "Many Rivers to Cross" (1981), is included in *On Call: Political Essays* (Boston: South End Press, 1985).

8. Jordan has since written a moving account of the marriage and breakup in "Love is Not the Problem" (1983); reprinted in *On Call.*

9. In my *Dictionary of Literary Biography* essay, I have discussed this poem's echoes of Shakespeare's Sonnet 116.

10. The one exception is "For Christopher" (Jordan's son), which is placed under the heading "For My Own," a section whose main focus is family.

June Jordan and Peter Erickson (interview date 1994)

SOURCE: Jordan, June, and Peter Erickson. "After Identity." *Transition,* no. 63 (1994): 132-49.

[*In this interview, Erickson considers the complexities of Jordan's conception of identity and politics as portrayed in her writings.*]

June Jordan is a poet, essayist, and political activist. Among her books of poetry are three volumes of selected poems: ***Things That I Do in the Dark*** (1977), ***Naming Our Destiny*** (1989), and ***Haruko/Love Poems,*** published this year with a foreword by Adrienne Rich. June Jordan's three collections of essays are: ***Civil Wars*** (1981), ***On Call*** (1985), and ***Technical Difficulties: African-American Notes on the State of the Union*** (1992). Since February 1989 she has written a column called "Just Inside the Door" for *The Progressive,* a monthly journal. On the occasion of the paperback printing of ***Technical Difficulties,*** Toni Morrison described June Jordan as "our premier black woman essayist."

Her poetry and prose both portray a passionately engaged conscience, yet a conscience that is also multifaceted, evolving, open to new possibilities. Her concerns range from power relations in a global context to individual love relations seen from a bisexual perspective. Her most fundamental commitment is to a rigorous scrutiny of democracy that focuses not only on its history of exclusions, but also on its potential for expansion. The keynote of her moral voice is the absolute refusal to be confined by fixed categories of identity, including race. One of the most interesting elements in her career is the complicated way in which she has negotiated black nationalism and come out on the other side. She continues to be resolute in her insistence on nothing less than full justice and empowerment for black Americans; but she is equally insistent about her transcendent human vision of political coalitions formed across racial lines.

[*Erickson*]: *Let's start with California. After living in New York for the first 53 years of your life, you moved to Berkeley in 1989 to begin your new position as*

Professor of African-American and Women's Studies. You are now in the middle of your fourth year in California. How has the move from New York to California affected your life? Has living in California had an impact on your vision of American society?

[Jordan]: California is completely different from the rest of the United States, to the best of my knowledge. But it's also the forecast for the rest of America, as far as changing demographics are concerned and what that implies. So I'm really excited to be here in the today of California and the tomorrow of the rest of America, both in the context of public education and the kinds of changes we'll have to undertake, and also especially because I feel my life has a quiet kind of sanity now as a result of the mix of people that I see on the streets and that I know in my own personal and professional life.

You were born in Harlem and you grew up in Bedford-Stuyvesant in Brooklyn, where your family moved when you were three. Both of your parents emigrated from Jamaica, though they met in New York. Did you have a specific sense of identity as a Jamaican-American?

As far as their views were concerned, my parents were, in today's lingo, nationalists and very much Jamaican nationalists. And there was a lot of concern about Jamaican food, which we ate most of the time and which occupied a lot of our family life—the preparation for it, the eating of it, the discussion of whether it was as good as so-and-so's. And all of my parents' friends that I can remember—well, not all of them, say 90% of them—were West Indians. And then there was maybe 10% of the people who were Americans, African-Americans.

Did your parents maintain contact with relatives in Jamaica? Did you have the feeling of a strong family connection between New York and Jamaica when you were growing up?

On my mother's side, there were photographs and visits with the cousins and their families and children. But my father's family was much more dispersed. In fact, a lot of his family resides in Panama and speaks only Spanish. And I have virtually lost that part of my family.

Do you have current contacts with Jamaica?

No, I just think of it as the homeland of my parents.

What were your parents' hopes for you?

My father was interested in having me become successful as a doctor, probably a brain surgeon or something like that. My mother was interested in having me marry a doctor or, preferably, a dentist. So they had quite different, you might even say gender-divided, expectations.

How did they communicate that?

I always had really pretty good grades. I can't even remember bringing home a whole lot less than an A. My father in particular would just say, you have to keep this up. It was always, you have to keep this up. And if you do, then you could become a doctor. He was quite straightforward—that makes it possible for you to become a doctor. He didn't ask me if I wanted to become a doctor. My mother would say things like, you don't need to go to this school or that school, which was usually the school I was already attending. She characterized it as too fancy or highfalutin. She would suggest something local—Brooklyn College, for example—where I would meet somebody whose parents we would probably know through the church and marry in a really quite local way.

What was the most important thing you received from your mother?

Oh dear. I don't know the answer to that.

What about your father?

My father imposed upon me a very keen sense of my intellectual aptitude, which he had tested when I was about two years old. So as the result of that, I knew from when I was very, very little that intellectually speaking, anyway, I didn't need to worry about anything. And I think that's been very helpful because as a girl and as a black person in this country there were a lot of ways in which people might have tried to make me feel inferior or unable. But I never felt inferior or unable on an intellectual level. That, in a perverse way, was something my father gave me. It didn't come from my mother—she was never interested in my report card, she wouldn't even look at that. And then my father also had a very passionate interest in beautiful things. He demonstrated that in a lot of ways. As a maniacal photographer. As a post-office worker who went to the Parke-Bernet auction gallery over in Manhattan and would choose a small but exquisitely beautiful object for our house like an umbrella stand. The music he loved and listened to—Beethoven, Bach, Brahms. His attention to detail as far as beauty is concerned—even in the backyard he always had a definite plan for the garden. He even colored the concrete for the pathways he laid down in the yard so that it was this distinctively beautiful, lovely rose color. He was obsessed with beauty. He's the one who took me to concerts and the planetarium and so on.

The other thing he did was to raise me pretty much as a boy. Physically I had the idea that I was supposed to be hearty. He would do things when I was just a toddler. I forget which bridge it was across the Harlem River and I was not more than 2½ years old and he would ask me

to try to hold my breath all the way across the bridge. Then he would say, "Well, everyday you try to hold your breath a little longer." Then he'd give me memory exercises that he had picked up in the army. So we're walking across the bridge and I'm holding my breath, he's also saying that he wants me to notice everything I possibly could and then we'd get to the other side of the bridge and he'd say, "OK, what'd you see?" And I'd have to say, it's a ferry or I didn't see one, I saw three people, da-da, da-da. The model was military. Because he had raised me in a lot of ways as a boy, it seemed perfectly natural to resist him when he was being abusive. At least at the time it was very unusual for a little girl to resist her father's beatings. It just never occurred to me not to do that, because he had taught me, don't let anybody pick on you. So in all those different ways he was, I would say, absolutely critical.

Do you trace your political convictions back to either of your parents, or were your political ideas a later development?

No, I wouldn't trace them to either of them. But the fact that my father and mother thought of themselves in a bitter way as some kind of interracial couple and the fact that they bitterly disputed my racial identity meant that I was predisposed to try and avoid a kind of either-or formulation and to try, rather, to be inclusive politically. Because otherwise I think I would feel I was choosing either my father or my mother, rather than managing to embrace both of them.

I don't know what this means about disputing your racial identity. What was the dispute?

Well, my father was sometimes what we would call today a black nationalist. Other times he acted as though he thought he was a white man. He looked white. When he was angry at my mother, he would call her "damn black woman." And he would say, "Where did that black child come from?" That was me. Because, he would say, obviously somebody like me could not come from him because of the kind of hair he had, the color, and all this. And she would say, "Well I don't know where she came from." So they would both disown me. Which left me nowhere. Which can be a kind of freedom.

Other than your parents, who were the significant people in your growing-up?

My Uncle Teddy, my aunt's husband, was very significant to me because he interfered with my father. He stopped my father from bullying me a lot. He also taught me to fight. And he had very high expectations of me as well. But it was different because my father imposed expectations upon me, but he did not expect me to do well, so it was kind of punitive—either you do really well or you're gonna get beaten. My uncle, on the other hand, was always expecting me to do really well—his name for me was Ace—so it was a completely different way of motivating me to excel. My uncle, who was an African American, spoke many languages within English—and the one he spoke to my greatest delight was Black English. He was a terrific, fabulous storyteller. And I always thought he was a great dresser, a great dancer, and a great singer. He had friends over sometimes and they would play for hours on the piano, they would play blues and he would sing. Or they would come over and play pinochle, and they would joke, and smoke, and eat, and play cards all night long. I just thought that was the most fascinating thing. Both he and my father were what I would call roosters, you know, extremely vain. They were both extremely interested in style, but they handled it differently.

What was your block like? What was the racial and ethnic mix of the immediate area and surrounding neighborhoods?

Most all of them were homeowners like my parents. That was about fifty-fifty West Indian and African American. Then there were the families, entirely African American, that rented cold-water flats. There was a real class difference. And then on the avenues it was entirely African American again and those families lived on top of stores. So economically the spread was from low-income working poor through lower middle income. So there would be somebody whose father was a garage mechanic and on the other hand there would be Father Coleman, our minister and the first black man on the New York City Board of Education, who lived across the street. It was quite a spread.

What were your experiences in school in the Bedford-Stuyvesant school system and at Midwood High School?

I don't remember a lot about school inside the classroom. Outside the classroom it was a real problem because I had to fight every day. There would be somebody waiting for me. Sometimes it would be a boy, though not often. So I had to fight just to get home. I didn't like that a whole lot. Eventually I actually joined a gang. I can remember times when my mother wanted me to run to the store and pick up some milk and I'd think, "Oh no!" At Midwood High School that was weird because, as I recollect, I was the only black student out of 3,000 students. That was really strange, because my whole universe was black and all of a sudden there I was the only person who was black. I don't remember a whole lot about it, except I didn't like that either. I didn't like traveling that much—it took forever, 1½ hours, to get there. I hated being the only person who was not white. I felt weird, and I felt I absolutely had to get A+s all down the line. In my own kid's way, I didn't think this was a great way to have a childhood.

I remember one of the things I did while I was there—which was only for a year—which was to develop a crush on this guy who played bass. And so I decided to try to learn how to play bass. That was pretty funny because I was like 4' 11" and he was about 6' 2". And he kept saying, "the bass? You want to play bass?" And I said, yeah, yeah.

How did it come about that you went to private school at Northfield School in Massachusetts? How did you find out about it? Who encouraged you to go?

Well, my father talked with Father Coleman and asked him what was the best prep school in the country and he recommended Northfield School for Girls. My father was interested to have me go there because he thought I was becoming a bit of a thug from hanging out in our neighborhood and fighting all the time. He didn't like the way I was talking. He thought I had a Brooklyn accent. And he had heard that Northfield was a finishing school for young ladies and he wanted me to be "finished." He apparently at this point had decided that I was a girl after all. So the school tested me and then I went.

The scholastic set-up at Northfield-Mt. Herman was first-rate. I loved it in that respect. I felt without question that I was in a world with my peers. I found most everybody very interesting. I was delighted to be there really in most ways. Even though the first year I was there I didn't open my mouth because I knew I didn't talk the "right way." But by the second year I was running at the mouth.

What was the most important thing that happened to you there?

It would be one of two things. One would be what would be the case for anybody who goes away to prep school, which is that because you live entirely with your peers day and night, Sunday to Sunday, all grown-ups become really peripheral to your experience. And so my sense of things was that however you acquitted yourself there was an absolutely reliable prediction of how you would do as an adult. It was excellent preparation for dealing with the world on a moral basis because the school was a religious school—at that time it was anyway—and there was a fundamental commitment to the idea of service, the idea of being of use in the world. And cooperation rather than competition. Those values and that kind of training and perspective, all of that has stayed with me in a very basic way.

The other thing I think was important was that I came to a racial identity because this was an all-white prep school. They didn't even have enough boys, as far as I was concerned, for a real decent choice of boyfriends, as far as black boys were concerned, because it was mostly white and there was no interracial dating. So when I went up there, everything I did—all the music I knew, the songs, the way I danced, the way I dressed—everything was "wrong." And by the middle of the year, I realized it wasn't wrong, it was black. I started thinking about it: everybody I knew at home danced like this and everybody I knew before I went there was black. So I began to realize that there were two worlds in this country. One was black and one was white. And for whatever reason my parents had decided to send me to a white world. But going to a completely different place where a lot of people looked at me as though I was from Mars helped me to understand who I was in a racial sense and also how I fit into this country.

How did you start writing? Did you begin writing completely on your own, or did you have someone who encouraged you? How did your parents feel about your writing?

It was on my own. I received encouragement from different teachers in school but not much at home. To the extent that my parents thought this meant I would do something other than become a doctor or lawyer, it was not a good sign.

You have many different writing identities: you are a journalist, an essayist, a poet, a dramatist. Which of these identities do your consider to be primary?

Poetry. And they're very separate activities. Poetry, I think, is about telling the truth. I'd say that essays are about trying to persuade people about something or other. And playwriting is moving into the realm of fiction.

What role did journalism play in giving you a start as a writer? Was journalism the mode in which you first imagined your career as a writer? To what extent do you still think of yourself as a journalist?

I am a working journalist. I have a press card. I don't think I'm a whole lot prouder of anything in my life than that press card I have with a San Francisco Police stamp on it. I didn't first think that I was going to be one; I thought of myself as a poet. But journalism had a lot of impact on my education in general because as a young woman that's how I met people such as Jimmy Hicks when he was the editor of *The Amsterdam News*. I knew everybody in Harlem, all the politicians, I knew Malcolm X, I knew all these people because I was a journalist, because I went around asking questions with my pen and my pad. As a result of functioning as a journalist, I got very addicted to facts, and listening to the way people say things, and what they actually say and don't say, and to seeing things for myself rather than waiting to hear second- and third-hand what supposedly happened some place.

You have written three dramas: **For the Arrow that Flies by Day, Bang Bang Uber Alles,** *and* **All These Blessings.** *What attracted you to this medium?*

I think it's my favorite kind of writing actually. I think it's the most challenging. It means I necessarily have to work with other people. The director is as important as I am, and I like that a lot. It takes you out of the loneliness. I think in one way or another I'm always trying to get away from being an only child, and theater is a great way to do it. It's alive and it's collective.

In what is presumably the first commentary on your poetry, Julius Lester wrote in the Introduction to **Some Changes** *(1971):*

> For some, her poetry may not qualify as "black poetry" because she doesn't rage or scream. No, she's quiet, but the intensity is frightening. Her poetry is highly disciplined, highly controlled. It's tight, like the Muddy Waters blues band is tight.

How does Lester's characterization of your early poetry strike you now? Would it be accurate to say that Lester's reference to "black poetry" can be considered a reaction against the expectations and strict conventions of a Black Aesthetic?

Well, at the time LeRoi Jones was writing in a certain way and a lot of people were imitating that. And I was just writing in my own way and not thinking about what was or was not really black, because I was in my own way really black. And as far as the rage not being there, that is interesting to look back on now because of course most people always said when they'd meet me for the first time they were very surprised that I'm not much bigger than I am and that they'd think of me as this huge woman who was raging all over the place. Certainly the poetry that he's talking about is coming from a place of rage, a whole lot of it.

In his Introduction to **Some Changes,** *Julius Lester pointedly addresses the question of audience: "Thus, the expression of the black experience should illuminate the consciousness of anyone who opens himself to it. Indeed, it affords nonblacks an opportunity to see themselves in a mirror which will not return to them the image they might want to see. And it affords blacks the same experience." In your Introduction to* **Soulscript: Afro-American Poetry,** *published the year before, in 1970, you speak of "the fabulous efflorescence of black literary art that we, Afro-American and white, can enjoy and honor with our lives." Could you comment on your conception of your readership at the outset of your career? Did your perception of audience include nonblacks from the start? How has this perception fluctuated over the past two decades?*

I think I had the idea when I started writing poetry in earnest that if I was a great poet, people in general would recognize that. Then the reality of racism in this country was something that I learned about in many different ways, including what happens to you as a poet and a writer. The people I was writing for and on behalf of and hoping to reach throughout the whole period published under the title *Some Changes* were black people. That was my community. And then the conclusion of the black nationalist period of my life around the mid-seventies changed my ideas about who I was writing for. I was writing for anybody I could reach.

What was your response to the black nationalist position in literature during the late sixties and early seventies? To what extent were you aware of The Black Aesthetic, *to use Addison Gayle's landmark title of 1971, as you began your career?*

I was very much a part of the black nationalist movement. As far as what Addison called the black aesthetic, you know, he's a critic, he's talking about stuff after the fact. You can call it whatever you want to call it. I was never part of a school. LeRoi Jones and I are, in age, contemporaries, so obviously he was not my leader. We were writing at the same time, yet we were different poets. Some things we did are similar, but a lot of things we did are not similar. That's all I'll say about it.

How did you meet Alice Walker?

Since I was teaching at Sarah Lawrence when she came through there, she and her husband at the time, Mel Leventhal, came to visit. Then a long time after that I went to Mississippi in 1969 to research a piece I called "Black Home in Mississippi" and when I got to Jackson, I interviewed her there. And in the course of that interview we became friends. [The article was published as **"Mississippi 'Black Home': A Sweet and Bitter Bluesong"** in *The New York Times Magazine,* October 11, 1970.]

In her Revolutionary Petunias & Other Poems *(1973), Walker cites you three times: as a dedicatee with Julius Lester at the beginning of the "Revolutionary Petunias" section, and in the epigraphs for two later sections. Can you give us the background for these references? Why did Walker find her connection with you particularly important at this moment?*

You'd have to ask Alice. We were very good friends, very close. I wrote to Alice from Rome where I was living for 1970-71 and I think I wrote to her beyond that.

Your first teaching job was at City College of New York starting in 1967. Among the extraordinary group of people teaching at City College during that period were Toni Cade Bambara, Barbara Christian, Addison Gayle, Jr., Audre Lorde, and Adrienne Rich. Can you describe what it was like to be there at that time? Was there a collective spirit, the sense of shared project?

Not right away but, I would say, by the end of the first year. There were two things that happened. One was that there was a woman named Mina Shaughnessy, who's an unsung educational giant in America. She had come up with these theories about how you could teach people to read and write. There was a program called SEEK that was entirely devoted to enabling students to read and write, and also to do mathematics so they could carry themselves independently in a college situation after a year of this kind of instruction. It was very demanding, the whole concept, because after whatever time, a semester, the students would be tested, and however many would get in, or not, on a completely competitive basis. So in that sense, you, the teacher, became really accountable. And so our goal was to get 100% of our students able to complete this exam and succeed at it. Everybody was very excited about this. We were all talking about it. The English department was discouraging. And then it was 1969 that the students decided we're going to have open admissions there at City University. So they just decided to take the university out and shut it down. During that time of extreme excitement and revolution, all of those people you mentioned got to know each other and also respect each other.

Toni Cade Bambara was like a mentor to me, not like a mother but a mentor. I remember my first class in the SEEK program. I thought, how does this thing work? Because accountability sounds great, but then when you're the one that's accountable, it's scary. She was never trained in teaching and she walked me all the way over to the building where my first class was going to take place, telling me, "you can do it." She told me what to concentrate on, what to think about. I don't think I could have done it without that because I was still very young and very scared. Toni Cade Bambara psyched me and prepared me. She wanted me to try to join the rest of the people there doing this stuff. And they were all in different ways very active during the student strike for open admissions. One of the things I did during that time was to write probably the first essay on Black Studies ["**Black Studies: Bringing Back the Person,**" 1969] to try to intellectually formulate a coherent way to understand the need for Black Studies. It's really exciting to think about how many people there at the same time you might say were rather distinguished writers and intellectuals. It was quite amazing. We didn't think of it as amazing. Everybody was just there and we thought that if we could make democracy come to City College that probably we could have an impact on the concept and perhaps even the practice of public education through the country. So there was a lot at stake.

Adrienne Rich was one of the people you first met while teaching at City College. In a letter to The New York Times Book Review *(April 19, 1987), you wrote that*

Rich "occupies a position of assured national honor as one of the few social thinkers of our time who has relentlessly dedicated herself to the fierce, honest engagement of the pivotal questions that torment contemporary life." Can you talk about different stages in your contact with Rich over the 25 years since that initial point at City College in 1967? Do you have the sense now of a renewed contact with Rich as part of a California community of writers?

I knew her first because her husband Al Conrad was a major spokesperson on the faculty at City College. I remember he was very eloquent and elegant both. And his wife was Adrienne Rich the poet. I didn't know her very well, but I remember just thinking they were, in the terms of those days, an ideal couple. I wasn't really very familiar with her work. I made myself more familiar as a result of our shared political commitment at City College. And then I got to know her when I came back from Rome. By then he had died [in October 1970] and she was now a single mother of three sons. She had become a lesbian separatist—I use the words we use now, but I don't really remember what terms exactly we used then. She was very different. As a matter of fact when she came to the door to see me in Brooklyn, I didn't know who it was because the last time I had seen her she looked so different. When she talked to me about her new concerns and values and so forth, I got very much into her work. This was around the time of *Diving into the Wreck* [1973] and *Of Woman Born* [1976]. It seemed to me that she was taking on a lot of things that nobody else would touch. I thought that, for example, as documented in *Diving into the Wreck,* her engagement with racism as well as with the rift between the sexes, men and women, was just startling in its honesty, her honesty about her life, and in its brilliance of articulation. At that point she occupied a really interesting role. I would see her once a week. We would go out for a dinner at an Indian restaurant around the corner from 93rd Street and people would come up to her and say, Thank you so much for your work. We just became very fast friends and we began to exchange poems.

And then we were in different places politically. [Compare, for example, the two 1976 essays, Rich's "It Is the Lesbian in Us . . ." and Jordan's **"Declaration of an Independence I Would Just as Soon Not Have."**] We were not coincident, but I respected the difference between us and she respected it too. And then we had a huge rift because in 1982 Israel invaded Lebanon. And right around that time, I think it was in June of '82, she appeared identifying herself as a Jewish lesbian. [Rich was one of seven signees of "An Open Letter to the Women's Movement" published under the heading "Anti-Zionism Is Anti-Semitism" in the June 1982 issue of *New Women's Times* as well as the May 29th *Gay Community News.*] Now until that

time, to my knowledge, both in her prose and poetry Adrienne had never identified herself as Jewish, let alone Zionist. I didn't know what the lag was between what she had written and when it had appeared, but the timing was that Israel invaded Lebanon and then this thing came out. And I was just stunned. To me it would be like if Idi Amin was rampaging, as he did, and until then I had never identified myself as black. Okay, for me to come out during the time he's exterminating one people or another, inside or outside of Uganda, and for me to announce myself as black and specifically support whatever the name of his party was. . . . In any event, I was shocked. It was a huge, deep, inconsolable loss that I felt because I felt there was no way we could be friends. So I composed a letter to challenge her on moral grounds. I sent it there to whatever this publication was and they said, Oh, we couldn't do this to Adrienne. And I said, What are you talking about? Adrienne is a big girl. They said, She's the mother of our movement. They wouldn't publish what I wrote to challenge her, so I sent it to her. I didn't hear from her for years. From my point of view at that time, I thought, All right, call it. That was that.

Years went by. During the interim I understand that, among other things, she went to Nicaragua. Anyway her perspective changed on politics outside the United States; her perspective also changed as far as Israel was concerned and the Palestinians. Oh, I don't know how long it was—at least three years later—it turned out that we were both participating in an anti-apartheid benefit poetry reading in New York. And I just thought that this is somebody I love and there must be some way we could get past this. So I went up to her and I just said—until then we had never spoken a word—I completely and absolutely detest your views on Israel and I love you. And she stood up and we hugged. And then that was that. And then I was coming out here to give the commencement address for the English department here at UC Berkeley [May 1986], and I let her know. Anyhow we had a fateful lunch over at the Claremont Hotel where I was staying, and she asked me to forgive her. And then since then we have been very good friends to the best of our abilities for each other. She's a great poet. Whether one agrees with her or not, you have to have enormous respect for her attempt to be a scrupulous, honest, engaged, moral human being in our time.

In your regular column for The Progressive *(**"Diversity or Death,"** June 1990), you reported on Berkeley's new requirement in American Cultures. How has the American Culture requirement worked out in practice? Has it been successful from your perspective?*

It has to succeed. These requirements have to be a success. All we are talking about here is requiring that people find out about most of the people who live on the earth as well as most of the people in California. If you're going to live in California in the 21st century, which is only six years away, all we're talking about is that you be required to know something about one of these majority populations out here, whether we're talking about the people from India, the second largest population on the planet, or Chinese, or African. You should know basically something about—something coherent, that is—about somebody who's really different from yourself. And you should be able to speak to somebody else in a language other than your own. I think these are minimal requirements for the 21st century.

I want to ask about your views on the revision of the literary canon, because you approach this issue from the double vantage point of someone who is both a teacher and a writer. What is your assessment of the present situation with regard to canon revision?

I think the revision of the canon is underway. But this is a huge country so you almost have to take it one department by one department, class by class, course by course. It's happening in a really haphazard way. It's not some kind of irreversible wave sweeping onto the shore of academics. But it is underway. And it must not fail. But how you ensure that, I don't even know, other than to just try to ask people to be reasonable and to notice as much as they possibly can who are the students in your classroom—let's see if we can just come up with a syllabus that is, on the face of it, related to the lives of the students you have to teach.

I also want to ask about multiculturalism as a conceptual framework for approaching literature. What associations—positive and/or negative—do you have with the term "multiculturalism"?

I don't really have any negative associations. It's a reality. We live in a multicultural, multiethnic, multiracial, multilingual republic, as well as world. That's real to me. The question is, what are we going to do about it as far as the curriculum is concerned and as far as political representation is concerned? I'm assuming that the curriculum on all levels of public education will increasingly reflect the diversity of the peoples sitting in our classrooms and honor, in other words, the multicultural nature of our body politic more and more. I don't know how it's going to happen exactly.

June, one criticism from the left is that multiculturalism in literature is not equivalent to multiculturalism in society, that multicultural curricular change becomes a substitute for and diversion from the more difficult problem of real social change. How would you respond to this charge?

It doesn't make any sense to me. Literature has never been "the same as" or "equivalent to" society. Part of

"real social change" happens as the result of what creative folks envision, and also creative folks reflect what's new, as that begins to materialize.

Virago Press has published collections of your poetry and of your essays. What has the reception of your work in England been like?

The reception of my work over there has been quite astounding. They have received me just the way rock stars are received. I'll never forget when I went over there and, first of all, **Lyrical Campaigns: Selected Poems** [1989], was number one on the bestseller book list. My face was on these posters all over town and it was just quite astounding. I haven't changed what I'm writing consciously in view of that reception. But I do have in mind, before I go over there again to England, and also to Ireland, to have written some poems, at least, that specifically reflect what I have seen and the people I have met.

Virago Press published **Haruko/Love Poems: New & Selected Love Poems** *in March 1993. How did the* **Haruko** *poems originate?*

Well, I fell in love with somebody named Haruko for one thing and I guess I started writing these poems in 1991. The poems were coming so fast it occurred to me that they might eventually mass into a book. Originally what I had in mind was to compose 20 poems in the tradition of Neruda [*Viente poemas de amor y una canción desesperada*; *Twenty Love Poems and a Song of Despair*, 1924]. In the tradition of Neruda they would be cheaply printed out and made available to people to use and to enjoy. That has not happened unfortunately, but that was my original idea. The reception for my **Haruko** poems in England and Ireland both has been overwhelming. When I was there last year, I was reading from the political essays [**Technical Difficulties**, 1992] as well as the love poems. During the question-and-answer period, a lot of people invariably asked political questions, one political question after another. But then when it was time to buy books and get them signed, the **Haruko** [**Haruko/Love Poems**] poems outsold the political essays at least two to one. That was very interesting to me. Men would buy it for their wives, wives would buy it for their husbands, a number of fathers bought it for their little girls. I could never have imagined that kind of response to love poetry in general. It was just very wonderful to witness.

Do you see the **Haruko** *poems as a new development in your work?*

Yeah, because that's a whole series of poems that document the trajectory of a love affair with one person as against a miscellany of poems about miscellaneous people. So in that sense it's completely new. And I think technically as well. For example, there's a *Taiko Dojo* poem in there. So you can see, let's call it, the transcultural or crosscultural reality of the relationship in the love poems.

Regarding the transcultural dimension, do you feel the image of African-American and Asian-American cultures intersecting is positive and successful, despite the love's failure or demise on an individual level?

In the **Haruko** poetry, yes! As one of the poems concludes, "So do we finally recover side by side / what we have loved enough to keep / in spite of passion or love's sorrow."

Could you talk about the role of music in your work? I'm thinking particularly of Bernice Reagon Johnson's singing versions of your poems and of your collaboration with Adrienne Torf on the musical drama **Bang Bang Uber Alles.** *Do you plan other such collaborations?*

Actually, Leonard Bernstein set my poetry to music as well. [Bernstein's *Song-fest* (1977) contains a duet with Langston Hughes's "I, Too, Sing America" and June Jordan's **"Okay 'Negroes.'"**] A number of composers this year have been in touch with me trying to get me to write specifically for them. And there are other composers who have taken my work and asked permission to set the words to music. It doesn't surprise me because I write poetry from a musical perspective as much as anything else. So I would imagine for a musician it's relatively easy to work with my stuff, rather than somebody else's poetry which might be more about visual imagery rather than sound, for example. At the moment I'm excited because I am about to enter into formal relationship with John Adams, who is an extremely distinguished American composer and musician [and] who has already put out such works as *Nixon in China, Death of Klinghoffer,* and so forth. He and I are going to collaborate on the writing of a new musical piece for the theater which will be a love story, and which will premiere in 1995 here in Berkeley actually. Peter Sellars will direct. Peter Sellars is the main producer of it, and he's already booked us into productions in L.A., New York, London, Paris, Frankfurt, and so on. It has already a kind of world tour set for it. Of course I haven't done any writing yet!

"Civil Wars" (1980), the final essay in your first essay collection of the same name, mentions your "continuing self-denial around the 'issue' of my bisexuality" and states your view of gay rights as civil rights. More recently, you published a major statement on bisexuality in The Progressive *called* **"A New Politics of Sexuality."** *Could you give us an overview of how your thinking about sexual identity has evolved?*

I think those two essays track the development of my thinking about bisexuality as well as anything else. At this point, I do view the issue of bisexuality, if you want to call it that, as integral to the struggle for sexual freedom per se. And I do view the struggle for sexual freedom as integral to the struggle for freedom per se. I don't see sexual freedom or issues such as bisexuality or lesbian and gay sexuality as in any way peripheral to my concept of freedom. It's all about freedom. Whether we're working on academic freedom or sexual freedom, for example, the first thing that we're working on is freedom. I want to try to fuse all issues depending upon freedom for their solution, I want to fuse them as effectively as I can in the public consciousness.

Could you elaborate on the passage in the 1976 essay in **Civil Wars** *in which you criticized "lecherous, exploitative, shallow, acting out, pathological behavior by women who term themselves lesbians—in much the same way that we, black people, once voluntarily called ourselves* niggas *out of a convoluted mood of defiance, a mood that proved to be heavily penetrated by unconscious, continuing self-hatred"?*

I'm pretty sure when I wrote that—which was of course a very long time ago—that I was coming from a place of serious idealism and some naiveté. I guess I thought back then that in affirming who you were—whether as someone who wasn't white or someone who wasn't conventional in a sexual sense—in a hateful environment, it was necessary to present yourself in an ideal way. So, for example, as a black person, I wouldn't present myself as a nigger because nigger means something despicable that originated in the mouths of people who hate black people. So I wouldn't want verbally to participate in that hatred of myself. As regards the kind of anger I was talking about on the part of lesbians, I guess what I was talking about was that I thought [for] those of us who love women that it behooves us to love in a way that is exemplary. According to my terms, that would mean, for example, not lecherous, and not exploitative, and not degrading, and not sadistic, and not masochistic: Not any of those kinds of things I have always regarded as disgusting, wherever they occur. And I thought that I'm not going to function outside a heterosexual context in ways that heterosexual relations have demonstrated to be inhuman.

Now I would have to qualify everything because I'm older and less naive. I don't know that I'm less idealistic, but I think I am less naive. I just have to say that for *me,* I feel it's important that as a black person, as a woman, as somebody who's interested in acquiring sexual freedom—along with the acquisition of all her other freedoms—I feel that it is really crucial that I conduct my life and my relationships in an exemplary way according to my moral code, and my code of honor, and my code of defensible conduct between people who have a lot of intimate impact on each other. And that would include how teachers should interact with students, doctors should interact with patients, parents should interact with children.

I don't regret having said that. I know, for example, with Urvashi Vaid [former executive director of the National Gay and Lesbian Task Force] that the question of right and wrong is just now arising inside the gay and lesbian community. And since that question is going to have a really tricky career, people seem really scared about saying, well I don't think this or that conduct is OK. My attitude about it is that I understand people being afraid, but I feel very, very strongly at this point that those of us who want to change the world, those of us who want to change ourselves in the context of changing the world in a positive, humane way have absolutely to be willing to call things right and call them wrong. And that includes, for example, criticizing anybody black, whether here or in Africa, if you think he or she is wrong or monstrous, you call it wrong and monstrous. And in the sexual realm, just because it's a gay couple doesn't mean it's a good couple. It just means it's the same sex. It doesn't necessarily mean it's a good or healthy relationship. I, anyway, believe that we have to get it together to call things right or wrong.

Can this passage be seen in the context of disagreements about tactics and strategy within the gay and lesbian political movement in the 1970s?

Back then I must say I was not really active or knowledgeable about the gay and lesbian community in America at that time. So I wasn't really trying to speak as some kind of omniscient person. I just think that I saw here and there women acting in ways that, if that woman was a man, everybody would be all upset about it, but because it was two women, nobody would say anything. It wasn't OK as far as I was concerned then, and it's not OK now.

Do you think the gay and lesbian movement has changed since then?

I think that there is a community now. You have people living and dying, getting up in the morning and going to bed at night, thinking politically about sexual freedom. I think it's the only movement out here at the moment. And I think there's a profound debate going on right now in the gay and lesbian community and the bisexual community. I have no idea how the debate's going to be settled or who's going to settle it, but some of the issues are about tactics. Act-Up, for example—is that the way to go in order to secure equal rights? Or assimilation—is that the way to go? There's also another debate about whether to pursue freedom and equal rights through traditional civilities, or to disrupt, and confront, and shock, and be in-your-face. And because there's such an enormous rise in violence against gay and lesbian and bisexual Americans today, and because there's this huge epidemic of AIDS affecting the gay community among many other communities here and around the world, the depth of the debate is gigantic.

Do you want to talk about your treatment for breast and lymphatic cancer?

No, not yet. I'm going to do a benefit for the Women's Resource Center here in Berkeley, and for that event I will write something that I hope I can present without breaking down. [See **"A Good Fight"** in the December 1993 *Progressive.*]

How are you managing?

The prognosis is very bad, but I'm very well. I'm taking this medicine which is in lieu of chemotherapy. I'm exercising, I've never been as fit as I am in my life before. I have less stamina than I did, but it's more than a lot of other people probably have available to them. I think that because the prognosis is what it is, and because cancer is what it is, and nobody really knows what they're doing, I think that the way I'm living my life is a lot more assertive and careful. I'm more careful about my health, but I'm also more careful about my happiness, I think, than I ever was before. And also I don't pull punches so much, at all, as I used to in committee meetings and so on. I really pretty much say exactly what I mean, and I don't really care the way I used to about whether people are hurt or upset. If you disagree, you can just disagree. Obviously I don't feel there's an endless amount of time on my side, so I just try to get things done and say things as clearly as possible, and be as useful and as productive as I can be, and also I try to stay healthy.

Is this a topic you feel able to write about in the tradition of Audre Lorde's Cancer Journals?

When I deal with the subject of breast cancer, I would be very surprised if I don't deal with it in a political way because that's the way I experience it, and I want to be part of the movement to put breast cancer into center-stage focus of the American consciousness. It is not OK that *The New York Times Magazine* recently gave as the most conservative estimate that more than 500,000 women will die of breast cancer in the 1990s. That is not an acceptable prospect as far as I'm concerned. We know that there is really just no clue about what causes it. It is not specific to any race or class, person or age, or women who nursed or didn't nurse, and so on. We need research to be undertaken as quickly as possible, and on as massive a scale as possible, to save lives. And I want to be part of that movement.

More generally, how do you think the post Reagan-Bush period is shaping up?

I don't know where this is going to come out, so I may change my mind about this. But at this point I feel extremely angry at Clinton. I feel he has betrayed in a

lot of ways the communities that put him into office—
that is, the peoples of color, gay and lesbian communities, people who have been worried about the Haitian
refugees, and people concerned about the genocide taking place in the former Yugoslavia. That's what I feel at
the moment. And I feel that overriding everything else
is our inertia where Bosnia is concerned, the systematic
rape of Muslim women there, the systematic pursuit of
ethnic cleansing in the Muslim communities inside
former Yugoslavia. I feel that Clinton's inertia in that
context is a stain that nothing else he may accomplish
that is helpful to people will ever eradicate. I cannot
forgive or forget anybody who has been inert in the
context of ethnic cleansing. He has been at the forefront,
as far as I'm concerned, of our national inertia. I feel
extreme shame to coexist with ethnic cleansing in my
lifetime. I would not vote for Clinton again.

*I'd like to read from Bernice Reagon Johnson's "Coali-
tion Politics: Turning the Century" (1981): "There was
a time when folks saw the major movement force coming out of the Black community. Then, the hottest thing
became the Native Americans and the next, students'
rights and the next, the anti-war movement or whatever.
The movement force just rolled around hitting various
issues. Now, there were a few people who kept up with
many of those issues. . . . They hold the key to turning
the century with our principles and ideals intact. They
can teach you how to cross cultures and not kill
yourself. . . . When it comes to political organizing,
and when it comes to your basic survival, there are a
few people who took the sweep from the 60's to the
80's and they didn't miss a step. They could stand it
all." I think this statement beautifully applies to your
lifework. Survival and resilience, driven and inspired by
the need for ever greater comprehensiveness and
inclusiveness, are keynotes. Your work keeps developing
and renewing itself out of the desire to confront, to
incorporate, to speak out about some new facet of your
own identity. I see this unfolding of multiple dimensions
as testimony to identity politics as a positive principle.
Since you have been critical of the dangers of an
identity politics that is narrow and rigid, I want to ask
whether you see, alongside the reductive negative version of identity politics, a more positive, complex version that emphasizes multiple dimensions rather than
one single monolithic element. A positive version that is
potentially empowering because it is constantly opening
out rather than closing in on itself. Doesn't this help to
explain why you did not become confined by a black
nationalist viewpoint, why you were able to move on to
a larger vision? A long question!*

I would agree that it's important to know yourself,
where you came from, your people, your history. But in
my lifetime I have not seen identity politics ever lead,
finally, anywhere I wanted to go. It seems to me again
and again it leads to an amoral position so that if the

man is black I vote for him, or if the person is gay that
person can speak on gay issues rather than anybody
who's dedicated to the principle of equal rights. I've
said in a number of different places now in writing—
and I mean it—that I'm really about what you do, rather
than who you are. I don't mean that therefore you
should remain ignorant of who you are. But finding out
who you are is only step one. And then once you know
who you are, you move into the world of other people
and make connections with other people that can have a
revolutionary potential.

I don't want to be mistaken and have everybody think
that I'm against people finding out about themselves at
all. That's not what I'm saying. I'm just saying that's
not the end of it. It would be like saying you're going
to go into personal therapy, because you want to go into
personal therapy. That would seem to me a ridiculous
ambition or concern and completely solipsistic. The
point about personal therapy is to change the way you
interact with other people in your life. In the same way,
you find out about yourself as a member of a group,
whatever that group is, if it's African American, Native
American, or whatever it is. The point is that then you
can, in a knowledgeable and intelligent way, undertake
to connect or intersect with other people's lives to some
political purpose having to do with the positive acquisition of new power.

Jacqueline Vaught Brogan (essay date 1997)

SOURCE: Brogan, Jacqueline Vaught. "From Warrior
to Womanist: The Development of June Jordan's
Poetry." In *Speaking the Other Self: American Women
Writers*, edited by Jeanne Campbell Reesman, pp. 198-
209. Athens: University of Georgia Press, 1997.

[*In the essay below, Brogan examines Jordan's development as a poet focusing particularly on* Naming Our
Destiny.]

While no single essay could begin to represent fairly
the full range of June Jordan's work (writing, as she
does, in so many different genres), nor even the full
range of voices and styles she moves among in her
poetry alone, it is fair to say that at its best Jordan's
verse combines the personal, the political, and the
aesthetic in an act of sustained "resistance" to the world.[1]
Hers is a resistance ultimately grounded in an appeal to
the "ethical not-yet" or the possibility of a redemptive
future, global in its magnitude, if we but have the courage to name (or re-name) our destiny.[2] Here I am, of
course, adapting the title of Jordan's most important
collection thus far—***Naming Our Destiny***.[3] And in the
last half of this essay I wish to take a close look at the
most important poem in that volume, the concluding

suite entitled **"War and Memory."** However, I begin this essay in something of a predicament. For readers already thoroughly familiar with Jordan's extensive corpus, much of what I say in the first half may be quite obvious. Yet, placing her work within the broad strokes of its own terms and development seems to me crucial, for it remains quite true that many people do not know her work at all.

There is, of course, a politics to this fact. Despite her productivity and prominence in contemporary writing, she is notably not in Gilbert and Gubar's *Norton Anthology of Literature by Women,* a fact I continue to find baffling.[4] Nor does she appear in Harris and Aguero's *An Ear to the Ground,* an anthology of contemporary ethnic poetries in America.[5] Nor does Jordan's work appear in the first *Heath Anthology of American Literature,* an anthology self-consciously as inclusive as possible, though three of her poems have been added to the second edition.[6] And yet Jordan has authored over a dozen different books, and her work has influenced any number of contemporary writers, including Adrienne Rich, Audre Lorde, and Alice Walker—to name only a few. In this sense what follows in the first part of this essay is intended not only to give an overview of June Jordan's work but also to encourage a more widespread knowledge and appreciation of this remarkable and important poet. Born in 1936, June Jordan is a playwright, novelist, essayist, professor, and political activist, as well as one of our nation's leading poets. From her earliest work, such as the novel *His Own Where* (1971), through such powerful collections as *New Days* (1974), *Things That I Do in the Dark: Selected Poetry* (1977), and *Civil Wars,* (essays, 1981), to her most recent work, *Naming Our Destiny* (poetry, 1989) and *Technical Difficulties* (essays, 1992), Jordan's various writings have been marked by an increasing inclusiveness (ranging from the early focus on blacks in America to concern with other countries, other ethnic groups, and women everywhere) and a consistent faith in the power of language to create nothing short of a redemptive world.[7] At the same time, this idealism, which we find repeated again and again in whatever genre within which she is working, is consistently tempered by an intensity that at time borders on militant ferocity. There is always something of the warrior in Jordan, no matter what the form. As she notes in **"White English/Black English: The Politics of Translation"** (1972), "As a poet and writer, I deeply love and I deeply hate words" (*CW* [*Civil Wars*], 68), the love stemming from human communication, even communion, the hate from the conscription that language inevitably means to individuals, groups, races who are not members of the "majority" who control, quite literally, the dominating sentence.

Jordan underscores this nearly irreconcilable division in her poetry later in the same essay: "As a human being,

I delight in this miraculous, universal means of communion," by which she means language, and yet, she continues, "as a Black poet and writer, I hate words that cancel my name and my history and the freedom of my future: I hate the words that condemn and refuse the language of my people in America" (*CW,* 69). She has given much attention, both in poetry and prose, to this internal, external, and seemingly eternal fight. To give but one example from her earliest poetry, a poem admittedly more complex in tone than I can discuss here,

> Teach me to sing
> Blackman Blacklove
> sing when the cops break your head
> full of song
> sing when the bullets explode in the back
> you bend over me
> Blacklove Blackman . . .
>
> (Poem: **"For My Brother,"** *NDays* [*New Days*], 109)

Despite such a critical division, Jordan's work is also marked by a certain thematic consistency, one might even say, integrity. As she notes in poem: **"From an Uprooted Condition,"** "sometimes the poem tends to repeat itself" (*NDays,* 70), a remark that could well apply to her entire corpus. Thus, we find throughout her work the recurring themes and motifs of love and desire (see *Passion: New Poems, 1977-1980*), of family, of social injustice, of suffering, and of joy.[8] Fittingly, several of these themes coalesce in the poem (first called **"Poem against a Conclusion"**) that concludes *New Days* and that becomes the title and opening poem for her selected poems, *Things That I Do in the Dark*:

> These poems
> they are things that I do
> in the dark
> reaching for you
> whoever you are
> and
> are you ready?
> These words
> they are stones in the water
> running away
> These skeletal lines
> they are desperate arms for my longing and love.
> I am a stranger
> learning to worship the strangers
> around me
> whoever you are
> whoever I may become.
>
> (*NDays,* 131)

However, given what I have said thus far, it is perhaps not surprising that her attention to the suffering of blacks and later to the suffering of other ethnic groups, and especially of women, often results in a "scream" (both in tone and language), while her attention to the possibility of creative redemption modulates toward a visionary faith.[9] It is quite to the point that recently Adrienne Rich includes Jordan in an article on poetic/

political activism entitled "The Hermit's Scream."[10] Here, I offer a brief example from Jordan's prose:

> I choose to exist unafraid of my enemies. . . . I choose to believe that my enemies can either be vanquished or else converted into allies, into Brothers. And I choose to disregard the death-obsessed, extravagantly depressed and depressing doom-sayers around. As a woman, as a Black woman, as a Black woman poet and writer, I choose to believe that we, women and Third World peoples, will in fact succeed in saving ourselves, *and* our traditional assassins, from the meaning of their fear and hatred. Even more deeply, I believe we can save ourselves from the power of our own fear and our own self-hatred.
>
> This is my perspective, and this is my faith.
>
> (*CW,* 129)

As may be obvious, Jordan's vision strikes a middle ground between those of Toni Morrison and Alice Walker (other Black writers who have much in common with Jordan), as well as between those of Malcolm X and Dr. Martin Luther King Jr. (The latter comparison she makes herself in an essay appropriately entitled **"Notes toward Balancing Black Love and Hatred"** [*CW,* 85].) However, I would also like to stress the fact that despite certain generalities we can make about her poetry, Jordan's work has proven neither stagnant nor predictable. As implied earlier, her work has evolved from a fairly tight focus on the predicaments of blacks (the "dream of the fourteenth amendment," as she calls it in **"War and Memory"**) to an increasingly inclusive embrace of all marginalized people (including, for example, Native Americans, Palestinians, Nicaraguans, people of the Third World, women, children, and most recently lesbians) and even of white men. As she notes in **"Thinking about My Poetry,"** "At this point in time, I refuse nothing" (*CW,* 129), a remark that, although made in 1977, seems increasingly true of her poetry. She even goes so far as to say, given her first "warriorist" tendencies in verse, "I do read and I do indeed listen to the poetry of white male poets" (*CW,* 129), no small achievement given her own vision and the actual political realities within which she is having to write and which, of course, she is trying to "right."

My last general remark is that despite this "catholicity of interest" (*CW,* 129), Jordan's most recent work moves into emphatically feminist, or perhaps more accurately, "womanist" concerns.[11] Hence the strength of the concluding line of **"War and Memory,"** the poem we shall look at momentarily, in which she imagines not simply a feminist but specifically a womanist invention of language, a language that clearly would not only sanction Jordan herself but possibly the world as well: "and I / invent the mother of the courage I require not to quit" (*ND* [*Naming Our Destiny*], 211). I should note that such an idea of invention, now feministically conceived as a new "mother tongue," may be traced

(however ironically) to Jordan's early childhood attraction to the creative power of words, as in the biblical passage, "In the beginning was the Word." In the foreword to *Civil Wars* she explains this fascination: "Early on, the scriptural concept that 'in the beginning was the Word and the Word was with God and the Word was God'—the idea that the word could represent and then deliver into reality what the word symbolized—this possibility of language, of writing, seemed to me magical and basic and irresistible" (x). This "thesis of John" (to quote a poem by Wallace Stevens) continually fuels Jordan's inherent optimism—if we are paying attention—an optimism or vision all the more courageous given the actual facts of life she so scrupulously notes, in poem after poem. Consider, for example, the following lines from her 1982 **"Moving Home,"** a poem that in style and theme notably anticipates some of the strategies in Adrienne Rich's *An Atlas of the Difficult World*:[12]

> Nor do I wish to speak about the nurse again and
> again raped
> before they murdered her on the hospital floor
> Nor do I wish to speak about the rattling bullets that
> did not
> halt on that keening trajectory
> Nor do I wish to speak about the pounding on the
> doors and
> the breaking of windows and the hauling of families
>   into
> the world of the dead
> I do not wish to speak about the bulldozer and the
> red dirt
> not quite covering all of the arms and legs. . . .
>
> (*LR* [*Living Room*], 142)

It is almost impossible, yet certainly consistent with Jordan's work, that she concludes such a difficult and painful poem with this remarkable line, "It is time to make our way home" (*LR,* 143). It is truly "remarkable," in both senses of the word, being both courageous in context and committed to a redemptive revision of the world.

As she clarifies in **"Thinking about My Poetry,"** and as may have been suggested by the preceding section, June Jordan has gone through several aesthetic stages and stances. She describes, for example, the stage between age seven and her mid-twenties as the stage when "poetry was the inside dictator" to which she "submitted" herself. Next was her commitment to craft, writing in the "manner of Herrick, Shelley, Eliot, or whoever" (*CW,* 123). Next came her decision to make her poetry of interest to others, necessitating the choosing of subjects of general and substantive consequence (largely the recurring motifs noted above). Later came the stage in which she decided "to aim for the achievement of a collective voice" (125), of which **"Gettin Down to Get Over: Dedicated to My Mother"** remains the finest example. I cite the opening lines:

MOMMA MOMMA MOMMA
momma momma
mammy
nanny
granny
woman
mistress
sista
luv

(*NDays,* 118)

However, the last stage Jordan describes is for my purposes both the most important and the most successful. In this stage, the best of her work demonstrates in praxis what has become almost idiomatic in feminist cultural theory: that is, the personal *really is* political. The triumph of **"War and Memory,"** the particular poem I wish to focus on for the remainder of this essay, is that Jordan makes this fact so compellingly clear while thematically and aesthetically evoking an evolution, a possible redemption, for a newly created world. It is a visionary poem, even as it is deeply historicized both in content and style.

However, I should first reiterate that in addition to her deep and obvious involvement with contemporary African American writers, Jordan is deeply involved with literary/linguistic history. To mention three obvious and relatively modern examples, one must have the mind of Elizabeth Bishop, or at least have her *North and South* in mind, to fully appreciate Jordan's poem **"Problems of Translation"** (*LR,* 37-41), or have Yeats's "Leda and the Swan" in mind to appreciate her alternative sonnet (both in form and content) such as **"The Female and the Silence of Man"** (*ND,* 190-91), or Robert Frost's "Mending Wall" in mind when reading her **"War Verse,"** which begins, quite ironically, with "Something there is that sure must love a plane" (*LR,* 112).[13] The same is even more true of **"War and Memory"** (*ND,* 204-11), where the aesthetic, the political, and the personal modulate from a saturated past (including the personal violence in her family) to a redemptive, reconstituted lineage. As such, this poem encapsulates the entire development of Jordan's work so far.

Consider the first few lines of section 1, a section that is at once deeply personal, autobiographical, while stylistically anticipating the structural move to follow in the poem toward the larger polis, the political, even cosmos-polis:

Daddy at the stove or sink. Large
knife nearby or artfully
suspended by his clean hand handsome
even in its menace
slamming the silverware drawer
open and shut / the spoons
suddenly loud as the yelling
at my mother

no (she would say) no
Granville no
about: would he
be late / had she
hidden away the Chinese laundry shirts
again / did she think
it right that he (a man in his own house)
should serve himself a cup of tea a plate
of food / perhaps she thought that he
should cook the cabbage and the pot roast
for himself as well?

In addition to the influence of alliteration and rhythm from African American sources of various kinds (including perhaps even rap), my ear at least finds a subversive flirtation with Anglo-Saxon alliteration, rhythm, and assonance. Such lines as "handsome / even in its menace / slamming the silverware drawer" and of course, is it "right that he (a man in his own house)" owe their success in part to their ability to evoke a literary and patriarchal legacy at odds with the action and tone of the poem. That is, the patriarchal legacy is certainly not venerated here, although just how culturally normalized this domineering patriarchy may be is made painfully clear through the nearly predictable phrases constituting these literal power lines.

There is simultaneously in the passage cited above an evocation of the kind of experimental writing characteristic of *How/(ever)* (an experimental feminist journal of poetry), as in the quasi-line breaks of lines 6, 12, 14, and 17. These self-consciously demarcated breaks complicate or defy the "normal" line ends, making them, by the way, very difficult to quote out of context. That, of course, is *the point,* as it is in much feminist and experimental poetry.

Section 2 works almost by way of medieval interlacing; the personal and gendered violence of the scene at home becomes both metonymy and metaphor for a world at war, in much the same way that Elizabeth Bishop's "In the Waiting Room" relates a personal experience to the violence of World War I.[14] I cite the last several lines of this section:

"The camps?" I asked them, eagerly: "The Nazis?"
I was quite confused, "But in this picture,
Daddy, I can't see nobody."
"*Any*body," he corrected me: "You can't see
anybody!" "Yes, but what," I persevered, "what
                                        is this a

picture of?"
"That's the trail of blood left by the Jewish girls
and women on the snow because the Germans
make them march so long."
"Does the snow make feet bleed, Momma?
Where does the bleeding come from?"

My mother told me I should put away
the papers and not continue to upset myself

about these things I could not understand
and I remember
wondering if my family was a war
going on
and if
there would soon be blood
someplace in the house
and where
the blood of my family would come from

Section 3 ["The Spanish Civil War: / I think I read about that one"] seems not-so-humorously indebted to the well-known Hemingway device of "omission," and appropriately so, both in theme and aesthetics, given the fact that omission (the difference between being an anybody and a nobody) is both the linguistic and the political argument of the preceding section just cited. Sections 4-6 work more like a collage than interlacing, moving from personal witnessing of North Korea, the Vietnam protest, and Kent State to the personal and painful choices necessitated by the now-twin subjects of personal betrayal and economic deprivation. I cite from the poem again at the point that a new, important stylistic trait enters:

Plump during The War on Poverty
I remember making pretty good
money (6 bucks an hour)
as a city planner and my former
husband married my best
friend and I was never positive
about the next month's rent but
once I left my son sitting
on his lunchbox in the early rain
waiting for a day-care pickup and I went
to redesign low-income housing for the Lower
East Side of Manhattan and three hours after that
I got a phone call from my neighbors
that the pickup never came
that Christopher was waiting
on the sidewalk
in his yellow slicker
on his lunchbox
in the rain.

Period. As opposed to the staccato-like snippets of section 5—"It was very exciting. The tear gas burned like crazy" (lines that sound much like Gertrude Stein when she is collapsing our notion of the hierarchy of foreground and background, of hierarchy in any form)—section 6 is also stylistically of necessity one sentence with multiple "lines," as it were, in which everything bears on everything else. This point is made at a terrible risk to the poem, for it is in such horrible contrast to the acute isolation of Christopher, whose neighbors presumably leave him in the rain (a synecdochic symbol of the breakdown of society's ethical memory that we all bear on one another).

At this point the poem is almost unbearably painful. However, in the section appropriately numbered "#VII" (here I appeal, however ironically, to the traditional numerological reading of "7" as creation, just as Jordan appealed to the feminist sense of possibilities latent in the phrase, "In the beginning was the Word"), African American literary devices of rhythm and repetition and even spiritual evangelism build to an incantatory evocation of a future, an expressly womanist world to come, that does not necessarily invert but rather redeems the obviously fallen patriarchal world (personally and politically) with which she began. Worried always about her mother, her father, this society, others, she creates an incantation that mesmerizes (in the old sense of the word):

And from the freedom days
that blazed outside my mind
I fell in love
I fell in love with Black men White
men Black
women White women
and I
dared myself to say The Palestinians
and I
worried about unilateral words like Lesbian or
                    Nationalist
and I tried to speak Spanish when I travelled
                    to Managua
and I
dreamed about The Fourteenth Amendment
and I
defied the hatred of the hateful everywhere
as best I could
I mean
I took long nightly walks to emulate the Chinese
        Revolutionaries
and I
always wore one sweater less than absolutely
                    necessary to
    keep warm
and I wrote everything I know how to write
                    against apartheid
and I thought I was a warrior growing up
and I
buried my father with all of the ceremony all of the
                    music
    I could piece together
and I
I lust for justice
and I
make that quest arthritic/pigeon-toed/however
and I invent the mother of the courage I require
                    not to quit

I suspect that these words, which conclude the volume entitled *Naming Our Destiny,* summarize the efforts of many other women writers we discussed at the Women Writers Symposium in San Antonio and, I hope, the efforts we make as critics as well. We should note that the poem ends without any concluding punctuation. The "sentence," as it were, is open. . . .

Notes

1. Since I have used the word "resistance" on numerous occasions to describe a political and ethical response

to violence (especially to World War II), I should clarify that, first, Jordan's "resistance" is fundamentally more activist than anything someone like Wallace Stevens wrote and that, second, their shared sense of the power of the word to create a world in which we can live is uncannily similar. See, for example, my "Wallace Stevens: Poems against His Climate," *Wallace Stevens Journal* 11.2 (1987): 75-93. For Stevens's sense of "resistance," see his "The Irrational Element in Poetry," in *Opus Posthumous,* ed. Samuel French Morse (New York: Alfred A. Knopf, 1972), 225.

2. Here I am paraphrasing Drucilla Cornell, "From the Lighthouse: The Promise of Redemption and the Possibility of Legal Interpretation," *Cardozo Law Review* 11 (1990): 1689. It is quite fitting, given how politically activist Jordan's verse is, to find such discourse circulating among legal activists.

3. *Naming Our Destiny: New and Selected Poems* (New York: Thunder's Mouth Press, 1989); hereafter abbreviated as *ND.* By way of an aside, I'm always tempted to call this book *Naming Our Destinies,* with emphasis on the plural, which is in a way very keeping with her vision. But the singularity she finds in the title she did choose is, in fact, finally more in keeping with what we might call her—now—fundamental sense of solidarity, far more in keeping with Adrienne Rich's *An Atlas of the Difficult World* (New York: W. W. Norton, 1991) than with Wallace Stevens's World War II volume, *Parts of a World* (New York: Alfred A. Knopf, 1945). Other works to be cited in the text include *Civil Wars* (Boston: Beacon Press, 1981; abbreviated as *CW*); *Living Room* (New York: Thunder's Mouth Press, 1985; abbreviated as *LR*); and *New Days* (New York: Emerson Hall, 1974; abbreviated as *NDays*).

4. Sandra M. Gilbert and Susan Gubar, eds., *The Norton Anthology of Literature by Women: The Tradition in English* (New York: W. W. Norton, 1985).

5. Marie Harris and Kathleen Aguero, eds., *An Ear to the Ground: An Anthology of Contemporary Poetry* (Athens: University of Georgia Press, 1989).

6. The first edition of *The Heath Anthology of American Literature,* ed. Paul Lauter et al. (Lexington, Mass: D.C. Heath, 1990) includes no mention of June Jordan. This omission has been partially rectified in the recent second edition (1994), vol. 2, which prints three of Jordan's poems: "Poem about My Rights," "To Free Nelson Mandela," and "Moving Towards Home."

7. *His Own Where* (New York: Thomas Crowell, 1971); *Things That I Do in the Dark: Selected Poetry* (New York: Random House, 1977); *Technical Difficulties: African-American Notes on the State of the Union* (New York: Pantheon, 1992).

8. *Passion: New Poems, 1977-1980* (Boston: Beacon Press, 1980).

9. See "Thinking about My Poetry" (1977), in *Civil Wars,* 122-25.

10. See Adrienne Rich, "The Hermit's Scream," *PMLA* (October 1983): 1157-64. It is worth noting, for points both made above and to follow, that Rich includes in this article, among others, Stevens, Walker, Lorde, and Bishop (as well as Jordan); the title of the article is borrowed from Bishop's "Chemin de Fer," a poem that has also figured in Drucilla Cornell's writings on legal jurisdiction.

11. Compare the following lines from the opening poem of Rich's *Atlas* with the lines cited from Jordan's work in the text above:

> I don't want to hear how he beat her after
>   the earthquake,
> tore up her writing, threw the kerosene
> lantern into her face waiting
> like an unbearable mirror of his own. I don't
> want to hear how she finally ran from the trailer
> how he tore the keys from her hands, jumped into
>   the truck
> and backed it into her.

(p. 4)

12. The parallels between Jordan's verse and that of Yeats and Frost are quite obvious, the first noted by herself (we are told to compare Jordan's subversive sonnet with "Leda and the Swan" in a postscript below the title), the second so ironic in its allusory stance. However, the similarity between Bishop and Jordan (not just in the instance mentioned in the text above) cannot be stressed enough. Not only does "Problems of Translation" refer directly to Bishop's poems "Roosters" and "The Map" from *North and South,* it also emulates strategies of Bishop's subsequent volumes *Questions of Travel* and *Geography III.*

13. Section 2 of "War and Memory" is so indebted to Bishop's "In the Waiting Room" that the subject is itself worthy of an article. However, in both, pictures taken or looked at during a time of war evoke in rather naive and "eager" young girls' profound questionings of personal identity, of the relationship between linguistic objectification and actual violence. For the child Elizabeth in "In the Waiting Room," the horror is learning that she is "one of *them,*" a linguistic subtlety much in keeping with that evoked by the difference between "anybody" and "nobody" in Jordan's poem.

14. See Joy Harjo, "An Interview with June Jordan," *High Plains Literary Review* 3.2 (1988): 60-76.

Scott MacPhail (essay date spring 1999)

SOURCE: MacPhail, Scott. "June Jordan and the New Black Intellectuals." *African American Review* 33, no. 1 (spring 1999): 51-71.

[*In the essay below, MacPhail addresses Jordan's place within African American intellectual circles.*]

In *Race Matters,* Cornel West states that "the time is past for black political and intellectual leaders to pose as *the* voice for black America." The contemporary black political and intellectual leader should "be a race-transcending prophet who critiques the powers that be . . . and who puts forward a vision of fundamental social change for all who suffer from socially induced misery" (70). If we are to believe a series of articles in popular American magazines,[1] a whole generation of African-American intellectuals is making the transition from experts on race matters to the more broadly defined role of the public, national intellectual, and in the process redefining "what it means to be an intellectual in the United States" (Bérubé 73). Whether or not these "new intellectuals," as Robert Boynton names them in *The Atlantic,* are or should be "race-transcending," or if they are reincarnations of the black spokespersons whose time West says is past, has spurred some acrimonious debate. Adolph Reed argues in *The Village Voice* that these public intellectuals trade on their blackness to gain authority with their white, academic audience, while blacks look to these intellectuals and their success at garnering a white audience for models of how to "make it" in the white world. Thus the new black intellectuals can use their roles as certified black spokespersons "to avoid both rigorous, careful intellectual work *and* protracted committed political action" (Reed 35). And Sean Wilentz similarly claims that these black writers are really a product of the needs of left-leaning white critics who find in the fact of their popular colleagues' blackness "the chance to affirm their anti-racist bona fides" (294). For Reed and Wilentz these "new" black intellectuals are not something new at all, but are rather the same old token blacks gaining prestige by explaining blackness to whites. Michael Bérubé, Robert Boynton, and others, however, argue that the sudden visibility of a group of black thinkers is a sign of changing American concerns and values, and the diversity of perspectives within this group signals a turn away from the Negro spokesperson to a new complexity in the role of the African-American intellectual. At the center of these competing interpretations of the media attention lavished on the "New Black Intellectuals" are different understandings of the African-American intellectuals' audience, purpose and, responsibilities.

Thirty years ago Harold Cruse, in *The Crisis of the Negro Intellectual,* argued that the role of the black intellectual is necessarily dual in nature: "The Negro intellectual must deal intimately with the white power structure and cultural apparatus, and the inner realities of the black world at one and the same time" (451). Cruse's call for a synthesis of the intellectual relationship with and responsibility to both a black and a white audience, like West's race-transcending prophet, echoes the turn-of-the-century argument and rhetorical project of Du Bois's *The Souls of Black Folk,* in which Du Bois famously defined the African American as possessing a double-consciousness, as being split between an essential sense of self and an identity reflected back through the power of the white gaze. Du Bois's difficult task, and the task of all African-American intellectuals that follow him, is to address both aspects of this definition. As Du Bois wrote in his critique of Booker T. Washington, racial inequality is not a problem that can be located within and solved by a single race, "when in fact the burden belongs to the nation, and the hands of none of us are clean if we bend not our energies to righting these great wrongs" (94). Du Bois's worry was that Washington was focusing too much on what blacks could do to address their situation, thus letting the white power structure ignore its responsibility for the "Negro Problem." Today, critics like Reed and Wilentz wonder if the new black intellectuals are gaining their national reputations at the expense of losing sight of the inner realities of the black world.

For me, the location of the ideas of the new black intellectuals cannot easily be graphed within this old binary, because their ideas are too diverse and too much in flux. Instead, as a way of raising some questions that this debate has ignored, I want to call attention to something, or more specifically some*one,* who has been left out of this debate about the shape and meaning of the new black intellectuals. If the need for a race-transcending prophet that can effectively advocate the ideas and goals of blacks to both black and white audiences were recognized at least as long ago as Du Bois's 1903 *The Souls of Black Folk,* why then must black intellectuals keep invoking this role as that which has not yet been achieved? Who has come closest to achieving this synthesis, and what models are available for the new crop of intellectuals? What has impeded black intellectuals from taking on this role, and what are the conditions necessary for it to be effected? In this essay, I pursue answers to these questions not in the reported or actual achievements of the new crop of black public intellectuals, but in the career of the artist, activist, and intellectual June Jordan, who has been excluded from the media representation of the new generation of African-American intellectuals, but who is nevertheless effecting a transition in the way that the black intellectual functions in American culture. First, however, I want to establish the models for an African-American intellectual available to Jordan as she embarked on her career.

From Negro Spokesperson to Black Artist

The mid- and late 1960s saw a radical transformation in the African-American Civil Rights Movement and a concomitant change in the expectations for what an African-American intellectual was to do. The 1963 March on Washington, the Civil Rights Act of 1963, and the Voting Rights Act of 1964 were the culmination of the non-violent crusade to guarantee the political rights of African Americans. Once these goals were achieved, some of the younger participants in the Movement, spurred by the realization that legislative and judicial reform did not necessarily lead to changes in the daily lives of African Americans, became more radical in their politics, and began to direct their activism more toward cultural practices than toward the government. William Van Deburg, in *New Day in Babylon,* his excellent study of Black Power as a cultural and political moment, traces the origins of this shift to the experiences of Student Non-Violent Coordinating Committee (SNCC) activists in Mississippi during the summers of 1964 and 1965. In Mississippi the SNCC workers became aware of the weak sense of community and lack of political and historical knowledge among rural Southern blacks. The young activists' response to this realization was to set up Freedom Schools to increase knowledge about black history and pride in the black community (Van Deburg 49-51). The goals of the SNCC activists, and those of the Black Power Movement that emerged in their wake, were in agreement with those articulated by Malcolm X in his June 1964 speech "Statement of Basic Aims and Objectives of the Organization of Afro-American Unity." Here Malcolm X called for a renewed attention to cultural issues in order to unify and raise the consciousness of African Americans: "We must recapture our heritage and our identity if we are ever to liberate ourselves from the bonds of white supremacy. . . . We must launch a cultural revolution to unbrainwash an entire people" (qtd. in Van Deburg 5). With the rise of the Black Power Movement and its focus on black identity and history rather than white responsibility for black victimization, the African-American social movements of the 1960s moved from the integrative political goals and peaceful protest strategies of King and the SCLC, to a cultural nationalism, born of Malcolm X and the experiences of SNCC, that began to adopt the language of revolution and separatism.

This shift in goals also signaled a shift in the relationship of the African-American intellectual to his audience. More specifically, his audience itself began to change, and as it changed so too did assumptions about the proper role of the African-American artist and intellectual. This shift can most easily be seen in a comparison of the intellectual and rhetorical strategies of James Baldwin and Amiri Baraka, writers whose precedents June Jordan negotiates in her work. The issues and questions that Baldwin takes up in his 1951 essay "Many Thousands Gone" constitute many of the typical moves for which he would be criticized in the 1960s:

> The story of the Negro in America is the story of America. . . . The Negro in America, gloomily referred to as that shadow which lies athwart our national life, is far more than that. He is a series of shadows, self-created, intertwining, which now we helplessly battle. One may say that the Negro in America does not really exist except in the darkness of our minds.

> (24-25)

Baldwin poses the "Negro Problem" as an American problem; the Negro is not a real person but rather a construct placed upon a group of people by the darkness of the American mind. Thus, for Baldwin, Du Bois's problem of the color line is less a problem of the social practices that divide whites from blacks than of the imaginative divide that threatens the coherence of the American identity. There is much force in Baldwin's argument. Like Du Bois he wants to stress the national responsibility for the Negro problem. By figuring the Negro as an imaginative construct that paradoxically both enables and endangers the successful articulation of an American identity, Baldwin argues that it is in America's best interest to confront the meaning and implications of this imagined Negro. But to simplify Baldwin's argument some, his rhetorical strategy is essentially to claim that the Negro is the product of the dominant, white components of American society, and thus to place the responsibility for solving the "Negro Problem" upon white America. But what of the other half of Du Bois's binary? The Negro corresponds to no real negroes, since his entire being is the product of an American imagination, and this seeming disregard for the agency of negroes in the development of their own identity is what Baldwin would be critiqued for in the 1960s.

Later in the same essay, Baldwin addresses the stereotype of the Uncle Tom: ". . . if we could boast that we understood [Negroes], it was far more to the point and far more true that they understood us" (28). Baldwin himself seems to be slipping into this role of the understanding Uncle Tom here. He becomes the Negro spokesperson, explaining to "us" how "we" have constructed him/the Negro in the process of guaranteeing our own identity; and thus, like Harriet Beecher Stowe's Tom, he rests hopes for the resolution to this problem on "us," on the white liberal readership of the *Partisan Review.*

Of course, how we read the "us" of this essay is not so simple as I have presented it, but this simplified version of Baldwin's thought is what was critiqued in the middle of the 1960s.[2] For instance, Harold Cruse attacked Baldwin and other intellectuals for, "trying to place the onus of their social predicament on white liberals" when the white liberals were "the real patrons and sponsors of their position as Negro intellectuals" and the Negro intellectuals were "unable to even hint at the outlines of another kind of program" beyond the integrationist one they were attacking (200). In other words, Cruse views Baldwin as a figure promoted by, and thus unable to think beyond, white liberal interests.

In 1967 Eldridge Cleaver went so far as to claim that Baldwin hated blacks and demonstrated "the most shameful, fanatical, fawning, sycophantic love of the whites that one can find in the writings of any black American writer" (qtd. in DeMott 157).

At the center of both Cleaver's and Cruse's attacks is a challenge to Baldwin's model for the African-American intellectual. With the advent of the Black Power Movement, and the accompanying Black Arts Movement, many African-American writers began to insist, at least rhetorically, that black artists and intellectuals should address only black issues and only black audiences.[3] Larry Neal's 1968 manifesto "The Black Arts Movement" exemplifies this trend:

> The Black Arts Movement is radically opposed to any concept of the artist that alienates him from his community. Black Art is the aesthetic and spiritual sister of the Black Power concept. As such, it envisions an art that speaks directly to the needs and aspirations of Black America . . . the Black American's desire for self-determination and nationhood. Both concepts are nationalistic. One is concerned with the relationship between art and politics; the other with the art of politics.
>
> (272)

The black artist's community is a singularity here: It is Black America. Where Baldwin spoke of Negroes in order to address their centrality to a national identity and audience, Neal argues that the black artist must speak specifically to blacks. The black artist and the black artwork serve the black audience's need to achieve self-representation: Rather than representing who blacks are, Black Art tells blacks who they should become. The black artist is not a realist, but a prophet. And the audience for this prophecy is a black audience that is expected to shape the goals and the product of black intellectual work by requiring that these goals and products serve the needs and desires of this audience. The black artist and intellectual must serve the audience appointed to them by birthright and shared suffering by reading and responding to the wants of this audience.

The work of Amiri Baraka (LeRoi Jones) offers the preeminent example of an attempt to fulfill the responsibilities of a Black Arts understanding of art. In a 1965 essay he offered a vision of the artist and intellectual that suggests the kinds of artistic and intellectual strategies that would produce a black art that black America "needs":

> The Black artist . . . is desperately needed to change the images his people identify with, by asserting Black feeling, Black mind, Black judgment. The black intellectual, in this same context, is needed to change the interpretation of facts towards the Black Man's best interests, instead of merely tagging along reciting white judgments of the world.
>
> (167)

The black artist does not simply respond to the needs of his audience, he forecasts these needs and asserts who this audience should become. Baraka's position is not so far from Baldwin's as it might at first seem. Baraka redirects, or at least narrows, Baldwin's sense of audience, but he still attempts a unifying representation of the people he speaks for—and now *to.* Like Baldwin, Baraka has at the core of his project the diagnosis of a "Negro Problem," and Baraka sees himself as the advocate of a community that is not accurately represented in a national discourse, but unlike Baldwin's focus on the Negro as a national, American, problem, Baraka seeks to transform African Americans into their own cultural nation. Baldwin adopts the traditional function of the intellectual as critic, addressing gaps in the national myth he inherits, whereas Baraka is more the prophet, trying to bring a new nation into being. Baraka wants to show African Americans the way out from beneath the defining gaze of an American culture so that they may become free subjects capable of finding their own essential selves.

Baraka's goals as a Black Power/Black Arts Movement intellectual are twofold: He must simultaneously reach and hold the attention of the African American, whose very existence enables a thing called Black Arts; and he must also write and speak in ways that will bring about this audience's transformation to their black selves. Baraka's struggle to find a single rhetoric to effect these dual goals can be seen in the poems he published in his famous 1969 book *Black Magic.* Take, for instance, the short poem titled "SOS":

> Calling black people
> Calling all black people, man woman
>   child
> Wherever you are, calling you, urgent,
>   come in
> Black People, come in, wherever you
>   are, urgent, calling
> you, calling all black people
> calling all black people, come in, black
>   people, come
> on in.
>
> (218)

This poem mutually constitutes a black poet and his black audience. At first the poem seems to be a distress call, an "SOS" that calls to black people to respond to the needs of the speaker. But with the addition of *on,* the position of the speaker shifts from a person in need of a response to the generous host of a party that black people must urgently join. In the essay "Black Art," Baraka writes that "poems are bullshit unless they are / teeth or trees or lemons piled / on a step" (219). "SOS" is an attempt to make a poem "do," and not simply "be." It links the black artist and black people, promising blackness to those who enter into the spell of its rhetoric. What makes this poem real, like teeth or trees or lemons, is that it has use value: It teaches black artists and listeners alike the way to find their blackness, and that way is to look to each other.

"SOS" is an invitation and a promise, but what exactly are the black "feeling," "judgment," and "mind" discovered in this Black Arts poetry? In "leroy" the speaker offers himself as source:

> When I die, the consciousness I carry I will
> to black people May they pick me apart and take the
> useful parts, the sweet meat of my feelings. And leave
> the bitter bullshit rotten white parts alone.
>
> (224)

Like "SOS" this poem looks to the future. It is about origins (the poem begins with a meditation on an old photograph of the poet's mother) and the continuity of cultural identity, but it is primarily a poem of incompleteness. An identity useful to black people is something that must be sifted from what obscures it. A national black identity is less a positive content in Baraka's writing than a future-oriented process.

In his essay "The Legacy of Malcolm X, and the Coming of the Black Nation," Baraka explains that "the Black Artist must demonstrate the sweet life, how it differs from the deathly grip of White Eyes" (167), and "Poem for HalfWhite College Students" questions if one might be too full of Elizabeth Taylor or Richard Burton. Blackness is what is not white, and Black Art is what names and polices what blackness is not. Baraka's poetry prods its auditors and readers to join the poet in the process of purification, to find the true black heart buried within both poet and audience. As Houston Baker has pointed out, Baraka's Black Arts articulation of blackness does "not point to any tangible referent" (135). The assertion of black feeling, judgment, and mind, the achieving of a black poem and a Black World, must await their disentanglement from the white discourse that has impeded their assertion.[4] Baraka avers this goal in "State/meant," in which he writes that the black artist must "teach the White Eyes their deaths, and teach the black man how to bring these deaths about" (169-70).

While the ultimate content of Baraka's asserted blackness may be difficult to ascertain except as a process of negation, his assertions in themselves are signs of the redefinition of the African-American intellectual which took place in the 1960s. In response to the calls of the Black Power Movement for a "cultural revolution" to "unbrainwash" an entire people, and in response to the shift among black activists from attempting to change white attitudes and laws affecting blacks to working for changes in the self-confidence, identity, and sense of community among African Americans, the new African-American intellectual attempted to work for the African-

American community by helping it define itself, rather than by representing that community to others. Baraka, in the 1960s, moves away from the role of the familiar Negro spokesperson to a more militant and separatist position marked by changing perceptions of the relationship between the African-American intellectual and his audience.

From Coming In to Coming Out: June Jordan

June Jordan follows through on Baraka's reform of our expectations for an African-American intellectual's responsibility to her audiences in her long and varied career as poet, essayist, playwright, novelist, teacher, activist, and journalist. While Baraka's most influential writings were published at the high point of the Black Power Movement, in the late 1960s and early 1970s, most of Jordan's major works have appeared in the past ten years.[5] And yet she is not often mentioned in the same breath as the new black intellectuals. Undoubtedly, she has benefitted from the recent vogue in African-American issues by moving up to a large publishing house for her latest collection of essays,[6] but she is not gaining so much mainstream press attention as are many other African-American writers and speakers. The reasons for this lack of attention are many and complex, but one factor that is important to consider, both in terms of her popularity and my argument that she reconfigures the role of the African-American intellectual, is her age. Jordan is almost a generation older than West, Henry Louis Gates, and the others linked by Bérubé and Boynton, and she falls between the division that Boynton makes in his generational model. But age here is almost a cover for a more ideological distinction, since it serves to marginalize those writers like Jordan who came of age during the heady time of the 1960s.

Boynton expands Bérubé's claim that black nationalism serves as the "springboard," "inspiration," and "antagonist" for the new intellectuals (75). Because the new intellectuals came of age after the deaths of Malcolm X and Martin Luther King, "they enjoyed the fruits of both the civil-rights and the black-nationalist vision without being entirely beholden to either" (Boynton 62). This is not quite Jordan's experience. As a young woman, she took part in a CORE freedom ride, witnessed and reported on the Harlem Riot of 1964, and was an occasional conversation partner of Malcolm X's after his split with the Nation of Islam.[7] Jordan's career as an activist thus might lead to the assumption that her work is "beholden" to her involvement in the Black Power Movement of the 1960s, and her writings are responsive and responsible to social and political concerns. Perhaps it is the importance of direct activism to Jordan's intellectual work that frightens off the mainstream press. This slighting obscures the important political function of an intellectual. The multiplicity of Jordan's commitments and strategies as an intellectual occasion a rethinking not only of the definition and the genealogy of the new African-American intellectuals of the 1990s, but also of the relationship of the intellectual and artist to the audiences and social movements to which she is aligned.

Like Baraka, June Jordan both struggles against the role of the black spokesperson and is highly conscious of her audience.[8] She manifests the Barakian mutually constitutive black audience/black artist relationship in some of her early essays and in her children's books, with their attempts to articulate a literary black English.[9] But one important difference between Jordan's early work and Baraka's Black Arts writings is that Jordan's invocations of her audience are not quite so monological as Baraka's, even when Jordan adopts some of Baraka's key rhetorical strategies. Take, for instance, her response to Baraka's "SOS," a poem Jordan titles **"Calling on All Silent Minorities"**:

HEY

C'MON
COME OUT

WHEREVER YOU ARE
WE NEED TO HAVE THIS MEETING
AT THIS TREE

AIN' EVEN BEEN
PLANTED
YET

(Naming [Naming Our Destiny] 24)

Jordan continues Baraka's attempts to produce, through the act of naming it, a community that only exists as a future projection, to give voice to a silent audience. But who is the audience that this poem calls on? The use of Black English marks the speaker (and thus the person who defines the "WE") as black, but the title suggests that Jordan is not interested in color or race or exclusion as a model for community building: She calls on *all* minorities to come out and play in the serious game of making their own voices heard. The substitution of a children's play call for the official, adult "SOS" puts the speaker outside of official channels and makes her less likely to be the source, rather than just the instigator, of what gets said at the meeting she calls for. She speaks loud, to wake up a complacent audience, to make it aware of itself as a coherent group, but calls her listeners "OUT," not "in." At least in this short poem Jordan seems wary of offering herself as the source for identity. She limits herself to pointing out the need for the next, communal step. Jordan is committed to many of the same cultural and political goals as Baraka and the Black Arts writers, to constitute an audience and thus a community by instilling an awareness of a sense

of community and its value, and yet the role of the artist in this project is more circumscribed for her.

Jordan's early essays, collected in *Civil Wars*, evidence the ways that she alternately adopts aspects of both Baldwin's and Baraka's notions of the black intellectual as they suit her strategic purposes. The *Civil Wars* essays stretch from one of Jordan's first published pieces (printed in 1964) to essays she placed in magazines like *Ms.* and *The New Republic* in the late 1970s. Here she addresses herself to white academics and black teachers and students alike to argue for the value of Black Studies to the curriculum at American universities; she calls on blacks to define a common culture through the study of Black English; and she argues that whites need to recognize the possibility that an African American can be more than the product of racist white America. One essay that attempts to reach a multiplicity of audiences is her 1964 **"Letter to Michael,"** in which she describes the 1964 Harlem Riots to her recently estranged husband, who lives in Chicago. Ostensibly to inform Michael of what has been going on in his absence, but published in this collection and thus a public document, it is meant to find a larger audience.[10] Jordan writes of the absurdities of police violence and the way that the violence both shocked a community and forced it to recognize itself as a community. This information is intended to counter the less truthful accounts of the riots that appeared in the mainstream press, and its effects upon its audiences are multiple: It is a protest to the white community that critiques both white police violence and white complicity in that violence, and it serves to affirm and reassure the African-American community that was the object of this violence that their suffering is real and that they do have a public voice with which to confront the immorality of their antagonists. There is a little bit of Baraka and Baldwin here. Baraka employs poetry (usually considered the medium of personal reflection/communication) and official genres, like the "SOS" message, for public, political, and oppositional ends, while Baldwin brings the truth of misperception to his white audience. Likewise, Jordan adapts the usually private genre of the letter to serve a public purpose, to record and give meaning to an experience that is too often co-opted or ignored by established channels of news and history making, and she attempts to represent the truth of black experience to a deceived white audience.[11] But she differs from both Baraka and Baldwin in the centrality she places on her own experience as that which both authenticates and limits her perspectives: She insists upon an individual voice that speaks from an African-American perspective rather than speaking for all African Americans.

Understanding June Jordan as an African-American intellectual does not come down to a simple choice between the models offered by Baraka and Baldwin, nor is it just a matter of fusing the two positions. Both the black spokesperson and the black prophet privilege race as a category of power, oppression, and identity, diminishing the importance of all other bases for identity, community, and political action. Jordan's experience of the importance of gender in the Black Power Movement complicates her relationship to this movement and her understanding of the role of the African-American intellectual. In fact, many of her professional activities of the late sixties and early seventies might be seen as stereotypically "feminine" interpretations of how to achieve the goals of the Black Power Movement: She published children's books, worked in the Teachers' and Writers' Collaborative in Brooklyn helping young inner-city children write poetry, became an instructor at City College, and raised her son. A question she asked of feminists in 1976 illustrates the value Jordan places on these nurturing, educational tasks: "Will we liberate ourselves so that the caring for children, the teaching, the loving, healing, person-oriented values that have always distinguished us will be revered and honored at least commensurate to the honors accorded bank managers, lieutenant colonels, and the executive corporate elite?" (*Civil Wars* 120). This is a question that Jordan could just as well have asked of the Black Power Movement—and, in effect, does when she presents the "ostensible leadership" of the Movement with the question, Why, when they talk "about the 'liberation of the Black man,' that is precisely, and only what they mean?" (*Civil Wars* 118).

In her poetry, Jordan begins to take on the task of sketching in what other liberations are needed. She offers a sample list of what gets left out of the official channels of the liberation movement in her long dramatic monologue *"From* **The Talking Back of Miss Valentine Jones:** *Poem # one."* As is almost always the case with Jordan, the title of the poem is central to establishing the work's rhetorical context. By emphasizing that this poem is both *"From"* a longer poem, and is the first in a series, Jordan offers the monologue as part of a species of many similar monologues. She also names the speaker in the title, letting us know that this voice is individual, and one among many who may come to speak. At one point Jordan has Valentine critique the naming strategies of "bodacious Blackm[e]n":

> and the very next bodacious Blackman
> call me queen
> because my life ain shit
> because (in any case) he ain been here to
>   share it
> with me
> (dish for dish and do for do and
> dream for dream)
> I'm gone scream him out my house

The context within the poem for this outburst is when "you (temporarily) shownup with a thing / you say's a

poem and you / call it / 'Will the Real Miss Black America Standup?'" (*Naming* 17). The larger context is the Black Arts Movement's poetry of invocation. The male "you" of the poem presumes that no "real Miss Black America" has stood up, and that his words are the ones that will stand her up (or stand in for her). Valentine responds to this male emptying out and then filling back in of a notion of black womanhood by listing all of the domestic routines that the bodacious Blackman fails to see or valorize. His aestheticized Black Woman knows nothing of the real daily work of black women that enable him to devote time to his poetry. Instead, he claims that the black women he knows are not "real," and he fails Valentine because, as she says, ". . . what I wanted was / your love / not pity" (17). Jordan is performing the same critique that West makes fifteen year later: She lets us know what gets lost when a black leader poses as *the* voice of black America. Yes, Baraka and the other Black Arts writers brought new attention to the meanings of blackness and the needs of a black audience, but changing the images black people identify with should also involve changing how images mean. Black intellectuals should not fall back on universal, idealizing images that ignore or devalue experience and difference. To do so only repeats the same kinds of images and effects that whites produced with their black stereotypes.

The poem **"Case in Point"** provides another powerful critique of masculine uses of power in the black community, but it is not just black men who are forced to confront their assumptions in this poem. It begins with "a friend of mine" who tells the speaker that "there is no silence peculiar / to the female." The speaker's "2¢" on this subject turn out to be the narration of her most recent rape by a "blackman actually / head of the local NAACP":

> Today is 2 weeks after the fact
> of that man straddling
> his knees either side of my chest
> his hairy arm and powerful left hand
> forcing my arms and my hands over
>   my head
> flat to the pillow while he rammed
> what he described as his quote big dick
> unquote into my mouth
> and shouted out: "D'ya want to swallow
> my big dick; well do ya?" . . .
>
> He was being rhetorical.
> My silence was peculiar
> to the female.
>
>   (*Naming* 81)

The man's question is "rhetorical" because he assumes that he already knows the answer to his question; his position of power allows him to construct an answer without needing the consent of his addressee. Here, as in **"Miss Valentine Jones"** [*"From* **The Talking Back** of Miss Valentine Jones: Poem # one"], Jordan is concerned with the ways that powerful male speakers presume to know what black women would say and how this presumption silences any different perspective that women would bring to a dialogue (be it political, social, or personal).

"Miss Valentine Jones" and **"Case in Point"** both critique the institutions of black protest from a feminist standpoint. The rhetoric of the NAACP head and the Black Arts poet are taken to task for silencing women and ignoring the debt that the institutions of black protest owe to women. But in its counter-argument to the friend's assertion that there is no silence peculiar to the female, **"Case in Point"** also registers another critique. Silence was an important idea in the wave of feminist thought and writings of the 1970s, and the friend who speaks at the beginning of the poem takes a familiar feminist stance. She is critiquing the cultural assumption that women are essentially passive and thus "naturally" silent about many things, including politics. But, of course, women are not naturally silent, and the ideology of silence was constructed by patriarchy to enforce gendered hierarchy.[12] What this argument fails to consider, and what Jordan points out, is that this strategy of a generalized, abstract response to silence, and the assumption that to reveal an ideology as a false consciousness is to disable it, does not take into account the real and differing material and political circumstances that contribute to the silencing of women, especially black women.

In her poems and essays, then, Jordan adopts a complex and shifting position. She shares many of the goals of the Black Arts Movement, working to give value to black experience and black culture. But she is not afraid to take issue with authoritative definitions when those definitions and their authorities are not responsive to experiences important to Jordan's sense of her own identity. Likewise, while her critiques of the Black Power Movement are primarily gendered critiques, she is also wary of a too easy identification with a feminist position when feminism does not account for the multiple ways that power is encoded in race and class, as well as gender. Jordan's multiple identifications and political affiliations lead her to articulate positions that try to defeat either/or reasoning. **"Case in Point"** is an instance of the "declaration of an independence I would just as soon not have," the title of an essay in which Jordan expresses the hope that "I can count on a sisterhood and a brotherhood that will let me give my life to its consecration, without equivocation, without sorrow" [*Civil* (*Civil Wars*) 121]). She declares her independence from narrowly defined versions of the Civil Rights and Women's Movements that seek to stifle her individual voice, while still trying to find a way to affirm the positive values of these movements.

The African-American intellectual is not a stable identity for June Jordan. She can neither wholeheartedly join Baraka and the Black Arts writers in their attempt to assert a Black Nation when this nation continues to silence African-American women, nor can she fully endorse a feminist perspective that obscures the real difference between women, like the absolute need for resistance to the racist power dynamics that contribute to the problems of black women. Baraka, Baldwin, and a narrowly defined feminism are all unsuitable models for Jordan because each attempts to define itself as the embodiment or representative of a singular audience. As a female African-American intellectual, Jordan cannot fit herself to the simplicity necessary to promote a traditional nationalist argument, but shifts her position and tactics in order to better serve the interest of all three terms of the hyphenated moniker "African-American Woman."

TECHNICAL DIFFICULTIES: LOCAL AND GLOBAL POLITICS

In July 1974, with Inez Smith Reid, Executive Director of the Black Women's Community Development Fund, June Jordan called for a "national meeting of Black media peoples" to respond to the crisis of the African famine in the Sahel. Jesse Jackson attended the meeting, and Fanny Lou Hamer and Roberta Flack, among others, donated time and effort to the Afro-Americans Against the Famine (AAAF) crusade that grew out of the meeting. Jordan describes this effort as "an exhausting, instructive, and unsuccessful campaign" (*Civil* 79) in which she learned that "it was as though Black nationalism meant only a preoccupation with your neighborhood conditions, a preoccupation incapable of making pragmatic connections to the continental African struggle" (80). This failed campaign would mark the beginning of another facet of Jordan's career. Her poems and essays begin to become more international in subject matter in the mid-1970s. For example, Jordan's essay **"Angola: Victory and Promise"** takes up the cause of Agostinho Neto, and introduces Americans to the first President of the People's Republic of Angola's poetry and politics, while several poems from this time period address the issue of South African Apartheid.[13]

In addition to bringing international issues to her domestic audience, Jordan's internationalism includes a broadening sense of her audience. In a 1989 interview Jordan explained how her poem **"Moving Towards Home,"** which had been translated into Arabic, was well known by Palestinians living in the West Bank: "As far as I'm concerned, that's the kind of validation of the usefulness of my work that's beyond anything I've ever dreamed of" (qtd. in Freccero 259). During this period, Jordan began to describe herself as a "dissident" poet (*On Call* 2), and her work began to align her with the goals of misrepresented or silenced peoples whose causes share much with her own needs and experiences as an African-American woman living in America.[14]

In her recent collection of essays *Technical Difficulties,* Jordan continues to focus on the misrepresented and silenced, and though the subject matter of these essays is more domestic than international, these assays of the local are her means to a broadly conceived project: the living and effecting of a moral, activist life. Jordan has given up the fixed relationship between spokesperson and constituency, presenting her voice as one among many that are fighting for power in the public forum. As she explains in an interview,

> "I make an effort in my political essays and poems to make it clear to people, this is just me speaking. I'm gonna put the best possible argument together to make you think about my point of view, but I'm not going to tell you that this is the truth, that all the important people in the world think this way, or whatever. I have tried to hinge everything I write to the truth of my personal experience, to give my writing a kind of anecdotal quality, because then people can see how I got there."

(qtd. in Nelson 51)

Jordan's political writings are honest attempts to grab and redirect power, and her most common rhetorical strategy of late has been an almost iconoclastic use of the occasional essay. Her essays are self-interested in the way they speak from and for Jordan's experiences, but also heterogeneous in the many outsider, or unheard from, positions they articulate. Most of the essays reprinted in *Technical Difficulties* were originally published as Jordan's regular contributions to *The Progressive* magazine, and as such they usually respond to something topical. What makes these essays almost iconoclastic is the way in which Jordan links the local to large political issues in surprising ways. In one essay she adopts the rhetoric of the traditional (male) African-American preacher to condemn both the U.S. government's and the black leadership's failure to rally to Anita Hill's side during the Clarence Thomas Supreme Court confirmation hearings. Jordan invokes the refrain *Can I get a witness?* and repeatedly asks questions to challenge the assumptions that allowed Thomas to use race to obscure an abuse of power along the axis of gender. She critiques the male black leadership's inability to live up to its own rhetoric. But this now familiar vigilant attention to the specific ways in which race disempowers women is placed alongside essays about Martin Luther King and Mike Tyson that find different lessons in the experiences of these two men.

Of Mike Tyson she writes a **"Requiem for the Champ"** that draws connections between Tyson's and Jordan's Brooklyn neighborhoods, and claims that the violent lifestyle that led Tyson to rape a woman originated in the spiritual and economic poverty of the world in which Tyson grew up. The only escape Tyson saw from this poverty lay in the monetary rewards our culture offers a violent response to this situation. For Tyson's limited options, and especially the limited constructions of masculinity available to him, Jordan finds herself, the Brooklyn community, and the American economic system responsible. "Who," Jordan asks, "would pay him to rehabilitate inner-city housing or to refurbish the bridge? Who would pay him that to study the facts of our collective history?" (226). There must be some way for our culture to reward a black man for something other than violence; there must be something else for a black man from the ghetto to do or be. Jordan articulates a similarly sympathetic and self-searching response to the failings of a black man when she writes of Martin Luther King in light of recent revelations that King was sexually opportunistic and deceitful, that he did not live up to the standard for a moral life that he preached. Jordan says that, while we should not "emulate the man who was not God," she will "follow after . . . this Black man of God" and is "thankful that he lived and that he loved us and that he tried so hard to be and to do good" (115-17). Jordan's most recent essays are thus a far cry from Baraka's "SOS," or even her own **"Calling on All Silent Minorities."** With her acute sense of the past's importance to the present and future, Jordan attempts to give the past a useful meaning, to recuperate it and build upon it rather than focus all energy toward the impossible goal of a totally new future. Jordan looks to a better future, but the path to this future is a healing of the divisions and wrongs of the present and the past.

A common critique of the media coverage of the new black intellectuals is the narrow context used to explain their supposedly sudden arrival. Their emergence is traced to America's post-Cold War turn from international issues to domestic concerns, or the repetition, for a new generation of thinkers who happen to be black, of the particular intellectual and institutional circumstances that produced the New York Intellectuals.[15] What these efforts to explain the newness of the new black intellectuals obscure is the long genealogy of the African-American intellectual tradition. Sam Fullwood reminds us that, "if the collective intellectual history of black Americans down the ages had been monitored by an electroencephalograph, the spikes might correspond to the periods of white people's attention. But the overlooked base line would record the steady, strong pulse of the body's resistance to oppression—a testament to African Americans' vitality" (32). June Jordan's work is this strong pulse that links the spikes of the Black Power Movement to today's current vogue. Her work translates the energy of Baraka's and Neal's writings in the service of a black community to a more complex and yet no less politically responsible accountability to the multiple grids of power and identity that shape a black audience and a black intellectual.

Michael Hanchard argues that what distinguishes the new black darlings of the press, and what disempowers them and thus makes them safe for public consumption, is that they "have no specific constituency or constellation of organizations to answer to, which would place their actions in a political context that speaks to both local and global communities" (23). Jordan's constituency is not specific in the sense that it is not singular. And yet in her work she is always aware of her audience and her responsibilities to that audience. She ties her writings to specific organizational goals,[16] and her work always seeks her audience's response, not just its passive acceptance of her words and definitions. She explains in an interview with Peter Erickson that "I'm really about what you do, rather than who you are." That is to say, she is not against finding out who you are as a personal therapy, but "the point is that then you can, in a knowledgeable and intelligent way, undertake to connect or intersect with other people's lives to some political purpose having to do with the positive acquisition of new power" (Erickson, **"After"** [**After Identity: A Conversation with June Jordan and Peter Erickson**] 149). In one sense, then, Jordan is not West's race-transcending prophet. One of her recurring concerns is how the politics of race have taken power away from people, and she writes to right this wrong. But at the same time she does transcend race when she draws on her experience of power inequalities—her experiences shaped by race, gender, and class—to address and attempt to redress all inequalities of political power that she encounters. To return to West's words, Jordan's work is characterized by a "vision of fundamental social change to all who suffer from socially induced misery" (70).

June Jordan's career thus inspires a broadening of our expectations for what an African-American intellectual can and should do, and how she can do it. Jordan addresses African-American concerns in a way that seeks to serve the best interests of the African-American community that she aligns herself with, a community that she recognizes as fluid and diverse, but which can be united in its opposition to the inequalities of power produced by the politics of race. She avoids the egotistical trap of the spokesperson model, and she shifts the Black Arts utopian vision to more pragmatic (and less oppressive) ends by seeking both to forward the interests of her multiple audiences and to elicit their responses. But if Jordan's career as a multiply aligned activist is the bridge to a new kind of African-American intellectual, one that begins to undertake the mission outlined by Du Bois, Cruse, and West, then why is she not enjoying so much public recognition as the "newer" intellectuals like Gates and West? Perhaps it has something to do with the explicitly political nature of

much of her writing, as compared to the more cultural and aesthetic focus of many of the more celebrated writers. Jordan suspects that editors find political writing by a black woman "presumptuous or simply bizarre," and Toni Morrison and bell hooks, the only women consistently linked with the new intellectuals, are decidedly cultural and literary in their focus (**On Call** 1). But I wonder if there might also be a little bit of fear involved in this response, a fear that comes with facing someone who does not back down.

In the introduction to **Civil Wars,** Jordan recounts how her uncle taught her how to stand up to bullies. He told her to remember, "It's a bully. Probably you can't win. . . . But if you go in there, saying to yourself, 'I may not win this one but it's going to cost you' . . . they'll leave you alone." Jordan may have lost a lot of fights in Bedford-Stuyvesant, but her uncle was right. ". . . nobody fought me twice," she observes. "They said I was 'crazy'" (**Civil** xi-xii). And Jordan has continued to fight the fight that began, for her, during the Harlem Riots of 1964, in which her response to the bloodshed on those nights was first to address immediate needs, to heal the wounded, and then to address the larger social, cultural, political, and economic wounds that led to that real blood. June Jordan is still fighting to heal these wounds, and her ability to stand up to bullies has contributed to many advances, such as the rise of the new black intellectuals who are following after her. But there is yet a ways to go before the fight is won.

Notes

1. Bérubé's *New Yorker* article and Boynton's cover story for *The Atlantic* have spearheaded a broader debate that has appeared on the pages of Sunday newspapers and weekly magazines. See, for example, Sam Fullwood's article in the *Los Angeles Times Magazine,* Michael Hanchard's in *The Nation,* Adolph Reed's in *The Village Voice,* Sean Wilentz's in *Dissent,* and Jacqueline Trescott's in *The Washington Post.*

2. For a more balanced treatment of Baldwin's conception of the black spokesperson, see Houston A. Baker's *The Journey Back,* in which Baker argues that "Baldwin's ideal black spokesperson . . . is 'socially responsible' to neither white nor black America . . . [and] cannot be easily categorized as 'integrationist' or 'assimilationist' since he is racing 'with all deliberate speed' to escape society" (61). In other words, Baldwin is an advocate for a politics of individual freedom.

3. One reading of Black Arts writing that disagrees with my interpretation is Phillip Brian Harper's claim that the violent rhetoric of "performative language predicates the status of Black Arts poetry as being heard by whites and overheard by blacks" (254). For

the purpose of this essay I am more interested in the effects Black Arts writing had upon understandings of the African-American intellectual than in the performative effect of the language as such. But Harper's argument does foreground the multiplicity of audiences and audience effects that the African-American intellectual must consider.

4. My process-oriented and future-looking reading of Baraka differs slightly from Baker's powerful reading. Baker claims that Baraka attempts to reach a primordial blackness "through sheer lyricism and assertiveness" (134-35).

5. Her major collection of poetry, *Naming Our Destiny,* was published in 1989. The essay collections *Technical Difficulties* and *On Call* were published in 1985 and 1994, respectively, and her important first collection of essays, *Civil Wars,* originally published in 1981, was reissued by Touchstone (a division of Simon & Schuster) in 1995.

6. *Technical Difficulties* was published by Vintage. Jordan's most recent poetry collection, *Kissing God Goodbye,* was brought out by Anchor, a subdivision of Bantam Doubleday Dell.

7. She tells of these experiences in the essays "Letter to Michael" and "One Way of Beginning This Book," both collected in *Civil Wars.* For more biographical information on Jordan, see her interview with Peter Erickson in *Transition* and Carla Freccero's article in *African American Writers.*

8. One sign of Jordan's discomfort with this role is her struggle over the title of one of her first published essays. *The Nation* renamed the essay "Spokesman for the Blacks" without Jordan's consent. When Jordan reprinted the essay, she used its original title—"On Listening: A Good Way to Hear" (*Civil* 39).

9. Jordan's campaign for the recognition of the value of Black English is one of the most visible markers of her black nationalist attempts to give voice to, and valorize, black cultural expression. Her second book-length publication, *His Own Where,* is a children's book written in Black English; many of her poems employ Black English; and several of her essays explain why she uses Black English and attempt to initiate a more rigorous study of it as a dialect. Her most interesting writings on this topic include the two essays "Nobody Mean More to Me Than You and the Future Life of Willie Jordan" (*On Call* 123-140) and "White English/Black English: The Politics of Translation" (*On Call* 59-73).

10. In her introduction to this essay in *Civil Wars,* she connects this piece to one she wrote for the *Herald Tribune* in the months before the riot. The editor asked Jordan "to determine whether or not there would be 'a long hot summer' in Harlem." Jordan's conclusion was that ". . . there would have to be/ that there *should* be a long hot summer because, as I titled my essay, 'nothing is new for the man uptown'" (16-17). The *Tribune* did not accept the essay.

11. At one level, Michael, a white graduate student in the Anthropology department of the University of Chicago, stands in for this white audience.

12. Besides de Beauvoir's classic argument against naturalized gender categories, two powerful critiques of the assumption that silence is natural for women are Adrienne Rich's *On Lies. Secrets and Silence* and Tillie Olson's *Silences.* Susan Griffin's *Pornography and Silence* is a later work (1981) which nicely sums up several arguments of the period. Especially important in light of Jordan's critique is Griffin's use of James Baldwin to suggest a parallel between the ways that the majority culture has obscured the real beauty of women and the way that it has constructed an imaginary black man. What does not occur to Griffin is what kind of effect this logic might have on the doubly silenced category of the black woman, and how her silences might be addressed.

13. See, for instance, "Poem for South African Women" and "Poem about My Rights" (*Naming* 89, 103). The essay about Neto is collected in *Civil Wars* (103-12).

14. An extended comparison of the careers of Baraka and Jordan, which is beyond my scope here, might usefully highlight the motives, means, and audiences of their efforts to become more international in scope. Jordan's broadening sense of subject matter, responsibility, and audience corresponds in some ways with Baraka's Third-World Marxist writings, though as usual Jordan keeps her critical distance from established categories of representation and political action by naming her project "First Worldism" and by continuing to employ the strategy that divides her from Baraka by insisting on differences and a multiplicity of audiences/voices.

15. The former is Boynton's explanation, and the latter is Bérubé's.

16. See, for instance, the description of her curricula for her creative writing class at UC-Berkeley which she published with Shanti Bright. Jordan's "Poetry for the People" project attempts to reform both the content and method of the college classroom in response to the changing demography of the U.S. university.

Works Cited

Baker, Houston. *The Journey Back: Issues in Black Literature and Criticism.* Chicago: U of Chicago P, 1980.

Baldwin, James. *Notes of a Native Son.* Boston: Beacon P, 1955

Baraka, Amiri. *The LeRoi Jones/Amiri Baraka Reader.* Ed. William J. Harris. New York: Thunder's Mouth P, 1991.

Bérubé, Michael. "Public Academy." *New Yorker* 9 Jan. 1995: 73-80.

Boynton, Robert S. "The New Intellectuals." *Atlantic* Mar. 1995: 53-69.

Carroll, Rebecca. *I Know What the Red Clay Looks Like: The Voice and Vision of Black Women Writers.* New York: Crown, 1994.

Cruse, Harold. *The Crisis of the Negro Intellectual.* New York: Morrow. 1967.

DeMott, Benjamin. "James Baldwin on the Sixties: Acts and Revelations." *James Baldwin: A Collection of Critical Essays.* Ed. Keneth Kinnamon. Englewood Cliffs: Prentice, 1974. 155-62.

Erickson, Peter. "After Identity: A Conversation with June Jordan and Peter Erickson." *Transition* 63 (1994): 132-49.

———. "June Jordan." *Afro-American Writers After 1955: Prose Writers and Dramatists.* Vol. 38 of *Dictionary of Literary Biography.* Ed. Thadious M. Davis and Trudier Harris. Detroit: Gale, 1985. 146-62.

Freccero, Carla. "June Jordan." *African American Writers.* Ed. Valerie Smith. New York: Scribner's, 1991, 245-61.

Fullwood, Sam. "Intellectuals in the Promised Land." *Los Angeles Times Magazine* 9 Apr. 1995: 10+.

Griffin, Susan. *Pornography and Silence.* New York: Harper, 1981.

Hanchard, Michael. "Intellectual Pursuit." *Nation* 19 Feb. 1996: 22-25.

Harper, Phillip Brian, "Nationalism and Social Division in Black Arts Poetry of the 1960s." *Critical Inquiry* 19 (1993): 234-55.

Jordan, June. *Civil Wars.* 1981. New York: Touchstone, 1995.

———. *His Own Where.* New York: Crowell, 1971.

———. *Kissing God Goodbye.* New York: Anchor, 1997.

———. *Naming Our Destiny: New & Selected Poems.* New York: Thunder's Mouth P, 1989.

———. *On Call: Political Essays.* Boston: South End P, 1985.

———. *Technical Difficulties.* New York: Vintage, 1994.

Neal, Larry. "The Black Arts Movement." *The Black Aesthetic.* Ed. Addison Gayle, Jr. New York: Doubleday, 1971. 272-90.

Nelson, Jill. "A Conversation with June Jordan." *Quarterly Review of Black Books* 1 (May 1994): 50-53.

Olander, Renee. "An Interview with June Jordan." *AWP Chronicle* Feb. 1995: 1+.

Reed, Adolph. "What are the Drums Saying, Booker?: The Current Crisis of the Black Intellectual." *Village Voice* 11 Apr. 1995: 31-36.

Van Deburg, William. *New Day in Babylon: The Black Power Movement and American Culture: 1965-1975.* Chicago: U of Chicago P, 1992.

West, Cornel. *Race Matters.* New York: Vintage, 1993.

Wilentz, Sean. "Race, Celebrity, and the Intellectuals: Notes on a Donnybrook." *Dissent* 42.3 (1995): 293-99.

Samiya A. Bashir (essay date September-October 2000)

SOURCE: Bashir, Samiya A. "June Jordan's True Grit." *Black Issues Book Review* 2, no. 5 (September-October 2000): 32-6.

[*In this essay, Bashir explores Jordan's background as related in* Soldier: A Poet's Childhood.]

> These poems
> they are things that I do
> in the dark
> reaching for you
> whoever you are
> and are you ready?

—June Jordan, from *Things That I Do in the Dark,* © 1980

> I think you better join with me to agitate
> and agitate for justice and
> equality we can eat
> and pay the rent with
> NOW.

—June Jordan, from **"Jim Crow: The Sequel"**

She hits you like an A-Bomb, and like the misunderstood atom, Jordan—slightly built, soft-voiced and with a sweetly infectious laugh—is often underestimated by those against whom she finds herself in opposition. Her new memoir, *Soldier: A Poet's Childhood* (Basic Civitas Books, May 2000) offers precious documentation of the consummate tough girl. Born in a Harlem heat wave in 1936 and raised first in the newly constructed Harlem projects then in the heart of the Bedford-Stuyvesant section of Brooklyn, Jordan's story is that of a vulnerable girl learning the survival strategies necessary to negotiate the hostile terrain of mid-twentieth century America.

Jordan is the only child of West Indian immigrant parents who had high ambitions for her. Her father was particularly strict, and allowed for nothing that might distract his only child from growing up to become the strong son he'd always wanted. "Regardless of any particulars about me, he was convinced that a 'Negro' parent had to produce a child who could become a virtual white man and, therefore, possess dignity and power," recalls Jordan in *Soldier* [*Soldier: A Poet's Childhood*], reflecting on the motivations of his pseudo-military method of childrearing. "Probably it seemed easier to change me than to change the meaning and complexion of power. He taught me everything from the perspective of a recruiting warrior. There was a war going on against colored people, against poor people. I had to become a soldier who would rise through the ranks and emerge a commander of men."

She was "that crazy Jordan girl" from a young age, never backing away from a fight with a neighborhood bully, no matter that they were all considerably bigger than she. Jordan began learning the important lessons of standing up for herself as a 4-year-old. "I was clear about one thing: A really excellent way to stop somebody from hitting you is to hit them back."

Soldier is Jordan's twenty-sixth book, marking her as the most frequently published African American writer in history. Yet it is hard to go into a bookstore and find her many volumes lining the shelves. Instead, one finds a conspicuously dismaying absence, perhaps a single copy of one or two titles. Her willingness to tell it like it is without apology keeps her work, no matter how widespread her critical acclaim, out of the mainstream.

Singled out as "our premiere Black woman essayist" by no less than Nobel laureate Toni Morrison, Jordan has had a rich literary career spanning over three decades. "When I came out with *Civil Wars* (reprinted by Simon & Schuster, August 1995), a million years ago," says Jordan, dotting her speech with her trademark conspiratorial laugh, "a lot of black writers that I know started thinking about writing essays. Toni Cade Bambara said she'd never thought about keeping track of what's going on in that way and [she said] maybe she was going to do that too."

We would he remiss, however, to label Jordan merely as a poet, or even an essayist, and leave it at that. Like many African American artists. Jordan uses her unique ability in a variety of forms. Jordan's resume reads like a who's who in literary honoraria from Rockefeller and NEA fellowships, to grants and awards from private and public organizations across the country. She has received the Prix de Rome Environmental Design Award and was recently given the American Institute of Architecture's Award for Architectural Design (1998) for a joint proposal for the African Burial Ground in New York City. She has even had her face depicted on a Ugandan postage stamp!

As professor in the African American Studies Department at the University of California at Berkeley, she established the wildly successful Poetry for the People program in 1991. It began as a two-part series of courses training selected students to become poetry teachers. Student teachers, myself included, tested their skills in a large-scale university course where they taught, under Jordan's direction, the power of poetry from a multicultural world view. Since then she has sent scores of these new trainees out into the world, expanding the program to include churches, high schools and community centers.

It's a warm spring afternoon in New York City as Jordan and I saunter slowly into a trendy new Euro-Asian restaurant. Over a delicately flavorful, remarkably overpriced lunch, we spoke about why someone who had led such a full and interesting life as Jordan would choose to limit her long-awaited memoir to her prepubescent years. "Childhood everywhere in the world is a political situation. Politics is about power; and if you are a child, you have no power," states Jordan, her agitation at the often-perilous plight of the least represented majority in the world clearly visible. "The childhood relationship to power is critical—if you're the child it's all about you not having any and the folks around you having it all. 'Let's have a relationship,' says this impossibly big man or woman. These are the beginning terms: you're completely dependent on me and I'm going to tell you what to do and you're going to do it."

A close look at her body of work reveals just how in sync with her political concerns and deep affection for children such an intensely personal undertaking actually was. Her earliest publications were the children's books she wrote and edited in the late '60s and early '70s including *His Own Where* (HarperCollins Children's Books, January 1971), the first American novel written wholly in Black English. With *Soldier,* Jordan returns to the realm of children, whom she classifies as the most universally powerless group of people on earth, and beginning with herself, gives them voice. "Every one of us has a childhood and each of us has to negotiate our place in that," says Jordan.

Soldier confides in her readers, sharing a frightening world for this little-girl-June, of whom we're instantly protective. Yet we are comforted by this marvelously strong child who maneuvers the twists and turns of her journey boldly offering readers an uncompromising gaze at all she finds. "I wanted to get [the story] right," she says, modestly eating her vegetables and reminiscing on the process of honestly telling the delicate story of her harsh upbringing. "So it was a bit scary. I was just fooling around for a while with different beginnings and storylines until finally I got the first sentence of the book, and then it kept pouring out."

What poured out, is uncompromising, poetic prose painted with hard brushes in soft colors. Her story is offered as a promise that we can become whole and carry others into wholeness with us. Readers watch this small young soldier in a poignant ending that is also a new beginning. "That was a very difficult ending to write, I didn't know until I wrote it just how hard it was because then I could really see her. I re-wrote that last section because I didn't want people to say 'oh, this is terrible.' This is the end of her childhood, and I wanted people to feel positive and hopeful while steadfast in the reality that this is the end—now what? *Black Boy, Brown Girl, Brownstones, Go Tell It On The Mountain,* those stories stop closer to childhood. I hope that this will stand beside them, that *Soldier* will spawn similar efforts among other people who never thought about doing this. It will make possible, if there are more of us doing this, for us to connect with each other in ways that we never seem really able to do. This is our story, much of your story and my story is the same, but we haven't taken the time to tell it yet."

At the end of this remarkably touching narrative there is a real sense of hope. Says Jordan, "I was looking forward definitely, not looking back . . . Hafla, to forget, is a sin in Islamic tradition. To remember is to praise God; I don't know how you can remember without some documentation. I hope that what folks will take away from the book is that we've made it, we're here. Here's my proof."

AnaLouise Keating (essay date 2000)

SOURCE: Keating, AnaLouise. "The Intimate Distance of Desire: June Jordan's Bisexual Inflections." In *'Romancing the Margins'?: Lesbian Writing in the 1990s,* edited by Gabriele Griffin, pp. 81-93. Binghamton, N.Y.: Harrington Park Press, 2000.

[*In the following essay, Keating comments on images of bisexuality in Jordan's poetry.*]

> These poems
> they are things that I do
> in the dark
> reaching for you

> whoever you are
> and are you ready?

> These words
> they are stones in the water
> running away

> These skeletal lines
> They are desperate arms for my longing and love.

> I am a stranger
> learning to worship the strangers
> around me

> whoever you are
> whoever I may become.

[**"Poem against a Conclusion"**] —June Jordan

In both her poetry and her prose, June Jordan enacts a complex process of interactional identity formation where self-change occurs only in the context of other people. Throughout her writing, Jordan uses her own self-naming process to illustrate the interrelational nature of individual and collective social change. Drawing connections between her personal experiences as a twentieth-century bisexual U.S. woman of Jamaican descent and the experiences of women from all ethnic backgrounds, colonized nations, gay men, and other oppressed groups, Jordan demonstrates that each person's self-determination entails recognizing and affirming both the commonalities and the differences between self and others. As she incorporates this mobile self-naming process into her poetry and prose, Jordan rejects restrictive notions of isolated, self-enclosed individual identities and creates intimate dialogues between herself and her readers. She invents an intersubjective, potentially transformational space that she invites her readers to share. Thus in the poem I have borrowed for my epigraph, Jordan employs ambiguous, shifting pronouns to generate new forms of identification and desire that break down without entirely erasing the boundaries between writer, readers, and the words on the page. Flesh becomes text (her poems are *'desperate arms for my longing and love'*) as she infuses the desire for connection and transformation into her words, embodying them.

I begin with this poem because it offers me a map, a model for interacting with Jordan's complex self-naming process. She adopts an opening, questioning position that she invites her readers—invites me—to adopt. In the first stanza as her words become concrete acts reaching outward, towards her readers—towards *'you / whoever you are'*—I identify with this 'you' and accept Jordan's challenge to change. Her words—tangible yet elusive (like *'stones in the water / running away'*)—seduce me, draw me into the poem, invite me to re-examine my own subject position. As I read her words on the page, I become the stranger Jordan describes, and this process of becoming-stranger begins to transform me, compels me to reach out, so that I too begin *'learning to worship the strangers / around me.'* Yet this worship of strangers—strangers who include both Jordan and me—entails an openness and, by extension, a willingness to take risks. By concluding this poem with two open-ended questioning statements that shift from second person to first, Jordan interpellates her readers—interpellates me—into a transitional place, where identification and desire converge, partially merging while remaining in some ways distinct.

As she inscribes herself into the words on the page, Jordan creates a transformational space—an intimate distance of desire—between herself and her readers. More specifically, by identifying both herself and her readers as strangers, she mobilizes new constellations of sameness and difference that make the development of commonalities possible. It is these new constellations I describe as an intimate distance of desire—a transitional place where the acceptance of differences leads through transformation to new forms of connection. I borrow the phrase *intimate distance* from Jordan, where it indicates open-ended potential, a meeting point between self and other. As she explains in her essay on Walt Whitman, 'the intimate distance between the poet and the reader is a distance that assumes that there is everything important, between them, to be shared' (**'People's Poetry'** [**'For the Sake of People's Poetry: Walt Whitman and the Rest of Us'**] 8). This shared space of difference acknowledges the separation between writer and reader yet redefines this potentially dualistic relation, creating a place where commonalities can arise. Inscribing this shared space of difference into her words, Jordan invites her readers to do so as well.

For Jordan, this intimate distance of desire opens up a bisexualized, intersubjective matrix—a nonspecific but gendered, sexualized space where new modes of identity can occur. Thus in the poem I began with she reaches out, through the darkness, toward her readers, reaches with *'longing and love,'* towards you—*'whoever you are.'* By oscillating between self and other, she enacts a bisexual inflection—an ethical, highly erotic vision that deploys mobile configurations of identification and desire to challenge restrictive labeling. These oscillations between sameness and difference (between 'I' and 'you') destabilize the binary system structuring sexual, gender, and ethnic categories, thus creating a space where alterations in consciousness and different modes of desire (can) occur.

But why describe this ethical vision and the shifting inflections Jordan employs as 'bisexual'? After all, in the poem I have adopted for my epigraph gender seems to be entirely irrelevant; the 'I' and the 'you' she refers to are unmarked by gender, sex, ethnicity, or any other system of difference. Moreover, other theorists who most definitely do not identify as bisexual express similar desires but use different terms. (Take, for example, Elizabeth Meese's (sem)erotics and lesbian:writing, or Gloria Anzaldúa's new mestiza queers: two theories of boundary-crossing invented by self-identified lesbian writers.) Is the bisexual inflection I find in Jordan's words simply the product of my own (bisexual) desires, reinforced by Jordan's open affirmation of *her* bisexual identity? Would other readers, who tell different stories about their lives, read Jordan's words differently? The concept of bisexuality is, itself, highly problematic—constantly evoked only to be ignored, erased, or in other ways dismissed as too ambivalent, elusive, and transitional to matter.[1] So why use the term 'bisexual'?

At this point, so many directions open up, many paths I could take in this essay: should I define and justify my use of the phrase bisexual inflections? (I could explain the ethical dimensions in the ambivalently gendered pronouns these inflections deploy.) Or should I continue with this personalized, self-reflective style of writing and tell you about my particular bisexual interactions with Jordan's poetry and prose? (I could narrate my personal experiences and explain how Jordan's self-declared bisexual politics speaks to my own, previously inarticulated desires and offered me a position—shifting, slippery, and elusive though it is—from which to think, speak, act, and love.) Or should I adopt a more scholarly approach? (I could begin by exploring Jordan's shifting identifications, draw on theoretical interpretations of bisexuality as an epistemological position, and argue that Jordan enacts an alternate mode of thinking that deconstructs binary oppositions from within.)

Perhaps, in the conclusion, I will return to my own story and to the questions I have raised concerning the (in)effectiveness of bisexual labels. Or perhaps I won't. But first I want to explore the transformational ambiguously gendered, multiply sexualized possibilities opened up by the intersubjective matrix Jordan's bisexual inflections create. More precisely, I want to examine the ways in which Jordan uses language to break down conventional boundaries between subject/object, writer/reader(s), and the material/psychic dimensions of writing and life. As she inscribes her self, her desires, and the intimate events from her life into her work, Jordan goes beyond dyadic relationships between 'me' and the words 'I' write to encompass 'you' as well—you reading me as I read Jordan. Together we (the at-least-three of us) enter into an intersubjective space, transformed by Jordan's textualized self-inscriptions.

As she writes her self, her desires, and the intimate events from her life into her work, Jordan develops an intricate interplay between sameness and difference that blurs the boundaries between writer, reader, and text. She challenges her readers—no matter how we identify, whether as male, female, heterosexual, homosexual, bisexual, lesbian, gay, black, white, or brown—to reexamine our own subject positions. Take, for example, **'A Short Note to My Very Critical Friends and Well-Beloved Comrades'** where she enacts a mobile self-naming process that challenges restrictive labeling. After defiantly outlining the numerous ways her well-meaning friends and comrades have tried unsuccessfully to classify her according to color, sexuality, age, and ideology, Jordan confidently reaffirms her ability to define herself as she sees fit:

> Make up your mind! They said. Are you militant
> or sweet? Are you vegetarian or meat? Are you straight
> or are you gay?
>
> And I said, Hey! It's not about *my* mind.
>
> *(Naming [Naming Our Destiny]* 98)

The implications of this final line are clear. Rejecting restrictive labels and the binary forms of thinking they so often entail, Jordan throws the responsibility back on her well-meaning questioners: they must reexamine their own desire for fixed labels and static categories of identity. These lines have a similar impact on readers; as Peter Erickson explains, 'Having aroused our irritation, the poem dares us to examine it, to probe our discomfort at being unable to pin down the poet's identity' (222). (What about you, reader: Do you agree with Erickson's statement? Are you, too, irritated with Jordan's flippant refusal to situate and name herself?) As she oscillates between apparently distinct categories of meaning, Jordan disrupts the boundaries between fixed identity locations. By destabilizing her own subjectivity, she destabilizes her readers' as well. She replaces the conventional, Enlightenment-based belief in isolated, self-contained identities with open-ended models of identity formation.

In the above lines, it is the way Jordan depicts sexuality that intrigues me. To begin with, by associating the binary opposition between straight and gay with political styles ('Are you militant / or sweet?') and eating habits ('vegetarian or meat?')—two aspects of life that we shape and change according to our needs, circumstances, and desires—she implies that sexuality also involves a degree of choice. And, by refusing to identify as either straight or gay, she refuses the limited choices we are generally offered, exposing the limitations in binary modes of thinking. She calls into question the conflict model of sexual identity that posits an irremedial difference between homosexual and heterosexual identities. This conflict model erases the middle ground and denies the possibility of hybrid sexualities that combine yet exceed hetero and homosexuality. (But

what might these possibilities be? Jordan leaves that to us—to you and me—to decide and live out for ourselves.)

As she goes beyond specific gender and ethnic categories of meaning, without denying their temporary historic significance, Jordan redefines identity as a constantly shifting internal process. As she asserts in **'Civil Wars,'**

> Neither race nor gender provides the final definitions of jeopardy or refuge. The final risk or final safety lies within each one of us attuned to the messy and intricate and unending challenge of self-determination. I believe the ultimate power of all the people rests upon the individual ability to trust and to respect the authority of the truth of whatever it is that each of us feels, each of us means.
>
> (187)

In emphasizing the messy, intricate, unending nature of this self-naming process, Jordan replaces conventional identity politics—or the tendency to base political actions on restrictive definitions of gender-, ethnic-, or sexual-specific identity categories—with her own fluid politics of self-determination. She points to the possibility of new types of identification based on each individual's interests and desires. Her words invite readers—invite me and (perhaps) you—to establish different ways of connecting with others, shaped by the particular situations we enter into and the specific individuals with whom we interact.

This fluid, open-ended politics of self-determination plays an important role in the bisexual inflections I find in Jordan's words. As she writes herself and particular events from her life into her poetry and prose, she oscillates between apparently distinct identities and locations. She employs open-ended pronouns that extend her experience outward, inventing a space her readers can share—an intimate distance of desire.

Jordan's bisexual inflections move the reader—move this reader, move me (and, perhaps, you?)—into and beyond an erotics of physical, heterosexual or homosexual pleasure and stimulate a desire for different connections. At this point, however, I won't even try to describe the particular forms these new connections might take (for you); they must be invented and lived out by each reader. All I can say is that the fluid—yet gendered—oscillations between sameness and difference open up new grounds for interchange and (e)merging desires.

Even love poems apparently addressed to male subjects—love poems presumably coded 'straight'—incorporate these bisexual inflections. Thus in **'For Dave: 1976'** Jordan briefly describes an afternoon of lovemaking between herself and another person named

'Dave,' a person I—and probably other readers as well—assume to be male. Yet this assumption is based solely on the title. There are no gender-specific markers in the text itself. Throughout this short poem Jordan employs ambiguous nongendered pronouns; nothing in her description definitively positions this afternoon lover as a man: there's 'the Army cap that spills your / hair below those clean-as-a-whistle ears nobody / knows how to blow so you hear them honest-to / God' and the '(red shirt / new shoes / the shower shining everywhere about you).' Unmarked by gendered labels, these references to 'you' are open to multiple interpretations. 'You' could be male or female, black, white, or any shade of brown; it could be me or you, reader. But to my mind, the important thing here is not the lover's gender but rather the intimate distance Jordan depicts between herself and 'you.' As in the poem I borrowed for my epigraph, she acknowledges the differences between 'me' and 'you' but uses the intimate distance this acknowledgment opens up to create new points of connection. Thus she concludes by stating

> And I accept again
> that there are simple ways of being joined
> to someone
> absolutely different from myself
>
>   (*Naming* 30)

It's this acceptance of simple interconnections despite—or at times perhaps because of—tremendous differences that makes possible the new forms of identification and desire I read in Jordan's words. But as in the poem I used for my epigraph, Jordan does not tell us what these simple ways of being joined to someone absolutely different might be; she simply points to the possibility of new types of connection through difference but leaves the specific details for readers—for us—to imagine and (perhaps) to begin living out with the bodies we encounter.

Significantly, **'For Dave'** is followed in *Naming Our Destiny* by **'Meta-Rhetoric,'** a poem addressed to an unnamed but most likely female subject, a potential lover referred to only as 'you.' Again Jordan employs shifting referents to blur the boundaries between reader and writer, between 'my body' and 'yours': 'your mouth on my mouth / your breasts resting on my own.' Each time I read this poem, identifying both with the 'I' and the 'you,' I oscillate between subject positions (Is it my mouth on yours? yours or mine?). To be sure, these lines can be read as an expression of lesbian desire (After all, both 'I' and 'you' have breasts.) To my mind, however, this lesbianized reading is too restrictive and simplifies the ambiguously gendered pronouns Jordan employs. Take, for example, the opening scene she describes between 'us':

> we sit apart
> apparently at opposite ends of a line

> and I feel the distance
> between my eyes
> between my legs
> a dry
> dust topography of our separation
>
>   (*Naming* 31)

Once again, Jordan opens up an intimate distance between herself and her reader, between 'me' and 'you.' However, by locating 'our separation' both within herself and between herself and 'you'—her potential lover—Jordan doubly embodies this intimate distance of desire, unsettling the binary opposition between self and other. As I identify both with the 'me' and the 'you' in Jordan's words, I too draw on my own memories of internal and external separation and experience the desire for connection through difference.

As in **'For Dave,'** Jordan's oscillations between 'me' and 'you' indicate bisexual inflections that trigger new forms of identity and desire. And again, Jordan concludes by pointing to an intimate distance of desire between 'me' and 'you':

> My hope is that our lives will declare
> this meeting
> open
>
>   (*Naming* 32)

These lines defer closure, shifting responsibility partially onto the reader, onto me or (perhaps) onto you. We are invited to enter into this shared embodied space of difference. If we do so, we too experience this partially expressed, perhaps only partially speakable desire.

In both poems, then, Jordan's pronouns create scenes—interactions between 'me' and 'you'—that seem gendered yet move beyond specific categories of identity. Her words are performative and move (us) from the page, from the fixed categories in our minds, into new ways of thinking and acting. If, as Marjorie Garber suggests, 'language can function *as* a sexual act, not just as a way of naming one' (144, her emphasis), Jordan's bisexual inflections seduce readers—seduce me and (perhaps) you. No matter how we label ourselves—whether as male, female, heterosexual, homosexual, bisexual, lesbian, gay, brown, black, white, or any variation among these terms—Jordan invites us to enter into this intersubjective matrix and enact new, sexualized encounters that go beyond familiar self-definitions, beyond conventional interactions between writer, reader, and text. She develops flexible models of subject positioning that enable her to establish points of similarity and difference with readers of diverse backgrounds. In these new constellations of reading/desire, gender becomes far less important than the desire for connection, for alternate forms of communication.

Do I read these poems—one (apparently) addressed to a man and one (apparently) to a woman—as bisexual because I read myself—my erotic attractions and desires—as bisexual? Would other readers who tell different stories about their lives read these poems differently? Or, do these questions even matter? After all, one of the points I want to make in this essay is that identity categories and labels can become far too restrictive, preventing us from establishing commonalities and points of connection with people who seem very different from ourselves. All too often, the labels others impose upon us, as well as the names we select for ourselves, shape the ways we perceive others and the ways we interact. This name-driven mode of perception compels us to read a poem (ostensibly) written by a woman to a man as 'heterosexual.' And this name-driven perception compels us to read a poem (ostensibly) written by a woman to a woman as 'lesbian.'

By reading **'For Dave'** and **'Meta-Rhetoric'** against their apparent codings, I attempt to resist this label-driven perception.

INTERLUDE; OR, THE PROBLEMS WITH NAMING

To be sure, this theory of bisexual inflections I try to invent as I read and interact with Jordan's words could be dismissed as what some might call my own over-identification with this openly bisexual writer. Remember: I write these words about this self-identified bisexual woman poet 'as' a bisexual. But what does it mean to desire bisexually, or to identify myself as 'bisexual'? Am I simply telling you that I have had both women and men as my lovers? Does bisexuality imply desiring—physically hungering for (lusting after) both women and men and doing so (hungering, lusting, desiring) in both masculine and feminine fashion or terms? When I identify myself as bisexual am I telling you that I incorporate both masculine and feminine energies within myself? Yet which of these definitions cannot also be applied to many people who identify as 'lesbian,' 'gay,' or 'straight'? Yes, this word—'bisexual'—disturbs me. With its reference to two it can easily—no matter how inadvertently—reinforce binary thinking and useless, dualistic definitions of bisexual identity—two sexes in one body, two sexual desires—one for women, one for men. Is it possible to escape these multiple forms of duality? These questions have no easy answers. Perhaps they have no answers at all.

To make matters even more confusing, as I seek alternate definitions for this sometimes dualistic term, I am torn between my own conflicting desires—no, not my erotic attractions to women and men. Rather, I am split by my desire for a politics of visibility—an affirmation of this elusive, so often erased bisexual

identity—and my desire to break the categories, to demonstrate the limitations that define/confine us as 'heterosexual,' 'lesbian,' 'man,' 'woman,' and so on. In our label-driven thinking, each label becomes a restriction, a limit to the many ways identification and desire (can) flow. For example, when I read Elizabeth Meese's description of the lesbian/body, must I limit myself to totally female encounters, to lesbianized interactions? Borrowing from Catherine Stimpson, Meese asserts that

> 'Lesbianism represents a commitment of skin, blood, breast, and bone' ([Stimpson] 164). But the literal body, however powerfully evoked, is a referential one, the 'skin' and 'bone' of textuality's absent lesbian, 'there,' and, literally speaking, not there at all, whose 'being' depends on the word's evocation. She is called forth, in the way that I see your figure on the page, make you present for me as I write my letter to you. Your body is only as 'literal' as the letter, the shade and angle of the marks on a page.
>
> (2)

Who is this 'you' Meese addresses? If I read this statement with the labels intact, I must visualize a female body, feminized letters sprawled out on the page. But these textualized marks say different things to me than they do to Meese (and probably to you). To be sure, the 'lesbian' body she refers to, the 'lesbian' bodies I have known, remain absent, 'not there at all.' Yet even in this absence these bodies are far more present than the bisexual body I know so well but so rarely, so very rarely, meet in print.

So how do I react? What do I read when I see *lesbian/body?* How do I embody, change, or desire these terms? Here, for example, is sidney matrix's take on lesbian/bodies and words:

> Writing embodied lesbian: theory means assembling myselves, not into a whole self, but into integrated selfhoods, encompassing all the scraps I was taught to overlook, lay by the wayside (un)necessarily. The notions of what a lesbian can be shape the way I think through myselves. Sometimes I rebel, resist, reject the ideal(s) of lesbianism, and sometimes I camp it up, flaunt it, work it for all it's worth. Within webs of cultural discourses—religious, medical, parental, heterosexist, feminist, lookist, intellectual, erotic, racist—I exist as a lesbian like this, lesbian like that. The lesbian *I* has always already been discursively constructed/constituted, and writes (re-writes / un-writes) according to what has been written, said, and imagined about lesbian experience(s).
>
> (71)

Like matrix, when I think about personalized inscriptions I assemble myselves, pulling together the scraps I was taught to overlook, as well as the scraps that have no name(s). However, I cannot say the same thing about 'the bisexual *I*.' This '*I*' does not-yet-exist. Not in print, anyway. It has not 'always already been discursively constructed/constituted.' It does not write (re-write / un-write) according to what has been written, said, and imagined about bisexual experience(s). Perhaps it will never exist. And maybe it shouldn't. Very little has been written about this bisexual *I,* or about bisexual bodies, bodies that can be male or female, mine or (maybe?) yours. And the small amount of material out there in print is so highly personal, so very body specific, that I must say 'No. That's not me.' Over and over again I say it.²

BISEXUAL INFLECTIONS: EMBODYING A MIDDLE GROUND

Let me emphasize: my goal in this essay, my goal in theorizing bisexual inflections, is not to negate the importance of developing a body of lesbian criticism. Nor am I adopting a 'me too' position—a defensive call for increased representation and respect for bisexuals. (At this point I could go into a diatribe on bi invisibility, but I'll spare you.) Rather, I want to break down the categories even further, and as I stated pages ago, I think Jordan's words provide one way to do so.

Jordan offers the clearest statement of the categorical breakdown she and I desire in **'A New Politics of Sexuality'** where she emphasizes the contextual, action-based nature of all self-naming:

> I will call you my brother, I will call you my sister, on the basis of what you *do* for justice, what you *do* for equality, what you *do* for freedom and not on the basis of who you are, even so I look with admiration and respect upon the new, bisexual politics of sexuality. This emerging movement politicizes the so-called middle ground: Bisexuality invalidates either/or formulation, either/or analysis. Bisexuality means I am free and I am as likely to want and to love a woman as I am likely to want and to love a man, and what about that? Isn't that what freedom implies? If you are free, you are not predictable and you are not controllable. To my mind, that is the keenly positive, politicizing significance of bisexual affirmation: To insist upon complexity, to insist upon the validity of all of the components of social/sexual complexity, to insist upon the equal validity of all the components of social/sexual complexity.
>
> (193)

The middle ground: a space often reserved for wishy-washy moderation. Straddling the fence, so to speak. Refusing to identify, refusing to take a stand. Jordan enters into and politicizes this ambivalent space without denying the ambivalence. She embodies it in her texts. By so doing, she loosens the labels that define—and, in defining confine 'us'—whoever this 'us' might be, whoever 'we' might become. Jordan's bisexual inflections create the sexualized, politicized middle ground she envisions, reminding us—reminding me, anyway—that we are all interconnected.

My point is not to argue that this intimate distance/bisexual inflection is *really* 'bisexual'—assuming that we could even agree on a single meaning for the term. Rather, I want to underscore the transformational dynamics that (can) occur in reading and writing, and I believe the bisexual inflections Jordan enacts in her poetry and prose provide a space (a nonbinary middle ground, perhaps?) in which to do so. It is the ambivalence generally associated with bisexual modes of identity and attraction that I find so appealing, for the oscillations between 'me' and 'you' disrupt existing categories of meaning. Bisexual inflections open multiple readings which in turn open multiple channels of desire. They break down without erasing conventional boundaries in sexually-specific labels and texts, leaving the next step to me and (perhaps) to you, reader: *'whoever you are / whoever I may become.'*

Notes

1. See, for example, Jo Eadie, Clare Hemmings, and Kenneth MacKinnon.

2. See, for example, the anthologies edited by The Bisexual Anthology Collective; Loraine Hutchins and Lani Kaahumanu; Naomi Tucker; and Rebecca Weise.

Works Cited

Anzaldúa, Gloria. 1991. 'To(o) queer the writer—*Loca, escritora y chicana.* In *Inversions: Writing by dykes, queers, and lesbians.* Ed. Betsy Warland. Vancouver: Press Gang. 249-64.

The Bisexual Anthology Collective, eds. 1995. *Plural desires: Writing bisexual women's realities.* Toronto: Sisters Vision.

Eadie, Jo. 1993. Activating bisexuality: Towards a bi/sexual politics. In *Activating theory: lesbian, gay, bisexual politics.* Eds. Joseph Bristow and Angelia R. Wilson. London: Lawrence & Wishart. 139-70.

Erickson, Peter. 1986. The love poetry of June Jordan. *Callaloo* 9: 221-34.

Hemmings, Clare. 1995. Locating bisexual identities: Discourses of bisexuality and contemporary feminist theory. In *Mapping desire: Geographies of sexuality.* Eds. David Bell and Gill Valentine. London and New York: Routledge. 41-55.

———. 1991. Resituating the bisexual body: From identity to difference. In Bristow and Wilson 118-38.

Hutchins, Loraine and Lani Kaahumanu, eds. 1991. *Bi any other name: Bisexual people speak out.* Boston: Alyson.

Jordan, June. 1981. *Civil wars.* Boston: Beacon P.

———. 1989. *Naming our destiny: New and selected poems.* New York: Thunder's Mouth P.

———. 1987. For the sake of people's poetry: Walt Whitman and the rest of us. In *On call: Political essays.* Boston: South End P. 5-15.

———. 1993. *Technical difficulties: African-American notions and the state of the union.* New York: Pantheon.

MacKinnon, Kenneth. 1993. Gay's the word—or is it? In *Pleasure principles: Politics, sexuality, and ethics.* Eds. Victoria Harwood, David Oswell et al. London: Lawrence & Wishart. 109-23.

matrix, sidney. 1995. Experiencing lesbian:theory, lesbian:writing: A personalist methodology. *Critical matrix*: 67-78.

Meese, Elizabeth A. 1992. *(Sem)Erotics theorizing lesbian: writing.* New York: New York UP.

Tucker, Naomi, ed. with Liz Highlyman and Rebecca Kaplan. 1995. *Bisexual politics: Theories, queries, and visions.* Binghamton, NY: Harrington Park P.

Weise, Elizabeth Reba, ed. 1992. *Closer to home: Bisexuality and feminism.* Seattle: Seal P.

Angela Ards (essay date September-October 2002)

SOURCE: Ards, Angela. "Tribute: The Faithful, Fighting, Writing Life of Poet-Activist June Jordan 1936-2002." *Black Issues Book Review* 4, no. 5 (September-October 2002): 63-4.

[*In the following essay, Ards eulogizes Jordan as poet and political activist.*]

Two years ago at a reading for **Soldier,** a poetic if unsettling memoir of June Jordan's childhood, Nobel laureate Toni Morrison described meeting the poet-activist when they were both young black women writers just starting out in the 1960s. June was a journalist who'd covered the struggle for civil rights down South, joining the freedom rides and becoming a protégé of Fannie Lou Hamer, all the while writing for film and theater, and her poetry. Morrison, then an editor at Random House, wondered, "which would give out first, her activism or her art." Too often, an artist who's political or an activist with no sense of grace produces only polemics, rhetorical outrage that is scripted and self-serving. But 40 years and 28 books of poetry, essays and plays later—thus making Jordan the most published African American author ever—her voice has lost neither its beauty nor its fire. What sustained her poetry and her activism was an indomitable spirit stoked by a love so fierce that it could have easily gone the other way.

After the Harlem Riots of 1964, provoked by another police killing of another unarmed black man, Jordan discovered she hated "everything and everyone white."

But "almost simultaneously," she wrote, "it came to me that this condition, if it lasted, would mean I had lost the point: not to resemble my enemies, not to dwarf my world, not to lose my willingness and ability to love." This stance was self-interested to be sure, not some turn-the-other-cheek goodness but necessary self-defense. And so she says she, "resolved not to run on hatred but, instead, to use what I loved, words, for the sake of the people I loved."

She deployed her words, lyrical and passionate missives that unfailing spoke truth to power, with the precision of the poet and the fierceness of a freedom fighter, which is to say that she said what she meant and meant exactly what she said. Jordan became an activist in, what she later described as "every sphere of voluntary—and involuntary—concern to me." That meant exploring literature, poetry, city planning, theater, teaching and breast cancer awareness. Who would constitute "the people I loved" grew beyond simplistic identity politics of "blackness" and "sisterhood."

Hers was a community forged "not according to ideology," she said. "Not according to group pressure. Not according to anybody's concept of 'correct.' . . . I will call you my brother, I will call you my sister, on the basis of what you do for justice, what you do for equality, what you do for freedom, and not on the basis of who you are." That each and every person—woman or man, Jew or Arab, gay or straight—can be freely and fully self-determining is at the heart of her writing.

"Poem about My Rights," perhaps her most well-known, and certainly most anthologized work articulated a model of personal and political resistance that infused her work, whether she was writing about rape, civil rights rollbacks, the sex police, terrorism or war:

> "I am not wrong: Wrong is not my name. / My name is my own my own my own / and I can't tell you who the hell set things up like this / but I can tell you that from now on my resistance / my simple and daily and nightly self-determination / may very well cost you your life."

Though she railed bitterly against "misbegotten American dreams," Jordan considered herself an "American dissident poet and writer"—a descendant of both Phillis Wheatley and Walt Whitman—"completely uninterested to run away from my country, my home." She spoke out unrelentingly about the country's failures of principle, because she so faithfully believed in the promise of its "democratic experiment."

The daughter of West Indian immigrants, she wrote, "perhaps there are other Americans as believing and as grateful and as loyal, but I doubt it." She was born in Harlem and raised in "Do or Die" Bed-Stuy, a black neighborhood in Brooklyn. "I grew up fighting. And I grew up and got out of Brooklyn because I got pretty good at fighting. And winning." A favorite uncle provided pointers on pugilistic defenses against bullies—namely her father, who was the first regular bully in her life. His nightmarish abuse and the misguided yet undeniable love that motivated it were detailed in *Soldier.* She came to believe that one must abandon "American delusions of individuality" to win an unfair fight against a bully, whether Congress or bodily disease or sociopathic hatred:

> "If we would name and say the source of our sorrow and scars, we would find a tender and a powerful company of others struggling as we do. . . . We would undertake collective political action founded on admitted similarities and grateful connection among us. . . ." It's the spirit of the fight that connects us and transcends us.

I came to New York wanting to be a writer like June Jordan. Within months of my arrival I was one of dozens crowded in a Greenwich Village bookstore to hear Jordan read from her then-latest works, *Technical Difficulties* and *Haruko/Love Poems.* I brought every Jordan book I owned at the time, which—after prompting me gently for my name, which I forgot overawed in her presence—she signed simply, "in faith." Later, in 1999, I profiled her for *MAMM,* a magazine dedicated to raising awareness and finding a cure for breast cancer.

"I call my own fight with breast cancer 'a good fight.' What I mean by that is that it is big," she said. "I feel the same way about it as I feel about justice, meaning that's a good fight, that's big. I might not win it—meaning we may not win it—but it's unimaginable to me that I wouldn't try to be a part of that fight."

The title of Jordan's last collection of essays, *Some of Us Did Not Die,* comes from an essay about September 11. It is both a rallying cry to the faithful and a warning to the enemies of freedom that our ranks are deep. It reminds friends and foes alike that, despite the devastation of terrorism, breast cancer, and all else that threatens the sanctity and joy of our lives, the fight for justice is still on. There are 40 essays in this volume, one for every year of her writing career. That this collection was to be her last lends it a definitive quality.

Jordan included tributes to Richard Wright and Zora Neale Hurston; Anita Hill ("the African beauty of her earnest commitment to do right and to be a good woman: a good black woman in this America"); and Mike Tyson ("I'm Black, Mike Tyson is Black. And neither one of us was ever supposed to win anything more than a fight between the two of us."); and two tributes to Martin Luther King Jr. ("he was not a saint, yet he lives on, miraculous: a mountain of a life.") Global concerns: the Middle East, South Africa, Nicaragua. The essays are assembled in reverse chronological order, beginning with her most recent—on

September 11, the murder of journalist Daniel Pearl, a young friend taking up the mantle of activism—to "greatest hits" from her previous four volumes of political writings: *Affirmative Acts, Technical Difficulties, On Call,* and *Civil Wars.* The very last essay in this volume is what had been the first: the introduction to *Civil Wars,* Jordan's first collection of political writings. The consistency, clarity, and in essence faithfulness of her voice and vision over forty years is the best testament and tribute to her faithful, fighting, writing life:

"My life seems to be an increasing revelation of the intimate face of universal struggle. You begin with your family and the kids on the block, and next you open your eyes to what you call your people and that leads you into land reform into Black English into Angola leads you back to your own bed where you lie by yourself, wondering if you deserve to be peaceful, or trusted or desired or left to the freedom of your own unfaltering heart. And the scale shrinks to the size of a skull: your own interior cage. And then if you're lucky, and I have been lucky, everything comes back to you. And then you know why one of the freedom fighters in the sixties, a young Black woman interviewed shortly after she was beaten up for riding near the front of the interstate bus—you know why she said, 'We are all so very happy.' It's because it's on. All of us and me by myself: we're on."

Jewelle Gomez (essay date 2002)

SOURCE: Gomez, Jewelle. "June Jordan." *Callaloo* 25, no. 3 (2002): 715-18.

[*In the following essay, Gomez surveys Jordan's life and work as a poet, academic, and activist.*]

> ". . . I got the idea that poetry could be useful."

June Jordan once recounted her Cyrano de Bergerac-like early literary career in an interview that both illuminated the depth of her artistic and political concerns and revealed her youthful entrepreneurial skills. Interviewed by David Barsamian for Alternative Radio in October of 2000 Jordan related how the child poet June used to reinterpret the emotional needs of her neighborhood friends—whether they were falling in or falling out of love. She would then, for a small fee, construct an effective poem that conveyed their heart's desire. In some ways this is what poet, essayist, and activist June Jordan did so successfully all of her career. She opened herself to our society's social needs and to the yearnings of the heart, then transformed them, most usefully, into cries for justice and celebrations of the human spirit.

Born in Harlem in 1936 June Jordan grew up in the Bedford Stuyvesant section of Brooklyn, and the rhythm of those two communities was often the back beat in her writing. She was the only child of Granville and Mildred Jordan, both immigrants to the United States—he from Jamaica, she from Panama. The distinct musicality which would have characterized their speech also underscored Jordan's work, lending her poems a sometimes unexpected lyricism and infusing her essays with the cadence of oratory.

Despite her childhood roots in traditionally Caribbean American and African American communities, Jordan often found herself making her way through institutions and situations that were dominated by non-Black cultural influences. She attended Northfield School for Girls in Massachusetts and graduated from Barnard College in 1957. While there she married a fellow student, Michael Meyer, and later, in 1958, gave birth to her son Christopher.

Her early career, like that of many authors, was a panoply of work experiences and her longest path led her through the halls of academia. Over the past 30 years she taught at Yale, City University of New York, Connecticut College, Sarah Lawrence College, the State University of New York at Stony Brook and most recently at the University of California at Berkeley, where she was a professor of African Studies.

Her first book of poetry, **Who Look at Me,** was published in 1969 and established the tenor of much of the work to follow. It held up to the light the harshness of Black life using unadorned verse that rang true. Jordan's insistence on looking and not turning away shaped everyone's perception of June Jordan and her work throughout her career.

She was called "the consummate tough girl" in *Black Issues Book Review* in 2000, in part because of her adept use of the vocabulary and rhythms of Black Urban America, but perhaps more because of her unflinching examination of the physical and psychological damage wrought by the *isms* that infect the United States.

But the toughness was not in Jordan, but rather in the situations she described. In her piece **"Poem about Police Violence"** (1974), she presages the anguish people of color would feel repeatedly in the coming decades with this question:

> Tell me something
> What you think would happen if
> everytime they kill a black boy
> then we kill a cop
> everytime they kill a black man
> then we kill a cop
> you think the accident rate would lower
> subsequently?

> (from **Passion**)

The shock of the question is deliberately provocative. But the poem's power lies in its status as inquiry. It's an intellectual hypothesis demanding we follow the corollaries out to the edge of the page. The result is a not-so-modest proposal that chills the blood.

Jordan's devotion to writing about the dangers inherent in a culture which tolerates the *isms*—racism, classism, sexism and heterosexism—might be seen as a direct outgrowth of her bi-cultural/outsider roots. Her parents' bi-cultural home, as well as her early interracial marriage provided her with a panoramic view from the richly diverse margins of U.S. culture. That confluence also sparked a combustible outrage at the social inequities she witnessed, as well as leavening her with a spirited sense of irony. The fact that **"Poem about Police Violence"** is set as a question, that the opening line and much of the rest is shaped so conversationally, does not convey a "tough girl" stance at all, really. When a reader is fortunate enough to have the distinctly plaintive sound of Jordan's voice in her head as she reads, even the harshest vocabulary fails to box Jordan into the category of tough. She was small and fierce and her laugh was a rolling giggle that seemed unstoppable. A more apt description of Jordan is fiery.

The passionate flame of justice burned deep inside and was always shining through in her essays, poems and activism. Yet the demands of that flame did not consume her. She remained connected to the political and social communities she championed and to the rigors of the intellect throughout her career. Her social world, too, was warmed by the deep fires of commitment.

The author of 26 books and three plays Jordan is probably the most published Black author in the United States. She was awarded the Prix de Rome in Environmental Design in 1970, beginning a life-long association with R. Buckminster Fuller. Her first novel, **His Own Where,** was nominated for a National Book Award. Among the many awards she received were a Rockefeller grant for creative writing, a National Endowment for the Arts fellowship, an Achievement Award for International Reporting from the National Association of Black Journalists, a Lila Wallace Reader's Digest Writers Award, and the Ground Breakers/Dream Makers Award from the Women's Foundation. The body of her work—poems and essays—that elicited these accolades is as wide-ranging as the issues that provoked her passions.

In her 1969 poem **"Memo to Daniel Pretty Moynihan,"** Jordan upbraids the senator for his superficial assessment of the role of Black women: "Don't you liberate me / from my female black pathology / I been working off my knees / I been drinking what I please . . ." (**Things That I Do in the Dark** 117). In response to the Nixon/Watergate scandal, Jordan wrote **"On**

Moral Leadership as a Political Dilemma" as a comic riff on the story about George Washington being unable to lie about chopping down a cherry tree.

Her poems and her essays were so very useful, whether conveying what it means for a small island such as Viecques to be continually bombed as target practice by the U.S. military; or insisting that "minorities" seek a common ground. She wrote: "HEY / C'MON / COME OUT / WHEREVER YOU ARE / WE NEED TO HAVE THIS MEETING / AT THIS TREE / AIN' EVEN BEEN / PLANTED / YET" (*Things That I Do in the Dark* 71).

In 1994 Jordan published *Haruko/Love Poems* (Serpent's Tail) and brought almost to full circle the idea of useful poems for the heart. In these verses she doesn't abandon the political framework that marks all of her work. Instead it is the love itself that is the political context. *Haruko/Love Poems* is a collection that illuminates love of many types, yet most especially the bisexuality of love threaded through the volume is what moves the reader to new understandings. In an untitled piece she writes:

> admittedly
> I do not forget
> the beauty of one braid
> black silk that fell
> as loose as it fell long
> and everlasting as the twilight
> anywhere
>
> (17)

Here as well as in other poems Jordan tells us that she is a lover of women, as well as the men who are a part of her past. At a time when middle-aged members of the radical left seem to have settled into a smoke-filled room of their own, it was critical for Jordan to say out loud with her poems: loving women is important.

Perhaps the most enduring legacy of the useful fire that burned inside June Jordan is her directorship of Poetry for the People at the University of California at Berkeley. Working with the widest array of students, Jordan carried the passion of writing and social consciousness through the classroom and into their hearts. For more than a decade she put any and all discussions on the table: children dying of hunger in the United States, Palestinians being confined to arid lands, religion as a cloak for oppression. Her students picked up the conversation enthusiastically and today write and teach with the same type of passionate commitment Jordan shared with them.

In that Alternative Radio interview Jordan was asked about the role of the poet in society. She answered that it was to "deserve the trust of people who know that what you do is work with words. The trust of other people that you will not miscarry what they mean and what they want." Her students, her readers and those for whom she advocated over the past 30 years would certainly say she'd earned that trust.

June Jordan's final book is called *Some of Us Did Not Die: New and Selected Essays* (2002). It is a prescient title, giving us the hope we need in these oddly nationalistic times. Forged by the activism of the Civil Rights, Anti-war and Women's Movements of the 1960s and 1970s, June Jordan did not fade into the comforts of academia or accommodation politics. She would never mistake U.S. militarism for a path toward freedom. Her poems and essays remain as vibrant and as useful today as they were when she first hurled them into the air around us. They reverberate there still. She did not die.

Richard Flynn (essay date 2002)

SOURCE: Flynn, Richard. "*Affirmative Acts*: Language, Childhood, and Power in June Jordan's Cross-Writing." *Children's Literature*, no. 30 (2002): 159-85.

[*In this essay, Flynn offers a reading of Jordan's poetics of childhood.*]

In a famous essay reprinted in *What is Found There*, Adrienne Rich meditates on the meaning of "The Hermit's Scream"—"'Love should be put into action!'"—in Elizabeth Bishop's poem "Chemin de Fer," and more particularly about the way poetry might serve as "a carrier of sparks" in a culture given over to "the language of therapy groups, of twelve-step programs, of bleached speech" (56-57).[1] Among the poems she discusses in the essay is June Jordan's **"For Michael Angelo Thompson"** (1973) about a thirteen-year-old boy, hit by a city bus, who died after being refused treatment at a Brooklyn hospital. In her discussion, Rich confesses that for a long time, "Race came between me and full reading of the poem: I wanted to believe the poet was elegiac, not furious":

> "Peace" is not the issue here, but the violent structures of urban class and racial power. The poem is a skin—luminous and resonant—stretched across a repetitive history of Black children's deaths in the cities, in a country that offers them neither hope nor respite.
>
> (67-68)

Learning to read Jordan's **"For Michael Angelo Thompson"** as "furious" rather than "elegiac" is tantamount to understanding "the difference between poetry and rhetoric," a phrase that is central to Audre Lorde's "Power," another poem Rich discusses in the essay (67-68). The univocal perspective of the "confession," Rich implies, is merely rhetoric, while "the double-edge, double-voicedness" she finds in **"Michael Angelo Thompson"** is poetry (67). From her first book, *Who Look at Me* (1969), a poem initially intended for children (and only later for adults), to her striking recent memoir *Soldier: A Poet's Childhood* (2000) Jordan has insisted on a poetics that interrogates private notions of childhood through activist, public positions.

Such a stance is unusual in contemporary poetry, and more unusual still in the now commonplace genre of the childhood memoir. Subverting the popular trope of the "traumatic childhood" Jordan insists in *Soldier* on "June's" agency, eschewing the pathos present in such works as Frank McCourt's *Angela's Ashes,* Tobias Wolff's *This Boy's Life,* or even Maya Angelou's *I Know Why the Caged Bird Sings.* As Patricia Pace argues, in her provocative article "All Our Lost Children: Trauma and Testimony in the Performance of Childhood," "the traumatized child" has become "a powerful locus of cultural anxiety" in contemporary memoirs (238). Using Mary Karr's *The Liar's Club* as her primary example, Pace shows that we are, perhaps, too adept at reading such accounts of childhood trauma. Just as the insights of so-called confessional poetry once seemed fresh but are now exhausted, "our experience with memoirs and other confessional texts" about childhood are by now so familiar that our "imaginative reconstructions" obscure the material circumstances of actual, rather than remembered, children. Furthermore, the power of a contemporary view of childhood "activated by sentimentality"—the "designation of the child to the private realm"—obscures the ways in which the child participates in our social, historical, and economic matrices (Pace 237-38).

By locating childhood victimization in the private sphere of a particular family, writers' testimony about that victimization tends to re-inscribe fictions of innocence violated rather than revealing the ways in which childhood and children are interpellated by the social. To testify against a broader ideology (in place since at least the eighteenth century) that views children contradictorily and often simultaneously as "little innocents and the limbs of Satan" (to use Fred Inglis's terms [70]) violates Romantic notions of authenticity and disturbs the Romantic and post-Romantic fiction that childhood is at once innocent and endangered.[2]

Jordan's approach to the memoir shares with other innovative works like Lyn Hejinian's *My Life* the view that "a child is a real person, very lively" (Hejinian 79). In other words, identity, including child identity (beyond that which is merely given), is complex. For the child, identity is formed from being in the world and negotiating that world, just as it is for adults. Rejecting the discourse of victimization as reductive, Jordan is also aware that such discourse ultimately serves to reinforce children's powerlessness. In a review of *Soldier* in the *Atlanta Journal-Constitution,* Valerie Boyd asserts that the book's "primary flaw" is that the writing resembles "a child's storybook rather than an adult's memoir of childhood." While praising Jordan for "refresh[ing] the form" of "the overused, much-maligned genre of memoir," she nevertheless criticizes the book's "creative, not-always-linear structure." But it is just this "poetic" quality—what Boyd praises as "the simple, direct language of a little girl"—that gives *Soldier* its power and distinguishes it from childhood memoirs that depict the child as victim rather than as agent. Jordan's consciously Joycean strategy of attempting to represent the child's perspective (the book was originally announced for publication as "Portrait of the Poet as a Little Black Girl") grows out of a lifelong commitment to experimenting with child language, and particularly with exploring the use of Black English as part of a powerful and longstanding commitment to teaching and promoting children's voices and children's poetry. In light of this career-long commitment, it should come as no surprise that Jordan distinguishes herself among contemporary poets with a decidedly unsentimental view of the child as a soldier-poet who wrests power over a literally paternal language.

Much of *Soldier* focuses on June's relationship with her father, Granville, who forced her to memorize poetry, raised her as a "boy soldier," and helped create the poet she is today. Granville, a Jamaican immigrant who had taught himself to read and write as an adult, was, Jordan writes, "loquacious, argumentative, and visionary" (*Soldier* 5). He also beat his daughter. But in a *New York Times* interview about *Soldier,* Jordan rejects the adjective "abusive" to characterize Granville. Although she doesn't excuse the beatings, she recognizes the cultural baggage that such an adjective carries and thus rejects simplistic explanations, as she has throughout her political and poetic career. Was her father abusive?[3] Jordan remarks, "Anyone can come up with an adjective, a pejorative. . . . I had committed myself to writing [*Soldier*] in the consciousness of a child, which meant making no judgments. I hope in a way this is very good news: I'm O.K. One can reasonably say some pretty dire things about my folks, but I love my father. I'm here to say, I'm here; I'm O.K." (qtd. in Lee).

In their introduction to a special issue of *Children's Literature,* Mitzi Myers and U. C. Knoepflmacher advance the useful term "cross-writing," a term that accurately describes Jordan's poetic project. "A dialogic mix of older and younger voices [that] occurs in texts too often read as univocal," cross-writing implies the "interplay and cross-fertilization rather than a hostile internal cross fire" (vii) that may be found in works intended for both children and adults and is often particularly pronounced in writers who address younger and older audiences with equal care and respect. Myers and Knoepflmacher see cross-writing as a way to "dissolve the binaries and contraries our culture has rigidified and fixed" (viii) and as a kind of versatile "critical Swiss Army knife" that will open the way to "children's cultural studies" (xv).

If June Jordan's success as a cross-writer lies first in her exploration of adult and child concerns dialogically (in writing for both adults and children), it is also articulated in her conscious theorizing about actual children in relation to historical and material concerns. This view has its origin in her early work with actual children, work that enriches her later focus on her own remembered childhood. Jordan's earliest publications either feature child writers whom she taught during the late sixties and early seventies or they are published as books for young people. Her early work and the circumstances of its publication demonstrate how much child-adult cross-writing is inflected by historical and material forces. Jordan's creative writing, political essays, and teaching are a model for the kind of Swiss Army knife called for by Myers and Knoepflmacher, and they remind us that children's cultural studies should concern itself with actual children as well as with literature and culture.

In order to appreciate *Soldier*'s fresh take on the genre of childhood memoir, one must turn to Jordan's career-long engagement as a child advocate and an understanding of her cross-fertilizing and testing of generic boundaries. Jordan's first volume of poetry for adults, *Some Changes* (1971), was published in Dutton's short-lived Black Poets Series, edited by Julius Lester; but it was preceded by three books of poetry either marketed for children—*Who Look at Me* (Crowell, 1969)[4]—or featuring children's writing—*Soulscript: Afro-American Poetry* (1970), part of Doubleday's Zenith series dedicated to "minority cultures," and, with Terri Bush, *The Voice of the Children* (Holt, Rinehart, 1970), an anthology of poetry by the children who had participated in their writing workshops in East Harlem and Brooklyn. In the preface to the *Soulscript* anthology, Jordan gives a contemporary account of an "Afro-American poetry" of "witness" that "until recently" had "suffered an alien censorship" (xviii). She opens the anthology with a selection of poems by children ages twelve to eighteen,[5] an unusual strategy that comes from a deep conviction that the "springs of poetry"—"reaction, memory, and dream" are available to children ("a four-year-old flows among them as fully as any adult" [xvi]) and out of a belief in the promise of social change: "when American classrooms change from confrontation to communion, black poetry will happen in the schools as well" (xvi). This optimism, unfortunately, has not been borne out today, when less African-American children's literature is being published than in the 1970s, when poetry has been further marginalized in American classrooms, and when the classrooms themselves have become symbols of violence and neglect. As Jordan herself has recently noted: "our children are compelled to attend school—day after day—in buildings that are not only disgraceful to see, but hazardous to occupy . . . and useless as far as what they impart" (Gilbert 3-4).

Nevertheless, Jordan's early optimism and refusal to underestimate children served to foster respect for children's voices as well as to instruct children in the rigors of craft and give them good poetic models in order to enable them to write "real poetry." In her provocative study *The Child as Poet: Myth or Reality?* noted children's poetry authority Myra Cohn Livingston praises Jordan as a "creative teacher" who exemplifies a "new mythology" that rejects prepackaged notions of childhood in order to foster meaningful children's writing (268-72). From Jordan's pioneer membership in the Teachers and Writers Collaborative (beginning in 1967) to her present position as professor at Berkeley where she has taught a course in "the Politics of Childhood" and established the very successful Poetry for the People program, Jordan has demonstrated a rare understanding of both children's poetry and the poetics and politics of childhood. On both theoretical and pragmatic levels, this engagement with childhood (or, more accurately speaking, childhoods) has been fruitfully complicated by Jordan's own sense of multiple "identities" (little girl, soldier-boy, daughter, mother, African American, bisexual, activist, teacher) and her investment in different kinds of language and literary genres (Black English, standard English, poetry, fiction, essays, plays, journalism, memoir, literature for children, adolescents, adults).

Indeed, Jordan's poetical and political interventions into childhoods actual and remembered involve the skillful negotiation of these various languages, genres, and identities. Jordan has thought deeply about children both as an audience for her writing and as writers themselves. While attuned to children's real suffering, she resists the ways in which the child (and particularly the "disadvantaged" child) is reified as an object of pity, preferring to emphasize children's agency by helping them to become writing subjects.

Jordan's response to the criticism of one of her child poets' work is illustrative here. In 1968 she was taken to task by Zelda Wirtshafter, the director of the Teachers and Writers Collaborative, for allowing her student Deborah Burkett to write a poem called "Travel" modeled on Robert Louis Stevenson's poem of the same title from *A Child's Garden of Verses*. The memo that occasioned Jordan's impassioned response has been "lost in the holes of time," according to Philip Lopate (*Journal* 113), but presumably it criticized Jordan for "foisting" Stevenson on the young black poet, rather than encouraging her to write in her own voice. Jordan's letter of reply of February 12, 1968, both insists on the importance of poetic craft for the young poet and criticizes the subtle racism in seeing black or poor children primarily as victims:

> Contrary to your remarks, a poet does not write poetry according to the way he talks. Poetry is a distinctively precise and exacting use of words—whether the poet is Langston Hughes or Bobby Burns.
>
> One should take care to discover racist ideas that are perhaps less obvious than others. For example, one might ask: Will I accept that a black child can write "creatively" and "honestly" and yet not write about incest, filth, violence, and degradations of every sort? Back of the assumption, and there is an assumption, that an honest and creative piece of writing by a black child will be ungrammatical, misspelled, and lurid titillation for his white teacher, is another idea. That black people are only the products of racist, white America and that, therefore, we can be and we can express only what racist white America has forced us to experience, namely: mutilation, despisal, ignorance and horror.
>
> Fortunately, however, we have somehow survived. We have somehow and sometimes survived the systematic degradation of America. And therefore there really are black children who dream, and who love, and who undertake to master such "white" things as poetry. There really are black children who are children as well as victims.
>
> (qtd. in Lopate, *Journal* 146)[6]

Already cognizant of what she would call in her essay about Phillis Wheatley **"The Difficult Miracle of Black Poetry,"** Jordan does not here advocate a capitulation to "the official language of the powerful" (*On Call* 36). But recognizing something of herself in Deborah Burkett, an "exceptional child" and a "clearly gifted writer," Jordan is loathe to discourage a child who "has been learning the streets and . . . learning in school and in the library" (Lopate, *Journal* 146). While Philip Lopate observes that Jordan's "training as a poet and the insistence on literary quality" sometimes conflicted with her "broad political and social goals," such as her early advocacy of Black English, it would be more accurate to say Jordan's commitment to "literary quality" reflects an equally strong commitment to a literary/linguistic theory that is inseparable from the political realm. As Jacqueline Vaught Brogan points out, "in addition to her deep and obvious involvement with contemporary African American writers, Jordan is deeply involved with literary/linguistic history" (203).[7]

Jordan's first book, **Who Look at Me** (1969), is a sophisticated poem about race and representation set in conversation with twenty-seven paintings by both black and white artists. Published as a children's book in 1969 and dedicated to her son Christopher, then eleven years old, the poem has been reprinted at the beginning of both of Jordan's volumes of selected poems. Though the poem works in its "text-only" version, it was

initially composed in conjunction with the paintings that were selected by her editor, Milton Meltzer,[8] and like all good picture books, it depends on the conversation between text and illustration to achieve its full impact. The title serves as a Black English refrain, a call followed by responses, a litany of the ways in which African Americans are represented or rather are not represented in white culture:[9]

> Who look at me?
>
> Who see the children
> on their street the torn down door the wall
> complete an early losing
> 	games of ball
> the search to find
> a fatherhood a mothering of mind
> a multimillion multicolored mirror
> of an honest humankind.
>
> (24)

This poetry (reminiscent of the early work of Gwendolyn Brooks) uses multiple address (black and white children; black and white adults; north and south), so that there is no subject position from which one can evade the speaker's command to:

> look close
> and see me black man mouth
> for breathing (North and South)
> A MAN
>
> (25)

This page of verse is followed by four portraits of black men: African-American artist John Wilson's *Self Portrait* (in color), Alice Neel's *Taxi Driver*, Symeon Shimin's *Boy* (black and white but reproduced in color on the front dust jacket) and Thomas Eakin's portrait of Henry O. Tanner (the first "Negro artist to be elected to the National Academy of Design" [96]). Following the portraits is a blank page, recto, and centered, verso, on page 31, a single line of verse: "I am black alive and looking back at you" so that looking close (demanded by the text and skillful layout) is answered by the text and portraits looking back at the reader in affirmation and accusation both. The poem continues as a succession of children "stranded in a hungerland / of great prosperity" are shown "reckless to succeed" but confined by a "solid alabaster space / inscribed keep off keep out don't touch / and Wait Some More for Half as Much" (36). "No doubt," says the speaker, "the jail is white where I am born / but black will bail me out," and the poem proceeds to journey back to the "complicated past" of the Middle Passage, the Amistad Revolt, the slave market, the Underground Railroad, the "lynchlength rope":

> so little safety
> almost nowhere like the place
> that childhood plans

in a pounding happy space

(60)

By insisting that African American history is "complicated," the poem and accompanying visual texts resist and subvert an Anglo-American version of history that defines the African American as an "absence"—a definition practiced even in the liberal discourse surrounding the civil rights movement. And black childhood, as the preceding passage suggests, was defined in sixties journalism and documentary photography as the absence of "normal" childhood. This trope of absence, popularized in photographs documenting the civil rights movement in such magazines as *Life, Look,* and *Newsweek* is both evoked and criticized by the poem:

Who see starvation at the table
lines of men no work to do
my mother ironing a shirt?

Who see a frozen midnight
of the winter and the hallway cold
to kill you like the dirt

where kids buy soda pop
in shoeshine parlors
barber shops so they can hear
some laughing

(23-24)

Significantly, this portion of the poem is not accompanied by images because the poet does not wish to reinforce the reified magazine images she wishes to disrupt. The most striking and effective disruption of the stereotypical view of African Americans and African-American children as victims or as absences occurs near the end of the poem in a double-page spread. The text:

Although the world
forgets me
I will say yes
AND NO

(84)

is opposite Romare Bearden's montage *Mysteries* (1964), a work that art historian Lee Glazer demonstrates is Bearden's response to the "well-known" journalistic "stereotype" of the "old, unpainted" southern shack (figure 8). In the work, argues Glazer, Bearden "confronts the received belief that black life and culture are unknowable and ultimately unrepresentable except as an absence" (423). Glazer describes Bearden's treatment of the figures and his "emphasis on faces, especially the eyes," as "a strategic use of direct confrontation" in which "the exchange of gazes . . . challenges the expected relationship between viewer and viewed" (423).

But *Mysteries* also disrupts the boundaries between child and adult, and this disruption is magnified when it is placed in the context of Jordan's children's book.

The figure in the center of the collage evokes the child as object of pathos (a face with large eyes on top of a diminutive body), but that pathos is disrupted by the spectral, almost translucent quality of the image, as well as by a second face peering out from behind her. Furthermore, though the image looks childlike, we can't be certain she is a child, just as the other figures appear to be composed of fragments of both children and adults, faces within faces. The indeterminacy of the figures allows them to resist the very stereotypes evoked by the "shack" in which they are placed, just as Bearden's manipulation of the gaze disrupts the viewer's potential for sentimentalizing condescension. Like Jordan's text, Bearden's collage explores the complexity of simultaneous presence and absence, of "yes / AND NO" (84).

Turning the page, that "NO" is reinforced:

NO
to a carnival run by freaks
who take a life
and tie it terrible
behind my back

(86)

Composed at about the same time as Jordan's angry letter to Zelda Wirtshafter, **Who Look at Me** uses poetic language in relation to visual images as a way of making many of the same points. Bearden's collage interrogates "racist ideas that are perhaps less obvious than others": liberal stereotypes that perpetuate a view of African Americans as less than human. Jordan's poetry emphasizes the way that Bearden's *Mysteries* appropriates the tropes of exoticism and freakishness historically forced on African Americans and turns them against the viewer. It tells us that those who perpetuate the fragmented and fragmenting images of African Americans as exotic freaks are themselves the real freaks; the collaboration between text and image in **Who Look at Me** becomes a way of seeking liberation from their carnival.

Insofar as it is a children's book, **Who Look at Me** reflects Jordan's understanding that child identities, even more than adult identities, are constructed by language as it is being learned. For any child, the power conferred by language mastery is not so much appropriated as it is wrested from those in authority (adults), and the material and emotional circumstances surrounding their attempt at language mastery are largely beyond children's control. For the African-American child, as Jordan points out in her 1972 essay **"White English/ Black English: The Politics of Translation,"** such disparities of power are even more pronounced: *"White power uses white English as a calculated, political display of power to control and eliminate the powerless"* (Jordan's italics; ***Civil*** [***Civil Wars***] 65). To demonstrate this point she contrasts a passage from *Romeo and Juliet* with a passage from her adolescent novel in Black English *His Own Where* neither of which "ain no kind of standard English":

> Both excerpts come from love stories about white and Black teenagers, respectively. But the Elizabethan, nonstandard English of *Romeo and Juliet* has been adjudged, by the powerful, as something students should tackle and absorb. By contrast, the Black, nonstandard language of my novel, *His Own Where,* has been adjudged, by the powerful, as substandard and even injurious to young readers.
>
> (*Civil* 71-72)

His Own Where, which was widely and favorably reviewed, nominated for the National Book Award, and named an ALA Best Book for Young Adults, nevertheless elicited criticism like the following 1980 "curriculum unit" from the Yale New Haven Teachers' Institute currently available on the World Wide Web:

> This book, even though the content would interest students, lacks many of the elements of a good novel. Therefore, the book will be used to illustrate how not to write. During the reading of *His Own Where,* you will find opportune time to teach sequence in writing, descriptive narrative writing, character development, and story line. Since it is written in Black English, it also affords an excellent exercise in translating paragraphs into proper grammar.
>
> [Exercise] 1. Choose one of the many poorly written sentences to show correct verb tense, double negatives, possessives, etc.
>
> ex: "Angela mother explain how Angela run out on her because she wouldn't hardly leave."
>
> (Petuch)

Although the novel's use of modernist techniques of narration, such as flashback and dream sequence, is also criticized as "deficient" by this teacher, it is the "unappropriateness" [*sic*] of Black English that is her primary target. This curriculum unit illustrates Jordan's claim that "the Black child is punished for mastery of his non-standard, Black English; . . . [that] America [has] decided that non-standard is substandard, and even dangerous, and must be eradicated" (*Civil* 65). And as the media reaction to the Oakland School Board Ebonics controversy demonstrates, even curricula that adopt a positive attitude toward Black English primarily in order to foster proficiency in standard English are deemed substandard and "unappropriate."[10]

In a 1998 essay, **"Affirmative Acts: Language, Information, and Power,"** in which she criticizes the dismantling of affirmative action and bilingual education in California, Jordan recalls the reaction to *His Own Where* shortly after its 1970 publication. She expresses surprise that her writing the novel in Black English became controversial while the controversial subject matter of the novel was ignored:

> As part of my story, I advocated sex education and the availability of free condoms in the sixteen-year-old hero's high school. And I presented the two young lovers, Buddy and his fourteen-year-old Angela as calmly and romantically planning to "make a baby" together.
>
> I thought I'd get some flak about the baby.
>
> I never expected what happened, instead: The book was banned in several cities and Black parents organized against it/me on the grounds that *His Own Where* would lead Black children into educational disaster. Black English was perceived to be the trigger to failure, not the public schools where shockingly high drop-out rates and shockingly low verbal aptitude scores held, as the norm, for these kids.
>
> (*Affirmative* [*Affirmative Acts: Political Essays*] 245-46)

Oddly enough, several favorable contemporary reviews pointed out the difficulty of the language in the novel. Christopher Lehmann-Haupt wrote in the *New York Times,* "The prose takes some getting used to" (67), and the anonymous reviewer for the *Center for Children's Books Bulletin* suggested that the "tell-it-like-it-is book in black talk, a poem in prose" was perhaps too sophisticated for all but the "special reader" (58). Although Jordan says that she chose to write *His Own Where* in Black English in order "to interest teenagers in reading it" so they could learn the "activist principles in urban design,"[11] it is most compelling for its linguistic power. Its use of the "home language" of black children is attractive to young readers, and the care and attention required to read it underscore the ways in which we both inhabit and are inhabited by language.[12] It is through language, the novel's refrain tells us, that the young protagonists and readers learn that "you be different from the dead" (*His Own Where* 1, 87). Jordan depicts material and political circumstances that conspire to deny life to the schools, the neighborhoods, the families in the African-American community. Buddy and Angela attempt to create a life for themselves (and to create a new life) by claiming their "own where" in the cemetery, an attempt that attests to the children's hopefulness and resiliency. They are able to construct a life "different from the dead" by asserting their right to speak and dream in a language that, far from being deficient, is complex and poetic. That language is also, like Buddy's and Angela's dwelling in the cemetery, makeshift—constructed of necessity as a means of survival.

In some ways, those objecting to the novel's Black English got it right in that they identified where the novel was truly subversive. By 1970 sensationalist subject matter had become practically de rigueur in the relatively new young adult genre. Jordan's demonstration that Black English is as much a vehicle for conveying the complex and the poetic as "so-called Standard English" (*Affirmative* 246) is ultimately far more radical than her depiction of two teenagers "planning to 'make a baby.'"

Another Jordan book for young people published in 1972 is, as Suzanne Rahn points out, "even more radically experimental in form and language than *His Own Where*" (251). In *Dry Victories,* Jordan presents a dialogue entirely in Black English between two young boys, Kenny and Jerome, as they compare the failures of Reconstruction to the failures of the civil rights movement. Their conversation is interspersed with documentary photographs and news clippings and framed by twin versions of the Declaration of Independence in positive and negative reproductions. There is also a frame within a frame: Jordan's preface written in Black English ("We taking the facts up front because the front is where we're at" [viii]) and an author's note at the back, written at the behest of the publisher, in "standard" English with Black English interpolations:

> The Publisher is worried. He wants me to write something, besides this book. Call it An Afterword. This whole book is an "afterword." It is written *after* the Civil War, *after* the Reconstruction Era, *after* the Civil Rights Era, *after* the assassination of Malcolm X, the Kennedys, Dr. King, little girls in a Birmingham Sunday School, and *after* the assassination of countless hopes and acts of faith.

> The Publisher is worried, but I'm not. I'm angry and you should be too. Then we can do something about this after-mess of aftermath, following on so much tragedy.

> (75)

"History," Jordan concludes, "don't stop to let nobody out of it." The truth as Jordan sees it can't be rendered in "no kind of Standard English."[13]

Soldier builds on this experiment with nonstandard discourses, not by employing Black English but by attempting to find a language whereby the adult can render the child's perspective with greater immediacy. By depicting the child as both incipient artist and incipient fighter, Jordan hopes to lend that fictional child agency: to be a soldier, she implies, is to refuse to be victim. Jordan's work for adults, as much as her work for children, provides the necessary preparation for finding the poetic voice for *Soldier* that can come close to accurately representing the child's experience. *Soldier* could not have been written without the insights developed in early poems, such as **"Gettin Down to Get Over"** (1972), **"Ah Momma"** (1975), **"Poem for Granville Ivanhoe Jordan"** (1974), and the fascinating prose poem **"Fragments from a Parable"** (written from 1958 to 1973). In this work, Jordan focuses on understanding the circumstances under which her parents, both of them West Indian immigrants, attempted to construct new lives as Americans and provide opportunities for her, their only daughter, and also on "wrestl[ing] my own language out of an enemy language" (Carroll 145). In the memoir, Jordan attempts to write "with the consciousness of a child, without the filter of adult perceptions and judgments," but that child's consciousness exists in dialogic (or perhaps dialectic) relationship to the adult poet and activist, one who understands that "childhood is the first, inescapable political situation each of us has to negotiate" (qtd. in Lee). Poetic language is particularly suited to this material, and Jordan's "prose" memoir regularly slides into verse. In fact, she asserts, "The whole thing should be a poem," but she "was afraid if it was poetry, people wouldn't read it" (qtd. in Lee).

Although Jordan does not excuse her father's erratic violence, she seems to have come to terms with it in various poems and essays and, most recently, in *Soldier.* Addressing the Northwest Regional Conference of the Child Welfare League in 1978, she explains, "it would not have helped me, it would not have rescued me, to know that one reason my father beat me to the extent of occasional scar tissue was because he himself felt beaten and he himself felt bullied and despised by strangers more powerful than he would ever be" (*Civil* 134). The complexity of her father's role in the family dynamic in relation to the outside world is explored in her fine **"Poem about My Rights"** (1980):

> and according to the *Times* this week
> back in 1966 the C.I.A. decided that they had this
>   problem
> and the problem was a man named Nkrumah so they
> killed him and before that it was Patrice Lumumba
> and before that it was my father on the campus
> of my Ivy League school and my father afraid
> to walk into the cafeteria because he said he
> was wrong the wrong age the wrong skin the wrong
> gender identity and he was paying my tuition and
> before that
> it was my father saying I was wrong saying that
> I should have been a boy because he wanted one/a
> boy and that I should have been lighter skinned and
> that I should have had straighter hair and that
> I should not be so boy crazy but instead I should
> just be one/a boy . . .

> (*Naming* [*Naming Our Destiny*] 103; *Passion* 87-88)

The father ironically feels displaced in his own gender identity at the Barnard cafeteria, and "before that" he has visited his feeling that he is "wrong" upon the speaker. He recognizes, if only intuitively, that the masculine identity that has been his only route to power is ineffectual in this female-dominated, white bastion of privilege. First person and masculine pronouns—"he" and "one/a boy"—dominate this part of the poem, but, like the father, they are out of place, are "wrong." Only in the conclusion of the poem will the speaker ultimately insist

> I am not wrong: Wrong is not my name
> My name is my own my own my own
> and I can't tell you who the hell set things up like this

but I can tell you that from now on my resistance
my simple and daily and nightly self-determination
may very well cost you your life

(*Naming* 104; *Passion* 89)

Explaining in *Soldier* that behind her father's determination was his conviction "that a Negro parent had to produce a child who could become a virtual whiteman and therefore possess dignity and power," Jordan concludes that, for Granville Jordan, "Probably it seemed easier to change me than to change the meaning and complexion of power" (18). **"Poem about My Rights,"** on the other hand, *does* try to change the meaning and complexion of power by refusing consent. The speaker refuses to capitulate to society's definition of her as "the history" and "the meaning of rape / . . . the problem everyone seeks to / eliminate by forced / penetration" as she connects the sanctity of her body with

the sanctity
of each and every desire
that I know from my personal and idiosyncratic
and indisputably single and singular heart.

(*Naming* 104; *Passion* 88-89).

Understanding her mother's role in family politics and the wider political sphere was far more difficult and painful. Jordan's mother, Mildred, committed suicide in 1966 after a debilitating stroke, but it was not until 1981, in an essay called **"Many Rivers to Cross"** that Jordan could write explicitly about her death (*On Call* 19-26). Even so, one senses the poet's continuing difficulty in coming to terms with her mother's legacy. As recently as 1994, in an interview with Peter Erickson, Jordan is able to discuss at length her father's legacy, that he gave her "a keen sense of my intellectual aptitude." But when Erickson asks, "What was the most important thing you received from your mother?" Jordan replies, "Oh dear. I don't know how to answer that." Nevertheless, since the late sixties, Jordan has written poetry in which she tries to understand and honor **"The Spirit of Mildred Jordan"** (1971, *Naming* 13-14; *Things* [*Things That I Do in the Dark*] 26-27). Indeed, it seems the very difficulty of understanding her mother leads Jordan to write some of her most important poetry, such as **"Gettin Down to Get Over,"** in which she interrogates tropes of black womanhood—from "bitch" to "Queen"—juxtaposing the sexist epithets:

MOMMA MOMMA
Black Momma
Black bitch
Black pussy
piecea tail
nice piecea ass

(*Naming* 67; *Things* 28)

with white rhetoric that described the black family as a "tangle of pathology." In her 1969 poem **"Memo to Daniel Pretty Moynihan"** Jordan, a single mother, had already declared, "Don't you liberate me / from my female black pathology" (*Things* 117).[14] In **"Gettin Down"** she is even more specific about the ways in which "black female pathology" is constructed by the intersection of sexist and racist rhetoric:

Black Woman
Black
Female Head of Household
Black Matriarchal Matriarchy
Black Statistical
Lowlife Lowlevel Lowdown
Lowdown and up
to be Low-down
Black Statistical
Low Factor
Factotem
Factitious Fictitious
Figment Figuring in Lowdown Lyin
Annual Reports

(*Naming* 68; *Things* 28)

Jordan here signifies on the kind of language contained in the 1963 Moynihan Report: bureaucratic language such as "Black / Female head of household" that is essentially a kinder and gentler way of implying "Lowlevel Lowlife Lowdown." Statistics, interpreted correctly, should indicate a call for political action, for social justice, but the "facts" that appear in "Lowdown Lyin / Annual Reports" become "Factitious Fictitious" as the "Black Matriarchal Matriarchy" is blamed for social problems whose root cause is a continuing history of racial and gender discrimination. Those "facts" become a "Factotem" (a portmanteau pun indicating a worship of "facts" and statistics that are ultimately designed to keep the black woman in the servile position of "factotum"). In contrast with this rhetoric, the speaker appeals directly to the mother in the poem's conclusion:

Teach me how to t.c.b./to make do
and be
like you
teach me to survive my
momma
teach me how to hold a new life
momma
help me
turn the face of history
to your face.

(*Naming* 75-76; *Things* 37)

In order to grow up, the little soldier of the memoir must learn to reject the objectifying discourse that would blame a mother like Mildred Jordan for the "breakdown" of the black family while ignoring the strength, sacrifice, and success of such women despite the great odds against them. In another poem, Jordan promises her mother that she will transform "the rhythms of your sacrifice, the ritual of your bowed head" into "an angry, an absolute determination that I would one day, prove myself to be, in fact your daughter" (**"Ah, Momma,"** *Naming* 15; *Things* 38-39; *Civil* 101-2).

As Jordan asserts in **"Thinking About My Poetry,"** "I have moved from an infantile reception of the universe, as given, into a progressively political self-assertion that is now reaching beyond the limitations of a victim mentality" (*Civil* 129). Paradoxically, however, this rejection involves understanding the ways "an infantile reception of the universe" contributed to Jordan's becoming a poet. She may have had trouble answering Peter Erickson's question about her mother in the 1994 interview, but she begins to answer the question in *Soldier.* Although Granville Jordan looms large as a presence in *Soldier* and the book is dedicated to him, Mildred Jordan's influence is just as important, despite her tendency to "more or less hide inside her 'little room,' where she would probably begin to pray" (xviii).

In fact, Jordan identifies her love of poetry as originating in relation to her mother, from those earliest experiences in which language is embodied: "Pretty soon my body had absorbed the language of all the Mother Goose nursery rhymes, and my mother's dramatization of the rhythms of these words filled me with regular feelings of agreeable intoxication" (*Soldier* 9). Jordan's pleasure in the rhythms of her mother's nursery rhymes and the rhythms of Bible stories, "the magical language and its repetition that left you feeling united and taken care of," is the bedrock upon which she constructs her later oppositional poetics, a poetics that arises from her resistance to her father's required reading. Forced to memorize and recite her father's "canon" through "compulsory reading assignments and next-day examinations" (45) that included Poe, Shakespeare, and Dunbar, as well as "The Ugly Duckling," *Rebecca of Sunnybrook Farm,* Zane Grey, and Sinclair Lewis, the rhythms and music that Jordan learned from her mother's nursery rhymes and Bible stories enabled her to perform "passages from memory, on demand," even when she didn't understand the meaning of what she was reciting, which "tended to placate, if not entirely satisfy, my father" (49). At an early age Jordan learned to question her father's canon, preferring the popular works of Zane Grey to the "serious" works of Sinclair Lewis, and even more tellingly, characterizing her first Broadway show, *The Member of the Wedding,* as "this play about a white girl and her Negro 'Mammy' looking after her" whose most striking moment occurs when "the girl uses this huge knife to slice at something on her foot" (259-60). Jordan taught herself to become a "resisting reader," the kind of child reader who questions as well as appreciates literature, as her reaction to her first storybook demonstrates:

> Why did the Ugly Duckling lose its mother?
> How could a duck turn into a swan?

> Why would that be a happy ending for a duck?
> The Ugly Duckling was depicted as a black baby duck.
> The swan was white.
> How did the black baby duck turn white?
> Why was that a happy ending?
>
> I thought I understood that story,
> and I didn't believe it,
> and I kept reading it to myself,
> over and over.
>
> I never wanted and I never got a Shirley Temple doll.
>
> (*Soldier* 23)

But as "June" comes to see herself at the center of her parents' arguments, Jordan writes, "My father' voice got loud":

> My mother didn't say much, but she never said, "All
>   right."
> She was fighting.
> They were fighting.
> They were fighting with each other.
> I had become the difference between them.
>
> (15-16)

In part 6, "More About My Father and My Mother: Fighting," her parents' argument centers on Mildred's insistence that her husband, who is arranging for June to attend a white boarding school where "she will rub elbows with the best: the sons of bankers, the sons of Captains of Industry," recognize that "June is not a Rockefeller boy. She have to become a Black woman!" Her father replies: "She will learn herself how to hold his own. She will come out the school a veritable prince. Among men." This argument rises to such a pitch, that her father slaps her "mother's face / from one side to the other" after which the child "tumbles down the stairs" to recite the ending of Kipling's "If": "And— which is more— / You'll be a Man, my son!" After Granville goes out to buy ice cream as a reward for the recitation, June pulls close to her mother, lays the Bible "across my mother's knees," and together ("you repeat it after me") they recite the Beatitudes.

Thus we see the origins of Jordan's adult verse, which combines rhythm and musicality with a critical and interrogating language. The recognition that even the most seemingly innocent uses of language are embedded in the social and the political, a recognition she first encountered as a child, inspires Jordan to tap into the "place of rage" with the subtle music of her mature poetry, that, nevertheless, is frequently attentive to the child's perceptions. Adult work, then, is incorporated in the childhood memoir, such as the first three sections of her major poem, **"War and Memory,"** the final six pages of part 3 of *Soldier.* The sections of **"War and Memory"** not reprinted, however, that concern adult experience make explicit that the child "warrior growing up" bears an important relation to the adult poet's quest:

and I
thought I was a warrior growing up
and I
buried my father with all of the ceremony all of the
    music
    I could piece together
and I
lust for justice
and I
make that quest arthritic/pigeon-toed/however
and I
invent the mother of courage I require not to quit

(*Naming* 210-11)

Jordan's recognition that she must pay attention to the "mother of courage" and the mother of invention, as much as the father's instruction, is an insight that translates into a richer portrait of the child's perspective in *Soldier.* Furthermore, inventing the "mother of courage" allows Jordan to discover her poetic form, her craft, learned first in her body, in early childhood from her mother's music and rhythms. Jordan calls this form "vertical rhythm," which, she explains, will "propel a listener or reader from one word to the next or one line to the next without possible escape" (qtd. in Muller 38).[15] The reader is required "not to quit."

Likewise, three separate accounts of a horrifying incident of police brutality remembered from childhood provide a stunning example of the powerful uses of cross-writing in showing the way that both adult and child perceptions may inform each other dialogically and intertextually. Jordan recalls the brutal disfigurement of her childhood friend, Jeffrey Underwood, when she was nine or ten, in an interview in Pratibha Parmar's 1991 film *A Place of Rage:*

> There was one boy, for example, named Jeffrey Underwood, who was really cute, and I liked him a lot. And the police went up on the roof after Jeffrey, and just beat him mercilessly. I mean everybody knew Jeffrey and his family—his parents were friends with my parents, and so on—this was really shocking. And it permanently disfigured him—in what was later explained as a kind of case of mistaken identity. And to see this boy that I idolized—who belonged to us, in the sense of our block and all of us—disfigured by these strangers who came in with all this force, and license to use that force, was really terrifying. And also it—it hardened me. I would say, early on. In a kind of place of rage, actually.

"Poem from Taped Testimony in the Tradition of Bernhard Goetz" is a poem Marilyn Hacker describes as "an ironically issue-oriented dramatic monologue." "Jordan's speaker," Hacker writes, "breathlessly appropriates to a black perspective the reasoning Goetz used to justify arming himself and firing on black youths in a New York City subway" (135). The irony Hacker identifies is complex in that not only does Jordan point out the faulty logic of accepting Goetz's testimony and

his claim, "This was not I repeat this was not a racial thing" (*Naming* 153), but that she continues to insist that we reject such logic, even after we discover the speaker of the poem is a black woman who offers far more compelling background stories than those of Goetz. Patricia Williams performs a similar analysis of Goetz's testimony in *The Alchemy of Race and Rights* (72-79), which corroborates Jordan's poetic performance, albeit somewhat less compellingly. One of the stories that makes **"Poem from Taped Testimony"** so effective is the story of Jeffrey Underwood, which appears as section 4:

> then the policeman beat Jeffrey
> unconscious and he/the
> policeman who was one of them he kicked
> Jeffrey's teeth out and I never wanted to see
> Jeffrey anymore but I kept seeing
> these policemen and I remember how
> my cousin who was older than I was I remember how
> she whispered to me, "That's what they
> do to you"

(*Naming* 155)

In *Soldier,* the child is spending an idyllic summer at a YWCA summer camp, and her version of the Jeffrey Underwood story is perhaps the most moving version:

> I felt so clean! I felt so safe!
>
> I felt myself far away from Valerie [Jordan's older cousin with whom she lived] and her beautiful, tall boyfriend, Jeffrey Underwood, when the cops busted up his face and kicked out his teeth because they were cops and they were white people and Jeffrey lived on our block and he hadn't done anything besides that besides live on our block because he belonged there on our block and then the cops chased him to the roof and they caught him and they messed everything up and nothing was the same after that: Nothing.

(*Soldier* 234-35)

The passage from *Soldier* certainly gains resonance placed next to the 1991 interview and the 1989 dramatic monologue, but the representation of the child's perspective is, in itself, striking. The "really terrifying" story that Jordan says "hardened" her is presented in the rush of a run-on sentence, but also in the context of the voice of the child soldier established in the 233 pages preceding it. It is not so much the "hardening" that impresses the reader as the way Jordan manages to tap into "a place of rage" as the child herself seems to have experienced it. And that place of rage is made productive. Like **"Poem from Taped Testimony,"** the memoir rejects victim mentality, refuses to participate in the logic of Bernhard Goetz. The poet's mining of childhood experience makes possible the deep ironies—"the double-edge, double-voicedness" that Rich identifies, or a Du Boisian "double-consciousness" (45)—employed in the poem for adults. And the sophisticated perspective in the poem for adults makes possible a way for the poet to represent a child's perspective, without sentimentality, in the memoir.

"Nothing was ever the same after that: Nothing," says the narrator of **Soldier**. The memoir itself ends with the young Jordan getting on the train to go to the Northfield School wondering whether, like Jackie Robinson, she would be a "first" (248). Her father tells her, "Okay! Little Soldier! G'wan! G'wan! / You gwine make me proud!" (261). It is, the section title tells us, "The Only Last Chapter of My Childhood," implying both the importance of this particular childhood for this particular child and the necessity of growing up. As the memoir's epigraph from Mark 5:42 suggests, Jordan is thereafter reborn like the "damsel" who arose "straightway," "for she was of the age of twelve years." "And they were astonished with a great astonishment," continues the passage from Mark; for Jordan, the astonishment involves "putting love into action."

Like the action of mentoring young poets in her Poetry for the People program at Berkeley or in teaching a class called "The Politics of Childhood," rechanneling "the pain of so much of the [students'] testimony" about their own childhoods into helping them form "a new organization advocating children's rights" (qtd. in Muller 5), adult-child cross-writing, then, has not only aesthetic but also practical value. A focus on children and childhood can either produce superficial, debilitating nostalgia and victim-consciousness, or it can produce an occasion for love put into action where real adult-child dialogue takes place. As in her stunning memoir, Jordan's writing, for children, for adults, and across what are ultimately artificial adult-child boundaries, recognizes the limits of the confessional and rejects the "bleached speech" of a therapeutic culture in favor of living language. By crossing genres, by recognizing the relationship between history and politics and the personal, and by promoting discovery rather than foreclosure, Jordan delineates a poetics that combats the regressive tropes of childhood embedded deep within our culture and proposes new tropes that may well be revolutionary.

Notes

1. In a striking uncollected essay, "Writing and Teaching" (1969), Jordan discusses the writing of her Upward Bound students ("mainly Black teenagers from economically impoverished backgrounds" [481]). Inspired by *Life* magazine photographs of starvation in Biafra, the students wrote "asking for action." "Quite apart from the political effectiveness of their campaign, which was no worse than our adult effectiveness," writes Jordan, "the students' writing leaped into an eloquent fluency that had never even been hinted at in their earlier work" (481). "Everything we read and everything we wrote," Jordan concludes, "quite literally, translated into action: it became part of our hopeful, conscious lives" (482). In a 1994 interview, Jordan says, "I make observations in my writing that will lead to action. I make suggestions for action" (Carroll 149).

2. For a discussion of the legacy of Romantic views of the child for contemporary poetry, see my "'Infant Sight': Romanticism, Childhood and Postmodern Poetry."

3. Jordan uses the adjective herself in the "After Identity" interview: "Because he had raised me in a lot of ways as a boy, it seemed perfectly natural to resist him when he was being abusive. At least at the time it was very unusual for a little girl to resist her father's beatings. It just never occurred to me not to do that, because he had taught me, don't let anybody pick on you" (Erickson, "After Identity" 135).

4. One may attribute the publication of Jordan's first volume of poetry, *Who Look at Me,* as a children's book at least in part to particular economic and historical circumstances that created a climate for black children's literature in the late sixties and early seventies (the same climate that facilitated the publication of children's literature by other major African-American poets such as Lucille Clifton). The surge in the publication of African-American writing for children by mainstream publishers during this period was largely a response to the Black Power or New Black Arts movement, as Dianne Johnson notes, in which "'black children's literature' gained weight and recognition within the publishing world, to a level which it has not enjoyed since" and in which that movement "was often exploited for its marketing value" (77). In her 1974 article "Black Children's Books: An Overview," Judy Richardson notes another impetus for the surge in African-American children's books—the passage of the Elementary and Secondary Education Act of 1965, which provided financial incentives to organizations to meet the needs of low-income, "educationally deprived children." According to Richardson, "Suddenly the [publishing] industry geared up to meet the challenge—be 'relevant' and try to get as much money as you can before it runs out" (389-90). Richardson then predicted that, although the publication of high-quality "black children's books [was] at an all-time high" many publishers were abandoning the market as a passing fad, and that recession and drastic Federal cutbacks threatened the "so-far upward trend" (399-400). According to Johnson, by 1990, "deplorably, less Black children's literature [was] being published than was published in the 1970s" (12). See also Suzanne Rahn, "The Changing Language of Black Child Characters in American Children's Books," which contains a discussion of Jordan's use of Black English in *His Own Where* and *Dry Victories.*

5. The young poets published in *Soulscript* had been Jordan's students. Among them were Julia Alvarez and Gayl Jones.

6. This letter and other entries are also reprinted as "The Voice of the Children" in *Civil Wars* (29-38). The fullest selection of Jordan's teaching journals, however, is in Lopate's *Journal of a Living Experiment.*

7. In her 1980 manifesto, "For the Sake of a People's Poetry: Walt Whitman and the Rest of Us," Jordan proclaims her allegiance to the "New World poetry" of "Walt Whitman, Pablo Neruda, Agostinho Neto, Gabriela Mistral, Langston Hughes, Margaret Walker, and Edward Brathwaite," dismissing unapologetically, the Anglo-American traditional poets "Emily Dickinson, Ezra Pound, T. S. Eliot, Wallace Stevens, Robert Lowell, or Elizabeth Bishop. If we are nothing to them," she proclaims, "they are nothing to us! Or, as Whitman exclaimed: 'I exist as I am, that is enough.'" However, Adrienne Rich has discussed Jordan's work in conjunction with Bishop's in "The Hermit's Scream" (*What Is Found* 54-71) and Brogan ("From Warrior" 198-209) has pointed out the common ground between Bishop's "Roosters" and Jordan's "Problems of Translation: Problems of Language" (*Living Room* 37-41) and "In the Waiting Room" and "War and Memory" (*Naming* 204-11). Brogan has also discussed the influence of Bishop and Stevens on Jordan and Rich ("Planets" 255-78).

8. According to Peter Erickson's *Dictionary of Literary Biography* entry on Jordan, the project was originally intended for Langston Hughes before his death in 1967 (page 149-50).

9. The "African-derived . . . call-response" form, as Geneva Smitherman points out, as practiced in African-American churches, occurs not only between the preacher and the congregation, but also among members of the congregation itself. It is "a basic organizing principle of Black American culture generally" derived from "the traditional African world view" that "does not dichotomize life into sacred and secular realms, you can find call-responses both in the church and on the street" (104). See also Smitherman, "Word from the Hood," esp. 208-10.

10. For a lively and cogent defense of the Oakland Ebonics Resolution, see Perry and Delpit, esp. part 4, 143-86.

11. Jordan was working at the time as an urban planner. With R. Buckminster Fuller, she had designed a plan for "the architectural redesign of Harlem" and on Fuller's recommendation she was awarded the 1970 Prix de Rome in Environmental Design largely on the strength of the novel that depicts its protagonist Buddy redesigning the apartment he shares with his father who is dying in the hospital after being hit by a car. See *Civil Wars* 23-28; 59-62.

12. *His Own Where* also reflects Jordan's experience teaching the children in her workshop: "my first novel, *His Own Where,* which was written entirely in Black English, was based upon two 'regulars' of our workshop, and, of course, upon my own, personal life as a child growing up in Bedford-Stuyvesant" (*Civil* 128-29).

13. While Jordan has continued to write children's books on occasion, her later books, such as *New Life: New Room* (1975) and *Kimako's Story* (1983), are neither as interesting as the earlier works nor as centrally related to her larger poetic project.

14. The phrase "tangle of pathology" appears in Daniel Patrick Moynihan's controversial 1963 report *The Negro Family: The Case for National Action.*

15. Jordan explains vertical rhythm in detail in Muller, 38-42.

15. This essay is dedicated in loving memory of my wife, Professor Patricia Pace (September 22, 1952 to November 17, 2000), my ardent companion in the fields of scholarship, as well as in the fields of love. This is the last essay of mine to have been enriched by her critical scrutiny and loving encouragement. Thanks also to Professor Aldon Nielsen for making suggestions about an earlier draft.

Works Cited

Brogan, Jacqueline Vaught. "From Warrior to Womanist: The Development of June Jordan's Poetry." In *Speaking the Other Self: American Women Writers.* Ed. Jeanne Campbell Reesman. Athens: University of Georgia Press, 1997. 198-209.

———. "Planets on the Table: From Wallace Stevens and Elizabeth Bishop to Adrienne Rich and June Jordan." *Wallace Stevens Journal* 19.2 (fall 1995): 255-78.

Boyd, Valerie. "'Soldier' Enlists Child's Memories." *Atlanta Journal and Constitution.* May 7, 2000. (Lexis-Nexis)

Carroll, Rebecca. *I Know What the Red Clay Looks Like: The Voice and Vision of Black Women Writers.* New York: Carol Southern Books, 1994.

Du Bois, W. E. B. *The Souls of Black Folk.* With a new introduction by Randall Kenan. New York: Signet Classic, 1995.

Erickson, Peter. "After Identity: A Conversation with June Jordan and Peter Erickson." *Transition* 63 (1994): 132-49.

———. "June Jordan 1936-" *Dictionary of Literary Biography* 38 (1985): 146-62.

———. "State of the Union." *Transition* 59 (1993): 104-9.

Gilbert, Derrick I. M. (a.k.a. D-Knowledge), ed. *Catch the Fire!!! A Cross-Generational Anthology of Contemporary African-American Poetry.* New York: Riverhead, 1998.

Glazer, Lee Stephens. "Signifying Identity: Art and Race in Romare Bearden's Projections." *Art Bulletin* 76 (1994): 411-26.

Hacker, Marilyn. "Provoking Engagement." Essay-review of *Naming Our Destiny,* by June Jordan. *The Nation* 250.4 (29 January 1990): 135-39.

Hejinian, Lyn. *My Life.* Los Angeles: Sun & Moon, 1991.

Inglis, Fred. *The Promise of Happiness: Value and Meaning in Children's Fiction.* Cambridge: Cambridge University Press, 1981.

Johnson, Diane. *Telling Tales: The Pedagogy and Promise of African American Literature for Youth.* New York: Greenwood, 1990.

Jordan, June. *Affirmative Acts: Political Essays.* New York: Anchor/Doubleday, 1998.

———. *Civil Wars.* Boston: Beacon, 1981.

———. *Dry Victories.* New York: Holt, Rinehart and Winston, 1972.

———. *His Own Where.* New York: Thomas Y. Crowell, 1971.

———. *Naming Our Destiny: New And Selected Poems.* New York: Thunder's Mouth, 1989.

———. *On Call.* Boston: South End, 1985.

———. *Passion: New Poems, 1977-1980.* Boston: Beacon, 1980.

———. *Soldier: A Poet's Childhood.* New York: Basic Civitas, 2000.

———. *Some Changes.* New York: E. P. Dutton, 1971.

———. *Technical Difficulties: African-American Notes on the State of the Union.* New York: Pantheon, 1992.

———. *Things That I Do in the Dark: Selected Poetry.* Boston: Beacon, 1981. Rpt. of 1st ed. New York: Random House, 1977.

———. *Who Look at Me. Illustrated with Twenty-Seven Paintings.* New York: Thomas Y. Crowell, 1969.

———. "Writing and Teaching." *Partisan Review* 36 (1969): 478-82.

Jordan, June, ed. *Soulscript: Afro-American Poetry.* New York: Zenith/Doubleday, 1970.

Jordan, June, and Terri Bush, eds. *The Voice of the Children.* New York: Holt, Rinehart, 1970.

Lee, Felicia R. "A Feminist Survivor with the Eyes of a Child." *New York Times.* July 4, 2000, page El. (Lexis-Nexis)

Lehmann-Haupt, Christopher. "A Children's Reading List." *New York Times.* December 16, 1971, page 67.

Livingston, Myra Cohn. *The Child as Poet: Myth or Reality?* Boston: Horn Book, 1984.

Lopate, Philip, ed. *Journal of a Living Experiment: A Documentary History of the First Ten Years of the Teachers and Writers Collaborative.* New York: Teachers and Writers, 1979.

Mostern, Kenneth. *Autobiography and Black Identity Politics: Racialization in Twentieth-Century America.* Cambridge: Cambridge University Press, 1999.

Muller, Lauren, and the Poetry for the People Collective, eds. *June Jordan's Poetry for the People: A Revolutionary Blueprint.* New York: Routledge, 1995.

Myers, Mitzi, and U. C. Knoepflmacher. "'Cross-Writing' and the Reconceptualizing of Children's Literary Studies." *Children's Literature* 25 (Special Issue on Cross-Writing Child and Adult) (1997): vii-xvii.

Pace, Patricia. "All Our Lost Children: Trauma and Testimony in the Performance of Childhood." *Text and Performance Quarterly* 18 (1998): 233-47.

Perry, Theresa, and Lisa Delpit, eds. *The Real Ebonics Debate: Power, Language, and the Education of African-American Children.* Boston: Beacon, 1998.

Petuch, Carol Ann. "I Hate to Read! An Assortment of Young Adult Literature." Yale New Haven Teachers Institute Curriculum Unit 80.01.06 <http://www.yale.edu/ynhti/curriculum/units/1980/1/80.01.06.x.html

A Place of Rage. Dir. Pratibha Parmar. With Angela Davis, June Jordan, Alice Walker, and Trinh T. Minh-ha. Women Make Movies, 1991. 52 min.

Rahn, Suzanne. "The Changing Language of Black Child Characters in American Children's Books." In *Infant Tongues: The Voice of the Child in Literature.* Ed. Elizabeth Good-enough, Mark A. Heberle, and Naomi Sokoloff. Detroit: Wayne State University Press, 1994. 225-58.

Review of *His Own Where,* by June Jordan. *Center for Children's Books Bulletin* 25 (December 1971): 58.

Rich, Adrienne. *What Is Found There: Notebooks on Poetry and Politics.* New York: Norton, 1993.

Richardson, Judy. "Black Children's Books: An Overview." *Journal of Negro Education* 43 (1974): 380-400.

Smitherman, Geneva. *Talkin and Testifyin: The Language of Black America.* Boston: Houghton Mifflin, 1977.

———. "Word from the Hood: The Lexicon of African-American Vernacular English." In *African-American English: Structure, History, and Use.* Ed. Salikoko S. Mufwene et al. London: Routledge. 1998. 203-25.

Williams, Patricia J. *The Alchemy of Race and Rights.* Cambridge: Harvard University Press, 1991.

Mary Eagleton (essay date 2002)

SOURCE: Eagleton, Mary. "Working Across Difference: Examples from Minnie Bruce Pratt and June Jordan." In *Caught Between Cultures: Women, Writing & Subjectivities,* edited by Elizabeth Russell, pp. 129-50. Amsterdam, The Netherlands: Rodopi, 2002.

[*In this essay, Eagleton contrasts the feminist stances of Jordan and Minnie Bruce Pratt.*]

> At a time when feminism has lost much of its political edge and is undergoing assaults from all sides, it is important that we learn to say 'I' and 'we' again, though 'I' and 'we' are not so simple.[1]

'I' and 'we' used to be simple words. 'I' was the oppressed female individual, struggling to cast off the restrictions of patriarchal society, to emerge whole and newly formed in a changing world. 'I' was victim, heroine, everywoman, role model. 'We' was the collective sisterhood of women across diverse cultures and throughout the centuries, united by common bonds and experiences, working together for a feminist future. Oh happy days—if they ever existed. Gayle Greene's suggestion, following her comment above, is that the terms 'I' and 'we' are now more complicated than second-wave feminism originally thought and, consequently, our use of the terms has become unsure and tentative: "contemporary theory has rendered suspect the view of personal experience as a site of authoritative discourse and exposed the essentialist, appropriative implications of saying 'we'."[2] In face of this, Greene believes, there is a political imperative to redefine the terms. Feminism wants both the individual and the collective female subject; but how are 'we' to speak them?

The need to say 'I' in a way that is ethical and politically productive is an issue that circulates throughout the texts we shall be considering. In *A Room of One's Own,* Virginia Woolf has problems with the letter 'I,' the 'I' of the literary male, "honest and logical; as hard as a nut, and polished for centuries by good teaching and good feeding." This 'I' casts a shadow across the page where, barely detectable behind it, stands the shapeless form of a woman with "not a bone in her body."[3]

Feminism has wanted to give substance and prominence to this elusive female figure. She should be visible, audible, an agent, self-aware; but she should not become the dominant and dominating ego of Woolf's male 'I'; nor should she become self-absorbed and self-dramatizing. It is all too easy to slide from one stance to another, from a legitimate concern with the self to situating that self at the center of some profound existential debate, the focus of deep emotions, agonizing about every action, word, and motive. Becoming an 'I' is full of pitfalls. There is the danger of neglecting the dialectical relation between the self and the larger formation, as if history will respond speedily and appropriately to one's carefully worked-out positioning. There is the danger of fooling oneself that one's identity can be fully known so that, with some moderate endeavor, the duplicity of memory, the psyche, and self-interest can be conquered and then, once fully known, that self can be cocooned from influence on or by others. There is, as always, the danger of immersion into an ever more refined intellectual process where the relation to political action becomes remote and unformulated. 'I' is the most beguiling word to lead one down these treacherous paths.

If 'I' is fraught, what constitutes 'we' and how to move between 'I' and 'we' are equally problematical. While, on the one hand, we may be alert to the dangers of universalizing, we still have to find ways of speaking to and with each other if feminism and internationalism and cross-cultural contact are to retain any meaning. As S. P. Mohanty asks: "How do we negotiate between my history and yours?".[4] Or as Audre Lorde says, "What do we want from each other / after we have told our stories."[5] To focus only on a personal voice is to retreat from dialog and engagement and, in the case of the privileged woman, to abrogate responsibility for the power she holds. This is what Adrienne Rich refers to as "a false transcendence, an irresponsibility towards the cultures and geopolitical regions in which we are rooted."[6] Yet movements out towards 'we' can become new strategies for domination. Minnie Bruce Pratt warns how, "in order to feel positively about ourselves, we may end up wanting not to *be* ourselves, and may start pretending to be someone else" or how "sometimes we don't pretend to *be* the other, but we take something made by the other and use it for our own."[7] In both cases the full implications of 'I' are not faced. We cannot presume that a quick foray into the relevant essays will give us an adequate insight into the condition of other women and a validation to speak for them; but, equally, we cannot dismiss all notions of collectivity as an oppressive eradication of important differences. Moreover, there are situations when speaking for others is inevitable, since, in Linda Alcoff's words, "certain political effects can be garnered in no other way."[8]

So integral are these arguments to questions of subjectivity and political action that one finds them surfacing in different ways across a variety of critical positions, positions which themselves overlap. Much of the early work in this area sprang from a radical-feminist stance and a concern with a more authentic selfhood; to speak for others was an act of appropriation. The influence of black and postcolonial feminists, questioning the race blindness of white feminism, the presumption of centrality by white feminists, and the construction of a monolithic 'Third World' woman—all this has been decisive, as has been the work of lesbian-feminists questioning heterosexual presumptions. Alongside this we have the analysis of Marxist feminists on ideology and the reasons why women might identify against their interests; the undermining by postmodernists of totalizing views of human society, the grand narratives, in favour of a more fragmented and discontinuous picture; the production by poststructuralists and psychoanalytic feminists of a subjectivity that appears unstable and fluid, constituted across a number of identities and subject positions. Under pressure from all quarters, the figure of a universal, female subject ready to embrace feminism after brushing off the last cobwebs of false consciousness has become untenable, at the same time as the deconstructed subject—without wholeness, without coherence, without fixed identity—has looked like a poor model for any successful political action. Where does this leave 'I' and 'we'?[9]

In this essay I want to concentrate the debate around a particular place and moment: the USA in the mid-1980s, and on the interest in feminist circles in notions of locatedness. Thus, it is evident that I am using the concept of the cross-cultural *within* the boundaries of a single nation. The recurrent metaphors for the USA of the melting pot and the quilt suggest different ways of crossing cultures; on the one hand, there is the subsuming of varied cultural identities within a common identity of 'Americanness' and, on the other, the vitality of difference, while the use of hyphenated categories (African-American, Italian-American) looks optimistically to an equitable balancing of identities. Locatedness has remained an important concept, since, at its best, it offers a workable strategy for bridging 'I' and 'we' and the multiple differences those figures embrace and, at the same time, is a possible route beyond the theoretical impasse between humanist and postmodern concepts of the subject. You will note the tentativeness of my claim—"at its best" and "possible"; with such a major undertaking, there are no easy solutions. The most effective writing on locatedness sees 'I' not, to quote Gayle Greene's words, as "a site of authoritative discourse" but rather as a site of critical questioning. The work has a self-reflexive quality, but one where the memory of past events acts as a stimulus to a new politics. Frequently the writing suggests a range of reference through time and space, but the broader concepts are always tied to specific moments often presented in the form of short, illustrative narratives that pose problems of response. With scrupulous effort, the authors try to unpick the multiple meanings of the events discussed. The structure of address in these essays is to women. In the familiar, but not uncritical, dialog which these authors establish with the reader, a sense of 'we' is created. As Shoshana Felman comments,

> An address is not merely an act of intellectual and emotional appeal. It is an *act of empowerment*. And such empowerment becomes possible only when women can transmit and grasp—their own metaphoricity to one another, only when each woman can become (however different) the metaphor for another woman.[10]

Felman's project is literary and psychoanalytic. She wants to listen to women and read women, to discover how women can know themselves and each other through their representations. She writes:

> Rather, I will here propose that we might be able to engender, or to access, our story only indirectly—by conjugating literature, theory, and autobiography together through the act of reading and by reading, thus, into the texts of culture, at once our sexual difference and our autobiography as missing.[11]

This interests me; but I am also interested in how the writers we shall consider here retain a firm sense of the political and the activist, how their writing struggles to move out of the literary, and how difficult that move is.

TEXTUAL EXPLORATIONS

With these possibilities and provisos in mind, I want to consider two textual examples from Minnie Bruce Pratt's "Identity: Skin Blood Heart" (1984) and June Jordan's **"Report from the Bahamas"** (1982). Just as, theoretically, the politics of location looks for a relation between the specific and the general, so the writing practice of these authors oscillates between particular incident and more abstract, reflective comment. The extracts are concerned with the widest sense of difference—cultural, but within that designation issues of race, class, sexuality, national identity feature prominently. In both cases, it is a physical move—to a new home in Pratt's case and a holiday destination in Jordan's—that makes the author particularly sensitive to her location. The writing is attentive to the self yet prepared to be self-critical—where necessary, humble. At the same time, there is always a turn towards other women, a search for dialog without dominance. Concurrently, two dynamics—the analytic and the introspective, on the one hand, and engagement in public debate and action, on the other—work alongside each other.

At the start of her essay "Identity: Skin Blood Heart," Pratt describes her geographical location in Washington DC, living in an area where she is almost the only white person:

> I've seen two other whites, women, in the year I've lived here. (This does not count white folks in cars, passing through. In official language, H St., NE, is

known as "The H Street Corridor," as in something to be passed through quickly, going from your place, on the way to elsewhere).[12]

A page or so into the essay, she debates one very small occurrence: namely, taking a walk down the street:

> I meet a white man on Maryland Avenue at ten at night, for instance. He doesn't look gay, and he's young and bigger than me. Just because he's wearing a three-piece suit, doesn't mean he won't try something. What's he doing walking here anyway? One of the new gentry taking over? Maybe that's what the Black neighbors think about me. If I speak, he'll probably assume it's about sex, not about being neighborly. I don't feel neighborly toward him, anyway. If he speaks to me, is that about sex? Or does he still think skin means kin. Or maybe he was raised someplace where someone could say, "I know your mama," if he didn't behave. But he's probably not going to think about her, when he does whatever he does *here*: better be careful.

> In the space of three blocks one evening, I can debate whether the young Black woman didn't speak because she was tired, urban-raised, or hates white women: and ask myself why I wouldn't speak to the young professional white woman on her way to work in the morning, but I do at night: and she doesn't speak at all: is it about who I think I may need for physical safety?

> And I make myself speak to a young Black man: if I don't, it will be the old racial-sexual fear. Damn the past anyway. When I speak directly, I usually get a respectful answer: is that the response violently extorted by history, the taboo on white women? Last week the group of Black men on 10th Street started in on "Can I have some?" when Joan and I walked by: was that because they were three? we were white? we were lesbian? Or because we didn't speak? What about this man? He is a man. And I would speak to him in the *day* time.

> After I speak and he speaks, I think how my small store of manners, how I was taught to be "respectful" of others, my middle-class, white-woman, rural Southern Christian manners, gave me no ideas on Sunday afternoon, in the northwestern part of the city, how to walk down the sidewalk by gatherings of Latinos and Latinas socializing there.

> And I think of how I'm walking to visit my Jewish lover. When we walk around the neighborhood together, we just look like two white women: except the ladies in my building say we look like sisters, because we're close and they can see we love each other. But I'm blonde and blue-eyed, she dark-haired and brown-eyed: we don't look a bit like sisters. If the white people and the Black people we meet knew she was Jewish as well as white, how would their speaking alter?[13]

Through the people Pratt encounters in the street, numerous identities are brought into play: relating to gender (male/female); race (black/white); sexuality (gay/straight, sexual threats); class (middle-class/working-class, professional/non-professional, the gentrification of the area); cultural identity (Latinos and Latinas). The term 'Jewish' could be operating as a cultural identity alongside Latino/a; or as a national identity signifying Israeli; or in an opposition of Jewish/Christian; or in an opposition of Semitic/anti-Semitic; or as a religious identity. The variety of geographical locations is notable: rural/urban; Southern States/Northern States; the meaning of 'neighborhood' and 'neighbor'; the different territories of "the northwestern part of the city" or a particular street or a number of blocks. The significance of time is also a factor: day/night; the historical legacy of black man/white woman relations—"Damn the past anyway"; a projection into the future and the supposition that future responses in the street would be different if it was known that her friend was Jewish. The title of Pratt's essay points us to the bodily; but that body is socially and politically placed, the repository of a complex sign system. Thus the importance of appearance is noted in Pratt's interpretation of the three-piece suit and of body size; how the two women are called "sisters" though they clearly do not look alike; the reference to a man who does not "look gay." The italics ("I would speak to him in the *day* time") indicate Pratt's awareness of the dangers of typecasting, at the same time as recognizing, with a kind of shorthand, that certain cultural signs in particular contexts can signify "gay." Though the passage suggests a number of binary pairings, these do not fix the debate in an oppositional mode, since all the identities and social relations mentioned are open to reinterpretation. She looks at and thinks about the people on the street; they look at and think about her. Neither Pratt nor the people she encounters, neither her behavior nor their behavior, can be simply explained, and the reader senses that the analysis, complicated though it is, could endlessly widen and deepen as more considerations are brought into play. On these journeys nothing is innocent; no look, no word, no gesture is trivial. They are, in one sense, archetypal journeys of self-discovery where Pratt learns what, previously, she might have recognized but not fully internalized.

In the extract from Pratt, we see her becoming acutely conscious of the everyday and how her experience of being almost the only white person in a black neighborhood provokes that defamiliarization. In June Jordan's essay as well, the usual accommodations with the everyday are no longer possible, to the extent that she is now both differently positioned and positions others differently. The essay starts with her description of her bargain-break Easter weekend at the Sheraton British Colonial hotel in the Bahamas:

> This is my consciousness of race as I unpack my bathing suit in the Sheraton British Colonial. Neither this hotel nor the British nor the long ago Italians nor the white Delta airline pilots belong here, of course. And every time I look at the photograph of that fool standing in the water with his shoes on I'm about to have a West Indian fit, even though I know he's no fool; he's

a middle-aged Black man who needs a job and this is his job—pretending himself a servile ancillary to the pleasures of the rich. (Compared to his options in life, I am a rich woman. Compared to most of the Black Americans arriving for this Easter weekend on a three nights four days' deal of bargain rates, the middle-aged waiter is a poor Black man.)

We will jostle along with the other (white) visitors and join them in the tee shirt shops or, laughing together, learn ruthless rules of negotiation as we, Black Americans as well as white, argue down the price of handwoven goods at the nearby straw market while the merchants, frequently toothless Black women seated on the concrete in their only presentable dress, humble themselves to our careless games:

"Yes? You like it? Eight dollar."

"Five."

"I give it to you. Seven."

And so it continues, this weird succession of crude intruders that, now, includes me and my brothers and my sisters from the North.

This is my consciousness of class as I try to decide how much money I can spend on Bahamian gifts for my family back in Brooklyn. No matter that these other Black women incessantly weave words and flowers into the straw hats and bags piled beside them on the burning dusty street. No matter that these other Black women must work their sense of beauty into these things that we will take away as cheaply as we dare, or they will do without food.

We are not white, after all. The budget is limited. And we are harmlessly killing time between the poolside rum punch and "The Native Show on the Patio" that will play tonight outside the hotel restaurant.

This is my consciousness of race and class and gender identity as I notice the fixed relations between these other Black women and myself. They sell and I buy or I don't. They risk not eating. I risk going broke on my first vacation afternoon.

We are not particularly women anymore: we are parties to a transaction designed to set us against each other.[14]

The hotel name is striking. Jordan sees tourism as part of a new wave of colonial enterprise and the hotel name brings together the history of British colonialism (apparently not a memory of shame for the hotel but a useful marketing strategy) and the current role in colonialism of the American multinational. Jordan adds herself to this history as included in "this weird succession of crude intruders." The opening paragraph of the essay refers to a photograph advertising the hotel in which a middle-aged black man, dressed as a waiter, is standing up to his calves in sea water, smiling and holding a tray of drinks. The message of the advert is that, in his eagerness to be of service to the hotel's guests, he will wade into the water with the drinks to serve the guests while they float on their inflatables. It is this photograph to which Jordan alludes in the first para-

graph, and her anger is tempered with the realization that here is someone who needs a job and will therefore do what is necessary to keep it.

Jordan cannot maintain any sense of moral superiority. She may be female, she may be black, she may have to earn her living, but in this situation she is not on the side of the angels. Bartering at the market to get the cheapest souvenirs to take home, she becomes in the eyes of the black Bahamians just another American tourist to whom they have to be "friendly" or "colourful" or "exotic" or "quaint" or any of those terms by which tourist brochures describe the indigenous population. The passage works its way consecutively through a series of problematical encounters: "This is my consciousness of race . . . This is my consciousness of class . . . This is my consciousness of race and class and gender. . . ." 'We' is variously constituted. Within a single sentence 'we' can be "black American" separate from "the (other) white visitors" but also 'we' as "black Americans as well as white" who together haggle over the price of goods at the market. At this juncture the distinction is not between black and white but between rich and poor, tourist and native, 'First World' and 'Third World.' Later Jordan tries to justify her actions by reference to race and economics and 'we' once again signifies, specifically, black Americans—"We are not white, after all. The budget is limited"—but the logic is suspect and the attempt fails, as she knows it will; running out of holiday spending money is not the same as being unable to buy food.

There is no "global sisterhood" as Robin Morgan would want it, no sense of a common identity, since the women are pitted against each other, unequally, in an economic transaction.[15] The Bahamian women in the market are, in fact, positioned by Jordan as "these other Black women" (the phrase is mentioned three times), different from herself and her family back home in Brooklyn and from the black American women on the trip. Also distinct from Jordan is "Olive," the black woman who cleans her hotel room. On the final day of her stay, Jordan picks up the report card, common now in hotels of a certain size and status, which asks her to rate the work of "Olive":

"Dear Guests:" it says, under the name "Olive." "I am your maid for the day. Please rate me: Excellent. Good. Average. Poor. Thank you."

I tuck this memento from the Sheraton British Colonial into my notebook. How would "Olive" rate *me*? What would it mean for us to seem "good" to each other? What would that rating require?[16]

"Olive" never gets out of her objectifying inverted commas. The network of internationalism that features here is not one of sisterhood or of anti-racism or of anti-colonialism but of the multinational hotel chain, trying to maintain world-wide an adequate level of customer care. Furthermore, as Jordan sardonically notes, it was precisely that factor which drew her to this particular hotel: "I calculated that my safety as a Black woman alone would be best assured by a multinational hotel corporation. In my experience, the big guys take customer complaints more seriously than the little ones."[17]

Jordan writes with a sharp, ironic edge: "And we are harmlessly killing time between the poolside rum punch and 'The Native Show on the Patio' that will play tonight outside the hotel restaurant." Of course, none of this is "harmless." The exploited black worker who brings the drinks or waits on in the restaurant, the servicing of the tourists' needs above or at the expense of all others, the transformation of the native culture into after-dinner entertainment, the importation of "the patio" or the validation of "the poolside rum punch" as signs of supposed elegant living—these are all familiar aspects of the new tourism. Elsewhere the rum punch might become a tequila and the patio, the sauna. Jordan's mocking irony is equally self-directed, and she is uncomfortably aware of the part she is playing in this scenario. In a number of ways, she is both *in* the situation and *out* of the situation. *In* it, in that, as we have seen, she readily falls into the role of 'tourist.' 'We,' meaning black tourists, sometimes with white tourists, sometimes not, are in opposition to the "toothless Black women" selling goods. But she is also *out* of the situation, critical and reflecting, aware of the politics, alert to the nascent creativity of the women who "weave words and flowers into the straw hats and bags." And yet, even so, she is still *in* the situation, positioned by forces that are beyond her control. The exploitative connotations inherent in the role of 'tourist' continue despite the personal goodwill or political awareness of well-meaning individuals, and in that situation gender, feminism, international feminism seem irrelevant. By the last sentence of the extract—"We are not particularly women anymore; we are parties to a transaction designed to set us against each other"—'we' carries no sense of collective identity.

FROM WORD TO WORK AND WORLD

Rosi Braidotti defines the politics of location as follows:

> But this recognition of a common condition of sister-hood in oppression cannot be the final aim; women may have common situations and experiences, but they are not, in any way, *the same*. In this respect, the idea of the politics of location is very important. This idea, developed into a theory of recognition of the multiple differences that exist among women, stresses the importance of rejecting global statements about all women and of attempting instead to be as aware as possible of the place from which one is speaking. Attention to the *situated* as opposed to the universalistic nature of statements is the key idea.[18]

That attention to "the place from which one is speaking" is revealed in an exemplary fashion in the extracts from Pratt and Jordan. At the same time, both evoke larger histories of racism, colonialism, international capitalism. When one thinks of these issues or of developments in information technology or of the internationalism of cultural signs (what does a world of McDonald's and Coca-Cola mean?) or of the potential world-wide consequences of environmental and, still, nuclear disasters, then, indeed, an understanding of the universal is also necessary. One of our most urgent needs is to re-affirm feminism as an international movement while trying to avoid all the sharks in the water: essentialism and idealism, relativism, fragmentation, privileging, defeatism, generalities. But the space between the local and the global or, for the individual, the psyche and the social is a most difficult territory to negotiate. Though fully conscious of the power of writing, both Pratt and Jordan are also keen for the words to get off the page and into a different order of activity; or, to put it another way, the words might be a conduit to a different order of activity.

Pratt is particularly astute in understanding ambiguity, how things can be at once true and false, good and bad. Hence, "we can experience this change as loss. Because it is: the old lies and ways of living, habitual, familiar, comfortable, fitting us like our skin, were *ours*."[19] She discovers in her own family a shameful history of slave ownership and segregation but her family continues to represent a place of childhood intimacy, community, 'home.' She cannot reject one without, seemingly, losing the other. Thus, knowledge of one's location is not simply a way of rationalizing the status quo, explaining why inequalities exist, worrying about them momentarily before moving on; what one learns demands a response. Pratt uses images of fierce bodily change: she is haunted by Edgar Allan Poe's story "The Fall of the House of Usher" and the figure of the incarcerated woman breaking out; she refers to a snake shedding its skin to suggest both the effort and the potential for "an expansion, some growth, and some reward for struggle and curiosity"; she fears that beneath "the wrappings of a shroud" she will find only "a disintegrating, rotting nothing."[20]

In writing on locatedness, there is for the privileged woman an uncertain line between a necessary sense of guilt at one's complicity and a dangerously indulgent self-laceration. Jordan avoids the danger in the selected passage through her use of ironic distancing; Pratt confronts the issue head-on, wanting to maintain a passionate involvement while aware of all the risks. At the end of the scene we have considered, she writes:

> By the amount of effort it takes me to walk these few blocks being conscious as I can of myself in relation to history, to race, to culture, to gender, I reckon the rigid

boundaries set around my experience, how I have been "protected." In this city where I am no longer of the majority by color or culture, I tell myself every day: In this *world* you aren't the superior race or culture, and never were, whatever you were raised to think: and are you getting ready to be *in* this world?

And I answer myself back; I'm trying to learn how to live, to have the speaking-to extend beyond the moment's word, to act so as to change the unjust circumstances that keep us from being able to speak to each other; I'm trying to get a little closer to the longed-for but unrealized world, where we each are able to live, but not by trying to make someone less than us, not by someone else's blood or pain: yes, that's what I'm trying to do with my living now.[21]

She certainly recognizes herself as of the *minority*. Yet such a recognition still carries the sense of an intellectual exercise where she has to convince herself that she is not special and to work against the ideology of her upbringing. The rational self and the politically egalitarian self might reject power; irrationally, memories of status and now-despised prejudices continue to surface. How inevitable, how overdetermined it is that the history of interracial sex should have featured earlier among her deliberations.

We can feel an anxiety and insistence in the short sentences, the frequent questions, the endless posing of new readings of events. No position is secure. But there is also the possibility that the analysis may become wearisome and disabling, so overscrupulous that every word or action is compromised. Certainly nothing could be spontaneous or disingenuous: "the amount of effort it takes me to walk these few blocks being conscious as I can of myself in relation to history, to race, to culture, to gender. . . ." Elsewhere she refers to her work on consciousness as "an exhausting process."[22] This response is utterly principled but, at the same time, the complaints are open to parody. Having the space for such extensive self-analysis is itself privileged. Like other writers involved in the politics of location, Pratt's solution for an introspection that is potentially inhibiting is to link the analysis with action: "to extend beyond the moment's word, to act so as to change the unjust circumstances that keep us from being able to speak to each other." This is in no way an easy answer. The final paragraph in the extract quoted above contains four instances of the word "trying." The term suggests effort, maybe hope, but no certainty. Indeed, if one has fully recognized the meaning of locatedness, then absolutism is impossible.

The move from word to work and world is most difficult at the endings of these essays. The nature of the rhetoric does not demand closure or resolution. In fact, a common motif is, precisely, the suggestion that the solution is not in sight. Pratt concludes her essay by describing a dream of reconciliation which can sustain

her as she continues "the struggle with myself and the world I was born in."[23] Jordan, thinking of the threat of nuclear war, insists she "must make the connection between me and these strangers everywhere."[24] Adrienne Rich, in probably the most important essay on locatedness, "Notes toward a Politics of Location" (1984), comments bluntly: "This is the end of the notes, but it is not an ending."[25] The abiding sense is always that nothing is finished and there is still work to be done. However, just as notably, the emotional effect of the endings is always positive, and this relies partly on a sense of intellectual satisfaction at having worked through material to deeper understandings and partly on a sense of energy and determination springing from a revived political commitment. It is also the product of the "metaphoricity" that Felman spoke of, how "each woman can become (however different) the metaphor for another woman"; hence the collective 'we' is a renewed possibility.

As with all writing, the success of the endings depends on that unstable relationship between author, reader and text. The ending of Jordan's essay is for me less successful than earlier parts. It concerns an episode from her teaching experience when she is asked for help by a black South African woman who is being beaten by her husband. The woman eventually gets aid through the intervention of Jordan and another student, Cathy, "a young Irish woman active in campus IRA activities."[26] I find a number of aspects of this narrative jarring. For instance, there is a passage of stilted dialogue when Jordan tells Cathy about the problem:

She asked for further details. I gave them to her.

"Her husband," Cathy told me, "is an alcoholic. You have to understand about alcoholics. It's not the same as anything else. And it's a disease you can't treat any old way."

I listened fearfully. Did this mean there was nothing we could do?

"That's not what I'm saying," she said. "But you have to keep the alcoholic part of the thing central in everybody's mind, otherwise her husband will kill her. Or he'll kill himself."

She spoke calmly, I felt there was nothing to do but to assume she knew what she was talking about.

"Will you come with me?" I asked, after a silence. "Will you come with me and help us figure out what to do next?"[27]

Improbably, Jordan seems unaware of what alcoholism is. Though the situation is undoubtedly urgent, I balk at Jordan's account of the events: the dramatic repetition—"Will you come with me . . ."—the significant silence and, a little later in this scene, the line "We were going to that room to try to save a life together." If this is too self-dramatizing, then the final image of the two young women together is too redolent of idealism:

I walked behind them, the young Irish woman and the young South African, and I saw them walking as sisters walk, hugging each other, and whispering and sure of each other and I felt how it was not who they were but what they both know and what they were both preparing to do about what they know that was going to make them both free at last.[28]

To be fair, the phrase "free at last" is not, in context, as grandiloquent as it might seem here. Jordan had noticed Cathy's car sticker, "BOBBY SANDS FREE AT LAST," and comments earlier in the passage on the curious conflation of Bobby Sands' name and Martin Luther King's words, all the more striking as Jordan had first been called "nigga" by the bullying Irish children with whom she grew up. The hope here that *both* the black South African woman and the Irish woman might be "free at last" rewrites that earlier incident. Yet the extract still poses political and literary problems. Jordan, in her eagerness to establish that connection across difference, loses the close detail of her earlier examples in the impact of the moment. Moreover, the difficulty of balancing a clear-eyed estimation of the present with a hopeful vision of the future is actually what makes this writing so uneasy and open to varied responses. The next reader could dismiss my interpretation as over-critical and miserably reluctant to recognize the significance of a transforming event. Which of us is right?

REASSESSING THE PRONOUNS

The move from word to work and world entails a reassessment of those pronouns 'I' and 'we' with which I started the essay. Jordan's phrasing, above, is significant. Her focus is not so much on "who they were"—ie the personal 'I' and the interpersonal 'we'—as on "what they both know and what they were both preparing to do about what they know": that is, the work and world. In a more recent interview, Jordan expresses some irritation with the interpersonal:

And I think, generally speaking, that relationships that include working together, you know, are just a whole lot healthier and sturdier [. . .] than just sitting around and talking about "relationships," I mean like in a void, in a vacuum. I'm talking about on a one-to-one level; and so I think if we look at this in a broader sense it makes sense as well, to start with the work, which as I say, again I want to reiterate, the work cannot wait, we have everything to do.[29]

Her qualifications are important. She is not dismissing questions of identity as irrelevant. Rather, she prefers to see them as interrelated with and a product of the work, while her sense of the urgency of the work ensures its priority. This strategy relates to what Jordan and others refer to as "coalition politics," a highly practical sense of making change on the basis of specific common interests but without presuming any personal affinity. It is a localized, grassroots approach. Bernice Johnson Reagon, in her definition of coalition work and the opposition of 'street' and 'home,' is even more trenchant and removes coalition work from feelings of personal gratification:

Coalition work is not work done in your home. Coalition work has to be done in the streets. And it is some of the most dangerous work you can do. And you shouldn't look for comfort. Some people will come to a coalition and they rate the success of the coalition on whether or not they feel good when they get there. They're not looking for a coalition; they're looking for a home! They're looking for a bottle with some milk in it and a nipple, which does not happen in a coalition. You don't get a lot of food in a coalition. You don't get fed in a coalition. In a coalition you have to give, and it is different from your home. You can't stay there all the time. You go to the coalition for a few hours and then you go back and take your bottle wherever it is, and then you go back and coalesce some more.[30]

Don't jeopardize the 'we' because you're so preoccupied with the needs of the 'I,' is the general gist.

Earlier in this essay I made a speculative claim for concepts of locatedness working across critical theories and making strange bedfellows of radical feminism and postmodernism. Coalition politics retains a strong, radical-feminist view of identity. As Jordan comments in her interview: "If anybody, if any numbers of people are going to change themselves, or diminish their specific identities, then we're not talking coalition anymore"[31] The suggestion is that there *is* a core identity which must remain intact and that coalition politics will not subsume it. From another perspective, though, there is a sense of 'I' and 'we' being produced performatively so that 'I' and 'we' are known afresh in the daily practice of coalition politics. The 'I' you are on 'the street' may not be the 'I' you are in 'the home' but neither is more or less authentic than the other. Equally, Pratt's imagery, discussed earlier, is not predicated, simply and naively, on the basis of a resolved 'I'— indeed, in one of the images that 'I' has disintegrated completely—but the desire for a more coherent self might be a motivating force for political work. Against the incapacitating selfhood of nervous scrutiny and confession, Pratt proposes "a positive process of recreating ourselves, or making a self that is not the negative, the oppressor."[32] Of course, this entails work; it cannot be mere wishful thinking or the product of a convenient amnesia about responsibility. Recreating oneself as not the oppressor is not simply an act of self-representation; it means *really not being the oppressor.* Pratt finds ways of connecting with her past which recognize both the inequities and how that past can provide resources for a better future. Thus, for example, her Presbyterian origins gave her "a comparative and skeptical way of thinking [. . .] which emphasized doubt and analysis: I saw that I had been using these skills all along as I tried to figure out my personal responsibility in a racist and anti-Semitic culture."[33] This is not a return to a 'true' self but a critical awareness of how the self is in constant production, the past and the present over-layering each other.

The imagery of connectedness, 'we,' has also shown some interesting correspondences across critical differences. Thus, in the work of Donna Haraway (1991) and Sadie Plant (1997), that most organicist image of social relation, the web, or the feminine imagery of tapestry making and weaving will be found alongside images of the Net, the integrated circuit, and the matrix, just as, in an episode of *The X-Files,* the Net as a mechanism for the exponential spread of important information was likened to Native American storytelling. Reference to "the World Wide Web" brings together these different models of connectedness, the organic and the techno-logical. Similarly, I doubt whether Rich had read the French original of Gilles Deleuze's and Félix Guattari's *Mille plateaux,* published four years before her "Notes Toward a Politics of Location" essay, when she produced her own wonderful image of the rhizome. Her critique of the space industry develops into a mode of poetic association and ends with an image of toxicity and pollution, and, equally, one of rebirth:

> On a split screen in my brain I see two versions of her story: the backward gaze through streaming weightless-ness to the familiar globe, pale blue and green and white, the strict and sober presence of it, the true intuition of relativity battering the heart: and the swiftly calculated move to a farther suburb, the male techno-crats and the women they have picked and tested, leav-ing the familiar globe behind: the toxic rivers, the cancerous wells, the strangled valleys, the closed-down urban hospitals, the shattered schools, the atomic desert blooming, the lilac suckers run wild, the blue grape hyacinths spreading, the ailanthus and kudzu doing their final desperate part—the beauty that won't travel, that can't be stolen away.[34]

A dystopian image of a fallen world is juxtaposed with an image that is organic and generative but also rhi-zomatic and nomadic. There is an attempt here to salvage something from dire and seemingly intractable circumstances. The physical movement at the end is not of space travel, from here to there and back, but of flowers spreading uncontrollably. Deleuze and Guattari claim that "a rhizome may be broken, shattered at a given spot, but it will start up again on one of its old lines, or on new lines."[35] Rich's rhizomatic syntax confronts the "given spot" of "the shattered schools"—both Rich and the translator of Deleuze and Guattari have made a serendipitous choice of the same word—but she will immediately "start up again [. . .] on new lines"; only a comma separates "the shattered schools" from "the atomic desert blooming." Thus the rhizome may offer us a further hopeful image for a movement across difference, with the caution always that for the word to become flesh necessitates work.

Notes

1. Gayle Greene, "Looking at History," in *Changing Subjects: The Making of Feminist Literary Criticism,* ed. Gayle Greene & Coppélia Kahn (London: Rout-ledge, 1993): 11.

2. Greene, "Looking at History." 11.

3. Virginia Woolf, *A Room of One's Own* (1929) in the combined volume *A Room of One's Own* and *Three Guineas,* ed. Michèle Barrett (Harmondsworth: Penguin. 1993): 90.

4. S. P. Mohanty, "Us and Them: On the Philosophical Bases of Political Criticism," *Yale Journal of Criti-cism* 2 (1989): 13.

5. Audre Lorde, *Our Dead Behind Us* (New York: W. W. Norton, 1986): 61.

6. Adrienne Rich, "Blood, Bread, and Poetry: The Loca-tion of the Poet," in *Blood, Bread, and Poetry. Selected Prose 1979-1985* (London: Virago, 1987): 183.

7. Minnie Bruce Pratt, "Identity: Skin Blood Heart," in *Yours in Struggle: Three Feminist Perspectives on Anti-Semitism and Racism,* Elly Bulkin, Minnie Bruce Pratt & Barbara Smith (Ithaca NY: Firebrand, 1984): 40-41.

8. Linda Alcoff, "The Problem of Speaking for Others," in *Who Can Speak? Authority and Critical Identity,* ed. Judith Roof & Robyn Wiegman (Urbana: U of Il-linois P., 1995): 107.

9. For further thoughts on speaking personally and impersonally, see Toril Moi, "'I Am a Woman': The Personal and the Philosophical," in Moi, *What Is a Woman? And Other Essays* (Oxford: Oxford UP, 1999): 121-250.

10. Shoshana Felman, *What Does a Woman Want? Read-ing and Sexual Difference* (Baltimore MD: Johns Hopkins UP, 1993): 127.

11. Felman, *What Does a Woman Want?* 14.

12. Pratt, "Identity: Skin Blood Heart," 11.

13. Pratt, "Identity: Skin Blood Heart," 12-13.

14. June Jordan, "Report from the Bahamas." in *Moving Towards Home: Political Essays* (London: Virago, 1989): 138.

15. Robin Morgan, ed. & intro. *Sisterhood is Global: The International Women's Movement Anthology* (Garden City NY: Doubleday/Anchor, 1984).

16. Jordan, "Report from the Bahamas," 143.

17. Jordan, "Report from the Bahamas," 139.

18. Rosi Braidotti, *Nomadic Subjects: Embodiment and Sexual Difference in Contemporary Feminist Theory* (New York: Columbia UP, 1994): 163.

19. Pratt, "Identity: Skin Blood Heart," 39.

20. Pratt, "Identity: Skin Blood Heart," 39.

21. Pratt, "Identity: Skin Blood Heart," 13.

22. Pratt, "Identity: Skin Blood Heart," 12.

23. Pratt, "Identity: Skin Blood Heart," 57.

24. Jordan, "Report from the Bahamas," 146.

25. Rich, "Notes toward a Politics of Location," in *Blood, Bread, and Poetry,* 231.

26. Jordan, "Report from the Bahamas," 145.

27. Jordan, "Report from the Bahamas," 145.

28. Jordan, "Report from the Bahamas," 146.

29. Margaret Christakos, "The Craft that the Politics Requires: An Interview with June Jordan," *Fireweed* 36 (Summer 1992): 32.

30. Bernice Johnson Reagon, "Coalition Politics: Turning the Century," in *Home Girls: A Black Feminist Anthology,* ed. Barbara Smith (New York: Kitchen Table, Women of Color Press, 1983): 59.

31. Christakos, "The Craft that the Politics Requires," 30.

32. Pratt, "Identity: Skin Blood Heart," 41.

33. Pratt, "Identity: Skin Blood Heart," 44.

34. Rich, "Notes toward a Politics of Location," 223.

35. Gilles Deleuze & Félix Guattari, *A Thousand Plateaus: Capitalism and Schizophrenia,* tr. Brian Massumi (*Mille plateaux: capitalisme et schizophrénie,* 1980; tr. London: Athlone. 1988): 9.

Works Cited

Alcoff, Linda. "The Problem of Speaking for Others," in *Who Can Speak? Authority and Critical Identity,* ed. Judith Roof & Robyn Wiegman (Urbana: U of Illinois P, 1995): 97-119.

Braidotti, Rosi. *Nomadic Subjects: Embodiment and Sexual Difference in Contemporary Feminist Theory* (New York: Columbia UP, 1994).

Christakos, Margaret. "The Craft that the Politics Requires: An Interview with June Jordan," *Fireweed* 36 (Summer 1992): 26-38.

Deleuze, Gilles, & Félix Guattari. *A Thousand Plateaus: Capitalism and Schizophrenia,* tr. Brian Massumi (*Mille plateaux: capitalisme et schizophrénie,* 1980; tr. London: Athlone, 1988).

Felman, Shoshana. *What Does a Woman Want? Reading and Sexual Difference* (Baltimore MD: Johns Hopkins UP, 1993).

Greene, Gayle. "Looking at History," in *Changing Subjects: The Making of Feminist Literary Criticism,* ed. Gayle Greene & Coppélia Kahn (London: Routledge, 1993): 4-27.

Haraway, Donna J. *Simians, Cyborgs, and Women: The Reinvention of Nature* (London: Free Association, 1991).

Jordan, June. "Report from the Bahamas," in *Moving Towards Home: Political Essays* (*On Call: Political Essays,* 1985: London: Virago, 1989): 137-46.

Lorde, Audre. *Our Dead Behind Us* (New York: W. W. Norton, 1986).

Mohanty, S. P. "Us and Them: On the Philosophical Bases of Political Criticism," *Yale Journal of Criticism* 2 (1989): 1-31.

Moi, Toril. "'I Am a Woman': The Personal and the Philosophical," in Moi, *What Is a Woman? And Other Essays* (Oxford: Oxford UP, 1999): 121-250.

Morgan, Robin, ed. & intro. *Sisterhood is Global: The International Women's Movement Anthology* (Garden City NY: Doubleday/Anchor, 1984).

Plant, Sadie. *Zeros + Ones: Digital Women + the New Technoculture* (London: Fourth Estate, 1997).

Pratt, Minnie Bruce. "Identity: Skin Blood Heart." in Elly Bulkin, Minnie Bruce Pratt & Barbara Smith, *Yours in Struggle: Three Feminist Perspectives on Anti-Semitism and Racism* (Ithaca NY: Firebrand, 1984): 9-63.

Reagon, Bernice Johnson. "Coalition Politics: Turning the Century," in *Home Girls: A Black Feminist Anthology,* ed. Barbara Smith (New York: Kitchen Table, Women of Color Press, 1983): 356-68.

Rich, Adrienne. *Blood, Bread, and Poetry: Selected Prose 1979-1985* (1986; London: Virago, 1987).

Woolf, Virginia. *A Room of One's Own* (1929) in the combined volume *A Room of One's Own* and *Three Guineas,* ed. Michèle Barrett (Harmondsworth: Penguin, 1993).

Rebecca Walsh (essay date 2002)

SOURCE: Walsh, Rebecca. "Where Metaphor Meets Materiality: The Spatialized Subject and the Limits of Locational Feminism." In *Exclusions in Feminist Thought: Challenging the Boundaries of Womanhood,* edited by Mary Brewer, pp. 182-202. Brighton, UK: Sussex Academic Press, 2002.

[*In the following essay, Walsh characterizes Jordan's feminism as multifaceted, specifically in terms of locational feminism.*]

Over the last few years, feminist theorists have increasingly turned to spatial models as a way to account for the multiple and shifting aspects of female identity neglected by previous feminisms. This emerging "locational feminism", as Susan Stanford Friedman has called it, gives spatial coordinates to the subject, whose complex, fluid and often contradictory relationships to gender, race, class, and sexuality are determined by the places she occupies (1998: 5). In large part, locational feminism owes its turn to geography to the work of women of color in the late 1970s and early 1980s, which criticized feminism's exclusionary academic practices, in particular its unexamined assumption that the experience of middle-class white women could serve as the barometer for *all* women's experience. Adrienne Rich's 1984 essay "Notes Toward a Politics of Location", for instance, is very much responsive to this critique as it puts into spatial terms an awareness of the vast differences among women and recognition of the multiple and interlocking nature of oppression. Rich asserts that what is important is "recognizing our location, having to name the ground we're coming from, the conditions we have taken for granted" (1986: 219) so that we may understand how racial and economic privilege affect female experiences. To embrace the variety of female perspectives, Rich urges us to "get back to earth—not as paradigm for 'women,' but as place of location" (1986: 214). This "grounded" analysis considers material contexts in which the female subject is located, thus avoiding "grandiose assertions" about the body or generalizations about universal female experience (Rich 1986: 215). Her foundational text lays out a valuable site-specific approach that considers multiple forms of alterity, or differences that are designated as "other" by dominant society, and situates them within a web of political alliances and disconnections. For literary critics and cultural theorists as well as geographers, then, place or location has provided a useful way to track the conjunctions and disjunctions among gender, race, class, and sexuality, without taking gender for granted as a privileged and insulated identity category.[1] Compared to prospects offered by temporally weighted, developmental models of identity such as Marxism or psychoanalysis, a locational approach opens up a much more complex understanding of the subject's protean relationship to difference and privilege.

However, this emergent paradigm also raises important questions about the kinds of female experience that often remain hidden by and in space. If attempts to locate a subject's multiple and shifting relationships to privilege necessarily involve reading and interpreting context, the temptation for locational feminism is to trust that difference is identifiable and mappable, and to assume that what is mappable is most determining, important, "real". As Patricia Yeager warns in *The Geography of Identity,* "One criterion of social space is its attempt to be thematic or real, to convince us of its

solidity or authenticity even when we are skeptics or disbelievers: to treat something as real is to endorse it. How do we deal with the devilish impenetrability of social space, with our bodies' temptation to misremember the categorical struggles that have founded our world?" (1996: 25). What I want to consider here are the difficulties inherent in trying to make identity "thematic" through the use of a geographical epistemology and its accompanying metaphors and tools. For somewhere in the attempt to map geography onto identity, or identity onto geography, locational feminism risks privileging and making more legitimate or, as Yeager puts it, "endorsing" those aspects of identity that are most easily seen. Friedman notes the shift that locational feminism has inaugurated "from an earlier emphasis on silence and invisibility" to "the geopolitics of identity within differing communal spaces of being and becoming" (1998: 3). However, the geographical strategies exhibited in essays by June Jordan and Minnie Bruce Pratt[2] indicate that the issue of (in)visibility remains a concern within locational feminism, and is in fact exacerbated by the very geographical mode that seeks to theorize beyond it.

The prominence of geography and visibility in Jordan and Pratt's texts reveals locational feminism's reliance upon the logic of visibility. This emphasis upon the seen at the expense of obscuring the unseen becomes particularly problematic when the female subject in question is bisexual or lesbian.[3] That some forms of race and homosexuality are not always performed on the body has been the subject of considerable discussion. While racial invisibility has been carefully addressed by others,[4] I focus on the complicated nature of the relationship between sexual alterity and metaphorical and material space as a way of indicating how locational feminism might consider more substantially the difference it makes that some kinds of difference are more visible than others. In charting gender, class, race, and desire, locational feminism needs to be more self-conscious about the nature of what it is trying to consider as well as how its project feeds into existing debates within the gay and lesbian community about issues of visibility, categorization, subversion, and the public sphere. What this involves, I want to suggest, is a resituating of the historical within locational analyses. For while few theorists would enforce a strict separation between time and space, the temporal in locational analysis has perhaps played a role too diminished to carefully consider identities that are dynamic, unstable, and/or in a state of constant becoming such as lesbian and bisexual subjectivities.

For many theorists, locational feminism's use of space as a flashpoint for understanding the complexities of difference has meant liberation from the difficulties of defining the subject and its role in identity politics. The noteworthy contributions of Rich and other theorists move us away from essentialist formulations of identity and embrace more flexible and contingent understandings of female experience. A number of scholars have taken up Rich's geographic rhetoric, commonly focusing on the subject's embeddedness in particular contexts and analyzing how these contexts call into play multiple and often paradoxical aspects of selfhood. While Donna Haraway thinks of this mathematically as a "geometrics of difference and contradiction" (1991: 170), Linda Alcoff, for instance, uses the apt metaphor of chess, conveying the complex and shifting power dynamics that grow out of each individual arrangement of the pieces; the pawn may be weak or strong depending upon its relation to other pieces. She observes that this positional approach circumvents essentialism since it makes the subject's identity "relative to a constantly shifting context, to a situation that includes a network of elements involving others, the objective economic conditions, cultural and political institutions and ideologies, and so on" (Alcoff 1988: 433).

On many fronts, essentialism has prevented feminism from being able to devote its energies to political mobilization, coalition building, and action. As Diana Fuss observes in *Essentially Speaking,* for lesbian feminists at least, the pressure to "claim" or "discover" one's true identity before going on to generate a political stance has created gridlock (1989: 100). This has led Michael Warner to wonder if the non-identity politics of queer theory is attractive, in part, because it releases this pressure to define the subject (1992: 17). Similar to queer theory's celebration of the freeing and potentially subversive nature of performance,[5] locational theory moves beyond arguments about identity *per se* to consider the conditions of space as determining identity. As Alcoff suggests, in focusing on position, and not essence, locational models register the need to analyze women's lack of power in social and political networks without constructing the female subject as naturally lacking agency (1988: 432). The relational field of women's studies thus remains sensitive to the shifting power dynamics that race, gender, class, or sexual desire might introduce into female coalition building, even while allowing room for women to actively engage with their environments.

And yet the spatial focus of locational feminism is tied to a politics of visibility that makes it difficult to track differences constituted by forms of female-female desire. Indeed, locational feminism is caught between two kinds of visibility often fused or conflated: political visibility (metaphor) and practical visibility (materiality). On a political level, visual metaphors are hard to avoid in describing the process by which an oppressed group asserts itself in the public arena and measures how well it has transformed hegemonic ideology and practice. Making one's identity manifest and highlighting particular forms of alterity in public

consciousness have become familiar strategies in oppositional politics. Such tactics participate in larger, firmly entrenched tendencies to link vision to power and knowledge.[6] Both Martin Jay (1992) and Jonathan Crary (1993) have discussed the "scopic" nature of western modernity, marked by competing ocular fields vying for truth. In the US, as in other western societies, this cultural trust in the palpable and perceptible is vested in the epistemological habits of natural history. What results from that discipline's scientific practices is an implicit faith that the truth will come from "objective" observation. This visual empiricism, accordingly, naturalizes what it sees and depends upon the fiction that visibility and reality come hand in hand.[7] The modern scopic regime pretends that the "truth" of differences can be noticed and that what is noticed represents the truth. The powerful role that has been afforded to vision has infiltrated even the most basic unit of being—the formation of the subject itself—in psychoanalytic theory.[8] And since establishing selfhood relies upon vision, taking control over the scopic regime becomes at its core a way to stake a claim for self-definition.

In this struggle to control what is seen and how it is seen in the cultural imagination, visibility politics has come to depend upon "real" visibility, making it extremely difficult to account for sexual alterity. As socially marginalized groups take charge of this scopic regime, they make difference visually noticeable on the body in order to reclaim the machinery by which cultural status is assigned. Real visible difference thus operates as the preferred route to political agency. As Lisa Walker observes, "privileging visibility has become a tactic of late twentieth-century identity politics, in which participants often symbolize their demands for social justice by celebrating visible signifiers of difference that have historically targeted them for discrimination" (1993: 868). Judith Butler provides a telling list of the ways in which queer-identified groups have used public performance to draw attention to and reclaim difference; die-ins by ACT UP, designed to make AIDS a publicly visible concern rather than a stigmatized issue for gays alone; kiss-ins by Queer Nation that move homosexuality out of the private sphere and into the public; as well as drag balls, instances of cross-dressing, and butch-femme performances, just to name a few (1993: 233). These scenes of activist intervention rely upon the ability of performance to disrupt and alter heterosexist ideology. For the lesbian, organized efforts such as staged, public performances of excess sexuality can successfully challenge the dominant discourse which has desexualized her, as Butler points out (1993: 233). Yet as important as public performance has become to queer politics and activism, many bisexuals and lesbians, femme lesbians in particular, find it quite challenging to use gender performance to subvert heterosexist and patriarchal discourse and, therein, alter the standard of vision or the frame of reference for what is seen and what can be seen.

This privileging of visibility in locational feminism—both on a political level and on the level of the body—can also lead to prioritizing race over sexuality, since the hierarchy of what is most visible tends to leave bisexuality and certain forms of lesbianism, such as the femme, in the shadows. Skin color functions as the most visible feature of alterity in the role it has come to play in racial categorization.[9] In the United States in particular, the black/white binary is so thoroughgoing that it is hard to consider forms of alterity other than color. Even theorists who attempt to analyze sexuality and race simultaneously have trouble preventing sexuality from slipping out of focus. Lisa Walker, in her analysis of the relationship between race, sexuality, and visibility, has demonstrated that theorists' attempts to consider race and sexuality together can end up privileging racial difference while relegating lesbianism to a supplementary position. Haraway's "A Manifesto for Cyborgs", for instance, tracks skin color as a definitive marker of alterity and under theorizes the equally important role that lesbianism plays in Cherrie Moraga's *Loving in the War Years* (Walker 1993: 872-3). Haraway concludes that Moraga's writing marks her body as colored, thereby preventing her, as a fair-skinned woman not visibly Chicana, from passing as white. Yet what this argument does not consider, Walker points out, is that Moraga sees her lesbianism as marked on her body first, a realization that then fuels her understanding of racial difference (1993: 871). This slippage of lesbian identity that occurs at the intersection of race and sexuality, Walker concludes, contributes to the triple erasure of women of color who are femme lesbians: they are seen first as women of color, not lesbians; their skin color makes them unrecognized within the white lesbian community; and their particular sexual style renders them unrecognizable within the general lesbian community (1993: 886). The convergence of these layers of invisibility hinges upon the assumption that visible markers of difference—skin color along with gender performance—constitute the presence of difference itself.

In texts upheld as exemplars of locational feminism, such as June Jordan's **"Report from the Bahamas,"** analysis becomes constrained when the axis of vision encounters female-female desire, though Jordan's essay does illustrate quite powerfully the dynamic and contradictory nature of identity, as well as the equally complicated task of forging alliances with others. In it, Jordan retraces her movements on a vacation in the Bahamas and details her life in New York as a professor at a public university; she narrates her experiences as a professor, feminist activist, single mother and as an African-American woman with West Indian roots, and charts her growing awareness of how social encounters in different locations pull various aspects of her identity into play. While in the Bahamas, she expects to find identification on the level of race and gender with the Afro-Caribbean women there However, Jordan feels discomfort at the thought of haggling with "these other Black women" over the price of the hand-woven tokens they sell as most American tourists—black and white—tend to do:

> This is my consciousness of race and class and gender identity as I notice the fixed relations between these other Black women and myself. They sell and I buy or I don't. They risk not eating. I risk going broke on my first vacation afternoon. We are not particularly women anymore; we are parties to a transaction designed to set us against each other.

(1985: 41)

What Jordan finds is dis-identification with the Bahamian women she encounters, as gender is undone by difference: they are not "particularly women anymore". Her separation from them is echoed by the repeated reference to "these other Black women" throughout this section of the essay. Here, the products of colonization, racism, and economic oppression become the salient characteristics of identification and the dictators of affiliation, effectively complicating the connections that Jordan and the Bahamian women would make with each other based on gender alone. The consciousness-raising produced by these encounters becomes a haunting refrain throughout the essay. Using the formula "this is my consciousness of race and class and gender identity" (Jordan 1985: 41) to describe each situation, she continually modulates the phrase to capture the new combinations of race, class, and gender specific to each new context in which she finds herself. Jordan is aware that mapping (dis)identification along and across the lines of difference requires careful attention to how multiple alterities interact; she warns against using race, class, and gender as "automatic concepts of connection", acknowledging that however much they can indicate shared pain, as absolute foundations for connection "they seem about as reliable as precipitation probability for the day after the night before the day" (1985: 46).

While the essay paints an important picture of the complexity of affiliation building, its geographic epistemology benefits from visuality because Jordan's heightened consciousness about difference depends upon the markers on the bodies that she encounters: accents, hairstyle, skin color, clothing. It is the "frequently toothless Black women seated on the concrete in their only presentable dress", humbling themselves to the American's "careless" games at haggling, that fuel Jordan's considerations of her positionality (1985: 40). Visible markers clearly compel her to consider race and class in her interactions with her maid, Olive, as well.

In the leisure space of her hotel room, Olive's working class status comes into stark contrast with Jordan's position as an American tourist. After all, Jordan notes, "Olive is older than I am and I may smoke a cigarette while she changes the sheets on my bed" (1985: 41). Economic difference colludes with national difference and imperialism; the relative lack of power in Olive's low paying job is only heightened by the fact that the hotel in which she cleans is the tellingly named Sheraton British Colonial, and Jordan seems to bump into statues of Christopher Columbus, the western hemisphere's ur-colonizer, at every turn.

Yet while Jordan carefully considers the intersections among gender, race, nationality, and class, issues of sexuality remain under interrogated by the text's locational analysis. Though Jordan ruminates "This is my consciousness of race and class and gender identity as I . . ." (1985: 41), sexuality is never part of the list of categories that form Jordan's consciousness of her identity. In the case of her maid Olive, such signs as skin, accent, name card, and uniform usefully signal to Jordan how she might connect or disconnect with her through race, class, nationality, or gender. But what if Olive is a lesbian? Nowhere in the essay does Jordan contemplate Olive's sexuality, or directly identify her own sexual orientation. Clearly, Olive's skin and dress do not encourage Jordan to think about the role sexual identity plays in their interaction in the same way that they do race and class; this gap is not one that the essay recognizes as hindering full analysis of Jordan's shifting positionality. In fact, though Olive never actually speaks to her, the comment Jordan imagines she would make draws upon heterosexual discourse to fill the gap between visibility and knowledge. Jordan presumes that Olive would ask her where her husband is, saying that she would "probably allow herself one indignant query before righteously removing her vacuum cleaner from my room; 'and why in the first place you come down you without your husband?'" (1985: 41). Not only is Olive constructed as straight, but her question works to inscribe Jordan into heterosexuality as well.[10] The "indignant" and "righteous" posture Olive strikes thereby allows her "heterotexuality" to take on a particularly aggressive form. In the absence of visual markers to indicate otherwise, Olive's sexual options are limited to heterosexuality, which allows Jordan to take on the oppositional power that Olive has represented up to this point.

The unmarked potential in the essay for Olive to participate in female-female desire illuminates the larger issues at stake for the bisexual or femme lesbian in locational feminism. The hot pursuit of political visibility via bodily difference reifies a new binary of visible/invisible in which the femme lesbian in particular cannot win. The femme has always struggled to carve out a legitimate space for her desire for other women. The

butch lesbian's readily apparent challenge to traditional gender roles, in contrast, has been celebrated by feminists and lesbians alike (Grahn 1984), and this particular articulation of lesbian sexuality is becoming increasingly popular in the media, if we are to take the success of figures like K. D. Lang as any indicator (Stein 1994: 12-13). Much to the frustration of critics like Biddy Martin, less political potential is seen in the femme because her ability to visually subvert traditional scripts of gender and sexual desire is "compromised" by her ability to pass as a heterosexual woman.[11] While some theorists argue that the femme lesbian can in fact challenge heterosexist discourse through the parodic mimicry of heterosexual desire,[12] she is only visible when accompanied by her butch partner whose presence can make her desire signify as queer. As JoAnn Loulan points out, positing the femme lesbian's subversive potential in these terms defines her through her partner, just as heterosexual women have been defined through their husbands in patriarchal discourse (1990: 90). Instances of excess femininity do not always succeed in signaling a lesbian identity to all audiences. Carole-Anne Tyler identifies the limits of queer performances that do not always signify as subversive, pointing out that middle-class audiences might take Dolly Parton for a female impersonator, but for working-class audiences she might be the finest embodiment of natural femininity (1991: 57). It all depends upon the specificity of context, determined in large part by the dynamics between performer and audience.

Jordan's essay seemingly passes over the active role that lesbian sexuality might play in coalition and action as it focuses on connections between women based on "what we can do for each other" (1985: 47). While Jordan and Olive's fictional conversation indicates the beguiling ease with which locational feminism can assume straightness in the absence of visible difference—gender performativity or signs of butch behavior—Jordan's elusive response to Olive's imagined question, however, illustrates the way in which the relative lack of epistemological control over sexual identity can jam locational feminism's determination to map positionality. For even as Olive's question, "why in the first place you come down you without your husband?", participates in heterosexual discourse, Jordan's answer, set apart in its own paragraph, undermines it: "I cannot imagine how I would begin to answer her" (1985: 41). Not an admission of divorce, nor a declaration of privacy, Jordan's confession hints that her account of her own sexual identity cannot fit into a traditional fixed model, heterosexual or otherwise. Just two years before publishing **"Report"** [**"Report from the Bahamas"**], Jordan points to her "continuing self-denial around the 'issue' of my bisexuality" in her essay **"Civil Wars"** (1980: 110), effectively putting her bisexual identification into public circulation. And yet here, Jordan's response admits a curious inability to express herself, which acknowledges and masks the alternative sexualities that would fall outside of the heterosexual default zone. The open-endedness of her answer confronts the overall nature of gay and lesbian identity and the challenges in self-definition and self-disclosure. As Eve Sedgwick argues, homosexual identity, unlike race in most cases, is a debatable issue, wherein others feel free to question whether it is "just a phase", or how one "really" knows one is gay. These challenges, she argues, "reveal how problematical at present is the very concept of gay identity, as well as how intensively it is resisted and how far authority over its definition has been distanced from the gay subject her- or himself" (1990: 79). So even while Jordan's text reveals locational feminism's reliance upon visibility for markers of difference, it also illustrates the epistemological problem that a lesbian or bisexual identity would pose to efforts to fix its existence and chart its location.

Perhaps in placing Olive within a fixed, heterosexual category, Jordan actually creates an opportunity to stage for us her active refusal of the narrow sexual options of the dominant discourse. Jordan's position here echoes Marilyn Frye, who celebrates lesbian desire as existing beyond definitions, in a "strange nonlocation beyond the pale", dancing around "a region of cognitive gaps and negative semantic spaces" (1983: 154). The passage becomes an occasion for Jordan to leave all sexual possibilities open for herself, a multiplicity that is preserved by the absence of visible markers that could be used to "fix" her as a lesbian or as a bisexual. As part of her passionate pursuit of political equality, she claims that any type of sexual oppression or limitation preempts freedom at its most basic level. Bisexuality, she has said, is a kind of sexual freedom that is inseparable from freedom in general (Erickson 1994: 145). Her essay **"Bisexuality and Cultural Pluralism"** proclaims her to be a "sexual pluralist" in her rejection of heterosexuality as the dominant, supposedly singular sexual option, celebrating instead the boundlessness of sexual freedom. Though Jordan appeals to the category of bisexuality in several other essays as well as her love poetry, she revels in the fluid continuum of sexual object choice that is performed stylistically by her text:

> Given men who desire women and women who desire men and men who desire men and women who desire women and men who want to become women and women who want to become men and men who desire men and women both, and women who desire women and men both, what else could I be, besides a sexual pluralist?

> (1998: 137)

Just as the long subordinated clause here articulates a multiplicity of desire, so her open-ended response to Olive refuses to fix her own sexuality within the positional framework she has set up in this encounter

between North and South, rich and poor, educationally privileged and educationally poor. In this respect, Jordan's resistance to categorizing her own sexuality in **"Report from the Bahamas"** offers a silent protest against the fixing tendencies of locational feminism.

Like Jordan, Minnie Bruce Pratt also explores the complex and geographically contingent nature of identity, and yet her essay, "Identity: Skin Blood Heart", offers a model of locational analysis more overtly self-conscious about the limitations of vision. Although most critics celebrate Pratt's essay for checking Western feminism's blindness to its indifference to the experiences of women of color and Third World women, I find that it is instrumental in indicating how to extend locational feminism's ability to account for the nonvisible. Pratt's essay records her geographical and ideological movement away from her white, bourgeois, Southern upbringing, a nexus of privilege linked to her father. What enables this careful interrogation of her own privilege, according to Martin and Mohanty (1986: 193), is the rigorous attention she pays to the geography and architecture of the communities she finds herself in. For example, Pratt's father's habit of surveying the architecture of their town with an air of propriety from the courthouse tower symbolizes his patriarchal, white entitlement; he wants Pratt to climb the tower to take visual possession of the town as he had done as a boy. Pratt declines, however, saying:

> What I would have seen at the top: on the streets around the courthouse square, the Methodist Church, the limestone building with the county Health Department, Board of Education, Welfare Department (my mother worked there), the yellow brick Baptist church, the Gulf station, the pool hall (no women allowed) . . . Dr. Nicholson's office, one door for whites, one for Blacks . . . Yet I was shaped by my relation to those buildings and to the people in those buildings, by ideas of who should be working in the Board of Education, who should be in the bank handling money, of who should have the guns and the keys to the jail, of who should be in the jail; and I was shaped by what I didn't see, or didn't notice, on those streets.

> (1984: 17)

Pratt's rejection of the white privilege that she might share with her father is one of many rejections of privilege she discusses. In beginning a lesbian relationship, her desire alienates her from her father, strains her relationship with her mother, and, through the process of divorce, reduces her relationship with her children to the occasional, supervised visitation. This precipitates her growing awareness of how her position as someone who is upper-middle class, educated, and white entitles her to privilege in some contexts, while her lesbian identity and her gender deny it in others. A white lesbian living in a predominantly Black neighborhood in Washington, D.C., she discusses her geographic and economic marginalization from the white community and her racial and sexual marginalization from her neighbors. These complex displacements, significantly, do not completely insulate her from the history of her relationship to her father's white privilege, which Pratt thinks of in spatialized terms: "Each of us carries around those growing-up places, the institutions, a sort of back-drop, a stage-set" (1984: 17).

Pratt's use of space as a way to address privilege, however, does not rely solely upon visible markers of difference. One of the lessons that she learns is the danger of viewing geography as static and fixed. In looking back on her memory of what she left behind in the rural south, Pratt notes that she was "shaped by what I didn't see, or didn't notice, on those streets" (1984: 17). After gathering details about the history of her hometown's cruelty and mistreatment of African Americans, she notes that she learned "a way of looking at the world that is more accurate, complex, multi-layered, multi-dimensioned, more truthful" (Pratt 1984: 17). Pratt goes on to say, "I feel the *need* to look differently" because "I've learned that what is presented to me as an accurate view of the world is frequently a lie" (1984: 17). Though she repeatedly points to the importance of vision and geography in shaping identity, her solution is to develop a way of seeing beyond the simple appearances presented by her surroundings.

The significant qualifications her essay places on vision inform an awareness of the non-visibility of particular kinds of difference—Jewish identity as well as lesbian identity. Sexual desire, rather than race or class, becomes the impetus for her careful attempts to strip away privilege of all kinds; Pratt's lesbianism "broke through the bubble of skin and class privilege around me" (1984: 20), allowing her to understand her connections to other women's struggles, particularly to those who are different from herself. Yet she realizes how those sympathetic connections might be hampered by misrecognition. In describing her movements in her predominantly African-American neighborhood, arm in arm with her lover, she points out the relative invisibility of her lover's Jewish identity. To the black women in her building, Pratt and her lover "look like sisters, because we're close and they can see that we love each other" (1984: 13), despite the contrast between Pratt's blond hair and blue eyes and her lover's darker features. She wonders how the knowledge of her lover's Jewish identity might dampen the warmth of her black neighbor women and the friendliness of the white people they encounter. The slipperiness of identity categorization thus exceeds the type of knowledge that comes from visible appearance alone; for her neighbors would not only assume that they are both white, but they would also interpret their closeness as familial, and not as sexual. Pratt's self-consciousness about her sexual identity makes strikingly clear the tenuous

relationship between knowledge and vision. As she considers the privileges that she has given up for her lesbianism, she bemuses that she could very easily hide her sexual desire for women and thereby pass to her neighbors, as well to as the readers of her essay. Pratt observes, "I fit neatly into the narrow limits of what is 'normal' in this country. Like most lesbians, I don't fit the stereotype of what a lesbian looks like; unless my hair is cut quite short and unless I am wearing the comfortable, sturdy clothes and shoes that are called 'masculine', I look quite stereotypically 'American', like the girl in the toothpaste ad" (1984: 20). Acknowl-edging the dominant but single-sided view of the butch, she steps back from examining her relationship to place and location to reflect on what sometimes does not present itself in space—articulations of lesbian identity. Self-reflection, in this case, seems to enable a locational feminism that stops short of conflating political vis-ibility with measurable physical difference. Rather, the gaps that Pratt recognizes help to mark the places where locational feminism might not be able to map formulations of sexual desire, as well as other alterities, that are not easily seen.

Beyond merely marking what might be unseeable, or in the case of Jordan, that which resists categorization, I want to suggest that locational feminism needs to foreground more strongly the role that the temporal plays in analysis of space; by focusing more explicitly on history in its interpretation of place and positionality, locational feminism might avoid relying upon visual epistemologies and reifying visibility politics so problematic for certain kinds of subjects. While feminist theorists readily note the historical and dynamic dimen-sions to space, very rarely have they pointed to the critical need to actively pursue the kinds of histories that might not be readily apparent or visible in the spatial scene, particularly in the interactions between specific bodies.[13] As Liz Bondi warns in her survey of the field, geographical metaphors of contemporary politics, in order to be useful, "must be informed by conceptions of space that recognize place, position, location, and so on as *created,* as *produced*" (1993: 99). If we conceptualize a lesbian identity as a continual process of becoming, as Shane Phelan has argued, then locating historical as well as spatial coordinates seems crucial for understanding how sexual identity might be determined by space. The role of history in Pratt's nar-rative about coming into her sexual desire in this way enhances locational feminism's ability to register differ-ence. As Martin and Mohanty mention, Pratt's "personal history acquires a materiality in the constant rewriting of herself in relation to shifting interpersonal and politi-cal contexts" (1986: 210), and this strategy, they argue, could translate into a larger political collectivity in which the range of female sexual desire might be recognized. For Rich, personal history is also important: "I need to understand how a place on the map is also a place in history" (1986: 212). Although "Notes Toward a Politics of Location" is not without its problems, one of its strengths, as Kathleen Kirby points out, is its ability to "incorporate into our theoretical framework personal history and the particular shaping forces of specific kinds of bodies" (1996: 29). However, this attention to the importance of the temporal needs to go beyond the mere historicizing of the subject, and requires searching for the histories of the people one is surrounded by; the full solution lies in uncovering the situated histories of the other pieces on the chessboard, to use Alcoff's metaphor, in order to track forms of difference that resist fixity, continually reconstitute themselves, or are otherwise not necessarily visible.

Recognizing the limitations that visibility puts on locational analysis and looking for the histories behind various subjectivities better prepares us to consider location without mistaking alternative sexualities for straight, or reducing the sexual options to straight or butch. However, if we consider how locational feminism might work best, we also need to remain sensitive to the complicated relationships that lesbians have to metaphorical and real spaces. Since space has always (over) determined lesbian and gay identity, forms of sexual alterity have a very different relationship to metaphorical space than other kinds of difference. On one level, metaphorical space for homosexual identities, as Diana Fuss points out, revolves around the cultural opposition between heterosexuality and homosexuality, philosophically and politically conceived as "inside" and "outside" (1991: 1). Yet, the "out" position is not only the marginalized position in the hetero/homo binary; it is also bound up with the metaphor of the closet, suggesting the processes of coming out, a "movement into a metaphysics of presence, speech, and cultural visibility" (Fuss 1991: 4). It is at this level that political space and the space of being and identity become so tangled as to make fixed space of any kind impossible: "To be out, in common gay parlance, is precisely to be no longer out; to be out is to be finally outside of exteriority and all the exclusions and deprivations such outsiderhood imposes. Or, put another way, to be out is really to be in—inside the realm of the visible, the speakable, the culturally intelligible" (Fuss 1991: 4); control even over this paradox is unstable. Rather than a simple inversion of inside/outside, there are actually multiple insides and outsides that are themselves mutable. For the queer subject, articulating one's sexual identity from a position of strategic outsiderhood is a difficult project indeed, as boundaries and spaces, insides and outsides, carry with them different valences. As a result, there's no luxury of centrality from which to idealize the outside (Fuss 1991: 5) and the fixed, visible position from which subversive performativity might take shape. And yet whatever strategic potential destabilized space offers is also a horizon from which lesbian and gay subjectivity can never fully be free. Fuss notes that the

"figure inside/outside cannot be easily or ever finally dispensed with; it can only be worked on and worked over—itself turned inside out to expose its critical operations and interior machinery" (1991: 1).

While Jordan's essay, for instance, refuses fixity on one level, its play with Jordan's sexuality necessarily negotiates the various and shifting levels of metaphorical space bound up with the terms of the closet. In answering Olive's question about her husband, Jordan's indeterminate response, "I cannot imagine how I would begin to answer her", may signify her bisexuality to those in her readership who already know, constituting her as "out" in this sense, but constituting her as "in" to those new to her work. For as several queer theorists have observed, speaking one's sexual identity or coming out, as Jordan in a sense does here, actually has the effect of creating more closets. As Butler notes, for gays and lesbians the work of complete self-assertion and circulation of public knowledge is never over (1991: 15-16). The effect of Jordan's essay is the prying open of these shifting and multiplying spaces, which are as difficult to see as they are to pinpoint and map.

Considering locational feminism in relation to cultural practice also requires that we theorize lesbians' and bisexuals' relationship to material space. For many lesbians, to be in a public space in the first place dictates that desire must be routed into the private sphere. Gill Valentine notes that a recent US survey found that heterosexuals commonly have no objection to homosexuals provided their sexuality is not flaunted in public. Yet this routing of homosexuality to the private sphere is based on the premise that the public sphere is neutral, that heterosexuality is also limited to private space. In fact, the heterosexual nature of public space is naturalized through repeated performances of heterosexual desire and culture, causing most lesbians and gays to veil their sexuality in public (Valentine 1996: 146). In the event that lesbians and gays do not, public order laws are often brought to bear on them in discriminatory ways or citizens use violence to "stabilize the heterosexuality of the street" (Valentine 1996: 148).

Even when lesbians do carve out a safe space for themselves in the public sphere, they expose themselves to health risks that are unique to their experience. The public spaces that lesbians claim for themselves often bring with them the dangers of alcoholism and substance abuse. In the US in the 1950s, lesbians were marginally successful at creating social institutions, such as softball leagues, that would offer socializing opportunities. Lesbian bars became an important meeting place, since they were public, roomy and yet separated out from the mainstream public enough so as to ensure privacy, where lesbians could socialize in a reasonably safe atmosphere (Faderman 1991: 161; Kennedy and Davis 1993: 29).[14] These bars fostered a sense of community and common culture, since lesbians often had to work together to identify which bars were problematic and which would be safe (Kennedy and Davis 1993: 65). Working-class lesbians in the 1950s experienced pressure to drink while at these bars; Faderman notes that "alcoholism was high among women who frequented the bars, much more prevalent, in fact, than among their heterosexual working-class counterparts" (1991: 163). Drinking and substance abuse became a particularly seductive outlet for many lesbians who had to endure the pressure of working at low-paying jobs at a time when few women were entering the workforce. Alcoholism continued in the 1970s despite the advances women made in the business world and, even with the successes of the "clean and sober" efforts of the 1980s (Faderman 1991: 282-3), it remains an important issue.

CONCLUSION

It is no wonder that locational feminism has used geography to expand its capabilities. As Friedman has observed, this approach has reinvigorated feminism as a singular movement unified around gender even as it wields viable explanatory power for a wide range of female experience (1998:4). Spatial rhetoric has retained a sustained focus on gender, but at the same time it facilitates considering the relationship between gender and other constituents of identity (Friedman 1998: 17). In the process, it encourages greater cross-pollinations of theory and experience based on different identity categories within the space of a single movement.

Not only does space concretize a coherent, inclusive feminism, but it also makes the strange familiar. As Smith and Katz observe, metaphor works by using one familiar meaning system, the source domain, to clarify another unfamiliar system. It is precisely the familiarity of space that makes it attractive as a metaphoric tool (1993: 69). This recourse to spatial metaphor is symptomatic of the inadequacy of language, which becomes an opportunity, as Kirby argues, for us to "flesh out" the materiality of the signified. Despite the fact that post-structuralist theorists have tried to "loosen the link between 'language' and the real'", language is nevertheless "predicated on, and enabled by, an idea of correspondence of words to 'things'—to objects, which are necessarily dimensional and necessarily exist in space, even when this substantiality appears only in the dimensionality of signifieds" (1996: 5).[15]

Yet in our intense longing for a problem-free language that would bring us closer to the objects of our theoretical inquiry, we need to confront the blindnesses that accompany spatial rhetoric. As Edward Soja points out in *Postmodern Geographies,* "[w]e must be insistently aware of how space can be made to hide consequences from us, how relations of power and discipline are inscribed into the apparently innocent spatiality of social life, how human geographies become filled with politics and ideology" (1989: 6). For locational feminism, the heft and feel of the familiar often masks the social and ideological challenges posed by the surroundings that we perceive. What is masked for aspects of lesbian desire is the fact that it is often unseeable in a specular economy that has come to prize queer performativity, and in the wake of attempts to make gay and lesbian desire visible to the public through gender inversion, the presence of the lesbian femme seems particularly precarious. More attention needs to be focused on the ways that locational feminism can account for aspects of sexuality that do not present difference by sight.

The attempt to map and mark difference hits on the tension in queer theory and lesbian studies between viewing the homosexual as a fixed, oppositional category, and viewing it as unstable, shifting, and erotically elusive. Whereas a gay sexuality posits a relatively stable identity, mappable onto fixed locations, queer sexuality, as Nancy Duncan notes, conveys a "destabilizing oppositional politics of sexuality which is associated with a fluid spatiality and multiplying and moveable sites or resistance" (1996: 246). Locational feminism seems caught between dual impulses, to both recognize fluidity when it is salient, and map positionality so as to make power relations visible, familiar. The use of space needs to be accompanied by a similar sensitivity to the way in which space (over)determines lesbian identities on multiple and mutable levels. Addressing these issues seems integral to constructing a singular feminism, geographically inflected, that is as careful in examining the intersections of sexuality with other forms of alterity as it has been in examining the intersections of gender with other forms of alterity.

Notes

1. For feminist theorists who draw upon ideas of location, see Anzaldúa (1987), Bondi (1993), Kaplan (1996), Duncan (1996), Friedman (1998), Higonnet (1994), McDowell (1996), and Rose (1993).

2. For discussion of the locational strategies in Jordan, see Friedman (1998: 48-51). For discussions of Pratt and location, see Martin and Mohanty (1986), Rose (1993: 156-9), Kirby (1996: 12), Friedman (1998: 50).

3. This paper targets the non-visible aspects of female-female desire and sexual behavior that the discourse and practice of location excludes. I do not assume that all lesbians fall into categories of either butch (which visually performs sexuality) or femme (which is visually indistinguishable from heterosexuality). However, the butch/femme binary is reified by the categories of visible/invisible maintained by the politics of visibility. Therefore, I use the terms "unseen" or "nonvisible" to recognize the range of sexual identities, but where I touch upon binarized butch/femme positions, I use the terms "visible" and "invisible".

4. For discussion of racial instability and passing, see Ahmed (1999).

5. See Butler (1993; 1991), de Lauretis (1993), and Case (1989).

6. See Foucault's *Discipline and Punish* for the role of surveillance (1979). This emphasis on vision resonates with a number of years of feminist theory, particularly the critique of the specular economy of western thought in Irigaray's *Speculum of the Other Woman* (1985), and the Lacanian feminist critique of the male gaze in film studies that we see advanced by Mulvey (1989) among others. For the role of the gaze in the visual arts in general, see Berger (1972), and for the connection between vision and colonialism, see M. L. Pratt (1992).

7. See Weigman (1995: 9), Fraser (1999: 110), and Phelan, P. (1993: 2).

8. Kathleen Kirby provides an overview in *Indifferent Boundaries* of the role vision plays in subject formation in psychoanalytic and film theory (1996: 122-45).

9. For discussion of the relationship between skin color and racial identification, see Ahmed (1998).

10. And yet, Olive's question about her husband might, on another level, operate as an indirect way to feel out Jordan's sexual preference. After all, if Olive were a man asking this question, alone in a hotel room with a female tourist, sexual attraction would be as likely a subtext as any. Olive's supposed impatience suggests this could be an erotic challenge to Jordan's presumed heterosexual status. However, Jordan's aligning of Olive with the loyal wife of the Talmudic scholar-father in Anzia Yezierska's *The Bread Givers* (1985: 42) links her to heterosexuality. Perhaps Olive's presumed heterosexuality reflects upon locational reading strategies, given the heterosexual imperative's strong foothold in some Afro-Caribbean cultures.

11. The femme lesbian has fared unfavorably when compared to the butch's more aggressive stance; since, as Pat Califia notes, femmes are sometimes seen by butch lesbians as passively finding a refuge from patriarchy in lesbianism (1992: 10-11). Biddy Martin defends the femme lesbian from assertions that, when not camped up, she is capitulating to patriarchy (1996: 73).

12. See Butler (1990: 123), Case (1989: 294), and Tyler (1991: 55).

13. Though Kaplan's work does not focus on the unique problems that sexuality poses, her recent study *Questions of Travel* astutely articulates the need for locational theory to consider history and process in order to address national, racial, economic, and gender differences in the global arena (1996). Mariam Fraser also focuses on the relationship between the spatial and temporal in her analysis of queer performativity and class (1999).

14. Karla Jay (1999) points out that though these bars did, in fact, provide a space in which lesbians could socialize, mafia ownership or control resulted in lesbians being overcharged or treated like perverts.

15. In Lacanian psychoanalysis, the "real" lies beyond signification and language, and yet can only be accessed through the signifiers that language gives us. Spatial theory, in Kirby's view, gives us the illusion of coming closer to the real by giving more body to the materiality of the signifiers themselves.

References

Ahmed, S. 1998: Animated Borders: Skin, Colour and Tanning. In M. Shildrick and J. Price (eds), *Vital Signs: Feminist Reconfigurations of the Bio/logical Body,* Edinburgh: Edinburgh University Press, 45-65.

———. 1999: She'll Wake Up One of These Days and Find She's Turned into a Nigger: Passing through Hybridity. *Theory, Culture, and Society* 16 (2), 87-106.

Alcoff, L. 1988: Cultural Feminism Versus Poststructuralism: The Identity Crisis in Feminist Theory. *Signs* 13 (3), 405-36.

Anzaldúa, G. 1987: *Borderlands/La Frontera: The New Mestiza.* San Francisco: Spinsters/Aunt Lute.

Berger, J. 1972: *Ways of Seeing.* London: Penguin.

Butler, J. 1990: *Gender Trouble: Feminism and the Subversion of Identity.* New York: Routledge.

———. 1991: Imitation and Gender Insubordination. In D. Fuss (ed.), *Inside/Out: Lesbian Theories, Gay Theories,* New York/London: Routledge, 13-32.

———. 1993: *Bodies that Matter: On the Discursive Limits of "Sex".* New York/London: Routledge.

Bondi, L. 1993: Locating Identity Politics. In M. Keith and S. Pile (eds), *Place and the Politics of Identity,* London/New York: Routledge, 84-101.

Califia, P. 1992: Clit Culture: Cherchez La Femme . . . *On Our Backs* 8 (4), 10-11.

Case, S. E. 1989: Toward a Butch-Femme Aesthetic. In L. Hart (ed.), *Making A Spectacle,* Ann Arbor, Michigan: University of Michigan Press, 282-99.

Crary, J. 1993: *Techniques of the Observer: On Vision and Modernity in the Nineteenth Century.* Cambridge, MA: MIT Press.

de Lauretis, T. 1993: Sexual Indifference/Lesbian Representation. In H. Abelove, M. A. Barale, and D. M. Halperin (eds), *The Gay and Lesbian Studies Reader,* New York/London: Routledge, 141-58.

Duncan, N. (ed.) 1996: *Bodyspace: Destabilizing Geographies of Gender and Sexuality.* London/New York: Routledge, 245-7.

Erickson, P. 1994: After Identity: A Conversation with June Jordan and Peter Erickson. *Transition* 63, 133-49.

Faderman, L. 1991: *Odd Girls and Twilight Lovers: A History of Lesbian Life in Twentieth-Century America.* New York: Penguin.

Foucault, M. 1979: *Discipline and Punish: The Birth of the Prison.* A. Sheridan (trans.). New York: Vintage.

Fraser, M. 1999: Classing Queer: Politics in Competition. *Theory, Culture & Society* 16 (2), 108-31.

Friedman, S. S. 1998: *Mappings: Feminism and the Cultural Geographies of Encounter.* Princeton, New Jersey: Princeton University Press.

Frye, M. 1983: *The Politics of Reality: Essays in Feminist Theory.* Trumansberg, New York: The Crossing Press.

Fuss, D. 1989: *Essentially Speaking: Feminism, Nature, and Difference.* New York: Routledge.

———. (ed.) 1991: *Inside/Out: Lesbian Theories, Gay Theories.* New York/London: Routledge, 1-12.

Grahn, J. 1984: *Another Mother Tongue: Gay Words, Gay Worlds.* Boston: Beacon.

Haraway, D. 1991: *Simians, Cyborgs, and Women: The Reinvention of Nature.* London: Free Association Books.

Higonet, M. and Templeton, J. (eds). 1994: *Reconfigured Spheres: Feminist Explorations of Literary Space.* Amherst: University of Massachusetts Press.

Irigaray, L. 1985: *Speculum of the Other Woman.* G. C. Gill (trans.). Ithaca, NY: Cornell University Press.

Jay, K. 1999: *Tales of the Lavender Menace: A Memoir of Liberation.* New York: Basic Books.

Jay, M. 1992: Scopic Regimes of Modernity. In S. Lash and J. Friedman (eds), *Modernity and Identity,* Oxford/Cambridge, MA: Blackwell, 178-95.

Jordan, J. 1985: Report from the Bahamas. In *On Call: Political Essays.* Boston: South End Press, 39-49.

———. 1989: Civil Wars. In *Moving Towards Home: Political Essays.* New York: Virago, 107-15.

———. 1998: On Bisexuality and Cultural Pluralism. In *Affirmative Acts: Political Essays.* New York: Anchor Books, 132-8.

Kaplan, C. 1996: *Questions of Travel: Postmodern Discourses of Displacement.* Durham, North Carolina: Duke University Press.

Kennedy, E. L. and Davis, M. D. (eds) 1993: *Boots of Leather, Slippers of Gold.* New York: Penguin.

Kirby, K. 1996: *Indifferent Boundaries: Spatial Concepts of Human Subjectivity.* New York: Guilford.

Loulan, J. 1990: *The Lesbian Erotic Dance: Butch, Femme, Androgyny and Other Rhythms.* San Francisco: Spinsters Press.

Martin, B. 1996: *Femininity Played Straight: The Significance of Being Lesbian.* New York/London: Routledge.

——— and Mohanty, C. T. 1986: What's Home Got to Do With It? In T. de Lauretis (ed.), *Feminist Studies/Critical Studies.* Bloomington, Indiana: Indiana University Press, 191-212.

McDowell, L. 1996: Spatializing Feminism: Geographic Perspectives. In N. Duncan (ed.), *Bodyspace: Destabilizing Geographies of Gender and Sexuality,* London/New York: Routledge, 28-44.

Mulvey, L. 1989: *Visual and Other Pleasures.* Bloomington, IN: Indiana University Press.

Phelan, P. 1993: *Unmarked: The Politics of Performance.* London/New York: Routledge.

Phelan, S. 1993: (Be)Coming Out: Lesbian Identity and Politics. *Signs* 18 (4), 765-90.

Pratt, M. L. 1992: *Imperial Eyes: Travel Writing and Transculturation.* London/New York: Routledge.

Pratt, M. B. 1984: Identity: Skin Blood Heart. In E. Bulkin, M. B. Pratt, and B. Smith (eds), *Yours in Struggle: Three Feminist Perspectives on Anti-Semitism and Racism.* Brooklyn, NY: Long Haul Press, 9-64.

Rich, A. 1986: Notes Toward a Politics of Location. In *Blood, Bread, and Poetry: Selected Prose, 1979-1985.* New York: Norton, 210-31.

Rose, G. 1993: *Feminism and Geography: The Limits of Geographical Knowledge.* Minneapolis, Minnesota: University of Minnesota Press.

Sedgwick, E. K. 1990: *The Epistemology of the Closet.* Berkeley, CA: University of California Press.

Smith and Katz, C. 1993: Grounding Metaphor: Towards a Spatialized Politics. In M. Keith and S. Pile (eds), *Place and the Politics of Identity.* London/New York: Routledge, 67-83.

Soja, E. 1989: *Postmodern Geographies: The Reassertion of Space in Critical Social Theory.* London: Verso.

Stein, A. 1994: Crossover Dreams: Lesbianism and Popular Music Since the 1970s. In D. Hamer and B. Budge (eds), *The Good, the Bad, and the Gorgeous: Popular Culture's Romance with Lesbianism,* London: Pandora, 15-27.

Tyler, C. A. 1991: Boys Will Be Girls: The Politics of Gay Drag. In D. Fuss (ed.), *Inside/Out: Lesbian Theories, Gay Theories,* New York/London: Routledge, 32-70.

Valentine, G. 1996: (Re)Negotiating the "Heterosexual Street": Lesbian Productions of Space. In N. Duncan (ed.), *Bodyspace: Destabilizing Geographies of Gender and Sexuality,* London/New York: Routledge, 146-55.

Walker, L. 1993: How to Recognize a Lesbian: The Cultural Politics of Looking Like What You Are. *Signs* 18 (4), 866-90.

Warner, M. 1992: From Queer to Eternity: An Army of Theorists Cannot Fail. *The Voice Literary Supplement* 37 (23), 17.

Weigman, R. 1995: *American Anatomies: Theorizing Race and Gender.* Durham, North Carolina: Duke University Press.

Yeager, P. (ed.) 1996: *The Geography of Identity.* Ann Arbor, Michigan: University of Michigan Press, 1-38.

Brian Norman (essay date 2004)

SOURCE: Norman, Brian. "June Jordan's Manifest New Destiny: Allegiance, Renunciation, and Partial Citizens, Claims on the State." *Michigan Feminist Studies,* no. 18 (2004): 77-96.

[*In the following essay, Norman evaluates Jordan's notions of citizenship and identity as expressed in her essays.*]

"I'm saying let's make it 84 percent turnout in two years, and then see what happens!"

. . . "Oh, yes! Vote! Dress yourself up, and vote! Even if you only go into the voting booth and pray. Do that!"

Bernice Johnson Reagon and Toni Morrison on the 2000 Presidential election in June Jordan's essay, **"The Invisible People: An Unsolicited Report on Black Rage"** (2001)[1]

June Jordan, noted Black feminist writer and activist, consistently called our attention to the lines that divide us—be they de facto racial segregation or rigorously policed national borders—throughout her poetry, essays, and novels that span the last thirty years. In her recent autobiography, she describes her experience of being one of the first African-Americans to enroll (on scholarship) at previously all white elite private schools, "I was the 'only' one . . . I felt outnumbered. I was surrounded by 'them.' And there was no 'we.' There was only 'me.' I didn't like it."[2] Her subsequent career is marked by attempts to build real collectivity amidst diverse constituents from her own experience of crossing social and political borders into potentially hostile terrain. In her third collection of essays, *Technical Difficulties: African-American Notes on the State of the*

Union (1992), Jordan proposes a Manifest New Destiny to achieve equity for those members of the American polity who often find themselves under siege by nativist and ethnocentric nationalist discourses, and sometimes by actions of the nation-state itself. Immigration scholar Mae Ngai chronicles how such outsiders within national borders construct the boundaries of American-ness itself, especially the figure of "alien citizens": persons who may be formal American citizens (whether by birth or by naturalization) but who are nevertheless presumed to be foreign by the mainstream of American culture and, at times, by state practices on the lookout for illegal aliens.[3] In response, rather than let invocations of the authority of the nation-state ensnare those who are caught inside its hostile borders, Jordan reclaims the very language of democracy. Jordan draws on the experiences of refugees, those once discussed as "The Negro Problem," American Japanese in the 1940s, and displaced Native Americans in her response to the violent expansionist project of American Manifest Destiny. Rather than solely protest the historical devastation of an American border that mowed down those who found themselves on its outward path, Jordan inhabits nationalist rhetoric to invoke an alternative "destiny that will carry us . . . into an educated, collective vision of a really democratic, really humane, a really good time."[4]

Jordan is aware in her essays that the state provides a powerful rhetorical apparatus to seek justice for those living within the nation-state, and perhaps for those not entirely circumscribed by its inclusive pronouncements of liberal democracy (refugees, second class citizens, new immigrants, formal or informal aliens, global citizens under the umber of American imperialism, etc.). In 1992, as the U.S. was just emerging from its first Iraq War, and having launched a new era of American imperialism, Jordan issued a collection of essays under the banner of an African-American State of the Union Address. Jordan was responding in part to George H. W. Bush's celebration of the ascendance of U.S. global hegemony in his 1992 State of the Union Address. "A world once divided into two armed camps," he opined, "now recognizes one sole and preeminent power the United States of America. And they regard this with no dread. For the world trusts us with power, and the world is right. They trust us to be fair and restrained. They trust us to be on the side of decency. They trust us to do what's right."[5] For Jordan, it was important not only to protest U.S. violence throughout the globe, but also to claim the very authority of speaking on behalf of a national people from a location outside the halls of power from which the Union is typically addressed.

In this article, I theorize the figure of the "partial citizen speaking" in order to understand the public space of dissent that writers like Jordan forge by simultaneously claiming and critiquing both the rhetoric and the forms of state pronouncements of full social and political membership for all. Squarely within the borders of the nation-state, Jordan stakes claims to the very national myths that often threaten her own existence and those for whom she speaks. Also, following Jordan's own entrance into political spokesmanship through a Black Arts Movement concerned with racial authenticity and self-determination, Jordan's constant focus on the specificity of her own experience allows us to underscore the variety of partial access to citizenship harbored by those swept up by universalist national myths and pronouncements—a variety both in terms of categories of identity familiar to feminist and critical race studies debates of the 1980s and 1990s about the need to address "difference," as well as to different manifestations of citizenship itself: as the ability to make formal claims upon the state, as legal status, as membership in a bounded community, as participation in civic activities and publics, and, most recently, as a diasporic connection to a community that crosses nation-state borders. More so than earlier conceptions of second-class citizenship which focused on identity-based barriers to full citizenship internal to the borders of the nation-state,[6] Jordan's determined focus on her own complex identity (as immigrant, as educated, as activist, as woman, as black, as queer, as writer) allows us to conceive of a theory of partial citizenship that accounts for specific histories and practices of subjugation and meted out privileges of specific groups or identities by the state. Whereas an older conception of citizenship simply as a formal legal status might presume the borders—geographic and ideological as much as legal—of the nation state, partial citizenship allows us to pay specific attention to how universalist conceptions of citizenship that exist amidst state practices of exclusion offer an apparatus of rhetorical power even to those the nation-state renders invisible under the umber of national pronouncements of achieved equality for all. For, even though full membership and participation in the political community may escape some of those who successfully cross U.S. borders, the universalist myths in operation within those borders may be taken up by those never meant to take such promises at face value.

I will begin by looking briefly at how the U.S. constructs and polices its borders, specifically at the site of the Citizenship Oath, in which a focus on external division suppresses or precludes internal division. While most studies of citizenship and the nation-state either focus on internal division or external exclusion, Jordan assumes a simultaneous glance outward and inward, both near and far sighted, both global and local. In this way, Jordan offers us a means of attending to both domestic inequality and imperial violence by acknowledging—and claiming—the enduring power of the nation-state.

I. To Cross Hostile Borders: Oaths of Citizenship[7]

On September 17, 2003, Citizenship Day, the U.S. was to adopt a new version of its Oath of Allegiance. The updated version would modernize the oath's rhetoric by removing cumbersome words like "abjure" and dropping anachronistic references like "potentate." Thus the oral recitation marking the entrance into citizenship would become more meaningful—and more manageable—for the millions of immigrants eligible for naturalization. The revised version, however, was quickly canned following a controversy in which conservative organizations, senators, and other loud political leaders decried what they saw as an attack on a "timeless" document and a weakening of the military obligation foundational to entrance into the American citizenry.[8] Reporter Shweta Govindarajan quotes Department of Homeland Security Director Tom Ridge, "'I am concerned that this construction diminishes and confuses the "true faith and allegiance" . . . necessary to foster a new citizen's ongoing attachment to this country,'"[9] The Heritage Foundation, one conservative think tank opposing the perceived "attack" on citizenship, issued an executive statement against "the Department of Homeland Security's misguided attempts to make U.S. citizenship more 'user-friendly' for those who want the benefits of our country, but don't care to accept the responsibility."[10]

Indeed, the thwarted attempt to make citizenship procedures more welcoming arose at a curious time. Iris Marion Young has tracked the recent manifestation of the long history of hostile U.S. borders that has resulted from the current presidential administration's fear mongering and vision of the government as masculinist protector of its citizens from external threat. For Young, focusing on external threat inscribes a tyrannical structure of dependence and an erosion of citizenship rights, which corresponds significantly to what an earlier generation of feminist scholars identified as the patriarchal family. Young explores how the rise of the current U.S. security state after fall 2001 "illuminates the meaning and effective appeal of a security state that wages war abroad and expects obedience and loyalty at home . . . To the extent that citizens of a democratic state allow their leaders to adopt a stance of protectors toward them, these citizens come to occupy a subordinate status like that of women in the patriarchal household."[11] The effect, according to Young, is the creation of a subordinate citizen: a citizen willing to give up her rights without hesitation in the name of security. In this world of masculinist protection, the Bush administration renamed the infamous INS[12] and placed it under the newly formed Department of Homeland Security. The consolidation of citizenship services and disparate border policing programs further bolsters the longstanding scrutiny of immigrants for their ideological commitment and adherence to going national ideals.

Naturalization procedures, inasmuch as they serve as an index of the permeability or rigidity of borders, require a uniform recitation of unhesitant adherence to official doctrines—and a stated commitment to fight and die for those ideals. The Citizenship Oath demonstrates how the figure of the immigrant undergoes rigorous scrutiny and thus defines the borders of America and, by extension, who is allowed to speak on behalf of the nation.[13] However, the specter of the immigrant also serves as an exculpatory device regarding preexisting inequities because it obscures internal division and dissent.[14] While immigrants perform allegiance publicly to obtain citizenship status, birthright citizens (whether by *ius soli* or *ius sanguinis*) are presumed to have been born with a natural allegiance that precludes multiple allegiances to ideologies, projects, or potentates outside national borders. What currently remains in the two versions of the citizenship oath, and what will surely remain in any accepted future version, is the idea that the entrance into full membership via naturalization requires a simultaneous oath of allegiance and renunciation. That is, entrance into the nation-state requires exit—ideological more than geographic—from the newly naturalized citizen's former home country. Though scholars of diasporic and cosmopolitan identities have attempted to dislodge the total decisiveness of the nation-state in the arena of citizenship,[15] official American articulations of citizenship adhere to a longstanding phenomenon where inclusion within the polity requires a simultaneous exclusion or renunciation.

Or, in the realm of rhetoric, any articulation of a "we" requires a simultaneous citation of a "not-we." At the heart of citizenship in particular, and collectivity in general, is a *cleavage*: a coming together made possible by a splitting apart. The border—whether open or closed, hostile or welcoming—continues to constitute the collective, as well as to suppress internal division. Ideas about the necessity of pairing exclusive ideological commitment with citizenship are as old as the American nation, notwithstanding the tremendous volume of announcements of a new world order in the wake of the attacks on the U.S. in Fall 2001. It is not mere historical curiosity that the notorious utterance of "We" in the Action of the Second Continental Congress popularly known as the Declaration of Independence is forged in direct opposition to a "He" (King George III)—repeated no less than nineteen times in the short document. In contrast, "we" appears only eleven times in the document designed to create an American people. What the Declaration shows, and what the Oath of Allegiance insists, is that the constitution of a bounded polity in America emphasizes external difference in order to create the semblance of an internally homoge-

neous "we." Thus arises the potency of national documents that announce equality amidst a decidedly unequal social order. These documents provide the ring of broad inclusion for what Rogers M. Smith has described as "civic myths": ideals of full equality that politicians and other leaders cite enthusiastically without worrying about the veracity of the myths for the everyday lives of the citizenry.[16]

Yet many have found authoritative "civic myths" quite useful for progressive calls for social justice. In this tradition arises a figure that threatens the fragile story of a finished "we" based on uniform allegiance: the partial citizen speaking.[17] The partial citizen speaking—from experience, on behalf of others—and addressing the real divisions within a national audience is situated at a strategic site at which to simultaneously claim and critique the inclusive pronouncements of the American Republic in order to make them real. A notable historical example is the ex-slave Frederick Douglass who, having been invited to celebrate the nation in 1848, capitalized on his tenuous claim to citizenship and delivered the speech "What to the Slave Is the Fourth of July?" In the speech, Douglass excoriates his audience in Rochester, New York on behalf of slaves who are absent because they are toiling on Southern plantations. To his "fellow-citizens" Douglass cries, "This Fourth of July is *yours* not *mine. You* may rejoice, *I* must mourn."[18]

Protest writers in Douglass' tradition speak on behalf of constituents who seek claim to the full social participation and equality promised by a national "we." In their Statement of Conscience, for instance, the Not In Our Name Coalition, a loose knit group formed in 2002 in direct response to Bush's plans for pre-emptive war in Iraq—and probably elsewhere—and his implicit arrogant use of a rhetoric of national unity for imperialist aggression, the real political capital of the ability to articulate a national "we" is at stake. The group declares, "We believe that people of conscience must take responsibility for what their own governments do—we must first of all oppose the injustice that is done in our own name."[19] In contradistinction to leaders' duplicitous uses of civic myths eschewed by Rogers M. Smith, protest writers like Jordan and the Not In Our Name Coalition use what claims to citizenship they might have in order to gain a toehold on the viable, but unfinished project of full democracy for all. They simultaneously claim and critique the potentially hollow rhetorical space of a national "we." And in doing so, the rhetorical space of "we" is able to foster real collectivity, be it at specific protest rallies or within political dialogue made more cautious and aware of the necessity of careful use of collective utterances. By claiming the essential American-ness of their projects, protest writers can work within national rhetoric in order to position their present projects as the fulfillment of previous national promises. In her study of foreigners' critiques of America, Bonnie Honig shows how "[Foreigners] make room for themselves by staging nonexistent rights, and by way of such stagings, sometimes, new rights, powers, and visions come into being."[20] By looking at Jordan's space of rhetorical address to a deeply divided nation, we can see similar "stagings" by those already *inside* presumed national borders who have been denied full access to, or enjoyment of civic, economic, and/or social rights. These partial citizens speaking and writing stage heretofore nonexistent rights by claiming preexisting civic myths by, for, and on behalf of voices that were never meant to speak such civic myths as truths.

II. SPEAKING WITHIN HOSTILE BORDERS: JUNE JORDAN'S STATE OF THE UNION ADDRESS

By presenting her essays under the banner of a response to a State of the Union Address, Jordan explicitly claims the language of democracy and the rhetorical forms of the state. At the same time that she inhabits state authority as a rightful heir, however, she attends to the location of speaking—her own or those for whom she speaks—as outside the intended limits of full membership in the nation-state: first generation West Indian immigrants, African-Americans living under the residue of second-class citizenship, political refugees, or anyone who has been constructed by official state discourse as "fringe or freak components of some theoretical nether land" (198)—the people who make up the inclusive nation she invokes her Manifest New Destiny. Though Jordan demands that we account for our specific locations and make use of our partial access to citizenship and the authority of the nation-state, the space she opens under the banner of "we", like its predecessor "We the people," allows access to a collective space precisely by attending to internal differences within the universalist-minded "we."

The theme of creating collectivity by *addressing* internal division and locational difference is constant throughout Jordan's long career. Much of Jordan's early work was published alongside other African-American women writers gaining recognition in the 1970s by a Black Arts movement and by an emergent feminist movement. Jordan directed much of her energy and early work toward black women, and she sustained a commitment to Black English. Jordan's particular rise to prominence is due in large part to feminists who valued creative work for its ability to bring the diverse personal experiences of women into the public sphere. Jordan's poetry in the 1970s exhibits a personal politics that places black women's experiences at the center of political analysis. In **"Poem about My Rights"** (1980),[21] one of her most anthologized poems, Jordan directly connects the speaker's experience of rape with the invasion of Namibia by South Africa. Jordan's early ability to

achieve geopolitical critique by attending to—and demanding—a specific location and experience of speaking are prescient to her later strategy of claiming the seemingly general pronouncements of the state from particular locations within its borders where inclusive pronouncements might prove untrue when measured against practice. If one partial citizen's experience or identity does not appear in Jordan's long but necessarily unfinished catalog of oppression and injustice, she nevertheless offers a blueprint on how to access the nation-state without erasing one's background.

Jordan became one of the first African American women to publish a book length collection of her own essays with the nation-state-minded title *Civil Wars* in 1981. In her four subsequent essay collections and regular columns in *The Progressive,* Jordan fashioned a "political essay" genre by writing about key national events from the specific perspective of an African American woman deeply committed to democracy, justice, and global solidarity. In her essays and speeches, Jordan is aware of her speaking voice as a "black spokesperson" addressing audiences divided along multiple and contradictory lines.[22] Jordan's strategic use of state-endorsed rhetoric of inclusion under girds her nationally focused work on civil rights and bisexual identity, for example, as well as her international focus on the Vietnam war, South African apartheid, Palestine, Nicaragua, Lebanon, the gulf war, and terrorism. At the same time that she celebrates lofty goals of democracy, Jordan rigorously seeks out voices of displaced peoples, both within the polity of the nation-state and beyond, and both within the groups that claim her as spokesperson and beyond.[23]

Jordan's focus on the creation of and identification with collectivity and particularized publics helps us to reimagine the relationship between citizenship and protest. The most obvious starting point for a project about a protest essay tradition might initially seem to be, say, Henry David Thoreau's "Civil Disobedience" (1849) as a precursor to, say, Martin Luther King's "A Letter from Birmingham City Jail" (1963). But given Jordan's goal of fostering collectivity in her African-American State of the Union Address, Thoreau's essay, originally titled "Resistance to Civil Government," and his rhetorical strategy of individualist protest becomes potentially suspicious. In response to those state-sponsored actions that he finds disagreeable (be it the Mexican War, the fugitive slave law, or government taxes in support of clergymen), Thoreau rails against an unthinking adherence to the state, and obedience that threatens "the progress toward a true respect for the individual"[24] (1719). Thoreau urges the questioning of the state from a position of privilege: choosing not to support financially those specific unacceptable state-sponsored endeavors by claiming a tradition greater than the immediate state (of natural rights, of democracy, of revolutionary independence). His strategy, though, is total refusal of civic participation via taxation generally; paradoxically, he calls for divestment within a public address. In short, Thoreau calls for individual protest in the form of retraction from collectivity. Following Thoreau, society itself becomes suspect as ultimately and only coercive.

Jordan questions the safety and the privilege of individual divestment as a dominant protest strategy that values political non-participation, and that holds up the individual as a "higher authority"[25] than the state. In her assessment of the place of African Americans in the Reagan-Bush era, Jordan explicitly inhabits Thoreau's space of solitude and meditation, or, as Jordan describes it, American "willful loneliness," in a borrowed cabin on her "pseudo-Walden Pond" in the selection **"Waking Up in the Middle of Some American Dreams."** In this address reprinted in an essay collection that explicitly claims the rhetorical podium of the Chief Executive of the United States, Jordan argues against the American myth of individuality that separates us as she builds on mid-twentieth-century protest movements that engaged coalitions as the basis of true democracy. The danger of Thoreau's isolation and divestment becomes clear when Jordan re-inserts a particularized body into the philosophical wanderings of the traditional essay. While writing in her rented drawing room on her quasi-Walden pond, the speaker is raped. As she considers the meaning of this violent event, in the public form of an essay, Jordan explains, "Someone had insinuated himself into that awkward, tiny shelter of my thoughts and dreams. He had dealt with me as egotistically as, in another way, I had positioned dealing with anyone besides myself. He had overpowered the supposed protection of my privacy, he had violated the boundaries of my single self" (14). To focus solely on the individual and personal experience in an essay tradition, for Jordan, represents a violent ripping apart of speaker and her audience, an isolating move not unlike the supposedly private experience of sexual violence. Jordan's feminist strategy of politicizing rape calls attention to the privileged space of the ostensibly dissociated essayistic "I" which, nevertheless, *still* exists in a real matrix of social and political power. Only those who already hold power to give up are allowed the luxury of social retraction as a protest strategy. The rhetorical and the social cannot be disassociated. And Jordan offers an alternative rhetorical and social space of protest: collectivity.

For Jordan, protest furthers the as yet unrealized dream of American democracy based on collectivity: "*Demos,* as in democratic, as in a democratic state, means people, not person" (19). For Jordan, people, not the state, constitute a nation. Against the liberal myth of individualism, Jordan deploys her essayistic exploration of competing American dreams to strive for—and create—

the "civilized metropolis that will validate the democratic state" (19). It is a *coming together,* not divestment, that can make good on the promises of American democratic traditions. Jordan's essay project is one of re-connection of the "I" with other subjects of the state, and beyond. The subjectivity at the heart of her protest essays, in the end, is a collective "we." It is only upon her *return* from isolation, an event signified within, but ultimately achieved outside of, the essay itself, that her American dream of a Manifest New Destiny will find realization. The "we" is signified within this essay and many others, but it can only be made real when accepted by a *demos*—her readership in this case.

Squarely within the boundaries of state rhetoric, Jordan turns consistently to locations and targets of American imperialism in order to draw connections between exclusion from full citizenship within the state and America's complicity with similar regimes or practices of imperial violence and social exclusion beyond the boundaries of the U.S. Throughout her notes on the State of the Union, Jordan provides a heightened polemical world where racialized landscapes become explicitly moral, and thereby she questions the moral authority of the state. For instance, to evidence of U.S. government efforts to quash, question, and quell the emergent non-white leadership of South Africa, Latin America, and the Gaza Strip, Jordan insists provocatively, "These were matters of wrong or white" (142). By speaking as a partial citizen, Jordan reflects a Manichean world in her essays where she makes visible how stark dividing lines of justice, morality, and equity fall along the color line as much as along national borders. However, Jordan presents this color line to a readership committed to the larger project of a fulfilled democracy *without* such dividing lines—be they hostile national borders or more circuitous internal lines of division (by race, ethnicity, sex, sexuality, nationality, etc.). The way out, for Jordan, is to occupy a position of moral authority that rejects, not formalizes, an identity-based line between friend and foe. For, Jordan asks, "If we are afraid to insist that we are right, then what?" (179). The question, like all of Jordan's questions, is not simply rhetorical; she takes the moralizing rhetoric of the state at face value and demands that inclusive pronouncements prove meaningful in practice. The answer to Jordan's call lies, in part, in a commitment to extend the work of those who came before. Just as Jordan's individual essays demand responses (often by ending with provocative questions like the one cited above), earlier social movements and state projects demand action in the present, and offer rhetorical tools to make that action happen.

III. COLLECTIVITY BUILDING AND PARTIAL CITIZENS' DISSENT

Sometime after September 11, 2001, President George W. Bush took the virtually unprecedented step of labeling U.S. citizens like Yasir Hamdi and José Padilla "enemy combatants" in order to circumvent the legal rights to counsel and trial afforded to all U.S. citizens. The arbitrary nullification of Hamdi's and Padilla's citizenship rights was not entirely new given that protest has often been seen as forfeiture of citizenship. In addition to the obvious example of the allegiance-renunciation pairing in the citizenship oath, we can turn to Emma Goldman's deportation to Russia in 1919 that some women's liberationists would signal as the end of the First Wave of a revolutionary feminism, or to the internment of Japanese citizens during World War II that Chester Himes would use as a haunting figure in his Black protest novel *If He Hollers Let Him Go* (1945), or to the odd favor with which the exit plans of Garveyites and their predecessors have been received, all before the House Unamerican Activities Committee (HUAC). Along with Thoreau's blueprint of civil disobedience that pairs protest with *withdrawal* from collectivity, many dominant notions of dissent have necessitated a *retraction* from participation in the public sphere. When we attend to the efficacy of the partial citizen speaking, however, there is another option; collectivity in the face of division. By addressing the lines of division within her audience, Jordan offers a space—often specifically a "we" without an antecedent—at which she wishes to make possible the collectivity promised by civic myths.

Many have argued that liberal democracy itself presents a paradoxical subject wherein inclusion is signified so that exclusion may be perpetrated; where "we, the people" provides a hegemonic promise of temporarily unequal participation with no real contractual obligation for fulfillment. Protesting writers like Jordan, however, solicit urgency in order to demand realization of past promises of future equality in the present. To do so, Jordan relies on the authority of the state both to legitimize and to shape her calls for full inclusion for all within the polity, and without. Nevertheless, inequality has continued to exist despite—or some argue because of—official doctrines of equality throughout American history. Many scholars have echoed Judith Shklar's claim that "black chattel slavery stood at the opposite social pole from full citizenship and so defined it."[26] In literary studies informed by critical race studies, Toni Morrison argues, for instance, that the "Africanist" presence of Black characters in American literature by white authors has served an analogous role: the free is defined by and against the unfree.[27] Jordan's response to this dilemma is to reclaim the language of citizenship, social participation, and collectivity through the vantage point of partial citizens. When Jordan articulates a "we," she calls for an actual collectivity as constitutive of the legacy of the incomplete projects of civil rights, women's liberation, the student movement, indeed, of modern democracy itself.

Protest writers like Jordan occupy the outposts of real publics that can deliver the ineffable social equality of the modern democratic state. Here, those whose very citizenship is in question are the ones to sift through the promises of the nation-state and to hold them against the evidence of experience—their own and that of others for whom they speak. If Toni Morrison would just as soon have us enter a polling station to pray as to vote; so, too, protesters demand hope amidst despairing situations of inequality—often state-sponsored. Jordan's project is never simply to unveil inconsistency between state promises and the experiences of subsets of its citizenry. Nor does she reside in a balkanized vision of internal group equality more easily achieved, as was the tendency of various self-determination movements such as Black Power. Jordan argues for an equitable state in which a comparison between promises and experience will not inevitably lead to charges of hypocrisy, broken contracts, and deceit as the heart of the modern subject of citizenship.

When Jordan died in June 2002 after a long battle with cancer, her death initiated various gatherings of a diverse range of writers, activists, students, and scholars. Rather than mourning, for instance, some came together to mark Jordan's passing in long poetry readings like those from her course in Poetry for the People.[28] Like her calls for realizing the stated goals of the democratic state, this diverse range of poets, admirers, and activists continued her project of giving voice to the people—all people. In her tribute to her activist poetics, Angela Davis described Jordan's legacy thus: "Politics was her life; collective pain, as well as collective resistance, was always something she felt in a deeply personal way."[29] What I find so astounding and fruitful is that Jordan assembled her personhood, in part, with the potentially hard and hollow rhetoric and discursive forms of the state.

By claiming a toehold on official aspirations of inclusion from a very personal, locational identity, Jordan demonstrated the way in which full, partial, or non-citizens are able to work within the borders of the nation-state—be they territorial, ideological, or discursive—by taking the inclusive promises of the state at face value. In more philosophical terms: the road to the universal is through the particular.[30] Though much work can and should be done to explore the variety of strategies different types of partial citizens employ to draw upon rhetorical tools of the nation-state, Jordan's particular location serves as the beginning of such a mapping project of how the particular can lead to a substantive universalism. In her State of the Union address, Jordan attends to divisions within the borders of the nation-state, as well as to the way those internal divisions serve to incapacitate collective responses to state-sponsored activities beyond the nation's borders. Rather than claim a space of protest outside the purview of the nation-state, Jordan recognized the unmatched potential of state rhetoric that may have been historically delivered in the service of imperialism and domestic inequality . . . but need not inherently be delivered along such paths. Jordan's unfinished project of a Manifest New Destiny always lay in the work of a collective, and never in the hands of an individual, or individualism. Jordan always understood her work as the reclamation of earlier unfinished projects: the establishment of a secular democracy begun in 1776, the demands for racial parity begun in the Civil Rights movement of the 1950s, the ground-shaking insight that the personal is political from 1970s women's liberation, or the promise of global self-determination and democracy begun in the overthrow of the South African apartheid regime in 1990. Jordan's use of authoritative pronouncements of the state connects the fervent projects of earlier writers and activists to the just futures envisioned by those writing today. And tomorrow.[31]

Notes

1. June Jordan, "The Invisible People: An Unsolicited Report on Black Rage," in *Some Of Us Did Not Die: New and Selected Essays of June Jordan* (New York: Basic Books, 2003), 17.

2. June Jordan, *Soldier: A Poet's Childhood* (New York: Basic Books, 2000), 248-9.

3. Mae Ngai, *Impossible Subjects: Illegal Aliens and the Making of Modern Americans* (Princeton: Princeton UP: 2004), esp. 2-3.

4. June Jordan, *Technical Difficulties: African-American Notes on the State of the Union* (New York: Pantheon, 1992), 211. Further citations will be given parenthetically.

5. George H. W. Bush, State of the Union Address, January 28, 1992. Text available at http://www.c-span.org/executive/stateoftheunion.asp

6. For an example of this internal-looking conception, see Judith N. Shklar, *American Citizenship and the Quest for Inclusion* (Cambridge: Harvard UP, 1991).

7. Part of sections I and III are adapted from an essay on citizenship that originally appeared in the 2004 issue on "Turf" of *M/C—Media/Culture* (http://media-culture.org.au/).

8. Shweta Govindarajan, "Criticism Puts Citizenship Oath Revision on Hold; Conservatives pan immigration officials' modernization of the long-used pledge," *Los Angeles Times* 19 Sept. 2003, sec. 1: 13.

9. Ibid., 13.

10. The Heritage Foundation, *First They Attacked the Pledge, Now the Oath*, Sept. 10, 2003 [newsletter on-line]; available from http://www.heritage.org/Research/HomelandDefense/meeseletter.cfm; Internet; accessed October 20, 2003. The language of

rights and obligations is certainly a hallmark of civic republican definitions of citizenship, but the controversy surrounding the citizenship oath presumes (enforces?) uniform allegiance within the native-born citizenry by baiting immigrants as freeloaders, as late-comers to foundational stories, and as the most likely potential threats to domestic security.

11. Iris Marion Young, "The Logic of Masculinist Protection: Reflections on the Current Security State," *Signs* 29.1 (Autumn 2003): 2.

12. The Bureau of Citizenship and Immigration Services.

13. For an excellent excavation of how the immigrant, or foreigner more generally, has served to define American-ness and citizenship, see Bonnie Honig, *Democracy and the Foreigner* (Princeton: Princeton UP, 2001).

14. For an alternative examination of African-Americans second-class citizenship, one that *removes* the question of immigrants and foreigners altogether, see Shklar. Recent multicultural literary studies, however, have placed migration and transnationalism at the center of American literature. See for example, Werner Sollors, ed., *Multilingual America: Transnationalism, Ethnicity, and the Languages of American Literature* (New York: New York UP, 1998); Amritjit Singh and Peter Schmidt, *Postcolonial Theory and the United States* (UP of Mississippi, 2000); and Wesley Brown and Amy Ling, eds., *Imagining America: Stories from the Promised Land* (New York: Persea Books, 2002).

15. See Arjun Appadurai, ed., *Globalization* (Durham, N.C.: Duke UP, 2001); Phengh Cheah and Bruce Robbins, eds., *Cosmopolites: Thinking and Feeling Beyond the Nation* (Minneapolis: U of Minnesota P, 1998); Brent Hayes Edwards, *The Practice of Diaspora: Literature, Translation, and the Rise of Black Internationalism* (Cambridge, Mass.: Harvard UP, 2003); and Aihwa Ong, *Flexible Citizenship: The Cultural Logic of Transnationality* (Durham, N.C.: Duke UP, 1999). For a study that places the state at the center of national identity, see Gregg D. Crane, *Race, Citizenship, and Law in American Literature* (Cambridge: Cambridge UP, 2002).

16. Rogers M. Smith, *Civic Ideals: Conflicting Visions of Citizenship in U.S. History* (New Haven: Yale UP, 1997). "[Leaders] worry less about whether their various appeals are true, or whether they fit together logically, than about whether they work politically. They thus simultaneously appeal to lofty rational moralities and thinly veiled greed and lust for power. But most have found irreplaceable the engaging, reassuring, inspiring, often intoxicating charm provided by colorful civic myths" (33). In his most recent work, Smith's disparagement of "civic myths" has evolved to value the work of people-building fostered by "stories of peoplehood," stories which are necessary for the formation of any robust political com-

munity. See his *Stories of Peoplehood: The Politics and Morals of Political Membership* (New York: Cambridge UP, 2003), esp. 9-15, 21-4, 74-6.

17. I choose the modifier "partial" to describe these orators' and speakers' relation to citizenship because, more so than two-tiered notions of "second-class citizenship" prominent in the citizenship debates of the past decade, the figure of "partial citizenship" is able to account for varying degrees of claims upon different forms of citizenship (as status, rights, membership, participation, or identity/recognition, etc.) in demands for the realization of assorted promises of full enjoyment of citizenship(s). My understanding of the contested, contingent arena of citizenship draws heavily from the work of Linda Bosniak on the relatively autonomous and often overlapping conceptions of citizenship, especially as seen through alienage and other forms of noncitizenship. See her "Citizenship," *The Oxford Handbook of Legal Studies* (Peter Can & Mark Tushnet, eds., New York: Oxford UP, 2003), 183-201.

18. Frederick Douglass, "What to the Slave Is the Fourth of July?" (1848), in *Oxford Frederick Douglass Reader,* Ed. William L. Andrews (New York: Oxford UP, 1996), 116.

19. Not In Our Name, "Statement of Conscience" (2001). In addition to the Xeroxed pamphlets handed out at rallies, the Statement of Conscience was first published in the U.S. press on September 19, 2002 as a full page in the *New York Times,* and subsequently was reprinted in *USA Today,* major African American newspapers like *Amsterdam News,* opinion journals like *The Nation,* and it has been translated in various languages and distributed by hand and by the internet innumerably.

20. Honig, 101.

21. June Jordan, "Poem about My Rights," in *Passion* (Boston: Beacon, 1980), 86-89.

22. For more on Jordan's status as spokesperson, see Scott MacPhail, "June Jordan and the New Black Intellectuals," *African American Review* 33.1 (Spring 1999): 57-71.

23. Parts of the previous two paragraphs borrow from my entry on Jordan in *An Encyclopedia of African American Literature,* ed. J. David Macey, Jr. and Hans A. Ostrom (Westport, Conn.: Greenwood, forthcoming).

24. Henry David Thoreau, "Resistance to Civil Government" in *The Norton Anthology of American Literature,* V. 1 (New York: Norton, 1994), 1719.

25. Thoreau's secular individualism: "There will never be a really free and enlightened State, until the State comes to recognize the individual as a higher and independent power, from which all its own power and authority are derived, and treats him accordingly" (1719).

26. Shklar, 16.

27. See *Playing in the Dark: Whiteness and the Literary Imagination* (New York: Vintage, 1992).

28. See Lauren Muller, et al., *June Jordan's Poetry for the People: A Revolutionary Blueprint* (New York: Routledge, 1995).

29. Angela Davis, "Tribute to June Jordan," *Meridians* 3.2 (2003): 1-2.

30. Iris Marion Young has explored how earlier conceptions of liberal/universalist citizenship tend to ignore internal difference, or require that people leave their particularity (ethnic heritage, most often) in a private space in order to gain access to public arenas of citizenship. Young has famously advocated against universal citizenship in favor of *addressing* group difference as a means of achieving substantive equality. See her "Polity and Group Difference: A Critique of the Ideal of Universal Citizenship," *Ethics* 99 (1989): 250-74.

31. Parts of the previous two paragraphs also borrow from my entry on Jordan in *An Encyclopedia of African American Literature* (op. cit.).

Christina Accomando (essay date 2004)

SOURCE: Accomando, Christina. "Exposing the Lie of Neutrality: June Jordan's *Affirmative Acts*." In *Still Seeking an Attitude: Critical Reflections on the Work of June Jordan,* edited by Valerie Kinloch and Margret Grebowicz, pp. 33-47. Lanham, Md.: Lexington Books, 2004.

[*In the following essay, Accomando evaluates Jordan's efforts as a political and social activist, examining the essays in* Affirmative Acts.]

The current civil rights climate in the United States is marked simultaneously by legal retrenchments *and* claims of progress and "color blindness." Attacks on affirmative action in particular are cloaked in the language of neutrality and *anti*-discrimination. Following a debate of intense ironies, California voters banned affirmative action through a 1996 ballot initiative, Proposition 209, which deliberately omitted the phrase "affirmative action." Proposition 209, strategically called the "California Civil Rights Initiative," in fact effectively dismantled civil rights policy in California by making affirmative action illegal. June Jordan taught for more than a decade at UC Berkeley, which owes its diversity largely to policies disallowed not only by Proposition 209, but also by a 1994 internal vote of the UC Regents. In the face of all this negative action, Jordan published in 1998 a collection of political essays with the unapologetic title *Affirmative Acts.*

June Jordan takes on a range of complex issues in this collection [*Affirmative Acts*], including the policies and politics of affirmative action. In *Affirmative Acts* Jordan offers a needed corrective to the deceptive rhetoric of current anti-civil rights discourse that undermines social justice policies while claiming support for equality. She makes visible the unmarked "norm" of whiteness, the unacknowledged history of white supremacy and the systemic nature of racism. Jordan deploys poetry, statistics, quotation, and anecdote in her analysis of the language, history, and law behind affirmative action. In so doing, she refuses the false neutralities of the debate and insists upon an accounting of history and a clear-eyed look at the present.

First, it is vital to explain briefly the history of affirmative action and identify the underlying mythologies and constructed fictions of the political debate. Affirmative action foes rely upon ahistorical, decontextualizing arguments that not only erase our long history of institutionalized racism and sexism, but also pretend that *but for* affirmative action, bias-free decisions would be rendered. Contemporary affirmative action is a fairly moderate gesture that came into being in the twentieth century as an acknowledgment that merely outlawing overt discrimination is not enough. Since prejudice and institutionalized discrimination run so deep, we need to take proactive steps—we need to act affirmatively—to ensure any genuine degree of equal opportunity. The term "affirmative action" first appeared in John F. Kennedy's 1961 executive order establishing the Committee on Equal Employment Opportunity. Four years later Lyndon B. Johnson signed Executive Order No. 11246, which required affirmative action in federal contracting. A 1941 executive order already had outlawed discrimination by federal contractors, but by the 1960s, equity still was nowhere in sight.[1] As President Johnson stated in a 1964 speech at Howard University:

> Freedom is the right to share fully and equally in American society. . . .
>
> But freedom is not enough. You do not wipe away the scars of centuries by saying: Now you are free to go where you want, do as you desire, and choose the leaders you please.
>
> We seek not just freedom but opportunity . . . not just equality as a right and a theory, but equality as a fact and as a result.[2]

Four decades ago, Johnson and other politicians and activists acknowledged that even with civil rights legislation barring discrimination, the United States did not offer an even playing field. Affirmative action is the idea that the state must take proactive measures[3] to addresses both the legacies of past discrimination and the continuing present-day discrimination that is embedded deep in our institutions in ways that will not always appear as overt and actionable bias.

Today, the United States has even more bans on overt discrimination, but inequities and injustices persist, in education, employment, wages, wealth, housing, criminal justice, public health, and numerous other areas. Racism and sexism are less likely to be overt and more likely to reside behind a cloak of color-blind and gender-blind language. Institutionalized discrimination means that individuals do not even have to hold bigoted views or take overtly racist or sexist measures for inequities to stay in place. Beverly Tatum defines racism as "a system of advantage based on race" and offers a powerful metaphor to explain the "ongoing cycle of racism," which she compares to a moving walkway at the airport. An active racist runs on the walkway, holding racist views and committing discriminatory acts. Passive racists stand still on the walkway, believing themselves nonracist, but still being moved along on the walkway. "No overt effort is made," but because of the ongoing cycle of racism, "the conveyor belt moves the bystanders along to the same destination as those who are actively walking."[4] Instead of any promise of "nonracism," Tatum offers white folks the option of being "actively antiracist"—turning around on the conveyor belt and walking actively in the opposite direction. The moving walkway metaphor vividly illustrates that inaction is decidedly *not* neutral. Affirmative action is one example of calling on institutions to turn around on the walkway and attempt to actively counter systemic racism. Tatum acknowledges that many people have a hard time accepting the notion of systemic racism, because it demolishes any notion of a fair, just, and color-blind meritocracy in the United States.

Opponents of affirmative action base their arguments precisely on the false premise of meritocracy and the fantasy of an even playing field. The myth of meritocracy pretends that everyone in America has an equal opportunity to succeed and that success depends upon merit and hard work alone (the corollary is that failure therefore reveals a lack of merit and hard work). This myth denies the existence of privilege and systemic inequalities. But opponents of affirmative action do not say they oppose equality; instead, they deploy a language of equality that masks the social inequalities that necessitate affirmative action policies. Affirmative action is redefined as "racial preference" or reverse discrimination, for example, and "angry white men" are painted as victims of discrimination. In this way, abolishing affirmative action can be redefined as "civil rights." Former California Governor Pete Wilson, who helped lead the charge against affirmative action and who attempted to use this wedge issue in his unsuccessful run for the presidency, offers one good example of this rhetoric. After celebrating Thomas Jefferson's founding principles of equal rights, and before the obligatory Martin Luther King Jr. quotation, Wilson writes:

[T]oday, that fundamental American principle of equality is being eroded, eroded by a system of preferential treatment that awards public jobs, public contracts, and seats in our public universities, not based on merit and achievement but on membership in a group defined by race, ethnicity or gender. That's not right. It's not fair. It is, by definition, discrimination. It's exactly what the civil rights movement sought to end.[5]

In a comparison to President Lincoln and the strife caused by slavery and civil war, Wilson asserts that "we are again in a house divided against itself. We are divided by a system that offers preferences and privileges to some at the expense of others."[6] While the divisive system eventually targeted by Abraham Lincoln was the system of human enslavement, for Wilson the oppressive present-day system is affirmative action, a fairly shocking parallel.[7]

Competing notions of history are a key element of these debates for Jordan and others. Cornel West argues that "Today's affirmative action policy is not the appropriate starting point for a substantive debate on affirmative action. Instead, we must begin with the larger historical and moral context of the recent controversy." Central to this context, for West and for Jordan, is "[t]he vicious legacy of white supremacy."[8] On the other hand, the cynical language games of the Right—appropriating civil rights rhetoric, recoding affirmative action as discrimination, fabricating color blindness, deploying a discourse of progress to conjure up a bias-free status quo—attempt to sever present conditions from their specific histories. What's past is past, the Right tells us. Jordan compels us to pay attention to historical context, and in particular the history and legacy of white supremacy, as she links past and present. She offers an unflinching narrative of the legal inequalities of the past and an open-eyed evaluation of the continuing legacies of slavery and discrimination in the present.

Exposing the ugly facts of history is key to exposing the false neutrality behind ahistorical notions like preference and color blindness. In the essay **"Affirmative Acts: Language, Information, and Power,"** Jordan critiques the inadequate national "dialogue" on race, saying that at best it "fogs the atmosphere" and at worst it "provokes appalling, ahistorical displays of disingenuous disinformation protected by the impertinent interposition of the word *preference*."[9] In this essay she links attacks on affirmative action and attacks on bilingual education, which also have been successful in California. Both debates are characterized by misinformation and masked racism. She asks how we can "publicly put to rest virulent and unsubstantiated allegations against affirmative action and against bilingual education." The first step is identifying "when and why huge national realities become racialized." Jordan brings us in one breath from the eighteenth century to the present:

Established by the violent exercise of white supremacist whim and wish, this same country that, in 1790, stipulated "white" as the race identity prerequisite to citizenship, this is that same staggering aggregate that today, on national network news, and in Supreme Court rulings, and out of the mouths of preselected so-called race-dialogue participants would have us believe that, really, ours is a colorblind/open-door society, and that anyone arguing to the contrary is just some weird malcontent harboring indefensible special interests opposed to the obvious, and obviously common, good.[10]

The myth of color blindness is deployed as an attack against efforts to create racial justice, erasing the profoundly color-conscious legal history that defined American citizenship as white.[11] In the 1790 Naturalization Law Jordan references here, the right to become a naturalized citizen was restricted to white persons only. This unabashedly racist law remained in effect until the second half of the twentieth century (and helped justify government actions such as racialized immigration bans and the internment of Japanese Americans). Despite this history of legalized white supremacy, ignoring present-day racial disparities is seen as color blindness and "common" interest, while addressing these disparities is coded as "special interest" politics. Once we see the inequities of the historical record, it is clear that doing nothing is actually advancing racism—in Beverly Tatum's terms, standing still is really moving along on the walkway of systemic racism. "It is a matter of reality," writes Jordan, "that institutionalized inequality enforced for hundreds of years will not diminish or disappear without seriously long-term institutional redress of those inequalities, and their consequences."[12] Justice requires not only an honest telling of history but also institutionally transformative affirmative acts.

History matters because it has an impact on the present. Jordan offers telling juxtapositions of past and present. **"An Angry Black Woman on the Subject of the Angry White Man"** begins with a very contemporary dedication, which is immediately juxtaposed with the erased historical context of the contemporary debate. The essay is *Dedicated to the Negro U.C. Regent, Ward Connerly, who gave more than $100,000 to the campaign of Governor Pete Wilson and who led the U.C. Regent attack on Affirmative Action, 1995."* She locates this historical discussion in a very specific present-day political and temporal moment, although the term *"Negro"* implies that Connerly's politics and demeanor come from an earlier era. The opening lines— "We didn't always need affirmative action / when we broke this crazy land into farms"—set up a discussion, in unrhymed verse, of the economic and human arrangements of slavery, expressed in often repetitious first-person plural declarations: "when we fed and clothed other people's children with the food we cooked and served to / other people's children wearing the garments that we fitted and we sewed together."[13] The twenty lines describing the labor of slavery emphasize not just the brutality of enslavement ("when we lived under the whip and in between the coffle and chains") but also the economic exploitation that benefited white Americans: "when we bleached and pressed linens purchased by the dollar blood profits from our / daily forced laborings." The vivid phrase "dollar blood profits" reminds us that white wealth in America came from unpaid black labor, setting up the debt that is due. The sickening dehumanization of slavery, however, makes this debt beyond financial recompense. How can such equations ever be repaid: "Like two-legged livestock we cost the bossman three hundred and fifteen dollars or six / hundred and seventy-five dollars and so he provided for our keep / like two-legged livestock / penned into the parched periphery of very grand plantation life." Here Jordan repeats and explains the opening statement that "we did not need affirmative action. No! We needed overthrow and a holy fire to purify / the air."[14] Affirmative action is not *too much* but *too little*.

Jordan addresses history in this essay/poem by acknowledging the contradictions of history. Rather than the simplistic picture of progress offered by the Right, Jordan problematizes great moments of progress, such as the legal abolition of slavery. While slavery meant unrelenting exploitation, freedom has meant unfulfilled promises and continuing inequality. Emancipation brought "freedom on a piece of paper," but not the end of white supremacy:

> And so we finally got freedom on a piece of paper.
> But for two hundred years in this crazy land the law
>   and the bullets
> behind the law
> continued to affirm
> the gospel of God-given white supremacy
> For two hundred years the law and the bullets
> behind the law and the money and the politics behind
>   that money
> behind the bullets
> behind the law affirmed the gospel of God-given white
>   supremacy
> God-given male
> white supremacy.[15]

Jordan exposes the violence, money, and politics behind the law that oppressed African Americans, even as other laws technically freed them. The repetitious language of "God-given white supremacy" hammer home the reality of the systemic racism that today's civil rights opponents erase.

This historical context explains the need for policies that go beyond merely ending officially sanctioned oppression:

> And so we needed affirmative action. We needed a
>   way into the big
> house

besides the back door. We needed a chance at the
  classroom and the
jobs and open
housing
in okay neighborhoods

> We need a way around the hateful heart of America
> We needed more than "freedom" because a piece of
>   paper
> ain't the same as opportunity or
> education.[16]

Legal and technical "freedom" are not the same as actual equality of opportunity or actual social justice, in areas like education, employment, and housing. "Freedom" might remove slavery but it does not, by itself, provide for anything in its place.

> And so thirty years ago we agitated
> and we agitated until the President declared,
> "I now decree our federal commitment
> to equality not
> just as a right
> but to equality
> in fact."[17]

This telling of the genesis of affirmative action credits, and quotes, Lyndon B. Johnson, but Jordan does not name this president, and she also emphasizes the role of African American activism ("we agitated / and we agitated") in exerting the pressure that led to the executive order. The promise now is not merely "freedom on a piece of paper" but "equality in fact." As it turns out, this promise too is largely unmet, which explains the continuing need for meaningful affirmative action.

Jordan illuminates history as a window to the present. While Jordan shows contemporary policies as inextricably linked to the history that produced them, she also demonstrates that we cannot simplistically tie affirmative action to the past. We err if we treat affirmative action as a tool that merely makes up for "past" discrimination. While often her essays become image-filled, anaphora-driven verse, the poetic form does not stop her from confronting us with contemporary statistics that reveal the endurance of racism. Poverty rates, prison populations, congressional populations, the makeup of the Forbes 400—these are a few of the dismal numbers that paint the present-day picture.

> But (three decades later) and come to find out
> we never got invited to the party
> we never got included in "the people"
> we never got no kind of affirmative action worth
> more than spit in the wind
> unless someone real articulate can up and explain to
>   me
> how come (in 1997)
> 39.9 percent of Black children living in poverty
> and in 1993
> the net worth of African-Americans averages
> $4,418 compared to $45,759 for whites.[18]

Present-day disparities tell us that discrimination persists and that affirmative action continues to be necessary and needs to be strengthened, not diminished. She references another unnamed Democratic president (Bill Clinton) in order to counter his pandering to the "angry white man" image:

> and yesterday
> the new man in the White House
>
> the new President
> he said, "What we have done for women and minori-
>   ties is a very
> good thing, but we
> must respond to those who feel discriminated
>   against. . . . This is a
>   psychologically difficult
> time for the so-called angry white man."[19]

In dominant discourse, the actual present-day inequities (detailed in Jordan's previous stanza) are compared to—and even made less current and less salient than—the *feeling* of discrimination experienced by white men. "Yesterday" and "new" tell us how current this old news is—it's a new day and a new president, but it's still the old story of white-centered white supremacy.

The history of white supremacy produces a present-day reality of white male dominance in arenas of economic and political power. Jordan confronts us with another set of rapid-fire statistics, this time illustrating the opposite end of the pyramid—the wealthy white men in power. While Jordan grimly presents the statistics of black oppression without punctuation, the even less-discussed facts of white dominance are marked with exclamation points.

> White men constitute 44 percent of the American labor
>   force but
>   white men occupy 95 percent
> of all senior management positions!
>
> And 80 percent of the congress, four fifths of tenured
>   university
>   faculty, nine tenths of the United States
> Senate—and 92 percent of the Forbes 400![20]

This juxtaposition of black poverty and white power exposes the lie of reverse discrimination and reveals the *feelings* of white male discrimination to be just that—feelings, not reality. To these misplaced feelings, Jordan replies with the lone stanza of direct address to the angry men:

> Hey guys, get a grip!
> You say you're angry?
> Who's angry?!!!

While she dedicates the essay to the "Negro U.C. Regent" who spearheaded California's attacks on affirmative action, she does not pretend that Connerly's

presence in this debate has in any way shifted the balance of power. The "you" she finally addresses are white men, the "guys" who are feeling angry at their imagined displacement, while still wielding the balance of power.

The image of the "angry white man" is exposed in several of Jordan's essays. The misleading image tells us to shift our attention to the pain of those in the dominant group who feel they have been disadvantaged by affirmative action policies, but Jordan insists on a clear-eyed view of who has a right to anger. "Who's angry?!!!" Jordan demands after the essay's long list of inequities. Her title names herself in opposition to this construction: **"An Angry Black Woman on the Subject of the Angry White Man."** She insists that if anyone has a right to anger it is women of color who experience the inequalities denied by the "angry white men" who are angry about giving up a small bit of their privilege. She demonstrates with stark imagery that the playing field was never even and that the inequalities of the past continue to structure the present. She closes the essay by declaring that the "problem with affirmative action" is not that it has been too effective, leaving white men as the new disadvantaged group, but rather that there has been "way too little action!" on behalf of Americans who are actually disadvantaged.[21]

The deceptive, misleading, and often downright Orwellian language in this debate allows dominant group members to be renamed as disadvantaged. In her political essays, Jordan not only corrects the history but also challenges the frustrating rhetoric of the debate. She takes on terms that are supposed to scare us off—from "political correctness" and "preference" to "angry white men" and "color blindness"—and refuses to be intimidated by those fictions. Today's opponents of civil rights appropriate the language of fairness and erase the context of the moving walkway of systemic racism. It is Jordan's task to make this context visible again. "There is a powerful hatred loose in the world," she writes. "And the most powerful practitioners of this hatred do not deploy a hateful rhetoric. They do not declare, 'I hate blackfolks,' or 'I hate women,' or 'I hate Jews,' or 'I hate Muslims,' or 'I hate homosexuals.' They make 'civil' pronouncements."[22] Jordan exposes the false neutrality and cynical civility in the opposition's "civil" pronouncements by dissecting their deceptive word choice and, in her own rhetoric, both playing with language and refusing euphemisms.

Jordan connects several different reactionary rhetorics. Her essay **"In the Land of White Supremacy"** exposes a range of ostensibly race-neutral terms as tools of white supremacy. As Jordan often does in her essays, she walks us through her own change in thinking. She begins by distinguishing between overtly "racist belief and behavior,"[23] which rest with hateful individuals, and her own more recent focus on "white supremacy," which is more everyday, ordinary, systemic, and insidious. She moves from her own change in terminology to an analysis of the deceptive terms of the national discourse: "I came to recognize media constructions such as 'The Heartland' or 'Politically Correct' or 'The Welfare Queen' or 'Illegal Alien' or 'Terrorist' or 'The Bell Curve' for what they were: multiplying scattershots intended to defend one unifying desire—to establish and preserve white supremacy as our national bottom line."[24] First she identifies these loaded terms as media constructions and political manipulations, not actual descriptions of real things. Then she does not merely expose the racialized nature of these seemingly race-neutral terms but goes further, linking these diverse "scattershots" as sharing one underlying motive: establishing and preserving white supremacy.

In order to critique the opposition, Jordan explains the justification for federal affirmative action policies, since the government has an obligation to provide security, and "you cannot provide for the security of a people without justice, without equality, without food, without education, without gainful employment, without housing." As she explains the logic of such policies, she also spells out the false logic of the backlash against these policies: "Hence, affirmative action, for example, is a federal government policy. Hence, the viciously orchestrated attack on 'affirmative [action]' for the sake of 'angry white men' who, statistics inform us, continue to occupy 95 percent of all senior management positions."[25] These attacks—"orchestrated" and not spontaneous—involve the cynical deployment of more loaded terms. Jordan dismantles the threat of the catch-phrase "angry white men," which is supposed to make us focus on white men as the new victims of reverse discrimination in an era of affirmative action. Jordan reminds us that these new victims in fact still dominate positions of power. And it is an analysis of power that is utterly missing in the anti-affirmative action discourse.

Jordan replaces the image of "angry white man" as victim with an image of victimizing white supremacy, by describing a literal image, a photograph of a violent white supremacist. She writes, "I guess that was the picture of one of those angry white men, that photograph of blond, white Timothy McVeigh. Is that the guy who bombed the federal office building and killed 167 human beings because something truly pissed him off? Is he one of those guys 'affirmative action' irritated like, so to speak, crazy?" Quoting the president, who emphasized the need to confront this "dark" force, Jordan writes:

> "Dark," Mr. President?
> On the contrary. White. White. American white
>   supremacist white.
> The monster is an "American-looking" white man.[26]

The media's focus on the victimized "angry white man" not only undermines efforts at affirmative action, but also blinds us to actual dangers in our midst. White is the unmarked norm in American society.[27] And so Jordan marks it over and over—five times in the seventeen-word paragraph above.

Attacks on affirmative action are not, of course, honestly articulated as defenses of white supremacy. These attacks shift the terms of the debate so that affirmative action sounds like the discriminatory policy. Jordan analyzes the cynical deployment of "preference" as a loaded redefinition that forces voters to recoil. In **"Justice at Risk,"** she describes the shift that occurred when "'racial preference' quickly eclipsed 'affirmative action,'" putting both phrases in quotes to remind these rhetorical choices matter gravely. She writes:

> So now the question put to white Americans changed to, "What do you think about job and college-admission policies that give preference to some racial groups over others? Do you think that's fair?"
>
> This double whammy, this model of loaded public inquiry, produced great excitement and front-page news: Gosh, no! White Americans didn't think "racial preference" was really "fair." And, as a matter of fact, once you redefined things like that, a whole lot of Black and Latino and Asian-Americans didn't think "racial preference" was really "fair," either.[28]

This narrative of media redefinitions brings us back again to that key obfuscating term, "angry white men." This phrase shifts the focus from the actually aggrieved party (African Americans and other people of color who have faced institutionalized racism since before the founding of the nation) to an imagined victim of too much racial justice:

> Soon our national press exploded with outcries from "angry white men" and a minicascade of first-person white student reports from universities overtaken by unqualified barbarians, politically correct thought police, and apologetic, but terrified, would-be employers who had truly wanted to hire the best white man for the job, but could not.[29]

She names race in the catch phrase "best man for the job" to remind us that the ostensibly neutral notion is already raced and gendered. Jordan's telling of this narrative culminates in the 1994 UC Regents vote to end affirmative action in the University of California. Jordan's description of the reaction exposes the unacknowledged white privilege embedded in the debate:

> And I suppose that everyone opposed to "racial preference" breathed easier as the prospect of preserving a mostly white Western curriculum for mostly white Western students who would later lead or join a mostly white labor force brightened a little bit. Obviously,

white Western curricular, educational, economic, and political hegemony does not translate into "racial preference." White Western hegemony is "fair!"[30]

The "racial preference" already quietly in place is white supremacy. Jordan exposes the lack of affirmative action as not neutrality but rather "White Western hegemony," which she makes visible in the curriculum, the student body, at the economic and political power structures. Her insistent repetition of "white Western" again names the bias in the falsely neutral unmarked norm of dominant discourse.

After redefining history and redefining terms throughout *Affirmative Acts,* Jordan closes her book with **"Break the Law!"** where she uses twentieth-century civil rights history to compel us to rethink the law. She demonstrates both the importance of the law as a tool for liberation and the need to break the law when it is an obstacle to liberation. Her argument here seems linked to the ideas of critical race theorists who examine legal constructions of race and who treat the law as a double-edged sword. Legal critic Mari Matsuda writes: "The struggle against racism is historically a struggle against and within law. The hard-won victories of that struggle demonstrate the duality of law: as subordination and law as liberation."[31] Critical race theory has emerged from "[s]cholars of color [who] have attempted to articulate a theoretical basis for using law while remaining deeply critical of it."[32] This duality is reflected in Jordan's juxtaposition of civil rights laws, including affirmative action, that attempt to equalize rights in America, and Proposition 209, which is another in a long series of unjust laws that need to be broken and overturned.

Jordan describes federal desegregation policy as the legal answer to the "shotgun-serious loathing of me and my kind" revealed in a Mississippi hotel's reluctance to allow African Americans in its rooms and its swimming pool.[33] This desegregation policy is paralleled with contemporary affirmative action policy, and both are juxtaposed with Proposition 209, which "eviscerated affirmative action"[34] and "effectively resegregates higher education."[35] She writes sarcastically that, under 209, "On a colorblind basis, we would now see who was really 'qualified' or not."[36] She clearly questions both "colorblind" and "qualified" here. Jordan provides detailed statistics about the new freshman class at UC Berkeley, under the new regime of Proposition 209. These numbers show declines, since the previous year, in students of color in the pool of admitted students: a 56.3 percent decline for Chicanos, 58.9 percent for Native Americans, and 64.3 percent for African Americans. Lest any reader think that this new policy merely allows the exclusion of students of color not "qualified" for entrance, Jordan offers italicized facts about who has been turned away: *"More than 800 minority*

students with a 4.0 grade point average as well as 1200 SAT scores had been 'turned away'" and *"More than 1300 minority students with grade point averages* above 4.0 *had also been 'turned away.'"*[37] For Jordan these numbers add up to injustice and resegregation. She articulates the chancellor's duty to break this unjust law through a chant-like reiteration of previous unjust laws:

> It was once against the law for Blackfolks to read and write.
> It was once against the law for Blackfolks to marry each other.
> It was once against the law for Blackfolks to vote.
> It was once against the law for Blackfolks to swim in indoor, or outdoor, public waters.[38]

This anaphora gives way to the justification for breaking unjust laws, from slavery time to the present:

> We had to break those laws or agree to the slaveholder's image of us: three fifths of a human being.
>
> When the law is wrong, when the law produces and enjoins manifest and undue injury to a people, when the law punishes one people and privileges another, it is our moral obligation to break the law!
>
> The law is not God-given![39]

A clear-eyed understanding of the past tells us that unjust laws had to be resisted for the legal practices of slavery and segregation to end. A clear-eyed understanding of the present tells us that the legacies of those practices are still with us, and so if the law does not stand firmly against entrenched racism, we must again break the law. Jordan dates this closing essay with great precision:

> *April 7, 1998*
>
> *1:05 A.M.*
>
> *Berkeley, California*[40]

She leaves no doubt about the contemporary nature and pressing urgency of this matter.

Jordan's precise and caustic use of language and her insistence upon the complexities of past and present provide a particularly lucid literary voice in this ongoing debate. Her essays teach us to read with skepticism the Right's cynical claims of color blindness and neutrality. Since the publication of *Affirmative Acts,* retrenchments have continued, and so has resistance to the backlash. While Jordan ties her work to specific moments and events, such as passage of Proposition 209, the political analysis and critical insights of Jordan's essays can apply to whatever new threats, and new opportunities, might arise.

Notes

1. George E. Curry, *The Affirmative Action Debate* (Cambridge: Perseus Books, 1996), xiv.

2. Lyndon B. Johnson, "To Fulfill These Rights," in *The Affirmative Action Debate,* ed. George E. Curry (Cambridge: Perseus Books, 1996), 17-18.

3. The proactive measures of affirmative action have not been rigid quotas, another red herring in the political debates, but rather goals and timetables to encourage efforts to create diversity where there has been none.

4. Beverly Tatum, *Why Are All the Black Kids Sitting Together in the Cafeteria, and Other Conversations about Race* (New York: Basic Books, 1997), 11.

5. Pete Wilson, "The Minority-Majority Society," in *The Affirmative Action Debate,* 168. Wilson goes on to cite the oft-quoted (and misused) passage from the 1963 "I Have a Dream" speech describing King's dream that one day his children will be judged not "by the color of their skin but by the content of their character." The Proposition 209 campaign created anti-affirmative action advertisements featuring King's image and this quotation. In fact, the late Dr. King supported affirmative action and most certainly would not have been on Wilson's side in this debate. As King wrote in "A Testament of Hope," in a passage quoted by Jordan but not by Proposition 209 partisans, "When millions of people have been cheated for centuries, restitution is a costly process. Inferior education, poor housing, unemployment, inadequate health care—each is a bitter component of the oppression that has been our heritage. Each will require billions of dollars to correct. Justice so long deferred has accumulated interest and its cost for this society will be substantial in financial as well as human terms. This fact has not been grasped, because most of the gains of the past decade were obtained at bargain prices" (quoted in June Jordan, *Affirmative Acts: Political Essays* [New York: Anchor Books, 1998], 50).

6. Wilson, "The Minority-Majority Society," 174.

7. Such comparisons actually are not that unusual among affirmative action foes. For example, attorney Todd Welch used such a parallel in his defense of the June 12, 1995, *Adarand* Supreme Court ruling, which greatly restricted affirmative action in federal contracting. Welch writes, "There have been times in our history when equality, although sought, was not realized by all citizens. One such time was before 1964 for most black Americans. Another time was between 1976 and June 12, 1995, for nonminorities" (Todd Welch, "The Supreme Court Ruled Correctly in *Adarand,*" in *The Affirmative Action Debate,* 158). Here he compares the lack of equality faced by African Americans before the 1964 Civil Rights Act, including slavery, Jim Crow segregation, and voting rights violations, to the lack of equality faced by white Americans during two decades of affirmative action.

8. Cornel West, "Affirmative Action in Context," in *The Affirmative Action Debate,* 31.

9. Jordan, *Affirmative Acts,* 243.

10. Jordan, *Affirmative Acts,* 250.

11. Ian Haney López offers a detailed study of U.S. citizenship law and the legal construction of white racial identity. Ian Haney López, *White by Law: The Legal Construction of Race* (New York: New York University Press, 1996).

12. Jordan, *Affirmative Acts,* 251.

13. Jordan, *Affirmative Acts,* 100.

14. Jordan, *Affirmative Acts,* 101.

15. Jordan, *Affirmative Acts,* 101.

16. Jordan, *Affirmative Acts,* 102.

17. Jordan, *Affirmative Acts,* 102.

18. Jordan, *Affirmative Acts,* 102-3.

19. Jordan, *Affirmative Acts,* 103.

20. Jordan, *Affirmative Acts,* 104.

21. Jordan, *Affirmative Acts,* 104. Cornel West and many others would agree that affirmative action has been too little. He writes, "The vicious legacy of white supremacy—institutionalized in housing, education, health care, employment, and social life—served as the historical context for the civil rights movement in the late 1950s and 1960s. Affirmative action was a *weak* response to this legacy" (West, "Affirmative Action in Context," 31).

22. Jordan, *Affirmative Acts,* 86. While my essay has focused on the role of race in the affirmative action debate, this long list of masked hatreds reminds us of Jordan's understanding of the interconnectedness of racism, sexism, homophobia, anti-Semitism, and anti-Arab hostility.

23. Jordan, *Affirmative Acts,* 113.

24. Jordan, *Affirmative Acts,* 113-14.

25. Jordan, *Affirmative Acts,* 115.

26. Jordan, *Affirmative Acts,* 115.

27. Haney López analyzes the "common sense" notion of whiteness as unmarked norm through the notion of "transparency" in his analysis of court rulings on U.S. citizenship. He writes, "Transparency, the tendency of Whites to remain blind to the racialized aspects of that identity, is omnipresent" (Haney López, *White by Law,* 157). This invisibility of whiteness helps to make it so difficult to interrogate race and its consequences in the United States. Part of Jordan's goal is to make whiteness and white supremacy visible.

28. Jordan, *Affirmative Acts,* 121.

29. Jordan, *Affirmative Acts,* 121-22.

30. Jordan, *Affirmative Acts,* 122.

31. Mari Matsuda, *Where is Your Body? and Other Essays on Race, Gender and the Law* (Boston: Beacon Press, 1996), 52.

32. Matsuda, *Where is Your Body,* 24.

33. Jordan, *Affirmative Acts,* 265.

34. Jordan, *Affirmative Acts,* 266.

35. Jordan, *Affirmative Acts,* 267.

36. Jordan, *Affirmative Acts,* 266.

37. Jordan, *Affirmative Acts,* 267.

38. Jordan, *Affirmative Acts,* 267.

39. Jordan, *Affirmative Acts,* 267.

40. Jordan, *Affirmative Acts,* 267.

Ramona Coleman (essay date 2004)

SOURCE: Coleman, Ramona. "Narrating Nation: Exploring the Space of Americanness and the Place of African American Women through the Works of June Jordan." In *Still Seeking an Attitude: Critical Reflections on the Work of June Jordan,* edited by Valerie Kinloch and Margret Grebowicz, pp. 49-66. Lanham, Md.: Lexington Books, 2004.

[*In this essay, Coleman offers a reading of Jordan's concepts of belonging and citizenship as expressed through her essays and other writings.*]

You can learn a great deal about belonging to a nation by standing in a grocery checkout line.[1] I learned several things. For one, I learned that my nation does not consider people who look like me one of the "One hundred and fifty most beautiful people" as indicated in the May 2002 *People* magazine.[2] On the front cover are Nicole Kidman and Jennifer Aniston (inside, the biracial and more white-skinned than dark-skinned Hale Berry and Alicia Keys top this list as well). Unlike the white man in front of me to whom the cashier says "have a nice day," the end of my transaction is concluded with silence and a "hello, how are you?" to the white woman in back of me. So, second, citizens of my nation can take my money without ever acknowledging that I gave it to them. Third, the newspapers at the end of the checkout lane construct a national imagery of Americanness that excludes people who look like me, for seldom are there pictures of people who look like me on the front page.

In a September 24, 2001 *Toledo Blade* story entitled "Face of America," the pictures that accompany this story contain only white faces and the back side of two black male athletes.[3] In fact, of the many front-page images of Americanness following the September 11, 2001 attack against the World Trade Center in New York City, I can recall only one picture of a black woman—a large dark-skinned woman with corn-rowed hair—who appears to be sewing a flag.[4] Lastly, my nation, in rearticulating what it means to be an American, still tells me that people who look like me are here to be poor and/or working-class mammies. There are several things problematic about this "grocery-lane" experience. This image of the black woman sewing the flag contributes to maintaining dominant structures of symbolic exclusion. Racialism continues to impact meditated images and messages in U.S. culture. The phenomenological existence of my black body continues to be a site that marks black subjectivity to a subordinate status by dominant ideological constructs. Exploring how the media racializes national identity combined with phenomenological inquiries of mediated constructions on national identity provide greater insight into notions of belonging for black women. Thus, for me standing in a checkout lane, my black body becomes a site through which gendered, racialized, and nationalized forms of exclusion are lived, negotiated, and resisted.

I understand what is going on, but I am more concerned about my twelve-year-old niece who follows behind me at the checkout lane and sees and hears the same things I do. How does this experience shape her notions of American citizenship? In what ways do generational shifts account for how my niece and I interpret the meanings of this "grocery-lane" experience—the magazine cover, newspaper images, and the cashier's behavior? Little has changed from my generation to hers. For example, she is being socialized into a culture where an aesthetic hierarchy of the female body in mainstream American culture privileges white skin and European features; therefore, this beauty aesthetic positions black women on the bottom, or worse renders them invisible. Because adolescence is a period of socialization—socialization involves learning the ways, rules, norms of society—the reality being constructed for her through mediated images normalizes whiteness and subordinates blackness, particularly black female bodies. Scholar Stuart Hall contends that the mass media is instrumental in maintaining ideological hegemony.[5] Theorist Roland Barthes reminds us how the mass media use images to construct a particular worldview—historically in the United States this has been white and male—as being natural or normal.[6] Writer, activist, educator June Jordan adds a phenomenological lens that enables me to explore national myths, ideological constructions, and the ways in which these myths and mediated social constructs affect the daily lived experiences of black women.

Given the power of mainstream media, I question the existence, or lack thereof, of public spaces that nurture the beautiful young black woman my niece is becoming while welcoming her to concepts of Americanness. Like Jordan, I too believe that "some of us must devise and improvise a million and one ways to convince young African-American and Chicana women that white skin and yellow hair and blue eyes and the thin thighs are not imperative attributes of beauty and loveliness."[7] Moreover, I must convince my young niece that she does belong to this nation even though visual narrative tells her otherwise. I am here to remind her that she too has every right to be here and that she too belongs to this nation. Since I cannot be with her at all times, while she stands in grocery lines, sits in classrooms, watches television—all those American places where black women, or issues concerning black women remain invisible—I leave with her the writings Jordan to remind her that there are spaces in America for her black female body. Even if she has to create the space as Jordan has done, there will be spaces for black, female bodies in American society. Like the post-September 11 images that establish spaces of containment for black female bodies or construct places where we should not be, the images in Jordan's examination reveal that such mediated constructions of national identity have always led to the oppression of black women. In fact, Jordan's analysis of American media has helped me to understand its function as a part of an epistemological system that constructs where black female bodies belong in the media's and state's construction of American national identity.

Since September 11, the United States (i.e., our government, various social and political groups) has rearticulated what it means to be an American. The media have created a discourse that engenders a common sense of nationhood. Yet in the midst of nation-(re)building, these images that I've collected from *BG News* (the Bowling Green State University newspaper), the *Toledo Blade* (the prime newspaper in Toledo, Ohio), and *USA Today* (The Nation's Newspaper), immediately following September 11, create a discourse of inclusion and exclusion. In the places I frequently visit, I could not help but see how these newspapers created a visual narrative wherein black women were physically erased; I began collecting these front-page pictures to visually read how these newspapers, combined, constructed what it means to be an American. As I studied these pictures, Jordan's voice rang loudly in my thoughts. For instance, in her essay **"A Powerful Hatred,"** she asks, "except for those occasions when the media smell a possible chance to pit blackfolks against other blackfolks, when do I get calls asking for my thoughts and opinions about anything whatsover?"[8] As the media paint a national imagery of America's citizens, I wondered where are the people—black women—who look like me?

Additionally, I began to critique articulations of race and gender in the post-September 11 efforts at nation building. These images and articulations allowed me to question the media's concerns to include black female bodies in the process of constructing American citizenship. In the representative newspapers, there was only one front-page photo of a black woman—a fairly large dark-skinned woman with hair parted in the middle and two thick corn-rolled plaits on each side. Allegedly, she is sitting at a table that is draped with the American flag; to her right is a sewing machine that, based on its positioning, offers the illusion that she is sewing an American flag that covers most of her body and chest. This image not only reduces the black female body to a mammified object, but it also renders the body to a historicized subject that perpetuates, on the one hand, enslavement, and on the other hand, a call for rescue from this quagmire. Such objectification begs the question, in what ways do mass media and public representations of humanity contribute to the oppression of African American women? Such a question can be interrogated through the political writings of Jordan.

Throughout her collection of essays—I focus on *Civil Wars: Observations from the Front Lines of America* (1981) to *Technical Difficulties: African-American Notes on the State of the Union* (1995) and *Affirmative Acts: Political Essays* (1998)—Jordan argues that the institutional bedfellows—the state and the media—reinscribe social hierarchies with their particular visions of U.S. nation and citizenry.[9] Both the media and the state are institutions that never leave Jordan's attention. In her 1979 article **"Black History as Myth,"** Jordan writes, "At the end of the 1960s, American mass media rolled the cameras away from black life and the quantity of print on the subject became too small to read."[10] From my collected images, I contend that little has changed in the way American mass media construct national identity. Not only has black life become too small to read, as Jordan argues, but black women must constantly confront identity erasure and/or misrepresentation from the national imagery of American media.

How Jordan links the terms state, nation, and citizenship is predicated upon how the nation-state imagines itself, given that the media collude with the state in its understanding of national identity. Scholar Benedict Anderson posits that nation "is an imagined political community and members are both inherently limited and sovereign."[11] Anderson elaborates on this idea of "imagined" by arguing that because members will never know most of their fellow-members, there still exists in the minds of each, the image of their communion. And it is imagined as a community because it is conceived as a deep, "horizontal comradeship."[12] The media's role, therefore, is to construct, particularly through visual images, the nation's conception of "horizontal comradeship"—community, and thus, communion.

However, as argued by Jordan, this ideal, "horizontal comradeship" is disrupted by America's legacy of racism and sexism. Jordan emphasizes that "White Western authorities on beauty and honor and courage and historical accomplishment have denied and denigrated whatever and whoever does not fit their white Western imagery."[13] In constructing national identity post-September 11, print media assumed the authority as to what bodies constitute American citizenship, and their nationally selected bodies fit a "white Western imagery" of Americanness. The photo on the front page of the September 22, 2001 issue of the *Toledo Blade* best captures this imagery. Pictured in the black and white photo are all-white males holding flags and waving to President Bush on the White House lawn. The photo appears to have been taken in the 1950s; their hairstyles and dress resemble that of the Ward Cleaver character from the television show *Leave It to Beaver*. The caption below the picture refers to the white males as "White House visitors." So in one way, I am led to believe that the men in the picture are not representative of a specific organization; quickly, I realize that the men are American citizens who are showing their support of President Bush as they defend his, and their, values. According to Jordan, "I came to recognize media constructions such as 'The Heartland' or 'Politically Correct' or 'The Welfare Queen' or 'Illegal Alien' or 'Terrorist' or 'The Bell Curve' for what they were: multiplying scattershots intended to defend one unifying desire—to establish and preserve white supremacy as our national bottom line."[14] This image of the all-white males on the White House lawn definitely signifies, through mediated construction of national identity, that white male supremacy is the bottom line. Therefore, if the imaginings of a nation are marked white and male, what are the implications for the nation's citizens who are not white and male? If nation is an imagined ideal, then both the state and the media materialize the imagined ideals of the nation, reinforcing identities that do not account for black women and that do not consider the plight of American citizens to be imagined as a nation. Women's material bodies are sties through which subordination is experienced and challenged.

The question "What must American citizens do to imagine and create 'nation' in light of public misrepresentations of racialized persons?" becomes multilayered. One way for such imagining to occur is through direct confrontation with the media's judgment of who embodies and is bestowed with American leadership. The photo of President Bush holding the flag while standing on top of a burned fire truck surrounded by white males is intended to capture such leadership.[15]

Jordan, in describing the advertised oppressive conditions of black people, reminds us of how national imagery in "these United States, where common nouns such as democracy and liberty have long known bumper-sticker popularity, the notion of a black man or a woman becoming the President remains a joke/a dopey idea/a theoretical construct of small or no plausibility."[16]

While I have lost count of how many times I have seen the image of President Bush standing atop a burned fire truck, I do remember first seeing this image on the front page of the *Toledo Blade*. At first sight, I recall thinking about representation, democracy, and liberty: What did this image mean for me, a racialized and gendered person? How can I read this image and think of democracy and liberty when the possibility of my niece or nephew remains a mere "theoretical construct of small or no plausibility"? Furthermore, how can I read this sign and imagine democracy and liberty when "black women continue to occupy the absolutely lowest rungs of the labor force in the United States, continue to receive the lowest pay of any group of workers, and endure the highest rate of unemployment"?[17] The terrorists attacks of September 11 produced a rhetoric that renewed the American spirit; however, I often wonder whose spirits are being renewed and how such a renewal is occurring in the presence of American capitalism and patriarchy. Can a picture of President Bush holding an American flag surrounded by white, male bodies "renew" my American spirit or the spirit of those citizens already disenfranchised because of race, ethnicity, and language? Is a picture of white males waving flags in one hand and motioning good-bye with the other to our president as he whisks away to Camp David going to send me and my family and my neighbors running out to buy an American flag to wave in "horizontal comradeship"?

The relationship between the media and the American presidency is nothing new, as evidenced in Jordan's essay **"America in Confrontation with Democracy."**[18] She remarks that the "national white media colluded with Democratic party bosses to silence, to slander, and finally, to stop Jesse Jackson."[19] She further adds, "White media moguls censored Jackson because they thought he just might accomplish 'the impossible' and become the Democratic nominee" for the American presidency.[20] In her evaluation of Jackson's campaign, Jordan focuses on the politics of American bodies, and what she reveals is the media's strategy of ridding the American body politic of its citizens of African descent. The success of Jackson's campaign challenged the notion of a racially homogeneous nation. Moreover, he articulated a vision that appealed beyond race, embracing workers, farmers, women, youth, gays, and others in a black-led movement for popular empowerment; as a result, "he had to be stopped."[21] Here was a black body defining national identity in political and social spaces. Historically in the American body politic, black bodies have occupied a space of confinement; however, Jackson in a populist uprising challenged white hegemonic imagery of the United States by defying this confinement.

After Jackson's victory in Michigan on March 26, where he took 55 percent of the votes, the "currently powerful went crazy," and "America was out of (their control)."[22] Unfortunately, Jackson's campaign success came to a halt in New York, and "the media made it happen."[23] It was the media's frenzy over Jackson's relationship to the Jews along with the media's biased and ultimately racist treatment of Jackson that sabotaged his campaign. Television and newspaper commentators solely focused on Jackson's relationship to the Jewish community: "Page one/top of the TV news/ubiquitous to the eyes and ears of New York residents, the fight for the Democratic party's nomination for the presidency of the United States had become a media-induced fight between two minorities: Jews and blacks."[24] Because Jackson did not win the Jewish vote in the New York Democratic primary, he lost the state, and thus New York via the media "cost him the Democratic party's nomination."[25] Jackson's run in the 1988 presidential campaign inspired "the least powerful and the most despised segments of our body politic."[26] Thus what does the sabotage of Jackson's campaign do for those who look just like him, those who speak his language, and those who work for inclusion, civil rights, representation in a society marked by waving flags and a false sense of renewed spirit?

Furthermore, how is my American spirit going to be renewed when the media continuously marginalizes black, female bodies and privileges white, female bodies? One newspaper photo (consequently, this same photo is pasted on a billboard that I pass daily) has a little white girl holding the American flag and sitting on a white man's shoulders surrounded by black and white males.[27] Another image contains a black male whose arm is wrapped around a white woman, and he appears to be consoling her while another white women, holding the American flag, stands in front of them; each woman is wearing an American flag bandanna.[28] Still there are no images of black women; hence, in constructing a national identity, the media signify that white, female bodies are to be elevated and protected meanwhile black women are excluded from dominant accounts of history. Black, female bodies are physically erased; thereby, these bodies do not need to be protected because they do not matter. And because they do not matter, it becomes impossible to establish an imagined community, an all-inclusive nation.

In turning to Jordan's writings, the obvious devaluation-turned-invisibility of black female bodies by white media is examined. The media's construction of American citizenship is just one part of a collaborative narrative in which both the state and the media write black women out of notions of belonging. The absence of black female bodies in the visions of the state and the media are reflective of a history of exclusion insofar as black women are concerned. As indicated by Jordan, the state and the American media locate the lives of women on the bottom of the nation's agenda while women of color are positioned even lower. One such example of this positioning of women on the national agenda is marked by the rampant increase of violence against women. In **"We Are All Refugees,"** Jordan points to American leadership and to the media in explaining how women are devalued in the United States because of the lack of attention paid to female violence. She links the "absence of a civilizing human leadership" to the murder of Elizabeth Alvarez.[29] A Latina mother of three children and married, Alvarez was killed by a ten-year-old boy and his "fourteen-year-old buddy." For Jordan, considering the various types of oppression coupled with the kind of presidential leadership ruling the United States, there is no wonder why these boys killed "a woman for eight dollars and the hell of it."[30]

In discussing the murder of Elizabeth Alvarez in **"We Are All Refugees,"** Jordan parallels the violence of women in the United States to people of color seeking asylum in the United States; in both cases, neither group can find sanctuary because white male leadership or "wannabe gatekeepers" construct a citizenship that "castigate[s] women and every one of the varieties of colored peoples seeking entry into our beloved American experiment of a multiracial/multiethnic/multicultural body politic."[31] Once again, the reminder that "our politicians and their media flunkies busily and viciously strive to resurrect an Old World in which there will be no safety, no asylum, for anybody but themselves"[32] comes as no surprise. The state and media maintain visions of national imagery through their treatment of human bodies within the United States and through the ways in which they control what bodies can and cannot enter the United States, the Land of the Free. From Bush to Clinton and back to a Bush, "these powerful white men now conspire to stop immigration to America by anybody who does not resemble themselves."[33]

Jordan also holds the media responsible for their collusion in the construction of a national identity whereby black women are constructed as second-class citizens. The media focused on the boys who killed her; "*The New York Times* devoted a whole page and a half to her killers," and all "you ever know about Elizabeth Alvarez is that she was pregnant, she was married, and she's dead."[34]

> As a woman, married or not, and pregnant or not, and
> mother of one/two/three, or none—where could she

find political or economic asylum that would mean safety and respect and equal access to freedom and to the power to guarantee her own safety and her own access to freedom?"[35]

Jordan points out the ways in which the media's complicity with devaluing the lives of black people and women perpetuates a system that privileges white male bodies. Powerfully, she writes of a "young Black woman, nineteen years old" who lived in "Brooklyn and she died there, gang-raped on a Brooklyn roof and thrown off, thrown down, screaming but inaudible."[36] To the state and the media, she is another "unidentified young Black woman, victim of unpardonable violence," whose death, to some, will mean very little because the state and the media treat black women as though their lives mean nothing. Scholar Kimberle Crenshaw also comments on this "forgotten victim"[37] by writing of how prosecutors describe this rape as "one of the most brutal in recent years."[38] This rape, along with the many others, was "virtually ignored by the media." Crenshaw attributes this lack of coverage to the attention given to the Central Park Jogger that occurred in the same week as she states, "the Central Park rape became a national rallying cause against random (read Black male) violence."[39] Crenshaw emphasizes that "because Black women face subordination based on both race and gender, reforms of rape law and judicial procedures that are premised on narrow conceptions of gender subordination may not address the devaluation of Black women."[40]

Both Crenshaw's claims and Jordan's observations illustrate why Jordan holds both the state and the media accountable for the assault on black women's bodies; Jordan strongly believes that something must be done about this domestic terrorism in the United States. These bodies belong to the many "unrecorded, unremembered" legions of black women "whose demise, whose violated bodies never lead to rallies/marching/vigilante vendettas/ legislation/loudspeaker-scale memorial services/ determined prosecution and community revenge."[41] These are just a few of the many women—most named and some unnamed—throughout Jordan's essays who are victims of violent acts perpetuated against women. The attention Jordan gives to these women is a call for the state to be attentive to this kind of violence. This call seeks more "legislation" and "determined prosecution" in efforts to protect women, given that inadequate protection reinforces a hetero-patriarchal citizenship in which women's bodies are devalued. Similarly, the connection between the devaluation of black women's bodies through visual imagery and their marginalization in social, political, economic, legal, and educational institutions is at the center of K. Sue Jewell's argument. In her book *From Mammy to Miss America and Beyond: Cultural Images and the Shaping of U.S. Social Policy,* Jewell posits "those who have a monopoly on power

and wealth use the mass media and societal institutions to ensure their privileged status through the maintenance of various systems of domination (i.e., race, sex and class inequality)."[42]

As evidenced in the writings of Jordan, Jewell, and many other scholars, the state is infamous in erasing the black body. Institutionalized racism has been one strategy used by the state to physically erase black, female bodies from national belonging. It hasn't been easy to imagine ourselves (i.e., black people in general, black women in particular) as part of national belonging when it is clear that "we can be killed, we can be sterilized. We can be kept out, pushed down, starved, shot, gassed, lynched, stunted, warped, and eliminated, altogether, from liberty, from our own pursuit of our own happiness. It's happened before. It's happening now."[43] Jordan's reference to sterilization has been well researched by Dorothy Roberts in *Killing the Black Body.* Roberts documents how the 1970s experienced an increase in sterilization as a predominant method of birth control—there were a reported 2,000,000 cases in 1970 as compared to 700,000 in 1980.[44] She states, "it was a common belief among Blacks in the South that Black women were routinely sterilized without their consent and for no medical reason."[45] Teaching hospitals performed "unnecessary hysterectomies on poor Black women as practice for their medical residents."[46] In other words, state apparatus uses means of force, violent atrocities included, to keep black people and women in their "place."

In addition, interlocking systems of oppression continue to place black women in the periphery of national identity, an argument clearly articulated in Jordan's analysis of the treatment of Anita Hill during the Clarence Thomas confirmation hearings. Before the 1995 publication of Geneva Smitherman's *African American Women Speak Out on Anita Hill-Clarence Thomas,* Jordan spoke out in 1991. In discussing the panoply of voices on the Thomas hearings in her introduction, Smitherman makes no mention of Jordan's response published in *The Progressive,* December 12, 1991.[47] Written in a call-and-response black rhetorical strategy, **"Can I Get a Witness"** reveals what happens to a black woman in America when she publicly testifies to a personal experience of sexual harassment; she gets ignored.[48] Hill was "trying to tell the truth in an arena of snakes and hyenas and dinosaurs and power-mad dogs."[49] As a result of this "televised victimization of Anita Hill, the American war of violence against women moved from the streets, moved from hip-hop, moved from multimillion-dollar movies into the highest chambers of the U.S. government."[50] Eager to protect Thomas, the fourteen white senators, prohibited expert testimony on sexual harassment, not a single psychiatrist or licensed psychologist was allowed to testify; therefore, Hill was "set up" and "slanderous suppositions" ensued. While Thomas vilified the hearings as a "high-tech lynching," Jordan wonders if there ever was a time in America that a black man got lynched because he was bothering a black woman? Historically, it was white female bodies that were protected, yet in this instance, the Senate Committee protected a black male body through which white power and authority were re-inscribed. Once again, the matrix of domination left, and continues to leave, black female bodies "isolated, betrayed, and abused."[51] Given that the "government will not protect and defend [Hill], and all black women, and all women, period in this savage country—if this government will not defend us from poverty and violence and contempt—then we will change the government." Jordan concludes her essay by calling out for witnesses to deliver on this warning because through solidarity women can empower themselves to force changes to take place. Furthermore, gender privilege is definitely at work in the Clarence Thomas judicial hearings. Also operating here is how the matrix of domination continues to oppress black women by first privileging whiteness, and next gender. Still, in a country where white privilege and male privilege allow for access to the nation's resources, black women remain subordinated.

Constructing a national identity that emphasizes male dominance is a part of the realities of many American women citizens. Jordan herself testifies to male dominance by recounting personal accounts of being raped; her accounts with and narration of these experiences amplify the devaluation of women's bodies in the American body politic. This devaluation of black, female bodies in American society privileges white hetero-patriarchal citizenship. As Jordan indicates, "our politicians and their media flunkies in these United States" remain "faithful to a Eurocentric, patriarchal history that drags a pretty poor track record into view."[52] This track record does not take seriously the violence against women, particularly rape. In 1986, Jordan writes of her first rape, "He had overpowered the supposed protection of my privacy, he had violated the boundaries of my single self."[53] She also questions, "What besides race and sex and class could block me from becoming a clearly successful American, A Great White Man?"[54] Ten years later, in 1996 Jordan tells "the second time [she] was raped the man was black—He was, in fact, head of the local NAACP."[55] In telling of her second rape, Jordan critically reflects back to the first time she was raped to provide chilling details of both experiences as "violent domination"[56] intended to physically and mentally disempower women into submissively and subordinate positions in American citizenry. This domination particularly informs public understandings of safety and protection (and the lack thereof) in the public and private spheres for women. The fact that these men "violated the boundaries" of Jordan's "single self" threatens the space of her existence as a black woman, as an American citizen, as a human being, as a member of America's imagined community and national identity.

In fact, "connections between rape and nation-making have important application to the United States."[57] In analyzing responses to rape by institutions such as the refugee/asylum system and the U.S. Border Patrol, Eithne Luibhéid illustrates ways that the state reinscribes exclusionary nationalism. Luibhéid's research shows how rape signifies forces and unwanted domination of the body at the same time that it represents local and national "social hierarchies of sexuality, gender, race, class, and legal status."[58] While Luibhéid's work heavily focuses on the rape of undocumented women crossing into the United States, her research has great implications for African American women and for notions of citizenship. In "Notes Toward a Model of Resistance," Jordan outlines implications for conceptualizing realities encountered by women much the same way the Luibhéid does in her own research.[59] While Luibhéid focuses on U.S. Border Patrol agents, Jordan examines specific state perpetrators such as the U.S. Marine Corps. She notes, "Marine Corps drill instructors still led training runs with chants like: 'One, two, three, four. Everyday we pray for war. Five, six, seven, eight. Rape. Kill. Mutilate.'"[60] In other words, the state prepares men for such violent, dehumanizing acts against the enemies, and oftentimes women are included on this list. Elsewhere, Jordan connects the actions of state perpetuators with the reality faced by many women in state-sanctioned positions: "Here are American women 50 percent more likely to be raped inside the military than in civilian life."[61]

In this essay, Jordan speaks not only to rape victims in the United States, but also to those women seeking asylum or U.S. citizenship. Drawing on her personal experience, Jordan offers a model of resistance applicable to her own survival in overcoming the fear and powerlessness brought about from rape. Jordan's argument is clearly significant: both women citizens and those women crossing into the United States must not let "brute domination" become the norm by which they live and come to understand American citizenship. Jordan knows that women "can never completely 'recover' from rape," yet we can "rescue any single girl or woman from lifelong, universal threats to her safe assertion of her human rights, her self-determination inside every moment and on every level."[62] For rape victims who remain silent, Jordan's model of resistance may not offer all the answers to combating the violence of rape, but it does suggest community-building grounded in hope. This hope, for Jordan, must materialize into action that demands our strength to fight back.

The imagining of the nation also materializes in the ways in which the state spends its money—budget. Throughout her essays, Jordan juxtaposes U.S. military spending and what the U.S. government could do with monies that have been used to "obliterate Iraq and its people and their leader."[63] In 1991, the White House and Pentagon, (i.e., "ruling white men") in less than three months "spent $56 billion" of American tax money, in their "armchair warfare."[64] In "rejoicing" the end of former President George Bush's administration in 1992, and in reflecting on the past twelve years of the presidency, Jordan insists that government spending could have been better served in other areas that would improve the lives of minority groups. For instance, Jordan contends that her tax dollars would be better spent if invested in the National Cancer Institute, an institution that is allocated only $90 million for research.[65] Jordan informs us that every single year, 175,000 American women learn they have breast cancer before informing us that in 1992 alone, 45,000 American women died of breast cancer.[66] We could have invested "the cost of three or four B-2 bombers into the complete, redemptive, onsite-resident rebuilding of our inner cities," or even possibly, "we could cure breast cancer."[67] Moreover, Bush can loan $400 million to new housing in Arab East Jerusalem, yet the Bush administration, according to Jordan, "has not guaranteed a $400 million anything for the homeless or low-income Americans who need shelter here."[68]

In turning to Clinton's presidency, Jordan's rejoicing is short-lived. In his budget speech to the nation, he expressed his interest to increase funding for AIDS, but he did not mention breast cancer.[69] So again, this "soft-spoken emergency" is not an item of national budget concern. In 1996, Jordan writes that "in the last twenty years in the United States, 3,660,000 women have perished from the disease known as breast cancer."[70] Overall, when it comes to black people, women, and the poor, the "almighty budget" has no money for job creation or for rescue and revitalization of public schools, for drug rehabilitation, for development and implementation of effective, grassroots community planning, or for social and psychological counseling: "No funds available in the Almighty Budget!"[71] Even the national budget available for welfare assistance in 1994 was less than one-half of one percent (Jordan notes that most recipients of welfare aid are white, not black). In short, Clinton and other powerful white men help those who are like themselves. Jordan emphasizes "to punish/ derogate/imprison/destroy," there are multibillions of dollars in hand, evidently, but to "salvage/teach/train/ enlighten/empower? No money in the Bank!"[72]

The construction of a national identity wherein black women remain on the periphery of American citizenship is a part of this nation's history. Black, female bodies in the American body politic have mattered little. In describing the relationship between American polity and black women, Jordan observes, "There is a terrible trouble across the land, in part, because we were never

the 'Men,' and because we were never the People: We were never the intended beneficiaries of the Founding Fathers of the Founding Documents of America."[73] Jordan traces notions of belonging back to America's founding fathers such as Thomas Jefferson who "did not suppose 'Men' to include anyone significantly different from himself: a white male aristocrat."[74] In placing dominant/subordinate relationships in a historical context, Jordan is then able to trace the struggle by black women who move from a group considered "not the people" to a group who proclaims "we are now the people."[75] In her brief overview of American history that covers the Gettysburg Address, Declaration of Independence, Constitution of 1787, Dred Scott Decision of 1857, Bill of Rights, and Constitutional Amendments 13, 14, 15, 19, and 24, Jordan provides a solid argument that America's relationship with African American women has not always ended happily ever after. Even though African American women were supposedly granted rights under constitutional amendments, Jordan questions the reasons why a Civil Rights Revolution in the Land of the Free needed to be waged more than 17 decades after legislative mandates of rights were passed. More important is Jordan's questioning of the rights and welfare of fighters for justice: "And, did we not, did we not have to, turn this country around, on and off international microphones and cameras, and risk multitude, and sacrifice far too many known and unknown heroic children and women and men—warriors for our civil rights, our 'equal protection under the law'"?[76]

Throughout her essays and throughout her activist life, Jordan wonders whether or not we are safe and free as she interrogates the basic premise of American democracy. For Jordan, not being safe and not being free means "certain human beings may be rightfully denied their land, their life, their liberty, and their pursuit of happiness."[77] Certain human beings have been denied access to full American citizenship and thus denied access to resources. And these certain human beings are not white, not male, and not heterosexual: "These powerful white men now conspire to stop immigration to America by anybody who does not resemble themselves. These same powerful white men are the ones who waffle on or ignore women's issues and who betray and/or attack gay and lesbian Americans."[78]

Constructions of national identity hurt people of color, women, and gays and lesbians given that America's national identity "is based upon a white supremacist ideology that determines domestic and foreign policies alike."[79] America's imagined notions of democracy and liberty are incongruent with the daily lives of most of American citizens; as a result, this incongruency translates to hypocrisy thus American national identity has both domestic and international consequences. Given the nation's domestic terrorism and position on international terrorism, I wonder if we can be a model for democracy given that our national identity is marked by exclusion, inequalities, and injustice.

National identity has not only been marked through race and gender, but also through sexuality. Jordan's essay **"A New Politics of Sexuality"** makes clear that the national imagery for American citizenship excludes blacks and women just as much as it excludes those whose identities are other than heterosexual.[80] Because the United States is "enforced by traditions of state-sanctioned violence plus religion and the law," to allow for "heterosexual institutionalization of rights and privileges" is to deny rights to men and women identified as homosexual.[81] Epistemological systems in the United States were first concerned with articulating American citizenship for white, male, heterosexual individuals; thus, it becomes difficult to form new epistemological notions of American citizenship representative and inclusive of sexual identities other than heterosexual. To be an American citizen, people should have the space to exist as they choose. When Jordan writes, "I am Black and I am female and I am a mother and I am bisexual and I am a nationalist and I am an antinationalist," she is imagining the acceptance of multi-identities without the presence of media constructs.[82]

Jordan asks, "Will we simply delete vast American communities from our national vision?"[83] In examining the ways in which U.S. institutions shape notions of belonging to American citizenship for black women, Jordan reveals that black people remain in the periphery of American citizenship. In insisting that America needs to be nationally restored (hence the emergence of a true democracy will then be possible), Jordan offers new possibilities of American citizenship in which the sum of her individual parts (i.e., race, gender, and sexuality) is protected by the nation-state. How the nation imagines itself reflects the political, civil, and social rights of American citizens. As long as national identity is marked white and male, all other bodies will remain on the lowest stratum in the nation's hierarchical citizenry. Despite what seems to be civil war all around, Jordan does not give up on a democracy wherein all peoples, be they black, women, bisexual, or refugees, enjoy life, liberty, and the pursuit of happiness.

As I tried to go along with the media's attempts to convince me, an American citizen, to commit to a flag-waving-America-the-beautiful-singing-land-where-my-fathers-died kind of spirit, the images reminded me of a history I had not forgotten.

Before turning to the politically charged writings of June Jordan, I wondered who will renew my American spirit? Before I was born, Jordan was talking about space. Before I moved out into the world, Jordan was

busy moving obstacles to make a place for other black, female bodies in her numerous writings and poetry, Jordan, the daughter of Jamaican immigrant parents, testifies to the struggles of being a U.S. citizen. Although I come from the lineage of black slave ancestry in America, Jordan and I share the same struggles of U.S. citizenship. Placed at the door to citizenship in America, there has not always been a welcome mat for black people. We could just touch the door handle and alarms would sound, sirens would ring, and dogs would bark. The citizenship Jordan envisions for black women and the lived experiences of American citizenship for black women are two different things, yet as an activist scholar, Jordan's self-determination insists on making the latter become the former—a citizenship that includes and protects all parts of her identity. Jordan's imagery of national identity forces the state and the media to seek new epistemologies that are not contingent on white, male bodies this would allow black people the rightful space in which to exist as American citizens in a democratized social order without harm. In terms of counterhegemony Jordan offers another vision of national imagery wherein bodies—in the American body politic—of blacks and women do matter. For democracy to truly exist the state must materialize a national imagery that is not just white, male, and heterosexual. In other words,

> where my life or the lives of African-Americans, Native Americans, Chicano-Americans, Latin-Americans, and Asian-Americans amount to arguable fringe or freak components of some theoretical netherland. We have become many peoples of this nation—nothing less than that. I do not accept that we, American peoples of color, signify anything optional or dubious or marginal or exotic or anything in any way less valuable, less necessary, less sacred than white America.[84]

National identity should materialize in the citizenship of all American peoples and not in the proliferation of mediated images that devalue black bodies Jordan reminds us that the people of the United States have a "need for freedom that does not omit any racial, gender, ethnic, sexual, or physical identity from its protection."[85] Her "self-constructed definitions of new spaces of culture, freedom, and identity" offer us new possibilities to American visions of national identity to which notions of belonging include black, female, bisexual bodies. Whether the American mainstream media and the state make an ideological shift to include such a national imagery Jordan envisions remains to be seen.

Notes

1. Ulf Hedetoft and Mette Hjort, *The Postnational Self: Belonging and Identity* (Minneapolis: University of Minnesota Press, 2002). Ulf Hedetoft and Mette Hjort note that "belonging constitutes a political and cultural field of global contestation (anywhere between ascriptions of belonging and self-constructed

definitions of new spaces of culture, freedom, and identity" summoning a range of pertinent issues concerning relations between individuals, groups, and communities.

2. *People,* May 2002.

3. *Toledo Blade,* September 24, 2001.

4. *USA Today,* September 26, 2001.

5. Stuart Hall, *Representation: Cultural Representations and Signifying Practices* (Newbury Park Calif.: Sage, 1997).

6. Roland Barthes, *Mythologies,* selected and translated from the French by Annette Lavers (New York: Hill & Wang, 1972).

7. June Jordan, *Affirmative Acts: Political Essays* (New York: Anchor Books, 1998), 207 See 9.

8. Jordan, *Affirmative Acts,* 82-83.

9. June Jordan, *Civil Wars: Observations From the Front Lines of America* (Boston: Beacon Press, 1981); *Technical Difficulties: African-American Notes on the State of the Union* (New York: Pantheon Books, 1992); *Affirmative Acts: Political Essays* (New York: Anchor Books, 1998).

10. Jordan, *Civil Wars,* 163.

11. Benedict Anderson, *Imagined Communities: Reflections on the Origin and Spread of Nationalism* (London: Verso, 1991), 5-7.

12. Anderson, *Imagined Communities,* 5-6.

13. Jordan, *Affirmative Acts,* 120.

14. Jordan, *Affirmative Acts,* 113-14.

15. *Toledo Blade,* September 15, 2001.

16. Jordan, *Affirmative Acts,* 91.

17. Jordan, *Civil Wars,* 115.

18. Jordan, *Technical Difficulties,* 119-33.

19. Jordan, *Technical Difficulties,* 122.

20. Jordan, *Technical Difficulties,* 122.

21. Jordan, *Technical Difficulties,* 125.

22. Jordan, *Technical Difficulties,* 125.

23. Jordan, *Technical Difficulties,* 129.

24. Jordan, *Technical Difficulties,* 130.

25. Jordan, *Technical Difficulties,* 131.

26. Jordan, *Technical Difficulties,* 120.

27. *Toledo Blade,* September 14, 2001.

28. *Toledo Blade,* September 15, 2001.

29. Jordan, *Affirmative Acts,* 91.

30. Jordan, *Affirmative Acts,* 92.

31. Jordan, *Affirmative Acts,* 94.

32. Jordan, *Affirmative Acts,* 93.

33. Jordan, *Affirmative Acts,* 85.

34. Jordan, *Affirmative Acts,* 92.

35. Jordan, *Affirmative Acts,* 93.

36. Jordan, *Technical Difficulties,* 147.

37. Kimberle Crenshaw, "Mapping the Margins: Intersectionality, Identity Politics, and Violence Against Women of Color," *Stanford Law Review,* vol. 43 (July 1991): 1241-99.

38. Crenshaw, "Mapping the Margins," 1268.

39. Crenshaw, "Mapping the Margins," 1268.

40. Crenshaw, "Mapping the Margins," 1270.

41. Jordan, *Technical Difficulties,* 147.

42. K. Sue Jewell, *From Mammy to Miss America and Beyond: Cultural Images & the Shaping of U.S. Social Policy* (London: Routledge, 1993).

43. Jewell, *From Mammy to Miss America and Beyond,* 30.

44. Dorothy Roberts, *Killing the Black Body: Race, Reproduction, and the Meaning of Liberty* (New York: Pantheon Books, 1997).

45. Roberts, *Killing the Black Body,* 90.

46. Roberts, *Killing the Black Body,* 90.

47. Geneva Smitherman, *African American Women Speak Out on Anita Hill-Clarence Thomas* (Detroit: Wayne State University Press, 1995).

48. Jordan, *Technical Difficulties,* 213-19.

49. Jordan, *Technical Difficulties,* 218.

50. Jordan, *Technical Difficulties,* 218.

51. Jordan, *Technical Difficulties,* 213.

52. Jordan, *Affirmative Acts,* 91.

53. Jordan, *Technical Difficulties,* 14.

54. Jordan, *Technical Difficulties,* 14.

55. Jordan, *Affirmative Acts,* 151.

56. Jordan, *Affirmative Acts,* 147.

57. Eithne Luibhéid, *Entry Denied: Controlling Sexuality at the Border* (Minneapolis: University of Minnesota Press, 2002), 105.

58. Luibhéid, *Entry Denied,* 133.

59. Jordan, *Affirmative Acts,* 143-56.

60. Jordan, *Affirmative Acts,* 155.

61. Jordan, *Affirmative Acts,* 37.

62. Jordan, *Affirmative Acts,* 153, 155.

63. Jordan, *Affirmative Acts,* 12.

64. Jordan, *Affirmative Acts,* 12.

65. Jordan, *Affirmative Acts,* 23.

66. Jordan, *Affirmative Acts,* 23.

67. Jordan, *Affirmative Acts,* 14, 17.

68. Jordan, *Affirmative Acts,* 6.

69. Jordan, *Affirmative Acts,* 35.

70. Jordan, *Affirmative Acts,* 160.

71. Jordan, *Affirmative Acts,* 84.

72. Jordan, *Affirmative Acts,* 84.

73. Jordan, *Technical Difficulties,* 57.

74. Jordan, *Technical Difficulties,* 57.

75. Jordan, *Technical Difficulties,* 57.

76. Jordan, *Technical Difficulties,* 59-60.

77. Jordan, *Technical Difficulties,* 57.

78. Jordan, *Affirmative Acts,* 85.

79. Jordan, *Affirmative Acts,* 85-86.

80. Jordan, *Technical Difficulties,* 187-93.

81. Jordan, *Technical Difficulties,* 188.

82. Jordan, *Technical Difficulties,* 189.

83. Jordan, *Technical Difficulties,* 95.

84. Jordan, *Technical Difficulties,* 198.

85. Jordan, *Affirmative Acts,* 61.

Kirsten Bartholomew Ortega (essay date 2004)

SOURCE: Ortega, Kirsten Bartholomew. "June Jordan's Radical Pedagogy: Activist Poetry in Public Education." In *Still Seeking an Attitude: Critical Reflections on the Work of June Jordan,* edited by Valerie Kinloch and Margret Grebowicz, pp. 189-208. Lanham, Md.: Lexington Books, 2004.

[*In this essay, Ortega comments on Jordan's role in developing public school poetry curricula.*]

Recently, I taught a writing class at the University of Florida in which education majors in the Pro-Teach Program were required to design a poetry curriculum for elementary school students. The assignment was required because the Education Department had determined that too few elementary educators teach poetry anymore. Initially, my students were intimidated by the assignment, claiming that they did not like poetry or understand it, so they were uncomfortable attempting to teach it. This reaction surprised me because the elements of poetry are an essential part of nursery rhymes and children's books. In fact, critically acclaimed poets such as Gertrude Stein, Gwendolyn Brooks, and more recently, June Jordan have all published children's books. For June Jordan, writing poetry that is accessible to children and general readers was essential to her vision of herself as both a poet and an educator.

June Jordan is often remembered as a beloved teacher. Since few writers are remembered for their teaching practices, Jordan's prioritization of pedagogy in her career reminds academics and artists that pedagogy and critical or artistic work are not mutually exclusive. Jordan's teaching practices not only provide a model of activist involvement in the community through the teaching of creative skills like poetry writing that employs 1960s and 1970s ideologies in addressing an activist pedagogy in the 1990s, but also anticipate the twenty-first-century need for radical change in public education at all levels. Jordan's greatest pedagogical triumph, the creation of the Poetry for the People program at the University of California at Berkeley, soon after she began teaching there in 1989, exemplifies this model. In 1995, those involved in the Poetry for the People program collectively published *June Jordan's Poetry for the People: A Revolutionary Blueprint,*[1] effectively making Jordan's poetry pedagogy accessible to all students and educators.

Recent government controls of public education evidence a general move away from the kinds of radical pedagogies that Jordan employed in her teaching a decade ago. At the primary and secondary levels, standardized testing is used to restrict teachers' autonomy and control the information that is disseminated to students. Such tests limit definitions of "knowledge" and restrict time and resources available for creative learning. School systems based on the "voucher" reward system, like those in Florida, prohibit the development of lower-income schools by punishing the teachers and students for their school's financial disadvantage. At the university level, open-admissions programs like the one that Jordan taught in at City College in New York have been discredited and dismantled. The bilingual education that Jordan fought for has been rescinded in California already, and the issue of Black English has been dismissed almost entirely. Preventing Jordan's work as an educator from being considered tangential to her work as a poet and social activist is crucial to renewing interest in the kinds of radical pedagogies that she practiced and proved are successful. We risk forgetting Jordan's urgent call to rescue public education from becoming a tool of inequality and oppression if we overlook her contributions to pedagogical theory and methodology.

In *Technical Difficulties,* Jordan challenges her readers to reevaluate the state of higher education in the United States today, clarifying the new, global demands of public school curricula and expectations.[2] "The challenge of higher education in the whole world of America is this: to lift the standards of the teachers and of the required core curriculum so that we who would teach can look into the eyes of those who would learn from us without shame and without perversions of ignorance disguised as Noble Mastery."[3] She characterizes the state of higher education through analogy to "finding a needle in the haystack."[4] According to Jordan, higher education is making the pointless effort of finding needles in a haystack instead of valuing the hay itself. She explains that a needle is something that has no use by itself. Hay, however, can serve a variety of functions, including providing food and shelter. Approaches to education that value "needles" over "hay" perpetually reward class privilege. Because class and race are often paralleled—whites having the majority of the wealth—this kind of classism perpetuates racial segregation as well. Those with more money become the "needles." The value of a university depends on how small the needle is, or how successfully it perpetuates class privilege.[5] Jordan fought this kind of elitist privileging of knowledge in her pedagogy by taking poetry off its academic pedestal and giving it back to "the people."

Although Jordan published descriptions of her experiences as a teacher, the best example of her methods are available in *June Jordan's Poetry for the People: A Revolutionary Blueprint,* which does what its title claims: it describes how Jordan and her students made their program work and how others can do the same. The program combines detailed instruction in poetry writing with community outreach. The poetry writing aspect of the program breaks down into three primary categories: reading, practice writing, and contact with published poet "colleagues." Even though the book provides bibliographic lists of the kinds of books Jordan and her students read in order to inform their own writing, it encourages teachers and students to determine together which texts are going to be most relevant. The literary background leads to the detailed assignment of poetry writing, including poems that require the demonstration of poetic forms. Finally, the program arranges to have various writers come to Berkeley to give public readings and hold discussions with the students.

The community outreach aspect of the program helps make the students' writing relevant to the world around them. While most academic studies occur in a vacuum created by the boundaries of the university, in "Poetry for the People," the "people" are not just academics. Each semester culminates in a public reading of each student's work, and throughout the semester students travel to local elementary schools, churches, and community centers to give readings and host poetry writing lessons. In Poetry for the People, writing is not restricted to the page. Rather, it becomes a social act, a contribution to different learning environments. Students' education moves from a passive acceptance of information to an active involvement with information. As the program proved to be successful at Berkeley, Jordan added further leadership possibilities for students by allowing them to become teaching assistants. After working in the program and proving their skill, students can become "student teacher poets" who provide personal instruction to the other students.[6] By creating the Poetry for the People program, Jordan provides a teaching model that gives students the kind of active role in their education of which she felt she had been deprived.

Jordan's personal struggle with education as a student gave her a unique perspective as a teacher. She comments that "[a]ll of my teaching life I have tried to remember how much I always, as a student, hated school, and why."[7] Although Jordan learned the value of education from her parents, the restrictions of "compulsory education," as she calls it, frustrated her. Despite the fact that Jordan was successful enough in her primary education to earn a scholarship to the Northfield Mount Hermon School, a prominent college preparatory school in Massachusetts, she still recognized the inability of school to validate her experiences from outside the school environment. She writes that:

> When I was going to school, too much of the time I found myself an alien body force-fed stories and facts about people entirely unrelated to me, or my family. And the regular demands upon me only required my acquiescence to a program of instruction predetermined without regard for my particular history, or future. I was made to learn about "the powerful": those who won wars or who conquered territory or whose odd ideas about poetry and love prevailed inside some distant country where neither my parents nor myself would find welcome.[8]

As phrases like "alien," "force-fed," and "required . . . acquiescence" indicate, Jordan recognized the ways that the education system stifled her personal growth. She was capable of learning the information required, but felt no personal connection to or interest in the information because her gender, race, and cultural background located her outside its boundaries. "Knowledge" was someone else's, not her own. For most students, this would be enough to turn them off of school completely. Fortunately, Jordan found refuge in reading and writing poetry. She expressed her frustrations in writing and social activism, but continued to read canonical works to inform those writings and acts. Despite her disillusionment with the education system, she continued to seek ways to educate herself, and established a concept of education and knowledge for herself that would eventually be the foundation of her teaching practices.

Jordan attended both Barnard College and the University of Chicago (without completing degrees) and found that the education regiments at those universities varied little from those at the institutions she had previously attended. She explains that she entered Barnard College with the hope that it "would either give me the connection between the apparently unrelated worlds of white and Black, or that this college would enable me to make that connection myself."[9] Jordan's goal in seeking education was to better understand the people and world around her. Her discoveries about the barriers that politics, culture, and race create between people frames both her political activism and her pedagogy, but she did not make those connections through analytical academic work. Instead, when she left Barnard, she attempted to connect the two worlds through an interracial marriage. Initially, she chose to explore race differences through her personal life rather than an academic life.

Jordan does not, however, totally reject traditional methods of teaching. She describes the survey courses at the University of Chicago as "excellent"[10] and values an understanding of literary history both as a writer and as a teacher. "[I]t's important to know, in a panoramic way, what's been done before you. I had always believed that, as a writer; it wasn't simply academic for me. I was curious. What had the poets before me done? We are *all* colleagues."[11] Jordan conscientiously familiarized herself with the literary canon and with poetic forms, putting knowledge of the traditions before experimentation with and distortion of them. Even though she describes having received harshly disparaging comments about her writing from Chicago professors, she refuses to not consider herself Walt Whitman's equal, whom she writes about in the introduction to *Passion: New Poems 1977-1980*.[12] By considering herself "colleagues" with canonical writers, Jordan bends the parameters of "literature" for both herself and her students, whom she implicitly considers writers as well. Jordan's complex perspective on education as a student—her belief that traditional education is both essential and inadequate—is crucial to understanding her perspective as a teacher because it justifies why she values her students' contributions to the classroom information. In Jordan's pedagogy, the teacher provides the students with access to context, history, and literary structure and examples, but the students are an essential factor in the construction of knowledge because they provide new insights and new forms of expression that keeps the literature alive.

Jordan addresses the problem of hegemonic standards of knowledge construction or "intelligence" in **"A Poem about Intelligence for My/ Brothers and Sisters."**[13] The poem confronts the issues of education outside the confines of institutionalized learning environments by raising such issues (standardized testing, for example) in comparison with the people in an average, working-class, black neighborhood. The poem reiterates Jordan's ideas about how important academic knowledge is or isn't in communities outside of academia, making it a useful lens through which to examine how her pedagogy reevaluates knowledge acquisition.

"A Poem about Intelligence for My/ Brothers and Sisters" opens by questioning the way standardized and I.Q. testing function to categorize African Americans as intellectually inferior:

> A few years back and they told me Black
> means a hole where other folks
> got brain/it was like the cells in the heads
> of black children was out to every hour on the hour
>   naps
> Scientists called the phenomenon the Notorious
> Jensen Lapse, remember?[14]

Because science is supposed to be based on fact determined from observation and experimentation, that scientists have labeled a "phenomenon" peculiar to black people gives it cultural credence in America. Jordan confronts and exposes ways that science has been manipulated to justify racist beliefs. After positioning herself as the victim of racist "scientific" testing, the speaker flips the roles and wonders what it would be like to be the one devising the tests that determine mental aptitude. She imagines possibly administering them to those who are in positions of the most power, such as the CIA.

> Anyway I was thinking
> about how to devise
> a test for the wise
> like a Stanford-Binet
> for the C.I.A.
> you know?[15]

By "thinking," the speaker is already disproving the misperception described at the beginning of the poem as the "Notorious Jensen Lapse." In suggesting that a new test be devised and given specifically to the CIA, Jordan not only singles out an organization that fits both rhythmically into the poem and into a burgeoning rhyme scheme, but she also calls attention to the CIA's association with thought-police, especially during the McCarthy era and the civil rights movement. The lines create a moment that is simultaneously dangerously close to threatening an overthrow of the established government and undermining itself in adopting the sing-song qualities of a nursery rhyme.

Employing the CIA as an example allows Jordan to suggest a parallel between standardized testing and control by surveillance. The problem of surveillance is one that Patricia Hill Collins addresses directly in *Fighting Words: Black Women and the Search for Justice*.[16] Collins explains that after slavery ended in the United States, "[t]wo strategies of control—racial segregation and surveillance—emerged to limit and in most cases to reverse newly gained citizenship rights."[17] Collins uses the example of white women watching their black domestic employees as a form of surveillance, before noting "[w]hereas racial segregation is designed to keep Blacks as a group or class *outside* centers of power, surveillance aims to control Black individuals who are *inside* centers of power."[18] For black women especially, because they often entered white homes—intimate, private spaces—to work, surveillance was a powerful force in manipulating their behavior and even attempting to control their thoughts. As Jordan describes it, the moment that black children enter a public school—especially if the teachers and administration are white—they are under a similar kind of surveillance. Teachers tell the students what is appropriate behavior, appropriate knowledge, and appropriate forms of communication. They have the ability to determine the students' future successes psychologically through praise or neglect and their literal progression in school through grading. The implication of surveillance is taken to the next level in **"A Poem about Intelligence for My/ Brothers and Sisters"** when Jordan proposes counter-surveillance in the form of standardized testing of the CIA.

The poem explicates the speaker's frustration with a system that defines intelligence irrationally and privileges Eurocentric ideas. Jordan uses Albert Einstein as an example of how the current definition of "genius" fails:

> Take Einstein
> being the most the unquestionable the outstanding
> the maximal mind of the century
> right?[19]

The hyperbolic use of "unquestionable," "outstanding," and "maximal" as descriptors of Einstein's place in intellectual/academic history are juxtaposed with a question of reassurance. While "right?" addresses an audience whom the speaker assumes will agree, it also suggests that the degree of Einstein's influence may still be open to interpretation. Naturally, the speaker continues by making this very kind of dissenting interpretation:

> And I'm struggling against this lapse leftover
> from my Black childhood to fathom why
> anybody should say so:
> *E = mc squared?*
> I try that on this old lady live on my block:[20]

The speaker sarcastically suggests that maybe "The Notorious Jensen Lapse" prevents her from understanding the value of "E = mc squared." It seems to her that the equation does not have immediate value in her daily life. Instead of seeking a solution to the "E = mc squared" problem in an academic setting, the speaker takes the question out of her front door and offers it to a neighbor, Mrs. Johnson. Here, the contrast between the setting of the poem and the nature of the question becomes almost humorous as the conversation ensues. That the question is out of place is, of course, part of the speaker's point. The question has no relevance to the lives of those in the working-class, black neighborhood, despite academic insistence on it being one of the most important intellectual theories of the century.

The narrative of the poem transitions to encompass Mrs. Johnson's world as she is busily sweeping off of her porch the stains of the neighbors' previous night of partying. The speaker's interruption of the morning is not welcomed by the old woman, especially since her question is irrelevant to the morning's work. In response to the speaker's first attempt, Mrs. Johnson attempts to divert attention away from the speaker's unseemly morning appearance and non-sequitur question by returning only a usual morning pleasantry. The speaker, however, is persistent:

> Then I tell her, "Well
> also this same guy? I think
> he was undisputed Father of the Atom Bomb!"
> "That right." She mumbles or grumbles, not too
>   politely
> "And dint remember to wear socks when he put on
> his shoes!" I add on (getting desperate)
> at which point Mrs. Johnson take herself and her
>   broom
> a very big step down the stoop away from me
> "And never did nothing for nobody in particular
> lessen it was a committee
> and
> used to say, 'What time is it?'
> and
> you'd say 'Six o'clock.'
> and
> he'd say, 'Day or night?'
> and
> and he never made nobody a cup a tea
> in his whole brilliant life!"
> "and
> (my voice rises slightly)
> and
> he dint never boogie neither: never!"[21]

The frenzy to which this passage builds ends this first and disproportionately long stanza, and is followed by a short, three-line stanza consisting only of Mrs. Johnson's reply to the speaker. Clearly, Mrs. Johnson either does not know who Einstein was, or she is not particularly interested in his inability to behave according to social expectations. The ambiguity of her response to the speaker's tirade simulates the kind of intellectual position into which most Americans have been lulled:

> "Well," say Mrs. Johnson, "Well, honey,
> I do guess
> that's genius for you."[22]

Mrs. Johnson's reply both accepts the definition of genius as something that doesn't make sense since it ignores common sense, and it acknowledges the uselessness of being a genius under the prevailing definition, exemplified by the speaker's description of Einstein.

Although Jordan's term "Notorious Jensen Lapse" is not used today, the implications of such beliefs are pervasive in the school system still. Parents are told now that their children have "emotional disabilities" when they do not behave "appropriately" in the classroom. Arts programs are removed from schools entirely when funding is cut. Pedagogical models like Jordan's are made obscure by time-consuming standards and test preparation that do not ensure students' success in college despite claims that they will. The public education system needs to be changed on a much larger scale than the simple updating of individual lesson plans. Jordan's pedagogy indicates one direction in which radical revision could head.

Jordan's instinct to resist hegemonic standards of knowledge construction pedagogically and her desire to insert the personal into the academic are reflected in **"A Poem about Intelligence for My/ Brothers and Sisters."** Although Jordan argues that her work is not theoretical, it fits the feminist genre recently exploded by writers such as Alice Walker, Gloria Wade Gayles, and bell hooks (among many others) who argue that black women's voices and experiences are excluded by an academic system that excludes the personal. Sometimes calling themselves black feminists, sometimes following Walker's rubric of womanism, these women demand that academic attention be given to the kinds of experiences and intelligence that black women have for centuries valued and cultivated, but that are systematically labeled "the personal" and therefore bereft of academic or aesthetic value. Like Jordan, these women include their personal experiences as well as those of their mothers, sisters, and friends in their theoretical writing. Alice Walker locates educational histories in the lost work of Zora Neale Hurston, whose literary work she helped resurrect.[23] Gloria Wade Gayles locates educational experiences in her "rememberings" of her childhood.[24] As Johnetta B. Cole explains in the foreword to Gayles's *Pushed Back to Strength: A Black Woman's Journey Home,* "The significance of such remembering, made public for all to hear and feel, is that the recollections of one black woman become the mirror into which each of us can see how alike and how different we are."[25] bell hooks locates educational

communities in the "home-place" and the "chitlin circuit" of the Southern black community of her youth.[26] Certainly the issue of the personal is still highly controversial in academia (for those who argue its value, at least), and Jordan's work helps redefine academic standards by valuing it. **"A Poem about Intelligence for My/ Brothers and Sisters"** confronts constructions of intelligence that employ narrow definitions of knowledge to exclude people and this political position, combined with Jordan's personal writing about her teaching experiences, demonstrate the degree of her dedication to actively revising the education system.

A commitment to education has historically accompanied a commitment to struggling for racial equality, so Jordan's position follows in the footsteps of her cultural foremothers and forefathers. Education has long been established by black men such as Frederick Douglass, Booker T. Washington, and W. E. B. Du Bois as a means to freedom. Collins clarifies black women's influence in this tradition as well. She explains how from slavery on, black women have been the backbones of African American communities by encouraging the education of their children and by serving the community as teachers. According to Collins, black women reject limited definitions of education because they recognize the ways that school could become an "agency of socialization into a White middle-class worldview" instead of functioning to empower black students.[27] Jordan's pedagogical writing clearly builds on a long tradition of black women educators, but it also contributes to an ongoing conversation about education between black poets.

Although Jordan did not address pedagogy directly in her poetry, other poets such as Langston Hughes and Audre Lorde did. Discussing Jordan's poetry in the context of the poetry of Langston Hughes and Audre Lorde is useful, for they demonstrate ways of addressing the problematic nature of black students and teachers working within a hegemonic system to which they are outsiders. As a lifelong student of poetry, Jordan was surely familiar with Hughes's writing. As colleagues and fellow teachers at City College, it is likely that Jordan and Lorde exchanged pedagogical and poetic ideas. If they did not, they were certainly responding in their work to a similar environment and sets of experiences.

Both Hughes and Lorde wrote poems that specifically address the inadequacies of public education and the need for reformation. In "Theme for English B" Hughes writes from the perspective of a college student who recognizes that his instructor's assignment ignores the perspectives of students of different cultural or racial backgrounds.[28] In "Blackstudies" Audre Lorde writes from the perspective of a teacher who revolutionizes her class by creating a new discipline relevant to her

African American college students.[29] I will briefly examine these two poems to demonstrate the kinds of specific critique that poets were offering of the school system and to provide context for Jordan's more general attack on hegemonic academic standards in **"A Poem about Intelligence for My/ Brothers and Sisters."**

In "Theme for English B," Langston Hughes resists the common belief that an instructor in a college classroom can give an assignment that will be understood by all of the students identically, regardless of racial or cultural background. Specifically, the speaker addresses the problem of an assignment in which the instructor advised the class to *"let the page come out of you— / Then, it will be true."*[30] The speaker is not sure what "truth" the instructor refers to since he seems sure that his truth is not the same as the instructor's. The speaker wonders, "Will my page be colored that I write? / Being me, it will not be white."[31] Then, the speaker takes the problem one step further: because the instructor and the student are a part of the same classroom, they are in a sort of educational conversation. The student turns writing in; the instructor responds to the writing. Because the student's work is always affected by the expectation of the teacher's comments and grade, the writing will be part of both of them. This writing is not coming directly from the student, but from the instructor's writing prompt:

> But it will be
> a part of you, instructor.
> You are white—
> yet a part of me, as I am a part of you.
> That's American.
>   . . .
>
> As I learn from you,
> I guess you learn from me—
> although you're older—and white—
> and somewhat more free.[32]

The speaker in the poem recognizes what the instructor could not: that "what is true" has a great deal to do with perspective, opinion, and historical context. The instructor thinks his power is benign because it is academic; he thinks it is outside of the historical oppression of voices like the poem's speaker's.

While the Hughes poem articulates the disconnects that exist among teacher, student, and instructional materials/ methods that June Jordan expresses in her prose, Audre Lorde's poem "Blackstudies" takes the next step in the progression from disenfranchised student to disenfranchised teacher. The poem is situated in the kind of scenario that Lorde and Jordan encountered as teachers at City College in the late 1960s, although Lorde taught at Hunter College as well and may have written the poem about a similar, although not identical, experience (fictional or factual).

The speaker of "Blackstudies" moves smoothly between metaphorical phrases like "chill winds sweeping high places," referring to academia's exposure to new perspectives as well as the remote classroom setting that was provided for the course, and specific concerns of teaching a class of students who wait outsider her door "on the 17th floor."[33] The speaker is attempting to convey a revisionist history and way of thinking to her students that includes the black perspective, exposing certain hypocrisies in the educational standards:

> by the weight of my remembered sorrows
> they will use my legend to shape their own language
> and make it ruler
> measuring the distance between my hunger
> and their own purpose.[34]

In this passage, Lorde implies the creation of a new language, the use of legend and memories to rewrite history, and by using "ruler" to mean both a measuring device and one who rules, she reevaluates positions of power in education. Although the speaker expresses fear in attempting such a radical endeavor, in the last stanza, she takes the risk, plunging head first into the educational reform. The speaker in Lorde's poem must create a pedagogy that has room for the kinds of unusual learning environments and expectations through and around which her students must navigate their knowledge construction. It stresses the value of their desires, their languages and histories that are not defined by or even allotted a place in traditional academics. Jordan's pedagogy responds to the needs of these kinds of students by valuing the different knowledges that they bring to the classroom from their different backgrounds.

Jordan's unique experience as a student enabled her to understand the importance of her students' contribution to the classroom, and therefore to create a radical pedagogy. She never allowed academic traditions to restrain her learning as a student, so she never utilized those traditions or standards in constructing her pedagogy. She was never limited by methods or rules of lesson planning taught by a certification program. In fact, Jordan openly dismisses the notion of her work as academic. She accuses academia of ignoring or excluding the very people to whom she wanted to speak. "I'm not writing for the academy. I don't give a shit about the academy. I'm writing for people who read. Mainly I try to reach college students, which is a huge, heterogeneous, and important audience to reach."[35] Jordan resolves the conflict between teaching in academia and resisting academic expectations by encouraging her students to interrogate academic standards. Like the student in Hughes's poem, Jordan remembers what it is like to have teachers who dictate the way knowledge will be constructed in a classroom, and, therefore, like the teacher in Lorde's poem, Jordan tries to find information that is relevant to her students and then to help them define the language in which to express their knowledge production.

Jordan's work within academia demonstrates her commitment to changing its role in determining what "education" is. Her discoveries about the way state universities and community colleges are funded forced her to realize that academia is not removed from the problems that public primary and secondary schools face.[36] She decided that academia cannot deny or allow for its participation in these problems of exclusion. Consequently, she created a pedagogy that moves beyond the walls of academia because she refuses to accept that some people deserve education and others do not—especially since the "others" are usually people of color or from minority backgrounds. As two of her former students explained in an article written after Jordan's death:

> June taught her students that the classroom extends far beyond the university. . . . She instilled in each of her University of California Berkeley students a sense of responsibility to community members who lacked access to privileged education, and who sometimes lacked any kind of economic or social power. By doing this, she dispelled myths about poetry and who had the right to read it. June believed, firmly, that every person has something significant and necessary to say.[37]

Specifically, Jordan used the teaching of poetry—her area of expertise, but also a form of writing accessible to all people—as a site of radical reformation of language education. Audre Lorde explains that poetry is the art form that is the most "economical" because it requires the least material and can be written or worked on in brief amounts of time, like on the subway.[38] The popularity of rap music today attests to the accessibility of poetry. Jordan felt that poetry offered an ideal vehicle for the unique, individual expression of students' thoughts and voices with the added benefit of a history of forms and styles with which to experiment. Yet, poetry is the literary form by which students and teachers alike are the most intimidated. While it is accessible, it is also intellectual, requiring multiple readings. The poetry's restrictions, however, are precisely what make Jordan's pedagogy applicable to other disciplines. Reading and writing poetry requires examination and manipulation of language in a way that improves communication, creativity, and logic skills.

What is most empowering about Jordan's pedagogical ideas is that they are practical instead of theoretical. She provides students with skills and then demonstrates how those skills are useful to them in their lives. Instead of writing about possibilities, she used every moment in the classroom as an experiment and then shared the results with others by publishing accounts of her teaching experiences. Without ever receiving certification or even training as a teacher, she carved out new approaches to classroom literacy programs from her life experience and her willingness to listen to her students' needs. Jordan explains that she was unprepared for her introduction to teaching and therefore able to approach it from a unique perspective. "In 1967, Herb Kohl, one of the founders of Teachers and Writers Collaborative asked me to join the program. For myself, this meant an unorthodox entry into unorthodox teaching. The idea was that of enablement: The encouragement of Black children to trust and then to express their own response to things."[39] Kohl's encouragement of "unorthodox" teaching made the offer an exciting one for Jordan despite her personal frustration with academia. In some of the teaching notes that she took while a part of the program, she describes the anxiety created by her students' illiteracy, their inability to make time for school, and the class's distant location from the students' homes. This first teaching experience introduced Jordan to the inadequacy of a traditional school's ability to address the conflict between academic expectations and the strains for students who have no space or time for reading, homework, or even attending class. From these notes we witness the beginning of Jordan's practical pedagogy.

Jordan's notes indicate her immediate realization upon beginning to teach that every teaching method must be tailored to specific classroom and student needs. She recognizes that by involving students in lessons, teachers value their knowledge and experience. In a classroom of diverse students, each needs to have a voice. In *Teaching to Transgress: Education as the Practice of Freedom,* bell hooks confirms the importance of students' hearing each other's voices, even in large classes.[40] Such a strategy requires that the teacher's curriculum be flexible enough to accommodate all of the students' needs. In highlighting the failure of academic/formal education to critically engage the interests of students, hooks explains that "any radical pedagogy must insist that everyone's presence is acknowledged" because "excitement is generated through collective effort."[41] A pedagogy that considers students' "excitement" an important factor in lesson planning reverses the usual expectation of teachers as suppliers of information and students as receptacles for that information. By requiring students to both write and publicly read their poetry, Jordan makes their individual voices a priority.

Despite Jordan's lack of formal training as an educator, her pedagogy indicates an awareness of criticism of the public school system at the time when she was teaching. Her pedagogy responds to the kinds of conditions Jonathan Kozol records in his studies of inner-city schools, connects with the radical pedagogy of Brazilian activist Paulo Freire, and anticipates the kind of radical education reformation that is necessary today. In order to help create a foundation of material available to black children about their cultural heritage, Jordan authored children's books. In *Civil Wars,* she also responded directly to the publication of Jonathan Kozol's *Death at an Early Age: The Destruction of the Hearts and Minds of Negro Children in the Boston Public Schools* when it was published in 1967.[42] Jordan praises and criticizes the observations Kozol made of inner-city schools and the children they fail to serve. Since Kozol's work has been invaluable to education reform by exposing the actual state of inner-city schools and giving voice to the silenced students and parents of the communities' schools, Jordan's engagement of the text indicates her investment in pedagogy. Jordan comments on Kozol's research as evidence of the complaints that black families have been vocalizing for years (long since the civil rights movement's attempt to integrate the schools):

> In an interview, Kozol observed, "There's nothing in my book that Negroes couldn't tell you themselves." Exactly. As regards ghetto public "education," there's nothing in his book that Negroes have not been *trying* to tell. That's what the busing was all about: an attempt, by Black parents, to dilute the consistency of an "education" serving to lower I.Q. scores and reading levels of Black children.[43]

Jordan returns to her critique of standardized tests here, phrasing her description of "'education' serving to lower I.Q. scores" so that it has a double meaning. The education both serves students who have low I.Q. scores here, which is certainly how it is characterized by administrators, and it serves to lower the students' I.Q. scores by refusing them adequate instruction. Jordan goes on to acknowledge the importance of Kozol's testimony to the validity of inner-city black parents' complaints. She hopes that his words, as a white man, will have more value to the other white men in power than the black parents' words had. Meanwhile, she continued to actively fight in her classrooms for the kinds of changes Kozol's text indicates are necessary.

Although Jordan may not have been familiar with Paulo Freire's work, her pedagogical ideas, as they are evidenced in the critique of Kozol, echo those in *Pedagogy of the Oppressed.*[44] Jordan positions public school students as victims of oppression since the system oppresses students by restricting the information that they receive. Although the term "oppression" is somewhat outdated today, the analogy between Freire's observations of oppressed people in Brazil and the conditions inner-city and poor public school children face is pertinent to both Jordan's pedagogy and today's school crisis. One of Freire's claims is that the oppressor will never free the oppressed. Such a situation is necessarily impossible because the oppressed develop an acceptance of their situation and resist any movements to threaten whatever little stability they might have. The task

requires a revolution that the people are neither willing nor equipped to begin. Freire explains that the way to motivate the oppressed people is to provide them with empowering education. He distinguishes between "systematic education," which he describes as the "banking" system of education in which students are receptacles for information from the teacher, and "educational projects," which involve students in the learning process and allow for development of critical skills that are necessary for recognition of the system's oppression and the students' ability to change their role in it.[45] Jordan's Poetry for the People is an example of such an educational project because she engages the students in deconstructing poetic traditions and in producing their own poetry. Freire argues that it is a necessity for a certain number of the oppressors to be willing to implement a revolutionary education that will enable the action of the oppressed. It is precisely this position to which Jordan attributes the value of Kozol's work—as a member of the oppressor class (an educated, middle-class white man) who begins to empower the oppressed (the children in the inner-city schools and projects that he studies) by giving them a credible public voice. Herbert Kohl functioned similarly in Jordan's life by giving her a job as a teacher.

By serving as an extension of the education system in the United States today, teachers often become complicit in the system's oppression of students from inner-city and poor areas and from minority cultures. Freire describes "oppression" as overwhelming control. Certainly the public education system has an overwhelming control over the dissemination of information to students, who are analogously oppressed by the system's inability to serve their needs. Jordan's success as a teacher demonstrates how it is not necessary for teachers to function as pawns of the system. Freire's theory suggests that teachers need to know how to empower students to resist the system by constructing their own concept of knowledge rather than just how to help them pass standardized tests. This is an especially viable proposal at the university level. Moreover, bell hooks clarifies that the call for change in academic classrooms is a cultural revolution in its own right. "The call for a recognition of cultural diversity, a rethinking of ways of knowing, a deconstruction of old epistemologies, and the concomitant demand that there be a transformation in our classrooms, in how we teach and what we teach, has been a necessary revolution— one that seeks to restore life to a corrupt and dying academy."[46] She suggests here that the kinds of "rethinking" and "transformation" that she is employing in her classrooms and that are requirements in Freire's pedagogy may already be happening at the academic level. By supplying students with the tools for poetry writing and public speaking, introducing them to published poets and local children as writers, encouraging them to develop their own curricula and then to take leadership roles as teachers in the Poetry for the People project, Jordan's pedagogy provides guidance, but not a required formula, for knowledge production that revolutionizes the students' education.

Because poetry is an expression in written and/or spoken language, it is the perfect vehicle for a radical pedagogy like the one hooks describes that also does not neglect a more traditional learning of language and literature. Jordan saw language as the center of learning and poetry as the clearest form of expression in language. For instance, Jordan was a vocal and active advocate for the recognition of Black English as a language, especially in the schools. She explains, "English language is steadily declining as the native tongue of our American citizenry. Fewer and fewer American children enter compulsory public schools with English-language fluency. Hence, there is now an educational crisis, nationwide, of enormous magnitude."[47] Jordan recognizes that for many students, their "native tongue" is Black English, which would prevent them from English as a Second Language instruction but means that they are often unskilled in Standard English. Even as someone who made part of her living by writing in Standard English, Jordan feels that it is the language of her "enemy" and recognizes why expecting children to adopt it uniformly threatens their individuality.[48] Not allowing students to write and learn in their primary languages denies their heritage and part of their identities. Moreover, learning about dominant cultures to the exclusion of personal history makes those histories invalid. Jordan recognizes that students who feel that education does not value them will not be inclined to value the education. Jordan's own poetry serves as a model of bilingualism for her students since she demonstrates skill in writing in Standard English and she values her primary language by writing in Black English.

Jordan encouraged her students to write in their own voices, including languages other than the dominant "standard" English, which positions her language instruction outside the accepted position of demanding that all students demonstrate adroit skill in the use of Standard English.[49] Jordan views compulsory language instruction as a central component to compulsory schooling's perpetuation of hegemonic standards. She reminds readers that by making public school a legal requirement, the government subjects the students— those who cannot afford to go elsewhere—to a form of education that might be hateful and harmful to their identities and cultures. In *Civil Wars,* Jordan writes:

> Education has paralleled the history of our Black lives; it has been characterized by the punishment of nonconformity, abridgement, withered enthusiasm, distortion, and self-denying censorship. Education has paralleled the life of prospering white America; it has been characterized by reverence for efficiency, cultiva-

> tion of competence unattended by concern for aim, big white lies, and the mainly successful blackout of Black life.[50]

Specifically, Jordan locates language instruction as one tool of the education system's oppression of nonwhite voices and knowledges.

> *White power uses white English as a calculated, political display of power to control and eliminate the powerless.* . . . Once inside this system, the white child is rewarded for mastery of his standard, white English: the language he learned at his mother's white and standard knee. But the Black child is punished for mastery of his non-standard Black English; for the ruling elite of America have decided that *non*-standard is *sub*-standard, and even dangerous and must be eradicated.[51]

That "non-standard" is considered "sub-standard" is the real key to Jordan's language argument. If Black English is substandard, then it not only needs to be ignored in school settings, but it needs to be eradicated for the children to have possible future successes. By encouraging her students to write in their primary voices, Jordan enables students to understand that different forms of communication all have value. It is important, however, to remember that Jordan's insistence on revolutionizing the standards of language education is not an attempt to lower the standards. In fact, her focus on poetry provides an intricately formalized writing instruction that, uniquely, allows room for personal expression, for resistance of prescribed structure, and for demonstration of knowledge.

As Jordan gained experience as a teacher, she discovered that her own prejudices could limit her abilities as an instructor. She realized that her pedagogical model needed to serve students of varying backgrounds, not just from backgrounds like her own. She explains that "it is not possible really to teach both Black and white students but to sustain a loving commitment only to some of them."[52] As she learned to view each of her students as individuals with valuable contributions to offer to her learning environment, Jordan became aware of the way that teaching was becoming a central focus of her life and career. "By 1974, teaching no longer seemed to me an accident, a stunt, or primarily a distraction from my real work as a poet. Teaching had begun to alter even the way I approached things as a writer."[53] Jordan's students served as a connection between the different aspects of her career and life. She learned to make teaching a priority in her social activism and poetic endeavors by connecting what she learned from her students (about them and herself) to her other work. She found connections between people of different races that she had previously been unable to find. Jordan's ability to revise her pedagogical position indicates her willingness to critique even herself in the context of the education system. This constant critique enabled her to continually improve her pedagogy.

Jordan's pedagogy of poetry, like the recent popularity of spoken word poetry that is evident in forums such as Russell Simmons's "Def Poetry" on HBO, takes poetry back from academia and returns it to the people, making it, literally, "Poetry for the People." Instead of neglecting poetry's decorated history, she shows her students how she used it to express her voice in a unique way and that they can too. Despite the fact that my elementary education students resisted poetry at the beginning of the semester, by the end they were sharing poetry discoveries with each other. They put their poetry curricula into action in the classrooms where they taught and reported back their astonishment at how successful the poetry unit was with their students. The students' writing revealed excellent comprehension of even difficult poetry and enthusiasm about expressing their own thoughts in poetry. The children had much less fear of the poetry than the teachers had. What seems like a contradiction, then, between traditional poetry and Jordan's pedagogy, is actually a productive incorporation and development for social and academic change.

Jordan reminds us that "each . . . one of us must consciously choose to become a willing and outspoken part of *the people* who, together, will determine our individual chances for happiness, and justice."[54] If we relegate the problems of inadequate public education—which determines individuals' ability to get out of poverty and seek the American Dream—to those who are poor, then we enable a system that perpetuates an increasing disparity between the wealthy and the poor. Jordan's writing about education and her lived model as an educator may end up being her most powerful and far-reaching work. Ideally, children and students everywhere can be touched by her education model—even if they don't know it—through their teachers' efforts and willingness to help make changes.

Notes

1. Lauren Muller and the Poetry for the People Collective. *June Jordan's Poetry for the People: A Revolutionary Blueprint* (New York: Routledge, 1995).

2. June Jordan, *Technical Difficulties: African-American Notes on the State of the Union* (New York: Pantheon Books, 1992), 89-101.

3. Jordan, *Technical Difficulties,* 100.

4. Jordan, *Technical Difficulties,* 90.

5. Jordan, *Technical Difficulties,* 90.

6. Muller, *June Jordan's Poetry for the People,* 55.

7. Muller, *June Jordan's Poetry for the People,* 4.

8. Muller, *June Jordan's Poetry for the People,* 20.

9. June Jordan, *Civil Wars* (Boston: Beacon Press, 1981), 84.

10. Molly McQuade, *An Unsentimental Education: Writers and Chicago* (Chicago: University of Chicago Press, 1995), 80.

11. McQuade, *An Unsentimental Education,* 80.

12. Jordan, June, *Passion: New Poems, 1977-1980* (Boston: Beacon Press, 1980).

13. Jordan, *Passion,* 37-38.

14. Jordan, *Passion,* 37.

15. Jordan, *Passion,* 37.

16. Patricia Hill Collins, *Fighting Words: Black Women and the Search for Justice* (Minneapolis: University of Minnesota Press, 1998).

17. Collins, *Fighting Words,* 17.

18. Collins, *Fighting Words,* 20.

19. Jordan, *Passion,* 37.

20. Jordan, *Passion,* 37.

21. Jordan, *Passion,* 38.

22. Jordan, *Passion,* 38.

23. Alice Walker, *In Search of Our Mothers' Gardens: Womanist Prose* (New York: Harvest Books, 1984), 83-116.

24. Gloria Wade Gayles, *Pushed Back to Strength: A Black Woman's Journey Home* (New York: Avon Books, 1993).

25. Gayles, *Pushed Back to Strength,* viii.

26. bell hooks, *Yearning: Race, Gender, and Cultural Politics* (Boston: South End Press, 1990), 33-49.

27. Patricia Hill Collins, *Black Feminist Thought: Knowledge, Consciousness, and the Politics of Empowerment* (New York: Routledge, 2000), 214.

28. Langston Hughes, *The Collected Poems of Langston Hughes,* ed. Arnold Rampersad and David Rossel (New York: Alfred Knopf, 2000), 409-10. Poem first published in 1949.

29. Audre Lorde, *The Collected Poems of Audre Lorde* (New York: Norton, 1997), 153-57. Poem first published in 1974.

30. Hughes, *The Collected Poems,* 409. Hughes's italics.

31. Hughes, *The Collected Poems,* 409.

32. Hughes, *The Collected Poems,* 409.

33. Lorde, *Collected,* 153.

34. Lorde, *Collected,* 154.

35. June Jordan, *I Know What the Red Clay Looks Like: The Voice and Vision of Black Women Writers,* ed. Rebecca Carroll (New York: Carol Southern Books, 1994), 150.

36. Jordan, *Technical Difficulties,* 89-101.

37. Soraya Sablo Sutton and Sheila Menezes, "In Remembrance of June Jordan, 1963-2002," *Social Justice* 29, no. 4 (2002): 205-6.

38. Audre Lorde, *Sister Outsider* (Freedom, Calif. Crossing Press, 1984), 116.

39. Jordan, *Civil Wars,* 29.

40. bell hooks, *Teaching to Transgress: Education as the Practice of Freedom* (New York: Routledge, 1994), 40-41.

41. hooks, *Teaching,* 8.

42. Jonathan Kozol, *Death at an Early Age: The Destruction of the Hearts and Minds of Negro Children in the Boston Public Schools* (New York: Bantam Books, 1967).

43. Jordan, *Civil Wars,* 42.

44. Paulo Freire, *Pedagogy of the Oppressed* (New York: Continuum, 1995). First published in 1970.

45. Feire, *Pedagogy,* 36.

46. hooks, *Teaching,* 29.

47. June Jordan, *Affirmative Acts: Political Essays* (New York: Anchor Books, 1998), 255.

48. Jordan, *I Know What the Red Clay Looks Like,* 145.

49. Janet Palmer Mullaney, *Truthtellers of the Times: Interviews with Contemporary Women Poets* (Ann Arbor: University of Michigan Press, 1998), 64.

50. Jordan, *Civil Wars,* 50.

51. Jordan, *Civil Wars,* 65. Jordan's italics.

52. Jordan, *Civil Wars,* 84.

53. Jordan, *Civil Wars,* 84.

54. Jordan, *Technical Difficulties,* 18.

Jane Creighton (essay date 2004)

SOURCE: Creighton, Jane. "Writing War, Writing Memory." In *Still Seeking an Attitude: Critical Reflections on the Work of June Jordan,* edited by Valerie Kinloch and Margret Grebowicz, pp. 243-55. Lanham, Md.: Lexington Books, 2004.

[*In the following essay, Creighton details Jordan's influence as a political activist.*]

> *Peace never meant a thing to me.*
>
> —June Jordan, **"War and Memory"**

I remember walking along the dirt road just west out of the village of Bumburet, Chitral Province, northwestern Pakistan, high in the Hindu Kush in 1977. Bumburet was, and apparently still survives as, a Kalash village, an ancient, polytheistic cultural community gravely threatened by the onslaught of modernity in the form of monotheistic Islam, nationalist politics, and, no doubt, tourists like ourselves. We had come to Bumburet after having spent several days in the provincial capital, lounging on mats and drinking tea in a hotel with Yanik and Sylvie, Swiss nationals with whom we'd been traveling for weeks, ever since drifting into conversation with them on the streets of Herat in western Afghanistan. We'd checked each other out for obnoxious nationalisms. Germans, we thought, were far too remote and efficient—they carried everything with them and avoided eating or drinking local products for fear of infection. Weren't the Swiss just like them? On the other hand, Americans were typically loud and boorish. They thought they knew it all, or worse, they thought their ignorance didn't matter. And for me there was that added element—Yanik and Sylvie at first sight had a kind of European hippie, beat gorgeousness that brought out in me a sense of myself as irrevocably blockish, a hardy, American, square-cut shrub. But that hipster coolness bled into warm, exploratory exchanges about where we all had been, and where we might go.

Altogether my companion and I had been on the road for several months. We'd flown to Switzerland on economy tickets, and immediately fled that pristine, orderly landscape for the south and east, loving and leaving Italy, then Greece, heading further into what was for us the intensely exotic and unknown otherness of central Asia. We wanted to go to India, overland. We wanted to see what we could see, get as far away as we could from everything that we knew, find ourselves, our common yet epic heroisms based in courage, adaptability, openness, and the ability not to be pinned down, fixed, shrunken into identities prepared for us by someone or something else. In the rhetoric of my 1977 this meant above all else I was conscious that I would not be framed by gender. I would not be told what was or was not for me. I would not settle down and begin planning a future based on gender-appropriate work or the availability of love. I would not fix myself in a narrow career, or a home life that pledged me to a less than radical undermining of the status quo. I was a poet riding waves radiating out from the Beats and Black Mountain College in the 1950s, from the civil rights struggle, radical movements against the Vietnam War and against racism that washed across the subsidence of my childhood, and then the feminism where I came of age. I was 25 years old, "not *that* young anymore" as my particularly crusty, Yankee aunt warned me when I seemed ill-disposed to make apparent use of the college education that had been unavailable to her or her sister, my mother who died when I was 17, four years after my father's fatal heart attack.

I could not yet recognize the oldness of this story. This trip, I thought, was about crossing out of my world into other worlds, escaping the radar of establishment America in pursuit of an alternative Americanness that, as the texts of Charles Olson I carried with me had it, thwarted classification and read the human body as agent in all perception, "so that *movement* or *action* is 'home'"[1] rather than, as I barely understood it, the stultifying nominative—a self without a verb, incapable of stepping out. I read Olson while traveling across Asia, read Melville's *Moby-Dick* in Herat and Kabul and thought about the greatness of language, Ahab's rage against that which he could not dominate, and then the industry itself, the grand and deadly chase giving way to the rendering of whales into product, lamplight oil and bony corsets cinching the bodies of middle- and upper-class women in the nineteenth century.

The oldness of this story: a young person ventures into strange lands in pursuit of the future and in an effort to escape the constraints of the past. She has a grand notion that, can she only give voice to it, she will somehow contribute to a new wave of liberatory aesthetic and political thought. She is very hopeful, but not yet aware of the perfect ironies that attend her reading of *Moby-Dick* as she crosses the frontiers of Turkey, Iran, Afghanistan, and Pakistan, countries whose histories and relations to the West she knows little. Nor is she yet capable of naming the most intimate, driving thing: she is in flight from death and its layers—the dead bodies of her parents, the extinguishing of their light, selves without verbs. She particularly mourns, though she hopes she is moving beyond this, the mother who appears to have succumbed to depression and death rather than survive being alone after her last child leaves home.

I headed East, then, a reasonably handsome young woman with a very beautiful young man, thinking myself androgynous and certainly unanchored, pursuing vastness, the great whale in a world larger than what I had known, hoping that the whale—a force moving across the great horizon of the world—would carry me with it and transform me into something better than I was. And I was transformed, challenged, taken down a notch or two. I began, just began to learn a great deal about my ignorance, what I didn't know of arguments over secularism and religion in Turkey, the history of American intervention in the Shah's Iran, or why 1977 was an interestingly virulent year to travel in the romantic bubble of American on-the-road adventurousness, knocked about on the streets of Tehran by men alternately eager to learn English and furious at my presence in the public eye, my Western face, and female body. I remember seeing some regime promo about how the Shah had relieved women of the veil, but sensed there was something missing from this story. I defended my androgyny in the absence of women's

faces and voices in the markets of Afghanistan, but whined about the heat and grew tentative, dependent on my companion for ventures out into the street. Like a girl, like an invalid, no longer rugged or heroic, a burden.

At least this is how I remember it, the way I thought at the time. I was grateful for Yanik and Sylvie, for the easy way they moved into the picture and kept us from imploding, because they, perhaps, saw us in ways we could no longer see ourselves. I was grateful that Sylvie, an inveterate traveler in search of spiritual connections everywhere she went, carried with her a picture of her long-dead mother as well as a sense of humor and a sensual regard for daily life that made even sitting on straw mattresses in the bare-bulbed light of village hotels an occasion for pleasurable conversation. I loved their rich laughter accented in French and German, their amused sparring, that they were European, so different from us yet still recognizable. Because of these Europeans, we broke out of our stupor and traveled well again for a time, following Sylvie's lead because Sylvie knew where to go—from Kabul to the remote lakes of Bandiamir, to the ancient, great, and now lost Buddhist statues in Bamian, across the Khyber Pass into Peshawar, Pakistan, and then the two-day trip north by bus and on top of brightly painted trucks over the 11,000-foot Lowari Pass, stopping on the edge of vertiginous canyons for smoky milk tea, then heading on into Chitral, all the time, and for thousands of miles now, watching the faces of men and sometimes women in the countryside and in cities, engaging through gestures and in clipped, aching English the business of acquiring food, a place to stay, and sometimes trinkets, maps, a book or two, interpreting them with a sense of inquiry but with very little knowledge beyond what I carried with me in the practice of my American life.

We heard of Bumburet on the international traveler grapevine. It was a rare place higher up in the mountains from the town of Chitral, one of several remaining villages of the Kalash, a people noted for having resisted Islam, and for the black robes and embroidered headdresses heavy with cowry shells and colorful beads that were worn by the Kalash women. We'd ridden up in a Jeep for a stay of several days in a settlement of wooden houses built into the steep inclines of the soaring Hindu Kush. Bumbur Khan kept a room in his house for the tourist trade and we stayed there, sleeping on string cots and eating the simple meals cooked for us over a fire by his wife. There were ladders for getting from the first to the second story, and in the night unmarred by electricity one could step out onto the roof into what felt like the heart of the sky, reading the darkness of the mountain against starlight. One room to the side of the house had intricately carved posts leading into it, and an opening in the ceiling that poured light over the tamped down dirt floor—a ceremonial center of some kind we thought, but we didn't know, were never going to know. Yet it was all so beautiful, so rugged and spare. Most moving to us was the open presence of women whose faces we could see and whose voices we could hear without apparent constraint.

This is what everyone said about it, what travelers who had been on the road for awhile seemed to hunger for—that the Kalash were colorful and showed their women, and wasn't it just great to see that. Most of us wouldn't venture much beyond this knowledge. What we did learn came from the chance meeting of a young Canadian anthropologist, a woman who spent months at a time living in the valley, dressed and lived as one of them. She spoke of things writ small and large across the village, that Bumbur Khan beat his first wife, for instance, and would be hard put to make a living without the tourists; that the communal life of the village was under immense stress caused not only by international tourism (harvest dances put on for our benefit, or the busload of Japanese tourists trying to take pictures of women near their menstrual hut) but also by the dominant Muslim culture of Pakistan, in a resurgence under the autocratic rule of General Zia. Men routinely flew up from the city to "experience" the Kalash women, to watch their dances and sometimes carry them off, for the night or forever. Multiple conversions occurred over time through violent physical coercion or economic pressure, while the Kalash and their culture were also "sold" as a tourist destination. A few thousand of them, that's all, a civilization that dates back maybe two thousand years. That's what's left.

When I remember these things, two images arise. They come to mind well before the beginning of this or any other variants of this narrative I've told over the years. As a matter of course, I've had to leave out significant moments in each telling, or select and shape them so that they bend to the task of supporting the point at hand, at times risking heavy-handed language, exaggeration, oversimplification—in short, the loss of lyric integrity. And so I risk these images here, because in their aliveness for me they are part of the point, the connection between my sitting down to write about June Jordan and the quick catapult to some days in August over twenty-five years ago, when I was walking along the dirt road just west out of Bumburet and passed at one point a woman and at another point a man. I no longer know in what order, or even if it was the same day, yet there they are and I am walking together with my companion, but also alone in sunlight and steep shadow. The images of the woman and of the man play back and over, like home movies of someone beloved, dead and gone. We see the woman a short distance away with a young child. She weeps, beseeching several village men for help of some kind. Whether they are Muslim or Kalash, I can't tell, nor can I tell which she is from the muted robe and headscarf she wears. They

reject her pleas almost casually, and turn back to their conversation. I've been trying to walk through the feeling I have that the valley's extraordinary beauty is cut with terrible losses among its people, all of that pitched against the finally unabating tension between me and my companion, my frustration at my weakness in the face of surrounding masculinities—his, but also the faces of the Pakistani men from Peshawar that I have seen for myself during our stay, leering in close circles around this Kalash woman or that. I am haunted by them, and haunted simultaneously by the distinct sense of my mother's body shadowing my own, her aching descent and death. The woman veers toward us, one arm around her child and the other reaching out. She is terribly distressed, almost frantic, but because I am frozen with doubt about my position, about hers, about the possibility that any exchange between one person and another might constitute a simple good, it is my companion who reaches into his pocket for the five-rupee note he gives her. Neither of us can bear it when she kneels to kiss his feet.

And then, I think I see my father. I think I see him in the face of a Kalash man, whose blue eyes and tentative smile mirror something I remember about my father's face soft with laughter. I can't remember his ever having a hard look about him, yet how would I know? It was so long ago, but the feeling of recognition is acute, and as the man walks softly by us I have to restrain myself from touching him. He has, it seems to me, looked kindly at us, and it's as if my father has come back to reassure me that whatever it is, somehow, it will be all right. Transfixed, I turn and watch him head on down the road. Just as he's passing a cluster of Muslim men, several of them kick up dust at him and spit, laughing among themselves. He seems then to hang his head, sidling off to a safer distance, and in that instant I am aware of what it might be to be this man in his own skin, despised in his own country, and of the possibilities of kinship beyond one's own blood.

> My mother told me I should put away
> the papers and not continue to upset myself
> about these things I could not understand
> and I remember
> wondering if my family was a war
> going on
> and if
> there would soon be blood
> someplace in the house
> and where
> the blood of my family would come from
>
> —June Jordan, **"War and Memory"**

I knew June Jordan over a period of years in the 1980s. I met her sometime in 1981 through Sara Miles, also a new friend I'd the luck of finding in on-the-edge feminist, wild girl poetry circles. So much detail floats away, but I remember the sweep of things, the great scope of Sara's smile, June's laughter melodic and infectious, a sometimes savage hilarity infusing the sense of purpose in conversations that fueled their activism. They were brilliant, generous, loyal to friends. Fierce about the responsibilities of citizenship, of finding a voice and making that voice heard in public discourse. Over and over again they worked the arteries linking the personal to the political, poetry to history.

I met them just as I was working to unearth these connections in the deepest part of myself. Travel across central Asia had opened in me a sharp and tactile sense of international bodies politic even as it had reawakened the intimacy of familial loss, the pulse of which I felt always, living in my skin. I had no clear understanding as to how, but each opened access to the other, and over the course of these friendships, I felt encouraged to explore that connection. Knowing Jordan and Miles led to my own activism among a group of writers, artists, and activists who over the course of the Reagan presidency wrote and organized in response to U.S. foreign policy relating to the Israeli invasion of Lebanon, the civil war in El Salvador, and the *contra* war in Nicaragua. For quite a while my own writing folded into the necessities of organizing—fliers, newsletters, press releases, letters to editors. It was hard to write anything else, particularly in the face of deadly U.S. covert military operations that were devastating the lives of people in these countries, some of whom I was coming to know personally. I hadn't the faith that poetry or personal testimony, at least my own, would do what needed to be done.

But through all that, there was Jordan's voice, on my phone, on the radio, in public gatherings and in print, exhorting, challenging, her laughter bringing a room to life and inviting more, more words, more poetry, more speaking up. Early on, somewhere around the massive June 12, 1982 antinuclear rally, I remember going to see her in the hospital. I can't remember why she was there, but I remember her expectant look as we came in, her interest in our report about the goings on outside, her own raucous and alert running commentary on the news more than a match for the fragility of lying in a hospital bed. I had not known her for so very long and still felt shy, still awed by her. She was, after all, June Jordan, the black poet and activist who kept it real, who spoke truth to power across decades of civil strife, who'd sat at a table with Malcolm X and planned visionary urban communities with R. Buckminster Fuller, who'd written poetry, essays, plays, and all of that time teaching and raising a child and still keeping track of what was going on in the neighborhood, in Mississippi, in Africa, and every place else. All of that, and so beautiful, too, it seemed impossible that I had gotten myself into such company. But whatever fears, self-effacements, whatever tender feelings of inadequacy I might have brought to that table pretty much didn't

matter. She was there, welcoming, engaged, happy to see us and always ready to talk in the great back and forth of friendship. She encouraged me by her warmth and her example—as she so clearly has for many others—to step out of self-consciousness and debilitating fear without feeling that I had to abandon the complexities that shaped me.

The way she always lived in the open engagement of daily life surges through poems filled with an egalitarianism as aware of love as it is of justice. Her achievement as a poet lies in a unique, lyric voice that is at once its own and also distinctly, emphatically identified with a roving, collective "we"—that is, anyone bent on love and justice and "fighting fair." She says it in **"Poem for a Young Poet"** from *Kissing God Goodbye*—

> I search for a face
> to believe and belong to
> a loosening mask
> with a voice
> ears
> and a consciousness
> breathing through
> a nose
> I can see
>
> . . .
> I search a face
> for obstacles to genocide
> I search beyond the dead
> and
> driven by imperfect visions
> of the living
> yes and no
> I come and go
> back to the yes
> of anyone
> who talks to me[2]

—and I remember it being like this in her company, *back to the yes* of speaking to one another in direct and open acknowledgment that we shared this world and could act together in it, no matter what aloneness we might feel. I hear her voice as a salve. I hear it rising and falling in disbelief, anger, and purpose, remembering the summer as it rolled into the Israeli invasion of Lebanon, drowning the anti-nuclear movement in the sound and sight of Beirut being bombed, a close and continual horror made distant, if you let it, by rituals of television watching where far-off plumes of smoke and nameless figures could be caught, framed, and reduced in news formats night after night, that is, on a schedule that belies the all-consuming nature of conflict, the days, weeks, months, and years of displacement, refugee status, occupation—lifetimes, in fact. Alone, I imagine I might have fallen into numbness, passivity. I mean, what could one do?

One could clearly raise one's voice, as Jordan did in one of the striking poems of that time, **"Moving Towards Home,"** which nearly tore apart a highly publicized 1982 reading given by Arab, Israeli, and American poets. Sara Miles and Kathy Engel organized the event, titled *Moving Towards Home* after Jordan's poem, as a UNICEF benefit for humanitarian relief in Lebanon. The way I recall it, almost all the poets worked the range between wrenching recognition of suffering on the ground in Lebanon and critique of Israeli policy and its U.S. backers, the Arab writers among them dealing with an intimate sense of conflagration, while the Americans wrestled with the dissonance streaming out of print and broadcast reportage, as Jordan's poem clearly does. Written in response to the massacre of Palestinians in the Sabra and Shatila refugee camps in Lebanon, the poem builds a litany of horrors based on extensive reporting from the camps. Its open identification with the Palestinians and its frank evocation of the Holocaust in terms of Israeli perpetrators, provoked an uproar in the aftermath of the reading when, she reports, she was surrounded by shouting white men, both Israeli and American.[3] In performing the poet's task of giving visage and voice—agency—to Palestinian subjects, Jordan also asserts, "I was born a Black woman / and now / I am become a Palestinian / against the relentless laughter of evil."[4] In doing so, she raises the provocative and, many would argue, terribly problematic notion that one can presume to know, and therefore stand in witness of, the truth about suffering across complex boundaries marking a cultural other. For some in her audience, to assert such identification while castigating the Israeli government for practices linked to the genocide of the Jews was an unpardonable reduction of history, not to mention an anti-Semitic act. And yet how could one respond to the massacre of Palestinian refugees at Sabra and Shatila, the annihilation of whole families carried out by Lebanese phalangists under the eye of the Israeli army, without thinking about the past? It is there, the elephant in the room, and Jordan's poem speaks to it in a catalogue of "unspeakable events"—executions, rapes, the bulldozing of bodies, the talk of purifying populations and reference to Arabs as "beasts with two legs"—all pulled from news reports and all attached to the refrain that she does not "wish to speak" of these things, yet clearly must in order to turn toward any hope of reconciliation and home. The echoes of the Holocaust must be acknowledged, the poem argues, in the way that history holds both Palestinians and Israelis in its grip. The poem shifts, then, toward what must be spoken of beyond political machinations, as Jordan poses crucial questions about what home is, what it might be, and where "living room" might be found. The poem's epigraph is the voice of a woman pulled from the *New York Times*: "'Where is Abu Fadi,' she wailed. / 'Who will bring me my loved one?'" Her lament, wrenching in its immediacy, is given its place in a news cycle that will just as rapidly bury it. But Jordan assumes the woman's

voice, inhabits it as an act that is less about appropriation than it is about solidarity. "I need to talk about living room," she writes,

> where I can sit without grief without wailing aloud
> for my loved ones
> where I must not ask where is Abu Fadi
> because he will be there beside me
> I need to talk about living room
> because I need to talk about home

She does so in such a way that one understands that the annihilation of families and homes a half a world away finds correspondences in the silencing of speech and in the passive receipt of televised news streaming into living rooms where identification with the other is at best only a matter of some sympathy. Jordan's effort here to "talk about living room" challenges all to be present, to be in dialogue, and to understand "living room" itself as a kind of consciousness under threat.

I think of the famous passage in *The Narrative of the Life of Frederick Douglass* where Douglass describes his severest moment of despair. It is a moment for the most part not comparable to the emotional predicament of the ordinary American consumer of world news coverage who, although she may be pinned to the couch by the weight of events, is nevertheless a free citizen, not subject to the institution of slavery. And yet, I think of Douglass while thinking about June Jordan and 1982 and the idea of living room. I think about the choices Douglass made in the way he narrated the events of his life, how he shaped his story in accord with his complex purpose—abolition wedded to the just claim of African Americans to full-fledged citizenship according to the principles of the Declaration of Independence and the Constitution. In the passage he is verging on a breakdown, having been sent as a consequence of his "spiritedness" to live for a year with the slave breaker, Edward Covey. Up to this point in his story he has been instructing his audience about the dreadful mechanics of slavery, what it does in both practical and spiritual ways to crush self-knowledge and agency in its central victims. He has also shown us himself evolving, gaining distance on the once total view of himself as an entity defined by the uses to which he is put by whites. In teaching himself to read, to argue, to resist, he has imagined himself surging across the horizons of enslavement and has made fundamental forays into self-definition as well as into his eventual escape. But Covey beats, bloodies, and works him to the point of exhaustion and senselessness. He institutes unpredictable and perpetual surveillance, making it impossible for any of the slaves to know where or when he might spring upon them, thus returning Douglass to the totalizing perspective of slavery. "My natural elasticity was crushed," Douglass says. "My intellect languished, the disposition to read departed, the cheerful spark that lingered about my eye died; the dark night of slavery closed in upon me," and in the ringing phrase that marks the nadir, he proclaims himself "a man transformed into a brute!"[5] But even as Douglass marks the enormity of the loss, he valorizes the capacity of the individual to fight back, reclaiming himself first through his fists, then through teaching others to read, through the building of community, through fighting to retain the wages of his own labor within slavery, and finally executing his escape from slavery itself in order to become a voice central to the argument for its demise. His *Narrative* wields his own experience as a rhetorical force against slavery, and provides a model for self-determination linked to communal uplift that he sees as a fundamental human right linked to the founding principles of the United States.

That the struggle to end slavery took many lifetimes, and that subsequent generations have and do continue to contend with the legacies of its aftermath are observations that, perhaps, float at a sobering distance, depending on who you are, and how you understand your circumstances. The same can be and will be said about the myriad forms of conflict no doubt inadequately characterized as the relationship between Islam and the West. It is quite possible to throw up one's hands in the contemplation of such enormity. But what comes through Douglass's work, particularly in every classroom where I have taught it, is the possibility of transformation and the understanding that what one does in response to unjust power radiates not just through one, but through many.

And this, to me, is what Jordan's work has always been about, making her arguments about love and justice through the recognition of intrinsic connections between individuals and history, between personal and public concerns. In 1987 I asked her to participate in a public reading series in Washington, D.C. for *War and Memory: In the Aftermath of Vietnam,* a three-month art exhibition sponsored by the Washington Project on the Arts for which I served as the literary curator. Her poem **"War and Memory,"** written in part as a response to that request, put into play ideas I had also been working on in my own writing—how the making of family culture moves in constant interaction with broader cultural history. In that poem, as in the broader field of play provided by her autobiography *Soldier: A Poet's Childhood,* she constructs a voice that is identifiably her own even as she resists, in the story she tells, any uniform assumptions about herself or her family that might be made according to race, her parents' immigrant status, or their respective roles as parents and child. **"War and Memory"** starts in the kitchen with her father holding a knife, slamming drawers and looking for something that his wife has not provided. It is the opening chord of a biting, complex conflict that inhabits a fluid geography. The love and terror of the young June's home mesh with battles just outside, in

Harlem, Bedford Stuyvesant, and beyond that to the German holocaust, all of it shifting toward a young adulthood marked by Vietnam and the war on poverty. Jordan gives an unstinting view of the unhappiness in the house, the violence of her father, and the meekness of a mother who attempts weak verbal comebacks that disappear under the struggle that ensues between Jordan and her father.

But there is no simple castigation here, no final pinning of blame on the oppressor father. Without, ever, excusing her father's violence, or her mother's passivity, Jordan brings forth those elements of their lives that are the making of herself and the hugeness of her appetite for justice. The Granville Ivanhoe Jordan of **"War and Memory"** and *Soldier* is the proud, intensely hard-working West Indian immigrant who is at the same time sharply aware of black status in the United States and what he and his family are up against. Jordan presents him in all his layers. He is the strict disciplinarian who trains her according to military codes, treats her as and even calls her the son who, American-born, will overcome all the social obstacles laid before them. He is teacher, drill instructor, master carpenter to whom she is apprenticed, and the intellectual who enforces the reading of Shakespeare. The king of the house, he is also the tyrant, explosive, a master of surveillance who wakes his child up in the middle of the night to beat her for some infraction, so that she must be ever watchful and vigilant. And vigilant she becomes, loving what she loves about him but also fighting when she has to, fighting him even when she knows she won't win, seeing not only the bigness of him, but also his limits, the range of hurts proffered him by the world. Those hurts, and the sense of a beautiful mother disappearing into pain and depression, must be spoken for. They must and do become a part of the full-blooded intelligence with which Jordan takes responsibility for her presence in the world in piece after piece, against the idea that nothing can be done about abuses of power that carry our names as citizens.

Because I met her and met Sara Miles at the time I did, I went to Nicaragua, came back and organized coffee brigades, worked against war, and felt the horizons open up on the subjects of my writing. Her voice was with me as I moved through graduate school toward teaching and into the very diverse, open-admissions university where she is part of my dialogue with students. I am just one of many, many people who have been moved, cheered, and challenged by her to carry themselves into the world full throttle, to assert the right of dialogue and argument against coercive, monologic tendencies in our national culture and to develop, somehow, a vibrantly engaged sense of self that resists the contemporary version of the ways in which people are classified by that national culture and deprived of access to public discourse and self-determination.

Jordan exhorts us to live, instead, for the self that claims the integrity of its own evolving voice, and for the multiple colorations that voice takes. I hear her when I teach the Aztec narratives, or Américo Paredes and resistance on the Mexican-American border. I hear her in the long tradition of fighting for American small "d" democracy in Frederick Douglass and in Walt Whitman: "Whoever degrades another degrades me . . . and whatever is done or said returns at last to me, / And whatever I do or say I also return" (*Song of Myself*).[6]

Long after time and geography took me out of her orbit, I have continued to hear her. The challenge of writing about her is the challenge of staying close to those things that keep me engaged—the synapses that join me with another and one set of conditions with another no matter how improbable or impossible such a joining might be. I use the term synapse with an emphasis on motion, the fluid moment of imagining the hope, the love, and the suffering of another through the opening provided by my own experience of these things. I do not suggest that disparate experiences can be rendered as equivalents, that, for instance, a Kalash woman in the Hindu Kush who is stricken by poverty, whose name, whose story, whose very language are unknown and who kisses the feet of a man who has given her pocket money, can be reduced to a pairing with my mother, depressed and dying, who nevertheless owned her own house. She cannot. But I can, in the deeply felt knowledge of one, recognize the contours of pain audible in the voice of the other and be changed by them. I can understand that the elements of my story, my mother's, my father's, exist in relationship to a world of stories that inform ours, that tell us something about the way stories are shaped by cultures, cataclysms, ordinary and extraordinary losses, by power, by violence, criminality and love. And in one way or another I can use the synapse, the recognition of kinship, to provide an opening for that woman's voice, for the fact of it, her sorrow, and her existence on earth.

Notes

1. Charles Olson, *Proprioception* (San Francisco: Four Seasons Foundation, 1965), 2.

2. June Jordan, "Poem for a Young Poet," in *Kissing God Goodbye: Poems, 1991-1997* (New York: Anchor Books/Doubleday, 1997), 1-4.

3. She describes this incident in "Life After Lebanon," in *On Call* (Boston: South End, 1985), 77-85.

4. June Jordan, "Moving Towards Home," in *Naming Our Destiny: New & Selected Poems* (New York: Thunder's Mouth Press, 1989), 142-43.

5. Frederick Douglass, *Narrative of the Life of Frederick Douglass, An American Slave,* with a foreword by Houston A. Baker Jr. (1845 reprint: New York: Penguin, 1986), 105.

6. See her discussion of Whitman in "For the Sake of People's Poetry," in *On Call*, 5-15.

Korina M. Jocson (essay date January 2005)

SOURCE: Jocson, Korina M. "Taking It to the Mic: *Pedagogy of June Jordan's Poetry for the People and Partnership with an Urban High School." English Education* 37, no. 2 (January 2005): 132-48.

[*In this essay, Jocson considers Jordan's influence on poetry curriculum.*]

For many youth whom I have encountered, poetry serves as a medium to speak about their experiences in ways often not censored by structures and rules. It is revered as an aesthetic form of expression with freedom to in/exclude elements of grammar and aspects of language. Noted in several National Council of Teachers of English publications, poetry lets students' imaginations run free while exposing them to a particular genre of writing (c.f., Somers, 1999; Michaels, 1999; Moon, 2000; Jago, 2002/1999). Accordingly, I recall classroom scenarios from my years as a high school teacher and college instructor—students with increased interest in poetry as compared to, say, essay or term papers. How could it be that poetry makes such a difference in students' interaction with writing? What follows (along with others in this issue) is an attempt to provide some possible answers.

For decades poetry has been a centerpiece of classroom curriculum and instruction. In the humanities it is commonplace to examine poetry as a genre of literature because it is deemed sophisticated, enduring, and revelatory of language use. Though usually more compact than prose, poetry makes intensive use of language and literary devices such as theme, tone, irony, and metaphor to influence its interpretation. More importantly for this paper, however, such use of language is key to the *construction* of poems as derived from creative differences and democratic engagement (see Kinloch, this issue). At times the relative distinction between "good" vs. "bad" poetry is set apart by criteria adhering to these devices and particular levels of intensity, craft, and precision. As I have found in my own experience as a student and later teacher in U.S. urban schools, the kinds of poetry used in many classrooms have relied heavily on the so-called "classics." With the exception of popular works by the likes of Langston Hughes or Maya Angelou, it has not been commonplace to see other poets of color's works incorporated in English reading and composition courses (Reed, 2003). Despite multiculturalism gaining some momentum in schools and inside classrooms over the last three decades, there still stands a hegemonic, hidden curriculum that advances the experience of historically privileged male-dominated whites (Apple, 1995/2000; Nieto, 2000). The focus largely remains, as pointed out to me by former students, on the experiences of "dead white men."

The prolific and most-published African American essayist and poet June Jordan knew about these kinds of limited textual representations. As professor in the African American Studies department at the University of California, Berkeley, she ventured to challenge these institutionalized Ivory Tower traditions and subsequently established a university program called Poetry for the People (P4P) in 1991. Such efforts to integrate literature courses with fresh material on the college level, however, still left many high school students in urban settings receiving traditional "classic" poetry in their English classes. In a joint effort to sustain artistic and political empowerment, Jordan and her students explored means to "democratize" poetry in and outside the confines of the university campus. They drew upon Dewey's (1916) notion of democracy through education to shape their role *and* the role of schools to develop a just society, in short, the essence behind *literocracy*. It was then that the partnership with Bellevue High School was born, becoming P4P's premiere educational project since its inception in 1996.

In this article I explore from a pedagogical standpoint June Jordan's Poetry for the People and its partnership with Bellevue High as one means to innovate the teaching and learning of poetry on the high school level. It is part of a larger qualitative study on poetry and literacy development in the lives of urban youth conducted in 2002. The perspectives I offer center on the "collaborative intervention" between high school English teachers, students, and college student-teacher-poets.

THEORETICAL FRAMEWORK

Poetry surfaces between the bounds of literacy and pedagogy, and involves one's ability to read, create, analyze, and criticize. This ability as a formulation of identity influences how we think, feel, and act—or on the basis of everyday interactions, how we live our lives within the very contexts we occupy. Embedded with meaning and experience, this ability is essential in validating as well as building upon knowledge and skills we already possess, whether we openly claim the title of poet or not. According to Greene (1988), a long-time advocate of the arts and other "spheres of freedom," it is this kind of ability that reflects our imagination, our exploration of alternative possibilities, in ways that can move us as members of a pluralistic society toward action. She draws explicit connections between education and freedom and notes the importance of "palpability." She writes, "It would mean the granting of audibility to numerous voices seldom heard before and, at once, an

involvement with all sorts of young people being provoked to make their own the multilinguality needed for restructuring of contemporary experience and thematizing lived worlds" (p. 127). Elsewhere, Greene (2000) also suggests that forms of expression such as poetry must exist as part of our lived worlds, in shared as well as public spaces. Poetry, taken from this perspective then, has the potential to defamiliarize or disclose aspects of experience ordinarily never seen, opening possibilities for critical awareness and reflection with self and others.

Feminist poet Adrienne Rich (1979) claims such disclosure to be instrumental to self-discovery. Making a distinction between fantasy and imagination, Rich describes the latter as being characterized by action. In a 1917 essay entitled "When We Dead Awaken: Writing as Re-Vision," she shares some pivotal moments in her young life that shaped both her life and poetry.

> Most, if not all, human lives are full of fantasy. . . . To write poetry or fiction, or even to think well, is not to fantasize, or to put fantasies on paper. For a poem to coalesce, for a character or an action to take shape, there has to be an imaginative transformation of reality which is in no way passive. And a certain freedom of the mind is needed—freedom to press on. . . . Moreover, if the imagination is to transcend and transform experience it has to question to challenge, to conceive alternatives. . . . For writing is re-naming.
>
> (p. 45)

Similarly, in conceptualizing the complexity of borderlands, feminist poet Gloria Anzaldúa (1987, 1999) places a high regard for naming the realities and using the language of Chicana/os who are neither Mexican nor Anglo-American, but rather a "synergy of two cultures." She as does Rich puts premium on imagination to produce poems with "feeling [that] have a palpable energy, a kind of power" allowing her to write *"con imágenes domo mi miedo . . . con palabras me hago piedra . . . todo lo que soy, todo lo que algún día seré"* (p. 93) [loosely translated "with imagery I dominate my fears . . . with words I become stone . . . all that I am, all that I will be someday"]. Hence, it isn't so much about what makes up a poem or what a poem may look like, but rather the "palpability" and the "visibility"—that which is also the (re)naming of experiences in the process of creating it. Poet Naomi Shihab Nye (2002) agrees and suggests, if necessary, the following evaluative criterion, "If it looks like a poem and you want to call it one, then it's a poem."

While poetry for some is about practicing one's imagination, for others it is about gaining voice. hooks (1989), for example, upholds poetry as a place for the "secret voice," a place in which the magic of transformation can emerge through its meaning and form, Poetry becomes the embodiment of the distinctive expression of an individual writer who comes into awareness capable of speaking in many voices. It means having a voice(s) with "a sense of versatility . . . [not] unilateral, monologist, or static, but rather multidimensional" (p. 11). Thus, it is through this multi-dimensional arena of poetry that hooks describes wherein lies the possibilities for empowerment; it is wherein lies the voices of a people.

In her essay entitled **"For the Sake of People's Poetry,"** Jordan (1985) problematizes the notion of democracy in America through an understanding of poetry as a site of struggle. She argues the importance of collective representation as an element of social change, identifying herself as "a stranger trying to figure out the system of language that excludes her name and all of the names of all her people" (p. 5). Her exclusion (and of others) proves useful in challenging and replacing "Old World concepts" about an elitist American literary establishment commonly found in American classrooms. She notes that even Walt Whitman, a White man and "father to American literature," had been punished for moral questions embodied in his poetry. How much more for non-White poets like "us"? According to Jordan, Whitman, a bohemian and a homosexual, afforded in his work a representation of "people's poetry" and "poets of the New World" who like him were condemned to peripheral status. She writes:

> New World does not mean New England. New World means non-European; it means new; it means big; it means heterogeneous; it means unknown; it means free; it means an end of feudalism, caste, privilege, and the violence of power. It means *wild* in a sense that a tree growing away from the earth enacts a wild event. It means *democratic*.
>
> (Jordan, 1985, p. 11)

Calling Whitman's poetry a "continent of consciousness," Jordan alludes to the ways in which poems can be used to change the privilege status of self-appointed Euro-centric literature in American society to something more heterogeneous, something more democratic. She pushes not only for poetry with "diction comprehensible to all," but also for poetry that is inclusive of "ordinary people." She reminds us about the ability of words to help embody the meaning of humanity, to enact that which is dynamic and accessible through "reverence for human life . . . an intellectual trust in sensuality as a means of knowledge" (p. 14). This sensuality between human beings, according to her, is potentially what can build a sense of collectivity to dislodge power from the hands of the privileged and on to the hands of the not-so privileged.

Indeed, past and current poets alike illustrate how poetry can be an empowering tool through which voice, access, and dialogue can co-exist, and possibly lead to social transformation. Poetry embraced in more critical ways becomes an arena for integrating "non-canonized" works in ivied spaces and acknowledging those who have been ignored by the dominant culture. Through the potential power of words, poetry offers a way for unrecognized cultural groups to imagine and (re)name their own experiences and assist in the (re)building of our multicultural understanding of literature. Poetry framed within *literocracy* in the context of Poetry for the People is one worth examining.

The Partnership and Collaborative Intervention

Bellevue High School is racially diverse with a student population of approximately 33% Black/African American, 37% White, 11% Chicano/Latino, 11% Biracial, and 8% Asian/Pacific Islander and/or Other. At the time of the study, Bellevue had two small learning communities, one of which (CARE) was active in sustaining the partnership. A total of eight English teachers, twelve different classes, and hundreds of students have been involved since 1996. Numerous printed readers and published anthologies including students' work exist today and reflect part of P4P's curricula during these years. Before delving into P4P's pedagogy and what has transpired inside Bellevue's classrooms, I begin with a definition of collaborative intervention.

What Is a Collaborative Intervention?

Resonating in focal teachers' retrospective interviews was the inconsistency in applying the term "collaboration" to their experience with Poetry for the People. These teachers described P4P generally arriving in each of their classrooms with a pre-determined set of topics and poems, with little to no input from them. "Collaboration" had somewhat become a misnomer for what seemed to be more closely related to the term "intervention." Due to this apparent dissent in naming this experience among teacher participants, I refer to the period of contact between teachers and P4P as a "collaborative intervention"—"collaborative" because several actors were involved in delivering a pre-determined curriculum, and "intervention" because P4P came in for a set period of time and used their own curricular model to ultimately provide a different approach to teaching and learning. P4P basically implemented its curriculum in a shared learning setting for purposes of "intervening," or rather in hopes of offering a different curricular and instructional approach that would positively influence students' learning processes and, in turn, writing development (cf. Mahiri & Sablo, 1996). I use "collaborative," however, with the understanding that actors such as teachers, student-teacher-poets (or STPs, a term which will be discussed more in a later section), and students were involved at various capacities, begging the question of what "true collaboration" in a learning setting means.

THE P4P READER AND CURRICULUM

Included in all course readers is P4P's "coda"—that is, "Poetry for the People is a program for political and artistic empowerment of students. It is motivated by the moral wish to prevent the invisibility and the imposed silence of those less privileged than we." This coda is found in the beginning pages of the reader with the "Table of Contents" and "Toolbox" sections, and is followed by three "groundrules that must be respected inside this experimental and hopeful society." These groundrules as originally conceived by Professor June Jordan consist of defining "the people," building a "community of trust," and creating connections among "strangers" (see Muller, 1995; Poetry for the People Reader, 1999, 2000, 2001, 2002; Sutton, 2003). Virtually all classes and workshops begin by reading and having a common understanding and "honoring this belief." It is intended to set the tone of the collaborative intervention, whether students agree or disagree at the outset.

Located in the first section of the printed reader, the "Groundrules" page is followed by several other pages that provide P4P's overall teaching approach. They include but are not limited to the following: *Poetry for the People Writing Guidelines, Technical Checklist, Examples of Guidelines, Writing Samples of a "Destroyed Martin Espada Poem," The No-No List or Overused and Tired Cliché Words, What the Heck is a Haiku Anyway???, Line Breaks, Rhythm + Rhyme + Reason,* and *Tips for Poetry Readings.* The remaining sections in the reader constitute the curriculum and weekly topics. Each section contains sample poems for instructional and writing workshop purposes, sometimes serving as prompts for group discussions and topical assignments. One example is Ruth Forman's (1993) "Young Cornrows Calling Out the Moon," which appears under the topic of bringing it home or emulation/self-affirmation; it is also an illustration of a poem with strong sensory details (see Appendix A). A first-time participant as a sophomore in the fall of 2000 collaborative intervention, focal student Damon, a 17-year-old Filipino/African American, remembered "Calling Out the Moon" as being about "the neighborhood"—his "childhood," his "block"—and added that its portrayal of everyday life influenced him to "be a better person." Similarly, another focal student Chante, a 17-year-old African American, described Forman's work as a "cool poem because it was showing different images . . . (like) we used to play this game . . . sit on the steps and get our hair braided, and stuff like that." She then completed the emulation/self-affirmation poem assignment as a junior in the spring of 2002 with a poem called "Where you from," notably adhering to the style and details in Forman's original poem.

> *Where you from*
> brothas got cornrows
> sistas got weaves

> we got rap
> Nas cappin Jay-Z
> Fallin n Alicia Keys
> B-high livin in diversity

> I got my Auntie's black eyed
> peas n macaroni n cheese

> I got Black Eyed Peas
> kickin new beats

> we got attitude
> we fiiine sistas

The parallel to Forman's incorporation of African American cultural referents is evident. Chante uses rap and R&B artists such as Nas, Jay-Z, and Alicia Keys (compared to "Rick James the Bump the Rock") and in so doing creates rhythm (also through "s" sounds) within and across lines. She even takes Forman's "black eye peas" to do a clever word play across stanzas, maintaining the "s" sounds throughout; in the third and fourth stanza, she refers to not only food, but also a musical group by the same name. Though short in length, she felt her ideas were clear, echoing Forman's exact words "we got attitude / we fiiine sistas" and reaffirming "brothas they cool."

Upon a closer examination of other poems reminiscent of Chante's emulation, I found that a mix of poetry written by novice to established poets filled the pages of the P4P reader. This deliberate mixture designated that a range of poems (including poetic styles) could co-exist and would have similar weight in the curriculum. It was also an indication of how P4P establishes grounds for a "safe space" to dialogue about various experiences and, consistent with its programmatic mission based on democratic ideals, to demonstrate that youth's voices are just as valuable as adults'. These poems, I noticed, often contained highly charged tones and differentiated styles, speaking with and to the interests of adolescents.

RHYTHM AND RHYME, HAIKU, AND OTHER SAMPLE POEMS

In spite of their incongruent definitions of "collaboration," focal teachers eventually became accustomed to the "collaborative" nature of the intervention. These teachers adopted and integrated P4P material into their own curriculum however it fit. Several of them kept a number of ideas and strategies for future classroom use. Ms. Tanner, for example, admitted that she set aside specific P4P materials from the 1998 collaboration that had been used time and again in her later Freshmen Writing and Senior Poetry classes. She spoke about the most recent 2002 collaborative intervention in her class and noted that what stood out the most for her (and she believed her students too) was a mini-lecture and its accompanying handout on "Rhythm and Rhyme." She was "not into hip hop," but recognized P4P's ability to make connections between poetry and rap and how important that was for students. Another focal teacher Ms. Best who has received P4P in her class at least three times pointed out its most influential effect on her practice:

> . . . Two years ago when I taught Haiku, I had pulled all this stuff up off the Internet about Haiku. And nothing was as succinct as the sheet that was in the reader. So I just . . . synthesized it with my own stuff and . . . basically stole Poetry for the People curriculum for use with my freshmen.

From such testimonies it is clear that focal teachers saw the value of some curricular material to adopt and claim them as their own. "Stealing" or not, their re-use of P4P's materials such as *Rhythm + Rhyme + Reason* and *What the Heck is a Haiku Anyway???* in other classroom settings was telling of an implicit kind of professional development that happened during the collaborative intervention. Curricular ideas were not only exchanged as part of the relationship between teachers and P4P, but also added to teachers' repertoire of literature, augmented their use of poetry in the classroom, and influenced what they did with poetry beyond the duration of the partnership.

CLASSROOM SCHEDULE AND ORGANIZATION

Collaborative interventions typically lasted about five to six weeks in each class. One unique instantiation was the four weeks in Ms. Tanner's 5th period Senior Poetry in the fall of 2002. P4P was present in this classroom three days a week—on Tuesdays, Wednesdays, and Fridays, a schedule that was pre-arranged to fit Ms. Tanner's curricular and instructional needs. Every Wednesday including P4P's initial arrival, STPs introduced a new topic through an interactive lecture and discussion of poems in the reader. Class time then culminated in an assignment, which students were expected to bring back on Friday. On Friday, a workshop day, STPs and students disbanded into their small groups. Depending on class size and the number of STPs available that particular day, the groups were small enough to have dialogue, share poems, and provide constructive feedback. Below is an excerpt taken from my field notes showing two STPs reminding students of what it means to "workshop":

> STP 1: Are we clear on the process of workshop? One reads, we give feedback, so that the poem can be revised, improved if necessary. Look at page 8. Guidelines of how to give constructive feedback. There's also a technical list. The verbs, how do we make them better, stronger? Adjectives, describe by showing, not naming. Keep these in mind when you read each others' poems.
>
> STP 2: Also, feel free to write on the paper. That's why we make copies so we can give comments back to the poet.

To form the groups, P4P relied heavily on a number of STPs available to participate; experienced and novice STPs were paired up to provide balance. In Ms. Tan-

ner's class, which consisted of 32 students, there were a total of 16 rotating STPs (including me). An average of seven to ten STPs showed up per day to facilitate the six small workshop groups, resulting in an average ratio of 1:3. Making copies of students' poems for group workshop became a front-end issue because many students forgot or did not have access to make their own. Ms. Tanner, for example, collected students' poems at the beginning of each class and ran off to the nearby teachers' lounge.

During actual group workshop, exchanges between students and STPs often centered around, or upon digression often connected back to, the topic of the week. At the end of this workshop, students received copies of their poems with sparse to extensive handwritten feedback. On Tuesday of the following week, a second round of group workshop took place. The cycle repeated itself on Wednesday with a new topic and a new assignment (see also Sutton, 2003).

THE ROLE OF STUDENT-TEACHER-POETS

To better understand the facilitation of the collaborative intervention is to understand the role of a student-teacher-poet. STP is more than a socially constructed acronym created as an element of the P4P program. It is by far one of the most unique multi-layered identity any college student could take on. As *students,* STPs have access to enroll in the large introductory P4P course (big class) where they begin or continue their exposure to particular kinds of and approaches to poetry while being exposed to P4P's coda and objectives. Similar to what high school students experience during a collaborative intervention, STPs undergo a learning process that, whether they agree or disagree with P4P's philosophies, seeks to affirm the poet in them, a kind of socialization process which Fisher (this issue) addresses in her current research on spoken word poetry inside classrooms.

Some of these college students who are convinced to do more proceed to the next phase, that is, to simultaneously take on the T (teacher) identity as members of another course on teaching poetry (small class). As *student-teachers* to each other in this small class and to other peers in the big class, STPs also retain their identity as *student-poets* and exercise their right to become more seasoned poets under the guidance of P4P's director (and then professorship of June Jordan) in the small class as well as continued exposure to visiting "Hot Shot" guest poets in the big class (see, for example, www.poetryforthepeople.org). Not without the other, these student, teacher, and poet identities blend into one, propelling for some a rare college experience to greater heights, becoming teachers, activists, authors, and more.

Developing Ways to Democratize the Teaching of Poetry

STPs play a major role in the program. In addition to taking on leadership roles on the university campus, they also utilize their knowledge and abilities to work with and serve high school students. They take on teacher-like responsibilities such as preparing daily or weekly lesson plans, teaching and engaging in active discussions, and facilitating in-class writing workshops. They also act as mentors and contribute to a college-going culture in the larger school by offering their camaraderie and support, including off-task conversations with students about college admissions, choices, and experiences. As an STP from the spring of 2000 to the fall of 2002, I witnessed and experienced how STPs met to discuss curricular plans and assignments, and used the STP Handbook prior to stepping foot on the high school grounds.

STPs ranged in age from their late teens and early twenties. Many, however, seemed to understand that working with high school students raised a new set of challenges than, say, working with college peers. Together, in what I call "pre-service" meetings, we brainstormed and role-played certain situations. For example, we discussed possible meanings of teaching and working with urban students. Pedagogical differences between democratic versus banking education, or implicit versus explicit instruction, became the basis for deriving the kinds of attitudes, expectations, and actions we would adhere to as "teachers." We built upon the concept of transformative pedagogy to address educational problematic dichotomies such as "saving" versus "making a difference." To bring it closer to home, we explored complexities in the lives of students who had been historically marginalized and made more evident reasons for the existing relationship between P4P and one of Bellevue's small learning communities (CARE). We also delved into topics that forced us to examine our political roles as teachers in this relationship. Basic assumptions about urban schooling became important points of departure to incorporate an approach that was not only in line with P4P's coda, but also was fresh and innovative. Interestingly, some of the suggestions came from our own schooling experiences in urban settings.

P4P's pre-service meetings also offered STPs a kind of professional development that resembled teacher education courses focused on classroom management. We addressed issues and challenges around classroom dynamic and interaction. One common scenario we used related to students' possible disinterest or reluctance in writing poetry. The question was, What do we do if/when that happens? Many of us agreed that the best response was usually to ask a personal question and engage students more actively in a conversation about things that interested them (e.g., what's your experience with writing been like?). In other words, the situation called for a student-centered approach that forced us as teachers to pay closer attention to students' experiences. Another issue we concerned ourselves with had to do with the specific type of language used to respond during small group workshops when students shared their poetry. For instance, how does an STP praise while critiquing student work at the same time? How does one provide constructive feedback without sounding abrasive? Since we understood its delicate nature from our own writing workshops, we established that language of critique had to be balanced with positive remarks set against a "safe" learning space. We role played different ways of stating such remarks and decided it was best to always begin with praises and then ask students specific questions about ideas or lines in the poem. Added concerns brought up in pre-service meetings related to possible ways of improvising conversations or topic discussions using P4P guidelines and poems found in the reader to supplement the interactions during group workshop. The overall message we went away with was the importance of voice in students' poetry and to illuminate it whenever possible in our oral as well as written speech, during and outside of group workshop.

Creating a "Safe Space" through Poetic Introductions

Establishing an authentic space for interaction relied on STPs introducing themselves and sharing what I call an "identity" poem in from of everyone on the first day of the collaborative intervention. This initial and quite personal interaction was significant in shaping the kind of "safe" space we hoped to build. Our apparent vulnerabilities became an important and deliberate way to convey our unique stances and views about the world, which we anticipated students would eventually share in their writing process.

STPs usually read from either a piece of paper or a page in a published anthology or reader, a kind of introduction that demonstrated to students that their words had been recorded and that they mattered enough in such a way to be written down, printed, and mass distributed (i.e., readers, chapbooks). The poems that STPs shared also provided model examples of the types of poetry that students would encounter in P4P. In the fall of 2002, one STP chose a poem about an Oakland Police scandal entitled "dancing on the head of a pin called probable cause," echoing what had been in recent local news media about Oakland homicides that many of the students in the class previously raised in their own conversations.

Preparing to Showcase Student Work

After several weeks of writing, revising, and interacting in small group workshops, students' efforts to produce polished poems culminated in an anthology and public reading. Students selected their "best" poem for the anthology and submitted a typed version in a timely manner in order to make press. Consistent with activities during the last week of the collaborative intervention, the day of the reading was set aside for final practice. This practice was, I noticed for many students, an opportunity to set off their fear and anxiety about being in the public eye. According to some experts, this "fear" had been a recurring social condition because youth and children are socialized to be silent (Fine, 1991; Weis & Fine, 1993), not "talk back" (hooks, 1989), or not have authority about what they say and be dominated by adults who do (Giroux, 2000).

Fear of speaking up—for fear of being ridiculed or opening up to vulnerabilities—was a condition that P4P attempted to challenge throughout the weeks of the collaborative intervention. Though oral performance always was second to the written construction of poetry, performing student poetry became P4P's main focus during the last week. "Taking it to the Mic" was important to calm students' fright and to practice for a night of successful public reading. Focal student Damon who dreaded the idea of public performance had the following to say about his experience:

> I mean people always try to tell me I'm a good writer, but I need a little bit of work. . . . I never really took their advice until this time when I had to and was happy with it. My memorable experience (was) reading in front of people. . . . I'll always remember that night.

That night Damon "busted out" with a poem called "Ode 2 My Moms." His mother had never heard or seen any of his work before because he never once shared. According to him, she was drowned in tears as he "spit" his ode, "nervous . . . and didn't want to mess up."

To better assist students, STPs shared moments of their own "scared" beginnings and carried out silly skits to illustrate that sometimes mistakes were inevitable but could be alleviated by adequate preparation. In a humorous way, several STPs in Ms. Tanner's fall of 2002 class (including myself) acted out different scenarios such as reading too fast or too slowly, reading while chewing gum, reading behind a piece of paper or book, reading while fidgeting or playing with one's hair, among others. STPs reminded students what the most important aspect in the whole public reading experience was—to own their words, deliver them with an air of confidence, and have fun with them. Spitting a poem on the mic with poise on the night of the reading finale, to be "in the moment," was what the week of preparation was all about. So students practiced "taking it to the mic"—in class, with each other, at home in front of the mirror, and other places.

On the day of the public reading in Ms. Tanner's class, the front of the classroom was transformed into a makeshift stage with a makeshift podium and microphone. Students and STPs randomly dispersed to the corners/sides of the room to project a standing-room-only environment, role-playing and creating an ambiance that consisted of wide-eyed audience members. Loud applause, cheery welcomes, and enthusiastic outbursts filled the room, in anticipation for what was to come that night.

CONCLUSION

In this article I have discussed the ways in which P4P carried out its artistic and political project in partnership with Bellevue High School. Using archival materials such as class readers and anthologies between 2000-2002 as well as interviews with teachers, I identified aspects of the program that revealed the complexities of what I call a "collaborative intervention." What became clear in laying out P4P's pedagogical practices inside several English classrooms was that different teachers had different experiences within the partnership. Moreover, the presence of P4P in the classroom, the implementation of its curriculum as a collaborative intervention model, the role of student-teacher-poets, and the program's culminating events together created a kind of learning environment that students, whether to their liking or not, were a part of. The finale, *vis a vis* the culmination of the collaborative intervention, was not so much about how poetry as a writing and learning process came to an end in the public reading; rather, it was about how a culminating experience both for teachers and students created possibilities for newer beginnings in and outside of the classroom. For some students, this unique experience further grounded their eventual participation in other youth poetry communities.

P4P's teaching practices and use of curricula reflected a kind of imagination that as Greene (1988) suggested explored alternative possibilities. For English language arts teachers and teacher educators, particularly in urban multicultural settings, P4P as a pedagogical model provides helpful ways of re-thinking the potential of poetry for invigorating classroom practice. For researchers and advocates of poetry, P4P and the collaborative intervention at Bellevue High School offers an instantiation that re-conceptualizes the value of university-school partnerships in order to better serve all students. It also demonstrates ways of bridging school and non-school literacy practices, tapping into the power of multiple voices, and bringing in both human and material resources to extend current pedagogies.

APPENDIX A

Young Cornrows Callin Out the Moon[1]
we don have no backyard
frontyard neither
we got black magic n brownstone steps
when the sun go down
we don have no backyard

no sof grass rainbow kites mushrooms butterflies
we got South Philly summer
when the sun go down

cool after lemonade n black eye peas
full after ham hocks n hot pepper greens
corn bread coolin on the stove
n more to watch than tv

we got double dutch n freeze tag n kickball
so many place to hide n seek n
look who here Punchinella Punchinella
look who here Punchinella inna zoo

we got the ice cream man

we got the corner store
red cream pop
red nails Rick James the Bump the Rock
n we know all the cheers

we got pretty lips
we got callous feet healthy thighs n ashy knees
we got fiiine brothas we r fiiine sistas
n
we got attitude

we hold mamma knees when she snap the naps out
we got gramma tell her not to pull so hard
we got sooo cleeen cornrows when she finish
n corn bread cool on the stove

so you know
we don really want no backyard
frontyard neither
cuz we got to call out the moon
wit black magic n brownstone steps

Ruth Forman

Note

1. From *We Are the Young Magicians,* Beacon Press, 1993, used by permission of the author.

References

Anzaldúa, G. (1987/1999). *Borderlands/la frontera: The new mestiza* (2nd ed.). San Francisco: Aunt Lute Books.

Apple, M. (1995/2000). *Official knowledge: Democratic education in a conservative age* (2nd ed.). New York: Routledge.

Dewey, J. (1916). *Democracy and education: An introduction to the philosophy of education.* New York: Free Press.

Fine, M. (1991). *Framing dropouts: Notes on the politics of an urban public high school.* Albany: State University of New York Press.

Fisher, M. T. (2005). From the coffeehouse to the schoolhouse: The promise and potential of spoken word poetry in school contexts. *English Education,* 37, 115-131.

Forman, R. (1993). *We are the young magicians.* Boston: Beacon.

Giroux, H. (2000). *Stealing innocence: Corporate culture's war on children.* New York: Palgrave.

Greene, M. (2000). Lived spaces, shared spaces, public spaces. In L. Weis & M. Fine (Eds.), *Construction sites: Excavating race, class, and gender among urban youth* (pp. 293-303). New York: Teachers College.

Greene, M. (1988). *The dialectic of freedom.* New York: Teachers College.

hooks, b. (1989). *Talking back: Thinking feminist, thinking black.* Boston: South End.

Jago, C. (2002). *Sandra Cisneros in the classroom: "Do not forget to reach."* Urbana, IL: National Council of Teachers of English.

Jago, C. (1999). *Nikki Giovanni in the classroom: "the same ol danger but a brand new pleasure."* Urbana, IL: National Council of Teachers of English.

Jordan, J. (1985). *On call: Political essays.* Boston: South End.

Kinloch, N. (2005). Poetry, literacy, and creativity: Fostering effective learning strategies in an urban classroom. *English Education,* 37, 96-114.

Mahiri, J., & Sablo, S. (1996). Writing for their lives: The non-school literacy of California's urban African American youth. *Journal of Negro Education,* 65(2), 164-180.

Michaels, J. (1999). *Risking intensity: Reading and writing poetry with high school students.* Urbana, IL: National Council of Teachers of English.

Moon, B. (2000). *Studying literature: New approaches to poetry and fiction.* Urbana, IL: National Council of Teachers of English.

Muller, L., & the Poetry for the People Blueprint Collective (Eds). (1995). *June Jordan's Poetry for the People: A revolutionary blueprint.* New York: Routledge.

Nieto, S. (1992/2000). *Affirming diversity: The sociopolitical context of multicultural education* (3rd ed.). New York: Longman.

Nye, N. S. (2002, November). Keynote address presented at the annual meeting of the National Council of Teachers of English, New Orleans, LA.

Poetry for the People. (2002). *Speak on it! Smash the state: The second coming.* Berkeley, CA: Author.

Poetry for the People. (2001). *Real talk 2002: Our world unveiled.* Berkeley, CA: Author.

Poetry for the People. (2000). *In a light this beautiful.* Berkeley, CA: Author.

Poetry for the People. (1999). *Witness: A collection of revolutionary poetry,* Berkeley, CA: Author.

Reed, I. (Ed.). (2003). *From totems to hip hop: A multicultural anthology of poetry across the Americas, 1900-2002.* New York: Thunder's Mouth.

Rich, A. (1979). *On lies, secrets, and silence: Selected prose, 1966-1978.* New York: W. W. Norton & Company.

Somers, A. (1999). *Teaching poetry in high school.* Urbana, IL: National Council of Teachers of English.

Sutton, S. S. (2003). *Writing our lives: An investigation of literacy, identity and poetry in an urban high school.* Unpublished doctoral dissertation, University of California, Berkeley.

Weis, L., & Fine, M. (Eds.). (1993). *Beyond silenced voices: Class, race, and gender in United States schools.* Albany: State University of New York Press.

FURTHER READING

Criticism

Brunot, Sally Ann, Lori M. Evans, Daniela Kocoska, Megan Quinn, and Carla Silva. "In Memoriam: June Jordan (1936-2002)." *Black Scholar* 32, no. 2 (summer 2002): 26-7.

> Provides recollections of Jordan from five different contributors.

Bush, Vanessa. Review of *Some of Us Did Not Die,* by June Jordan. *Booklist* 98, no. 22 (August 2002): 1895.

> Lauds *Some of Us Did Not Die* as provocative in the best sense of the word.

Ciolkowski, Laura. "Rage, Rage: in a Posthumous Essay Collection, June Jordan Champions the Fight against a Host of Tyrannies." *New York Times Book Review* 107, no. 38 (22 September, 2002): 16.

Characterizes the essays in *Some Of Us Did Not Die* as lacking complexity.

DeVeaux, Alexis. "A Conversation with June Jordan." *Essence* (September 2000): 102.

> Brief interview in which Jordan discusses various aspects of her autobiographical work *Soldier: A Poet's Childhood.*

McDowell, Deborah E. "Favorite Son." *Women's Review of Books* 18, no. 2 (November 2000): 1.

> Provides a laudatory review of the memoir *Soldier: A Poet's Childhood,* commenting on Jordan's "spare and reticent" style in this work as compared to that of her other writings.

Priest, Myisha. "Mourning Vital Links to Our Culture." *Crisis* 111, no. 2 (March-April 2004): 54.

> Considers Jordan's career in context of scholarship by African American Women.

Rothschild, Matthew. "Editor's Note." *Progressive* 66, no. 8 (August 2002): 4.

> Provides a poignant reminiscence of Jordan by Rothschild, editor of the *Progressive,* where Jordan contributed a monthly column.

St. John, Janet. Review of *Directed by Desire,* by June Jordan. *Booklist* 102, no. 1 (1 September 2005): 43.

> Provides a positive review of the early poems in *Directed by Desire.*

"Remembering June Jordan." *Women's Review of Books* 20, no. 1 (October 2002): 15.

> Ruth Forman, Sara Miles, Marilyn Hacker, Alexis DeVeaux, Laura Flanders, and others provide prose and poetry reminiscing about Jordan—a friend, colleague, and mentor.

Additional coverage of Jordan's life and career is contained in the following sources published by Thomson Gale: *African American Writers,* **Eds. 1, 2;** *Authors and Artists for Young Adults,* **Vols. 2, 66;** *Black Literature Criticism Supplement;* *Black Writers,* **Eds. 2, 3;** *Children's Literature Review,* **Vol. 10;** *Contemporary Authors,* **Vols. 33-36R, 206;** *Contemporary Authors New Revision Series,* **Vols. 25, 70, 114, 154;** *Contemporary Literary Criticism,* **Vols. 5, 11, 23, 114;** *Contemporary Poets,* **Eds. 3, 4, 5, 6, 7;** *Contemporary Women Poets;* *Dictionary of Literary Biography,* **Vol. 38;** *DISCovering Authors Modules: Multicultural Authors, Poets;* *Gay & Lesbian Literature,* **Ed. 2;** *Literature and Its Times,* **Vol. 5;** *Literature Resource Center;* *Major Authors and Illustrators for Children and Young Adults,* **Eds. 1, 2;** *Major 20th-Century Writers,* **Ed. 1;** *Poetry Criticism,* **Vol. 38;** *Something About the Author,* **Vols. 4, 136;** *St. James Guide to Young Adult Writers.*

Alan Moore
1953-

English graphic novelist and novelist.

The following entry provides an overview of Moore's career through 2005.

INTRODUCTION

One of the most renowned and prolific writers of graphic novels, Moore popularized the genre with his groundbreaking series *Watchmen* (1987), which received a Hugo Award and a Locus Award. He has earned distinction due to the widespread assertion that his "comic book" writing, or graphic novel scripting, particularly that of *Watchmen,* can be considered as works of literature. Moore has garnered numerous accolades, including the British Eagle Award for Best Comics Writer in 1982 and 1983.

BIOGRAPHICAL INFORMATION

Born on November 18, 1953, in Northampton, England, Moore grew up in a working-class family. His father worked as a brewery worker and his mother worked as a printer. As a child Moore read extensively, including books about Robin Hood, Greek and Norse mythology, and British comic books. Expelled from school at the age of seventeen, Moore was employed at various jobs before finding a position as a cartoonist for the weekly magazine *Sounds.* After publishing a comic detective story titled "Roscoe Moscow" in *Sounds,* Moore focused more serious attention on writing. He contributed pieces—including the comics "D. R. & Quinch," and "The Ballad of Halo Jones"—to the British magazines *Doctor Who Weekly, 2000 A.D.,* and *Warrior* in 1983 and 1984. Moore earned recognition for two of the series that he began in *Warrior* in the early 1980s—*Marvelman* (titled *Miracleman* in the United States) and *V for Vendetta,*—with critics suggesting that his writing had developed to resemble that of a novelist. In 1984, Moore started working for DC Comics, an American publishing company. Moore wrote stories for the struggling series *Saga of Swamp Thing,* dramatically increasing the title's circulation, and also contributed on "Tales of the Green Lantern Corps." Moore later founded his own comic imprints Mad Love Publishers in 1988 and America's Best Comics in 1999. He has also released several spoken word and music albums and staged multimedia performance pieces.

MAJOR WORKS

Moore collaborated with illustrator Dave Gibbons to develop *Watchmen.* This work, which deconstructed the typical superhero, follows superheroes who must cope with their own human emotions and limitations. The story describes how the protagonists, based on old characters from Charlton Comics, have played roles in key moments in American history, including World War II and the Vietnam War. The story begins as the United States faces the brink of nuclear war and a superhero is murdered; the remaining superheroes suspect that their lives are also in danger from a mysterious killer. *Batman: The Killing Joke* (1988) is a dark, grisly depiction of Batman's relationship with his rival The Joker, treating such subjects as institutionalization and treatments for the criminally insane. A documentary graphic novel *Brought to Light* (1989) explores the United States's involvement with the sale and smuggling of drugs and weapons. Based on information from a lawsuit brought against the government, this work contains two separate stories: *Shadowplay: The Secret Team* and *Flashpoint: The LA Penca Bombing.* Set in the near-future in a fascist, government-controlled Great Britain, *V for Vendetta* (1990), follows "V,"—a man disguised as Guy Fawkes, the failed seventeenth-century British insurrectionist—who terrorizes and kills officials who are connected with a secret concentration camp. Moore conducted extensive research in order to write *From Hell* (1991-96), his version of the Jack the Ripper story. Moore's tale proposes that Dr. William Gull, a royal physician, committed the Ripper murders in an attempt to cover up a scandal involving the heir to the throne. *The League of Extraordinary Gentlemen* (2001) features characters from nineteenth-century works of literature, including Edward Hyde and Dr. Henry Jekyll (from the novel by Robert Louis Stevenson), Captain Nemo (from *20,000 Leagues under the Sea,* by Jules Verne), Hawley Griffin (from H. G. Welles's *Invisible Man*), and Allan Quatermain (from *King Solomon's Mines,* by H. Rider Haggard). Published by America's Best Comics, *Promethea* (2001) centers on a female hero with magical powers, and *Tom Strong* (2001-02) concerns a superhero, his wife and his daughter, each possessing extraordinary mental and physical capabilities. Moore's *The Mirror of Love* (2003), a lengthy poem that examines the history of homosexuality, originally appeared in 1988 in *Artists Against Rampant Government Homophobia* (*AARGH*). Moore wrote this piece in protest of a controversial anti-homosexual British law.

Top 10 (2000) and *Top 10: The Forty-Niners* (2005) focus on a police department located in a city created as a home for people with superpowers. Three of Moore's works have been adapted to film: *From Hell,* in 2001, *The League of Extraordinary Gentlemen* in 2003, and *V for Vendetta* in 2005.

CRITICAL RECEPTION

Numerous critics have lauded Moore's writing, asserting that his comic books and graphic novels encompass the same levels of mature subject matter, complex plot and character development, and attention to detail that serious novelists include in their works. *From Hell,* for instance, contains thorough footnotes demonstrating Moore's extensive research into historical facts and circumstances surrounding the Ripper killings. In 2005 *Time Magazine* charted *Watchmen* on its list of the Top 100 English-language novels from 1923 to the present. Steve Rose remarked that *Watchmen* is "a dense, meticulous deconstruction of the whole superhero game that received mainstream 'literary' acclaim." Furthermore, Rose and other critics posit that Moore's works transcend the limitations of the "comic book" genre, and continue to chart new ground, breaking boundaries and exploring new methods of telling stories. Moore's work has, according to Mark Bernard and James Bucky Carter, "helped set apart sequential art as a unique and viable art form deserving of more critical respect than is currently attributed to it in relation to the whole of twentieth century accomplishment." Bernard and Carter have lavished further praise on Moore, claiming that "[H]is work illustrates how sequential art is the most precise culmination of ideas and forms that more established and recognized artistic and literary genres of the twentieth century strove to realize."

PRINCIPAL WORKS

Shocking Futures (graphic novel) 1986

Saga of the Swamp Thing [illustrated by Steve Bissette and John Tottleben; originally published in *Saga of the Swamp Thing,* issues 21-27 in 1984] (graphic novel) 1987

Twisted Times (graphic novel) 1987

Watchmen [illustrated by Dave Gibbons] (graphic novel) 1987

Batman: The Killing Joke [illustrated by Brian Bolland and John Higgins] (graphic novel) 1988

Brought to Light [illustrated by Bill Sienkiewicz] (graphic novel) 1989

Big Numbers [illustrated by Bill Sienkiewicz] (graphic novel) 1990

*Marvelman [illustrated by Gary Leach and Alan Davis; originally published in serial form in *Warrior* in 1982-84, later published as *Miracleman* in the U.S.] (graphic novel) 1990

V for Vendetta [illustrated by David Lloyd; originally published in serial form in *Warrior* in 1982-1985] (graphic novel) 1990

The Complete Ballad of Halo Jones [originally published in serial form in *2000 A.D.* in 1984] (graphic novel) 1991

Lost Girls [illustrated by Melinda Gebbie] (graphic novel) 1995

Saga of the Swamp Thing: Love and Death [illustrated by Bissette, Tottleben, and Shawn McManus; originally published in *Saga of the Swamp Thing,* issues 28-34 and Annual 2 in 1984-1985] (graphic novel) 1995

Voice of the Fire (novel) 1996

Superman: Whatever Happened to the Man of Tomorrow? [illustrated by Curt Swan and George Perez; originally presented in serial form in *Superman* 423 and *Action Comics* 583 in 1986] (graphic novel) 1997

From Hell [illustrated by Eddie Campbell; originally published in serial form in *Taboo* and then by Kitchen Sink Press in 1991-96] (graphic novel) 1998

†*The Birth Caul* [illustrated by Eddie Campbell] (comic book) 1999

Bloodfeud (graphic novel) 1999

Saga of the Swamp Thing: The Curse [illustrated by Bissette and Tottleben; originally published in *Saga of the Swamp Thing,* issues 35-42 in 1985] (graphic novel) 2000

Top Ten [illustrated by Gene Ha and Zander Cannon] (graphic novel) 2000

The Complete D. R. & Quinch [illustrated by Alan Davis; originally published in serial form in *2000 A.D.* in 1983] (graphic novel) 2001

The League of Extraordinary Gentlemen [illustrated by Kevin O'Neill] (graphic novel) 2001

Promethea Book 1 (graphic novel) 2001

Promethea Book 2 (graphic novel) 2001

Saga of the Swamp Thing: A Murder of Crows [illustrated by Bissette, Tottleben, and others; originally published in *Saga of the Swamp Thing,* issues 43-50 in 1985-1986] (graphic novel) 2001

‡*Snakes and Ladders* [illustrated by Campbell] (comic book) 2001

Tom Strong Book 1 (graphic novel) 2001

Captain Britain [illustrated by Alan Davis] (graphic novel) 2002

Mr. Majestic (graphic novel) 2002

Saga of the Swamp Thing: Earth to Earth [illustrated by Rick Veitch, Alfredo Alcala, and others; originally published in *Saga of the Swamp Thing,* issues 51-56 in 1986-1987] (graphic novel) 2002

Tomorrow Stories (graphic novel) 2002

Judgment Day (graphic novel) 2003

The Mirror of Love [illustrated by José Villarrubia] (poem) 2003

Supreme: The Return (graphic novel) 2003

Saga of the Swamp Thing: Reunion [illustrated by Veitch, Bissette, Tottleben, Alcala, and others; originally published in *Saga of the Swamp Thing,* issues 57-64 in 1987] (graphic novel) 2003

America's Best Comics [scriptwriter] (graphic novel) 2004

Tomorrow Stories (graphic novel) 2004

Top 10: The Forty-Niners [illustrated by Gene Ha] (graphic novel) 2005

§*Lost Girls* [illustrated by Melinda Gebbie] (graphic novel) 2006

*Published in England as *Marvelman*; republished and continued serially as *Maricleman* by American publisher Eclipse Comics in 1985.

†This work was originally staged as a performance piece by Moore in 1995.

‡This work was originally staged as a performance piece by Moore in 1999.

§This work is an expanded version, now presented in three oversized volumes, of the one-volume work begun as the *Lost Girls* graphic novel in 1995.

CRITICISM

Brent Fishbaugh (essay date fall 1998)

SOURCE: Fishbaugh, Brent. "Moore and Gibbons's *Watchmen*: Exact Personifications of Science." *Extrapolation* 39, no. 3 (fall 1998): 189-98.

[*In this essay, Fishbaugh considers the origins and context of* Watchmen.]

Comic books seem to be eternally stigmatized as garbage for children's minds and sources of potential revenue for the toy market; however, every decade or so a comic book or visionary creator enters the medium, taking the comic world in a different, more adult direction. In the fifties, in his book *Seduction of the Innocent* and in his testimony before Congress, Fredric Wertham, a child psychologist, made people aware of the adult themes that could be transmitted through this so-called kiddie-lit. In the sixties, Robert Crumb rose to prominence with his underground stories—comics that he and others would use to explore such issues as sexual liberation and drug use. These sporadic and often missed explosions of seriousness in the medium, however, have always paled in comparison to the esteem many European and Asian countries give to their graphic literature. But in 1985, two works appeared that would change the way many Americans would view comic books: Frank Miller's *Batman: The Dark Knight Returns,* a dark and violent view of Batman in his fifties, and *Watchmen,* by Alan Moore and Dave Gibbons,

which examines, in a science fiction setting similar to George Orwell's *1984,* the cost of achieving world peace. Moore, as the writer, uses his superhero characters—if they can truly be called "heroes"—as symbolic representations of hard and soft sciences and of their potential, shaped by human failings, to create a utopia.

The origins of *Watchmen* stem from Moore's desire to do a comic series about superheroes and the effect they might have if they were placed in a "real world" setting; there would be real, contemporary issues, such as graphic street crime, the controversy over nuclear disarmament, and human sexual relations; many of these topics would be based around historical events, such as the New York City murder of Kitty Genovese in 1964 or the repercussions of the Vietnam War. Moore already had some success as a writer in his native England and had managed to rejuvenate a tired horror comic, *Swamp Thing,* for DC Comics by turning it from conventional horror and superhero fare to a more introspective examination of the human condition. DC had recently purchased another company's comic book universe, which amounted to roughly seven not-so-famous heroes from the sixties and early seventies. Moore hoped to twist these characters to fit his plans; however, the editors at DC were unwilling to let their properties be turned to a project so dark and untried as what Moore suggested. This led to a decision by Moore and Gibbons to create characters based on those they had hoped to use. Both agreed later that this was for the best; it allowed them to explore avenues of development they had previously ignored. Many of the characters' idiosyncrasies came from this necessity to reconstruct them along the frames of the previous characters' personas. As inspiration will usually have it, this led to the development of traits previously unplumbed by the creators and served to further—albeit haphazardly—the "real world" aspect the creators sought to evoke.

Likewise, as the characters developed somewhat unsystematically, the story did the same as the writer and artist bounced ideas off each other, continually adding to the depth of the book. The work began to take on a much more postmodern feel as the layers of the book began to deepen. Small stories within the main story began to take place, and the New York City environment itself became as crucial a character in its revelations about the so-called heroes as the actual human characters did. By examining the setting, one sees clues that point toward the eventual outcome of the book. Seemingly insignificant props placed in the background play a crucial role, shaping the tone and narrative of the work; the creator stumbled upon many of these, such as the factually based "smiling crater" on Mars, coincidentally, but this only served to strengthen their resolve that they were indeed on the right track. Posters promoting such films as *The Day the Earth Stood Still* and *Things to Come* on the placard for the "Utopia Theater" lend hints as to the method the series mastermind will use to achieve his ultimate goal. The theme of the Gordian Knot and how it runs from a locksmith to Mars to Alexander the Great also points to the architect of the mystery behind the plot and to his motives. A dual storyline in the novel, detailed in a comic book about pirates read by the child at the newsstand, parallels one man's decent into the abyss in order to create peace on Earth—a modern-day Dr. Frankenstein. As these story characteristics begin to take shape in a seemingly unplanned manner, the authors sought to use the last few pages of each installment similarly. In most comic books, these pages are reserved for letters sent by readers commenting on previous issues or chapters as they hit the newsstands. With merely twelve issues in which to tell their story, and since responses would not begin arriving until the third or fourth issue/chapter, Moore and Gibbons opted to forego a letters column and instead fill those pages—at least in the initial issues—with chapters of an imaginary autobiography mentioned in the main story. This worked so well for them and added so much to their narrative that they decided to exclude the letters section from future chapters as well; in its place would be such seemingly inconsequential and unrelated items as articles on ornithology or a police report and psychiatric evaluations of one of the characters. Interviews with or articles about the main players in the story were developed in these sections and further served to define the characters and the bleak world they inhabited.

It was to be something of an experiment for Moore and Gibbons, but it grew beyond anything they had imagined as they opened a door to an idea, only to be drowned in the possibilities it released. The astounding aspects of this novel are that the creators managed to include most of these ideas—such as the Hiroshima lovers' graphitti silhouette and the murder of Kitty Genovese—and, as admitted by the pair, that there were such coincidences in the way these details, like the smiley face crater on Mars and Rorschach's smiley-face button, interlocked and supported one another. The authors admit to incredible fluke occurrences in their research for the book, and they took these as omens for their success; even as they watched, somewhat helpless in the flood of ideas they were discovering, the novel was evolving into much more than they had envisioned. It continues to surprise them and most readers with each examination.

The importance of science is made clear from the beginning of the novel when, in the first chapter, the reader is immediately made aware of the advanced science at play in the story. Moore immediately and subtly lays out the advanced technology used by the characters in their 1985—a 1985 where Nixon is still president, a 1985 where people drive electric cars and eat at a chain of Indian restaurants instead of burger joints. Cars are electric; readers learn later that one of the heroes has

made this possible. Airships travel the skies between buildings much like those in the film *Blade Runner.* It is in the heroes themselves, however, that Moore proposes his primary question: Is humanity responsible and humane enough to properly use science? As such, he personifies the sciences within the major characters and through the text, asks the reader if placing the power of various sciences in the hands of the subject morality and wisdom of human beings is a wise idea. In the minor characters, Moore demonstrates to some extent the results of applied science. Both instances serve to prove that mankind is unable to responsibly handle the power of science.

The story begins with the masked adventurer Rorschach investigating the death of a man he learns to be the Comedian, a former comrade and current government operative. Rorschach immediately jumps to the conclusion that this may be some sort of vendetta against adventurers of the past decades, most of whom were forced to retire or go underground when a law banning the fad of masked adventuring restricted all but those for whom the government had use. Rorschach sets out to warn his former friends and, as he does, he introduces the reader to the remainder of the leading cast: Nite Owl, a.k.a. Daniel Drieberg, a wealthy ornithologist; Ozymandias, a.k.a. Adrian Veidt, "the smartest man in the world," a billionaire industrialist and philanthropist; the Silk Spectre, a.k.a. Laurie Juspeczyk, a woman forced into the role of hero by her mother. Laurie is also the girlfriend of Dr. Manhattan, a.k.a. Jon Osterman, a nuclear physicist and the only real "superhero" in the book, with amazing extrahuman abilities, used by the government as a weapon against the communists. None take Rorschach's assumptions very seriously, since he has a reputation as a paranoid rebel; suddenly, however, coincidences begin to take shape that support Rorschach's claims. Dr. Manhattan is accused of unknowingly giving cancer to his close associates; he leaves Earth out of guilt. Rorschach is framed for the murder of one of his old adversaries and is captured by the police, who have wanted him for more than a decade due to his violent methods. Adrian is the target of an attempted assassination. Dan and Laurie break Rorschach out of prison, and they discover the person behind the plots against them, plots linked to a grander one involving mass murder as a way of frightening the nations of the world into unity and peace. This mastermind wants to save the world from itself and, to do so, will kill all of New York City if he must. During this search for the truth, the characters each discover smaller truths about themselves: Laurie comes to a realization about her father, Jon about what it means to be human, Dan about his feelings for Laurie, etc. These "learned truths" reveal much about the aspect science plays in the representations of three characters: Rorschach, Dr. Manhattan, and Ozymandias.

Rorschach, Walter Kovacs, as he investigates the death of the Comedian, is the first character encountered by the reader. Like his name implies, his link to the sciences comes through psychology. He wears a mask that resembles a Rorschach test itself—a black fluid trapped between a layer of white and a layer of transparent material, with the black constantly changing its pattern to feature test upon test upon test. While he is the link that initially joins the main characters as he seeks out each to deliver the news of the Comedian's death, his own link—besides the obvious symbolic one of his name—is not truly explored until chapter six, after he has been captured by the police. In this chapter, a psychologist comes to examine the imprisoned Rorschach, the man now revealed to be the nameless man in the background who has, up until this point, walked the streets carrying a sign announcing that "The End is Nigh," his true identity unknown to the reader.

This examination of Rorschach and the revelation of his true identity and past are the most obvious links of this character to the soft sciences. Rorschach was created entirely by his environment, and it is that environment which has driven him to the extreme behavior he so often demonstrates. At first, the psychiatrist uses Rorschach tests to examine the patient, but the reader sees what the doctor cannot; Rorschach lies in his responses. What Kovacs sees are not the simple, pleasant images that lead the doctor to believe his patient is making progress but images from Walter Kovacs's past, which reveal his motivations for becoming Rorschach, Walter's truest identity, and memories that pushed him into his obsessive behavior. Walter sees in the ink spots his prostitute mother turning a trick, a trick which skipped out on full payment for her services, a trick Walter was beaten for interrupting. He was removed from his mother's custody and placed in an orphanage until he left during his late teens to work as an unskilled laborer in the garment industry. When he was twenty-two, a woman failed to pick up a dress made of an experimental fabric, "Viscous fluids between two layers of latex, heat and pressure sensitive. . . . Black and white. Moving. Changing shape . . . but not mixing. No gray." The woman who ordered the dress never collected it; she thought it was ugly. The young Walter put the dress away and forgot about it and her for two years. In 1964 she turned up dead, raped and murdered in an alley while almost forty neighbors listened to her screams or watched her torture; her name was Kitty Genovese, and she presents still another example of how Moore draws the horror of reality into the story. This is a spark that proves to be the ignition of Walter's real life, the ignition but not the full flame. Walter cut up the dress and made it into "a face that [he] could bear to look at in the mirror" (Moore and Gibbons 6:10).[1]

He joins the fad of costumed crimefighting not for fun, but out of guilt—guilt over what his entire race has become, guilt spawned not just from the events surrounding Kitty Genovese's death but from his own misbegotten upbringing. In 1975, Walter has an epiphanal experience that will overwrite his Kovacs personality into that of Rorschach. In that year, a child is kidnapped under the false assumption that she is related to a wealthy family; Rorschach promises to return her safely. He tracks the criminal to his home, only to discover the man has killed the child and fed her to his German shepherds rather than admit his mistake. "Walter as Rorschach" silently examines the chopping block and the tools, the potbellied stove where a few scraps of the girl's clothes remain, and a thighbone over which the dogs fight. Walter closes his eyes when he kills the dogs and has fully become Rorschach when he opens them; these images of the dogs, heads split by his blows, resurface during his testing by the psychiatrist. It proves to be the turning point in his life. He no longer "mollycoddles" the criminals by allowing them to live and kill again or by walking away from the encounter with his foes merely bound. The kidnapper and murderer of the child is faced with a choice upon his capture: Cut off his arm with a hacksaw to escape his handcuffs, or burn to death in the building Rorschach sets afire. From this point forth, Kovacs becomes a mask for Rorschach instead of the converse as it had been. He is no longer "soft" on criminals, as he puts it; he is more often than not, ready and willing to kill them to rid society of their filth (6:14-26).

This leads to a conclusion at the end that will cost Rorschach his life. There is no compromise when it comes to evil; it must be cut out and destroyed like the cancer it is. At the novel's end and faced with the decision whether or not to expose the hoax which has frightened the world into peace, he chooses truth, knowing that the other heroes will kill him to protect their grand lie. Those who disagree with him justify the act in that millions have already died for world unity; would Rorschach make their sacrifices in vain? However, Rorschach will not lie, and the others kill him to protect the peace: "Joking, of course. . . . No. Not even in the face of Armageddon. Never compromise. . . . Evil must be punished. People must be told" (12:20, 23).

Rorschach is the epitome of soft science not only in his obvious connection to psychology but in his subtle connections to it as well. Two easily recognized examples of this link are revealed in his relationship with his psychiatrist and in the way he is shaped by his environment. The former begins when Rorschach is captured by the police and is given a psychiatric exam involving, ironically, Rorschach tests. The subject knows the game, though, and gives safe, pat answers to the doctor's questions. The doctor is initially pleased with Rorschach's seeming progress but is troubled later by the easy answers as he studies Rorschach's file, so he chooses to review the same ink blots the following day. On the second showing, Rorschach reveals to the doctor what he truly sees and tells the psychiatrist that the knowledge will cost him more than the fame he gains from his patient is worth. Rorschach reveals the abuse through which his mother put him as a child and the inhumanity of the man who fed the child to his dogs (6:9-26). Kovacs is no more, and the doctor sees the validity of Rorschach's existence; he sees the necessity of the vigilante's ruthless presence, and it cannot help but color his view of the world from that point forth. Instead of the doctor helping Rorschach, Rorschach has brought the doctor around to his way of thinking. And this new outlook on the world is visible in the psychiatrist's later actions in the book where he now has no choice but to involve himself in the violence; he cannot look the other way (6:27; 11:20).

Secondly, the whole "nurture versus nature" debate is reawakened with Rorschach's examination. How much of the violence he exhibits is inherited from his prostitute mother and unknown father? On the other hand, this violent behavior may be due to the childhood home and the environment in which he continues to develop. He grows to adolescence in an abusive home and knows Kitty Genovese, the victim of a brutal rape and murder. He witnesses the barbarity of a man who killed a child for no reason and fed her to animals—animals he seemed to love more than other humans. The senseless violence hits too close to home. Is the violence a gene in Rorschach's family, carried by all those of his line, or does it spring from society's ills? Both are represented in Rorschach and his retributive outrage towards crime.

Dr. Manhattan, or Jon, is at the opposite end of the science spectrum; where Rorschach represents the soft, personal, somewhat subjective sciences, Jon represents the cold, hard, true mathematical and chemical sciences. He begins his life wanting to be a watchmaker like his father; however, while Jon is in his late teen years, the first atomic bomb is dropped, and Jon's father sees no future in watchmaking. Jon becomes a nuclear physicist and, one day in the laboratory, is caught on the wrong side of an experiment that removes the intrinsic field from objects. Months later, Jon manages to reintegrate his body, but he now has great control over matter and energy. The government immediately capitalizes on this and names him "Dr. Manhattan," making him a very public deterrent to the cold-war Russians. The heroes from the fifties begin to feel outclassed by Jon and his incredible abilities; however, Jon is satisfied simply to have a place in which to continue his experiments. Separated as he is from normal humans by his neon blue appearance and god-like powers, Jon begins to distance himself from humanity. He now has to guess at what things a "human" woman such as Laurie might want from a mate and does not see that he is failing to meet a need for her in

the area of human spiritual connection. During a television interview, Jon is accused of unwittingly giving cancer to many of his past associates and leaves Earth for Mars to ponder his existence. He returns for Laurie and brings her back to the red planet in an effort to rediscover his lost humanity; he manages to do this to some extent and comes to realize the gulf his power must cause between him and humanity. He returns to Earth too late to save New York from Veidt's plan, but it is these newly discovered qualities that lead him to question the methods by which peace has been forced on the planet.

Jon is the ultimate scientist—so much so that he loses touch with real life and the applications of knowledge beyond the theoretical. Until Laurie reawakens his humanity towards the end of the book, Jon is on a downward slide of his disassociation from the human race. Moore relates this in his notes:

> Try to imagine what it would be like to be [Dr. Manhattan]. The desk you're sitting at and the chair you're sitting on give less of an impression of reality and solidity to you if you know you can walk though them. . . . Everything around you is somehow more insubstantial and ghostly, including the people you know and love. . . . While most of us are intellectually aware of that both our bodies and the reality surrounding us are composed of billions of gyrating waves or particles or whatever the current quantum theory states, we can forget this disconcerting fact quite easily. . . . [Dr. Manhattan] would not be so fortunate. He would know himself and the world about him from a perspective far more alien than that of the most rabid quantum theorist. He would experience the paradoxes of reality at a quantum scale of existence: that all things can exist in two places at the same time, that certain particles [tachyons] can travel backwards through time and exhibit physical properties that are exactly the reverse of normal physical laws. . . . [Dr. Manhattan] is no longer human enough to be driven mad by the experience, he is no longer human enough to feel an attachment to the world and its concerns. . . .

> **(*Watchmen: Special Edition*, "Minutes")**

After his transformation, Jon, like God, experiences every minute of time simultaneously. In 1959, he knows what will happen in 1969 because he is already there; he knows about JFK's assassination at his rebirth because he was already experiencing it, unable to change the course of history:

> Janey: So what you're saying is you knew he'd get shot? Jon, I . . . I mean, if you're serious, I mean, why didn't you do something?

> Jon: I can't prevent the future. To me, it's already happening. . . . In 1959, I could hear you shouting here, now in 1963. Soon we make love.

> Janey: Just like that? Like I'm a puppet? Jon, you know how everything in this world fits together except people. Your prediction's way off mister.

Jon: "No. We make love right after Wally arrives with the earrings I ordered for you." [Janey interrupts, but Wally comes to the door.]

(*Watchmen* 4:16)

He declines dinner with his friends to locate a "gulino" which would validate his "supersymetrical theory." He creates a double of himself so he can make love to Laurie and continue working on an experiment; Laurie is noticeably upset at his lack of attention (1:23; 3:4, 5). He is obsessed with the abstract principles of the universe and, only at the end of the novel, is he interested in how they apply to life—Veidt: "But you've regained interest in human life." Jon: "Yes. I think I'll *create* some" (Moore's emphasis, 12:27).

If Rorschach is the ultimate personification of the soft sciences and Jon is the totality of the hard ones, Adrian Veidt, Ozymandias, is the perfect melding of the two. He is born wealthy and orphaned young, but he gives away all of his inheritance in order to prove that he can achieve greatness on his own, without any head-start. Idolizing Alexander the Great, Veidt retraces his hero's path and tries to understand how Alexander, at so young an age, had come to rule and unite most of the civilized world. Veidt, too, becomes a costumed adventurer during the late sixties, but he foresees the end of the fad and retires two years before costumed vigilantism is banned in 1977. He is more interested in the future than the present, more interested in the big world picture than the local one; the "smartest man in the world," he sees the growing escalation of nuclear armament and realizes before anyone else the probable coming holocaust. It is then—years before the events of the book take place—that he begins to implement his plans for saving the world through uniting it without anyone knowing how or why the new world order has arrived. He is not out to conquer the world but rather to save it from itself. It is not power or fame that he sought, for his part in the united world will never be known; he has killed to protect that secret, but his pride, his limitless hubris in the belief that only he could save the world, leads to his possible failure. No one will know that he saved the world, but Veidt will emphasize the belief to those that discover his secret that only he could ever accomplish such a task.

Veidt is the embodiment of the soft science; however he manipulates the hard ones to achieve his plans. He manipulates the future by analyzing the past. He studies Alexander and Ramses II to acquire the wisdom they used to bring peace to their enormous kingdoms (11:8, 10). He studies the backgrounds and weaknesses—both physical and psychological—of those liable to interfere with or pose a threat to his goals, such as Jon and the Comedian, in order to plan for their removal (11:19, 24-26). Adrian analyzes the sociology and trends of the present; he builds his fortune on knowing the psychol-

ogy of people. He sits before his wall of television screens, analyzes what he sees and plans accordingly (8:7, 8). He knows the audience to which he plays in both his business- and peace-related goals. Like Rorschach, he knows the value of appearance, violence, and reputation, and he knows how to make the most of them. Like Jon, Veidt genetically builds an "alien" which he will teleport—technology gained from Jon—to New York City. The enormous monster will die on arrival, but using cloned genes from a psychic sensitive, the creation will send psychic shockwaves around the world, killing millions in the immediate vicinity and causing brain damage and nightmares worldwide. When Veidt implements his plan, he achieves the result he knew he would. The world sees this as an alien invasion; hostilities between nations halt in order to combat what they believe is a greater menace. Veidt achieves world peace by frightening the countries into working together, much like the alien visitor does in *The Day the Earth Stood Still*. It seems that Veidt has taken everything into account—everything but the fact that neither Alexander's empire nor the works of Shelley's poetic Ozymandias survived the kings' deaths. Adrian is a perfect melding of the sciences, but in the end he is still human.

While Rorschach, Dr. Manhattan, and Ozymandias are one-sided representations of science, the other major cast members, the Silk Spectre and Nite Owl, demonstrate the affects of these sciences on "ordinary" people. Laurie, the Silk Spectre, can easily be seen as a character containing all of the psychological conflicts personified in Rorschach. Sally, her mother and the original Silk Spectre of the forties, seeks to relive her youth vicariously through her daughter and compensate for all of the deficiencies she possessed as a hero. Sally trains her teen daughter mercilessly, yet she will not allow Laurie to be included in discussions of the older heroes; she actively seeks to suppress certain information concerning her own past—both as a heroine and a mother—for there are incidents in it that may frighten her daughter from the path Sally has chosen for her. These missing pieces of Laurie's life will be revealed in chapter 9, when she realizes the truth about her father, a truth hidden from her by those closest to her and repressed by herself. While Rorschach raises the question of "nature versus nurture," Laurie answers it to some extent when she breaks free of her mother's conditioning and begins to make realizations and choices for herself.

If Laurie is like a humanized Rorschach, Nite Owl can similarly be compared to Dr. Manhattan. While Jon is interested in science for science's sake—he wants to know merely to know—Dan is interested in science for the sake of its beauty and for its value to the heroic human spirit. He is an ornithologist and, in his essay, "Blood from the Shoulder of Pallas," at the end of chapter 7, he reflects that it is possible to study birds so closely that the wonder of them is lost.

> Is it possible, I wonder, to study a bird so closely, to observe and catalogue its peculiarities in such detail, that it becomes invisible? Is it possible that while fastidiously calibrating the span of its wings or the length of its tarsus, we somehow lose sight of its poetry? That in our pedestrian descriptions of a marbled or vermiculated plumage we forfeit a glimpse of living canvases, cascades of carefully toned browns and golds that would shame Kadinsky, misty explosions of color to rival Monet? I believe that we do. I believe that in approaching our subject with the sensibilities of statisticians and dissectionists, we distance ourselves increasingly from the marvelous and spell-binding planet of imagination whose gravity drew us to our studies in the first place.
>
> (7:29-30)

This reflects exactly what has happened to Jon, who has become a scientist to the extent of losing his humanity, his appreciation for the beauty of science. Dan recognizes the danger of such a mindset and continues to expound upon it when, in the same chapter, he explains how technology—represented in his prototype exoskeleton—can be dangerous when not tempered with humanity. With this realization, he becomes a humanized Jon—seeing all the wonder and potential of science but also its risks and responsibilities.

Although Moore and Gibbons give exact personifications of the potential uses of science, they are also quick to illustrate the need for emotion and humanity in decisions concerning the morality of such uses and the weaknesses these same human traits bring to any such implementation. Rorschach is all passion and no reason while Jon is the exact opposite. Rorschach will not change and thus is killed. Jon accepts Veidt's plan for the sake of those already dead and regains some of his humanity. Veidt, a blend of the two extremes, is conquered by that same humanity—too much pride; he sees himself as the only possible messiah for which mankind can hope, and he believes that in the universe his work alone is eternal. In this book, science has become a moral object lesson from the authors, working on many levels.

Note

1. Since the story was initially released as a monthly series, each of the book's chapters begins with page 1. Thus, references are given here with the chapter number followed by the page number(s). For example, this reference concerns chapter 6, page 10.

Works Cited

Daniels, Les. *Comix: A History of Comic Books in America.* New York: Bonanza, 1971.

Eisner, Will. *Graphic Storytelling.* Tamarac, FL: Poorhouse, 1995.

Feiffer, Jules. *The Great Comic Book Heroes.* New York: Dial, 1965.

Gibbons, Dave. "Pebbles in a Landscape." *Comics Journal* (July 1987): 97-103.

Horn, Maurice. *Sex in the Comics.* New York: Chelsea House, 1985.

Inge, M. Thomas. *Comics as Culture.* Jackson: U of Mississippi P, 1990.

McCloud, Scott. *Understanding Comics: The Invisible Art.* Northampton, MA: Kitchen Sink, 1993.

Moore, Alan. "Sychronicity and Symmetry." *Comics Journal* (July 1987): 89-96.

Moore, Alan, and Dave Gibbons. *Watchmen.* New York: DC Comics/Warner Books, 1987.

———. "Minutes." *Watchmen: Special Edition.* New York: DC Comics/Warner Books and Graphitti Designs, 1987.

———. "A Portal to Another Dimension." *Comics Journal* (July 1987): 80-88.

Steranko, James. *The Steranko History of Comics.* 2 vols. Reading, PA: Supergraphics, 1970-72.

Waugh, Couton. *The Comics.* New York: Macmillan, 1947.

Wertham, Fredric. *Seduction of the Innocent.* 1954. Port Washington, N.Y.: Kennikat Press, 1972.

Curt Holman (essay date 26 October 1999)

SOURCE: Holman, Curt. "From Hell." *Salon.com* (26 October 1999).

[*In the following essay, Holman provides a brief overview of Moore's career to date.*]

If comic books have a *Citizen Kane,* the clear choice is **Watchmen,** written by Alan Moore and drawn by Dave Gibbons. Just as Orson Welles' kaleidoscopic biography of a newspaper tycoon invariably tops cinematic best-ever lists, Moore and Gibbons' apocalyptic yet intimate superhero tale commands a similar status in its medium. And as the flashbacks from Charles Foster Kane's estranged loved ones come together to form a tragic portrait on film, so do the distinct voices and aspirations of Moore's Watchmen coalesce into engrossing and credible human beings—never mind the cowls and capes. **Watchmen** proves that a story published in "funny book" form can be as perceptive, relevant and mature as any novel, film or television series.

When DC Comics published *Watchmen*'s 12 issues in the mid-1980s, comics were viewed as the bottom of the pop culture barrel, no more than adolescent fantasies of brightly-costumed characters in never-ending, rock 'em-sock 'em fight scenes. But *Watchmen* proved as far removed from standard superhero fare as *Trainspotting* is from *Reefer Madness,* and gave adventurous readers a brand-new addiction, *Watchmen* and its contemporaries not only popularized the term "graphic novel," they made it a necessary distinction that set these new, deeper works apart from juvenile-sounding "comic books."

Other comics depicted alienated supermen and antiheroic vigilantes before *Watchmen,* but never before had they seemed so much like people of flesh and blood, instead of ink and pulp. *Watchmen* also made the ordinary lives of street-corner bystanders as crucial as the doings of its atom-age *übermensch,* and could intercut fate-of-the-world confrontations in Antarctica with quiet, awkward moments of middle-aged romance. Dr. Manhattan, the book's only "super-powered" individual, becomes so detached he grows to prefer the surface of Mars to the company of his lover or colleagues. Like Billy Pilgrim in *Slaughterhouse-Five,* he perceives time from all angles, flashing backwards and forwards, from scenes of love and teamwork in his youth to his perfect isolation on Mars' airless deserts.

Welles didn't invent the landmark filmic techniques (as well as the ideas from radio and live theater) that he used in *Citizen Kane,* but he gave them an electrifying new showcase. Likewise, Moore drew diverse cinematic, literary and cartooning styles together in a style unprecedented in comics. But creating an encore to an instant classic is a tricky business, and Welles never equaled *Kane.* After *Watchmen,* the Moore's most significant graphic novel is *From Hell,* an epic autopsy of the Jack the Ripper slayings, serialized through the 1990s and now finally being published in book form by Eddie Campbell Comics.

As ambitious and affecting as anything ever rendered in pictures and word balloons, *From Hell* combines an intricate mystery, insightful social criticism and unflinching brutality capable of unnerving the most desensitized pop audience. It's publication as a book promises to give it a new lease on life. That's what happened with Art Spiegelman's Pulitzer-Prize winning *Maus,* which was originally published in installments in the arty comic *Raw.* *From Hell* is the only graphic novel since *Maus* to rival its ambition and historical depth.

One of the rare comic book masters who's solely a writer, Moore first made his mark in the 1980s with serials in British comic book anthologies. But he became a sensation when he took over DC Comics'

Swamp Thing. With Moore at the helm, the lurid horror title about a shambling plant man offered Hitchcockian thrills, debates about hot-button issues from gun control to incest and visual flights worthy of psychedelic rock album covers.

Swamp Thing shook up staid DC Comics, home of Batman and Superman, and became the first mainstream comic book to be published without the seal of the industry's self-censoring Comics Code Authority. Moore began catching up with his earlier serials, including the British dystopian tale *V For Vendetta* and the first of his revisionist hero books, *Miracleman.* His work for DC culminated with the 12 issues of *Watchmen,* which perfected a cinematic writing style replete with jump cuts, "tracking shots" and close attention to recurring symbols; each issue had its own equivalents to the famous "Rosebud" sled and shattered snow-globe from *Kane.*

Alan Moore and Jon B. Cooke (interview date 16 June 2000)

SOURCE: Moore, Alan, and Jon B. Cooke. Transcribed by Jon B. Knutson. "Toasting Absent Heroes." *Comic Book Artist* 9 (August 2000).

[*In the following interview, also available at http:// twomorrows.com, Cooke talks with Moore about the genesis of the graphic novelists' characters in* Watchmen.]

To admit I felt decidedly out of place calling one of comics' best writers to discuss—ugh! of all topics!— comic book characters is a drastic understatement, but the sheer coolness of having a chat with Mr. Alan Moore eased the prospect considerably. The self-professed anarchist is plainly a nice guy and we spent more time talking about a real-life character—Steve Ditko—than, say, the relationship between Judomaster and Tiger. Alan currently rules the marketplace with his critically-successful and popular America's Best Comics line, his and Eddie Campbell's **From Hell** *collection is flying off bookstore shelves, and life seems pretty good for the British writer. And, yes, good reader, there really is a connection with the wildly-popular scribe and Charlton Comics. This interview took place via phone on June 16, 2000. (Special thanks to JBK for the speedy transcription.)*

[*Cooke*]: *Did you read Charlton comics as a kid?*

[Moore]: Yes, I did. It was kind of pecking order situation, with the distribution of all American comics being very spotty in England. I believe they were originally brought over as ballast on ships, which meant there'd be sometimes a whole month of a particular comic, or even a whole lot of comics that I just missed. So, consequently, I'd buy my favorites early in the month, and then a little later, I'd probably buy my second favorites [laughter] . . . and by the end of the month, I'd be down to *Casper, the Friendly Ghost* just to keep my comic habit fulfilled. Somewhere along the way there, I'd see the Archie/MLJ/Mighty super-hero comics, the Tower comics that were around at the time. . . .

Was Charlton at the bottom of the list for you?

They'd vary, it would depend. Charlton would be at some points low on the list, but then, there was a wonderful period which I later realized was when Dick Giordano was having a great deal of creative say in the Charlton books, when they became very high on the list. There's still one of the books, *Charlton Premiere*—sort of a Showcase title—and I remember in the second or third issue of that, there was this wonderful thing called "Children of Doom" by Pat Boyette, who died recently. It was an incredibly sort of progressive piece of storytelling. He was obviously, I'd imagine, looking at artists like Steranko that were coming up and messing around with the form and sort of experimenting. Pat decided to pitch his own hat into the ring, apparently.

Prior to that golden period when Dick was editor, I very much enjoyed the Steve Ditko stuff—Captain Atom and the Charlton monster books—so the main reason that I liked Charlton would've been probably Steve Ditko, originally. Not to say that there weren't other great artists and writers, but the ace of it all was, Ditko was the only one that I really noticed, until that period when Dick took over.

I remember there was a very short-lived strip that I think was probably based on Harlan Ellison's "Repent, Harlequin! Said the Tick-Tock Man" that was about a kind of futuristic jester character drawn by Jim Aparo. He might've even been called the Harlequin or something like that, but I remember it was drawn by Jim Aparo, it lasted for a couple of episodes, probably written by Steve Skeates or somebody.

There were some very good little strips, and then of course, there was that big Charlton revamp where we got the new Blue Beetle, the new Captain Atom, and so forth, which was a shot in the arm. All of these things contributed in pushing Charlton higher up my league title of which comics to buy first. They never quite ousted Marvel or DC, but during that golden period, Charlton was up there with the best of them.

Do you recall The Question?

Yes, I do. That was another very interesting character, and it was almost a pure Steve Ditko character, in that it was odd-looking. *The Question* didn't look like any

other super-hero on the market, and it also seemed to be a kind of mainstream comics version of Steve Ditko's far more radical *Mr. A,* from witzend. I remember at the time—this would've been when I was just starting to get involved in British comics fandom—there was a British fanzine that was published over here by a gentleman called Stan Nichols (who has since gone to write a number of fantasy books). In Stan's fanzine, *Stardock,* there was an article called "Propaganda, or Why the Blue Beetle Voted for George Wallace." [laughter] This was the late-'60s, and British comics fandom had quite a strong hippie element. Despite the fact that Steve Ditko was obviously a hero to the hippies with his psychedelic *Dr. Strange* work and for the teen angst of *Spider-Man,* Ditko's politics were obviously very different from those fans. His views were apparent through his portrayals of Mr. A and the protesters or beatniks that occasionally surfaced in his other work. I think this article was the first to actually point out that, yes, Steve Ditko did have a very right-wing agenda (which of course, he's completely entitled to), but at the time, it was quite interesting, and that probably led to me portraying [*Watchmen* character] Rorschach as an extremely right-wing character.

When you read some of Ditko's diatribes in The Question *and in some issues of* Blue Beetle, *did you read it with bemusement or disgust?*

Well . . .

A mix of both?

Well, no. I can look at Salvador Dali's work and marvel at it, despite the fact that I believe that Dali was probably a completely disgusting human being [laughter] and borderline fascist, but that doesn't detract from the genius of his artwork. With Steve Ditko, I at least felt that though Steve Ditko's political agenda was very different to mine, Steve Ditko had a political agenda, and that in some ways set him above most of his contemporaries. During the '60s, I learned pretty quickly about the sources of Steve Ditko's ideas, and I realized very early on that he was very fond of the writing of Ayn Rand.

Did you explore her philosophy?

I had to look at *The Fountainhead.* I have to say I found Ayn Rand's philosophy laughable. It was a "white supremacist dreams of the master race," burnt in an early-20th century form. Her ideas didn't really appeal to me, but they seemed to be the kind of ideas that people would espouse, people who might secretly believe themselves to be part of the elite, and not part of the excluded majority. I would basically disagree with all of Ditko's ideas, but he has to be given credit for expressing these political ideas. I believe some feminists regard Dave Sim in much the same light; they might disagree with everything he says, but at least there is some sort of sexual-political debate going on there. So I've got respect for Ditko.

A few years ago, I was in a local rock band called "The Emperors of Ice Cream," and one of our numbers that always went down very well live, was a thing called, "Mr. A." The beat and the tune of it were completely stolen from "Sister Ray" by the Velvet Underground, but the lyrics were all about Steve Ditko.

"Right/wrong, black/white"? [laughter]

One of the verses was, "He takes a card and shades one-half of it in dark, so he can demonstrate to you just what he means / He says, 'There's wrong and there's right, there's black and there's white, and there is nothing, nothing in-between.' That's what Mr. A says." [laughter] And then we'd go into the chorus. Yeah, it was a Velvet Underground thrash, but with lyrics about Steve Ditko, which were very sympathetic, because at that time, I'd heard that Steve Ditko was pretty much harmless, living at the YMCA or something like that. This was, I think, during Spider-Man's anniversary year, and I thought that was criminal.

Steve Ditko is completely at the other end of the political spectrum from me. I wouldn't say that I was far left in terms of Communism, but I am an anarchist, which is 180° away from Steve Ditko's position. But I have a great deal of respect for the man, and certainly respect for his artwork, and the fact that there's something about his uncompromising attitude that I have a great deal of sympathy with. It's just that the things I wouldn't compromise about or that he wouldn't compromise about are probably very different.

Even if they have morals you don't agree with, a person with strong moral code is a person who has a big advantage in today's world.

You wrote in the introduction to the **Watchmen Graphitti** *special edition that you reached a point doing* **Watchmen,** *when you were able to purge yourself of the nostalgia for super-hero characters, in general, and your interest in real human beings came to fore. Do you think that Steve Ditko's work retains substance compared to most anything else that was produced at the time with Charlton?*

I wouldn't want to claim there was any sort of deep or great worthy philosophy in those Charlton strips; it was just that I always have a fondness for Ditko because of his line—irrespective of what he was drawing—and Steve Ditko didn't always draw super-heroes. My favorite Steve Ditko work was the stuff he did for Warren, "Collector's Edition." He was using wash and grey

tones, and that was marvelous. But yeah, Steve Ditko, whatever he was drawing, if it was a Gorgo monster strip, or some sort of Atlas super-hero, it was all terrific stuff.

I always had a suspicion there was an element of the MLJ characters—The Hangman, The Shield, etc.—within **Watchmen,** *and upon recently reading your intro to the* **Graphitti Watchmen** *special edition, I read that my inkling was indeed true. You were exposed to the MLJ characters, such as The Mighty Crusaders, and so on?*

Right. That was the initial idea of **Watchmen**—and this is nothing like what **Watchmen** turned out to be—was it was very simple: Wouldn't it be nice if I had an entire line, a universe, a continuity, a world full of super-heroes—preferably from some line that has been discontinued and no longer publishing—whom I could then just treat in a different way. You have to remember this was very soon after I'd done some similar stuff, if you like, with Marvelman, where I'd used a pre-existing character, and applied a grimmer, perhaps more realistic kind of world view to that character and the milieu he existed in. So I'd just started thinking about using the MLJ characters—the Archie super-heroes—just because they weren't being published at that time, and for all I knew, they might've been up for grabs. The initial concept would've had the 1960s-'70s rather lame version of the Shield being found dead in the harbor, and then you'd probably have various other characters, including Jack Kirby's Private Strong, being drafted back in, and a murder mystery unfolding. I suppose I was just thinking, "That'd be a good way to start a comic book: have a famous super-hero found dead." As the mystery unraveled, we would be lead deeper and deeper into the real heart of this super-hero's world, and show a reality that was very different to the general public image of the super-hero. So, that was the idea.

When Dick Giordano had acquired the Charlton line, Dave Gibbons and I were talking about doing something together. We had worked together on a couple of stories for *2000 A. D.*, which we had a great deal of fun with, and we wanted to work on something for DC. (We were amongst that first wave of British expatriates, after Brian Bolland, Kevin O'Neil, and I was the first writer, and we wanted to work together.) One of the first ideas was that perhaps we should do a Challengers of the Unknown mini-series, and somewhere I've got a rough penciled cover for a Martian Manhunter mini-series, but I think it was the usual thing: Other people were developing projects regarding those characters, so DC didn't want us to use them. So, at this point, I came up with this idea regarding the MLJ/Archie characters, and it was the sort of idea that could be applied to any pre-existing group of super-heroes. If it had been the Tower characters—the T. H. U. N. D. E. R. Agents—I could've done the same thing. The story was about super-heroes, and it didn't matter which super-heroes it was about, as long as the characters had some kind of emotional resonance, that people would recognize them, so it would have the shock and surprise value when you saw what the reality of these characters was.

So, Dick had purchased the Charlton characters for DC, and he was looking for some way to use them, and Dave and I put forth this proposal which originally was designed around a number of the Charlton characters. I forget how much of the idea was in place then, but I think that it would start with a murder, and I pretty well knew who would be guilty of the murder, and I've got an idea of the motive, and the basic bare-bones of the plot—all of which actually ended up being about the least important thing about **Watchmen.** The most powerful elements in the final book was more the storytelling and all the stuff in-between, bits of the plot. When we were just planning to do an extreme and unusual super-hero book, we thought the Charlton characters would provide us with a great line-up that had a lot of emotional nostalgia, with associations and resonance for the readership. So, that was why we put forward this proposal for doing this new take on the Charlton characters.

So you mailed this proposal in to Dick?

Something like that, and I forget the details—it was such a long time ago—but I remember that at some point, we heard from Dick that yes, he liked the proposal, but he didn't really want to use the Charlton characters, because the proposal would've left a lot of them in bad shape, and DC couldn't have really used them again after what we were going to do to them without detracting from the power of what it was that we were planning.

If we had used the Charlton characters in **Watchmen,** after #12, even though the Captain Atom character would've still been alive, DC couldn't really have done a comic book about that character without taking away from what became **Watchmen.** So, at first, I didn't think we could do the book with simply characters that were made-up, because I thought that would lose all of the emotional resonance those characters had for the reader, which I thought was an important part of the book. Eventually, I realized that if I wrote the substitute characters well enough, so that they seemed familiar in certain ways, certain aspects of them brought back a kind of generic super-hero resonance or familiarity to the reader, then it might work.

So, we started to reshape the concept—using the Charlton characters as the jumping-off point, because those were the ones we submitted to Dick—and that's what the plot involved. We started to mutate the characters,

and I began to realize the changes allowed me so much more freedom. The only idea of Captain Atom as a nuclear super-hero—that had the shadow of the atom bomb hung around him—had been part of the original proposal, but with Dr. Manhattan, by making him kind of a quantum super-hero, it took it into a whole new dimension, it wasn't just the shadow of the nuclear threat around him. The things that we could do with Dr. Manhattan's consciousness and the way he saw time wouldn't have been appropriate for Captain Atom. So, it was the best decision, though it just took me a while to realize that.

As you were writing the series itself, suddenly by #4, you realized you had more freedom?

Oh, before #1, once I started actually writing it, I thought, "Actually, this is sort of cool!" By the time I was writing the first issue, I was sold on the idea. It was in preparation when I had my doubts. But once we decided on that course of action, and once there'd been some feedback between me and Dave, and I was starting to see Dave's sketches and ideas, yeah, by the time I started writing #1, I'd already gotten the characters and they seemed solid and strong in my head. I was able to sort of work that into the script, and it was with the very first page of #3 when I'd realized we'd actually gotten more than we bargained for. I suddenly thought, "Hey, I can do something here where I've got this radiation sign being screwed on the wall on the other side of the street, which will underline the kind of nuclear threat; and I can have this newspaper guy just ranting, the way that people on street corners with a lot of spare time sometimes do; and I can have the narrative from this pirate comic that the kid's reading; and I can have them all bouncing off each other; and I can get this really weird thing going where things that are mentioned in the pirate story seem to relate to images in the panel, or to what the newsman is saying . . ." And that's when **Watchmen** took off; that's when I realized that there was something more important going on than just a darker take on the super-hero, which after all, I'd done before with **Marvelman.**

Was one element in the genesis of **Watchmen** *the appearance of the Justice League in* **Swamp Thing,** *where the reader never saw the super-heroes' faces, they never called each other by names, with that very ominous, sinister feeling?*

Like I said, **Marvelman**—later **Miracleman**—had been my first attempt to restructure the super-hero, and to do something that was very adult and quite strong in places. Although they admired **Marvelman,** and it was obvious I could do a good super-hero-type story, when DC first brought me over, I think the reason they gave me **Swamp Thing** was probably because they might have been a little reticent to actually turn me loose upon one of their traditional characters, [laughter] for fear it might end up like *Marvelman,* with strong language and childbirth all over the place. [laughter]

The horror! [laughs]

DC felt that, with *Swamp Thing,* I would work out fine, because it was a horror strip anyway with a more adult aura around it. When I was doing *Swamp Thing,* it occurred to me that, "Well, actually Swamp Thing exists in the same universe with all these other DC characters, so I can let that be a limitation, or something I always steered clear of, or I could just tackle it full-on, and see if I can stick a big, colorful super-hero group like the Justice League into *Swamp Thing,* and make it work without disturbing the atmosphere of the title." So, right, we don't show their faces very much because I wanted the readers to think, "I know who that is!" [laughter] We weren't letting them use their names, just stripping all the familiar trappings away, and our intention was to get the readers to look at super-heroes in a different way. I was quite pleased with how that went, and it showed me, yeah, I could take established super-heroes and write them in a way that would not violate their essential character, and yet which would give them a kind of freshness. But, in terms of *Watchmen,* where the characters are entirely self-created, it owed more to *Marvelman* than to that specific issue of *Swamp Thing.*

Just to map this out: The prototype for Rorshach was The Question, right?

The Question was Rorschach, yep. Dr. Manhattan and Captain Atom were obviously equivalent. Nite-Owl and the new Blue Beetle—well, the Ted Kord Blue Beetle—were equivalent. Because there was a pre-existing, original Blue Beetle in the Charlton cosmology, I thought it might be nice to have an original Nite-Owl. I can't really say that Nightshade was a big inspiration. I never thought she was a particularly strong or interesting female character. The Silk Spectre was just a female character because I needed to have a heroine in there. Since we weren't doing the Charlton characters anymore, there was no reason why I should stick with Nightshade, I could take a different sort of super-heroine, something a bit like the Phantom Lady, the Black Canary, generally my favorite sort of costume heroines anyway. The Silk Spectre, in that she's the girl of the group, sort of was the equivalent of Nightshade, but really, there's not much connection beyond that. The Comedian was The Peacemaker, we had a greater degree of freedom, and we decided to make him slightly right-wing, patriotic, and we mixed in a little bit of Nick Fury into The Peacemaker make-up, and probably a bit of the standard Captain America patriotic hero-type. So, yeah, these characters started out like that, to fill gaps in the story that had been left by the Charlton

heroes, but we didn't have to strictly stick to that Charlton formula. In some places, we stuck to it more closely, and in some places, we didn't.

Adrian Veidt was Peter Cannon, Thunderbolt; I always quite liked Pete Morisi's *Thunderbolt* strip . . . there was something about the art style, almost bordering on kind of Alex Toth style, though it was never as good as Toth, but it sometimes had a pleasing sensibility and a nice design sense about it that I was quite taken by. And I quite like the idea of this character using the full 100% of his brain and sort of having complete physical and mental control. Adrian Veidt did grow directly out of the Peter Cannon, Thunderbolt character.

When I was a kid, I grew up in a rather left-wing environment, and I remember seeing The Peacemaker *with the tag-line "He loves peace so much he's willing to fight for it." I thought, "Ugh. Too reactionary for me," and I passed it by.*

When I first read that, I thought, "Well, that's stupid!" [laughter] I was only about 10 or so, and I hadn't really grown up in a left-wing family—my family voted labor, and that was back when Labor was a socialist party—but it was a working-class family, probably not a very well-educated one, and so their political opinions didn't run very deep, but even so, yeah, the idea that "He loves peace so much he's willing to fight for it," [laughter] I could see the holes in that one straightaway.

Keith Giffen modified the tag line to read "He loves peace so much he's willing to kill for it." [laughs]

Bomb, murder, assassinate! Because we're not doing *The Peacemaker* or *The Question,* we could be much more extreme with all these characters. We probably couldn't have had The Question living in a completely filthy slum room and being mentally disturbed, who had a personal odor problem, and be a little guy who was ugly—you would've had to have had Vic Sage, successful TV commentator.

I noticed, when I was a teenager, that Ditko had got some fixation about the letter K, probably because it occurs in his own name. It's sort of "Kafka," and "Ditko," and there seemed to be a lot of Ditko characters with prominent Ks . . . Ted Kord . . . Ditko seemed very fond of that sort of sound, so in some half-assed way, that observation influenced me in giving Rorschach the name Walter Kovacs.

With our Peacemaker character, Dave and I were saying, "This is a guy who's a comedian," and I believe I took the name from Graham Greene's book, *The Comedians.* At that point, I'd done quite a bit of research upon various kind of CIA and intelligence community dirty tricks, so Dave and I saw him as a kind of Gordon Liddy character, only a much bigger, tougher guy. [laughter] *[laughs] Gordon Liddy as a "bigger, tougher guy"? [laughter]*

Sure, Gordon Liddy is a tough guy, but he's not that huge and imposing physically. But if Liddy had comic book muscles . . . and with Liddy espousing all that Nietzsche philosophy, and the bullocks of holding his hand in a candle flame and not feeling the pain, even though it's searing. So yeah, bits of Liddy worked into The Comedian's make-up, those sort of barking-mad, right-wing adventurists.

Are you ever going to deal with other people's characters again?

I don't really want to, to tell the truth. Mind you, I might change me mind, you know.

You're writing super-hero comics again.

My super-hero comics are very different, I think. After I finished doing **Watchmen,** I said that I had gotten a bit tired of super-heroes, and I didn't have the same nostalgic interest in them, and that's still very true to a certain degree. Even if I was actually writing for DC Comics again (and I often read *Superman*), I haven't got any interest in Superman now. I'd gotten interested in the character when I wrote it, but it wouldn't work for me now—the characters are different, the whole world is different. [laughs]

But you were able to purge yourself pretty quick, right? You didn't write that many, maybe four or five Superman stories?

And that was enough. Those were ones I wanted to write, but since then, most characters have changed so much that they no longer feel to me like the characters I knew. So, I wouldn't have that kind of nostalgic interest in those sort of characters anymore. At the time, I was also saying I didn't feel that if there was some strong political message I wanted to get over, probably super-hero comics were not the best place to do it. If I wanted to do stuff about the environment, that there didn't need to be a swamp monster there, for instance. When I did **Brought to Light,** about the CIA activities in World War II, that story would not have been greatly enhanced by a guy with his underwear outside his trousers, you know. And also, there did seem to be a rash of quite heavy, frankly depressing and overtly pretentious super-hero comics that came out in the wake of **Watchmen,** and I felt to some degree responsible for bringing in a fairly morbid Dark Age. Perhaps I overburdened the super-hero, made it carry a lot more meaning than the form was ever designed for. So, for a while, I went off to do stuff that was very non-super-hero, and going into other areas I was interested in.

The super-heroes I'm doing now are not carrying strong political messages, and that's intentional. They're entertainment, and I think there are very few genres actually as entertaining as the super-hero genre. And entertainment can be emotionally affecting and intelligent, but I don't really want to lecture in the same way I did when I was younger. I'm not trying to break or transcend the boundaries of mainstream comics, because mainstream comics is in pieces, you know?

Well, you're about the only one left standing, I would think. [laughs]

There's no point in trying to transcend the boundaries of something that's already shattered, you know? [laughter] The thing to try and do is to surely try and come up with a strong form of mainstream comics, with some occasionally transcendent elements, but not, "Let's smash the envelope!" Perhaps I have more of a constructive approach than deconstructive.

*Is your current work on America's Best Comics, in the wake of that "morbid Dark Age" you mentioned, a reaction to **Watchmen**?*

It's not so much of a reaction to **Watchmen** because I've got the greatest respect for that book—it was a great piece of work—and Dave and I did a good job there, and I'm proud of it.

It's still in print, right?

Oh, yeah, and there's going to be a great big 15th anniversary edition coming out next year. [laughter] I don't know why 15th. In terms of marriages, I mean, that's like your papier-mâché anniversary or something. There is going to be sort of a big souvenir edition, and I've got Mr. Gibbons coming up here to little old Northampton early next week, and we're going to do some sort of video, because they can't get me to leave Northampton to appear at conventions, and they're gonna see if I actually do show up on film. [laughter] We will try and film Dave and I together.

Watchmen is a work that I've still got a great deal of fondness for, and it was quite ground-breaking, there was a range of techniques that Dave and I developed specifically for the book, but by the time I finished **Watchmen,** they already felt like a cliché to me. You know what I mean? I didn't want my next work to have those same storytelling techniques, so that's why **Big Numbers, Lost Girls,** and **From Hell,** have no captions, and no contrived, clever scene-changes. It's just hard cuts, which felt to me like a more natural way of doing it. I mean, I love the convolution of **Watchmen**—it is a lovely Swiss watch piece, a mechanism, you know?

Wasn't it exhausting to write?

Yes, absolutely exhausting. To do something with that level of complexity—and where the complexity's on the surface—I thought, "Well, I never want to do this again." I have done things that are as complex; *From Hell,* in its own way, is as complex as *Watchmen,* but the complexities of *From Hell* are more in the narrative. It's not as flashy, and I didn't want to ever have to do anything as flashy as *Watchmen* again. I think that the other project I did during the same time, *The Killing Joke* [*Batman: The Killing Joke*], suffered. Brian's artwork is beautiful, but it's probably one of my least favorite works in terms of my writing. It was too close to the storytelling techniques of *Watchmen,* and if I'd done it two years earlier or later—when I wasn't so much under the spell of what we were doing in *Watchmen*—it would've probably been a different and, perhaps, a better book, at least in the writing.

The ABC stuff at the moment is not a denial of *Watchmen,* it's just a recognition that, hey, *Watchmen* was 1986, that was almost 15 years ago, and today's a completely different time. With ABC, I want to do stories with a sense of exhilaration about them, a kind of freshness and effervescence, a feeling that the people doing them are loving it.

Fun!

Exactly, and I think that shows. I'm not sure how it shows, but enthusiasm always makes the difference. The reason why *Watchmen* was good was because Dave and I were loving it, doing stuff we'd never done before, and it was really exciting. We were talking to each other, and were charged up, and it's the same for most of these ABC strips. In that sense, they're very similar to *Watchmen,* even though they look different and read different. They're very similar in that the level of commitment given to them and the amount of fun we're having with them.

You're saying the ABC comics are primarily entertainment for the sake of entertainment. Can you see returning to doing work of more substance?

Oh, yeah! The thing is, comics is not all I do. I wrote a novel a couple of years ago, and when I've got the time, I'm going to do another one. I've got two or three CDs out now of spoken-word performances, which are full of substance, with no super-heroes. In terms of comic work, at the moment we're finishing up *Lost Girls,* which I believe is a work of substance—it's a pornography, [laughter] but it's my kind and Melinda's kind of pornography, and I think it has meaning, social weight, and political value.

So you can have your cake and eat it, too!

Oh, absolutely! [laughter] Yeah, and with that still going on, another CD, I've just been in the studio doing the final mix on a CD that I think Dave Severin will be bringing out later in the year, the guy who used to be in Siouxsie and the Banshees.

Y'know, readers don't call your books "super-hero books"; they call them "The Alan Moore books." [laughs] That's pretty cool.

The Alan Moore books, yes, I'm happy with that. You know, I'm hoping in the future we're going to be able to do the stranger stuff. I'd like to do westerns and all these old genres they used have in comics and we suddenly decided to get rid of for some reason. I remember fondly when there used to be war comics and western comics and teenage comics and friendly ghost comics and things like that. Or Herbie—Herbie was one of my all-time passions when I was growing up, and you couldn't have a character like that in comics these days. He's too eccentric, it's too original! So, that part of Jack B. Quick is kind of trying to fill the hole that Herbie has left in the comics industry.

I suppose ABC comics is sort of an attempt to build an ark, where all of my favorite concepts, things that I think should be included in comics, you know, can maybe survive the deluge.

Alan Moore and Sridhar Pappu (interview date 18 October 2000)

SOURCE: Moore, Alan, and Sridhar Pappu. "We Need Another Hero." *Salon.com* (18 October 2000).

[*In the interview below, Pappu considers Moore's place within the comics industry.*]

Alan Moore spun a tornado into motion 14 years ago, and now he wants to repair the damage—with a talking gorilla.

In 1986 the legendary comic book author changed the genre forever with *Watchmen,* a 12-part serial in which superheroes turned rapists, racists and flunkies of Richard Nixon are hunted down in the days before World War III. This series was read by people who'd never read comics before and never would again. It influenced a generation of comic book writers to turn cowled and caped men into emotional invalids who were fighting crime in lieu of substantive psychotherapy.

It was also what turned Moore into the medium's first pop star, bigger than the characters on the page. Now, he is using that status on his latest endeavor: a whole line of comics meant to reconstruct the superhero, to make him and her again worthy of our attention.

This is not just an aesthetic concern. Having established the "direct market" in the 1980s to better serve the existing readership, giving comic shops earlier access to books than newsstands, the comic book industry set out on a decade-long pursuit of self-destruction. Between 1990 and 1993, the number of comic shops in North America rose from 3,000 to 10,000, fueled by customers' misguided hopes of financial reward. Forty-eight million comics were sold in April 1993, helping sales for that year to reach $850 million.

Sales booms, when based on products largely inessential to our own breathing, invariably end. By January 1994, 1,000 comic shops, or a 10th of all such stores in North America, went out of business, followed by 11 of the 12 distributors set up to serve them. Marvel, the home of *Spider-Man* and *The Hulk,* which had collected revenues of $415 million in 1993, saw its stock lose 90 percent of its value, forcing the company to file for Chapter 11. Last year, the industry as a whole averaged about 7 million copies a month in sales.

More troubling is that comics lost their sense for self-preservation. They became the nearly exclusive domain of specialty shops, they grew exorbitantly expensive compared with other forms of entertainment and their story lines relied on 10 or more years of previous reading for one to understand. Once, we came to comics early in life, still able to believe in a scientist from a doomed planet delivering us a boy who could change the course of rivers and outrun bullets. Without that early exposure, the form that gave Clark Kent life has become the one in need in saving.

Waiting for Moore in the lobby of the Grand Hotel in Northampton, England, I'm prepared to be scared. This readiness comes from nothing other than an unnerving examination of his publicity photos, the most haunting of which depicts Moore leering up at the camera, his long beard flowing into darkness, with only the left side of his face visible, as if he's hanging off the perch of a benighted void. Moreover, I know that he makes no personal appearances, doesn't associate with "fan boys" and doesn't attend comic book conventions. He takes a scant view of TV appearances and very rarely leaves the country.

So I've flown from my home in Chicago to London, then taken a train for an hour and a half across the English countryside to a place only 68 miles from the U.K.'s social and political heart but, at first glance, as foreign and removed as Guam. Established by the Saxons in 700, it's a factory town, but all cobblestone at its center. It's the kind of place where the fading limestone and weathered arches of the All Saints Church look across the street to an electronics shop, a community where it's difficult to find anyone under 30 after dark. Leave your window open at night and you hear post-pub-closing romantic quarrels and fisticuffs until 4 in the morning.

All of this leaves me with what *Harper*'s editor Lewis Lapham once described as the "desperate innocence" of a true believer, willing to go any distance to sit near the feet of a near spiritual being. This is what **Watchmen** made of Moore in the eyes of comic fandom: the man who made comics that disapproving nonreaders enjoyed. An Alan Moore comic in hand earned you a bit of redemption.

Set in mid-1980s New York, **Watchmen** asks what would have happened to us if costumed heroes had appeared in reality around the same time they appeared in the American pop consciousness: the 1930s. It shows heroes getting old and losing faith in the public, against the backdrop of an imminent nuclear war. The series received startling acclaim in *Time, Rolling Stone* and the *Nation.* A headline in the *Chicago Tribune* declared it "a comic book as gripping as Dickens," but warned readers to "think twice before you show it to your kids."

Moore, 6-foot-2, with hair way past his shoulders and a beard that appears to reach his chest, arrives. Yes, he dresses completely in black and carries a walking stick in the shape of a snake. He has thick metal rings on all his fingers, but also the air of a rosy-cheeked English barrister back from the Continent, waving his snake in circles as he talks, a storyteller trying to lay out the places he has seen on the map of his imagination.

Over lunch in a basement pizza parlor, Moore says that his current endeavor—*America's Best Comics* (ABC)—came to him "almost mystically," after the 1998 collapse of Awesome Entertainment, the publisher of his project **Supreme.** In thinking about what would come next, Moore opened up one of the notebooks in which he occasionally scribbles dialogue for his characters in longhand, and there he found a list of names.

Tom Strong. Promethea. Greyshirt. Jack B. Quick. **The League of Extraordinary Gentlemen. Top 10.** He hadn't remembered writing these, but they were in his hand. And it seemed to him that the names themselves had a certain degree of resonance, that they wanted to reflect an earlier time in comics history, before Superman's creators, Jerry Siegel and Joe Shuster, by accident really, changed America for good and forever.

Essence was what he was interested in here—taking just the plain nub of what makes superheroes appealing and "fusing it with a progressive sensibility—something that can be retrograde and avant-garde at the same time. So you get the best of what comics were, sort of distilled in some way to make the fuel for what comics *will* be."

"Not," he adds, "to sound too high flatulent about something that's just a crap superhero book."

Moore himself favors nonhero, small-press work to the dozens of books he receives each month in his "big box of shit" from DC Comics. He says he would prefer the diversity of comics in the 1950s, where one could find everything, from the most benign subjects—cowboys and Martians and funny animals—to the most morally aphasic characters, within the 24-page pamphlet. He would rather not write about superheroes, but he feels that he must do what he can to save the mainstream marketplace and, in so doing, embolden the only subject anyone in the mainstream has any interest in reading about.

In trying to pull the locomotive from peril, then, Moore has chosen to use all of his available hours to write and bring together a horde of artists giddy at the prospect of working with him. He produces five books, including *Tom Strong* and *The League of Extraordinary Gentlemen,* in which Captain Nemo, Bram Stoker's Mina Murray, Allan Quatermain, Henry Jekyll and the Invisible Man team up to fight the forces of darkness at the end of the 19th century.

In *Tom Strong,* Moore reaches for the hero at his most archetypal, trying to reel, as he puts it, "the tape of the superhero" back before Superman. In the tape before Superman are the pulp characters that inspired him— Doc Savage, Solomon Kane—as well as the charm and freshness of Tintin. Moore wanted Strong to have a Victorian origin but still be around today, wanted him married because "married superheroes are somehow sexier" and knew, in some way, that the hero should be friends with a talking gorilla.

What's appealing about Tom Strong is precisely how unrealistic he is, how very little attempt there is to link him to the drudgery of daily life. Little if any concern is given to the fact that Tom is 100 years old and looks 39, or to the fact that, when called upon, he will be sent back into time and travel to Venus. Moreover, Tom Strong acts not out of a desire to feed his ego or a pathological need to hurt but out of what Plato, in his *Republic,* deemed "justice": each person in a society performing the role to which he is most suited.

"He's got a fantastic visual imagination, and no comic book writer ever tried to communicate that to an artist before," says longtime Moore collaborator Rick Veitch. "What most comic book writers did was give you the most simplified, bare-bones description of an act that was supposed to take place on a panel, like 'Superman fights Bizzaro,' [whereas] Alan goes into the motivations of all the characters while they're doing that. He's setting up tiny little images, telling you, 'Oh yeah,

there's a picture on the wall back there of Bizzaro when he's a young kid.' He's tracing it in all these different levels—and some artists can't handle that."

"I'm not interested so much in whether they're clever or profound," Moore says of his comics. "If they happen to be occasionally, fine. But I'm mainly concerned with whether they're fresh or not. It's just been kind of stale—'For Christ's sake, will somebody open a window?'—for the comics industry for 10 years. I just wanted a bit of fresh air."

After lunch Moore and I walk around the streets of Northampton. He seems out of place here, though he has never really been anywhere else. Born here in 1953, he was raised in a neighborhood with houses from the 19th century, owned and rented out by the Town Council. The maternal grandmother with whom he and his family lived had no indoor toilet, while his other grandmother had indoor plumbing, all right, but no electric light.

"Looking back on it," he says, "it sounds like I'm describing something out of Dickens. I mean, I'm talking 1955, but 1955 in England. I've seen *Happy Days* on television. Maybe the American '50s were like that, but that wasn't what the British '50s were like. It was all sort of monochrome, and it was all indoors."

The escapes Moore found were all in the form of imaginative forces—in mythology, first, with the children's versions of the Greek and Norse legends, the children's Robin Hood and Hiawatha. There were comics, of course, but these were British comics, works that depicted the travails of uniformed boys in public school. Black and white, they focused mainly on jokes about headmasters and corporal punishment, and appeared to Moore then not as an escape but as a cackling mirror of the problems he faced.

Then came Superman and the Flash—modern-day extensions of his beloved myths. And they were even more fantastic for their presence in America, a place drawn in color, with huge buildings Northampton just couldn't offer.

"I got my morals more from Superman than I ever did from my teachers and peers," he says. "Because Superman wasn't real—he was incorruptible. You were seeing morals in their pure form. You don't see Superman secretly going out behind the back and lying and killing, which, of course, most real-life heroes tend to be doing."

After dealing acid (something Clark Kent might frown upon) and getting thrown out of school at 17, Moore traded his childish flights for grown-up rigor. He went to work at a sheep-skinning plant on the outskirts of town for 6 pounds (now equal to $8.66) a week, then cleaned toilets at the Grand Hotel, where we're meeting. It was after moving up to an office job at the local gas company that he hit his crossroads: He decided that if he didn't act soon on his more creative impulses, he'd have to face himself in the mirror when he was 40, and decide whether to slit his wrists.

In truth, he didn't know exactly what he wanted to do. So he went on public assistance and, with a pregnant wife, spent a year starting impossibly big projects (a 20-part space opera, of which he wrote only a page, for example). Finally, he got work as a cartoonist for British music weekly *Sounds.*

His work became known in British comic magazines *Warrior* and *2000 A.D.* In 1984, DC Comics tapped him to take over one of its least successful books, **Swamp Thing.** Unconventional and serious, he turned the book into a tool for exploring social issues, using it to discuss everything from racism to environmental affairs. In return, he quickly drew a devoted following and raised the monthly sales of the comic from 17,000 to 100,000 copies.

"Nobody," he says, "wanted to actually say, 'But he's talking rubbish.' They all sort of said, 'He's an English genius, and you must be a fool if you don't see it,' which did me well for a while."

After **Swamp Thing,** everyone saw the genius with **Watchmen,** which, along with Frank Miller's *The Dark Knight Returns,* a depiction of Batman's older, alcoholic, calamitous self, spawned a slew of imitators. For the better part of five years, every book seemed to feature deconstructed bad guys turned mildly good who, dredged up from the sewers, say very little and kill very readily.

Having become the comics' first "star writer," Moore was mobbed at conventions and asked to appear on TV, and he soon swore off both. He and artist Dave Gibbons fought with DC over money. Then DC, in response to evangelical pressure, slapped some of its titles with "Mature Readers Only" labels. In response, Moore walked away from DC, from "mainstream comics" and even from superheroes forever.

Moore threw all of the **Watchmen** money into his own publishing company, and began his ill-fated magnum opus. It was called "Big Numbers," and it was supposed to be a 12-part, 480-to-500-page work, with 40 characters. The script was huge. Moore, his wife and their mutual girlfriend would spend whole days photographing scenes for long tracking shots that were meant to last for four or five pages.

Our most ambitious endeavors are the ones most prone to great failure. Artist Bill Sienkiewicz started turning in his artwork later and later, and then quit after the second issue. His replacement, Al Columbia, worked on one issue and then disappeared. In the course of things, Moore's marriage ended, and he lost nearly all of the money he'd earned from **Watchmen.**

"I don't think it was misguided at all," says Gary Groth, editor of the *Comics Journal.* "I think it was the best thing Alan could have done—for himself and for comics. That it failed was a real tragedy."

Moore's response was to return to the superhero, but not through the same door. He now believed that talking about an issue such as the environment in comics was perfectly all right, but using a swamp monster to do so trivialized the matter. Moreover, by attaching a self-consciousness to superheroes, a belief that they had to be grounded in what is often an awful reality, one was throwing away their fundamental greatness: the uncanny ability to lift our spirits, to bring us closest to the primordial setting of the storyteller "sitting around the campfire, making up impromptu stories about the guy who can fly."

Moore's reclamation project began in 1996, when he took over a "very, very, very, very, very" lame superhero named Supreme. Created by artist Rob Liefeld, Supreme had been drawn and written as a brooding, musclebound oaf, a crusader who said largely incomprehensible things like "Foolish pup! Back to your mother!" Moore threw away this severity by refashioning the hero's origin and recycling elements that had been discarded by DC Comics' various Superman revisionists. He filled the book with silly, wonderful components, and converted the central character into a moral paragon. **Supreme** was the jumping-off point for Moore's current idea of saving the comics industry, one that has led him back to the financial auspices of DC. By August of 1998, Moore had begun work on a major project for Wildstorm Comics, developing story outlines and commissioning artists, when he received a visit from then Wildstorm owner Jim Lee and the company's editor in chief, Scott Dunbier. Over lunch Lee told Moore that because of the instability of the market, he had agreed to sell Wildstorm to the behemoth Moore had walked away from more than 10 years before. Moore thought about dropping the project altogether, but he was reassured that he'd be working directly under Wildstorm's editors in California, not those at the Time Warner (DC's parent company) building in New York.

"Alan's got as much input as he wants," Dunbier says. "He will always have as much input as he wants. But he trusts us. I mean, he trusts us a lot more so than a lot of other publishers."

It's hard to say whether all of Moore's efforts will succeed. Retailers have complained that the ABC books are consistently late, and in February, the seventh issue of *Top 10* ranked 59th, with 32,000 copies sold on the direct market, while *Promethea* had sold 29,000, good for 70th place. These numbers are profitable, but they're nowhere near good enough to resuscitate comic shops that have taken to selling toys, memorabilia and even adult publications to stay afloat.

"Did Alan say he's trying to save comics?" asks Groth, who loathes superhero comics and has yet to read any of Moore's ABC books. "Good lord, it sounds like desperate hyperbole. Why would anyone want to save mainstream comics?"

There are many things about the industry Moore cannot change. All he can do is hope for new fans, and hope that the old ones who watched him take apart the superhero 14 years ago will return to see the myth reassembled.

"What I could do is what everyone wants me to do," Moore says over coffee, having come back with me to the lounge of the hotel where he once scrubbed toilets, "and to ignore the fact the popular market is going down the toilet. I could do something really obscure. I'd get critical appeal and sell 1,500 copies and incidentally go broke and earn the respect of Gary Groth, and the comics industry would completely fall to pieces. Even if it all happens, and comics does fall to pieces, at least I did my best."

Lisa Coppin (essay date January 2003)

SOURCE: Coppin, Lisa. "Looking Inside Out: The Vision as Particular Gaze in *From Hell* (Alan Moore & Eddie Campbell)." *Image & Narrative,* no. 5 (January 2003).

[*In this essay, Coppin considers issues of perspective in* From Hell.]

Some people see images from another reality. We mostly consider them crazy, although in the past some of them used to be called prophets. Perhaps, as it is suggested in following passage from *From Hell,* visions are all but a sign of madness and most people may miss half of reality. Maybe there is more than what the common mortal can see. Sometimes, images from a repressed unconscious return, through dreams, apparitions, visions. In *From Hell* this kind of optical apparitions bring the characters in contact with the supernatural.

In *The interpretation of dreams* (1900), Freud defines the unconscious as a picture story, a sort of catalogue of images that is acted in dreams. Images from dreams make a link between the unconscious and the conscious,

but, so Freud contends, we cannot simply translate these images into meaningful words, since there will always remain a tension between image and interpretation because of the radically different nature of both: visual versus textual material. In his review of Freud's ideas about the visual representation in dreams, Jay says:

> Although there were visual representations in dreams, they had to be rearticulated in linguistic form before they could become available for analysis. In addition, Freud admitted that even the most thorough exegesis of dreams confronted a blind spot, which he called its "navel": a place "which has to be left obscure . . . the spot where it reaches down into the unknown."
>
> (Jay: 334)

Therefore, the original images need to be translated into language in order to be useful as analysis material. Still, because of their specific nature, these images will continue to resist to the interpretation. *From Hell* is a picture story in the literal sense of the word, it combines image and word. The uncanny effect that will undeniably affect the reader is to a large extent due to visual devices. Thematically as well as formally—as a comic—the work is a reflection on the statute of reality, to which the gaze provides one of the privileged accesses. Critics speak of a "graphic novel";[1] technically speaking, it is a comic, but the topics and particularly the way they are treated and put into words used to be traditionally ascribed to the novel. This double, ambiguous nature makes *From Hell* a very interesting study object.

As Miller states in *La fantasmagorie,* there are three main reasons why a psychoanalytically inspired literary criticism or a psycho-criticism[2] should be interested in optic phenomena. In the first place, the optic is one of the privileged accesses to reality. It is a commonly known fact that "the eye deceives"—optic effects and disorders of the psyche—can deform images. Depending on whether the power and truthfulness of images are stressed, or on the contrary, their deceptive or transitory nature, the idea of imagination has been put into question in different ways. Moreover, theoretical changes in the conception of the visual, induced by the theory of Lacan, have resulted in a stronger stress on what optical models can tell us about the statute of the subject and the regime of desire. In this context, the visual relation is seen as the place of encounter between the individual and the cultural sphere, in as far as the imagination power of the writer is not only tributary to the available cultural material, but also, and in no less extent, to the way the culture of a given period represents or visualises that material. In the third place, literature is a modality of "showing" and disposes of a whole arsenal of optic tools that can be meaningful for the functioning of the text. The framing, the perspective, the relief and the exposure of a story not only have a relation to the subject and his desire, but constitute the elements that make a text into a "machine à faire voir" (Milner: 7).

In this essay we will explore two of the three tracks of investigation indicated by Milner. In a thematic analysis we will investigate the status of reality and imagination as they are created through the gaze of the characters and in the second place we pay attention to the way this is brought into image in *From Hell.* This will lead us to the question that is at the basis of our essay: *How is the uncanny created?* In the first place and in a preponderating way this happens via visual effects, and in this respect we deal with a particular way of looking that is focused in *From Hell,* the vision. A second procedure in the creation of the uncanny concerns the repetition of both images and text. The structure of this essay is inspired by the thematic analysis. In a first part we will concisely situate our study object, paying specific attention to the underlying opinions of the authors that are included in the realisation of their creative project. In part two, the relation of some of the main characters with the physical and supernatural reality through their gaze will be discussed. Part three offers a thorough analysis of the evolution of the particular visual relation the protagonist Dr. William Gull maintains with the material and supernatural reality.

1. A GRAPHIC NOVEL

In the autumn of 1888 London is stirred by the murder of five prostitutes in the neighbourhood of Whitechapel. The girls of easy virtue are found with their throat cut and disembowelled, and the conclusion of the public and the investigators of the murders is unanimous: this must be the work of a particularly cold-blooded serial murderer. The police are not able to unmask the author of the cruelties who enters history under the name of "Jack the Ripper". Now, a 120 years later, the story continues to appeal to the imagination of writers, film-makers and other artists who are fascinated by the killer's calculating way of acting, his precision and his astonishing knowledge of anatomy. Above all we keep on wondering what was the motive of Jack the Ripper, why did he proceed in such a cruel way and why did he suddenly stop after five perfect murders?

In *From Hell* Alan Moore gives his own interpretation of the facts, based mainly on the book of Stephen Knight *Jack the Ripper: The Final Solution* (1977). William Gull, doctor at the Court of Queen Victoria, is pointed as the guilty one. The motive: Queen Victoria discovers Crown Prince Eddy has a child with an ordinary woman and charges William Gull with the mission to avoid the leaking of this secret that could mean the ruin of the empire that is already in distress. Gull takes his task seriously and eliminates all the women knowing about the royal baby. This of course reveals nothing about why the Ripper behaves in such a bloodthirsty way. Moore himself tries to answer this question in chapter four, where William Gull explains his ideological motives.

From Hell arose from the cooperation of script author Alan Moore and illustrator Eddie Campbell. The drawings as well as the text are based upon thorough historic investigation that was conducted in order to create a comic as truthful as possible. We get a detailed image of what London looked like by the end of the 19th century and Moore overwhelms us in the appendices with a profusion of evidence material and erudition making it, even in spite of his warnings, hard to believe that things did not happen the way he presents them. However nothing is less sure. In *From Hell,* the border between fiction and reality is continuously played with: almost every detail is supported with possible evidence, and yet, the conclusions drawn by Moore remain conjectures. The title of the book refers to the signature in one of the letters supposedly coming from Jack the Ripper that arrived at the police office, in which the author refers to his supernatural mission: he does not write the police from earthly reality but "from hell".

If one expects to read a pleasant, colourful comic, *From Hell* is bound to disappoint. The abundance of violence, sex and especially a lot of blood make reading the work into a real hardship. Moreover, illustrator Eddie Campbell visualizes all this raw material in a very rough manner; his drawings are all but a caress for the eye with their hard and angry pen strokes. Critics sometimes suggest that Campbell's style would be "unworthy" of Moore's screenplay. However, a graphic style always has to be judged according to its integration and commitment to the artistic project as a whole and according to the extent in which structural links of congruency or rivalry between text and image are realised.[3] Campbell's work in *From Hell* definitely meets up to this ideal, reflecting the contents and contributing to the creation of the atmosphere that makes the book into a masterpiece. The above-mentioned structural links will be central in our analysis of the uncanny in *From Hell.*

From Hell is not a traditional detective story. From the beginning it is obvious who is responsible for the murders and what his motives are. The uncanny effect produced by *From Hell* has little or nothing to do with suspense or with withholding information. On the contrary, Moore overwhelms us with detailed information of which we can mostly only understand the point afterwards. This procedure corresponds to a particular conception of the course of history. In an interview, Moore states:

> I began to play with the idea that the 1880s were a sort of microcosm of what was going to happen in the 20th century—scientifically, artistically, politically. So could

you say that the Ripper murders were a microcosm of the 1880s? Could you make it seem—just poetically, I mean—that this was the seed event of the 20th century?

(Jackson)

In *From Hell,* Moore gives us successive views of the social unrest that led to two world wars, including the begetting of Hitler and the growing anti-Semitism. Furthermore, Jack the Ripper was also the first "media murderer": the press spread his story as never before and the sensation illustrates the increasing power of the media. Moore's conception of the murders as a prefiguration of the 20th century are echoed in the world vision of the protagonist Dr. Gull who believes in the existence of a fourth dimension. This fourth dimension is understood as an architecture of time wherein different time levels are related to each other. His good friend Hinton communicates this idea to Gull:

—Fourth dimensional patterns within eternity's monolith would, (. . .), seem merely random events to third dimensional percipients . . . events rising to an inevitable convergence like an archway's lines. Let us say something peculiar happens in 1788. A century later related events take place. Then again, 50 years later . . . then 25 years . . . then 12 1/2 . . . An invisible curve rising through the centuries.

—Can history then be said to have an architecture Hinton? The notion is most glorious and most horrible.

(Moore and Campbell, ch 2: 15)

Later on, the importance of this idea of a fourth dimension for the construction of the comic will become clear.

2. THE VISION AS PARTICULAR GAZE

DEFINITIONS

Let us begin in the same way Freud does in his article "Das Unheimliche" (1919) and concentrate on the definition the *Webster's New Collegiate Dictionary* gives for the entrance "vision":

Vision 1 a: something *seen in a dream, trance or ecstasy*; specific: a *supernatural appearance* that conveys a revelation b: an object of *imagination* c: a manifestation to the senses of something immaterial <look, not at ~s but at reality -Edith Wharton 2 a: the act or power of imagination b (1): mode of seeing or conceiving (2) *unusual* discernment or fore*sight* <a man of ~s c: direct *mystical* awareness of the *supernatural* usu. *in visible form* 3 a: the act or power of *seeing*: SIGHT b: the special sense by which the qualities of an object (as color, luminosity, shape and size) constituting its appearance are perceived and which is mediated by the eye 4 a: something seen b: a lovely or charming sight.[4]

(*Webster's New Collegiate Dictionary* 1979: 1299)

A vision is a particular way of seeing, an internal view that gives someone a glance on something one "experiences" as prophetic, mystic or supernatural. Notice that this says very little about the nature of the images one would come to see. Part of the description already suggests the uncanny: a vision can be frightening, it is an unusual discernment or foresight. Vidler also insinuates already in the introduction of *The Architectural Uncanny. Essays in the modern unhomely* (1992) that the uncanny is not an intrinsic characteristic of an object—in his thematic, this is space—, but rather the representation of a certain state of mind:

the "uncanny" is not a property of the space itself nor can it be provoked by any particular spatial conformation; it is, in its aesthetic dimension, a representation of a mental state of projection that precisely elides the boundaries of the real and the unreal to provoke a disturbing ambiguity, a slippage between waking and dreaming.

(Vidler: 11)

This is why the effect of the uncanny for a great part depends on one's look upon the world that surrounds him. In this context, it becomes important to point out which elements constitute a particular look upon the world, and how that look becomes substantial. Vidler talks about "a mental state of projection" and hereby again refers to an optical operation, and this is, of course, not a coincidence. Since the Enlightenment, the gaze is one of the most important ways to come into contact with the world. In *From Hell* this acknowledgement is successfully exploited.

THE CHARACTERS IN *FROM HELL* AND THEIR LOOK UPON REALITY

In *From Hell,* the very divergent reactions of several characters facing the supernatural via their gaze are confronted. In this essay, the specific relation of the characters to the physical and supernatural world will be analysed. The denomination "physical world" refers to the surrounding environment that can be observed with the naked eye and that is usually called "reality". The "supernatural" is used to talk about the images that reach us coming from elsewhere, as in dreams, rapture, déjà-vu and other similar phenomena. The opposition real versus unreal is intentionally avoided, for precisely this opposition will be put into question in *From Hell.*

MISTER LEES

Mister Lees is the professional visionary of the story. He helps Queen Victoria to come into contact with her deceased husband and leads the police to Jack the Ripper. Lees pretends to stand in contact with the supernatural world. He however fails to ever really see something; he in fact feigns all his raptures, as he confesses to his friend Abberline when he is an old man. The reader sees the confession scene in the prologue, therefore he/she knows that Lees' predictions do not correspond to real visions. The fact that what he pretends to see really turns out to be true, astonishes Lees as much as it astonishes the reader. It gives him an uncanny feeling that reaches its paroxysm when Gull appears to be the real perpetrator of the murders, even though for Lees pointing him out as the guilty person was just a way of making him pay for a previous offence. At that occasion, Gull whispers him in the ear: "Tell me, Mr. Lees, have you ever TRULY had a VISION? A REAL vision? (. . .) No? I didn't THINK so . . . but I have." (Moore and Campbell, ch. 12: 13). Very striking is also the graphic presentation of Lees pretended visions, as when he has a so-called talk with Prince Albert, who's body is represented by Campbell. Lees does not believe that the prince is present at all and he deceives the queen, but the picture suggests that a spirit is really hanging over them. This time the uncanny feeling is situated exclusively on the side of the reader.

In the epilogue we meet Mr. Lees again, when he is telling Abberline about a frightening dream he had. It appears to be the same dream that the mother of Adolf Hitler had during his begetting, announcing the Second World War and the persecution of the Jews. This dream, in which both Klara Hitler and Mister Lees see the church of Hawksmoor in Whitechapel, a Jewish neighbourhood, flooding with blood and Jews fleeing in all directions, had been visualised earlier in the book. The dream not only predicts the Second World War but also links the intensification of the persecution of the Jews at the end of the 19th century with the Ripper murders, which were committed in the Jewish neighbourhood of London. Moore shows how during the investigation the hatred for the Jews in London strongly flared up. Slanderers indeed pretended from the first victim that the Jewish community was responsible for the murders.

Queen Victoria

The queen wants to look further but fails to do so. She believes in another reality, but misses visual contact with it. It is striking that she seldom or never looks the reader straight into the eyes. She looks aside, absent-minded, feeling superior to others and does not look at them in an attempt to guard distance. In *From Hell* she is the one who orders the murders, but the reader cannot but feel pity for her because of her loneliness and the way she is manipulated by those surrounding her. Mister Lees makes use of her superstition by pretending that she can come in contact with the ghost of her deceased husband. William Gull transgresses the orders of the queen and exploits her confidence. Where she wanted to avoid a scandal in the first place, she now is confronted with incidents that may cast a dark shadow over the British throne. Because of her public image she cannot but keep silent. The inability of the queen to come in contact with the physical world via her look isolates her and alienates her from reality. The only consolation left are the pretended contacts with her deceased husband where she, as mentioned before, fails to see anything.

Polly

The first prostitute to be murdered, Polly, has ominous dreams that warn her if something dreadful is going to happen. Her friends do not take the prophecies serious; they are "but dreams". When the fire Polly saw in one of her dreams really happens, this is graphically visualised as the melting together of the images of vision and reality: Polly runs in the middle of the flames (as she saw in her dream), while she in fact finds herself in another part of the city (Moore and Campbell, ch. 5: 23). The fact that Polly is murdered shortly afterwards gives her omen an even more morbid character.

Inspector Abberline

Abberline, the police inspector in charge of the investigation of the murders, has a matter-of-fact and analytic view on the case. When a boy from the crowd points to the magic nature of the murders, he severely denounces this attitude (Moore and Campbell, ch. 9: 4). Abberline adopts the scientific approach we would expect from Doctor Gull and seems to completely shut himself off from impressions of a supernatural kind. In spite of this, under pressure of the circumstances, he accepts Mister Lees' visions (after all they lead him to the real murder) and sometimes he drifts back to the past in his dreams, e.g., when he is transported to his childhood, observing his father at work as a little boy. Later on, his visual and analytic capacities will ironically turn out to be rather useless: when he finally sees clear into the true circumstances of the murders, he is forced to keep silent and is forced to retire so that he will never be able to use his talent anymore.

3. William Gull

William Gull, the protagonist, is the only character of the comic who has a real relationship to the supernatural. Three stages can be distinguished in his visual relation to respectively the physical and supernatural world that can be schematically represented as follows:

	PHASE 1	PHASE 2	PHASE 3
Physical World	Looks	Looks	~~Looks~~
	Sees	~~Sees~~	~~Sees~~
Supernatural World	~~Looks~~	~~Looks~~	Looks
	~~Sees~~	Sees	Sees

In the first phase Gull has an optical relation only to the physical reality, although his concern with the supernatural is not totally absent. In the second phase, he has one foot in the physical reality and the other in the supernatural, a situation that will finally bend him towards madness. Shortly before his death, in the third phase, Gull leaves the material world completely and is left with his mere visual contact with the supernatural.

First optic stage

The second chapter begins with the symbolic birth of William Gull, who, as a child in a boat with his father,[5] approaches the light at the end of a tunnel. In this scene the reader gets many indications about William Gull's later life. It is suggested that experiences of his early childhood will strongly determine his forthcoming life and the importance of the gaze is emphasised by its position in this "primal scene". The graphic design of this scene goes from complete darkness to bright light in a gradually widening of the visual range of the spectator. The scene moreover displays graphic similarities with other scenes that put the eye on the foreground.[6] William's odd question to his father makes clear that the boy believes that his physical apparition is related to his mother's gaze:

> - Mother says that when she were with child after Waterloo, the pictures of Napoleon everywhere impressed fearfully on her mind and that's why I look like him. Is that so father?
>
> - Well, it is a medicinal fact that such things may occur. How it accords with Scripture I know not.
>
> (Moore and Campbell, ch. 2: 2)

A second important influence in Gull's life is the Holy Bible. His father is a very religious man and gives his son continuous citations from the Holy Scriptures. The question "What does the Lord expect from you?" concerns the boy most of all. He dreams that the Lord has chosen him for a great task and waits for Him to reveal that task.

The first stage in Gull's relation to reality can be called 'the formation phase' and occupies the first seventy years of his life. During this period the protagonist solely has a relation to the physical reality. William Gull observes the environment with a scientifically interested look that excludes any kind of sympathy: it is cold, matter-of-fact and cruel. When his father dies, little William opens the eyes of the body and looks into them. This scene undoubtedly refers to William's professional choice and to his early passion for human anatomy, but there is more. It is possible that William opens the eyes of the body because he wants to know the last image perceived by his father before dying. Maybe he even wonders what lies behind the earthly reality and if the dead have a view on the supernatural. Also his meeting with Merrick, the elephant man, reveals many things about his character and his gaze. Unlike most people, Gull feels no disgust at his encounter with Merrick, not even *tremendum et fascinosum* applies to him. His interest is purely scientific and therefore he greets Merrick with the words: "Mr. Merrick, you are the most dreadfully deformed human being I have ever encountered. It's a great privilege to make your acquaintance" (Moore and Campbell, ch. 2: 22). For Merrick it is stirring news that his visitor does not start screaming nor look aside and he feels quite comfortable in the presence of Gull. Because of his similarity with the Hindu god Ganesa (a human being

with an elephant head), in India Merrick would be a god among the human race, so Gull tells him. Indeed in India someone like Merrick is worshipped and his sleep is studied: when the man-god has a restless sleep, this means social unrest or war, a quiet sleep means peace. The Hindus believe just like Gull in the existence of a supernatural world that has its influence on material reality. And as the druids used to observe signs,[7] they interpret tokens of the Indian incarnation of Ganesa. Gull's interest for the elephant man is perhaps also related to Merrick's possible connection with the supernatural. In other words, Gull sees Merrick as an in-between being, as someone having a privileged access to the supernatural.

In the second chapter, which mostly corresponds to the formation phase, the reader literally comes to see the world through Gull's eyes. The camera takes his perspective, making the voice of the first person coincide with his perception of the world. Often we see hands at work as the protagonist must see them; sometimes there is darkness when his eyes are blinded. In comics, characters talking in the first person are usually pictured as a third person whom we see acting. The original camera position in this part of ***From Hell*** forces us to enter the body of Gull, creating thus a particular link between the reader and the main character, for whom we would normally feel little sympathy. At the end of the chapter, our perspective suddenly changes from Gull to the character of Annie Crook[8] to finally fade away together with her. This particular position of the camera will reappear: when Annie, the second prostitute, is murdered, during the dissection of Mary Kelly, at William's own trial and in the last vision he has before his death.

Second optic stage

During the second stage that can be distinguished in Gull's visual relation to the environing world, he still looks at earthly reality, but in fact he only really sees the supernatural. This phase starts when Gull gets a first vision during a cardiac arrest.[9] The architect Nicholas Hawksmoor,[10] his father, his deceased friend Hinton and God successively appear to him. Gull asks the ghost of his father what is now really his task in life since God still has not given him one. The apparition of God in the shape of Yabulon, the three-headed god of the freemasons, is the apotheosis of this first vision. Yabulon nevertheless does not speak to him and remains image without sound. Gull does not seem to be surprised about having this vision, on the contrary, he is happy that God finally decides to show him the way and that he at least gets to see what he has been waiting for since so long. At the same time God reminds him that He is watching him. This reflexivity is an important theme in the Jewish-Christian tradition: when God makes himself visible to a subject, this act refers to the look of the Other defining the subject over and over again:

Une fois visible, les jeux sont faits: il sera virtuelle-
ment regardé de toutes parts et son regard ne pourra à
son tour "se poser" sur le monde qu'en déchaînant les
pouvoirs du visible qui le cerne autant qu'il "l'incarne"

(Assoun: 9)

When Gull is called shortly afterwards to Queen Victoria for an extremely delicate task, he soon interprets
this task as his divine mission. From that moment in the
story Gull will correspond to the profile that Freud
defines as "paranoia": he lives in an illusionary world
where God has chosen him for an important task. From
the moment of the vision, the whole universe is oriented
towards the accomplishment of that task.

In the fourth chapter Gull holds a long monologue
explaining the deeper motives for the murders to Netley, his coachman, who becomes his accomplice or better, his "slave", because he in fact gets trapped in a
situation that surpasses his capacities. Gull intends to
save the world from the decay caused by women and
by doing so, he definitively wants to consolidate the
age of Reason, or in other words, the patriarchy. In
order to save patriarchy, one has to recognise again the
ongoing war between the sun (the male element, light
of knowledge, personified in the Greek god Apollo) and
the moon (the female element, dark, creative, since the
beginning of patriarchy personified in the Greek god
Dionysus). This war has been going on for centuries
and traces of the Dionysus worship can be found
everywhere, for example in the architecture of Nicholas
Hawksmoor and in the poetry and pictures of William
Blake. Gull is afraid that the omnipotence of Reason
will be defeated if Reason fails to give its unconscious
antagonist a place. Trying to balance the dark powers,
he falls back on an animistic vision of the world
wherein magic and reality intersect. Netley is Gull's
only confidant, precisely because the coachmen will not
understand the deeper motives that drive him: "You realise that I only share these thoughts in recognition of
your lack of cognisance?" (Moore and Campbell, ch. 4:
33) Netley is a simple man who has never come in
contact with magic and Gull's conceptions strongly
disturb his carefully protected everyday life. Up till
then, Netley had never felt the need to see any further
than the end of his nose. Not only does Netley not
understand Gull's explanation, he also rejects it
impulsively. Gull then points out the figures of the sun
around the horses' necks that symbolise the male force
of the god Apollo, making clear that whether he wants
it or not, Netley is also involved in the conflict between
reason and the unconscious. Gull's words make such a
deep impression on Netley that fear makes him suffer
physically and he throws up in the gutter. It is not a
coincidence that the coachmen had kidneys for lunch,
since they are the same organs the Romans used to read
the future from.

The description of Gull contains at least two seeds for
the uncanny. Freud states: "an uncanny experience occurs either when infantile complexes which have been
repressed [here: what does the Lord expect from you?]
are once more revived by some impression [here: the
cardiac affection with aphasia], or when primitive
beliefs which have been surmounted seem once more to
be confirmed." (Freud: 249). Freud more particularly
links these primitive beliefs with our ancestor's
animistic conception of the universe that is "characterised by the idea that the world was peopled with the
spirits of human beings; by the subject's narcissistic
overvaluation of his own mental processes; by the belief
in the omnipotence of thoughts and the technique of
magic based on that belief, by the attribution to various
outside persons and things of carefully graded magical
powers (. . .)" (Freud: 240). According to Freud, in our
normal development we all have been through a stage
corresponding to the animistic world conception of
primitive men, so that everything that strikes us now as
uncanny "fulfils the conditions of touching those
residues of animistic mental activity within us and
bringing them to expression." (Freud: 241). All these
elements mentioned by Freud can be observed in Gull's
conceptions and acts. For Freud, this return of repressed
material seems to bear a rather negative connotation, as
something "we did not yet overcome". In the opinion of
William Gull, however, the return is highly necessary
for it is the only possible way to save reason, not
surprisingly symbolised by light (the sun) and the capacity to see. Since the age of reason also corresponds to
patriarchy, we can argue that Gull's story also brings
castration fear on stage. The protagonist is stimulated
by a greed for optic effects—after each vision he longs
for a new one—that is closely linked to the fear never
to be able to see again. Freud defends in his analysis of
"The Sandman" that the fear to lose one's capacity to
see symbolises castration fear. This explanation can be
useful when interpreting the mortal scene of Gull that
pictures his eye as a solar eclipse that later on changes
into a veiled moon (symbol of Dionysus and the dark
powers) at the moment of dying.

Each successful murder and mutilation is accompanied
by a particular vision. The dissection of the corpses is
fundamental for the intensity of the visions. Jan Baetens proposes an auto-reflexive lecture of the return of
dissection and autopsy, which would offer a metaphor
for the activity of the reader:

Car si métaphore il y a, elle concerne en tout premier
lieu le geste même du lecteur, lequel à force de vouloir
arracher au livre les sécrets supposés, finit par mettre
en pièces ce qu'il est censé de rassembler en un tout
cohérent, étayé par un faisceau d'interprétations soi-
gneusement vérifiées.

(Baetens: 111)

Because of the excess of information, the dissection
becomes a performative act: it is a showing that is at

the same time an acting. By contrast, for Gull, the dissection is rather an acting that also implicates a showing: only in the expectation of, or at the moment of the mutilation, images are shown to him. His visions become longer and more intense, in the end involving him personally. As Moore points out in the appendices, it is quite common for serial murderers and psychopaths to have visions before, during and/or after killing. Moreover, the desire to see (to have a vision) and to be seen (by God) cannot be disconnected. Gull is fascinated by his visions and every time again he wants to see; and therefore he has to continue the killing. Since he is also acting according to God's wishes, he wants God to look at him, and to admire him in the accomplishment of his difficult task. Later on, at his trial, Gull will repeat that God has chosen him for the job and that He is the only one to call him to account.

In the beginning, Gull does not experience his visions as being uncanny. The visions of the first three murders refer to the future and show images that above all fascinate him. However, he has no personal link with those images and they do not yet implicate him directly. For the reader, on the contrary, the visions are uncanny indeed: not only do they correspond to possible real situations in the 20th century—so he sees for example a TV-set and electric lamps in a living room—, but, as the appendices teach us, the people in his visions later testify to having seen him as well.[11] This reflexive proceeding reaches its paroxysm in Gull's mortal vision.

For Gull himself the visions only become uncanny when he starts seeing images from the past and repetition begins to operate. In the cruellest scene of the book, showing the dissection of the last victim during 30 unbearable pages, Gull experiences various connected visions in which he talks for the first time, though the characters do not yet perceive him. He is suddenly fully affected by an uncanny feeling when his deceased friend Hinton appears to him, for it is the first time he gets a vision of something recognisable from his personal past. As a reaction, he looks around in anguish to see if his friend is really there. For Freud, the uncanny precisely hides itself in the "return of the same" (Freud: 227) and it is frightening because "something repressed (which) recurs" (Freud: 241). From that moment on the images from the past succeed each other and Gull gradually loses his mind. The transition to the third optical stage, where Gull will get snared in the supernatural world, starts from here.

3.3 TRANSITION TO THE SECOND AND THIRD PHASE

When Gull is cited to appear before the court of freemasons, he finds himself for the first time in a situation he has seen in a vision before. Graphically this is presented by a chiasm: what during the dissection was part of the vision now becomes reality. When Gull realises what happens, he sees himself imprisoned in the crossing and unconsciously lifts his hand as if he still held the knife that he used for the dissection. This confrontation with the uncanny nature of his own visions is what drives Gull to insanity, a process that reaches its culmination just before his death, when he enters a scene he already saw in a vision and which symbolises the negation and the loss of his identity. The same procedure of a graphic chiasm is used here, making clear that Gull has become unable to distinguish vision and reality.

THIRD OPTIC STAGE

Just before his death, when Gull has been left in a madhouse by the freemasons, he has definitively lost his capacity to look (he does not even remark on the couple making love in his view range), and the only thing he still sees is what goes on before his spiritual eye. This is what according to Freud characterises the behaviour of neurotics: "the over-accentuation of physical reality in comparison with material reality—a feature closely allied to the belief in the omnipotence of thoughts" (Freud: 187). The mighty Gull we could admire for his genius is now reduced to an old child, his fancy suits have been replaced by asylum togs. Campbell visualises the situation in a very oppressive way: Gull's once so lucid gaze now only reaches the top of his nose.

The mortal vision heralds Gull's last optic stage and the uncanny feeling strikes the reader most intensely in this scene. For the second time we get a close-up of Gull's eye, an image that Campbell reserves for the most oppressive visions[12], and through the eye we enter Gull's world of visions. In this scene, Moore ties all the ends together and shows the link between many elements he brought to the reader's notice in a subtle or less subtle way during the story. An example of one of those details is the return of the painting *The Ghost of a Flea* from William Blake that represents a frightening monster. In his monologue Gull already referred to this terrifying painting that is said to be the representation of a ghost that appeared to the poet. The reader also gets a glance of this painting in the middle of the book when Gull menaces the poet Yeats in a scene that does not seem to have a specific function at that time. In the final vision it appears that Gull himself is the monster that Blake sees and draws, which means that Gull travels through time: William Blake indeed lived a century earlier.

The images that William Gull gets to see from the past and the future, link the Ripper murders with other serial murderers throughout time. Moreover, the future apparitions in which Gull is the object of the vision of others correspond to existing testimonies. In this last vision, together with the protagonist, the reader seems to access the fourth dimension of time. We alternatively see what Gull sees and how he is perceived, in the past as well as in the future. In this way, Moore seems to suggest the possibility that the hypothesis of a fourth dimension in the structure of time might be right. The visions in this book are not subjective, unique experiences but they are all linked to each other. A good example is the dream shared by Mister Lees and Klara Hitler. Everything that occurs in history is related. Nil novi sub sole.

4. CONCLUSIONS

How does the form of the message contribute to the creation of uncanny effects on the reader? Or, to put it in other words: why can **From Hell** not be conceived otherwise than as a comic?

1. Moore and Campbell focus in the construction of their book precisely on the return of both textual and visual elements to create an uncanny feeling. Hereby they skilfully make use of their knowledge that our visual memory does not stock images in the same way our conscious memory stocks words. Images remain brand-marked on our retina in a subtle, often unconscious way. The coca-cola advertisements that show a coca-cola bottle during a few hundredths of a second in between film images are a well-known example of this phenomenon. It is therefore all but a coincidence that Freud used to define the unconscious as a picture story. Maybe in the beginning of the 21st century, he would have compared it to a comic, maybe even after reading **From Hell.**

2. The obsessive return of elements is ideologically justified in the conception of history as a "fourth dimension" that we defined before as an architecture of time wherein different time levels are related to each other. Via visual procedures such as the positioning of the camera and the graphic melting together of vision and reality, the reader gets drawn into the story, what contributes to the efficiency of the uncanny. Moreover, the appendices, full of data to confirm the veracity of the story, implicate us in a direct way in the creative process of the writer. The reader gets the impression to be drawn along in a frenzied search for the truth and might forget that his perception of the case is manipulated. All the pieces of the puzzle fit together in an almost too perfect way and precisely that is what makes us shudder. Or as a critic puts it: "this book is a black hole" (Hausler).

Notes

1. "The term graphic novel is used to distinguish so-called literary illustrated narratives from their more frivolous brethren known as the comic book." (Hausler)

2. Milner defines psycho criticism as follows: "une critique d'inspiration psychanalytique dont la visée essentielle est d'identifier, dans les oeuvres qu'elle prend en considération, les processus inconscients dont Freud a révélé l'existence en étudiant le psychisme individuel" (1982: 5)

3. Jan Baetens, "Une dialectique à l'oeuvre". (112)

4. My italics.

5. It is not a coincidence that his father is present in this symbolic scene for the ghost of his young deceased father will follow Gull for the rest of his life. Besides, the mother figure is strikingly absent in the education of the young Gull. After the death of his father, his mother trusts him to rector Harisson, who makes sure that William gets the best education and is able to study to become a doctor. Women are also absent in his early adulthood years, except as patients. The freemasonry, which will strongly influence his life, is a community of men. The absence of women in his life might have a direct relationship with his later misogyny and the ideological motives for the murders. This remains, of course, a mere conjecture.

6. See also phase 3.

7. Gull uses the example of the druids in his monologue (cf. second phase).

8. Annie Crook is the lover of Prince Eddy and the mother of his child. In order to force her to silence, Gull makes her undergo a brain surgery that makes her insane.

9. In the footnotes Moore points out that the cardiac arrest striking Gull in October 1887 resulted into recurrent aphasia. Aphasia causes all kinds of weird hallucinations to the patient.

10. In *From Hell,* buildings from the 17th century architect Hawksmoor, with in the first place the cathedral of Whitechapel, occupy an important place. *From Hell* would be a perfect example for the study of the uncanny in architecture; this is certainly a precious research track. A particularly uncanny description of Christchurch can be found in footnote 32 of the second chapter.

11. The way Moore in this section creates an uncanny effect by providing extra information in the notes illustrates very well the point we made earlier in the first section.

12. The second close-up is found in the chapter describing the dissection of the fifth and last victim, Mary Kelly.

References

Assoun, Paul-Laurent. 1995. *Leçons psychoanalytiques sur Le Regard et la Voix.* Paris: Anthropos.

Baetens, Jan. 2001. "Une dialectique à l'oeuvre" in *Neuvième Art. Les cahiers du musée de la bande dessinée* 6. 108-113.

Freud, Sigmund. [1919] 1955. "The 'Uncanny'." *The Standard Edition of the Complete Psychological works of Sigmund Freud. Volume XVII.* London: The Hogarth Press: 217-256.

Hausler, Pete. 2000. "From Hell by Alan Moore; Illustrated by Eddie Campbell" *Village Voice http://www.villagevoice.com/issues/0009/gehr.php*

Jackson, Kevin. 2000. "Old Moore's ripping yarns Alan Moore's ambitious and soon-to-be-filmed comic book novel traces the roots of the 20th century to Jack the Ripper." *http://www.invisibilia.co.uk/articles/article191.htm*

Jay, Martin. 1993. *Downcast Eyes. The Denigration of Vision in Twentieth-century French Thought.* Berkeley/Los Angeles/London: University of California Press.

Milner, Max. 1982. *La fantasmagorie. Essai sur l'optique fantastique.* Paris: Puf.

Moore, Alan, and Eddy Campbell. 1999. *From Hell. Being a melodrama in sixteen parts.* Northhampton: Kitchen Sink Press.

Vidler, Anthony. 1992. "Introduction" in *The Architectural Uncanny. Essays in the modern unhomely.* Cambridge: MIT Press.

Alan Moore and Frank Beaton (interview date 31 March 2003)

SOURCE: Moore, Alan, and Frank Beaton. "Snake Charmer: An Interview with Alan Moore Part One." *NinthArt.com* (31 March 2003).

[*In this interview, Beaton speaks with Moore about his performance art piece* Snakes and Ladders.]

In 1994, Alan Moore announced to the world that he was dedicating his life to magic and had begun worshipping a snake. Amid puzzled looks from fanboys patiently awaiting a sequel to **Killing Joke** [**Batman: The Killing Joke**] and scoffs from the magic-with-a-'K' community, Moore embarked on a string of new projects, including a full-length novel (**Voice of the Fire**) and a series of powerful mixed-media performances.

With a troupe of like-minded individuals that he dubbed "The Grand Egyptian Theatre of Marvels" (which included New Age musician Tim Perkins and former Bauhauser David J), Moore began constructing elaborate multimedia happenings, often inspired by the exact place and time of the performance itself. The shows were sensory experiences, featuring fiercely experimental music, *avant-garde* film collages and Middle Eastern dancers, and even a ghost, though that only made the rehearsals.

Over time, it became clear that the performances had become Moore's chosen medium for expressing his spiritual beliefs and philosophies in their purest form, undiluted by narrative restrictions or editorial guidelines. These were stark works—labyrinthine prose poems that attempted to explain the very nature of the universe itself. They were beautifully constructed, emotionally charged, and more than a little creepy.

His latest performance piece, the North London-inspired **Snakes and Ladders,** has just been released on CD through *Steven Severin's Re:Records.*

Snakes and Ladders is a story of spiritual awakening told through the eyes of 19th century pulp novelist Arthur Machen. Where did the fascination with Machen come from, and what inspired the piece itself? "With the **Snakes and Ladders** piece, it was a daylong event, a 'symposium of real magic'—although I think I'll be the judge of that—and we decided to try and do one of our performances that was entirely based on the place where the event would be taking place, which happened to be Red Lion Square in Holborn."

"Working on my basic assumption, which is that every square metre on the planet is probably a repository of wonderful things if you dig deeply enough, we got to work researching the square—trying to find out what, if anything, was interesting about it."

"So we started to dig up all this stuff, the stuff about the disinterment of Oliver Cromwell, and how his body was laid out in Red Lion Fields overnight; the fact that at least two or three of the major Pre-Raphaelites had lived there during one period; all of these other little threads, and the fact that Arthur Machen had been living on the Gray's Inn Road, which leads directly onto the square, just at the point where his wife had died and where, according to his autobiography, he'd had these peculiar visions, or shifts of state, probably brought on by the depression that followed his wife's death."

"The thing that's interesting about all of these performances, or at least interesting to me, is that you start with a fairly mundane area of London or Northampton or Newcastle or wherever you're doing it, and the unique character and essence of that area reveals itself to you. It's quite striking. I mean, Highbury is only a couple miles away from Holborn—they're both areas of North London—and yet when we started to dig into Highbury's past we found all of these very different kinds of energies represented."

"We found that there'd been freak shows, that there'd been an awful lot of people, from Aleister Crowley to the record producer Joe Meek, who'd been taking quite a lot of drugs. We found that this even extended to the 1925 Arsenal team, who had apparently been taking some sort of speed—must have been a prototype. They referred to them as 'courage pills'. We found that there was an awful lot of drugs, phantasmagoria, freak shows, ghost shows—there was a *freakish* atmosphere to Highbury. In Holborn, it seemed mostly to be about Death and Resurrection."

And love is a big theme in that one as well. "Love and Death and Resurrection. It's a different character. The character of Highbury is kind of freakish, garish, drugged, phantasmagoric. Holborn and Red Lion Square seem to have this natural Pre-Raphaelite palette, where it's all these images of love and death and resurrection. I don't think it's something we imposed upon the area; I think it's something that we revealed through our research into the area."

"It's really interesting doing these things, you find that places definitely do have their own unique essence, made up of their history all of the rumours and legends about them—all of the people who passed through there, leaving a kind of historical imprint. You've just got layers and layers of historical meaning and mythological meaning that somehow go together to make the place what it is."

What are the advantages to performing these works live, as opposed to just writing a book? "Well, that's partly to do with how the things originated. About ten years ago now, in 1993, when I turned 40, I suddenly decided to announce that I'd become a magician, just for a bit of a laugh really. But everyone took me seriously, so then I had to actually do some magic. I had initial experiences which seemed, at least in my book, to be magical experiences."

"As with most things in my life, I will try to process them in some creative way. Having had all of this extraordinary new information pouring into my head as a result of this magical experience, my first thought was 'How do I process *this*?' Following a kind of instinct, along with a couple of other friends who were experimenting with magic of a similar bent, it kind of felt that the most natural way to express some of the ideas I was receiving on account of the magic was in some sort of mixed-media performance."

"At the time I hadn't realised that a lot of significant magicians in the past had done exactly the same thing. Aleister Crowley did a kind of theatrical, musically-accompanied, mixed media ritual called The Rites of Eleusis, SL MacGregor Mathers had performed The

Rites of Isis—even John Dee back in the 16th century had frightened everybody with a mechanical flying beetle he had produced for one of the Greek dramas."

Moore noted that this practice was even more widespread than he thought. "The biggest thing that I found out was that Opera itself originated as an outgrowth of alchemy. That people like Monteverde, who were basically the fathers of opera—they were alchemists. They'd conceived opera as kind of an *ultimate* art form because it included all of the others. There'd be a libretto, so that there'd be words; there'd be music; there'd be painted sets; there'd be costumes; there'd be theatrical drama."

"Apparently, this is also why so many of the early operas have alchemical themes. Whether it's *The Ring Cycle,* with all the trolls and the gold in the North, or *The Magic Flute,* opera originated as kind of a mixed-media performance vehicle to get across magical ideas. It seems like it's a natural way that people came up with to express magic—in these kinds of *overwhelming* performances."

Will an audience listening to a CD of an Alan Moore performance be sufficiently overwhelmed, not having the benefit of the multimedia aspects? "Well, obviously, it would be better if they saw the whole performance. But I think that, because there is so much in the words and the music—those *are* the main parts of the performance—that it's still easy to get an approximation of the night. Yes, it probably would have been more powerful if they had a fire-breather in their living room with them. That probably would have gotten them to sit up and pay attention. But they can probably get the gist of it with a CD."

"I think this kind of multimedia thing is entirely natural, thinking about it, because if you look at most of our religions—the Catholic Church, for example—in the kind of 'high ritual' Catholic Mass; you can see a multimedia performance there. You've got the incantations, you've got the impressive, resonant music; you've got the light show of the stained glass window; you've got the perfumed incense. We use incense at some of our performances, just to try to engage and, to a degree, *overload* all of the senses."

"The actual experience is very much like psychedelic drugs, like your head is suddenly receiving information on sixteen channels at once. It's a bit like listening to a musical fugue, where if you try to follow just one of the voices, you can't hear the overall music. So the best way to deal with a fugue, or the sort of 'fugue state' that LSD provokes, is to just not worry about processing it in your normal linear way. Just let it wash over you."

"I think that there's things in common between the sort of things that we do, opera, and high Catholic ritual. It's all working upon similar principles."

How comfortable is Alan performing these pieces for an audience that may or may not get it, for people that might have just have come because he's the guy who wrote **Watchmen**? "I'm very comfortable in practice, because actually, these performances . . . I don't know if you do get the full effect off of the CD, but they're quite *riveting*. I'm sure there have been members of those audiences who have come along because I wrote **Watchmen,** but you can generally get a pretty good feel as to how the audience is receiving it."

"As yet, there's not been a bad performance. If you're in a rock band and you're performing the same set every night, you're going to have good nights and you're going to have bad nights. But there just seems to be something about these one-off performances, where you're never going to do it again and you haven't rehearsed it countless times before—there seems to be something that gives an intensity and an immediacy to the performance, just by virtue of the fact that it is a completely unique event that will not be repeated. [The audience] seem to be fairly spellbound."

"During a lot of these performances, there have been a lot of other performances that they probably came to see. During the William Blake performance there was Billy Bragg and Jah Wobble and Deepspace and this weird supergroup that was made up of Glen Matlock from the Sex Pistols, Dave Rowntree from Blur, and Ewan McGregor. The people at these events—a lot of them haven't come to see me at all."

"But I think we're getting quite good at this performance business. We can generally hold an audience and—I *think*—captivate them for 40 minutes or an hour or however long the performance takes. And if they did enjoy **Watchmen,** and came to see what I was like in the flesh, then hopefully they'd have gotten an experience that in many ways was every bit as interesting as **Watchmen.** That's what I hope anyway."

Alan Moore and Frank Beaton (interview date 7 April 2003)

SOURCE: Moore, Alan, and Frank Beaton. "Snake Charmer: An Interview with Alan Moore Part Two." *NinthArt.com* (7 April 2003).

[*In this interview, Beaton talks with Moore about his stature in the comics industry and the rumors that surround him as a result.*]

It's hard not to be intimidated by Alan Moore. In addition to being an acclaimed and hugely influential writer, Moore is also a big scary man with an enormous beard and an absolutely *biblical* voice. He's also been the subject of more urban legends than any author since JD Salinger. I'm sure we've all heard them:

Alan Moore hasn't left his bedroom in over a decade.

Alan Moore has tea with the ghost of Aleister Crowley every second Tuesday.

Alan Moore is wanted by the CIA. *No one knows why.*

Alan Moore sacrifices things in his basement. Usually journalists.

Having acquired a reputation as the Mad Genius of Comic Books, you have to wonder what Alan Moore himself thinks of the Alan Moore stories. "I'd probably like it if they were more elaborate. People are not fantasising hard enough. They can come up with better stuff than that. I probably don't even hear most of these rumours because I tend to just stay here in my kind of— well, I wouldn't say it was *normal*—my slightly unusual terraced house in Northampton. I don't venture far outside. I mean, even the other end of the living room is a bit of a mystery to me, so I tend not to hear much of that."

What about the Howard Hughes-style recluse stories: 'Alan Moore hasn't left his house in twenty years,' etc.? Alan laughs. "Well, Alan Moore goes out nearly every day, if only to walk downtown. For example, today I went and took my laundry to the launderette where the really nice ladies always return it to me nicely pressed and folded."

"I don't really leave the *country* anymore, that's true. I can't be bothered; don't really have the time. I leave Northampton very seldom. I'll go to London if there's pressing business that needs attending, or go up north to see my daughters, but Northampton's got pretty much everything I could possibly need, obscurity and silence being two of the most attractive features."

And what about the more sinister rumours? "Yeah, I have heard the rumours about how I'm not allowed to visit America because the CIA are still cross with me about **Brought to Light.** That's not true. The reason I can't visit America is that I haven't got my passport renewed, and getting one doesn't really sound like something I can see myself doing at the moment."

"Apathy is the key to an awful lot of my behaviour. It's the reason I've got this ridiculous beard and haircut. It's just simple laziness. I can't be bothered to shave every morning like ordinary people do. I can't be bothered going to the barbers or places like that. I could be sitting here writing my silly-arse comic books or composing some new incomprehensible magical tract, which is much preferable to me."

Alan's first full-length novel, *Voice of the Fire,* is finally getting a mass-market release. What does he think of the new edition? "It's going to get an American release via Top Shelf, and this will be this new lavish edition with the José Villarrubia illustrations. José has done an awful lot of stuff in comics, and he's a *master* of digital artwork. He did a wonderful digital section in one of the early *Promethea*s [issue #7, **"Rocks and Hard Places"**] where he'd actually found models that looked like the various characters. I thought it was one of the best comics sequences I've seen, it had some marvellous things in it."

"José is a wonderful photographer. He's doing an adaptation of **"The Mirror of Love"**, which is a poem that I wrote for an anti-government homophobia magazine back in the late 80s as a protest for some anti-gay legislation that the conservatives were trying to bring in. I'd written this fairly comprehensive, if condensed, history of gay culture, and I'd squeezed it into about eight pages. What José's going to do is expand that into an 80-page book, with one verse on one page, and one of his images on the other page."

"At the same time he suggested this, he suggested doing an American edition of *Voice of the Fire,* with him doing a series of twelve of his digitally-manipulated photo images, with one image to represent each of the different narrators in the book. So he'll be doing an image of the eleventh century crusader, the 1930s burning car murderer, the Jacobean head on a spike."

"One of the big advantages—and probably why I really agreed to it—is that I'm the writer of the last chapter, so he had to take a glamorous-looking picture of me. I think my extraordinary physical beauty really does deserve a full-page picture, instead of one of those little panels on the back cover. I'm looking forward to that. I still don't know if anyone will be able to make heads or tails of the novel itself, but when they find the text incomprehensible, they can always sit and stare at the pictures for an hour or two."

"José is a great performer [as well]. He did a performance of *The Mirror of Love* at some kind of queer fest or something in Boston—sort of a queer film festival. José did a performance which he sent us a video of, which he performed entirely naked. And I've got to say, you know, nice arse."

How has Moore's performance work gone over with the occult community? "The only time that we've done one specifically for the occult community at large was the *Snakes and Ladders* performance, and the audience as a whole seemed to love it. The magicians that I met there—at least the ones that I have *respect* for—seemed to be quite bowled over, because nobody in magic does

this. Nobody in performance does stuff involving magic in the way we do, and nobody in magic does stuff involving performance in quite the way we do. It's a fairly new idea for them."

"The occult community is as easily impressed as anyone is in these matters, you know. The days of Crowley doing his performances are long gone. People haven't seen anything like this since the 20s or 30s; so, consequently, the reception in the occult community has been very, very encouraging. I think to a lot of them it might be like a breath of fresh air."

Artist and long-time friend Eddie Campbell has done a few comic book adaptations of Alan Moore's performances, and some have criticized them for being too literal. Moore disagrees. "I love it. I think it was with *The Birth Caul* that Eddie first asked if he could turn something into a comic book adaptation, and I genuinely hadn't considered turning one of these performances into a comic strip. But I've obviously got a very good relationship with Eddie and I tend to trust his instincts."

"I was very pleased with the way he had interpreted *The Birth Caul,* so when he asked if he could interpret *Snakes and Ladders* as well, I said 'Yeah, I've got no problem with that,' mainly because I didn't actually have to do anything—I didn't have to write out a script, or anything like that, I can just leave it all to Eddie."

"[The *Snakes and Ladders* adaptation] is very much his work, his interpretation of the piece, and there were some very poetic images in there. Particularly the way that he cleverly used all of Rosetti's angels from that golden staircase picture—he'd managed to fit that exactly onto the DNA spiral, so you've got a whole bunch of Rosetti's angels walking down a double-helix. Very poetic, very lovely."

Moore has great admiration for Campbell's adaptation skills. "I think that these are probably difficult works to adapt, when it's just sort of a string of sometimes semi-disconnected ideas. Sometimes you might have to make choices; to handle one section in a more impressionistic way, another section in a more strictly literal fashion—these are the choices that Eddie has to make. But by and large, I've been very happy with the choices that Eddie's made."

A lot of the themes and symbols used in Moore's magical performances—especially *Snakes and Ladders*—are echoed in his comic *Promethea,* including the idea of Imagination personified as a woman. How closely would he say the two works are related? "Well, they're both outgrowths of my thinking during this stretch of my life. The performances seem to be a natural way of expressing magical ideas, and since I know my way around writing a comic, it seemed natural to try to express magical ideas through *Promethea* as well."

"I suppose the reason for doing both is that there are things you can do in the comics medium that you simply can't do in performance, and vice-versa. In some of the issues of *Promethea* we've done quite complex interplays of words and images, or complex structures, things that are a novelty for the comic book that you couldn't do in any medium *other* than in a comic book."

"Most of my ideas these days tend to be heavily coloured by a magical world view. You get similar ideas finding their way out and expressing themselves in different terms—in comics or in performance or in the CDs, or whatever I happen to be doing."

Moore plays around a bit with the comics world on *Snakes and Ladders,* making sly references to "back continuities" and talking about the time he claims to have actually met John Constantine. Does Alan Moore the magician ever feel the need to distance himself from Alan Moore the comic book writer? "Funny you should ask that," he says with a laugh.

"I'm certainly not *ashamed* of the work I've done in comics. *Snakes and Ladders* [contains] the only specific reference I've made to the fact that I'm a comic writer, because it was relevant in terms of what we were talking about. Not that I'm ashamed of the comics, or that in the comics I'm ashamed of the magic stuff. I'm pretty open about all of it."

So what does the magician have up his sleeve at the moment? "What I'm trying to do at the moment is finish off all of the mainstream comics work around the end of this year, at which point having retired effectively from mainstream comics, I want to play around with things I've been neglecting. Like, I used to quite enjoy drawing at one point, and although I could never draw quickly enough to actually have a career as an artist, it would be nice to have the freedom to play around with a bit more artwork, some sculpture, more performance work."

"There will probably still be comics in the mix somewhere, almost certainly. It's a medium that I have a great deal of fondness for, and that I feel there's still a lot of potential in."

"But, yes, I will be putting distance between my mainstream comics career and my magical work, simply by closing down my mainstream comics career and becoming a full-time magician."

Alan Moore and Mark Askwith (interview date July 2003)

SOURCE: Moore, Alan, and Mark Askwith. "In League with Alan Moore." *Locus: The Magazine of The Science Fiction And Fantasy Field* 51, no. 1 (July 2003): 81-2.

[*In this interview, Moore comments on his career in comics.*]

Alan Moore is the author of several of the most celebrated comic books in modern history, and he continues to pioneer the graphic novel form. Born November 18, 1953 in Northampton, England, Moore began his career as a cartoonist in 1979, but by the early 1980s was best known as a writer. For Warrior Magazine, *Moore began two serialized strips—***Marvelman** (*later released in the US as* **Miracleman**), *and* **V for Vendetta.** *He won the British Eagle Award for Best Comics Writer in 1982 and 1983.*

Moore's first American series, **The Saga of the Swamp Thing**—*revived by Vertigo in 1983 with issue #20 and Moore as writer—debuted to great acclaim. In the mid-'80s, Moore teamed up with artist Dave Gibbons on a 12-issue super-hero story,* **Watchmen**—*the first comic book to win a Hugo Award; it also won a Locus Award. In 1988, Moore began two series for Stephen Bissette's* Taboo *anthology series (1988-95):* **Lost Girls** *with artist Melinda Gebbie, and* **From Hell,** *a re-examination of the Jack the Ripper murders, with artist Eddie Campbell. A year later, Moore collaborated with artist Bill Sienkiewicz to tell the secret history of American covert operations in* **Brought to Light.** *In 1996, he published a novel* **Voice of the Fire** (*the first US edition of which is due this summer with an introduction by Neil Gaiman*).*

Currently, Moore has his own imprint, America's Best Comics (ABC), created in 1999, and is writing several titles, including **Promethea** (*begun 1999*) *and Stoker Award-winning* **The League of Extraordinary Gentlemen** (*begun 2000*); *the latter will be published as a special edition this spring accompanied by Moore's expansive scripts, and has been adapted as a major motion picture to be released this summer.*

Moore has two grown daughters by first wife Phyllis, and currently lives in Northampton, England with girlfriend and collaborator Melinda Gebbie. He plans to "retire" this year on his 50th birthday, when he will end his work on ABC comics (except for **The League of Extraordinary Gentlemen**), *and hopes to work on performance art and novels.*

Interview conducted by Mark Askwith.

* * *

"In 25 years writing comics, I have failed to exhaust their possibilities by a considerable distance. I could probably continue working in comics as a medium forever."

"As far as I can make out, comics, or something very much like the comic strip (by which I mean a sequential progression of images that tell a story, or convey some meaning), would seem to be about the earliest form of written language. If you are talking about Egyptian hieroglyphics, or the ancient Chinese pictograms, it seems to me the impulse to convey meaning or information in a sequence of pictures is probably our earliest impulse. You could take this back much further than hieroglyphics or ancient Chinese pictograms—just take a look at the cave walls of Lascaux, which have kind of primitive comic strips decorating them, a progression of images. It would seem to me the comic-strip form, being one of the earliest forms of written communication, must be something we as a species find ourselves drawn to quite naturally."

"The fact that the comic strip, or something like it, tends to survive throughout mankind's history is also a testament to its staying power. As to why the comic strip should have this power, I suppose I'd have to say that it may be, and I stress this is only speculation, that the comic strip is one of the few art forms that engages both halves of the brain and sets them to the same task. This might account for the ability of the medium not only to transmit information, but to do so in a form that can be completely retained and remembered. There seems to be in comic strips a very primal form of technology at work, a profoundly powerful technology that we have yet to scratch the surface of."

"When I was working on CIA exposé **Brought to Light** in the late '80s with Joyce Brabner, Bill Sienkiewicz, and Tom Yeates, we uncovered a Pentagon document referring to the comic strip that was part of a Pentagon investigation as to which form of presentation best conveyed information that could be clearly understood and retained by the recipient. They tried various permutations: straight-forward text, text with photographs, photographs with captions, text with illustrations, and comic strips. They found that the comic strip provided a means of transmitting information clearly, simply, and in a way that would in all likelihood be retained by the person reading it. Now that's interesting, and it raises the question—why should this be?"

"With the comic strip, words are only one track of the kind of multi-track information you are providing, so you can get an awful lot of information across concisely with simply the visuals. You can add detail and texture with the words. I've found you can do *anything* with comics. Anything that has any visual or verbal content, anything that has an element of time in it, or not—I'm sure you could do an excellent comic-book still life, where nothing moved. There are endless possibilities."

"I would not want to single out any particular thing the medium does particularly well. It has, in all of the areas and genres it embraces, different and unique strengths. In the fantasy genre, for example, it has obvious advantages in that you can accomplish almost any kind of conceivable special effect cheaply and quickly. If dealing with historical or documentary subjects, it has advantages in that complex issues, as with the **Brought to Light** story, can be illuminated with easy to understand, intelligent illustrations that can underline and transform even the driest point."

"Comics will always be, I am sure, a major part of my artistic output just because it is such a rich medium. It's a medium where you are looking at a lot of virgin snow, even given the excellent works that have been accomplished in the medium thus far. We are still only talking about a hundred years tops, so I have no doubt that a lot of the great comic books have yet to be written."

"I've no objection to the term 'graphic novel,' as long as what it is talking about is actually some sort of graphic work that could conceivably be described as a novel. My main objection to the term is that usually it means a collection of six issues of *Spider-Man,* or something that does not have the structure or any of the qualities of a novel, but is perhaps roughly the same size."

"When the opportunity arose to do things that were longer than a two- or three-issue run of a 24-page comic, it was just a case of imagining the structures. With **Watchmen,** a 12-issue miniseries seemed to be a fairly popular length. Dave Gibbons and I were able to work out a story that fit comfortably into that 12-issue length. Admittedly, that was probably the first time I'd attempted anything like that, so I probably misjudged the amount of plot that would fill 12 issues. I probably got six issues of plot when I started **Watchmen,** When I realized that, at the end of the first issue, we solved the problem by interspersing the more plot-driven issues with issues that gave kind of a biographical portrait of one of the main characters."

"After finishing **Watchmen,** and having wrapped up *V for Vendetta* and **Marvelman** (which were started before **Watchmen,** but finished shortly afterwards), I decided to see if I could change as many of the parameters as possible. So I tried to rid my thinking of a lot of the imposed limitations or formats that had sprung up in my work in mainstream comics."

"With *From Hell,* we decided not to do something that was about superheroes, that didn't conform to the standard dramatic rules of adventure comics, and decided there was no reason to actually conceive of it as a certain number of episodes at a given length. To give it some sort of overall structure and to provide a kind of beginning, middle, and end, at the very start of the project I worked out that it would take about 16 chapters, including a prologue and an afterword, to tell the entire story as I understood it from my preliminary research. It was a finite story that took place over a certain period of the 1880s. Sixteen episodes were enough to tell the story; however, I was aware I would be doing a lot more research over the course of this work, which might provide information that took the story off into new areas. So I stated up front it was going to be 16 chapters long, but we left the length of the chapters completely open so they could range from eight pages up to 50 or 60 pages, which was a much more organic way of structuring it. Rather than build it as 12 predetermined 24-page-long units, this allowed the work to breathe and expand, and it was an interesting experiment."

"With *Lost Girls,* we decided that in order to keep the story tightly structured, it would perhaps be best to write it in eight-page installments, but to have 30 of them so it would build up into a 240-page story. Different works seem to demand different working methods, and I'm always up for trying anything new. If it looks viable, if my instincts tell me this is something that could actually work, then I throw myself into it without hesitation."

"The initial idea with *The League of Extraordinary Gentlemen* was simply putting together a kind of superhero team composed of striking characters from the fantastic fiction of the late Victorian period. At the time, I was musing about what could be done with the superhero team book, which always looks like such a good idea when you see the cover, but actually seldom lives up to that promise. Most superhero team books are too crammed with characters to allow any of the characters to emerge, or be important. So I was thinking about this, and I started to consider the roots of these superhero characters. My musings led me back through the pulp characters of the 1930s (which obviously influenced the subsequent comic-book heroes), back through the characters of the Golden period of the American newspaper strip after the turn of the century; but inexorably it led me back to the fantastic characters of late 19th-, early 20th-century science fiction, who in

some ways provided the archetypes, or templates, from which a lot of later superheroes found their careers. The obvious example would be that the Incredible Hulk is a kind of 1960s irradiated Jekyll and Hyde. All invisible characters in comics owe a great deal to H. G. Wells's *The Invisible Man* A great many of the scientific adventurers, the techno-heroes and techno-villains for that matter, probably owe a great deal to Captain Nemo—the world's first techno-pirate. So, thinking along these lines, it eventually occurred to me there might be something interesting to be done with taking a lot of fairly well-known characters of the fiction of that period and creating a Victorian superhero team, and seeing what happened. What I was originally envisaging was a very high-spirited romp where I'd get the chance to write a lot of the characters that have interested me since childhood."

"The idea of getting Kevin O'Neill on board as artist occurred to me almost immediately, because Kevin's art style is so uniquely English. Kevin was largely influenced by British comics rather than American comics, thus in Kevin's work you can see this incredible British tradition of exaggerated, often grotesque satire that runs right back through Beano and Dandy, back to the traditions of Hogarth and Gilray, the vicious British political cartoonists of the 18th and 19th centuries. There's something so extreme about Kevin's work that although it's not photographically realistic, there's a kind of emotional realism he achieves by exaggerating it beyond the confines of the strictly realistic."

"We started to work this thing up, and as with *Watchmen* and a lot of my other work, it took me till the end of the first issue before I started to get a feel of what it was really about. I think it was when I realized I'd gotten Robert Louis Stevenson's Mr. Hyde murdering Emile Zola's Nana on Edgar Allan Poe's Rue Morgue that I started to realize this was something I could conceivably have a lot of fun with. I resolved upon the spot not to have any characters anywhere in *The League of Extraordinary Gentlemen* referred to by name who were not characters either from or related to the fiction of that period, or perhaps back-engineered characters where we have taken somebody from a later work and retro-fitted a father or grandfather into our narrative."

"So, all of the characters are related to the fiction of that period. This started to become very interesting once we'd made this decision because it suddenly suggested all sorts of amusing possibilities—like the idea that the Invisible Man might be hiding at a pornographic girls' school from the *Pearl* (a British pornographic magazine from the late 19th century); so we had characters from that pornographic magazine mixed up with Pollyanna, characters from Henry James, *Rebecca of Sunnybrook Farm,* and Katy Carr from *What Katy Did Next.* This connecting-the-dots between fictional characters isn't new—A. Gordon Pym set out in a whaler from Nantucket in Edgar Allan Poe's *Narrative of Arthur Gordon Pym of Nantucket* only to end up in a story by Jules Verne called *The Sphinx of the Ice Fields,* which Verne wrote after reading Poe's original story, and of course you had H. P. Lovecraft using references to the *Narrative of Arthur Gordon Pym* in his *At the Mountains of Madness* In some ways you could almost get the impression that these individual writers were actually trying to link up their stories in a common big world, so we've been able to extend that; out of that thinking the entire strip has emerged."

"We decided the world we would be showing, the world of 1898, would not be the world of 1898 as it was, but as it would have been if their fantastic inventors and their creations had actually existed. We, Kevin really, managed to find quite a lot of ridiculous architectural schemes of the 19th century for grandiose buildings that were never actually constructed because they were too mad, but they obviously existed in the public imagination. For example, there were various schemes to build a bridge connecting London and France. None of these were ever attempted, but in our first issue of the first volume of **The League of Extraordinary Gentlemen,** we open with a conversation at the end of the almost-completed Channel causeway."

"We've shown buildings of an imaginary London that are based upon proposals for architecture that were floating around the collective imagination at the time and never got realized. We are depicting an entire planet of human fictions as if they all existed in the same world. Now, this was pretty advanced by the end of the first volume, but with the second volume I'm afraid the mania has progressed. We decided for the text feature at the rear of the book we didn't want to simply do another pastiche of a Penny Dreadful serial as we'd done in our first volume. While that had been enjoyable, we'd done it once, and we wondered if the space could be used for anything more interesting. We hit upon the idea of coming up with this massive and extensive fictitious travelogue in which we would provide 'A New Travelers Almanac' that would move around all over the world's major land masses issue by issue, and would detail all of the fictitious locales that had ever been alleged to exist. So we started off with the British Isles, and we've got the Arthurian remnants and ruins. We've got places like Baskerville Hall, various sites connected with Alice in Wonderland, and references to stories by

people as diverse as H. P. Lovecraft, Graham Greene, John Steinbeck, and William Morris—dozens and dozens of authors we've linked up to this imaginary geography."

"By the end of the second volume we'll have charted, as well as we are able, the entire planet of fiction. I don't know whether there is any more to this than just another one of my deranged obsessions, but it feels as if there is. The more I've thought about this, it occurs to me that as long as there's been a world we have been creating an imaginary counterpart to that world with different places, different people, different history, and to some degree that phantom world of the imagination has co-existed with our own. All of us, at various points in our lives, have found ourselves spending more time on that imaginary planet than we have upon our own world. We may well find in the later stages of our life that there are places from that imaginary world that we remember more vividly than actual physical locations we have visited. We may find that fictional characters, the inhabitants of that world, are more familiar, more dear to us, more memorable than a lot of the real flesh and blood people who may have been our acquaintances."

"There is obviously something important in this. If we did not have some kind of biological or cultural need to create these imaginary spaces and these imaginary beings, I really don't think nature would have given us the capacity to do it. Nature doesn't generally provide a lot of things that are purely there for decoration or entertainment. Most things have to do with the quite stark issues of survival, and I've got no reason to suppose the human capacity for art and fiction and imagination is not in that category."

"There is something quite wonderful about linking up these various fictitious stories that were possibly never meant to be linked up. There's plenty of gleeful vandalism you can enjoy in pulling down the picket fences that divide one writer's world and characters from that of another. You can have Frankenstein's monster rampaging berserk through a garden party thrown by Louisa May Alcott's Little Women. You can do all sorts of things. In the Africa section of the Almanac, for example, we decided that since Joseph Conrad's rogue ivory trader Mr. Kurtz obviously was situated in the Belgian Congo and would presumably have been in elephant territory, I decided to put him smack in the middle of territory populated by the people of *Babar the Elephant.* There's just something very appealing about putting Babar next to Mr. Kurtz. 'The Horror! The Horror! Exterminate all the brutes!' These sorts of juxtapositions can be quite startling. Near the end of the second volume, there's a juxtaposition of two different characters that makes perfect sense and yet it's hilarious and horrifying and deeply upsetting all at the same time."

"Whether it's low art or high art, that is part of the subversive thrill of putting things from the most despised lower reaches of the artistic spectrum next to the most revered cultural icons. I think, surprisingly, both can be enhanced by the juxtaposition. We could write stories that go hundreds of years back in the past, and thousands of years into the future, simply because the fictional world extends into the future as well as the past. And since we have claimed this entire fictional world as our territory and colonized it, that is the kind of area we have to play with. Although it's a very simple initial concept, the possibilities of *The League of Extraordinary Gentlemen* could keep Kevin and me in work for the rest of our lives."

Douglas Wolk (essay date 17 December 2003)

SOURCE: Wolk, Douglas. "Please Sir, I Want Some Moore: The Lazy British Genius who Transformed American Comics." *Slate.com* (17 December 2003).

[*In the following essay, Wolk analyzes Moore's significance within the field of American comic books and graphic novel writing.*]

You wouldn't necessarily think that an anarchist Gnostic who worships the Roman snake-god Glycon would be at the top of his field, but Alan Moore is universally acknowledged as the most important mainstream comics writer of the last three decades. The second volume of *The League of Extraordinary Gentlemen,* his collaboration with artist Kevin O'Neill, was published early this month; given his recent announcement of his impending retirement, it's worth looking at how this very English writer has shaped American comics. Moore is comics' Orson Welles: a genius formalist with a natural collaborative impulse and a habit of taking on overambitious projects. His work is alternately groundbreaking and painfully lazy; he often coasts on his cleverness for a quick paycheck. The question of whether he's a fountain of imagination or just bats has never arisen: He's both, and his ability to see familiar ideas from an alien perspective is one of his best tricks.

Moore is best-known for a pair of furiously dark graphic novels, *Watchmen* and *From Hell.* Even so, he's dismissed the "grim and gritty" school of comics writing he fathered as the unwanted result of "a bad mood I was in 15 years ago," and his recent work is much lighter in tone. His writing has more to do with his fascination with Gnosticism: He's interested in investigating the inner workings of everything that affects him strongly (violence, sexual fantasy, mystical experience, old Superman comics). Hence the Glycon thing, about which he is both dead serious and very funny.

But he's also spent his career as the bellwether for comics' path between commerce and art. Moore's debut, in the early '80s, roughly coincided with the rise of the independent comics movement and the schism between the mainstream (the superhero genre-fiction comics industry) and indie publishers (which concentrate on cartoonist "auteurs" who both write and draw). Despite a flirtation with indie art-comics around 1990, Moore is basically a mainstream reformer: He's made an explicit decision to work in genre comics but to try to do something broadly entertaining with a lot of craft. He doesn't draw the stories he writes, although he's notorious for obsessively detailed scripts that play to his artist-collaborators' individual strengths but give them very little latitude. Even if your sympathies lie with the art-comics side of the debate, it's pretty damn hard to complain about the depth and ingenious construction of *Watchmen* or *Promethea.* And even Moore's early work was about teasing out the subtexts of third-rate superhero and horror comics that gave them power and meaning: the Nietzschean fantasy of the hero who remakes the world in his image, the varieties of body-terror and sleep-of-reason that produce monsters.

Brought up in a working-class family in Northampton, England, where he still lives, Moore began his career writing short gag stories and serials for British anthology comics in the early '80s. His commercial breakthrough came in 1983, when he took over *Saga of the Swamp Thing,* a terrible American comic book; Moore took the opportunity to show off the range of his technique, which resulted in a certain amount of purple prose ("Clouds like plugs of bloodied cotton wool dab ineffectually at the slashed wrists of the sky") and a lot of thrilling formal experiments that had never been tried in mainstream comics before. His success led directly to American comics' "British invasion" of writers, notably Neil Gaiman (*The Sandman*), Grant Morrison, Garth Ennis, and Warren Ellis, all of whom have made much of his castoffs.

In the late '80s, Moore briefly forswore the mainstream and started writing a handful of hugely audacious independent projects, none of which worked out quite as planned. The still fondly remembered *Big Numbers* ran aground after two issues. A few chapters of *Lost Girls,* a tenderly pornographic riff on classic children's literature (drawn by American underground cartoonist

Melinda Gebbie, who is now Moore's girlfriend), and *From Hell,* a brutal autopsy of Victorian England and the nature of misogyny, were serialized in a short-lived small-press anthology, *Taboo.* Fortunately for Moore, flashy, tacky cartoonists like Todd McFarlane and Rob Liefeld threw wads of money at him to bang out superhero comics like *Spawn* and *Supreme* for them—lightweight at best, pretentious codswallop at worst. He reserved his actual effort for *From Hell,* which was being published in very occasional installments, and, apparently, *Lost Girls,* which wasn't being published anywhere. (It will appear in mid-2004.)

* * *

Moore hit his prime with *Watchmen,* drawn by Dave Gibbons and published in 1985-86. A densely orchestrated story about a world on the verge of nuclear annihilation, *Watchmen* is a high-modernist triumph: It's an astonishing piece of structural clockwork, an allegorical critique and history of the comics medium, and an adventure story that systematically undermines the whole premise of adventure stories. Meanwhile, Moore and artist David Lloyd returned to finish their incomplete early project *V for Vendetta,* recently adapted into a screenplay by *The Matrix*'s Wachowski brothers. (Unsurprisingly, the film has yet to be optioned: Moore's story concerns a heroic British anarchist terrorist who blows up Parliament.)

From Hell was collected as a single book in 1999 (published by its artist, Eddie Campbell) and filmed as a Johnny Depp vehicle that bore very little resemblance to its source. By then, Moore had begun his current project, the sardonically named America's Best Comics line: four allegedly monthly series and a handful of other projects, all initially written by him. It's often been noted that Moore does better with other writers' characters than with his own, and *The League of Extraordinary Gentlemen* lets him play with a cast drawn from Victoriana and early pulp fiction and their attendant subtext and colorful detail. (Moore has a particular affinity for the way Victorian culture and literature invested everything with symbolic meaning, and for the Victorian habit of describing quotidian or ghastly things in jeweled language.) Almost all the other ABC titles have fallen way behind schedule or been handed over to other writers, and he's clearly just phoning them in these days.

The one exception is *Promethea,* a thinly veiled exegesis of Moore's obsession with magic and the occult, which implausibly went from decent to terrific when he halted the plot to spend 12 issues explaining the Kabala. As with a lot of his work, it's sometimes

showoffishly clever: One issue is a single image extended across 24 pages, in the course of which the major arcana of the tarot deck are presented as an allegorical history of human civilization (in rhyming couplets, no less), in parallel with a joke told by Aleister Crowley, not to mention a different apropos anagram of *Promethea* spelled out in Scrabble tiles on every page. Moore says he plans to become a full-time magician—not the rabbit-from-a-hat kind—once he wraps up his current commitments in comics. Although he's not entirely washing his hands of the medium (he's promised a third *League of Extraordinary Gentlemen* project at some point), he's quitting while he's ahead. Better snake-god-worshipping rituals than Paul Masson wine commercials.

Marc Singer (essay date spring 2004)

SOURCE: Singer, Marc. "Unwrapping *The Birth Caul*: Word, Performance, and Image in the Comics Text." *International Journal of Comic Art* 6, no. 1 (spring 2004): 236-49.

[*In the following essay, Singer evaluates Moore's worldview as presented in the performance piece and comic adaptation* The Birth Caul.]

> *Having become more familiar with magic, I eventually learned that magic was what Aleister Crowley referred to as 'a disease of language,' and came to understand that magic is indeed mostly a linguistic phenomenon and was therefore what had been lying at the end of the path beyond mere craft all along . . .*
>
> —Alan Moore, interview with Eddie Campbell, p. 4

Alan Moore has seemingly always been preoccupied by language. From the breathless futurist slang of Halo Jones to the melodious Rannian dialect in *Swamp Thing* to the sinister Lovecraftian grammar of **"The Courtyard,"** his genre work has explored the pleasure and the power of language since well before he publicly dedicated himself to the study of magic. But one of his richest investigations of this linguistic theme has come in one of his magical performance pieces, *The Birth Caul,* a "shamanism of childhood" (Moore and Campbell, 1999a:1) that examines the connections between our language, our identity, and our perceptions of the world.[1] First performed at the Old County Court in Newcastle-upon-Tyne on November 18, 1995, and later adapted into comic book form by Moore's *From Hell* collaborator Eddie Campbell, *The Birth Caul* is a moving meditation on the loss of Moore's mother and on the myriad other losses that come with time and maturity.

In *The Birth Caul,* Moore claims that contemporary adults have lost some primal understanding of and connection to the world, a loss he attempts to undo by reversing time in a sequence of narrative flashbacks. These flashbacks first illustrate a history of Newcastle, then offer a series of more personal vignettes that depict the stages of development in a regression from early adulthood to adolescence, childhood, infancy, and finally back to prenatal existence. (In Campbell's adaptation these flashbacks illustrate the life of an audience member at Moore's Old County Court performance, creating a communal narrative that matches Moore's use of the collective "we" in his narration of these scenes,) Through these flashbacks, *The Birth Caul* presents an essentially gnostic view of child development in which each earlier stage possesses an intuitive perception of the world that its successors have long forgotten.

To recover this primeval consciousness, Moore must reverse not only our stages of development but also our faculties of language and self-awareness. Paradoxically, *The Birth Caul* uses language to erase language, a seemingly self-defeating proposition that it must negotiate both as a performance and as a comic. Significantly, although both these media offer nonverbal means of communication, neither one fully releases *The Birth Caul* from its reliance on language—they merely underscore the centrality of language to Moore's shamanic project and his literary technique. Yet Moore nevertheless manages to reverse time and language, and he does so in a manner surprisingly consistent with some of the preeminent models of cognitive development. These models can potentially resolve Moore's linguistic contradictions; conversely, Moore's narrative also offers some important revisions of these theories. Ultimately Moore's writing—particularly in its most arcane and metaphorical aspects—proves ideally suited to his goals of reversing time, self, and language.

WORD

Like *From Hell,* which Moore was writing at the time of his performance, *The Birth Caul* presents an essentially Romantic view of history as a tragic fall into modernity. Both works depict the modern world as numbed, desensitized, and degraded because it has lost some vital connection to its raw and violent past. In Chapter 10 of *From Hell,* Sir William Gull, transported by his murderous rituals into a vision of his future—our anesthetized present—hectors a crowd of unseeing, unhearing office-park drones, telling them, "Your days were born in blood and fires, whereof in you I may not see the meanest spark! Your past is pain and iron! Know yourselves! . . . I am with you always!" (1999b: 10.21). With a disturbing similarity, *The Birth Caul* presents the history of Newcastle as a long tumble from the mysteries of the Votadini tribes, who "blew upon the flames and made the rocks weep iron 800 years before Rome's golden bracelet was upon us" (6), to a pestilent profusion of McDonalds and Pizza Huts. Moore stresses how far he and his peers have fallen and then, like Gull, looks to a bloody anatomical symbol to rediscover the primitive energy and meaning they have lost. He tells his audience,

> In this present moment we are either smaller than we were or else are on our knees. These hollow days, these strangers in the bathroom mirror. Flinching and diminished. We have wandered too far from some vital totem . . . something central to us that we have misplaced and must find our way back to . . . guided by some ancient bloodstained chart.
>
> (8)

That totem, that bloodstained chart, is his mother's birth caul.

But *The Birth Caul* is far more than just a recapitulation of ideas that Moore has presented elsewhere. His Romantic and tragic concept of *cultural* history prepares the audience for an equally Romantic, tragic view of *personal* development—if all of English society has fallen from some primitive state of grace, then so too have all of us as individuals, over the course of our own lives. In his brief introduction to Campbell's adaptation, Moore says the birth caul "documents a personal Atlantis, a pre-verbal dreamtime, a naive shamanic state rich with abandoned totems" (1); he spends much of the rest of the work attempting to recover these totems by regressing his narrative consciousness to a state that predates language. This theme first comes to prominence in the flashback episode on pages 28 to 33, in which Moore and Campbell depict the tribulations of preadolescence. The episode opens with a child staring at a butcher's window and at "the ritual centrepiece, a massive ox-tongue" that Moore employs, appropriately enough, as a totem of language: "the symbol of our power, of the divide between us and the other beasts, severed and dressed upon this public altar" (28; Figure 1). Because its sacrifice insures humanity's linguistic power, Moore uses the tongue to initiate *The Birth Caul*'s most detailed exploration of the mysteries of language.[2]

The remainder of the episode focuses primarily on the prices we pay for our mastery of language. Moore describes the child's acquisition of language—although possibly he refers to his own, since he writes this passage in the first-person singular rather than the more communal plural that marks most of the flashbacks narration—in violent, mythic terms similar to those he has used to describe the ox-tongue: "They hanged me from a tree branch by my wrists and this is how I learned the words. They caved the underground den in on top of me and crawling like a lugworm through the smothering black dirt . . . I learned the words" (31). From the rituals of premature burial and Odin-like hanging, Moore gains the power of words.

The next two pages, however, abandon these mythological metaphors to describe a more realistic and conventional process of language acquisition, one that instructs children in socialization and obedience. In a passage that Campbell illustrates with images of childhood trials and schoolroom punishments, Moore writes,

> the language of a larger world is on us. We absorb its glossary of smack and panic . . . Sat knock-kneed at desks, we master an unmentioned alphabet of retribution and approval, become fluent in the lexicon of cross and tick and gold adhesive star. And this is how the tongue is severed, dressed, made fit for public consumption.
>
> (32)

Here Moore adds some more common sacrifices to the metaphors of ox-tongue and gallows-tree; for children, learning language frequently means learning a punitive code of behavior. It also means losing the private language of home, as "Words we are allowed at home are confiscated. We become aware that the terrain behind our front door is unnervingly unique" (32). Language instructs the child in difference and separation, a theme to which *The Birth Caul* will soon return.

But language also carries an even more fundamental loss, one that Moore says we incur long before school and its torments. He writes, "Already something has been lost; a certain sight, a certain voice. Unable to recall more than the vaguest shape or flavour now as it recedes from us into that speechless fog before we knew the dazzle of the word, when form was all of our vocabulary" (33). In the next flashback episode, Moore attempts to illuminate that speechless fog by projecting the narrative back into the preverbal state of infancy. With creatively mangled syntax, and with Campbell providing appropriately disjointed layouts and scribbled handwriting to complement him, Moore attempts to reproduce a preverbal consciousness that recognizes objects but not grammar. Many of the infant's insights are merely childlike misperceptions that invest mundane objects with animistic power: lawn ornaments that can talk (38), for example, or the underside of a simple table transformed into "Worldwood roof of undertable" (37), both a Tree of Life and a vault of heaven.

More boldly, though, Moore also claims that prelinguistic children perceive time quite differently than adults, implying that our sense of linear chronology is learned,

if not outright imposed, by language or experience. The infant in *The Birth Caul* has not yet learned to recognize the divisions between past, present, and future. He senses "already that we are living long ago, like waistcoat whisker men the light got in and spoiled"—here Campbell introduces a fading nineteenth-century photograph (39)—and he possesses a remarkable presentiment of mortality. The child thinks,

> dead is birthday party . . . day one gran is be dead and just to think of it is almost now, day one is dad and mum be dead and it is now we cry and cry, and day one is a thing worse that we not can think about and cry and cry and cry and it is now and it is now.
>
> (40)

Either this child is perceiving all time as the present, foreseeing future events—including his own death—or he has attained some more subtle awareness of time as a state of constant decay, a message in keeping with Moore's tragic conception of cultural and personal development.

Either way, it's probably safe to say that we don't commonly attribute this level of insight to a toddler. Yet Moore argues that we have simply lost our memory of these preverbal realizations, because of language but also because of an even more basic act of division whose precise moment in our development he attempts to capture: this forgetting happens "one sudden morning when us first think that we thinking and before it what we can't remember in the nothing came from" (41). The first moment of reflexive self-awareness also prompts our first amnesia, our loss of the gnosis that precedes not only our language but our most basic sense of self.

Moore's attempt to rediscover a state of consciousness unhindered by the divisions of language, self, and symbol leads to the innermost moment in his narrative regression (though not its earliest one), a recollection of consciousness before birth. Campbell's art and Moore's narration depict the first flicker of fetal consciousness from inside the womb, where Moore can pronounce that "the birth caul is the honest silence of ourselves" (42)—that is, a state that predates language and therefore a state where people "only are" (42), a state of being without any object or qualifier. The next page continues the depiction of a prelingual Eden; Moore describes the birth caul, amidst a torrent of metaphors, as "our sole identifying luggage label in the waiting room before they call our name and being named we are no more a part of everything" (43). Thus language not only destroys the infant's heightened awareness of past and future, it also sets the first boundaries around the self through the act of naming. The birth caul is a remnant of that last moment before language is imposed upon us, before we are delivered into the world where "self and time surrounds us" (44).

Yet even this moment before birth does not satisfy Moore as the origin of the self, and so he presses still farther back in time. *The Birth Caul* reverts through the stages of fetal development, past conception, beyond even copulation, back into some mysterious phylogenetic swamp from which Moore speculates we have arisen. This non-place (which Campbell can depict only metaphorically through quotations from Bosch, Escher, and Hokusai) is the source of our creation, a river or sea whose waters Moore now pushes backwards over the "ocean wall of definition separating *us* from *other*—dashing it aside as if it were no more than words" (47). In fact, throughout the narrative that wall *has* been nothing more than words, as Moore has argued that language severs self from other, past from present. By reversing time and unspooling language, Moore hopes to undo the most basic boundaries of our selfhood as "verse by verse the song unwrites itself back to the word, the syllable . . . The cold white page" (47). In this total absence of language humanity can regain—or, at least, Moore can imagine—its first gnosis, the first unity that existed before the self. Moore's reversal of time and language therefore carries us back down the evolutionary ladder, back to our component elements, to the creation of those elements, to the creation of the universe and finally to the void that preceded it, in which we might finally understand "where we are come from" (48).

At this moment, however, when we might finally learn the ultimate source of our creation, when Moore twice promises to reveal the birth caul's final meaning, language fails Moore and his audience alike: "And our lips are . . . sealed" (48). What is remarkable about this failure is not its ill timing, however, but that it has not happened sooner. Moore has been describing a state of consciousness before birth for nearly a sixth of his narrative, states before language for nearly a third, but only at the end does his own language fail to represent that prelingual gnosis that should by definition be unrepresentable. The true mystery, then, is not only what lies behind the final, unspoken unveiling of the birth caul, but also how Moore's writing has so long sustained a narrative whose goal is to shed all language.

The richness of Moore's narration only exacerbates this internal contradiction; it is both ironic and unsurprising that the same work that tries to undo language should feature such a characteristically Moorish command of it. The same vocabulary that Moore struggles so fiercely to discard furnishes him with a cornucopia of insights, such as his pithy and unforgivingly accurate characterizations of teenage lovers' spats: "Embittered slanging matches that occur nowhere save on some spite streaked astral plane, until these acid dregs seem almost sweeter than the wine" (21). Or pubic hair: "the insignia of a forbidden order, a werewolf freemasonry from which

we are as yet excluded" (31). Or this ultimate statement on adolescence: "We confuse rebellion with a hairstyle" (23). For all that Moore tries to unwrite his language, *The Birth Caul* is utterly dependent on it—never more so than when the narrative regresses back to the primal seas of creation, a state so unimaginable and unrepresentable it can only be rendered metaphorically through Moore's full linguistic power.

PERFORMANCE AND IMAGE

Fortunately, *The Birth Caul* exists in two different media that both permit nonverbal means of communication: through its physical, visual, and aural presence as a performance piece and through its adaptation by Eddie Campbell into a comic book. But although Moore and Campbell deftly exploit the formal potentials of both these media, neither version of *The Birth Caul* wholly eradicates or supplants language.

Moore's public readings capitalize on the physical presence (and ephemerality) of performance, constantly reminding the audience of "this present moment" as they watch the show (4). In a short essay written on *The Birth Caul*, Moore states that each of his public rituals

> is considered a unique event to be performed on one occasion only, at a specified location that is felt to be appropriate to the intention of the work, on a specific date considered to be equally significant. . . . The energy of the performance here is undiluted by all subsequent or previous repetitions, standing as a singular event with its initial force intact. (n.d.:Essay)

Yet while this immediacy and ephemerality lend the performances a singular energy, they do not reduce their reliance upon language; Moore even identifies the words and music as "the main parts of the performance" (2003:part 1).

The Birth Caul in particular stands in a peculiar sort of tension to its own performance. While Moore initially roots his audience in the present moment of Newcastle in 1995, a moment that "skewers our attention . . . and will not let us be; will not allow us to be anything but now but us" (5), the rest of his narrative attempts to transcend those limitations. The piece tries to remove its audience from that present moment and transport them back to their own past and to a collective unconscious, a mass regression it can enact only through Moore's words. In fact, Moore's repeated emphasis on the confining presence of "this present moment" suggests that the singularity of performance actually *opposes* his temporal project, that only his shamanic language and not his performative staging can "set the action in reverse" and "turn back the world's blunt engine" (17).

The printed medium of the comic book, because it is not limited to a single moment in time—because it can, in fact, rearrange, distort, and transcend time through its simultaneous arrangement of images—affords Eddie Campbell more options in his adaptation of *The Birth Caul*.[3] His art transforms a singular and ephemeral event into a permanent, mass-produced visual text that can freely move backwards and forwards in time without recourse to words. But Campbell also attempts to simulate the performative presence of the original piece, preserving the performance for those who were not present to witness it firsthand (including Campbell himself). He depicts Moore's performance space at the Old County Court several times, most prominently when Moore seeks to ground his audience in "This present moment" (4, 5, 8, 9); Campbell replicates this grounding for those far distant from Newcastle and 1995, following Moore's lead as both images and words root the audience in the performance's immediate physical and temporal surroundings before beginning the narrative regression.

Campbell also employs other, more interpretive and interactive means of recreating the experience of attending Moore's performance. One of his most significant contributions to *The Birth Caul* is his creation of an audience surrogate whose memories, apparently stirred by Moore's performance, will comprise the visual storyline of most of the adaptation. This surrogate first appears on the last panel of page 5, a thin box outlining his head to draw him to the readers' attention. He also appears in the last panel of page 11, initiating the readers into the first flashback and suggesting that the images to follow will be his own reveries. Campbell's decision to frame the flashbacks through this man implies that Moore's performance has found some personal resonance with his audience; it also models a similar reaction for the comic book's readers, allowing them to inhabit the spectator's position and become part of the original audience, part of the performance itself.

Campbell's use of this surrogate is governed by his own interpretation of Moore's text. He generally assigns the surrogate's image to those general reflections on youth that Moore narrates in the communal first-person plural; memories more specific to Moore, such as his first-person singular recollections of his mother's and grandmother's deaths, are accompanied by illustrations of Moore himself and are frequently (though not always) lettered in a cursive script quite distinct from the black-box captions that narrate the scenes of the audience surrogate. With these differentiations of image and text, Campbell separates Moore's individual history from his communal musings, a division hardly as distinct in Moore's words alone. Campbell's art creates a virtual second storyline with a second protagonist,

even if he follows Moore's verbal cues in distinguishing this tale from the narrative's more autobiographical elements. Campbell has created a parallel narrative, then, but still not a wholly nonlinguistic one. While he cleverly solves the problems of adapting the immediacy and singularity of performance into the permanence of text, he does not address the narrative's more fundamental dependence on language.

MIND

It would be a mistake, however, to place too much emphasis on the paradox of the text's concurrent rejection of and reliance upon language. Rather than undermine Moore's work, this apparent contradiction exposes many of his boldest arguments about symbolic reasoning and the human self—arguments that are surprisingly consistent with some of the twentieth century's most prominent and influential theories of psychoanalysis and developmental psychology.

At first glance, the myriad oppositions of *The Birth Caul* bear some striking similarities to Jacques Lacan's claim that two orders, the "imaginary" and the "symbolic," alienate us from the "real" order of direct, traumatic presence.[4] The imaginary order is marked, Lacan argues, by the child's formation of ego and self-image during the "mirror stage" of first self-awareness; the symbolic order follows by introducing children to signification, teaching them the difference between signifiers and the objects they signify. Signification and selfhood both separate children from the real, ushering them into a world of difference and alienation (Lacan, 1977:65; see also Evans, 1996:159-60). While Moore does not strictly adhere to Lacan's theories, he nevertheless provides an interesting case study for them in his attempt to revert to a state of consciousness unhindered by these symbolic divisions.

Lacanian theory might therefore help explain some of the contradictions that underwrite Moore's gnostic concept of childhood. According to Lacan, *The Birth Caul*'s recovery of an undivided, presymbolic subject can *only* be attempted through the symbolic realm of language, because we can only imagine prior orders of consciousness through the lens of the symbolic (Evans, 1996: 97-98, 202-203). However, Lacan also argues that language can never hope to represent the real, since the real belongs to another order entirely, "outside language and inassimilable to symbolisation" (Evans 159). To the extent that Moore declines to represent the prenatal experience, hinting at it only through the blank spaces of the "cold white page" (47) or the dark and silent void in which eyes, ears, and lips are sealed (48), he would appear to agree that language can never truly convey the real.

But Moore is hardly beholden to Lacanian psychoanalysis; in fact, he departs from Lacan in a number of other key areas. Perhaps most significantly, and refreshingly, Moore does not base his narrative of child development on any Oedipal struggles over the presence or lack of the phallus. Lacan regards the phallus as a "privileged signifier," the initiator of the symbolic order and the only absolute guarantor of meaning in a world whose symbols are otherwise relational and unfixed (Evans, 1996:143): Moore, on the other hand, creates a counter-sign that can undo its symbolic power. The birth caul functions as a kind of anti-phallus, passed down to Moore from his late mother and stained with his "grandmother's birth-blood" (3). This maternal, matrilineal totem enables him to reverse the symbolic divisions of self and other, signifier and signified that Lacan assigns to the phallus. Interestingly, Moore also opposes the birth caul to another totem, the aforementioned ox-tongue, which he describes in overtly phallic terms as a "veined and purple underhang, the symbol of our power" (28). By overtaking the ox-tongue, by effacing the linguistic power that it symbolizes, the birth caul creates the possibility for a return to the states of consciousness that existed before language, signification, and self-awareness divided us from each other and from our world.

Neither is Moore's narrative wholly anti-Lacanian, however, for it also reifies these very same divisions. By presenting language as the breach that separates humanity from nature and gnosis, Moore reinforces Lacan's idea that the symbolic order performs a separation from the unfiltered, undifferentiated experience of the real; by presenting a phallic tongue as the marker of this separation, he reinforces the concept of the phallus as symbolic divider and privileged signifier. Furthermore, this contrast between the phallic ox-tongue and maternal birth caul also reinforces the text's already heavily reified if unspoken sense of gender difference. Although Moore presents *The Birth Caul* as a narrative of general experience, its protagonists—Moore himself, Campbell's audience surrogate, and perhaps even the communal "we" of Moore's narration—are exclusively male. Moore may seek to capitalize on the totemic powers of the feminine birth caul, and to reverse the phallus/ ox-tongue's symbolic power, but he still presents this symbolic division as a universal stage in a universally male narrative.

Fortunately, Lacanian psychoanalysis is not the only model that might explain the contradictions of *The Birth Caul*; developmental psychology can also reconcile some of Moore's most eccentric observations on time and language with his narrative technique. In *The Child and Reality* (1973), Jean Piaget outlines four stages of cognitive development, claiming that children begin life in a stage of "sensorimotor intelligence" (10) in which they have no symbolic or linguistic faculties and draw no distinctions between subject and object,

self and other. Piaget also argues in "The Child's Conception of Time" (1946) that children do not easily grasp temporal concepts or distinguish them from spatial ones because they have a static concept of time (564). He terms this a "temporal egocentrism" (565) which, like the sensorimotor egocentrism that fails to distinguish between self and other, projects the child's sense of self forwards and backwards across time. In the words of historiographer Hayden White, at the earliest stages of development "there is only the timeless, spaceless experience of the Same" (1978:8). While Piaget's account of preverbal timelessness differs from Moore's—the psychologist describes a lack of awareness of time, not preternatural perceptions across it— both authors claim that this timeless experience is lost after children gain the powers of speech and symbolic operations.

But this explanation still doesn't resolve the apparent contradiction of using language to revert to a prelingual gnosis. However, Hayden White points to a potential resolution in his analysis of Piaget's model of cognitive development. In his introduction to *Tropics of Discourse* (1978). White considers the possibility of rhetorically reversing Piaget's model, of reverting to earlier modes of intelligence, in terms that prove startlingly prescient of **The Birth Caul**:

> To be sure, an unconscious or unintended lapse into a prelogical mode of comprehending reality would merely be an error or, more correctly, a regression . . . But such lapses, when undertaken in the interest of bringing logical thinking itself under criticism and questioning either its presuppositions, its structure, or its adequacy to an existentially satisfying relationship to reality, would be poetry . . . Metaphorical consciousness may be a primitive form of knowing in the ontogenesis of human consciousness in its passage from infancy to maturity, but insofar as it is the fundamental mode of poetic apprehension in general, it is a mode of situating language with respect to the world every bit as authoritative as logic itself.
>
> (10)

This is precisely what Moore has done in **The Birth Caul,** regressing his own language back to presymbolic, metaphoric modes of consciousness in order to critique language for its separation of self from other. If this regression is still paradoxical, relying on language to unmake language, White at least demonstrates how such paradoxes are perfectly consistent within Piaget's model.

In other words, Moore does not need to abandon all language when language itself can excavate earlier states of consciousness. Piaget "stresses that in the process of development, a given mode of cognition is not so much obliterated as preserved, transcended, and assimilated to the mode that succeeds it" (White, 1978:10), sustaining the trace of the older forms and thereby making possible White's (and Moore's own) speculations on the potential of reverting to earlier, prelogical and prelinguistic modes of consciousness. Moreover, in White's model the first and most fundamental mode of consciousness—corresponding to Piaget's infantile, sensorimotor stage—is that of metaphor (White, 1978:5, 12), the same tactic to which Moore resorts in the final, prenatal pages of *The Birth Caul.* Because Moore cannot represent this primal state through any more literally descriptive, metonymic modes of language, he appropriately relies upon the earliest mode that White and Piaget describe. Under White's reading of Piaget, then, Moore's linguistic command in *The Birth Caul* is not a logical impossibility but rather the only feature that makes his narrative possible, as Moore's metaphoric gifts are the nearest means of approximating the earliest modes of human consciousness.

This final testimony to the power, rather than the paradoxes, of Moore's language seems an appropriate note on which to end this article. In a narrative that constantly posits a radical separation between the individual and the world, these contradictions redeem language by demonstrating how it can also recuperate the undivided self. Language is no longer only the vehicle of adult alienation and amnesia, but also the best hope for recovering the unities and gnoses of childhood. Therefore, whatever form *The Birth Caul* should take, whatever medium to which it is adapted, language remains both its central concern and its primary asset. Alan Moore may indeed be unable to escape his language in *The Birth Caul,* and for that we should all be grateful.

Notes

1. Unless otherwise noted, all parenthetical references are to Moore and Campbell, 1999a, *The Birth Caul,* Eddie Campbell Comics. For clarity's sake I have assigned page numbers to the unpaginated comic book, beginning the labeling with the first page of text and creators' credits.

2. The CD recording of *The Birth Caul* labels this episode "The Dressing of the Tongue," underscoring the symbol's importance to the section and to the work as a whole.

3. For more on comics' potential to restructure time, see Scott McCloud, *Understanding Comics,* ch. 4, and *Reinventing Comics,* pp. 200-07, 215-20; Spiros Tsaousis, "Postmodern Spatiality and the Narrative Structure of Comics"; and my own "Invisible Order: Comics, Time, and Narrative."

4. Don Ault discusses how these three orders translate onto the comics page, and how comics innately break down distinctions between the orders, in "'Cutting Up' Again Part II: Lacan on Barks on Lacan." Ault's chapter suggests that the comics form is well suited to blurring or transcending these Lacanian categories.

4. Portions of this article appeared previously in *Alan Moore: Portrait of an Extraordinary Gentleman* (Abiogenesis Press, 2003: 41-46), a tribute volume celebrating Moore's fiftieth birthday. Reprinted by permission, and with many thanks to editor Gary Spencer Millidge.

References

Ault, Don. 2000. "'Cutting Up' Again Part II: Lacan on Barks on Lacan." In *Comics and Culture,* edited by Anne Magnussen and Hans-Christian Christiansen, pp. 123-140. Copenhagen: Museum Tusculanum Press.

Evans, Dylan. 1996. *An Introductory Dictionary of Lacanian Psychoanalysis.* London: Routledge.

Lacan, Jacques. 1977. *Écrits. A Selection.* Translated by Alan Sheridan. London: Tavistock.

McCloud, Scott. 1993. *Understanding Comics.* Northampton, MA: Kitchen Sink.

McCloud, Scott. 2000. *Reinventing Comics.* New York: DC Comics.

Moore, Alan. n.d. Essay. <http://www.locusplus.org.uk/amess.html

Moore, Alan. 2002. "Alan Moore, Interviewed by Eddie Campbell." In *Eddie Campbell's Egomania 2,* pp. 1-32. Paddington, Australia: Eddie Campbell Comics.

Moore, Alan. 2003. "Snake Charmer: An Interview with Alan Moore." 2 parts. *Ninth Art.* <http://www.ninthart.com/display.php?article=532

Moore, Alan and Eddie Campbell. 1999a. *The Birth Caul.* Paddington, Australia: Eddie Campbell Comics.

Moore, Alan and Eddie Campbell. 1999b. *From Hell.* Paddington, Australia: Eddie Campbell Comics.

Piaget, Jean. 1946. "The Child's Conception of Time." Translated by A. J. Pomerans. In *The Essential Piaget.* 1977, edited by Howard E. Gruber and J. Jacques Vonéche, pp. 547-575. New York: Basic Books.

Piaget, Jean. 1973. *The Child and Reality: Problems of Genetic Psychology.* Translated by Arnold Rosin. New York: Grossman.

Singer, Marc. 1999. "Invisible Order: Comics, Time, and Narrative." *International Journal of Comic Art.* 1.2:29-40.

Tsaousis, Spiros. 1999. "Postmodern Spatiality and the Narrative Structure of Comics." *International Journal of Comic Art.* 1.1:205-218.

White, Hayden. 1978. "Introduction: Tropology, Discourse, and the Modes of Human Consciousness." In *Tropics of Discourse,* pp. 1-25. Baltimore: Johns Hopkins University Press.

Mark Bernard and James Bucky Carter (essay date fall 2004)

SOURCE: Bernard, Mark and James Bucky Carter. "Alan Moore and the Graphic Novel: Confronting the Fourth Dimension." *ImageTexT* 1, no. 2 (fall 2004).

[*In the following essay, Bernard and Carter consider Moore's role in expanding the influence and boundaries of the graphic novel genre.*]

Though comic books and graphic novels are earning more serious academic consideration than ever, in relation to one of the foremost goals of twentieth century art and literature, comic books may be more important and innovative than even the most open-minded of scholars have yet to realize. Comics, graphic novels, and sequential art belong to a rich artistic and literary tradition due in no small part to their ability to utilize the techniques of cubism and futurism. This is not a new assertion. Will Eisner (*Comics and Sequential Art*; *Graphic Storytelling and Visual Narrative*) and Scott McCloud (*Understanding Comics*), among many others, have examined comic art's multiple influences from forms and movements considered "high" or fine art. What has hitherto been unexplored, however, is how purely sequential art forms utilize aspects of these movements to fulfill the elusive goals and ideals of many of cubism and futurism's most renowned creators via a unique relationship with the space-time continuum. Indeed, no media before or after the comic book, and more specifically, the graphic novel, has fully bridged the fourth dimension as well. Comics and graphic novels, we argue, constitute the 20th century culmination of the goals of these other pivotal modern and postmodern genres.

Before moving this argument forward, it is imperative to establish an understanding of what is meant herein by the term "fourth dimension." The term to us refers to a special relationship with space and time wherein the two conflate such that infinite multiple dimensionalities become simultaneously present. When the reader's interaction, his or her own space-time, is accounted for, this evocation of space-time becomes quite literal and expands exponentially. The fourth dimension is bridged by human experience and interaction. The spontaneous, real-time interplay of all these forces at once create an ethereal dimension of its own, also what we refer to as the fourth dimension. Therefore, the fourth dimension is defined as simultaneous, multitudi-

nous dimensionality deeply entwined in and part of individual experience. There is special artistry in sequential art and narratives in the relationship of this metaphorical and literal space-time continuum. This artistry does not make the comic book or graphic novel superior to all art, but unique in its absolute expression of ideals that modernist writers and artists sought independently (and therefore less successfully) in their writings and sketches.

Concerns with the space-time continuum and fourth dimensionality are a reoccurring theme in the work of one of comics' most acclaimed and prolific writers, Alan Moore. He is the Picasso of his art when it comes to bridging the fourth dimension and therefore worth particular consideration. Examining samples of Moore's work from his seminal and groundbreaking graphic novels **Watchmen** and **From Hell** show how he is able to use the cubist and futurist tendencies of the comics medium to superbly explore notions of space and time.

Before examining Moore's works, we should consider first some of the basic principles of cubism and futurism. Edward F. Fry describes the cubist notions of Pablo Picasso that began to emerge at the turn of the twentieth century as a reaction against "one-point perspective" (14) and claims that Picasso's strongest cubist works strive to "[combine] multiple view points into a single form" (15). An observer of said works does not see an object from one side or one angle, but is subjected to simultaneous, multitudinous angles from which the object or objects (or persons, or ideas) could be viewed. The end result in terms of flat canvas is a meshing of "selfness" that is more truly the object than any one fixed perspective could provide. Indeed, Picasso can be said to be presenting a version of art more true to the "thing itself" in that he strives to express many states of being at once. When the viewer interacts with the work, time, space, and real-time experience meld. Hence, quite literally, dimensions cross: there is a concrete positioning of the viewer in his or her own space and time added into the already interdimensionality of the work itself. The object is in time, in space on flat canvas, yet simultaneously viewed and experienced via multiple depictions (/directions/dimensions) expressing the object within space-time.

For example, *Guernica* (1937), which can be seen as a sequential magnum opus in one frame, explores a large span of time within a relative small space and surveys the horrid destruction of the town not from any one literal angle, but not from one *perspective* as well. The horse, the bull, the disembodied people: all express elementally the totality of the subject being portrayed. When the viewer digests all of these perspectives, he or she completes the bridge, if the work is successful, by being with everyone and everything at once, both everywhere and engaged in the present simultaneously.

Fry also discusses the cubist paintings of Cézanne, explaining that "In painting a motif Cézanne would [. . .] organize his subject according to the separate acts of perception he had experienced" (14). Basically, cubism strove to dissolve conventional notions of time, space, and the single, static image by showing an object observed and perceived from a multitude of viewpoints at different points in time. Even the most successful of these works, however, lack the power of graphic novels to bridge fully that fourth dimensional gap.

In her book *Futurism and its Place in the Development of Modern Poetry,* Zbigniew Folejewski claims, "Cubism, with its insistence on decomposing the shape of things and rearranging it into a new multidimensional vision, was one of the earliest manifestations of the tendencies which were developed into a coherent programme by Futurism" (5). Take, for example, Umberto Boccioni's *Unique Forms Of Continuity in Space* (1913) [original essay contains a graphic of this sculpture]. The anthropomorphic bronze cast appears to represent a figure in motion, a figure not here or there, but both and everywhere in between: simultaneous dimensionality. Dynamic curves fuse with twists and discombobulations to give the essence of speedy movement, yet Boccioni strives, just as Picasso so often does, to show the figure en masse from every angle by which it could be moving. This both creates the blur effect that many are familiar with via photography and displaces the form and the observer from one stationary perspective to one of many. Of course, within this being of many spaces at once, the figure and the observer are literally still in one station. Marcel Duchamp's *Nude Descending a Staircase* (1912) [original essay contains a graphic of this painting] is perhaps a better example of art transcending time and space. In terms of the graphic novel, the painting appears to be a multitude of sequential panels overlapped to explore the full idea of a brief movement. The observer, in his or her own time and space, transcends placement by noticing the various different motions over time—frozen in oil on canvas—concerned with a simple action.

Cubism's occupation with multiple perspectives led to futurism and its examination of movement, growth, and time. The concepts behind these two movements are found in a literary incarnation through artists such as Gertrude Stein. According to Malcolm Bradbury, Stein wanted "to find [cubism's] equivalent in fiction" (240) and sought to create a "new composition" with the written word that would be a product of the new space-time continuum with which the cubists and futurists were experimenting. One of the novels that emerged from Stein's experimentations, *Three Lives,* she claimed as "the first definite step away from the Nineteenth and into the Twentieth Century in literature" (250). In this novel, Stein uses her ideas on collective consciousness to create an original literature that breaks down common notices of time and place, just as Picasso, a friend of hers, and the other cubists were doing in the visual arts. An example of Stein's exploration of the space-time continuum is Melanctha, a character from *Three Lives*; Melanctha is supposed to live in the "continuous present," and Stein hoped that this concept would displace conventional past tense narrative by somehow making the past, present, and future into a continual state of always, already omnipresence, or, again, a sort of dimensional simultaneity.

While this novel and other works by Stein and the other literary cubists were great efforts, the written word, in and of itself, was too limited to offer an all-new exploration of the space-time continuum. What was needed was a genre with a unique interplay of words and images. A step into the literary fourth dimension couldn't truly take place without a return to where Stein originally drew her inspiration: the visual arts. Thus, the literary cubists and futurists could find an artistic successor in the most unlikely of places: sequential art, a dynamic combination of texts and visuals. While comic strips printed in book form had been around since the 1930s, the modern graphic novel evolved throughout the twentieth century and began to be recognized as a cogent genre (disputably) by the 1960s or 70s. The graphic novel is an art form that finally has the adequate tools to transcend written text and to create the appropriate medium necessary for entering the fourth dimension.

Will Eisner's *A Contract With God and Other Tenement Stories* from 1978 is one example where we see a successful bridge of the space-time continuum. Through Eisner's use of his characters' memories and flashbacks, the involved partaker is truly able to be at more than one place in time at one time. Take, for example, the account of the childhood of Frimme Hersh's adopted daughter in "A Contract With God." While the narrator's voice through the text keeps us grounded in the present, the past comes alive vividly through the drawings (placed side-by-side with the text) [original essay contains a graphic from *A Contract with God and Other Tenement Stories*], and this combination allows for a true "continuous present." Just as in Picasso's *Guernica,* this continuous present enables the audience to consider the totality of a thing; in this case, the "thing" in question is Frimme Hersh's intense love and devotion for his daughter, shown through various scenes from her childhood, presented all at once on one page. Eisner's technical mastery is apparent here, but what is also noteworthy is how Eisner is able to use joining of space and time to create an emotional resonance. By presenting the life of Hersh and his daughter in such a whirlwind, all-at-once manner, the reader is devastated when, on the very next page, an illness attacks his daughter "suddenly and fatally." Her death is the axis around which this whole tale revolves, and Eisner's use of sequential storytelling makes this tragic event jarring and memorable. What the narrator makes clear as an event in the past happens as he speaks it, forcing a new relationship with "now" and "then" in which the two not only coincide, but coexist.

Eisner's pioneering work in the graphic novel led the way for other comic book writers and artists to exploit more fully the fourth dimensional possibilities of the graphic novel, but he was far from the only influence. In the early twentieth century, Winsor McCay's (*Little Nemo in Slumberland,* etc.) dynamic panel work broke up the "beat-by-beat segmentation of time and space of earlier comics, reminiscent of a slide show of successive still images" (Carey). As well, throughout his long career, Harvey Kurtzman (perhaps most known for helping to create *Mad*) created comic works that express a skillful, precise manipulation of narrative time, for example. However, Alan Moore, a disciple of Kurtzman's style, who emerged from Britain in the early 1980s, would be the figure to refine the space-time exceptionality of comics to an overtly intentional creative force rarely paralleled. Like Eisner, Moore's comic work also makes use of sequential art's ability to create a continuous present. What makes Moore's work so interesting, however, is that he not only expertly uses sequential art's ability to simulate the fourth dimension in the telling of his stories, but he is also preoccupied with the space-time continuum as a theme. Moore is deliberate in his utilization of techniques unique to sequential art that deal with space-time, and his calculated interplay provides his own commentary on the possibility of a fourth dimension. Further, he strives to express how the discovery of this dimension affects human existence. As he explains it:

> I try to see things in four dimensions. I feel that if we regard Time as a fourth dimension, then in order to have any sense of what we as individuals mean, what our lives mean, we really have to know where those lives came from, how we got to this current position whether as personally or in terms of cultures, nations, you know, entire histories running back to the Paleae-olithic. All these things seem fascinating to me [. . .].
>
> (Millidge 111-12)

As artists and writers before him saw objects from multiple posits, Moore sees people as simultaneous beings and grants them the possibility of consciousness thereof. When those "simultaneous beings" are readers of his deliberate comic narratives, their experiences further conflate the simultaneous, multitudinal dimensionality that he sees as omnipresent.

A good place to begin a discussion of Moore and the fourth dimension is with his graphic novel from 1986-87 *Watchmen,* a collaboration with artist Dave Gibbons and a major touchstone of comic book storytelling. Much has been made of Moore and Gibbons' skillful use of such literary devices as flashback and foreshadowing in *Watchmen,* but what is perhaps more interesting is how the usage of these techniques allows Moore and Gibbons to create a text in which the present and the past merge together with enough fluidity to make even the best cubists and futurists envious. From the very opening pages of *Watchmen,* it is clear that the reader is in for a virtuoso bridging of space and time, made all the more complete by his or her own role.

For example, while two detectives investigate the apartment where the Comedian, a costumed adventurer, has been murdered, we are able both to hear about the murder through their dialogue and to see it through Gibbons' graphic illustrations of the crime that are spliced in-between the detectives' examination of the murder scene. Through the combination of texts and visuals, we, the readers, are truly in both places at the same time as well as in our own space; this amazing bridge of the space-time continuum is, we argue, particular to sequential art, certainly the culmination of major goals of twentieth century art, and perfectly expressed by Moore. Also, just as with Eisner, this yoking together of space and time is much more than just a neat technical trick. Discussing the relationship between past and present, Moore explains, "I think that if we are to value the present and to really get as much as we can out of each present moment, it would help if we understood how this moment has arisen, if we understood how incredibly rich and savage and beautiful our history can be" (Millidge 112). In this opening scene, Moore and Gibbons are not only able to show the present moment juxtaposed beside the violence that created it, but they also "get as much as they can out of each present moment" by conveying how violence and "savagery" from the past can continue both to rupture the present (notice how, in one panel, the elevator operator announces "Ground floor comin' up" in the present as the panel shows the Comedian being thrown out of the window of his high-rise apartment in the past [original essay contains a graphic from *Watchmen*]) and to reverberate throughout the space-time continuum.

Moore and Gibbons continue to explore the potentials of comic book storytelling in the second chapter of *Watchmen.* The main focus of this chapter is the funeral of the Comedian, a gathering attended by most of the main characters. The reader learns about the Comedian's life through the flashbacks of these characters. For example, as Dr. Manhattan, an atomic and quantum powered superhero, stands by the Comedian's graveside, Gibbons' panels pull in tighter on him [original essay contains a graphic from *Watchmen*], and we notice a man holding a bouquet of flowers standing just over his shoulder. In the next panel, the bouquet transforms into a blast of fireworks, and we are suddenly in Vietnam right after the war, experiencing Dr. Manhattan's disturbing memory of the Comedian's murder of his pregnant Vietnamese girlfriend. Just as in the opening scene with the detectives, Moore and Gibbons show how the historic is able to manifest itself with facility in the present, and no other medium beside the comics page, where images are presented simultaneously on a grid, could present this dilemma with such ease and precision. The reader is engaged in simultaneous, multitudinous placement: the funeral, various events from Vietnam, and in his or her own real space. In *Watchmen* Moore and Gibbons create what Stein longed for: a "continuous present."

One of Moore and Gibbons' most powerful and innovative bridgings of the space-time continuum takes place at the end of this chapter. As Rorschach, an obsessive hero bent on solving the Comedian's murder, meditates on the bitter ironies and the cruelty of human existence, the reader is privy both to his narrative in the captions and to spliced-together memories of the Comedian's life taken from all the flashbacks from the chapter in the panels. While Rorschach's words keep the audience grounded in the present, they can see different brutal scenes from the Comedian's life, disparate images taken from different points in time that now occupy the same space on a grid. In her book, *The Futurist Moment*, Marjorie Perloff claims that one of the mediums in which futurism has found its most powerful means of expression is the collage, an artistic form that "incorporates directly into the work an actual fragment of the referent, thus forcing the reader or viewer to consider the interplay between preexisting message or material and the new artistic composition that results from the graft" (viii), and this collage of the Comedian's life, coupled with Rorschach's text, creates an intimate, horrifying, and poignantly sad portrait of the Comedian's life in a way that only sequential art is able. The reader absorbs images of the Comedian raping the Silk Spectre, the Comedian fearlessly brandishing a riot gun amidst a cloud of tear gas, the Comedian being attacked and disfigured by his Vietnamese girlfriend, the Comedian weeping and clutching a bottle of liquor, and the Comedian being humiliated, beaten, and murdered by Ozymandias. The interplay between these images forces the reader to consider the Comedian in his horrifying totality (i.e *Guernica* [original essay contains a graphic of Pablo Picasso's *Guernica*]) and to notice how the Comedian's choices have created shockwaves that ripple throughout his entirety. In order to achieve this effect, Moore and Gibbons have truly made time a tangible dimension on this comic page. Hence, we see that neither Stein nor Picasso nor Boccioni had it exactly right: neither art nor literature could successfully bridge the fourth dimensions on its own, but a medium utilizing both in tandem accomplishes their goals with an astonishing ease worthy of respectful, critical attention.

No discussion of the space-time continuum in *Watchmen* would be complete without emphasis given to Dr. Manhattan, a superhero granted God-like powers by an atomic accident. Dr. Manhattan can transform the molecular structure of any object, teleport to anywhere in the universe, and is slowly becoming omnipotent. Throughout the graphic novel, Manhattan struggles with his humanity; he seems to be losing touch with human experience as we know it due to his amazing ability to never age and to be aware always of the past, present, and the future. Again, Moore and Gibbons are able to allow the reader to see the world through Dr. Manhattan's eyes as only sequential art can by exploiting fully its fourth dimensional powers. Chapter Four of *Watchmen,* in which Dr. Manhattan exiles himself to Mars and considers his origin, is a tour-de-force in comics storytelling. In the first panel on the first page of the chapter, the reader sees Dr. Manhattan's hand holding a photograph of him and his ex-girlfriend. Manhattan's captions read, "The photograph is in my hand. It is the photograph of a man and a woman. They are at an amusement park, in 1959" [original essay contains a graphic of *Watchmen*]. In the next panel, the reader sees the photograph lying on the red Martian terrain, surrounded by footprints that signify that Manhattan has dropped the photo and wondered off. Manhattan states, "In twelve seconds time, I drop the photograph to the sand at my feet, walking away. It's already lying there, twelve seconds into the future." The reader finds the photo back in Manhattan's hand in the next panel as Manhattan reveals that he "found it in a derelict bar at the Gila Flats test base, twenty-seven hours ago." The reader is at the bar with Manhattan in the next panel, looking at the photo as he duly notes, "It's still there [. . .]. I'm still there looking at it."

This sequence would be of little note if it were played out in a novel or film; after all, most everyone is familiar with stream of consciousness in prose and crosscutting (moving back and forth between two or more scenes) in film. When sequential art is used as the medium, however, this sequence is an exceptional experience. As the audience ingests the comics page as a whole, they are with Dr. Manhattan every step of the way. When the setting turns back to Manhattan at the derelict bar, the reader is there with him, just as the reader is, at the same time, back on Mars with him. After all, while observing the panel that shows Manhattan in the bar, the panel showing Manhattan on Mars is still within eyeshot. This all combines with the reader's actual space to bridge dimensional relations. It could be argued that a novel could achieve similar results (after all, all the words on a page are observable all at the same time), and by this same token, one could claim this same feat could be performed in film through the usage of split-screen. What gives comics advantage over these other mediums, however, is that while literature and film must use obtrusive techniques (ruptures in the text, split screen) to create a tangible fourth dimension, this manipulation of the space-time continuum is so much part and parcel with the very nature of sequential art that this bridging of space and time is virtually seamless. The only way a film can achieve the same fourth dimensional effects that a comic can is through the usage of split screen, an effect that takes the audience out of the film and is very distracting and self-aware. Even in movies that try to use split screen techniques derivative of comics panels (Ang Lee's *Hulk,* for example), it is extremely disconcerting and ostentatious simply because it is not what viewers are used to experiencing. In comics, there is none of this tension. It is natural, seamless, and it is a huge theoretical (and space/time) leap that the reader can take with relative ease. In comics, even when panels separate actions, seemingly creating a "fracture of both time and space" the reader's experience forces a sort of closure that "allows us to connect these moments and mentally construct a continuous, unified reality" (McCloud 67). That continuous reality, though, is saturated in interdimensionality, multiple realities, moments, and experiences.

This situation recalls Slavoj Zizek's location of a break between modernism and postmodernism, a break that "affects *the very status of interpretation*" (1). Zizek explains, "A modernist work is by definition 'incomprehensible': it functions as a shock, as the irruption of a trauma which undermines the complacency of our daily routine and resists being integrated into the symbolic universe of the prevailing ideology" (1). Whenever the cubists and futurists ruptured or fragmented a text, the reader or observer's attention is almost always called to its initial complexity, if not preliminary incomprehensibility. Likewise, whenever split screen is used in film, the audience cannot help but take note and immediately began to speculate on the filmmaker's reasons for utilizing this technique. On the other hand, Zizek claims that "What postmodernism does, however, is the very opposite: its objects *par excellence* are products with a distinctive mass appeal [. . .]—it is for the interpreter to detect in them an exemplification of the most esoteric theoretical finesses of Lacan, Derrida or Foucault. [. . .] [T]he aim of the postmodernist treatment is to estrange its very initial homeliness" (1-2). Considering that comics have long been viewed as children's literature or books for adults not intelligent enough to read "real" books, few art forms have a more "distinctive mass appeal" than comics, and since this bridging of space and time is so imbedded in sequential art's basic language system, causing little to no noticeable "irruption" in the text, comics may very well be, by Zizek's definition, the epitome of postmodern art.

And the power and essence of this postmodernity is embodied perfectly in Dr. Manhattan. Indeed, the true genius of Dr. Manhattan is that he seems to be a metaphor for the art of the graphic novel in and of itself as well as for the graphic novel experience. He is everywhere all the time as well as where he is presently. He is not most like any other character in the book, but most like the reader himself in that he transcends transience, simple being, via not displacement, but *multi*placement, of being many places at once, mentally and, in the storyline, physically as well. His character is the fullest, most essential fourth dimensional relationship in the genre to date. It is fitting that at the conclusion of **Watchmen,** Manhattan decides to leave the galaxy of Watchmen for another, where he hopes to create some human life of his own, just as the reader always has the power to leave the **Watchmen** galaxy by simply closing the book. In addition, both Manhattan and the reader also have the power to forge life elsewhere: Manhattan, through his molecular powers, and the reader, by picking up another book or graphic novel of his or her choosing and thus beginning the interaction between reader and text all over again. Manhattan leaves Ozymandias (and the galaxy) behind with the ominous proclamation that "Nothing ever ends," and with **Watchmen,** Moore and Gibbons prove his final words to be true both by creating a fourth dimension in which the reader can witness the reoccurring ripples of history and by embodying sequential art's relationship with the reader, a relationship that can be repeated *ad infinitum.*

It is clear that Moore's work with the fourth dimension and the space-time continuum is stimulating and empowering for his audience, but Moore can also use this aspect of sequential storytelling to shock and frighten his readers in new and unique ways. When Moore deals with the horrifying ramifications of the possible existence of a fourth dimension, his place in a rich artistic tradition again becomes apparent as he falls in line with some of the darker, more cynical futurist ideologies. Zbigniew Folejewski sees futurism largely as "a reaction, in which cynicism and nihilism alternated with the desire to seek new beliefs and forge new values" (5), and Moore (who is, interestingly enough, a self-proclaimed anarchist) often displays this same ambivalent attitude as he creates and explores fourth dimensional time and the architecture of history, most notably in another of his major works, **From Hell.** In this graphic novel, a mammoth collaboration with artist Eddie Campbell that took around eight years (1988-96) to complete, the two presuppose that Jack the Ripper was Sir William Gull, one of Queen Elizabeth's surgeons on a mission to destroy those who attempted to blackmail the royal family, and the graphic novel is a harrowing chronicle of the cultural and historical aftershocks of the Ripper murders and Gull's descent into madness, an insanity abetted by his growing ability to experience the fourth dimension. At its very heart, **From Hell** is a horror story (it began its publishing history in Stephen Bissette's *Taboo,* an anthology that was, at least, intended to be a horror anthology), and it is all the more unnerving since the reader is able to partake fully of Gull's fourth dimensional hallucinations via the power of sequential art.

Gull's eventual madness is foreshadowed early in the novel in Chapter Two, "A State of Darkness." The first page of this chapter consists of eight panels, all of which are solid black and contain only word balloons [original essay contains a graphic of *From Hell*]. The caption in the first panel establishes the setting as "The Limehouse Cut. July 1827," but the dialogue in the subsequent panels makes no narrative sense. The only continuing thread throughout the page is a question that is repeated three times: "What is the fourth dimension?" The reader is, quite literally, left "in the dark" as to how all these bits of dialogue supposedly fit together, and the question of the fourth dimension goes unanswered. As the chapter progresses, however, the reader learns that the narrative begins in July 1827 with Gull as a young child, and the rest of the chapter recounts Gull's life and experiences. Perhaps when the reader is about half through reading the chapter, he will realize that all those bits of dialogue that appear on the first page of the chapter are actually bits of conversation that arise at different points of Gull's life. Therefore, it is clear that the mysterious first page of the chapter was, in fact, a spliced together collage of snippets from Gull's life presented on a grid, and the audience, by slowly orienting themselves with how space and time are being manipulated here, is an absolute essential ingredient in bridging the gap between space and time. The reader moves from a state of darkness in which the fourth dimension is present all around them but is elusive and invisible to a point where he is slowly becoming aware of this fourth dimension, just as Gull does. For this very reason, it is important that a majority of this chapter is told from Gull's perspective, the panels revealing to the reader Gull's point of view. As he moves in and out of the darkness and light, the reader moves along with him, and the readers' experience is nearly as subjective as Gull's.

At one point in this chapter, Gull has a conversation with his friend, James Hinton, who discusses some of the ideas of his mathematician son, Howard Hinton. James tells Gull of his son's theories on time and space, explaining that Howard's ideas "suggest time is a human illusion . . . that all times co-exist in the stupendous whole of eternity. [. . .] Fourth dimensional patterns within Eternity's monolith would, he suggests, seems merely random events to third dimensional percipients . . . events rising towards inevitable convergence like an archway's lines." Gull reacts to these ideas by asking, "Can history then be said to have an architecture? This notion is most glorious and most horrible."

The "glorious and horrible" architecture of time continues to reveal itself slowly as the story unfolds and Gull commences on his murderous missions. During his various murders, he begins to receive brilliant flashes of the future, but it isn't until Chapter 10, "The Best of All Tailors," which details Gull's ritualistic and horrific butchering of prostitute Mary Kelly, his last murder, that Gull plunges headlong into fourth dimensional awareness. As the mutilation of Kelly's body becomes more and more severe, Gull travels back into the past (briefly becoming a Babylonian alchemist) and sees into his immediate future and beyond. In his appendix notes for this chapter, Moore discusses some of his influences when composing this bizarre and disturbing chapter, explaining:

> In his splendid book of essays, *Mortal Lessons,* Dr. Richard Seltzer (from whom many of Gull's detailed medical pronouncements in this episode were lifted) talks about the view of life that doctors have, almost that they alone have been elected to that priesthood that may look upon the mysteries inside us. It is a similar state of God-like disassociation from the obvious horror of the flesh that I hoped to create within the reader's mind by the portrayal of events here.
>
> (Appendix 35)

Sequential art allows Moore and Campbell to conceive a true "God-like disassociation" in this chapter by giving the reader a perspective (Gull's warped perspective) that flirts with total omnipotence. Just as with Dr. Manhattan in *Watchmen,* when Gull travels into the future, the reader travels with him, whilst still remaining with Gull in that blood soaked room in the surrounding panels. Near the conclusion of this massacre, Gull cuts Kelly's heart from her carcass and places it in a kettle over the fire. As the heart burns, a blinding light explodes from the fireplace, and Gull and the reader, who had both begun this narrative of *From Hell* in darkness and ignorance of the fourth dimension, are moving closer to omnipotence. (Curiously, in the first printing of this chapter by Kitchen Sink Press in 1995, when Gull stares into the blinding light emanating from the fireplace, he whispers "God?" In the first collected edition of *From Hell* [published in 1999], however, this line has been omitted.)

The final chapter of *From Hell,* entitled "Gull, Ascending," takes place eight years after the Ripper murders and finds Gull, now a near comatose lunatic, locked up in an insane asylum. In the last moments of his life, Gull's consciousness travels back and forth through time and manifests itself in various time periods until he ascends to godhood in the heavens [original essay contains a graphic of *From Hell*]. Just as with Chapter Two, a great deal of this final chapter is told directly from Gull's point of view, so Gull and the reader complete their rise from darkness into the light of omnipotence here. As Gull finally reaches the climax of his journey, everything unravels, the panels of the grid dissolve away, and the only thing remaining is a completely white, blank page with the tiny words, "God and then I . . ." (14.24). Moore and Campbell lead the reader to a catharsis so great, an omnipotence so overwhelming, that their artistic medium breaks down. The upswing is that the catharsis of being so intertwined within the process of bridging the fourth dimension—it is the reader's consciousness that makes all this possible, after all—need not affect readers in the same manners of intensity as expressed by Moore's characters. Yet it can not be underscored that the fourth dimensional play can and does not fully culminate without the reader interacting with the texts, visual and literal, in much the same way as a Gull or Dr. Manhattan.

This study is by no means exhaustive. We have only briefly mentioned some of Moore's influential space-time savvy predecessors, and there are many other examples of how Moore explores the space-time continuum in his own oeuvre. For instance, in **Batman: The Killing Joke,** a collaboration with Brian Bolland from 1988, Moore uses many of the same techniques used in **Watchmen** to fuse together the past and the present. Also, in his work on **Supreme** and the unfinished 1963 mini-series (both published during the 90s by Image Comics), Moore further considers the mystery and danger surrounding the possible existence of a fourth dimension, at which we have only hinted. When discussing the nature of comic art in an essay written in 1985, Moore asked:

> Rather than seizing upon the superficial similarities between comics and films or comics and books in the hope that some of the respectability of those media will rub off upon us, wouldn't it be more constructive to focus our attention upon those ideas where comics are special and unique? Rather than dwelling upon film techniques that comics can duplicate, shouldn't we perhaps consider comic techniques that films can't duplicate?
>
> (4)

However, this study, we hope, will help bridge the gap in our current space-time exigency: one where comics and sequential art are still struggling to garner the respect they deserve. Considering Moore's groundbreaking work in using comics to bridge the gap between space and time and, as a result, finally succeeding, it is obvious that he has helped set apart sequential art as a unique and viable art form deserving of more critical respect than is currently attributed to it in relation to the whole of twentieth century accomplishment. His work illustrates how sequential art is the most precise culmination of ideas and forms that more established and recognized artistic and literary genres of the twentieth century strove to realize. Though he recently announced his retirement from comics, it is hard to

conceive of any future works of his not creating the "continuous present," as comics and graphic novels so perfectly do, proving their unmitigated success as the one unmitigated twentieth century art form to bridge the fourth dimension.

References

Bradbury, Malcolm and Richard Ruland. *From Puritanism to Postmodernism: The Story of American Literature.* London: Routledge, 1991.

Carey, Mike. *Comics and film. Pop Thought. <http://www.popthought.com/display_column.asp?DAID=156.* 7 Jul, 2004.

Eisner, Will. *Comics and Sequential Art.* Tamarac, FL: Poorhouse Press, 1985.

———. *A Contract With God and Other Tenement Stories.* NY: DC Comics, 2000.

———. *Graphic Storytelling and Visual Narrative.* Tamarac, FL: Poorhouse Press, 1996.

Folejewski, Zbigniew. *Futurism and Its Place in the Development of Modern Poetry: A Comparative Study and Anthology.* Ottawa: U of Ottawa P, 1980.

Martini, Omar. "The Dark Side of the Moore: An Interview." *Alan Moore: Portrait of an Extraordinary Gentleman.* Eds. smoky man and Gary Spencer Millidge. LEIGH-ON-SEA, England: Abiogenesis, 2003. 107-117.

McCloud, Scott. *Understanding Comics: The Invisible Art.* New York: HarperPerennial, 1994.

Moore, Alan and Eddie Campbell. *From Hell.* Paddington Q, Australia: Eddie Campbell Comics, 1999.

Moore, Alan and Dave Gibbons. *Watchmen.* NY: DC Comics, 1986-1987.

Moore, Alan. *Writing For Comics.* Urbana, IL: Avatar, 2003.

Perloff, Marjorie. *The Futurist Moment: Avant-garde, Avant Guerre, and the Language of Rupture.* Chicago, IL: U of Chicago P, 1986.

Zizek, Slavoj. "Alfred Hitchcock, or, The Form and its Historical Meditation." *Everything You Always Wanted to Know About Lacan (But Were Afraid to Ask Hitchcock).* London: Verso, 1992. 1-12.

Annalisa Di Liddo (essay date spring/summer 2005)

SOURCE: Di Liddo, Annalisa. "Transcending Comics: Crossing the Boundaries of the Medium in Alan Moore and Eddie Campbell's *Snakes and Ladders.*" *International Journal of Comic Art* 7, no. 1 (spring/summer 2005): 530-45.

[*In the essay below, Di Liddo addresses the different approaches taken in some of Moore's works.*]

INTRODUCTION

The aim of this paper is to discuss some aspects and recent developments in the work of Alan Moore. These involve in particular his mixed media performance works, two of which—***The Birth Caul*** (1995) and ***Snakes and Ladders*** (1999)—have been released on CD, and additionally interpreted and turned into comic books by Eddie Campbell. While Moore's "magical" and performative turn has been widely investigated in review articles and interviews, in relation to his overall opinion on the creative process, to the well-known series ***Promethea*** or to the general ideas underpinning his live acts, the comic book adaptations of the performances have always been mentioned but, at the same time, they have also been dismissed as minor results (with the exception of Marc Singer's comprehensive study of ***The Birth Caul***; see References). On the contrary, my purpose here is to demonstrate how, in those adaptations, the approach to magic at the core of Moore's performances brings about some interesting outcomes as regards the use of the comics medium. The paper will focus primarily on ***Snakes and Ladders,*** performed on April 10, 1999, in London and published as a comic book by Eddie Campbell in 2001. But before moving on to a brief analysis of some aspects of this work, it is necessary to make some preliminary remarks about the key concepts of magic, psychogeography, and performance.

MAGIC, PSYCHOGEOGRAPHY, PERFORMANCE

More than ten years have passed since Alan Moore decided to declare himself a magician in November 1993. He asserts that the process which led him to allow for the existence of magic was triggered by the realization of a series of odd coincidences and concurrences between his art and his life and by the necessity of answering questions as to the nature of consciousness and inspiration (Campbell, 2002:3). He claims (4) to have established first contact with the irrational while writing the character of Dr. William Gull in ***From Hell*** and having him say that, "The one place Gods inarguably exist is in our minds where they are real beyond refute, in all their grandeur and monstrosity" (Moore and Campbell, 2000: ch. 4, 18). This sentence forced him to come to terms with the idea that what seems to lie beyond the boundaries of human rational thinking is nothing but the product of human thinking itself—therefore, in the ultimate analysis, fiction. After resuming and refashioning Aleister Crowley's notion of magic as "a disease of the language" and integrating it with this concept, Moore now considers magic as an essentially "linguistic phenomenon" (Campbell, 2002:4) and has elaborated a complex theory that branches out to include the Tarot deck and the Kabbalah as related to fractal mathematics and genetics, and that eventually identifies magic with imagination and creativity. If magic is a linguistic system, then, it will provide us with a vocabulary to read and interpret the world surrounding us:

> The world is kind of pregnant with revelation if you're somebody who comes equipped with the right kind of eyes and the right kind of phrase book . . . for decoding. Magic is, in a sense, a kind of language with which to read the universe.
>
> (Babcock, 2002)

This acknowledgement leads directly to the concept of "psychogeography," defined by Moore as "a means of divining the meaning of the streets in which we live and pass our lives (and thus our own meaning, as inhabitants of those streets)" (Campbell, 2002:7). In Moore's production, the traces of this process date back as far as 1990: in the first issue of ***Big Numbers,*** Mr. Slow, a history teacher, is shown while explaining to his students the importance of recognizing Hampton's—a fictional equivalent of Moore's own native Northampton—historical and cultural substratum in order to understand their own place in society (Moore and Sienkiewicz, 1990:28-29). Psychogeographical practice is common to other artists, above all to British writer and director Iain Sinclair.[1] By means of walking and of researching places, the psychogeographical writer becomes not an author as much as a channel for the cultural legacy of place to emerge through the mass of historical coordinates and anthropological memories he gathers from the geographical—often urban—experience; therefore, he uses physical space as a palimpsest for outlining a path on a subjective and yet universal fictional map in which the reader can recognize his own identity and cultural references. The same approach also lies at the core of the novel ***Voice of the Fire*** (1996), in its attempt to cover a span of 5000 years of British history through the fictional voices—including Moore's own—of characters located within ten miles of Northampton. However, the best-known example of psychogeographical writing by Alan Moore is certainly chapter 4 in ***From Hell,*** which depicts Dr. Gull and coachman Netley's route through the streets of London in search of evidence of the city's Masonic structure, where the historical reminiscences of places overlap with Gull's own perception of reality (Moore and Campbell, 2000: ch. 4, 4-38).

The interest in psychogeography, together with ritual and magical practice, evolved into the idea of mixed media performances, designed with the aid of musicians and collaborators Tim Perkins and David Jay. The reason for the choice of performance as a form of expression is the will to convey the considerable amount of information accumulated in the ritual/shamanic process through creating a multi-sensory experience, which is supposed to overwhelm the senses of the audience, thus involving it in the experience itself. The declaration of intent Moore wrote in his short explanatory essay about *The Birth Caul* can apply to all of his performance acts:

> I've attempted to construct a process and a context for performance art and poetry that builds on and makes use of the shamanic worldview to direct the audience through a structured mental landscape to a predetermined level of awareness. Each performance that emerges from this process is considered a unique event to be performed on one occasion only, at a specified location that is felt to be appropriate to the intention of the work, on a specific date considered to be equally significant.
>
> (Moore, 2001)

Again, as in the case of psychogeography, performance has proved to be an old concern of Moore's: in the early 1970s, when he was about 17, he spent a period of artistic apprenticeship at the Northampton Arts Lab, an experience he has defined as seminal in his intellectual development, not much in terms of acquiring high technical skills, as in those of adopting an open attitude towards the potential boundlessness of artistic practice. The activities of the Lab included performance poetry readings, independent theater, music, and multimedia installations, and it was through the Lab that Moore had the chance to meet "Principal Edward's Magic Theatre," an experimental band based in a Northampton commune whose live acts mixed music with stage performance and dance (Khoury, 2003). Even though there is no trace of any precise theoretical point of reference on the part of the Lab, it is reasonable to trace its approach to artistic creation back to the influence of thinkers and directors such as Peter Brook, Jerzy Grotowski, and Eugenio Barba, who all tried to bring theater back to its original collective and ritual status, and whose pervasive effect was strongly felt in most militant theatrical groups and institutions in the 1970s. In his 1968 collection of essays, *The Empty Space,* Peter Brook advocates a return to Antonin Artaud's notion of theater as a site for magic and totemic evocation, and the idea of "a cry from the womb" (Brook, 1978[1968]:54), clearly referring to the attempt to evoke the audience's prenatal consciousness, seems to foreshadow the conception of Moore's *Birth Caul.* Jerzy Grotowski's *Towards a Poor Theatre* (1968) is even more radical in reasserting the nature of the stage act as a vehicle for spiritual knowledge; the Polish director maintains that the ideal theatrical performance is a communal psychic experience in which the audience's mental blocks are removed by means of the actors' formal discipline, and of the control of the structure of the act, resulting in a universal, mythical experience which allows each partaker to acquire a higher perception of his/her own personal awareness.[2] This view very palpably tallies with the notion Moore expresses in the essay about *The Birth Caul* quoted above, with the difference that, in Moore's works, the

"structured mental landscape" (Moore, 2001) perceived by the audience comes not so much from the actors' use of the body, as from the web of psychogeographical references woven by the author throughout the stage act. Therefore, Moore's performances can be seen as a part of what is now a well-established theatrical tradition; in addition to this, Moore himself has appealed to some performative magic rituals of the past, particularly to those by Aleister Crowley, MacGregor Mathers, and—back in the 16th century—John Dee, and then again to Claudio Monteverde and the origins of opera (Beaton, 2003).

Being the fourth of the five performances carried out so far,[3] *Snakes and Ladders* was staged at Conway Hall, Red Lion Square, London, UK. on April 10, 1999; the psychogeographical suggestions of the London Holborn area, mainly concerning Oliver Cromwell, the Pre-Raphaelites and most of all *fin de siècle* fantastic fiction writer Arthur Machen, provided the leitmotifs for a five-part reflection on life, place, and the function of art. The CD recording of the performance was made available only later, after the appearance of Campbell's comic book adaptation, published in 2001. Obviously excluding the possibility of attending the performance, there remains for most of us a threefold possibility of approach *Snakes and Ladders,* i.e. 1. listening to the recording; 2. listening to the recording and, with Moore's voice as a guide, following Campbell's adaptation in print; 3. reading the printed version only. Due to the scarce availability of the limited edition CD, the easiest way to access this work is the volume, which is the element I am going to focus on in order to demonstrate how, while reading an adaptation is unquestionably different from attending a live act and cannot substitute the whole multimedia experience, the comic book proves effective in itself and opens the way for some useful remarks.

FROM PERFORMANCE TO COMICS: SNAKES AND LADDERS, A SECTION-TO-SECTION ANALYSIS

In the essay about *The Birth Caul* quoted above, Moore explains that "the energy of the performance . . . is undiluted by all subsequent or previous repetitions, standing as a singular event with its initial force intact" (Moore, 2001): it may thus be argued that transferring a one-off event into comic book form is a questionable choice. The unrepeatability of the performance is taken here as an essential feature which comics, permanently fixed on paper and allowing as many readings as one wishes, can only fail to represent. Nevertheless, there are various reasons why Campbell's adaptation can be considered worthwhile. First of all, if on the one hand the printed version loses the element of uniqueness and instantaneousness, on the other, it noticeably gains another aspect, i.e. the possibility for the reader to dwell upon details and to delve deep into the text and pictures.

Secondly, the medium of comics engages all of the reader's senses and requires a very high level of interaction on his/her part (McCloud, 1994 [1993]:88, 92); as a consequence, it gets close to the sort of strong personal involvement and synaesthetic experience which, through the stimulation of various sensory faculties at a time, Moore sets as the goal of his performative experiments (Campbell, 2002: 9-10; Beaton, 2003).

Moreover, as Alasdair Watson has remarked, some artists achieve interesting results "when they're working against some kind of imposed limitation, as they try and find ways to work with it and around it" (Watson, 2001); such is the case of landmark genre fiction, to quote a pretty straightforward example. As a consequence, the choice to represent the impact of the live performance and to convey the core of Moore's esoteric experience has compelled Campbell to devise some interesting visual strategies in his adaptation. Therefore, the following analysis will focus on the most relevant issues connected to the manipulation of the medium in each section of *Snakes and Ladders.*

One of the crucial features in determining the visual layout of *Snakes* [*Snakes and Ladders*] is the narrating voice's continuous, non-linear movement from personal to collective experience and backwards: hence Campbell renders the free flow of words by means of very loose page layouts, where there is no precise panel framing but mostly a juxtaposition of images which differ in size and arrangement. In the first section, "The Gate of Tears" (Moore and Campbell, 2001:2-11), the first three paragraphs of the monologue conjure up a dark vision of the end of the 20th century—a century filled with "the smoking wrecks of ideologies" (2), compared to smashed cars with broken-down wheels and shattered radios, and seething with clammy, muddy filth percolating through the fissures in the once-solid soil of the collective certainties of Western civilization. The background of pages 2 and 3 is an entirely grey area that seems stained by an undefined organic matter, on top of which, on page 3, Campbell has pasted a reworking of a photograph—its edges tattered as if it were torn off a newspaper page—of the Berlin Wall, cracked and covered with faded graffiti announcing the "Millennium" and pleading for "Freiheit" (freedom); in front of the wall lies a pile of wrecked cars, while in the heap of junk that occupies the foreground, a copy of *Vogue* magazine with Lady Diana Spencer on its cover stands out, emblematically exposing massive commodification of misfortune as a sign of last century's ideological decadence. In these same paragraphs, Moore intertwines this all-inclusive view on turn-of-the-century anguish with the time-specific, site-specific nature of the performance:

> It's 1999. . . . It's April 10th; we find ourselves in Red Lion Square . . . caught in the crosshairs of geography and time like sitting ducks. . . . Fluttering

attention pinned to where we are and when and who we are. The honey-trap of our personal circumstance, of our familiar bodies restless in these chairs.

(2-3)

Campbell aptly represents the simultaneous presence of universality and spatial/temporal specificity by placing a panel depicting Moore addressing his audience onto the "organic" background of page 2, and by completing page 3 with a view of Red Lion Square. The narrative movement continues on pages 4 and 5, this time starting again from personal experience:

> From this complex lace of moment, all our strands of individual information stretch away towards their different points of origin, through how we got here, winding back to where we're from. In my case, that would be Northampton, an unprepossessing blur on the M1 halfway to Birmingham.

(4)

Moore goes on to weave a network of references to Oliver Cromwell, Arthur Machen, and Francis Crick, who all spent some time in Northampton or in its surroundings, and whose connection to the Holborn area will be revealed through the monologue's psychogeographical journey. But the narrating voice, seemingly not knowing which reference to start from, decides to "start with the basics. Best make sure we're all on the same page," (5) and therefore moves again to the universal dimension, rising to speak about the origin of the cosmos and then descending once more to locate Red Lion Square, to expand on the history of its construction and on the characters who inhabited it through the centuries, mostly focusing on Cromwell and the Pre-Raphaelites. In his attempt to reproduce the multiplicity of references and factual correspondences which crowd Moore's script, Campbell makes a substantial use of collage, placing his own drawings side by side with photographs, portraits, and maps (4-5, 7) or reproductions of Pre-Raphaelite paintings (9). In order to represent the shift to the cosmic plane, he makes use of a splash page where the words are set in a column and three quarters of the space is occupied by a starry sky which, with its vastness, overhangs a small building.

Another interesting example of Campbell's treatment of the performance material is the second section, "Stars and Garters" (12-23). The section opens with a reproduction of a pamphlet, fully designed and written in 19th century fashion, inviting the audience to attend the performance by Mr. Moore and his collaborators. The setting of the following pages is a late Victorian or Edwardian stage where a woman—according to the monologue, the incarnation of imagination—carries out a dance with a puppet snake steered by a hooded figure. As the snake—which, in the performance, was a prop moved by Frank Ryan (see the CD booklet for credits)—

appears on page 16, the narrating voice starts to list creation legends and stories involving the serpent, eventually connecting it to the DNA. The words wind on the page in a single line that loops in a spiral around the head of the reptile, thus visually symbolizing the coils of the snake's body and the rhythmic curls of the narration in its persistent shifting from past to present and from singular to universal. The dance with the snake puppet was originally performed by Paula van Vijngaarden: Campbell reproduces the act in his adaptation, being careful to emphasize not only the thread tied to the reptile's head but also the machinery on stage and the presence of the people who operate it (22-23), thus clearly reasserting Moore's theory about magic as a purely fictional product of the human mind, and also referring to Moore's own tongue-in-cheek worship of the fake 2nd century Roman snake divinity Glycon.[4] The same topic appears again in section three where, with further irony and self-referentiality, Moore himself enters *Snakes and Ladders* as a character and meets the occultist John Constantine from *Swamp Thing,*[5] who reveals the secret of magic to him: "Any cunt could do it" (31).

Campbell brings his visual strategies to further expansion in the "Baghdad" section (24-31), where the use of the collage technique is made even more significant and where the simple juxtaposition of visuals is often placed side by side with the superimposition of images. Baghdad is the name Machen gave to the imaginary lunar landscape he claimed to have visited in the nightmarish state of mind that followed his wife's death. Moore identifies it with "Yesod" (27), which he associates with the descent into the unconscious and into the realm of dream, the dark repository of images and fantasies underlying any act of creation—hence underlying art, thought, and life. Moore elucidates the topic of the connection between the lunar territory of Yesod, death, and imagination in his magical manifesto *Promethea,* where, in Issue 14 (**"Moon River"**), Promethea crosses the Styx, the river that leads to the underworld, and reaches the Moon. Charon, her guide, immediately tells her that "the Moon governs the dreams and the unconscious. The unconscious, in a way, is the underworld" (Moore, Williams, and Gray, 2002:32). Before observing the lunar citadel (46-47), whose clock towers and little bridges slightly resemble those of Campbell's Baghdad (Moore and Campbell, 2001: 26-27). Promethea reads the word "Yesod" carved into the archway at the entrance, and exchanges the following views with Charon:

Promethea:

It's a Hebrew word, meaning Foundation. I guess it implies that spirituality is founded in imagination.

Charon:

Naturally, Before journeying to higher spheres, man must first reach the Moon. From here, armed with imagination's vision, man need only look up.

(Moore, Williams, and Gray, 2002:46)[6]

This is the same progression Machen goes through in *Snakes and Ladders* as, after crossing Baghdad, he ascends to the enlightened state of "Syon" (Moore and Campbell, 2001:38-48). But let us go back to Campbell and to his representation of Baghdad and its inhabitants: page 38, by means of a dense collage of images in various styles, conveys the sense of marvellous vision and of a plunge into collective imagination in both its beauty and horror. The pictures range from a watercolor depicting an exotic, monstrous elephant-like creature to a series of photographs of actresses such as Marilyn Monroe and Brigitte Bardot, rising in the form of soap bubbles blown out of a pipe. A sketch of Vlad Tepes, the historical figure at the root of the legend of Count Dracula, and of his victims, here impaled on flowers, is placed not far from a lifelike portrait of 19th century British fairy painter Richard Dadd, and from a freeze frame from George Meliès's *Voyage dans la Lune* (1902). Then, the monologue reaches a decisive turning point in connecting imagination with life, and thus with genetics:

Everyone knows this Moontown, that has ever dreamed or wondered. In our reveries we windowshop at its emporiums and in our fevers ride wild, steaming horses down its avenues. . . . Machen and Morris, Burne-Jones and Rossetti, J. D. Watson, co-discoverer with Francis Crick of the dual helix, dreams of interwoven stairwells and the structure of the DNA is suddenly made clear. These are not tourists in the moonsoaked mews of the unconscious, but explorers.

(28-29)

It is at this point, on page 29, that Campbell portrays the common root of all creation by superimposing Edward Burne-Jones' angels walking down the steps in his 1880 painting *The Golden Stairs* onto the pattern of the DNA dual helix. In the upper part of the picture, a further image overlaps with these two, i.e. a line of tiny black silhouettes representing the characters quoted in the text: one holds a painting brush, another a pen, and the bent silhouette we identify as Watson is picking up the DNA pattern, seemingly fallen from the windblown tie of Crick, who appears wearing a tie with that same pattern on page 4. Last but not least, the bottom right corner of the page is occupied by a small reproduction of a panel from Winsor McCay's "Little Nemo in Slumberland," thus highlighting again the theme of dream and reminding the reader that comics have the right to be included in the field of artistic creation. Moreover, it might be worth remarking that in 1914, Winsor McCay used his first animated sequence for "Gertie the

Dinosaur" for performing in a vaudeville stage show, where he pretended to interact with the animal on the screen, eventually even pretending to walk into the very film.[7] For this reason, we could consider the reference to "Nemo" as a homage not only to one of the fathers of comics and animation, but also to a distinguished predecessor in connecting comic art and performance, although of a different kind.[8] The surface of the following page is occupied by other superimposed visuals, as the narration focuses here on Machen's meeting with the characters from his own work *The Three Impostors* (1895): "In Baghdad, Machen . . . is engaged in conversation with his own creations. . . . The written page becomes too frail a barrier. Things start to tear their way from the other side" (30). Campbell represents the crossing of the blurred border between fiction and reality by reproducing a torn fragment of a page from the *Impostors* and overlaying it with the figure of Machen and of the other characters enumerated by Moore's voice.

Section 4, (32-37) goes on in its development of the reflection on imagination to prepare the audience and the reader to their—and Machen's—final ascent to artistic ecstasy and the golden reign of Syon. This part of the monologue is centered on the difficulty of reaching the semi-divine, orgasmic state of mind to be identified with Syon, a state that can be attained only when silver and gold, i.e. lunar imagination and vision, and solar determination and radiance—also standing for traditional representations of the feminine and masculine principles—are intertwined and then totally blended into each other. The six pages which form this section are characterized by a peculiar layout: much of the available space is left empty and white, the drawings are bigger in size and this time there is no collage, no visual barrage as it often happened in the previous sections: this compensates for the increasing complexity and lyrical intensity of the script, and paves the way for the moment when "we step out in the white-hot streets of Syon. And in their radiance, we know ourselves" (37). Each page is occupied by a single image, which not only relates to the monologue, but which also expands and elaborates on the theme presented in the previous page. The section opens with a reproduction of the Tarot card for "Art" designed by Lady Frieda Harris:[9] the card depicts a two-faced woman whose dress is embroidered with snakes, as she bends over a goblet, side by side withe a lion and an eagle (32). The next page follows the monologue's reflection on man's imperative to rise and go beyond his earthly condition through imagination, inspired by the endless spiral of the DNA, and shows us two snakes, inextricably coiled as in Promethea's caduceus. Campbell fills the space between the coils with three images: the bars of the terrestrial prison in the lower part, the moon in the middle, and the sun in the higher part. Page 34 resumes the theme of the spiral and represents it in the form of a gold-and-silver chain—accompanied by the figures of

the lion and the eagle; "the burnished chain of difficult ideas our shaking ladder has become" (34) represents man's path toward Syon, and it becomes an actual ladder on page 35. As a consequence, pages 36 and 37 depict a small Machen, who finally reaches Syon after going through all the ups and downs of his existence—visually, after climbing a ladder on a huge Snakes and Ladders board, while the narrating voice, in accordance with the pattern it has followed throughout the work, reminds its audience that this abstract, universal experience is also *their* personal experience, taking place in *that* precise moment:

> It's April . . . all of us dragged from the vaults of the earth to see the sun again. . . . We remember what we are. . . . We are each other, are the dead and the living. We are Arthur Machen. . . . We are Dante Gabriel Rossetti. . . . And it is Now, and we are by this heat distilled, and it is Now forever (36-37).

The final "Syon" section (38-49) brings the movement between universality and historical/geographical specificity to its apex and conclusion. The initial description of the heavenly city is accompanied by an illustration which covers two full pages. The skyline of Syon, made both of historical and of industrial buildings rising on a pavement of York stone (38), is silhouetted in the distance against a white sky. The only characters on the pavement are a flower-girl and a customer, quoted in the monologue (39), and a reproduction of Botticelli's Venus, which can be seen as a symbol of birth, art, and creation. The massive shape of an insect stands out on the stone paving, probably the ant mentioned in the script—an obscure reference we might interpret as referring to the mythological figure of the ant as capable of communicating with the gods, as in Aztec and Tagalog cultures, or as the first human being, as in Hopi creation myths, which are but two of the many symbolic implications ascribed to insects throughout myth and history (Cherry and Kritsky, 2000). Finally conflating timelessness and history, the narrating voice then moves on to an overview on a space-time where "decade and distance are collapsed to a magnificent carnelian of Here and Now" (Moore and Campbell, 2001:40), thus placing Cain and Abel in contemporary London, evoking the Roman empire together with Dresden, Carthage, and Nagasaki, and finally shifting to King George the Fifth's funeral procession, which took place in Holborn in 1936 (40-41), to move on to a reflection on the Christian symbol of the cross and of the sacrifice of Christ, which in Western culture personifies the ultimate emblem for the fusion of the divine and the human, and for the path that reaches ecstasy through sacrifice (42-43).[10] These issues, once again, are visually rendered through the juxtaposition of panels in different styles and through the employment of photographs, while in the last pages of the book, Machen's progression towards mystic awakening after his descent into hallucination is mirrored by the gradual increase of white areas and by the respective decrease of words. The process culminates in the very last page, which contains neither words nor pictures, but only a blurred photograph of Red Lion Square—in color, so as to finally bring the reader back to his own time and reality (49) and to complete the audience and the reader's psychogeographical journey into man's existence.

CONCLUSION

The examples discussed in this short survey do not wholly account for the extreme complexity and density of **Snakes and Ladders.** However, they hopefully give some hints as to the main features of this comic book. Campbell's adaptation, therefore, must not be read as an attempt to substitute the performance, but as an alternative and just as effective way to convey the multi-sensory experience of the live act. Comics in **Snakes and Ladders** are really "transcending"; and, just like **Snakes and Ladders,** the title of this paper encompasses different layers of meaning. Reaching the apex of a long development which began in comics, with his reflection on psychogeography as related to identity, Moore has come to *transcend* the matter of much of his previous production, crossing the boundaries of story-telling to move into the field of narrative as connected to ideas and magic. He has then *transcended* the form of comics by shifting to the multimedia sphere: and **Snakes and Ladders,** thanks to Campbell's skillful interpretation, has moved back to comics, where after assimilating the multimedia experience, the medium is stretched, altered, and made to cross the borders of its formal conventions to try out its newly professed capabilities. **Snakes and Ladders,** therefore, can be seen as an example of Moore and Campbell's unflagging commitment to the expansion and innovation of the expressive potential of comics.

Notes

1. The reference to Iain Sinclair is particularly relevant, because he and Moore have now been acquainted for a long time and their interests often seem to run on parallel tracks. Moore has apparently drawn inspiration from Sinclair's *White Chappell, Scarlet Tracings* (1987) to outline Dr. Gull's route across London in *From Hell.* Moreover, Sinclair comes from a multimedia background in experimental filmmaking, and he has professed a deep fascination with the figure of Arthur Machen (Pilkington and Baker, 2001)—both features that connect him once again to Moore, as the following part of this essay will show.

2. Other interesting details on theater as an all-absorbing practice emerge from the theories elaborated by Eugenio Barba during his work with the Odin Teatret in Holstebro, Denmark. My reference, on this occasion, has been Taviani's *Il Libro dell' Odin: Il Teatro-Laboratorio di Eugenio Barba*; as an alternative, as there is no English translation of this volume. I would recommend Ian Watson's *Towards a Third Theatre: Eugenio Barba and the Odin Teatret* (see References).

3. Besides the two performances I have already mentioned, the others are *The Moon and Serpent Grand Egyptian Theater of Marvels* (1994), *The Highbury Working* (1997), and *Angel Passage* (2000). Additional information appears in the detailed bibliography to be found in the collection edited by George Khoury (2003:202-221).

4. For additional information on Moore's ironic cult of Glycon, see Campbell (2002:5).

5. Moore's legendary run of *Swamp Thing* went from 1983 to 1987 and is now published in collected volumes by DC Comics.

6. Of course, both these representations are part of a longer, older tradition of fantastic lunar journeys, starting with Lucian of Samosata's (AD 120-180) account of his *Trips to the Moon.* Lucian and other authors appear on the houseboat by the Moon citadel in *Promethea* Issue 14 (Moore, Williams, and Gray, 2002:44).

7. An excellent resource on Winsor McCay's (1869-1934) animation movies and art is the DVD *Animation Legend: Winsor McCay* (see References).

8. There is a long tradition of contacts between comics and performance, going from McCay through the "chalk talk" comic artists to experimental groups such as the Chicago-based *Live Action Cartoonists* (see References). As regards references on the connection between comics and live acts, I am indeed indebted to the comments and suggestions I got from Jeet Heer, both in his e-mails and in his contribution in panel discussions in the Comics Section at the PCA/ACA Conference, San Antonio, TX, April 7-10, 2004, where this paper was originally presented.

9. Lady Frieda Harris (1877-1962), a friend and collaborator of Aleister Crowley, designed and painted for him the set of Tarot cards known as the "Thoth deck."

10. Again, *Promethea* provides us with useful reference. In Issue 17, Promethea and her travelling companions witness the crucifixion and comment on Christ's sacrifice: "Crucifixion, it wasn't just, like, executin' somebody. It was something you'd do to a dog. . . . That's us up there, man" (Moore, Williams, and Gray, 2002:133). This same idea resonates, in more lyrical terms, in *Snakes and Ladders*—"In Syon, every incident is symbol, every symbol is immediate and real. . . . The symbol of divinity within mankind is crucified, a dog's death. . . . Oh Christ. Oh Christ in all of us" (Moore and Campbell, 2001:42-43).

References

Babcock, Jay. 2002. "The Rational Shaman." *LA Weekly.* <www.laweekly.com.

Beaton, Frank. 2003. "Snake Charmer: An Interview with Alan Moore." Part 1 & 2. *NinthArt.* <www.ninthart.com.

Blackton, Stuart, dir. 1997. *Animation Legend: Winsor McCay.* DVD. B/w, col., Lumivision.

Brook, Peter. 1978 [1968]. *The Empty Space.* New York: Atheneum. Campbell, Eddie. 2002. *Egomania.* 2:1-32.

Cherry, Ron and Gene Kritsky. 2000. *Insect Mythology.* New York: Writers Club Press.

Crafton, Donald. 1984 [1982]. *Before Mickey: The Animated Film. 1898-1928.* Cambridge, MA: The MIT Press.

Grotowski, Jerzy. 1975 [1968]. *Towards a Poor Theatre.* London: Methuen.

Khoury, George, ed. 2003. *The Extraordinary Works of Alan Moore.* Raleigh: Tomorrows.

Live Action Cartoonists. 2003. "Have Markers. Will Travel: Live Action Cartoonists in the Age of Multimedia Performances and Online Comics." *International Journal of Comic Art.* Spring:355-365.

McCloud, Scott. 1994 [1993]. *Understanding Comics: The Invisible Art.* New York: HarperCollins.

Meliès, George. 2002 [1902]. "Voyage dans la Lune". *The Movies Begin Vol. 1: The Great Train Robbery and Other Primary Works.* VHS. Dir. Edwin S. Porter, b/w, col., Kino Video.

Moore, Alan. 1996. *Voice of the Fire.* London: Gollancz.

Moore, Alan. 2001. "The Birth Caul" (essay). *Locus.* <www.locusplus.org

Moore, Alan and Eddie Campbell. 2000. *From Hell.* London: Knockabout.

Moore, Alan and Eddie Campbell. 1999. *The Birth Caul: A Shamanism of Childhood.* Originally staged at the Old County Court, Newcastle, UK. November 18, 1995. Paddington: Eddie Campbell Comics.

Moore, Alan and Eddie Campbell. 2001. *Snakes and Ladders.* Originally staged at Conway Hall, Red Lion Square, London, UK, April 10, 1999. Paddington: Eddie Campbell Comics.

Moore, Alan and Tim Perkins. 2003. *Snakes and Ladders.* Audio CD. Re: Records.

Moore, Alan and Bill Sienkiewicz. 1990. *Big Numbers.* Issue I. Northampton: Mad Love.

Moore, Alan, J. H. Williams III. and Mick Gray, 1999. *Promethea: Book 1.* La Jolla: America's Best Comics.

Moore, Alan, J. H. Williams III, and Mick Gray. 2001. *Promethea: Book 2.* La Jolla: America's Best Comics.

Moore, Alan, J. H. Williams III, and Mick Gray. 2002. *Promethea: Book 3.* La Jolla: America's Best Comics.

Moore, Alan, J. H. Williams III, and Mick Gray. 2003. *Promethea: Book 4.* La Jolla: America's Best Comics.

Pilkington, Mark and Baker, Phil. 2001. "City Brain: Iain Sinclair Interview." *Fortean Times,* <www.forteantimes.com/articles/147_iainsinclair.shtml.

Singer, Marc. 2003. "Unwrapping the Birth Caul," in smoky man and G. S. Millidge, eds. *Alan Moore: Portrait of an Extraordinary Gentleman.* Leigh-on-Sea: Abiogenesis, 41-46. And in: *International Journal of Comic Art.* Spring, 2004:236-249.

Taviani, Ferdinando, ed. 1975. *Il Libro dell' Odin: Il Teatro-Laboratorio di Eugenio Barba.* Milano: Feltrinelli.

Watson, Alasdair. 2001. "Camera Obscura: Charming the Snake." *NinthArt.* <www.ninthart.com.

Watson, Ian. 1993. *Towards a Third Theatre: Eugenio Barba and the Odin Teatret.* London and New York: Routledge.

FURTHER READING

Criticism

Ali, Barash. "The Violence of Criticism: The Mutilation and Exhibition of History in *From Hell.*" *Journal of Popular Culture* 38, no. 4 (2005): 605-31.

Provides a discussion of the differences between criticism aimed at traditional literature and that aimed at graphic novels, including an in-depth analysis of *From Hell.*

Cavanaugh, Tim. "Alan Moore Comes Like a Thief in the Night: A Writer With a Libertarian Following Delivers Some Flaccid Porn." *Reason* 38, no. 6 (November 2006): 78-9.

Pans Moore's *Lost Girls.*

Duralde, Alonso. "Awakenings: Alan Moore and Melinda Gebbie's *Lost Girls* Recasts *Alice in Wonderland, The Wizard of Oz,* and *Peter Pan* as Sexual Coming-of-Age Stories." *Advocate* 968, (15 August 2006): 76-7.

Review praises Moore's *Lost Girls.*

Flagg, Gordon. Review of *Top 10: Beyond the Farthest Precinct,* by Paul Di Filippo and illustrated by Jerry Ordway. *Booklist* 103, no. 1 (1 September 2006): 69.

Laments Moore's departure as author of the *Top 10* series.

Khoury, George, et al. *The Extraordinary Works of Alan Moore.* Raleigh, N.C., 2003, 224 p.

Provides a detailed overview of Moore's life and career, including interviews, tributes by colleagues, sketches, early stories, scripts, and other materials.

Mangels, Andy. From Queer to Eternity." *Advocate* (16 March 2004): 52-4.

Discusses the history of the creation of *The Mirror of Love*—originally a stage piece that accompanied Moore's poem—now adapted into book form with photographic pieces by José Villarrubia.

McConnell, Frank. "Comic Relief: From *Gilgamesh* to *Spider-Man*." *Commonweal* 119, no. 4 (28 February 1992): 21-2.

Asserts that some of the best contemporary literature is being presented in the form of comic books—or "graphic novels"—discussing *Dark Knight Returns*, by Frank Miller, *Sandman*, by Neil Gaiman, and *Watchmen*, by Moore, in support of this view.

Moore, Alan. "On Writing for Comics: Part One." *Comics Journal*, no. 119 (January 1988): 91-5.

The first of a three-part installment, slightly revised from its original form in Fantasy Advertiser, in which Moore discusses the craft of writing good stories.

———, and Gary Groth. "Alan Moore: Last Big Words." *Comics Journal*, no. 140 (February 1991): 72-85.

Provides an extensive interview in which Moore discusses *Marvelman, Watchmen, From Hell, V for Vendetta*, and other works.

———, and Gary Groth. "Mainstream Comics Have, at Best, Tenuous Virtues." *Comics Journal*, no. 152 (August 1992): 89-100.

Extensive interview in which Moore discusses the state of mainstream comics, the competing major comic-book publishers, leading titles, and other comic works, writers, and artists.

———, Guy Lawley, and Steve Whitaker, et al. "Writer: Alan Moore." *Comics Interview*, no. 12, (June 1984): 5-25.

Extensive interview in which Moore discusses *Marvelman, Swamp Thing*, horror comics, *V for Vendetta*, and other topics.

———, and Christopher Sharrett. "Writer: Alan Moore Interview." *Comics Interview*, no. 65 (1988): 5-23.

Extensive, in-depth interview in which Moore discusses major themes, political implications, morality, and other topics in *Watchmen*, as well as his relationship with Frank Miller and other creators in the comic book industry.

———, and Bhob Stewart. "Synchronicity and Symmetry." *Comics Journal*, no. 116 (July 1987): 89-95.

Interview in which Moore discusses various aspects of the story-within-a-story told in *Watchmen*, along with a brief commentary on the "Pog" storyline from *Swamp Thing*.

Raiteri, Steve. Review of *Supreme: The Story of the Year*, by Alan Moore, et al. *Library Journal* 128, no. 4 (1 March 2003): 75.

Applauds Moore's lovingly satiric look at the comics industry.

———. Review of *The League of Extraordinary Gentlemen, Vol. 2*, by Alan Moore; illustrated by Kevin O'Neill. *Library Journal* 129, no. 4 (1 March 2004): 62.

Praises the second volume of *The League of Extraordinary Gentlemen* but finds the work less compelling than the first volume.

Roberts, Jason. "V vs. V: Book or Movie?" *America's Intelligence Wire* (22 March 2006).

Provides a summary of the *V for Vendetta* graphic novel which served as source material for the movie, praising both book and film, but asserting that the book is ultimately superior and more satisfying.

Rodi, Rob. "Cruel Britannia." *Comics Journal*, no. 142 (June 1991): 41-7.

Provides positive reviews of *The New Adventures of Hitler*, by Grant Morrison, and *From Hell*, by Moore, praising each for attention to historical detail.

Wolk, Douglas. "Alan Moore's 'Literary Pornography.'" *Publishers Weekly* 235, no. 18 (1 May 2006):22-3.

Provides an overview of the history of the writing and creation of *Lost Girls*, the controversy surrounding the pornographic content of this work, and the decisions and companies involved in publishing it.

Additional coverage of Moore's life and career is contained in the following sources published by Thomson Gale: *Authors and Artists for Young Adults*, Vol. 51; *Contemporary Authors*, Vol. 204; *Contemporary Authors New Revision Series*, Vol. 138; *Dictionary of Literary Biography*, Vol. 261; *Literature Resource Center*; *Major 21st-Century Writers*, (eBook) 2005; and *St. James Guide to Science Fiction Writers*, Ed. 4.

Quentin Tarantino
1963-

(Full name Quentin Jerome Tarantino) American screenwriter and director.

The following entry provides an overview of Tarantino's career through 2006. For additional information on his life and works, see *CLC*, Volume 125.

INTRODUCTION

Among the most successful American filmmakers to have emerged in the 1990s, Tarantino gained his reputation directing offbeat, darkly satiric films including *Reservoir Dogs* (1992), *Pulp Fiction* (1994), and *Jackie Brown* (1997), in addition to more recent films: *Kill Bill, Vol. 1* (2003) and *Kill Bill, Vol. 2* (2004). Initially considered a new renegade force in Hollywood, Tarantino has earned large box office receipts and cult adoration. Critics and audiences have grown to recognize his use of extraordinary (but sometimes humorously rendered) violence, long sequences of dialogue in which characters examine mundane subjects in exhaustive detail, and a glorification of popular culture in general and B-movies in particular. Aside from the quality of his movies, Tarantino has attracted attention due to his success outside of the Hollywood mainstream as a video store clerk-cum-independent filmmaker. As such he has inspired other aspiring filmmakers and has enjoyed enormous financial and critical rewards—*Pulp Fiction* won the Palme d'Or at the Cannes Film Festival and the Academy Award for Best Screenplay Written Directly for the Screen, among other prizes. Tarantino has emerged, as he observed somewhat derisively in a 1997 interview with *New York Times Magazine,* as "an adjective": "Every third script out there," he has said, "is described as 'Tarantino-esque.'"

BIOGRAPHICAL INFORMATION

Born in 1963 in Knoxville, Tennessee, and reportedly named for Burt Reynolds's character "Quint Asper" in the 1950s television series *Gunsmoke,* Tarantino grew up in California. In 1965 his mother separated from his father and moved west, bringing two-year-old Tarantino with her. Tarantino's mother, who would later become a corporate executive, settled in Harbor City, a middle-class neighborhood. The city bordered on less affluent areas, including the town of Carson where Tarantino

regularly attended movies. Though considered a bright child, Tarantino suffered from hyperactivity and performed poorly in school. Finally, having failed several grades, he dropped out of the ninth grade and then worked as an usher at a pornographic movie theatre. He studied acting, but with the exception of a brief part as an Elvis impersonator on the television show *The Golden Girls* in 1990, he achieved little success as an actor. Though he has since acted in a number of movies, most of these roles have been either in his own films or as cameos in those of others. At age twenty-two, Tarantino worked at Video Archives, a video store in the Los Angeles area. The job, which he held for five years, gave him exposure to a wide variety of films, and he and coworker Roger Avary—another future filmmaker who co-wrote the screenplay for *Pulp Fiction*—would often watch four movies a day. In 1990, Tarantino and Avary left to work with producer John Langley, a regular customer of the video store, and moved to Hollywood. There they began developing key contacts, most notably with producer Lawrence Bender. After raising $1.5 million—in film terms, a shoestring budget—they made *Reservoir Dogs,* which subsequently earned many times that sum. The resulting critical attention propelled Tarantino to stardom on a level seldom enjoyed by those outside of mainstream Hollywood. Director Tony Scott bought one of Tarantino's screenplays which became the film *True Romance* (1993). Tarantino also wrote the story for Oliver Stone's *Natural Born Killers* (1994), although he later disagreed with Stone's interpretation and disclaimed all involvement in the resulting film. Tarantino managed to make his next film, *Pulp Fiction,* with the relatively small budget of $8 million. The release of this film brought Tarantino even greater critical and commercial success. Along with his emerging notoriety, Tarantino began to establish himself as a capable Hollywood businessman. Having formed A Band Apart in 1991—a production company—he later created commercial and music subsidiaries, and in 1995 established Rolling Thunder, a specialty distribution company. During the mid-1990s, Tarantino played small roles in the making of several films, including an uncredited rewrite on Scott's *Crimson Tide* in 1995. He also worked with Robert Rodriguez on the film *From Dusk Till Dawn* (1996). Rodriguez is an independent filmmaker best known for the film *El Mariachi.* The U.S. version of the film *Desperado* also featured a cameo by Tarantino. In 1997, Tarantino released his third movie as screenwriter and director,

Jackie Brown, based on Elmore Leonard's 1992 novel *Rum Punch.* In 2003 Tarantino wrote his first novel, *Kill Bill,* and adapted the story to film in two parts: *Kill Bill, Vol. 1* and *Kill Bill, Vol. 2.* Tarantino ventured into television in 2005, writing and directing a season finale for "CSI: Crime Scene Investigation."

MAJOR WORKS

Tarantino's films often acknowledge other directors' work; for example, reviewers have drawn connections between *Reservoir Dogs* and Stanley Kubrick's *The Killing* (1956), also a dispassionate postmortem of a robbery. In Tarantino's film, an aging crime boss gathers a group of criminals, giving them color-coded names—Mr. Blonde, Mr. Pink, Mr. Brown, et. al.—in order to protect their identities. The criminals plan a jewelry store robbery not knowing that one member of the group is an undercover police officer. The robbery, which is never depicted, goes terribly wrong. The film plays with time, shifting backward and forward, from a long scene in a pancake house before the robbery to a short vignette of a horribly wounded gangster just after it. After a series of temporal disjunctions, the action ultimately returns to a warehouse where the robbers have gathered to square off against one another in an attempt to find the traitor. The film's stylistic touches include brutal violence played out against a 1970s musical soundtrack; the use of matching anonymous black suits by the color-designated robbers; and long quasi-philosophical discussions which take place in the stage-like warehouse, offering notable counterpoints. *True Romance* similarly involves a crime, or series of crimes, that have gone wrong; but whereas *Reservoir Dogs* revolves around a world of men without the benefit of female characters, a love story lies at the center of *True Romance.* The central figures are Clarence and a prostitute named Alabama who fall in love. When Clarence kills Alabama's pimp and steals a bag containing a fortune in cocaine, the couple is forced on a cross-country race to evade federal agents and escape a crime boss determined to retrieve the drugs and eliminate them. Like *Reservoir Dogs, True Romance* concludes with a violent and bloody "Mexican standoff," a common feature of Tarantino's films. *Pulp Fiction,* in contrast, actually begins with events leading up to a standoff, but in a "Tarantino-esque" inversion of time sequence, the viewer will not return to the opening scene, and thus see the consequences of the standoff, until the very end of the movie. Several plots comprise *Pulp Fiction,* most of them surrounding a drug lord named Marsellus. One major subplot involves two hitmen, Vincent Vega (played by John Travolta), and Jules Winnfield (played by Samuel L. Jackson), who are employed by Marsellus (Ving Rhames). Another plot centers on Marsellus's alluring wife who suffers a near-fatal heroin overdose while out on a date with Vega;

and yet another sequence involves a boxer named Butch (played by Bruce Willis) who double-crosses Marsellus and flees for his life, only to find himself in a position to save the man who wants him killed. In the final scene, Jules makes a decision to leave his life of crime; the audience has already seen a segment that takes place later in time in which Vincent Vega confronts the results of his own refusal to do the same. Tarantino and three other directors each created segments for *Four Rooms* (1995). Tarantino's section, "The Man from Hollywood," revolves around an attempt to reenact a hair-raising scene from an Alfred Hitchcock television show in which Steve McQueen bets Peter Lorre his little finger than he can get his lighter to light ten times in a row. In *From Dusk Till Dawn* Tarantino's tale presents an unusual combination of a straightforward bank robber getaway story with a tale of Mexican vampires. His next film, *Jackie Brown,* features an underpaid flight attendant, Jackie (Pam Grier) who earns extra money by helping an arms dealer, Ordell (played by Samuel Jackson), launder money. When the police catch Jackie, Ordell fears that she will turn him in, and he wants to eliminate her. Several other subplots focus on a tender-hearted bail bondsman who comes to Jackie's rescue, and federal agents who goad her into helping them. All of her adversaries underestimate Jackie, as a sequence surrounding the transfer of a bag containing money—a scene shot from three different points of view—serves to illustrate. Despite this experimental use of time, the film follows an essentially linear progression of events, relying upon fewer temporal shifts and more complex character development than *Reservoir Dogs* and *Pulp Fiction.* The films *Kill Bill, Vol. 1* and *Kill Bill, Vol. 2* center on a character known as The Bride (Uma Thurman), a former member of a group of female assassins called the Deadly Viper Assassination Squad, or DIVAS. The Bride's colleagues have massacred her family and friends on her wedding day, leaving her for dead. The two films follow her as she seeks revenge against the other assassins and hunts down Bill (played by David Carradine), the head of the organization. The pictures pay homage to various genres including martial arts films, westerns, blaxploitation films, and anime.

CRITICAL RECEPTION

Many reviewers have criticized Tarantino for what they consider an excessive use of violence in his films. As critics widely note, one of the shocking moments in *Reservoir Dogs* is a gruesome scene in which Mr. Blonde slices off a police officer's ear while the 1970s musical hit "Stuck in the Middle with You" is heard in the background. Likewise, *Pulp Fiction* features a brutal sado-masochistic rape scene, and a long list of murdered cast members. Tarantino's penchant for violence and degradation has prompted certain critics to compare his early work to French dramatist Antonin Artaud's

Theater of Cruelty. Some reviewers have responded to criticism of the gratuitous violence in Tarantino's films by pointing out that the bloodshed reflects the underlying themes of his movies. Theresa Duncan stated "For Tarantino, violent genre films seemed to respond with honesty and immediacy to a culture undergoing wrenching social change." Duncan continues by referencing Tarantino's latest work, asserting that "[T]he constant slashing, stabbing, beating, chopping, slicing, beheading, disemboweling, kicking, and crushing of *Kill Bill* forms a sort of 4/4 backbeat as thirty years of Hollywood culture are updated in a breathless rush." Critics have also observed that Tarantino's attitude towards pop culture, including B-movies, old TV shows, and other paraphernalia of mass media, wavers between veneration and satire. The opening scene of *Reservoir Dogs,* in which Mr. Brown (played by Tarantino himself) offers a memorable exegesis of Madonna's 1985 hit song "Like a Virgin," and the long discussion about cheeseburgers between the two hitmen in *Pulp Fiction* are frequently cited as emblematic of his style. Tarantino's contributions to *True Romance* and *Four Rooms* were panned by most reviewers, and *From Dusk Till Dawn* received mixed assessment. While Tarantino's detractors dismiss his work as derivative, sensational, and nihilistic, others have praised his films, asserting they contain eccentric humor, biting wit, and unpretentious democratic perspective. As Tarantino commented in a 1997 interview with the *New York Times Magazine*: "I don't believe in elitism. I don't think the audience is this dumb person lower than me. I am the audience." Critics have also celebrated Tarantino's style, with Stephen Weinberger noting "it seems that style is what attracts the attention of critics, scholars, and actors. Tarantino's gift for writing remarkable dialogue, his use of violence, his nonlinear chronology, and his ability to create rich and interesting characters are so striking and powerful that they dominate the discussion."

PRINCIPAL WORKS

Reservoir Dogs [screenwriter with Roger Avary] (film) 1992

True Romance [screenwriter] (film) 1993

Natural Born Killers [story] (film) 1994

Pulp Fiction [screenwriter with Roger Avary; director] (film) 1994

Four Rooms [screenwriter and director with Alexandre Rockwell, Allison Anders, and Robert Rodriguez] (film) 1995

From Dusk Till Dawn [screenwriter with Robert Kurtzman] (film) 1996

Jackie Brown [screenwriter and director] (film) 1997

Kill Bill, Vol. 1 [screenwriter and director] (film) 2003

Kill Bill, Vol. 2 [screenwriter and director] (film) 2004

CRITICISM

Fred Botting and Scott Wilson (essay date 1998)

SOURCE: Botting, Fred, and Scott Wilson. "By Accident: The Tarantinian Ethics." *Theory, Culture & Society* 15, no. 2 (1998): 89-113.

[*In the following essay, Botting and Wilson explore Tarantino's conceptualization of ethics via psychoanalytic theory.*]

> . . . the question of ethics is to be articulated from the point of view of the location of man in relation to the real.
>
> (Lacan, 1992: 11)

HOLY SHIT

'Holy shit.' Butch Coolidge, returning to his apartment to collect his father's watch, notices a Czech M61 submachine gun on his kitchen counter. Gingerly, he picks it up. Then his toilet flushes. Butch freezes. The bathroom door opens and Vincent Vega comes out fastening his trousers. They lock eyes in an unexpected stand-off: two mute protagonists and one silenced machine gun. But nothing happens.

Suddenly two 'Pop Tarts' are ejected from the toaster, Butch's finger hits the trigger and the gun unloads a muffled volley of bullets into Vincent. It is Vincent's last encounter with the shock of accidental discharge.

But not his first, which also involves an unexpected emergence from a bathroom. This near-fatal encounter happens in the conclusion to the scene which immediately follows *Pulp Fiction*'s credit sequence, when Jules and he repossess Marsellus Wallace's briefcase. The conclusion is played out much later in the movie, after the fatal encounter with Butch. Having apparently finished their job in an explosion of retributive violence Vincent and Jules prepare to leave, but a 'Fourth Man' dashes from the bathroom screaming 'die . . . die . . . die . . . die . . . !' and discharges every bullet from his revolver. Astonishingly, neither Jules nor Vincent are hit. As confused as the fourth man, they nonetheless retaliate with greater accuracy. The fourth man's miss, however, provokes consternation in Jules: 'We should be fuckin' dead!', he repeats. Evidently unexplainable by reason, Vincent appeals to chance: 'Yeah, we were lucky.' But luck is not sufficient for Jules: 'That shit wasn't luck. That shit was somethin' else.' For Jules, all doubt vanishes; it is clearly a case of divine intervention. While Vincent shrugs it off and prepares to leave, Jules insists:

> Don't do that! Don't fuckin' do that! Don't blow this shit off! What just happened was a fuckin' miracle!

VINCENT

> Chill the fuck out, Jules, this shit happens.

JULES

> Wrong, wrong, this shit doesn't just happen.
>
> (Tarantino, 1994b: 139)

The shit constitutes a moment of sacred excess, holy shit. For Vincent, the inexplicability of the event is put down, with professional equanimity, to chance and accident; for Jules it becomes a revelatory moment that alters his life for good. While he is normally a terrifying, if indifferent, embodiment of Old Testament justice, Jules decides, as a result of God's divine intervention, to paradoxically renounce His law by quitting what he now perceives to be a 'shit job'. In the final scene of *Pulp Fiction,* still discussing the implications of the 'miracle', Jules determines to walk the earth 'until God puts me where he wants me to be'. And God, psychoanalysis makes plain, is unconscious.

While Jules gives up on the law, he does not give up on himself or his desire: 'I'll just be Jules, Vincent—no more, no less' (1994b: 174). Jules's ethical turn means, for his partner, that he will become a 'bum', a 'piece of shit' outside the proper social order of 'job, residence or legal tender'. Jules, however, is serenely beyond the reach of these materialist reservations. Abruptly, Vincent interrupts the discussion in the diner in order to visit, appropriately enough, the bathroom: leaving Jules alone, he inadvertently gives him the opportunity to complete his first ethical act.

The diner in which Jules and Vincent are breakfasting turns out to be the very one which opens the movie, scene of Pumpkin's and Honey Bunny's robbery. Confronting Jules, Pumpkin demands the briefcase and, while mesmerized by its contents, finds Jules's gun in his face. But Jules holds his fire. Normally Pumpkin and his partner would be by now, as Jules notes, as 'dead as fuckin' chicken'. However, he happens to be, as he says, in a 'transitional period' and wants to help them. Nonetheless, he refuses to hand over the case: 'I went through too much shit this morning on account of this case to just hand it over to your ass' (1994b: 183). Some things, it appears, are not exchangeable. He resolves the stand-off by giving money to Pumpkin so that he is not obliged to kill him. An economic exchange is substituted for the absolute expenditure heralded by

the words attributed to the book of Ezekiel 25: 17. The chilling speech that previously announced the violent explosion of execution is now reinterpreted by Jules: he calls the fatal words of moral law into question, a questioning that underlines his ethical action. The miraculous encounter and its ethical conclusion chart the righteous path determined by 'holy shit'.

Shit, of course, is not always holy. It pervades *Pulp Fiction* in diverse ways, signifying both the sacred dimension that transforms Jules's life and gives it meaning and the excrescence of the profane or abject world inhabited by the secular Vincent. For the latter shit connotes those objects cast out by the everyday sphere of existence: the faeces which he expels with such regularity, the accidental splatter of Marvin's brains which needs to be cleaned up and the bum that Jules intends to become. Shit, moreover, interrupts the predictable course of his existence, fatally, with Vincent's last bowel movement. Excluded, shit nonetheless dominates everyday existence, the word is applied to the commodities of conventional and prohibited satisfaction: the 'same shit' embraces burgers, colas, cocaine and heroin, and glazes the consummate object of desire, Marsellus' briefcase itself, with an indescribable faecal attraction. Shit, marker of desire and consumption, figures as an excess that pervades the same, a heterogeneous point of a-valuation integral to junk culture. It applies, moreover, to the symbolic as much as to the consumer and the black economies represented in the movies, pertaining, also, to names and meanings: in America, Butch informs his taxi driver, 'names don't mean shit'. Shit, then, articulates the everyday, symbolic reality dominated by consumption with something else, something excessive, wasteful, unpredictable, something that both interrupts and causes action. Fatally, for Vincent, it is the sudden ejection of Pop Tarts that triggers the explosive discharge of the machine gun's 'holy shit'.

'Accidents happen', is Clarence's tolerant reaction to having popcorn spilt on him in *True Romance.* 'What a wonderful philosophy', Alabama observes (Tarantino, 1995: 38). Accidents dominate and direct Tarantino's narratives. In *Pulp Fiction* accidents, from the ejection of Pop Tarts, to the forgetting of a gold watch and the various guns that, almost by themselves, go off, cause unpredictable narrative turns. In *True Romance* the recovery of the wrong suitcase precipitates the entire action while in *Natural Born Killers* the prison riot becomes the lucky or fateful aid to escape, just as the late night noise in Mickey Knox's house causes him to make his visit to a gun shop, a visit that becomes, retrospectively, a determining moment, one that, as with Jules's revelation by (gun)fire, alters his life irrevocably. In *Reservoir Dogs,* too, events do not follow a planned, predictable course: the robbery goes catastrophically awry in a manner that shapes the course of the story. Accidents happen, the unexpected occurs to transform, and also constitute, the diegetical order of things. Taran-tino's narratives, then, hardly follow a conventional narrative course: disparate scenes only belatedly tell the story through the articulation of accident and misadven-ture. The various threads that are eventually knotted together accentuate the retrospective significance of the unexpected events and interruptions: meaning always comes later, subordinated to the chains of discrete and associated images.

But *Tarantinian Ethics*? Tarantino *and* ethics? Tarantino and ethics *and* psychoanalysis? These appear strange conjunctions to say the least, given the movies' presentations of shocking violence which, for some, is taken to the point of sadism and amorality; their strange-ness is only exacerbated by the apparent distance between the ethical concern with the good and the focus of psychoanalysis on desire. Is this connection purely perverse? Possibly. However, the violent yoking of heterogeneous topics, overriding their apparent incom-mensurability, begins to disclose the heterogeneity and strangeness at the core of ethical and psychoanalytical questioning. Both discourses address the Other, just as both turn on an encounter that is simultaneously disrup-tive and constitutive, an encounter experienced as traumatic that takes the form of an unexpected accident or calamity which shatters even as it founds subjectivity in relation to something intimate yet inexplicable, something in and in excess of the subject.

In recent years, the work of the French philosopher Emmanuel Levinas has become central to ethical think-ing, displacing the conventional concerns of ethics with moral agency, with rights and justice, on to the singular-ity of the demand of responsibility towards the ultimate unknowability of 'the other'. For Levinas, the encounter with the utter alterity of the other person also happens by chance, an accident that then has determining ef-fects: 'one approaches the other perhaps in contingency, but henceforth one is not free to move away from him' (1989a: 117). Ethics depends on this unpredictable, ac-cidental encounter with something Other for it consti-tutes an absolute ethical difference from the realm of morality and law. Levinas makes the difference explicit:

> By morality I mean a series of rules relating to social behaviour and civic duty. But while morality thus oper-ates in the socio-political order of organizing and improving our human survival, it is ultimately founded on an ethical responsibility towards the other. As *prima philosophia*, ethics cannot itself legislate for society or produce the rules of conduct whereby society might be revolutionized or transformed. It does not operate at the level of the manifesto or *call to order*; it is not a *savoir vivre*.
>
> (1986: 29)

Ethics takes the form of a 'dis-interestedness' opposed to the 'interestedness' of the world of political and social exchanges ruled by morality. Beyond morality,

however, ethical norms provide the foundation for judgement and discrimination; as foundational, they are exterior, heterogeneous points in excess of moral and political laws. Surprisingly perhaps, ethics are a-moral, a-political, the 'a' marking the point of exclusion that indicates a locus altogether different from the laws governing everyday activity in the world: 'ethics is not a moment of being; it is otherwise and better than be-ing, the very possibility of the beyond' (1989b: 179). The glimpse of the beyond as something sublime and elevating happens in the traumatic encounter with the Other: 'the proximity of the neighbour in its trauma does not only strike up against me, but exalts and elevates me . . .' (1989a: 113-14).

In psychoanalysis the traumatic encounter and the pres-ence of the Other make themselves felt in a similar way. Everyday reality, the world inhabited by individual subjects, is regulated by symbolic codes through signi-fiers of difference, desire and prohibition that are structured in relation to a gap, the real and an object— *objet petit a*—which fills it. For Jacques Lacan, reality is not the real: the latter remains unsymbolizable even though it has disarming effects. The real is experienced only as trauma, chance, accident, an unpredictable ir-ruption (into the symbolic world of ordered existence or the imaginary sense of individual unity) of an event that cannot be accounted for and can only be belatedly explained. Thus the ejection of Pop Tarts functions as a little piece of the real that breaks into the frozen and ordered stand-off between Butch and Vincent. The unbelievable miss-firing of the fourth man becomes a traumatic experience that causes Jules to reassess his old life and begin anew. The real introduces something other into symbolic or imaginary orders, exceeding their capacity for representation and the command of the paternal figure at their apex. Accidents, chance and excess lie beyond the world of regulated desire and law to remain unpresentable, occupying a hollow within and without the desires and laws they found.

Ethical questions surrounding the law and the unpre-sentable have become more pressing since Jean-François Lyotard diagnosed the crisis resulting from the general 'incredulity towards metanarratives' that characterizes 'the postmodern condition' (1984: xxiv). The incredulity signals a separation between conven-tional systems of meaning—science, rationality, moral-ity, history—and the subjects for whom these 'grand narratives' once established a place, an identity and a direction. The separation which devolves into a series of disparate and competing small narratives testifies to a rift, an unpresentable sublime rupture in the narrative orders of knowledge, being, culture and society. Ethics has come to the fore then, precisely because of the ad-dress to what is most at stake in a post- or hyper-modern society. Ethical enquiry, for John Rajchman, in an essay on ethics and psychoanalysis, 'involves a "suspiciousness" about received values' (1991: 175). Ethics raises the question of 'how to be "at home" in a world where our identity is not given, our being-together in question, our destiny contingent and uncertain: the world of the violence of our self-constitution' (1991: 144). If contemporary spectres of contingency, uncertainty and violence turn on questions of identity, being and society, those questions inevitably receive numerous conflicting responses.

Zygmunt Bauman concludes his account of postmodern ethics, which throughout argues for a morally responsible self, by contrasting moral matters with 'the ethics of socially conventionalized and rationally "founded" norms', reversing the meaning of the distinction given to morality and ethics by Levinas. To reject socially sanctioned ethics, he argues, need not contradict the importance of morality: 'far from excluding each other, the two can be accepted or rejected only together. If in doubt—consult your conscience' (1993: 250). Even the most sophisticated critiques of post/modernity cannot help but appeal, in the most unsophisticated way, to a centre, a homogenized and homogenizing self that is grounded in experience and self-knowledge, intimately sure of the truth of its own moral conscience. From a psychoanalytical perspective, however, the return to conscience, the point of individual suture with the moral law, presents an invocation of the superego, a figure that powerfully subjects beings to the imperatives of the symbolic order. Which is to say that, in psychoanalysis, the superego remains manifestly unethical. Slavoj Zizek argues that Lacan resists the truism that binds the superego to ethics as conscience. In opposition to the superegoic obedience to morality, an obedience which may occlude an underlying 'obscene enjoyment', ethics, while violating moral norms, may, nonetheless, distinguish actions adhering to higher principles and a refusal to give up on one's desire. Hence the 'radical exclusion' between ethics and the superego in which the latter dominates a 'vicious cycle': 'the more we submit ourselves to the superego imperative, the greater its pressure, the more we feel guilty' (1993: 67). There is no exit from this guilty cycle:

> . . . our sacrificing to the superego, our paying tribute to it, only corroborates our guilt. For that reason our debt to the superego is unredeemable: the more we pay it off, the more we owe. Superego is like the extortioner slowly bleeding us to death—the more he gets, the stronger his hold on us.

> (Zizek, 1993: 68)

This describes what Rajchman eloquently calls 'the *gourmandise* of the super-ego—the more you feed it the more it wants' (1991: 58). Desire, in its superegoic manifestation, thus offers an image that conjoins consumption and capitalism in terms of an insistent, voracious want.

Psychoanalysis offers a different perspective on ethics, a perspective that turns on desire but glimpses 'something in our desire that goes beyond what would direct us to what we think we want for ourselves' (Rajchman, 1991: 36). Here, for Rajchman, lies the difficulty and the strangeness of the relation between ethics and psychoanalysis: 'For Freud, our *eros* is at odds with our *ethos*; its occurrence in our lives is always *unheimlich*' (1991: 47). For Lacan, moral law 'is simply desire in its pure state' (1977c: 275). The implications of the conjunction of desire and law present difficulties which Rajchman contends are a matter of ethics, a demonstration of the ethical problem of how to speak truly of oneself. With the introduction of the unconscious, Freud's thought reveals itself as an ethical 'event'. Characterizing the unconscious as gap, impediment, split, Lacan dissociates it from being: 'the status of the unconscious, which, as I have shown, is so fragile on the ontic plane, is ethical' (1977c: 133). Psychoanalytical ethics, Rajchman suggests, does not set out to distinguish passion and reason:

> . . . for its aim is not to make us more virtuous citizens or more productive workers. It is not an attempt to insure that our actions contribute to the good of all, or of determining which principles we cannot rationally disagree with. It is not an aim that can be realized through the institution of positive laws or moral sanctions.

> (1991: 20-1)

Departing from the traditional trajectory of ethical concerns with virtue, the good or obligation, psychoanalysis discloses something that ceaselessly troubles consciousness, 'something that goes "beyond" what the mind conceives or calculates as its good' (1991: 25-6). This is Lacan's point:

> . . . namely that ethics cannot derive from pure obligation. Man in his acts tends towards a good. Analysis puts desire back into favor as the principle of ethics. Even censorship, at first the only thing of desire to figure as morality, draws all its energy from it. There is no other root of ethics.

> (Rajchman, 1991: 31)

By way of an illustration, what follows is a reading of *Reservoir Dogs* that pursues the moebial unfolding of desire and the law as it circulates around the void disclosed by accident: the trauma to which the movie's narrative continually returns, the irruption of the real that demands an ethical response.

BLACK SCREEN

Disorientation. The opening sequence of *Reservoir Dogs* in Uncle Bob's Pancake House shows a series of banal, ribald and comic exchanges between eight men dressed in black suits: professional men. They pay the bill and leave to the purposeful backbeat of 'Little Green Bag': 'Let's go to work.' Credits roll, the screen goes black and the screaming starts.

Something has gone wrong.

Between the familiarity of the first scene and the agony of the second a gulf has emerged, a gap, a black screen determining the structure of the movie. The unspeakable and unseen event—the job gone wrong—remains unrepresented. The event constitutes the point of trauma as it introduces something unexpected and profoundly disorientating into the workaday world of ordinary life and the everyday work of visual narrative: 'this is so fucked up' (Tarantino, 1994a: 41). The order sustaining continuity and intelligibility has fragmented. Instead of a single sequence of predictable scenes, there looms only the blackness of the inexplicable demanding to be understood, demanding to be reconstructed so that the narrative can be restored and positions, meanings and actions recognizably plotted. Panic, violence and paranoia take centre stage as a variety of interpretations of events are offered and various courses of action are suggested: the probability of a betrayal, the abandonment of the plan, immediate flight, conspire to undermine the rules of this particular professional game. The aftermath of the catastrophic robbery only allows for the emergence of fragments, flashbacks, partial histories, all limited attempts to chart a sequence of events whose cause is unknown.

Black screen, site for an unvisualizable projection, a gap constitutive of visibility. The real emerges in the gap determining the course of the movie. As that which 'resists symbolization absolutely' (Lacan, 1988: 39), the real only appears as a blackness, that empty screen to which the drama repeatedly returns. The fissure in visual representation is itself without fissure, continuous in its blackness. It functions, in the experience of ***Reservoir Dogs,*** as in psychoanalytical experience, 'in the form of that which is *unassimilable* in it—in the form of trauma, determining all that follows, and imposing on it an apparently accidental origin' (Lacan, 1977c: 55). As *tuché* 'the real is beyond the *automaton,* the return, the coming-back, the insistence of signs, by which we see ourselves governed by the pleasure principle. The real is that which lies behind the *automaton . . .*' (Lacan, 1977c: 53-4). ***Reservoir Dogs*** stages and restages the insistence of signs as they repeatedly return to the point of trauma, the failed heist. Experienced as trauma, the real engenders repetition, a repetition of signifiers in the form of theories about traitors, arguments and apportionings of blame and efforts at explaining events. The partial, repetitive, retroactive reconstructions fail to deliver any truth, origin or meaning, but disclose a sequence of accidents: the alarm is triggered, Blonde starts shooting, a woman dies, the police appear in numbers, robbers are shot or flee. Further accidents

testify to the utter disintegration of the plan, as envisaged both by the robbers and the police, for a successful robbery and unimpeded arrival at the warehouse: members of the gang and the LAPD die; Orange, the undercover cop, is shot by and kills a woman during the escape; Blonde arrives at the warehouse with a 'surprise'—a uniformed policeman, bound and gagged in the trunk of his car. The world of professional men, police and criminals alike, encounters the real in the form of accidents, unpredicted events which only retrospectively assume meaning in the scripted scheme of things.

The non-sense of the accidental, which irrupts during and after the job, distinguishes a realm beyond reason and order that cannot be contained or fully explained. That there is a madness to this non-sense emerges in the significance of the psychotic Mr Blonde. His trigger-happy response to the alarm is, if not irrational, certainly unprofessional. It also triggers the general madness of shooting. But before anything like an intelligible sequence of events can be established, the action of the film undergoes a series of loops around the real, a hole in representation. Linked to the drive, the accidents, noises and small bits of reality that puncture conventional sequential narrative disclose 'the other reality hidden behind the lack of that which takes the place of representation' (Lacan, 1977c: 60). These loops take the form of a series of narrative, temporal and psychological regressions. As in a conventional cinematic narrative, the flashbacks return to scenes prior to both the opening of the movie and the trauma of the robbery. They belatedly develop 'character' and suggest motives and explanations, looking for some cause to the narration. A pre-history of the catastrophe is sketched in for the audience, a history that starts to fill in the gaps, that begins to piece together some meaning in the form of an identification of possible reasons, a reconnection of the symbolic threads binding the protagonists together.

The retrospective movement that is concerned with cause and character, a movement around a central gap, foregrounds the writerliness of Tarantino's movies. In an interview Tarantino explicitly compares his script-writing to the work of a novelist:

> I wanted the whole movie to be about an event we don't see, and I wanted it to take place at the rendezvous at the warehouse—what would normally be given ten minutes in a heist film. I wanted the whole movie to be set there and to play with a real-time clock as opposed to a movie clock ticking. I also wanted to introduce these guys in a series of chapters. Like, when you're reading a book. . . .

> (1994a: xiii)

In ***Reservoir Dogs,*** the writerly movement is driven by the trauma that is only retroactively, and partially, explained: the repeated efforts that, in the wake of the disintegration of the boss's plan, try to repair the torn fabric of the symbolic order with more and more signification, returning to something, some 'thing' that remains beyond rationalization or control. The lack in representation determines the course of the narrative: it is both ruptured and caused by an unknown something; its originary form appears as repetition. The black screen, then, describes 'the place of the real, which stretches from the trauma to the phantasy—insofar as the phantasy is never anything more than the screen that conceals something quite primary, something determinant in the function of repetition . . .' (Lacan, 1977c: 60). The screen's blackness, a representation of the absence of representation, thus stands in place of the unsymbolizable real, assuming the place of the Thing. For Lacan, the Thing is the 'beyond-of-the-signified', the 'extimate' object 'situated in the relationship that places man in the mediating position between the real and the signifier' (1992: 52, 129).

PROFESSIONAL ETHICS

'I can only know of the Thing by means of the Law', suggests Lacan (1992: 83). Law, claimed Freud, originates, mythically, in crime. And crime is a family affair, committed against the father. In **Reservoir Dogs** the paternal role is performed by Joe Cabot. Like God the father, he bestows names:

> Okay, quickly.
>
> *(pointing at the men as he gives them a name)*
>
> Mr Brown, Mr White, Mr Blonde, Mr Blue, Mr Orange, and Mr Pink.
>
> (Tarantino, 1994a: 91)

The use of colour names is 'a matter of business'. No one other than himself and his son, Eddie, 'know who the members of the team are' (1994a: 90). The conjunction of commercial and sporting references indicates the intention of getting a job done, of executing a plan as efficiently as possible by sticking to a defined set of rules. Nonetheless, there is a brief flurry of resistance to the nominal act of paternal law: 'Why am I Mr Pink?', 'Why can't we pick out our own color?' The childish 'why' questions test the boss's law. The questions repeat the trauma of castration, of being subjected to the father's law, as it engenders a series of anxious responses attendant on encountering the desire of the Other.

The 'why' question, of course, culminates, not with an adequate and final reason, but with the enunciation of law, to which the only response is a paternal 'because I say so'. In Joe's case, the law is laid down in equally undemocratic terms: 'Look, this ain't a goddamn fuckin' city council meeting! Listen up Mr Pink. We got two ways here, my way or the highway' (1994a: 92). The law is absolute, its ultimate reason, its final answer remains the assertion of its own authority.

The symbolic law established by Joe in his act of renaming is designed to regulate and differentiate through signifiers, not meanings. These functions have to be spelt out before members of the gang accept their given names. Initially, objections arise from a misapprehension of the function of names, a misunderstanding informed by the conventional associations and meanings of colours: 'Yeah, but Mr Brown? That's too close to Mr Shit'; 'Yeah, Mr Pink sounds like Mr Pussy'. While there are better positions in the hierarchy of cool colours, black, for instance, there are also worse, yellow. The colour names are imagined to have meanings already attached to them; they are misread as signs, signifiers irrevocably bound to signifieds. Joe's law, as he makes plain, is different: names are purely signifiers differentiating robbers from each other within an arbitrary system. Though arbitrary in its bestowal of names, the system refuses freedom of choice, as Pink discovers when he asks and independently renames himself Mr Purple: 'You're not Mr Purple, somebody from another job's Mr Purple. You're Mr Pink' (1994a: 92). The proper name is non-negotiable and non-exchangeable: 'Nobody's trading with anybody!' Law, in its differentiation of subjects in and between jobs, remains absolute.

The meanings of names, moreover, inhibit the smooth functioning of Joe's system, causing problems that law sets out to forestall. Indeed, Joe explains why he selects the names, rather than allowing individual choice: 'I tried that once, it don't work. You get four guys fighting over who's gonna be Mr Black. Since nobody knows anybody else, nobody wants to back down' (1994a: 91). Investing colours with meanings and identifying with the one possessing the most prestigious, coolest, conventional criminal significance, threatens Joe's law by calling up another law of differentiation; it does not work because imaginary investment in the name overrides all other considerations, to the point of death. No one wants to back down in the standoff over being Mr Black, the master name of canonical criminality, because the desire for prestige demands the risk of one's life: Mr Black, the criminal ego-ideal, of course, is the one who never backs down. So, in the absence of any other knowledge or means of regulation, the desire to be master will prevail, risking the fatal expenditure with which **Reservoir Dogs** climaxes. The name remains what one risks one's very being for unless the boss makes the decision. And, of course, like the title **Reservoir Dogs,** naming is not about meanings, but about effects. The role of the boss's law is to intervene and regulate misapprehensions over the position of master, ascertaining beyond doubt the position of the father as the desire of the Other, the very figure who differentiates and subjects individuals.

Paternal law operates by means of prohibition in order to ensure its power. Indeed the *nom du père* (name of the father) is always tied to the *non du père* (the no of the father). Before he names the gang members with colours, Joe utters an absolute injunction on the use of any other name, enacting what amounts to the repression of anything personal. Repression and prohibition work together. In **Reservoir Dogs** the strongest prohibition relates to the real, Christian name:

> Under no circumstances are you to tell one another your real name or anything else about yourself. That includes where you're from, your wife's name, where you might have done time, about a bank in St Petersburg you might have robbed. You guys don't say shit about who you are, where you have been or what you might have done.

> (1994a: 90)

With the real name there trails a host of other, metonymically linked, signifiers of identity that have to be repressed: the very details that add up to one's life, being, origins, history. In the interests of business, all personal details are replaced with a different, if limited, network of signifiers: colour, the bank job and, of course, the anonymous web of popular culture. In the context of the movie, the chain of signifiers associated with the real name, now rendered unspeakable, banished from all discourse, becomes the unconscious: 'since Freud, the unconscious has been a chain of signifiers that somewhere (on another stage, in another scene, he wrote) is repeated, and insists on interfering in the breaks offered it by the effective discourse and the cogitation that it informs' (Lacan, 1977b: 297). Aware of the insistence of unconscious signifiers, Joe repeats his prohibition, underscoring it within the punitive threat of law: 'But once again, at the risk of being redundant, if I even think I hear somebody telling or referring to somebody by their Christian name . . . *(Joe searches for the right words)* . . . you won't want to be you' (1994a: 90-1).

While there are good professional reasons for the process of renaming group members with aliases on a need-to-know basis, the subjection of individuals has other implications for the position of the paternal figure. Renaming means no one knows enough to incriminate the others, except, of course, Joe. The paternal figure is situated in excess of his own law, leaving him at the apex of knowledge and power:

> . . . this way you gotta trust me. I like that. I set this up and picked the men I wanted for it. None of you came to me, I approached all of you. I know you. I know your work, I know your reputation. I know you as men.

> (1994a: 91)

What matters is his pleasure, his desire, his knowledge. Moreover, the knowledge of job history, status and character veils the threat that underlies paternal power,

and the assumption of such power places the father beyond his own symbolic law. He knows their real names and they know his, but it is not an equal exchange: he remains unconcerned; his system places him imaginarily above the law in that it challenges any traitor to prove his guilt, and to achieve that they must know the others' names. Moreover, the knowledge he possesses about them demands, as he notes with satisfaction, their trust: as the organizing figure holding the various threads together, his knowledge demands something more than simple obedience, their subjection to his system requires a degree of belief, of trust. He lies simultaneously within and beyond the symbolic contract enacted by naming, the position of the master signifier: their positions are dependent on his for, without him, there would be no plan, no order, only criminals joking and fighting among themselves and ultimately languishing in jail.

Regulated by an impersonal paternal regime, the planning of the job is executed with professional efficiency. Professionalism becomes the standard by which everyone is judged. As the newest recruit, Orange is introduced to the rules of this particular game. He is shown being initiated into the ways of the profession by Mr White who explains how to deal with employees who go beyond the call of duty and profession:

> Now if it's a manager, that's a different story. The managers know better than to fuck around. So if one's givin' you static, he probably thinks he's a real cowboy. So what you gotta do is break that son-of-a-bitch in two. If you wanna know something and he won't tell you, cut off one of his fingers. The little one. Then you tell 'im his thumb's next. After that he'll tell ya if he wears ladies underwear. I'm hungry, let's get a taco.

> (1994a: 96)

Mr Orange listens to all this with a degree of queasy incredulity, but it is important to note that White's description of the torture of employees is purely clinical and business-like. There is no gratuitous, sadistic enjoyment here of the sort the audience has already seen Blonde exhibit back in the warehouse when he severs the cop's ear for no good reason. White is purely interested in information. He knows that the minimum amount of mutilation, removing the little finger, will be all that is necessary to produce the maximum effect. He will merely have to threaten the amputation of a thumb for the information to be forthcoming. However, for all his professional experience, and skill with management, Mr White retains something that, for Mr Pink, signifies an unprofessional attitude: there is something ethical in his relationship with Mr Orange.

When things go awry the authority of Joe's law and the viability of his plan are open to serious question. Early in the movie, after White, Orange and Pink have arrived at the warehouse rendezvous, they begin to narrate the disastrous course of events, to explain precisely what went wrong and discover the cause of the misadventures. In the course of trying to make sense of the chaos, various theories are offered and evidence analysed. Pink's conclusion, that someone has betrayed them, casts serious doubts on the obligation to continue according to plan: 'I say the plan became null and void once we found out we got a rat in the house' (1994a: 27). The symbolic contract with Joe is no longer binding. Nonetheless, White and Orange try to remain calm, the loss of 'cool' being a major breach of professional ethics. As they recount their fragmentary memories of the robbery, they compare scorecards: Pink has killed a couple of cops, White a few. Significantly neither have shot any 'real people'. At this point Mr Blonde's actions are subjected to bewildered scrutiny: his 'insane' and indiscriminate shooting nearly hit his colleagues but killed an innocent bystander, a young black girl. The death is perceived, however, not as a sign of human tragedy, but as a damning marker of Blonde's poor professional skills: 'what you're supposed to do is act like a fuckin' professional. A psychopath is not a professional. You can't work with a psychopath, 'cause ya don't know what those sick assholes are gonna do next' (1994a: 25-6). Blonde's actions, flagrantly ignoring the code, are condemned from the position of productive efficiency and predictability; they constitute another sign of the utter disintegration of the plan.

Having impeached the authority of the plan and caused desperate levels of incredulity among the gang, the indeterminate sequence of events and accidents becomes too traumatic for even the coolest of professionals to deal with. The professional code unravels in the encounter with things it can neither predict nor rationalize. In the arguments and the fighting that dominate the warehouse scenes, the breakdown of relations is described as childish or unprofessional: 'you're acting like a first-year thief. I'm actin' like a professional. They get him, they can get you, they get you, they get closer to me, and that can't happen' (1994a: 41), Pink tells White as accusations and counter-accusations fly, threatened by the unravelling of Joe's chain of professional conduct and discreet anonymity. The paranoia culminates in the deadlock of another standoff, this time between White and Pink. It is interrupted by the arrival of Blonde: 'You kids don't play so rough. Somebody's gonna start crying' (1994a: 41). Although the arrival of Blonde activates another round of aggressive posturing, he also occupies the position of the third term and, indifferent to their collective plight, calls for continued adherence to the plan. This scene culminates in White and Pink losing their cool in a descent into unprofessionalism that is accompanied by the regressive behaviour akin to childish 'why' questions caused by the trauma of paternal naming and prohibition. One sign of symbolic disintegration directly concerns the prohibition on real names. It emanates from White who,

trapped in the same crisis as Pink, betrays the emergence of a personal bond in his appeal to forgo professional names: 'Look, enough of this "Mr White" shit' he declares. Pink, however, will have none of it. The very idea remains unconscionable, his vigorous rebuttal insisting on the letter, the name, of the law: 'Don't tell me your name, I don't want to know! I sure as hell ain't gonna tell ya mine' (1994a: 22). The most professional among the crooks, Pink countenances no transgression of the taboo on real names. True to Joe's law, he is quick to reiterate to White the problem that the latter has created: 'And you, you motherfucker, are lookin' at me like it's my fault. I didn't tell him my name. I didn't tell him where I was from. I didn't tell him what I knew better than to tell him' (1994a: 41). Superegoically invoking the judgement of Joe's law, Pink moralistically affirms the rectitude of his position and displays his utter subservience to the rules in a suppression of his earlier, panic-induced, desire for escape. His professional ethics, like his paranoia, remain bound to self-interest and self-preservation. But White has already succumbed to the demand of names other than those prescribed by proper professionalism: his allegiance to Joe's law has been unwound by something of which he is neither fully aware nor can control.

UNPROFESSIONAL ETHICS

'Larry, I'm gonna kill him', Joe purposefully declares, deciding the fate of Orange (1994a: 105). Significantly Joe has broken his own rule in his statement to White: he has used the latter's Christian name. The slip, which goes unnoticed in the final and fatal confrontation at the climax of the movie, indicates that things are no longer strictly a matter of business: the issue is now personal. With professionalism, personality is excluded by performance, but Joe's vengeance discloses something of the 'un' haunting an ethics of professionalism: the job has become a matter of pride, prestige and honour. At stake is Joe's 'character' and reputation, his person and life invested totally in maintaining his paternal name, a distinctly unprofessional attachment. In breaking his own rule, Joe has let himself down, has failed to live up to his own standards. The use of the personal name follows a greater oversight, a failure to listen to his own better judgement. Joe reproaches himself on these grounds:

> . . . he [Orange] was the only one I wasn't a hundred per cent on. I should have my head examined for goin' forward when I wasn't hundred per cent. But he seemed like a good kid, and I was impatient and greedy and all the things that fuck you up.
>
> (1994a: 106)

Economic gratification short-circuits the regulated system of symbolic relations, fucking up the moral order sustaining Joe's position. Significantly, however, Joe appeals to intuition: something unspecifiable was awry with Orange, something that failed to add up, something other than appearance. Imaginarily the picture was incomplete. What remained invisible to Joe, the object in his gaze which he could not see, was Orange in the form of traitor, as *objet a*. The resolution necessary to restore his symbolic authority is evident however: the immediate and murderous expulsion of 'that piece of shit' is required, 'this lump of shit' having interrupted the efficient running of his plan (1994a: 104).

White has other ideas: the matter has become personal for him as well. He refuses to allow the execution of Orange, raising his pistol against the erstwhile figure of law and thus facing death on behalf of another. The fight for recognition, for prestige, and the risk of death integral to it, forms a far more volatile and entrenched encounter than the standoff for the honorary title of Mr Black mentioned earlier in Joe's cautionary scenario about names. Lives are staked in White's identification with Orange and Joe's bid to regain mastery. With the latter's law impeached by the course of events, nobody is prepared to back down. However, White, split between an old friendship with Joe and an apparently unbreakable bond with Orange, who he insists is a 'good kid', tries to bridge the impasse. After claiming Joe is wrong, White calls for trust and declares his knowledge of 'this man' (Orange) thereby re-enacting the paternal position Joe occupied in the scene of naming. White goes further, however: calling for reason and understanding he puts himself before the law by requesting evidence from Joe. However, in this trial of Joe's law there is no knowledge and no evidence to offer, nor need of it: Joe's intuition is enough. White responds, incredulous, for the defence: 'That's your proof?' But Joe's law has something other than proof for its guarantee: 'You don't need proof when you got instinct' (1994a: 106). Joe's position of 'knowledge', like White's, is purely imaginary. Without a recognized law to regulate the differences or bridge the gaps of imaginary identification and investment, the possibility of backing down is occluded. One law is left, the explosive expenditure that delivers the absolute Other, death.

The final confrontation and exchange of fire in the warehouse exceeds exchange, giving, instead, that which remains non-returnable or negotiable. It goes beyond that good in a material sense, serving no purpose and sacrificing life for a symbolic good which cannot be enjoyed. The good, it seems, is never restrictively economic, becoming, for the subject, a matter of honour, of the signifier, that remains more intense than a feeling for life itself. When the good that is defined and sustained through reference to the symbolic order is put in question by the subject, the relation to 'the Thing' (*das Ding*) alters. Lacan suggests that 'The question of *das Ding* is . . . attached to

whatever is open, lacking, or gaping at the center of our desire' (1992: 84). As the locus where the phallus is lacking, the gap presents an impeachment of the authority of law; it constitutes a hole in the symbolic structures; the disconnection, rather than the connection between the law and the Thing is announced. Instead of functioning as cause and support of desire, the Thing interrupts, breaks the structures of law:

> . . . in its search for justification, for a base and support, in the sense of reference to the reality principle, ethics encounters its own stumbling block, its failure—I mean there where an aporia opens up in that mental articulation we call ethics'.
>
> (Lacan, 1992: 79)

Ethics, binding a subject to networks of law, is nonetheless open to a different relation to the real, one that lies in the gap itself as precisely a gap, a rupture and encounter with a fundamental split.

The Thing and the gap wherein it appears works as excess, remainder and the very point of unworking. It is precisely the leftover, the reserve that determines the course and relations of *Reservoir Dogs,* both in the way it represents the operation and breakdowns of the paternal (moral) law and in its opening up of a relation between subjects and that law, an opening that verges on the ethical. For Lacan, 'the summit of the ethical imperative . . . ends up being articulated in a way that is strange or even scandalous for some people as "Thou shalt love thy neighbour as thyself"'. He continues, 'this is because the law of the relation of the subject to himself that he makes himself his own neighbour, as far as his relationship to his desire is concerned' (1992: 76). The imperative introduces the uncanny, the strangeness of the double, the *Nebenmensch,* at once distanced from and close to the subject: the other that is and is not the subject, the Thing that is within and without.

In *Reservoir Dogs* this ethical demand to love thy neighbour remains a question for the cinema audience: who do we love? Who are we supposed to love? With whom should we identify? The movie never presents the audience with a stable figure of identification, and through this uncertainty, this absence of an omniscient view, denies a secure moral position: it is precisely the gaps, the blanks, that the narrative reconstructions slowly fill. The subject of the movie in *Reservoir Dogs* is also uncertain. The chain of stories offers too many perspectives, disparate points of view shift too rapidly within scenes, so that a stable position, or a simple identification become impossible. While the movie centres on the respective pasts and present of the robbers, White and Blonde in particular, at its core lies the story of the undercover cop, 'our boy' for the police, a 'good kid' for White and a 'piece of shit' to Joe. For the audience, his true identity is only belatedly revealed, amid a variety of substitutions.

According to the professional ethics of the movie, identification, in the form of personal attachment, is no more than an unprofessional sentiment that gets in the way of business. But identification nonetheless persists: the movie turns, precisely, on the inevitability of identification as a form of imaginary misrecognition. Orange, abandoned for much of the time in a corner of the warehouse, left to writhe in the blood oozing from his blasted gut, is central to this process: he retains a double significance as object of attraction and repulsion, constituting the cause of the breakdown of the plot and its final denouement. Orange is not so much the subject of the story in the sense of being its main protagonist, he is, rather, its *objet a,* its Thing. As the point around which the drama turns, Orange functions as a gap in the course of events, one that is only retrospectively identified. Central to the plot yet also excluded from it, drifting in and out of consciousness, the undercover cop only occasionally intervenes, for instance, when he shoots Blonde. Nonetheless, silent or groaning off camera, he introduces something other into the proceedings. For White this other is that bit of the human law that remains and returns in the shape of the real name. For Joe, this other is something intangible and barely evident, something that sticks in the throat, blocks his plans and leaves only a trace, a feeling that the apparently 'good kid' is not 100 percent: the *a* signals that something is lacking in paternal law.

The strongest imaginary investment in the movie is manifested, of course, in White's attachment to Orange. His identification, an effect of the traumatic breakdown of the plan and the unravelling of Joe's law, is clearly disclosed by the eschewal of the symbolic prohibition on real names. The dominance of the imaginary in White's outlook is noticed by Pink as he refuses to be drawn on the sharing of names: 'Fuck, fifteen minutes ago, you almost told me your name. You, buddy, are stuck in a situation you created. So, if you wanna throw bad looks somewhere, throw 'em at a mirror' (1994a: 41). Uttered in the name of the law, the statement discloses how it is, indeed, the mirror that governs the relationship between White and Orange, an identification tied to a profoundly human yet deceptive form of imaginary recognition, a form that creates the situation in which White finds himself ever more tightly 'stuck'.

The use of real names, in contravention of the orders of professional law, signifies the return of the chain of signifiers that Joe prohibited. The relationship between White and Orange has become distinctly personal. Emerging most powerfully in the wake of the traumatic irruption of the real, it signals a return of the repressed. The return of the real name, the breaking of the prohibition, is structured for White around the particular figure who becomes the double of himself, a figure distinct from him but who discloses something in him more than him, the symptom he can neither integrate nor

control. Orange remains a 'good kid'; White will accept no other version, from Joe or Pink: 'that kid in there is dying from a fuckin' bullet that I saw him take. So don't be calling him a rat' (1994a: 28). His vigorous, categorical denial, based on his witnessing of an authenticity guaranteed by pain, indicates the extent of White's imaginary misrecognition. For him the object, Orange, has become absolutely determining, to the point of being a part of himself that he cannot forgo.

There is something in his relationship with Orange that he cannot control; it is indicated in his account of the exchange of real names: 'What the fuck was I supposed to tell him, "Sorry, I can't give out that information, it's against the rules. I don't trust you enough?" Maybe I shoulda, but I couldn't' (1994a: 36). An involuntary emotional attachment overrides the obligations of professional conduct, in opposition to the symbolic law embodied by Joe. In Orange, White imagines his own manhood. But the imaginary subject is not only duplicated, it is, in the shape of Orange, duplicitous. White utterly misrecognizes Orange, seeing him as the reflection of the subject he would like to be, a matter of love. For White, Orange is identified, ethically, as the other, the neighbour and double, that one loves as oneself. Until the very end, White remains blind to the true and duplicitous nature of this relationship; his actions centre on an unquestioning belief in Orange as the very image of himself. His identity, his very being, is staked on this other to the point of death: nothing causes him to deviate from the object of his identification, protection and love.

Of all the 'characters' in **Reservoir Dogs,** Mr White and Mr Orange most closely approximate the status of conventional human subjects. Beyond the rules and the prohibition on uttering real names, at the very point of death, a distinctly human bond emerges: guilt, compassion and trust lead inexorably to honesty and truth, distinguishing a particularly human imaginary against a purely professional symbolic order, a law that it defines by transgression:

> We had just gotten away from the cops. He just got shot. It was my fuckin' fault he got shot. He's a fuckin' bloody mess—he's screaming. I swear to God, I thought he was gonna die right then and there. I'm tryin' to comfort him, telling him not to worry, he's gonna be okay, I'm gonna take care of him. And he asked me what my name was. I mean, the man was dyin' in my arms. What the fuck was I supposed to tell him, 'Sorry, I can't give out that information, it's against the rules. I don't trust you enough?' Maybe I shoulda, but I couldn't.
>
> (1994a: 36)

The element that White cannot control, that exceeds regulation and the need-to-know, draws out a remarkably human chain of signification. Guilt signifies

White's personal investment in Orange's pain and the imminence of death calls inexorably for compassion and trust. Indeed, pain and death take both subjects beyond the restricted orders of law, towards a fully human relation. Pink understands this discourse, but remains unimpressed: 'Oh, I don't doubt it was quite beautiful' (1994a: 38), he sarcastically comments. The sarcasm, however, only briefly punctures the romantic illusion of human relationship. Moreover, the irony bestowed on the touching human moment is double: an unshot scene from the screenplay makes it clear that Orange already knows White's name. But the truth is withheld from White until the very end.

Reinforced by the feeling for the other's pain, consumed by the proximity of death, the image of the good kid continues to dominate White's psychic economy, to a fatal extent: the identification with Orange causes him to question the authority of Joe's paternal law, sacrificing himself for the other, sacrificing himself to the image of himself and the law of the absolute Other, death. In this moment, in this relation to both the other—the double he loves as himself—and the absolute Other White briefly accedes to the human, to the honour of that name and the honour of its image. Cruelly, the truth of this human position is revealed as betrayal. The last scene demonstrates the reversible relation of the subject and the Thing. From being an object of attraction, a good kid, Orange becomes an object to be expelled as a traitor, an enemy, an object disclosing White's self-betrayal precisely at the point where he thought he was being most true to himself. For Orange the reverse happens: in spite of his job, his business to uncover the crime and secure the capture of Joe, his apology and confession discloses an identification with White that reaches beyond their respective professional codes in an ethical gesture towards a truth imagined as fully human. The feeling for the other, even an impostor, is what defines the human and leads to truth and betrayal. It is the same unaccountable feeling that informs the more suspicious intuitions of Pink and Joe and leads to violent expulsion. Indeed, by confessing and apologizing, Orange repeats and condemns the human discourse enacted earlier by White: truth, honesty, guilt and concern are exchanged along with the real name and death.

'I find what passes between Mr White and Mr Orange at the end of ***Reservoir Dogs*** very moving and profound in its morality and its human interaction', comments the director (1994a: xvi). Or, as Mr Pink has observed of their relationship in an earlier scene, 'I don't doubt it was quite beautiful.' Both banal and profound, empty and ethical, the final moments remain ambivalent in respect of their humanity and morality. In telling the truth, Orange discloses the lie of his human relationship with White in a distinctly human gesture.

Orange's confession is unnecessary: he has already, professionally, completed his task. Indeed, his successful enaction of his duty has already meant he has risked his life for the Other in the shape of law and society, living and, possibly, dying, in honour of his symbolic mandate to 'protect and serve'. Something else, something more, emerges in his recognition of White's tragically ethical sacrifice. Unnecessary though his confession of the truth is in professional terms, it remains something he is compelled to do, something, precisely, in him and more than him which he cannot control. The other's pain, the other's sacrifice for another who he does not know, draws the subject beyond the laws of commercial self-interest. Freddy's confession, a sacrifice of himself to a human and yet personal truth, the truth of an individual relation, is performed in full cognizance of its implications and thus constitutes an absolutely ethical gift, a consummate act of expenditure from which he can expect no return.

MADONNA'S PAIN AND THE EAR OF THE OTHER

Pain, the other's pain, underlines the simultaneously human and inhuman relation between White and Orange: it culminates in a tragically human and inescapably ethical sacrifice of life for the other. Through pain one reaches the limit, the Thing, that articulates ethics and desire:

> In brief, Kant is of the same opinion as Sade. For in order to reach *das Ding* absolutely, to open the flood gates of desire, what does Sade show us on the horizon? In essence, pain. The other's pain as well as the pain of the subject himself, for on occasions they are simply one and the same thing. To the degree that it involves forcing an access to the Thing, the outer extremity of pleasure is unbearable to us.
>
> (Lacan, 1992: 80)

It is pain that guarantees the human relationship. For White, pain proves the authenticity of Orange. Pain draws the subject to the point of death and thereby draws out the truth, just as it does when White's sacrifice places him in an identical position to Orange.

The ethical question of the other's pain is raised at the beginning of the movie by Mr Brown in his infamous 'Madonna speech'. His interpretation highlights the function of metaphor by suggesting, emphatically, that 'the whole song is a metaphor for big dicks'. In so doing, his reading of 'Like a Virgin' squarely refutes the version offered by Mr Blonde who proposes, romantically, that 'it's about a girl who is very vulnerable and she's been fucked over a few times. Then she meets some guy who's really sensitive . . .' (1994a: 3). Dismissing this, Brown underscores the crucial experience of pain:

> Now she's gettin' this serious dick action, she's feelin' something she ain't felt since forever. Pain. . . . It

hurts like the first time. The pain is reminding a fuck machine what it was like to be a virgin. Hence, 'Like a Virgin'.

(1994a: 4-5)

The pain differentiates machine from human, innocent from habitué, recalling something that has been lost. At its crudest, the reading of 'Like a Virgin' affirms phallic law in its most brutal, literal rendering of a subjection. But the loss of an innocent, virginal state as a result of this encounter metaphorically signifies, for the position of the interpreter, a different traumatic, castrating encounter with phallic law. What is raised in the interpretation is the spectre of lack, of subjection to law. For the woman, the experience of pain broaches the Thing at the extremity of pleasure, a pleasure enjoyed, not by the interpreter, Mr Brown, but by another, the Other:

> The real father, Freud tells us, is a castrating father. In what way? Through his presence as real father who effectively occupies that person with whom the child is in a state of rivalry, namely, the mother. Whether or not that is the case in experience, in theory there is no doubt about it: the real father is elevated to the rank of Great Fucker—though not, believe me, in the face of the Eternal, which isn't even around to count the number of times. Yet doesn't this real and mythical father fade at the moment of the decline of the oedipus complex into the one whom the child may easily have already discovered at the relatively advanced age of five years old, namely, the imaginary father, the father who has fucked the kid up.

(Lacan, 1992: 307-8)

'Like a Virgin' is about the 'Great Fucker': 'it's about some cooze who's a regular fuck machine. I mean all the time, morning, day, night, afternoon, dick, dick, dick, dick, dick, dick, dick, dick, dick, dick, dick' (1994a: 4). As 'fuck machine' the woman testifies to the *jouissance* demanded by the Other, the great fucker and castrating father. The myth of the phallus as embodiment of the Other's *jouissance* is thus promoted in this reading of 'Like a Virgin'. It is a reading endorsed by the director who, as actor, performs the speech:

> I have no doubt in my mind she [Madonna] is going to come to me and say: 'Quentin, you're a hundred per cent right, that's exactly what the song's about. And I was laughing my ass off when all these fourteen-year-old girls were singing it.'

The certainty, however, even as it anticipates authorization, was deluded: Madonna inscribed a copy of her album *Erotica* 'To Quentin—it's about love, not dick' (Bernard, 1995: 193). The interpretation, countermanded by an inscription of authority, discovers itself to be fantastical.

But what the interpretation discloses, significantly, is the realm of fantasy determined by the Thing: 'Freud placed in the forefront of ethical enquiry the simple relationship between man and woman. Strangely enough, things haven't been able to move beyond that point' (Lacan, 1992: 87). For Lacan, the relation between the sexes is a nonrelation, a relation only to the *objet a* which is, precisely, not one, but *'something of the One'* (1982: 139). Indeed, the non-relation between Madonna's and Tarantino's versions of the song charts an insurmountable difference between male and female fantasy: the myth of the phallus embodied or literalized, is opposed to the myth of romantic union, the phallus idealized. It is a point that, strangely, cannot be surmounted since it figures the gap between the sexes as Thing. Sexual difference is the point on which symbolic castration turns, the point of lack, the very gap, the site of loss and separation marked by the *objet a*. The differentiating effects of the castrating father thus enjoin the male subject to, and bar him from, the *jouissance* of the Other.

Since ***Dogs*** [***Reservoir Dogs***] is framed by the elevation of the great fucker at the beginning of the film and the Other's explosive assertion of power at its end, in the shape of the LAPD, the position of Joe appears tenuous. Throughout the film, he assumes the role of paternal metaphor: the one who lays down the law, who knows the robbers 'as men', who knows their real names, and who is invoked as the one that will take care of things. But his plan is ruined by one Thing: his blindness to Orange. His authority is questioned, his rules broken, his law collapses, the supposed father killed. What Orange introduces and the film dramatizes is this collapse, its implosion. The fragmentation, the repetitions and regressions circulate around the central absence that Joe's law cannot fill. For Lacan, it is 'the foreclosure of the Name-of-the-Father' in the place of the Other and 'the failure of the paternal metaphor' that defines psychosis:

> We will take *Verwerfung,* then, to be *foreclosure* of the signifier. To the point at which the Name-of-the-Father is called—we shall see how—may correspond to the Other, then, a mere hole, which, by the inadequacy of the metaphoric effect will provoke a corresponding hole at the place of the phallic signification.

(1977a: 201)

It is precisely around such a hole that ***Reservoir Dogs*** turns.

But there is one figure for whom there are no holes: Mr Blonde. 'I guarantee we've got a rat in the house', says Pink. 'What would ever make you think that?' replies Blonde. Supremely indifferent to their predicament and unconcerned about his part in it, he replies to the accusations about his trigger-happy response to the alarm sounding with a statement of fact: 'I told 'em not to touch the alarm. They touched it. I blew 'em full of holes. If they hadn't done what I told 'em not, they'd still be alive today' (1994a: 59). Callously indifferent, 'a fucking psycho', he has one thing in his favour, as Pink observes: 'Right now, Mr Blonde is the only one I completely trust. He's too fuckin' homicidal to be workin' with the cops' (1994a: 44). Pink's vote of confidence is subsequently underscored by the flashback entitled 'Mr Blonde'. With an almost filial relation to Joe and a fraternal relation to Eddie, the loyalty of Blonde is beyond question: '. . . you don't lie to a man who's just done four years in the slammer for ya', Joe comments to Eddie (1994a: 50). Unimpeachable in the eyes of the Other, Joe and Pink, Blonde is distinguished as psychotic: he has foreclosed any relation to the Other, 'his shooting spree in the store' defining him as a subject of pure expenditure. Without reference to a reality or any law, his actions situate him beyond reason, subject only to his own sovereign pleasure. 'First off, I don't have a boss', he informs the captured cop. He then goes on:

> Now I'm not gonna bullshit you. I don't really care about what you know or don't know. I'm gonna torture you for a while regardless. Not to get information, but because torturing a cop amuses me. There's nothing you can say, I've heard it all before. There's nothing you can do. Except pray for a quick death, which you ain't gonna get.
>
> (1994a: 61)

Without point, use or purpose beyond the value of amusement, the torture scene presents psychosis as that which is detached from any reference to law, usefulness or meaning. Hence the importance of the organ he severs from the body of the captured cop. The ear is what connects the subject to the voice of the Other: in *Reservoir Dogs* it is presented as an ethical, human organ, the one that, in the absence of visual orientation, connects others to the screaming voice of Orange's pain. Moreover, the ear is what connects subjects in the film to the Other, the world outside the drama which intrudes from the airwaves in the form of K-Billy's voice. Blonde switches on the radio, before opening his razor: 'Clowns to the left of me, jokers to the right. Here I am, stuck in the middle with you' (1994a: 63), he mouths, assuming the place, the words of the Other. These words signify, for the psychotic, the redundancy of the Other: there is no law, no paternal metaphor, only jokers and clowns. Blonde, moreover, is deaf to the cop's pleading. Without compassion, he has no relation to the other or the Other and, by severing the other's ear situates the cop in an identical position, cut off from all law or protection. *'Mr Blonde just stares into the cop's/our face, singing along with the seventies hit. Then he reaches out and cuts off the cop's/our ear'* (1994a: 63). The script includes the audience in this scene of utter subjection to irrational, tyrannical and ruthless violence. However, in the movie, the camera pans away, separating the cop from 'us' as 'we' effectively turn away from the amputation in an act that

may produce relief in not seeing, having no mirror to see an unbearable infliction of pain.

But the moment is heard. It is an ethical moment, opening morality to its own desire. 'Was that as good for you as it was for me?' Blonde asks the cop off screen, but it is to 'us' that the disembodied voice is really addressed, as we-the-camera stare into the vacant space at the back of the warehouse. Well was it? Yes, clearly, but in a different way. For the audience the (missed) spectacle of the ear amputation is a moral moment that calls up and frustrates moral desire, activating a prurience in withdrawal and disappointment; it is ethical in the way it opens a gap in the moral gaze, leaving an imaginary residue and a sound when it is the real thing that is wanted, the point of abhorrence that is also the place of absolute moral enjoyment and execration.

Tarantino explains just how deliberate, and deliberately moral, was his seduction and thwarting of the audience during this scene. It appears to have been designed precisely to produce this sort of disturbance between desire, morality and the law. As he says in the interview featured on the video of *Reservoir Dogs*:

> In the infamous 'torture' scene the use of the song 'Stuck in the Middle with You'—which is a kind of bouncy, kinda cool song—not only does it not lighten up the scene, it makes the scene even harder to watch. You're sitting there and you're watching it, then all of a sudden this tune comes on and you're tapping your toes, it's real catchy and everything, Michael Madsen starts doing his little dance, and then . . . BOOM! The hard stuff starts. You're sitting there watching this [hard] stuff, but it's already too late, you're already a co-conspirator. You enjoyed the song, you enjoyed his dance, now you've got to take the hard stuff. And *that's* what makes it so disturbing.

The 'hard stuff' introduces the kernel, the hard core, of subjective existence, that which remains least avowable to the subject, the *objet a*. The scene is so traumatic because its use of the song calls up an unconscious self-reproach in the audience that invites an aggressive response that, furthermore, takes its support in a disappointed prurience. Perhaps that is why this scene has become notorious, has been singled out with so much moral outrage and so many calls for censorship: and yet it is all directed towards an act that is missing, *that has already been censored.*

Aesthetic violence, then, becomes ethical if it opens a gap within representation thereby questioning the complicity of desire and law. Aesthetic violence and the violence of aesthetics manifests both a hole in the real and a corresponding rupture in the fabric of the symbolic, the locus of law. In the encounter with the hole all (paternal) metaphors appear inadequate as, in the figure of Blonde, reason fails and meaning falters in the face of an absolute negativity that goes beyond, even as it constitutes, the possibility of ethics. The negativity that comes to the fore in **Reservoir Dogs** pertains to desire that is moral insofar as it appears useless and ineffective: 'the desire of the Other is apprehended by the subject in that which does not work, in the lacks of the discourse of the Other . . .' (Lacan, 1977c: 214). Desire surpasses the position of the one supposed to be master, Joe. In a similar vein, Pink's professionalism is unworked by desire: the desire for the money prevents him walking away from the job. Desire exceeds the Other, it seems, as it raises the problem of the Good alongside that of goods; desire serves no purpose, accedes to no law other than that of desire, attenuating another economy beyond that of meaning and regulated exchange.

This other economy is one of pure expenditure, the explosive expenditure on which the movie climaxes. In Blonde's irrational, amoral, purposeless violence, it mimics the consumption of commodified culture; it is 'a shooting spree in the store', the absolute expenditure, without return, of the consumer's shopping spree. Excessive expenditure leaves the subject of desire wanting only to the extent that it wants for nothing or, in Guattari's words, wants only the absolute Other, the 'diamond of unnamable desire', the point of its own extravagant consumption and non-return (1984: 8). The exorbitance of the subject's desire charts a trajectory that is heterogeneous: toward a transcendent point and enmired in utter profanity, a locus of shit and the sacred. Indeed, if **Reservoir Dogs** has any reference it is, perhaps, to the condition of sovereignty and abjection, to what, in a restricted economy of use and exchange, is held in reserve, the surplus, the profit and the value that serves no useful function, unemployable and unworkable, the dogs, the remains, leftovers of another world of desire, the thieving rabble, the detritus and utter waste of expenditure.

References

Bauman, Zygmunt (1993) *Postmodern Ethics*. Oxford: Blackwell.

Bernard, Jami (1995) *Quentin Tarantino: The Man and the Movies*. London: Harper Collins.

Guattari, Felix (1984) *Molecular Revolution: Psychiatry and Politics*, trans. Rosemary Sheed. Harmondsworth: Penguin.

Lacan, Jacques (1977a) 'On a Question Preliminary to any Possible Treatment of Psychosis', pp. 179-225 in *Ecrits*, trans. Alan Sheridan. London: Tavistock.

Lacan, Jacques (1977b) 'The Subversion of the Subject and the Dialectic of Desire in the Freudian Unconscious', pp. 292-325 in *Ecrits*, trans. Alan Sheridan. London: Tavistock.

Lacan, Jacques (1977c) *The Four Fundamental Concepts of Psychoanalysis,* ed. Jacques-Alain Miller, trans. Alan Sheridan. London: Penguin.

Lacan, Jacques (1982) 'God and the *Jouissance* of the Woman', pp. 138-48 in Juliet Mitchell and Jacqueline Rose (eds) *Feminine Sexuality: Jacques Lacan and the école freudienne*. Basingstoke and London: Macmillan.

Lacan, Jacques (1988) *The Seminar of Jacques Lacan Book I: Freud's Papers on Technique 1953-1954,* ed. Jacques-Alain Miller, trans. John Forrester. Cambridge: Cambridge University Press.

Lacan, Jacques (1992) *The Ethics of Psychoanalysis 1950-60,* ed. Jacques-Alain Miller, trans. Dennis Porter. London: Routledge.

Levinas, Emmanuel (1986) 'Dialogue with Emmanuel Levinas', in Richard A. Cohen (ed.) *Face to Face with Levinas*. Albany, NY: SUNY Press.

Levinas, Emmanuel (1989a) 'Substitution', pp. 88-125 in Sean Hand (ed.) *The Levinas Reader.* Oxford: Blackwell.

Levinas, Emmanuel (1989b) 'God and Philosophy', pp. 166-89 in Sean Hand (ed.) *The Levinas Reader.* Oxford: Blackwell.

Lyotard, Jean-François (1984) *The Postmodern Condition,* trans. Geoff Bennington and Brian Massumi. Manchester: Manchester University Press.

Rajchman, John (1991) *Truth and Eros: Foucault, Lacan and the Question of Ethics*. London: Routledge.

Tarantino, Quentin (1994a) *Reservoir Dogs*. London: Faber.

Tarantino, Quentin (1994b) *Pulp Fiction*. London: Faber.

Tarantino, Quentin (1995) *True Romance*. London: Faber.

Zizek, Slavoj (1993) *Tarrying with the Negative: Kant, Hegel and the Critique of Ideology.* Durham, NC: Duke University Press.

Caroline Jewers (essay date spring 2000)

SOURCE: Jewers, Caroline. "Heroes and Heroin: From *True Romance* to *Pulp Fiction*." *Journal of Popular Culture* 33, no. 4 (spring 2000): 39-61.

[*In the essay below, Jewers connects Tarantino's work to medieval literary traditions.*]

When Marsellus Wallace, the black godfather of Quentin Tarantino's **Pulp Fiction** (1994), is about to exact revenge on Zed, one of the two redneck captors recently responsible for his rape, he declares ominously: "I'm gonna git Medieval on your ass" (108), a line which drew an instant comic response from the audiences I observed.[1] This film has become an instant classic, exerting a curious appeal that goes deeper than the movie's glossy packaging and dizzying narrative speed: its appeal lies in a capacity to strike several allusive and interpretive chords simultaneously. While it would be productive to explicate the film as a reflection of contemporary politics and mores, I am interested in the generic roots of *Pulp Fiction*'s mass appeal, and the distant formal ancestor that, on analysis, proves to be a close relative. My intention is to "git medieval" and explore the complex connection between literature and film. What interests me here is film as narrative, and the subsequent relationship of film as narrative and literary genre. Most particularly, I would like to explore *Pulp Fiction* and pulp fiction, that is to say the specific narrative of the film, and the film as emblematic of a broader category belonging to popular culture, and its relationship to the first great modern manifestation of popular fiction since antiquity—the medieval romance of chivalry. While I suggest there are similarities between elements of the film and elements found in specific romance texts, the aim is to highlight generic parallels that are in turn indicative of a narrative continuity that begins eight hundred years ago. By definition, what follows will thus appear both metonymic and metaphoric, in the hope of conveying that in significant ways bright celluloid and highly decorated manuscripts are both vehicles for glamorized archetypal plots that reflect the hopes, fears, and material aspirations of respective contemporary cultures, and how they both assimilate and aestheticize violence—to show that in their respective and consonant ways they "perform" culture. The point of comparing the two is not to detract from the post-modern novelty of Tarantino's film by placing it within some rigid canonic tradition, or to illustrate the dull truism that history—even literary history—is destined merely to repeat itself. However, I wish to illustrate how genres and texts resonate across cultural and temporal boundaries, and how the speculation they generate can challenge our perceptions. Their dialogic juxtapositions reveal new ways of illuminating our understanding of our own contested culture and that of the past. My example of quintessential medieval fiction will be mostly drawn from the works of Chrétien de Troyes (fl.1160-85), who is the great stylist of Arthurian romance, and about whom little is known beyond his vivid and fashionable texts. His ability to shape his narratives to contemporary tastes and fantasies puts him in a similar category (and, it must be said, higher class) to Tarantino.

In context, the surface medieval allusion made by Wallace at first strikes us as curiously anachronistic, except that it evokes a stereotypical, violent, comic-book Middle Ages parodied in that kinky, inquisitional torture scene: to "git medieval" is patently synonymous with achieving a level of physical violence grim even by the exacting standards of the vicious model of society created by Tarantino. On reflection, this is the least of the ways in which we might view the film as imbued with a certain medievalism, or rather, apt to recycle elements of fiction that stretch back beyond the recent cultural past. The justification for embarking on an analysis that makes a connection between the two is the author/ director himself, who through his title and opening dictionary definition invites us to consider extra- and metatextual issues related to literary/cinematographic form and substance, in order to explore the inner depths and extradiegetic possibilities of genre: "PULP (pulp) n.1. A soft, moist, shapeless mass of matter. 2. A magazine or book containing lurid subject matter and being characteristically printed on rough, unfinished paper" (foreword).

In this supremely visually literate film, there is an initial identification with, and post-modern, reflexive awareness of literariness. It is a labyrinth of verbal and visual intertexts, and even defines itself as a book, albeit in the form of that lowest common denominator of generic taste. One of Tarantino's many visual gags underscores this: the copy of the cheap thriller *Modesty Blaise* that Vincent Vega, played by John Travolta, carries on his significant trips to the bathroom provides a playful reminder of the nature, substance, depth, and throwaway value of mass-market adventure stories: pulp fiction is the subject and the object of filmic reflection. Vega's particular choice of book is inspired by a distinctly B-movie remake by Joseph Losey (1966) from Peter O'Donnell's original cartoon strip, characterized by its gaudy violence and bodice-ripper kitsch. It serves, in Lucien Dällenbach's terms, as a mirror in the text, or *mise-en-abyme,* as a narcissistic reflection of the whole work. We could compare an analogous, although more dignified, scene from Chrétien de Troyes' twelfth-century romance *Yvain,* in which on arriving at the Château de Pesme Aventure (the Castle of Worst Adventure) the hero encounters the lord and lady of the castle listening to their daughter reading a chivalric romance in a garden, a replication of the enunciated text that sets up an intellectual game of mirrors. At the heart of the medieval romance we find a modern preoccupation with literature as a self-referential and intertextual polished replica of reality and of itself, just as we do in Tarantino's film: in the turbulent world of violent proving and adventure there is a calm, self-ironic, bookish eye, and in a more overtly humorous way, *Modesty Blaise* fulfills the same function of blurring the line between art and illusion, while its conceit mimics and draws in the outside consumer of the narrative in parodic play.

The French medieval romance, as many commentators have observed, springs to the forefront of literary activity at precisely the time when feudalism tightens its efficient and often ruthless grip on the socio-political and economic state during the twelfth and thirteenth centuries. The first modern, leisured, and materialistic urban culture since antiquity enjoys enough relative stability to embark on internal territorial wars largely designed to consolidate wealth and political ambition, and exterior Crusades that sought to reinforce strategic policies and ideological supremacy. In a period of intense productivity on all fronts, confluent cultural forces see the Romanesque give way to Gothic, and the building of increasingly sophisticated castles and cathedrals; at the same time there is the emergence of an urban and urbane burgeoning mercantile class that grew expert in the generation of great wealth and new technology, and a flowering intellectual pre-Renaissance in ever-mushrooming centers of art and thought. A general sense of social dynamism manifests itself in hybristic self-confidence, and in the certainty of moral virtue and religious belief. Yet at the same time, there is a dark side that expresses itself through the iconography of art and literature as the deep fear of imminent chaos: the cavernous, monumental cathedrals whose spires reflect the lofty aspirations of the society that built them are covered with grotesques, and with men and angels wrestling demons, or being devoured by the forces of evil. Serene Virgins and images of an ordered world compete with sadistic scenes of torture and dismemberment: nature and human nature run riot in carnivalesque humor and dark, sardonic satire. Curious and frightened faces gaze down from corbels, gargoyles, and capitals: bearing the weight of heavy stone, they also reveal the burden and menace that sickness, violence, and death bring as ever-present forces that threaten to engulf and overwhelm progress and prosperity. Perhaps it is a condition of every society to fear that it is on the verge of violent collapse, but the sombre iconography of medieval popular culture suggests a link with the disturbing images of modern times.

From the developing ethos of feudal chivalry in France, two main literary genres emerge, the feudal epic *(chanson de geste)* and the romance. While the former may be considered an outgrowth of the epic, its narrative parameters are not always quite those of the national epic, represented by texts like the *Chanson de Roland* or *Beowulf.* The feudal epic mixes the ethos of military conquest with regional and family politics, and makes its protagonists often less than heroic, as in texts like *Raoul de Cambrai* (last quarter of the twelfth century), in which the struggle between good and evil is displaced into a typical conflict between the legitimate and illegitimate rivals for family lands. Raoul himself is not above haranguing nuns in the most graphic language before burning and pillaging neighbouring town and convent alike in his quest for a just inheritance. Such vivid and violent texts present a world of knightly adventure with little encroachment into the magic realm of fantasy or of love. Its purposeful roots are founded in a limited form of realism perhaps best described as socio-political verisimilitude. National epics like *Roland* tend to exclude women altogether, except as peripheral figures or decoration. The feudal epic makes slightly more room for them, although they play no substantial role, except as sisters, heiresses, and conduits to wealth.

The courtly romance blends elements of epic heroism and feudal knighthood, but locates them in a more feminized lyrical universe influenced by the contemporary fashion for troubadour verse from Occitania, which (under the influence of the sophisticated Southern courts, Ovid, Arabic literature from North Africa and Spain, and of the spreading cult of Marianism) placed the lady at the center of a literary, amorous feudal hierarchy. Knights in lyric and courtly romance were at the command not of a lord or king, but of the often distant and imperious object of their affections. This charming conceit permeates imaginative literature throughout the medieval period and long after its demise. Chivalric romance, as Erich Köhler suggests, was destined to encourage the landless noble young knights to seek their fortunes and glory. It is most often a literature of self-improvement through physical trial and combat, leading to fame and often marriage. The valorization of women gave it an appeal to both sexes, and as a genre it extols the virtues of prowess, faithful love, and material gain.

Three heroes of Chrétien reflect different prismatic refractions of this form of exemplary idealized knighthood: Yvain (in *Le Chevalier au lion,* c.1177-81) begins as the shallow, ambitious loner who learns by his own folly and literal madness that altruism is a better model than selfishness for integration into the privileged world of the court. Chrétien is the originator of Lancelot (*Le Chevalier de la Charrette,* also 1177-81), who must combat pride and humble himself to the commands of Guenevere in order to become a worthy courtly lover. Lastly, Perceval (*Le conte du Graal,* c.1181-85) makes the transition from a secular to a religious code of knighthood that takes him from being a clumsy ingénu to being an instrument of grace. All three have separate trajectories that lead them from the court either singly, or in pairs in counterpoint to Gawain, who becomes the yardstick of their progress, and in each case some form of egotistical self-interest has to be overcome.

Their adventures are stereotypical: a concatenated series of literal and allegorical episodes, designed as moral tests or physical combats, set in a symbolic, alternate world of signs varying from the more realistic to the entirely supernatural, from the secular to the religious. Rather after the fashion of a board game, they advance at a varying pace, quickened and delayed by sudden obstacles, information, or challenges, towards a personal goal that usually includes the love and reward. Vast cycles of romances proliferated throughout the Middle Ages in series of prequels (rather like the *Phantom Menace*) and sequels rather like popular films: many are second-rate recyclers of a few basic premises. The greatest exempla, like the works of Chrétien, test the limits of the narrative paradigm. Some of the greatest examples are anonymous: the *Queste del Saint Graal* and *La Mort le roi Artu* (*The Quest for the Holy Grail* and *The Death of King Arthur*, 1225-30) show the final stage in the development of the genre, with its two possible means of demise. In the *Queste*, finding the Grail brings an end to the telos of chivalry: there are no more adventures to be had. In the *Mort*, we see secular chivalry straying from its moral path and finding incestuous conflagration in bloody civil war. The possibility of damnation and redemption is often a part of the romance: the greatest heroes are those that carry the capacity for change as well as the seeds of their own undoing.

The adventure landscape is an important narrative element, merging backdrops that splice natural and cultured settings in the form of castles, tournaments, concealing forests, and ravaged wastelands. Eventually, Yvain and Lancelot find return from an otherworld landscape and integration to court, while Chrétien's Perceval remains in suspense in the unfinished story, spawning prolific lesser sequels to his adventures: however, in the best Grail narrative, the *Quest*, even Perceval is superseded by the flawless Galahad, who has no choice but to become a religious hermit and die after having achieved the ultimate quest. In this text, women figure both as temptresses and morally improving inspirers of heroic deeds, and in the many medieval romances to post-date Chrétien, such fundamentals remain consistent. However, in contrast with the feudal epic, the chivalric romance generally gives a more prominent place to women, even if (reflecting their historical status) they only enjoy a limited form of power to captivate and inspire.

Although the audience of chivalric romances was relatively narrow, restricted to the upper classes who commissioned literature, to the social mix of those who lived and served in castles and courts, and to the socially-climbing merchant classes, such texts were nonetheless the popular fiction of their time. Nowadays we define popular culture as that which appeals to the largest, unrestricted number of people that can consume it: in medieval times a mass material culture was oral, and does not exist in the same way, since such a large percentage of the population was illiterate, and engaged in the production but not in the consumption of wealth. Culture was elitist: but chivalric romances (and the feudal epics with which they coexisted) still qualify as the equivalent of popular fiction, since they had the broadest appeal to the social strata who had access to them.

The very plasticity of the fundamental form of the romance makes it the most enduring of all genres, and its popularity has never faded: on the contrary, it has undergone myriad rebirths. It is a short step from the chivalric hero of romance to *Gargantua* and *Don Quixote*, thence to the picaresque hero, Voltaire's *Candide*, the eighteenth-century libertine, and the heroes and anti-heroes of the nineteenth-century novel. Whether in the hands of Virginia Woolf, David Lodge, Umberto Eco, or Italo Calvino, or in the form of board- or video-games, the basic pattern of romance is still with us. Its love-narrative inspires operas, bodice-ripping novels, soap operas and songs. Most accessibly, perhaps, it inspires films. Curiously, many Arthurian films are less than successful. While John Boorman's *Excalibur* (1981) and Bresson's *Lancelot du Lac* (1974) enjoy critical success, others like *First Knight* (Jerry Zucker, 1995) somehow fail to capture the lively spirit of the original texts even if they reproduce the desired period on screen. Ironically, some of the more successful attempts update the romance rather than seek to reproduce the medieval original. Here one could point to *The Fisher-King* (Terry Gilliam, 1991), *The Voyager* (Volker Schlöndorff, 1991), and *The Natural* (Barry Levinson, 1984) as examples. Best of all, and in a class of its own, is *Pulp Fiction*, which captures all the elements of experimental narrative and familiar episodic structure and combines them in an original and intelligent way.

As a film auteur, Tarantino has already toyed with a form of romance in **True Romance** (1993), but in **Pulp Fiction**, he apes its literary model with skill in the remixing and realignment of clichés and conventions, and goes one step further. This is not to suggest that Tarantino had medieval literature in mind when penning **Pulp Fiction**, but since one underpinning of the film is to speculate on metanarrative, and the déjà-vu and déjà-dit generated by reworking convention, then the temptation to pursue those resonances as far as possible inevitably results. Inspired by Tarantino's stylistic exercise, I would like to attempt a reading of **Pulp Fiction** as an inverted, subversive courtly romance, and most particularly one with elements of a Grail romance twisted and embedded in it, exploiting the dangerous sense of self-destruction and redemption inherent in the best romance tradition. First, it is useful to set out a few considerations about Tarantino's other cult classic, **Reservoir Dogs** (1992), in order to show how it illustrates elements of feudal epic, so that we can then go on to distinguish more clearly how its elements blend with the traits of the romance apparent in **Pulp Fiction**.

Reservoir Dogs contains many elements found subsequently in **Pulp Fiction**, and is, essentially, a contemporary form of feudal epic, stripped of the veneer of nationally or socially redemptive ideals found in texts like the *Chanson de Roland*.[2] Even in the case of *Roland*, the theme of internal strife and violence offsets and frames the apocalyptic conflagration of the conflict between Christian and Saracen, making the story as much an incestuous rivalry for power as a narrative of exemplary Christian knighthood. *Reservoir Dogs* tells a not dissimilar simple story of honor, betrayal, greed, and a "hit" gone wrong, leading to the self-destruction of the gang of assassins who have been infiltrated by an undercover police officer, also the victim of their brutality. Perhaps more like *Raoul de Cambrai,* it portrays a feudal world of struggle and self-interest, where strength and the ability to wield weaponry determines survival and status. Centered on loyalty and treachery, and on the struggle between good and evil in a grey world where wealth is seized and not earned, set on the violent margins of something resembling "normal" society, *Reservoir Dogs* sketches its individualistic characters with economy, burying the outward signs of their personalities in formal black ties and suits of the kind worn by Jules and Vincent in *Pulp Fiction,* suits described by Tarantino in a recent interview as being like armor.[3] The band of errant hit-men in *Reservoir Dogs* appear in the opening shot of the film seated at a parodic Round Table banquet scene, situated in the kind of diner that seems to be a trademark of Tarantino's films. Sleazy, plastic, domestic, tasteless, and essentially American, the diners are places of human intersection, where the real and familiar meet the strange and surreal, and they function as the banquet scenes in Arthurian romance do in providing a springboard for action.

Like Jules and Vincent, the hit-men's characters are mostly defined by function, and share a closed, monologic, idiomatic language that mixes tough profanity with an incongruous, almost genteel sensibility. Jules and Vincent, however, live in a romance world that broadens their language and range of registers to include discussions on the ethics of foot-massage, the terminology for hamburgers in France, and the unfortunate gastronomic habits of pigs.

Similar to medieval literary knights, Tarantino's hit-men emerge from nowhere, without personal history, into a slightly anachronistic representation of the present. For Chrétien de Troyes, the Arthurian setting fulfills this same representational function, with its nostalgia for a material, glamorous world that never was, while in Tarantino's films, the celluloid and vinyl '50s, '60s, and '70s seem to coexist with, and add artificial luster to, contemporary reality. In both cases, the audience enters an altered plane, where surrealism and the mysterious workings of magic are suddenly possible, whether in the form of narrative surprises or special effects.

Tarantino's characters have little bond between them other than a curious code of chivalry that has a recognizable morality at its core, a certain courtliness, and a sense that society is structured by power and governed by violence. In *Reservoir Dogs,* the hitmen cloak themselves with pseudonyms, using simple colors like Mr. White and Mr. Pink, recalling, perhaps, the striking mixture of personal names and color epithets found in medieval fiction. Why, after all, are some knights Red Knights and others Black Knights? In the case of heroes, it is when they wish to appear temporarily incognito, but most often colors are found ascribed to impersonal adversarial figures, to characters who are no more than chess pieces, murderous obstacles that constitute a narrative problem to be solved by the hero. A tense humor pervades Tarantino's choice of palette, since colors like pink and orange do little to conjure a portrait of epic machismo, and throw the general shadiness of the hitmen's world into sharp relief. However, their nominative softness is sharply at odds with their physical hardness. A secondary effect of their anonymity is to distance us from them, so that to the viewer they are more or less like automata and cannot be identified with on human terms.

Tarantino's films are pervaded with an almost surreal, sickening, yet fascinating and aestheticized form of ritualized violence that becomes a literary device, or as he puts it glibly: "Violence in real life is terrible; violence in the movies can be cool. It's just another colour to work with" (O'Hagen 13). It is only the phenomenon of distancing emotion that makes the scenes acceptable and even enjoyable. Whether this justifies the kind of violence and torture that Tarantino exploits is another matter, but it is clear that he taps a rich vein of fascination for both filmmakers and audiences alike. At the end of *Reservoir Dogs,* the hitmen slaughter each other, a fitting end for a group whose implosive and explosive world-view merits self-destruction. Outside the popular culture of the late twentieth century, a close comparable phenomenon occurs in the Middle Ages. Looking, for example, at the violence inherent in the *Chanson de Roland* and many other medieval poems, we find graphic scenes that make the ear-slicing episode of *Reservoir Dogs* look tame, as here:

> Olivier realises he is mortally wounded. He grips Hauteclaire, whose blade was bloody, and strikes Marganice on his pointed, gold-adorned helmet; flower decorations and precious stones fall to the ground; he cuts through the head from here to the back teeth and twists the blade in the wound.[4]

In the world of the feudal epic, brains spill out, bodies are split in two, limbs are lost in a welter of bloody slaughter, knights are disemboweled and dismembered, and yet the narrator can describe such episodes as marvelous and even beautiful, tinged with patent homoeroticism. When Harvey Keitel, as Mr. White, caresses the face of the dying Mr. Orange, there is a symbolic link with Roland and Olivier and countless male-bonded epic heroes. Moreover, in a moment of ludicrous absurdity, filled with pathos and self-absorption, the dying policeman Marvin asks Freddy how he looks, and we are propelled back to the familiar, narcissistic epic ethos. For a further medieval correlative to epic violence, one only has to look at the embroidered borders of the Bayeux tapestry, structured very much like the frames of a film, where in the climactic battle scene the margins mirror the physical disintegration on the field and the dismembering of the feudal body politic that causes the conflict. There is little description beyond the ritualized portrayal of battle: bodies lie twisted, and become increasing naked, distorted, abstract, and grotesque until the viewer has the impression that where the panels break off, the artists became too overwhelmed by their own work to finish. The Normans are indistinguishable from the English, and all that remains is violence and confusion.

If *Reservoir Dogs* is in epic style, taking place in a monolithic setting that excludes women, save for a little peripheral sentimentality and invocation of the eternally feminine (the initial discussion of Madonna's lyrics, for example, or the discussion about the hard life of waitresses, paralleling the minimal role of ladies Aude and Bramimonde in *Roland*), then *Pulp Fiction* follows the pattern of the feminized chivalric romance.

In lighter tone and style, it uses carefully spliced episodes that constitute a visual correlative of textual narrative interlace, and following the traditional paradigm of knightly adventure, we see the same feudal world, governed this time by Marsellus Wallace (Ving Rhames), who acts as a twisted parody of King Arthur, or perhaps the incapacitated Fisher-King of Grail romances. The Fisher-King is mysteriously handicapped and redeemable. Wallace is neither, unless the Band-Aid he wears on the back of his neck is more than a metaphor for his moral flaws, or an outward sign he has lost or sold his soul. He wields power, controls the local economy, and dispenses rough justice, without involving himself in the action unless forced to do so by circumstance, and his very name implies an uneasy combination of imperial might and materialism. In *Reservoir Dogs,* the crimelord is the stereotypical white, mafioso-style character, whereas in *Pulp Fiction* he is black, his color intensified by the whiteness of his Band-Aid, perhaps indicating that in an unjust society, the disfigured gangland underworld where Marsellus is king is the only realm over which he can govern. The palette of colors used by Tarantino is pared down to black and white, with problematic implications for the theme of race in the film. By exclusion and default, Tarantino does not overtly introduce the issue of race into *Reservoir Dogs,* where color operates on such a different level, but blatant and subtle commentary about who has power, and how it is wielded, comes across at many points there and in *Pulp Fiction.* Serious critiques can be made of Tarantino on grounds of racism in *Pulp*

Fiction, although even if the underworld kingpin is black, so is the redemptive hero: it is unfortunate that he emblematizes and parodies gangland black vigilante heroes like Shaft. The nature of representation is open for critique: however, under-representation in such a seedy universe may be flattering rather than insulting. The act of rape that incites Marsellus to "git medieval" is the most shocking in the film, and that it is perpetrated on him is significant in that it acts as a metaphor for racial exploitation. Quite how one interprets the Gimp is another matter. At the same time, it is clear that Tarantino takes far greater pleasure in exacting revenge on the redneck captors.

As well as recalling the many paired knights of medieval fiction, Jules and Vincent illustrate the topos of black and white "buddies" that has been an enduring part of American popular culture since James Fenimore Cooper and Mark Twain, and like everything else in this film, there is an original twist, since Jules (Samuel L. Jackson) is the one to survive, whereas our expectation, for at least some of the time, is that Vincent (John Travolta) will be redeemed, and most likely by the sacrifice of his partner. The driving forces in *Pulp Fiction* are race, class, and power; as well as being black and white, life is grey, and a more important distinction between those immoral and amoral parameters is that which distinguishes victors from victims. Wallace presides over a shady court that functions as an anti-Round Table, in a feudal world tempered with female sensuality that lends the illusion of shifting the center of power and interest from men to women, just as the masculine poles of epic shift towards the feminine in chivalric fiction under the influence of the aesthetics of courtly love.

Chief among Wallace's minions are Jules Winnfield and Vincent Vega, who function as Chrétien's heroes do. While the name Vincent Vega suggests something of the jaunty picaresque, and could apply to a whole range of characters including a mafia assassin, Jules Winnfield evokes precious stones, the world of the tournament, and the ethos of medieval chivalry. Vega conjures up the lone path of the aimless wanderer, but Jules' name is reminiscent of the ritualized joust, and the notion of somehow "winning the field." Jules and Vincent are an unlikely Galahad and Lancelot, while Butch Coolidge (Bruce Willis) fills the role of a Gawain figure, a successful, worldly, chivalrous loner, trying to survive in an environment where the staged fight has supplanted the joust, and where feudal duty can mean collecting payment and self-sacrifice of a less honorable kind. No less than the Arthurian court, Marsellus' gaudy clubland relies on indentured service to ensure its stability. Butch will never be a Grail-knight: the closest he can come to grace is in the form of a Harley-Davidson chopper of the same name, but he has an innate sense of honor, revealed with great humor when he selects a weapon with which to avenge himself on Zed and Maynard, bypassing lowly hammer and vulgar chainsaw for a more dignified samurai sword. The recognized dignity of some arms over others is a topos that goes back at least as far as the medieval period: losing weapons can humble a haughty knight or provide a comic incident to be later echoed in a serious combat scene, in which the knight recoups his honor—as does Chrétien's Lancelot.

The characters' intersecting stories, along with the framing narrative of the irritating ingénus Hunny-Bunny and Pumpkin (a modern-day pair of courtly lovers with a sideline in armed robbery), interlace rather in the same complex way that medieval works of fiction do. The diner and the nightclub replace the court setting, and the mysterious forest that is the locus for adventure in the medieval romance is transformed into something between an urban jungle and an archetypal Wasteland, of the kind first encountered as the *gaste forest* (waste forest) of Chrétien's *Conte du Graal,* and seen subsequently in Eliot's poetic reworking: a sterile environment in perpetual decline and therefore in constant need of redemption.

Nor is **Pulp Fiction** without its essential share of damsels, in distress or otherwise: as a set of archetypes, they recall the female figures in medieval romance. Some act as adjuvants, like the sultry and exotic taxi-driver, Esmarelda Villalobos, a marginal figure, whose twilight existence is enhanced as she and Butch drive through town, and the back projection is seen in evocative and disjunctive black and white. In medieval fiction, there are usually liminal figures that act as signposts, who randomly appear to change the course of adventures. As well as adding a tinge of mystery, such characters often take the form of ugly maidens, or young women abandoned by a lover, and their worldly and otherworldly presence serves to reinforce the virtual reality of the romance setting. In a similar fashion, Raquel, the daughter of the junkyard owner, Monster Joe, is a distant relative of the accommodating daughter of the minor noble, whose function is to make the hero comfortable, to act as a potential bride that he can refuse, and provide him with a change of horse.[5] While the filmscript has some less than courtly descriptions of Raquel, portrayed as the Wolf's unlikely consort, the film version shows him referring to her as "m'lady" (142) and handing her into his expensive car as they drive off to breakfast.[6]

Butch's girlfriend Fabian conforms to yet another stereotype found in medieval fiction, that of the fragile female; beautiful, vulnerable, exasperating, and brainless. Her main function is to reveal the soft underside of the hard-bitten boxer, to elicit a syrupy courtliness from him. Whatever her needs and demands, whatever she does wrong (i.e., forgetting the gold watch), it is never her fault. She has many counterparts in medieval

fiction, and uses the same qualities to exert power and influence over surrounding male characters.

The final, and most crucial medieval archetype, is found in the central figure of Mia (Uma Thurman), who is surely cast in the Queen Guenevere mold of French chivalric fiction. The short possessive adjective that makes up her name belies a fierce sense of independence: the world belongs to her as much as she belongs to any part of it. There is more heroin than there are heroines in this film, but if there is one, it is she; seductive, charming, spoilt, and married to the feudal lord, Mia finds a champion in Vincent Vega. Drawn together as much by circumstance and the seductiveness of power as by physical attraction, there is a parallel for their kind of relationship in Chrétien's Lancelot and Guenevere, as Lancelot is obliged to demean himself in all sorts of ways (chiefly by leaping onto a cart) to go off to the mysterious realm of Gorre in search of his captured love. This realm is a distorted mirror-world of reality (the "normal" courtly world in this text as in others is Logres, the land of ogres, suggesting a curious sublimation of feudal society), and the setting far removed from Arthur's court where the lovers can act on their feelings with a greater sense of freedom. Lancelot undergoes many trials to win and rescue Guenevere, including deliberately throwing a tournament to prove his obedience. Even incarcerated in her tower prison, Guenevere exerts a curious power over Lancelot and her captors, as if she were orchestrating events.

Romance settings abound in **Pulp Fiction,** where the seedy glamor of Los Angeles and the mirrorworld of the suburbs around Hollywood function as a back-lot Camelot; we have the memorable scene when Vincent arrives (to escort Mia to dinner and an unforgettable twist contest that has no counterpart in medieval fiction), where she observes and directs him through the artificial eyes of the video security system. Her cold, controlling, predatory gaze is very much Guenevere's, and like Lancelot, Vincent almost needs protecting from her more than he needs to protect her.

Of particular interest is the romance-type use of time and space configured in the film. At the surreal diner Jackrabbit Slim's, Mia and Vincent enter a timeless mythical space, where the infernal inanity of Hollywood fuses with a Dante-esque fast-food Limbo, lit by a neon sign proclaiming it, prophetically for the purposes of this thesis, to be the "Next best thing to a time machine" (38A, recto). As if to remind us that nothing is real, Mia designates Vincent a square by drawing a dotted box on screen, just as they are about to enter the restaurant, recalling the many narrative framing devices and moments of authorial intervention used in medieval fiction that pull us back to the realization that we are dealing with text, texture, and image, and thus with a self-conscious, artificial representation of reality as a charmed conceit. Time and space enter a different dimension in *Pulp Fiction,* an adventure-time rather like that described by M. M. Bakhtin when referring to medieval chivalric romance, as an artfully constructed space almost conscious of its unreal intersecting parameters:

> Time breaks down into a sequence of adventure fragments, within which it is organized abstractly and technically; the connection of time to space is also merely technical. We encounter here the same simultaneities and disjunctions in time, the same play with distance and proximity, the same retardations. . . . We also find oriental and fairy-tale motifs that are ultimately linked to the issue of identity: enchantments of every sort, which temporarily take a man out of the ordinary course of events and transport him to a strange world.
>
> (Bakhtin 151)

Tarantino exploits this twilight world of adventure-time, and pokes fun at its linear, rigid, limited counterpart. To see what happens to normal, linear, heroic-epic time in this film, one only has to contemplate the sordid and uncomfortable fate of Butch's family heirloom during his father's unfortunate incarceration as a prisoner of war. The choice of the watch is a deliberate and symbolic one for the way it deals with popular culture and the Vietnam War, and provides a commentary on the subgenre of films dealing with battle narratives and personal history so prevalent in the last twenty years in works like *The Deer Hunter* (Michael Cimino, 1986). The most important target of the satire of this scene is directed not so much at war per se but at the artistic enshrinement of it in exaggerated epic style. In an excellent essay on the Indiana Jones trilogy, Susan Aronstein points out that Spielberg's return to the heroic defiance of Nazi tyranny is a revealing one. The setting for Indiana's quests has the effect and advantage of bypassing the Vietnam period, allowing for the easier construction of an all-American hero: "The trilogy returns America to the time when the Allies fought against Nazi Germany, free from the shadow of Vietnam and as secure as ever Arthur's court was in the moral right of its cultural code" (7). Aronstein shows how Indiana's career waxes and wanes with Ronald Reagan's. Her enlightening analysis shows how the Grail narrative and Spielberg's use of it illustrate a double quest the lost father and sense of nation. In Tarantino's vision, the orphaned boy's visit with Captain Koons is an awful parody of the father-quest and the search for national identity, and Tarantino's protagonists thus play out the conceptual problem of heroism in the post-Reagan, post-Bush years. Aronstein says of Oliver North that "in spite of his plain green uniform and his Boy Scout sincerity, [he] appeared to many to be an Indiana Jones who had thrown his lot in with the Belloqs [i.e., the French archaeologist who collaborates with the Nazis in the retrieval of the Ark of the Covenant] of this world" (19). For her, this demystification of a heroic ideal leads

to the final Grail quest necessary to redeem a tired ethos with a new spiritual reorientation. And indeed, Tarantino bears out her hypothesis and seems to take up American cultural history where Spielberg leaves off—until we get to *Private Ryan,* that is—addressing the very heart of darkness that Spielberg's trilogy sidesteps. Christopher Walken's character, Captain Koons, is an Oliver in both implications of the name who has lost his Roland and his Charlemagne, but who clings to ideals that have become as tarnished as the watch he guards. Epic heroism in the post-Vietnam era seems a problematic concept, and is embedded at the very core of *Pulp Fiction.* The monologic and monolithic epic frame is abandoned in favor of the dialogism of romance, a less rigidly ideological form that proves to be a looser genre in all aspects.

This satiric digression into epic stands out set against the charmed world and world-upside-down of the romance. On returning to her house after dinner with Vincent, the atmosphere is charged with eroticism as Mia soliloquizes to music in the dining room, while he rehearses a chaste and chivalrous speech about morality and loyalty in the bathroom mirror, in order to convince himself that no subsequent seduction is to take place. Artificial escapism in the form of heroin displaces the magic and erotic tension of this romantic episode, but Mia still needs to be saved from the otherworld, which in this case is the twilight zone of the trip, a feat requiring skill with a hypodermic rather than a sword or lance. The only magic here is the "magic" marker used to indicate the point of the needle's entry, but Vincent effects an absurd, chivalrous rescue of sorts, where the ill—but suggestively—named Lance, the drug dealer, fails. The twisted code of chivalry at the heart of *Pulp Fiction* manifests itself throughout Vega's scenes with Lance, especially in the initial encounter at his house, where Vega buys heroin that he later shoots up on the premises: here, in the midst of the patent sordidness and illegality of drug culture, a bizarre discussion concerning the outrage Vincent feels at having his car paintwork vandalized (33) confirms the existence of a rigid set of rules, a form of behavioral *bienséance* comically at odds with the criminal activities of most of the characters, but recalling the ritual taboos of knighthood pertaining to the sanctity of equipment and horses.

I am not suggesting that medieval romance provides the most obvious connection with the narrative elements described in the film. After all, reviewers, commentators, and the author himself draw attention to the many sources, visual quotations and homages in it. The list of film genres it draws from is impressive: samurai films, the spaghetti Western and its traditional counterpart, vigilante films, musicals, kung fu films (referred to amusingly by some reviewers as chopsocky), the blaxploitation films of the '70s, Hitchcock-style horror films, and film noir.[7] But whether one takes *Le Samouraï*

(Jean-Pierre Melville, 1967), *The Good, the Bad, and the Ugly* (Sergio Leone, 1966), or *The Maltese Falcon* (Rey del Ruth, 1931, and John Huston, 1941), a narrative pattern emerges that has been with us, at the heart of literary culture, since the twelfth century, and stretching back to classical antiquity.

In my opinion, although it could be argued many ways, the basic blueprint of films like *The Maltese Falcon* is at the heart of **Pulp Fiction,** since one image and object dominates the unravelling of the narrative, and visually links disparate pasts of the story: the briefcase. A classic example is to be found in Robert Aldrich's classic film noir *Kiss Me Deadly* (1955), which transforms a pulp novel of Micky Spillane's. While Tarantino uses a similar motif in **True Romance,** the other obvious correlative of Marsellus' briefcase is the sinister attaché case from *Repo Man* (Alex Cox, 1984), which contains an unearthly force of destruction, and is the center of a hot pursuit by the main characters, but the meaning and implication of Tarantino's case gives it much more in common with Dashiell Hammett's Falcon, created in 1930. In **Pulp Fiction,** the combination of the case is 666, a number with biblical and apocalyptic implications, but its contents fascinate more than they terrify. Vincent first sees it in the first scenes of the film, when he and his partner are reclaiming Marsellus' property from some doomed college boys who are tragically out of their depth in a hit-man's world. The script notes: "We can't see what's inside, but a small glow emits from the case. Vincent just stares at it, transfixed" (22). We never see the case actually returned to Marsellus at Sally LeRoy's club (and here the regal and medieval resonances of the name are apparent, since *le roy* is "the king") in the second scene of the film, which is chronologically the last, and it reappears in the final restaurant scene that occurs earlier according to the "real" timeline.

Here, Pumpkin, who holds up the restaurant with his accomplice, is particularly drawn to the case, described in the directions: "Jules flips the locks and opens the case revealing it to Pumpkin, but not to us. The same light SHINES from the case. Pumpkin's expression goes to amazement" (153). He then asks, "Is that what I think it is?," to which the reply from Jules is affirmative. "It's beautiful," he replies, but neither the characters in the film nor the audience ever get to see it, and it remains ineffable to Vincent, Jules, and Pumpkin, who are the only ones to have seen inside. This indescribable beauty sits ill with the other description of the contents as Marsellus' dirty laundry, for there is something mystical and spiritually purifying about the case. Is it Marsellus's lost soul (is that what the Band-Aid means?), and Jules's redemption? In this regard, it recalls both the Maltese Falcon and its distant ancestor, the Grail. Inspired by crusader legend, the Falcon is the last symbolic vestige of the Templar order,

a valuable statuette that becomes the object of a worldly quest. The tarnished object is also symbolic of the possibility of redemption: dark and rough-cast on the outside, and solid gold on the inside, it is a metaphor for the true character of its avenging hero, played by Humphrey Bogart, and inspires a luminous morality in the acquisitive darkness of the criminal underworld. Its medieval associations are the vital, redemptive element, and it functions much as the Grail does.

The Grail is always an incongruous, anachronistic presence in medieval literature, and its religious connotations are dissonant with the materialistic and secular wish-fulfillment fantasy of chivalric fiction. Aside from its potential for redeeming a tired and clichéd world of convention from itself, the Grail's chief property is to function in a very modern way to decenter the narrative by making its *telos* the ever-present pursuit of an impossible textual absence, and thus to destabilize the central characters, their values and their world-view. Among those elected to seek it, only a chosen few will approach or look upon it, and for the Grail-knight—Perceval in Chrétien's tale, Galahad in the anonymous *Quest,* and Jules Winnfield in **Pulp Fiction**—it means separation from worldly things and a life spent in solitary meditation, or being, as Vincent puts it, "like Caine in *Kung Fu,*" and essentially "a bum" (148). Chrétien's tale breaks off before Perceval can finally ask the right question and achieve grace; Galahad dies a hermit, caught up in the ecstatic contemplation of divine mysteries; Jules Winnfield decides to quit his chosen profession and wander the earth. Tarantino's *Grail* is not religious, but it is somehow spiritual, inspiring sometimes ironic philosophical and moral reflection, but reflection nevertheless. It is Jules who is obsessed with Ezekiel 25:17:

> The path of the righteous man is beset on all sides by the iniquities of the selfish and the tyranny of evil men. Blessed is he who, in the name of charity and goodwill, shepherds the weak through the valley of darkness, for he is truly his brother's keeper and the finder of lost children. And I will strike down upon thee with great vengeance and furious anger those who attempt to poison and destroy my brothers. And you will know my name is the Lord when I lay my vengeance upon you.
>
> (25)

This Old Testament severity is his prologue to killing, until after we relive the end of the initial hit in the apartment, where Jules and Vincent are repeatedly fired upon, but the bullets lodge in the wall behind them without causing injury. Whatever its status as a latter-day Pandora's box, the inference is that the presence of the case is somehow protective of its guardians, and while in the ensuing discussion, Vincent is convinced that it is all coincidence, Jules sees a miracle. In the final restaurant scene, realization has been superseded by revelation: "Yeah, I was just sitting here drinking my coffee, eatin' my muffin, playin' the incident in my head, when I had what alcoholics refer to as a moment of clarity" (148). Jules reconfigures his interpretation of who is the righteous man, who are the evil men, and reassesses the identity of the weak and of the shepherd. In a wry exegesis of the Bible passage, he concludes: "The truth is that you're the weak. And I'm the tyranny of evil men. But I'm tryin'. I'm tryin' real hard to be the shepherd" (158). Contact with the case has altered an otherwise rigidly ordered universe, with the result that the light emitted from its shiny contents has allowed the passage from moral blindness to insight. There is a moment of generic introspection that reveals the flawed nature of the twisted chivalric underworld, an instant where fiction turns in on itself to reveal a dark core. The brilliance of *Pulp Fiction* is ultimately similar to the originality of the Grail narratives, to bring a suggestive center to an essentially decentered narrative. This phenomenon has been best characterized by Tzvetan Todorov. Using the *Quest* as a model, he argues that the text contains its own commentary and typology; the narrative text implies another text, the signified reveals the signifier, and the dynamism of the story derives from the play between the two competing and complementary discourses. The knights' adventures reflect the presence of these two codes: some characters have run-of-the-mill adventures that are purely narrative, while Galahad's can be termed ritualistic (70), or belonging to a symbolic order that points to a higher, more complex meaning. In the simultaneity of personal quests, the interesting knights in Grail texts are those weak and human characters, like Lancelot, who fall between salvation and damnation, and who have everything to gain, and nothing to lose. Galahad's unblemished record makes him of less exemplary value than his more earthly counterparts.

On a lesser scale, the same can be argued for *Pulp Fiction,* with similar interpretive implications for producing a transcendent form: Vincent is the doomed, worldly figure we are meant to compare with the ambiguous, but potentially redeemed Jules, and their divergent paths point to the literal and figurative planes they open in the text. The mere presence of Jules, and the suggestion of greater, although in this case not necessarily deeper, meaning takes *Pulp Fiction* beyond the parameters it establishes for itself in the opening frames, such that the soft, moist, shapeless matter becomes not so much formless as protean, capable of being molded into some new, original shape. In essence, what was once pulp becomes *papier mâché,* an original form made up of a plethora of disparate texts. The elements adhere thanks to the fundamental form of the romance, which lends its archetypal characterization and symbolic landscape, as well as its "code" of love and adventure, and a superficially casual yet finely wrought structure that is ever-experimental in its use of time and space.

The point of the preceding arguments is to show that the chivalric romance form has been with us since the twelfth and thirteenth centuries: the narrative pattern it created in the form of the questing hero in a symbolic landscape, not to mention a whole paradigm of conventions, springs from a deep necessity that is still apparently meaningful even to modern audiences who have never read Chrétien de Troyes or his contemporaries. If the signification of such texts has changed, the conceptual form and narrative parameters have not altered greatly with each new complex refabrication. Moral, linguistic, and cultural codes evolve, but if the tenor alters, the vehicle remains recognizably the same. In *Pulp Fiction,* a strong sense of generic intertextuality resonates far beyond its own time and literary space. This is not to say that it "means" the same as a medieval romance does: works like Chrétien's tend towards the resolution of chaos into order and integration, whereas in the filmic representation of Tarantino, the reverse is true. When he takes the figure of a feudal lord, and introduces errant knights, damsels, and a quest motif, the result is quite different: just as the title suggests, he explodes the form outwards towards meta-narrative. And yet the reason that the film has such a particular impact is that it transcends the clichéd "B" movie in the way that medieval romance writers made their fiction so much more than the articulation of convention: in addition to being deeply intertextual, they always manage to alter the audience's horizon of expectation, a conspiracy in which each small element takes part from setting to characterization. The casual teleology of romance masks precise narrative aims. The genre as a whole played itself out in two main ways, by tending toward the moral resolution of the Grail quest, and by making the Arthurian world implode under its own self-generative weight in an immoral resolution. The dialectic wavering between damnation and redemption is an essential part of the romance: *Pulp Fiction* is an excellent example of how the resulting moral dynamism can still be used efficiently.

Marsellus Wallace declares his anachronistic intentions to "git medieval" *de profundis*: he is, of course, unaware of the appropriateness of his words. Better than any other genre, the romance of chivalry recognises that Hell needs to be harrowed before any personal transfiguration can take place. The older and wiser hero will not be Vincent or Wallace, but Jules Winnfield, who departs like a street-wise Galahad to walk the earth in search of enlightenment, and where the briefcase finishes up, the audience never knows.

Notes

1. All references to the text of the film are drawn from the paperback edition of the filmscript. I would like to thank Dr. Beth Schultz of the University of Kansas for encouraging this project.

2. In defining epic, I am thinking in particular of Bakhtin's formulation in "Epic and Novel," pp. 3-40, in *The Dialogic Imagination.*

3. "Quentin Tarantino on *Pulp Fiction*": "When Jean-Pierre Melville was making his crime films, he talked about how it was important that his characters have a suit of armor. . . . The black suits in *Pulp Fiction,* that's my armor" (17).

> 4. Oliver sent que a mort est ferut.
> Tient Halteclere, dunt li aciers fut bruns,
> Fiert Marganices sur l'elme a or, agut,
> E flurs e cristaus en acraventet jus;
> Trenchet la teste d'ici qu'as denz menuz,
> Brandist sun colp, si l'ad mort abatut.
>
> *(laisse* 146, 100)

5. In the movie, transportation is still an issue, but it is to be disposed of rather than provided, in the form of the car in which Vincent has accidentally shot Marvin, and which has just been cleaned up at Jimmie's house with the assistance of the mysterious Mr. Wolf. In the filmscript, Vincent fires twice at Marvin. The first is a careless shot, but the second is designed to "put him out of his misery" (117). It is a deliberate act of violence that leads to blood being splattered over the interior of the car. The film version, which presents the incident as an accident during a conversation that opposes fate and acts of God against the random, haphazard nature of existence, works much better visually and verbally.

6. As for Mr. Wolf himself, we might look on him as a part-knight, part-Merlin figure, since he possesses the ability to make things magically disappear, and is the omniscient intelligence behind the unfolding of events.

7. As if to underline the fundamental filmic intertextuality of Tarantino's films, in a review in the London *Sunday Times* (1 Oct. 1995), director Ken Russell reviews two recent studies of Tarantino and mentions the contentious discovery of the Urquelle of *Reservoir Dogs*: "Who would have guessed that the inspiration for *Reservoir Dogs* was an obscure gangster movie called *City of Fire,* made in Hong Kong by one Ringo Lam?" (5).

Works Cited

Aronstein, Susan. "Not Exactly a Knight: Arthurian Narrative and Recuperative Politics in the Indiana Jones Trilogy." *Cinema Journal* 34.4 (Summer 1995).

Bakhtin, M. M. "Forms of Time and Chronotope in the Novel: Notes Toward a Historical Poetics." *The Dialogic Imagination: Four Essays by M. M. Bakhtin.* Ed. and trans. Michael Holquist and Caryl Emerson. Austin: U of Texas P, 1981. 84-258.

Calin, William C. *La Chanson de Roland.* New York: Appleton-Century-Crofts, 1968.

Dällenbach, Lucien. *Le Récit spéculaire: Essai sur la mise-en-abyme.* Paris: Seuil, 1977.

O'Hagen, Sean. "X Offender." *The Times Magazine* (London) 15 Oct. 1994: 10, 13-14.

Pauphilet, Albert, ed. *La Queste del Saint Graal.* Paris: Champion/CFMA 33 (1978).

Staines, David, trans. *The Complete Romances of Chrétien de Troyes.* Bloomington & Indianapolis: Indiana UP, 1990.

Tarantino, Quentin. *Pulp Fiction: A Quentin Tarantino Screenplay.* New York: Miramax Books/Hyperion, 1994.

———. "Quentin Tarantino on Pulp Fiction." *Sight and Sound* 4.11 (1994): 16-18.

Todorov, Tzvetan. "La quête du récit: Le Graal." *La Poétique de la Prose.* Paris: Seuil, 1971. 59-80.

Devin Anthony Ogreron (essay date summer 2000)

SOURCE: Ogreron, Devin Anthony. "Scatological Film Practice: *Pulp Fiction* and a Cinema in Movements." *Post Script* 15, no. 3 (summer 2000): 29-40.

[*In the essay below, Ogreron proposes a scatological model for Tarantino's* Pulp Fiction.]

> *Temporal immortality must be looked for in refuse, in excrement and nowhere else . . . I am dumbfounded by how little philosophical and metaphysical importance the human mind has attached to the capital subject of excrement.*
>
> Salvador Dali, *Diary of a Genius* (1965)

Dali's words are a fertile starting point for this exploration of Quentin Tarantino and what I will be calling a "cinema in movements." Dali critically links excrement and temporality, hinting at that other biological clock that ticks somewhere in the lower intestines. Dali's connection is made visual in his painting "The Persistence of Memory" in which shit-like fluid clocks/watches melt on the desolate landscape of "timelessness." What Dali understands is the amazing control the urge to defecate has upon our daily schedules, so much control that a clear distinction has developed over the past one hundred years between "regularity" and "irregularity." If the language here sounds decidedly like the language of neurosis, it is because of a neurotic cultural fascination with the anal; a neurotic fascination that Quentin Tarantino makes "cinematic" in his 1994 film *Pulp Fiction.*

I have been struck by how little "good" criticism there is out there on *Pulp Fiction* and have decided that there is something specific about Tarantino's cinema that creates a critical impasse. This impass(age) is precisely what the film is supposed to create. Critical constipation is the end result of a diarrheic cinema. In *The Excremental Sublime: The Postmodern Literature of Blockage and Release* Roberto Maria Dainotto discusses, through Neil Hertz, the postmodern practice of citation and the "accumulation of secondary discussion" and suggests that this brings the postmodern author to a condition of constipation (150). Quentin Tarantino is a postmodernist in at least this sense. His self-willed moments of narrative retention and release, and his formal practice of citation not only mark him or his films as anal sadistic but, more importantly, seem to have constipated the director and the critic alike.

This essay will examine Tarantino's *Pulp Fiction* using the logic of excrement—a scato-logic. The term "scatological" describes the visually and dialogically "obscene" (particularly the excremental); however, it will also focus on the "logical" portion of the scatological, and its relation not only to filmic narrative, but what can loosely be called Tarantino's cinematic world, which extends beyond the few films he has directed. The excremental metaphor will allow for an examination of the film's (and the filmmaker's) thematic scatological obsessions. It will also allow for a more general exploration of the postmodern world that both gave rise to and has been transformed by the film. This article hopes to foreground a special affinity between the excremental and the postmodern.

Freud might seem like an unusual link to the concept of postmodernity. Freud is useful to this examination, however, in that he theorizes a psychology (in the Wolfman case and elsewhere) that has lost control of itself and seeks, in the form of neurotic attachments, to maintain an illusion of control elsewhere. Tarantino's cinematic world exposes a culture that has similarly lost control of itself and its own "output." *Pulp Fiction* is about the randomness of events and is thus in the not-so-grand tradition of pulp fiction. It is also about the randomness of late-millennial culture. The film's organization, then, its cultural references, and most evidently its thematic preoccupation with the scatological functions can usefully be explored as neurotic attempts to maintain order in the midst of postmodern disorder.

This author's original elation at what he took to be "his generation's" filmmaker has died down since 1994. In a sense I've been "retaining" my criticism of Tarantino's cinematic logic, hoping that in the years that followed the film I could amass more evidence. Perhaps my own retention and Tarantino's equally limited "output" make this article more relevant, a more accurate assessment of Tarantino's career (*Jackie Brown* [1997] is his only feature film since *Pulp Fiction*), and a more telling statement about the postmodern condition of the cinematic arts and its attending criticism as we near the

end of the millennium. In many ways postmodern cinema denies the critic. It invites his attention and then leaves him to contemplate its emptiness. A scatological understanding of the postmodern, however, implicates the critic. The critic and everything he or she produces in response to the postmodern text is simply a part of the increasingly undifferentiated postmodern mass.

PLUMBING THE POSTMODERN

Manohla Dargis defines pulp fiction (as opposed to *Pulp Fiction*) in the following way: "Although the name originates from the groundwood paper on which the magazines were printed, the christening was felicitous given the condition of the heroes and miscreants by the stories' end . . . Every so often the pulps made it on to film, where the gore was stanched and the sex turned down to a careful simmer (Dargis 6)."[1] Dargis continues to make the insightful and correct observation that Tarantino's "(b)one shattering, skin-splitting, blood spurting . . . cinema of viscera" (6) represents a new era in pulp. But Tarantino's specifically postmodern pulpism needs to be interrogated. Postmodernism, it seems, breeds in the world of pulp. Tarantino offers the following:

> If you're going to get historical, then the whole idea of pulp, what it really means, is a paperback you don't really care about. You read it, put it in your back pocket, sit on the bus, and the pages start coming out, and who gives a fuck? When you're finished it (*sic*) you hand it to someone else to read, or throw it away. You don't put it in your library . . . Pulp sneaked in through the cracks.
>
> (qtd. in Dargis 10)

Tarantino has identified the disposability of his own tradition and has forecasted, perhaps guaranteed his own eventual failure, as pulp is something *"you don't really care about."* This brings us back to the idea of refuse. However, other remarks he's made about the film indicate his conflicting desire to create, with *Pulp Fiction,* an enduring and timeless film—recalling Dali, who asks us to look for immortality in this very refuse.[2]

As Tarantino points out, pulp fiction is handed down from one person to another: if the pages come out it doesn't really matter, they can be put back in any order because we already "know" the story. This is precisely what happens to the temporal world in Tarantino's film whose scenes have fallen out and been put back together, only out of order. This idea of time re-ordered is the basis of editing itself. However, Tarantino's use of this tactic is motivated by an anal sadistic playfulness—he retains and releases his narrative like the child in Freud's Fort/Da game.[3] In fact, Tarantino's original idea was to release the film in fragments at festivals, and amass these pieces until they amounted to a feature-length film (Tarantino 10). The recyclability of pulp fiction, the idea that it represents an undifferentiated mass of the "stuff" of popular culture ordered, re-ordered, retained and released by the creator, is precisely what marks it as postmodern.

Tarantino's conceptualization of this recyclability, however, is also curiously biological. Tarantino, like any good twenty/thirty-something American, has consumed popular culture. His cinematic practice has been to foreground that process of consumption—he gives back, in digested form, the culture that he has consumed. This is most apparent in his "recycling" of actors. In an interview in *Sight and Sound*, Tarantino defends his decision to use Bruce Willis for the part of Butch in the film: "One of the things that Bruce Willis brings to the part is that his role as the boxer Butch is similar to some of the characters he's played, except that they've never had to run the gauntlet Butch does. I wanted him to be a complete fucking asshole . . . I wanted him to be a bully and a jerk" (Tarantino 10). Later in the self-conducted interview, Tarantino claims that what "excites (him) is the idea of putting people together" (Tarantino 10). By choosing Willis to play the part of Butch, Tarantino establishes a connection to another film in which Willis and co-star John Travolta worked together, sort of: *Look Who's Talking* (1990). In the film, Willis is the spermatic, embryonic and infantile voice of Mikey, an illegitimate child who forms a special attachment to the cab driver (John Travolta) who facilitates his birth. The film is otherwise of no interest, but this seems to be the point. Tarantino's cross-referencing isn't especially discriminating; its silliness is part of the joke. His lack of discrimination is also fundamentally postmodern—he simply "enjoys" putting people together.

The character Butch in the film is very much a "baby" or child of sorts, connecting Willis to his verbal role in *Look Who's Talking*. His girlfriend Fabienne (Maria de Medeiros) and he have a decidedly "infantile" relationship and Tarantino tells us that it is only with her that Butch is anything else but a "complete fucking asshole" (Tarantino 10). They constantly babytalk with one another and transform their sexuality, one of the few moments of it in the film, into an episode of juvenile sexual experimentation: Fabienne—"Will you give me oral pleasure?"; Butch—"Will you kiss it?" This infantile behavior is rivaled only by the other "real" couple in the film—Honey Bunny and Pumpkin—whose very names give them away.

The Vietnam film tradition is also implicated by Christopher Walken's character, Colonel Koons. In *Pulp Fiction* Walken plays a fully uniformed soldier delivering a watch to young Butch. Of course the "story" behind the watch is of interest here, but Christopher Walken is more importantly testament to Tarantino's referential mind-set. As Colonel Koons, Walken exists

in the film as a rather direct reference to *The Deer Hunter* (1979), a film that also figures the Vietnamese prison camp within its narrative. In *The Deer Hunter* Walken plays Nick, the never-to-return soldier who gets caught up in the underground world of Vietnamese gambling. Susan Jeffords discusses the reproductive confusion in *The Deer Hunter* and specifically illustrates the feminization of the Walken character. In *Pulp Fiction,* Colonel Koons is similarly feminized, here through the implied anal birthing of the watch given to him by Butch's father in Vietnam, a watch that he designates as Butch's birthright (Jeffords 94-102). *The Deer Hunter* is also crucially concerned with temporality, randomness (the roulette game), loyalty and the male homosocial bond—ideas that also govern the logic of *Pulp Fiction.*

Such references to other films create the illusion that characters are able to step out of the screens of their previous roles and enter Tarantino's narrative complete with their previous cinematic "baggage." Through Walken's character the watch becomes a symbol for the "looseness" of temporal constraints on these multiply and repeatedly signifying characters. They are what Dali would identify as "immortal" because of the immortality of film—its ability to "freeze" time and image, and its postmodern capacity for sustaining images of the past. Another example of this cross-referentiality is the Jack Rabbit Slim's sequence, which, in its attention to dancing, is an obvious reference to Travolta's breakthrough role in *Saturday Night Fever.* The fact that the sequence takes place in this particular location, a theme restaurant specializing in the recycling of pop-cultural icons (Monroe, Dean, Mansfield, etc.), emphasizes the point even further. Even the name Vincent recalls Travolta's major run as Vinny Babarino of television's *Welcome Back Kotter.* On a more subtle level, the "wordiness" of the film, its reliance on dialogue, suggests a connection to Brian De Palma's *Blow Out,* a film about dialogical excess and obsession that also stars Travolta.

Pulp Fiction, then, is a sort of waste product of popular culture; a digested and changed mass of signifiers released at the "producer's" discretion. This defecatory analogy, however, is not simply a playful one that will allow the critic to label any postmodern work *a piece of shit.* At its core can be detected the very dilemma of the postmodern condition: the problem of indulgence and waste. Tarantino has repeatedly and readily acknowledged his own indulgence in popular culture. His self-conscious *thematic* reliance on the digestive metaphor, however, suggests that the filmmaker is interested in exploring and exposing this indulgence and waste. More critically, it suggests the postmodern desire to control and nurture the undifferentiated mass—to re-order it and impose a pleasurable narrative sense upon it. This desire is both perverse and infantile, for it uncovers a miscomprehension that Freud acknowledges in his work on the infantile activity of the anal zone. In *Three Essays on Sexuality,* Freud observes that children understand the waste products of the bowels first as a gift (not unlike the gold watch) and then as a baby (children, he explains, believe that babies are acquired by eating and are birthed through the bowels).[4] Tarantino similarly conflates the processes of defecation, gifting, and birthing in *Pulp Fiction.*

DIARRHEA OF THE MOUTH

PULP (pulp) n. 1. A soft, moist, shapeless mass of matter. 2. A magazine or book containing lurid subject matter and being characteristically printed on rough, unfinished paper.

Opening Intertitle, *Pulp Fiction*

This section is entitled "Diarrhea of the Mouth" because it explores the connections between orality (both profilmic and directorial) and anality—connections that we are begged to make from the very opening of *Pulp Fiction.* The first definition of "pulp" is very much like a standard definition of loose fecal matter. The second definition is of "the other" kind of pulp that is specifically communicative or literary. Tarantino draws the cinematic line at the border between the excremental and the linguistic, conveying, in written form, the scatological logic upon which the film depends.

There is nothing particularly radical in imagining a cinema based on a linguistic model—Sergei Eisentein did as much some fifty years before Tarantino in "Dickens, Griffith, and the Film Today." But what is interesting in *Pulp Fiction* is a reliance on this very specific linguistic model in which most of the references and most of the referents are obscene, shocking, repulsive, frightening or uncomfortably amusing. Tarantino exploits this scatologically based linguistic form not only in the dialogue or visual content of the film, which many of his predecessors have done, but formally through a temporal logic based on the same psychological manipulations. *Pulp Fiction* is a film about consumption and expulsion at both the thematic and formal levels. It is natural, then, that food should arise as one of the film's fundamental motifs.

One of the most quotable and quoted moments of dialogue in the film revolves around the national differences between hamburgers: "A lotta the same shit we got here, they got there, but they're a little different" says Vincent (John Travolta) before embarking on the overly quoted "Royale with Cheese" speech.[5] Directly following this scene, the men make their first hit. Jules (Samuel Jackson), however, takes some time out to enjoy his soon-to-be victim's Big Kahuna Burger, reciting the story of the Royale with Cheese and then the Shepherd's story before killing him. Tarantino self-

consciously combines the processes of consumption (eating) and this particular type of expulsion (storytelling) repeatedly in the film. Fundamental to our scatological understanding of these scenes, however, is the fact that the bathroom itself figures prominently in their logic. During these oral exchanges between Jules and his victim, there is also an unseen and unseeing spectator who, like Vincent later in the film, emerges from the bathroom only to find himself in a deadly narrative space.

A key element to pulp fiction is repetition—the same stories are recycled in cheap paperback after cheap paperback. This compulsion to repeat is central to the narrative of *Pulp Fiction* where much emphasis is given to the recyclability of "the story." The Royale with Cheese story, the Tony Rocky Horror story, Jules' shepherd story and, by implication, the watch in the ass story, all undergo several translations in the film and are performed for several audiences. The film itself is highly talkative, relying as heavily on dialogical excesses as on visual excesses. There is an uncontrollable, diarrheic "flow" of words in the film that compounds the scatological connection between the linguistic and the excremental.

These oral/anal connections are advanced further in the "Vincent Vega and Marsellus Wallace's Wife" portion of the film. On their first and only "date," Mia (Uma Thurman) describes her distaste for "uncomfortable silences" asking, "Why do we feel it's necessary to yak about bullshit in order to be comfortable?" Mia then goes to the bathroom in order to allow enough time for the dialogical flow to resume, excusing herself to "powder [her] nose" and asking Vincent to "sit here and think of something to say." Narrative flow is once again facilitated by the relationship between language, food, and excrement, with the bathroom acting as a catalyst for conversation. A later symbolic cessation and flow of dialogue occurs when Mia holds out on telling a joke, despite Vincent's pleas, until after she's overdosed—revealing a narrative retention in which the story-telling is deferred until things "loosen up" between them. Vincent almost refuses to discuss what's been on his mind since she asked him to think of something to say. These are mandatory "uncomfortable silences" that echo the narrative retention and release practiced by the director himself. Mia in fact refers to silences as "uncomfortable" and thereby like the discomfort of constipation in its lack of "normal" or necessary flow—in Mia's case, the dialogic flow of conversation. She has the same difficulty, however, with "yakking" about *bullshit* in order to compensate for these narrative stoppages. Despite the fact that Mia is critical of "yakking about bullshit," both she and Vincent, whenever they are separated, fill in for the narrative silence through monologue—Mia punctuating her drug consumption with a chorus and Vincent chatting to himself in the mirror while Mia overdoses. Even Roger, who Vincent and Jules riddle with bullets, is not content with his safe though *silent* position, and bursts forth from the bathroom screaming. Despite the fact that the bathroom is a place one escapes to for comfort, its privacy is uncomfortable precisely because it creates an impossibility for narrative dialogue and because its location is necessarily removed from the action. These bathroom moments are directly related to the filmic spectator who "misses out" on a good deal of narrative should he or she make an excremental exit during the film.

Upon her return from the bathroom Mia asks Vincent "Don't you just love it when you come back from the bathroom and you find your food waiting for you?" She thereby immediately resumes the conversation by "yakking" about bullshit in order to correct their former dialogic constipation. Mia's question is also ironic, for when Vincent comes back from his multiple bathroom visits over the course of the film he finds everything *but* his food waiting for him—he finds a half-dead Mia, a hold-up in progress, and finally, his own gun pointed at himself. Like the spectator in need of a bathroom trip who is disoriented upon returning to a narrative which has continued to progress without him/her, Vincent misses out on the "action" of the film and finds himself in a new and uncomfortable narrative space.

Since silences are uncomfortable in this film, it is not surprising that to avoid such discomfort several of the characters enact personal verbal narrations often revolving around the excremental functions. Returning to Mia's home after their date, Vincent announces that he has to "take a piss." His need to vocalize his urges makes clear Vincent's own confusion between bodily functions and narrative—the "flow" of both are critical, it seems, for this character's comfort. Vincent's narration is fundamentally scatological, tending toward a "boyish" fascination with the obscene. But Vincent's logic also becomes the motivational logic for the film itself, which progresses in relation to his *movements*. Successful or not, Vincent's moments in the bathroom are, in an animalistic way, themselves communicative. Walter Ong, in *Orality and Literacy: The Theorizing of the Word* tells us that some "investigations of writing which take 'writing' to mean any visible or sensible mark with an assigned meaning merge writing with purely biological behavior. When does a footprint or a deposit of feces or urine (used by many species of animals for communication—Wilson 1975, 228-9) become 'writing'?" (Ong 84).

Vincent leaves his deposits as territorial markers and he rarely enters a new location without first "marking" it. This primitive form of communication illustrates the ways in which this film links the oral and the anal. Vincent's attachment to the toilet as a site for obtaining knowledge (he reads, makes critical decisions, etc.)

further confirms the primacy of this location both to Vincent and, implicitly, Tarantino. The bathroom is also a space where Vincent consumes his own pulp fiction— he is reading *Modesty Blaise* at two of these "seatings." The narrative itself thus relies not only on Vincent's continuing consumption, but his continuing expulsion as well.

The Gold Watch sequence shares a similar preoccupation with the scatological, emphasizing the logical in its attention to real time and timepieces. A young Butch (later played by Bruce Willis) gets a visit from Captain Koons of the US army who comes bearing a gift. Koons tells Butch the story of the boy's "birthright," a watch that has been hidden in two rectums before making its stateside appearance in Butch's living room. The anus and storytelling are linked through several exchanges; most importantly the passage of the watch and its story to Koons from Butch's father, which takes place literally from asshole to asshole, and the passage of the watch and its story form Koons to Butch. Excrement and storytelling are virtually the same thing here, as the watch only exists and has meaning though the mediation of the anus and the telling of the story. The double release of anal and oral, of watch and story, shows precisely how the "scato" and the "logic" of this film are united. Toilets and Temporality: Narrative Laxativity.

This essay began with a quote from Salvador Dali that seeks to establish links between narrative, immortality, temporality and excrement. The watch in the ass, as explored above, is the point at which Tarantino makes that connection most clearly. This sequence in the film sets the precedent for the way in which the film as a whole needs to be read. It suggests the arbitrariness of time—time is literally shoved up the ass—while also demonstrating the need, even in the face of death, to cling to this antiquated device. In the end, Butch's desire is to maintain control over both the processes of narrative (the story that is attached to the watch) and time (the watch itself). This is also the task of the film, which is similarly embroiled in a battle between the postmodern age of informational and temporal anarchy and a desire to control and direct those processes. The watch itself represents a patrilinearly exchanged memento of male birth, rebirth and immortality—it is shoved up the ass in order to be "re-born" later. But the process of re-birth is insignificant without the elaborate storytelling which accompanies it. It is the story that makes sense out of the patriarchal chain.

This process of time-conscious retention and rebirth also informs the formal structure of the film. The film itself is made up of three "separate" stories that, through some creative and self-conscious editing, have been melded together to form not a *seamless* whole, but a whole all the same. Tarantino remarks:

When I started **Pulp Fiction** I was trying to figure out a way to get a feature going and I came up with the idea of writing a crime short story, shooting it as a short film, then doing another and another and putting them together like a crime-film anthology. It seemed like a good idea because it would be something I could manage: finish it, take it to festivals, get notoriety, feel like a film-maker. It could be a thing in itself, and I could keep building on it until it was a feature. I wasn't a filmmaker then, and I was trying to do something.

(Tarantino 10)

Of course, the film came out "all at once." If pulp fiction is to be equated with refuse, waste, the disposable or even shit, what do we make of Tarantino's decision to "let it all out at once"? Consider the following thoughts Freud offers on the subject of character and anal eroticism:

As infants, they seem to have belonged to the class who refuse to empty their bowels when they are put on the pot because they derive a subsidiary pleasure from defecating; for they tell us that even in somewhat later years they enjoyed holding back their stool, and they remember—though more readily about their brothers and sisters than about themselves—doing all sorts of unseemly things with the faeces that had been passed.

(Freud 170)

Tarantino, then, retains the three narratives only to expel them in one larger narrative. Tarantino's is a scatological film practice founded on the neurosis of the anal sadistic. The anal sadist seeks sexual satisfaction in the control over the sphincter muscle. Tarantino's desire to "hold back" until he was "good and ready" is a moment of analogous control and retention. Tarantino's anal sadism, however, is also specifically postmodern in its attempt to control and release the flow of *culture.* This fascination with retention and expulsion does not occur exclusively at the level of the directorial impulse to create the film in the form in which it exists. It is largely responsible for the spatial, formal, and temporal logic of the film—its postmodern scatology. As the "Gold Watch" sequence progresses it becomes increasingly difficult to remember that a gold watch is the motivating factor behind the series of events that unfolds thereafter. Indeed, by the end of this segment, the story has located itself back in the same location that began the film, with Vincent's implied presence in the bathroom at the coffee shop. **Pulp Fiction,** in fact, opens and closes in the same space (and approximate temporal moment)—the coffee shop where we are initially introduced to Pumpkin and Honey Bunny and where Vincent takes his final shit. This spatial framing sets up the connection between the anal and the oral: the coffee shop is the space for planning (Honey Bunny and Pumpkin), it is the place for conversations about filth and pig shit (Vincent and Jules) and finally it is a location for non-domestic defecation (Vincent takes an extended seating here). Over cigarettes and coffee,

Honey Bunny (Amanda Plummer) and Pumpkin (Tim Roth) plan their robbery at the coffee shop:

HONEY BUNNY:

This place? A coffee shop?

PUMPKIN:

What's wrong with that? Nobody ever robs restaurants. Why not? Bars, liquor stores, gas stations—you get your head blown off sticking up one of them. Restaurants, on the other hand, *you catch with their pants down.* They're not expecting to get robbed. Not as expecting, anyway. (italics mine)

Pumpkin has helped considerably in drawing the connections between the oral and the anal. Restaurants are the location of food consumption and expulsion—"you catch them with their pants down"—which is precisely what occurs by film's end when, after taking his final shit, Vincent comes out of the rest room with his gun aimed. In this single scene Tarantino establishes the connection between excrement, food, and temporality. There is a very deliberate relationship between the anal and the oral, and in this relationship both are figured as uncontrollable, excessive, diarrheic. Such logic extends to the film's recycling of popular culture and Tarantino's understanding of the increasingly undifferentiated mass of postmodern life.

This is so much the case in **Pulp Fiction,** that toilets mediate and frame virtually every action in the film. In fact, *every* time Vincent takes a shit, the *shit goes down.* This "narrative in movements" is actually divided or punctuated by Vincent's bowel movements or by the intertitles with which they become analogous. The irregularity of the film's narrative is connected to the irregularity (or hyper-regularity) of Vincent who seems to have a bit of a problem with being too "lax." It is, however, never revealed whether or not Vincent's trips to the toilet are actually successful, though there is a very telling "flush before dying"—a flush which gives him away to Butch in the apartment sequence. His fondness for rich foods (as compared to Jules who is "almost" a vegetarian) could be the cause of constipation and his trips could simply be desperate attempts at release. In a related discussion of the postmodern condition, Roberto Daimotto offers the following comments on blockage:

But is "appetite" enough for the individual's survival? Cannot eating rather be, as Baudrillard's discussion on "The Obese" insinuates, a "fatal strategy," or simply produce a blockage? "As a child," Kingston tells us, "I pictured a naked child sitting on a modern toilet desperately trying to perform until it died of congestion" (86). Cannot the introjection of social structures, literary traditions, and Aesop's moralities, actually paralyze the childlike postmodern imagination in some sort of congestion? Or a compulsion to repeat? Indeed, the rather heavy meal can create digestive disorder, a rampant dysperia, a metabolic chaos. The "urgent message" of the postmodern author is hindered. The author "squats hastily, breeches down. Ah!, what a plunging weight!"

(Daimotto 146-7)

Whether successful or not, Vincent's biological/scatological "clock" governs the movements of the film itself. The film's much discussed irregularity in its sequentialization can be attributed to this character's own irregularity. However, because the film is pulp fiction, these trips to the toilet can be re-ordered so that Vincent's final on-screen emergence from the toilet is victorious (he assists Jules in stopping a robbery in progress and the two walk out of the restaurant) and not tragic. Tarantino has controlled his character's lack of control and has hinted at the arbitrariness of time in the post modern, pulp fictional world.

Since so much of the film's narrative is concerned with the anal sadistic and the way this stage might be said to inform Tarantino's narrative structure, it would be remiss not to address the most literal moment of anal sadism in the film; the anal rape in Zed and company's pawn shop. In the scene, Marsellus Wallace (Ving Rhames) catches up with Butch and the two men are held prisoner by a group of sadistic pawnshop dwellers. Butch manages to escape. Marsellus Wallace's violation at the hands of these men, however, holds interesting implications, along with Butch's watch, for the film process itself. The anal sadism being inflicted upon Marsellus represents a reverse in the direction of the film—it is an insertion, a blockage, rather than an exiting, which accounts for why this scene both looks and feels so disruptive to the narrative. In fact Butch has to go back into the pawn shop and "save." Marsellus from this "backwards" motion in order for the narrative to continue, creating a literal detour in his forward narrative progression. Tarantino's temporal play is here transformed into something not only anal, but violent as well. Marsellus also implies a temporal regression, a turning back of the clock, when he states in the end, "I'm gonna get Medieval on your ass."

A final sequence that illustrates the centrality of forward-moving time is "The Bonnie Situation." After blowing Marvin's (one of the kids in the apartment where Jules and Vincent make their first hit) face off in the car, Vincent and Jules go to Jimmy's (Quentin Tarantino) house to "clean up" the situation. The job is too big for them to coordinate on their own so Marsellus sends Winston "The Wolf" (Harvey Keitel) to assist them in the job. In name alone, "The Wolf" invites comparison to Freud's Wolfman, an enema addict whose post enema stools become the basis for much of the Freudian thinking regarding fecal symbolism.[6] Taranti-

no's Wolf basically performs, or orders Jules and Vincent to perform, an "enema" on the brain be-splattered car.

Jules and Vincent compliment Jimmy on his coffee (the recurrent Tarantino laxative) and Jimmy gets frustrated saying that his wife, Bonnie, will be home in an hour and a half and they have to hurry up. The Wolf, who is all speed *and* control, is the personification of criminal anal retention—he is neatly dressed, impeccably detail oriented, and has others perform the "dirty" work. The Wolf's temporal obsessions are clearly connected to his anality. This is radically contrasted by Jules and Vincent, who are constantly hanging back and letting time run its own course. The Wolf enters the narrative as a primary (and successful) example of neurotic anality. His arrival at Jimmy's house is preceded by a subtitle indicating the *exact* time his drive from point A to point B has taken, illustrating his character's anal obsession with time. He is also interested in the details of Jules' and Vincent's story and wants them delivered in an orderly and timely fashion. His sense of order, however, is too much for Vincent who questions his logical approach and, not coincidentally, winds up arguing with Jules in the bathroom about the etiquette of post-murder hand-cleaning. Vincent's position in this episode in the narrative is telling, for he represents disorder, chaos, and lack of control. He is, in short, a walking, talking representative of the postmodern who, once again, ends up in the bathroom.

Since this article has attempted to demonstrate the ways that Tarantino employs a scatologically based film practice as a means of confronting the postmodern, it seems appropriate to look for an equally postmodern conclusion to this analysis. The most appropriate coda to this examination occurs not in the film itself but rather at the 1995 Academy Awards. At the podium to accept their award for best screenplay, Tarantino and Roger Avary (the co-writer) summed up the scatological film technique in a way that seemed torn from the pages of **Pulp Fiction.** Tarantino began by stating that he had been "saving up" (words? a speech? ideas? emotions?) for "so long" for this moment. However, instead of reading from his "script," Tarantino briefly thanked the audience. Tarantino's decision to retain his planned narrative, not unlike his own practice in **Pulp Fiction** is another moment of verbal blockage. Avary, mimicking the obnoxiously over-quoted and award-sweeping Forest Gump simply said, "I gotta pee." The on-stage reference to *Forest Gump* acknowledges the inescapability of the postmodern and of "culture" generally. In addition, Avary's acknowledgment of an excremental impulse makes public the urges that drive and organize the narrative of **Pulp Fiction**. It reveals that the cross referentiality of the very film they were accepting an award for cuts beyond the level of the film itself and into the realm of dialogue "about" the film. It contributes, as I suppose this article does, to the *soft, moist, shapeless mass of matter* that is the postmodern condition.

Notes

1. This rather anal attention to the grade of paper used in pulp fiction is fascinating, especially when paralleled with Paul Spinrad's history of wiping in his *RE/Search Guide to Bodily Fluids,* which has almost too much to say about the subject:

> Daily news journals became most popular during the 1700s, and as a result printed matter soon became Western Europe and America's favorite wipe . . . German composer Max Reger responded to the critic Rudolph Louis in a famous letter, "I am sitting in the smallest room in my house. I have your review before me. In a moment it will be behind me." Similar sentiments lie behind the English slang term "bump," meaning "worthless stuff," and originating from the phrase "bum fodder" . . .
>
> . . . The use of toilet paper caught on gradually, but just as writing paper had been used for wiping, this specially-manufactured toilet paper doubled in duty to carry the written word.

(Spinrad, 22)

Spinrad's genealogy of toilet paper makes literal the connection between language and excrement. Implicit in this genealogy is that not only does literature share a very special relationship with the anus but, more crucially, *criticism,* as exemplified by the Max Reger letter, is particularly suited to do the duty, so to speak.

2. Like Paul Spinrad's genealogy of toilet paper, pulp represents "worthless stuff." But this "worthless stuff" lives on through its own recyclability.

3. In *Beyond the Pleasure Principle* Freud discusses this game, invented by a one and a half year old, involving a spool and string. The child, controlling the comings and goings of the spool by hurtling it out of sight, would ecstatically yell "fort" (gone). Upon reeling the missing object back in, he'd yell with pleasure "da" (there). The tiny event is significant to Freud in its metaphorical relationship to the child's developing activity and his desire to *control* events through the process of retention and release. In his work on infantile sexuality, Freud builds a similar model around the child's retention and release of the fecal mass.

4. See "Infantile Sexuality," particularly page 52.

5. Paul Spinrad states that "food becomes excrement, and in this way the two are closely related, but in many old recipes, excrement also becomes food. Many foods we like also remind us of excrement, and we sometimes even name them or present them in ways that reinforce the connection" (Spinrad 107). Hamburger is certainly one of those foods.

6. See Freud's case history of the "Wolf Man" in *Three Case Histories.*

Works Cited

Blow Out. Dir. Brian De Palma. 1981.

Dargis, Manohla. "Pulp Instincts." *Sight and Sound* May 1994: 6-9.

Dainotto, Roberto Maria. "The Excremental Sublime: The Postmodern Literature of Blockage and Release." *Essays in Postmodern Culture.* Oxford: Oxford UP, 1983. 133-172.

Eisenstein, Sergei. "Dickens, Griffith, and The Film Today." *Film Form.* Ed. & Trans. Jay Leyda. New York: 1977, 195-255.

Freud, Sigmund. *Beyond the Pleasure Principle.* Trans. James Strachey. New York: W. W. Norton & Company, 1989.

———. "Character and Anal Erotism." *The Standard Edition of The Complete Psychological Works of Sigmund Freud.* Vol 9. Trans. James Strachey. London: The Hogarth Press and The Institute of Psycho-Analysis, 1959. 167-175.

———. "From the History of an Infantile Neurosis (1918)." *Three Case Histories.* Ed. Philip Rieff. New York: Macmillan, 1963, 187-297.

———. *Three Essays on the Theory of Sexuality.* Trans. James Strachey. New York: Basic Books, Inc., 1962.

James, Mike. "Stayin' Alive." *The Washington Post* 26 March 1995, F: 1-4.

Jeffords, Susan. *The Remasculinization of America: Gender and the Vietnam War.* Bloomington and Indianapolis: Indiana UP, 1989.

Kermode, Mark. "Endnotes." *Sight and Sound* Feb. 1995: 62

Look Who's Talking. Dir. Amy Heckerling. 1990.

Ong, Walter J. *Orality & Literacy: The Technologizing of the Word.* New York: Routledge, 1982.

Pulp Fiction. Dir. Quentin Tarantino. 1994.

Reservoir Dogs. Dir. Quentin Tarantino, 1992.

Saturday Night Fever. Dir. John Badham. 1977.

Spinrad, Paul. *The RE/Search Guide to Bodily Fluids.* San Francisco: RE/Search Publications, 1994.

Tarantino, Quentin. "'Pulp Fiction' Script Extract." *Sight and Sound* May 1994: 11.

———. "Quentin Tarantino on 'Pulp Fiction.'" *Sight and Sound* May 1994: 10.

The Deer Hunter. Dir. Michael Cimino. 1979.

Sharon Willis (essay date 2000)

SOURCE: Willis, Sharon. "'Style,' Posture, and Idiom: Tarantino's Figures of Masculinity." In *Reinventing Film Studies,* edited by Christine Gledhill and Linda Williams, pp. 279-95. London: Oxford University Press, 2000.

[*In the following essay, Willis explores Tarantino's images of maleness in* Reservoir Dogs, Pulp Fiction, *and other films.*]

If Quentin Tarantino has been celebrated as the embodiment of 'cool', it may be because his tightly crafted films offer a distinctive blend of affective forces—combining astonishing violence with explosive hilarity—while carefully calibrated irony allows them to push relentlessly at aesthetic and discursive boundaries. Such a structure offers the thrill of transgression with the promise that the ironic frame will manage and contain it. If irony is an unmistakably social and inter-subjective form, however, the world of affective intensities seems inevitably linked to privacy and subjective interiority. That world is also, of course, the world of fantasy. And when we speak of fantasy, our most flexible interpretive tool may be psychoanalysis.

Long-standing and often implicit debates within film studies and cultural studies concern suspicions that psychoanalytic readings invariably understand social conflict through models of individual subjectivity, thus reducing the social to the psychic. However, I want to argue that, in fact, popular representations themselves elaborate social anxieties through fantasmatic structures that are apparently 'private'. Collective or public fantasies about social difference, then, take shape through representations that seem to draw on private or subjective intensities. To the extent that social difference continues to provide some of the most striking material for the collective fantasies elaborated in cultural representations, we cannot really afford to dispense with psychoanalytic tools. From this perspective, Quentin Tarantino's work offers a case in point since the steadfastly oedipal framing of his dramas works to 'privatize' his violent images and to evaporate any historical specificity or social referentiality from them. Articulating the fantasies it deploys through signature stylistic effects, *Pulp Fiction* (1994) codes them as 'subjective', as emanating from and ultimately referring to only the director himself.

A close reading of *Pulp Fiction* that remembers *Reservoir Dogs* (1991) and Tony Scott's (1993) *True Romance,* for which Tarantino wrote the screenplay, may allow us to chart Tarantino's consistent construction of blackness, and especially of black males, as a specific cultural icon. However, we must also examine the production of Tarantino's vivid authorial style in the consumer context of promotion and reception. By exploring our current working conceptions of an 'auteur' and their social meanings, we may disclose the discursive interactions that shape audiences in relation to a specific authorial persona. Closely linked to the consolidation of audiences as taste cultures, the contemporary auteur figures as an embodiment of 'style'. But this emphasis on style often obscures the social and cultural situation that underwrites it. This reading of *Pulp Fiction* seeks to discern the social side of style by exploring the ways that 'race' works for Tarantino and for his imagined audience, particularly in relation to gender identity, erotics, and fantasy. In discussing fantasy here, I mean to explore the unstable and obscure intersection where collective or public fantasies remain tightly bound in reciprocally shaping relations with the private ones that we consider to be the product of a particular subjectivity.

Quentin Tarantino's characters spend a lot of time in the bathroom, and because they do, the bathroom acquires a dramatic centrality in his work. The bathroom is an ambivalent site, since the activities that take place there become in these films structurally both world-making and earth-shattering. In *Pulp Fiction* the bathroom anchors a dense nexus that connects blood and violence to anal eroticism and smearing. It thus permits delicate intersections that connect aggressive soiling impulses with tense efforts to consolidate, to clean, and to retain, at the literal level, and, at the figurative level, with social hygienic dreams of sanitizing a word such as 'nigger'. In the process, the bathroom also realigns cultural authority in relation to refuse, or trash, on the one hand, and to 'race', on the other.

To read the relationship between private and public fantasy in Tarantino's work, however, we must look at the privy and the threat of exposure. Often, like *Pulp Fiction*'s Vincent Vega (John Travolta), Tarantino's characters get caught with their pants down. We might even understand that as the film's central metaphor. Not only does Vince Vega get killed as a consequence of an untimely visit to the john, but the anal rape of Marsellus Wallace is the most deeply embedded episode in its interlocked plot structure. Wallace (Ving Rhames), Vega's boss, is the central figure who organizes all the characters diegetically, and who orchestrates the narratives' intertwining. So, in some sense, the film is about catching the big boss with his pants down literally, even as the other characters strive to keep from being caught that way.

Getting caught with one's pants down seems to be the prevailing effect these films aim to produce in the spectator as well. Tarantino addresses this effect—provocatively—in connection with his film's most discussed scene. Tarantino tells Dennis Hopper in an interview:

> The thing that I am really proud of in the torture scene in *Dogs* with Mr. Blonde, Michael Madsen, is the fact that it's truly funny up until the point that he cuts the cop's ear off. While he's up there doing that little dance to 'Stuck in the Middle with You' I pretty much defy anybody to watch and not enjoy it . . . And then when he starts cutting the ear off, that's not played for laughs. . . . So now you've got his coolness and his dance, the joke of talking into the ear and the cop's pain, they're all tied up together, and that's why I think that scene caused such a sensation, because you don't know how you're supposed to feel when you see it.
>
> (1994a: 17)

To be caught laughing when something horrific happens, gasping at the mismatch between our affective state and the next image, reproduces or recalls the embarrassment, or even shame, of being caught in a breach of social discipline. Tweaking our internal social censorship mechanisms through such uncomfortable intersections of the funny and the horrifying, these films leave us to manage that affective excess, which we may do by turning shock into embarrassment, or by taking satisfaction in the alibi they provide for us to get away with laughing when we should not.

Curiously, the film-maker addresses this kind of excess through references to taste, food, and consumption, a category definitively mismatched with the bathroom and its functions. '"Funniness and scariness", in the words of the film geek-turned-auteur are "two great tastes that taste great together"' (Kennedy, 1994; 32). By appropriating a jingle this way, Tarantino mimes the discourse of *Pulp Fiction,* a film that, like *Reservoir Dogs,* self-consciously speaks fragments of popular culture. As these films consume the soundtrack of daily life and recycle it, bits of discourse, figures, and fragmented texts from television, radio, and print become found objects that circulate as residue or trash. That circulation may be linked to the films' metaphorics of shit.

Part of the reason that bloodletting can be humorous in Tarantino's work is that blood really operates like feces, so that the spilling of blood is very much like smearing. In all its evocation of infantile activity, smearing not only provokes laughter, but also implies violence. Though this connection between blood and shit might seem at first farfetched, a look at Tarantino's signature effects suggests that it is not. While the celebratory clamor about his emergence as the American auteur for the 1990s turns on his wizardry with violence and its eroticized possibilities, the film-maker's own appearance as a figure in his films is as closely associated with shit as with violence. Tarantino's character in *Reservoir Dogs* loudly proclaims this in so many words. Complaining to his boss about his alias, Mr Brown, he asserts: 'Brown, that's a little too close to shit.'

Soiling and cleaning are, of course, the central subject of episode titled 'The Bonnie Situation'. This sequence's sustained comic gag means to rewrite and contain the film's violence as entirely 'over the top', and thereby to ironize retroactively much of what has gone before. Vince Vega precipitates 'the Bonnie situation' when he accidently shoots Marvin, the only survivor of the opening confrontation, in the face, blowing blood, skull, and brain matter all over the back seat and into his and Jules's (Samuel L. Jackson's) hair. This moment echoes one of *Reservoir Dogs*'s central images, as Mr Orange (Tim Roth) spends most of the film's duration writhing and slipping in an ever growing pool of blood. Here, the image of blood veers away from the violence that produces it, and begins to refer more definitively to the shocking aesthetic effects the smears of red on white background produce.

Tarantino's character, Jimmy, who appears only in this episode, is frantic to clean up all the bloody evidence of Jules's and Vince's visit to his home. In a central and particularly hilarious moment, Jules, clearly the film's best cleaner, as well as its most articulate speaker, is infuriated by Vince's poor bathroom habits, since he leaves the washcloth stained with blood, and looking like a 'maxipad'. As this sequence foregrounds hygiene in an uproarious way, its structural link between blood and the bathroom reinforces our sense that bloodletting is Tarantino's way of 'smearing'. Soiling and cleaning, then, become central organizing processes for these films—at the literal and the figurative levels.

What can happen inside the bathroom? Somebody can, for instance, consolidate his position or his image, as Vince Vega does when he spends several minutes in Mia's (Uma Thurman's) bathroom posing before her mirror and earnestly talking himself out of sleeping with her. Of course, when Vince returns from his trip to the bathroom he finds a full-blown crisis: Mia is comatose, drooling and bleeding from the nose. Similarly, in the closing segment of the film's framing sequence, Vince emerges from the bathroom to find the Hawthorne Diner in the middle of a full crisis. In *Pulp Fiction,* emerging from the bathroom sometimes has the status of an emergency. With striking frequency, people return from the john to find that the world has changed in their absence, as the situation has exploded or imploded.

But the bathroom's relationship to anality and aggression is, of course, what underlies its connection to emergencies, to world-making and earth-shattering change. The infantile lining to the fantasies Tarantino's films mobilize around this site discloses itself across the story, 'The Gold Watch', the second of *Pulp Fiction*'s three embedded narratives. From its opening this story establishes both its pleasures and its shocks as rooted in infantile regression to anal sadism and the satisfactions of producing a 'gift'. The gift is, of course, the father's watch, the gold watch of the title.

This sequence opens with a cartoon image that fills the screen, later to be matched on the television in the child Butch Coolidge's living room. As spectators, then, we are watching Coolidge's childhood television of the 1960s. Butch becomes the character the film links most closely to the television; for instance, the sound of automatic weapons fire from the television is ambient when Butch wakes up in his motel room. This soundtrack recalls the opening of the story, where the child Butch receives his dead father's watch from a Viet Nam war buddy, Captain Koons, played by Christopher Walken.

Walken himself operates as an icon of 1970s' readings of the Viet Nam war, through his performance in *The Deer Hunter* (1978). As he tells Butch the story of the watch's itinerary through family history, and through men's bodies—explaining to Butch that the watch is a paternal legacy that goes back to his great-grandfather, and that passes from father to son as an amulet to protect them in war—he reproduces the deranged voice and look of his character in the earlier film. He recounts that the watch's most recent passage from man to man has transpired in the prisoner-of-war camp where Koons and the senior Coolidge have been incarcerated. There, Koons tells Butch, with blunt force, his father hid the watch 'up his ass'. When the father dies of dysentery (the inability to retain anything at all), Koons installs the watch in his own rectum—for two years. So the adored fetish for which Butch risks his life later in this episode is a gift that issues from the father's ass. Metaphorically, then, this is a gift from the very site of the father's death, and one that passes from man to man in an exchange forcefully coded as anal. Here the relentless focus on the anal indicates the persistence of pre-oedipal impulses underlying the oedipal structures. Indeed, as *Pulp Fiction* unfolds, we might see it as producing an increasingly tense friction between oedipal organization and ferocious pre-oedipal impulses.

At the level of dialogue, this scene is quite funny, especially as Walken's character moves from solemn reverence about his war buddy and his own surrogacy in fulfilling the paternal legacy to a vulgar diatribe about the discomforts of carrying a watch in one's rectum. Equally ironic, the father surrogate's appearance is heralded by a television image, and the television continues to play throughout this sequence. Television and televised visions of the Viet Nam war have come to coincide with the figure of the father. It is as if the television, and war movies of the 1970s, were Butch's father, at least to the extent that the television inscribes the father's images as endless reruns. That is, Butch has Viet Nam war movies and video footage in place of the absent father. And when Captain Koons enters the living room, we see Christopher Walken in his function as an image retrieved from a repertoire of 1970s' television and movie versions of ruined masculinity in search of rehabilitation.

In this sequence the gray light of the television presiding over the scene seems to inscribe a ghostly paternal gaze. Where the previous sequences have unfolded under Marsellus's absent but ambient gaze, this story substitutes a paternal gaze emerging from the concreteness of the television set, the site of a different kind of unlocalizable gaze. But even more important, figurally, this effect coheres with a reading of the film's overarching project as a drive to turn shit into gold. That might also be a way of describing the project of redeeming and recycling popular culture, especially the popular culture of one's childhood, as is Tarantino's inclination. To follow out this logic, then, Walken himself is part of the detritus that is being recycled here, as are John Travolta, Dennis Hopper in ***True Romance,*** and Harvey Keitel, both as Winston Wolf in this film, and as Mr White in ***Reservoir Dogs.***

Harvey Keitel figures an interesting link between the well-known actors of this generation who function to anchor both the ensembles of these films and the popular culture of Tarantino's own past that circulates through and animates their narrative and image repertoires. Keitel, however, also figures as a father. Not only is he the co-producer of Tarantino's first film, ***Reservoir Dogs,*** but his character incarnates a certain paternal authority of experience. Likewise, his character in ***Pulp Fiction,*** Winston Wolf, who orchestrates the clean-up in Jimmy's house, brings a certain paternal force to bear on the situation, instructing and ordering Jules and Vince to perform their tasks, reassuring Jimmy about his ability to restore order to the suburban home. He is also, of course, in this sequence, a director figure, orchestrating the action, and referring to the people involved as 'the principals'. It is surely no accident that this kind of director figure appears to discipline and reassure the character played by Tarantino himself here, a man desperate with anxiety that he will not be able to fulfill domestic responsibilities presumably set out by his wife, Bonnie. Tarantino's person, then, figures as irresponsible in ways that have interesting resonances for the rest of the film, particularly concerning his repeated use of the word 'nigger', a term that the film keeps in volatile circulation. But this sequence also evokes the director-as-auteur, his persona for the press.

What is interesting about Tarantino in this connection is that he provides both a phantom presence within the film and an extratextual commercial performance—which is probably why he has emerged so spectacularly as the auteur of the 1990s. This ability to combine two types of authorial function is no doubt part of Tarantino's debt to the French New Wave, and part of his appeal to 'art' audiences. In this regard, he fulfills what

James Naremore describes as the 'two faces' of auteurism. 'Marginalized social groups,' he writes, 'can declare solidarity and create a collective identity by adopting authors as culture heroes—names that signify complex, coded meanings.' 'Once these same culture heroes have been established and widely recognized, however,' Naremore continues, 'they can become icons of mass memory or touchstones in a "great tradition"' (1990: 21). Tarantino's function as an icon of mass memory like those he recycles is certainly worth serious attention. But this should be understood in the context of his appeal to cult and fan formations, and perhaps most particularly because he presents himself as a superfan.

In this respect, the rapidity with which Tarantino has developed a huge fandom may have to do with what Timothy Corrigan describes as the increasing importance of cult viewing in relation to auteurship, where the auteur operates 'as a commercial strategy for organizing audience reception, as a critical concept bound to distribution and marketing aims that identify and address the potential cult status of an auteur' (Corrigan, 1991: 103). And perhaps this is why Tarantino is so intent on inscribing himself, multiply, in his films.

Butch Coolidge is only one of a series of characters who all represent some defiance of paternal authority, such as Clarence Worley, Mr Orange, Vince Vega, Vic Vega (Mr Blonde), and, of course, the characters Jimmy and Mr Brown, whose presence inscribes the author as the kind of 'fanboy'—a film buff drawn to a collective male youth culture that he both identifies with and seeks to attract. Tarantino's auteur status is closely coincident with his cult status because both his persona and his films embody a nostalgia for a 1970s that is continually circulating in television, video, and radio.

This is the popular culture that formed the previous generation—the parent generation—now the shapers of dominant critical discourse about popular culture. And if that generation experienced as children the formative effects of a popular culture whose nostalgia and recollection were seeking to make some sense, through cultural artifacts and repetitions, of the 1960s, later appropriations of the products of the 1970s recycle them as a kind of nostalgia to the second degree: nostalgia for nostalgia. Tarantino's work stresses the absolute contemporaneity—the contemporaneity of the always already 'missed'—that television and radio recycling posit for these cultural artifacts. And this artificial contemporaneity operates as a kind of utopian eternal present. In relying on these artifacts as central organizing devices, his films offer the perfect salvage operation, redeeming a past for the generation that inhabited it, but that also 'missed' it. To redeem a previous generation's trash may be, metaphorically, to turn its shit into gold, and to posit a certain reversibility of

cultural authority in the process. At the same time, we need to explore how this obsessive return to oedipal narratives and images for processing a cultural history produces a powerful—even structuring—equation in Tarantino's work between African-American masculinity and popular culture.

Butch circulates through episodic structures that are governed by another figure who also emerges under the sign of the father and of the law. This is Marsellus Wallace, the 'big man', the boss that Jules and Vince keep referring to in the preceding sequence. While Marsellus is absent from all but the opening scene of this segment, he is clearly constructed as the ultimate authority in Jules and Vince's work-world, as well as the central narrative organizing principle, to the extent that he holds all the plot lines together. Operating as the intersection of plots, Marsellus himself is the link that connects the divergent episodes and initially unrelated characters. Having established him as the unseen law of this world, the film introduces his physical presence at the beginning of 'Vince Vega and Marsellus Wallace's Wife', in a sequence that we will later understand to be a snippet of the 'Gold Watch' segment.

At first Marsellus is only a voice instructing Butch Coolidge. When he does appear, we see only the back of his head, dilated to fill most of the frame. In place of a face, we see the blank screen of his shaved head, a surface interrupted only by the risible mark of a bandaid, of that pinkish beige color that white people often once called 'flesh'. This puny and familiar little object, placed as it is in the middle of the back of Marsellus's skull, operates as a blemish, a mark that highlights this character's skin tone in a world that is white-bound at the level of the most banal everyday object. This scene, which turns on Marsellus's transaction with Butch, paying him to lose a boxing match, also establishes his relationship to Vince and Jules. Upon noticing Vince at the bar, Marsellus greets him jauntily as 'my nigger'. Where Jules, the avenging angel, is the character who first employs this term, and thus associates its use with his own moral/spiritual authority, Marsellus is the character with the lexical authority to displace its reference, making it apply to Vince, a white guy.

However, to understand the many functions of Marsellus as authority or law, we must first read him as a disembodied figure who is most powerful in his absence—as, for instance, a voice on the phone. Though he is initially invisible, since Marsellus is soon transformed into a spectacular body, we must explore the resources and effects of this embodiment. It does not seem accidental that the two white 'hillbillies' in the gun shop-surplus store choose Marsellus as their rape victim. It seems all the less accidental as the film establishes these characters as racist through their recitation of 'eeny-meeny miney moe, catch a nigger by the toe'. Intentionally or not, this moment establishes the non-accidental character of the very chance that is invoked here. And, as we will see, part of the reason this is not an accident is that *Pulp Fiction* depends ambiguously and ambivalently on the very racism it wishes to establish as its own outside, or its 'elsewhere'. Consequently, it is worth considering how the film's apparently critical edge of suggested anti-racism, which is built as much out of interviews with its author as out of its diegetic handling of racial material, is implicated with the racist discourse it seeks to dislodge or hold up for our examination.

The smugly superior distance the film provides on these 'hillbilly' characters—for itself and for us—may be more than slightly akin to the concept of 'white guilt' and its social functioning that Judith Butler describes in *Bodies that matter*:

> For the question . . . is whether white guilt is itself the satisfaction of racist passion, whether the reliving of racism that white guilt constantly performs is not itself the very satisfaction of racism that white guilt ostensibly abhors . . . for white guilt . . . *requires* racism to sustain its sanctimonious posturing. . . . Rooted in the desire to be exempted from white racism, to produce oneself as the exemption, this strategy virtually requires that the white community remain mired in racism; hatred is merely transferred outward, and thereby preserved, but it is not overcome.
>
> (1993: 227, note 14)

The emphasis in *Pulp Fiction* clearly lies more on the side of the will to exemption than on the posture of guilt, but the two seem deeply interrelated. The substitution of an acrimonious, ironic, and aggressive posture for a sanctimonious one hardly slips the social knot that ties together guilt and a desire to exempt oneself from racism.

In their effort to humiliate Marsellus before they rape him, these characters reduce the 'big man' by calling him 'boy'. And this may be the point at which the embedded symbolics of the film's most anxious and horrifying moment of suspense emerge, because the reduction of man to boy in the context of this anal aggression returns us to the problem of fathers and sons, and to the oedipal-pre-oedipal tonality with which the whole film, like Tarantino's work in general, is tinged. As spectators, we are implicated in this scene's construction as a primal scene; we are required to wait anxiously, staring at the closed green door while we hear groans of bodily strain that could easily be confused with sexual sounds. We might find in this position a certain analogy with a curious child outside his or her parents' bedroom, or waiting outside the bathroom door. Straining to see beyond the wall, but fearing the moment of disclosure, we find ourselves in a position which might put us in mind of the film's

opening sequence, where, at a certain point, the screen goes black, and we anxiously await the return of the image. When it does, we are looking up at Vince and Jules, and we retroactively locate the camera in the trunk of the car. This is the position that Marvin's body will soon occupy, once Vince has accidentally blown his head off. So *Pulp Fiction*'s spectator position might resemble that of the victim abducted and thrown in the gangster's trunk.

At the same time, the rape scene emphatically replays the familiar Tarantino effect: it catches us laughing inappropriately. While Marsellus is concealed in the closed room, Butch manages to get free. In a visible, but unaccountable, 'change of heart' that is a familiar move for Tarantino's characters, he goes to seek a weapon with which to rescue Marsellus. Our enjoyment of Butch's slow, deliberate choice of weapon, ending up with the least appropriate, the samurai sword, is abruptly interrupted by the revelation of the rape in progress behind the door. So we get caught laughing at an anal rape; we are caught, figuratively, at the very moment when Marsellus is caught with his pants down literally.

The violence and aggression that attend this literalization produce an affective force that is somewhat hard to localize, and this may be because of the reversibility suggested by our own position as spectators—caught off guard and rendered vulnerable. In the sadomasochistic economy that drives the film's most gleefully violent sequences, the spectator seems subject to a constant oscillation between the position of subject and object of violence, an oscillation in which we are at constant risk of being caught out. It is as if the film were addressing an audience whose visual and aural appetite for knowledge—curiosity—were the unmistakable counterpart of that anal aggressivity.

Another indication that *Pulp Fiction*'s fantasies are steadfastly infantile is that in its universe everything is reversible. As soon as he is freed, Marsellus retaliates by shooting his rapist, Zed, in the crotch, and by threatening him with distinctly racialized violence: 'I'll get a couple of hard pipe fitting niggers to go to work on Mr. Rapist here with a blowtorch and pliers'. If the film had any ambition to sanitize the anal rape of its racial overcodings, this moment certainly reinstates the racialized edge to this homoerotophobic attack.

On the other hand, I think the image of this anal rape becomes only fully legible if we set it in the context of the obsessional patterns that emerge around the bathroom, and around violence not only in relation to race, but to sexuality, paternity, and culture in Tarantino's films. In *Pulp Fiction*'s elaborate performances, race is coded as culture, through its figuration as pure linguistic expression. 'Race' becomes a kind of switch point here, lying at the center of a knot that condenses oedipal rivalry with homoerotophobic attraction—repulsion, an attraction and repulsion that is also aligned with anxieties and desires about feminization. In this vortex of reversible infantile fantasies of anal aggression, raping the father reverts to being raped by him. At the same time, however, 'race' becomes a transformative term, placed at the border where identification rubs against murderous hostility.

This is because the obsessive rehearsal of oedipal structures—and of the pre-oedipal ones that underlie and break through them—intersects with ambivalent racial meanings with suspicious frequency, as it does in the figure of Marsellus Wallace. Such intersections produce negotiations that often flip-flop between idealization and abjection, two processes that may operate in a dialectical interplay around the father and extend to other figures as well. But is Daddy black or white? We might be moved to ask about the fantasmatic father's race and its impact on the oedipal dramas the film is playing out its their collisions of cultural artifacts. *Pulp Fiction* seems to channel an ambivalent mix of desire and hostility through recourse to adolescent, 'boyish', bathroom humor. And both desire and hostility seem to be directed at fathers, in attacks staged to win the approval of women and black men. Notably, in many instances, the father figures are represented as popular culture icons in films that depend centrally on a structure that repeatedly effects a displacement and substitution of authority between an idealized absent black male peer—represented by a figure such as Marsellus Wallace—and the white father, frequently associated with the popular culture industry, as either its star, or its abject or residue, such as Travolta and Walken.

The over-the-top hilarity and adolescent glee at merging racial slur with sexual insult between the two smirking characters here combine the pleasure of transgressive hate speech in the safe container of highly staged artifice—performance—with the pleasure of having Daddy for an audience. Part of the power of the scene's effect is its ambiguity about what its primary point is. That ambiguity is bound to the possible satisfactions and pleasures in hearing spoken elsewhere what remains censored and unavailable to speech. It depends, that is, on imagining that some of us—individually or collectively—must be working to censor such speech. It imagines, in other words, something like a cultural id that functions on an analogy with individual unconscious processes.

Tarantino's films seem to map social differences as competing cultures, where icons of African-American culture are constructed as an intervention, a critical challenge to Daddy's culture of the 1970s. Racial difference, figured as cultural capital or expressivity, operates fantasmatically to interrupt white paternal author-

ity, as young white men watch their white father under the intervening gaze of an imaginary black male, either alternate father or rival brother.[1]

In *Pulp Fiction,* the father's watch—his gift, his excrement—is a source of obsessive fascination that reminds us of the gaze and surveillance as well; it is as if the watch, like the television, and popular culture in general, were an instrument of the reversible gaze. In this web of reversible infantile fantasies, authority and its gaze are linked to shit. But which father is watching? If the repetition of oedipalized couplings of men perhaps provides us some clue about the address of the masculine posturings that emerge as the central subjects of Tarantino's films, this may suggest that the point of address is as important as the performance itself.

To understand Marsellus Wallace's function as a paternal figure, saturated with racial meanings, we need to see this figure in relation to *Pulp Fiction*'s other black male authority: Jules. Jules the avenger, quoting redemptive verses from Ezekiel to his victims, is the only character who judges the universe these characters inhabit. Finding it insufficient, he retreats from it. Effectively, by exiting when he does, he puts an end to the potentially endless series of episodes that might unfold here. If Jules is the ultimate judge, and the would-be redeemer of Honey Bunny and Pumpkin, he is also the film's most consistent viewpoint and mouthpiece; he sees and analyzes everything. By contrast, we never see things from Marsellus's point of view directly. This effect helps to establish his perspective as omniscient and unsituated, as the patriarchal god who commands and judges, where Jules mediates and redeems. There is one exception to the Law of Marsellus's indirect point of view, however, one shot that seems anchored to and governed by his gaze. This is the moment when Jimmy's absent wife, Bonnie, is given to our sight, as Marsellus, talking on the phone with Jules about the 'situation', imagines her coming home to find the disarray. This shot, assigned to Marsellus's knowledge or fantasy, establishes Bonnie as a black woman.

If Marsellus Wallace may figure the law of the film, his authority is superseded by that of the black woman, Jimmy's wife, whose image, after all, he supplies for us. Whereas the other women in *Pulp Fiction* appear as narrative agents only to the extent that they produce accidents for the men to handle—Fabian's forgetting Butch's watch, for instance, or Mia's heroin overdose—the woman is the whole point of the Bonnie situation. The segment is conditioned by and addressed to her absence. When Jules and Vince retreat to Jimmy's suburban house to clean their car and to dispose of Marvin's body, the situation goes into comic overdrive as Marsellus calls in a specialist, Mr Wolf, to mobilize the bumbling group in a desperate cleaning binge. As this segment devotes itself entirely to the men's anxiety about a woman's anger, it is shaped by a parodic address to Mommy.

This very address shows the father to be deficient. The figure of the black woman interrupts his authority, since even Marsellus fears Bonnie. Of course, this is part of the segment's comic effect: all these violent, aggressive males, including the most hypermasculinized, Marsellus, are intimidated by the absent, unseen nurse—the phallic Mommy. And we know this because the fantasy of Bonnie's return to catch the boys in the act is visualized from Marsellus's point of view. Hence, the black father is completed and complemented by an address to an absent black woman. And the phallic overtones assigned to racial inflection are the most significant symptoms of the specific racial fetishism that conditions Tarantino's filmic universe.

We've seen this before: the men's behavior in the Bonnie situation echoes the fumbling band of boy fans who fetishize blaxploitation heroine Pam Grier in *Reservoir Dogs.* These guys may remind us that *Pulp Fiction*'s male group at Jimmy's house is like a bunch of fans. And perhaps the fans in the films, and the fans imagined to be in the audience, are a group of guys that it's fun to hang out with, but that you would not want Mom to see? Perhaps this is why the Bonnie situation is so compellingly essential to the narrative intricacies of *Pulp Fiction,* because it discloses a central motivation for the film's excesses, playing with what you wouldn't want Mom to see or hear: shit, genitals, and obscene language. Such a reading is consistent with the status of feminine authority in the Bonnie situation. This status, in turn, is consistent with the film's gendered universe, where all challenges to authority are marked as oedipally addressed: to Mommy or Daddy.

But there is another aspect to this authority as well. Tarantino's character expresses his rage and anxiety in a characteristic riff where dialogue comes close to pure performance. He rants on and on: 'What do you think this is? Dead nigger storage?' This explosive eruption, coming from the white actor, and repeated four times, is clearly meant to shock. In the context of this episode and the absent authority who presides over it, the film aims to place racist epithet at the same level as obscenities. Everything proceeds as if, by figuring Jimmy's wife as African-American, the film could insulate the director's own image from the racist edge of his discourse. Bonnie functions, then, as his alibi; she is supposed to exempt him from cultural rules, from ordinary whiteness. This alibi function is consistent with many popular cultural representations of interracial relationships, where each partner's racial identity is imagined to be interrupted, realigned, and exempted from its own category by virtue of the other partner's difference.

Given the way the film sets her up as the ultimate judge of the men's housekeeping operation, Bonnie both authorizes this moment of verbal smearing and spewing, and symbolically cleans it up, or sanitizes it. Thus, this moment emerges as contained by the female authority to whom it is addressed. Equally important, the condensation of aggression, abjection, and authority here constitutes the implosion of the oedipal narrative into the pre-oedipal figure it both addresses and wards off, the phallic mother. A central address to absent feminine authority might explain some of the pleasures of Tarantino's films for the young males who largely constitute his fan audience. But it may also account for an appeal to certain female spectators as well. Tarantino's films are nothing if not symptomatic. If the absence of women in *Reservoir Dogs,* for example, or in 'The Bonnie Situation' does not put off female spectators, it may be because Tarantino's films display a masculinity whose worst enemy is itself. Or, it may be because the film interpellates women spectators into the reassuring posture of judge, adjudicator, or evaluator. In this case, self-deconstructing adolescent white masculinity is on parade before the discerning, and perhaps satisfied, feminine gaze, a gaze that can take its distance from a transgressive eruption designed precisely to provoke her.

In this particular structural sense, it is worth considering that the viewing pleasures that Tarantino's films mobilize resemble pornographic ones. That is, they may draw on some of the same energies that are at play for the presumed masculine addressees of certain versions of heterosexual pornography, and, specifically, on the structure of the fourth look. Paul Willemen describes this fourth look and its effects as follows. The possibility of the 'overlooking-look' that haunts our exercise of the scopic drive, he argues:

> gains in force when the viewer is looking at something she or he is not supposed to look at, either according to an internalized censorship (superego) or an external, legal one (as in clandestine viewings) or, as in most cases, according to both censorships combined.

> (1992: 174)

The fourth look, then, articulates internal psychic processes with a social dimension. Interestingly, for Willemen, there is reason to speculate that the fourth look is most often imagined as a feminine spectator overlooking the male viewer. It may be specifically in relation to the possibility of a feminine fourth look catching the viewer unawares that his pleasure emerges.

In the viewing structures Tarantino's films offer us, the pleasures of transgressive viewing are secured in the framework that mobilizes a judging gaze, which both threatens the spectator with exposure and also guarantees a certain containment. The figure of the woman overlooking the scene, like Bonnie, for instance, represents the social and its censoring demands, while she also serves as a reproachful addressee. Consequently, within the pleasurable structures of reversibility that allow the viewer to be both subject and object of the look, she might be imagined to be the origin as well as the addressee of the fantasies, and specifically the fantasy of the phallic woman who can manage all the men.

At the same time, the film inscribes an address to two audiences, the one performing for the other. If the fourth look is assigned to women and African-Americans, mostly males, the specular aggressive posturing and display that animates the gang in *Reservoir Dogs,* much as it does the group in the Bonnie situation, seems designed to capture the fascinated and transgressive identifications of white male fans. Tarantino's films imagine a fandom for 'boys' that would recognize itself through an identification with a bad boy fan auteur. The films and the fandom, however, depend upon a reinscription of sexual and racial difference to mark the border that sets this band apart. [We remember that Tarantino's films appear under the logo 'band apart' films, in a reference to Godard's *Bande à part* (*Band of Outsiders*) (1964).]

Outsiders become insiders in view of a virtual gaze overlooking their specular posturing for each other, and overhearing the stream of insults and obscenities with which they amuse themselves. We might ask how this circuit of specularities and identifications is linked to *Pulp Fiction*'s drive to lift the word 'nigger' out of its web of social meanings, and how its ruse that this is a simple lifting of repression, like any other, can only fail. One reason for this failure is, of course, that the pleasurable charges the film means to mobilize as the word erupts from its characters are structurally associated with obscenity and anal aggression.

Within the rather resolute oedipality of these structures, Bonnie figures as the ultimate condensation of gendered and racialized authority, an authority that seems to preside over the circulation of racial epithets as a form of transgressiveness that is exactly equivalent to obscenity. But this is a false analogy, and we need to inquire why obscenity and aggression continually accumulate at the borders of racial difference. This overcharged friction around racial difference seems to blend abjecting and idealizing impulses, just as it mingles fetishism—in the fantasy that blackness is phallic—with projective identifications. Part of what Bonnie authorizes, I want to suggest, is white male posturing in imitation of *images* of black men. Of course, Jimmy's 'dead nigger storage' riff is a paradigmatic example of this posturing.

Tarantino's universe seems to depend intimately on just such an iconic construction of African-American masculinity. This is the universe in which *Pulp Fiction*

posits that the term 'nigger' can be neutralized through a generalized circulation in which it designates anyone at all, of whatever race. Race plays similarly in *Reservoir Dogs.* One of the more hilarious moments in that film involves a problem of color and naming. As Joe Cabot prepares his men for 'the job', he assigns them aliases: Brown, Blonde, Blue, Orange, Pink, and White. Pink's name is the subject of much joking and of dissatisfaction to its bearer: 'pink, faggot, pussy'. One character demands to know why they cannot pick their own names. 'It doesn't work out', Cabot replies. 'Put four guys in a room and let them pick their own colors, everybody wants to be Mr Black.' 'Black' is the coolest name, and, for these characters, the only other 'cool-sounding' name is 'white'. It is this boyish association of 'blackness' with 'cool' that forms the context in which we may examine the circulation of the word 'nigger' among the interlocutors who inhabit *Pulp Fiction.*

Through white men's identifications with them, black men become icons, gestural repertoires, and cultural artifacts, as the threads of cross-racial identification wind around a white body that remains stable. Perhaps more important, these fantasmatic identifications maintain an aggressive edge: the white subject wants to be in the other's place, without leaving its own. These are identifications that still operate through a gaze that is imagined to remain stable before the volatile image it wants to imitate. What results is a re-inscription of black masculinity as an image, a cultural icon, seen through white eyes. And this why neither Bonnie nor Marsellus Wallace really has a point of view.

In a commentary for the *Chicago Tribune,* Todd Boyd examines and contests the use of the word 'nigger' in *Pulp Fiction.* For Boyd, in our current cultural context, 'the recurrent use of the N-word has the ability to signify the ultimate level of hipness for white males who have historically used their perception of black masculinity as the embodiment of cool' (1994: 2C). This use of the word, Boyd contends, allows for persistent reference to 'one's own whiteness without fear of compromise'. In effect, Tarantino's films seem to re-territorialize and re-stabilize whiteness. In the process, however, they offer up explicit anxieties about race for critical scrutiny. Such anxieties clearly emerge in the fascination invested in a masculinity that expresses itself as racialized *and* as constituted by the exclusions it continually memorializes.[2] But, in the context of ongoing cultural work that remakes 'race' both for and against racism, we need to entertain the possibility that *Pulp Fiction* might re-secure racialized representations for a racist imaginary, even as it tries to work them loose from it.

Pulp Fiction parades an identificatory delirium, where white men posture as 'talking black', and thus confuse speaking as and speaking with their objects of identification. Like its author, the film seems to believe there is a certain inoculating effect to code mixing and repetition.[3] What the film forgets to remember is that social force of words cannot be privatized, that it cannot cite the word 'nigger' outside a context formed by its enunciative conditions, which include the author's social location, as well as the word's history. Indeed, the word functions to highlight the ways the very racism the film discourse wants to abject instead forms the border against which it takes shape. Equally important, this dream of sanitation ignores the force of the unconscious speaking through us. But what if, in a spectacular misfire, that word becomes the signifier that organizes all the others, much the way Marsellus Wallace's body seems to organize all the other bodies? What if the word itself remembers history? It then remembers *for* the film, and it acts like the film's unconscious.

Given the public enthusiasm with which the author persona connects his 'will to cool' with his desire to imitate his own cultural fantasy of black males, Todd Boyd's analysis of the uses of 'the N-word' seems all the more compelling. As he indicates, this word also circulates frequently through a wide variety of African-American authored popular culture. This circulation may be precisely what allows Tarantino to appropriate the term as an artifact from the culture with which his films seem to entertain a playful and admiring rivalry. Tarantino's use of the word has as much to do with the wish to mark himself as a cultural 'outsider' with the privilege of an 'insider' within the 'outsider' culture he fetishizes. And the word stands as the mark of precisely that fetishization.

The steadfastly oedipal nature of the author's relations to popular culture—so that he can pick the term up as found object and combine it with an address to the fantasmatic black male rival through display and impersonation—may be what allows him to go on insisting on the politically progressive possibilities in his 'sanitizing' project. Similarly, his recourse to blaxploitation images, for instance, operates as a false social anchor, a mere referencing in a universe where all artifacts have equal weight. For the world of Tarantino's films is a world without history—a world where all culture is simultaneous, where movies only really watch other movies. *Pulp Fiction* is relentless in its refusal to inhabit any specific historical moment; its very collision of styles and signs undermines any effort to stabilize it historically. A variety of details recall recent decades in a dense jumble—from the twist scene and the club in which it takes place as iconic of the 1960s, to Bruce Willis's '1950s' face', to Samuel L. Jackson's incoherent hair—combining 1970s' sideburns with 1980s' jheri curls.[4]

Tarantino's characters, like his films, live in no community, none but the public space that is built into television, radio, and videotapes—a community of popular culture users and cult viewers. As Timothy Corrigan has described cult films:

> these movies by definition offer themselves for endless reappropriation: their worn out tropes become the vehicles not for original connotations but for the viewer's potentially constant re-generation of connotations, through which the audience reads and re-reads itself rather than the film.
>
> (1991: 90)

In a world of equal 'users', like Tarantino's, we are allowed to imagine that the meanings of a word in popular circulation can be interrupted and reshaped by a set of individual speech events. Similarly, the films which seek to disalign body from speech, names, and race forget their own dependence on the bodies of actors—familiar and often iconic faces and gestures—recycled and reprocessed. The same cinematic moves that figure history as cultural nostalgia, as generational trash to be collected and recombined, produce a fantasy that 'race' could be susceptible to private manipulations, as videos are to private screenings.

Pulp Fiction knows that no one 'owns' race, or culture, either individually or collectively. But it does not quite own up to the differences in the ways that we, as specific social subjects, remain dispossessed of the very processes of racialization that nevertheless circumscribe our cultural locations. And that is why all its efforts to render 'race' as performance, much as they symptomatically highlight the instability of 'race' as a category, and much as they challenge any imaginary coherence between appearance and identity, cannot escape capture in a circuit of cultural meanings that strive to restabilize race. More important, *Pulp Fiction* depends on the fantasy that the category of white men is meaning-free in order to cast it as the blank screen upon which racial meanings may be written—and voluntarily at that. Even in a filmic world which seeks to disarticulate meaning from appearance, white men figure as not meaning anything by themselves or to themselves or to anyone else. And what a privilege this is.

In Tarantino's privatized public sphere, memory and history become entirely contemporary in the user's use. It is as if these films offered history as the screen for one's own fantasies. What kind of identification does one make with this screen? In the end, the obsession to organize history oedipally upholds the powerful and curious equation that structures Tarantino's filmic universe: the equation of African-American masculinity and popular culture. So we need to ask why his films map the sphere of popular culture as thoroughly oedipalized. Their insistently oedipal account of cultural production and exchange displaces or erases social conflicts in favor of the drama of fathers and sons.

Pulp Fiction dreams of offering a screen beyond history, since history is figured in the textures of recycled and replayed popular music, television and movies, sound and image tracks we all share, and whose continual contemporariness functions as the mark of a nostalgia untethered from a historical moment. How should we take its aggressive figuration of a cultural legacy and history as refuse, a refuse whose emblem is surely the father's gold watch stashed in his rectum? It is precisely an oedipal imaginary that seems to govern this work's relation to the popular culture debris it gathers and redistributes. If popular culture artifacts are stepchildren to be adopted, Tarantino as auteur presents himself as a stepson, claiming fathers such as Oliver Stone, or Jean-Luc Godard, and seeking to be affectionately adopted by his male fans.

So, Tarantino's films seem to posit that we might read history by sifting through the father's waste. But then they do not go on to read what they find there. If they posit, likewise, that history is what catches you with your pants down, they do not examine the social context in which such an event takes on meanings. Still, their symptomatic edge extends in several directions. For better, and for worse, these are white-authored films that understand masculinity as racialized, and that understand their own context as multicultural. These may be the first films of their genre to play so explicitly and self-consciously on a multicultural field.

We may not like ***Pulp Fiction,*** or we may not *want* to like it. But, then, films are rarely about what we say we want, or what we consciously want. Instead, they tend to produce what works on us by appealing to our pleasure, our anger, fear, or anxiety, or by appealing to what we do not want to own. And this is why it is worth exploring the stunning asymmetry of the equation that seems to underlie Tarantino's aggressive identifications with the icons of African-American masculinity that he presents as exact equivalents of Elvis, for example, or 1970s music. Such an equation emerges at a moment when the dominant white culture might begin to take seriously the ongoing historical conversations with African-American cultural production that have always been centrally structuring to its very fabric.[5] Tarantino's ahistorical reading of these conversations is deeply fetishistic. But other readings, respecting history, might ask what US culture would look like without this conversation, saturated with struggle though it has been. Critically analyzing and contesting the work that acknowledges this conversation may be our best means of owning up to the ways in which we do not own culture.

Notes

1. For a study that may help to set Tarantino's borrowings of 'style' in a long history of white appropriations of African-American cultural forms, see Carole Clover's brilliant essay, 'Dancin' in the rain' (*Critical Inquiry* 1995, 21: 4). Clover contends that *Singin' in the Rain*'s symptomatic moments of unacknowleged borrowing from African-American dance styles may be characterized as: '"memories" in the framework of "forgetting"' (1995: 737).

2. Amy Taubin has analyzed the fascination with rap culture that emerges in *Reservoir Dogs* and has theorized what underlies it, specifically in connection to Tarantino's violence.

   > If the unconscious of the film is locked in competition with rap culture, it's also desperate to preserve screen violence as a white male privilege. It's the privilege of white male culture to destroy itself, rather than to be destroyed by the other.

   (1992: 5)

3. On the relationship of self-consciousness to African-American vernacular styles and their consequent susceptibility to a variety of appropriations, see Kobena Mercer (1994).

4. See 'Pulp Instincts', for Tarantino's take on this: 'Bruce has the look of a 50s actor. I can't think of any other star that has that look, he reminds me of Aldo Ray in Jacques Tourneur's *Nightfall*' (1994b: 10). Meanwhile, Jackson shed his jheri curl wig for the film's publicity still, increasing its effects of incoherence.

5. Paul Gilroy makes a sustained and detailed argument about the centrality of the African or black diaspora to Western culture, most particularly in the USA and England, in *The black Atlantic: modernity and double consciousness* (1993).

References

Boyd, Todd 1994: Tarantino's mantra, *Chicago Tribune,* 6 November, p. 2C.

Butler, Judith 1993: *Bodies that matter: on the discursive limits of 'sex'.* New York and London: Routledge, 277.

Corrigan, Timothy 1991: *A cinema without walls.* New Brunswick, NJ: Rutgers University Press.

Gilroy, Paul 1993: *The black Atlantic: modernity and double consciousness.* Cambridge, MA: Harvard University Press.

Kennedy, Lisa 1994: Natural born filmmaker. *Village Voice* (25 October) 32.

Mercer, Kobena 1994: *Welcome to the jungle.* New York and London: Routledge.

Naremore, James 1990: Authorship and the cultural politics of film criticism. *Film Quarterly,* 20.

Tarantino, Quentin 1994a: Blood lust snicker snicker in wide screen. Dennis Hopper interviews Quentin Tarantino. *Grand Street* 49 (Summer).

Tarantino, Quentin 1994b: Pulp Instincts. Interview. *Sight and Sound* (May) 10.

Taubin, Amy 1992: The men's room. *Sight and Sound* 2 (December): 8.

Willemen, Paul 1992: Letter to John. *The sexual subject.* London and New York: Routledge.

Ken Garner (essay date 2001)

SOURCE: Garner, Ken. "'*Would You Like to Hear Some Music?*': Music In and Out of Control in the Films of Quentin Tarantino." In *Film Music: Critical Approaches,* edited by K. J. Donnelly, pp. 188-205. New York, N.Y.: Continuum International Publishing, 2001.

[*In the following essay, Garner explores Tarantino's use of music in such films as* Reservoir Dogs, Pulp Fiction, *and others.*]

> 'One of the things I do when I'm thinking about starting a movie, is, I'll go through my record collection and just start playing songs.'
>
> Quentin Tarantino interview, included on *The Tarantino Connection* (1996)

Music clearly means a lot to Quentin Tarantino. It also matters to the characters in his films. Even when they are not playing music, they like to talk about it, along with fast food, television and the rest of popular culture. Tarantino himself, as Mr Brown, opens *Reservoir Dogs* (1995) with a debate about the meaning of Madonna's *Like a Virgin*. In a scene written for *Pulp Fiction* (1995), but later cut during filming and replaced with another, Mia asks if Vincent Vega is related to Suzanne Vega 'the folk singer'; to which Vincent replies, 'Suzanne Vega's my cousin. If she's become a folk singer, I sure as hell don't know nothin' about it' (Tarantino 1994a). Bail bondsman Max Cherry asks the heroine of *Jackie Brown* (1998) why she 'never got into the CD revolution', to which she replies 'I can't afford to start all over again. I got too much time and money invested in my records.' 'You can't get new stuff on vinyl,' says Max. 'I don't buy new stuff that often,' says Jackie (Tarantino 1998).

But that last piece of dialogue also forms part of a scene of a type common to each of Tarantino's three major films (*Reservoir Dogs, Pulp Fiction* and *Jackie Brown*): a scene in which a central character is seen selecting music and then playing it, whether it be an LP record on a turntable, an audio-cassette in a car stereo, a reel-to-reel tape recorder, or by turning on and tuning a radio to a favourite station.

There is, of course, nothing original in having actors show the source of diegetic music, music from within the world of the film, in this way. Nor is it unusual for music that thus emerges from the hi-fi, car or radio to recur non-diegetically, on the soundtrack, playing over scenes from which it can't possibly be emanating. Filmmakers have long used such techniques to either fill the world of the film with the affect of a carefully crafted composed score, or draw the audience into the emotional character or situation cues provided by diegetic music at crucial moments. What is different about the use of such diegetic music in Tarantino's films is that this act, the actors appearing to take control of the score, is explicitly celebrated. The process of music selection is foregrounded. It is the choice of this-music or that-music in these particular circumstances, its switching on and off—rather than just the music itself—which is made indicative of character or situation.

That scene in *Jackie Brown* where Max and Jackie discuss records versus CDs provides a good example. It begins with Jackie opening the door to Max and him walking in, the camera cuts to his point of view, and the first thing his gaze falls on is her turntable and pile of LP records in their sleeves. In between Max's saying 'You can't get new stuff on records,' and Jackie's reply 'I don't buy new stuff' we see an extreme close-up of the record needle dropping into the groove of the record. As the intro to The Delfonics' *Didn't I Blow Your Mind This Time* wells up, Jackie lights a cigarette, then performs a brief musical gesture with both hands in appreciation of the arrangement. He says it's 'pretty', asks her who it is, she tells him, 'it's nice,' he comments.

This use of music and music culture is the only aspect of this scene not present in chapter 12 of Tarantino's source for the film, Elmore Leonard's novel *Rum Punch* (Leonard 1998). Allowing for cuts, Tarantino's visualisation here is otherwise faithful to the spirit of the original. Not long after, we see an extreme close-up of a vertical rack of cassette spines labelled 'Best of the Delfonics', then Max going to the record-shop counter to buy the song he discovered from Jackie. Later, he mouths along to the lyrics while listening to *Didn't I Blow Your Mind This Time* in his car. He is still listening to this song on his car cassette player as he drives up to the Del Amo Mall to play his part in the plot's sting. Finally, and most comically, the song sweeps out of his car stereo once more, as tense Ordell, driving them to the dramatic denouement at Max's office where who-is-shafting-whom will finally be revealed, punches the cassette into the system. 'I didn't know you liked the Delfonics,' he says. 'They're pretty good,' says Max.

A fair conclusion from this example might be that this foregrounding of music control is wholly attributable to Tarantino, and a device of which he is particularly fond. It performs a number of functions. The film theorist in us spots the case with which it enables a particular piece of music emanating from the diegesis to recur.

Music fans can appreciate Tarantino's knowledgeable plundering of the back catalogue, here choosing a Philly sound hit from 1970, close enough to the era of the blaxploitation movies of the early 1970s, to which *Jackie Brown* is in part a homage, to provide aural consistency to the tribute. More importantly, however, the sound of *Didn't I Blow Your Mind* is given four new, different signifying functions within the specific context of this particular diegesis. As Jackie drifts into a brief reverie at its prompting, we cannot but see the song as signifying for Jackie general memories, probably of her youth. Secondly, her decision to play such a record to Max is itself a performative act of display of identity. To Max, the record and her reaction signifies to him that this is indeed a woman with a particular identity and past. Finally, Max's subsequent frequent replaying of the song in his car is a sign to the audience of his connection with Jackie.

It is this that makes its final recurrence simultaneously tense and comic. Surely Ordell will now realise the extent of Max's intimacy with Jackie, and realise he's being set up? But his question reveals that although thinking himself a cool guy, he, unlike us, does not realise how significant this song is. Instead, his black man's question merely draws attention for the first time to our preconception of the apparent absurdity of a middle-aged white man digging old Philly soul. We laugh with nervous relief, and at our own taste-culture prejudices.

What is noticeable about these various significations is that at no point is the song's meaning fixed. What it means precisely to Jackie and Max remains unclear. Clearly, what matters most about much of the music in Tarantino's films—all of it culled from existing records and movies—is the situational use his characters make of it. But before exploring further why this has helped his films' soundtracks touch a chord with young cinema audiences, it must be acknowledged that this is just one of the locations for music in his films of which there are three.

(I) MUSIC FOR MAIN THEMES AND SCORING

These are the records Tarantino selects to play over the main credits at the beginning (and end), as well as music that is played over certain scenes—in lieu of a composed score—which does not emanate from the world of the film. With the exception of *Reservoir Dogs'* use of the device of having almost all its music supposedly played on the radio station *K-Billy*'s 'Super Sounds of the Seventies Weekend', this music remains largely non-diegetic, outside the world of the film.

(II) UNSELECTED, INCIDENTAL DIEGETIC MUSIC

Occasional instances of music playing mainly in public places—shops, bars, coffee shops—which the leading characters have not chosen. Examples include Al

Green's *Let's Stay Together* playing as Marsellus briefs Butch in his club, near the beginning of *Pulp Fiction*; and *(Holy Matrimony) Letter to the Firm,* by Foxy Brown, playing in the record shop as Max buys his Delfonics tape in *Jackie Brown.* These fill out and humanise these spaces; act as a caesura in the film's mood (the Al Green coming immediately after the opening execution scene in *Pulp Fiction*); and additionally enable Tarantino to offer a wider range of styles of music for inclusion on the soundtrack CD, than those which he selects for particular reasons for (i) above, and (iii) below. A unique exception to these common functions of unselected diegetic music is provided by the Jack Rabbit Slim's sequence in *Pulp Fiction,* as discussed later.

(III) DIEGETIC MUSIC SELECTED BY CHARACTERS

These scenes, as described above, provide the key, striking scenes in each of the three films under discussion; the scenes which if asked about Tarantino's use of music, most audiences think of immediately: Max's use of the Delfonics, as described above, in *Jackie Brown*; Mia, first, playing Dusty Springfield's *Son of a Preacher Man* as Vincent arrives at her house, then dancing to Urge Overkill's *Girl, You'll Be a Woman Soon* before overdosing, in *Pulp Fiction*; and Mr Blonde's slicing off the cop's ear to Stealer's Wheel's *Stuck in the Middle with You* on the radio in *Reservoir Dogs.*

All the music Tarantino chooses for his main themes and scoring shares three common characteristics: it is old; it is referential to distinct musical, film or media genres; and the opening credit music features what Richard Middleton (1984), developing the ideas of Philip Tagg (1982), has called musematic repetition, rather than discursive, or melodic repetition of longer phrases. In other words, Tarantino chooses records for his opening credits whose first few seconds are characterised by repetition of short rhythmic units, or 'riffs'. Middleton says the effects of such repetition are 'epic-recursive', 'achieving a resonance with primary energy flow, setting it in motion'. In addition, this repetition in each theme is played by a unique instrument or voice, unmistakably expressive of a singular musical personality.

This last quality explains a lot. If his credit themes were only characterised by their age and referentiality, it would be tempting to see his use of music as exclusively post-modern in effect. By deliberately not choosing contemporary recordings for his themes for films set in the present, he eschews not only current pop-soundtrack standard practice (assemble a selection of new recordings that target the film's audience demographic), but also the approach of such directorial masters of appropriation of past records to locate their film's action or characters temporally, culturally or psychologically, as Scorsese, Kubrick and Allen. What he offers instead, a dated musical style, perhaps referring to film genres, might suggest the audience is intended to lean back and smirk at his knowingness.

But these undeniable characteristics are both limited in their effect by the degree of popular music and film expertise of the audience (not everyone knows the records, or what genres or movies this music comes from), and held in balance by the sheer 'epic' energy of the credit themes' musematic repetition, a quality Tarantino acknowledges he strives for (*The Tarantino Connection,* 1996: track 1, interview). For example, it is possible—if unlikely—to be familiar with soul legend Bobby Womack's career; to recognise the opening credit music to **Jackie Brown** as his theme song for the 1972 Barry Shear American thriller *Across 110th Street* (1972); and to sense that the film will therefore be in part a homage to blaxploitation movies of those years; and yet become wholly involved in this particular story from the moment Womack starts singing.

His is the first voice of the film. As light fades up on the 1970s wall mosaics inside Los Angeles airport, he moans a wordless, descending figure, twice, with a slight variation. Its melodic fall, in two successive triplets, is expressive of endless lament. It says, in effect, 'bad things will always happen, and they're about to happen again'. Then the verse, the main melody, begins as Jackie Brown appears; and the camera (tracking Jackie's progress along the travelator), the narrative and the lyric all start to move simultaneously. But her mature, blank face is still. It is thus inevitably connected with Womack's voice at the centre of the soundtrack's stereo imaging, a fixed point in the midst of his trademark chattering rhythm guitars and clavinet keyboard. The details of the lyric don't quite fit, but when he sings 'You don't know whatcha do until you're put under pressure' we know this middle-aged woman is going to have to do something bad. But she has survived before, the sequence says, and she will again. The music's datedness thus serves to authenticate her identity. Far from offering post-modern irony, the homage lays the foundation stone of Jackie's character. In the film *Across 110th Street* Womack's song had accompanied shots of a large black Cadillac driving through rough-looking areas of New York before arriving in Harlem, establishing the environment and world of the film. Tarantino, however, sharpens its focus onto a single character, drawing on the music's cultural associations to locate both his actress' performed past, and her character's background.

Something rather different is happening with the music in the opening credit sequence of *Reservoir Dogs.* The fact that K-Billy's 'Super Sounds of the Seventies' has already been mentioned—and praised—in the opening, pre-credit scene, means when the voice of Steven

Wright as the DJ is heard as the screen fades to black as the men get up to leave the restaurant, we know the music we hear and its source has some meaning in the lives of these characters. The George Baker Selection's *Little Green Bag* is not so much a detached, authorial commentary on these men, as a musical emanation of the world as they hear it.

Tarantino himself has spoken of his intent to use the 'sugariness, catchiness, lightness' of early 1970s bubble-gum pop singles throughout this film to either 'lighten up' some scenes, 'making it funnier', or to make the torture scene 'even more disturbing' (Dawson 1995: 79-81). Elsewhere he has been quoted describing this as providing 'ironic counterpoint' to the visual action (Ciment and Niogret 1998: 21), a conventional terminology which other critics have been happy to seize on to explain the function of the **Reservoir Dogs** soundtrack (Barnes and Hearn 1996: 102). However, Claudia Gorbman has persuasively pointed out the limitations of this critical description of narrative/music relationships in film studies, restricting music's function to providing either 'parallelism' or 'counterpoint': these notions 'erroneously assume the image is autonomous' (Gorbman 1987: 15). She offers instead 'mutual implication'. This too implies commentary, but crucially, reciprocity between visuals and music. The film sound theoretician Michel Chion goes further, arguing that genuine 'audio-visual counterpoint' is rare in film, because 'sound and image fall into different sensory categories', so to apply the term at all is 'an intellectual speculation rather than a workable concept' (Chion 1994: 36). He goes on to suggest that what most film critics actually mean by 'counterpoint' is merely a contrast, which he defines as 'audiovisual dissonance, counterpoint-as-contradiction' (Chion 1994: 37-9). Counterpoint, however, in its strict musicological meaning, refers to two or more independent melodic lines that have independent musical life, each with its own rhythm; when individual notes in each line meet at the same point in time, we call that harmony (see Cummings 1995: 139; Burt 1994: 6; Chion 1994: 36). The writer and film composer George S. Burt argues that film and music can interact contrapuntally, with each medium perceived independently, but combining to 'make a statement that is larger than each of the component parts' (Burt 1994: 6). It is perhaps this kind of audio-visual harmony which characterises the main titles of **Reservoir Dogs.**

The images of the **Reservoir Dogs** titles sequence are hardly autonomous, because they are very obviously manipulated by Tarantino to fit the music. Why is everything in slow motion? Why are the men shown walking from right to left together, then towards the camera individually, then in longshot from behind walking away together? An obvious, practical answer to the first question is that slowing the sequence down means it's long enough to allow a full hearing of both the main themes of *Little Green Bag.* This is not as cynical as it might sound. Under Steven Wright's DJ announcement and the fade-to-black we hear the first statement on solo bass guitar of the first theme, or riff, of *Little Green Bag,* with tambourine. Over the repetition, now with drums and extra half-notes within the bass riff, seeming to up the urgency to double-time, we see the group from side-on, moving into shot in slow motion from screen right. But from the start of the vocal, we move to a sequence of slow motion head-on shots of the cast, with each actor getting two bars exactly of credit-time each: the edits fall on the first beat of every other bar. These shots of the eight players consequently neatly fill the entire sixteen bars of the complete statement of this theme. With the jump to the second, more melodic and light hearted seeming theme, played over a swinging Latino *La Bamba* rhythm, the image jumps to the long shot, from the rear, of the men walking away, with the film's title scrolling up. At the end of the vocal statement of this theme, the screen goes black and the remaining credits scroll up over its instrumental repetition.

The music's rhythmic and thematic structure is thus foregrounded throughout by the visual editing. Chion has categorised such 'synchronous cuts in both sound and image track' as examples of what he calls 'synchpoints', which are 'salient moments of an audiovisual sequence during which a sound event and a visual event meet in synchrony' (Chion 1994: 58-9). With visuals and music locked together at the beginnings and ends of musical measures, song-parts and different points-of-view shots, then perhaps we can for once—acknowledging Chion's warning—apply counterpoint as a metaphor. The two independent melodic lines in this composition are the slo-mo men's legs, faces and backs; and George Baker's two-part song. The harmony between audio and visual lies in the synch-points.

As Tarantino rightly acknowledges, credits are frequently the only 'mood-time' films allow themselves (*The Tarantino Connection* 1996: 1). Slow motion here, then, encourages us to linger a moment, really look at these men, perhaps hinting that it's our last chance to see them all together. Indeed, the pre-credit scene, in which they argue violently over Madonna's *Like a Virgin* and attitudes to tipping, has already revealed the tensions within the group. The first theme of 'Little Green Bag' is another distinctively individual solo voice, this time on the bass guitar, playing an 'epic' riff which seems to set the action in motion. But its recursive nature, going over the same small musical territory time and again, combined with slow motion and the close-up for two measures on each face, suggests the self-absorption of these men, each individual bound up in an image of himself as a black-suited, sunglass-

wearing villain. Then the second musical theme reveals the track's initial grooviness as phony, replaced as it is by a pale, third-hand imitation of Latino sophistication.

Combined with the long shot of the men's backs, a mundane reworking of a Hollywood cliché—the heroes walking off into the setting sun—it's hard not to suppress a smirk. The film has hardly begun, and we are being invited to wave these men goodbye. The story is already over, this sequence says: stay watching only to find out how it ended. Factor-in the lyrics about an absurd, paranoid search for lost drugs, and the comedy is complete. Look at these losers, says Tarantino, just listen to their music. Again, this credit sequence does not so much use music as 'ironic counterpoint', but as part of a synchronic—and thus harmonic—narrative whole, a mini audio-visual pageant.

So the music in the opening credits of both *Jackie Brown* and *Reservoir Dogs* is drawn from the diegesis, and is used to say something about character: at the end of *Jackie Brown* we see her driving away in Ordell's car, mouthing along to the Bobby Womack song, so the connection with her character is made explicit. By contrast, despite its impact on *Pulp Fiction*'s soundtrack CD sales (up to June 1999, *Pulp Fiction: Music from the Motion Picture,* had sold over 1 million copies in the UK alone, compared to *Reservoir Dogs*' 300,000, and *Jackie Brown*'s 100,000, according to MCA Records and Maverick/Warner; and *Pulp Fiction* has sold more than 3 million copies in the USA [Smith 1998: 195]). Dick Dale's surf guitar instrumental *Misirlou* is used in a more straightforward way, to make a directorial statement of intent about the tone and mood of the film as a text or experience. This is sustained by the use of other surf instrumentals throughout the film. The characters do not—with one exception—listen to surf music themselves; it is not meant to represent their taste. Instead, as Tarantino says, it functions as 'rock n' roll Ennio Morricone music, rock n' roll spaghetti western music' (Dargis 1998: 69). It supplies a distinct kind of musical intensity of style, to complement the film's verbal and visual exaggeration.

This is especially true of the opening. Pumpkin and Honey-Bunny discuss the idea of robbing the coffee shop, with liberal use of the 'f' word. As they begin the robbery, Honey-Bunny screams 'Any of you fuckin' pricks move and I'll execute every motherfuckin' last one of you!' To underline the extreme language, at this moment the action freeze-frames on their outstretched, pointing guns, and Dick Dale's unique electric guitar sound surges in for the main titles.

In this case, unique is the right word. As his followers, the 'Dick-heads' know, Dale's sound was formed by the experimental demands he made of the legendary American guitar and amplification engineer Leo Fender in the early 1960s. These led to the production models eventually known as the Fender Dual Showman amplifier and the Fender Reverb unit, but these models never recreated the exact parts and construction methods of Fender's prototypes for Dale, which the guitarist still uses. There is also the matter of the very heavy string gauges Dale prefers, with a '16 thou' for the top E string, for example (most guitarists use 8-10 thou). The tune Tarantino chose, the one he personally told Dale he could not do the film without, *Misirlou,* was Dale's first recording with this exact technical configuration of Dual Showman and Fender Reverb prototypes, in March 1962 (see Dale 1996; Blair 1989; Blair 1996; dickdale-.com 1999).

Misirlou itself was a Greek standard of the 1940s, which remains popular at slow tempo for dancing the tango. Dale had learnt it from his Lebanese father. To say the tune has an epic, recursive quality is an understatement. In Dale's performance, it is not just recursive melodically, but also as an extreme, minimalistic performative gesture. Dale had incorporated the tune into his live act when a fan challenged him to play a tune on one string only (Blair 1996). As anyone who has seen him perform live can confirm, and as attested by a recent tablature analysis of his fingering (tomwbell 1995), he plays the tune once through on the open, bottom E string; and a second time, with the same fingering, two octaves higher on the open, top E string. An electric guitar had never been fingered or sounded like this before, and no other has since: Dale is 'King of the Surf Guitar'.

Cinema audiences may have become used to extreme language and exaggerated visuals, but very few were aware of Dick Dale before *Pulp Fiction.* It is not therefore unreasonable to suggest that, thanks to the unique style of Dale's guitar, it is the musical communication code of *Pulp Fiction* that is the most distinctive of the film's three such codes, dialogic, visual and musical. Subsequent uses of three other famous surf instrumentals as scoring over later scenes—as well as three rock instrumentals—are carried along in the wake of Dale's opening onslaught, without quite ever matching its impact. The Tornadoes' *Bustin' Surfboards* seems to be playing when Vincent visits his drug dealer Lance, but its diegetic status is fluid, fading in and out without any obvious sign of a source. It is perhaps useful as a mood bridge between Al Green (over Marsellus and Butch) and what follows, the brief pop-video-like sequence—edited to *Bullwinkle pt II* by The Centurions—comprising extreme close-ups of Vincent shooting-up, cut with the immediate effect: his driving to Mia's while obviously high. After this sequence, surf/instrumental rock music only recurs briefly towards the end of the film: The Revels' *Comanche* plays over Maynard and Zed's rape of Marsellus—although Tarantino originally wanted The Knack's *My Sharona* (Mooney 1994: 73)—and The Lively Ones'

Surf Rider plays Vincent and Jules out of the diner and then over the end credits. Tarantino is using it as a simple code, its extreme reverberation, spartan instrumentation and epic melodies serving as a musical equivalent of visual action that dwells on bodily abuse and excess. The surface texture of surf music—its electro-acoustic dynamics, its tempo, its sheer volume—is intensely arousing; but its melodic recursiveness allows no lyrical, narrative development or commentary function. So in the surf music-scoring of *Pulp Fiction,* unlike a film with an original composed score, Tarantino makes no comment on the particular emotional content on screen. The music only communicates the degree or intensity of emotion present in the abstract. He merely wishes to elevate the audience to the heightened state of arousal of his characters. This is why the shooting-up-to-The Centurions sequence is simultaneously exciting and uncomfortable to watch, an attempt at audio-visual emulation of a narcotic experience. Our intense level of arousal is out with our control.

A less disturbing but remarkably accomplished piece of scoring-with-records is constructed by Tarantino for the 'Money Exchange—For real this time' twenty-four-minute sequence in the third reel of *Jackie Brown.* The mood and narrative is opened and sustained by the extensive use of three tracks from Roy Ayers' soundtrack to one of Tarantino's favourite blaxploitation films, *Coffy* (1973), also one of star Pam Grier's most famous roles (Ayers 1973; Keough 1998). But these recontextualised, non-diegetic pieces—*Aragon, Escape* and *Vittroni's Theme/King is Dead*—are interspersed with three diegetic tracks listened to by the characters in their cars as they drive up to the Mall to play their role. Jackie, for example, is playing Randy Crawford's version of The Crusaders' *Street Life.* Technically, the frequent return to the Ayers riffs achieves several things. They give the sequence a feeling of coherence and organic drive: at first viewing, most, like me, will not consciously spot that they are different tracks at all. The fact that they stop and start again at key moments and after other diegetic songs have been heard embodies on the soundtrack the recursive temporal sequencing: we see what happens over a few minutes that afternoon from several characters' perspectives, one after another. The main two pieces—the funky brass riff of *Aragon,* and the edgy bongos of *Escape*—are used for precise, specific scoring functions: *Aragon* is an opening and ending theme, associated specifically with the object of the sting—the money—playing while Jackie hides the money under the towels, and when Max calmly walks out with the bag near the end; while *Escape* is the mood piece for tension, whether Jackie's or Ordell's. Finally, these pieces collectively serve as another homage to Tarantino's blaxploitation models for the films. But they are structurally prevented from seeming dated or too self-conscious by the integration of the snatches of diegetic music from various styles and periods. It is as if all this groovy music just might be found in one person's eclectic record collection.

The one noteworthy scene in the three films under consideration when diegetic music not specifically selected by the characters has more than passing influence is the extended 'Jack Rabbit Slim's' sequence in **Pulp Fiction.** It is not simply that the playing of 1950s rock n' roll records in the retro-theme restaurant is a natural sound for the diegesis. But, just like Mia and Vincent's dialogue (they teasingly call each other 'daddy-o' and 'kitty-cat', 'cowboy' and 'cowgirl'), the art direction (1950s cars, lurid primary colours) and costume (Vincent's bootlace tie, Mia's tail-fin cuffs, the waiters dressed as 1950s film and music stars), the performance of the music is another piece of dressing-up, playing with possible identities. Ricky Nelson impressionist Gary Sharelle is doing a passable imitation of the star's hit *Waitin' in School* as Mia and Vincent enter. As they eat, we hear Ricky Nelson's record of *Lonesome Town* and two classic Link Wray guitar instrumentals, *Rumble* and *Ace of Spades*. Coming after Sharelle's performance, these oldies are clearly located as emanating from the scene; and for the only time in the film, the sound of loud guitar instrumentals—elsewhere used solely as arousing scoring—is heard as offering a possible taste choice in the characters' own world, as immediately available sounds to stimulate their arousal, not ours. This function is made explicit by Mia and Vincent's stylised dancing to Chuck Berry's *You Never Can Tell* in the Jack Rabbit Slim's Twist Contest. In word, image and music, the entire sequence is an elaborate, masqued ritual, in which self-image for the purposes of sexual display is made both possible and yet safe, by being lifted piecemeal off the cultural shelf or record rack.

But all this takes place within the context of the precise emerging relationship between the characters of Mia and Vincent, which is what this whole section of the film is about. Jack Rabbit Slim's is merely the comic centrepiece of this story, the middle-eight of a twenty-minute sequence set to almost continuous pop music, in which the first verse-and-chorus and reprise form two of the most striking, memorable uses of music by characters in Tarantino's work: Mia watching Vincent arrive on closed-circuit TV as she listens to Dusty Springfield's *Son of a Preacher Man*; and, later, after their date at Jack Rabbit Slim's, dancing and then overdosing, to the accompaniment of Urge Overkill's cover version of Neil Diamond's *Girl, You'll Be A Woman Soon.*

Both scenes, in an alluring reversal of established gender roles in hi-fi history (see Keightley 1996), foreground the central female character's music selec-

tion and control of the aural environment, by featuring extreme close-ups on her music technology: the needle lifting from the groove of Mia's copy of the *Dusty in Memphis* LP; her finger pressing rewind then play on her reel-to-reel tape recorder. Tarantino's original script had the Dusty album more plausibly being played from a CD (Tarantino 1994a: 45), but the stopping-and-starting of a CD's internal laser cannot be shown as a physical, fetishised act. The scene as edited emphasises Mia's desire to exercise remote control over her and Vincent's first meeting. She selected and is playing Dusty's LP; she watches and directs Vincent's movements from another room by closed-circuit security camera. Her only words to him in person are imperative: 'Let's go'. Like Vincent, the audience is not permitted to see Mia's face. The extreme close-ups—Mia's razor blade and mirror as she snorts cocaine, Vincent's grasping the whisky bottle, Mia's hand guiding the camera joystick, the turntable needle—present music as just another social stimulant, depressant or technology for taking the up-close tension out of sexual encounters. The fact that we see these images of detachment while Dusty is singing about 'looking into the eyes of her lover,' 'stealing kisses' and 'learning from each other' is amusing and yet arousing. The music, the only direct manifestation of Mia's character and mood that Vincent and the audience are granted at first, is explicitly suggestive of illicit sexual relations, in both its lyrics and performative style. It is not certain, but the 'son of a preacher man' in the song might well be a black man. We already know from previous scenes that Mia is married to a jealous black gangster and Vincent is fearful of getting involved. In the circumstances, what more provocative a come-on record could Mia possibly have played? If we could only shut out the melodic and rhythmic drive of the record, offering tantalising glimpses of sexual fulfilment and narrative closure ('yes, he was, he was, oh yes he was'), we might find it easier to laugh or be concerned by Mia's detached, control-freak mentality. But like Vincent's blood, the music is booming too loud in our ears. In total, the scene suggests this is how sexual and power relations are conducted today: remotely, under the influence of narcotics. Mia appears to be playing a sophisticated game, surfing her own scene on a wave of cocaine and funk.

When they return from Jack Rabbit Slim's, things go very differently. Playing Urge Overkill's straightforward cover of Neil Diamond's hit *Girl, You'll Be A Woman Soon* on her tape recorder, Mia launches into a solo, self-obsessed dance while Vincent is in the bathroom. In his coat pocket she discovers what she imagines is cocaine, overdoses and collapses into a coma. The song fades out to silence, the screen fades to black. Like *Son of a Preacher Man,* Mia's second chosen song also lyrically promises female maturity and fulfilment. But much as any of us might in private, she also mimes along with the epicly recursive, three-note falling guitar riff (preserved from the original) which punctuates the chorus title line: 'Wow, wow, wow,' she wails on her air guitar. It acts like a new drug to get her started.

It is precisely at this moment of *Pulp Fiction*—Mia's near-death—that the real, moral action of the story begins. And it is noticeable that whereas most of this story 'Vincent Vega and Marsellus Wallis' Wife', occupying from twenty minutes to one hour into the film, is set to music, rising in concentration and intensity to Mia's overdose (fifty); by contrast, after this, there is no music whatsoever for thirty minutes, and it only recurs at all in the remaining eighty minutes of the film as two brief fragments of diegetic car-radio music, and two scored scenes. Just as Mia is snapped out of drug-induced coma, so is the audience rudely awoken from its musical haze. Suddenly everyone realises that all actions have consequences. In visual terms, an equivalence is established between the extreme close-ups of Vincent's heroin injection, Mia's turntable arm and needle and the adrenalin shot Vincent administers straight to Mia's heart. The only truly penetrating experiences available here are drugs, music and more drugs. Each seems to offer control of one's environment, and the ability to assume any desired sexual identity. But just as Mia takes too much of one, the audience is made to overdose on the other.

The potency of these foregrounded music-selection scenes for audiences is not simply a result of their shocking outcomes on screen. Tarantino is also dramatising the dominant music situational-use practices of his youth audience. As the music psychologist John A. Sloboda has argued, 'Music listening is . . . intensely situational. One cannot begin to give a full account of the cognitive, affective, or aesthetic response of a listener, without paying detailed attention to the reasons why the person is listening to that particular music at that particular time'. His review of recent findings suggests that most music listening accompanies domestic, solitary activity; and listening behaviour is 'ranged along a particularly important dimension, that of control, related to choice and autonomy . . . listeners must make very definite choices about the precise track to accompany activities'. The younger the listener, the more domestic activities there are which are accompanied by self-chosen music (Sloboda 1999). Several other studies confirm that music listening is the most popular leisure activity of older adolescents, used by them most commonly to alter mood and enhance emotional states; and that this listening is primarily a solitary activity (see for example Zillman and Gan 1997; Christenson and Roberts 1998: 33-53). Young audiences watching Tarantino's films are seeing adults in their rooms and cars doing what they themselves do with music; but, excitingly, seeking to project their private mood-enhancement on to other characters as well.

These psychological studies might even partly explain why the infamous scene in *Reservoir Dogs* in which Mr Blonde slices off a cop's ear to Stealer's Wheel's *Stuck in the Middle with You* is so disturbing. On one level, it is Mr Blonde's self-absorption in the music and detachment from the brutality of his treatment of the cop which is so shocking. If most of us turned on the radio while preparing to do some housework and heard *Stuck in the Middle with You,* we might perhaps turn it up a bit to 'moderate our arousal' in keeping with the low complexity of the task at hand, according to the theories of Konecki (see the summary of his work in Hargreaves and North 1997: 84-103). But other studies have shown that in some activities we deliberately choose continuously arousing music (arousing most likely by virtue of its volume, rather than its complexity)—a good example being for aerobics classes. North and Hargreaves sum this up by suggesting 'people prefer typical musically-evoked levels of arousal which help them to achieve a particular situational goal' (see Crozier 1997; Hargreaves and North 1997). We know Mr Blonde's goal is to torture the cop for fun; perhaps his conduct is so disturbing because we see him self-consciously topping-up his high state of arousal, dancing around to the music, much as we might in executing more innocent tasks. This characterises our everyday use of the radio for arousal purposes as a morally neutral act: arousal doesn't know what it's for, only we do.

There's something else this psychological perspective might help clarify: why Tarantino's soundtrack albums have sold so well. Among respondents to a mass observation mailing on music in 1997, those who reported more mood-enhancing functions for their self-chosen music also reported 'greater levels of liking' of music in public places. This is a promising indication, says Sloboda, that 'patterns of music use in high-control contexts have implications for attitudes towards music in low-control contexts' (Sloboda 1999). Watching a movie at the cinema must qualify as 'low-control'. You cannot alter the film music, no matter how annoying. If cinema audiences are comprised mostly of that youthful section of the public for whom solitary, mood-enhancing musical use is most important, they are likely not only to recognise the way Tarantino's characters use music, but also to discover something they like on his soundtracks. 'The use of music as a cue to reminiscence is the single most frequent use reported', says Sloboda. The person who buys and puts on a Tarantino soundtrack CD in the privacy of their room is taking pleasure in reminiscing over acts which transgressed the normal patterns of musical arousal. To do so is to act a bit like Tarantino's characters: in control enough to choose; yet choosing music which just might drive you out of control.

Bibliography, Filmography, Discography

Across 110th Street Soundtrack (1997) Rykodisc/MGM Entertainment RCD 10706.

Ayers, Roy (1973) *Coffy: Original Motion Picture Soundtrack.* Polydor Records PD5048.

Barnes, Alan and Marcus Hearn (1996) *Tarantino A to Zed: The films of Quentin Tarantino.* London: Batsford.

Bernard, Jami (1995) *Quentin Tarantino: The Man and His Movies.* London: Harper-Collins.

Blair, John (1989) Sleeve notes to *King of the Surf Guitar: The Best of Dick Dale and His Del-Tones.* Rhino Records CD R2 75756.

Blair, John (1996) Sleeve notes to *Cowabunga! The Surf Box Rhino Records 4-CD set of surf music 1960-1995.* R2 72418.

Burt, George S. (1994) *The Art of Film Music.* Boston: Northeastern University Press.

Chion, Michel (1994) *Audio-Vision: Sound on Screen* (trans. Claudia Gorbman). New York: Columbia University Press.

Christenson, Peter G. and Donald F. Roberts (1998) *It's Not Only Rock & Roll: Popular Music in the Lives of Adolescents.* New York: Hampton Press.

Ciment, Michel and Hubert Niogret (1998) 'Interview at Cannes' [1992] in Gerald Peary (ed.) *Quentin Tarantino: Interviews.* Jackson: University of Mississippi Press.

Crozier, W. Ray (1997) 'Music and social influence' in David J. Hargreaves and Adrian C. North (eds) *The Social Psychology of Music.* Oxford: Oxford University Press.

Cummings, David (ed.) (1995) *The Hutchinson Encyclopedia of Music.* Oxford: Helicon Publishing.

Dale, Dick (1996) Foreword to sleeve notes to *Cowabunga! The Surf Box Rhino Records 4-CD set of surf music 1960-1995,* R2 72418.

Dargis, Manohla (1998) 'Quentin Tarantino on *Pulp Fiction*' in Gerald Peary (ed.) *Quentin Tarantino: Interviews.* Jackson: University of Mississippi Press.

Dawson, Jeff (1995) *Tarantino: Inside Story.* London: Cassell.

.dickdale.com (1999) http://www.dickdale.com/ history.html, 'The Official Dick Dale Homepage', downloaded 27 June 1999.

du Gay, Paul, Stuart Hall, Linda Janes, Hugh Mackay and Keith Negus (1997) *Doing Cultural Studies: The Story of the Sony Walkman.* London: Sage/Open University.

Gorbman, Claudia (1987) *Unheard Melodies: Narrative Film Music.* London: BFI.

Hargreaves, David J. and Adrian C. North (1997) *The Social Psychology of Music.* Oxford: Oxford University Press.

Jackie Brown: Widescreen special edition (1998) Miramax Home Entertainment, D888016 PAL/VHS.

Jackie Brown: Music from the Miramax Motion Picture (1997) Maverick/A Band Apart, 9362-46841-2.

Keightley, Keir (1996) 'Turn it down! She shrieked: Gender, domestic space, and high fidelity, 1948-59'. *Popular Music,* vol. 15, no. 2.

Keough, Peter (1998) Press conference on *Jackie Brown* [1997] in Gerald Peary (ed.) *Quentin Tarantino: Interviews.* Jackson: University of Mississippi Press.

Leonard, Elmore (1998) *Rum Punch* (film tie-in edition, first published 1992). London: Penguin.

Middleton, Richard (1984) 'Play it again Sam': Some notes on the productivity of repetition in popular music. *Popular Music,* vol. 3.

Mooney, Joshua (1994) Interview with Quentin Tarantino, in Gerald Peary (ed.) *Quentin Tarantino: Interviews.* Jackson: University of Mississippi Press.

North, Adrian C. and David J. Hargreaves (1997) 'Experimental aesthetics and everyday music listening,' in David J. Hargreaves and Adrian C. North (eds) *The Social Psychology of Music.* Oxford: Oxford University Press.

Peary, Gerald (ed.) (1998) *Quentin Tarantino: Interviews.* Jackson: University of Mississippi Press.

Pulp Fiction: Special widescreen edition (1995) Touchstone Home Video, D400172 PAL/VHS.

Pulp Fiction: Music from the Motion Picture (1994) MCA Records, MCD 11103.

Reservoir Dogs (1995) Polygram Filmed Entertainment, 6379523 VHS/PAL.

Reservoir Dogs: Music from the Motion Picture Soundtrack (1992) MCA Records, MCD 10793.

Sloboda, John (1999) Everyday uses of music listening: A preliminary study' in S. W. Yi (ed.) *Music, Mind and Science.* Seoul: Western Music Research Institute.

Smith, Jeff (1998) *The Sounds of Commerce: Marketing Popular Film Music.* New York: Columbia University Press.

Tagg, Philip (1982) Analysing popular music: theory, method and practice. *Popular Music,* vol. 2.

Tarantino, Quentin (1994a) *Pulp Fiction.* London: Faber and Faber.

Tarantino, Quentin (1994b) *Reservoir Dogs.* London: Faber and Faber.

Tarantino, Quentin (1998) *Jackie Brown.* London: Faber and Faber.

The Tarantino Connection (1996) MCA Records, MCD 80325.

———. tomwbell (1995, rev. 1997), 'Miserlou tablature', members.aol.com/tomwbell/music/ Miserlou.html, downloaded 27 June 1999.

Woods, Paul A. (1996) *King Pulp: The Wild World of Quentin Tarantino.* London: Plexus.

Zillman, Dolf and Su-Lin Gan (1997) 'Musical taste in adolescence' in David J. Hargreaves and Adrian C. North (eds) *The Social Psychology of Music.* Oxford: Oxford University Press.

Donald R. Ross & Marcus Favero (essay date fall 2002)

SOURCE: Ross, Donald R. and Marcus Favero. "The Experience of Borderline Phenomena through Cinema: Quentin Tarantino's *Reservoir Dogs, True Romance,* and *Pulp Fiction.*" *Journal of the American Academy of Psychoanalysis* 30, no. 3 (fall 2002): 489-507.

[*In the essay below, Ross and Favero offer a psychological examination of Tarantino's work, focusing on* True Romance, Reservoir Dogs, *and* Pulp Fiction.]

Creative productions are one of the well-travelled roads to understanding the experience of others through empathic or vicarious immersion. Psychiatry has made use of this to expand the clinician's appreciation of psychopathological phenomenology and to understand the complex dynamic meanings of pathological actions, symptoms, and character. Freud (1900) appreciated this as evidenced in his analysis of *Oedipus Rex* and *Hamlet* in *The Interpretation of Dreams.* Later, Freud (1907, 1910) expanded this use of literature in analyzing Jensen's *Gravida,* and used Leonardo da Vinci's artistic productions to weave an interpretation of his character. Freud knew nothing of cinema, a medium that lends itself to vicarious experiences of sensations and emotions with great immediacy and power. Gabbard (1985, 1999) has been a pioneer in the use of film to explore various psychopathological states and their meanings.

Perhaps more than any other art form, cinema provides a multisensory "assault" on the viewer. Movies offer a unique opportunity to vicariously experience such phenomena as the mixture of drives, the dissociation of time and space, and the loosening of ego boundaries between fantasy and reality. Movies also offer the traditional realms of narrative and character development, giving the viewer an inside look at another's structural deformations, object relational world, and self experience. In other words, movies let the viewer both vicariously experience and empathically understand something about the inner world of another individual.

Some movies are very powerful in bringing to the viewer the experience of a different psychic structure. Quentin Tarantino's trilogy of **Reservoir Dogs, True Romance,** and **Pulp Fiction** captures much that is essential in the inner world of the borderline personality. As outlined by Woods (1998), these three films were produced over a short period of time and brought Tarantino to prominence in Hollywood. In our opinion, they have thematic and technical similarities that justify their grouping as a trilogy. Together, they present a compelling exploration of five key borderline themes: (1) fluidity of drive derivatives, (2) discontinuous experience of time and space, (3) conflicts in the search for an idealized parent, (4) specific antisocial distortions of the superego, and (5) the critical role of a central "romance" or fantasy in holding the borderline self together.

Borderline personality has engaged (and frustrated) psychiatrists for over 50 years. There are many insightful clinical and theoretical writings in this area, including some fine recent reviews, in particular by Gunderson and Zanarini (1987) and Gabbard (2001). The work of Otto Kernberg (1974, 1975, 1980, 1984) stands out as a coherent and articulate foundation that has penetrated deeply, comprehensively, and perceptively into the world of the borderline patient. The self-psychological perspectives of Kohut (1971, 1972, 1977, 1984) and Adler (1989) and the unique contributions of Grotstein (1990) provide additional dimensions. Most movies and psychoanalytic writings that depict borderline personalities do so with female characters. In contrast, Tarantino's movies focus predominately on the male borderline experience. Here, guilt is less in play and antisocial pathology is more prominent.

Tarantino may have perceived intuitively that "pulp" is a metaphor for the ego structure of the borderline personality. At the beginning of **Pulp Fiction,** the viewer is given the dictionary definition of pulp—"a mash, a paste, flash and marrow; or a tabloid of yellow journalism that may have pornographic content." In our clinical experience, this captures the pathognomonic experience of the borderline—a chaotic, soup-like existence, with islands of solid material that congeal into both pornographic and violent content, and at other times is empty and void.

The Fluid Nature of Drive Expression

One of the most striking aspects of borderline pathology is the rapid shift of drive discharge—from perverse sexuality to violence to voracious eating—which occurs in some patients particularly when they are under stress. An example not infrequently seen is the patient who, enraged by a slight from her boyfriend, gets drunk, picks up a man at the bar (often choosing one who has a violent streak), engages in sex, perhaps gets hit or hits the partner, leaves feeling empty, and returns home to binge, vomit, or cut on her wrists. It is as if the borderline is in the midst of an emotional storm and any and every port will do to escape from the overwhelming nature of it. On a more day-to-day basis, the borderline's expression of drive derivatives is frequently in mixed form, with elements of oral aggression fusing with conflicted dependency yearnings and/or genital sexual arousal.

This fluidity of drives, the mixture of sex, violence, and eating, is a prominent theme in Tarantino's trilogy. In *True Romance,* the action opens in a bar where Clarence is trying to pick up a woman to keep him from feeling alone on his birthday. He talks to her about his attraction to Elvis, saying, "If I had to fuck a man, I'd fuck Elvis." Already the fluidity of his sexual drive is apparent. In the next breath, he offers to treat her to three violent kung fu movies. He's excited by the prospect, but it's not her idea of a fun date and she declines. The next scene has him alone in the theater, fully identified with the violent action on the screen. Now, Alabama makes her entrance. She is a call girl paid to help him celebrate his birthday, loaded with ripe breasts and a king-size bucket of popcorn. She spills the popcorn all over him; they share it and the movie, and later go for pie and finish the night with sex. The combination of violent movies, food, and sex (along with a visit to the comic bookstore where Clarence works) leads to their falling in love. It is the ideal of a true borderline romance, and they are married the next day.

But Clarence is disturbed by the idea that another man has a claim to Alabama. He develops a rage toward Drexel, her pimp. In a mini-psychotic reverie in which he talks to Elvis, he decides he has to kill Drexel. This leads to another scene full of mixed drives and rapid shifts in action. When he confronts Drexel, he is invited to "sit and eat some Chinese food." The table is overflowing with greasy cartons half eaten. Pounding rock music is playing. Drexel sets the overhead lamp swinging and the viewer feels the building tension with a sense of vertigo. Both men are full of primitive drives and the storm is about to break. Suddenly, there is a struggle and Drexel, wearing only his underwear, sits on top of Clarence, pounding him in the face, telling him how he is going to "fuck him up." Blood and grease

are smeared all over them both. Just as quickly, the tables are turned. Clarence has his gun out and shoots Drexel in the genitals and then in the face. He leaves and returns home to Alabama with a bag of greasy hamburgers. He's excited, talking rapidly, and wants to have sex with her. When she expresses anxiety and concern about his beaten face, he offers her a bite from his burger and says, "Eat this, you'll feel better." She tells him that what he did is the most romantic thing she has ever heard and wraps herself around him.

This mixture or rapid alternation of drives, with a preponderance of oral sexualized aggression, also is prominent in *Pulp Fiction,* One example is the scene in which Vincent and Jules are sent to murder the young men who tried to double cross their boss, Marsellus. As they walk to the apartment where they will carry out their killings, they talk about whether a foot massage is equivalent to oral sex with a woman. Then they break down the door and hold their victims at gunpoint. Jules notices that the leader is having a greasy hamburger for breakfast and asks to have a bite. The camera moves to an extreme close-up of Jules chewing the burger with enthusiasm, saying, "This is one hell of a good burger." He then partakes of the young man's soft drink, slurping it through the straw, as the tension builds. Only after he is finished with his feast does Jules commence the killing. He starts with a biblical quote, which builds in violent grandiloquent intensity until he and Vincent pull the triggers on their guns in a sort of orgasmic finale.

Reservoir Dogs is the most tightly scripted of the three movies. The tension builds as hired gunmen meet at a rendezvous point after a botched jewelry heist. The potential for violence is high and the viewer is invited to ride waves of violent tension throughout the entire movie. But even here sex and food commingle in characteristically borderline ways. When Mr. Blond arrives, he is eating french fries. Immediately, Blond and Mr. White verbally pounce upon each other, with taunts that include a homosexual overtone. This quickly escalates to the verge of physical violence before Mr. Pink steps in and stops things. Blond looks slightly flushed and says how excited he was by the encounter. He then beckons them to his car, where he shows them a bound policeman he has taken hostage. All three men ease up and smile—and then take out their tension by beating the captured cop. But Blond takes it further in a chilling, sadomasochistic scene where he dances to rock music as he caresses and then cuts off the cop's ear and prepares to light him on fire.

What is behind this fluidity of drives in the borderline personality? Structural theory points in two directions. The first is a hypothesized preponderance of oral aggressive drives in the borderline, which may be constitutional or the result of excessive oral frustrations.

The second involves a study of the ego deficits of the borderline. Specifically, there is a dearth of subliminatory channels and a paucity of affective buffering capacity. This leads to the creation of highly charged and unstable states when the borderline is stressed with internal or external stimuli. There is little internal capacity to hold the tension that results. The ego cannot bind the drive energy effectively and so must look for outlets. Discharge is more important than what is discharged. Once drive discharge begins, it tends toward a few common pathways—sex, violence, and eating. The drive tensions are quickly spread over these available channels, looking for the quickest way to discharge. The borderline lacks well-differentiated ego structures or pathways to route the drive discharge onto specific objects, action patterns, or fantasies. Instead, the flow of affects and actions is like a flash flood after a rainstorm in territory where there is little infrastructure to handle the surging water.

Object relations theory emphasizes the borderline's affectively intense but otherwise impoverished inner world. Ogden (1979, 1989), expanding on Kemberg (1975), demonstrates that primitive affects retain their irradiating quality for the borderline, taking precedence over the boundary between self and objects. Objects (internal representations of other people) are all good or all bad, and usually they are bad. The object's malevolent and dangerous qualities are significantly augmented by the projected inner badness of the borderline self. The borderline experiences the other as persecutory. The bad object must be avoided or (counter) attacked. This paves the way for violent drive discharge, with a sense of self-righteous justification. When the other is killed or destroyed, the borderline experiences a "manic triumph" which overrides prohibitions against indulging in other drive discharge behavior. Sex, eating, or further violence is permitted in this manicky, celebratory state. Adding to this lack of drive containment is the fact that other people lack the psychological weight of whole, ambivalently held objects to the borderline. They give no pause to violent attack because they have no meaning, no shared history, and no substance. Objects are interchangeable so long as they have the right valence, all good or all bad, which makes them easy targets for sex or aggression.

Self psychology explains uncontrolled drive expression as a breakdown product of an endangered self. The self structure of the borderline is vulnerable under stress to severe disintegration anxiety. The borderline patient feels an unbearable tension and acute dysphoria as if he or she will fall apart. The desperate pursuit of drive discharge is in the service of diverting this disintegration. Alternatively, the borderline is prey to periods of feeling dead inside. This devitalized sense of self is also intolerable, and sexual and aggressive drive expression is sought to give a sense of energy and life. The

catastrophic drug scene in *Pulp Fiction* is an example of this latter situation. Mia, Marsellus's wife, is working hard to avoid an inner deadness, to feel alive. While out with Vincent, she indulges in greasy food and "a $5 milkshake," then exhibitionistic dancing, and finally snorting an unknown drug she finds in Vincent's coat pocket. This almost kills her. Only a syringe of adrenaline, shot directly into her heart, saves her life. At the end of this evening of adventure, Mia tells Vincent a joke that unconsciously captures her psychological imperative. She tells of a tomato who is told he'd better hurry or he will be "ketchup"—in other words he will be dead, will lose his form and structure and become an amorphous pulp. To avoid this, the specific drive or combination of drives pursued is of secondary importance so long as they fulfill the emergency function of maintaining the integrity of the self.

THE DISJUNCTIVE NATURE OF LIVED EXPERIENCE

One of the most dramatic aspects of Tarantino's trilogy of movies is the experience of dislocation in time and space. This is accomplished by rapid scene shifts between past and future events, and across the narratives of separate but intersecting characters. *Reservoir Dogs* opens in a confusion of violent language and a sense of urgency as three criminals arrive at a meeting place after fleeing a botched and bloody jewelry heist. One is shot in the gut and has passed out from shock. The two who are conscious are frantically trying to figure out what went wrong, what happened to the other players, and what to do next. The tale unfolds in incomplete narratives, which move backwards to vivid scenes from the planning of the robbery, to the frenetic flight that led them to the rendezvous, and forward as new players arrive and new developments occur. As the action moves back and forth, it weaves an increasingly complex web that tries to capture what went wrong. They decide they were set up by an insider, a rat, but can't sort out whom. Paranoid by nature and life experience, each character suspects every other character. The key segment, the robbery itself, is never played out in the movie. The viewer is required to piece it together from the surrounding elements. The effect is a series of brief, dramatic, and unforgettable scenes that live in their own right, but fail to form a coherent narrative for any of the characters. The secondary process thinking and reasoning required to make sense of things continually breaks down under the barrage of violent threats, paranoid conjectures, and unexpected actions.

Pulp Fiction has much the same structure. The movie opens with an impulsive, nerve-jangling robbery attempt of a diner by a man and woman. Over the next two hours of movie watching, several tangentially interconnected narratives are introduced and partially developed through a dozen key characters. This is done via "random access" to one dramatic scene after another, until the movie returns to the finale of the restaurant robbery. However, the viewer experiences this attempt to "tie up loose ends" as dislocating, since one of the main characters in the scene (Vincent) has already been killed in a "previous" scene. The experience of the viewer is like that of the characters—each scene is lived in the moment and only held together as a coherent whole when conscious secondary process thinking is directed to it. The narrative flow has nothing of the power of the individual scenes it contains.

True Romance has less of this dislocation in time and space built into its structure. This makes it easier for the viewer to follow the narrative flow with Clarence and Alabama. Still, the viewer senses that time and space are not continuous for these two borderline characters. For example, Clarence visits his father after an absence of a number of years—to introduce him to his bride, seek some information, and then head off to California. This lack of regular contact is accepted as normal. After that scene, the father ceases to exist as part of Clarence's story. Only the viewer is aware that later that day, the father is brutally tortured and murdered by mobsters who are looking for Clarence. The father's sacrifice is not even heroic within a meaningful context. The best that happens is he gets off a good joke under extreme pressure at the expense of his torturer and is killed. He dies, not knowing that he left his son's forwarding address on the refrigerator door.

This experience of discontinuity in time and space is a common feature of borderline patients. Some of this can be explained through *dissociation,* a common feature of borderline personality, described by Loewenstein and Ross (1992). Dissociation is defined by the American Psychiatric Association's DSM-IV (1994) as "a disruption in the usually integrated functions of consciousness, memory, identity, or perception of the environment." Hinsie and Campbell (1970) expand on this definition, saying, "dissociation generally means a loss of the usual interrelationships between various groups of mental processes with resultant almost independent functioning of the one group that has been separated from the rest" (p. 22). It is used frequently by borderline and other primitive personalities to fend off traumatic or conflicted experiences, compartmentalizing these in discrete, incompletely communicating memory traces. Dissociation is used most extensively in patients with post-traumatic stress disorder, which may be acute or chronic. The characters in Tarantino's movies experience many violent episodes that the viewer would label as "traumatic." The lack of anxiety about these experiences is presumptive evidence that the characters have had a number of such experiences in the past and

already employ dissociative or numbing defenses. One aspect of this tendency toward dissociation is a relative weakness in continuous experience of self and others over time.

A second psychodynamic cause of this experience of discontinuity is the borderline's extensive use of *splitting defenses.* Gabbard (2000) defines splitting as, "an unconscious process that actively separates contradictory feelings, self-representations, or object representations from one another" (p. 415). Melanie Klein (1946) saw splitting as the fundamental mechanism of the "paranoid-schizoid position" in which the infant (and primitive adult patient) separates good objects from bad objects, keeping the good within him- or herself and projecting the bad into the environment where it can be feared and/or controlled. The borderline patient remains stuck in this position much of the time, unable to integrate "good" with "bad" and thus unable to neutralize aggression. This results in classical borderline experiences described in DSM-IV such as "unstable and intense interpersonal relationships characterized by alternating between extremes of idealization and devaluation, . . . unstable self-image . . . impulsivity, affective instability, . . . and inappropriate, intense anger or difficulty controlling anger" (p. 650). Furthermore, as Kernberg (1975, 1984) points out, splitting is a prominent source of ego weakness in the borderline, circumventing the development of more sophisticated intrapsychic structures that would bind anxiety and allow for ambivalent and complex relationships with guilt, remorse, empathy, and a wish to repair damage done to another. Splitting protects the borderline from intolerable anxiety, but dooms him to a life of rather shallow, stereotyped, and action-oriented "scenes" based on all good versus all bad self and object representations. Such experience accumulates in memory much like a Tarantino movie—disjointed scenes that diminish any sense of a coherent, internally consistent narrative thrust or self-identity.

Finally, this disjunctive nature of the borderline experience can be explained as the result of recurrent "black hole experiences," a concept developed by Grotstein (1990). Many borderline patients describe experiences where "the floor drops out" from under them, and they suddenly find themselves in the realm of "terror of nothingness and boundarilessness on the one end and that of implosive, claustrophobic engulfment and entrapment on the other" (p. 30). These black hole experiences are the result of neurobiological processes beyond the borderline's conscious or unconscious control—for example, neurotransmitter-driven mood shifts or impingements that exceed the psyche's stimulus barrier. They are the stuff of the "micro-psychotic episodes" that borderline patients experience. The borderline person who suffers these experiences has to adapt to them. He or she can do so by defensively fragmenting experience so that these "black holes" are not so disorienting, but only another "scene" or episode in an already chaotic (but no longer terrifying) life. Whatever psychological meaning is attributed to these terror-filled episodes, it is secondary and becomes another way to cope with them to avoid the full impact of their random, chaotic, and meaningless nature. In these three Tarantino films, the viewer, like the borderline patient, is required to make mental efforts to pull together disparate scenes, to make sense of senseless violence, or to distance him- or herself from it. The example *par excellence* is the scene in **Pulp Fiction** where the young African-American man has his head shot off unexpectedly in the back seat of the car. There is no meaningful explanation, and as Vincent and Jules try to figure it out, they become more and more irritable until they can barely contain themselves. Finally, Mr. Wolf takes charge, organizes the clean up, and attributes a secondary meaning to the "accident." It becomes a "problem" of how to get rid of the body before Bonnie gets home.

THE CONFLICTED SEARCH FOR AN IDEALIZED FATHER FIGURE

In each movie of this trilogy, Tarantino depicts a central relationship, based largely on fantasy, between a main character and an idealized father figure.

In **True Romance,** Clarence has Elvis, "The King," to whom he turns for advice and reassurance about his self-worth. At crucial moments, Clarence hallucinates Elvis while gazing at himself in the bathroom mirror and commences a dialog that assuages his anxieties. (This happens just before he leaves to kill Drexel to establish his right to have the woman, Alabama; it happens again when he is about to become a success by consummating the drug deal with Lee.) Each time, Elvis tells him he is acting like a real man and leaves him with his trademark comment. "I like you Clarence. I always did, I always will." Clarence then can go forth with courage and confidence.

In **Pulp Fiction,** Butch has a complex relationship to the father he has never seen through the transitional object of his father's watch. As a child, his dead father's war buddy tells him that this watch has traveled with Butch's great grandfather through World War I, with his grandfather into World War II, and then with his father through years of being a POW in Vietnam. This watch was hidden in his father's rectum to preserve it for his unseen newborn son. Death and hardship have followed this watch, but cannot prevent it from returning to young Butch as his "birth-right"—as a stand-in for his heroic father. Surrounding the fateful prize-fight in which Butch double-crosses Marsellus, Butch awakens twice from nightmares related to losing the watch or his father. When he cannot find the watch among the things his girlfriend retrieved from the apartment, he becomes

unglued. He *must* have this watch, and so he returns to the apartment, kills Vincent who was stationed there to kill him, and retrieves it. He places it on his wrist and soon is humming a song and feeling invulnerable. With the watch on his wrist, he survives the subsequent bizarre encounter with Marsellus, Zed, and the sado-masochistic rape. With his father close to him, Butch overcomes his nightmares, acts honorable and brave, and lives happily ever after.

In **Reservoir Dogs,** Mr. White becomes the idealized, protecting father figure to the badly injured Mr. Orange. He is thrust into this position with Orange from the opening scene of the movie, when Orange is gut-shot and sure he is going to die. White gives him his hand and tells him his real name as a talisman and guarantee against death. White quickly becomes so committed to this protective father role that he refuses to see the evidence that Orange is the police informant. In the penultimate scene. White holds a gun on the "father" of the criminal operation and threatens to shoot him if Orange is shot. The standoff ends with a series of shots fired and everyone injured or killed. White cradles Orange in his arms, and at that moment Orange admits he is the informer. White cannot survive this disillusionment. Moaning like a wounded animal, he slowly brings his gun to Orange's head and shoots him, then allows himself to be shot by the converging police.

The importance of an idealized father figure is a prominent theme for Kohut (1971, 1977, 1984), as it forms one of the nuclei for the development of selfobject transferences and healthy self-esteem. Kohut posits a universal need for a parental figure that the child can idealize and thus merge with for safety and comfort. A stable sense of self depends upon it. In healthy development, these functions are internalized and become part of the self—available to reestablish a sense of cohesion and stability. However, the need for an idealized father figure is never completely outgrown, especially in times of external stress.

This need is particularly acute and unmodified (primitive) when there has been the lack of a real father to fulfill and gradually (nontraumatically) disappoint the growing child. No internalization of a soothing presence has taken place. Consequently, the narcissistic and borderline patient is more vulnerable to external pressures that challenge his or her sense of self-cohesion and self-worth. When a solid internalized father figure is lacking, other resources are employed. For example, Clarence has immersed himself in the culture of comic book heroes and pop icons. When he requires the reassurance of an idealized father figure, he resorts to dissociative hallucinations of a dialog with Elvis—a variant of the micropsychotic episodes characteristic of borderline patients. It is of significance that Clarence's real father had been an alcoholic who left the family early in Clarence's childhood. Another potential solution is overdependence upon a transitional object, first described by Winnicott (1953) and later elaborated by Lewin and Schulz (1992). Butch, who never saw his father (but was filled with heroic myths about him), transfers these selfobject needs onto the precious watch. With the watch, he feels himself merged with his guardian angel father on some primitive level. With Mr. White, the viewer knows nothing about his developmental background, but clearly he was pulled into the role of the idealized father and identified with it. Presumably this is so because it filled a deep need within him. This is an example of "role responsiveness" as described by Sandler, Holder, and Dare (1970), but without any self-awareness and with a subsequent loss of critical judgment. Until that point in time, White was the consummate professional criminal, without attachments or illusions. His ready acceptance of the idealized parental role demonstrates its emotional power.

A secondary function of the idealized father role is to deflect and defend against acute rivalry with the older, stronger male. In *Reservoir Dogs,* when Blond shows no inclination to respect the older White, the interchange quickly escalates to the verge of one having to kill the other. Blond had no use for White in the idealized parental role; he already has an idealized father figure in the boss of the operation, the man to whom he was loyal throughout his time in prison and to whom he returned upon his release. It takes Pink to break the tension and prevent a killing by making an appeal to the ego—reminding White and Blond that they are "professionals" and refocusing them on their current, shared dilemma.

Borderline patients share a vulnerability to self-fragmentation with narcissistic personality disordered patients. While the narcissistic patient readily forms minoring and/or idealizing transferences in dynamic psychotherapy, Adler (1989) points out that the development of cohesive selfobject transferences (such as an idealizing transference to the therapist) is usually a later manifestation in therapy with borderline patients. Before idealization takes center stage, the borderline patient needs to work through some of his or her acute abandonment fears, primitive rage and guilt, and develop a stronger alliance with the therapist. This results in a stronger capacity for libidinal object constancy. Still, we often see that borderline patients find creative ways *in vivo* to recreate the idealized father, and to use that imago to shore up their sense of self in times of stress.

DISTORTIONS OF THE SUPEREGO

Tarantino's cinematic characters articulate and demonstrate a particular set of moral and ethical values that are typical of the borderline with antisocial features.

The fundamental value is loyalty. Justice is based upon "an eye for an eye." There is great concern about not being "fucked." If one is wronged, the perpetrator must be eliminated regardless of cost. There is little or no guilt for the most severe aggression and no concern for the victim's life. Moral reflections revolve around the proportionality or fairness of the revenge. Reference to ambiguous situations may be sought from outside sources such as the Old Testament or an older, wiser man. The moral structure as a whole lacks internal solidity, complexity, and subtlety. Rather, it consists of poorly integrated islands of strongly held beliefs that may give way to other disconnected strongly held beliefs under the stress of other circumstances.

True Romance is about loyalty right from the beginning. Alabama tells Clarence that once she promises herself to him, she is "true blue 100 percent." The fact that she is a call girl and they met that night is irrelevant, swept away. She is offering him her unconditional loyalty. And Clarence is primed to accept it and return it in the same degree. He tells her that if she is lying he will simply die. And so they get married later that day and go forward on that basis of blind trust in each other, a "true romance" in which they remain loyal to each other even through beatings and while facing death.

A version of primitive justice is played out in *True Romance* in almost literal fashion within the complex relationship between Clarence and Drexel. Clarence must kill Drexel because he has sexually "owned" Alabama. In order for Clarence to claim his right to her, Drexel must cease to exist, must not be allowed to even "breathe the same air." He shoots him in the genitals before shooting him in the face to kill him. At the end of the movie, Clarence is shot in the face and loses an eye. Drexel had the same injury (a damaged eye) when Clarence killed him. Clarence must take on Drexel's deformity along with his ownership of Alabama.

Reservoir Dogs opens with all the criminals sitting in a diner discussing the right or wrong of giving a tip to the waitress. Is it fair that female waitresses get tipped while male laborers don't? The relative values of social convention, gender stereotyping, the right to earn a living in America, fair payment for services rendered, and even a hint of empathy for the waitress herself are raised. But this is all swept aside by the boss of the operation. When he returns from paying the bill and is told what the discussion is about, he tells everyone to put in a dollar and shut up. The ethical discussion has shifted to a "higher level." It is not lost on the viewer that this discussion about tipping is in the context of planning a major robbery in which people may, and in fact do, get killed. The ethical implications of armed robbery and murder don't concern this group of primitive personalities.

Pulp Fiction is by far the richest of the three films in depicting the distorted superego of the criminal mind. Vincent and Jules enter into an intense and sophisticated dialog about whether a foot massage given to Marsellus's wife was adequate provocation for Marsellus to throw the perpetrator off a fourth story balcony. They become so involved in this discussion that they leave the very doorway of the young men they are there to kill, and go down the hall to finish it. Later in that sequence, Jules fires up with righteous rage, quoting the Old Testament prophet Ezekiel about vengeance against "the tyranny of evil men." It is his prelude to the killing. But a hidden victim springs on them with a gun, fires six shots at short range, but misses. Jules sees it as a miracle. Now he has to struggle with the meaning of Ezekiel's words. In the movie's last scene, he is still puzzled and discusses it at gunpoint with a man he would normally have just killed.

In another sequence from *Pulp Fiction,* Marsellus is enraged that Butch has doublecrossed him by not throwing the prizefight as planned. (There is no concern that throwing the fight would have been wrong.) He orders all the resources of his organization to be devoted to finding Butch and killing him. Later, he is sodomized by Zed, but saved by Butch. His rage shifts to Zed, and he tells Butch that he plans to "get some of the brothers with pliers and blowtorches to take this place apart." He plans "to get medieval" with Zed and his cronies. In contrast, he and Butch are square. It is not that the debt is wiped away and Butch is forgiven. Rather, to Marsellus, that relationship no longer exists. "There is no you and me," he says. Butch must simply disappear and never show up again.

In one final example, Vincent's gun accidentally goes off while Jules is driving, the bullet instantly killing their informant in the back seat and splattering his blood and brains all over the car. They don't know how to think about this—their superegos give them no help with this situation. Vincent feels he should be instantly and totally forgiven because he said he was sorry and it was a mistake. Jules is upset because he has to clean up the mess and has imposed upon a friend to hide the car. The friend is upset because his wife, Bonnie, is coming home and will cause trouble for him. No one is concerned about the dead boy who was killed in the most meaningless way possible. All that is said of him is, "No one will be missed." This "problem" of moral ambiguity is finally resolved by calling in Mr. Wolf. He is an older man, a professional at taking charge of "clean ups." He reframes the problem from existential or moral to logistical, and quickly calms both Vincent and Jules with his presence, authority, and decisiveness.

Moral and ethical values are the province of the superego, a concept originating with Freud (1923) and so beautifully expanded by Brenner (1982). In normal development, the superego forms coincident with the resolution of the Oedipal conflict, with the prohibition against murder and incest forming the joint cornerstones of the internal moral system. However, a successful Oedipal resolution implies the capacity for libidinal object constancy toward both a mother and father figure, something that is sorely lacking in borderline and other primitive character disordered patients. Consequently these individuals have typical deviations in their superego formation. It is not that they lack a superego, but rather the specific content of it, its coherence, and its power to provide safety and support for the ego are changed. This is compounded when the person has antisocial traits.

Loyalty is such a central value in the superego of the borderline patient because the borderline has such a problem with abandonment fears. He or she has learned to distrust others, in part out of experience with unreliable parents, and in part out of aggressive wishes that originate inside but are projected onto the other person. In such a paranoid inner and outer world, another person who is "true blue 100 percent" is invaluable.

Likewise, because the borderline patient "lives" in the paranoid position, the constant focus is on protecting oneself from being penetrated by dangerous, bad objects. This specific danger is captured in the fear of being "fucked," which is damaging to the integrity of the self and humiliating, destroying self-esteem. The borderline, especially the antisocial borderline, counterattacks preemptively, feeling self-righteous and justified. Empathy for the other person (which is a feature of the more advanced "depressive position") has never developed, and so there is no concern for harming or even killing the other. If one is "fucked," the injury provokes an intense narcissistic rage response in which, according to Kohut (1972), the other must be totally erased to undo the injury.

The borderline patient, especially the female patient, often feels tremendous guilt in association with his or her destructive rage. This is missing from the characters in Tarantino's movies. Most likely this is because they are predominately male and have antisocial distortions of their superego as well. Only Alabama demonstrates some guilt when she makes her tearful confession to Clarence that she has deceived him, that actually she is a call girl sent to spend the night with him as a birthday gift. It is the deception, the implied disloyalty for which she feels guilty. She follows this up by vehemently declaring she is "no Florida trailer trash"—clearly something she fears she is and needs to deny. Guilt requires some sense of inner badness that is not fully projected onto object representations of the persecuting others.

Finally, external sources of moral authority are necessary for borderlines during times of indecision or stress because the superego lacks sufficient internal authority. When Mr. Wolf is sent to "rescue" Jules and Vincent, they idealize him and bestow upon him the magic of higher authority. This problem merges with the borderline's problem of finding an idealized father figure, discussed in an earlier section.

The Organizing Power of Romantic Fantasy

Finally, Tarantino cinematically demonstrates the power of romantic fantasy in organizing the inner life of the borderline. Fantasy is a powerful organizer of motivated behavior for everyone. On the macroscopic level, we can look at the power to shape our world of the fantasy of one group of religious fanatics (namely—the ideal of a pan-Islamic fundamentalist world) in conflict with the secular fantasy of the American Dream (that is—the ideal of liberty, justice, and happiness for each individual.) On an intrapsychic level, we see the power of fantasy in shaping the specific goals, ambitions, and behaviors of our patients, whether neurotic, borderline, or psychotic. As Arlow (1969a, 1969b) points out, unearthing the nucleus of our patient's neurosis is the same as discovering his or her central unconscious fantasy.

In its essence, the movie *True Romance* is the story of the power of a romantic fantasy between two borderline individuals. It is a childlike romance, with magical belief in the power of each other and their love. It is filled with allusions to childhood magic. There is the visit to the comic bookstore, where Clarence reverently shows Alabama *Spiderman #1.* They make love in front of a statue of Elvis, which sits by the bed like a shrine. They drive across America, from the slums of Detroit to Hollywood California, having sex in a phone booth on the road. They go to the amusement park, ride the roller coaster, and get into a drug deal with a movie producer. Alabama admits to Clarence that, when she feels worried, she looks at him and says, "Baby, you are so cool." Clarence confesses to her that he always dreamed of flying away on one of those planes that flew over his house by the Detroit airport. If this isn't romantic love, what is? What makes the movie so compelling is that, each time the viewer thinks the fantasy has to end in brutality or disillusionment, it doesn't. In the climactic scene where bullets are flying amidst feathers floating on the air; where police, mafia, and bodyguards are shooting each other; Clarence and Alabama limp out of the bloodbath with the suitcase of money and drive in their purple Cadillac to an idyllic future in Mexico. With nothing going for them except their mutual romantic fantasy, they triumph over the badness and ugliness of the world.

In *Pulp Fiction,* Butch has the unconscious fantasy of rescuing his father, and the more-or-less conscious fantasy of making him proud. When he is being

instructed to throw the prizefight, Marsellus tells him, "Forget pride. Pride fucks with your head." But pride is central to Butch's romantic fantasy. He hopes to join the list of proud men in his family, to be worthy of his father. So he bets on himself, kills the other fighter in the ring, and plans to live off the winnings after escaping Los Angeles. But his girlfriend forgets to pack his father's watch. There is no question about leaving the watch behind. He goes back for it with a sense of mission, going through the "jungle" of a deserted lot, like he is about to penetrate a Vietcong prisoner camp to rescue his father. It is this sense of living out a fantasy that allows him to act without fear. The childlike nature of the fantasy continues as he puts Pop-Tarts in the toaster once he enters the apartment. He finds his watch where he left it—on a small bedside figurine of a kangaroo that looks like a cross between a comic book character and a child's night-light. He retrieves the watch, the toaster pops, and he kills Vincent who is "guarding" the apartment. He looks at it all—the blood, the watch, and the Pop-Tarts—in amazement. He has fulfilled his fantasy enactment and reminds himself that "they" are always underestimating him. He puts on the watch in a giddy, manicky state, and drives away, singing and drumming on the steering wheel a song about a kangaroo.

Romantic fantasy is less obvious in *Reservoir Dogs,* but even in this movie about hardened and dangerous men, it is there. Each of the professional thieves is given an alias, the name of a color, which is to serve as his identity throughout the operation. Mr. Pink almost whines as he expresses dissatisfaction with his name. He wants to be Mr. Black or Mr. Purple, something that sounds more dangerous and romantic. Ironically, even he, the most professional and level-headed of the criminals, is sensitive to the fantasy aspect of his self identity.

Finally, the romantic fantasy aspect inherent throughout these three movies comes across in the background music. The music is soft, melodic, and full of yearning with themes that stir up images from childhood. Or the music is a montage of "golden oldies" from the rock and roll of the 60s and 70s, full of energy and nostalgia at the same time. These songs are a counterpoint to the chaotic scene changes across time and space, the violence, the splattered brains and severed ears, the profanity, the vertiginous moments of drives about to explode into devastating action. At critical times, it is the romantic music of the soundtrack that holds the movie together and allows the viewer to experience it without overwhelming anxiety.

Borderline fantasies have defining characteristics that help clinicians understand better the borderline condition. The fantasies of borderlines often are closer to conscious awareness than the fantasies of neurotics. To the borderline, they often feel more real than reality. They have a romantic structure like many simple fairy tales. The themes tend to be of rescue, reunion, and finding a soul mate who substitutes for the longed-for idealized parent. They involve heroic struggles over impossible obstacles. They have a felt quality of being hopeless and compelling at the same time. Like all unconscious fantasies, the fantasies of borderlines are compromise formations as demonstrated by Brenner (1982) and Abend, Porder, and Willick (1983). They contain elements of drive satisfaction, superego prohibition, anxiety, and ego defense. As such, they reflect the specific strengths and deficits of the borderline id, ego, and superego. Likewise, they are reworked versions of an unfulfilled object relationship, which, for the borderline, often involves the missing good mother or heroic father. And, like all fantasies, the borderline's fantasies capture a sense of self that is grandiose, alive, and secure, although for the borderline, this may be a degree more intense and primitive. Finally, the borderline individual often puts more of his or her eggs in this basket. He or she relies upon the romantic fantasy to keep afloat psychologically. Damage to the fantasy can lead to suicide. As Clarence tells Alabama when she offers to be his true love, "If you are lying to me it will kill me."

CONCLUSION

Quentin Tarantino has created a trilogy of films that bring to life a number of essential features of the borderline experience. He graphically depicts the borderline's fluidity of drive expression, especially regarding the close connection between sex, violence, and gorging on food. He captures the borderline's experience of life as islands of intense action and emotion with only tenuous connections through time and space—an experience that is disorienting to narrative flow and self-identity. He articulates important content in the borderline's inner world. In particular, he shows the viewer the central importance of primitive romantic fantasies that deal with "true love" and the search for an idealized parent. These fantasies fill vital object relational and selfobject needs that help hold the borderline together in the midst of inner chaos. Finally, he exposes a specific superego structure and content for the antisocial borderline that has dominant themes of distrust versus loyalty, being "fucked" versus seeking revenge. When the moral dilemmas are ambiguous or complex, he shows how the borderline desperately looks to a "higher authority" for answers outside his or her self. Each of these characteristics is seen clinically in the psychotherapy of borderline patients. Tarantino brings them to life on the screen in a way that is creative, complex, compelling, and worthy of our attention.

References

Abend, S. M., Porder, M. S., and Willick M. S. (1983), *Borderline Patients: Psychoanalytic Perspectives,* International Universities Press, New York.

Adler, G. (1989), Uses and limitations on Kohut's self-psychology in the treatment of borderline patients, *Journal of the American Psychoanalytic Association, 37.* 761-785.

American Psychiatric Association (1994), *Diagnostic and Statistical Manual of Mental Disorders, 4th Edition,* American Psychiatric Press, Washington, DC.

Arlow, J. A. (1969a), Unconscious fantasy and disturbances of conscious experience, *Psychoanalytic Quarterly,* 38, 1-27.

Arlow, J. A. (1969b), Fantasy, memory, and reality testing, *Psychoanalytic Quarterly,* 38, 28-51.

Brenner, C. (1982), *The Mind in Conflict,* International University Press, Madison, CT.

Freud, S. (1900), The Interpretation of Dreams, *Standard Edition,* vol. 4 and 5.

Freud, S. (1907), Delusions and Dreams in Jensen's Gravida, *Standard Edition,* vol. 9, pp. 1-95.

Freud, S. (1910), Leonardo da Vinci and a Memory of his Childhood, *Standard Edition,* vol. 11, pp. 57-137.

Freud, S. (1923), The Ego and the Id. *Standard Edition,* vol. 19, pp. 3-66.

Gabbard, G. O., and Gabbard, K. (1985), Countertransference in the movies, *Psychoanalytic Review,* 72, 171-184.

Gabbard, G. O. (1999), *Psychiatry and the Cinema,* 2nd Edition, American Psychiatric Press. Washington, DC.

Gabbard, G. O. (2000). Cluster B personality disorders, borderline, in *Psychodynamic Psychiatry in Clinical Practice,* 3rd Edition, American Psychiatric Press, Washington, DC, pp. 411-462.

Gabbard, G. O. (2001), Psychodynamic psychotherapy of borderline personality disorder. a contemporary approach, *Bulletin on the Menninger Clinic,* 65, 41-57.

Grotstein, J. S. (1990), The "black hole" as the basic psychotic experience, some newer psychoanalytic and neuroscience perspectives on psychosis. *Journal of the American Academy of Psychoanalysis,* 18, 29-46.

Gunderson, J. G., and Zanarini, M. C. (1987), Current overview of the borderline diagnosis, *Journal of Clinical Psychiatry,* 48, Supplement, 5-14.

Hinsie, L. E., and Campbell, R. J. (1970), *Psychiatric Dictionary,* 4th Edition, Oxford University Press, New York.

Kernberg, O. (1974), Barriers to falling and remaining in love. *Journal of the American Psychoanalytic Association,* 22, 486-511.

Kernberg, O. (1975), *Borderline Conditions and Pathological Narcissism,* Jason Aronson, New York.

Kernberg, O. (1980), *Internal World and External Reality, Object Relations Theory Applied,* Jason Aronson, New York.

Kernberg, O. (1984), *Severe Personality Disorders, Psychotherapeutic Strategies,* Yale University Press, New Haven.

Klein, M. (1946), Notes on some schizoid mechanisms. In *Envy and Gratitude and Other Works.* 1946-1963, Free Press, New York, 1975, pp. 1-24.

Kohut, H. (1971), *The Analysis of the Self,* International University Press, New York.

Kohut, H. (1972), Thoughts on narcissism and narcissistic rage. *Psychoanalytic Study of the Child,* 27, 360-400.

Kohut, H. (1977), *The Restoration of the Self,* International University Press, Madison, CT.

Kohut, H. (1984), *How Does Analysis Cure?* University of Chicago Press, Chicago.

Lewin, R. A., and Schulz, C. G. (1992), *Losing and Fusing, Borderline Transitional Object and Self Relations,* Aronson, Northvale, NJ.

Loewenstein, R. J., and Ross, D. R. (1992), Multiple personality and psychoanalysis, an introduction, *Psychoanalytic Inquiry* 12, 3-48.

Ogden, T. H. (1979), On projective identification, *International Journal of Psychoanalysis,* 60, 357-373.

Ogden, T. H. (1989), *The Primitive Edge of Experience,* Aronson, Northvale, NJ.

Sandler, J., Holder, A., and Dare, C. (1970), Basic psychoanalytic concepts IV, counter-transference, *British Journal of Psychiatry,* 117, 83-88.

Winnicott, D. W. (1953), Transitional objects and transitional phenomena, a study of the first not-me possession, in *Playing and Reality,* Basic Books, New York, 1971, pp. 1-25.

Woods, P. A. (1998), *King Pulp, the Wild World of Quentin Tarantino,* 2nd Edition, Plexus Publishers, New York.

Joshua Fausty and Edvige Giunta (essay date 2002)

SOURCE: Fausty, Joshua and Edvige Giunta. "Quentin Tarantino: An Ethnic Enigma." In *Screening Ethnicity: Cinematographic Representations of Italian Americans in the United States,* edited by Anna Camaiti Hostert and Anthony Julian Tamburri, pp. 210-21. Boca Raton, Florida: Bordighera Press, 2002.

[*In the essay below, Fausty and Giunta examine representations of Italian American ethnicity in Tarantino's films.*]

> ***Pulp Fiction*** is a film . . . that leaves you with the distinct impression that Tarantino has thrown everything but the proverbial kitchen sink into the celluloid melting pot.
>
> (*Empire*)

> [*Playboy*]: *What's the difference between Los Angeles Italians and New York Italians?*
>
> [Tarantino]: There really is no such thing as a Los Angeles Italian. In New York there are Italian neighborhoods. In Los Angeles there aren't. There is no ethnicity here. You just are who you are. Of course, most of that Italian stuff is learned from movies like *Mean Streets* anyway. . . . But can I tell the genuine article Italian from the poseur Italian? No. [laughs] To me they all seem like poseurs.
>
> (*Playboy*)

> Truthfulness—verism—is an adolescent affectation. No one presents himself directly, even among friends. Everyone is more or less fictional, made up, constructed.
>
> (James Monaco, quoted in Gamson 10)

When we first started working on this essay on Quentin Tarantino, it seemed convenient to think of Tarantino as the latest in a list of contemporary Italian American directors that includes Francis Ford Coppola, Martin Scorsese, Brian De Palma, Michael Cimino, Nancy Savoca, John Turturro, and Robert De Niro. Film is one area in which Italian Americans have flourished, both commercially and artistically, on the American pop-culture scene. So we decided to trust the name. After all, with a name like Tarantino, he's gotta' be Italian. Soon, though, we had to face the real question of Tarantino's origins.

We turned for help to a friend who works on the David Letterman show, where Tarantino appeared as a guest when *Pulp Fiction* hit the screens. We tried to find legitimacy for this not-too-traditional research method in the fact that Toni, despite her non-Italian last name, is Italian American. She was also at one point offered a position as Martin Scorsese's personal assistant, and since Scorsese is one of Tarantino's idols and models, we felt the "stars" were with us. While she could not shed light on the ethnic enigma, she sent us a file, full of articles, reviews, interviews, and reports collected and prepared by Letterman's research team—none of which represent the type of source regularly consulted in serious scholarly research. All of the material—much of which reproduces almost verbatim information found in just about every source—testifies to the quick notoriety reached by Tarantino in the mid-1990s—one achieved through a carefully orchestrated publicity that Tarantino himself was heavily involved in creating.

Following the release of *Pulp Fiction* and its huge popularity, Tarantino engaged in the construction of an image of himself not only by appearing in each of his movies—including one he wrote but did not direct—but also by appearing in commercial introductions to videotapes of his movies on such popular TV shows as *Late Night with David Letterman,* and by allowing himself to be photographed in the company of other celebrities—not to mention the wide gallery of Tarantino portraits in the glossy pages of magazines like *Empire, Sky,* and *Premiere.* His movies quickly became cult movies, and the scripts of *Pulp Fiction, True Romance* and *Reservoir Dogs* were published, and placed in prominent view in large-selling bookstores as well as advertised with the soundtracks of his movies on Blockbuster video tapes. Tarantino's quick success seems rooted in his self-fascination and self-promotion, and in his love affair with the movies and celebrity—matched in intensity only by Hollywood's, and the public's, fascination with his movies, and with him. If in the Hollywood star system Tarantino represents the young, off-beat, unconventional director who can pride himself on having made blockbusters *and* won the Palme d'Or at the Cannes Film Festival, he has also achieved the kind of fame sanctioned by a number of biographies.

Tarantino's supposed quick rise from rags to riches makes him even more endearing to the American public. Every journalist will tell the story of how, in order to support himself while studying acting, Tarantino worked for several years in a video store, an occupation that allowed him to indulge his fascination with film. A high-school drop-out, Tarantino did not actually come to success all-of-a-sudden. His long-time involvement in show business ranged from writing scripts to playing an Elvis impersonator on *The Golden Girls,* an appropriate role for Tarantino since he is originally from Tennessee. (Elvis in fact makes a few cameo appearances in *True Romance.*)

But what about Tarantino's *ethnic* origins? Although Tarantino has repeatedly been compared to Coppola and Scorsese, none of his movies advertise themselves as "ethnic," nor do they reveal a specific concern with Italian American culture. Tarantino's mysterious ethnic origins and the little emphasis he places on his ethnicity raise questions about identity politics and subjectivity, not to mention the legitimacy of Tarantino himself as a subject matter for Italian American studies.

By 1996, Tarantino's four movie scripts (only two of which he directed as feature films) seemed to typify the evolution of a certain kind of ethnic cycle. *True Romance,* his first script to become a feature film, contains the most explicit references to Italians, that is, Sicilians. Scagnetti, the name of the detective who hunts down Mickey and Mallory in *Natural Born Killers,* is unmistakably Italian. And Scagnetti is a name Tarantino uses for Mr. Blonde's parole officer in *Reservoir Dogs,* which opens with a long conversation about the meaning of the Madonna song "Like a Virgin," the video of which was notably filmed in Venice, where Tarantino finished drafting *True Romance. Pulp Fiction* treats the question of ethnic identity in a distinctly postmodern fashion. In the tortured world of this film, racial, ethnic, sexual, linguistic, and narrative borders are continuously crossed, creating a story in which multiple sub-plots intersect in unpredictable ways. This is a strategy that derails the narrative even as it gathers its scattered threads. The multifaceted story of *Pulp Fiction* is brimming with allusions to myriad films, TV shows, and other artifacts of American popular culture.

There is a certain coherence established by the fragmented and multilayered plots, the plethora of incongruous and disparate allusions, the rootlessness of the characters themselves, and the absurd or gratuitous explosions of violence. Quoting Sergio Leone, in an interview with Dennis Hopper, Tarantino contrasted the American public's response to his movies with the response of Italian spectators to violence: "Italians tend to laugh at violence. They don't take violence seriously. . . . The only people in America that take that attitude are Black people" (Hopper 140). The stereotyping of Tarantino's off-handed comment establishes a cultural connection between Italians and Blacks, one that is emphasized and magnified in *True Romance.* The Sicilian interlude in *True Romance,* directed by Tony Scott, captures feelings of racial discrimination and self-hatred, and problematizes questions of origins and identity, which are crucial to a discussion of Tarantino as an Italian American auteur.

Tarantino has a special attachment to this scene: "as far as I am concerned," he told Dennis Hopper, "[it] . . . should go into a time capsule for future generations to look at" (Hopper 21). While Tarantino does not quite explain why this scene is so important, his emphasis on future generations underscores the role of origins and heritage. The scene also raises issues of paternity and racial and cultural crossings. Don Vincenzo Coccotti (played by Christopher Walken), during his interrogation of Clarence's father Cliff (played by Dennis Hopper), claims the authority and power of the lie: "Sicilians are great liars. The best in the world. I'm a Sicilian. And my old man was the world heavyweight champion of Sicilian liars" (147-148). Coccotti believes that by demonstrating his "inherited" ability to tell when someone is lying or telling the truth, he will be able to extract Clarence's whereabouts from Cliff: "What we got here is a little game of show and tell. You don't wanna show me nothing'. But you're tellin' me everything. Now I know you know where they are. So tell me, before I do some damage you won't walk away from" (148). If Coccotti claims the authority of the lie, Cliff instead claims the authority of "history"—an overtly white history that figures Sicilians as Blacks.

Accepting his own death as the only alternative to betraying his son's location, and having given up all hope of survival—he knows by now that lying will get him nowhere but dead—Cliff makes the decision to strike an unexpected blow while he still has the chance. Cliff: "So you're a Sicilian, huh?" Coccotti answers, intensely, "Uh-huh." Cliff continues:

> You know I read a lot. Especially about things that have to do with history. I find that shit fascinating. In fact, I don't know if you know this or not, Sicilians were spawned by niggers.
>
> (148)

At this point in the script, "All the men stop what they are doing and look at Cliff, except for Tooth-Pick Vic, who doesn't speak English and isn't insulted. Coccotti can't believe what he is hearing" (148). Cliff goes on:

> It's a fact. Sicilians have nigger blood pumpin' through their hearts. If you don't believe me, look it up. You see, hundreds and hundreds of years ago the Moors conquered Sicily. And Moors are niggers. Way back then. Sicilians were like the wops in northern Italy. Blond hair, blue eyes. But, once the Moors moved in there, they changed the whole country. They did so much fuckin' with the Sicilian women, they changed the blood-line for ever, from blonde hair and blue eyes to black hair and dark skin. I find it absolutely amazing to think that to this day, hundreds of years later, Sicilians still carry that nigger gene. I'm just quotin' history. It's a fact. It's written. Your ancestors were niggers. Your great, great, great, great, great-grandmother fucked a nigger, and she had a half-nigger kid. That is a fact. Now tell me, am I lyin'?
>
> (149)

Cliff's history lesson leads Coccotti to kill Cliff—to kill with his own hands for the first time in years. The gravity of the insult is taken for granted by all present: the characters' laughter as Cliff recounts the story of their people is chilling, yet humorous, as it becomes increasingly out of place given the unfolding of the scene. Everyone knows—including Cliff—that his death is imminent, and this increases the seriousness of the situation—the story and its ultimately grave reception. It is through this story of historical "truth" that cannot be denied—after all, it is "written"—that Cliff is able to reassert his own authority, even during this confrontation to the death. It is the historical "truth" of Cliff's lesson that makes it so troubling for the self-proclaimed connoisseur of liars, who is implicitly forced to admit

that he has been given what he has asked for—he has been told the "truth," but at his own expense. Coccotti's only response is to shoot Cliff in the head: he has been beaten at his own game of "show and tell"; there is nothing left to be said.

But what is the status of Cliff's and Don Vincenzo's prejudice? The racism of Tarantino's characters works in complex ways. Cliff's offensive use of the word "nigger" and his bigoted account of the "contamination" of Sicilian blood problematizes any sympathy or compassion the spectator feels for this character. But it is precisely his use of this bit of "history" in the face of certain death that makes him most admirable. A helpless victim, he finds the strength to spit in the face—so to speak—of the bad guy. The explicitly racial hatred of his otherwise noble performance (while enduring torture, we should add) does little to weaken his character. Don Vincenzo's reaction, on the other hand, provides the outlet for whatever judgement and tension we may have been building up. His inevitable, brutal response to Cliff's insult is to inflict injury—the kind of "damage" you don't "walk away from."

Tarantino's treatment of racism is self-consciously executed yet at the same time, totally unself-critical.[1] Cliff is likeable, unmistakably the good guy, in contrast to his gangster foe Don Vincezo. But unless we go out of our way to read his frequent and comfortable use of the word "nigger" as completely strategic—it is intended to humiliate Don Vincenzo when all is lost—Cliff is also unmistakably racist. The juxtaposition of the Sicilians as "great liars" and victims of the Moor conquest and rape intensifies the conflict between torturer and tortured: for a moment it even reverses the dynamics of power. Interestingly, the example is one that performs another sort of reversal, in which Africans colonize Europeans.

Although Tarantino does not know Italian, he indicated in the script for *True Romance* that the characters should speak Italian, and Tony Scott remained faithful to the script in this case. Far from conveying a realistic portrayal, though, the use of Sicilian dialect in this scene articulates the twilight—better, the disintegration—of Italian American ethnicity. These gangsters, for example, are not modeled on the Al Capones of American history. They are distilled from the mafia characters of Coppola's and Scorsese's cinema. If ethnicity is never a tangible entity, but rather a kind of posture, performance, or self-representation, in Tarantino's cinema, ethnicity is an even more highly mediated form of representation—it is the representation of representation. These gangsters, who seem to come from another era and another world, shed light on the problematic narrative of origins and identity that haunts Tarantino.

Tarantino walks the line between an overt and persistent bigotry and an implicit critique of prejudice. Yet while his cinema brings to the forefront a racism pervasive in American society, Tarantino does not declare a social commitment of any kind. He problematizes essentialized notions of identity—racial, ethnic, gender, and sexual—without ever aligning himself with a specific political position. If it is difficult to identify a clear ethical stance anywhere in his films, this is because Tarantino assumes an ambiguous moral posture akin to what Linda Hutcheon characterizes as the postmodern "complicitous critique": "Postmodernism," she argues, "ultimately manages to install and reinforce as much as undermine and subvert the conventions and presuppositions it appears to challenge" (1-2). Tarantino's motivation is rather dictated by considerations of film-making and the conventions of cinema, which he both draws upon and undermines. In the interview with Dennis Hopper, Tarantino said:

> [A]s far as I'm concerned, if you're going to make a revenge movie, you've got to let the hero get revenge. There's a purity in that. You can moralize after the fact all you want, but people paid seven dollars to see it. So you set it up and the lead guy gets screwed over. And then, you want to see him kill the bad guys—with his bare hands, if possible. They've got to pay for their sins.
>
> (19)

The language in the passage is telling: not only is there a "purity" in letting the "hero get revenge," but the "bad guys" have to "pay for their sins" by getting killed with the "bare hands" of the "lead guy." Cinema becomes a sort of religion for this director, who couches his ethics of revenge film-making in religious terms of "purity" and "sin," but assigns "moralizing" a low priority compared to giving his audience "what [it] paid for." Hutcheon argues that "complicitous critique . . . situates the postmodern squarely within both economic capitalism and cultural humanism, two of the major dominants of much of the western world" (13). Tarantino's "ethic" takes shape through the language of capitalist exchange. His morality is derived from Hollywood economics.

Tarantino's fascination is with film itself, and with representation. According to Graham Fuller, Tarantino is interested in what has already "been mediated or predigested" (9), for example, in the opening scene of **Reservoir Dogs,** he is not so much concerned with Madonna "but [with] what Madonna has come to represent" (Graham Fuller ix). What interests Tarantino is not Italian American ethnicity as such, but what Italian American ethnicity has come to represent in American culture and, more specifically, in Hollywood cinema—hence the Sicilian interlude. There is no doubt that in Hollywood cinema, Coppola and Scorsese have produced—and, with De Niro, have become them-

selves—the most impressive icons of Italian American ethnicity. Of his pals in acting school, Tarantino says: "They all wanted to work with Robert De Niro or Al Pacino—and I would have loved to work with them too—but what I really wanted was to work with the directors. I wanted to work with Francis Ford Coppola. I wanted to work with Brian De Palma, and I would have learned Italian to work with Argento" (Hopper 50).

Although here, Tarantino does not identify himself as an Italian American auteur, he conveys the sense of a certain longing for Italian identity, aligning himself with Italian American actors, and Italian American and Italian directors. Talking about his notorious fascination with board games, Tarantino said: "I'm in a position now, as a kind of celeb, that I could look up the people that were in these shows and these movies, and play these games with them. I played the *Welcome Back Kotter* game and the *Grease* game with John Travolta. I had him sign the game and who won and what the date was and everything. . . . I've got a *Batman Returns* game that I can play with Danny De Vito, and I can play the *Laverne and Shirley* game with Penny Marshall, because I know Penny" (*Premiere* 1994). Need we add that all of these players have one thing in common besides the honor of having "played" their own characters in board games with Tarantino? Every one of them is Italian American.

While a director like Martin Scorsese, whom Tarantino often alludes to, grew up during the twilight of both cinema and ethnicity, and infuses a sense of loss and nostalgia for both in his films, Tarantino belongs to a different generation. In Tarantino's work, the mystification of the commodity value of cinema is replaced by a self-conscious flaunting of the power of the ultimate commodity created by the film industry: the videotape. The rewinding and fast-forwarding afforded by this postmodern form emerges in *Pulp Fiction* through complex editing that disrupts the conventions of linear and chronological development. As Tarantino himself put it, **Pulp Fiction** is three films for the price of one.

The kind of violent brutality Tarantino frequently depicts in his films often becomes funny—and not only when it's an accident. In the Hopper interview, Tarantino says, "I think it's humorous, but it's not all one big joke. I want the work to have complexity. So it's hah-hah-hah . . . until I don't want you to laugh at all. . . . And then you might even have to think about why you were laughing. And then I want to try to get you to start laughing again" (17). Scorsese's fascination with violence represents one of the most important allusive layers of Tarantino's cinema. In many ways, **Pulp Fiction** pays tribute to its Scorsesian antecedent, *Goodfellas,* and Jules is a parodic descendant of Max Cady in *Cape Fear,* with whom he shares a concern with biblical exegesis and revenge, or vengeance. If, as Robert Casillo argues, in the world of Scorsese violence is linked to the sacred in a Girardian sense, in Tarantino's world, violence is utterly decontextualized and deprived of any ritualistic function (although Jules's recital of the bible passage is ritualistic). The exception is perhaps *Natural Born Killers.* The film carries the unmistakable signature of its director, Oliver Stone (Tarantino was so disconcerted with what Stone had done with his script that he expressed his desire to have the credits changed from "script by" to "original story by Tarantino"). Even though most of the violence in *Natural Born Killers* is senseless and gratuitous (by most standards), the film is infused with a heavy moral vision completely absent in the Tarantino scripts and films. Mickey's accidental shooting of the innocent Indian, who embodies a connection with the past, with a mythologically rooted history, causes Mallory's vehement reaction: "Bad, bad, bad, bad, bad." But in Tarantino's films, things are different: the accidental murder of Marvin in the unforgettable *Pulp Fiction* car scene causes roaring laughter. In contrast to Stone's treatment, here there is no serious consideration of the reality of death, the loss of life. Even Joe Pesci's absurd violence in Scorsese's *Goodfellas* seems less senseless, and elicits at least a semblance of moral indignation in his not-so-moral partners in crime. But in Tarantino's world of quick consumption, lives become interchangeable, disposable.

While Tarantino seems to place himself in this multigenerational community of Italian Americans, and while Cliff does his best to protect his son Clarence from the mob, there is no nostalgia in this world for the comfort of either the ethnic neighborhood or the extended family: they have both disintegrated beyond traditional recognition. As ethnic and cultural assimilation and other social and political consequences of late capitalism and globalization, lead to the continued breakdown of multiple barriers and borders, and hasten the arrival of diverse, multiethnic, transnational identities and cultural hybridity, certain questions come up for scholars of ethnic studies. The emergence of an author/director such as Tarantino, whose ethnic identification is somewhat problematic, forces us to ask questions concerning the inclusion of such authors as subject matter for Italian American studies. It also becomes imperative to interrogate the validity of current methodologies in ethnic studies in general. If Italian American and other ethnic studies are to remain viable fields in a rapidly changing cultural milieu, what changes will these fields need to register, and how will the acknowledgment of the necessity for change be implemented in actual scholarly practices?

* * *

Before concluding, we feel the obligation to revisit our initial question: Is Quentin Tarantino Italian American?

This is what we found out: "He was born on March 27, 1963 in Knoxville, Tennessee. His mother, Connie Zastoupil, is . . . a native of that state but was raised in Cleveland, Ohio before going to high school in Los Angeles, the town she has always considered home" (Dawson 96). Tarantino's mother turns out to be "half Cherokee," though she says "you wouldn't know it" (Dawson 96).[2] She became pregnant when she was sixteen, but by the time she found out about her pregnancy, she had already separated from her husband, Tony Tarantino—and "never even contacted him" (98). Quentin was named after the character "Quint Asper" in the TV series *Gunsmoke* (played by Burt Reynolds), but he was also named after Quentin in *The Sound and the Fury.* When he was two years old, mother and son moved to Los Angeles, where he was adopted by Kurt Zastoupil, his mother's second husband. Quentin took his surname, but after quitting school he again began using the name Tarantino, that of his biological father, with whom he had had no contact. When asked about his father, Tarantino answered "flatly": "I have his name." According to one of his friends, Tarantino "took back his biological father's name . . . because he couldn't stand being called Zastoupil—'In school they had called him disaster peel'" (Bernard 102). Tarantino's onomastic narrative effectively captures the very themes that are played out in his movies: reflexivity, gender and sexual ambiguity, ethnic and racial crossings, name play, and multiple identities.[3] If, as Rosi Braidotti argues, the "nomadic subject" is someone with "no mother tongue, only a succession of translations, of displacements, of adaptations to changing conditions" (Braidotti 1), then Tarantino's films—and perhaps his life—represent a sort of parodic rendition of intellectual and cultural (artistic?) nomadism. The epistemological crisis often associated with postmodernism is indeed reflected in the crisis of identity in Tarantino's cinema—a crisis that was, perhaps, first played out in his own life.

We began writing an article about Tarantino's cinema, but our primary concern turns out to be the question of whether or not—and how—to write about Tarantino himself. As Tarantino demonstrates, writing about Italian American ethnicity, and ethnicity in general, can no longer be done unproblematically: What is a real Italian American? How do we decide who belongs? What is the object—or the subject—of Italian American studies? If Tarantino never met his father, and, for whatever reason, only adopted the name as a teenager, then what else—other than "blood"—is Italian American about Quentin Tarantino?

Notes

1. This is not true of his treatment of homosexuality, in *Pulp Fiction* or in the other three films, which is not only unself-conscious but homophobic: every mention, or instance, of anal sex between men takes the

form of, as one reviewer of *Pulp Fiction* uncritically put it, "a fate worse than death" [Corliss 73]).

2. Tarantino's mother is Catholic (*Premiere*, November 1994, 102), but since her maiden name does not appear anywhere in the press, her ethnic identity remains enigmatic—even more so than her son's.

3. Other aspects of Tarantino's films serve similar ends: hero-characters like Marsellus (another powerful crime boss) and Jules (who undergoes the radical transformation from assassin to devout, and ethically oriented, biblical scholar): inter-racial marriages like those of Marsellus and Mia, and the one between Tarantino's character and his African American wife, and even that between Butch (Bruce Willis) and his Bora Boran girlfriend Fabian, serve, as notable additions to the racially liberal though critically problematic dimension of many of Tarantino's characterizations.

Works Cited

Bernard, Jaime. "Quentin Tarantino: The Man and His Movies." *Sky Magazine* (September 1995): 101-08.

Braidotti, Rosi. *Nomadic Subjects: Embodiment and Sexual Difference in Contemporary Feminist Theory.* New York: Columbia UP, 1994.

Casillo, Robert. "Scorsese and Girard at Cape Fear." *Italian Americana* 12 (Summer 1994): 201-25.

Dawson, Jeff. "Revenge of the Nerd." *Empire* (October 1995): 96-100.

Fuller, Graham. "An Interview with Quentin Tarantino." *Quentin Tarantino: Reservoir Dogs and True Romance.* New York: Grove Press, 1994, ix-xviii.

Gamson, Joshua. *Claims to Fame: Celebrity in Contemporary America.* Berkeley: U of California P, 1984.

Hopper, Dennis. "Interview with Quentin Tarantino." *Grand Street Magazine* 13.1 (Summer 1994): 10-22.

Natural Born Killers. Dir. Oliver Stone. Story by Quentin Tarantino. Screenplay by David Veloz and Richard Rutowski. Warner Bros., 1994.

Pulp Fiction. Dir. Quentin Tarantino. Writing Credits, Quentin Tarantino (stories), Roger Avary. Warner Bros., 1994.

Reservoir Dogs. Dir. Quentin Tarantino. Writing Credits, Roger Avary, Quentin Tarantino. Warner Bros., 1994.

Tarantino, Quentin. *Pulp Fiction.* New York: Hyperion, 1994.

———. *Reservoir Dogs and True Romance.* New York: Grove Press, 1994.

True Romance. Dir. Tony Scott. Writing Credits, Quentin Tarantino. Warner Bros., 1994.

Glen Creeber (essay date 2002)

SOURCE: Creeber, Glen. "TV Ruined the Movies: Television, Tarantino, and the Intimate World of *The Sopranos*." In *This Thing of Ours: Investigating* The Sopranos, edited by David Lavery, pp. 124-34. New York, N.Y.: Columbia University Press, 2002.

[*In the following essay, Creeber argues that the works of Tarantino, among others, have brought a television aesthetic to film.*]

"It won't be cinematic."

Patsy Parisi to Gloria Trillo as he points a gun to her chest and describes how she will be killed if she continues to stalk Tony Soprano ("Amour Fou"/3012)

INTRODUCTION

Surprisingly perhaps for the creator of *The Sopranos* (what one American critic has referred to as "the best television drama ever made" [Holden ix]), David Chase seems to hold a less than favorable view of the medium in which he works. "All my life I wanted to do movies," he explained to Bill Carter in the *New York Times*. "I just resented every moment I spent in television . . . for me it was always cinema, cinema, cinema" (90). Despite previous credits to his name such as *The Rockford Files, Northern Exposure* and *I'll Fly Away,* Chase seems to regard television as cinema's poor cousin, unable to ever capture its magnitude and visual spectacle. "There's so much more to the movie experience," he told the British journalist Alex Blimes, "music and pictures and rhythm. I miss that" (169). Chase clearly feels that cinema has inevitably suffered for allowing itself to be increasingly influenced by its small screen rival. "I saw television take over cinema," he told Allen Rucker. "I saw TV executives moving into movies. I saw the pandering, cheerleading, family entertainment shit dominate everything. Low attention span stuff. It all came from TV. TV ruined the movies . . ."

As this suggests, Chase seems to resent the increasing influence of television on a new generation of filmmakers and cinema-goers. Quentin Tarantino's own much-hyped employment in a video store perhaps most famously suggests such a trend, revealing a writer, director, and actor as openly influenced as much by the small screen as the big. As Roger Avary, Tarantino's friend, co-worker, and (frequently over-looked) co-writer *of **Pulp Fiction*** (1994), points out: "We were the video store generation, right after the film school generation, the first generation of people who wanted to be filmmakers who had grown up alongside computers, videos, the information highway" (cited by Botting & Wilson 7). Indeed, the phenomenal success of Tarantino's ***Reservoir Dogs*** (1992) on video is sometimes cited as evidence that the aesthetics of cinema and television are perhaps gradually beginning to merge.[1] According to *New York Times* film critic Vincent Canby:

> Since the videocassette recorder has become, in effect, the second run of the theatrical film, there has been a televisionization in the look of movies. An interesting number of today's theatrical movies give the impression of being photographed almost entirely in the close-ups and medium shots that register best on the small screen.

(Cited by Wasko 166)

Few genres perhaps illustrate this trend towards "televisionization" as perfectly as the gangster genre. While movie critics like Peter Cowie have praised *The Godfather* (1972) for epitomizing the "classical style" of modern film-making (209-23), newer gangster movies such as ***Reservoir Dogs, Pulp Fiction,*** or more recently *Lock, Stock and Two Smoking Barrels* (1998) have often been associated with the type of "cartoon imagery" and "MTV aesthetics" more generally associated with TV. Indeed, *Lock, Stock* was recently made into a British television series, quickly cashing in on its big screen success.[2] For many critics, then, cinema's apparent movement towards adopting televisual aesthetics has produced a new breed of gangster film, one that is inherently different in style, form, and content from its big screen predecessor.

In this essay, I will argue that *The Sopranos* implicitly critiques the "televisionization" of the gangster genre—parodying its gradual development (Chase might say decline) from cinematic epic to standard video or television fare. In particular, I will illustrate how its constant self-reflexive referencing to its own generic history reveals a television narrative desperately trying to re-invent and re-examine itself; searching for the means by which it can both deconstruct and possibly reconstruct its own narrative dynamics. By critiquing the very medium it both utilizes and exploits, the drama ironically produces a complex and sophisticated narrative structure that simultaneously denigrates and celebrates its own inherent potential and artistic possibilities. Above all, then, *The Sopranos* can be seen as an investigation of genre, not only an attempt to "modernize" the portrayal of the Mob, but also an attempt to look back longingly to a genre that was once perhaps more morally stable and secure than it can ever be today.

A FEAR OF INTIMACY

It is clear, even to the most casual of viewers, that *The Sopranos* self-consciously positions itself (however ironically) as part of a long and illustrious cinematic tradition. As Caryn James points out, "One man has a car horn that blares out the first bars of *The Godfather* theme; another routinely impersonates Al Pacino as

Michael Corleone" (29). As other essays in this volume demonstrate the drama seems intent, even in areas such as casting, on offering reminders of an earlier generic tradition. This implicit referencing to an earlier generic tradition seems to be paralleled by Tony Soprano's own longing to return to a now forgotten era. "Out there it's the 1990s," the Prozac munching Mobster tells his children, "in here, it's 1954" ("Nobody Knows Anything"/1011). In particular, this depressed Mafia boss seems obsessed with the standards and the values epitomized by an earlier generation of gangsters. "He never reached the heights like me," he says of his father, "but in a lot of ways he had it better. He had his people. They had their standards. They had pride. Today, what have we got?" As this suggests, Tony appears to believe that the world of organized crime is clearly less noble and respected than it once was in its Golden Age.

This notion of a "Golden Age" could refer as much to the *dramatic universe* Tony inhabits as it does to the reality of the Mob itself. For it has been argued that, like the Mob, the contemporary gangster movie has also rejected the traditional conventions of *its* past. Interestingly, a TV mob expert suggests ("46 Long"/ 1002) that the Mafia itself is partly to blame for its own decline, particularly for turning its back on the "rules which once served the old Dons so well." Indeed, such a statement could equally refer to a *genre* that has perhaps similarly rejected its own (cinematic) heritage, disregarding a set of moral "standards" and aesthetic "rules" that once governed it in the past. Seen in this light, Tony's depression is symptomatic of a character who unconsciously feels he exists at the wrong end of a long and illustrious tradition (literally, in the form of the Mob and metaphorically, in the form the gangster genre). "Lately I've been getting the feeling that I came in at the end," he tells his psychiatrist. "The best is over."

As such, Tony Soprano is clearly meant to represent an earlier *generic* tradition, a world that still remembers the "rules" and the "standards" that once "served the old Dons so well." In cinematic terms, this perhaps most famously refers to Coppola's classic portrayal of the Mafia, particularly Marlon Brando's modern (yet inherently old-school) Don Vito Corleone.[3] According to his wife Carmela, her husband "watches *The Godfather* all the time." On his new laser disk, she adds, "he says the camera work looks as good as in the movie theater." Consequently, Tony's choice of film and his specific appreciation of the genre appears to reflect a particular cinematic tradition, a time when the gangster movie had not yet succumbed to the increasing influence of television. In contrast to more recent examples of the genre, critics have argued that Coppola's original movie was made primarily for cinema and therefore can never be fully appreciated on the small screen. As film critic Anton Wilson puts it:

Coppola created the magnificent "underworld" texture by extensively exploiting the shadow detail capability of film. Most of the action in many of the interior scenes existed in the lowest regions of the exposure curve. In my opinion this subtle feel of the texture was lost when the film appeared on television as the medium could not cope with the range of exposure, especially the shadow details.

(cited by Wasko 167)[4]

As this suggests, Tony Soprano epitomizes the "classical" gangster genre, one that was inherently at home on the big screen.[5] As such, it is no wonder that he finds it difficult to adjust to the smaller dimensions of television. In what is now regarded as one of the founding texts of Television Studies, Horace Newcomb argued that television could never emulate the sheer "expansiveness" of the cinema. Instead, the small screen (particularly through its use of close-up and medium shots) achieves a more *personal* and *intimate* view of the world (243-64).[6] Tony's tragic predicament can be viewed as an essentially cinematic creation, desperately trying to conform to the apparently *intimate* dynamics of the small screen. Looking like extras from *The Godfather,* his crew are deposited uncomfortably into a world of soap operas, docu-soaps, and confessional talk shows—forced to take their personalities beyond their traditional generic boundaries. "Nowadays," Tony complains, "everybody's gotta go to shrinks, and counselors and go on *Sally Jessy Raphael* and talk about their problems" ("The Sopranos"/1001). As such, Tony's long-running battle with therapy implicitly parallels the narrative's own struggle with the personal requirements of television. Frustrated by the constant need to express his feelings, this Mafia boss is not simply resisting the contemporary preoccupation with self-analysis but also struggling to adapt to television's obsession with the *private* and *personal* dynamics of human experience.

It comes as no surprise, then, that he frequently longs to escape from this "intimate" world and return to the traditional conventions of classical Hollywood. "Whatever happened to Gary Cooper, the strong silent type?" he asks his psychiatrist. "He wasn't in touch with his feelings. He just did what he had to do." In this context, it is clear that Tony's fear of *intimacy* is not just a symptom of his *psychological* condition but is also perhaps an inevitable reaction against his own *generic* confinement.

In contrast, Tony's impetuous nephew, Christopher Moltisanti, is clearly meant to represent a new breed of both gangster and genre. Brought up on a steady diet of television, videos and computer games, he is, as the *New York Times* puts it, "a soldier of the MTV generation." Tony clearly feels his nephew has been spoiled, citing his $60,000 Lexus automobile as an example of a generation that has been over-indulged ("The Sopranos"/

1001). However, both men do seem to share a love of the movies, although for Christopher it is a passion that threatens to almost overcome his allegiance to the Mob. Indeed, he secretly enrolls in an acting class and begins (with the help of *How to Write a Movie in 21 Days*) to write a screenplay. "You Bite, I Bark" is based on his experiences in the Mob, although as Holden points out, "his stolen laptop seems to come without a spell checker" (129). Later Christopher even visits a movie set with his cousin's girlfriend who just happens to have worked for Tarantino.[7] As this might suggest, Christopher's perspective on the cinema perhaps reflects the cultural attitude of a new generation of filmmakers and movie buffs. Although clearly obsessed with film, his local video store is as near as he actually gets to the cinematic experience. "I love movies," he tells his girlfriend Adriana. "That smell at Blockbuster, that candy and carpet smell, I get high off" ("The Legend of Tennessee Moltisanti"/1008).

As a symbol of the new "video store" generation, Christopher clearly seems to reflect the contemporary genre's more violent and perhaps increasingly "amoral" sensibilities. He certainly seems unable to disconnect movies from his real life, frequently reacting self-reflexively to volatile situations. "This is the *Scarface* final scene," he shouts at Tony and the crew, "Fucking bazookas under each arm. Say hello to my little friend" ("Pax Soprano"/1006). However, his older colleagues seem unimpressed by his uncontrolled outbursts of anger. "Always with the scenarios," Pussy comments sarcastically. As this implies, this new "video store" generation simply fails to appreciate many of the more subtle ingredients of the classic gangster movie. Even when Christopher travels to Naples with Tony and the crew, he spends most of his time in his hotel room doing drugs; missing a rare chance to see and experience his ancestral homeland. Not surprisingly, then, he also seems unable to fully grasp the details of his own cinematic heritage, even managing to misquote from Coppola's original masterpiece. This contrast between Tony and Christopher's viewing habits clearly reveal characters at different ends of the same generic spectrum—perhaps representative of the old "film school" and new "video store" generations respectively. While both characters are clearly corrupt, dangerous, and violent individuals, they appear to represent a fundamentally different set of moral and ethical values.

"They Just Don't Give a Damn"

Some critics argue that the new gangster movie is representative of a "new brutalism" in modern cinema. Julia Hallam and Margaret Marshment argue that rather than constructing "narratively adequate motivations . . . for violent acts," these films tend to portray *natural* born killers who are not apparently motivated by any "narrative causality" (225). Similarly, in his discussion of *Reservoir Dogs,* the film critic Geoff Andrew argues that "Tarantino does not appear to be concerned with the moral implications of the film; rather, it is primarily a stylish variation on traditional genre conventions, designed to thrill, shock, amuse and surprise" (323). This apparent "amorality" has certainly helped to characterize this new breed of gangster film, distinguishing it from the kind of realism that critics have associated with the genre in the past. As Hallam and Marshment put it:

> By the 1980s and the 1990s, the gangster film's roots in any antecedent discourse of social reality is largely obscured by "high concept" aesthetics that foreground stylistic excess, its entertainment value articulated through accrued layers of generic self-reflexivity and intertextuality.
>
> (92)

Consequently, it has been argued that these new films are inevitably more concerned with creating intricate aesthetic worlds, rather than with exploring the wider *moral* and *ethical* considerations of the genre. For some critics it is a cinematic tendency seen in the contemporary depiction of crime and violence as a whole. According to Philip L. Simpson, "the popular 1990s films that mythologize serial murderers' exploits are unremittingly conservative in many aspects and generally dispense with social critique in favor of apocalyptic (as opposed to cathartic) levels of violence" (120). As a TV psychiatrist says of Mickey and Mallory (the postmodern Bonnie and Clyde of *Natural Born Killers* [1992]): "They know the difference between right and wrong. They just don't give a damn." According to Phil Hardy's introduction to the *BFI Companion to Crime,* "These [new] films are deeply pessimistic and very violent." Comparing Scorsese's *Mean Streets* (1973) with *Pulp Fiction,* Hardy argues that "for all his freneticism" Harvey Keitel's character (perhaps like Tony) "has a secure sense of society." This is in stark contrast to John Travolta's who (perhaps like Christopher) "can only innocently wonder about the odd thread that connects the events of his life . . ."

(23)

Put crudely, then, it could be argued that there has been a tendency in the contemporary gangster genre—embodied in the contrast between Tony and Christopher—to swap its classical sense of realism with "cartoon style" violence and "high concept aesthetics." In this sense, the new gangster movie may have taken on many of the most excessive characteristics of the television action series, replacing ethics with exhibition and personality with spectacle. As Toby Miller has recently put it, "Several genres within US and UK [television] drama focus on action rather than character [such as] police programs that feature violence rather than detection . . . war shows that stress fighting over politics . . . and action packed historical . . . and science fiction epics" (17-18). As such, films like *Reservoir Dogs* have been criticized for glamorizing a similar

televisual tradition, carefully tuning into and articulating the stereotyped themes and repressed motifs of the classic 1970s television action and crime series. As Taubin puts it:

> What makes *Reservoir Dogs* such a 90s film is that it's about the return of what was repressed in the television version of 70s masculinity—a paranoid, homophobic fear of the other that explodes in hate speech, in kicks and blows, in bullets and blades. *Reservoir Dogs* is an extremely insular film—women get no more than thirty seconds of screen time, people of color get zero—yet not a minute goes by without some reference to coons and jungle bunnies, to jailhouse rape (black semen shooting up white asses), to the castration threat of "phallic" women like Madonna or that 70s icon Pam Grier.
>
> (124)

Seen in this light, *The Sopranos* ultimately offers the viewer a critique of the "classic" TV action series, particularly in the way this TV genre has now infiltrated and "contaminated" the narrative dynamics of the "classical" gangster movie. The repressed sexism, racism, and homophobia present in such programs become the subject of a television serial that seeks to re-invent and re-position its own narrative point of view and generic construction. However, rather than blatantly renew and reinvigorate the stereotypes of the past, it could be argued that *The Sopranos* re-employs these very tropes so that both Tony and the genre itself become the subjects of analysis. In this way, the viewer may be forced to reconsider the hidden and repressed desires that have produced and manufactured them both.

In "D-Girl" (2007), for instance, Christopher meets up with film development girl Amy Safir and actor Jon Favreau. Clearly sophisticated and middle-class, this Hollywood pair simply engineer to use Christopher (and his script) to help them with their next project, *Crazy Joe*—based on the life of the real gangster, Crazy Joe Gallo. "Mob theme stories," as Amy tells Christopher, "are always hot." Visibly turned on by his Mob connections, she begins an affair with him that she clearly has no intention of continuing beyond her hotel room. Later, both she and Favreau become excited when Christopher tells them real stories from the Mob, secretly hoping to appropriate them for their own screenplay. One tale revolves around a gangster who unknowingly has sex with a transsexual and is horrified when he discovers she still has male genitalia. In retaliation he buys a can of acid and seeks her out. He "burns everything" Christopher explains, "pours it on her arms, on her face . . . on her prick." Favreau is clearly shocked; forced to confront the reality of a type of violence he prefers to think of only in cinematic terms. However, the hard-nosed Amy is simply concerned that the story lacks originality and mentions *The Crying Game* (1992). "This is a true story," Favreau has to quickly remind her. In this way, the exploitative tendencies of the new gangster genre are clearly satirized, contrasting the comfortable lives of these two affluent filmmakers with the people they depict, stereotype, and inherently use.

COMPLICATED SHADOWS

An implicit critique of the contemporary gangster genre is discernible in the style of *The Sopranos* as a whole, particularly in the way that it appears to deliberately echo the mise en scene of the "classical" gangster movie. The narrative, for example, frequently employs the technique most famously used in *The Godfather* of cross-cutting (as Holden puts it) "between scenes of extreme violence and domestic warmth" (xiii). At the end of Coppola's movie the innocence of a family christening and a number of brutal murders are carefully edited together. As Michael Corleone renounces the devil in his role as Godfather to his sister's child, so his role as a Mafia Godfather is graphically foregrounded by the cold-blooded murders that we see carried out in his name. The end of episode three of the first season ("Denial, Anger, Acceptance"/1003) clearly borrows this technique, mixing the killing of Brendan and the mock execution of Christopher with a choral recital from Meadow's school concert. This kind of montage gives an important moral and ethical context to the story, graphically revealing the hypocrisy that lies beneath the Mafia's respectable veneer.

A similar technique is loosely applied in "College" (1005). When Tony visits Maine with his daughter Meadow for a college tour, he accidentally comes across a notorious "rat" now living under the pseudonym Fred Peters. As a result, the normality of this everyday trip is suddenly juxtaposed with a bloody tale of Mafia revenge. As with Brendan's death, Tony's brutal strangling of "Fred" from behind is also reminiscent of a scene from *The Godfather,* the infamous murder of Luca Brasi. Such a treatment of violence is clearly meant to unsettle viewers, forcing them to contemplate the different facets of Tony's life and personality. As if to reinforce such a reading, Tony himself spies a plaque on a wall while waiting for Meadow to be interviewed at Bowdoin. "No man can wear one face to himself and another to the multitude," it reads, "without finally getting bewildered as to which may be true" (Hawthorne in *The Scarlet Letter*). In this way, rather than allowing Tony's Mafia persona to dominate the narrative point of view, the viewer is given a number of contrasting perspectives (father/parent/husband/mobster) from which to view the action. This offers a complexity of characterization seldom witnessed in movies such as *Reservoir Dogs,* where colors replace even the names of its principal characters. As Stephen Prince puts it: "Tarantino is drawn to violence because he knows it as a movie style, and it is one that he finds compelling.

The style itself is the subject and form of his work. Accordingly, he has not moved to explore the psychological and emotional dynamics of violence in terms that might reference life apart from the movies" (241).

A similar approach can be detected in *The Sopranos'* use of music. Although the series frequently employs popular songs, they generally lack the catchy intensity of the music that so often punctuates more recent examples of the genre. Indeed, the low-key beat of Nick Lowe's "The Beast in Me" or Elvis Costello's "Complicated Shadows" is in direct contrast with the frenetic dance beat of *Pulp Fiction*'s "Jungle Boogie" (Kool & The Gang) or the infectious pop of *Reservoir Dogs'* "Stuck in the Middle with You" (Stealer's Wheel). Consequently, the choice of music tends to avoid constructing the sort of rapidly edited sequences that have become associated with the new sub-genre. Instead, the series' use of music frequently helps to create a mood and an atmosphere that is reminiscent of Coppola's famously languid pace, perhaps echoing the classical eloquence of Nino Rota's memorable theme tune.

The second season of *The Sopranos,* for instance, begins with the lazy and melancholic tones of Frank Sinatra performing Ervin Drake's "It Was a Very Good Year." As the song plays, so we are given a long and leisurely paced selection of apparently unconnected scenes. Sequences such as Livia lying motionless and depressed in her hospital bed, Carmela baking at home, Silvio trying on a new pair of shoes, AJ self-consciously combing his hair, and Tony and Paulie making love with their girlfriends/prostitutes provide an essentially "domestic" montage. However, the music fails to extenuate or exaggerate the pace of the action (as, for example, George Baker's "Little Green Bag" famously does at the opening of *Reservoir Dogs*). Instead, Sinatra's unhurried and mournful ballad (played in its full four and a half minutes) explicitly heightens the scene's leisurely construction, deliberately slowing down the story's narrative pace and transforming the generic spectacle of the modern gangster genre into an essentially domestic and intimate display.[8]

This leisurely pace and implicit sense of intimacy is further heightened by the drama's deliberate excursions away from the traditional world of the gangster genre. If, as I have argued, Tony finds himself implicitly trapped in the relatively restricting dynamics of television, it is not surprising that televisual aesthetics are frequently employed to break up and fragment the narrative's more traditionally "cinematic" images and techniques. As in the domestic (sitcom-like) story lines surrounding Tony's family, the psychiatry sessions seem to deliberately utilize some of the essential elements of the small screen. Relatively static (at least, compared to the "high concept" techniques favored in newer examples of the genre), the emphasis here is on dialogue, close-ups, and human interaction, employing what many critics regard as some of the most basic ingredients of television drama (see, for example, Jacobs 7-8).

Indeed, these scenes are perhaps more reminiscent of the conventional TV chat show or the "head-to-head" political interview than they are of the contemporary gangster or action movie. In this way, the therapy sequences appear to deliberately fragment the series narrative dynamic, perhaps forcing the viewer to stand back for a moment from Tony's exotic (and perhaps essentially "cinematic") life-style so that they can briefly distance themselves from the genre's historically seductive appeal.[9] Like Tony, then, the aesthetic intimacy of the small screen is unexpectedly thrust upon the viewer and the narrative expectations of the genre suddenly denied.

The first episode, for instance, opens with Tony sitting alone and in silence for a full twenty seconds in Melfi's waiting room. Once in her office, it is another thirty seconds before she finally breaks the silence, a bravely austere opening for a pilot episode of a gangster series.[10] Compare this, for example, with the hectic opening sequence of *Lock, Stock and Two Smoking Barrels,* or the famously seductive credit sequence of **Reservoir Dogs.**[11] Later in the episode, Dr. Melfi interrupts one of Tony's recollections to get, as she puts it, "some ethical ground-rules out of the way." This interruption similarly breaks up the narrative pace of the action, while the rock soundtrack that accompanies Tony's violent memory is suddenly replaced by the abrupt silence of Mefli's office. In this way the therapy sessions unexpectedly forces the viewer to take time out from the traditional attractions of the gangster genre, giving a possibly "ethical" and spatially contrasting perspective from which to view the events taking place. As a result, the typically high powered conventions of the genre are temporarily suspended and the audience given a brief moment away from its visual and audio excitement.

In this way, *The Sopranos* implicitly reflects the use of the psychiatry narrative as employed in a television series like *The Singing Detective* (Potter/Amiel, BBC 1986).[12] In a manner seldom matched by cinema (hence perhaps the more comedic inflection of a film like *Analyze This!*), the sheer breadth of the television series (what Newcomb refers to as its tendency towards "continuity") enables the inherently slow and *gradual* process of psychotherapy to be more realistically represented and explored. Like Dennis Potter's equally reluctant patient in *The Singing Detective,* Tony's therapy appears to progress slowly, operating in a timeframe clearly not affordable in the relatively limited time-span of the cinema. It is not until "Down Neck" (1007), for example, that we are given our first direct glimpse (in the form of a flashback) of his childhood. As a young boy in 1967 we see him discover (for the first time) his father's involvement in the Mob, accidentally witnessing him and his Uncle Junior "beat the crap" out of a man from the neighborhood.

Interestingly, the way this scene is shot is strikingly reminiscent of the childhood trauma at the heart of *The Singing Detective,* when Marlow (as a young boy) accidentally comes across his mother having sex in the woods. Like Marlow, Tony stands at the foot of a tree, voyeuristically witnessing the action from a concealed spot, both repulsed and excited by what he secretly witnesses.[13] The echo of this famous scene perhaps implicitly pays homage to the depth of characterization that the cumulative narrative of a television series like *The Singing Detective* can achieve. Tony is ultimately struggling with the claustrophobic dynamics of television but (despite its apparently limiting restrictions) may ironically gain a greater understanding of himself— and perhaps the genre in which he unknowingly exists—through serialized drama's gradual excavation of character, desire, and perhaps even unconscious motivation.[14]

By reluctantly allowing the "intimate" world of television into the more "masculine" world of the gangster genre, both Tony and the drama itself are gradually forced to recognize the limitations of their own restricting worlds. This employment of televisual techniques may seem contradictory (especially for a drama that implicitly critiques the impact of television on an essentially cinematic genre), but the critique of a certain type of television remains intact. Indeed, Tony's therapy sessions are a world away from the classic action series, of "cartoon violence" and "MTV aesthetics." In this way, the drama critiques not the medium itself (of which it is clearly now an important exponent) but the refusal of the medium to utilize its basic strengths and inherent possibilities.

CONCLUSION

Tony Soprano is clearly sexist, homophobic, and unashamedly racist, but in his journey through psychoanalysis we learn some of the reasons for his complex condition (a psychological journey that, as we have seen, is seldom equaled in the new gangster genre). As such, we are given the means by which we can start to unravel the historical and personal dynamics by which this character has arrived at such a complex and neurotic state. *The Sopranos* does not pretend to resolve these problems for Tony—indeed, in the process of therapy little real change seems to have been made either to his mental health, life-style or personal views. However, the series does attempt to examine its own narrative desires, asking difficult and uncomfortable questions that simultaneously harness and investigate the genre that Tony both inhabits and ultimately subverts.

As such, Tony's continual nostalgia for his father's long forgotten "moral" standards can be partly regarded as a yearning to return to the age of the "classical" gangster genre—certainly before the rise of the "new brutalism" and the increasing influence of television on this apparently "most cinematic" of all genres. The clash between these two opposing worlds is most clearly played out in the conflict that exists between Tony and his impetuous young protégé, Christopher. While Tony's "traditional" sensibilities appear to represent Coppola's old "film school" generation (represented by the series' own homage to "classical" film aesthetics), Christopher clearly encapsulates the new priorities of Tarantino's "video store" generation, particularly its apparent obsession with the forms and moral aesthetics of the television action series. However, this "televisionization" of the genre is clearly both critiqued and celebrated by the series that both deliberately employs and subverts the intimate dimensions of the small screen, forcing its cinematic heroes into strangely intimate and uncomfortably private situations. In the way, the drama simultaneously modernizes and parodies a genre that has seemingly lost touch with a heritage that was perhaps more morally stable and secure than it can ever appear today.

It is clearly ironic that *The Sopranos* attempts to do all this on the very medium that it implicitly set out to examine and critique. However, by incorporating both elements of television and cinematic practice into its essentially hybrid form, the drama implicitly forces the viewer to confront the very means by which the narrative is produced, contained and finally received. In this way, Chase and his team of writers and directors have created a form of drama that transcends traditional generic boundaries, but still retains the moral framework upon which the gangster genre was originally (if not ambiguously) based. In doing so, the narrative self-consciously satirizes and subverts the changes and developments that have recently taken place in the gangster genre as whole. Perhaps the overriding message of *The Sopranos* is that we are all capable of overcoming and transcending our inherent prejudices and "generic" limitations; that heroism and tragedy resides not just in the epic and the spectacular but also in the personal and the everyday. A view of the world, it could be argued, that is more successfully examined and explored within the inherently "intimate" dynamics of television.

Notes

1. In an interview that accompanied the film's video release, Tarantino (1992) argued that it was the sort of movie that would do well in video shops. "Having worked in a video store I know what happens in there," he explained to his anonymous interviewer.

"This is the sort of movie that, in particular, the young kids who work in the video store are going to like . . . so I think it's going to get a big in-store push . . ."

2. The TV series was later released on video in the UK (*Lock, Stock . . . the Television Series*: Ska/Ginger Productions: 2000).

3. As an old-school Mafia don, Don Vito is disgusted by the modern spread of narcotics and refuses an invitation to get his "business" involved in dealing drugs. This refusal eventually leads to a Mafia war that results in his attempted assassination.

4. Curiously we never discover Tony's view of *Good-Fellas* (1990). When Father Phil asks Carmela where her husband stands on the film, a suspected burglar immediately interrupts them. (Father Phil's shocked reaction to the gun that Carmela instantly acquires also offers a clear juxtaposition between his reaction to "screen" and "real" violence). Similarly, when Meadow tells Tony that her friends think that the Mafia is "cool," he seems shocked and surprised when she suggests the reason is *Casino,* apparently oblivious to *The Godfather.* Tony himself makes no comment ("College"/1005)

5. In the second episode of the third season of *The Sopranos* we see Tony watch *Public Enemy* (1931) on a number of occasions, clearly enthralled by this more "innocent" view of gangster life, particularly Tom Powers' (James Cagney) relationship with his mother.

6. This notion of intimacy appears in most early discussions of the medium. See, for instance, Ellis 132.

7. The movie Christopher visits is called *Female Suspects* and stars Janeane Garofalo and Sandra Bernhard, who both guest star as themselves in the episode.

8. Likewise, Sinatra's infamous association with the Mafia (the character of Johnny Fontane in *The Godfather* was rumored to be based on the singer and actor) further reminds the viewer of an earlier generic tradition—a world before the "amoral" onslaught on the new "brutalized" gangster movie, perhaps epitomized by the more contemporary rhythms of rock, pop and funk.

9. For example, critics have chastised *The Godfather* for implicitly mythologizing and glamorizing its portrayal of the Mob In "Myth & Meaning: Francis Ford Coppola and Popular Response to the *Godfather* Trilogy," David Ray Papke has explained how the director was first amazed when people seemed to be *attracted* to many of the elements of the original movie. In particular, he was reported to be shocked that viewers thought he had intentionally "romanticized" Michael Corleone (Al Pacino). This was in stark contrast with his own belief that Michael was represented "as a monster" by the end of the movie

(9). Ironically, the Mafia itself also seemed to be among some of the film's most enthusiastic supporters. As Papke points out, "According to anonymous reports, the old-fashioned and largely abandoned custom of kissing the hands of powerful Mafia leaders revived because of its portrayal in the film" (6). Indeed, according to the British journalist Ben Macintyre, recent transcripts of wire-tapped conversations from within the Mob show that *The Sopranos* itself is now similarly beginning to effect the behavior and discourse of the real Mafia, with Mobsters discussing the drama and repeating the characters' own hang-ups and concerns. According to Macintyre, "What these and other Mafia tapes show is not just that art mirrors life, but that the life of the mobster is in some ways controlled by art" (24).

10. Compare their portrayal, for example, with the psychiatry sessions in a movie like *Analyze This!* (1999), a film (often compared with *The Sopranos* because of its narrative similarities) where there is still a great deal of action and slapstick even in the meetings between patient and psychiatrist.

11. Although the series' own credit sequence employs both fast editing techniques and rock music (A3's "Woke Up This Morning"), it is frequently brought to a sudden halt when the drama itself begins, an inversion of Tarantino's familiar technique, where banal conversation usually precedes a dynamic opening credit sequence

12. This is not the first time the series has been compared with *The Singing Detective*. "In its leisurely use of the form," Caryn James has argued, "it is strangely like *Brideshead Revisited, The Singing Detective* and *I Claudius*" (26). At the 2001 *Console-ing Passions: Television, Video, Feminism and New Media* conference, connections were also drawn by Roger Sorkin's "Murderous Matriarch: Liva Soprano."

13. Like Potter's Marlow, Tony's mother is clearly a powerful and domineering woman. Indeed, the similarities between the two women are significant, not least their strangely Oedipal relationship with their young sons (Livia even threatens to poke out Tony's eyes with a fork during one of the flashbacks to his childhood). Earlier, in episode four of the first season Tony dreams he is in Dr. Melfi's office, a woman he is sexually attracted to. After watching Silvio and a lap dancer have sex in the waiting room, he turns back to Melfi. However, as she turns around it is revealed to be his mother in the chair. (To make the connection with British television drama even more pronounced, Livia is also the name of the ruthless, scheming wife in *I, Claudius* [BBC 1976]— although it was also significantly the name of Chase's own mother). For a consideration of the role of the mother in *The Singing Detective,* see Creeber 166-78.

14. 'Soprano' usually refers either to the highest adult female voice or the voice of a young boy before puberty. It is perhaps worth noting that both these television dramas refer to the act of singing in their titles. It is as if these quintessentially masculine genres (*film-noir* in the case of *The Singing Detective*) were being forced to take on board the more "feminine" characteristics traditionally associated with genres such as the soap opera or the confessional talk show. While "singing" is sometimes used as street-slang for the act of "grassing" to the police (or even, appropriately enough, *confession*), the surname Soprano refers to the female or adolescent section of a choir (an indication perhaps of the drama's own examination of a genre more commonly equated with the tenor or the mature male voice generally).

Bibliography

Botting, Fred and Scott Wilson. *The Tarantinian Ethics.* London: Sage, 2001.

Ellls. John. *Visible Fictions: Cinema, Television, Video.* London: Routledge, 1982.

Hallam, Julia, with Margaret Marshment. *Realism and Popular Cinema.* Manchester: Manchester UP, 2000.

Hawthorne, Nathaniel. *The Scarlet Letter* Ed. Ross C. Murfin. Case Studies in Contemporary Criticism. Boston: Bedford Books of St. Martin's Press, 1991.

Holden, Stephen "The Sopranos an Introduction." *The New York Times on The Sopranos.* xi-xix.

Jacobs, Jason. *The Intimate Screen: Early British Television Drama.* New York: Oxford UP, 2001.

James, Caryn. "Addicted to a Mob Family Potion." *The New York Times on The Sopranos.* 23-31.

Miller Toby. "The Action Series." *The Television Genre Book.* Ed. Glen Creeber. London: BFI, 2001. 17-19.

Newcomb, Horace. *TV: The Most Popular Art.* New York: Anchor Books, 1974.

Papke, David Ray. "Myth & Meaning: Francis Ford Coppola and Popular Response to the *Godfather* Trilogy" *Legal Reelism: Movies as Legal Texts.* Ed. John Denvir. Urbana: U Illinois P, 1996. 1-22.

Prince, Stephen. *Savage Cinema: Sam Peckinpah and the Rise of Ultraviolent Movies.* London: Athlone Press, 1998.

Tarantino, Quentin. *Reservoir Dogs* (CD featuring interview with Tarantino on the making of the movie). Dog Eat Dog Productions, Universal Pictures, UK, 1992.

Taubin, Amy. "The Men's Room." *Action/Spectacle Cinema: A Sight & Sound Reader.* Ed. José Arroyo. London: BFI, 2000.

Wasko, Janet. *Hollywood in the Information Age: Beyond the Silver Screen.* Cambridge: Polity Press, 1994.

Quentin Tarantino and Mark Olsen (interview date October 2003)

SOURCE: Tarantino, Quentin, and Mark Olsen. "Turning On a Dime." *Sight & Sound* 13, no. 10 (October 2003): 12-15.

[*In the following interview, Olsen discusses the* Kill Bill *films with Tarantino.*]

Winding up the long drive that leads to Quentin Tarantino's secluded Hollywood Hills home, visitors are greeted by the bright-yellow Pussy Wagon, a customised truck driven by Uma Thurman in volume one of the director's new film *Kill Bill.* Tarantino's devotion to the memorabilia, minutiae and mythology of his own films is legendary, and seems perfectly in tune with the fervour and anticipation with which his fans still await each new release.

His previous outing, 1997's *Jackie Brown,* caused consternation in some quarters for its wilfully quiet character sketches and the dignity and grace the director brought to the seedy goings-on, filtering his own voice through novelist Elmore Leonard's. If *Jackie Brown*'s leisurely pacing took a few viewings to attune to, *Kill Bill* is an immediate, high-energy experience, an explosion of colour, music and mayhem. A crazed amalgam of exploitation-revenge pictures and Shaw Brothers-style kung-fu films, it's as over-the-top as *Jackie Brown* was understated.

Left for dead on her wedding day by her former associates, a team of assassins known as the Deadly Viper Assassination Squad, The Bride (Thurman) awakens from a five-year coma determined to avenge her betrayal. One by one she stalks those she once considered her allies (played by Daryl Hannah, Michael Madsen, Vivica A. Fox and Lucy Liu). At the end of the road waits Bill, played by David Carradine with the grizzled appeal of Lee Van Cleef.

Shooting in China, Japan, Mexico and the US and riffing on anime, Italian giallos, blaxploitation and other subgenres, Tarantino set out to make his ultimate "movie-movie", the movie he himself would most like to see. Eventually the epic scale became too much for one film to hold, so Harvey Weinstein, head of Miramax, suggested splitting it in half and releasing it as two pictures. The House of Blue Leaves sequence, a baroque battle that forms the climax of volume one, took eight weeks to shoot; all of *Pulp Fiction* took only ten.

Where Tarantino is widely recognised for the way he has redefined pop chestnuts—who can hear 'Stuck in the Middle with You' or 'Didn't I (Blow Your Mind This Time)' and not think of scenes from his films?—here he steals score music from other movies, re-using pieces by Bernard Herrmann, Ennio Morricone, Isaac Hayes, Quincy Jones and Luis Bacalov to stunning effect. Working with kung-fu-ologist The RZA, the production mastermind behind hip-hop group Wu-Tang Clan, he has woven an amazing aural quilt that's a step beyond his previous efforts. His mobilisation of disreputable genre tropes is not entirely dissimilar from the way passages of Bob Dylan's recent *Love and Theft* album were paraphrased from Japanese writer Junichi Saga's *Confessions of a Yakuza.* If Dylan distills the essence of Asian gangster cool and transports it to a landscape of dustbowl drifters, so Tarantino brings the wild imagery and out-of-control narratives of the exploitation-revenge picture and kung-fu film into new territory. The iconic grandeur of Sergio Leone's spaghetti Westerns was lifted from Kurosawa's brooding samurai films, which were in turn inspired by American cowboy pictures. Tarantino seems determined to claim them back once and for all.

Tarantino says he has cut together about 40 per cent of volume two of *Kill Bill,* and while hesitant to give away too much, he promises the next instalment will feature more story and character and more of the "Quentin dialogue" that's notably absent from volume one. While one can't help but adopt a wait-and-see attitude to the work as a whole, the inspired delirium of this first movie is more than enough to whet the appetite.

[*Olsen*]: *As you move from the gangster picture to blaxploitation to revenge pictures and kung fu, are your movies following your own interests as a viewer?*

[Tarantino]: I would go along with that. To me, movie-watching and movie-making are intertwined. From the beginning I've been a fan not so much of genre as of subgenre. *Reservoir Dogs* isn't just a gangster movie, it's a heist film, which is a subgenre of its own. I think the movie fan in me gets hung up on this or that subgenre for a while. And those obsessions intersect with what I want to do next. If I ever lost my interest in watching movies I'd lose everything I have to offer in terms of film-making. There's part of me that wants to make an Italian giallo, a European sex movie, a women-in-prison movie, a Filipino blood-island movie, a Dirty Dozen movie or my own spaghetti Western. Which I keep making anyway—it's just I've yet to do it as a Western.

Why did you break up **Kill Bill** *into two movies?*

Initially it was because of the length—Harvey [Weinstein] just wanted to tame it. I always hoped to get it down to two and a half hours—90 minutes for the first half and an hour for the second. It was probably never going to happen, but that's what was in my mind. It sounded crazy to suggest it could be two movies until Harvey proposed it. And it's understandable when you see the way the movie is done, because I've already cut out the boring scenes.

In the editing?

In the writing. It's a question of how I can go from strength to strength. If **Kill Bill: Vol. 1** were an album it would be a greatest-hits album: there's nothing there just to round it out. And there is an element of let's go through all these genre movies, drop the scenes we had to suffer through and just go for the good stuff. As a movie junkie I could handle a three-and-a-half-hour version of it. But unless you're a mainline movie junkie like me you'd probably overdose from that much **Kill Bill.** The time between the weekend coming up, when volume one opens, and the release of volume two early next year is unique in the life of **Kill Bill.** From that point on it'll be on video and DVD, and if you want to see it as a three-hour movie you have your whole life to do that.

One of the more surprising elements in volume one is how terse the dialogue is. At times there's very little talking at all.

I wanted it to be a burst of adrenaline. We're getting The Bride on her way, and we don't want to get lost. We're also setting up how she can't be stopped. One of my favourite shots is her in that wheelchair: she wakes up, she kills these guys, her bottom half doesn't work but that's not going to stop her.

Sequences aren't built on comic rhythms and digressions in their full, back-and-forth poetic glory. But I'm proud of the back and forth between Vernita Green [Vivica A. Fox] and The Bride, and of the speech by O-Ren Ishi [Lucy Liu] in the Boss Tanaka scene (actually the Boss Tanaka scene is Quentin dialogue, but in Japanese, as is the fantastic verbiage in the snow-garden scene). But this is an action movie, it doesn't need that dialogue. What's there is good, and you'll get more of it in the second movie, but I don't have to live or die by it. I'm giving you something I haven't given you before and it's got to be good so that you don't miss the dialogue.

The long section at the House of Blue Leaves is remarkable. Towards the end, The Bride goes into a blue room and there's a shift where the flooring and lighting change and it seems as if you're suddenly outside the reality of the movie, which then leads to the strange beauty of the snow garden.

It's not about being realistic, it's about being theatrical, operatic. I tried to deal with that in the prose of the script: that this is not real, it's a set. The biggest

problem with most Hong Kong movies is that the fights at the end go on too long. So I wanted to have a massive battle but with different layers. The silhouette against the big colourful background is less Japanese, more an old-school kung-fu thing. Many Shaw Brothers or Golden Harvest opening-credits sequences start out with a character silhouetted against a big colourful background doing kung-fu moves to music.

Is the snow garden influenced by Seijun Suzuki or Kenji Fukasaku, to whom you dedicated the film?

Not that I was really thinking about this, but I'd consider the blue-wall silhouette fight in the kabuki room more like Seijun Suzuki. But it's as much from a Zhang Che opening-credits sequence or Yuen Wo-Ping's opening-credits sequence to *The Snake in the Eagle's Shadow* as anything else. The snow-garden fight is more Fukasaku meets Sergio Leone. I play the Japanese elements—the honour and such like—very straight: there's no irony there, though I always felt a wink in Suzuki's portrayal of that stuff. I've wanted to do a Leone sequence literally forever, for years before I directed anything, and my Mexican stand-offs were always modern-day, unpretentious versions of Leone. So I finally do one, and I make it Japanese.

If that sequence didn't work as strongly as it does then the movie could never be two movies—for my money, it's a pretty terrific climax that almost demands the respect of being the climax of a movie. Every time I've watched it with an audience and we get to that sequence, it's pin-drop time. I've got them right where I want them. If I'd worn my welcome out in any one of the sequences before that the quiet wouldn't be as quiet, I wouldn't have them in the middle of my hand.

I think the use of music from other movies is phenomenal, really different and really effective.

To me what's really cool about it is that that's where my directing started, with buying soundtrack albums. Before video, when I was a kid and in love with *Dressed to Kill* or whatever, I'd get the soundtrack album and put on the music for the museum sequence and remember it in my mind as I listened to the music. And sometimes you could even, in your own mind, make it better. You'd misremember it and when you saw it again you'd think, I like my version more. That's where making movies in my head started.

But what also led me to go this way is that this is what the Shaw Brothers' movies did—took soundtrack cuts off the goddamn soundtrack album and laid them right into the movie. And the composers couldn't do much about it because they'd have to go to Hong Kong to sue them. Some of those uses are far more inventive than in the movies or TV shows they're originally from. *Queen*

Boxer has an opening-credits sequence that uses the *Shaft* theme and is so exhilarating you just keep rewinding the tape to watch it again. Watching something like *Sting of the Dragon Masters* for the fiftieth time, you suddenly realise this is Bernard Herrmann's theme to *North by Northwest.*

The music heightens the out-of-time quality all your movies have.

That even goes down to using whatever quality of recording we had available. We had a master recording for every few of the pieces so often I decided to go straight from my soundtrack album, not even a CD version. I liked hearing the pops and crackles and thinking, hey, that's my record, the record I bought.

You've said your first two films took place in the Quentin Tarantino universe and **Jackie Brown** *took place in Elmore Leonard's universe. Where would you place* **Kill Bill**?

I've always considered I have two universes. There's the normal Quentin universe, which to me has all the fun of a movie-movie but in fact is more real than real life. You take all the fun of a genre movie and then you throw real life smack against the conventions and have fun out of that. I can't say I made it up—it was Elmore Leonard's process, which I used to read in his books and I turned into a movie thing. That's the world which **Reservoir Dogs** takes place in, and **Pulp Fiction** and my script for **True Romance.**

Then I have another universe, which is the movie-movie universe. It's not about real life, it's just about the movies. The only way it exists in the other Quentin universe is to be the movies people see in that universe. It really exists only on the screen and in the projector. **Kill Bill** is the first movie I've directed inside that universe, but my scripts for **Natural Born Killers** and **From Dusk Till Dawn** exist in that world. The most accurate way to describe the differences between the two universes is to say that when the characters in **True Romance** or **Reservoir Dogs** or **Pulp Fiction** go to the movies, these are the movies they see.

Kill Bill *is very violent yet it's so outlandish it doesn't seem real. Sofie Fatale in a pool of blood is a long way from Mr. Orange in a pool of blood.*

To tell you the truth, Sofie Fatale getting her arm cut off is one of the scenes where I play the violence for the pain of it. I'm not playing up the shock appeal, playing up the pain the way I normally do, with the exception of that scene. Otherwise it's so obviously coming off the pop-samurai style I think of when I think of Japanese movies, not the Kurosawa doom style but a Zatoichi or *Baby Cart from Hell* movie where characters

have garden hoses for veins. To me it's an aesthetic thing and you have to go with it. I wouldn't use the word cartoonish, but there are all these distancing devices. There's never a moment when I'm telling you this is happening in the real world, when you're not aware you're watching a movie. Nobody is getting killed, this isn't real blood and if you don't like it you mustn't like the colour red because you know it's not real. It couldn't more obviously be a movie.

Do you worry that the more outlandish elements make it harder for the viewer to shift back to the character-driven scenes?

That's my job. To be able to turn on a dime. Not on a dollar, on a dime. And it's for the beholder to say if I achieved it or not. I think I did it the way I wanted to—to make it hurt and then right at the moment it hurts, get you to laugh. My job is to pull that off.

Theresa Duncan (essay date February 2004)

SOURCE: Duncan, Theresa. "Twin Bills." *ArtForum* 42, no. 6 (February 2004): 45-6.

[*In the essay below, Duncan posits that Tarantino brings a female aesthetic and point of view to his work.*]

At first glance, Sofia Coppola's melancholy love story *Lost in Translation* and Quentin Tarantino's brazen splatterfest *Kill Bill: Vol. 1* don't seem to have much in common beyond their similarly lavish Oscar campaigns. But then a peculiar set of coincidences begins to emerge. Both are set in a dreamlike, pop-palette Tokyo, the action in both pivots on the marital troubles of a female protagonist, and the films each sport a key scene in which the heroine rides along a hospital corridor in a wheelchair. Even some of the finer points are identical, like both films' featuring a minor Japanese character nicknamed Charlie Brown. The chain of happenstance starts to look like the "eerie" coincidences connecting the assassinations of Abraham Lincoln and John F. Kennedy. (You know, Lincoln's secretary was named Kennedy. Kennedy's secretary was named Lincoln . . .) But while these young, talented filmmakers' most recent works may bear similar details, they intersect only briefly at a set of opposing cultural currents. If the X marking Coppola and Tarantino's generation stands for a crossroads, then one director is helping to maintain the status quo while the other emerges as American film's first truly great female director.

Toni Morrison famously declared Bill Clinton the first black president: and by lights of a similar set of sociological shifts and personal circumstances, Quentin Tarantino has become the first "female" director to reach

American film's commercial and artistic pinnacles. While Sofia Coppola has a matter-of-fact Hollywood pedigree. Tarantino (like fellow hick striver Clinton) had no father. Born in Knoxville, Tennessee, he was raised by a single teenage mom in Long Beach, California, eventually trading his shit job at the local video-rental mart for Cannes and a Palme d'Or, Also like Clinton, Tarantino grew up to be an accomplished and authoritative white man who can consider the subjectivities of women and minorities without breaking into a cold sweat. Beginning with Uma Thurman's Mia Wallace in *Pulp Fiction* (1994) and Pam Grier's *Jackie Brown* (1997), Tarantino has demonstrated an unselfconscious empathy with and ability to write strong, dynamic roles for women that no female director in America has yet matched.

Kill Bill: Vol. 1 centers on a woman's quest for justice. The title character Bill, played in *Vol. 2* [*Kill Bill: Vol. 2*] by David Carradine, is here an invisible figure looming over the story. We know Bill is the head of an elite, all-female group called the Deadly Viper Assassination Squad, or DIVAS. *Vol. 1* [*Kill Bill: Vol. 1*] opens with Bill and his DIVAS gunning down a wedding party. The pregnant woman in the blood-soaked wedding dress, the Bride (Uma Thurman), is also known as Black Mamba, the most lethal Viper of them all. Bill and the Vipers leave the Bride for dead, but she is actually comatose. Cut to four years later. Suddenly awakening in a hospital, the Bride efficiently dispatches the hospital orderly who has been pimping her inert body (slamming a door repeatedly on his skull), steals his custom-built hot rod emblazoned with foot-high pink letters reading "Pussy Wagon," and sets off on a ferociously focused mission of revenge. In *A Thousand Plateaus*, Deleuze and Guattari said that a hole is just a vagina traveling at the speed of light. For years I had no inkling what that gnomic pronouncement could possibly mean—and then I saw Uma Thurman hurtling around in the Pussy Wagon.

Sam Peckinpah's masterpiece of American screen violence *Straw Dogs* (1971) was famously called a "fascist work of art" by Pauline Kael; *Kill Bill*'s hallucinatory violence and rivers of gore have elicited similarly hysterical commentary. The *New Republic*'s Gregg Easterbrook went so far as to accuse Harvey Weinstein, one of the film's producers, of promoting terrorism. In conversation, Tarantino praises violent films for their "honesty" and for being "true to themselves." While Tarantino is a fan of nearly all violent cinema, from mainstream directors like Peckinpah to spaghetti westerns to Hong Kong action films, he claims that the primary influence for *Kill Bill* was a string of decades old genre and exploitation films. "I had a whole list of these films. *The Doll Squad* [1973] by Ted V. Mikels, Burt Kennedy's *Hannie Caulder* [1971], *I Spit on Your Grave* by Meir Zarchi [1978]—

there are tons of them." These cheaply made films, produced predominantly in the '70s, acted as a sort of cinematic unconscious for mainstream Hollywood. Genre films often featured black or female protagonists on the losing end of aggressive scenarios who then come back to bloodily triumph over their tormentors. For Tarantino, violent genre films seemed to respond with honesty and immediacy to a culture undergoing wrenching social change. The constant slashing, stabbing, beating, chopping, slicing, beheading, disemboweling, kicking, and crushing of *Kill Bill* forms a sort of 4/4 backbeat as thirty years of Hollywood culture are updated in a breathless rush.

The punishing damage the Bride inflicts is also oddly, startlingly funny, Watching *Kill Bill* is a cathartic experience, like a great rock show, with the desire and aggression at the film's heart seeming to originate within the audience. From the Little Tramp to Jim Carrey, physical comedy has long been a way for male comedians to express social and sexual anxiety. *Kill Bill*'s woman-on-woman martial-arts brutality updates slapstick for the twenty-first century, claiming it as a female genre for the first time. As if to underscore the mayhem's metaphorical nature, Tarantino gives his gore a deliberately virtual look. Perhaps the film's closest cousin in mixing humor, artifice, quotation, and aggression is *The Itchy and Scratchy Show*, the crazily violent cartoon-within-a-cartoon parody of *Tom and Jerry* on *The Simpsons*. While the look of *Kill Bill* is often patently fake, Tarantino's updings of convention comment on real cultural undercurrents. Like genre films and Peckinpah's more mainstream *Straw Dogs, Kill Bill* uses violence to examine and describe seismic social shifts.

Straw Dogs is frequently read as an allegory of Vietnam, but the real violence being done is to conventions of white working-class masculinity. The film is based on Gordon M. Williams's 1969 novel *The Siege of Trencher's Farm*, with the siege seeming to occur when thuggish workmen come after a physically meek mathematician and his wife in their Irish country home. But, as in *Junior Bonner* the following year. Peckinpah seems to be describing an assault on the working class by the assent of a more economically and intellectually agile white-collar male. As film scholar Stephen Prince has commented, it is Dustin Hoffman's urbane mathematician who is the interloper in the Irish village, arriving in a convertible sports car with the local sexpot, whom he has married and carried off to the United States. The "siege" of the farm is by the cosmopolitan math professor, who doesn't physically work the land as has been done by village men for centuries but instead uses it as a place of leisure. By film's end the professor succeeds in defending his pleasurable lifestyle with the use of extreme violence.

Whereas Peckinpah used slow motion to balletic effect, it is Tarantino's lunatic kineticism and breakneck pop referencing that tends *Kill Bill*'s violence its often breathtaking formal beauty. Like the new pop musical form "mashups," where existing songs are digitally combined to make new hits, Tarantino rapidly calls up decades of films and of a host of film genres, often within the same scene. Trying to spot the filmmaker's references is part of the fun, if a seemingly infinite task. The director was particularly excited about casting David Carradine from the *Kung Fu* TV series as Bill because the actor evokes so many different genres. "*Kung Fu,* yeah, but he was one of the Long Riders too," the director says. "You've got a great thing with David because *Bill* really is a mix of Asiatic influences and genuine American western influences." When asked about using the actress Chiaki Kuriyama from the radically violent Japanese teen satire *Battle Royale* (2000) as *Kill Bill*'s Go Go Yubari, Tarantino responds with an anecdote delivered in his machine-gun rhetorical style:

> I went out to dinner with Kinji Fukasaku [director of *Battle Royale,* who died last year] and his son Kenta. I was going, "I love this movie! I love the scene where the girls are shooting each other." And Kenta laughs and goes, "The author of the original *Battle Royale* novel would be glad to hear that you liked that scene." And I go "Why?" And he says, "Well, because it's from *Reservoir Dogs*!" Even when I was watching it I was going, "God, these fourteen year-old girls are shooting each other just like in *Reservoir Dogs*!"

The director travels so far in his reference making that often he winds up where he started—face to face with himself.

Just as Lincoln and Kennedy were both succeeded by presidents named Johnson. Tarantino's and Coppola's Tokyo stories both feature "Bill" at their center. Whereas Tarantino's Bill goes unseen, the actor Bill Murray occupies most of *Lost in Translation*'s screen time. In contrast to Tarantino's speed, Sofia Coppola's partly improvised film unfolds rather lackadaisically. *Lost in Translation* follows Charlotte, a young woman in an unhappy marriage who falls for a melancholy actor old enough to be her father while they are staying in the same hushed and dim Tokyo hotel. Charlotte is the only character in the movie who is in Tokyo for leisure rather than work. Many have celebrated *Lost in Translation* as a breakthrough for this clearly promising director, but there's a point in the semiautobiographical film when Charlotte ridicules the older man for having stopped making good movies in the 1970s and the breezy love story starts to feel like a queasy oedipal transaction. Compare Coppola's film, where the confused May-December couple are still idly orbiting each other at film's end, to Mike Nichols's landmark 1967 youth anthem *The Graduate.* Would Nichols's film be celebrated now if Benjamin hadn't wised up

and decided to shuck his torpid life spent floating in his parents' pool and dump the gnarly Mrs. Robinson? Placing the image of Tarantino's battered Bride struggling alone in her wheelchair, desperately trying to leave the hospital, alongside Coppola's droll Charlotte being wheeled into an emergency room (for a stubbed toe no less) by her older love interest is a telling juxtaposition. Coppola's Charlotte seems to prefer being pushed around, while Tarantino's Bride understands that we had to crawl before we could walk, and walk before we could disembowel our mortal enemies with supercool samurai moves. "That's the world that this movie takes place in," the director says. "*Everybody* has a samurai sword," Like many of his generation, Tarantino was not socialized to see the father as the center of the family—or of the culture. With his democratic vision of a samurai sword for every man, woman, and child, Tarantino abolishes established hierarchies on which elitism, superiority, and exclusion are built. If "Bill" represents a decaying social order, then Coppola's Charlotte comes to praise Bill, and Tarantino's Bride to bury him. *Kill Bill* is not your father's action movie.

Kent L. Brintnall (essay date spring 2004)

SOURCE: Brintnall, Kent L. "Tarantino's Incarnational Theology: *Reservoir Dogs,* Crucifixions and Spectacular Violence.'" *CrossCurrents* 54, no. 1 (spring 2004): 66-75.

[*In the essay below, Brintnall posits that* Reservoir Dogs *fits within and borrows from traditional Christian theology and imagery.*]

Writing about *Reservoir Dogs,* Quentin Tarantino's 1995 directorial and screenwriting debut, Manohla Dargis observed:

> A history of American cinema could be traced on the bruised, besieged male body, from westerns to gangster sagas to male weepies to war films. . . . [F]ilm after film features men . . . at risk who can only find redemption through pain, theirs or someone else's.[2]

Whether or not these observations about American cinema are accurate, Dargis's summary most assuredly captures the spirit of the vast majority of Christian theology. The Christian theological imaginary traces quite precisely the outlines of a particular brutalized male body and the redemptive significance of the suffering that it endured. Indeed, the theological fact may explain the cinematic one: insofar as Christianity has dominated the Euro-American cultural imagination for a millennium or so, the mystery of physical brutality, and its possible redemptive power, has been in the air, ready to be scripted, interrogated, displayed and deployed time and time again. Given that both American cinema and the Christian narrative give pride of place to brutality against the male body, it seems likely that an interdisciplinary conversation about such violence may be productive.

In this article, I will explore the ethical and erotic dimensions of physical brutality against the male body as they appear in theological discourses and cinematic texts, relying on film theory to help unpack certain dynamics related to the crucifixion. With such an exploration, I hope to accomplish two things. First, I seek to contribute certain insights to Christian theological understandings of the significance and meaning of the crucifixion. By attending specifically to the figure of the brutalized body on the cross, certain issues related to gender and eroticism open up around the space of the crucifixion. Second, I seek to make a methodological intervention in the arena of religion and film scholarship. Theological discourses can benefit from taking up film theory as a full, legitimate and independent conversation partner—a form of "worldly wisdom" which must be interwoven with the faith tradition. With this article I hope to demonstrate how a truly interdisciplinary methodology between theology and film studies is both possible and productive for constructive theological discourses. In sum, this article could be read as an essay in constructive theology, as an essay in method for the study of religion and film, or—most appropriately—as both.

This article is intended solely as a starting point for both the substantive and the methodological inquiries. As an initial gesture, it invokes concerns about the relationship between religious discourses and visual culture, the ethical and theological value of spectacular violence, the erotic dimension of physical brutality, and the maturity of method in religion and film scholarship which I will not be able to address with the depth and precision that such questions deserve.

For simplicity's sake, I will keep the scope of comparison relatively limited. To examine the dynamics surrounding representations of brutality against the male body and how they relate to narratives of the crucifixion, I will focus my attention on Julian of Norwich's *Showings* and Quentin Tarantino's ***Reservoir Dogs.*** Although there are a number of reasons for decrying a comparison of these two artifacts—they are from radically different historical periods, generated for different reasons, produced in disparate mediums, by "authors" with remarkably different commitments—I hope that by the conclusion of my examination the structural and thematic similarities between the texts will be sufficiently apparent so as to justify my choice.

The theological writings of the fourteenth-century mystic and visionary Julian of Norwich are justifiably renowned for their originality, their elegance, their

emphasis on the limitless mercy of an all-loving God, and their description of the maternal aspects of Jesus' character. Any reader of Julian's writings, however, will also be struck by her fascination with the gruesome details of the body of the crucified Christ. While the feminine imagery for Christ and the boundless character of God's love in Julian's writings have received much critical attention, the violence that pervades her texts has not. Here is a representative passage in which Julian describes one of her visions:

> And after this as I watched, I saw the body bleeding copiously in the furrows made by the scourging, and it was thus. The fair skin was deeply broken into the tender flesh through the vicious blows delivered all over the lovely body. The hot blood ran out so plentifully that neither skin nor wounds could be seen, but everything seemed to be blood. And as it flowed down to where it should have fallen, it disappeared. Nonetheless, the bleeding continued for a time, until it could be plainly seen. And I saw it so plentiful that it seemed to me that if it had in fact and in substance been happening there, the bed and everything all around it would have been soaked in blood.[3]

The vivid details in this passage echo throughout Julian's writings. Moreover, the majority of her visions take the crucified body as their object. In fact, the brutalized body of Jesus serves as the foundational inspiration for Julian's theological musings. Julian states clearly and explicitly that all of her writings relate back to her visions of the Passion of Jesus—to its violence and brutality, to His suffering and pain.

Just as the figure of Jesus is the brutalized body around which Julian's theological writings are organized, the wounded body of Mr. Orange (Tim Roth) lies at the heart, quite literally, of Tarantino's ***Reservoir Dogs.*** In the second scene of the film, after its first break in temporal continuity, Mr. Orange is shown screaming and writhing in the back seat of a car, the victim of a gun-shot wound to the belly. This image of pain is magnified by the vividness and simplicity of its colors— Mr. Orange is dressed in black and white, lying on a white vinyl car seat, which forcefully propels the vibrant red of the copious amounts of his blood at the audience. The temporal discontinuity of this scene contributes to its unsettling nature. Not only is the viewer forced to watch a bleeding man writhe in pain, but the viewer is compelled to attend to this image carefully to gather clues as to what has happened and why. In this way, Tarantino combines form and content masterfully to increase the visual assault of the images he has assembled. As the movie progresses, and as the narrative jumps between present and past, Mr. Orange's body remains virtually motionless on the floor of the warehouse where the hoodlum characters are supposed to reconnoiter. Whenever the camera returns to his body, however, the amber pool surrounding it has enlarged. Throughout the movie, the actions of Mr. White (Harvey

Keitel) are motivated primarily by his concern for Mr. Orange's well-being and the movie culminates in a scene of violence focused primarily on the characters' differential positioning toward Mr. Orange. In both texts, then, a wounded, bleeding, brutalized body organizes and controls the discourse.

While the gruesome details of Julian's texts often go unremarked, Tarantino's status as auteur is distinguished by the graphic character of violence in his films. In **Reservoir Dogs,** the body count is truly Shakespearean. By the end of the film, all of the named characters are dead. Most of these deaths have taken place on screen. In addition, at least four other characters—three police officers and a young mother—are killed on screen. Another woman is dragged through the driver's side window of her car and beaten. All of the deaths that we see are marked by intense violence, extensive gun-play, and large amounts of blood. And, most infamously, before being killed, one of the police officers is tortured, in a session that involves the removal of his ear with a straight-edge razor, to the sounds of a seventies bubble-gum pop hit, "Stuck in the Middle with You."

How does Tarantino respond to charges that this film is gratuitously violent? For the most part, flippantly.

> To me, violence is a totally aesthetic subject. Saying you don't like violence in movies is like saying you don't like dance sequences in movies. I do like dance sequences in movies, but if I didn't, it doesn't mean I should stop dance sequences from being made.[4]

So, with a smirk and a shrug of his shoulders, Tarantino justifies graphic violence as a mere aesthetic choice. In one interview, however, he lets it be known,

> For all the wildness that happens in my movies, I think that they usually lead to a moral conclusion. For example, I find what passes between Mr. White and Mr. Orange at the end of **Reservoir Dogs** very moving and profound in its morality and its human interaction.[5]

What does happen between Mr. White and Mr. Orange at the end of the film? After every other character but the two of them has been killed, Mr. Orange lies bleeding to death, cradled like a baby by Mr. White, and divulges that he is an undercover cop—that he is, in fact, the person responsible for most of the carnage that has taken place. Commenting on this final scene, Robert Hilferty writes, "I have never seen such tenderness between two men in an ostensibly straight crime film."[6]

While Tarantino's film blurs the line between tenderness and violence—even between comedy and violence—Julian's visions, and her theological commentary, link compassion and brutality more explicitly. Julian wrote at a time when graphic depictions of the crucified Jesus were on the rise, both in written theological reflection and in Christian pictorial represen-

tation. The assumption was that meditating on the suffering of Jesus would increase compassion in the believer. Remembering the prayers of her youth—for a sickness unto death that would draw her into a full understanding of Jesus' passion—Julian writes

> And suddenly it came into my mind that I ought to wish . . . that our Lord, of his gift and of his grace, would fill my body full with recollection of his blessed Passion, as I had prayed before that his pains might be my pains, with compassion which would lead to longing for God. . . . I desired to suffer with him, living in my mortal body, as God would give me grace. And at this, suddenly, I saw the red blood trickling down from under the crown, all hot, flowing freely and copiously, a living stream, just as it seemed to me that it was at the time when the crown of thorns was thrust down upon his blessed head.[7]

Julian's goal is greater compassion; the means to this end is contemplation of the spectacle of a wounded body. Her writings, then, indicate a relationship between spectacular violence and a response in the viewer that seeks to understand, participate in the alleviation of, and overcome that violence through compassion. **Reservoir Dogs,** for all of its violence and male bravado, also has an ethical dimension. Tarantino's film is, on one reading, a *reductio ad absurdum* on the cult of masculinity. It shows a world of powerful men at its absolute, and self-destructive, worst. The film portrays a hermetically sealed, claustrophobic world of gun-loving, trash-talking, violence-prone men and the carnage they leave in their wake. The care-taking, physically intimate bond that Mr. Orange and Mr. White embody is portrayed as something alternative, unusual, and superior within this harsh world. This bond, however, is only possible given the violence enacted against Mr. Orange's body. Both Julian's and Tarantino's work, then, calls its audience to a place of compassion and empathy, but the mechanism for this ethical call is the display of a brutalized body.

Tarantino's critique of culturally dominant scripts of gender identity finds a possible echo in Julian's text. At the same time, the precise gender dynamics in the two texts are markedly different. The gender of Julian's Jesus is ambiguous. With her description of Jesus as Mother, Julian marks the body on the cross as female, while retaining male-gendered pronouns for the person of Jesus. Jesus is mother not merely because of His compassion and loving care, but primarily because He gives birth to the Church from the wound in His side and sustains believers with the blood from His wounds. The power of Jesus to love, redeem and sustain believers is related to Jesus' *feminine* energy; this feminine energy, however, is located in a body consistently imagined and addressed as male. Similarly, Mr. Orange and Mr. White retain their identities as male, but their behavior toward one another violates the norms of traditional masculine behavior. Specifically, Mr.

Orange's emotional outbursts and Mr. White's physical tenderness lie outside traditional macho interaction patterns. Thus, both characters are feminized and rendered ambiguous in terms of gender and erotic identity. Resolving these ambiguities, articulating the precise dynamics of the allure of a wounded male body versus a wounded female body, and interpreting the meaning of wounds associated with the generation of life as opposed to those which threaten the continuation of life are tasks which lie outside the scope of this article. For the purposes of my argument, it is enough to note the *fact* of the fascination: desire and perceptual transformation are somehow bound up with the improper and unclean body, regardless of gender.

Both visions then—Julian's mystical one and Quentin's directorial one—use representations of the bloody, wounded, human figure as a mechanism for generating ethical critique, moral judgment and possible social transformation. Both visions, moreover, have a notion about the fluidity and instability of gender at their heart. The crucifixion, the brutalized body, spectacular violence serve as sites for interrogating and deconstructing prevailing gender norms and imaging different ways of organizing bodies, desire, and erotic attachment. Not only does physical brutality enable and generate an ethical critique, but this critique has a very specific content in both Julian's and Tarantino's work. This understanding of the relationship between the brutalized body, ethical response, and gender critique may open up very different conceptions of the salvific nature of Jesus' death.

These representations, it must also be noted, are vivid, detailed, and gruesome; the violence is significant, moving, real. Again, Tarantino discussing *Reservoir Dogs*:

> The reason [the film] freaks out people is that it's not theatrical, it's realistic. When somebody gets shot in the stomach that way, they bleed to death. . . . It's a horrible, horrible pain, until you get too numb to feel it. Yes, the blood in that scene is realistic. We had a medic on the set controlling the pool, saying, "Okay, one more pint and he's dead."[8]

To make an ethical demand, violence cannot be fantastic; theatrical, cartoonish violence is too easily deflected and dismissed. Realistic violence may also be a source of disgust and discomfort, but it draws us into the drama of the events represented more fully and completely.

It is interesting to note, with this observation in mind, that unlike the rest of Tarantino's films, *Reservoir Dogs* has no redemptive or restorative *denouement*. At the end of a very violent and bloody film, all the characters are dead. Fade to black. Similarly, in Julian's text, although there are fleeting references to Christ in glory, there is no explicit mention of the resurrection and no

sustained attention to the post-crucifixion Jesus. If violent spectacle is capable of making an ethical demand and directing our moral attention, then what is lost when we avert our gaze from images of brutality? What is the cost when Jesus becomes a great moral teacher instead of a victim of public torture? What happens when cinematic violence is stripped from narrative, or sanitized, or moved off-screen? Without violence in our theology and our entertainment, are we left with fewer resources to deal with the violence that is very much a part of our lived reality?

What else might we miss if we avert our gaze from brutality directed against the male body? In his essay, "Masculinity as Spectacle," Steve Neale seeks to extend Laura Mulvey's work on the male gaze and to challenge her assertion that the male or male-identified spectator can never look upon the male body as an erotic object.[9] To challenge Mulvey's assertion, Neale identifies the mechanisms mainstream Hollywood cinema uses to represent the male body as erotic. One way of doing this, Neale argues, is by making the male body the target of violence. In the war film, a soldier can hold his buddy—as long as his buddy is dying on the battlefield. In the western, Butch Cassidy can wash the Sundance Kid's naked flesh—as long as it is wounded. In the boxing film, a trainer can rub the well-developed torso and sinewy back of his protegé—as long as it is bruised. In the crime film, a mob lieutenant can embrace his boss like a lover—as long as he is riddled with bullets. Violence makes the homoeroticism of many "male" genres invisible; it is a structural mechanism of plausible deniability.

In *Reservoir Dogs*, this representational strategy is most evident in a scene near the beginning of the film where we first see Mr. White caring for Mr. Orange after Mr. Orange has been shot. The scene begins with Mr. White dragging Mr. Orange into the warehouse from the car. Mr. Orange is sobbing, gasping, rambling incoherently and Mr. White is doing everything he can to comfort him. Mr. White tells Mr. Orange it is okay for him to stop being brave. In addition, he cleans his face, combs his hair, and cradles him like an infant—or a lover. Here, in violation of the masculine code that controls his actions throughout the rest of the film, Mr. Orange shows his emotions, his fear, his terror. Mr. White holds him, holding him tighter and more closely after Mr. Orange desperately requests that he do so. The camera stays tight on the two men's faces, increasing the viewer's sense that there is a violation of traditional rules of appropriate physical distance. There are moments where it almost looks like the two men will kiss. In a move that would be absolutely *verboten* in any other context, the presumably heterosexual Mr. White unbuckles the presumably heterosexual Mr. Orange's belt and opens his trousers. All of this—the emotionality, the physical intimacy, the violation of traditional gender codes—is justified, deflected and explained by the fact of Mr. Orange's brutalization. But for the bullet in Mr. Orange's belly, none of this would be possible; because of the bullet in Mr. Orange's belly, all of this is possible and is permissibly interpreted as asexual.

This link between violence and eroticism is not as apparent in Julian's text, but it still makes an appearance. Compared to other medieval mystics who wrote about the crucifixion, Julian's writing is the least erotically charged. It is interesting to note, however, in the vast majority of her descriptions of the crucified Christ, she is quick to point out that the brutality of the crucifixion and its attendant horrors deformed and disfigured a beautiful, attractive, appealing body. Given my earlier comments about how Julian depicts the body of Jesus as a female body, the circuit of desire and contemplation in Julian's text could be described as one of female homoeroticism. Regardless, even in this text, the erotic bursts through crucified flesh to make an appearance. Violence can attempt to cover and divert erotic energy, but it can never fully extinguish it.

Although I have discovered no extended religious or theological analysis of **Reservoir Dogs,** several commentators on the film characterized the staging of Mr. Orange and Mr. White's bodies as strongly reminiscent of the *Pietà*. The figure of the *Pietà* is interesting for the comparison that I am making. The *Pietà*—the image of Mary holding the body of her dead son, Jesus—first appears in the fourteenth century, near the time that Julian had her visions and wrote her theological treatises. The pathos of this image is seconded only by its eros. Death and sensuality are bound in the smooth lines of Mary's cloak and Jesus' flesh in most examples of the *Pietà*. Moreover, Mary is usually depicted as a young maiden in the *Pietà,* ignoring the age she would be if the corpse in her arms was in its thirties; the similarity in age between "mother" and "child" works to further mark the two figures as contemporaries and lovers. Just as Julian often observed the dying Christ through the eyes of Mary in her visions, Tarantino represents the homoeroticized hyper-masculinity of *Reservoir Dogs* through a *Pietà*-like pose which invokes the figure of Mary. In all of these artifacts, then, death, broken bodies, sensuality, pathos, and eros are bound together in a complex, mutually implicated, multiply reinforcing web.

After tracing these structural and thematic relationships between these texts, trying to describe how they fit together, and offering suggestions as to the questions a comparative analysis might raise, I must stop. Partly, this is for reasons of space. Primarily, this is for reasons of theoretical acumen—or lack thereof.

It seems clear to me that a text as non-theological as Tarantino's and a disciplinary field as a-religious as film studies can provide useful analytical tools to Christian theologians. Film studies includes sophisticated work about the meaning and function of violent spectacle—how it affects spectators, how it relates to gender and sexuality. Given the centrality of a specific violent spectacle in the Christian narrative, this body of theoretical work should be of interest to those of us still contemplating the meaning and importance of that narrative. Specifically, representations of violence have an ethical import because they can focus our attention and generate our sympathy in particular ways. As Tarantino's work and Julian's writings demonstrate, the violence may need to have a certain realistic character before this ethical effect can reach fruition. Cartoon violence simply will not do. Understanding how and why and when and in what way violence can stir ethical reflection will be vital to articulations of the Christian narrative and to the work for a non-violent world. Moreover, violence both conceals and reveals something erotic at the heart of Christianity. Insofar as violent images are a strategy for camouflaging homoerotic desire, Christian theologians may need to ask: What has been covered by centuries of veneration of images of a nearly naked, badly beaten male figure? The erotic heart of Christianity does erupt from time to time in theological discourse, but this energy is too easily forgotten in moments of sexual panic.

Where I remain puzzled, however, is why these three elements—violent spectacle, ethical reflection, erotic response—are connected and how they reinforce each other. This must remain the task of future work. In addition, how the gender of the object of violence and the gender of its spectator affects these dynamics are also questions which must wait for another day.

Hopefully, what I have accomplished is to articulate how the crucifixion can be understood and appropriated as part of a very different conversation than the one in which it is traditionally situated. The conversation I have in mind is a conversation that would be familiar to certain Christian mystics of the Middle Ages; this conversation understands the violent spectacle of the crucifixion as an erotic spectacle. What I would hope for is a re-articulation of this erotic understanding of the central event of the Christian narrative as a means to open up Christianity to those who have been excluded on the basis of their gender and erotic identities. Moreover, I hope to have demonstrated that cinematic texts and the discourses of film theory are useful conversation partners in the theological task of understanding the significance and meaning of the death of Jesus. Although the task is barely begun, for the moment, hopefully, we are left with sufficient reason to attend to those great pictorialists—Catherine of Siena, Richard Rolle, St. John of the Cross, Julian of Norwich—as well as those neo-theologians—Sam Peckinpah, Martin Scorsese, Francis Ford Coppola, Quentin Tarantino—as we seek to make sense of representations of violence, their nature, their value, their ethics, their erotics, their relationship to the Christian theological imagination.

Notes

1. This article is based on a conference paper presented at the 2003 SBL/AAR annual meeting. The paper has benefited immensely from the comments and suggestions of Emily Holmes and Rick Warner.

2. Manohla Dargis, "Who's Afraid of Red Yellow and Blonde?," *Artforum International* 31, no. 3 (1992): 11.

3. Julian of Norwich, *Showings,* trans. Edmund Colledge and James Walsh (Mahwah, NJ: Paulist Press, 1978), Long Text, chapter 12, 199-200.

4. Gerald Peary, ed., *Quentin Tarantino: Interviews* (Jackson: University of Mississippi, 1998), 60.

5. Peary, *Quentin Tarantino: Interviews,* 60.

6. Robert Hilferty, "Reservoir Dogs," *Cinéaste* 19, no. 4 (1993): 79.

7. Julian of Norwich, *Showings,* Short Text, chapter 3, 129.

8. Peary, *Quentin Tarantino: Interviews,* 17.

9. Steve Neale, "Masculinity as Spectacle," in Screen, *The Sexual Subject: A Screen Reader in Sexuality* (New York: Routledge, 1992 [1983]), 277-87; see also Laura Mulvey, "Visual Pleasure and Narrative Cinema," in Laura Mulvey, *Visual and Other Pleasures* (Bloomington: Indiana University Press, 1989 [1975]), 14-26.

Stephen Weinberger (essay date 2004)

SOURCE: Weinberger, Stephen. "It's Not Easy Being Pink: Tarantino's Ultimate Professional." *Literature/Film Quarterly* 32, no. 1 (2004): 46-50.

[*In the essay below, Weinberger reflects on the ways in which* Reservoir Dogs *comments on professionalism.*]

When discussing the films of Quentin Tarantino, it seems that style is what attracts the attention of critics, scholars, and actors. Tarantino's gift for writing remarkable dialogue, his use of violence, his nonlinear chronology, and his ability to create rich and interesting characters are so striking and powerful that they dominate the discussion. In describing his response to the script of **Pulp Fiction,** Samuel L. Jackson said:

> I sat down, read the script straight through, which I normally don't do, took a breath, and read it again, which I never do, just to make sure it was true. That it was the best script I'd ever read . . . When people see

killers for hire they think that they sit at home, they clean their guns . . . and all these other things. But Quentin takes you into a world where you actually find out that they gossip. They talk about their lives outside of what they do. He has the facility for creating every day language and sensibilities for his characters.

(Dawson 106-07)

And Jeffrey Dawson, the author of *Quentin Tarantino: The Cinema of Cool,* echoed Jackson's views:

> That such characters (especially Jules and Vincent) can exist so vividly is an uncommon thing in the world of modern cinema and beyond anything else—beyond the structure, the acting, the dialogue, the popular culture, the filmic references or anything else, it is, in the opinion of this author—the overwhelming reason why Tarantino as a filmmaker has achieved such remarkable success.

(Dawson 189-90)

Yet, while acknowledging these obvious qualities, is there more to Tarantino's films? What about substance? Does he address important issues about the human condition, or should we simply be grateful for the exhilarating ride he provides, and leave it at that? Tarantino himself seems to opt for the ride. Some years ago, he observed:

> My stuff, so far, has definitely fallen into what I would consider pulp fiction. If you're going to get historical, then the whole idea of pulp, what it really means, is a paperback you don't really care about. You read it, put it in your back pocket, sit on it in the bus, and the pages start coming out, and who gives a fuck? When you're [sic] finished it, you hand it to someone else, or you throw it away. You don't put it in your library.

(Woods 102)

Yet, we might reasonably ask whether Tarantino's films do more than their creator realized? Does anything of value remain after the viewers have recovered their breath? In answering this question we might consider how **Reservoir Dogs** deals with the issue of professionalism. What does it mean to be a professional? Is this a commendable quality worthy of praise? What causes people to become unprofessional? And when this does happen, is it something to be condemned, or do other, perhaps more admirable, qualities emerge?

The term "professional" is commonly used as an expression of praise. To refer to people as "professionals" is to do more than identify their employment or even indicate that they have mastered a certain type of work. The term also involves living according to a particular set of values. The "true professional" is one who can minimize emotional involvements with colleagues, and can subordinate personal likes and dislikes, as well as the claims of family, friends, and organizations, to the demands of his employment. As they structure the priorities in their lives, those who live according to this ethic elevate the ideals of the workplace over all others.

The values of professionalism seem to dominate the first part of **Reservoir Dogs.** The early scenes involve the planning of a jewelry store heist and then bring together the men who will carry this out. All of these men are career criminals. The organizer, Joe Cabot (Lawrence Tierney), is the head of a crime syndicate. For this particular robbery, Cabot and his devoted son, Nice Guy Eddie (Chris Penn), have selected six men they know well, but who do not know one another. To ensure that they remain anonymous from one another, Joe instructs them to reveal nothing about their personal lives, not even their names. Instead, he assigns a color to each man as the sole means of identification.

These robbers convey the impression that they are all serious, mature men. Some, at least, have served jail terms. While they can engage in interesting small talk, such as the meaning of Madonna's "Like a Virgin," these are grim, no-nonsense men who have come together to commit a robbery and then disperse.

At this point in the film, the only character one might have questions about is Mr. Pink (Steve Buscemi). In the company of these solid, self-possessed men, Pink stands out as high-strung, irritable, and petty. When Joe Cabot assigns the color identities, Pink complains at length about his color, which he regards as unmanly. And, later, at the gathering in the coffee shop, he alone refuses to leave a tip, complaining that this practice is just one more way society unfairly manipulates people. Pink remains adamant, despite being roundly criticized by the others, and only acquiesces when a frustrated Joe Cabot finally asserts his authority.

Although **Reservoir Dogs** excludes scenes of the jewelry heist, Tarantino develops the film in such a way that his viewers have a vivid picture of what has occurred. In the course of the robbery an alarm is set, prompting Mr. Blonde (Michael Madsen) to execute several store employees. This in turn causes the police to move in. In the ensuing shootouts, Mr. Brown and Mr. Blue are killed and Mr. Orange (Tim Roth) is shot in the stomach.

The real drama of the film begins when the surviving robbers arrive at the rendezvous, an abandoned warehouse. From this point on, the professionalism, which had been so apparent earlier, has largely disappeared. While the primary concern had been to conduct an efficient and successful robbery and to keep personal relations at an absolute minimum, these considerations are now no longer the priority. Instead, a series of intensely emotional and volatile relationships dominates the following scenes. Dividing the jewels and eluding the police have become lesser considerations.

Among the various robbers, Blonde's loss of professionalism takes the most disturbing form. Judged strictly by the early scenes, he emerges as a fundamentally

decent "standup guy." He chose to serve a four-year prison term for robbery rather than give evidence against Joe Cabot. And in the coffee shop, he joins the others in criticizing Pink's "no tip policy." Yet, with the robbery, he also reveals himself to be a violent and sadistic psychopath. Blonde systematically executes the store employees in the jewelry store not out of panic, but as a punishment for setting off the alarm. Not only is this a pointless act, since the damage has already been done, but it also places all of the robbers in much graver legal jeopardy. Blonde turns what has begun as armed robbery into mass murder. Furthermore, his torture of Marvin, the captive policeman, is pure sadism. The others also abuse Marvin, but they do so to force him to reveal the identity of the undercover agent. Blonde has no such interest. For him, this is about the sheer pleasure he derives from inflicting pain and terror.

While Blonde reveals a dark and disturbing nature, Mr. White (Harvey Keitel) is very much the opposite, showing himself to be highly principled and compassionate. Abandoning his earlier professionalism, he now acts on the basis of powerful emotions and a deeply felt sense of right and wrong. He blames himself for Orange's stomach wound and risks capture to bring him back to the warehouse. In the highly charged escape scene, he discards his color identity and reveals his name as he desperately tries to calm the hysterical Orange. Once inside the warehouse, when Pink wants to leave the bleeding man to die, the highly emotional White explains, "That bullet in his belly is my fault. Now that might mean jack shit to you, but it means a hell of a lot to me."

White goes even further toward the end of the film, putting his life on the line to protect Orange from Joe and Eddie Cabot. Joe Cabot correctly concludes that Orange is a police undercover agent, and is about to execute him when White draws his own gun. Despite his long and respectful relationship with the father and son, he refuses to let them shoot a man to whom he is committed, and whom he believes is innocent. "Joe, you're making a terrible mistake. I'm not going to let you make it."

In contrast to the dramatic and abrupt changes Blonde and White have undergone, Joe Cabot maintains his professionalism almost to the very end. His approach to crime is very much that of a successful CEO, taking meticulous care with planning and selecting personnel to ensure a successful outcome. At one point, when the robbers appear too lighthearted for his liking, the rather crusty Joe Cabot is quick to lecture them about the dangers of not taking their work seriously.

However, toward the end of the film, the outraged Cabot, accompanied by his son, storms into the warehouse, determined to mete out justice to Orange.

"That lump of shit is working with the LAPD." When White rises to defend Orange, Joe Cabot's anger and pride prevent him from lowering his gun. Cabot certainly could have handled the matter differently without letting Orange escape punishment. He might have tried to reason with White and perhaps convince him of Orange's treason. Or, he could have postponed dealing with Orange to focus on the pressing matters of business—salvaging the robbery and escaping from the police. Instead, his obsession with punishing the man who has infiltrated his operations has become paramount at this point. Indeed, for justice, Cabot willingly puts his own life on the line, and those of his son and White, a man he has long respected and liked. The resulting three-way showdown, which could have been avoided, ends in a bloodbath.

Of all the main characters, none goes to greater lengths to maintain his professionalism than does the undercover policeman, Orange. He successfully wins Joe Cabot's confidence and is accepted by the other robbers. Beginning with the botched robbery, several violent incidents could drive Orange to reveal his identity and stop further bloodshed, yet he holds back. He makes no effort to stop Blonde from executing the store employees. He then watches in shocked silence as White kills two policemen who are coming to the robbery scene. Indeed, he himself ends up participating in the carnage. When the driver of the car he stops at gunpoint shoots him, he instinctively shoots back, killing her. He remains steadfast, keeping his criminal persona intact, despite all the slaughter he witnesses and commits.

It is only in the warehouse, after Blonde has tortured Marvin and is about to set him aflame, that Orange reveals his identity by shooting the sadist. Yet, even here, despite all that he and Marvin have suffered, Orange insists that they remain where they are and endure the pain. "Marvin, I need you to hold on. We are not going to make a move till Joe Cabot shows up. . . . We are just going to sit here and bleed till Joe Cabot sticks his fuckin' head through that door."

Orange does not abandon his professionalism until the very end of the film. Having seen White kill the Cabots in order to protect him, Orange reveals his identity to his wounded defender. Orange can no longer keep his humanity in check, even though he knows that this will mean his own death. He is so profoundly moved by White's sacrifice that his professionalism finally gives way to his personal and private values. As the bleeding White cradles his head, Orange reaches back to embrace him and apologetically reveals the truth. "I'm sorry, I'm so sorry. I'm a cop. I'm sorry. I'm sorry. I'm sorry."

Pink stands out as the only character who retains his professional values from beginning to end. He alone remains in control of himself, analyzing each situation clearly and rationally; all of the others ultimately allow their private values to control their actions. While the other robbers have begun to relate to one another on an emotional and personal level, only Pink insists on the original agreement of anonymity and distance. In the warehouse, he criticizes White for revealing his own name to Orange. For White, however, there seems to be no point in retaining the color identities and he responds angrily:

> He asked me what my name was. I mean, the man was dying in my arms. What the fuck was I supposed to do; tell him "I'm sorry. I can't give out that information. It's against the rules. I don't trust you enough."

White then suggests that they all drop the color names. In light of all that has occurred, it seems foolish to continue to refer to one another by a color, but Pink adamantly refuses. "Don't tell me your fuckin' name, man. Jesus Christ. I don't want to know it. I'm not going to tell you mine."

Pink then goes on to explain that White's seemingly humane act toward Orange means that they cannot leave the wounded man at a hospital. Since he now knows White's identity, Orange can put all of the robbers at risk. The wounded man will unfortunately have to remain where he is and bleed to death. "Some fellows are lucky and some aren't."

If Pink refuses to show compassion, he also displays none of the rage that the others feel toward one another. He certainly would have been justified in feeling the same anger that White has toward Blonde for the carnage at the jewelry store, or that Joe Cabot feels toward Orange. Yet, those emotions never emerge. When White and Blonde seem ready to come to blows, Pink steps in, acting as the voice of reason. "Am I the only professional?"

And while White rages on about Blonde's excesses, Pink merely says, "He went crazy in the store, but he seems alright now." For Pink, what matters is addressing the practical problems of the present, not holding on to past resentments.

Pink is also the one who has the presence of mind to salvage the proceeds of the robbery. Despite the hail of bullets and the ensuing panic and carnage, he not only escapes, but also manages to take the diamonds with him. Even more impressive, he is clearheaded enough not to bring the diamonds back to the warehouse. "I stashed them," he explains, "to make sure this place wasn't a police station."

Furthermore, it is Pink who accurately analyzes what has occurred at the jewelry store. While the emotional White is obsessing about Blonde's murderous rampage and his own bad luck, Pink calmly and logically explains that the robbers were "set up." It was not the alarm that brought the police. The police were already outside waiting for them. They knew ahead of time about the robbery. He not only convinces the incredulous White that "we got a rat in our house" but the Cabots as well.

Toward the end of the film, when White and the Cabots become involved in a three-way standoff, Pink again remains the voice of reason. Shocked at what he sees, he urges them to lower their guns and regain control of themselves. "Nobody wants this. We're supposed to be fuckin' professionals," Realizing that passions have taken control, Pink seeks cover. While justice and protecting innocent people one cares about might be admirable values, unlike the Cabots and White, he is not willing to die or kill for them.

Following the shootout, Pink crawls out of his hiding place. Clearly shaken by the senseless slaughter, he quickly walks past the bleeding bodies, picks up the diamonds, and leaves. Once outside, the police, who have surrounded the building, confront him. The sound of shooting makes clear that despite his best efforts, Pink ends up like the other robbers.

In considering the sweep of events in *Reservoir Dogs,* it seems that Tarantino has done more than present a powerful drama of a robbery gone wrong. He also has explored the interaction between two essentially incompatible value systems that exists within each person: "the professional" that requires self-awareness and self-control, and "the personal" that is instinctual and unreflective.

This distinction is perhaps best summed up in Joe Cabot's monologue. Just before assigning the color identities, Joe delivers a stinging rebuke to the playful and casual attitude the robbers are displaying:

> You guys like to tell jokes and giggle and kid around, huh . . . When this caper is over . . . we'll go down to the Hawaiian Islands and I'll roar and laugh with all of ya. You'll find me a different character down there. Right now, it's a matter of business.

He then orders them not to reveal any personal information at all to one another. "All I want you guys to talk about, if you have to talk, is what you are going to do."

These instructions seem perfectly reasonable. Until the robbery is completed, everyone must adopt professional ethics and suppress their natural desires for sociability and conviviality. And it would seem that in the normal course of events, mature adults should be able to exercise that degree of restraint.

What this film then demonstrates is how each robber, with the exception of Pink, abandons his professionalism. Under the pressures of the botched robbery and the

realization that one of their group is an undercover agent, the powerful natural or instinctual values gradually take over—Blonde's sadism, White's sense of loyalty and honor, and Joe Cabot's need for revenge.

Only Pink's professionalism endures to the very end. Throughout everything—the executions in the bank, the betrayal by Orange, and the senseless shootout between White and the Cabots—Pink is the voice of reason and common sense. He is the one who tries to keep the robbers from turning on one another, and it is he who shows that the robbery has been compromised from the very beginning. It would seem, therefore, that he should emerge as the most admirable of the group. And, yet, in many ways, he is arguably the most unlikable.

Perhaps the explanation for this lies in his failure or inability to ever allow a personal side to emerge. While the others, with the exception of Blonde, eventually abandon their professionalism, they also reveal their humanity and idealism. The Cabots, White, and Orange display deeply held personal values that, in the end, are more important than a successful robbery. Pink, by contrast, seems to have possessed no idealism. Instead, he is distant, pragmatic, calculating, and unsentimental. He remains throughout a professional, thoroughly suppressing any traces of humanity.

Work Cited

Dawson, Jeff. *Quentin Tarantino: The Cinema of Cool.* New York: Applause Theatre, 1995.

Woods, Paul A. *King of Pulp: The Wild World of Quentin Tarantino.* London: Plexus, 1996.

Dave Brown (essay date 2006)

SOURCE: Brown, Dave. "Tarantino and the Re-Invention of the Martial Arts Film." *Metro Magazine* 148 (2006): 100-04.

[*In the essay below, Brown comments on the manner in which Tarantino has re-imagined the martial arts genre in* Kill Bill.]

Every frame is full of cinematic references: the Italian gore of *City of the Living Dead* (Lucio Fulcí, 1980) and the brutal feminist vengeance of *Thriller: A Cruel Picture* aka *They Call Her One Eye* (Bo Arne Vibenius, 1974) loom large, but it's from the martial arts film that Tarantino draws most of his inspiration. From modern classics like *Battle Royal* (Kinji Fukasaku, 2000) and the films of Takashi Miike to the old classics of The Shaw Brothers and Sonny Chiba, along with *Lady Snowblood* (Toshiya Fujita, 1973) and the *Lone Wolf and Cub* series, Quentin Tarantino's tribute to 1970s' grindhouse classics is a smorgasbord of blood-soaked references. These influences are modernized and streamlined, but Tarantino never loses sight of the essence of what made them so memorable in the first place. In casting some of his heroes, he again accentuates the similarities between his film and its predecessors, and helps *Kill Bill* join the legacy of martial arts motion pictures he was so desperate to emulate—or recreate.

Hiring the legendary Sonny Chiba as the swordmaker Hattori Hanzo was a masterstroke. Since starring in a succession of wonderful kung fu films in the seventies, including the *Streetfighter* series, Chiba has rarely been seen on the big screen. In fact when *The Streetfighter* (Shigehiro Ozawa, 1974)—along with its sequels *Return of the Streetfighter* (Shigehiro Ozawa, 1974) *The Streetfighter's Last Revenge* (Teruo Ishii, 1974) and *Sister Streetfighter* (Kazuhiko Yamaguchi, 1974)—was released on laserdisc in the nineties, it was Tarantino's quote extolling the film's virtues that graced the sleeve, "*The Streetfighter* . . . It's been a long time coming, I speak for all my friends when I say thank God the wait is over." It was the continuation of a love affair between Tarantino and martial arts films, and the beginning of his attempts to bring them to a modern Western audience. Tarantino had been a huge fan of The Shaw Brothers, Bruce Lee and Chiba, and now he was giving something back. The first release on his Rolling Thunder DVD label was *The Mighty Peking Man* (Meng-Hwa Ho, 1977) a giant-monkey-on-the-rampage movie by the Shaws, and it is also no coincidence that Uma Thurman wears a yellow and black tracksuit in *Kill Bill, Vol. 1*'s House of the Blue Leaves massacre, replicating Bruce Lee's attire in *Game of Death* (Robert Clouse, 1978).

David Carradine, the actor playing Bill, has been even more influential in bringing martial arts to Western audiences. Carradine is known to millions as Kwai Chang Caine from the seventies' TV sensation *Kung-Fu* (Jerry Thorpe, 1972). The show blended westerns and martial arts epics like *The Water Margin* (various, 1977)[1] and Carradine's flute-playing sensei became a poster icon for the decade, joining Bruce Lee on many a teenager's wall. Carradine lent a graceful beauty to his kung fu style and went on to make such classics as *The Silent Flute* (Richard Moore, 1978). After years in the wilderness, Tarantino has resurrected the legend's career; his position in the film as a great man with an illustrious kung fu fighting past helps draw the audience in and is perfect casting. However, when I spoke to Carradine I got a different explanation:

> There's a lot more to Tarantino than his love of those genres, and a lot more to our working relationship. We are both alien visitors from other planets, and possibly, both some kind of genius, forced to associate with mere

> mortals. Main thing, though, we both have a mission, like The Blues Brothers (*John Landis, 1980*). And, yeah, it worked.[2]

Surprisingly, Tarantino's first choice for the role of Bill was Warren Beatty. As you watch Carradine lead the Bride (Uma Thurman) to meet her tutor Pai Mei (Gordon Lu), you could not imagine Beatty ever fighting the white-haired teacher. In a scene cut from the final version of *Kill Bill, Vol. 2,* you get to see Bill strut his stuff killing a gang with his trusty samurai sword; again, Beatty would have been ridiculous in this scene.

An interesting side note is the existence of an alternative Japanese version of *Kill Bill, Vol. 1.* The version seen in Western cinemas was a sanitized glimpse of Tarantino's vision, whereas the full-strength, no-holds-barred Japanese film was made for Eastern audiences accustomed to ultra-violent anime and the outrageous movies of Takashi Miike. The differences in hindsight are slight, but show a major difference between what is acceptable in mainstream cinema in terms of violence and sexual gratification. The differences occur in a few separate scenes. Our introduction to Go Go (Chiaki Kuriyama) now features a gutsy pay-off as she eviscerates her potential suitor. In the anime section, as a young O-Ren Ishii (Lucy Liu) wreaks revenge on the yakuza boss who killed her parents, now results in a pan over his ruptured innards as the young girl straddles his lifeless form. This sequence would have had Western censors in a fury if it had been shot in live action; the combination of cute young Japanese girls, paedophiles and bloody carnage pushes buttons that Japanese cinema frequently touches, and Tarantino's use of anime to portray O-Ren Ishii's fury takes the modern Western audience to a place so dark it rarely visits. The other differences involve the Bride removing an additional appendage from the car-booted Sofie Fatale (Julie Dreyfus) and, more importantly, the House of the Blue Leaves massacre is now shown in its full technicolour glory rather than fading into black and white. Despite the fact that the moment when Tarantino's switches to monochrome is a piece of cinematic genius, the longer, more violent Japanese fight scene includes more gags, more gore and more of the incredible skills of Gordon Lu.[3]

If Chiba and Carradine represent two of the old-school kung fu fighters Tarantino adores, then Gordon Lu is the new guard. Starring in a plethora of martial arts classics like *5 Masters of Death* (Cheh Chang, 1974) and *Drunken Master 3* (Chia-Liang Liu, 1994), he is a huge star in Hong Kong and Tarantino knows exactly how to use him. He is given two roles in *Kill Bill*: the leader of the assassination hit squad The Crazy 88, and Pai Mei, the Bride's camp tutor. In the latter role, with his flowing white hair, always arched eyebrow and ever-flicking beard, he marks the major comic moment in both films. During the eighties and the video boom, most martial arts films shown to Western audiences were badly dubbed, poorly shot action films in which the fighting talents of the cast completely outweighed the acting talent required. Tarantino tries to recreate this viewing 'pleasure' using a combination of dubbing, downgrading film stock and some outrageous acting from Lu. Pai Mei's scenes also pave the way for the Bride to learn how to use the five-point-palm exploding heart technique that will help her to finally kill Bill. This rather preposterous move will seem ridiculous to many but familiar to anyone with a penchant for 1970s kung fu, where the moniker for a kung-fu move was almost as important as the act of violence itself.

Kill Bill's use of **Pulp Fiction**'s (Quentin Tarantino, 1994) technique of multi-level plotting is a modern conceit, but the tale of a woman scorned is a staple of exploitation and martial arts cinema. Two films in particular, Toshiya Fujita's *Lady Snowblood* and its sequel *Lady Snowblood 2: Love Song of Vengeance* (1974), are the blueprint for **Kill Bill.** Lady Snowblood tells the story of a young girl Yuki (Meiko Kaji) who is brought up as an unfeeling assassin after her mother is killed in prison, and many of the major elements of **Kill Bill** are present in it: vengeance, swordplay, the female protagonist, along with snow-covered battle scenes that probably inspired the final battle between the Bride and O-Ren Ishii. The links with *Lady Snowblood* are enhanced by the use of the song *Flower of Carnage*[4] from the film during **Kill Bill**'s closing moments. By giving the Bride a samurai sword as her chief weapon, Tarantino has once again given his movie a connection with the past, but his style is still very modern in its technique. He may downgrade film stock to give certain elements of **Kill Bill, Vol. 2** a vintage aesthetic, but it's done in a very knowing fashion that turns previously serious footage into high-camp slapstick. This knowing humour is also present during the film's violence. As in the *Lone Wolf and Cub* series, the bloodletting is so over the top it turns the carnage into a blood-soaked ballet, almost beautiful in its choreographed mayhem. The wirework by Woo-ping Yuen, the KNB FX—everything is done 'old school', no CGI here. It all results in a stylized slaughter that harks back to the seventies yet is modern in its execution.

Snow-covered mayhem also plays a part in one of the episodes of another Japanese classic. The *Lone Wolf and Cub* series follow the lives of Ogami Itto (Tomisaburo Wakayama), a dishonoured samurai, and his son Daigoro (Fumio Watanabe). Travelling across the Japanese countryside, they are under constant attack from the ranks of Ogami's former leader, but all he has in his clouded mind is a venomous need to avenge the death of his wife. He pushes his son in a fully armed pram across beautiful vistas; the films are quite serene in their beauty until the attacks take place. Bloody,

brutal and shocking: limbs fly, blood sprays in huge arterial geysers and the dying give themselves epic eulogies as they fall victim to a swift sword. In a clever marketing move that I would bet enabled Tarantino to see the films in the first place, US producer Robert Houston edited the first two episodes, *Sword of Vengeance* (Kenji Misumi, 1972) and *Babycart at the River Styx* (Kenji Misumi, 1972) together. He also removed many of the quieter moments, rescored the film and released it as the rip-roaring *Shogun Assassin* (Robert Houston, 1980) giving the film a new, garish tagline 'Lone wolf and son. The greatest team in the history of mass slaughter.'

This perfectly sums up Tarantino's method when making **Kill Bill.** He took a much-loved genre and recreated it for a modern audience. By referencing the films of his youth, he has given us a modern classic that passionately displays his loves, but also rises above its fan-boy origins to become a film that exudes everything that is wonderful in modern martial arts cinema. Those tempted to the genre by the gentle thrills of *Crouching Tiger, Hidden Dragon* (Ang Lee, 2000) will be shocked at how 'in your face' Tarantino's tribute is, but anyone who references the halcyon days of the Shaw Brothers as the zenith of the genre will find much to enjoy in Tarantino's love letter to the martial arts film.

Notes

1. Image Entertainment's NTSC laserdisc.

2. Writer's interview with David Carradine for *Filmink Magazine,* Oct 2004.

3. The full length Japanese version is presently only available on the Region 3 DVD.

4. *Flower of Carnage (Shura No Hana).* written by Kazuo Koike, Masaaki Hirao, Koji Ryuzaki; Teichiku Entertainment, Inc.

FURTHER READING

Criticism

Berg, Charles Ramirez. "A Taxonomy of Alternative Plots in Recent Films: Classifying the 'Tarantino Effect.'" *Film Criticism* 31, nos. 1-2 (fall-winter 2006): 5-61.

Details Tarantino's influence on non-linear narrative techniques in contemporary filmmaking.

Corliss, Richard. "Quentin Tarantino: The Value of Teen-Boy Fixations." *Time* 165, no. 16 (18 April 2005): 132.

Extols Tarantino's film choices.

Indiana, Gary, bell hooks, Jeanne Silverthorne, Dennis Cooper, and Robert Paul Wood. "Pulp the Hype on the Q.T. True Fiction: Killers Romance Dogs." *Artforum International* 33, no. 7 (March 1995): 62-6, 104, 108.

Critical viewings of Tarantino's work offered by contemporary artists and writers.

Richmond, Ray. Review of *CSI: Crime Scene Investigation,* "Grave Danger" directed by Quentin Tarantino. *Hollywood Reporter* 389, no. 12 (19 May 2005): 18.

Applauds Tarantino's turn to television.

Additional coverage of Tarantino's life and career is contained in the following sources published by Thomson Gale: *Authors and Artists for Young Adults,* **Vol. 58;** *Contemporary Authors,* **Vol. 171;** *Contemporary Authors New Revision Series,* **Vol. 125;** *Contemporary Literary Criticism,* **Vol. 125; and** *Literature Resource Center.*

How to Use This Index

The main references

Calvino, Italo
1923-1985 .... **CLC 5, 8, 11, 22, 33, 39,
73; SSC 3, 48**

---

list all author entries in the following Thomson Gale Literary Criticism series:

AAL = Asian American Literature
BG = The Beat Generation: A Gale Critical Companion
BLC = Black Literature Criticism
BLCS = Black Literature Criticism Supplement
CLC = Contemporary Literary Criticism
CLR = Children's Literature Review
CMLC = Classical and Medieval Literature Criticism
DC = Drama Criticism
FL = Feminism in Literature: A Gale Critical Companion
GL = Gothic Literature: A Gale Critical Companion
HLC = Hispanic Literature Criticism
HLCS = Hispanic Literature Criticism Supplement
HR = Harlem Renaissance: A Gale Critical Companion
LC = Literature Criticism from 1400 to 1800
NCLC = Nineteenth-Century Literature Criticism
NNAL = Native North American Literature
PC = Poetry Criticism
SSC = Short Story Criticism
TCLC = Twentieth-Century Literary Criticism
WLC = World Literature Criticism, 1500 to the Present
WLCS = World Literature Criticism Supplement

The cross-references

See also CA 85-88, 116; CANR 23, 61;
DAM NOV; DLB 196; EW 13; MTCW 1, 2;
RGSF 2; RGWL 2; SFW 4; SSFS 12

---

list all author entries in the following Thomson Gale biographical and literary sources:

AAYA = Authors & Artists for Young Adults
AFAW = African American Writers
AFW = African Writers
AITN = Authors in the News
AMW = American Writers
AMWR = American Writers Retrospective Supplement
AMWS = American Writers Supplement
ANW = American Nature Writers
AW = Ancient Writers
BEST = Bestsellers
BPFB = Beacham's Encyclopedia of Popular Fiction: Biography and Resources
BRW = British Writers
BRWS = British Writers Supplement
BW = Black Writers
BYA = Beacham's Guide to Literature for Young Adults
CA = Contemporary Authors
CAAS = Contemporary Authors Autobiography Series
CABS = Contemporary Authors Bibliographical Series
CAD = Contemporary American Dramatists
CANR = Contemporary Authors New Revision Series
CAP = Contemporary Authors Permanent Series
CBD = Contemporary British Dramatists
CCA = Contemporary Canadian Authors
CD = Contemporary Dramatists
CDALB = Concise Dictionary of American Literary Biography

CDALBS = Concise Dictionary of American Literary Biography Supplement
CDBLB = Concise Dictionary of British Literary Biography
CMW = St. James Guide to Crime & Mystery Writers
CN = Contemporary Novelists
CP = Contemporary Poets
CPW = Contemporary Popular Writers
CSW = Contemporary Southern Writers
CWD = Contemporary Women Dramatists
CWP = Contemporary Women Poets
CWRI = St. James Guide to Children's Writers
CWW = Contemporary World Writers
DA = DISCovering Authors
DA3 = DISCovering Authors 3.0
DAB = DISCovering Authors: British Edition
DAC = DISCovering Authors: Canadian Edition
DAM = DISCovering Authors: Modules
   DRAM: Dramatists Module; **MST:** Most-studied Authors Module;
   MULT: Multicultural Authors Module; **NOV:** Novelists Module;
   POET: Poets Module; **POP:** Popular Fiction and Genre Authors Module
DFS = Drama for Students
DLB = Dictionary of Literary Biography
DLBD = Dictionary of Literary Biography Documentary Series
DLBY = Dictionary of Literary Biography Yearbook
DNFS = Literature of Developing Nations for Students
EFS = Epics for Students
EXPN = Exploring Novels
EXPP = Exploring Poetry
EXPS = Exploring Short Stories
EW = European Writers
FANT = St. James Guide to Fantasy Writers
FW = Feminist Writers
GFL = Guide to French Literature, Beginnings to 1789, 1798 to the Present
GLL = Gay and Lesbian Literature
HGG = St. James Guide to Horror, Ghost & Gothic Writers
HW = Hispanic Writers
IDFW = International Dictionary of Films and Filmmakers: Writers and Production Artists
IDTP = International Dictionary of Theatre: Playwrights
LAIT = Literature and Its Times
LAW = Latin American Writers
JRDA = Junior DISCovering Authors
MAICYA = Major Authors and Illustrators for Children and Young Adults
MAICYAS = Major Authors and Illustrators for Children and Young Adults Supplement
MAWW = Modern American Women Writers
MJW = Modern Japanese Writers
MTCW = Major 20th-Century Writers
NCFS = Nonfiction Classics for Students
NFS = Novels for Students
PAB = Poets: American and British
PFS = Poetry for Students
RGAL = Reference Guide to American Literature
RGEL = Reference Guide to English Literature
RGSF = Reference Guide to Short Fiction
RGWL = Reference Guide to World Literature
RHW = Twentieth-Century Romance and Historical Writers
SAAS = Something about the Author Autobiography Series
SATA = Something about the Author
SFW = St. James Guide to Science Fiction Writers
SSFS = Short Stories for Students
TCWW = Twentieth-Century Western Writers
WLIT = World Literature and Its Times
WP = World Poets
YABC = Yesterday's Authors of Books for Children
YAW = St. James Guide to Young Adult Writers

Literary Criticism Series
Cumulative Author Index

Alexeyev, Constantin Sergeivich
See Stanislavsky, Constantin
Alexeyev, Konstantin Sergeyevich
See Stanislavsky, Constantin
Alexie, Sherman 1966- .... **CLC 96, 154;
NNAL; PC 53**
See also AAYA 28; BYA 15; CA 138;
CANR 65, 95, 133; CN 7; DA3; DAM
MULT; DLB 175, 206, 278; LATS 1:2;
MTCW 2; MTFW 2005; NFS 17; SSFS
18
al-Farabi 870(?)-950 .... **CMLC 58**
See also DLB 115
Alfau, Felipe 1902-1999 .... **CLC 66**
See also CA 137
Alfieri, Vittorio 1749-1803 .... **NCLC 101**
See also EW 4; RGWL 2, 3; WLIT 7
Alfonso X 1221-1284 .... **CMLC 78**
Alfred, Jean Gaston
See Ponge, Francis
Alger, Horatio, Jr. 1832-1899 .... **NCLC 8, 83**
See also CLR 87; DLB 42; LAIT 2; RGAL
4; SATA 16; TUS
Al-Ghazali, Muhammad ibn Muhammad
1058-1111 .... **CMLC 50**
See also DLB 115
Algren, Nelson 1909-1981 ..... **CLC 4, 10, 33;
SSC 33**
See also AMWS 9; BPFB 1; CA 13-16R;
103; CANR 20, 61; CDALB 1941-1968;
CN 1, 2; DLB 9; DLBY 1981, 1982,
2000; EWL 3; MAL 5; MTCW 1, 2;
MTFW 2005; RGAL 4; RGSF 2
**al-Hariri, al-Qasim ibn 'Ali Abu
Muhammad al-Basri**
1054-1122 .... **CMLC 63**
See also RGWL 3
Ali, Ahmed 1908-1998 .... **CLC 69**
See also CA 25-28R; CANR 15, 34; CN 1,
2, 3, 4, 5; DLB 323; EWL 3
Ali, Tariq 1943- .... **CLC 173**
See also CA 25-28R; CANR 10, 99
Alighieri, Dante
See Dante
See also WLIT 7
al-Kindi, Abu Yusuf Ya'qub ibn Ishaq c.
801-c. 873 .... **CMLC 80**
Allan, John B.
See Westlake, Donald E.
Allan, Sidney
See Hartmann, Sadakichi
Allan, Sydney
See Hartmann, Sadakichi
Allard, Janet .... **CLC 59**
Allen, Edward 1948- .... **CLC 59**
Allen, Fred 1894-1956 .... **TCLC 87**
Allen, Paula Gunn 1939- .... **CLC 84, 202;
NNAL**
See also AMWS 4; CA 112; 143; CANR
63, 130; CWP; DA3; DAM MULT; DLB
175; FW; MTCW 2; MTFW 2005; RGAL
4; TCWW 2
Allen, Roland
See Ayckbourn, Alan
Allen, Sarah A.
See Hopkins, Pauline Elizabeth
Allen, Sidney H.
See Hartmann, Sadakichi
Allen, Woody 1935- .... **CLC 16, 52, 195**
See also AAYA 10, 51; AMWS 15; CA 33-
36R; CANR 27, 38, 63, 128; DAM POP;
DLB 44; MTCW 1; SSFS 21
Allende, Isabel 1942- ... **CLC 39, 57, 97, 170;
HLC 1; SSC 65; WLCS**
See also AAYA 18, 70; CA 125; 130; CANR
51, 74, 129; CDWLB 3; CLR 99; CWW
2; DA3; DAM MULT, NOV; DLB 145;
DNFS 1; EWL 3; FL 1:5; FW; HW 1, 2;
INT CA-130; LAIT 5; LAWS 1; LMFS 2;

MTCW 1, 2; MTFW 2005; NCFS 1; NFS
6, 18; RGSF 2; RGWL 3; SATA 163;
SSFS 11, 16; WLIT 1
Alleyn, Ellen
See Rossetti, Christina
Alleyne, Carla D. .... **CLC 65**
Allingham, Margery (Louise)
1904-1966 .... **CLC 19**
See also CA 5-8R; 25-28R; CANR 4, 58;
CMW 4; DLB 77; MSW; MTCW 1, 2
Allingham, William 1824-1889 ...... **NCLC 25**
See also DLB 35; RGEL 2
Allison, Dorothy E. 1949- .... **CLC 78, 153**
See also AAYA 53; CA 140; CANR 66, 107;
CN 7; CSW; DA3; FW; MTCW 2; MTFW
2005; NFS 11; RGAL 4
Alloula, Malek .... **CLC 65**
Allston, Washington 1779-1843 .... **NCLC 2**
See also DLB 1, 235
Almedingen, E. M. .... **CLC 12**
See Almedingen, Martha Edith von
See also SATA 3
Almedingen, Martha Edith von 1898-1971
See Almedingen, E. M.
See also CA 1-4R; CANR 1
Almodovar, Pedro 1949(?)- .... **CLC 114, 229;
HLCS 1**
See also CA 133; CANR 72, 151; HW 2
Almqvist, Carl Jonas Love
1793-1866 .... **NCLC 42**
**al-Mutanabbi, Ahmad ibn al-Husayn Abu
al-Tayyib al-Jufi al-Kindi**
915-965 .... **CMLC 66**
See Mutanabbi, Al-
See also RGWL 3
Alonso, Damaso 1898-1990 .... **CLC 14**
See also CA 110; 131; 130; CANR 72; DLB
108; EWL 3; HW 1, 2
Alov
See Gogol, Nikolai (Vasilyevich)
al'Sadaawi, Nawal
See El Saadawi, Nawal
See also FW
al-Shaykh, Hanan 1945- .... **CLC 218**
See Shaykh, al- Hanan
See also CA 135; CANR 111; WLIT 6
Al Siddik
See Rolfe, Frederick (William Serafino
Austin Lewis Mary)
See also GLL 1; RGEL 2
Alta 1942- .... **CLC 19**
See also CA 57-60
Alter, Robert B(ernard) 1935- .... **CLC 34**
See also CA 49-52; CANR 1, 47, 100
Alther, Lisa 1944- .... **CLC 7, 41**
See also BPFB 1; CA 65-68; CAAS 30;
CANR 12, 30, 51; CN 4, 5, 6, 7; CSW;
GLL 2; MTCW 1
Althusser, L.
See Althusser, Louis
Althusser, Louis 1918-1990 .... **CLC 106**
See also CA 131; 132; CANR 102; DLB
242
Altman, Robert 1925-2006 .... **CLC 16, 116**
See also CA 73-76; CANR 43
Alurista .... **HLCS 1; PC 34**
See Urista (Heredia), Alberto (Baltazar)
See also CA 45-48R; DLB 82; LLW
Alvarez, A. 1929- .... **CLC 5, 13**
See also CA 1-4R; CANR 3, 33, 63, 101,
134; CN 3, 4, 5, 6; CP 1, 2, 3, 4, 5, 6, 7;
DLB 14, 40; MTFW 2005
Alvarez, Alejandro Rodriguez 1903-1965
See Casona, Alejandro
See also CA 131; 93-96; HW 1
Alvarez, Julia 1950- .... **CLC 93; HLCS 1**
See also AAYA 25; AMWS 7; CA 147;
CANR 69, 101, 133; DA3; DLB 282;

LATS 1:2; LLW; MTCW 2; MTFW 2005;
NFS 5, 9; SATA 129; WLIT 1
Alvaro, Corrado 1896-1956 .... **TCLC 60**
See also CA 163; DLB 264; EWL 3
Amado, Jorge 1912-2001 ... **CLC 13, 40, 106;
HLC 1**
See also CA 77-80; 201; CANR 35, 74, 135;
CWW 2; DAM MULT, NOV; DLB 113,
307; EWL 3; HW 2; LAW; LAWS 1;
MTCW 1, 2; MTFW 2005; RGWL 2, 3;
TWA; WLIT 1
Ambler, Eric 1909-1998 .... **CLC 4, 6, 9**
See also BRWS 4; CA 9-12R; 171; CANR
7, 38, 74; CMW 4; CN 1, 2, 3, 4, 5, 6;
DLB 77; MSW; MTCW 1, 2; TEA
Ambrose, Stephen E. 1936-2002 .... **CLC 145**
See also AAYA 44; CA 1-4R; 209; CANR
3, 43, 57, 83, 105; MTFW 2005; NCFS 2;
SATA 40, 138
Amichai, Yehuda 1924-2000 .. **CLC 9, 22, 57,
116; PC 38**
See also CA 85-88; 189; CANR 46, 60, 99,
132; CWW 2; EWL 3; MTCW 1, 2;
MTFW 2005; PFS 24; RGHL; WLIT 6
Amichai, Yehudah
See Amichai, Yehuda
Amiel, Henri Frederic 1821-1881 .... **NCLC 4**
See also DLB 217
Amis, Kingsley 1922-1995 . **CLC 1, 2, 3, 5, 8,
13, 40, 44, 129**
See also AITN 2; BPFB 1; BRWS 2; CA
9-12R; 150; CANR 8, 28, 54; CDBLB
1945-1960; CN 1, 2, 3, 4, 5, 6; CP 1, 2,
3, 4; DA; DA3; DAB; DAC; DAM MST,
NOV; DLB 15, 27, 100, 139, 326; DLBY
1996; EWL 3; HGG; INT CANR-8;
MTCW 1, 2; MTFW 2005; RGEL 2;
RGSF 2; SFW 4
Amis, Martin 1949- ... **CLC 4, 9, 38, 62, 101,
213**
See also BEST 90:3; BRWS 4; CA 65-68;
CANR 8, 27, 54, 73, 95, 132; CN 5, 6, 7;
DA3; DLB 14, 194; EWL 3; INT CANR-
27; MTCW 2; MTFW 2005
Ammianus Marcellinus c. 330-c.
395 .... **CMLC 60**
See also AW 2; DLB 211
Ammons, A.R. 1926-2001 .. **CLC 2, 3, 5, 8, 9,
25, 57, 108; PC 16**
See also AITN 1; AMWS 7; CA 9-12R;
193; CANR 6, 36, 51, 73, 107, 156; CP 1,
2, 3, 4, 5, 6, 7; CSW; DAM POET; DLB
5, 165; EWL 3; MAL 5; MTCW 1, 2; PFS
19; RGAL 4; TCLE 1:1
Ammons, Archie Randolph
See Ammons, A.R.
Amo, Tauraatua i
See Adams, Henry (Brooks)
Amory, Thomas 1691(?)-1788 .... **LC 48**
See also DLB 39
Anand, Mulk Raj 1905-2004 ...... **CLC 23, 93**
See also CA 65-68; 231; CANR 32, 64; CN
1, 2, 3, 4, 5, 6, 7; DAM NOV; DLB 323;
EWL 3; MTCW 1, 2; MTFW 2005; RGSF
2
Anatol
See Schnitzler, Arthur
Anaximander c. 611B.C.-c.
546B.C. .... **CMLC 22**
Anaya, Rudolfo A. 1937- .... **CLC 23, 148;
HLC 1**
See also AAYA 20; BYA 13; CA 45-48;
CAAS 4; CANR 1, 32, 51, 124; CN 4, 5,
6, 7; DAM MULT, NOV; DLB 82, 206,
278; HW 1; LAIT 4; LLW; MAL 5;
MTCW 1, 2; MTFW 2005; NFS 12;
RGAL 4; RGSF 2; TCWW 2; WLIT 1

Andersen, Hans Christian
1805-1875 .... **NCLC 7, 79; SSC 6, 56; WLC 1**
See also AAYA 57; CLR 6, 113; DA; DA3; DAB; DAC; DAM MST, POP; EW 6; MAICYA 1, 2; RGSF 2; RGWL 2, 3; SATA 100; TWA; WCH; YABC 1

Anderson, C. Farley
See Mencken, H(enry) L(ouis); Nathan, George Jean

Anderson, Jessica (Margaret) Queale
1916- .... **CLC 37**
See also CA 9-12R; CANR 4, 62; CN 4, 5, 6, 7; DLB 325

Anderson, Jon (Victor) 1940- .... **CLC 9**
See also CA 25-28R; CANR 20; CP 1, 3, 4, 5; DAM POET

Anderson, Lindsay (Gordon)
1923-1994 .... **CLC 20**
See also CA 125; 128; 146; CANR 77

Anderson, Maxwell 1888-1959 .... **TCLC 2, 144**
See also CA 105; 152; DAM DRAM; DFS 16, 20; DLB 7, 228; MAL 5; MTCW 2; MTFW 2005; RGAL 4

Anderson, Poul 1926-2001 .... **CLC 15**
See also AAYA 5, 34; BPFB 1; BYA 6, 8, 9; CA 1-4R; 181; 199; CAAE 181; CAAS 2; CANR 2, 15, 34, 64, 110; CLR 58; DLB 8; FANT; INT CANR-15; MTCW 1, 2; MTFW 2005; SATA 90; SATA-Brief 39; SATA-Essay 106; SCFW 1, 2; SFW 4; SUFW 1, 2

Anderson, Robert (Woodruff)
1917- .... **CLC 23**
See also AITN 1; CA 21-24R; CANR 32; CD 6; DAM DRAM; DLB 7; LAIT 5

Anderson, Roberta Joan
See Mitchell, Joni

Anderson, Sherwood 1876-1941 ... **SSC 1, 46, 91; TCLC 1, 10, 24, 123; WLC 1**
See also AAYA 30; AMW; AMWC 2; BPFB 1; CA 104; 121; CANR 61; CDALB 1917-1929; DA; DA3; DAB; DAC; DAM MST, NOV; DLB 4, 9, 86; DLBD 1; EWL 3; EXPS; GLL 2; MAL 5; MTCW 1, 2; MTFW 2005; NFS 4; RGAL 4; RGSF 2; SSFS 4, 10, 11; TUS

Anderson, Wes 1969- .... **CLC 227**
See also CA 214

Andier, Pierre
See Desnos, Robert

Andouard
See Giraudoux, Jean(-Hippolyte)

Andrade, Carlos Drummond de ..... **CLC 18**
See Drummond de Andrade, Carlos
See also EWL 3; RGWL 2, 3

Andrade, Mario de .... **TCLC 43**
See de Andrade, Mario
See also DLB 307; EWL 3; LAW; RGWL 2, 3; WLIT 1

Andreae, Johann V(alentin)
1586-1654 .... **LC 32**
See also DLB 164

Andreas Capellanus fl. c. 1185- .... **CMLC 45**
See also DLB 208

Andreas-Salome, Lou 1861-1937 ... **TCLC 56**
See also CA 178; DLB 66

Andreev, Leonid
See Andreyev, Leonid (Nikolaevich)
See also DLB 295; EWL 3

Andress, Lesley
See Sanders, Lawrence

Andrewes, Lancelot 1555-1626 .... **LC 5**
See also DLB 151, 172

Andrews, Cicily Fairfield
See West, Rebecca

Andrews, Elton V.
See Pohl, Frederik

Andrews, Peter
See Soderbergh, Steven

Andreyev, Leonid (Nikolaevich)
1871-1919 .... **TCLC 3**
See Andreev, Leonid
See also CA 104; 185

Andric, Ivo 1892-1975 .... **CLC 8; SSC 36; TCLC 135**
See also CA 81-84; 57-60; CANR 43, 60; CDWLB 4; DLB 147, 329; EW 11; EWL 3; MTCW 1; RGSF 2; RGWL 2, 3

Androvar
See Prado (Calvo), Pedro

Angela of Foligno 1248(?)-1309 .... **CMLC 76**

Angelique, Pierre
See Bataille, Georges

Angell, Roger 1920- .... **CLC 26**
See also CA 57-60; CANR 13, 44, 70, 144; DLB 171, 185

Angelou, Maya 1928- ... **BLC 1; CLC 12, 35, 64, 77, 155; PC 32; WLCS**
See also AAYA 7, 20; AMWS 4; BPFB 1; BW 2, 3; BYA 2; CA 65-68; CANR 19, 42, 65, 111, 133; CDALBS; CLR 53; CP 4, 5, 6, 7; CPW; CSW; CWP; DA; DA3; DAB; DAC; DAM MST, MULT, POET, POP; DLB 38; EWL 3; EXPN; EXPP; FL 1:5; LAIT 4; MAICYA 2; MAICYAS 1; MAL 5; MBL; MTCW 1, 2; MTFW 2005; NCFS 2; NFS 2; PFS 2, 3; RGAL 4; SATA 49, 136; TCLE 1:1; WYA; YAW

Angouleme, Marguerite d'
See de Navarre, Marguerite

Anna Comnena 1083-1153 .... **CMLC 25**

Annensky, Innokentii Fedorovich
See Annensky, Innokenty (Fyodorovich)
See also DLB 295

Annensky, Innokenty (Fyodorovich)
1856-1909 .... **TCLC 14**
See also CA 110; 155; EWL 3

Annunzio, Gabriele d'
See D'Annunzio, Gabriele

Anodos
See Coleridge, Mary E(lizabeth)

Anon, Charles Robert
See Pessoa, Fernando (Antonio Nogueira)

Anouilh, Jean 1910-1987 ..... **CLC 1, 3, 8, 13, 40, 50; DC 8, 21**
See also AAYA 67; CA 17-20R; 123; CANR 32; DAM DRAM; DFS 9, 10, 19; DLB 321; EW 13; EWL 3; GFL 1789 to the Present; MTCW 1, 2; MTFW 2005; RGWL 2, 3; TWA

Anselm of Canterbury
1033(?)-1109 .... **CMLC 67**
See also DLB 115

Anthony, Florence
See Ai

Anthony, John
See Ciardi, John (Anthony)

Anthony, Peter
See Shaffer, Anthony; Shaffer, Peter

Anthony, Piers 1934- .... **CLC 35**
See also AAYA 11, 48; BYA 7; CA 200; CAAE 200; CANR 28, 56, 73, 102, 133; CLR 118; CPW; DAM POP; DLB 8; FANT; MAICYA 2; MAICYAS 1; MTCW 1, 2; MTFW 2005; SAAS 22; SATA 84, 129; SATA-Essay 129; SFW 4; SUFW 1, 2; YAW

Anthony, Susan B(rownell)
1820-1906 .... **TCLC 84**
See also CA 211; FW

Antiphon c. 480B.C.-c. 411B.C. .... **CMLC 55**

Antoine, Marc
See Proust, (Valentin-Louis-George-Eugene) Marcel

Antoninus, Brother
See Everson, William (Oliver)
See also CP 1

Antonioni, Michelangelo 1912- .... **CLC 20, 144**
See also CA 73-76; CANR 45, 77

Antschel, Paul 1920-1970
See Celan, Paul
See also CA 85-88; CANR 33, 61; MTCW 1; PFS 21

Anwar, Chairil 1922-1949 .... **TCLC 22**
See Chairil Anwar
See also CA 121; 219; RGWL 3

Anzaldua, Gloria (Evanjelina)
1942-2004 .... **CLC 200; HLCS 1**
See also CA 175; 227; CSW; CWP; DLB 122; FW; LLW; RGAL 4; SATA-Obit 154

Apess, William 1798-1839(?) .... **NCLC 73; NNAL**
See also DAM MULT; DLB 175, 243

Apollinaire, Guillaume 1880-1918 .... **PC 7; TCLC 3, 8, 51**
See Kostrowitzki, Wilhelm Apollinaris de
See also CA 152; DAM POET; DLB 258, 321; EW 9; EWL 3; GFL 1789 to the Present; MTCW 2; PFS 24; RGWL 2, 3; TWA; WP

Apollonius of Rhodes
See Apollonius Rhodius
See also AW 1; RGWL 2, 3

Apollonius Rhodius c. 300B.C.-c. 220B.C. .... **CMLC 28**
See Apollonius of Rhodes
See also DLB 176

Appelfeld, Aharon 1932- ... **CLC 23, 47; SSC 42**
See also CA 112; 133; CANR 86; CWW 2; DLB 299; EWL 3; RGHL; RGSF 2; WLIT 6

Apple, Max (Isaac) 1941- .... **CLC 9, 33; SSC 50**
See also CA 81-84; CANR 19, 54; DLB 130

Appleman, Philip (Dean) 1926- .... **CLC 51**
See also CA 13-16R; CAAS 18; CANR 6, 29, 56

Appleton, Lawrence
See Lovecraft, H. P.

Apteryx
See Eliot, T(homas) S(tearns)

Apuleius, (Lucius Madaurensis) c. 125-c. 164 .... **CMLC 1, 84**
See also AW 2; CDWLB 1; DLB 211; RGWL 2, 3; SUFW; WLIT 8

Aquin, Hubert 1929-1977 .... **CLC 15**
See also CA 105; DLB 53; EWL 3

Aquinas, Thomas 1224(?)-1274 ...... **CMLC 33**
See also DLB 115; EW 1; TWA

Aragon, Louis 1897-1982 .... **CLC 3, 22; TCLC 123**
See also CA 69-72; 108; CANR 28, 71; DAM NOV, POET; DLB 72, 258; EW 11; EWL 3; GFL 1789 to the Present; GLL 2; LMFS 2; MTCW 1, 2; RGWL 2, 3

Arany, Janos 1817-1882 .... **NCLC 34**

Aranyos, Kakay 1847-1910
See Mikszath, Kalman

Aratus of Soli c. 315B.C.-c. 240B.C. .... **CMLC 64**
See also DLB 176

Arbuthnot, John 1667-1735 .... **LC 1**
See also DLB 101

Archer, Herbert Winslow
See Mencken, H(enry) L(ouis)

Archer, Jeffrey 1940- .... **CLC 28**
See also AAYA 16; BEST 89:3; BPFB 1; CA 77-80; CANR 22, 52, 95, 136; CPW; DA3; DAM POP; INT CANR-22; MTFW 2005

Archer, Jeffrey Howard
    See Archer, Jeffrey
Archer, Jules 1915- .... **CLC 12**
    See also CA 9-12R; CANR 6, 69; SAAS 5;
    SATA 4, 85
Archer, Lee
    See Ellison, Harlan
Archilochus c. 7th cent. B.C.- .... **CMLC 44**
    See also DLB 176
Arden, John 1930- .... **CLC 6, 13, 15**
    See also BRWS 2; CA 13-16R; CAAS 4;
    CANR 31, 65, 67, 124; CBD; CD 5, 6;
    DAM DRAM; DFS 9; DLB 13, 245;
    EWL 3; MTCW 1
Arenas, Reinaldo 1943-1990 .. **CLC 41; HLC
    1**
    See also CA 124; 128; 133; CANR 73, 106;
    DAM MULT; DLB 145; EWL 3; GLL 2;
    HW 1; LAW; LAWS 1; MTCW 2; MTFW
    2005; RGSF 2; RGWL 3; WLIT 1
Arendt, Hannah 1906-1975 .... **CLC 66, 98**
    See also CA 17-20R; 61-64; CANR 26, 60;
    DLB 242; MTCW 1, 2
Aretino, Pietro 1492-1556 .... **LC 12**
    See also RGWL 2, 3
Arghezi, Tudor .... **CLC 80**
    See Theodorescu, Ion N.
    See also CA 167; CDWLB 4; DLB 220;
    EWL 3
Arguedas, Jose Maria 1911-1969 .... **CLC 10,
    18; HLCS 1; TCLC 147**
    See also CA 89-92; CANR 73; DLB 113;
    EWL 3; HW 1; LAW; RGWL 2, 3; WLIT
    1
Argueta, Manlio 1936- .... **CLC 31**
    See also CA 131; CANR 73; CWW 2; DLB
    145; EWL 3; HW 1; RGWL 3
Arias, Ron 1941- .... **HLC 1**
    See also CA 131; CANR 81, 136; DAM
    MULT; DLB 82; HW 1, 2; MTCW 2;
    MTFW 2005
Ariosto, Lodovico
    See Ariosto, Ludovico
    See also WLIT 7
Ariosto, Ludovico 1474-1533 ... **LC 6, 87; PC
    42**
    See Ariosto, Lodovico
    See also EW 2; RGWL 2, 3
Aristides
    See Epstein, Joseph
Aristophanes 450B.C.-385B.C. .... **CMLC 4,
    51; DC 2; WLCS**
    See also AW 1; CDWLB 1; DA; DA3;
    DAB; DAC; DAM DRAM, MST; DFS
    10; DLB 176; LMFS 1; RGWL 2, 3;
    TWA; WLIT 8
Aristotle 384B.C.-322B.C. .... **CMLC 31;
    WLCS**
    See also AW 1; CDWLB 1; DA; DA3;
    DAB; DAC; DAM MST; DLB 176;
    RGWL 2, 3; TWA; WLIT 8
Arlt, Roberto (Godofredo Christophersen)
    1900-1942 .... **HLC 1; TCLC 29**
    See also CA 123; 131; CANR 67; DAM
    MULT; DLB 305; EWL 3; HW 1, 2;
    IDTP; LAW
Armah, Ayi Kwei 1939- . **BLC 1; CLC 5, 33,
    136**
    See also AFW; BRWS 10; BW 1; CA 61-
    64; CANR 21, 64; CDWLB 3; CN 1, 2,
    3, 4, 5, 6, 7; DAM MULT, POET; DLB
    117; EWL 3; MTCW 2; WLIT 2
Armatrading, Joan 1950- .... **CLC 17**
    See also CA 114; 186
Armin, Robert 1568(?)-1615(?) .... **LC 120**
Armitage, Frank
    See Carpenter, John (Howard)

Armstrong, Jeannette (C.) 1948- .... **NNAL**
    See also CA 149; CCA 1; CN 6, 7; DAC;
    SATA 102
Arnette, Robert
    See Silverberg, Robert
**Arnim, Achim von (Ludwig Joachim von
    Arnim)** 1781-1831 .. **NCLC 5, 159; SSC
    29**
    See also DLB 90
Arnim, Bettina von 1785-1859 ...... **NCLC 38,
    123**
    See also DLB 90; RGWL 2, 3
Arnold, Matthew 1822-1888 ..... **NCLC 6, 29,
    89, 126; PC 5; WLC 1**
    See also BRW 5; CDBLB 1832-1890; DA;
    DAB; DAC; DAM MST, POET; DLB 32,
    57; EXPP; PAB; PFS 2; TEA; WP
Arnold, Thomas 1795-1842 .... **NCLC 18**
    See also DLB 55
Arnow, Harriette (Louisa) Simpson
    1908-1986 .... **CLC 2, 7, 18**
    See also BPFB 1; CA 9-12R; 118; CANR
    14; CN 2, 3, 4; DLB 6; FW; MTCW 1, 2;
    RHW; SATA 42; SATA-Obit 47
Arouet, Francois-Marie
    See Voltaire
Arp, Hans
    See Arp, Jean
Arp, Jean 1887-1966 .... **CLC 5; TCLC 115**
    See also CA 81-84; 25-28R; CANR 42, 77;
    EW 10
Arrabal
    See Arrabal, Fernando
Arrabal (Teran), Fernando
    See Arrabal, Fernando
    See also CWW 2
Arrabal, Fernando 1932- ... **CLC 2, 9, 18, 58**
    See Arrabal (Teran), Fernando
    See also CA 9-12R; CANR 15; DLB 321;
    EWL 3; LMFS 2
Arreola, Juan Jose 1918-2001 .... **CLC 147;
    HLC 1; SSC 38**
    See also CA 113; 131; 200; CANR 81;
    CWW 2; DAM MULT; DLB 113; DNFS
    2; EWL 3; HW 1, 2; LAW; RGSF 2
Arrian c. 89(?)-c. 155(?) .... **CMLC 43**
    See also DLB 176
Arrick, Fran .... **CLC 30**
    See Gaberman, Judie Angell
    See also BYA 6
Arrley, Richmond
    See Delany, Samuel R., Jr.
Artaud, Antonin (Marie Joseph)
    1896-1948 .... **DC 14; TCLC 3, 36**
    See also CA 104; 149; DA3; DAM DRAM;
    DFS 22; DLB 258, 321; EW 11; EWL 3;
    GFL 1789 to the Present; MTCW 2;
    MTFW 2005; RGWL 2, 3
Arthur, Ruth M(abel) 1905-1979 ..... **CLC 12**
    See also CA 9-12R; 85-88; CANR 4; CWRI
    5; SATA 7, 26
Artsybashev, Mikhail (Petrovich)
    1878-1927 .... **TCLC 31**
    See also CA 170; DLB 295
Arundel, Honor (Morfydd)
    1919-1973 .... **CLC 17**
    See also CA 21-22; 41-44R; CAP 2; CLR
    35; CWRI 5; SATA 4; SATA-Obit 24
Arzner, Dorothy 1900-1979 .... **CLC 98**
Asch, Sholem 1880-1957 .... **TCLC 3**
    See also CA 105; EWL 3; GLL 2; RGHL
Ascham, Roger 1516(?)-1568 .... **LC 101**
    See also DLB 236
Ash, Shalom
    See Asch, Sholem

Ashbery, John 1927- ... **CLC 2, 3, 4, 6, 9, 13,
    15, 25, 41, 77, 125, 221; PC 26**
    See Berry, Jonas
    See also AMWS 3; CA 5-8R; CANR 9, 37,
    66, 102, 132; CP 1, 2, 3, 4, 5, 6, 7; DA3;
    DAM POET; DLB 5, 165; DLBY 1981;
    EWL 3; INT CANR-9; MAL 5; MTCW
    1, 2; MTFW 2005; PAB; PFS 11; RGAL
    4; TCLE 1:1; WP
Ashdown, Clifford
    See Freeman, R(ichard) Austin
Ashe, Gordon
    See Creasey, John
Ashton-Warner, Sylvia (Constance)
    1908-1984 .... **CLC 19**
    See also CA 69-72; 112; CANR 29; CN 1,
    2, 3; MTCW 1, 2
Asimov, Isaac 1920-1992 ..... **CLC 1, 3, 9, 19,
    26, 76, 92**
    See also AAYA 13; BEST 90:2; BPFB 1;
    BYA 4, 6, 7, 9; CA 1-4R; 137; CANR 2,
    19, 36, 60, 125; CLR 12, 79; CMW 4;
    CN 1, 2, 3, 4, 5; CPW; DA3; DAM POP;
    DLB 8; DLBY 1992; INT CANR-19;
    JRDA; LAIT 5; LMFS 2; MAICYA 1, 2;
    MAL 5; MTCW 1, 2; MTFW 2005;
    RGAL 4; SATA 1, 26, 74; SCFW 1, 2;
    SFW 4; SSFS 17; TUS; YAW
Askew, Anne 1521(?)-1546 .... **LC 81**
    See also DLB 136
Assis, Joaquim Maria Machado de
    See Machado de Assis, Joaquim Maria
Astell, Mary 1666-1731 .... **LC 68**
    See also DLB 252; FW
Astley, Thea (Beatrice May)
    1925-2004 .... **CLC 41**
    See also CA 65-68; 229; CANR 11, 43, 78;
    CN 1, 2, 3, 4, 5, 6, 7; DLB 289; EWL 3
Astley, William 1855-1911
    See Warung, Price
Aston, James
    See White, T(erence) H(anbury)
Asturias, Miguel Angel 1899-1974 .... **CLC 3,
    8, 13; HLC 1**
    See also CA 25-28; 49-52; CANR 32; CAP
    2; CDWLB 3; DA3; DAM MULT, NOV;
    DLB 113, 290, 329; EWL 3; HW 1; LAW;
    LMFS 2; MTCW 1, 2; RGWL 2, 3; WLIT
    1
Atares, Carlos Saura
    See Saura (Atares), Carlos
Athanasius c. 295-c. 373 .... **CMLC 48**
Atheling, William
    See Pound, Ezra (Weston Loomis)
Atheling, William, Jr.
    See Blish, James (Benjamin)
Atherton, Gertrude (Franklin Horn)
    1857-1948 .... **TCLC 2**
    See also CA 104; 155; DLB 9, 78, 186;
    HGG; RGAL 4; SUFW 1; TCWW 1, 2
Atherton, Lucius
    See Masters, Edgar Lee
Atkins, Jack
    See Harris, Mark
Atkinson, Kate 1951- .... **CLC 99**
    See also CA 166; CANR 101, 153; DLB
    267
Attaway, William (Alexander)
    1911-1986 .... **BLC 1; CLC 92**
    See also BW 2, 3; CA 143; CANR 82;
    DAM MULT; DLB 76; MAL 5
Atticus
    See Fleming, Ian; Wilson, (Thomas) Wood-
    row
Atwood, Margaret 1939- . **CLC 2, 3, 4, 8, 13,
    15, 25, 44, 84, 135; PC 8; SSC 2, 46;
    WLC 1**
    See also AAYA 12, 47; AMWS 13; BEST
    89:2; BPFB 1; CA 49-52; CANR 3, 24,

33, 59, 95, 133; CN 2, 3, 4, 5, 6, 7; CP 1, 2, 3, 4, 5, 6, 7; CPW; CWP; DA; DA3; DAB; DAC; DAM MST, NOV, POET; DLB 53, 251, 326; EWL 3; EXPN; FL 1:5; FW; GL 2; INT CANR-24; LAIT 5; MTCW 1, 2; MTFW 2005; NFS 4, 12, 13, 14, 19; PFS 7; RGSF 2; SATA 50, 170; SSFS 3, 13; TCLE 1:1; TWA; WWE 1; YAW

Atwood, Margaret Eleanor
See Atwood, Margaret

Aubigny, Pierre d'
See Mencken, H(enry) L(ouis)

Aubin, Penelope 1685-1731(?) .... **LC 9**
See also DLB 39

Auchincloss, Louis 1917- ..... **CLC 4, 6, 9, 18, 45; SSC 22**
See also AMWS 4; CA 1-4R; CANR 6, 29, 55, 87, 130; CN 1, 2, 3, 4, 5, 6, 7; DAM NOV; DLB 2, 244; DLBY 1980; EWL 3; INT CANR-29; MAL 5; MTCW 1; RGAL 4

Auchincloss, Louis Stanton
See Auchincloss, Louis

Auden, W(ystan) H(ugh) 1907-1973 . **CLC 1, 2, 3, 4, 6, 9, 11, 14, 43, 123; PC 1; WLC 1**
See also AAYA 18; AMWS 2; BRW 7; BRWR 1; CA 9-12R; 45-48; CANR 5, 61, 105; CDBLB 1914-1945; CP 1, 2; DA; DA3; DAB; DAC; DAM DRAM, MST, POET; DLB 10, 20; EWL 3; EXPP; MAL 5; MTCW 1, 2; MTFW 2005; PAB; PFS 1, 3, 4, 10; TUS; WP

Audiberti, Jacques 1899-1965 .... **CLC 38**
See also CA 25-28R; DAM DRAM; DLB 321; EWL 3

Audubon, John James 1785-1851 . **NCLC 47**
See also AMWS 16; ANW; DLB 248

Auel, Jean M(arie) 1936- .... **CLC 31, 107**
See also AAYA 7, 51; BEST 90:4; BPFB 1; CA 103; CANR 21, 64, 115; CPW; DA3; DAM POP; INT CANR-21; NFS 11; RHW; SATA 91

Auerbach, Berthold 1812-1882 .... **NCLC 171**
See also DLB 133

Auerbach, Erich 1892-1957 .... **TCLC 43**
See also CA 118; 155; EWL 3

Augier, Emile 1820-1889 .... **NCLC 31**
See also DLB 192; GFL 1789 to the Present

August, John
See De Voto, Bernard (Augustine)

Augustine, St. 354-430 .... **CMLC 6; WLCS**
See also DA; DA3; DAB; DAC; DAM MST; DLB 115; EW 1; RGWL 2, 3; WLIT 8

Aunt Belinda
See Braddon, Mary Elizabeth

Aunt Weedy
See Alcott, Louisa May

Aurelius
See Bourne, Randolph S(illiman)

Aurelius, Marcus 121-180 .... **CMLC 45**
See Marcus Aurelius
See also RGWL 2, 3

Aurobindo, Sri
See Ghose, Aurabinda

Aurobindo Ghose
See Ghose, Aurabinda

Austen, Jane 1775-1817 ...... **NCLC 1, 13, 19, 33, 51, 81, 95, 119, 150; WLC 1**
See also AAYA 19; BRW 4; BRWC 1; BRWR 2; BYA 3; CDBLB 1789-1832; DA; DA3; DAB; DAC; DAM MST, NOV; DLB 116; EXPN; FL 1:2; GL 2; LAIT 2; LATS 1:1; LMFS 1; NFS 1, 14, 18, 20, 21; TEA; WLIT 3; WYAS 1

Auster, Paul 1947- .... **CLC 47, 131, 227**
See also AMWS 12; CA 69-72; CANR 23, 52, 75, 129; CMW 4; CN 5, 6, 7; DA3; DLB 227; MAL 5; MTCW 2; MTFW 2005; SUFW 2; TCLE 1:1

Austin, Frank
See Faust, Frederick (Schiller)

Austin, Mary (Hunter) 1868-1934 . **TCLC 25**
See also ANW; CA 109; 178; DLB 9, 78, 206, 221, 275; FW; TCWW 1, 2

Averroes 1126-1198 .... **CMLC 7**
See also DLB 115

Avicenna 980-1037 .... **CMLC 16**
See also DLB 115

Avison, Margaret (Kirkland) 1918- .. **CLC 2, 4, 97**
See also CA 17-20R; CANR 134; CP 1, 2, 3, 4, 5, 6, 7; DAC; DAM POET; DLB 53; MTCW 1

Axton, David
See Koontz, Dean R.

Ayckbourn, Alan 1939- ...... **CLC 5, 8, 18, 33, 74; DC 13**
See also BRWS 5; CA 21-24R; CANR 31, 59, 118; CBD; CD 5, 6; DAB; DAM DRAM; DFS 7; DLB 13, 245; EWL 3; MTCW 1, 2; MTFW 2005

Aydy, Catherine
See Tennant, Emma (Christina)

Ayme, Marcel (Andre) 1902-1967 ... **CLC 11; SSC 41**
See also CA 89-92; CANR 67, 137; CLR 25; DLB 72; EW 12; EWL 3; GFL 1789 to the Present; RGSF 2; RGWL 2, 3; SATA 91

Ayrton, Michael 1921-1975 .... **CLC 7**
See also CA 5-8R; 61-64; CANR 9, 21

Aytmatov, Chingiz
See Aitmatov, Chingiz (Torekulovich)
See also EWL 3

Azorin .... **CLC 11**
See Martinez Ruiz, Jose
See also DLB 322; EW 9; EWL 3

Azuela, Mariano 1873-1952 .. **HLC 1; TCLC 3, 145**
See also CA 104; 131; CANR 81; DAM MULT; EWL 3; HW 1, 2; LAW; MTCW 1, 2; MTFW 2005

Ba, Mariama 1929-1981 .... **BLCS**
See also AFW; BW 2; CA 141; CANR 87; DNFS 2; WLIT 2

Baastad, Babbis Friis
See Friis-Baastad, Babbis Ellinor

Bab
See Gilbert, W(illiam) S(chwenck)

Babbis, Eleanor
See Friis-Baastad, Babbis Ellinor

Babel, Isaac
See Babel, Isaak (Emmanuilovich)
See also EW 11; SSFS 10

Babel, Isaak (Emmanuilovich) 1894-1941(?) . **SSC 16, 78; TCLC 2, 13, 171**
See Babel, Isaac
See also CA 104; 155; CANR 113; DLB 272; EWL 3; MTCW 2; MTFW 2005; RGSF 2; RGWL 2, 3; TWA

Babits, Mihaly 1883-1941 .... **TCLC 14**
See also CA 114; CDWLB 4; DLB 215; EWL 3

Babur 1483-1530 .... **LC 18**

Babylas 1898-1962
See Ghelderode, Michel de

Baca, Jimmy Santiago 1952- . **HLC 1; PC 41**
See also CA 131; CANR 81, 90, 146; CP 6, 7; DAM MULT; DLB 122; HW 1, 2; LLW; MAL 5

Baca, Jose Santiago
See Baca, Jimmy Santiago

Bacchelli, Riccardo 1891-1985 .... **CLC 19**
See also CA 29-32R; 117; DLB 264; EWL 3

Bach, Richard 1936- .... **CLC 14**
See also AITN 1; BEST 89:2; BPFB 1; BYA 5; CA 9-12R; CANR 18, 93, 151; CPW; DAM NOV, POP; FANT; MTCW 1; SATA 13

Bach, Richard David
See Bach, Richard

Bache, Benjamin Franklin 1769-1798 .... **LC 74**
See also DLB 43

Bachelard, Gaston 1884-1962 ...... **TCLC 128**
See also CA 97-100; 89-92; DLB 296; GFL 1789 to the Present

Bachman, Richard
See King, Stephen

Bachmann, Ingeborg 1926-1973 .... **CLC 69**
See also CA 93-96; 45-48; CANR 69; DLB 85; EWL 3; RGHL; RGWL 2, 3

Bacon, Francis 1561-1626 ... **LC 18, 32, 131**
See also BRW 1; CDBLB Before 1660; DLB 151, 236, 252; RGEL 2; TEA

Bacon, Roger 1214(?)-1294 .... **CMLC 14**
See also DLB 115

Bacovia, George 1881-1957 .... **TCLC 24**
See Vasiliu, Gheorghe
See also CDWLB 4; DLB 220; EWL 3

Badanes, Jerome 1937-1995 .... **CLC 59**
See also CA 234

Bagehot, Walter 1826-1877 .... **NCLC 10**
See also DLB 55

Bagnold, Enid 1889-1981 .... **CLC 25**
See also BYA 2; CA 5-8R; 103; CANR 5, 40; CBD; CN 2; CWD; CWRI 5; DAM DRAM; DLB 13, 160, 191, 245; FW; MAICYA 1, 2; RGEL 2; SATA 1, 25

Bagritsky, Eduard .... **TCLC 60**
See Dzyubin, Eduard Georgievich

Bagrjana, Elisaveta
See Belcheva, Elisaveta Lyubomirova

Bagryana, Elisaveta .... **CLC 10**
See Belcheva, Elisaveta Lyubomirova
See also CA 178; CDWLB 4; DLB 147; EWL 3

Bailey, Paul 1937- .... **CLC 45**
See also CA 21-24R; CANR 16, 62, 124; CN 1, 2, 3, 4, 5, 6, 7; DLB 14, 271; GLL 2

Baillie, Joanna 1762-1851 ...... **NCLC 71, 151**
See also DLB 93; GL 2; RGEL 2

Bainbridge, Beryl 1934- ...... **CLC 4, 5, 8, 10, 14, 18, 22, 62, 130**
See also BRWS 6; CA 21-24R; CANR 24, 55, 75, 88, 128; CN 2, 3, 4, 5, 6, 7; DAM NOV; DLB 14, 231; EWL 3; MTCW 1, 2; MTFW 2005

Baker, Carlos (Heard) 1909-1987 .... **TCLC 119**
See also CA 5-8R; 122; CANR 3, 63; DLB 103

Baker, Elliott 1922- .... **CLC 8**
See also CA 45-48; CANR 2, 63; CN 1, 2, 3, 4, 5, 6, 7

Baker, Jean H. .... **TCLC 3, 10**
See Russell, George William

Baker, Nicholson 1957- .... **CLC 61, 165**
See also AMWS 13; CA 135; CANR 63, 120, 138; CN 6; CPW; DA3; DAM POP; DLB 227; MTFW 2005

Baker, Ray Stannard 1870-1946 .... **TCLC 47**
See also CA 118

Baker, Russell 1925- .... **CLC 31**
See also BEST 89:4; CA 57-60; CANR 11, 41, 59, 137; MTCW 1, 2; MTFW 2005

Bakhtin, M.
See Bakhtin, Mikhail Mikhailovich

Binchy, Maeve 1940- .... **CLC 153**
   See also BEST 90:1; BPFB 1; CA 127; 134;
   CANR 50, 96, 134; CN 5, 6, 7; CPW;
   DA3; DAM POP; DLB 319; INT CA-134;
   MTCW 2; MTFW 2005; RHW
Binyon, T(imothy) J(ohn)
   1936-2004 .... **CLC 34**
   See also CA 111; 232; CANR 28, 140
Bion 335B.C.-245B.C. .... **CMLC 39**
Bioy Casares, Adolfo 1914-1999 ... **CLC 4, 8,
   13, 88; HLC 1; SSC 17**
   See Casares, Adolfo Bioy; Miranda, Javier;
   Sacastru, Martin
   See also CA 29-32R; 177; CANR 19, 43,
   66; CWW 2; DAM MULT; DLB 113;
   EWL 3; HW 1, 2; LAW; MTCW 1, 2;
   MTFW 2005
Birch, Allison .... **CLC 65**
Bird, Cordwainer
   See Ellison, Harlan
Bird, Robert Montgomery
   1806-1854 .... **NCLC 1**
   See also DLB 202; RGAL 4
Birkerts, Sven 1951- .... **CLC 116**
   See also CA 128; 133; 176; CAAE 176;
   CAAS 29; CANR 151; INT CA-133
Birney, (Alfred) Earle 1904-1995 .. **CLC 1, 4,
   6, 11; PC 52**
   See also CA 1-4R; CANR 5, 20; CN 1, 2,
   3, 4; CP 1, 2, 3, 4, 5, 6; DAC; DAM MST;
   POET; DLB 88; MTCW 1; PFS 8; RGEL
   2
Biruni, al 973-1048(?) .... **CMLC 28**
Bishop, Elizabeth 1911-1979 ..... **CLC 1, 4, 9,
   13, 15, 32; PC 3, 34; TCLC 121**
   See also AMWR 2; AMWS 1; CA 5-8R;
   89-92; CABS 2; CANR 26, 61, 108;
   CDALB 1968-1988; CP 1, 2, 3; DA;
   DA3; DAC; DAM MST; DLB 5;
   169; EWL 3; GLL 2; MAL 5; MBL;
   MTCW 1, 2; PAB; PFS 6, 12; RGAL 4;
   SATA-Obit 24; TUS; WP
Bishop, John 1935- .... **CLC 10**
   See also CA 105
Bishop, John Peale 1892-1944 ..... **TCLC 103**
   See also CA 107; 155; DLB 4, 9, 45; MAL
   5; RGAL 4
Bissett, Bill 1939- .... **CLC 18; PC 14**
   See also CA 69-72; CAAS 19; CANR 15;
   CCA 1; CP 1, 2, 3, 4, 5, 6, 7; DLB 53;
   MTCW 1
Bissoondath, Neil (Devindra)
   1955- .... **CLC 120**
   See also CA 136; CANR 123; CN 6, 7;
   DAC
Bitov, Andrei (Georgievich) 1937- ... **CLC 57**
   See also CA 142; DLB 302
Biyidi, Alexandre 1932-
   See Beti, Mongo
   See also BW 1, 3; CA 114; 124; CANR 81;
   DA3; MTCW 1, 2
Bjarme, Brynjolf
   See Ibsen, Henrik (Johan)
Bjoernson, Bjoernstjerne (Martinius)
   1832-1910 .... **TCLC 7, 37**
   See also CA 104
Black, Benjamin
   See Banville, John
Black, Robert
   See Holdstock, Robert P.
Blackburn, Paul 1926-1971 .... **CLC 9, 43**
   See also BG 1:2; CA 81-84; 33-36R; CANR
   34; CP 1; DLB 16; DLBY 1981
Black Elk 1863-1950 .... **NNAL; TCLC 33**
   See also CA 144; DAM MULT; MTCW 2;
   MTFW 2005; WP
Black Hawk 1767-1838 .... **NNAL**
Black Hobart
   See Sanders, (James) Ed(ward)

Blacklin, Malcolm
   See Chambers, Aidan
Blackmore, R(ichard) D(oddridge)
   1825-1900 .... **TCLC 27**
   See also CA 120; DLB 18; RGEL 2
Blackmur, R(ichard) P(almer)
   1904-1965 .... **CLC 2, 24**
   See also AMWS 2; CA 11-12; 25-28R;
   CANR 71; CAP 1; DLB 63; EWL 3;
   MAL 5
Black Tarantula
   See Acker, Kathy
Blackwood, Algernon (Henry)
   1869-1951 .... **TCLC 5**
   See also CA 105; 150; DLB 153, 156, 178;
   HGG; SUFW 1
Blackwood, Caroline (Maureen)
   1931-1996 .... **CLC 6, 9, 100**
   See also BRWS 9; CA 85-88; 151; CANR
   32, 61, 65; CN 3, 4, 5, 6; DLB 14, 207;
   HGG; MTCW 1
Blade, Alexander
   See Hamilton, Edmond; Silverberg, Robert
Blaga, Lucian 1895-1961 .... **CLC 75**
   See also CA 157; DLB 220; EWL 3
Blair, Eric (Arthur) 1903-1950 .... **TCLC 123**
   See Orwell, George
   See also CA 104; 132; DA; DA3; DAB;
   DAC; DAM MST, NOV; MTCW 1, 2;
   MTFW 2005; SATA 29
Blair, Hugh 1718-1800 .... **NCLC 75**
Blais, Marie-Claire 1939- ... **CLC 2, 4, 6, 13,
   22**
   See also CA 21-24R; CAAS 4; CANR 38,
   75, 93; CWW 2; DAC; DAM MST; DLB
   53; EWL 3; FW; MTCW 1, 2; MTFW
   2005; TWA
Blaise, Clark 1940- .... **CLC 29**
   See also AITN 2; CA 53-56, 231; CAAE
   231; CAAS 3; CANR 5, 66, 106; CN 4,
   5, 6, 7; DLB 53; RGSF 2
Blake, Fairley
   See De Voto, Bernard (Augustine)
Blake, Nicholas
   See Day Lewis, C(ecil)
   See also DLB 77; MSW
Blake, Sterling
   See Benford, Gregory (Albert)
Blake, William 1757-1827 . **NCLC 13, 37, 57,
   127, 173; PC 12, 63; WLC 1**
   See also AAYA 47; BRW 3; BRWR 1; CD-
   BLB 1789-1832; CLR 52; DA; DA3;
   DAB; DAC; DAM MST, POET; DLB 93,
   163; EXPP; LATS 1:1; LMFS 1; MAI-
   CYA 1, 2; PAB; PFS 2, 12, 24; SATA 30;
   TEA; WCH; WLIT 3; WP
Blanchot, Maurice 1907-2003 .... **CLC 135**
   See also CA 117; 144; 213; CANR 138;
   DLB 72, 296; EWL 3
Blasco Ibanez, Vicente 1867-1928 . **TCLC 12**
   See Ibanez, Vicente Blasco
   See also BPFB 1; CA 110; 131; CANR 81;
   DA3; DAM NOV; EW 8; EWL 3; HW 1,
   2; MTCW 1
Blatty, William Peter 1928- .... **CLC 2**
   See also CA 5-8R; CANR 9, 124; DAM
   POP; HGG
Bleeck, Oliver
   See Thomas, Ross (Elmore)
Blessing, Lee (Knowlton) 1949- .... **CLC 54**
   See also CA 236; CAD; CD 5, 6; DFS 23
Blight, Rose
   See Greer, Germaine
Blish, James (Benjamin) 1921-1975 . **CLC 14**
   See also BPFB 1; CA 1-4R; 57-60; CANR
   3; CN 2; DLB 8; MTCW 1; SATA 66;
   SCFW 1, 2; SFW 4
Bliss, Frederick
   See Card, Orson Scott

Bliss, Reginald
   See Wells, H(erbert) G(eorge)
Blixen, Karen (Christentze Dinesen)
   1885-1962
   See Dinesen, Isak
   See also CA 25-28; CANR 22, 50; CAP 2;
   DA3; DLB 214; LMFS 1; MTCW 1, 2;
   SATA 44; SSFS 20
Bloch, Robert (Albert) 1917-1994 .... **CLC 33**
   See also AAYA 29; CA 5-8R, 179; 146;
   CAAE 179; CAAS 20; CANR 5, 78;
   DA3; DLB 44; HGG; INT CANR-5;
   MTCW 2; SATA 12; SATA-Obit 82; SFW
   4; SUFW 1, 2
Blok, Alexander (Alexandrovich)
   1880-1921 .... **PC 21; TCLC 5**
   See also CA 104; 183; DLB 295; EW 9;
   EWL 3; LMFS 2; RGWL 2, 3
Blom, Jan
   See Breytenbach, Breyten
Bloom, Harold 1930- .... **CLC 24, 103, 221**
   See also CA 13-16R; CANR 39, 75, 92,
   133; DLB 67; EWL 3; MTCW 2; MTFW
   2005; RGAL 4
Bloomfield, Aurelius
   See Bourne, Randolph S(illiman)
Bloomfield, Robert 1766-1823 ..... **NCLC 145**
   See also DLB 93
Blount, Roy (Alton), Jr. 1941- .... **CLC 38**
   See also CA 53-56; CANR 10, 28, 61, 125;
   CSW; INT CANR-28; MTCW 1, 2;
   MTFW 2005
Blowsnake, Sam 1875-(?) .... **NNAL**
Bloy, Leon 1846-1917 .... **TCLC 22**
   See also CA 121; 183; DLB 123; GFL 1789
   to the Present
Blue Cloud, Peter (Aroniawenrate)
   1933- .... **NNAL**
   See also CA 117; CANR 40; DAM MULT
Bluggage, Oranthy
   See Alcott, Louisa May
Blume, Judy (Sussman) 1938- .... **CLC 12, 30**
   See also AAYA 3, 26; BYA 1, 8, 12; CA 29-
   32R; CANR 13, 37, 66, 124; CLR 2, 15,
   69; CPW; DA3; DAM NOV, POP; DLB
   52; JRDA; MAICYA 1, 2; MAICYAS 1;
   MTCW 1, 2; MTFW 2005; NFS 24;
   SATA 2, 31, 79, 142; WYA; YAW
Blunden, Edmund (Charles)
   1896-1974 .... **CLC 2, 56; PC 66**
   See also BRW 6; BRWS 11; CA 17-18; 45-
   48; CANR 54; CAP 2; CP 1, 2; DLB 20,
   100, 155; MTCW 1; PAB
Bly, Robert (Elwood) 1926- .... **CLC 1, 2, 5,
   10, 15, 38, 128; PC 39**
   See also AMWS 4; CA 5-8R; CANR 41,
   73, 125; CP 1, 2, 3, 4, 5, 6, 7; DA3; DAM
   POET; DLB 5; EWL 3; MAL 5; MTCW
   1, 2; MTFW 2005; PFS 6, 17; RGAL 4
Boas, Franz 1858-1942 .... **TCLC 56**
   See also CA 115; 181
Bobette
   See Simenon, Georges (Jacques Christian)
Boccaccio, Giovanni 1313-1375 ... **CMLC 13,
   57; SSC 10, 87**
   See also EW 2; RGSF 2; RGWL 2, 3; TWA;
   WLIT 7
Bochco, Steven 1943- .... **CLC 35**
   See also AAYA 11, 71; CA 124; 138
Bode, Sigmund
   See O'Doherty, Brian
Bodel, Jean 1167(?)-1210 .... **CMLC 28**
Bodenheim, Maxwell 1892-1954 .... **TCLC 44**
   See also CA 110; 187; DLB 9, 45; MAL 5;
   RGAL 4
Bodenheimer, Maxwell
   See Bodenheim, Maxwell
Bodker, Cecil 1927-
   See Bodker, Cecil

Bodker, Cecil 1927- .... **CLC 21**
See also CA 73-76; CANR 13, 44, 111;
CLR 23; MAICYA 1, 2; SATA 14, 133

Boell, Heinrich (Theodor)
1917-1985 ..... **CLC 2, 3, 6, 9, 11, 15, 27,
32, 72; SSC 23; WLC 1**
See Boll, Heinrich (Theodor)
See also CA 21-24R; 116; CANR 24; DA;
DA3; DAB; DAC; DAM MST, NOV;
DLB 69; DLBY 1985; MTCW 1, 2;
MTFW 2005; SSFS 20; TWA

Boerne, Alfred
See Doeblin, Alfred

Boethius c. 480-c. 524 .... **CMLC 15**
See also DLB 115; RGWL 2, 3; WLIT 8

Boff, Leonardo (Genezio Darci)
1938- .... **CLC 70; HLC 1**
See also CA 150; DAM MULT; HW 2

Bogan, Louise 1897-1970 .... **CLC 4, 39, 46,
93; PC 12**
See also AMWS 3; CA 73-76; 25-28R;
CANR 33, 82; CP 1; DAM POET; DLB
45, 169; EWL 3; MAL 5; MBL; MTCW
1, 2; PFS 21; RGAL 4

Bogarde, Dirk
See Van Den Bogarde, Derek Jules Gaspard
Ulric Niven
See also DLB 14

Bogosian, Eric 1953- .... **CLC 45, 141**
See also CA 138; CAD; CANR 102, 148;
CD 5, 6

Bograd, Larry 1953- .... **CLC 35**
See also CA 93-96; CANR 57; SAAS 21;
SATA 33, 89; WYA

Boiardo, Matteo Maria 1441-1494 .... **LC 6**

Boileau-Despreaux, Nicolas 1636-1711 . **LC 3**
See also DLB 268; EW 3; GFL Beginnings
to 1789; RGWL 2, 3

Boissard, Maurice
See Leautaud, Paul

Bojer, Johan 1872-1959 .... **TCLC 64**
See also CA 189; EWL 3

Bok, Edward W(illiam)
1863-1930 .... **TCLC 101**
See also CA 217; DLB 91; DLBD 16

Boker, George Henry 1823-1890 . **NCLC 125**
See also RGAL 4

Boland, Eavan 1944- ... **CLC 40, 67, 113; PC
58**
See also BRWS 5; CA 143, 207; CAAE
207; CANR 61; CP 1, 6, 7; CWP; DAM
POET; DLB 40; FW; MTCW 2; MTFW
2005; PFS 12, 22

Boll, Heinrich (Theodor)
See Boell, Heinrich (Theodor)
See also BPFB 1; CDWLB 2; DLB 329;
EW 13; EWL 3; RGHL; RGSF 2; RGWL
2, 3

Bolt, Lee
See Faust, Frederick (Schiller)

Bolt, Robert (Oxton) 1924-1995 ...... **CLC 14;
TCLC 175**
See also CA 17-20R; 147; CANR 35, 67;
CBD; DAM DRAM; DFS 2; DLB 13,
233; EWL 3; LAIT 1; MTCW 1

Bombal, Maria Luisa 1910-1980 .... **HLCS 1;
SSC 37**
See also CA 127; CANR 72; EWL 3; HW
1; LAW; RGSF 2

Bombet, Louis-Alexandre-Cesar
See Stendhal

Bomkauf
See Kaufman, Bob (Garnell)

Bonaventura .... **NCLC 35**
See also DLB 90

Bonaventure 1217(?)-1274 .... **CMLC 79**
See also DLB 115; LMFS 1

Bond, Edward 1934- .... **CLC 4, 6, 13, 23**
See also AAYA 50; BRWS 1; CA 25-28R;
CANR 38, 67, 106; CBD; CD 5, 6; DAM
DRAM; DFS 3, 8; DLB 13, 310; EWL 3;
MTCW 1

Bonham, Frank 1914-1989 .... **CLC 12**
See also AAYA 1, 70; BYA 1, 3; CA 9-12R;
CANR 4, 36; JRDA; MAICYA 1, 2;
SAAS 3; SATA 1, 49; SATA-Obit 62;
TCWW 1, 2; YAW

Bonnefoy, Yves 1923- . **CLC 9, 15, 58; PC 58**
See also CA 85-88; CANR 33, 75, 97, 136;
CWW 2; DAM MST, POET; DLB 258;
EWL 3; GFL 1789 to the Present; MTCW
1, 2; MTFW 2005

Bonner, Marita . **HR 1:2; PC 72; TCLC 179**
See Occomy, Marita (Odette) Bonner

Bonnin, Gertrude 1876-1938 .... **NNAL**
See Zitkala-Sa
See also CA 150; DAM MULT

Bontemps, Arna(ud Wendell)
1902-1973 .. **BLC 1; CLC 1, 18; HR 1:2**
See also BW 1; CA 1-4R; 41-44R; CANR
4, 35; CLR 6; CP 1; CWRI 5; DA3; DAM
MULT, NOV, POET; DLB 48, 51; JRDA;
MAICYA 1, 2; MAL 5; MTCW 1, 2;
SATA 2, 44; SATA-Obit 24; WCH; WP

Boot, William
See Stoppard, Tom

Booth, Martin 1944-2004 .... **CLC 13**
See also CA 93-96, 188; 223; CAAE 188;
CAAS 2; CANR 92; CP 1, 2, 3, 4

Booth, Philip 1925- .... **CLC 23**
See also CA 5-8R; CANR 5, 88; CP 1, 2, 3,
4, 5, 6, 7; DLBY 1982

Booth, Wayne C. 1921-2005 .... **CLC 24**
See also CA 1-4R; 244; CAAS 5; CANR 3,
43, 117; DLB 67

Booth, Wayne Clayson
See Booth, Wayne C.

Borchert, Wolfgang 1921-1947 .... **TCLC 5**
See also CA 104; 188; DLB 69, 124; EWL
3

Borel, Petrus 1809-1859 .... **NCLC 41**
See also DLB 119; GFL 1789 to the Present

Borges, Jorge Luis 1899-1986 ... **CLC 1, 2, 3,
4, 6, 8, 9, 10, 13, 19, 44, 48, 83; HLC 1;
PC 22, 32; SSC 4, 41; TCLC 109;
WLC 1**
See also AAYA 26; BPFB 1; CA 21-24R;
CANR 19, 33, 75, 105, 133; CDWLB 3;
DA; DA3; DAB; DAC; DAM MST,
MULT; DLB 113, 283; DLBY 1986;
DNFS 1, 2; EWL 3; HW 1, 2; LAW;
LMFS 2; MSW; MTCW 1, 2; MTFW
2005; RGHL; RGSF 2; RGWL 2, 3; SFW
4; SSFS 17; TWA; WLIT 1

Borowski, Tadeusz 1922-1951 .... **SSC 48;
TCLC 9**
See also CA 106; 154; CDWLB 4; DLB
215; EWL 3; RGHL; RGSF 2; RGWL 3;
SSFS 13

Borrow, George (Henry)
1803-1881 .... **NCLC 9**
See also BRWS 12; DLB 21, 55, 166

Bosch (Gavino), Juan 1909-2001 ..... **HLCS 1**
See also CA 151; 204; DAM MST, MULT;
DLB 145; HW 1, 2

Bosman, Herman Charles
1905-1951 .... **TCLC 49**
See Malan, Herman
See also CA 160; DLB 225; RGSF 2

Bosschere, Jean de 1878(?)-1953 ... **TCLC 19**
See also CA 115; 186

Boswell, James 1740-1795 ... **LC 4, 50; WLC
1**
See also BRW 3; CDBLB 1660-1789; DA;
DAB; DAC; DAM MST; DLB 104, 142;
TEA; WLIT 3

Bottomley, Gordon 1874-1948 ..... **TCLC 107**
See also CA 120; 192; DLB 10

Bottoms, David 1949- .... **CLC 53**
See also CA 105; CANR 22; CSW; DLB
120; DLBY 1983

Boucicault, Dion 1820-1890 .... **NCLC 41**

Boucolon, Maryse
See Conde, Maryse

Bourdieu, Pierre 1930-2002 .... **CLC 198**
See also CA 130; 204

Bourget, Paul (Charles Joseph)
1852-1935 .... **TCLC 12**
See also CA 107; 196; DLB 123; GFL 1789
to the Present

Bourjaily, Vance (Nye) 1922- .... **CLC 8, 62**
See also CA 1-4R; CAAS 1; CANR 2, 72;
CN 1, 2, 3, 4, 5, 6, 7; DLB 2, 143; MAL
5

Bourne, Randolph S(illiman)
1886-1918 .... **TCLC 16**
See also AMW; CA 117; 155; DLB 63;
MAL 5

Bova, Ben 1932- .... **CLC 45**
See also AAYA 16; CA 5-8R; CAAS 18;
CANR 11, 56, 94, 111, 157; CLR 3, 96;
DLBY 1981; INT CANR-11; MAICYA 1,
2; MTCW 1; SATA 6, 68, 133; SFW 4

Bowen, Elizabeth (Dorothea Cole)
1899-1973 . **CLC 1, 3, 6, 11, 15, 22, 118;
SSC 3, 28, 66; TCLC 148**
See also BRWS 2; CA 17-18; 41-44R;
CANR 35, 105; CAP 2; CDBLB 1945-
1960; CN 1; DA3; DAM NOV; DLB 15,
162; EWL 3; EXPS; FW; HGG; MTCW
1, 2; MTFW 2005; NFS 13; RGSF 2;
SSFS 5, 22; SUFW 1; TEA; WLIT 4

Bowering, George 1935- .... **CLC 15, 47**
See also CA 21-24R; CAAS 16; CANR 10;
CN 7; CP 1, 2, 3, 4, 5, 6, 7; DLB 53

Bowering, Marilyn R(uthe) 1949- .... **CLC 32**
See also CA 101; CANR 49; CP 4, 5, 6, 7;
CWP

Bowers, Edgar 1924-2000 .... **CLC 9**
See also CA 5-8R; 188; CANR 24; CP 1, 2,
3, 4, 5, 6, 7; CSW; DLB 5

Bowers, Mrs. J. Milton 1842-1914
See Bierce, Ambrose (Gwinett)

Bowie, David .... **CLC 17**
See Jones, David Robert

Bowles, Jane (Sydney) 1917-1973 ..... **CLC 3,
68**
See Bowles, Jane Auer
See also CA 19-20; 41-44R; CAP 2; CN 1;
MAL 5

Bowles, Jane Auer
See Bowles, Jane (Sydney)
See also EWL 3

Bowles, Paul 1910-1999 ..... **CLC 1, 2, 19, 53;
SSC 3**
See also AMWS 4; CA 1-4R; 186; CAAS
1; CANR 1, 19, 50, 75; CN 1, 2, 3, 4, 5,
6; DA3; DLB 5, 6, 218; EWL 3; MAL 5;
MTCW 1, 2; MTFW 2005; RGAL 4;
SSFS 17

Bowles, William Lisle 1762-1850 . **NCLC 103**
See also DLB 93

Box, Edgar
See Vidal, Gore
See also GLL 1

Boyd, James 1888-1944 .... **TCLC 115**
See also CA 186; DLB 9; DLBD 16; RGAL
4; RHW

Boyd, Nancy
See Millay, Edna St. Vincent
See also GLL 1

Boyd, Thomas (Alexander)
1898-1935 .... **TCLC 111**
See also CA 111; 183; DLB 9; DLBD 16,
316

Boyd, William (Andrew Murray)
1952- .... **CLC 28, 53, 70**
See also CA 114; 120; CANR 51, 71, 131;
CN 4, 5, 6, 7; DLB 231

Boyesen, Hjalmar Hjorth
1848-1895 .... **NCLC 135**
See also DLB 12, 71; DLBD 13; RGAL 4

Boyle, Kay 1902-1992 .... **CLC 1, 5, 19, 58,
121; SSC 5**
See also CA 13-16R; 140; CAAS 1; CANR
29, 61, 110; CN 1, 2, 3, 4, 5; CP 1, 2, 3,
4, 5; DLB 4, 9, 48, 86; DLBY 1993; EWL
3; MAL 5; MTCW 1, 2; MTFW 2005;
RGAL 4; RGSF 2; SSFS 10, 13, 14

Boyle, Mark
See Kienzle, William X.

Boyle, Patrick 1905-1982 .... **CLC 19**
See also CA 127

Boyle, T. C.
See Boyle, T. Coraghessan
See also AMWS 8

Boyle, T. Coraghessan 1948- ..... **CLC 36, 55,
90; SSC 16**
See Boyle, T. C.
See also AAYA 47; BEST 90:4; BPFB 1;
CA 120; CANR 44, 76, 89, 132; CN 6, 7;
CPW; DA3; DAM POP; DLB 218, 278;
DLBY 1986; EWL 3; MAL 5; MTCW 2;
MTFW 2005; SSFS 13, 19

Boz
See Dickens, Charles (John Huffam)

Brackenridge, Hugh Henry
1748-1816 .... **NCLC 7**
See also DLB 11, 37; RGAL 4

Bradbury, Edward P.
See Moorcock, Michael
See also MTCW 2

Bradbury, Malcolm (Stanley)
1932-2000 .... **CLC 32, 61**
See also CA 1-4R; CANR 1, 33, 91, 98,
137; CN 1, 2, 3, 4, 5, 6, 7; CP 1; DA3;
DAM NOV; DLB 14, 207; EWL 3;
MTCW 1, 2; MTFW 2005

Bradbury, Ray 1920- ... **CLC 1, 3, 10, 15, 42,
98; SSC 29, 53; WLC 1**
See also AAYA 15; AITN 1, 2; AMWS 4;
BPFB 1; BYA 4, 5, 11; CA 1-4R; CANR
2, 30, 75, 125; CDALB 1968-1988; CN
1, 2, 3, 4, 5, 6, 7; CPW; DA; DA3; DAB;
DAC; DAM MST, NOV, POP; DLB 2, 8;
EXPN; EXPS; HGG; LAIT 3, 5; LATS
1:2; LMFS 2; MAL 5; MTCW 1, 2;
MTFW 2005; NFS 1, 22; RGAL 4; RGSF
2; SATA 11, 64, 123; SCFW 1, 2; SFW 4;
SSFS 1, 20; SUFW 1, 2; TUS; YAW

Braddon, Mary Elizabeth
1837-1915 .... **TCLC 111**
See also BRWS 8; CA 108; 179; CMW 4;
DLB 18, 70, 156; HGG

Bradfield, Scott 1955- .... **SSC 65**
See also CA 147; CANR 90; HGG; SUFW
2

Bradfield, Scott Michael
See Bradfield, Scott

Bradford, Gamaliel 1863-1932 .... **TCLC 36**
See also CA 160; DLB 17

Bradford, William 1590-1657 .... **LC 64**
See also DLB 24, 30; RGAL 4

Bradley, David (Henry), Jr. 1950- .... **BLC 1;
CLC 23, 118**
See also BW 1, 3; CA 104; CANR 26, 81;
CN 4, 5, 6, 7; DAM MULT; DLB 33

Bradley, John Ed 1958- .... **CLC 55**
See also CA 139; CANR 99; CN 6, 7; CSW

Bradley, John Edmund, Jr.
See Bradley, John Ed

Bradley, Marion Zimmer
1930-1999 .... **CLC 30**
See Chapman, Lee; Dexter, John; Gardner,
Miriam; Ives, Morgan; Rivers, Elfrida
See also AAYA 40; BPFB 1; CA 57-60; 185;
CAAS 10; CANR 7, 31, 51, 75, 107;
CPW; DA3; DAM POP; DLB 8; FANT;
FW; MTCW 1, 2; MTFW 2005; SATA 90,
139; SATA-Obit 116; SFW 4; SUFW 2;
YAW

Bradshaw, John 1933- .... **CLC 70**
See also CA 138; CANR 61

Bradstreet, Anne 1612(?)-1672 .... **LC 4, 30,
130; PC 10**
See also AMWS 1; CDALB 1640-1865;
DA; DA3; DAC; DAM MST, POET; DLB
24; EXPP; FW; PFS 6; RGAL 4; TUS;
WP

Brady, Joan 1939- .... **CLC 86**
See also CA 141

Bragg, Melvyn 1939- .... **CLC 10**
See also BEST 89:3; CA 57-60; CANR 10,
48, 89; CN 1, 2, 3, 4, 5, 6, 7; DLB 14,
271; RHW

Brahe, Tycho 1546-1601 .... **LC 45**
See also DLB 300

Braine, John (Gerard) 1922-1986 . **CLC 1, 3,
41**
See also CA 1-4R; 120; CANR 1, 33; CD-
BLB 1945-1960; CN 1, 2, 3, 4; DLB 15;
DLBY 1986; EWL 3; MTCW 1

Braithwaite, William Stanley (Beaumont)
1878-1962 .... **BLC 1; HR 1:2; PC 52**
See also BW 1; CA 125; DAM MULT; DLB
50, 54; MAL 5

Bramah, Ernest 1868-1942 .... **TCLC 72**
See also CA 156; CMW 4; DLB 70; FANT

Brammer, Billy Lee
See Brammer, William

Brammer, William 1929-1978 .... **CLC 31**
See also CA 235; 77-80

Brancati, Vitaliano 1907-1954 .... **TCLC 12**
See also CA 109; DLB 264; EWL 3

Brancato, Robin F(idler) 1936- .... **CLC 35**
See also AAYA 9, 68; BYA 6; CA 69-72;
CANR 11, 45; CLR 32; JRDA; MAICYA
2; MAICYAS 1; SAAS 9; SATA 97;
WYA; YAW

Brand, Dionne 1953- .... **CLC 192**
See also BW 2; CA 143; CANR 143; CWP

Brand, Max
See Faust, Frederick (Schiller)
See also BPFB 1; TCWW 1, 2

Brand, Millen 1906-1980 .... **CLC 7**
See also CA 21-24R; 97-100; CANR 72

Branden, Barbara .... **CLC 44**
See also CA 148

Brandes, Georg (Morris Cohen)
1842-1927 .... **TCLC 10**
See also CA 105; 189; DLB 300

Brandys, Kazimierz 1916-2000 .... **CLC 62**
See also CA 239; EWL 3

Branley, Franklyn M(ansfield)
1915-2002 .... **CLC 21**
See also CA 33-36R; 207; CANR 14, 39;
CLR 13; MAICYA 1, 2; SAAS 16; SATA
4, 68, 136

Brant, Beth (E.) 1941- .... **NNAL**
See also CA 144; FW

Brant, Sebastian 1457-1521 .... **LC 112**
See also DLB 179; RGWL 2, 3

Brathwaite, Edward Kamau
1930- .... **BLCS; CLC 11; PC 56**
See also BRWS 12; BW 2, 3; CA 25-28R;
CANR 11, 26, 47, 107; CDWLB 3; CP 1,
2, 3, 4, 5, 6, 7; DAM POET; DLB 125;
EWL 3

Brathwaite, Kamau
See Brathwaite, Edward Kamau

Brautigan, Richard (Gary)
1935-1984 .... **CLC 1, 3, 5, 9, 12, 34, 42;
TCLC 133**
See also BPFB 1; CA 53-56; 113; CANR
34; CN 1, 2, 3; CP 1, 2, 3, 4; DAM
NOV; DLB 2, 5, 206; DLBY 1980, 1984;
FANT; MAL 5; MTCW 1; RGAL 4;
SATA 56

Brave Bird, Mary .... **NNAL**
See Crow Dog, Mary

Braverman, Kate 1950- .... **CLC 67**
See also CA 89-92; CANR 141

Brecht, (Eugen) Bertolt (Friedrich)
1898-1956 ..... **DC 3; TCLC 1, 6, 13, 35,
169; WLC 1**
See also CA 104; 133; CANR 62; CDWLB
2; DA; DA3; DAB; DAC; DAM DRAM,
MST; DFS 4, 5, 9; DLB 56, 124; EW 11;
EWL 3; IDTP; MTCW 1, 2; MTFW 2005;
RGHL; RGWL 2, 3; TWA

Brecht, Eugen Berthold Friedrich
See Brecht, (Eugen) Bertolt (Friedrich)

Bremer, Fredrika 1801-1865 .... **NCLC 11**
See also DLB 254

Brennan, Christopher John
1870-1932 .... **TCLC 17**
See also CA 117; 188; DLB 230; EWL 3

Brennan, Maeve 1917-1993 ... **CLC 5; TCLC
124**
See also CA 81-84; CANR 72, 100

Brenner, Jozef 1887-1919
See Csath, Geza
See also CA 240

Brent, Linda
See Jacobs, Harriet A(nn)

Brentano, Clemens (Maria)
1778-1842 .... **NCLC 1**
See also DLB 90; RGWL 2, 3

Brent of Bin Bin
See Franklin, (Stella Maria Sarah) Miles
(Lampe)

Brenton, Howard 1942- .... **CLC 31**
See also CA 69-72; CANR 33, 67; CBD;
CD 5, 6; DLB 13; MTCW 1

Breslin, James 1930-
See Breslin, Jimmy
See also CA 73-76; CANR 31, 75, 139;
DAM NOV; MTCW 1, 2; MTFW 2005

Breslin, Jimmy .... **CLC 4, 43**
See Breslin, James
See also AITN 1; DLB 185; MTCW 2

Bresson, Robert 1901(?)-1999 .... **CLC 16**
See also CA 110; 187; CANR 49

Breton, Andre 1896-1966 .. **CLC 2, 9, 15, 54;
PC 15**
See also CA 19-20; 25-28R; CANR 40, 60;
CAP 2; DLB 65, 258; EW 11; EWL 3;
GFL 1789 to the Present; LMFS 2;
MTCW 1, 2; MTFW 2005; RGWL 2, 3;
TWA; WP

Breton, Nicholas c. 1554-c. 1626 .... **LC 133**
See also DLB 136

Breytenbach, Breyten 1939(?)- .. **CLC 23, 37,
126**
See also CA 113; 129; CANR 61, 122;
CWW 2; DAM POET; DLB 225; EWL 3

Bridgers, Sue Ellen 1942- .... **CLC 26**
See also AAYA 8, 49; BYA 7, 8; CA 65-68;
CANR 11, 36; CLR 18; DLB 52; JRDA;
MAICYA 1, 2; SAAS 1; SATA 22, 90;
SATA-Essay 109; WYA; YAW

Bridges, Robert (Seymour)
1844-1930 .... **PC 28; TCLC 1**
See also BRW 6; CA 104; 152; CDBLB
1890-1914; DAM POET; DLB 19, 98

Bridie, James .... **TCLC 3**
See Mavor, Osborne Henry
See also DLB 10; EWL 3

Brown, William Hill 1765-1793 .... **LC 93**
See also DLB 37

Brown, William Wells 1815-1884 ...... **BLC 1;
DC 1; NCLC 2, 89**
See also DAM MULT; DLB 3, 50, 183,
248; RGAL 4

Browne, (Clyde) Jackson 1948(?)- ... **CLC 21**
See also CA 120

Browne, Sir Thomas 1605-1682 .... **LC 111**
See also BRW 2; DLB 151

Browning, Robert 1812-1889 . **NCLC 19, 79;
PC 2, 61; WLCS**
See also BRW 4; BRWC 2; BRWR 2; CD-
BLB 1832-1890; CLR 97; DA; DA3;
DAB; DAC; DAM MST, POET; DLB 32,
163; EXPP; LATS 1:1; PAB; PFS 1, 15;
RGEL 2; TEA; WLIT 4; WP; YABC 1

Browning, Tod 1882-1962 .... **CLC 16**
See also CA 141; 117

Brownmiller, Susan 1935- .... **CLC 159**
See also CA 103; CANR 35, 75, 137; DAM
NOV; FW; MTCW 1, 2; MTFW 2005

Brownson, Orestes Augustus
1803-1876 .... **NCLC 50**
See also DLB 1, 59, 73, 243

Bruccoli, Matthew J(oseph) 1931- ... **CLC 34**
See also CA 9-12R; CANR 7, 87; DLB 103

Bruce, Lenny .... **CLC 21**
See Schneider, Leonard Alfred

Bruchac, Joseph 1942- .... **NNAL**
See also AAYA 19; CA 33-36R; CANR 13,
47, 75, 94, 137; CLR 46; CWRI 5; DAM
MULT; JRDA; MAICYA 2; MAICYAS 1;
MTCW 2; MTFW 2005; SATA 42, 89,
131, 172

Bruin, John
See Brutus, Dennis

Brulard, Henri
See Stendhal

Brulls, Christian
See Simenon, Georges (Jacques Christian)

Brunetto Latini c. 1220-1294 .... **CMLC 73**

Brunner, John (Kilian Houston)
1934-1995 .... **CLC 8, 10**
See also CA 1-4R; 149; CAAS 8; CANR 2,
37; CPW; DAM POP; DLB 261; MTCW
1, 2; SCFW 1, 2; SFW 4

Bruno, Giordano 1548-1600 .... **LC 27**
See also RGWL 2, 3

Brutus, Dennis 1924- ... **BLC 1; CLC 43; PC
24**
See also AFW; BW 2, 3; CA 49-52; CAAS
14; CANR 2, 27, 42, 81; CDWLB 3; CP
1, 2, 3, 4, 5, 6, 7; DAM MULT, POET;
DLB 117, 225; EWL 3

Bryan, C(ourtlandt) D(ixon) B(arnes)
1936- .... **CLC 29**
See also CA 73-76; CANR 13, 68; DLB
185; INT CANR-13

Bryan, Michael
See Moore, Brian
See also CCA 1

Bryan, William Jennings
1860-1925 .... **TCLC 99**
See also DLB 303

Bryant, William Cullen 1794-1878 . **NCLC 6,
46; PC 20**
See also AMWS 1; CDALB 1640-1865;
DA; DAB; DAC; DAM MST, POET;
DLB 3, 43, 59, 189, 250; EXPP; PAB;
RGAL 4; TUS

Bryusov, Valery Yakovlevich
1873-1924 .... **TCLC 10**
See also CA 107; 155; EWL 3; SFW 4

Buchan, John 1875-1940 .... **TCLC 41**
See also CA 108; 145; CMW 4; DAB;
DAM POP; DLB 34, 70, 156; HGG;
MSW; MTCW 2; RGEL 2; RHW; YABC
2

Buchanan, George 1506-1582 .... **LC 4**
See also DLB 132

Buchanan, Robert 1841-1901 .... **TCLC 107**
See also CA 179; DLB 18, 35

Buchheim, Lothar-Guenther 1918- .... **CLC 6**
See also CA 85-88

Buchner, (Karl) Georg
1813-1837 .... **NCLC 26, 146**
See also CDWLB 2; DLB 133; EW 6;
RGSF 2; RGWL 2, 3; TWA

Buchwald, Art 1925- .... **CLC 33**
See also AITN 1; CA 5-8R; CANR 21, 67,
107; MTCW 1, 2; SATA 10

Buchwald, Arthur
See Buchwald, Art

Buck, Pearl S(ydenstricker)
1892-1973 .... **CLC 7, 11, 18, 127**
See also AAYA 42; AITN 1; AMWS 2;
BPFB 1; CA 1-4R; 41-44R; CANR 1, 34;
CDALBS; CN 1; DA; DA3; DAB; DAC;
DAM MST, NOV; DLB 9, 102, 329; EWL
3; LAIT 3; MAL 5; MTCW 1, 2; MTFW
2005; RGAL 4; RHW; SATA 1, 25; TUS

Buckler, Ernest 1908-1984 .... **CLC 13**
See also CA 11-12; 114; CAP 1; CCA 1;
CN 1, 2, 3; DAC; DAM MST; DLB 68;
SATA 47

Buckley, Christopher 1952- .... **CLC 165**
See also CA 139; CANR 119

Buckley, Christopher Taylor
See Buckley, Christopher

Buckley, Vincent (Thomas)
1925-1988 .... **CLC 57**
See also CA 101; CP 1, 2, 3, 4; DLB 289

Buckley, William F., Jr. 1925- ..... **CLC 7, 18,
37**
See also AITN 1; BPFB 1; CA 1-4R; CANR
1, 24, 53, 93, 133; CMW 4; CPW; DA3;
DAM POP; DLB 137; DLBY 1980; INT
CANR-24; MTCW 1, 2; MTFW 2005;
TUS

Buechner, Frederick 1926- ..... **CLC 2, 4, 6, 9**
See also AMWS 12; BPFB 1; CA 13-16R;
CANR 11, 39, 64, 114, 138; CN 1, 2, 3,
4, 5, 6, 7; DAM NOV; DLBY 1980; INT
CANR-11; MAL 5; MTCW 1, 2; MTFW
2005; TCLE 1:1

Buell, John (Edward) 1927- .... **CLC 10**
See also CA 1-4R; CANR 71; DLB 53

Buero Vallejo, Antonio 1916-2000 ... **CLC 15,
46, 139, 226; DC 18**
See also CA 106; 189; CANR 24, 49, 75;
CWW 2; DFS 11; EWL 3; HW 1; MTCW
1, 2

Bufalino, Gesualdo 1920-1996 .... **CLC 74**
See also CA 209; CWW 2; DLB 196

Bugayev, Boris Nikolayevich
1880-1934 .... **PC 11; TCLC 7**
See Bely, Andrey; Belyi, Andrei
See also CA 104; 165; MTCW 2; MTFW
2005

Bukowski, Charles 1920-1994 ... **CLC 2, 5, 9,
41, 82, 108; PC 18; SSC 45**
See also CA 17-20R; 144; CANR 40, 62,
105; CN 4, 5; CP 1, 2, 3, 4, 5; CPW; DA3;
DAM NOV, POET; DLB 5, 130, 169;
EWL 3; MAL 5; MTCW 1, 2; MTFW
2005

Bulgakov, Mikhail 1891-1940 .... **SSC 18;
TCLC 2, 16, 159**
See also BPFB 1; CA 105; 152; DAM
DRAM, NOV; DLB 272; EWL 3; MTCW
2; MTFW 2005; NFS 8; RGSF 2; RGWL
2, 3; SFW 4; TWA

Bulgakov, Mikhail Afanasevich
See Bulgakov, Mikhail

Bulgya, Alexander Alexandrovich
1901-1956 .... **TCLC 53**
See Fadeev, Aleksandr Aleksandrovich;
Fadeev, Alexandr Alexandrovich; Fadeyev,
Alexander
See also CA 117; 181

Bullins, Ed 1935- ... **BLC 1; CLC 1, 5, 7; DC
6**
See also BW 2, 3; CA 49-52; CAAS 16;
CAD; CANR 24, 46, 73, 134; CD 5, 6;
DAM DRAM, MULT; DLB 7, 38, 249;
EWL 3; MAL 5; MTCW 1, 2; MTFW
2005; RGAL 4

Bulosan, Carlos 1911-1956 .... **AAL**
See also CA 216; DLB 312; RGAL 4

**Bulwer-Lytton, Edward (George Earle
Lytton)** 1803-1873 .... **NCLC 1, 45**
See also DLB 21; RGEL 2; SFW 4; SUFW
1; TEA

Bunin, Ivan
See Bunin, Ivan Alexeyevich

Bunin, Ivan Alekseevich
See Bunin, Ivan Alexeyevich

Bunin, Ivan Alexeyevich 1870-1953 ... **SSC 5;
TCLC 6**
See also CA 104; DLB 317, 329; EWL 3;
RGSF 2; RGWL 2, 3; TWA

Bunting, Basil 1900-1985 ...... **CLC 10, 39, 47**
See also BRWS 7; CA 53-56; 115; CANR
7; CP 1, 2, 3, 4; DAM POET; DLB 20;
EWL 3; RGEL 2

Bunuel, Luis 1900-1983 ... **CLC 16, 80; HLC
1**
See also CA 101; 110; CANR 32, 77; DAM
MULT; HW 1

Bunyan, John 1628-1688 .. **LC 4, 69; WLC 1**
See also BRW 2; BYA 5; CDBLB 1660-
1789; DA; DAB; DAC; DAM MST; DLB
39; RGEL 2; TEA; WCH; WLIT 3

Buravsky, Alexandr .... **CLC 59**

Burckhardt, Jacob (Christoph)
1818-1897 .... **NCLC 49**
See also EW 6

Burford, Eleanor
See Hibbert, Eleanor Alice Burford

Burgess, Anthony . **CLC 1, 2, 4, 5, 8, 10, 13,
15, 22, 40, 62, 81, 94**
See Wilson, John (Anthony) Burgess
See also AAYA 25; AITN 1; BRWS 1; CD-
BLB 1960 to Present; CN 1, 2, 3, 4, 5;
DAB; DLB 14, 194, 261; DLBY 1998;
EWL 3; RGEL 2; RHW; SFW 4; YAW

Burke, Edmund 1729(?)-1797 .... **LC 7, 36;
WLC 1**
See also BRW 3; DA; DA3; DAB; DAC;
DAM MST; DLB 104, 252; RGEL 2;
TEA

Burke, Kenneth (Duva) 1897-1993 ... **CLC 2,
24**
See also AMW; CA 5-8R; 143; CANR 39,
74, 136; CN 1, 2; CP 1, 2, 3, 4, 5; DLB
45, 63; EWL 3; MAL 5; MTCW 1, 2;
MTFW 2005; RGAL 4

Burke, Leda
See Garnett, David

Burke, Ralph
See Silverberg, Robert

Burke, Thomas 1886-1945 .... **TCLC 63**
See also CA 113; 155; CMW 4; DLB 197

Burney, Fanny 1752-1840 .... **NCLC 12, 54,
107**
See also BRWS 3; DLB 39; FL 1:2; NFS
16; RGEL 2; TEA

Burney, Frances
See Burney, Fanny

Collingwood, R(obin) G(eorge)
1889(?)-1943 .... **TCLC 67**
See also CA 117; 155; DLB 262

Collins, Billy 1941- .... **PC 68**
See also AAYA 64; CA 151; CANR 92; CP
7; MTFW 2005; PFS 18

Collins, Hunt
See Hunter, Evan

Collins, Linda 1931- .... **CLC 44**
See also CA 125

Collins, Tom
See Furphy, Joseph
See also RGEL 2

Collins, (William) Wilkie
1824-1889 .... **NCLC 1, 18, 93; SSC 93**
See also BRWS 6; CDBLB 1832-1890;
CMW 4; DLB 18, 70, 159; GL 2; MSW;
RGEL 2; RGSF 2; SUFW 1; WLIT 4

Collins, William 1721-1759 ...... **LC 4, 40; PC**
72
See also BRW 3; DAM POET; DLB 109;
RGEL 2

Collodi, Carlo .... **NCLC 54**
See Lorenzini, Carlo
See also CLR 5, 120; WCH; WLIT 7

Colman, George
See Glassco, John

Colman, George, the Elder
1732-1794 .... **LC 98**
See also RGEL 2

Colonna, Vittoria 1492-1547 .... **LC 71**
See also RGWL 2, 3

Colt, Winchester Remington
See Hubbard, L. Ron

Colter, Cyrus J. 1910-2002 .... **CLC 58**
See also BW 1; CA 65-68; 205; CANR 10,
66; CN 2, 3, 4, 5, 6; DLB 33

Colton, James
See Hansen, Joseph
See also GLL 1

Colum, Padraic 1881-1972 .... **CLC 28**
See also BYA 4; CA 73-76; 33-36R; CANR
35; CLR 36; CP 1; CWRI 5; DLB 19;
MAICYA 1, 2; MTCW 1; RGEL 2; SATA
15; WCH

Colvin, James
See Moorcock, Michael

Colwin, Laurie (E.) 1944-1992 .... **CLC 5, 13,**
23, 84
See also CA 89-92; 139; CANR 20, 46;
DLB 218; DLBY 1980; MTCW 1

Comfort, Alex(ander) 1920-2000 .... **CLC 7**
See also CA 1-4R; 190; CANR 1, 45; CN
1, 2, 3, 4; CP 1, 2, 3, 4, 5, 6, 7; DAM
POP; MTCW 2

Comfort, Montgomery
See Campbell, (John) Ramsey

Compton-Burnett, I(vy)
1892(?)-1969 .... **CLC 1, 3, 10, 15, 34;**
TCLC 180
See also BRW 7; CA 1-4R; 25-28R; CANR
4; DAM NOV; DLB 36; EWL 3; MTCW
1, 2; RGEL 2

Comstock, Anthony 1844-1915 ...... **TCLC 13**
See also CA 110; 169

Comte, Auguste 1798-1857 .... **NCLC 54**

Conan Doyle, Arthur
See Doyle, Sir Arthur Conan
See also BPFB 1; BYA 4, 5, 11

Conde (Abellan), Carmen
1901-1996 .... **HLCS 1**
See also CA 177; CWW 2; DLB 108; EWL
3; HW 2

Conde, Maryse 1937- ..... **BLCS; CLC 52, 92**
See also BW 2, 3; CA 110, 190; CAAE 190;
CANR 30, 53, 76; CWW 2; DAM MULT;
EWL 3; MTCW 2; MTFW 2005

Condillac, Etienne Bonnot de
1714-1780 .... **LC 26**
See also DLB 313

Condon, Richard (Thomas)
1915-1996 .... **CLC 4, 6, 8, 10, 45, 100**
See also BEST 90:3; BPFB 1; CA 1-4R;
151; CAAS 1; CANR 2, 23; CMW 4; CN
1, 2, 3, 4, 5, 6; DAM NOV; INT CANR-
23; MAL 5; MTCW 1, 2

Condorcet .... **LC 104**
See Condorcet, marquis de Marie-Jean-
Antoine-Nicolas Caritat
See also GFL Beginnings to 1789

Condorcet, marquis de
Marie-Jean-Antoine-Nicolas Caritat
1743-1794
See Condorcet
See also DLB 313

Confucius 551B.C.-479B.C. .... **CMLC 19, 65;**
WLCS
See also DA; DA3; DAB; DAC; DAM
MST

Congreve, William 1670-1729 ... **DC 2; LC 5,**
21; WLC 2
See also BRW 2; CDBLB 1660-1789; DA;
DAB; DAC; DAM DRAM, MST, POET;
DFS 15; DLB 39, 84; RGEL 2; WLIT 3

Conley, Robert J(ackson) 1940- .... **NNAL**
See also CA 41-44R; CANR 15, 34, 45, 96;
DAM MULT; TCWW 2

Connell, Evan S., Jr. 1924- .... **CLC 4, 6, 45**
See also AAYA 7; AMWS 14; CA 1-4R;
CAAS 2; CANR 2, 39, 76, 97, 140; CN
1, 2, 3, 4, 5, 6; DAM NOV; DLB 2;
DLBY 1981; MAL 5; MTCW 1, 2;
MTFW 2005

Connelly, Marc(us Cook) 1890-1980 . **CLC 7**
See also CA 85-88; 102; CAD; CANR 30;
DFS 12; DLB 7; DLBY 1980; MAL 5;
RGAL 4; SATA-Obit 25

Connor, Ralph .... **TCLC 31**
See Gordon, Charles William
See also DLB 92; TCWW 1, 2

Conrad, Joseph 1857-1924 ..... **SSC 9, 67, 69,**
71; TCLC 1, 6, 13, 25, 43, 57; WLC 2
See also AAYA 26; BPFB 1; BRW 6;
BRWC 1; BRWR 2; BYA 2; CA 104; 131;
CANR 60; CDBLB 1890-1914; DA; DA3;
DAB; DAC; DAM MST, NOV; DLB 10,
34, 98, 156; EWL 3; EXPN; EXPS; LAIT
2; LATS 1:1; LMFS 1; MTCW 1, 2;
MTFW 2005; NFS 2, 16; RGEL 2; RGSF
2; SATA 27; SSFS 1, 12; TEA; WLIT 4

Conrad, Robert Arnold
See Hart, Moss

Conroy, Pat 1945- .... **CLC 30, 74**
See also AAYA 8, 52; AITN 1; BPFB 1;
CA 85-88; CANR 24, 53, 129; CN 7;
CPW; CSW; DA3; DAM NOV, POP;
DLB 6; LAIT 5; MAL 5; MTCW 1, 2;
MTFW 2005

Constant (de Rebecque), (Henri) Benjamin
1767-1830 .... **NCLC 6**
See also DLB 119; EW 4; GFL 1789 to the
Present

Conway, Jill K(er) 1934- .... **CLC 152**
See also CA 130; CANR 94

Conybeare, Charles Augustus
See Eliot, T(homas) S(tearns)

Cook, Michael 1933-1994 .... **CLC 58**
See also CA 93-96; CANR 68; DLB 53

Cook, Robin 1940- .... **CLC 14**
See also AAYA 32; BEST 90:2; BPFB 1;
CA 108; 111; CANR 41, 90, 109; CPW;
DA3; DAM POP; HGG; INT CA-111

Cook, Roy
See Silverberg, Robert

Cooke, Elizabeth 1948- .... **CLC 55**
See also CA 129

Cooke, John Esten 1830-1886 .... **NCLC 5**
See also DLB 3, 248; RGAL 4

Cooke, John Estes
See Baum, L(yman) Frank

Cooke, M. E.
See Creasey, John

Cooke, Margaret
See Creasey, John

Cooke, Rose Terry 1827-1892 ...... **NCLC 110**
See also DLB 12, 74

Cook-Lynn, Elizabeth 1930- .... **CLC 93;**
NNAL
See also CA 133; DAM MULT; DLB 175

Cooney, Ray .... **CLC 62**
See also CBD

Cooper, Anthony Ashley 1671-1713 .. **LC 107**
See also DLB 101

Cooper, Dennis 1953- .... **CLC 203**
See also CA 133; CANR 72, 86; GLL 1;
HGG

Cooper, Douglas 1960- .... **CLC 86**

Cooper, Henry St. John
See Creasey, John

Cooper, J. California (?)- .... **CLC 56**
See also AAYA 12; BW 1; CA 125; CANR
55; DAM MULT; DLB 212

Cooper, James Fenimore
1789-1851 .... **NCLC 1, 27, 54**
See also AAYA 22; AMW; BPFB 1;
CDALB 1640-1865; CLR 105; DA3;
DLB 3, 183, 250, 254; LAIT 1; NFS 9;
RGAL 4; SATA 19; TUS; WCH

Cooper, Susan Fenimore
1813-1894 .... **NCLC 129**
See also ANW; DLB 239, 254

Coover, Robert 1932- .. **CLC 3, 7, 15, 32, 46,**
87, 161; SSC 15
See also AMWS 5; BPFB 1; CA 45-48;
CANR 3, 37, 58, 115; CN 1, 2, 3, 4, 5, 6,
7; DAM NOV; DLB 2, 227; DLBY 1981;
EWL 3; MAL 5; MTCW 1, 2; MTFW
2005; RGAL 4; RGSF 2

Copeland, Stewart (Armstrong)
1952- .... **CLC 26**

Copernicus, Nicolaus 1473-1543 .... **LC 45**

Coppard, A(lfred) E(dgar)
1878-1957 .... **SSC 21; TCLC 5**
See also BRWS 8; CA 114; 167; DLB 162;
EWL 3; HGG; RGEL 2; RGSF 2; SUFW
1; YABC 1

Coppee, Francois 1842-1908 .... **TCLC 25**
See also CA 170; DLB 217

Coppola, Francis Ford 1939- ... **CLC 16, 126**
See also AAYA 39; CA 77-80; CANR 40,
78; DLB 44

Copway, George 1818-1869 .... **NNAL**
See also DAM MULT; DLB 175, 183

Corbiere, Tristan 1845-1875 .... **NCLC 43**
See also DLB 217; GFL 1789 to the Present

Corcoran, Barbara (Asenath)
1911- .... **CLC 17**
See also AAYA 14; CA 21-24R; 191; CAAE
191; CAAS 2; CANR 11, 28, 48; CLR
50; DLB 52; JRDA; MAICYA 2; MAIC-
YAS 1; RHW; SAAS 20; SATA 3, 77;
SATA-Essay 125

Cordelier, Maurice
See Giraudoux, Jean(-Hippolyte)

Corelli, Marie .... **TCLC 51**
See Mackay, Mary
See also DLB 34, 156; RGEL 2; SUFW 1

Corinna c. 225B.C.-c. 305B.C. ...... **CMLC 72**

Corman, Cid .... **CLC 9**
See Corman, Sidney
See also CAAS 2; CP 1, 2, 3, 4, 5, 6, 7;
DLB 5, 193

Corman, Sidney 1924-2004
See Corman, Cid
See also CA 85-88; 225; CANR 44; DAM POET

Cormier, Robert 1925-2000 .... **CLC 12, 30**
See also AAYA 3, 19; BYA 1, 2, 6, 8, 9; CA 1-4R; CANR 5, 23, 76, 93; CDALB 1968-1988; CLR 12, 55; DA; DAB; DAC; DAM MST, NOV; DLB 52; EXPN; INT CANR-23; JRDA; LAIT 5; MAICYA 1, 2; MTCW 1, 2; MTFW 2005; NFS 2, 18; SATA 10, 45, 83; SATA-Obit 122; WYA; YAW

Corn, Alfred (DeWitt III) 1943- .... **CLC 33**
See also CA 179; CAAE 179; CAAS 25; CANR 44; CP 3, 4, 5, 6, 7; CSW; DLB 120, 282; DLBY 1980

Corneille, Pierre 1606-1684 ... **DC 21; LC 28**
See also DAB; DAM MST; DFS 21; DLB 268; EW 3; GFL Beginnings to 1789; RGWL 2, 3; TWA

Cornwell, David
See le Carre, John

Cornwell, Patricia 1956- .... **CLC 155**
See also AAYA 16, 56; BPFB 1; CA 134; CANR 53, 131; CMW 4; CPW; CSW; DAM POP; DLB 306; MSW; MTCW 2; MTFW 2005

Cornwell, Patricia Daniels
See Cornwell, Patricia

Corso, Gregory 1930-2001 .... **CLC 1, 11; PC 33**
See also AMWS 12; BG 1:2; CA 5-8R; 193; CANR 41, 76, 132; CP 1, 2, 3, 4, 5, 6, 7; DA3; DLB 5, 16, 237; LMFS 2; MAL 5; MTCW 1, 2; MTFW 2005; WP

Cortazar, Julio 1914-1984 ... **CLC 2, 3, 5, 10, 13, 15, 33, 34, 92; HLC 1; SSC 7, 76**
See also BPFB 1; CA 21-24R; CANR 12, 32, 81; CDWLB 3; DA3; DAM MULT, NOV; DLB 113; EWL 3; EXPS; HW 1, 2; LAW; MTCW 1, 2; MTFW 2005; RGSF 2; RGWL 2, 3; SSFS 3, 20; TWA; WLIT 1

Cortes, Hernan 1485-1547 .... **LC 31**

Corvinus, Jakob
See Raabe, Wilhelm (Karl)

Corwin, Cecil
See Kornbluth, C(yril) M.

Cosic, Dobrica 1921- .... **CLC 14**
See also CA 122; 138; CDWLB 4; CWW 2; DLB 181; EWL 3

Costain, Thomas B(ertram) 1885-1965 .... **CLC 30**
See also BYA 3; CA 5-8R; 25-28R; DLB 9; RHW

Costantini, Humberto 1924(?)-1987 . **CLC 49**
See also CA 131; 122; EWL 3; HW 1

Costello, Elvis 1954- .... **CLC 21**
See also CA 204

Costenoble, Philostene
See Ghelderode, Michel de

Cotes, Cecil V.
See Duncan, Sara Jeannette

Cotter, Joseph Seamon Sr. 1861-1949 .... **BLC 1; TCLC 28**
See also BW 1; CA 124; DAM MULT; DLB 50

Couch, Arthur Thomas Quiller
See Quiller-Couch, Sir Arthur (Thomas)

Coulton, James
See Hansen, Joseph

Couperus, Louis (Marie Anne) 1863-1923 .... **TCLC 15**
See also CA 115; EWL 3; RGWL 2, 3

Coupland, Douglas 1961- .... **CLC 85, 133**
See also AAYA 34; CA 142; CANR 57, 90, 130; CCA 1; CN 7; CPW; DAC; DAM POP

Court, Wesli
See Turco, Lewis (Putnam)

Courtenay, Bryce 1933- .... **CLC 59**
See also CA 138; CPW

Courtney, Robert
See Ellison, Harlan

Cousteau, Jacques-Yves 1910-1997 .. **CLC 30**
See also CA 65-68; 159; CANR 15, 67; MTCW 1; SATA 38, 98

Coventry, Francis 1725-1754 .... **LC 46**

Coverdale, Miles c. 1487-1569 .... **LC 77**
See also DLB 167

Cowan, Peter (Walkinshaw) 1914-2002 .... **SSC 28**
See also CA 21-24R; CANR 9, 25, 50, 83; CN 1, 2, 3, 4, 5, 6, 7; DLB 260; RGSF 2

Coward, Noel (Peirce) 1899-1973 . **CLC 1, 9, 29, 51**
See also AITN 1; BRWS 2; CA 17-18; 41-44R; CANR 35, 132; CAP 2; CBD; CD-BLB 1914-1945; DA3; DAM DRAM; DFS 3, 6; DLB 10, 245; EWL 3; IDFW 3, 4; MTCW 1, 2; MTFW 2005; RGEL 2; TEA

Cowley, Abraham 1618-1667 .... **LC 43**
See also BRW 2; DLB 131, 151; PAB; RGEL 2

Cowley, Malcolm 1898-1989 .... **CLC 39**
See also AMWS 2; CA 5-8R; 128; CANR 3, 55; CP 1, 2, 3, 4; DLB 4, 48; DLBY 1981, 1989; EWL 3; MAL 5; MTCW 1, 2; MTFW 2005

Cowper, William 1731-1800 ..... **NCLC 8, 94; PC 40**
See also BRW 3; DA3; DAM POET; DLB 104, 109; RGEL 2

Cox, William Trevor 1928-
See Trevor, William
See also CA 9-12R; CANR 4, 37, 55, 76, 102, 139; DAM NOV; INT CANR-37; MTCW 1, 2; MTFW 2005; TEA

Coyne, P. J.
See Masters, Hilary

Cozzens, James Gould 1903-1978 . **CLC 1, 4, 11, 92**
See also AMW; BPFB 1; CA 9-12R; 81-84; CANR 19; CDALB 1941-1968; CN 1, 2; DLB 9, 294; DLBD 2; DLBY 1984, 1997; EWL 3; MAL 5; MTCW 1, 2; MTFW 2005; RGAL 4

Crabbe, George 1754-1832 .... **NCLC 26, 121**
See also BRW 3; DLB 93; RGEL 2

Crace, Jim 1946- .... **CLC 157; SSC 61**
See also CA 128; 135; CANR 55, 70, 123; CN 5, 6, 7; DLB 231; INT CA-135

Craddock, Charles Egbert
See Murfree, Mary Noailles

Craig, A. A.
See Anderson, Poul

Craik, Mrs.
See Craik, Dinah Maria (Mulock)
See also RGEL 2

Craik, Dinah Maria (Mulock) 1826-1887 .... **NCLC 38**
See Craik, Mrs.; Mulock, Dinah Maria
See also DLB 35, 163; MAICYA 1, 2; SATA 34

Cram, Ralph Adams 1863-1942 ..... **TCLC 45**
See also CA 160

Cranch, Christopher Pearse 1813-1892 .... **NCLC 115**
See also DLB 1, 42, 243

Crane, (Harold) Hart 1899-1932 .... **PC 3; TCLC 2, 5, 80; WLC 2**
See also AMW; AMWR 2; CA 104; 127; CDALB 1917-1929; DA; DA3; DAB; DAC; DAM MST, POET; DLB 4, 48; EWL 3; MAL 5; MTCW 1, 2; MTFW 2005; RGAL 4; TUS

Crane, R(onald) S(almon) 1886-1967 .... **CLC 27**
See also CA 85-88; DLB 63

Crane, Stephen (Townley) 1871-1900 ...... **SSC 7, 56, 70; TCLC 11, 17, 32; WLC 2**
See also AAYA 21; AMW; AMWC 1; BPFB 1; BYA 3; CA 109; 140; CANR 84; CDALB 1865-1917; DA; DA3; DAB; DAC; DAM MST, NOV, POET; DLB 12, 54, 78; EXPN; EXPS; LAIT 2; LMFS 2; MAL 5; NFS 4, 20; PFS 9; RGAL 4; RGSF 2; SSFS 4; TUS; WYA; YABC 2

Cranmer, Thomas 1489-1556 .... **LC 95**
See also DLB 132, 213

Cranshaw, Stanley
See Fisher, Dorothy (Frances) Canfield

Crase, Douglas 1944- .... **CLC 58**
See also CA 106

Crashaw, Richard 1612(?)-1649 .... **LC 24**
See also BRW 2; DLB 126; PAB; RGEL 2

Cratinus c. 519B.C.-c. 422B.C. ..... **CMLC 54**
See also LMFS 1

Craven, Margaret 1901-1980 .... **CLC 17**
See also BYA 2; CA 103; CCA 1; DAC; LAIT 5

Crawford, F(rancis) Marion 1854-1909 .... **TCLC 10**
See also CA 107; 168; DLB 71; HGG; RGAL 4; SUFW 1

Crawford, Isabella Valancy 1850-1887 .... **NCLC 12, 127**
See also DLB 92; RGEL 2

Crayon, Geoffrey
See Irving, Washington

Creasey, John 1908-1973 .... **CLC 11**
See Marric, J. J.
See also CA 5-8R; 41-44R; CANR 8, 59; CMW 4; DLB 77; MTCW 1

Crebillon, Claude Prosper Jolyot de (fils) 1707-1777 .... **LC 1, 28**
See also DLB 313; GFL Beginnings to 1789

Credo
See Creasey, John

Credo, Alvaro J. de
See Prado (Calvo), Pedro

Creeley, Robert 1926-2005 .... **CLC 1, 2, 4, 8, 11, 15, 36, 78; PC 73**
See also AMWS 4; CA 1-4R; 237; CAAS 10; CANR 23, 43, 89, 137; CP 1, 2, 3, 4, 5, 6, 7; DA3; DAM POET; DLB 5, 16, 169; DLBD 17; EWL 3; MAL 5; MTCW 1, 2; MTFW 2005; PFS 21; RGAL 4; WP

Creeley, Robert White
See Creeley, Robert

Crenne, Helisenne de 1510-1560 .... **LC 113**
See also DLB 327

Crevecoeur, Hector St. John de
See Crevecoeur, Michel Guillaume Jean de
See also ANW

Crevecoeur, Michel Guillaume Jean de 1735-1813 .... **NCLC 105**
See Crevecoeur, Hector St. John de
See also AMWS 1; DLB 37

Crevel, Rene 1900-1935 .... **TCLC 112**
See also GLL 2

Crews, Harry 1935- .... **CLC 6, 23, 49**
See also AITN 1; AMWS 11; BPFB 1; CA 25-28R; CANR 20, 57; CN 3, 4, 5, 6, 7; CSW; DA3; DLB 6, 143, 185; MTCW 1, 2; MTFW 2005; RGAL 4

Crichton, Michael 1942- ..... **CLC 2, 6, 54, 90**
See also AAYA 10, 49; AITN 2; BPFB 1; CA 25-28R; CANR 13, 40, 54, 76, 127; CMW 4; CN 2, 3, 6, 7; CPW; DA3; DAM NOV, POP; DLB 292; DLBY 1981; INT CANR-13; JRDA; MTCW 1, 2; MTFW 2005; SATA 9, 88; SFW 4; YAW

Author Index

Author Index

Author Index

Farmer, Philip Jose 1918- .... **CLC 1, 19**
See also AAYA 28; BPFB 1; CA 1-4R;
CANR 4, 35, 111; DLB 8; MTCW 1;
SATA 93; SCFW 1, 2; SFW 4

Farquhar, George 1677-1707 .... **LC 21**
See also BRW 2; DAM DRAM; DLB 84;
RGEL 2

Farrell, J(ames) G(ordon)
1935-1979 .... **CLC 6**
See also CA 73-76; 89-92; CANR 36; CN
1, 2; DLB 14, 271, 326; MTCW 1; RGEL
2; RHW; WLIT 4

Farrell, James T(homas) 1904-1979 . **CLC 1,
4, 8, 11, 66; SSC 28**
See also AMW; BPFB 1; CA 5-8R; 89-92;
CANR 9, 61; CN 1, 2; DLB 4, 9, 86;
DLBD 2; EWL 3; MAL 5; MTCW 1, 2;
MTFW 2005; RGAL 4

Farrell, Warren (Thomas) 1943- ...... **CLC 70**
See also CA 146; CANR 120

Farren, Richard J.
See Betjeman, John

Farren, Richard M.
See Betjeman, John

Fassbinder, Rainer Werner
1946-1982 .... **CLC 20**
See also CA 93-96; 106; CANR 31

Fast, Howard 1914-2003 .... **CLC 23, 131**
See also AAYA 16; BPFB 1; CA 1-4R, 181;
214; CAAE 181; CAAS 18; CANR 1, 33,
54, 75, 98, 140; CMW 4; CN 1, 2, 3, 4, 5,
6, 7; CPW; DAM NOV; DLB 9; INT
CANR-33; LATS 1:1; MAL 5; MTCW 2;
MTFW 2005; RHW; SATA 7; SATA-
Essay 107; TCWW 1, 2; YAW

Faulcon, Robert
See Holdstock, Robert P.

Faulkner, William (Cuthbert)
1897-1962 ..... **CLC 1, 3, 6, 8, 9, 11, 14,
18, 28, 52, 68; SSC 1, 35, 42, 92;
TCLC 141; WLC 2**
See also AAYA 7; AMW; AMWR 1; BPFB
1; BYA 5, 15; CA 81-84; CANR 33;
CDALB 1929-1941; DA; DA3; DAB;
DAC; DAM MST, NOV; DLB 9, 11, 44,
102, 316, 330; DLBD 2; DLBY 1986,
1997; EWL 3; EXPN; EXPS; GL 2; LAIT
2; LATS 1:1; LMFS 2; MAL 5; MTCW
1, 2; MTFW 2005; NFS 4, 8, 13, 24;
RGAL 4; RGSF 2; SSFS 2, 5, 6, 12; TUS

Fauset, Jessie Redmon
1882(?)-1961 .. **BLC 2; CLC 19, 54; HR
1:2**
See also AFAW 2; BW 1; CA 109; CANR
83; DAM MULT; DLB 51; FW; LMFS 2;
MAL 5; MBL

Faust, Frederick (Schiller)
1892-1944 .... **TCLC 49**
See Brand, Max; Dawson, Peter; Frederick,
John
See also CA 108; 152; CANR 143; DAM
POP; DLB 256; TUS

Faust, Irvin 1924- .... **CLC 8**
See also CA 33-36R; CANR 28, 67; CN 1,
2, 3, 4, 5, 6, 7; DLB 2, 28, 218, 278;
DLBY 1980

Fawkes, Guy
See Benchley, Robert (Charles)

Fearing, Kenneth (Flexner)
1902-1961 .... **CLC 51**
See also CA 93-96; CANR 59; CMW 4;
DLB 9; MAL 5; RGAL 4

Fecamps, Elise
See Creasey, John

Federman, Raymond 1928- .... **CLC 6, 47**
See also CA 17-20R, 208; CAAE 208;
CAAS 8; CANR 10, 43, 83, 108; CN 3,
4, 5, 6; DLBY 1980

Federspiel, J(uerg) F. 1931- .... **CLC 42**
See also CA 146

Feiffer, Jules (Ralph) 1929- ...... **CLC 2, 8, 64**
See also AAYA 3, 62; CA 17-20R; CAD;
CANR 30, 59, 129; CD 5, 6; DAM
DRAM; DLB 7, 44; INT CANR-30;
MTCW 1; SATA 8, 61, 111, 157

Feige, Hermann Albert Otto Maximilian
See Traven, B.

Feinberg, David B. 1956-1994 .... **CLC 59**
See also CA 135; 147

Feinstein, Elaine 1930- .... **CLC 36**
See also CA 69-72; CAAS 1; CANR 31,
68, 121; CN 3, 4, 5, 6, 7; CP 2, 3, 4, 5, 6,
7; CWP; DLB 14, 40; MTCW 1

Feke, Gilbert David .... **CLC 65**

Feldman, Irving (Mordecai) 1928- ..... **CLC 7**
See also CA 1-4R; CANR 1; CP 1, 2, 3, 4,
5, 6, 7; DLB 169; TCLE 1:1

Felix-Tchicaya, Gerald
See Tchicaya, Gerald Felix

Fellini, Federico 1920-1993 .... **CLC 16, 85**
See also CA 65-68; 143; CANR 33

Felltham, Owen 1602(?)-1668 .... **LC 92**
See also DLB 126, 151

Felsen, Henry Gregor 1916-1995 ..... **CLC 17**
See also CA 1-4R; 180; CANR 1; SAAS 2;
SATA 1

Felski, Rita .... **CLC 65**

Fenno, Jack
See Calisher, Hortense

Fenollosa, Ernest (Francisco)
1853-1908 .... **TCLC 91**

Fenton, James Martin 1949- .... **CLC 32, 209**
See also CA 102; CANR 108; CP 2, 3, 4, 5,
6, 7; DLB 40; PFS 11

Ferber, Edna 1887-1968 .... **CLC 18, 93**
See also AITN 1; CA 5-8R; 25-28R; CANR
68, 105; DLB 9, 28, 86, 266; MAL 5;
MTCW 1, 2; MTFW 2005; RGAL 4;
RHW; SATA 7; TCWW 1, 2

Ferdowsi, Abu'l Qasem
940-1020(?) .... **CMLC 43**
See Firdawsi, Abu al-Qasim
See also RGWL 2, 3

Ferguson, Helen
See Kavan, Anna

Ferguson, Niall 1964- .... **CLC 134**
See also CA 190; CANR 154

Ferguson, Samuel 1810-1886 .... **NCLC 33**
See also DLB 32; RGEL 2

Fergusson, Robert 1750-1774 .... **LC 29**
See also DLB 109; RGEL 2

Ferling, Lawrence
See Ferlinghetti, Lawrence

Ferlinghetti, Lawrence 1919(?)- .... **CLC 2, 6,
10, 27, 111; PC 1**
See also BG 1:2; CA 5-8R; CAD; CANR 3,
41, 73, 125; CDALB 1941-1968; CP 1, 2,
3, 4, 5, 6, 7; DA3; DAM POET; DLB 5,
16; MAL 5; MTCW 1, 2; MTFW 2005;
RGAL 4; WP

Ferlinghetti, Lawrence Monsanto
See Ferlinghetti, Lawrence

Fern, Fanny
See Parton, Sara Payson Willis

Fernandez, Vicente Garcia Huidobro
See Huidobro Fernandez, Vicente Garcia

Fernandez-Armesto, Felipe .... **CLC 70**
See Fernandez-Armesto, Felipe Fermin
Ricardo
See also CANR 153

Fernandez-Armesto, Felipe Fermin Ricardo
1950-
See Fernandez-Armesto, Felipe
See also CA 142; CANR 93

Fernandez de Lizardi, Jose Joaquin
See Lizardi, Jose Joaquin Fernandez de

Ferre, Rosario 1938- ...... **CLC 139; HLCS 1;
SSC 36**
See also CA 131; CANR 55, 81, 134; CWW
2; DLB 145; EWL 3; HW 1, 2; LAWS 1;
MTCW 2; MTFW 2005; WLIT 1

Ferrer, Gabriel (Francisco Victor) Miro
See Miro (Ferrer), Gabriel (Francisco
Victor)

Ferrier, Susan (Edmonstone)
1782-1854 .... **NCLC 8**
See also DLB 116; RGEL 2

Ferrigno, Robert 1948(?)- .... **CLC 65**
See also CA 140; CANR 125

Ferron, Jacques 1921-1985 .... **CLC 94**
See also CA 117; 129; CCA 1; DAC; DLB
60; EWL 3

Feuchtwanger, Lion 1884-1958 .... **TCLC 3**
See also CA 104; 187; DLB 66; EWL 3;
RGHL

Feuerbach, Ludwig 1804-1872 ..... **NCLC 139**
See also DLB 133

Feuillet, Octave 1821-1890 .... **NCLC 45**
See also DLB 192

Feydeau, Georges (Leon Jules Marie)
1862-1921 .... **TCLC 22**
See also CA 113; 152; CANR 84; DAM
DRAM; DLB 192; EWL 3; GFL 1789 to
the Present; RGWL 2, 3

Fichte, Johann Gottlieb
1762-1814 .... **NCLC 62**
See also DLB 90

Ficino, Marsilio 1433-1499 .... **LC 12**
See also LMFS 1

Fiedeler, Hans
See Doeblin, Alfred

Fiedler, Leslie A(aron) 1917-2003 ..... **CLC 4,
13, 24**
See also AMWS 13; CA 9-12R; 212; CANR
7, 63; CN 1, 2, 3, 4, 5, 6; DLB 28, 67;
EWL 3; MAL 5; MTCW 1, 2; RGAL 4;
TUS

Field, Andrew 1938- .... **CLC 44**
See also CA 97-100; CANR 25

Field, Eugene 1850-1895 .... **NCLC 3**
See also DLB 23, 42, 140; DLBD 13; MAI-
CYA 1, 2; RGAL 4; SATA 16

Field, Gans T.
See Wellman, Manly Wade

Field, Michael 1915-1971 .... **TCLC 43**
See also CA 29-32R

Fielding, Helen 1958- .... **CLC 146, 217**
See also AAYA 65; CA 172; CANR 127;
DLB 231; MTFW 2005

Fielding, Henry 1707-1754 .... **LC 1, 46, 85;
WLC 2**
See also BRW 3; BRWR 1; CDBLB 1660-
1789; DA; DA3; DAB; DAC; DAM
DRAM, MST, NOV; DLB 39, 84, 101;
NFS 18; RGEL 2; TEA; WLIT 3

Fielding, Sarah 1710-1768 .... **LC 1, 44**
See also DLB 39; RGEL 2; TEA

Fields, W. C. 1880-1946 .... **TCLC 80**
See also DLB 44

Fierstein, Harvey (Forbes) 1954- ..... **CLC 33**
See also CA 123; 129; CAD; CD 5, 6;
CPW; DA3; DAM DRAM, POP; DFS 6;
DLB 266; GLL 1; MAL 5

Figes, Eva 1932- .... **CLC 31**
See also CA 53-56; CANR 4, 44, 83; CN 2,
3, 4, 5, 6, 7; DLB 14, 271; FW; RGHL

Filippo, Eduardo de
See de Filippo, Eduardo

Finch, Anne 1661-1720 .... **LC 3; PC 21**
See also BRWS 9; DLB 95

Finch, Robert (Duer Claydon)
1900-1995 .... **CLC 18**
See also CA 57-60; CANR 9, 24, 49; CP 1,
2, 3, 4, 5, 6; DLB 88

Fornes, Maria Irene 1930- .... **CLC 39, 61, 187; DC 10; HLCS 1**
See also CA 25-28R; CAD; CANR 28, 81; CD 5, 6; CWD; DLB 7; HW 1, 2; INT CANR-28; LLW; MAL 5; MTCW 1; RGAL 4

Forrest, Leon (Richard)
1937-1997 .... **BLCS; CLC 4**
See also AFAW 2; BW 2; CA 89-92; 162; CAAS 7; CANR 25, 52, 87; CN 4, 5, 6; DLB 33

Forster, E(dward) M(organ)
1879-1970 ...... **CLC 1, 2, 3, 4, 9, 10, 13, 15, 22, 45, 77; SSC 27; TCLC 125; WLC 2**
See also AAYA 2, 37; BRW 6; BRWR 2; BYA 12; CA 13-14; 25-28R; CANR 45; CAP 1; CDBLB 1914-1945; DA; DA3; DAB; DAC; DAM MST, NOV; DLB 34, 98, 162, 178, 195; DLBD 10; EWL 3; EXPN; LAIT 3; LMFS 1; MTCW 1, 2; MTFW 2005; NCFS 1; NFS 3, 10, 11; RGEL 2; RGSF 2; SATA 57; SUFW 1; TEA; WLIT 4

Forster, John 1812-1876 .... **NCLC 11**
See also DLB 144, 184

Forster, Margaret 1938- .... **CLC 149**
See also CA 133; CANR 62, 115; CN 4, 5, 6, 7; DLB 155, 271

Forsyth, Frederick 1938- .... **CLC 2, 5, 36**
See also BEST 89:4; CA 85-88; CANR 38, 62, 115, 137; CMW 4; CN 3, 4, 5, 6, 7; CPW; DAM NOV, POP; DLB 87; MTCW 1, 2; MTFW 2005

Forten, Charlotte L. 1837-1914 .... **BLC 2; TCLC 16**
See Grimke, Charlotte L(ottie) Forten
See also DLB 50, 239

Fortinbras
See Grieg, (Johan) Nordahl (Brun)

Foscolo, Ugo 1778-1827 .... **NCLC 8, 97**
See also EW 5; WLIT 7

Fosse, Bob 1927-1987
See Fosse, Robert L.
See also CA 110; 123

Fosse, Robert L. .... **CLC 20**
See Fosse, Bob

Foster, Hannah Webster
1758-1840 .... **NCLC 99**
See also DLB 37, 200; RGAL 4

Foster, Stephen Collins
1826-1864 .... **NCLC 26**
See also RGAL 4

Foucault, Michel 1926-1984 . **CLC 31, 34, 69**
See also CA 105; 113; CANR 34; DLB 242; EW 13; EWL 3; GFL 1789 to the Present; GLL 1; LMFS 2; MTCW 1, 2; TWA

Fouque, Friedrich (Heinrich Karl) de la Motte 1777-1843 .... **NCLC 2**
See also DLB 90; RGWL 2, 3; SUFW 1

Fourier, Charles 1772-1837 .... **NCLC 51**

Fournier, Henri-Alban 1886-1914
See Alain-Fournier
See also CA 104; 179

Fournier, Pierre 1916-1997 .... **CLC 11**
See Gascar, Pierre
See also CA 89-92; CANR 16, 40

Fowles, John 1926-2005 .... **CLC 1, 2, 3, 4, 6, 9, 10, 15, 33, 87; SSC 33**
See also BPFB 1; BRWS 1; CA 5-8R; 245; CANR 25, 71, 103; CDBLB 1960 to Present; CN 1, 2, 3, 4, 5, 6, 7; DA3; DAB; DAC; DAM MST; DLB 14, 139, 207; EWL 3; HGG; MTCW 1, 2; MTFW 2005; NFS 21; RGEL 2; RHW; SATA 22; SATA-Obit 171; TEA; WLIT 4

Fowles, John Robert
See Fowles, John

Fox, Paula 1923- .... **CLC 2, 8, 121**
See also AAYA 3, 37; BYA 3, 8; CA 73-76; CANR 20, 36, 62, 105; CLR 1, 44, 96; DLB 52; JRDA; MAICYA 1, 2; MTCW 1; NFS 12; SATA 17, 60, 120, 167; WYA; YAW

Fox, William Price (Jr.) 1926- .... **CLC 22**
See also CA 17-20R; CAAS 19; CANR 11, 142; CSW; DLB 2; DLBY 1981

Foxe, John 1517(?)-1587 .... **LC 14**
See also DLB 132

Frame, Janet .. **CLC 2, 3, 6, 22, 66, 96; SSC 29**
See Clutha, Janet Paterson Frame
See also CN 1, 2, 3, 4, 5, 6, 7; CP 2, 3, 4; CWP; EWL 3; RGEL 2; RGSF 2; TWA

France, Anatole .... **TCLC 9**
See Thibault, Jacques Anatole Francois
See also DLB 123, 330; EWL 3; GFL 1789 to the Present; RGWL 2, 3; SUFW 1

Francis, Claude .... **CLC 50**
See also CA 192

Francis, Dick
See Francis, Richard Stanley
See also CN 2, 3, 4, 5, 6

Francis, Richard Stanley 1920- ... **CLC 2, 22, 42, 102**
See Francis, Dick
See also AAYA 5, 21; BEST 89:3; BPFB 1; CA 5-8R; CANR 9, 42, 68, 100, 141; CD-BLB 1960 to Present; CMW 4; CN 7; DA3; DAM POP; DLB 87; INT CANR-9; MSW; MTCW 1, 2; MTFW 2005

Francis, Robert (Churchill)
1901-1987 .... **CLC 15; PC 34**
See also AMWS 9; CA 1-4R; 123; CANR 1; CP 1, 2, 3, 4; EXPP; PFS 12; TCLE 1:1

Francis, Lord Jeffrey
See Jeffrey, Francis
See also DLB 107

Frank, Anne(lies Marie)
1929-1945 .... **TCLC 17; WLC 2**
See also AAYA 12; BYA 1; CA 113; 133; CANR 68; CLR 101; DA; DA3; DAB; DAC; DAM MST; LAIT 4; MAICYA 2; MAICYAS 1; MTCW 1, 2; MTFW 2005; NCFS 2; RGHL; SATA 87; SATA-Brief 42; WYA; YAW

Frank, Bruno 1887-1945 .... **TCLC 81**
See also CA 189; DLB 118; EWL 3

Frank, Elizabeth 1945- .... **CLC 39**
See also CA 121; 126; CANR 78, 150; INT CA-126

Frankl, Viktor E(mil) 1905-1997 ...... **CLC 93**
See also CA 65-68; 161; RGHL

Franklin, Benjamin
See Hasek, Jaroslav (Matej Frantisek)

Franklin, Benjamin 1706-1790 .... **LC 25; WLCS**
See also AMW; CDALB 1640-1865; DA; DA3; DAB; DAC; DAM MST; DLB 24, 43, 73, 183; LAIT 1; RGAL 4; TUS

Franklin, (Stella Maria Sarah) Miles (Lampe) 1879-1954 .... **TCLC 7**
See also CA 104; 164; DLB 230; FW; MTCW 2; RGEL 2; TWA

Franzen, Jonathan 1959- .... **CLC 202**
See also AAYA 65; CA 129; CANR 105

Fraser, Antonia 1932- .... **CLC 32, 107**
See also AAYA 57; CA 85-88; CANR 44, 65, 119; CMW; DLB 276; MTCW 1, 2; MTFW 2005; SATA-Brief 32

Fraser, George MacDonald 1925- ...... **CLC 7**
See also AAYA 48; CA 45-48; 180; CAAE 180; CANR 2, 48, 74; MTCW 2; RHW

Fraser, Sylvia 1935- .... **CLC 64**
See also CA 45-48; CANR 1, 16, 60; CCA 1

Frayn, Michael 1933- .... **CLC 3, 7, 31, 47, 176; DC 27**
See also AAYA 69; BRWC 2; BRWS 7; CA 5-8R; CANR 30, 69, 114, 133; CBD; CD 5, 6; CN 1, 2, 3, 4, 5, 6, 7; DAM DRAM, NOV; DFS 22; DLB 13, 14, 194, 245; FANT; MTCW 1, 2; MTFW 2005; SFW 4

Fraze, Candida (Merrill) 1945- .... **CLC 50**
See also CA 126

Frazer, Andrew
See Marlowe, Stephen

Frazer, J(ames) G(eorge)
1854-1941 .... **TCLC 32**
See also BRWS 3; CA 118; NCFS 5

Frazer, Robert Caine
See Creasey, John

Frazer, Sir James George
See Frazer, J(ames) G(eorge)

Frazier, Charles 1950- .... **CLC 109, 224**
See also AAYA 34; CA 161; CANR 126; CSW; DLB 292; MTFW 2005

Frazier, Ian 1951- .... **CLC 46**
See also CA 130; CANR 54, 93

Frederic, Harold 1856-1898 ... **NCLC 10, 175**
See also AMW; DLB 12, 23; DLBD 13; MAL 5; NFS 22; RGAL 4

Frederick, John
See Faust, Frederick (Schiller)
See also TCWW 2

Frederick the Great 1712-1786 .... **LC 14**

Fredro, Aleksander 1793-1876 .... **NCLC 8**

Freeling, Nicolas 1927-2003 .... **CLC 38**
See also CA 49-52; 218; CAAS 12; CANR 1, 17, 50, 84; CMW 4; CN 1, 2, 3, 4, 5, 6; DLB 87

Freeman, Douglas Southall
1886-1953 .... **TCLC 11**
See also CA 109; 195; DLB 17; DLBD 17

Freeman, Judith 1946- .... **CLC 55**
See also CA 148; CANR 120; DLB 256

Freeman, Mary E(leanor) Wilkins
1852-1930 .... **SSC 1, 47; TCLC 9**
See also CA 106; 177; DLB 12, 78, 221; EXPS; FW; HGG; MBL; RGAL 4; RGSF 2; SSFS 4, 8; SUFW 1; TUS

Freeman, R(ichard) Austin
1862-1943 .... **TCLC 21**
See also CA 113; CANR 84; CMW 4; DLB 70

French, Albert 1943- .... **CLC 86**
See also BW 3; CA 167

French, Antonia
See Kureishi, Hanif

French, Marilyn 1929- .. **CLC 10, 18, 60, 177**
See also BPFB 1; CA 69-72; CANR 3, 31, 134; CN 5, 6, 7; CPW; DAM DRAM, NOV, POP; FL 1:5; FW; INT CANR-31; MTCW 1, 2; MTFW 2005

French, Paul
See Asimov, Isaac

Freneau, Philip Morin 1752-1832 .. **NCLC 1, 111**
See also AMWS 2; DLB 37, 43; RGAL 4

Freud, Sigmund 1856-1939 .... **TCLC 52**
See also CA 115; 133; CANR 69; DLB 296; EW 8; EWL 3; LATS 1:1; MTCW 1, 2; MTFW 2005; NCFS 3; TWA

Freytag, Gustav 1816-1895 .... **NCLC 109**
See also DLB 129

Friedan, Betty 1921-2006 .... **CLC 74**
See also CA 65-68; 248; CANR 18, 45, 74; DLB 246; FW; MTCW 1, 2; MTFW 2005; NCFS 5

Friedan, Betty Naomi
See Friedan, Betty

Friedlander, Saul 1932- .... **CLC 90**
See also CA 117; 130; CANR 72; RGHL

Friedman, B(ernard) H(arper)
1926- .... **CLC 7**
See also CA 1-4R; CANR 3, 48
Friedman, Bruce Jay 1930- ...... **CLC 3, 5, 56**
See also CA 9-12R; CAD; CANR 25, 52, 101; CD 5, 6; CN 1, 2, 3, 4, 5, 6, 7; DLB 2, 28, 244; INT CANR-25; MAL 5; SSFS 18
Friel, Brian 1929- .... **CLC 5, 42, 59, 115; DC 8; SSC 76**
See also BRWS 5; CA 21-24R; CANR 33, 69, 131; CBD; CD 5, 6; DFS 11; DLB 13, 319; EWL 3; MTCW 1; RGEL 2; TEA
Friis-Baastad, Babbis Ellinor
1921-1970 .... **CLC 12**
See also CA 17-20R; 134; SATA 7
Frisch, Max 1911-1991 ...... **CLC 3, 9, 14, 18, 32, 44; TCLC 121**
See also CA 85-88; 134; CANR 32, 74; CD-WLB 2; DAM DRAM, NOV; DLB 69, 124; EW 13; EWL 3; MTCW 1, 2; MTFW 2005; RGHL; RGWL 2, 3
Fromentin, Eugene (Samuel Auguste)
1820-1876 .... **NCLC 10, 125**
See also DLB 123; GFL 1789 to the Present
Frost, Frederick
See Faust, Frederick (Schiller)
Frost, Robert 1874-1963 . **CLC 1, 3, 4, 9, 10, 13, 15, 26, 34, 44; PC 1, 39, 71; WLC 2**
See also AAYA 21; AMW; AMWR 1; CA 89-92; CANR 33; CDALB 1917-1929; CLR 67; DA; DA3; DAB; DAC; DAM MST, POET; DLB 54, 284; DLBD 7; EWL 3; EXPP; MAL 5; MTCW 1, 2; MTFW 2005; PAB; PFS 1, 2, 3, 4, 5, 6, 7, 10, 13; RGAL 4; SATA 14; TUS; WP; WYA
Frost, Robert Lee
See Frost, Robert
Froude, James Anthony
1818-1894 .... **NCLC 43**
See also DLB 18, 57, 144
Froy, Herald
See Waterhouse, Keith (Spencer)
Fry, Christopher 1907-2005 ... **CLC 2, 10, 14**
See also BRWS 3; CA 17-20R; 240; CAAS 23; CANR 9, 30, 74, 132; CBD; CD 5, 6; CP 1, 2, 3, 4, 5, 6, 7; DAM DRAM; DLB 13; EWL 3; MTCW 1, 2; MTFW 2005; RGEL 2; SATA 66; TEA
Frye, (Herman) Northrop
1912-1991 .... **CLC 24, 70; TCLC 165**
See also CA 5-8R; 133; CANR 8, 37; DLB 67, 68, 246; EWL 3; MTCW 1, 2; MTFW 2005; RGAL 4; TWA
Fuchs, Daniel 1909-1993 .... **CLC 8, 22**
See also CA 81-84; 142; CAAS 5; CANR 40; CN 1, 2, 3, 4, 5; DLB 9, 26, 28; DLBY 1993; MAL 5
Fuchs, Daniel 1934- .... **CLC 34**
See also CA 37-40R; CANR 14, 48
Fuentes, Carlos 1928- .. **CLC 3, 8, 10, 13, 22, 41, 60, 113; HLC 1; SSC 24; WLC 2**
See also AAYA 4, 45; AITN 2; BPFB 1; CA 69-72; CANR 10, 32, 68, 104, 138; CDWLB 3; CWW 2; DA; DA3; DAB; DAC; DAM MST, MULT, NOV; DLB 113; DNFS 2; EWL 3; HW 1, 2; LAIT 3; LATS 1:2; LAW; LAWS 1; LMFS 2; MTCW 1, 2; MTFW 2005; NFS 8; RGSF 2; RGWL 2, 3; TWA; WLIT 1
Fuentes, Gregorio Lopez y
See Lopez y Fuentes, Gregorio
Fuertes, Gloria 1918-1998 .... **PC 27**
See also CA 178, 180; DLB 108; HW 2; SATA 115
Fugard, (Harold) Athol 1932- . **CLC 5, 9, 14, 25, 40, 80, 211; DC 3**
See also AAYA 17; AFW; CA 85-88; CANR 32, 54, 118; CD 5, 6; DAM DRAM; DFS

3, 6, 10; DLB 225; DNFS 1, 2; EWL 3; LATS 1:2; MTCW 1; MTFW 2005; RGEL 2; WLIT 2
Fugard, Sheila 1932- .... **CLC 48**
See also CA 125
Fujiwara no Teika 1162-1241 .... **CMLC 73**
See also DLB 203
Fukuyama, Francis 1952- .... **CLC 131**
See also CA 140; CANR 72, 125
Fuller, Charles (H.), (Jr.) 1939- .... **BLC 2; CLC 25; DC 1**
See also BW 2; CA 108; 112; CAD; CANR 87; CD 5, 6; DAM DRAM, MULT; DFS 8; DLB 38, 266; EWL 3; INT CA-112; MAL 5; MTCW 1
Fuller, Henry Blake 1857-1929 .... **TCLC 103**
See also CA 108; 177; DLB 12; RGAL 4
Fuller, John (Leopold) 1937- .... **CLC 62**
See also CA 21-24R; CANR 9, 44; CP 1, 2, 3, 4, 5, 6, 7; DLB 40
Fuller, Margaret
See Ossoli, Sarah Margaret (Fuller)
See also AMWS 2; DLB 183, 223, 239; FL 1:3
Fuller, Roy (Broadbent) 1912-1991 ... **CLC 4, 28**
See also BRWS 7; CA 5-8R; 135; CAAS 10; CANR 53, 83; CN 1, 2, 3, 4, 5; CP 1, 2, 3, 4, 5; CWRI 5; DLB 15, 20; EWL 3; RGEL 2; SATA 87
Fuller, Sarah Margaret
See Ossoli, Sarah Margaret (Fuller)
Fuller, Sarah Margaret
See Ossoli, Sarah Margaret (Fuller)
See also DLB 1, 59, 73
Fuller, Thomas 1608-1661 .... **LC 111**
See also DLB 151
Fulton, Alice 1952- .... **CLC 52**
See also CA 116; CANR 57, 88; CP 5, 6, 7; CWP; DLB 193
Furphy, Joseph 1843-1912 .... **TCLC 25**
See Collins, Tom
See also CA 163; DLB 230; EWL 3; RGEL 2
Fuson, Robert H(enderson) 1927- .... **CLC 70**
See also CA 89-92; CANR 103
Fussell, Paul 1924- .... **CLC 74**
See also BEST 90:1; CA 17-20R; CANR 8, 21, 35, 69, 135; INT CANR-21; MTCW 1, 2; MTFW 2005
Futabatei, Shimei 1864-1909 .... **TCLC 44**
See Futabatei Shimei
See also CA 162; MJW
Futabatei Shimei
See Futabatei, Shimei
See also DLB 180; EWL 3
Futrelle, Jacques 1875-1912 .... **TCLC 19**
See also CA 113; 155; CMW 4
Gaboriau, Emile 1835-1873 .... **NCLC 14**
See also CMW 4; MSW
Gadda, Carlo Emilio 1893-1973 ...... **CLC 11; TCLC 144**
See also CA 89-92; DLB 177; EWL 3; WLIT 7
Gaddis, William 1922-1998 ... **CLC 1, 3, 6, 8, 10, 19, 43, 86**
See also AMWS 4; BPFB 1; CA 17-20R; 172; CANR 21, 48, 148; CN 1, 2, 3, 4, 5, 6; DLB 2, 278; EWL 3; MAL 5; MTCW 1, 2; MTFW 2005; RGAL 4
Gaelique, Moruen le
See Jacob, (Cyprien-)Max
Gage, Walter
See Inge, William (Motter)
Gaiman, Neil 1960- .... **CLC 195**
See also AAYA 19, 42; CA 133; CANR 81, 129; CLR 109; DLB 261; HGG; MTFW 2005; SATA 85, 146; SFW 4; SUFW 2

Gaiman, Neil Richard
See Gaiman, Neil
Gaines, Ernest J. 1933- .. **BLC 2; CLC 3, 11, 18, 86, 181; SSC 68**
See also AAYA 18; AFAW 1, 2; AITN 1; BPFB 2; BW 2, 3; BYA 6; CA 9-12R; CANR 6, 24, 42, 75, 126; CDALB 1968-1988; CLR 62; CN 1, 2, 3, 4, 5, 6, 7; CSW; DA3; DAM MULT; DLB 2, 33, 152; DLBY 1980; EWL 3; EXPN; LAIT 5; LATS 1:2; MAL 5; MTCW 1, 2; MTFW 2005; NFS 5, 7, 16; RGAL 4; RGSF 2; RHW; SATA 86; SSFS 5; YAW
Gaitskill, Mary 1954- .... **CLC 69**
See also CA 128; CANR 61, 152; DLB 244; TCLE 1:1
Gaitskill, Mary Lawrence
See Gaitskill, Mary
Gaius Suetonius Tranquillus
See Suetonius
Galdos, Benito Perez
See Perez Galdos, Benito
See also EW 7
Gale, Zona 1874-1938 .... **TCLC 7**
See also CA 105; 153; CANR 84; DAM DRAM; DFS 17; DLB 9, 78, 228; RGAL 4
Galeano, Eduardo (Hughes) 1940- . **CLC 72; HLCS 1**
See also CA 29-32R; CANR 13, 32, 100; HW 1
Galiano, Juan Valera y Alcala
See Valera y Alcala-Galiano, Juan
Galilei, Galileo 1564-1642 .... **LC 45**
Gallagher, Tess 1943- .... **CLC 18, 63; PC 9**
See also CA 106; CP 3, 4, 5, 6, 7; CWP; DAM POET; DLB 120, 212, 244; PFS 16
Gallant, Mavis 1922- ..... **CLC 7, 18, 38, 172; SSC 5, 78**
See also CA 69-72; CANR 29, 69, 117; CCA 1; CN 1, 2, 3, 4, 5, 6, 7; DAC; DAM MST; DLB 53; EWL 3; MTCW 1, 2; MTFW 2005; RGEL 2; RGSF 2
Gallant, Roy A(rthur) 1924- .... **CLC 17**
See also CA 5-8R; CANR 4, 29, 54, 117; CLR 30; MAICYA 1, 2; SATA 4, 68, 110
Gallico, Paul (William) 1897-1976 ..... **CLC 2**
See also AITN 1; CA 5-8R; 69-72; CANR 23; CN 1, 2; DLB 9, 171; FANT; MAICYA 1, 2; SATA 13
Gallo, Max Louis 1932- .... **CLC 95**
See also CA 85-88
Gallois, Lucien
See Desnos, Robert
Gallup, Ralph
See Whitemore, Hugh (John)
Galsworthy, John 1867-1933 .... **SSC 22; TCLC 1, 45; WLC 2**
See also BRW 6; CA 104; 141; CANR 75; CDBLB 1890-1914; DA; DA3; DAB; DAC; DAM DRAM, MST, NOV; DLB 10, 34, 98, 162, 330; DLBD 16; EWL 3; MTCW 2; RGEL 2; SSFS 3; TEA
Galt, John 1779-1839 .... **NCLC 1, 110**
See also DLB 99, 116, 159; RGEL 2; RGSF 2
Galvin, James 1951- .... **CLC 38**
See also CA 108; CANR 26
Gamboa, Federico 1864-1939 .... **TCLC 36**
See also CA 167; HW 2; LAW
Gandhi, M. K.
See Gandhi, Mohandas Karamchand
Gandhi, Mahatma
See Gandhi, Mohandas Karamchand
Gandhi, Mohandas Karamchand
1869-1948 .... **TCLC 59**
See also CA 121; 132; DA3; DAM MULT; DLB 323; MTCW 1, 2

Gann, Ernest Kellogg 1910-1991 ..... **CLC 23**
See also AITN 1; BPFB 2; CA 1-4R; 136; CANR 1, 83; RHW

Gao Xingjian 1940- .... **CLC 167**
See Xingjian, Gao
See also MTFW 2005

Garber, Eric 1943(?)-
See Holleran, Andrew
See also CANR 89

Garcia, Cristina 1958- .... **CLC 76**
See also AMWS 11; CA 141; CANR 73, 130; CN 7; DLB 292; DNFS 1; EWL 3; HW 2; LLW; MTFW 2005

Garcia Lorca, Federico 1898-1936 ...... **DC 2; HLC 2; PC 3; TCLC 1, 7, 49, 181; WLC 2**
See Lorca, Federico Garcia
See also AAYA 46; CA 104; 131; CANR 81; DA; DA3; DAB; DAC; DAM DRAM, MST, MULT, POET; DFS 4, 10; DLB 108; EWL 3; HW 1, 2; LATS 1:2; MTCW 1, 2; MTFW 2005; TWA

Garcia Marquez, Gabriel 1928- ... **CLC 2, 3, 8, 10, 15, 27, 47, 55, 68, 170; HLC 1; SSC 8, 83; WLC 3**
See also AAYA 3, 33; BEST 89:1, 90:4; BPFB 2; BYA 12, 16; CA 33-36R; CANR 10, 28, 50, 75, 82, 128; CDWLB 3; CPW; CWW 2; DA; DA3; DAB; DAC; DAM MST, MULT, NOV, POP; DLB 113, 330; DNFS 1, 2; EWL 3; EXPN; EXPS; HW 1, 2; LAIT 2; LATS 1:2; LAW; LAWS 1; LMFS 2; MTCW 1, 2; MTFW 2005; NCFS 3; NFS 1, 5, 10; RGSF 2; RGWL 2, 3; SSFS 1, 6, 16, 21; TWA; WLIT 1

Garcia Marquez, Gabriel Jose
See Garcia Marquez, Gabriel

Garcilaso de la Vega, El Inca 1539-1616 .... **HLCS 1; LC 127**
See also DLB 318; LAW

Gard, Janice
See Latham, Jean Lee

Gard, Roger Martin du
See Martin du Gard, Roger

Gardam, Jane (Mary) 1928- .... **CLC 43**
See also CA 49-52; CANR 2, 18, 33, 54, 106; CLR 12; DLB 14, 161, 231; MAICYA 1, 2; MTCW 1; SAAS 9; SATA 39, 76, 130; SATA-Brief 28; YAW

Gardner, Herb(ert George) 1934-2003 .... **CLC 44**
See also CA 149; 220; CAD; CANR 119; CD 5, 6; DFS 18, 20

Gardner, John, Jr. 1933-1982 ... **CLC 2, 3, 5, 7, 8, 10, 18, 28, 34; SSC 7**
See also AAYA 45; AITN 1; AMWS 6; BPFB 2; CA 65-68; 107; CANR 33, 73; CDALBS; CN 2, 3; CPW; DA3; DAM NOV, POP; DLB 2; DLBY 1982; EWL 3; FANT; LATS 1:2; MAL 5; MTCW 1, 2; MTFW 2005; NFS 3; RGAL 4; RGSF 2; SATA 40; SATA-Obit 31; SSFS 8

Gardner, John (Edmund) 1926- ..... **CLC 30**
See also CA 103; CANR 15, 69, 127; CMW 4; CPW; DAM POP; MTCW 1

Gardner, Miriam
See Bradley, Marion Zimmer
See also GLL 1

Gardner, Noel
See Kuttner, Henry

Gardons, S. S.
See Snodgrass, W.D.

Garfield, Leon 1921-1996 .... **CLC 12**
See also AAYA 8, 69; BYA 1, 3; CA 17-20R; 152; CANR 38, 41, 78; CLR 21; DLB 161; JRDA; MAICYA 1, 2; MAICYAS 1; SATA 1, 32, 76; SATA-Obit 90; TEA; WYA; YAW

Garland, (Hannibal) Hamlin 1860-1940 .... **SSC 18; TCLC 3**
See also CA 104; DLB 12, 71, 78, 186; MAL 5; RGAL 4; RGSF 2; TCWW 1, 2

Garneau, (Hector de) Saint-Denys 1912-1943 .... **TCLC 13**
See also CA 111; DLB 88

Garner, Alan 1934- .... **CLC 17**
See also AAYA 18; BYA 3, 5; CA 73-76, 178; CAAE 178; CANR 15, 64, 134; CLR 20; CPW; DAB; DAM POP; DLB 161, 261; FANT; MAICYA 1, 2; MTCW 1, 2; MTFW 2005; SATA 18, 69; SATA-Essay 108; SUFW 1, 2; YAW

Garner, Hugh 1913-1979 .... **CLC 13**
See Warwick, Jarvis
See also CA 69-72; CANR 31; CCA 1; CN 1, 2; DLB 68

Garnett, David 1892-1981 .... **CLC 3**
See also CA 5-8R; 103; CANR 17, 79; CN 1, 2; DLB 34; FANT; MTCW 2; RGEL 2; SFW 4; SUFW 1

Garnier, Robert c. 1545-1590 .... **LC 119**
See also DLB 327; GFL Beginnings to 1789

Garrett, George (Palmer, Jr.) 1929- . **CLC 3, 11, 51; SSC 30**
See also AMWS 7; BPFB 2; CA 1-4R, 202; CAAE 202; CAAS 5; CANR 1, 42, 67, 109; CN 1, 2, 3, 4, 5, 6, 7; CP 1, 2, 3, 4, 5, 6, 7; CSW; DLB 2, 5, 130, 152; DLBY 1983

Garrick, David 1717-1779 .... **LC 15**
See also DAM DRAM; DLB 84, 213; RGEL 2

Garrigue, Jean 1914-1972 .... **CLC 2, 8**
See also CA 5-8R; 37-40R; CANR 20; CP 1; MAL 5

Garrison, Frederick
See Sinclair, Upton

Garrison, William Lloyd 1805-1879 .... **NCLC 149**
See also CDALB 1640-1865; DLB 1, 43, 235

Garro, Elena 1920(?)-1998 .. **HLCS 1; TCLC 153**
See also CA 131; 169; CWW 2; DLB 145; EWL 3; HW 1; LAWS 1; WLIT 1

Garth, Will
See Hamilton, Edmond; Kuttner, Henry

Garvey, Marcus (Moziah, Jr.) 1887-1940 ... **BLC 2; HR 1:2; TCLC 41**
See also BW 1; CA 120; 124; CANR 79; DAM MULT

Gary, Romain .... **CLC 25**
See Kacew, Romain
See also DLB 83, 299; RGHL

Gascar, Pierre .... **CLC 11**
See Fournier, Pierre
See also EWL 3; RGHL

Gascoigne, George 1539-1577 .... **LC 108**
See also DLB 136; RGEL 2

Gascoyne, David (Emery) 1916-2001 .... **CLC 45**
See also CA 65-68; 200; CANR 10, 28, 54; CP 1, 2, 3, 4, 5, 6, 7; DLB 20; MTCW 1; RGEL 2

Gaskell, Elizabeth Cleghorn 1810-1865 .... **NCLC 5, 70, 97, 137; SSC 25**
See also BRW 5; CDBLB 1832-1890; DAB; DAM MST; DLB 21, 144, 159; RGEL 2; RGSF 2; TEA

Gass, William H. 1924- . **CLC 1, 2, 8, 11, 15, 39, 132; SSC 12**
See also AMWS 6; CA 17-20R; CANR 30, 71, 100; CN 1, 2, 3, 4, 5, 6, 7; DLB 2, 227; EWL 3; MAL 5; MTCW 1, 2; MTFW 2005; RGAL 4

Gassendi, Pierre 1592-1655 .... **LC 54**
See also GFL Beginnings to 1789

Gasset, Jose Ortega y
See Ortega y Gasset, Jose

Gates, Henry Louis, Jr. 1950- ... **BLCS; CLC 65**
See also BW 2, 3; CA 109; CANR 25, 53, 75, 125; CSW; DA3; DAM MULT; DLB 67; EWL 3; MAL 5; MTCW 2; MTFW 2005; RGAL 4

Gatos, Stephanie
See Katz, Steve

Gautier, Theophile 1811-1872 .. **NCLC 1, 59; PC 18; SSC 20**
See also DAM POET; DLB 119; EW 6; GFL 1789 to the Present; RGWL 2, 3; SUFW; TWA

Gay, John 1685-1732 .... **LC 49**
See also BRW 3; DAM DRAM; DLB 84, 95; RGEL 2; WLIT 3

Gay, Oliver
See Gogarty, Oliver St. John

Gay, Peter 1923- .... **CLC 158**
See also CA 13-16R; CANR 18, 41, 77, 147; INT CANR-18; RGHL

Gay, Peter Jack
See Gay, Peter

Gaye, Marvin (Pentz, Jr.) 1939-1984 .... **CLC 26**
See also CA 195; 112

Gebler, Carlo 1954- .... **CLC 39**
See also CA 119; 133; CANR 96; DLB 271

Gee, Maggie 1948- .... **CLC 57**
See also CA 130; CANR 125; CN 4, 5, 6, 7; DLB 207; MTFW 2005

Gee, Maurice 1931- .... **CLC 29**
See also AAYA 42; CA 97-100; CANR 67, 123; CLR 56; CN 2, 3, 4, 5, 6, 7; CWRI 5; EWL 3; MAICYA 2; RGSF 2; SATA 46, 101

Gee, Maurice Gough
See Gee, Maurice

Geiogamah, Hanay 1945- .... **NNAL**
See also CA 153; DAM MULT; DLB 175

Gelbart, Larry
See Gelbart, Larry (Simon)
See also CAD; CD 5, 6

Gelbart, Larry (Simon) 1928- .... **CLC 21, 61**
See Gelbart, Larry
See also CA 73-76; CANR 45, 94

Gelber, Jack 1932-2003 ...... **CLC 1, 6, 14, 79**
See also CA 1-4R; 216; CAD; CANR 2; DLB 7, 228; MAL 5

Gellhorn, Martha (Ellis) 1908-1998 .... **CLC 14, 60**
See also CA 77-80; 164; CANR 44; CN 1, 2, 3, 4, 5, 6 7; DLBY 1982, 1998

Genet, Jean 1910-1986 .. **CLC 1, 2, 5, 10, 14, 44, 46; DC 25; TCLC 128**
See also CA 13-16R; CANR 18; DA3; DAM DRAM; DFS 10; DLB 72, 321; DLBY 1986; EW 13; EWL 3; GFL 1789 to the Present; GLL 1; LMFS 2; MTCW 1, 2; MTFW 2005; RGWL 2, 3; TWA

Genlis, Stephanie-Felicite Ducrest 1746-1830 .... **NCLC 166**
See also DLB 313

Gent, Peter 1942- .... **CLC 29**
See also AITN 1; CA 89-92; DLBY 1982

Gentile, Giovanni 1875-1944 .... **TCLC 96**
See also CA 119

Gentlewoman in New England, A
See Bradstreet, Anne

Gentlewoman in Those Parts, A
See Bradstreet, Anne

Geoffrey of Monmouth c. 1100-1155 .... **CMLC 44**
See also DLB 146; TEA

George, Jean
See George, Jean Craighead

George, Jean Craighead 1919- .... **CLC 35**
See also AAYA 8, 69; BYA 2, 4; CA 5-8R;
CANR 25; CLR 1; 80; DLB 52; JRDA;
MAICYA 1, 2; SATA 2, 68, 124, 170;
WYA; YAW

George, Stefan (Anton) 1868-1933 . **TCLC 2, 14**
See also CA 104; 193; EW 8; EWL 3

Georges, Georges Martin
See Simenon, Georges (Jacques Christian)

Gerald of Wales c. 1146-c. 1223 ... **CMLC 60**

Gerhardi, William Alexander
See Gerhardie, William Alexander

Gerhardie, William Alexander
1895-1977 .... **CLC 5**
See also CA 25-28R; 73-76; CANR 18; CN
1, 2; DLB 36; RGEL 2

Gerson, Jean 1363-1429 .... **LC 77**
See also DLB 208

Gersonides 1288-1344 .... **CMLC 49**
See also DLB 115

Gerstler, Amy 1956- .... **CLC 70**
See also CA 146; CANR 99

Gertler, T. .... **CLC 34**
See also CA 116; 121

Gertsen, Aleksandr Ivanovich
See Herzen, Aleksandr Ivanovich

Ghalib .... **NCLC 39, 78**
See Ghalib, Asadullah Khan

Ghalib, Asadullah Khan 1797-1869
See Ghalib
See also DAM POET; RGWL 2, 3

Ghelderode, Michel de 1898-1962 ..... **CLC 6, 11; DC 15**
See also CA 85-88; CANR 40, 77; DAM
DRAM; DLB 321; EW 11; EWL 3; TWA

Ghiselin, Brewster 1903-2001 .... **CLC 23**
See also CA 13-16R; CAAS 10; CANR 13;
CP 1, 2, 3, 4, 5, 6, 7

Ghose, Aurabinda 1872-1950 .... **TCLC 63**
See Ghose, Aurobindo
See also CA 163

Ghose, Aurobindo
See Ghose, Aurabinda
See also EWL 3

Ghose, Zulfikar 1935- .... **CLC 42, 200**
See also CA 65-68; CANR 67; CN 1, 2, 3,
4, 5, 6, 7; CP 1, 2, 3, 4, 5, 6, 7; DLB 323;
EWL 3

Ghosh, Amitav 1956- .... **CLC 44, 153**
See also CA 147; CANR 80; CN 6, 7; DLB
323; WWE 1

Giacosa, Giuseppe 1847-1906 .... **TCLC 7**
See also CA 104

Gibb, Lee
See Waterhouse, Keith (Spencer)

Gibbon, Edward 1737-1794 .... **LC 97**
See also BRW 3; DLB 104; RGEL 2

Gibbon, Lewis Grassic .... **TCLC 4**
See Mitchell, James Leslie
See also RGEL 2

Gibbons, Kaye 1960- .... **CLC 50, 88, 145**
See also AAYA 34; AMWS 10; CA 151;
CANR 75, 127; CN 7; CSW; DAM
POP; DLB 292; MTCW 2; MTFW 2005;
NFS 3; RGAL 4; SATA 117

Gibran, Kahlil 1883-1931 . **PC 9; TCLC 1, 9**
See also CA 104; 150; DA3; DAM POET,
POP; EWL 3; MTCW 2; WLIT 6

Gibran, Khalil
See Gibran, Kahlil

Gibson, Mel 1956- .... **CLC 215**

Gibson, William 1914- .... **CLC 23**
See also CA 9-12R; CAD; CANR 9, 42, 75,
125; CD 5, 6; DA; DAB; DAC; DAM
DRAM, MST; DFS 2; DLB 7; LAIT 2;
MAL 5; MTCW 2; MTFW 2005; SATA
66; YAW

Gibson, William 1948- .... **CLC 39, 63, 186, 192; SSC 52**
See also AAYA 12, 59; AMWS 16; BPFB
2; CA 126; 133; CANR 52, 90, 106; CN
6, 7; CPW; DA3; DAM POP; DLB 251;
MTCW 2; MTFW 2005; SCFW 2; SFW 4

Gide, Andre (Paul Guillaume)
1869-1951 ...... **SSC 13; TCLC 5, 12, 36, 177; WLC 3**
See also CA 104; 124; DA; DA3; DAB;
DAC; DAM MST, NOV; DLB 65, 321,
330; EW 8; EWL 3; GFL 1789 to the
Present; MTCW 1, 2; MTFW 2005; NFS
21; RGSF 2; RGWL 2, 3; TWA

Gifford, Barry (Colby) 1946- .... **CLC 34**
See also CA 65-68; CANR 9, 30, 40, 90

Gilbert, Frank
See De Voto, Bernard (Augustine)

Gilbert, W(illiam) S(chwenck)
1836-1911 .... **TCLC 3**
See also CA 104; 173; DAM DRAM, POET;
RGEL 2; SATA 36

Gilbert of Poitiers c. 1085-1154 .... **CMLC 85**

Gilbreth, Frank B(unker), Jr.
1911-2001 .... **CLC 17**
See also CA 9-12R; SATA 2

Gilchrist, Ellen (Louise) 1935- .. **CLC 34, 48, 143; SSC 14, 63**
See also BPFB 2; CA 113; 116; CANR 41,
61, 104; CN 4, 5, 6, 7; CPW; CSW; DAM
POP; DLB 130; EWL 3; EXPS; MTCW
1, 2; MTFW 2005; RGAL 4; RGSF 2;
SSFS 9

Giles, Molly 1942- .... **CLC 39**
See also CA 126; CANR 98

Gill, Eric .... **TCLC 85**
See Gill, (Arthur) Eric (Rowton Peter
Joseph)

Gill, (Arthur) Eric (Rowton Peter Joseph)
1882-1940
See Gill, Eric
See also CA 120; DLB 98

Gill, Patrick
See Creasey, John

Gillette, Douglas .... **CLC 70**

Gilliam, Terry 1940- .... **CLC 21, 141**
See Monty Python
See also AAYA 19, 59; CA 108; 113; CANR
35; INT CA-113

Gilliam, Terry Vance
See Gilliam, Terry

Gillian, Jerry
See Gilliam, Terry

Gilliatt, Penelope (Ann Douglass)
1932-1993 .... **CLC 2, 10, 13, 53**
See also AITN 2; CA 13-16R; 141; CANR
49; CN 1, 2, 3, 4, 5; DLB 14

Gilligan, Carol 1936- .... **CLC 208**
See also CA 142; CANR 121; FW

Gilman, Charlotte (Anna) Perkins (Stetson)
1860-1935 ...... **SSC 13, 62; TCLC 9, 37, 117**
See also AMWS 11; BYA 11; CA 106; 150;
DLB 221; EXPS; FL 1:5; FW; HGG;
LAIT 2; MBL; MTCW 2; MTFW 2005;
RGAL 4; RGSF 2; SFW 4; SSFS 1, 18

Gilmour, David 1946- .... **CLC 35**

Gilpin, William 1724-1804 .... **NCLC 30**

Gilray, J. D.
See Mencken, H(enry) L(ouis)

Gilroy, Frank D(aniel) 1925- .... **CLC 2**
See also CA 81-84; CAD; CANR 32, 64,
86; CD 5, 6; DFS 17; DLB 7

Gilstrap, John 1957(?)- .... **CLC 99**
See also AAYA 67; CA 160; CANR 101

Ginsberg, Allen 1926-1997 .... **CLC 1, 2, 3, 4, 6, 13, 36, 69, 109; PC 4, 47; TCLC 120; WLC 3**
See also AAYA 33; AITN 1; AMWC 1;
AMWS 2; BG 1:2; CA 1-4R; 157; CANR
2, 41, 63, 95; CDALB 1941-1968; CP 1,
2, 3, 4, 5, 6; DA; DA3; DAB; DAC; DAM
MST, POET; DLB 5, 16, 169, 237; EWL
3; GLL 1; LMFS 2; MAL 5; MTCW 1, 2;
MTFW 2005; PAB; PFS 5; RGAL 4;
TUS; WP

Ginzburg, Eugenia .... **CLC 59**
See Ginzburg, Evgeniia

Ginzburg, Evgeniia 1904-1977
See Ginzburg, Eugenia
See also DLB 302

Ginzburg, Natalia 1916-1991 .... **CLC 5, 11, 54, 70; SSC 65; TCLC 156**
See also CA 85-88; 135; CANR 33; DFS
14; DLB 177; EW 13; EWL 3; MTCW 1,
2; MTFW 2005; RGHL; RGWL 2, 3

Giono, Jean 1895-1970 .... **CLC 4, 11; TCLC 124**
See also CA 45-48; 29-32R; CANR 2, 35;
DLB 72, 321; EWL 3; GFL 1789 to the
Present; MTCW 1; RGWL 2, 3

Giovanni, Nikki 1943- ...... **BLC 2; CLC 2, 4, 19, 64, 117; PC 19; WLCS**
See also AAYA 22; AITN 1; BW 2, 3; CA
29-32R; CAAS 6; CANR 18, 41, 60, 91,
130; CDALBS; CLR 6, 73; CP 2, 3, 4, 5,
6, 7; CSW; CWP; CWRI 5; DA; DA3;
DAB; DAC; DAM MST, MULT, POET;
DLB 5, 41; EWL 3; EXPP; INT CANR-
18; MAICYA 1, 2; MAL 5; MTCW 1, 2;
MTFW 2005; PFS 17; RGAL 4; SATA
24, 107; TUS; YAW

Giovene, Andrea 1904-1998 .... **CLC 7**
See also CA 85-88

Gippius, Zinaida (Nikolaevna) 1869-1945
See Hippius, Zinaida (Nikolaevna)
See also CA 106; 212

Giraudoux, Jean(-Hippolyte)
1882-1944 .... **TCLC 2, 7**
See also CA 104; 196; DAM DRAM; DLB
65, 321; EW 9; EWL 3; GFL 1789 to the
Present; RGWL 2, 3; TWA

Gironella, Jose Maria (Pous)
1917-2003 .... **CLC 11**
See also CA 101; 212; EWL 3; RGWL 2, 3

Gissing, George (Robert)
1857-1903 ...... **SSC 37; TCLC 3, 24, 47**
See also BRW 5; CA 105; 167; DLB 18,
135, 184; RGEL 2; TEA

Gitlin, Todd 1943- .... **CLC 201**
See also CA 29-32R; CANR 25, 50, 88

Giurlani, Aldo
See Palazzeschi, Aldo

Gladkov, Fedor Vasil'evich
See Gladkov, Fyodor (Vasilyevich)
See also DLB 272

Gladkov, Fyodor (Vasilyevich)
1883-1958 .... **TCLC 27**
See Gladkov, Fedor Vasil'evich
See also CA 170; EWL 3

Glancy, Diane 1941- .... **CLC 210; NNAL**
See also CA 136; 225; CAAE 225; CAAS
24; CANR 87; DLB 175

Glanville, Brian (Lester) 1931- .... **CLC 6**
See also CA 5-8R; CAAS 9; CANR 3, 70;
CN 1, 2, 3, 4, 5, 6, 7; DLB 15, 139; SATA
42

Glasgow, Ellen (Anderson Gholson)
1873-1945 .... **SSC 34; TCLC 2, 7**
See also AMW; CA 104; 164; DLB 9, 12;
MAL 5; MBL; MTCW 2; MTFW 2005;
RGAL 4; RHW; SSFS 9; TUS

Hebert, Anne 1916-2000 .... **CLC 4, 13, 29**
See also CA 85-88; 187; CANR 69, 126; CCA 1; CWP; CWW 2; DA3; DAC; DAM MST, POET; DLB 68; EWL 3; GFL 1789 to the Present; MTCW 1, 2; MTFW 2005; PFS 20

Hecht, Anthony (Evan) 1923-2004 .... **CLC 8, 13, 19; PC 70**
See also AMWS 10; CA 9-12R; 232; CANR 6, 108; CP 1, 2, 3, 4, 5, 6, 7; DAM POET; DLB 5, 169; EWL 3; PFS 6; WP

Hecht, Ben 1894-1964 ..... **CLC 8; TCLC 101**
See also CA 85-88; DFS 9; DLB 7, 9, 25, 26, 28, 86; FANT; IDFW 3, 4; RGAL 4

Hedayat, Sadeq 1903-1951 .... **TCLC 21**
See also CA 120; EWL 3; RGSF 2

Hegel, Georg Wilhelm Friedrich 1770-1831 .... **NCLC 46, 151**
See also DLB 90; TWA

Heidegger, Martin 1889-1976 .... **CLC 24**
See also CA 81-84; 65-68; CANR 34; DLB 296; MTCW 1, 2; MTFW 2005

Heidenstam, (Carl Gustaf) Verner von 1859-1940 .... **TCLC 5**
See also CA 104; DLB 330

Heidi Louise
See Erdrich, Louise

Heifner, Jack 1946- .... **CLC 11**
See also CA 105; CANR 47

Heijermans, Herman 1864-1924 .... **TCLC 24**
See also CA 123; EWL 3

Heilbrun, Carolyn G(old) 1926-2003 .... **CLC 25, 173**
See Cross, Amanda
See also CA 45-48; 220; CANR 1, 28, 58, 94; FW

Hein, Christoph 1944- .... **CLC 154**
See also CA 158; CANR 108; CDWLB 2; CWW 2; DLB 124

Heine, Heinrich 1797-1856 .... **NCLC 4, 54, 147; PC 25**
See also CDWLB 2; DLB 90; EW 5; RGWL 2, 3; TWA

Heinemann, Larry 1944- .... **CLC 50**
See also CA 110; CAAS 21; CANR 31, 81, 156; DLBD 9; INT CANR-31

Heinemann, Larry Curtiss
See Heinemann, Larry

Heiney, Donald (William) 1921-1993
See Harris, MacDonald
See also CA 1-4R; 142; CANR 3, 58; FANT

Heinlein, Robert A. 1907-1988 .. **CLC 1, 3, 8, 14, 26, 55; SSC 55**
See also AAYA 17; BPFB 2; BYA 4, 13; CA 1-4R; 125; CANR 1, 20, 53; CLR 75; CN 1, 2, 3, 4; CPW; DA3; DAM POP; DLB 8; EXPS; JRDA; LAIT 5; LMFS 2; MAICYA 1, 2; MTCW 1, 2; MTFW 2005; RGAL 4; SATA 9, 69; SATA-Obit 56; SCFW 1, 2; SFW 4; SSFS 7; YAW

Helforth, John
See Doolittle, Hilda

Heliodorus fl. 3rd cent. - .... **CMLC 52**
See also WLIT 8

Hellenhofferu, Vojtech Kapristian z
See Hasek, Jaroslav (Matej Frantisek)

Heller, Joseph 1923-1999 . **CLC 1, 3, 5, 8, 11, 36, 63; TCLC 131, 151; WLC 3**
See also AAYA 24; AITN 1; AMWS 4; BPFB 2; BYA 1; CA 5-8R; 187; CABS 1; CANR 8, 42, 66, 126; CN 1, 2, 3, 4, 5, 6; CPW; DA; DA3; DAB; DAC; DAM MST, NOV, POP; DLB 2, 28, 227; DLBY 1980, 2002; EWL 3; EXPN; INT CANR-8; LAIT 4; MAL 5; MTCW 1, 2; MTFW 2005; NFS 1; RGAL 4; TUS; YAW

Hellman, Lillian 1906-1984 . **CLC 2, 4, 8, 14, 18, 34, 44, 52; DC 1; TCLC 119**
See also AAYA 47; AITN 1, 2; AMWS 1; CA 13-16R; 112; CAD; CANR 33; CWD; DA3; DAM DRAM; DFS 1, 3, 14; DLB 7, 228; DLBY 1984; EWL 3; FL 1:6; FW; LAIT 3; MAL 5; MBL; MTCW 1, 2; MTFW 2005; RGAL 4; TUS

Helprin, Mark 1947- .... **CLC 7, 10, 22, 32**
See also CA 81-84; CANR 47, 64, 124; CDALBS; CN 7; CPW; DA3; DAM NOV, POP; DLBY 1985; FANT; MAL 5; MTCW 1, 2; MTFW 2005; SUFW 2

Helvetius, Claude-Adrien 1715-1771 .. **LC 26**
See also DLB 313

Helyar, Jane Penelope Josephine 1933-
See Poole, Josephine
See also CA 21-24R; CANR 10, 26; CWRI 5; SATA 82, 138; SATA-Essay 138

Hemans, Felicia 1793-1835 ..... **NCLC 29, 71**
See also DLB 96; RGEL 2

Hemingway, Ernest (Miller) 1899-1961 .... **CLC 1, 3, 6, 8, 10, 13, 19, 30, 34, 39, 41, 44, 50, 61, 80; SSC 1, 25, 36, 40, 63; TCLC 115; WLC 3**
See also AAYA 19; AMW; AMWC 1; AMWR 1; BPFB 2; BYA 2, 3, 13, 15; CA 77-80; CANR 34; CDALB 1917-1929; DA; DA3; DAB; DAC; DAM MST, NOV; DLB 4, 9, 102, 210, 308, 316, 330; DLBD 1, 15, 16; DLBY 1981, 1987, 1996, 1998; EWL 3; EXPN; EXPS; LAIT 3, 4; LATS 1:1; MAL 5; MTCW 1, 2; MTFW 2005; NFS 1, 5, 6, 14; RGAL 4; RGSF 2; SSFS 17; TUS; WYA

Hempel, Amy 1951- .... **CLC 39**
See also CA 118; 137; CANR 70; DA3; DLB 218; EXPS; MTCW 2; MTFW 2005; SSFS 2

Henderson, F. C.
See Mencken, H(enry) L(ouis)

Henderson, Sylvia
See Ashton-Warner, Sylvia (Constance)

Henderson, Zenna (Chlarson) 1917-1983 .... **SSC 29**
See also CA 1-4R; 133; CANR 1, 84; DLB 8; SATA 5; SFW 4

Henkin, Joshua .... **CLC 119**
See also CA 161

Henley, Beth .... **CLC 23; DC 6, 14**
See Henley, Elizabeth Becker
See also AAYA 70; CABS 3; CAD; CD 5, 6; CSW; CWD; DFS 2, 21; DLBY 1986; FW

Henley, Elizabeth Becker 1952-
See Henley, Beth
See also CA 107; CANR 32, 73, 140; DA3; DAM DRAM, MST; MTCW 1, 2; MTFW 2005

Henley, William Ernest 1849-1903 .. **TCLC 8**
See also CA 105; 234; DLB 19; RGEL 2

Hennissart, Martha 1929-
See Lathen, Emma
See also CA 85-88; CANR 64

Henry VIII 1491-1547 .... **LC 10**
See also DLB 132

Henry, O. . **SSC 5, 49; TCLC 1, 19; WLC 3**
See Porter, William Sydney
See also AAYA 41; AMWS 2; EXPS; MAL 5; RGAL 4; RGSF 2; SSFS 2, 18; TCWW 1, 2

Henry, Patrick 1736-1799 .... **LC 25**
See also LAIT 1

Henryson, Robert 1430(?)-1506(?) ..... **LC 20, 110; PC 65**
See also BRWS 7; DLB 146; RGEL 2

Henschke, Alfred
See Klabund

Henson, Lance 1944- .... **NNAL**
See also CA 146; DLB 175

Hentoff, Nat(han Irving) 1925- .... **CLC 26**
See also AAYA 4, 42; BYA 6; CA 1-4R; CAAS 6; CANR 5, 25, 77, 114; CLR 1, 52; INT CANR-25; JRDA; MAICYA 1, 2; SATA 42, 69, 133; SATA-Brief 27; WYA; YAW

Heppenstall, (John) Rayner 1911-1981 .... **CLC 10**
See also CA 1-4R; 103; CANR 29; CN 1, 2; CP 1, 2, 3; EWL 3

Heraclitus c. 540B.C.-c. 450B.C. ... **CMLC 22**
See also DLB 176

Herbert, Frank 1920-1986 ... **CLC 12, 23, 35, 44, 85**
See also AAYA 21; BPFB 2; BYA 4, 14; CA 53-56; 118; CANR 5, 43; CDALBS; CPW; DAM POP; DLB 8; INT CANR-5; LAIT 5; MTCW 1, 2; MTFW 2005; NFS 17; SATA 9, 37; SATA-Obit 47; SCFW 1, 2; SFW 4; YAW

Herbert, George 1593-1633 . **LC 24, 121; PC 4**
See also BRW 2; BRWR 2; CDBLB Before 1660; DAB; DAM POET; DLB 126; EXPP; RGEL 2; TEA; WP

Herbert, Zbigniew 1924-1998 ..... **CLC 9, 43; PC 50; TCLC 168**
See also CA 89-92; 169; CANR 36, 74; CDWLB 4; CWW 2; DAM POET; DLB 232; EWL 3; MTCW 1; PFS 22

Herbst, Josephine (Frey) 1897-1969 .... **CLC 34**
See also CA 5-8R; 25-28R; DLB 9

Herder, Johann Gottfried von 1744-1803 .... **NCLC 8**
See also DLB 97; EW 4; TWA

Heredia, Jose Maria 1803-1839 .... **HLCS 2**
See also LAW

Hergesheimer, Joseph 1880-1954 ... **TCLC 11**
See also CA 109; 194; DLB 102, 9; RGAL 4

Herlihy, James Leo 1927-1993 .... **CLC 6**
See also CA 1-4R; 143; CAD; CANR 2; CN 1, 2, 3, 4, 5

Herman, William
See Bierce, Ambrose (Gwinett)

Hermogenes fl. c. 175- .... **CMLC 6**

Hernandez, Jose 1834-1886 .... **NCLC 17**
See also LAW; RGWL 2, 3; WLIT 1

Herodotus c. 484B.C.-c. 420B.C. .. **CMLC 17**
See also AW 1; CDWLB 1; DLB 176; RGWL 2, 3; TWA; WLIT 8

Herr, Michael 1940- .... **CLC 231**
See also CA 89-92; CANR 68, 142; MTCW 1

Herrick, Robert 1591-1674 .... **LC 13; PC 9**
See also BRW 2; BRWC 2; DA; DAB; DAC; DAM MST, POP; DLB 126; EXPP; PFS 13; RGAL 4; RGEL 2; TEA; WP

Herring, Guilles
See Somerville, Edith Oenone

Herriot, James 1916-1995 .... **CLC 12**
See Wight, James Alfred
See also AAYA 1, 54; BPFB 2; CA 148; CANR 40; CLR 80; CPW; DAM POP; LAIT 3; MAICYA 2; MAICYAS 1; MTCW 2; SATA 86, 135; TEA; YAW

Herris, Violet
See Hunt, Violet

Herrmann, Dorothy 1941- .... **CLC 44**
See also CA 107

Herrmann, Taffy
See Herrmann, Dorothy

Hersey, John 1914-1993 .. **CLC 1, 2, 7, 9, 40, 81, 97**
See also AAYA 29; BPFB 2; CA 17-20R; 140; CANR 33; CDALBS; CN 1, 2, 3, 4, 5; CPW; DAM POP; DLB 6, 185, 278,

Hochwalder, Fritz
  See Hochwaelder, Fritz
  See also EWL 3; RGWL 2
Hocking, Mary (Eunice) 1921- .... **CLC 13**
  See also CA 101; CANR 18, 40
Hodgins, Jack 1938- .... **CLC 23**
  See also CA 93-96; CN 4, 5, 6, 7; DLB 60
Hodgson, William Hope
  1877(?)-1918 .... **TCLC 13**
  See also CA 111; 164; CMW 4; DLB 70,
  153, 156, 178; HGG; MTCW 2; SFW 4;
  SUFW 1
Hoeg, Peter 1957- .... **CLC 95, 156**
  See also CA 151; CANR 75; CMW 4; DA3;
  DLB 214; EWL 3; MTCW 2; MTFW
  2005; NFS 17; RGWL 3; SSFS 18
Hoffman, Alice 1952- .... **CLC 51**
  See also AAYA 37; AMWS 10; CA 77-80;
  CANR 34, 66, 100, 138; CN 4, 5, 6, 7;
  CPW; DAM NOV; DLB 292; MAL 5;
  MTCW 1, 2; MTFW 2005; TCLE 1:1
Hoffman, Daniel (Gerard) 1923- . **CLC 6, 13,
  23**
  See also CA 1-4R; CANR 4, 142; CP 1, 2,
  3, 4, 5, 6, 7; DLB 5; TCLE 1:1
Hoffman, Eva 1945- .... **CLC 182**
  See also AMWS 16; CA 132; CANR 146
Hoffman, Stanley 1944- .... **CLC 5**
  See also CA 77-80
Hoffman, William 1925- .... **CLC 141**
  See also CA 21-24R; CANR 9, 103; CSW;
  DLB 234; TCLE 1:1
Hoffman, William M.
  See Hoffman, William M(oses)
  See also CAD; CD 5, 6
Hoffman, William M(oses) 1939- ..... **CLC 40**
  See Hoffman, William M.
  See also CA 57-60; CANR 11, 71
Hoffmann, E(rnst) T(heodor) A(madeus)
  1776-1822 .... **NCLC 2; SSC 13, 92**
  See also CDWLB 2; DLB 90; EW 5; GL 2;
  RGSF 2; RGWL 2, 3; SATA 27; SUFW
  1; WCH
Hofmann, Gert 1931-1993 .... **CLC 54**
  See also CA 128; CANR 145; EWL 3;
  RGHL
Hofmannsthal, Hugo von 1874-1929 ... **DC 4;
  TCLC 11**
  See also CA 106; 153; CDWLB 2; DAM
  DRAM; DFS 17; DLB 81, 118; EW 9;
  EWL 3; RGWL 2, 3
Hogan, Linda 1947- ..... **CLC 73; NNAL; PC
  35**
  See also AMWS 4; ANW; BYA 12; CA 120,
  226; CAAE 226; CANR 45, 73, 129;
  CWP; DAM MULT; DLB 175; SATA
  132; TCWW 2
Hogarth, Charles
  See Creasey, John
Hogarth, Emmett
  See Polonsky, Abraham (Lincoln)
Hogarth, William 1697-1764 .... **LC 112**
  See also AAYA 56
Hogg, James 1770-1835 .... **NCLC 4, 109**
  See also BRWS 10; DLB 93, 116, 159; GL
  2; HGG; RGEL 2; SUFW 1
Holbach, Paul-Henri Thiry
  1723-1789 .... **LC 14**
  See also DLB 313
Holberg, Ludvig 1684-1754 .... **LC 6**
  See also DLB 300; RGWL 2, 3
Holcroft, Thomas 1745-1809 .... **NCLC 85**
  See also DLB 39, 89, 158; RGEL 2
Holden, Ursula 1921- .... **CLC 18**
  See also CA 101; CAAS 8; CANR 22
Holderlin, (Johann Christian) Friedrich
  1770-1843 .... **NCLC 16; PC 4**
  See also CDWLB 2; DLB 90; EW 5; RGWL
  2, 3

Holdstock, Robert
  See Holdstock, Robert P.
Holdstock, Robert P. 1948- .... **CLC 39**
  See also CA 131; CANR 81; DLB 261;
  FANT; HGG; SFW 4; SUFW 2
Holinshed, Raphael fl. 1580- .... **LC 69**
  See also DLB 167; RGEL 2
Holland, Isabelle (Christian)
  1920-2002 .... **CLC 21**
  See also AAYA 11, 64; CA 21-24R; 205;
  CAAE 181; CANR 10, 25, 47; CLR 57;
  CWRI 5; JRDA; LAIT 4; MAICYA 1, 2;
  SATA 8, 70; SATA-Essay 103; SATA-Obit
  132; WYA
Holland, Marcus
  See Caldwell, (Janet Miriam) Taylor
  (Holland)
Hollander, John 1929- .... **CLC 2, 5, 8, 14**
  See also CA 1-4R; CANR 1, 52, 136; CP 1,
  2, 3, 4, 5, 6, 7; DLB 5; MAL 5; SATA 13
Hollander, Paul
  See Silverberg, Robert
Holleran, Andrew .... **CLC 38**
  See Garber, Eric
  See also CA 144; GLL 1
Holley, Marietta 1836(?)-1926 .... **TCLC 99**
  See also CA 118; DLB 11; FL 1:3
Hollinghurst, Alan 1954- .... **CLC 55, 91**
  See also BRWS 10; CA 114; CN 5, 6, 7;
  DLB 207, 326; GLL 1
Hollis, Jim
  See Summers, Hollis (Spurgeon, Jr.)
Holly, Buddy 1936-1959 .... **TCLC 65**
  See also CA 213
Holmes, Gordon
  See Shiel, M(atthew) P(hipps)
Holmes, John
  See Souster, (Holmes) Raymond
Holmes, John Clellon 1926-1988 ...... **CLC 56**
  See also BG 1:2; CA 9-12R; 125; CANR 4;
  CN 1, 2, 3, 4; DLB 16, 237
Holmes, Oliver Wendell, Jr.
  1841-1935 .... **TCLC 77**
  See also CA 114; 186
Holmes, Oliver Wendell
  1809-1894 .... **NCLC 14, 81; PC 71**
  See also AMWS 1; CDALB 1640-1865;
  DLB 1, 189, 235; EXPP; PFS 24; RGAL
  4; SATA 34
Holmes, Raymond
  See Souster, (Holmes) Raymond
Holt, Victoria
  See Hibbert, Eleanor Alice Burford
  See also BPFB 2
Holub, Miroslav 1923-1998 .... **CLC 4**
  See also CA 21-24R; 169; CANR 10; CD-
  WLB 4; CWW 2; DLB 232; EWL 3;
  RGWL 3
Holz, Detlev
  See Benjamin, Walter
Homer c. 8th cent. B.C.- .... **CMLC 1, 16, 61;
  PC 23; WLCS**
  See also AW 1; CDWLB 1; DA; DA3;
  DAB; DAC; DAM MST, POET; DLB
  176; EFS 1; LAIT 1; LMFS 1; RGWL 2,
  3; TWA; WLIT 8; WP
Hongo, Garrett Kaoru 1951- .... **PC 23**
  See also CA 133; CAAS 22; CP 5, 6, 7;
  DLB 120, 312; EWL 3; EXPP; RGAL 4
Honig, Edwin 1919- .... **CLC 33**
  See also CA 5-8R; CAAS 8; CANR 4, 45,
  144; CP 1, 2, 3, 4, 5, 6, 7; DLB 5
Hood, Hugh (John Blagdon) 1928- . **CLC 15,
  28; SSC 42**
  See also CA 49-52; CAAS 17; CANR 1,
  33, 87; CN 1, 2, 3, 4, 5, 6, 7; DLB 53;
  RGSF 2
Hood, Thomas 1799-1845 .... **NCLC 16**
  See also BRW 4; DLB 96; RGEL 2

Hooker, (Peter) Jeremy 1941- .... **CLC 43**
  See also CA 77-80; CANR 22; CP 2, 3, 4,
  5, 6, 7; DLB 40
Hooker, Richard 1554-1600 .... **LC 95**
  See also BRW 1; DLB 132; RGEL 2
hooks, bell 1952(?)- .... **CLC 94**
  See also BW 2; CA 143; CANR 87, 126;
  DLB 246; MTCW 2; MTFW 2005; SATA
  115, 170
Hope, A(lec) D(erwent) 1907-2000 .... **CLC 3,
  51; PC 56**
  See also BRWS 7; CA 21-24R; 188; CANR
  33, 74; CP 1, 2, 3, 4, 5; DLB 289; EWL
  3; MTCW 1, 2; MTFW 2005; PFS 8;
  RGEL 2
Hope, Anthony 1863-1933 .... **TCLC 83**
  See also CA 157; DLB 153, 156; RGEL 2;
  RHW
Hope, Brian
  See Creasey, John
Hope, Christopher (David Tully)
  1944- .... **CLC 52**
  See also AFW; CA 106; CANR 47, 101;
  CN 4, 5, 6, 7; DLB 225; SATA 62
Hopkins, Gerard Manley
  1844-1889 .... **NCLC 17; PC 15; WLC 3**
  See also BRW 5; BRWR 2; CDBLB 1890-
  1914; DA; DA3; DAB; DAC; DAM MST,
  POET; DLB 35, 57; EXPP; PAB; RGEL
  2; TEA; WP
Hopkins, John (Richard) 1931-1998 .. **CLC 4**
  See also CA 85-88; 169; CBD; CD 5, 6
Hopkins, Pauline Elizabeth
  1859-1930 .... **BLC 2; TCLC 28**
  See also AFAW 2; BW 2, 3; CA 141; CANR
  82; DAM MULT; DLB 50
Hopkinson, Francis 1737-1791 .... **LC 25**
  See also DLB 31; RGAL 4
Hopley-Woolrich, Cornell George 1903-1968
  See Woolrich, Cornell
  See also CA 13-14; CANR 58, 156; CAP 1;
  CMW 4; DLB 226; MTCW 2
Horace 65B.C.-8B.C. .... **CMLC 39; PC 46**
  See also AW 2; CDWLB 1; DLB 211;
  RGWL 2, 3; WLIT 8
Horatio
  See Proust, (Valentin-Louis-George-Eugene)
  Marcel
Horgan, Paul (George Vincent
  O'Shaughnessy) 1903-1995 .. **CLC 9, 53**
  See also BPFB 2; CA 13-16R; 147; CANR
  9, 35; CN 1, 2, 3, 4, 5; DAM NOV; DLB
  102, 212; DLBY 1985; INT CANR-9;
  MTCW 1, 2; MTFW 2005; SATA 13;
  SATA-Obit 84; TCWW 1, 2
Horkheimer, Max 1895-1973 .... **TCLC 132**
  See also CA 216; 41-44R; DLB 296
Horn, Peter
  See Kuttner, Henry
Horne, Frank (Smith) 1899-1974 ...... **HR 1:2**
  See also BW 1; CA 125; 53-56; DLB 51;
  WP
Horne, Richard Henry Hengist
  1802(?)-1884 .... **NCLC 127**
  See also DLB 32; SATA 29
Hornem, Horace Esq.
  See Byron, George Gordon (Noel)
Horney, Karen (Clementine Theodore
  Danielsen) 1885-1952 .... **TCLC 71**
  See also CA 114; 165; DLB 246; FW
Hornung, E(rnest) W(illiam)
  1866-1921 .... **TCLC 59**
  See also CA 108; 160; CMW 4; DLB 70
Horovitz, Israel (Arthur) 1939- .... **CLC 56**
  See also CA 33-36R; CAD; CANR 46, 59;
  CD 5, 6; DAM DRAM; DLB 7; MAL 5
Horton, George Moses
  1797(?)-1883(?) .... **NCLC 87**
  See also DLB 50

Horvath, odon von 1901-1938
See von Horvath, Odon
See also EWL 3

Horvath, Oedoen von -1938
See von Horvath, Odon

Horwitz, Julius 1920-1986 .... **CLC 14**
See also CA 9-12R; 119; CANR 12

Horwitz, Ronald
See Harwood, Ronald

Hospital, Janette Turner 1942- .... **CLC 42,
145**
See also CA 108; CANR 48; CN 5, 6, 7;
DLB 325; DLBY 2002; RGSF 2

Hostos, E. M. de
See Hostos (y Bonilla), Eugenio Maria de

Hostos, Eugenio M. de
See Hostos (y Bonilla), Eugenio Maria de

Hostos, Eugenio Maria
See Hostos (y Bonilla), Eugenio Maria de

Hostos (y Bonilla), Eugenio Maria de
1839-1903 .... **TCLC 24**
See also CA 123; 131; HW 1

Houdini
See Lovecraft, H. P.

Houellebecq, Michel 1958- .... **CLC 179**
See also CA 185; CANR 140; MTFW 2005

Hougan, Carolyn 1943- .... **CLC 34**
See also CA 139

Household, Geoffrey (Edward West)
1900-1988 .... **CLC 11**
See also CA 77-80; 126; CANR 58; CMW
4; CN 1, 2, 3, 4; DLB 87; SATA 14;
SATA-Obit 59

Housman, A(lfred) E(dward)
1859-1936 .... **PC 2, 43; TCLC 1, 10;
WLCS**
See also AAYA 66; BRW 6; CA 104; 125;
DA; DA3; DAB; DAC; DAM MST,
POET; DLB 19, 284; EWL 3; EXPP;
MTCW 1, 2; MTFW 2005; PAB; PFS 4,
7; RGEL 2; TEA; WP

Housman, Laurence 1865-1959 .... **TCLC 7**
See also CA 106; 155; DLB 10; FANT;
RGEL 2; SATA 25

Houston, Jeanne Wakatsuki 1934- .... **AAL**
See also AAYA 49; CA 103, 232; CAAE
232; CAAS 16; CANR 29, 123; LAIT 4;
SATA 78, 168; SATA-Essay 168

Howard, Elizabeth Jane 1923- ..... **CLC 7, 29**
See also BRWS 11; CA 5-8R; CANR 8, 62,
146; CN 1, 2, 3, 4, 5, 6, 7

Howard, Maureen 1930- .... **CLC 5, 14, 46,
151**
See also CA 53-56; CANR 31, 75, 140; CN
4, 5, 6, 7; DLBY 1983; INT CANR-31;
MTCW 1, 2; MTFW 2005

Howard, Richard 1929- .... **CLC 7, 10, 47**
See also AITN 1; CA 85-88; CANR 25, 80,
154; CP 1, 2, 3, 4, 5, 6, 7; DLB 5; INT
CANR-25; MAL 5

Howard, Robert E 1906-1936 .... **TCLC 8**
See also BPFB 2; BYA 5; CA 105; 157;
CANR 155; FANT; SUFW 1; TCWW 1,
2

Howard, Robert Ervin
See Howard, Robert E

Howard, Warren F.
See Pohl, Frederik

Howe, Fanny (Quincy) 1940- .... **CLC 47**
See also CA 117; 187; CAAE 187; CAAS
27; CANR 70, 116; CP 6, 7; CWP; SATA-
Brief 52

Howe, Irving 1920-1993 .... **CLC 85**
See also AMWS 6; CA 9-12R; 141; CANR
21, 50; DLB 67; EWL 3; MAL 5; MTCW
1, 2; MTFW 2005

Howe, Julia Ward 1819-1910 .... **TCLC 21**
See also CA 117; 191; DLB 1, 189, 235;
FW

Howe, Susan 1937- .... **CLC 72, 152; PC 54**
See also AMWS 4; CA 160; CP 5, 6, 7;
CWP; DLB 120; FW; RGAL 4

Howe, Tina 1937- .... **CLC 48**
See also CA 109; CAD; CANR 125; CD 5,
6; CWD

Howell, James 1594(?)-1666 .... **LC 13**
See also DLB 151

Howells, W. D.
See Howells, William Dean

Howells, William D.
See Howells, William Dean

Howells, William Dean 1837-1920 ... **SSC 36;
TCLC 7, 17, 41**
See also AMW; CA 104; 134; CDALB
1865-1917; DLB 12, 64, 74, 79, 189;
LMFS 1; MAL 5; MTCW 2; RGAL 4;
TUS

Howes, Barbara 1914-1996 .... **CLC 15**
See also CA 9-12R; 151; CAAS 3; CANR
53; CP 1, 2, 3, 4, 5, 6; SATA 5; TCLE 1:1

Hrabal, Bohumil 1914-1997 ...... **CLC 13, 67;
TCLC 155**
See also CA 106; 156; CAAS 12; CANR
57; CWW 2; DLB 232; EWL 3; RGSF 2

Hrabanus Maurus 776(?)-856 .... **CMLC 78**
See also DLB 148

Hrotsvit of Gandersheim c. 935-c.
1000 .... **CMLC 29**
See also DLB 148

Hsi, Chu 1130-1200 .... **CMLC 42**

Hsun, Lu
See Lu Hsun

Hubbard, L. Ron 1911-1986 .... **CLC 43**
See also AAYA 64; CA 77-80; 118; CANR
52; CPW; DA3; DAM POP; FANT;
MTCW 2; MTFW 2005; SFW 4

Hubbard, Lafayette Ronald
See Hubbard, L. Ron

Huch, Ricarda (Octavia)
1864-1947 .... **TCLC 13**
See also CA 111; 189; DLB 66; EWL 3

Huddle, David 1942- .... **CLC 49**
See also CA 57-60; CAAS 20; CANR 89;
DLB 130

Hudson, Jeffrey
See Crichton, Michael

Hudson, W(illiam) H(enry)
1841-1922 .... **TCLC 29**
See also CA 115; 190; DLB 98, 153, 174;
RGEL 2; SATA 35

Hueffer, Ford Madox
See Ford, Ford Madox

Hughart, Barry 1934- .... **CLC 39**
See also CA 137; FANT; SFW 4; SUFW 2

Hughes, Colin
See Creasey, John

Hughes, David (John) 1930-2005 ..... **CLC 48**
See also CA 116; 129; 238; CN 4, 5, 6, 7;
DLB 14

Hughes, Edward James
See Hughes, Ted
See also DA3; DAM MST, POET

Hughes, (James Mercer) Langston
1902-1967 ..... **BLC 2; CLC 1, 5, 10, 15,
35, 44, 108; DC 3; HR 1:2; PC 1, 53;
SSC 6, 90; WLC 3**
See also AAYA 12; AFAW 1, 2; AMWR 1;
AMWS 1; BW 1, 3; CA 1-4R; 25-28R;
CANR 1, 34, 82; CDALB 1929-1941;
CLR 17; DA; DA3; DAB; DAC; DAM
DRAM, MST, MULT, POET; DFS 6, 18;
DLB 4, 7, 48, 51, 86, 228, 315; EWL 3;
EXPP; EXPS; JRDA; LAIT 3; LMFS 2;
MAICYA 1, 2; MAL 5; MTCW 1, 2;
MTFW 2005; NFS 21; PAB; PFS 1, 3, 6,
10, 15; RGAL 4; RGSF 2; SATA 4, 33;
SSFS 4, 7; TUS; WCH; WP; YAW

Hughes, Richard (Arthur Warren)
1900-1976 .... **CLC 1, 11**
See also CA 5-8R; 65-68; CANR 4; CN 1,
2; DAM NOV; DLB 15, 161; EWL 3;
MTCW 1; RGEL 2; SATA 8; SATA-Obit
25

Hughes, Ted 1930-1998 . **CLC 2, 4, 9, 14, 37,
119; PC 7**
See Hughes, Edward James
See also BRWC 2; BRWR 2; BRWS 1; CA
1-4R; 171; CANR 1, 33, 66, 108; CLR 3;
CP 1, 2, 3, 4, 5, 6; DAB; DAC; DLB 40,
161; EWL 3; EXPP; MAICYA 1, 2;
MTCW 1, 2; MTFW 2005; PAB; PFS 4,
19; RGEL 2; SATA 49; SATA-Brief 27;
SATA-Obit 107; TEA; YAW

Hugo, Richard
See Huch, Ricarda (Octavia)

Hugo, Richard F(ranklin)
1923-1982 .... **CLC 6, 18, 32; PC 68**
See also AMWS 6; CA 49-52; 108; CANR
3; CP 1, 2, 3; DAM POET; DLB 5, 206;
EWL 3; MAL 5; PFS 17; RGAL 4

Hugo, Victor (Marie) 1802-1885 .... **NCLC 3,
10, 21, 161; PC 17; WLC 3**
See also AAYA 28; DA; DA3; DAB; DAC;
DAM DRAM, MST, NOV, POET; DLB
119, 192, 217; EFS 2; EW 6; EXPN; GFL
1789 to the Present; LAIT 1, 2; NFS 5,
20; RGWL 2, 3; SATA 47; TWA

Huidobro, Vicente
See Huidobro Fernandez, Vicente Garcia
See also DLB 283; EWL 3; LAW

Huidobro Fernandez, Vicente Garcia
1893-1948 .... **TCLC 31**
See Huidobro, Vicente
See also CA 131; HW 1

Hulme, Keri 1947- .... **CLC 39, 130**
See also CA 125; CANR 69; CN 4, 5, 6, 7;
CP 6, 7; CWP; DLB 326; EWL 3; FW;
INT CA-125; NFS 24

Hulme, T(homas) E(rnest)
1883-1917 .... **TCLC 21**
See also BRWS 6; CA 117; 203; DLB 19

Humboldt, Alexander von
1769-1859 .... **NCLC 170**
See also DLB 90

Humboldt, Wilhelm von
1767-1835 .... **NCLC 134**
See also DLB 90

Hume, David 1711-1776 .... **LC 7, 56**
See also BRWS 3; DLB 104, 252; LMFS 1;
TEA

Humphrey, William 1924-1997 .... **CLC 45**
See also AMWS 9; CA 77-80; 160; CANR
68; CN 1, 2, 3, 4, 5, 6; CSW; DLB 6, 212,
234, 278; TCWW 1, 2

Humphreys, Emyr Owen 1919- .... **CLC 47**
See also CA 5-8R; CANR 3, 24; CN 1, 2,
3, 4, 5, 6, 7; DLB 15

Humphreys, Josephine 1945- ..... **CLC 34, 57**
See also CA 121; 127; CANR 97; CSW;
DLB 292; INT CA-127

Huneker, James Gibbons
1860-1921 .... **TCLC 65**
See also CA 193; DLB 71; RGAL 4

Hungerford, Hesba Fay
See Brinsmead, H(esba) F(ay)

Hungerford, Pixie
See Brinsmead, H(esba) F(ay)

Hunt, E(verette) Howard, (Jr.)
1918- .... **CLC 3**
See also AITN 1; CA 45-48; CANR 2, 47,
103; CMW 4

Hunt, Francesca
See Holland, Isabelle (Christian)

Hunt, Howard
See Hunt, E(verette) Howard, (Jr.)

Karl, Frederick R(obert)
1927-2004 .... **CLC 34**
See also CA 5-8R; 226; CANR 3, 44, 143

Karr, Mary 1955- .... **CLC 188**
See also AMWS 11; CA 151; CANR 100;
MTFW 2005; NCFS 5

Kastel, Warren
See Silverberg, Robert

Kataev, Evgeny Petrovich 1903-1942
See Petrov, Evgeny
See also CA 120

Kataphusin
See Ruskin, John

Katz, Steve 1935- .... **CLC 47**
See also CA 25-28R; CAAS 14, 64; CANR
12; CN 4, 5, 6, 7; DLBY 1983

Kauffman, Janet 1945- .... **CLC 42**
See also CA 117; CANR 43, 84; DLB 218;
DLBY 1986

Kaufman, Bob (Garnell)
1925-1986 .... **CLC 49; PC 74**
See also BG 1:3; BW 1; CA 41-44R; 118;
CANR 22; CP 1; DLB 16, 41

Kaufman, George S. 1889-1961 ...... **CLC 38;
DC 17**
See also CA 108; 93-96; DAM DRAM;
DFS 1, 10; DLB 7; INT CA-108; MTCW
2; MTFW 2005; RGAL 4; TUS

Kaufman, Moises 1964- .... **DC 26**
See also CA 211; DFS 22; MTFW 2005

Kaufman, Sue .... **CLC 3, 8**
See Barondess, Sue K(aufman)

Kavafis, Konstantinos Petrou 1863-1933
See Cavafy, C(onstantine) P(eter)
See also CA 104

Kavan, Anna 1901-1968 .... **CLC 5, 13, 82**
See also BRWS 7; CA 5-8R; CANR 6, 57;
DLB 255; MTCW 1; RGEL 2; SFW 4

Kavanagh, Dan
See Barnes, Julian

Kavanagh, Julie 1952- .... **CLC 119**
See also CA 163

Kavanagh, Patrick (Joseph)
1904-1967 .... **CLC 22; PC 33**
See also BRWS 7; CA 123; 25-28R; DLB
15, 20; EWL 3; MTCW 1; RGEL 2

Kawabata, Yasunari 1899-1972 ..... **CLC 2, 5,
9, 18, 107; SSC 17**
See Kawabata Yasunari
See also CA 93-96; 33-36R; CANR 88;
DAM MULT; DLB 330; MJW; MTCW 2;
MTFW 2005; RGSF 2; RGWL 2, 3

Kawabata Yasunari
See Kawabata, Yasunari
See also DLB 180; EWL 3

Kaye, M.M. 1908-2004 .... **CLC 28**
See also CA 89-92; 223; CANR 24, 60, 102,
142; MTCW 1, 2; MTFW 2005; RHW;
SATA 62; SATA-Obit 152

Kaye, Mollie
See Kaye, M.M.

Kaye-Smith, Sheila 1887-1956 .... **TCLC 20**
See also CA 118; 203; DLB 36

Kaymor, Patrice Maguilene
See Senghor, Leopold Sedar

Kazakov, Iurii Pavlovich
See Kazakov, Yuri Pavlovich
See also DLB 302

Kazakov, Yuri Pavlovich 1927-1982 . **SSC 43**
See Kazakov, Iurii Pavlovich; Kazakov,
Yury
See also CA 5-8R; CANR 36; MTCW 1;
RGSF 2

Kazakov, Yury
See Kazakov, Yuri Pavlovich
See also EWL 3

Kazan, Elia 1909-2003 .... **CLC 6, 16, 63**
See also CA 21-24R; 220; CANR 32, 78

Kazantzakis, Nikos 1883(?)-1957 .... **TCLC 2,
5, 33, 181**
See also BPFB 2; CA 105; 132; DA3; EW
9; EWL 3; MTCW 1, 2; MTFW 2005;
RGWL 2, 3

Kazin, Alfred 1915-1998 ..... **CLC 34, 38, 119**
See also AMWS 8; CA 1-4R; CAAS 7;
CANR 1, 45, 79; DLB 67; EWL 3

Keane, Mary Nesta (Skrine) 1904-1996
See Keane, Molly
See also CA 108; 114; 151; RHW

Keane, Molly .... **CLC 31**
See Keane, Mary Nesta (Skrine)
See also CN 5, 6; INT CA-114; TCLE 1:1

Keates, Jonathan 1946(?)- .... **CLC 34**
See also CA 163; CANR 126

Keaton, Buster 1895-1966 .... **CLC 20**
See also CA 194

Keats, John 1795-1821 ...... **NCLC 8, 73, 121;
PC 1; WLC 3**
See also AAYA 58; BRW 4; BRWR 1; CD-
BLB 1789-1832; DA; DA3; DAB; DAC;
DAM MST, POET; DLB 96, 110; EXPP;
LMFS 1; PAB; PFS 1, 2, 3, 9, 17; RGEL
2; TEA; WLIT 3; WP

Keble, John 1792-1866 .... **NCLC 87**
See also DLB 32, 55; RGEL 2

Keene, Donald 1922- .... **CLC 34**
See also CA 1-4R; CANR 5, 119

Keillor, Garrison 1942- ..... **CLC 40, 115, 222**
See also AAYA 2, 62; AMWS 16; BEST
89:3; BPFB 2; CA 111; 117; CANR 36,
59, 124; CPW; DA3; DAM POP; DLBY
1987; EWL 3; MTCW 1, 2; MTFW 2005;
SATA 58; TUS

Keith, Carlos
See Lewton, Val

Keith, Michael
See Hubbard, L. Ron

Keller, Gottfried 1819-1890 .... **NCLC 2; SSC
26**
See also CDWLB 2; DLB 129; EW; RGSF
2; RGWL 2, 3

Keller, Nora Okja 1965- .... **CLC 109**
See also CA 187

Kellerman, Jonathan 1949- .... **CLC 44**
See also AAYA 35; BEST 90:1; CA 106;
CANR 29, 51, 150; CMW 4; CPW; DA3;
DAM POP; INT CANR-29

Kelley, William Melvin 1937- .... **CLC 22**
See also BW 1; CA 77-80; CANR 27, 83;
CN 1, 2, 3, 4, 5, 6, 7; DLB 33; EWL 3

Kellogg, Marjorie 1922-2005 .... **CLC 2**
See also CA 81-84; 246

Kellow, Kathleen
See Hibbert, Eleanor Alice Burford

Kelly, Lauren
See Oates, Joyce Carol

Kelly, M(ilton) T(errence) 1947- ...... **CLC 55**
See also CA 97-100; CAAS 22; CANR 19,
43, 84; CN 6

Kelly, Robert 1935- .... **SSC 50**
See also CA 17-20R; CAAS 19; CANR 47;
CP 1, 2, 3, 4, 5, 6, 7; DLB 5, 130, 165

Kelman, James 1946- .... **CLC 58, 86**
See also BRWS 5; CA 148; CANR 85, 130;
CN 5, 6, 7; DLB 194, 319, 326; RGSF 2;
WLIT 4

Kemal, Yasar
See Kemal, Yashar
See also CWW 2; EWL 3; WLIT 6

Kemal, Yashar 1923(?)- .... **CLC 14, 29**
See also CA 89-92; CANR 44

Kemble, Fanny 1809-1893 .... **NCLC 18**
See also DLB 32

Kemelman, Harry 1908-1996 .... **CLC 2**
See also AITN 1; BPFB 2; CA 9-12R; 155;
CANR 6, 71; CMW 4; DLB 28

Kempe, Margery 1373(?)-1440(?) ... **LC 6, 56**
See also BRWS 12; DLB 146; FL 1:1;
RGEL 2

Kempis, Thomas a 1380-1471 .... **LC 11**

Kendall, Henry 1839-1882 .... **NCLC 12**
See also DLB 230

Keneally, Thomas 1935- .... **CLC 5, 8, 10, 14,
19, 27, 43, 117**
See also BRWS 4; CA 85-88; CANR 10,
50, 74, 130; CN 1, 2, 3, 4, 5, 6, 7; CPW;
DA3; DAM NOV; DLB 289, 299, 326;
EWL 3; MTCW 1, 2; MTFW 2005; NFS
17; RGEL 2; RGHL; RHW

Kennedy, A(lison) L(ouise) 1965- ... **CLC 188**
See also CA 168, 213; CAAE 213; CANR
108; CD 5, 6; CN 6, 7; DLB 271; RGSF
2

Kennedy, Adrienne (Lita) 1931- .... **BLC 2;
CLC 66; DC 5**
See also AFAW 2; BW 2, 3; CA 103; CAAS
20; CABS 3; CAD; CANR 26, 53, 82;
CD 5, 6; DAM MULT; DFS 9; DLB 38;
FW; MAL 5

Kennedy, John Pendleton
1795-1870 .... **NCLC 2**
See also DLB 3, 248, 254; RGAL 4

Kennedy, Joseph Charles 1929-
See Kennedy, X. J.
See also CA 1-4R, 201; CAAE 201; CANR
4, 30, 40; CWRI 5; MAICYA 2; MAIC-
YAS 1; SATA 14, 86, 130; SATA-Essay
130

Kennedy, William 1928- ... **CLC 6, 28, 34, 53**
See also AAYA 1; AMWS 7; BPFB 2; CA
85-88; CANR 14, 31, 76, 134; CN 4, 5, 6,
7; DA3; DAM NOV; DLB 143; DLBY
1985; EWL 3; INT CANR-31; MAL 5;
MTCW 1, 2; MTFW 2005; SATA 57

Kennedy, X. J. .... **CLC 8, 42**
See Kennedy, Joseph Charles
See also AMWS 15; CAAS 9; CLR 27; CP
1, 2, 3, 4, 5, 6, 7; DLB 5; SAAS 22

Kenny, Maurice (Francis) 1929- ..... **CLC 87;
NNAL**
See also CA 144; CAAS 22; CANR 143;
DAM MULT; DLB 175

Kent, Kelvin
See Kuttner, Henry

Kenton, Maxwell
See Southern, Terry

Kenyon, Jane 1947-1995 .... **PC 57**
See also CA 118; 148; AMWS 7; CA 118; 148;
CANR 44, 69; CP 6, 7; CWP; DLB 120;
PFS 9, 17; RGAL 4

Kenyon, Robert O.
See Kuttner, Henry

Kepler, Johannes 1571-1630 .... **LC 45**

Ker, Jill
See Conway, Jill K(er)

Kerkow, H. C.
See Lewton, Val

Kerouac, Jack 1922-1969 ...... **CLC 1, 2, 3, 5,
14, 29, 61; TCLC 117; WLC**
See Kerouac, Jean-Louis Lebris de
See also AAYA 25; AMWC 1; AMWS 3;
BG 3; BPFB 2; CDALB 1941-1968; CP
1; CPW; DLB 2, 16, 237; DLBD 3;
DLBY 1995; EWL 3; GLL 1; LATS 1:2;
LMFS 2; MAL 5; NFS 8; RGAL 4; TUS;
WP

Kerouac, Jean-Louis Lebris de 1922-1969
See Kerouac, Jack
See also AITN 1; CA 5-8R; 25-28R; CANR
26, 54, 95; DA; DA3; DAB; DAC; DAM
MST, NOV, POET, POP; MTCW 1, 2;
MTFW 2005

Kerr, (Bridget) Jean (Collins)
1923(?)-2003 .... **CLC 22**
See also CA 5-8R; 212; CANR 7; INT
CANR-7

Author Index

Lamming, George (William) 1927- ... **BLC 2; CLC 2, 4, 66, 144**
    See also BW 2, 3; CA 85-88; CANR 26, 76; CDWLB 3; CN 1, 2, 3, 4, 5, 6, 7; CP 1; DAM MULT; DLB 125; EWL 3; MTCW 1, 2; MTFW 2005; NFS 15; RGEL 2

L'Amour, Louis 1908-1988 .... **CLC 25, 55**
    See also AAYA 16; AITN 2; BEST 89:2; BPFB 2; CA 1-4R; 125; CANR 3, 25, 40; CPW; DA3; DAM NOV, POP; DLB 206; DLBY 1980; MTCW 1, 2; MTFW 2005; RGAL 4; TCWW 1, 2

Lampedusa, Giuseppe (Tomasi) di
    .... **TCLC 13**
    See Tomasi di Lampedusa, Giuseppe
    See also CA 164; EW 11; MTCW 2; MTFW 2005; RGWL 2, 3

Lampman, Archibald 1861-1899 ... **NCLC 25**
    See also DLB 92; RGEL 2; TWA

Lancaster, Bruce 1896-1963 .... **CLC 36**
    See also CA 9-10; CANR 70; CAP 1; SATA 9

Lanchester, John 1962- .... **CLC 99**
    See also CA 194; DLB 267

Landau, Mark Alexandrovich
    See Aldanov, Mark (Alexandrovich)

Landau-Aldanov, Mark Alexandrovich
    See Aldanov, Mark (Alexandrovich)

Landis, Jerry
    See Simon, Paul

Landis, John 1950- .... **CLC 26**
    See also CA 112; 122; CANR 128

Landolfi, Tommaso 1908-1979 .... **CLC 11, 49**
    See also CA 127; 117; DLB 177; EWL 3

Landon, Letitia Elizabeth
    1802-1838 .... **NCLC 15**
    See also DLB 96

Landor, Walter Savage
    1775-1864 .... **NCLC 14**
    See also BRW 4; DLB 93, 107; RGEL 2

Landwirth, Heinz 1927-
    See Lind, Jakov
    See also CA 9-12R; CANR 7

Lane, Patrick 1939- .... **CLC 25**
    See also CA 97-100; CANR 54; CP 3, 4, 5, 6, 7; DAM POET; DLB 53; INT CA-97-100

Lane, Rose Wilder 1887-1968 ...... **TCLC 177**
    See also CA 102; CANR 63; SATA 29; SATA-Brief 28; TCWW 2

Lang, Andrew 1844-1912 .... **TCLC 16**
    See also CA 114; 137; CANR 85; CLR 101; DLB 98, 141, 184; FANT; MAICYA 1, 2; RGEL 2; SATA 16; WCH

Lang, Fritz 1890-1976 .... **CLC 20, 103**
    See also AAYA 65; CA 77-80; 69-72; CANR 30

Lange, John
    See Crichton, Michael

Langer, Elinor 1939- .... **CLC 34**
    See also CA 121

Langland, William 1332(?)-1400(?) .... **LC 19, 120**
    See also BRW 1; DA; DAB; DAC; DAM MST, POET; DLB 146; RGEL 2; TEA; WLIT 3

Langstaff, Launcelot
    See Irving, Washington

Lanier, Sidney 1842-1881 . **NCLC 6, 118; PC 50**
    See also AMWS 1; DAM POET; DLB 64; DLBD 13; EXPP; MAICYA 1; PFS 14; RGAL 4; SATA 18

Lanyer, Aemilia 1569-1645 .... **LC 10, 30, 83; PC 60**
    See also DLB 121

Lao Tzu c. 6th cent. B.C.-3rd cent.
    B.C. .... **CMLC 7**

Lao-Tzu
    See Lao Tzu

Lapine, James (Elliot) 1949- .... **CLC 39**
    See also CA 123; 130; CANR 54, 128; INT CA-130

Larbaud, Valery (Nicolas)
    1881-1957 .... **TCLC 9**
    See also CA 106; 152; EWL 3; GFL 1789 to the Present

Lardner, Ring
    See Lardner, Ring(gold) W(ilmer)
    See also BPFB 2; CDALB 1917-1929; DLB 11, 25, 86, 171; DLBD 16; MAL 5; RGAL 4; RGSF 2

Lardner, Ring W., Jr.
    See Lardner, Ring(gold) W(ilmer)

Lardner, Ring(gold) W(ilmer)
    1885-1933 .... **SSC 32; TCLC 2, 14**
    See Lardner, Ring
    See also AMW; CA 104; 131; MTCW 1, 2; MTFW 2005; TUS

Laredo, Betty
    See Codrescu, Andrei

Larkin, Maia
    See Wojciechowska, Maia (Teresa)

Larkin, Philip (Arthur) 1922-1985 ... **CLC 3, 5, 8, 9, 13, 18, 33, 39, 64; PC 21**
    See also BRWS 1; CA 5-8R; 117; CANR 24, 62; CDBLB 1960 to Present; CP 1, 2, 3, 4; DA3; DAB; DAM MST, POET; DLB 27; EWL 3; MTCW 1, 2; MTFW 2005; PFS 3, 4, 12; RGEL 2

La Roche, Sophie von
    1730-1807 .... **NCLC 121**
    See also DLB 94

La Rochefoucauld, Francois
    1613-1680 .... **LC 108**

Larra (y Sanchez de Castro), Mariano Jose de 1809-1837 .... **NCLC 17, 130**

Larsen, Eric 1941- .... **CLC 55**
    See also CA 132

Larsen, Nella 1893(?)-1963 .... **BLC 2; CLC 37; HR 1:3**
    See also AFAW 1, 2; BW 1; CA 125; CANR 83; DAM MULT; DLB 51; FW; LATS 1:1; LMFS 2

Larson, Charles R(aymond) 1938- ... **CLC 31**
    See also CA 53-56; CANR 4, 121

Larson, Jonathan 1960-1996 .... **CLC 99**
    See also AAYA 28; CA 156; DFS 23; MTFW 2005

La Sale, Antoine de c. 1386-1460(?) . **LC 104**
    See also DLB 208

Las Casas, Bartolome de
    1474-1566 .... **HLCS; LC 31**
    See Casas, Bartolome de las
    See also DLB 318; LAW

Lasch, Christopher 1932-1994 .... **CLC 102**
    See also CA 73-76; 144; CANR 25, 118; DLB 246; MTCW 1, 2; MTFW 2005

Lasker-Schueler, Else 1869-1945 ... **TCLC 57**
    See Lasker-Schuler, Else
    See also CA 183; DLB 66, 124

Lasker-Schuler, Else
    See Lasker-Schueler, Else
    See also EWL 3

Laski, Harold J(oseph) 1893-1950 . **TCLC 79**
    See also CA 188

Latham, Jean Lee 1902-1995 .... **CLC 12**
    See also AITN 1; BYA 1; CA 5-8R; CANR 7, 84; CLR 50; MAICYA 1, 2; SATA 2, 68; YAW

Latham, Mavis
    See Clark, Mavis Thorpe

Lathen, Emma .... **CLC 2**
    See Hennissart, Martha; Latsis, Mary J(ane)
    See also BPFB 2; CMW 4; DLB 306

Lathrop, Francis
    See Leiber, Fritz (Reuter, Jr.)

Latsis, Mary J(ane) 1927-1997
    See Lathen, Emma
    See also CA 85-88; 162; CMW 4

Lattany, Kristin
    See Lattany, Kristin (Elaine Eggleston) Hunter

Lattany, Kristin (Elaine Eggleston) Hunter
    1931- .... **CLC 35**
    See Hunter, Kristin
    See also AITN 1; BW 1; BYA 3; CA 13-16R; CANR 13, 108; CLR 3; CN 7; DLB 33; INT CANR-13; MAICYA 1, 2; SAAS 10; SATA 12, 132; YAW

Lattimore, Richmond (Alexander)
    1906-1984 .... **CLC 3**
    See also CA 1-4R; 112; CANR 1; CP 1, 2, 3; MAL 5

Laughlin, James 1914-1997 .... **CLC 49**
    See also CA 21-24R; 162; CAAS 22; CANR 9, 47; CP 1, 2, 3, 4, 5, 6; DLB 48; DLBY 1996, 1997

Laurence, Margaret 1926-1987 ..... **CLC 3, 6, 13, 50, 62; SSC 7**
    See also BYA 13; CA 5-8R; 121; CANR 33; CN 1, 2, 3, 4; DAC; DAM MST; DLB 53; EWL 3; FW; MTCW 1, 2; MTFW 2005; NFS 11; RGEL 2; RGSF 2; SATA-Obit 50; TCWW 2

Laurent, Antoine 1952- .... **CLC 50**

Lauscher, Hermann
    See Hesse, Hermann

Lautreamont 1846-1870 .. **NCLC 12; SSC 14**
    See Lautreamont, Isidore Lucien Ducasse
    See also GFL 1789 to the Present; RGWL 2, 3

Lautreamont, Isidore Lucien Ducasse
    See Lautreamont
    See also DLB 217

Lavater, Johann Kaspar
    1741-1801 .... **NCLC 142**
    See also DLB 97

Laverty, Donald
    See Blish, James (Benjamin)

Lavin, Mary 1912-1996 . **CLC 4, 18, 99; SSC 4, 67**
    See also CA 9-12R; 151; CANR 33; CN 1, 2, 3, 4, 5, 6; DLB 15, 319; FW; MTCW 1; RGEL 2; RGSF 2; SSFS 23

Lavond, Paul Dennis
    See Kornbluth, C(yril) M.; Pohl, Frederik

Lawes, Henry 1596-1662 .... **LC 113**
    See also DLB 126

Lawler, Ray
    See Lawler, Raymond Evenor
    See also DLB 289

Lawler, Raymond Evenor 1922- .... **CLC 58**
    See Lawler, Ray
    See also CA 103; CD 5, 6; RGEL 2

Lawrence, D(avid) H(erbert Richards)
    1885-1930 .... **PC 54; SSC 4, 19, 73; TCLC 2, 9, 16, 33, 48, 61, 93; WLC 3**
    See Chambers, Jessie
    See also BPFB 2; BRW 7; BRWR 2; CA 104; 121; CANR 131; CDBLB 1914-1945; DA; DA3; DAB; DAC; DAM MST, NOV, POET; DLB 10, 19, 36, 98, 162, 195; EWL 3; EXPP; EXPS; LAIT 2, 3; MTCW 1, 2; MTFW 2005; NFS 18; PFS 6; RGEL 2; RGSF 2; SSFS 2, 6; TEA; WLIT 4; WP

Lawrence, T(homas) E(dward)
    1888-1935 .... **TCLC 18**
    See Dale, Colin
    See also BRWS 2; CA 115; 167; DLB 195

Lawrence of Arabia
    See Lawrence, T(homas) E(dward)

Madach, Imre 1823-1864 .... **NCLC 19**

Madden, (Jerry) David 1933- .... **CLC 5, 15**
See also CA 1-4R; CAAS 3; CANR 4, 45;
CN 3, 4, 5, 6, 7; CSW; DLB 6; MTCW 1

Maddern, Al(an)
See Ellison, Harlan

Madhubuti, Haki R. 1942- ... **BLC 2; CLC 6, 73; PC 5**
See Lee, Don L.
See also BW 2, 3; CA 73-76; CANR 24,
51, 73, 139; CP 6, 7; CSW; DAM MULT,
POET; DLB 5, 41; DLBD 8; EWL 3;
MAL 5; MTCW 2; MTFW 2005; RGAL
4

Madison, James 1751-1836 .... **NCLC 126**
See also DLB 37

Maepenn, Hugh
See Kuttner, Henry

Maepenn, K. H.
See Kuttner, Henry

Maeterlinck, Maurice 1862-1949 ..... **TCLC 3**
See also CA 104; 136; CANR 80; DAM
DRAM; DLB 192; EW 8; EWL 3; GFL
1789 to the Present; LMFS 2; RGWL 2,
3; SATA 66; TWA

Maginn, William 1794-1842 .... **NCLC 8**
See also DLB 110, 159

Mahapatra, Jayanta 1928- .... **CLC 33**
See also CA 73-76; CAAS 9; CANR 15,
33, 66, 87; CP 4, 5, 6, 7; DAM MULT;
DLB 323

Mahfouz, Naguib 1911(?)-2006 ..... **CLC 153; SSC 66**
See Mahfuz, Najib
See also AAYA 49; BEST 89:2; CA 128;
CANR 55, 101; DA3; DAM NOV;
MTCW 1, 2; MTFW 2005; RGWL 2, 3;
SSFS 9

Mahfouz, Naguib Abdel Aziz Al-Sabilgi
See Mahfouz, Naguib

Mahfuz, Najib .... **CLC 52, 55**
See Mahfouz, Naguib
See also AFW; CWW 2; DLBY 1988; EWL
3; RGSF 2; WLIT 6

Mahon, Derek 1941- .... **CLC 27; PC 60**
See also BRWS 6; CA 113; 128; CANR 88;
CP 1, 2, 3, 4, 5, 6, 7; DLB 40; EWL 3

Maiakovskii, Vladimir
See Mayakovski, Vladimir (Vladimirovich)
See also IDTP; RGWL 2, 3

Mailer, Norman 1923- ... **CLC 1, 2, 3, 4, 5, 8, 11, 14, 28, 39, 74, 111**
See also AAYA 31; AITN 2; AMW; AMWC
2; AMWR 2; BPFB 2; CA 9-12R; CABS
1; CANR 28, 74, 77, 130; CDALB 1968-
1988; CN 1, 2, 3, 4, 5, 6, 7; CPW; DA;
DA3; DAB; DAC; DAM MST, NOV,
POP; DLB 2, 16, 28, 185, 278; DLBD 3;
DLBY 1980, 1983; EWL 3; MAL 5;
MTCW 1, 2; MTFW 2005; NFS 10;
RGAL 4; TUS

Mailer, Norman Kingsley
See Mailer, Norman

Maillet, Antonine 1929- .... **CLC 54, 118**
See also CA 115; 120; CANR 46, 74, 77,
134; CCA 1; CWW 2; DAC; DLB 60;
INT CA-120; MTCW 2; MTFW 2005

Maimonides, Moses 1135-1204 ..... **CMLC 76**
See also DLB 115

Mais, Roger 1905-1955 .... **TCLC 8**
See also BW 1, 3; CA 105; 124; CANR 82;
CDWLB 3; DLB 125; EWL 3; MTCW 1;
RGEL 2

Maistre, Joseph 1753-1821 .... **NCLC 37**
See also GFL 1789 to the Present

Maitland, Frederic William
1850-1906 .... **TCLC 65**

Maitland, Sara (Louise) 1950- .... **CLC 49**
See also BRWS 11; CA 69-72; CANR 13,
59; DLB 271; FW

Major, Clarence 1936- ... **BLC 2; CLC 3, 19, 48**
See also AFAW 2; BW 2, 3; CA 21-24R;
CAAS 6; CANR 13, 25, 53, 82; CN 3, 4,
5, 6, 7; CP 2, 3, 4, 5, 6, 7; CSW; DAM
MULT; DLB 33; EWL 3; MAL 5; MSW

Major, Kevin (Gerald) 1949- .... **CLC 26**
See also AAYA 16; CA 97-100; CANR 21,
38, 112; CLR 11; DAC; DLB 60; INT
CANR-21; JRDA; MAICYA 1, 2; MAIC-
YAS 1; SATA 32, 82, 134; WYA; YAW

Maki, James
See Ozu, Yasujiro

Makine, Andrei 1957- .... **CLC 198**
See also CA 176; CANR 103; MTFW 2005

Malabaila, Damiano
See Levi, Primo

Malamud, Bernard 1914-1986 .. **CLC 1, 2, 3, 5, 8, 9, 11, 18, 27, 44, 78, 85; SSC 15; TCLC 129; WLC 4**
See also AAYA 16; AMWS 1; BPFB 2;
BYA 15; CA 5-8R; 118; CABS 1; CANR
28, 62, 114; CDALB 1941-1968; CN 1, 2,
3, 4; CPW; DA; DA3; DAB; DAC; DAM
MST, NOV, POP; DLB 2, 28, 152; DLBY
1980, 1986; EWL 3; EXPS; LAIT 4;
LATS 1:1; MAL 5; MTCW 1, 2; MTFW
2005; NFS 4, 9; RGAL 4; RGHL; RGSF
2; SSFS 8, 13, 16; TUS

Malan, Herman
See Bosman, Herman Charles; Bosman,
Herman Charles

Malaparte, Curzio 1898-1957 .... **TCLC 52**
See also DLB 264

Malcolm, Dan
See Silverberg, Robert

Malcolm, Janet 1934- .... **CLC 201**
See also CA 123; CANR 89; NCFS 1

Malcolm X .... **BLC 2; CLC 82, 117; WLCS**
See Little, Malcolm
See also LAIT 5; NCFS 3

Malebranche, Nicolas 1638-1715 .... **LC 133**
See also GFL Beginnings to 1789

Malherbe, Francois de 1555-1628 .... **LC 5**
See also DLB 327; GFL Beginnings to 1789

Mallarme, Stephane 1842-1898 ...... **NCLC 4, 41; PC 4**
See also DAM POET; DLB 217; EW 7;
GFL 1789 to the Present; LMFS 2; RGWL
2, 3; TWA

Mallet-Joris, Francoise 1930- .... **CLC 11**
See also CA 65-68; CANR 17; CWW 2;
DLB 83; EWL 3; GFL 1789 to the Present

Malley, Ern
See McAuley, James Phillip

Mallon, Thomas 1951- .... **CLC 172**
See also CA 110; CANR 29, 57, 92

Mallowan, Agatha Christie
See Christie, Agatha (Mary Clarissa)

Maloff, Saul 1922- .... **CLC 5**
See also CA 33-36R

Malone, Louis
See MacNeice, (Frederick) Louis

Malone, Michael (Christopher)
1942- .... **CLC 43**
See also CA 77-80; CANR 14, 32, 57, 114

Malory, Sir Thomas 1410(?)-1471(?) . **LC 11, 88; WLCS**
See also BRW 1; BRWR 2; CDBLB Before
1660; DA; DAB; DAC; DAM MST; DLB
146; EFS 2; RGEL 2; SATA 59; SATA-
Brief 33; TEA; WLIT 3

Malouf, David 1934- .... **CLC 28, 86**
See also BRWS 12; CA 124; CANR 50, 76;
CN 3, 4, 5, 6, 7; CP 1, 3, 4, 5, 6, 7; DLB
289; EWL 3; MTCW 2; MTFW 2005;
SSFS 24

Malraux, (Georges-)Andre
1901-1976 .... **CLC 1, 4, 9, 13, 15, 57**
See also BPFB 2; CA 21-22; 69-72; CANR
34, 58; CAP 2; DA3; DAM NOV; DLB
72; EW 12; EWL 3; GFL 1789 to the
Present; MTCW 1, 2; MTFW 2005;
RGWL 2, 3; TWA

Malthus, Thomas Robert
1766-1834 .... **NCLC 145**
See also DLB 107, 158; RGEL 2

Malzberg, Barry N(athaniel) 1939- ... **CLC 7**
See also CA 61-64; CAAS 4; CANR 16;
CMW 4; DLB 8; SFW 4

Mamet, David 1947- .. **CLC 9, 15, 34, 46, 91, 166; DC 4, 24**
See also AAYA 3, 60; AMWS 14; CA 81-
84; CABS 3; CAD; CANR 15, 41, 67, 72,
129; CD 5, 6; DA3; DAM DRAM; DFS
2, 3, 6, 12, 15; DLB 7; EWL 3; IDFW 4;
MAL 5; MTCW 1, 2; MTFW 2005; RGAL
4

Mamet, David Alan
See Mamet, David

Mamoulian, Rouben (Zachary)
1897-1987 .... **CLC 16**
See also CA 25-28R; 124; CANR 85

Mandelshtam, Osip
See Mandelstam, Osip (Emilievich)
See also EW 10; EWL 3; RGWL 2, 3

Mandelstam, Osip (Emilievich)
1891(?)-1943(?) .... **PC 14; TCLC 2, 6**
See Mandelshtam, Osip
See also CA 104; 150; MTCW 2; TWA

Mander, (Mary) Jane 1877-1949 ... **TCLC 31**
See also CA 162; RGEL 2

Mandeville, Bernard 1670-1733 .... **LC 82**
See also DLB 101

Mandeville, Sir John fl. 1350- ..... **CMLC 19**
See also DLB 146

Mandiargues, Andre Pieyre de .... **CLC 41**
See Pieyre de Mandiargues, Andre
See also DLB 83

Mandrake, Ethel Belle
See Thurman, Wallace (Henry)

Mangan, James Clarence
1803-1849 .... **NCLC 27**
See also RGEL 2

Maniere, J.-E.
See Giraudoux, Jean(-Hippolyte)

Mankiewicz, Herman (Jacob)
1897-1953 .... **TCLC 85**
See also CA 120; 169; DLB 26; IDFW 3, 4

Manley, (Mary) Delariviere
1672(?)-1724 .... **LC 1, 42**
See also DLB 39, 80; RGEL 2

Mann, Abel
See Creasey, John

Mann, Emily 1952- .... **DC 7**
See also CA 130; CAD; CANR 55; CD 5,
6; CWD; DLB 266

Mann, (Luiz) Heinrich 1871-1950 ... **TCLC 9**
See also CA 106; 164, 181; DLB 66, 118;
EW 8; EWL 3; RGWL 2, 3

Mann, (Paul) Thomas 1875-1955 . **SSC 5, 80, 82; TCLC 2, 8, 14, 21, 35, 44, 60, 168; WLC 4**
See also BPFB 2; CA 104; 128; CANR 133;
CDWLB 2; DA; DA3; DAB; DAC; DAM
MST, NOV; DLB 66; EW 9; EWL 3; GLL
1; LATS 1:1; LMFS 1; MTCW 1, 2;
MTFW 2005; NFS 17; RGSF 2; RGWL
2, 3; SSFS 4, 9; TWA

Mannheim, Karl 1893-1947 .... **TCLC 65**
See also CA 204

Martinez Sierra, Gregorio
See Martinez Sierra, Maria
Martinez Sierra, Gregorio
1881-1947 .... **TCLC 6**
See also CA 115; EWL 3
Martinez Sierra, Maria 1874-1974 .. **TCLC 6**
See also CA 250; 115; EWL 3
Martinsen, Martin
See Follett, Ken
Martinson, Harry (Edmund)
1904-1978 .... **CLC 14**
See also CA 77-80; CANR 34, 130; DLB
259; EWL 3
Martyn, Edward 1859-1923 .... **TCLC 131**
See also CA 179; DLB 10; RGEL 2
Marut, Ret
See Traven, B.
Marut, Robert
See Traven, B.
Marvell, Andrew 1621-1678 .... **LC 4, 43; PC
10; WLC 4**
See also BRW 2; BRWR 2; CDBLB 1660-
1789; DA; DAB; DAC; DAM MST,
POET; DLB 131; EXPP; PFS 5; RGEL 2;
TEA; WP
Marx, Karl (Heinrich)
1818-1883 .... **NCLC 17, 114**
See also DLB 129; LATS 1:1; TWA
Masaoka, Shiki -1902 .... **TCLC 18**
See Masaoka, Tsunenori
See also RGWL 3
Masaoka, Tsunenori 1867-1902
See Masaoka, Shiki
See also CA 117; 191; TWA
Masefield, John (Edward)
1878-1967 .... **CLC 11, 47**
See also CA 19-20; 25-28R; CANR 33;
CAP 2; CDBLB 1890-1914; DAM POET;
DLB 10, 19, 153, 160; EWL 3; EXPP;
FANT; MTCW 1, 2; PFS 5; RGEL 2;
SATA 19
Maso, Carole 1955(?)- .... **CLC 44**
See also CA 170; CANR 148; CN 7; GLL
2; RGAL 4
Mason, Bobbie Ann 1940- ... **CLC 28, 43, 82,
154; SSC 4**
See also AAYA 5, 42; AMWS 8; BPFB 2;
CA 53-56; CANR 11, 31, 58, 83, 125;
CDALBS; CN 5, 6, 7; CSW; DA3; DLB
173; DLBY 1987; EWL 3; EXPS; INT
CANR-31; MAL 5; MTCW 1, 2; MTFW
2005; NFS 4; RGAL 4; RGSF 2; SSFS 3,
8, 20; TCLE 1:2; YAW
Mason, Ernst
See Pohl, Frederik
Mason, Hunni B.
See Sternheim, (William Adolf) Carl
Mason, Lee W.
See Malzberg, Barry N(athaniel)
Mason, Nick 1945- .... **CLC 35**
Mason, Tally
See Derleth, August (William)
Mass, Anna .... **CLC 59**
Mass, William
See Gibson, William
Massinger, Philip 1583-1640 .... **LC 70**
See also BRWS 11; DLB 58; RGEL 2
Master Lao
See Lao Tzu
Masters, Edgar Lee 1868-1950 ...... **PC 1, 36;
TCLC 2, 25; WLCS**
See also AMWS 1; CA 104; 133; CDALB
1865-1917; DA; DAC; DAM MST,
POET; DLB 54; EWL 3; EXPP; MAL 5;
MTCW 1, 2; MTFW 2005; RGAL 4;
TUS; WP
Masters, Hilary 1928- .... **CLC 48**
See also CA 25-28R, 217; CAAE 217;
CANR 13, 47, 97; CN 6, 7; DLB 244

Mastrosimone, William 1947- .... **CLC 36**
See also CA 186; CAD; CD 5, 6
Mathe, Albert
See Camus, Albert
Mather, Cotton 1663-1728 .... **LC 38**
See also AMWS 2; CDALB 1640-1865;
DLB 24, 30, 140; RGAL 4; TUS
Mather, Increase 1639-1723 .... **LC 38**
See also DLB 24
Mathers, Marshall
See Eminem
Mathers, Marshall Bruce
See Eminem
Matheson, Richard (Burton) 1926- .. **CLC 37**
See also AAYA 31; CA 97-100; CANR 88,
99; DLB 8, 44; HGG; INT CA-97-100;
SCFW 1, 2; SFW 4; SUFW 2
Mathews, Harry (Burchell) 1930- ..... **CLC 6,
52**
See also CA 21-24R; CAAS 6; CANR 18,
40, 98; CN 5, 6, 7
Mathews, John Joseph 1894-1979 .. **CLC 84;
NNAL**
See also CA 19-20; 142; CANR 45; CAP 2;
DAM MULT; DLB 175; TCWW 1, 2
Mathias, Roland (Glyn) 1915- .... **CLC 45**
See also CA 97-100; CANR 19, 41; CP 1,
2, 3, 4, 5, 6, 7; DLB 27
Matsuo Basho 1644(?)-1694 ...... **LC 62; PC 3**
See Basho, Matsuo
See also DAM POET; PFS 2, 7, 18
Mattheson, Rodney
See Creasey, John
Matthews, (James) Brander
1852-1929 .... **TCLC 95**
See also CA 181; DLB 71, 78; DLBD 13
Matthews, Greg 1949- .... **CLC 45**
See also CA 135
Matthews, William (Procter III)
1942-1997 .... **CLC 40**
See also AMWS 9; CA 29-32R; 162; CAAS
18; CANR 12, 57; CP 2, 3, 4, 5, 6; DLB
5
Matthias, John (Edward) 1941- .... **CLC 9**
See also CA 33-36R; CANR 56; CP 4, 5, 6,
7
Matthiessen, F(rancis) O(tto)
1902-1950 .... **TCLC 100**
See also CA 185; DLB 63; MAL 5
Matthiessen, Peter 1927- ... **CLC 5, 7, 11, 32,
64**
See also AAYA 6, 40; AMWS 5; ANW;
BEST 90:4; BPFB 2; CA 9-12R; CANR
21, 50, 73, 100, 138; CN 1, 2, 3, 4, 5, 6,
7; DA3; DAM NOV; DLB 6, 173, 275;
MAL 5; MTCW 1, 2; MTFW 2005; SATA
27
Maturin, Charles Robert
1780(?)-1824 .... **NCLC 6, 169**
See also BRWS 8; DLB 178; GL 3; HGG;
LMFS 1; RGEL 2; SUFW
Matute (Ausejo), Ana Maria 1925- .. **CLC 11**
See also CA 89-92; CANR 129; CWW 2;
DLB 322; EWL 3; MTCW 1; RGSF 2
Maugham, W. S.
See Maugham, W(illiam) Somerset
Maugham, W(illiam) Somerset
1874-1965 .. **CLC 1, 11, 15, 67, 93; SSC
8, 94; WLC 4**
See also AAYA 55; BPFB 2; BRW 6; CA
5-8R; 25-28R; CANR 40, 127; CDBLB
1914-1945; CMW 4; DA; DA3; DAB;
DAC; DAM DRAM, MST, NOV; DFS
22; DLB 10, 36, 77, 100, 162, 195; EWL
3; LAIT 3; MTCW 1, 2; MTFW 2005;
NFS 23; RGEL 2; RGSF 2; SATA 54;
SSFS 17
Maugham, William Somerset
See Maugham, W(illiam) Somerset

Maupassant, (Henri Rene Albert) Guy de
1850-1893 . **NCLC 1, 42, 83; SSC 1, 64;
WLC 4**
See also BYA 14; DA; DA3; DAB; DAC;
DAM MST; DLB 123; EW 7; EXPS; GFL
1789 to the Present; LAIT 2; LMFS 1;
RGSF 2; RGWL 2, 3; SSFS 4, 21; SUFW;
TWA
Maupin, Armistead 1944- .... **CLC 95**
See also CA 125; 130; CANR 58, 101;
CPW; DA3; DAM POP; DLB 278; GLL
1; INT CA-130; MTCW 2; MTFW 2005
Maupin, Armistead Jones, Jr.
See Maupin, Armistead
Maurhut, Richard
See Traven, B.
Mauriac, Claude 1914-1996 .... **CLC 9**
See also CA 89-92; 152; CWW 2; DLB 83;
EWL 3; GFL 1789 to the Present
Mauriac, Francois (Charles)
1885-1970 .... **CLC 4, 9, 56; SSC 24**
See also CA 25-28; CAP 2; DLB 65; EW
10; EWL 3; GFL 1789 to the Present;
MTCW 1, 2; MTFW 2005; RGWL 2, 3;
TWA
Mavor, Osborne Henry 1888-1951
See Bridie, James
See also CA 104
Maxwell, William (Keepers, Jr.)
1908-2000 .... **CLC 19**
See also AMWS 8; CA 93-96; 189; CANR
54, 95; CN 1, 2, 3, 4, 5, 6, 7; DLB 218,
278; DLBY 1980; INT CA-93-96; MAL
5; SATA-Obit 128
May, Elaine 1932- .... **CLC 16**
See also CA 124; 142; CAD; CWD; DLB
44
Mayakovski, Vladimir (Vladimirovich)
1893-1930 .... **TCLC 4, 18**
See Maiakovskii, Vladimir; Mayakovsky,
Vladimir
See also CA 104; 158; EWL 3; MTCW 2;
MTFW 2005; SFW 4; TWA
Mayakovsky, Vladimir
See Mayakovski, Vladimir (Vladimirovich)
See also EW 11; WP
Mayhew, Henry 1812-1887 .... **NCLC 31**
See also DLB 18, 55, 190
Mayle, Peter 1939(?)- .... **CLC 89**
See also CA 139; CANR 64, 109
Maynard, Joyce 1953- .... **CLC 23**
See also CA 111; 129; CANR 64
Mayne, William (James Carter)
1928- .... **CLC 12**
See also AAYA 20; CA 9-12R; CANR 37,
80, 100; CLR 25; FANT; JRDA; MAI-
CYA 1, 2; MAICYAS 1; SAAS 11; SATA
6, 68, 122; SUFW 2; YAW
Mayo, Jim
See L'Amour, Louis
Maysles, Albert 1926- .... **CLC 16**
See also CA 29-32R
Maysles, David 1932-1987 .... **CLC 16**
See also CA 191
Mazer, Norma Fox 1931- .... **CLC 26**
See also AAYA 5, 36; BYA 1, 8; CA 69-72;
CANR 12, 32, 66, 129; CLR 23; JRDA;
MAICYA 1, 2; SAAS 1; SATA 24, 67,
105, 168; WYA; YAW
Mazzini, Guiseppe 1805-1872 .... **NCLC 34**
McAlmon, Robert (Menzies)
1895-1956 .... **TCLC 97**
See also CA 107; 168; DLB 4, 45; DLBD
15; GLL 1
McAuley, James Phillip 1917-1976 .. **CLC 45**
See also CA 97-100; CP 1, 2; DLB 260;
RGEL 2

Author Index

MTFW 2005; RGEL 2; RGSF 2; SATA
29; SSFS 5, 13, 19; TCLE 1:2; WWE 1
Munro, H(ector) H(ugh) 1870-1916
See Saki
See also AAYA 56; CA 104; 130; CANR
104; CDBLB 1890-1914; DA; DA3;
DAB; DAC; DAM MST, NOV; DLB 34,
162; EXPS; MTCW 1, 2; MTFW 2005;
RGEL 2; SSFS 15
Murakami, Haruki 1949- .... **CLC 150**
See Murakami Haruki
See also CA 165; CANR 102, 146; MJW;
RGWL 3; SFW 4; SSFS 23
Murakami Haruki
See Murakami, Haruki
See also CWW 2; DLB 182; EWL 3
Murasaki, Lady
See Murasaki Shikibu
Murasaki Shikibu 978(?)-1026(?) .. **CMLC 1,
79**
See also EFS 2; LATS 1:1; RGWL 2, 3
Murdoch, Iris 1919-1999 .. **CLC 1, 2, 3, 4, 6,
8, 11, 15, 22, 31, 51; TCLC 171**
See also BRWS 1; CA 13-16R; 179; CANR
8, 43, 68, 103, 142; CBD; CDBLB 1960
to Present; CN 1, 2, 3, 4, 5, 6; CWD;
DA3; DAB; DAC; DAM MST, NOV;
DLB 14, 194, 233, 326; EWL 3; INT
CANR-8; MTCW 1, 2; MTFW 2005; NFS
18; RGEL 2; TCLE 1:2; TEA; WLIT 4
Murfree, Mary Noailles 1850-1922 .. **SSC 22;
TCLC 135**
See also CA 122; 176; DLB 12, 74; RGAL
4
Murglie
See Murnau, F.W.
Murnau, Friedrich Wilhelm
See Murnau, F.W.
Murnau, F.W. 1888-1931 .... **TCLC 53**
See also CA 112
Murphy, Richard 1927- .... **CLC 41**
See also BRWS 5; CA 29-32R; CP 1, 2, 3,
4, 5, 6, 7; DLB 40; EWL 3
Murphy, Sylvia 1937- .... **CLC 34**
See also CA 121
Murphy, Thomas (Bernard) 1935- ... **CLC 51**
See Murphy, Tom
See also CA 101
Murphy, Tom
See Murphy, Thomas (Bernard)
See also DLB 310
Murray, Albert L. 1916- .... **CLC 73**
See also BW 2; CA 49-52; CANR 26, 52,
78; CN 7; CSW; DLB 38; MTFW 2005
Murray, James Augustus Henry
1837-1915 .... **TCLC 117**
Murray, Judith Sargent
1751-1820 .... **NCLC 63**
See also DLB 37, 200
Murray, Les(lie Allan) 1938- .... **CLC 40**
See also BRWS 7; CA 21-24R; CANR 11,
27, 56, 103; CP 1, 2, 3, 4, 5, 6, 7; DAM
POET; DLB 289; DLBY 2001; EWL 3;
RGEL 2
Murry, J. Middleton
See Murry, John Middleton
Murry, John Middleton
1889-1957 .... **TCLC 16**
See also CA 118; 217; DLB 149
Musgrave, Susan 1951- .... **CLC 13, 54**
See also CA 69-72; CANR 45, 84; CCA 1;
CP 2, 3, 4, 5, 6, 7; CWP
Musil, Robert (Edler von)
1880-1942 .... **SSC 18; TCLC 12, 68**
See also CA 109; CANR 55, 84; CDWLB
2; DLB 81, 124; EW 9; EWL 3; MTCW
2; RGSF 2; RGWL 2, 3
Muske, Carol .... **CLC 90**
See Muske-Dukes, Carol (Anne)

Muske-Dukes, Carol (Anne) 1945-
See Muske, Carol
See also CA 65-68, 203; CAAE 203; CANR
32, 70; CWP; PFS 24
Musset, Alfred de 1810-1857 . **DC 27; NCLC
7, 150**
See also DLB 192, 217; EW 6; GFL 1789
to the Present; RGWL 2, 3; TWA
Musset, Louis Charles Alfred de
See Musset, Alfred de
Mussolini, Benito (Amilcare Andrea)
1883-1945 .... **TCLC 96**
See also CA 116
Mutanabbi, Al-
See al-Mutanabbi, Ahmad ibn al-Husayn
Abu al-Tayyib al-Jufi al-Kindi
See also WLIT 6
My Brother's Brother
See Chekhov, Anton (Pavlovich)
Myers, L(eopold) H(amilton)
1881-1944 .... **TCLC 59**
See also CA 157; DLB 15; EWL 3; RGEL
2
Myers, Walter Dean 1937- .. **BLC 3; CLC 35**
See Myers, Walter M.
See also AAYA 4, 23; BW 2; BYA 6, 8, 11;
CA 33-36R; CANR 20, 42, 67, 108; CLR
4, 16, 35, 110; DAM MULT, NOV; DLB
33; INT CANR-20; JRDA; LAIT 5; MAI-
CYA 1, 2; MAICYAS 1; MTCW 2;
MTFW 2005; SAAS 2; SATA 41, 71, 109,
157; SATA-Brief 27; WYA; YAW
Myers, Walter M.
See Myers, Walter Dean
Myles, Symon
See Follett, Ken
Nabokov, Vladimir (Vladimirovich)
1899-1977 .... **CLC 1, 2, 3, 6, 8, 11, 15,
23, 44, 46, 64; SSC 11, 86; TCLC 108;
WLC 4**
See also AAYA 45; AMW; AMWC 1;
AMWR 1; BPFB 2; CA 5-8R; 69-72;
CANR 20, 102; CDALB 1941-1968; CN
1, 2; CP 2; DA; DA3; DAB; DAC; DAM
MST, NOV; DLB 2, 244, 278, 317; DLBD
3; DLBY 1980, 1991; EWL 3; EXPS;
LATS 1:2; MAL 5; MTCW 1, 2; MTFW
2005; NCFS 4; NFS 9; RGAL 4; RGSF
2; SSFS 6, 15; TUS
Naevius c. 265B.C.-201B.C. .... **CMLC 37**
See also DLB 211
Nagai, Kafu .... **TCLC 51**
See Nagai, Sokichi
See also DLB 180
Nagai, Sokichi 1879-1959
See Nagai, Kafu
See also CA 117
Nagy, Laszlo 1925-1978 .... **CLC 7**
See also CA 129; 112
Naidu, Sarojini 1879-1949 .... **TCLC 80**
See also EWL 3; RGEL 2
Naipaul, Shiva 1945-1985 .... **CLC 32, 39;
TCLC 153**
See also CA 110; 112; 116; CANR 33; CN
2, 3; DA3; DAM NOV; DLB 157; DLBY
1985; EWL 3; MTCW 1, 2; MTFW 2005
Naipaul, V.S. 1932- .. **CLC 4, 7, 9, 13, 18, 37,
105, 199; SSC 38**
See also BPFB 2; BRWS 1; CA 1-4R;
CANR 1, 33, 51, 91, 126; CDBLB 1960
to Present; CDWLB 3; CN 1, 2, 3, 4, 5,
6, 7; DA3; DAB; DAC; DAM MST,
NOV; DLB 125, 204, 207, 326; DLBY
1985, 2001; EWL 3; LATS 1:2; MTCW
1, 2; MTFW 2005; RGEL 2; RGSF 2;
TWA; WLIT 4; WWE 1
Nakos, Lilika 1903(?)-1989 .... **CLC 29**
Napoleon
See Yamamoto, Hisaye

Narayan, R.K. 1906-2001 ...... **CLC 7, 28, 47,
121, 211; SSC 25**
See also BPFB 2; CA 81-84; 196; CANR
33, 61, 112; CN 1, 2, 3, 4, 5, 6, 7; DA3;
DAM NOV; DLB 323; DNFS 1; EWL 3;
MTCW 1, 2; MTFW 2005; RGEL 2;
RGSF 2; SATA 62; SSFS 5; WWE 1
Nash, (Frediric) Ogden 1902-1971 . **CLC 23;
PC 21; TCLC 109**
See also CA 13-14; 29-32R; CANR 34, 61;
CAP 1; CP 1; DAM POET; DLB 11;
MAICYA 1, 2; MAL 5; MTCW 1, 2;
RGAL 4; SATA 2, 46; WP
Nashe, Thomas 1567-1601(?) .... **LC 41, 89**
See also DLB 167; RGEL 2
Nathan, Daniel
See Dannay, Frederic
Nathan, George Jean 1882-1958 .... **TCLC 18**
See Hatteras, Owen
See also CA 114; 169; DLB 137; MAL 5
Natsume, Kinnosuke
See Natsume, Soseki
Natsume, Soseki 1867-1916 .... **TCLC 2, 10**
See Natsume Soseki; Soseki
See also CA 104; 195; RGWL 2, 3; TWA
Natsume Soseki
See Natsume, Soseki
See also DLB 180; EWL 3
Natti, (Mary) Lee 1919-
See Kingman, Lee
See also CA 5-8R; CANR 2
Navarre, Marguerite de
See de Navarre, Marguerite
Naylor, Gloria 1950- ..... **BLC 3; CLC 28, 52,
156; WLCS**
See also AAYA 6, 39; AFAW 1, 2; AMWS
8; BW 2, 3; CA 107; CANR 27, 51, 74,
130; CN 4, 5, 6, 7; CPW; DA; DA3;
DAC; DAM MST, MULT, NOV, POP;
DLB 173; EWL 3; FW; MAL 5; MTCW
1, 2; MTFW 2005; NFS 4, 7; RGAL 4;
TCLE 1:2; TUS
Neal, John 1793-1876 .... **NCLC 161**
See also DLB 1, 59, 243; FW; RGAL 4
Neff, Debra .... **CLC 59**
Neihardt, John Gneisenau
1881-1973 .... **CLC 32**
See also CA 13-14; CANR 65; CAP 1; DLB
9, 54, 256; LAIT 2; TCWW 1, 2
Nekrasov, Nikolai Alekseevich
1821-1878 .... **NCLC 11**
See also DLB 277
Nelligan, Emile 1879-1941 .... **TCLC 14**
See also CA 114; 204; DLB 92; EWL 3
Nelson, Willie 1933- .... **CLC 17**
See also CA 107; CANR 114
Nemerov, Howard 1920-1991 .... **CLC 2, 6, 9,
36; PC 24; TCLC 124**
See also AMW; CA 1-4R; 134; CABS 2;
CANR 1, 27, 53; CN 1, 2, 3; CP 1, 2, 3,
4, 5; DAM POET; DLB 5, 6; DLBY 1983;
EWL 3; INT CANR-27; MAL 5; MTCW
1, 2; MTFW 2005; PFS 10, 14; RGAL 4
Neruda, Pablo 1904-1973 .. **CLC 1, 2, 5, 7, 9,
28; HLC 2; PC 4, 64; WLC 4**
See also CA 19-20; 45-48; CANR 131; CAP
2; DA; DA3; DAB; DAC; DAM MST,
MULT, POET; DLB 283; DNFS 2; EWL
3; HW 1; LAW; MTCW 1, 2; MTFW
2005; PFS 11; RGWL 2, 3; TWA; WLIT
1; WP
Nerval, Gerard de 1808-1855 ... **NCLC 1, 67;
PC 13; SSC 18**
See also DLB 217; EW 6; GFL 1789 to the
Present; RGSF 2; RGWL 2, 3
Nervo, (Jose) Amado (Ruiz de)
1870-1919 .... **HLCS 2; TCLC 11**
See also CA 109; 131; DLB 290; EWL 3;
HW 1; LAW

Nesbit, Malcolm
See Chester, Alfred

Nessi, Pio Baroja y
See Baroja, Pio

Nestroy, Johann 1801-1862 .... **NCLC 42**
See also DLB 133; RGWL 2, 3

Netterville, Luke
See O'Grady, Standish (James)

Neufeld, John (Arthur) 1938- .... **CLC 17**
See also AAYA 11; CA 25-28R; CANR 11,
37, 56; CLR 52; MAICYA 1, 2; SAAS 3;
SATA 6, 81, 131; SATA-Essay 131; YAW

Neumann, Alfred 1895-1952 .... **TCLC 100**
See also CA 183; DLB 56

Neumann, Ferenc
See Molnar, Ferenc

Neville, Emily Cheney 1919- .... **CLC 12**
See also BYA 2; CA 5-8R; CANR 3, 37,
85; JRDA; MAICYA 1, 2; SAAS 2; SATA
1; YAW

Newbound, Bernard Slade 1930-
See Slade, Bernard
See also CA 81-84; CANR 49; CD 5; DAM
DRAM

Newby, P(ercy) H(oward)
1918-1997 .... **CLC 2, 13**
See also CA 5-8R; 161; CANR 32, 67; CN
1, 2, 3, 4, 5, 6; DAM NOV; DLB 15, 326;
MTCW 1; RGEL 2

Newcastle
See Cavendish, Margaret Lucas

Newlove, Donald 1928- .... **CLC 6**
See also CA 29-32R; CANR 25

Newlove, John (Herbert) 1938- .... **CLC 14**
See also CA 21-24R; CANR 9, 25; CP 1, 2,
3, 4, 5, 6, 7

Newman, Charles 1938-2006 .... **CLC 2, 8**
See also CA 21-24R; 249; CANR 84; CN
3, 4, 5, 6

Newman, Charles Hamilton
See Newman, Charles

Newman, Edwin (Harold) 1919- ...... **CLC 14**
See also AITN 1; CA 69-72; CANR 5

Newman, John Henry 1801-1890 . **NCLC 38,
99**
See also BRWS 7; DLB 18, 32, 55; RGEL
2

Newton, (Sir) Isaac 1642-1727 ...... **LC 35, 53**
See also DLB 252

Newton, Suzanne 1936- .... **CLC 35**
See also BYA 7; CA 41-44R; CANR 14;
JRDA; SATA 5, 77

New York Dept. of Ed. .... **CLC 70**

Nexo, Martin Andersen
1869-1954 .... **TCLC 43**
See also CA 202; DLB 214; EWL 3

Nezval, Vitezslav 1900-1958 .... **TCLC 44**
See also CA 123; CDWLB 4; DLB 215;
EWL 3

Ng, Fae Myenne 1957(?)- .... **CLC 81**
See also BYA 11; CA 146

Ngema, Mbongeni 1955- .... **CLC 57**
See also BW 2; CA 143; CANR 84; CD 5,
6

Ngugi, James T(hiong'o) . **CLC 3, 7, 13, 182**
See Ngugi wa Thiong'o
See also CN 1, 2

Ngugi wa Thiong'o
See Ngugi wa Thiong'o
See also CD 3, 4, 5, 6, 7; DLB 125; EWL 3

Ngugi wa Thiong'o 1938- ... **BLC 3; CLC 36,
182**
See Ngugi, James T(hiong'o); Ngugi wa
Thiong'o
See also AFW; BRWS 8; BW 2; CA 81-84;
CANR 27, 58; CDWLB 3; DAM MULT,
NOV; DNFS 2; MTCW 1, 2; MTFW
2005; RGEL 2; WWE 1

Niatum, Duane 1938- .... **NNAL**
See also CA 41-44R; CANR 21, 45, 83;
DLB 175

Nichol, B(arrie) P(hillip) 1944-1988 . **CLC 18**
See also CA 53-56; CP 1, 2, 3, 4; DLB 53;
SATA 66

Nicholas of Cusa 1401-1464 .... **LC 80**
See also DLB 115

Nichols, John 1940- .... **CLC 38**
See also AMWS 13; CA 9-12R, 190; CAAE
190; CAAS 2; CANR 6, 70, 121; DLBY
1982; LATS 1:2; MTFW 2005; TCWW 1,
2

Nichols, Leigh
See Koontz, Dean R.

Nichols, Peter (Richard) 1927- .... **CLC 5, 36,
65**
See also CA 104; CANR 33, 86; CBD; CD
5, 6; DLB 13, 245; MTCW 1

Nicholson, Linda ed. .... **CLC 65**

Ni Chuilleanain, Eilean 1942- .... **PC 34**
See also CA 126; CANR 53, 83; CP 5, 6, 7;
CWP; DLB 40

Nicolas, F. R. E.
See Freeling, Nicolas

Niedecker, Lorine 1903-1970 ..... **CLC 10, 42;
PC 42**
See also CA 25-28; CAP 2; DAM POET;
DLB 48

Nietzsche, Friedrich (Wilhelm)
1844-1900 .... **TCLC 10, 18, 55**
See also CA 107; 121; CDWLB 2; DLB
129; EW 7; RGWL 2, 3; TWA

Nievo, Ippolito 1831-1861 .... **NCLC 22**

Nightingale, Anne Redmon 1943-
See Redmon, Anne
See also CA 103

Nightingale, Florence 1820-1910 ... **TCLC 85**
See also CA 188; DLB 166

Nijo Yoshimoto 1320-1388 .... **CMLC 49**
See also DLB 203

Nik. T. O.
See Annensky, Innokenty (Fyodorovich)

Nin, Anais 1903-1977 ..... **CLC 1, 4, 8, 11, 14,
60, 127; SSC 10**
See also AITN 2; AMWS 10; BPFB 2; CA
13-16R; 69-72; CANR 22, 53; CN 1, 2;
DAM NOV, POP; DLB 2, 4, 152; EWL
3; GLL 2; MAL 5; MBL; MTCW 1, 2;
MTFW 2005; RGAL 4; RGSF 2

Nisbet, Robert A(lexander)
1913-1996 .... **TCLC 117**
See also CA 25-28R; 153; CANR 17; INT
CANR-17

Nishida, Kitaro 1870-1945 .... **TCLC 83**

Nishiwaki, Junzaburo 1894-1982 .... **PC 15**
See Junzaburo, Nishiwaki
See also CA 194; 107; MJW; RGWL 3

Nissenson, Hugh 1933- .... **CLC 4, 9**
See also CA 17-20R; CANR 27, 108, 151;
CN 5, 6; DLB 28

Nister, Der
See Der Nister
See also EWL 3

Niven, Larry 1938-
See Niven, Laurence VanCott
See also CA 21-24R, 207; CAAE 207;
CAAS 12; CANR 14, 44, 66, 113, 155;
CPW; DAM POP; MTCW 1, 2; SATA 95,
171; SFW 4

Niven, Laurence VanCott .... **CLC 8**
See Niven, Larry
See also AAYA 27; BPFB 2; BYA 10; DLB
8; SCFW 1, 2

Nixon, Agnes Eckhardt 1927- .... **CLC 21**
See also CA 110

Nizan, Paul 1905-1940 .... **TCLC 40**
See also CA 161; DLB 72; EWL 3; GFL
1789 to the Present

Nkosi, Lewis 1936- .... **BLC 3; CLC 45**
See also BW 1, 3; CA 65-68; CANR 27,
81; CBD; CD 5, 6; DAM MULT; DLB
157, 225; WWE 1

Nodier, (Jean) Charles (Emmanuel)
1780-1844 .... **NCLC 19**
See also DLB 119; GFL 1789 to the Present

Noguchi, Yone 1875-1947 .... **TCLC 80**

Nolan, Christopher 1965- .... **CLC 58**
See also CA 111; CANR 88

Noon, Jeff 1957- .... **CLC 91**
See also CA 148; CANR 83; DLB 267;
SFW 4

Norden, Charles
See Durrell, Lawrence (George)

Nordhoff, Charles Bernard
1887-1947 .... **TCLC 23**
See also CA 108; 211; DLB 9; LAIT 1;
RHW 1; SATA 23

Norfolk, Lawrence 1963- .... **CLC 76**
See also CA 144; CANR 85; CN 6, 7; DLB
267

Norman, Marsha (Williams) 1947- . **CLC 28,
186; DC 8**
See also CA 105; CABS 3; CAD; CANR
41, 131; CD 5, 6; CSW; CWD; DAM
DRAM; DFS 2; DLB 266; DLBY 1984;
FW; MAL 5

Normyx
See Douglas, (George) Norman

Norris, (Benjamin) Frank(lin, Jr.)
1870-1902 .... **SSC 28; TCLC 24, 155**
See also AAYA 57; AMW; AMWC 2; BPFB
2; CA 110; 160; CDALB 1865-1917; DLB
12, 71, 186; LMFS 2; MAL 5; NFS 12;
RGAL 4; TCWW 1, 2; TUS

Norris, Leslie 1921-2006 .... **CLC 14**
See also CA 11-12; 251; CANR 14, 117;
CAP 1; CP 1, 2, 3, 4, 5, 6, 7; DLB 27,
256

North, Andrew
See Norton, Andre

North, Anthony
See Koontz, Dean R.

North, Captain George
See Stevenson, Robert Louis (Balfour)

North, Captain George
See Stevenson, Robert Louis (Balfour)

North, Milou
See Erdrich, Louise

Northrup, B. A.
See Hubbard, L. Ron

North Staffs
See Hulme, T(homas) E(rnest)

Northup, Solomon 1808-1863 ...... **NCLC 105**

Norton, Alice Mary
See Norton, Andre
See also MAICYA 1; SATA 1, 43

Norton, Andre 1912-2005 .... **CLC 12**
See Norton, Alice Mary
See also AAYA 14; BPFB 2; BYA 4, 10,
12; CA 1-4R; 237; CANR 2, 31, 68, 108,
149; CLR 50; DLB 8, 52; JRDA; MAI-
CYA 2; MTCW 1; SATA 91; SUFW 1, 2;
YAW

Norton, Caroline 1808-1877 .... **NCLC 47**
See also DLB 21, 159, 199

Norway, Nevil Shute 1899-1960
See Shute, Nevil
See also CA 102; 93-96; CANR 85; MTCW
2

Norwid, Cyprian Kamil
1821-1883 .... **NCLC 17**
See also RGWL 3

Nosille, Nabrah
See Ellison, Harlan

Nossack, Hans Erich 1901-1977 .... **CLC 6**
See also CA 93-96; 85-88; CANR 156;
DLB 69; EWL 3

Powell, Padgett 1952- .... **CLC 34**
See also CA 126; CANR 63, 101; CSW;
DLB 234; DLBY 01
Powell, (Oval) Talmage 1920-2000
See Queen, Ellery
See also CA 5-8R; CANR 2, 80
Power, Susan 1961- .... **CLC 91**
See also BYA 14; CA 160; CANR 135; NFS
11
Powers, J(ames) F(arl) 1917-1999 ..... **CLC 1,
4, 8, 57; SSC 4**
See also CA 1-4R; 181; CANR 2, 61; CN
1, 2, 3, 4, 5, 6; DLB 130; MTCW 1;
RGAL 4; RGSF 2
Powers, John J(ames) 1945-
See Powers, John R.
See also CA 69-72
Powers, John R. .... **CLC 66**
See Powers, John J(ames)
Powers, Richard 1957- .... **CLC 93**
See also AMWS 9; BPFB 3; CA 148;
CANR 80; CN 6, 7; MTFW 2005; TCLE
1:2
Pownall, David 1938- .... **CLC 10**
See also CA 89-92, 180; CAAS 18; CANR
49, 101; CBD; CD 5, 6; CN 4, 5, 6, 7;
DLB 14
Powys, John Cowper 1872-1963 ... **CLC 7, 9,
15, 46, 125**
See also CA 85-88; CANR 106; DLB 15,
255; EWL 3; FANT; MTCW 1, 2; MTFW
2005; RGEL 2; SUFW
Powys, T(heodore) F(rancis)
1875-1953 .... **TCLC 9**
See also BRWS 8; CA 106; 189; DLB 36,
162; EWL 3; FANT; RGEL 2; SUFW
Pozzo, Modesta
See Fonte, Moderata
Prado (Calvo), Pedro 1886-1952 ... **TCLC 75**
See also CA 131; DLB 283; HW 1; LAW
Prager, Emily 1952- .... **CLC 56**
See also CA 204
Pratchett, Terry 1948- .... **CLC 197**
See also AAYA 19, 54; BPFB 3; CA 143;
CANR 87, 126; CLR 64; CN 6, 7; CPW;
CWRI 5; FANT; MTFW 2005; SATA 82,
139; SFW 4; SUFW 2
Pratolini, Vasco 1913-1991 .... **TCLC 124**
See also CA 211; DLB 177; EWL 3; RGWL
2, 3
Pratt, E(dwin) J(ohn) 1883(?)-1964 . **CLC 19**
See also CA 141; 93-96; CANR 77; DAC;
DAM POET; DLB 92; EWL 3; RGEL 2;
TWA
Premchand .... **TCLC 21**
See Srivastava, Dhanpat Rai
See also EWL 3
Prescott, William Hickling
1796-1859 .... **NCLC 163**
See also DLB 1, 30, 59, 235
Preseren, France 1800-1849 .... **NCLC 127**
See also CDWLB 4; DLB 147
Preussler, Otfried 1923- .... **CLC 17**
See also CA 77-80; SATA 24
Prevert, Jacques (Henri Marie)
1900-1977 .... **CLC 15**
See also CA 77-80; 69-72; CANR 29, 61;
DLB 258; EWL 3; GFL 1789 to the
Present; IDFW 3, 4; MTCW 1; RGWL 2,
3; SATA-Obit 30
Prevost, (Antoine Francois)
1697-1763 .... **LC 1**
See also DLB 314; EW 4; GFL Beginnings
to 1789; RGWL 2, 3
Price, Reynolds 1933- .. **CLC 3, 6, 13, 43, 50,
63, 212; SSC 22**
See also AMWS 6; CA 1-4R; CANR 1, 37,
57, 87, 128; CN 1, 2, 3, 4, 5, 6, 7; CSW;

DAM NOV; DLB 2, 218, 278; EWL 3;
INT CANR-37; MAL 5; MTFW 2005;
NFS 18
Price, Richard 1949- .... **CLC 6, 12**
See also CA 49-52; CANR 3, 147; CN 7;
DLBY 1981
Prichard, Katharine Susannah
1883-1969 .... **CLC 46**
See also CA 11-12; CANR 33; CAP 1; DLB
260; MTCW 1; RGEL 2; RGSF 2; SATA
66
Priestley, J(ohn) B(oynton)
1894-1984 .... **CLC 2, 5, 9, 34**
See also BRW 7; CA 9-12R; 113; CANR
33; CDBLB 1914-1945; CN 1, 2, 3; DA3;
DAM DRAM, NOV; DLB 10, 34, 77,
100, 139; DLBY 1984; EWL 3; MTCW
1, 2; MTFW 2005; RGEL 2; SFW 4
Prince 1958- .... **CLC 35**
See also CA 213
Prince, F(rank) T(empleton)
1912-2003 .... **CLC 22**
See also CA 101; 219; CANR 43, 79; CP 1,
2, 3, 4, 5, 6, 7; DLB 20
Prince Kropotkin
See Kropotkin, Peter (Aleksieevich)
Prior, Matthew 1664-1721 .... **LC 4**
See also DLB 95; RGEL 2
Prishvin, Mikhail 1873-1954 .... **TCLC 75**
See Prishvin, Mikhail Mikhailovich
Prishvin, Mikhail Mikhailovich
See Prishvin, Mikhail
See also DLB 272; EWL 3
Pritchard, William H(arrison)
1932- .... **CLC 34**
See also CA 65-68; CANR 23, 95; DLB
111
Pritchett, V(ictor) S(awdon)
1900-1997 ... **CLC 5, 13, 15, 41; SSC 14**
See also BPFB 3; BRWS 3; CA 61-64; 157;
CANR 31, 63; CN 1, 2, 3, 4, 5, 6; DA3;
DAM NOV; DLB 15, 139; EWL 3;
MTCW 1, 2; MTFW 2005; RGEL 2;
RGSF 2; TEA
Private 19022
See Manning, Frederic
Probst, Mark 1925- .... **CLC 59**
See also CA 130
Procaccino, Michael
See Cristofer, Michael
Proclus c. 412-c. 485 .... **CMLC 81**
Prokosch, Frederic 1908-1989 ...... **CLC 4, 48**
See also CA 73-76; 128; CANR 82; CN 1,
2, 3, 4; CP 1, 2, 3, 4; DLB 48; MTCW 2
Propertius, Sextus c. 50B.C.-c.
16B.C. .... **CMLC 32**
See also AW 2; CDWLB 1; DLB 211;
RGWL 2, 3; WLIT 8
Prophet, The
See Dreiser, Theodore
Prose, Francine 1947- .... **CLC 45, 231**
See also AMWS 16; CA 109; 112; CANR
46, 95, 132; DLB 234; MTFW 2005;
SATA 101, 149
Protagoras c. 490B.C.-420B.C. ...... **CMLC 85**
See also DLB 176
Proudhon
See Cunha, Euclides (Rodrigues Pimenta)
da
Proulx, Annie
See Proulx, E. Annie
Proulx, E. Annie 1935- .... **CLC 81, 158**
See also AMWS 7; BPFB 3; CA 145;
CANR 65, 110; CN 6, 7; CPW 1; DA3;
DAM POP; MAL 5; MTCW 2; MTFW
2005; SSFS 18, 23
Proulx, Edna Annie
See Proulx, E. Annie

**Proust, (Valentin-Louis-George-Eugene)
Marcel** 1871-1922 ..... **SSC 75; TCLC 7,
13, 33; WLC 5**
See also AAYA 58; BPFB 3; CA 104; 120;
CANR 110; DA; DA3; DAB; DAC; DAM
MST, NOV; DLB 65; EW 8; EWL 3; GFL
1789 to the Present; MTCW 1, 2; MTFW
2005; RGWL 2, 3; TWA
Prowler, Harley
See Masters, Edgar Lee
Prudentius, Aurelius Clemens 348-c.
405 .... **CMLC 78**
See also EW 1; RGWL 2, 3
Prus, Boleslaw 1845-1912 .... **TCLC 48**
See also RGWL 2, 3
Pryor, Aaron Richard
See Pryor, Richard
Pryor, Richard 1940-2005 .... **CLC 26**
See also CA 122; 152; 246
Pryor, Richard Franklin Lenox Thomas
See Pryor, Richard
Przybyszewski, Stanislaw
1868-1927 .... **TCLC 36**
See also CA 160; DLB 66; EWL 3
Pteleon
See Grieve, C(hristopher) M(urray)
See also DAM POET
Puckett, Lute
See Masters, Edgar Lee
Puig, Manuel 1932-1990 .... **CLC 3, 5, 10, 28,
65, 133; HLC 2**
See also BPFB 3; CA 45-48; CANR 2, 32,
63; CDWLB 3; DA3; DAM MULT; DLB
113; DNFS 1; EWL 3; GLL 1; HW 1, 2;
LAW; MTCW 1, 2; MTFW 2005; RGWL
2, 3; TWA; WLIT 1
Pulitzer, Joseph 1847-1911 .... **TCLC 76**
See also CA 114; DLB 23
Purchas, Samuel 1577(?)-1626 .... **LC 70**
See also DLB 151
Purdy, A(lfred) W(ellington)
1918-2000 .... **CLC 3, 6, 14, 50**
See also CA 81-84; 189; CAAS 17; CANR
42, 66; CP 1, 2, 3, 4, 5, 6, 7; DAC; DAM
MST, POET; DLB 88; PFS 5; RGEL 2
Purdy, James (Amos) 1923- .... **CLC 2, 4, 10,
28, 52**
See also AMWS 7; CA 33-36R; CAAS 1;
CANR 19, 51, 132; CN 1, 2, 3, 4, 5, 6, 7;
DLB 2, 218; EWL 3; INT CANR-19;
MAL 5; MTCW 1; RGAL 4
Pure, Simon
See Swinnerton, Frank Arthur
Pushkin, Aleksandr Sergeevich
See Pushkin, Alexander (Sergeyevich)
See also DLB 205
Pushkin, Alexander (Sergeyevich)
1799-1837 .... **NCLC 3, 27, 83; PC 10;
SSC 27, 55; WLC 5**
See Pushkin, Aleksandr Sergeevich
See also DA; DA3; DAB; DAC; DAM
DRAM, MST, POET; EW 5; EXPS; RGSF
2; RGWL 2, 3; SATA 61; SSFS 9; TWA
P'u Sung-ling 1640-1715 .... **LC 49; SSC 31**
Putnam, Arthur Lee
See Alger, Horatio, Jr.
Puttenham, George 1529(?)-1590 ..... **LC 116**
See also DLB 281
Puzo, Mario 1920-1999 .... **CLC 1, 2, 6, 36,
107**
See also BPFB 3; CA 65-68; 185; CANR 4,
42, 65, 99, 131; CN 1, 2, 3, 4, 5, 6; CPW;
DA3; DAM NOV, POP; DLB 6; MTCW
1, 2; MTFW 2005; NFS 16; RGAL 4
Pygge, Edward
See Barnes, Julian
Pyle, Ernest Taylor 1900-1945
See Pyle, Ernie
See also CA 115; 160

Author Index

DLB 45, 63; EWL 3; EXPP; MAL 5;
MTCW 1, 2; MTFW 2005; RGAL 4; TUS
Rao, Raja 1908-2006 .... **CLC 25, 56**
See also CA 73-76; CANR 51; CN 1, 2, 3,
4, 5, 6; DAM NOV; DLB 323; EWL 3;
MTCW 1, 2; MTFW 2005; RGEL 2;
RGSF 2
Raphael, Frederic (Michael) 1931- ... **CLC 2,
14**
See also CA 1-4R; CANR 1, 86; CN 1, 2,
3, 4, 5, 6, 7; DLB 14, 319; TCLE 1:2
Ratcliffe, James P.
See Mencken, H(enry) L(ouis)
Rathbone, Julian 1935- .... **CLC 41**
See also CA 101; CANR 34, 73, 152
Rattigan, Terence (Mervyn)
1911-1977 .... **CLC 7; DC 18**
See also BRWS 7; CA 85-88; 73-76; CBD;
CDBLB 1945-1960; DAM DRAM; DFS
8; DLB 13; IDFW 3, 4; MTCW 1, 2;
MTFW 2005; RGEL 2
Ratushinskaya, Irina 1954- .... **CLC 54**
See also CA 129; CANR 68; CWW 2
Raven, Simon (Arthur Noel)
1927-2001 .... **CLC 14**
See also CA 81-84; 197; CANR 86; CN 1,
2, 3, 4, 5, 6; DLB 271
Ravenna, Michael
See Welty, Eudora
Rawley, Callman 1903-2004
See Rakosi, Carl
See also CA 21-24R; 228; CANR 12, 32,
91
Rawlings, Marjorie Kinnan
1896-1953 .... **TCLC 4**
See also AAYA 20; AMWS 10; ANW;
BPFB 3; BYA 3; CA 104; 137; CANR 74;
CLR 63; DLB 9, 22, 102; DLBD 17;
JRDA; MAICYA 1, 2; MAL 5; MTCW 2;
MTFW 2005; RGAL 4; SATA 100; WCH;
YABC 1; YAW
Ray, Satyajit 1921-1992 .... **CLC 16, 76**
See also CA 114; 137; DAM MULT
Read, Herbert Edward 1893-1968 ..... **CLC 4**
See also BRW 6; CA 85-88; 25-28R; DLB
20, 149; EWL 3; PAB; RGEL 2
Read, Piers Paul 1941- .... **CLC 4, 10, 25**
See also CA 21-24R; CANR 38, 86, 150;
CN 2, 3, 4, 5, 6, 7; DLB 14; SATA 21
Reade, Charles 1814-1884 .... **NCLC 2, 74**
See also DLB 21; RGEL 2
Reade, Hamish
See Gray, Simon (James Holliday)
Reading, Peter 1946- .... **CLC 47**
See also BRWS 8; CA 103; CANR 46, 96;
CP 5, 6, 7; DLB 40
Reaney, James 1926- .... **CLC 13**
See also CA 41-44R; CAAS 15; CANR 42;
CD 5, 6; CP 1, 2, 3, 4, 5, 6, 7; DAC;
DAM MST; DLB 68; RGEL 2; SATA 43
Rebreanu, Liviu 1885-1944 .... **TCLC 28**
See also CA 165; DLB 220; EWL 3
Rechy, John 1934- ..... **CLC 1, 7, 14, 18, 107;
HLC 2**
See also CA 5-8R; 195; CAAE 195; CAAS
4; CANR 6, 32, 64, 152; CN 1, 2, 3, 4, 5,
6, 7; DAM MULT; DLB 122, 278; DLBY
1982; HW 1, 2; INT CANR-6; LLW;
MAL 5; RGAL 4
Rechy, John Francisco
See Rechy, John
Redcam, Tom 1870-1933 .... **TCLC 25**
Reddin, Keith 1956- .... **CLC 67**
See also CAD; CD 6
Redgrove, Peter (William)
1932-2003 .... **CLC 6, 41**
See also BRWS 6; CA 1-4R; 217; CANR 3,
39, 77; CP 1, 2, 3, 4, 5, 6, 7; DLB 40;
TCLE 1:2

Redmon, Anne .... **CLC 22**
See Nightingale, Anne Redmon
See also DLBY 1986
Reed, Eliot
See Ambler, Eric
Reed, Ishmael 1938- ..... **BLC 3; CLC 2, 3, 5,
6, 13, 32, 60, 174; PC 68**
See also AFAW 1, 2; AMWS 10; BPFB 3;
BW 2, 3; CA 21-24R; CANR 25, 48, 74,
128; CN 1, 2, 3, 4, 5, 6, 7; CP 1, 2, 3, 4,
5, 6, 7; CSW; DA3; DAM MULT; DLB
2, 5, 33, 169, 227; DLBD 8; EWL 3;
LMFS 2; MAL 5; MSW; MTCW 1, 2;
MTFW 2005; PFS 6; RGAL 4; TCWW 2
Reed, John (Silas) 1887-1920 .... **TCLC 9**
See also CA 106; 195; MAL 5; TUS
Reed, Lou .... **CLC 21**
See Firbank, Louis
Reese, Lizette Woodworth
1856-1935 .... **PC 29; TCLC 181**
See also CA 180; DLB 54
Reeve, Clara 1729-1807 .... **NCLC 19**
See also DLB 39; RGEL 2
Reich, Wilhelm 1897-1957 .... **TCLC 57**
See also CA 199
Reid, Christopher (John) 1949- .... **CLC 33**
See also CA 140; CANR 89; CP 4, 5, 6, 7;
DLB 40; EWL 3
Reid, Desmond
See Moorcock, Michael
Reid Banks, Lynne 1929-
See Banks, Lynne Reid
See also AAYA 49; CA 1-4R; CANR 6, 22,
38, 87; CLR 24; CN 1, 2, 3, 7; JRDA;
MAICYA 1, 2; SATA 22, 75, 111, 165;
YAW
Reilly, William K.
See Creasey, John
Reiner, Max
See Caldwell, (Janet Miriam) Taylor
(Holland)
Reis, Ricardo
See Pessoa, Fernando (Antonio Nogueira)
Reizenstein, Elmer Leopold
See Rice, Elmer (Leopold)
See also EWL 3
Remarque, Erich Maria 1898-1970 . **CLC 21**
See also AAYA 27; BPFB 3; CA 77-80; 29-
32R; CDWLB 2; DA; DA3; DAB; DAC;
DAM MST, NOV; DLB 56; EWL 3;
EXPN; LAIT 3; MTCW 1, 2; MTFW
2005; NFS 4; RGHL; RGWL 2, 3
Remington, Frederic S(ackrider)
1861-1909 .... **TCLC 89**
See also CA 108; 169; DLB 12, 186, 188;
SATA 41; TCWW 2
Remizov, A.
See Remizov, Aleksei (Mikhailovich)
Remizov, A. M.
See Remizov, Aleksei (Mikhailovich)
Remizov, Aleksei (Mikhailovich)
1877-1957 .... **TCLC 27**
See Remizov, Alexey Mikhaylovich
See also CA 125; 133; DLB 295
Remizov, Alexey Mikhaylovich
See Remizov, Aleksei (Mikhailovich)
See also EWL 3
Renan, Joseph Ernest 1823-1892 . **NCLC 26,
145**
See also GFL 1789 to the Present
Renard, Jules(-Pierre) 1864-1910 .. **TCLC 17**
See also CA 117; 202; GFL 1789 to the
Present
Renart, Jean fl. 13th cent. - .... **CMLC 83**
Renault, Mary .... **CLC 3, 11, 17**
See Challans, Mary
See also BPFB 3; BYA 2; CN 1, 2, 3;
DLBY 1983; EWL 3; GLL 1; LAIT 1;
RGEL 2; RHW

Rendell, Ruth 1930- .... **CLC 28, 48**
See Vine, Barbara
See also BPFB 3; BRWS 9; CA 109; CANR
32, 52, 74, 127; CN 5, 6, 7; CPW; DAM
POP; DLB 87, 276; INT CANR-32;
MSW; MTCW 1, 2; MTFW 2005
Rendell, Ruth Barbara
See Rendell, Ruth
Renoir, Jean 1894-1979 .... **CLC 20**
See also CA 129; 85-88
Resnais, Alain 1922- .... **CLC 16**
Revard, Carter 1931- .... **NNAL**
See also CA 144; CANR 81, 153; PFS 5
Reverdy, Pierre 1889-1960 .... **CLC 53**
See also CA 97-100; 89-92; DLB 258; EWL
3; GFL 1789 to the Present
Rexroth, Kenneth 1905-1982 .... **CLC 1, 2, 6,
11, 22, 49, 112; PC 20**
See also BG 1:3; CA 5-8R; 107; CANR 14,
34, 63; CDALB 1941-1968; CP 1, 2, 3;
DAM POET; DLB 16, 48, 165, 212;
DLBY 1982; EWL 3; INT CANR-14;
MAL 5; MTCW 1, 2; MTFW 2005;
RGAL 4
Reyes, Alfonso 1889-1959 .... **HLCS 2; TCLC
33**
See also CA 131; EWL 3; HW 1; LAW
Reyes y Basoalto, Ricardo Eliecer Neftali
See Neruda, Pablo
Reymont, Wladyslaw (Stanislaw)
1868(?)-1925 .... **TCLC 5**
See also CA 104; EWL 3
Reynolds, John Hamilton
1794-1852 .... **NCLC 146**
See also DLB 96
Reynolds, Jonathan 1942- .... **CLC 6, 38**
See also CA 65-68; CANR 28
Reynolds, Joshua 1723-1792 .... **LC 15**
See also DLB 104
Reynolds, Michael S(hane)
1937-2000 .... **CLC 44**
See also CA 65-68; 189; CANR 9, 89, 97
Reznikoff, Charles 1894-1976 .... **CLC 9**
See also AMWS 14; CA 33-36; 61-64; CAP
2; CP 1, 2; DLB 28, 45; RGHL; WP
Rezzori, Gregor von
See Rezzori d'Arezzo, Gregor von
Rezzori d'Arezzo, Gregor von
1914-1998 .... **CLC 25**
See also CA 122; 136; 167
Rhine, Richard
See Silverstein, Alvin; Silverstein, Virginia
B(arbara Opshelor)
Rhodes, Eugene Manlove
1869-1934 .... **TCLC 53**
See also CA 198; DLB 256; TCWW 1, 2
R'hoone, Lord
See Balzac, Honore de
Rhys, Jean 1890-1979 .... **CLC 2, 4, 6, 14, 19,
51, 124; SSC 21, 76**
See also BRWS 2; CA 25-28R; 85-88;
CANR 35, 62; CDBLB 1945-1960; CD-
WLB 3; CN 1, 2; DA3; DAM NOV; DLB
36, 117, 162; DNFS 2; EWL 3; LATS 1:1;
MTCW 1, 2; MTFW 2005; NFS 19;
RGEL 2; RGSF 2; RHW; TEA; WWE 1
Ribeiro, Darcy 1922-1997 .... **CLC 34**
See also CA 33-36R; 156; EWL 3
Ribeiro, Joao Ubaldo (Osorio Pimentel)
1941- .... **CLC 10, 67**
See also CA 81-84; CWW 2; EWL 3
Ribman, Ronald (Burt) 1932- .... **CLC 7**
See also CA 21-24R; CAD; CANR 46, 80;
CD 5, 6
Ricci, Nino (Pio) 1959- .... **CLC 70**
See also CA 137; CANR 130; CCA 1

Rice, Anne 1941- .... **CLC 41, 128**
  See Rampling, Anne
  See also AAYA 9, 53; AMWS 7; BEST
    89:2; BPFB 3; CA 65-68; CANR 12, 36,
    53, 74, 100, 133; CN 6, 7; CPW; CSW;
    DA3; DAM POP; DLB 292; GL 3; GLL
    2; HGG; MTCW 2; MTFW 2005; SUFW
    2; YAW
Rice, Elmer (Leopold) 1892-1967 ...... **CLC 7,**
  49
  See Reizenstein, Elmer Leopold
  See also CA 21-22; 25-28R; CAP 2; DAM
    DRAM; DFS 12; DLB 4, 7; IDTP; MAL
    5; MTCW 1, 2; RGAL 4
Rice, Tim(othy Miles Bindon)
  1944- .... **CLC 21**
  See also CA 103; CANR 46; DFS 7
Rich, Adrienne 1929- ..... **CLC 3, 6, 7, 11, 18,**
  36, 73, 76, 125; PC 5
  See also AAYA 69; AMWR 2; AMWS 1;
    CA 9-12R; CANR 20, 53, 74, 128;
    CDALBS; CP 1, 2, 3, 4, 5, 6, 7; CSW;
    CWP; DA3; DAM POET; DLB 5, 67;
    EWL 3; EXPP; FL 1:6; FW; MAL 5;
    MBL; MTCW 1, 2; MTFW 2005; PAB;
    PFS 15; RGAL 4; RGHL; WP
Rich, Barbara
  See Graves, Robert
Rich, Robert
  See Trumbo, Dalton
Richard, Keith .... **CLC 17**
  See Richards, Keith
Richards, David Adams 1950- .... **CLC 59**
  See also CA 93-96; CANR 60, 110, 156;
    CN 7; DAC; DLB 53; TCLE 1:2
Richards, I(vor) A(rmstrong)
  1893-1979 .... **CLC 14, 24**
  See also BRWS 2; CA 41-44R; 89-92;
    CANR 34, 74; CP 1, 2; DLB 27; EWL 3;
    MTCW 2; RGEL 2
Richards, Keith 1943-
  See Richard, Keith
  See also CA 107; CANR 77
Richardson, Anne
  See Roiphe, Anne
Richardson, Dorothy Miller
  1873-1957 .... **TCLC 3**
  See also CA 104; 192; DLB 36; EWL 3;
    FW; RGEL 2
Richardson (Robertson), Ethel Florence
  Lindesay 1870-1946
  See Richardson, Henry Handel
  See also CA 105; 190; DLB 230; RHW
Richardson, Henry Handel .... **TCLC 4**
  See Richardson (Robertson), Ethel Florence
    Lindesay
  See also DLB 197; EWL 3; RGEL 2; RGSF
    2
Richardson, John 1796-1852 .... **NCLC 55**
  See also CCA 1; DAC; DLB 99
Richardson, Samuel 1689-1761 ...... **LC 1, 44;**
  WLC 5
  See also BRW 3; CDBLB 1660-1789; DA;
    DAB; DAC; DAM MST, NOV; DLB 39;
    RGEL 2; TEA; WLIT 3
Richardson, Willis 1889-1977 .... **HR 1:3**
  See also BW 1; CA 124; DLB 51; SATA 60
Richler, Mordecai 1931-2001 .... **CLC 3, 5, 9,**
  13, 18, 46, 70, 185
  See also AITN 1; CA 65-68; 201; CANR
    31, 62, 111; CCA 1; CLR 17; CN 1, 2, 3,
    4, 5, 7; CWRI 5; DAC; DAM MST, NOV;
    DLB 53; EWL 3; MAICYA 1, 2; MTCW
    1, 2; MTFW 2005; RGEL 2; RGHL;
    SATA 44, 98; SATA-Brief 27; TWA
Richter, Conrad (Michael)
  1890-1968 .... **CLC 30**
  See also AAYA 21; BYA 2; CA 5-8R; 25-
    28R; CANR 23; DLB 9, 212; LAIT 1;

MAL 5; MTCW 1, 2; MTFW 2005;
    RGAL 4; SATA 3; TCWW 1, 2; TUS;
    YAW
Ricostranza, Tom
  See Ellis, Trey
Riddell, Charlotte 1832-1906 .... **TCLC 40**
  See Riddell, Mrs. J. H.
  See also CA 165; DLB 156
Riddell, Mrs. J. H.
  See Riddell, Charlotte
  See also HGG; SUFW
Ridge, John Rollin 1827-1867 ...... **NCLC 82;**
  NNAL
  See also CA 144; DAM MULT; DLB 175
Ridgeway, Jason
  See Marlowe, Stephen
Ridgway, Keith 1965- .... **CLC 119**
  See also CA 172; CANR 144
Riding, Laura .... **CLC 3, 7**
  See Jackson, Laura (Riding)
  See also CP 1, 2, 3, 4, 5; RGAL 4
Riefenstahl, Berta Helene Amalia 1902-2003
  See Riefenstahl, Leni
  See also CA 108; 220
Riefenstahl, Leni .... **CLC 16, 190**
  See Riefenstahl, Berta Helene Amalia
Riffe, Ernest
  See Bergman, (Ernst) Ingmar
Riggs, (Rolla) Lynn
  1899-1954 .... **NNAL; TCLC 56**
  See also CA 144; DAM MULT; DLB 175
Riis, Jacob A(ugust) 1849-1914 ..... **TCLC 80**
  See also CA 113; 168; DLB 23
Riley, James Whitcomb 1849-1916 .... **PC 48;**
  TCLC 51
  See also CA 118; 137; DAM POET; MAI-
    CYA 1, 2; RGAL 4; SATA 17
Riley, Tex
  See Creasey, John
Rilke, Rainer Maria 1875-1926 .... **PC 2;**
  TCLC 1, 6, 19
  See also CA 104; 132; CANR 62, 99; CD-
    WLB 2; DA3; DAM POET; DLB 81; EW
    9; EWL 3; MTCW 1, 2; MTFW 2005;
    PFS 19; RGWL 2, 3; TWA; WP
Rimbaud, (Jean Nicolas) Arthur
  1854-1891 ... **NCLC 4, 35, 82; PC 3, 57;**
  WLC 5
  See also DA; DA3; DAB; DAC; DAM
    MST, POET; DLB 217; EW 7; GFL 1789
    to the Present; LMFS 2; RGWL 2, 3;
    TWA; WP
Rinehart, Mary Roberts
  1876-1958 .... **TCLC 52**
  See also BPFB 3; CA 108; 166; RGAL 4;
    RHW
Ringmaster, The
  See Mencken, H(enry) L(ouis)
Ringwood, Gwen(dolyn Margaret) Pharis
  1910-1984 .... **CLC 48**
  See also CA 148; 112; DLB 88
Rio, Michel 1945(?)- .... **CLC 43**
  See also CA 201
Rios, Alberto 1952- .... **PC 57**
  See also AAYA 66; AMWS 4; CA 113;
    CANR 34, 79, 137; CP 6, 7; DLB 122;
    HW 2; MTFW 2005; PFS 11
Ritsos, Giannes
  See Ritsos, Yannis
Ritsos, Yannis 1909-1990 .... **CLC 6, 13, 31**
  See also CA 77-80; 133; CANR 39, 61; EW
    12; EWL 3; MTCW 1; RGWL 2, 3
Ritter, Erika 1948(?)- .... **CLC 52**
  See also CD 5, 6; CWD
Rivera, Jose Eustasio 1889-1928 ... **TCLC 35**
  See also CA 162; EWL 3; HW 1, 2; LAW

Rivera, Tomas 1935-1984 .... **HLCS 2**
  See also CA 49-52; CANR 32; DLB 82;
    HW 1; LLW; RGAL 4; SSFS 15; TCWW
    2; WLIT 1
Rivers, Conrad Kent 1933-1968 .... **CLC 1**
  See also BW 1; CA 85-88; DLB 41
Rivers, Elfrida
  See Bradley, Marion Zimmer
  See also GLL 1
Riverside, John
  See Heinlein, Robert A.
Rizal, Jose 1861-1896 .... **NCLC 27**
Roa Bastos, Augusto 1917-2005 ...... **CLC 45;**
  HLC 2
  See also CA 131; 238; CWW 2; DAM
    MULT; DLB 113; EWL 3; HW 1; LAW;
    RGSF 2; WLIT 1
Roa Bastos, Augusto Jose Antonio
  See Roa Bastos, Augusto
Robbe-Grillet, Alain 1922- .... **CLC 1, 2, 4, 6,**
  8, 10, 14, 43, 128
  See also BPFB 3; CA 9-12R; CANR 33,
    65, 115; CWW 2; DLB 83; EW 13; EWL
    3; GFL 1789 to the Present; IDFW 3, 4;
    MTCW 1, 2; MTFW 2005; RGWL 2, 3;
    SSFS 15
Robbins, Harold 1916-1997 .... **CLC 5**
  See also BPFB 3; CA 73-76; 162; CANR
    26, 54, 112, 156; DA3; DAM NOV;
    MTCW 1, 2
Robbins, Thomas Eugene 1936-
  See Robbins, Tom
  See also CA 81-84; CANR 29, 59, 95, 139;
    CN 7; CPW; CSW; DA3; DAM NOV,
    POP; MTCW 1, 2; MTFW 2005
Robbins, Tom .... **CLC 9, 32, 64**
  See Robbins, Thomas Eugene
  See also AAYA 32; AMWS 10; BEST 90:3;
    BPFB 3; CN 3, 4, 5, 6, 7; DLBY 1980
Robbins, Trina 1938- .... **CLC 21**
  See also AAYA 61; CA 128; CANR 152
Roberts, Charles G(eorge) D(ouglas)
  1860-1943 .... **SSC 91; TCLC 8**
  See also CA 105; 188; CLR 33; CWRI 5;
    DLB 92; RGEL 2; RGSF 2; SATA 88;
    SATA-Brief 29
Roberts, Elizabeth Madox
  1886-1941 .... **TCLC 68**
  See also CA 111; 166; CLR 100; CWRI 5;
    DLB 9, 54, 102; RGAL 4; RHW; SATA
    33; SATA-Brief 27; TCWW 2; WCH
Roberts, Kate 1891-1985 .... **CLC 15**
  See also CA 107; 116; DLB 319
Roberts, Keith (John Kingston)
  1935-2000 .... **CLC 14**
  See also BRWS 10; CA 25-28R; CANR 46;
    DLB 261; SFW 4
Roberts, Kenneth (Lewis)
  1885-1957 .... **TCLC 23**
  See also CA 109; 199; DLB 9; MAL 5;
    RGAL 4; RHW
Roberts, Michele (Brigitte) 1949- .... **CLC 48,**
  178
  See also CA 115; CANR 58, 120; CN 6, 7;
    DLB 231; FW
Robertson, Ellis
  See Ellison, Harlan; Silverberg, Robert
Robertson, Thomas William
  1829-1871 .... **NCLC 35**
  See Robertson, Tom
  See also DAM DRAM
Robertson, Tom
  See Robertson, Thomas William
  See also RGEL 2
Robeson, Kenneth
  See Dent, Lester

Sacastru, Martin
See Bioy Casares, Adolfo
See also CWW 2

Sacher-Masoch, Leopold von
1836(?)-1895 .... **NCLC 31**

Sachs, Hans 1494-1576 .... **LC 95**
See also CDWLB 2; DLB 179; RGWL 2, 3

Sachs, Marilyn 1927- .... **CLC 35**
See also AAYA 2; BYA 6; CA 17-20R; CANR 13, 47, 150; CLR 2; JRDA; MAICYA 1, 2; SAAS 2; SATA 3, 68, 164; SATA-Essay 110; WYA; YAW

Sachs, Marilyn Stickle
See Sachs, Marilyn

Sachs, Nelly 1891-1970 .... **CLC 14, 98**
See also CA 17-18; 25-28R; CANR 87; CAP 2; EWL 3; MTCW 2; MTFW 2005; PFS 20; RGHL; RGWL 2, 3

Sackler, Howard (Oliver)
1929-1982 .... **CLC 14**
See also CA 61-64; 108; CAD; CANR 30; DFS 15; DLB 7

Sacks, Oliver 1933- .... **CLC 67, 202**
See also CA 53-56; CANR 28, 50, 76, 146; CPW; DA3; INT CANR-28; MTCW 1, 2; MTFW 2005

Sacks, Oliver Wolf
See Sacks, Oliver

Sackville, Thomas 1536-1608 .... **LC 98**
See also DAM DRAM; DLB 62, 132; RGEL 2

Sadakichi
See Hartmann, Sadakichi

Sa'dawi, Nawal al-
See El Saadawi, Nawal
See also CWW 2

Sade, Donatien Alphonse Francois
1740-1814 .... **NCLC 3, 47**
See also DLB 314; EW 4; GFL Beginnings to 1789; RGWL 2, 3

Sade, Marquis de
See Sade, Donatien Alphonse Francois

Sadoff, Ira 1945- .... **CLC 9**
See also CA 53-56; CANR 5, 21, 109; DLB 120

Saetone
See Camus, Albert

Safire, William 1929- .... **CLC 10**
See also CA 17-20R; CANR 31, 54, 91, 148

Sagan, Carl 1934-1996 .... **CLC 30, 112**
See also AAYA 2, 62; CA 25-28R; 155; CANR 11, 36, 74; CPW; DA3; MTCW 1, 2; MTFW 2005; SATA 58; SATA-Obit 94

Sagan, Francoise .... **CLC 3, 6, 9, 17, 36**
See Quoirez, Francoise
See also CWW 2; DLB 83; EWL 3; GFL 1789 to the Present; MTCW 2

Sahgal, Nayantara (Pandit) 1927- .... **CLC 41**
See also CA 9-12R; CANR 11, 88; CN 1, 2, 3, 4, 5, 6, 7; DLB 323

Said, Edward W. 1935-2003 .... **CLC 123**
See also CA 21-24R; 220; CANR 45, 74, 107, 131; DLB 67; MTCW 2; MTFW 2005

Saint, H(arry) F. 1941- .... **CLC 50**
See also CA 127

St. Aubin de Teran, Lisa 1953-
See Teran, Lisa St. Aubin de
See also CA 118; 126; CN 6, 7; INT CA-126

Saint Birgitta of Sweden c.
1303-1373 .... **CMLC 24**

Sainte-Beuve, Charles Augustin
1804-1869 .... **NCLC 5**
See also DLB 217; EW 6; GFL 1789 to the Present

Saint-Exupery, Antoine de
1900-1944 .... **TCLC 2, 56, 169; WLC**
See also AAYA 63; BPFB 3; BYA 3; CA 108; 132; CLR 10; DA3; DAM NOV; DLB 72; EW 12; EWL 3; GFL 1789 to the Present; LAIT 3; MAICYA 1, 2; MTCW 1, 2; MTFW 2005; RGWL 2, 3; SATA 20; TWA

Saint-Exupery, Antoine Jean Baptiste Marie Roger de
See Saint-Exupery, Antoine de

St. John, David
See Hunt, E(verette) Howard, (Jr.)

St. John, J. Hector
See Crevecoeur, Michel Guillaume Jean de

Saint-John Perse
See Leger, (Marie-Rene Auguste) Alexis Saint-Leger
See also EW 10; EWL 3; GFL 1789 to the Present; RGWL 2

Saintsbury, George (Edward Bateman)
1845-1933 .... **TCLC 31**
See also CA 160; DLB 57, 149

Sait Faik .... **TCLC 23**
See Abasiyanik, Sait Faik

Saki .... **SSC 12; TCLC 3; WLC 5**
See Munro, H(ector) H(ugh)
See also BRWS 6; BYA 11; LAIT 2; RGEL 2; SSFS 1; SUFW

Sala, George Augustus 1828-1895 . **NCLC 46**

Saladin 1138-1193 .... **CMLC 38**

Salama, Hannu 1936- .... **CLC 18**
See also CA 244; EWL 3

Salamanca, J(ack) R(ichard) 1922- .. **CLC 4, 15**
See also CA 25-28R; 193; CAAE 193

Salas, Floyd Francis 1931- .... **HLC 2**
See also CA 119; CAAS 27; CANR 44, 75, 93; DAM MULT; DLB 82; HW 1, 2; MTCW 2; MTFW 2005

Sale, J. Kirkpatrick
See Sale, Kirkpatrick

Sale, John Kirkpatrick
See Sale, Kirkpatrick

Sale, Kirkpatrick 1937- .... **CLC 68**
See also CA 13-16R; CANR 10, 147

Salinas, Luis Omar 1937- ...... **CLC 90; HLC 2**
See also AMWS 13; CA 131; CANR 81, 153; DAM MULT; DLB 82; HW 1, 2

Salinas (y Serrano), Pedro
1891(?)-1951 .... **TCLC 17**
See also CA 117; DLB 134; EWL 3

Salinger, J.D. 1919- . **CLC 1, 3, 8, 12, 55, 56, 138; SSC 2, 28, 65; WLC 5**
See also AAYA 2, 36; AMW; AMWC 1; BPFB 3; CA 5-8R; CANR 39, 129; CDALB 1941-1968; CLR 18; CN 1, 2, 3, 4, 5, 6, 7; CPW 1; DA; DA3; DAB; DAC; DAM MST, NOV, POP; DLB 2, 102, 173; EWL 3; EXPN; LAIT 4; MAICYA 1, 2; MAL 5; MTCW 1, 2; MTFW 2005; NFS 1; RGAL 4; RGSF 2; SATA 67; SSFS 17; TUS; WYA; YAW

Salisbury, John
See Caute, (John) David

Sallust c. 86B.C.-35B.C. .... **CMLC 68**
See also AW 2; CDWLB 1; DLB 211; RGWL 2, 3

Salter, James 1925- .. **CLC 7, 52, 59; SSC 58**
See also AMWS 9; CA 73-76; CANR 107; DLB 130

Saltus, Edgar (Everton) 1855-1921 . **TCLC 8**
See also CA 105; DLB 202; RGAL 4

Saltykov, Mikhail Evgrafovich
1826-1889 .... **NCLC 16**
See also DLB 238:

Saltykov-Shchedrin, N.
See Saltykov, Mikhail Evgrafovich

Samarakis, Andonis
See Samarakis, Antonis
See also EWL 3

Samarakis, Antonis 1919-2003 .... **CLC 5**
See Samarakis, Andonis
See also CA 25-28R; 224; CAAS 16; CANR 36

Sanchez, Florencio 1875-1910 .... **TCLC 37**
See also CA 153; DLB 305; EWL 3; HW 1; LAW

Sanchez, Luis Rafael 1936- .... **CLC 23**
See also CA 128; DLB 305; EWL 3; HW 1; WLIT 1

Sanchez, Sonia 1934- .... **BLC 3; CLC 5, 116, 215; PC 9**
See also BW 2, 3; CA 33-36R; CANR 24, 49, 74, 115; CLR 18; CP 2, 3, 4, 5, 6, 7; CSW; CWP; DA3; DAM MULT; DLB 41; DLBD 8; EWL 3; MAICYA 1, 2; MAL 5; MTCW 1, 2; MTFW 2005; SATA 22, 136; WP

Sancho, Ignatius 1729-1780 .... **LC 84**

Sand, George 1804-1876 ..... **NCLC 2, 42, 57, 174; WLC 5**
See also DA; DA3; DAB; DAC; DAM MST, NOV; DLB 119, 192; EW 6; FL 1:3; FW; GFL 1789 to the Present; RGWL 2, 3; TWA

Sandburg, Carl (August) 1878-1967 . **CLC 1, 4, 10, 15, 35; PC 2, 41; WLC 5**
See also AAYA 24; AMW; BYA 1, 3; CA 5-8R; 25-28R; CANR 35; CDALB 1865-1917; CLR 67; DA; DA3; DAB; DAC; DAM MST, POET; DLB 17, 54, 284; EWL 3; EXPP; LAIT 2; MAICYA 1, 2; MAL 5; MTCW 1, 2; MTFW 2005; PAB; PFS 3, 6, 12; RGAL 4; SATA 8; TUS; WCH; WP; WYA

Sandburg, Charles
See Sandburg, Carl (August)

Sandburg, Charles A.
See Sandburg, Carl (August)

Sanders, (James) Ed(ward) 1939- .... **CLC 53**
See Sanders, Edward
See also BG 1:3; CA 13-16R; CAAS 21; CANR 13, 44, 78; CP 1, 2, 3, 4, 5, 6, 7; DAM POET; DLB 16, 244

Sanders, Edward
See Sanders, (James) Ed(ward)
See also DLB 244

Sanders, Lawrence 1920-1998 .... **CLC 41**
See also BEST 89:4; BPFB 3; CA 81-84; 165; CANR 33, 62; CMW 4; CPW; DA3; DAM POP; MTCW 1

Sanders, Noah
See Blount, Roy (Alton), Jr.

Sanders, Winston P.
See Anderson, Poul

Sandoz, Mari(e Susette) 1900-1966 .. **CLC 28**
See also CA 1-4R; 25-28R; CANR 17, 64; DLB 9, 212; LAIT 2; MTCW 1, 2; SATA 5; TCWW 1, 2

Sandys, George 1578-1644 .... **LC 80**
See also DLB 24, 121

Saner, Reg(inald Anthony) 1931- .... **CLC 9**
See also CA 65-68; CP 3, 4, 5, 6, 7

Sankara 788-820 .... **CMLC 32**

Sannazaro, Jacopo 1456(?)-1530 .... **LC 8**
See also RGWL 2, 3; WLIT 7

Sansom, William 1912-1976 . **CLC 2, 6; SSC 21**
See also CA 5-8R; 65-68; CANR 42; CN 1, 2; DAM NOV; DLB 139; EWL 3; MTCW 1; RGEL 2; RGSF 2

Santayana, George 1863-1952 .... **TCLC 40**
See also AMW; CA 115; 194; DLB 54, 71, 246, 270; DLBD 13; EWL 3; MAL 5; RGAL 4; TUS

Sheridan, Richard Brinsley
1751-1816 . **DC 1; NCLC 5, 91; WLC 5**
See also BRW 3; CDBLB 1660-1789; DA;
DAB; DAC; DAM DRAM, MST; DFS
15; DLB 89; WLIT 3

Sherman, Jonathan Marc 1968- .... **CLC 55**
See also CA 230

Sherman, Martin 1941(?)- .... **CLC 19**
See also CA 116; 123; CAD; CANR 86;
CD 5, 6; DFS 20; DLB 228; GLL 1;
IDTP; RGHL

Sherwin, Judith Johnson
See Johnson, Judith (Emlyn)
See also CANR 85; CP 2, 3, 4, 5; CWP

Sherwood, Frances 1940- .... **CLC 81**
See also CA 146, 220; CAAE 220

Sherwood, Robert E(mmet)
1896-1955 .... **TCLC 3**
See also CA 104; 153; CANR 86; DAM
DRAM; DFS 11, 15, 17; DLB 7, 26, 249;
IDFW 3, 4; MAL 5; RGAL 4

Shestov, Lev 1866-1938 .... **TCLC 56**

Shevchenko, Taras 1814-1861 .... **NCLC 54**

Shiel, M(atthew) P(hipps)
1865-1947 .... **TCLC 8**
See Holmes, Gordon
See also CA 106; 160; DLB 153; HGG;
MTCW 2; MTFW 2005; SCFW 1, 2;
SFW 4; SUFW

Shields, Carol 1935-2003 .. **CLC 91, 113, 193**
See also AMWS 7; CA 81-84; 218; CANR
51, 74, 98, 133; CCA 1; CN 6, 7; CPW;
DA3; DAC; MTCW 2; MTFW 2005; NFS
23

Shields, David 1956- .... **CLC 97**
See also CA 124; CANR 48, 99, 112, 157

Shiga, Naoya 1883-1971 .... **CLC 33; SSC 23;**
TCLC 172
See Shiga Naoya
See also CA 101; 33-36R; MJW; RGWL 3

Shiga Naoya
See Shiga, Naoya
See also DLB 180; EWL 3; RGWL 3

Shilts, Randy 1951-1994 .... **CLC 85**
See also AAYA 19; CA 115; 127; 144;
CANR 45; DA3; GLL 1; INT CA-127;
MTCW 2; MTFW 2005

Shimazaki, Haruki 1872-1943
See Shimazaki Toson
See also CA 105; 134; CANR 84; RGWL 3

Shimazaki Toson .... **TCLC 5**
See Shimazaki, Haruki
See also DLB 180; EWL 3

Shirley, James 1596-1666 .... **DC 25; LC 96**
See also DLB 58; RGEL 2

Sholokhov, Mikhail (Aleksandrovich)
1905-1984 .... **CLC 7, 15**
See also CA 101; 112; DLB 272; EWL 3;
MTCW 1, 2; MTFW 2005; RGWL 2, 3;
SATA-Obit 36

Shone, Patric
See Hanley, James

Showalter, Elaine 1941- .... **CLC 169**
See also CA 57-60; CANR 58, 106; DLB
67; FW; GLL 2

Shreve, Susan
See Shreve, Susan Richards

Shreve, Susan Richards 1939- .... **CLC 23**
See also CA 49-52; CAAS 5; CANR 5, 38,
69, 100; MAICYA 1, 2; SATA 46, 95, 152;
SATA-Brief 41

Shue, Larry 1946-1985 .... **CLC 52**
See also CA 145; 117; DAM DRAM; DFS
7

Shu-Jen, Chou 1881-1936
See Lu Hsun
See also CA 104

Shulman, Alix Kates 1932- .... **CLC 2, 10**
See also CA 29-32R; CANR 43; FW; SATA
7

Shuster, Joe 1914-1992 .... **CLC 21**
See also AAYA 50

Shute, Nevil .... **CLC 30**
See Norway, Nevil Shute
See also BPFB 3; DLB 255; NFS 9; RHW;
SFW 4

Shuttle, Penelope (Diane) 1947- .... **CLC 7**
See also CA 93-96; CANR 39, 84, 92, 108;
CP 3, 4, 5, 6, 7; CWP; DLB 14, 40

Shvarts, Elena 1948- .... **PC 50**
See also CA 147

Sidhwa, Bapsi 1939-
See Sidhwa, Bapsy (N.)
See also CN 6, 7; DLB 323

Sidhwa, Bapsy (N.) 1938- .... **CLC 168**
See Sidhwa, Bapsi
See also CA 108; CANR 25, 57; FW

Sidney, Mary 1561-1621 .... **LC 19, 39**
See Sidney Herbert, Mary

Sidney, Sir Philip 1554-1586 .... **LC 19, 39,**
131; PC 32
See also BRW 1; BRWR 2; CDBLB Before
1660; DA; DA3; DAB; DAC; DAM MST,
POET; DLB 167; EXPP; PAB; RGEL 2;
TEA; WP

Sidney Herbert, Mary
See Sidney, Mary
See also DLB 167

Siegel, Jerome 1914-1996 .... **CLC 21**
See Siegel, Jerry
See also CA 116; 169; 151

Siegel, Jerry
See Siegel, Jerome
See also AAYA 50

Sienkiewicz, Henryk (Adam Alexander Pius)
1846-1916 .... **TCLC 3**
See also CA 104; 134; CANR 84; EWL 3;
RGSF 2; RGWL 2, 3

Sierra, Gregorio Martinez
See Martinez Sierra, Gregorio

Sierra, Maria de la O'LeJarraga Martinez
See Martinez Sierra, Maria

Sigal, Clancy 1926- .... **CLC 7**
See also CA 1-4R; CANR 85; CN 1, 2, 3,
4, 5, 6, 7

Siger of Brabant 1240(?)-1284(?) . **CMLC 69**
See also DLB 115

Sigourney, Lydia H.
See Sigourney, Lydia Howard (Huntley)
See also DLB 73, 183

Sigourney, Lydia Howard (Huntley)
1791-1865 .... **NCLC 21, 87**
See Sigourney, Lydia H.; Sigourney, Lydia
Huntley
See also DLB 1

Sigourney, Lydia Huntley
See Sigourney, Lydia Howard (Huntley)
See also DLB 42, 239, 243

Siguenza y Gongora, Carlos de
1645-1700 .... **HLCS 2; LC 8**
See also LAW

Sigurjonsson, Johann
See Sigurjonsson, Johann

Sigurjonsson, Johann 1880-1919 ... **TCLC 27**
See also CA 170; DLB 293; EWL 3

Sikelianos, Angelos 1884-1951 .... **PC 29;**
TCLC 39
See also EWL 3; RGWL 2, 3

Silkin, Jon 1930-1997 .... **CLC 2, 6, 43**
See also CA 5-8R; CAAS 5; CANR 89; CP
1, 2, 3, 4, 5, 6; DLB 27

Silko, Leslie 1948- ...... **CLC 23, 74, 114, 211;**
NNAL; SSC 37, 66; WLCS
See also AAYA 14; AMWS 4; ANW; BYA
12; CA 115; 122; CANR 45, 65, 118; CN
4, 5, 6, 7; CP 4, 5, 6, 7; CPW 1; CWP;

DA; DA3; DAC; DAM MST, MULT,
POP; DLB 143, 175, 256, 275; EWL 3;
EXPP; EXPS; LAIT 4; MAL 5; MTCW
2; MTFW 2005; NFS 4; PFS 9, 16; RGAL
4; RGSF 2; SSFS 4, 8, 10, 11; TCWW 1,
2

Sillanpaa, Frans Eemil 1888-1964 ... **CLC 19**
See also CA 129; 93-96; EWL 3; MTCW 1

Sillitoe, Alan 1928- .. **CLC 1, 3, 6, 10, 19, 57,**
148
See also AITN 1; BRWS 5; CA 9-12R, 191;
CAAE 191; CAAS 2; CANR 8, 26, 55,
139; CDBLB 1960 to Present; CN 1, 2, 3,
4, 5, 6; CP 1, 2, 3, 4, 5; DLB 14, 139;
EWL 3; MTCW 1, 2; MTFW 2005; RGEL
2; RGSF 2; SATA 61

Silone, Ignazio 1900-1978 .... **CLC 4**
See also CA 25-28; 81-84; CANR 34; CAP
2; DLB 264; EW 12; EWL 3; MTCW 1;
RGSF 2; RGWL 2, 3

Silone, Ignazione
See Silone, Ignazio

Silver, Joan Micklin 1935- .... **CLC 20**
See also CA 114; 121; INT CA-121

Silver, Nicholas
See Faust, Frederick (Schiller)

Silverberg, Robert 1935- .... **CLC 7, 140**
See also AAYA 24; BPFB 3; BYA 7, 9; CA
1-4R, 186; CAAE 186; CAAS 3; CANR
1, 20, 36, 85, 140; CLR 59; CN 6, 7;
CPW; DAM POP; DLB 8; INT CANR-
20; MAICYA 1, 2; MTCW 1, 2; MTFW
2005; SATA 13, 91; SATA-Essay 104;
SCFW 1, 2; SFW 4; SUFW 2

Silverstein, Alvin 1933- .... **CLC 17**
See also CA 49-52; CANR 2; CLR 25;
JRDA; MAICYA 1, 2; SATA 8, 69, 124

Silverstein, Shel 1932-1999 .... **PC 49**
See also AAYA 40; BW 3; CA 107; 179;
CANR 47, 74, 81; CLR 5, 96; CWRI 5;
JRDA; MAICYA 1, 2; MTCW 2; MTFW
2005; SATA 33, 92; SATA-Brief 27;
SATA-Obit 116

Silverstein, Virginia B(arbara Opshelor)
1937- .... **CLC 17**
See also CA 49-52; CANR 2; CLR 25;
JRDA; MAICYA 1, 2; SATA 8, 69, 124

Sim, Georges
See Simenon, Georges (Jacques Christian)

Simak, Clifford D(onald) 1904-1988 . **CLC 1,**
55
See also CA 1-4R; 125; CANR 1, 35; DLB
8; MTCW 1; SATA-Obit 56; SCFW 1, 2;
SFW 4

Simenon, Georges (Jacques Christian)
1903-1989 .... **CLC 1, 2, 3, 8, 18, 47**
See also BPFB 3; CA 85-88; 129; CANR
35; CMW 4; DA3; DAM POP; DLB 72;
DLBY 1989; EW 12; EWL 3; GFL 1789
to the Present; MSW; MTCW 1, 2; MTFW
2005; RGWL 2, 3

Simic, Charles 1938- .... **CLC 6, 9, 22, 49, 68,**
130; PC 69
See also AMWS 8; CA 29-32R; CAAS 4;
CANR 12, 33, 52, 61, 96, 140; CP 2, 3, 4,
5, 6, 7; DA3; DAM POET; DLB 105;
MAL 5; MTCW 2; MTFW 2005; PFS 7;
RGAL 4; WP

Simmel, Georg 1858-1918 .... **TCLC 64**
See also CA 157; DLB 296

Simmons, Charles (Paul) 1924- .... **CLC 57**
See also CA 89-92; INT CA-89-92

Simmons, Dan 1948- .... **CLC 44**
See also AAYA 16, 54; CA 138; CANR 53,
81, 126; CPW; DAM POP; HGG; SUFW
2

Simmons, James (Stewart Alexander)
1933- .... **CLC 43**
See also CA 105; CAAS 21; CP 1, 2, 3, 4,
5, 6, 7; DLB 40

Smith, Johnston
See Crane, Stephen (Townley)
Smith, Joseph, Jr. 1805-1844 .... **NCLC 53**
Smith, Kevin 1970- .... **CLC 223**
See also AAYA 37; CA 166; CANR 131
Smith, Lee 1944- .... **CLC 25, 73**
See also CA 114; 119; CANR 46, 118; CN 7; CSW; DLB 143; DLBY 1983; EWL 3; INT CA-119; RGAL 4
Smith, Martin
See Smith, Martin Cruz
Smith, Martin Cruz 1942- .. **CLC 25; NNAL**
See also BEST 89:4; BPFB 3; CA 85-88; CANR 6, 23, 43, 65, 119; CMW 4; CPW; DAM MULT, POP; HGG; INT CANR-23; MTCW 2; MTFW 2005; RGAL 4
Smith, Patti 1946- .... **CLC 12**
See also CA 93-96; CANR 63
Smith, Pauline (Urmson)
1882-1959 .... **TCLC 25**
See also DLB 225; EWL 3
Smith, Rosamond
See Oates, Joyce Carol
Smith, Sheila Kaye
See Kaye-Smith, Sheila
Smith, Stevie 1902-1971 .... **CLC 3, 8, 25, 44; PC 12**
See also BRWS 2; CA 17-18; 29-32R; CANR 35; CAP 2; CP 1; DAM POET; DLB 20; EWL 3; MTCW 1, 2; PAB; PFS 3; RGEL 2; TEA
Smith, Wilbur 1933- .... **CLC 33**
See also CA 13-16R; CANR 7, 46, 66, 134; CPW; MTCW 1, 2; MTFW 2005
Smith, William Jay 1918- .... **CLC 6**
See also AMWS 13; CA 5-8R; CANR 44, 106; CP 1, 2, 3, 4, 5, 6, 7; CSW; CWRI 5; DLB 5; MAICYA 1, 2; SAAS 22; SATA 2, 68, 154; SATA-Essay 154; TCLE 1:2
Smith, Woodrow Wilson
See Kuttner, Henry
Smith, Zadie 1975- .... **CLC 158**
See also AAYA 50; CA 193; MTFW 2005
Smolenskin, Peretz 1842-1885 ...... **NCLC 30**
Smollett, Tobias (George) 1721-1771 ... **LC 2, 46**
See also BRW 3; CDBLB 1660-1789; DLB 39, 104; RGEL 2; TEA
Snodgrass, W.D. 1926- .... **CLC 2, 6, 10, 18, 68; PC 74**
See also AMWS 6; CA 1-4R; CANR 6, 36, 65, 85; CP 1, 2, 3, 4, 5, 6, 7; DAM POET; DLB 5; MAL 5; MTCW 1, 2; MTFW 2005; RGAL 4; TCLE 1:2
Snorri Sturluson 1179-1241 .... **CMLC 56**
See also RGWL 2, 3
Snow, C(harles) P(ercy) 1905-1980 ... **CLC 1, 4, 6, 9, 13, 19**
See also BRW 7; CA 5-8R; 101; CANR 28; CDBLB 1945-1960; CN 1, 2; DAM NOV; DLB 15, 77; DLBD 17; EWL 3; MTCW 1, 2; MTFW 2005; RGEL 2; TEA
Snow, Frances Compton
See Adams, Henry (Brooks)
Snyder, Gary 1930- . **CLC 1, 2, 5, 9, 32, 120; PC 21**
See also AMWS 8; ANW; BG 1:3; CA 17-20R; CANR 30, 60, 125; CP 1, 2, 3, 4, 5, 6, 7; DA3; DAM POET; DLB 5, 16, 165, 212, 237, 275; EWL 3; MAL 5; MTCW 2; MTFW 2005; PFS 9, 19; RGAL 4; WP
Snyder, Zilpha Keatley 1927- .... **CLC 17**
See also AAYA 15; BYA 1; CA 9-12R; CANR 38; CLR 31; JRDA; MAICYA 1, 2; SAAS 2; SATA 1, 28, 75, 110, 163; SATA-Essay 112, 163; YAW
Soares, Bernardo
See Pessoa, Fernando (Antonio Nogueira)

Sobh, A.
See Shamlu, Ahmad
Sobh, Alef
See Shamlu, Ahmad
Sobol, Joshua 1939- .... **CLC 60**
See Sobol, Yehoshua
See also CA 200; RGHL
Sobol, Yehoshua 1939-
See Sobol, Joshua
See also CWW 2
Socrates 470B.C.-399B.C. .... **CMLC 27**
Soderberg, Hjalmar 1869-1941 ...... **TCLC 39**
See also DLB 259; EWL 3; RGSF 2
Soderbergh, Steven 1963- .... **CLC 154**
See also AAYA 43; CA 243
Soderbergh, Steven Andrew
See Soderbergh, Steven
Sodergran, Edith (Irene) 1892-1923
See Soedergran, Edith (Irene)
See also CA 202; DLB 259; EW 11; EWL 3; RGWL 2, 3
Soedergran, Edith (Irene)
1892-1923 .... **TCLC 31**
See Sodergran, Edith (Irene)
Softly, Edgar
See Lovecraft, H. P.
Softly, Edward
See Lovecraft, H. P.
Sokolov, Alexander V(sevolodovich) 1943-
See Sokolov, Sasha
See also CA 73-76
Sokolov, Raymond 1941- .... **CLC 7**
See also CA 85-88
Sokolov, Sasha .... **CLC 59**
See Sokolov, Alexander V(sevolodovich)
See also CWW 2; DLB 285; EWL 3; RGWL 2, 3
Solo, Jay
See Ellison, Harlan
Sologub, Fyodor .... **TCLC 9**
See Teternikov, Fyodor Kuzmich
See also EWL 3
Solomons, Ikey Esquir
See Thackeray, William Makepeace
Solomos, Dionysios 1798-1857 .... **NCLC 15**
Solwoska, Mara
See French, Marilyn
Solzhenitsyn, Aleksandr I. 1918- .. **CLC 1, 2, 4, 7, 9, 10, 18, 26, 34, 78, 134; SSC 32; WLC 5**
See Solzhenitsyn, Aleksandr Isayevich
See also AAYA 49; AITN 1; BPFB 3; CA 69-72; CANR 40, 65, 116; DA; DA3; DAB; DAC; DAM MST, NOV; DLB 302; EW 13; EXPS; LAIT 4; MTCW 1, 2; MTFW 2005; NFS 6; RGSF 2; RGWL 2, 3; SSFS 9; TWA
Solzhenitsyn, Aleksandr Isayevich
See Solzhenitsyn, Aleksandr I.
See also CWW 2; EWL 3
Somers, Jane
See Lessing, Doris
Somerville, Edith Oenone
1858-1949 .... **SSC 56; TCLC 51**
See also CA 196; DLB 135; RGEL 2; RGSF 2
Somerville & Ross
See Martin, Violet Florence; Somerville, Edith Oenone
Sommer, Scott 1951- .... **CLC 25**
See also CA 106
Sommers, Christina Hoff 1950- ...... **CLC 197**
See also CA 153; CANR 95
Sondheim, Stephen (Joshua) 1930- . **CLC 30, 39, 147; DC 22**
See also AAYA 11, 66; CA 103; CANR 47, 67, 125; DAM DRAM; LAIT 4
Sone, Monica 1919- .... **AAL**
See also DLB 312

Song, Cathy 1955- .... **AAL; PC 21**
See also CA 154; CANR 118; CWP; DLB 169, 312; EXPP; FW; PFS 5
Sontag, Susan 1933-2004 ... **CLC 1, 2, 10, 13, 31, 105, 195**
See also AMWS 3; CA 17-20R; 234; CANR 25, 51, 74, 97; CN 1, 2, 3, 4, 5, 6, 7; CPW; DA3; DAM POP; DLB 2, 67; EWL 3; MAL 5; MBL; MTCW 1, 2; MTFW 2005; RGAL 4; RHW; SSFS 10
Sophocles 496(?)B.C.-406(?)B.C. .... **CMLC 2, 47, 51, 86; DC 1; WLCS**
See also AW 1; CDWLB 1; DA; DA3; DAB; DAC; DAM DRAM, MST; DFS 1, 4, 8; DLB 176; LAIT 1; LATS 1:1; LMFS 1; RGWL 2, 3; TWA; WLIT 8
Sordello 1189-1269 .... **CMLC 15**
Sorel, Georges 1847-1922 .... **TCLC 91**
See also CA 118; 188
Sorel, Julia
See Drexler, Rosalyn
Sorokin, Vladimir .... **CLC 59**
See Sorokin, Vladimir Georgievich
Sorokin, Vladimir Georgievich
See Sorokin, Vladimir
See also DLB 285
Sorrentino, Gilbert 1929-2006 .... **CLC 3, 7, 14, 22, 40**
See also CA 77-80; 250; CANR 14, 33, 115, 157; CN 3, 4, 5, 6, 7; CP 1, 2, 3, 4, 5, 6, 7; DLB 5, 173; DLBY 1980; INT CANR-14
Soseki
See Natsume, Soseki
See also MJW
Soto, Gary 1952- ... **CLC 32, 80; HLC 2; PC 28**
See also AAYA 10, 37; BYA 11; CA 119; 125; CANR 50, 74, 107, 157; CLR 38; CP 4, 5, 6, 7; DAM MULT; DLB 82; EWL 3; EXPP; HW 1, 2; INT CA-125; JRDA; LLW; MAICYA 2; MAICYAS 1; MAL 5; MTCW 2; MTFW 2005; PFS 7; RGAL 4; SATA 80, 120; WYA; YAW
Soupault, Philippe 1897-1990 .... **CLC 68**
See also CA 116; 147; 131; EWL 3; GFL 1789 to the Present; LMFS 2
Souster, (Holmes) Raymond 1921- .... **CLC 5, 14**
See also CA 13-16R; CAAS 14; CANR 13, 29, 53; CP 1, 2, 3, 4, 5, 6, 7; DA3; DAC; DAM POET; DLB 88; RGEL 2; SATA 63
Southern, Terry 1924(?)-1995 .... **CLC 7**
See also AMWS 11; BPFB 3; CA 1-4R; 150; CANR 1, 55, 107; CN 1, 2, 3, 4, 5, 6; DLB 2; IDFW 3, 4
Southerne, Thomas 1660-1746 .... **LC 99**
See also DLB 80; RGEL 2
Southey, Robert 1774-1843 .... **NCLC 8, 97**
See also BRW 4; DLB 93, 107, 142; RGEL 2; SATA 54
Southwell, Robert 1561(?)-1595 .... **LC 108**
See also DLB 167; RGEL 2; TEA
Southworth, Emma Dorothy Eliza Nevitte
1819-1899 .... **NCLC 26**
See also DLB 239
Souza, Ernest
See Scott, Evelyn
Soyinka, Wole 1934- .. **BLC 3; CLC 3, 5, 14, 36, 44, 179; DC 2; WLC 5**
See also AFW; BW 2, 3; CA 13-16R; CANR 27, 39, 82, 136; CD 5, 6; CDWLB 3; CN 6, 7; CP 1, 2, 3, 4, 5, 6 ,7; DA; DA3; DAB; DAC; DAM DRAM, MST, MULT; DFS 10; DLB 125; EWL 3; MTCW 1, 2; MTFW 2005; RGEL 2; TWA; WLIT 2; WWE 1
Spackman, W(illiam) M(ode)
1905-1990 .... **CLC 46**
See also CA 81-84; 132

Symonds, John Addington
1840-1893 .... NCLC 34
See also DLB 57, 144
Symons, Arthur 1865-1945 .... TCLC 11
See also CA 107; 189; DLB 19, 57, 149;
RGEL 2
Symons, Julian (Gustave)
1912-1994 .... CLC 2, 14, 32
See also CA 49-52; 147; CAAS 3; CANR
3, 33, 59; CMW 4; CN 1, 2, 3, 4, 5; CP 1,
3, 4; DLB 87, 155; DLBY 1992; MSW;
MTCW 1
Synge, (Edmund) J(ohn) M(illington)
1871-1909 .... DC 2; TCLC 6, 37
See also BRW 6; BRWR 1; CA 104; 141;
CDBLB 1890-1914; DAM DRAM; DFS
18; DLB 10, 19; EWL 3; RGEL 2; TEA;
WLIT 4
Syruc, J.
See Milosz, Czeslaw
Szirtes, George 1948- .... CLC 46; PC 51
See also CA 109; CANR 27, 61, 117; CP 4,
5, 6, 7
Szymborska, Wislawa 1923- ... CLC 99, 190;
PC 44
See also CA 154; CANR 91, 133; CDWLB
4; CWP; CWW 2; DA3; DLB 232; DLBY
1996; EWL 3; MTCW 2; MTFW 2005;
PFS 15; RGHL; RGWL 3
T. O., Nik
See Annensky, Innokenty (Fyodorovich)
Tabori, George 1914- .... CLC 19
See also CA 49-52; CANR 4, 69; CBD; CD
5, 6; DLB 245; RGHL
Tacitus c. 55-c. 117 .... CMLC 56
See also AW 2; CDWLB 1; DLB 211;
RGWL 2, 3; WLIT 8
Tagore, Rabindranath 1861-1941 .... PC 8;
SSC 48; TCLC 3, 53
See also CA 104; 120; DA3; DAM DRAM,
POET; DLB 323; EWL 3; MTCW 1, 2;
MTFW 2005; PFS 18; RGEL 2; RGSF 2;
RGWL 2, 3; TWA
Taine, Hippolyte Adolphe
1828-1893 .... NCLC 15
See also EW 7; GFL 1789 to the Present
Talayesva, Don C. 1890-(?) .... NNAL
Talese, Gay 1932- .... CLC 37
See also AITN 1; CA 1-4R; CANR 9, 58,
137; DLB 185; INT CANR-9; MTCW 1,
2; MTFW 2005
Tallent, Elizabeth 1954- .... CLC 45
See also CA 117; CANR 72; DLB 130
Tallmountain, Mary 1918-1997 .... NNAL
See also CA 146; 161; DLB 193
Tally, Ted 1952- .... CLC 42
See also CA 120; 124; CAD; CANR 125;
CD 5, 6; INT CA-124
Talvik, Heiti 1904-1947 .... TCLC 87
See also EWL 3
Tamayo y Baus, Manuel
1829-1898 .... NCLC 1
Tammsaare, A(nton) H(ansen)
1878-1940 .... TCLC 27
See also CA 164; CDWLB 4; DLB 220;
EWL 3
Tam'si, Tchicaya U
See Tchicaya, Gerald Felix
Tan, Amy 1952- ...... AAL; CLC 59, 120, 151
See also AAYA 9, 48; AMWS 10; BEST
89:3; BPFB 3; CA 136; CANR 54, 105,
132; CDALBS; CN 6, 7; CPW 1; DA3;
DAM MULT, NOV, POP; DLB 173, 312;
EXPN; FL 1:6; FW; LAIT 3, 5; MAL 5;
MTCW 2; MTFW 2005; NFS 1, 13, 16;
RGAL 4; SATA 75; SSFS 9; YAW
Tandem, Carl Felix
See Spitteler, Carl

Tandem, Felix
See Spitteler, Carl
Tanizaki, Jun'ichiro 1886-1965 ... CLC 8, 14,
28; SSC 21
See Tanizaki Jun'ichiro
See also CA 93-96; 25-28R; MJW; MTCW
2; MTFW 2005; RGSF 2; RGWL 2
Tanizaki Jun'ichiro
See Tanizaki, Jun'ichiro
See also DLB 180; EWL 3
Tannen, Deborah 1945- .... CLC 206
See also CA 118; CANR 95
Tannen, Deborah Frances
See Tannen, Deborah
Tanner, William
See Amis, Kingsley
Tante, Dilly
See Kunitz, Stanley
Tao Lao
See Storni, Alfonsina
Tapahonso, Luci 1953- .... NNAL; PC 65
See also CA 145; CANR 72, 127; DLB 175
Tarantino, Quentin (Jerome)
1963- .... CLC 125, 230
See also AAYA 58; CA 171; CANR 125
Tarassoff, Lev
See Troyat, Henri
Tarbell, Ida M(inerva) 1857-1944 . TCLC 40
See also CA 122; 181; DLB 47
Tarkington, (Newton) Booth
1869-1946 .... TCLC 9
See also BPFB 3; BYA 3; CA 110; 143;
CWRI 5; DLB 9, 102; MAL 5; MTCW 2;
RGAL 4; SATA 17
Tarkovskii, Andrei Arsen'evich
See Tarkovsky, Andrei (Arsenyevich)
Tarkovsky, Andrei (Arsenyevich)
1932-1986 .... CLC 75
See also CA 127
Tartt, Donna 1964(?)- .... CLC 76
See also AAYA 56; CA 142; CANR 135;
MTFW 2005
Tasso, Torquato 1544-1595 .... LC 5, 94
See also EFS 2; EW 2; RGWL 2, 3; WLIT
7
Tate, (John Orley) Allen 1899-1979 .. CLC 2,
4, 6, 9, 11, 14, 24; PC 50
See also AMW; CA 5-8R; 85-88; CANR
32, 108; CN 1, 2; CP 1, 2; DLB 4, 45, 63;
DLBD 17; EWL 3; MAL 5; MTCW 1, 2;
MTFW 2005; RGAL 4; RHW
Tate, Ellalice
See Hibbert, Eleanor Alice Burford
Tate, James (Vincent) 1943- ..... CLC 2, 6, 25
See also CA 21-24R; CANR 29, 57, 114;
CP 1, 2, 3, 4, 5, 6, 7; DLB 5, 169; EWL
3; PFS 10, 15; RGAL 4; WP
Tate, Nahum 1652(?)-1715 .... LC 109
See also DLB 80; RGEL 2
Tauler, Johannes c. 1300-1361 ...... CMLC 37
See also DLB 179; LMFS 1
Tavel, Ronald 1940- .... CLC 6
See also CA 21-24R; CAD; CANR 33; CD
5, 6
Taviani, Paolo 1931- .... CLC 70
See also CA 153
Taylor, Bayard 1825-1878 .... NCLC 89
See also DLB 3, 189, 250, 254; RGAL 4
Taylor, C(ecil) P(hilip) 1929-1981 .... CLC 27
See also CA 25-28R; 105; CANR 47; CBD
Taylor, Edward 1642(?)-1729 . LC 11; PC 63
See also AMW; DA; DAB; DAC; DAM
MST, POET; DLB 24; EXPP; RGAL 4;
TUS
Taylor, Eleanor Ross 1920- .... CLC 5
See also CA 81-84; CANR 70

Taylor, Elizabeth 1912-1975 ..... CLC 2, 4, 29
See also CA 13-16R; CANR 9, 70; CN 1,
2; DLB 139; MTCW 1; RGEL 2; SATA
13
Taylor, Frederick Winslow
1856-1915 .... TCLC 76
See also CA 188
Taylor, Henry (Splawn) 1942- .... CLC 44
See also CA 33-36R; CAAS 7; CANR 31;
CP 6, 7; DLB 5; PFS 10
Taylor, Kamala 1924-2004
See Markandaya, Kamala
See also CA 77-80; 227; MTFW 2005; NFS
13
Taylor, Mildred D. 1943- .... CLC 21
See also AAYA 10, 47; BW 1; BYA 3, 8;
CA 85-88; CANR 25, 115, 136; CLR 9,
59, 90; CSW; DLB 52; JRDA; LAIT 3;
MAICYA 1, 2; MTFW 2005; SAAS 5;
SATA 135; WYA; YAW
Taylor, Peter (Hillsman) 1917-1994 .. CLC 1,
4, 18, 37, 44, 50, 71; SSC 10, 84
See also AMWS 5; BPFB 3; CA 13-16R;
147; CANR 9, 50; CN 1, 2, 3, 4, 5; CSW;
DLB 218, 278; DLBY 1981, 1994; EWL
3; EXPS; INT CANR-9; MAL 5; MTCW
1, 2; MTFW 2005; RGSF 2; SSFS 9; TUS
Taylor, Robert Lewis 1912-1998 .... CLC 14
See also CA 1-4R; 170; CANR 3, 64; CN
1, 2; SATA 10; TCWW 1, 2
Tchekhov, Anton
See Chekhov, Anton (Pavlovich)
Tchicaya, Gerald Felix 1931-1988 .. CLC 101
See Tchicaya U Tam'si
See also CA 129; 125; CANR 81
Tchicaya U Tam'si
See Tchicaya, Gerald Felix
See also EWL 3
Teasdale, Sara 1884-1933 .... PC 31; TCLC 4
See also CA 104; 163; DLB 45; GLL 1;
PFS 14; RGAL 4; SATA 32; TUS
Tecumseh 1768-1813 .... NNAL
See also DAM MULT
Tegner, Esaias 1782-1846 .... NCLC 2
Teilhard de Chardin, (Marie Joseph) Pierre
1881-1955 .... TCLC 9
See also CA 105; 210; GFL 1789 to the
Present
Temple, Ann
See Mortimer, Penelope (Ruth)
Tennant, Emma (Christina) 1937- .. CLC 13,
52
See also BRWS 9; CA 65-68; CAAS 9;
CANR 10, 38, 59, 88; CN 3, 4, 5, 6, 7;
DLB 14; EWL 3; SFW 4
Tenneshaw, S. M.
See Silverberg, Robert
Tenney, Tabitha Gilman
1762-1837 .... NCLC 122
See also DLB 37, 200
Tennyson, Alfred 1809-1892 ... NCLC 30, 65,
115; PC 6; WLC 6
See also AAYA 50; BRW 4; CDBLB 1832-
1890; DA; DA3; DAB; DAC; DAM MST,
POET; DLB 32; EXPP; PAB; PFS 1, 2, 4,
11, 15, 19; RGEL 2; TEA; WLIT 4; WP
Teran, Lisa St. Aubin de .... CLC 36
See St. Aubin de Teran, Lisa
Terence c. 184B.C.-c. 159B.C. ...... CMLC 14;
DC 7
See also AW 1; CDWLB 1; DLB 211;
RGWL 2, 3; TWA; WLIT 8
Teresa de Jesus, St. 1515-1582 .... LC 18
Teresa of Avila, St.
See Teresa de Jesus, St.
Terkel, Louis .... CLC 38
See Terkel, Studs
See also AAYA 32; AITN 1; MTCW 2; TUS

Tiptree, James, Jr. .... **CLC 48, 50**
See Sheldon, Alice Hastings Bradley
See also DLB 8; SCFW 1, 2; SFW 4

Tirone Smith, Mary-Ann 1944- .... **CLC 39**
See also CA 118; 136; CANR 113; SATA
143

Tirso de Molina 1580(?)-1648 .... **DC 13;
HLCS 2; LC 73**
See also RGWL 2, 3

Titmarsh, Michael Angelo
See Thackeray, William Makepeace

Tocqueville, Alexis (Charles Henri Maurice
Clerel Comte) de 1805-1859 .. **NCLC 7,
63**
See also EW 6; GFL 1789 to the Present;
TWA

Toer, Pramoedya Ananta
1925-2006 .... **CLC 186**
See also CA 197; 251; RGWL 3

Toffler, Alvin 1928- .... **CLC 168**
See also CA 13-16R; CANR 15, 46, 67;
CPW; DAM POP; MTCW 1, 2

Toibin, Colm 1955- .... **CLC 162**
See also CA 142; CANR 81, 149; CN 7;
DLB 271

Tolkien, J(ohn) R(onald) R(euel)
1892-1973 .... **CLC 1, 2, 3, 8, 12, 38;
TCLC 137; WLC 6**
See also AAYA 10; AITN 1; BPFB 3;
BRWC 2; BRWS 2; CA 17-18; 45-48;
CANR 36, 134; CAP 2; CDBLB 1914-
1945; CLR 56; CN 1; CPW 1; CWRI 5;
DA; DA3; DAB; DAC; DAM MST, NOV,
POP; DLB 15, 160, 255; EFS 2; EWL 3;
FANT; JRDA; LAIT 1; LATS 1:2; LMFS
2; MAICYA 1, 2; MTCW 1, 2; MTFW
2005; NFS 8; RGEL 2; SATA 2, 32, 100;
SATA-Obit 24; SFW 4; SUFW; TEA;
WCH; WYA; YAW

Toller, Ernst 1893-1939 .... **TCLC 10**
See also CA 107; 186; DLB 124; EWL 3;
RGWL 2, 3

Tolson, M. B.
See Tolson, Melvin B(eaunorus)

Tolson, Melvin B(eaunorus)
1898(?)-1966 .... **BLC 3; CLC 36, 105**
See also AFAW 1, 2; BW 1, 3; CA 124; 89-
92; CANR 80; DAM MULT, POET; DLB
48, 76; MAL 5; RGAL 4

Tolstoi, Aleksei Nikolaevich
See Tolstoy, Alexey Nikolaevich

Tolstoi, Lev
See Tolstoy, Leo (Nikolaevich)
See also RGSF 2; RGWL 2, 3

Tolstoy, Aleksei Nikolaevich
See Tolstoy, Alexey Nikolaevich
See also DLB 272

Tolstoy, Alexey Nikolaevich
1882-1945 .... **TCLC 18**
See Tolstoy, Aleksei Nikolaevich
See also CA 107; 158; EWL 3; SFW 4

Tolstoy, Leo (Nikolaevich)
1828-1910 . **SSC 9, 30, 45, 54; TCLC 4,
11, 17, 28, 44, 79, 173; WLC 6**
See Tolstoi, Lev
See also AAYA 56; CA 104; 123; DA; DA3;
DAB; DAC; DAM MST, NOV; DLB 238;
EFS 2; EW 7; EXPS; IDTP; LAIT 2;
LATS 1:1; LMFS 1; NFS 10; SATA 26;
SSFS 5; TWA

Tolstoy, Count Leo
See Tolstoy, Leo (Nikolaevich)

Tomalin, Claire 1933- .... **CLC 166**
See also CA 89-92; CANR 52, 88; DLB
155

Tomasi di Lampedusa, Giuseppe 1896-1957
See Lampedusa, Giuseppe (Tomasi) di
See also CA 111; DLB 177; EWL 3; WLIT
7

Tomlin, Lily 1939(?)-
See Tomlin, Mary Jean
See also CA 117

Tomlin, Mary Jean .... **CLC 17**
See Tomlin, Lily

Tomline, F. Latour
See Gilbert, W(illiam) S(chwenck)

Tomlinson, (Alfred) Charles 1927- .... **CLC 2,
4, 6, 13, 45; PC 17**
See also CA 5-8R; CANR 33; CP 1, 2, 3, 4,
5, 6, 7; DAM POET; DLB 40; TCLE 1:2

Tomlinson, H(enry) M(ajor)
1873-1958 .... **TCLC 71**
See also CA 118; 161; DLB 36, 100, 195

Tonna, Charlotte Elizabeth
1790-1846 .... **NCLC 135**
See also DLB 163

Tonson, Jacob fl. 1655(?)-1736 .... **LC 86**
See also DLB 170

Toole, John Kennedy 1937-1969 ..... **CLC 19,
64**
See also BPFB 3; CA 104; DLBY 1981;
MTCW 2; MTFW 2005

Toomer, Eugene
See Toomer, Jean

Toomer, Eugene Pinchback
See Toomer, Jean

Toomer, Jean 1894-1967 .. **BLC 3; CLC 1, 4,
13, 22; HR 1:3; PC 7; SSC 1, 45;
TCLC 172; WLCS**
See also AFAW 1, 2; AMWS 3, 9; BW 1;
CA 85-88; CDALB 1917-1929; DA3;
DAM MULT; DLB 45, 51; EWL 3; EXPP;
EXPS; LMFS 2; MAL 5; MTCW 1, 2;
MTFW 2005; NFS 11; RGAL 4; RGSF 2;
SSFS 5

Toomer, Nathan Jean
See Toomer, Jean

Toomer, Nathan Pinchback
See Toomer, Jean

Torley, Luke
See Blish, James (Benjamin)

Tornimparte, Alessandra
See Ginzburg, Natalia

Torre, Raoul della
See Mencken, H(enry) L(ouis)

Torrence, Ridgely 1874-1950 .... **TCLC 97**
See also DLB 54, 249; MAL 5

Torrey, E(dwin) Fuller 1937- .... **CLC 34**
See also CA 119; CANR 71

Torsvan, Ben Traven
See Traven, B.

Torsvan, Benno Traven
See Traven, B.

Torsvan, Berick Traven
See Traven, B.

Torsvan, Berwick Traven
See Traven, B.

Torsvan, Bruno Traven
See Traven, B.

Torsvan, Traven
See Traven, B.

Tourneur, Cyril 1575(?)-1626 .... **LC 66**
See also BRW 2; DAM DRAM; DLB 58;
RGEL 2

Tournier, Michel 1924- .... **CLC 6, 23, 36, 95;
SSC 88**
See also CA 49-52; CANR 3, 36, 74, 149;
CWW 2; DLB 83; EWL 3; GFL 1789 to
the Present; MTCW 1, 2; SATA 23

Tournier, Michel Edouard
See Tournier, Michel

Tournimparte, Alessandra
See Ginzburg, Natalia

Towers, Ivar
See Kornbluth, C(yril) M.

Towne, Robert (Burton) 1936(?)- ..... **CLC 87**
See also CA 108; DLB 44; IDFW 3, 4

Townsend, Sue .... **CLC 61**
See Townsend, Susan Lilian
See also AAYA 28; CA 119; 127; CANR
65, 107; CBD; CD 5, 6; CPW; CWD;
DAB; DAC; DAM MST; DLB 271; INT
CA-127; SATA 55, 93; SATA-Brief 48;
YAW

Townsend, Susan Lilian 1946-
See Townsend, Sue

Townshend, Pete
See Townshend, Peter (Dennis Blandford)

Townshend, Peter (Dennis Blandford)
1945- .... **CLC 17, 42**
See also CA 107

Tozzi, Federigo 1883-1920 .... **TCLC 31**
See also CA 160; CANR 110; DLB 264;
EWL 3; WLIT 7

Tracy, Don(ald Fiske) 1905-1970(?)
See Queen, Ellery
See also CA 1-4R; 176; CANR 2

Trafford, F. G.
See Riddell, Charlotte

Traherne, Thomas 1637(?)-1674 .. **LC 99; PC
70**
See also BRW 2; BRWS 11; DLB 131;
PAB; RGEL 2

Traill, Catharine Parr 1802-1899 .. **NCLC 31**
See also DLB 99

Trakl, Georg 1887-1914 .... **PC 20; TCLC 5**
See also CA 104; 165; EW 10; EWL 3;
LMFS 2; MTCW 2; RGWL 2, 3

Trambley, Estela Portillo .... **TCLC 163**
See Portillo Trambley, Estela
See also CA 77-80; RGAL 4

Tranquilli, Secondino
See Silone, Ignazio

Transtroemer, Tomas Gosta
See Transtromer, Tomas (Goesta)

Transtromer, Tomas (Gosta)
See Transtromer, Tomas (Goesta)
See also CWW 2

Transtromer, Tomas (Goesta)
1931- .... **CLC 52, 65**
See Transtromer, Tomas (Gosta)
See also CA 117; 129; CAAS 17; CANR
115; DAM POET; DLB 257; EWL 3; PFS
21

Transtromer, Tomas Gosta
See Transtromer, Tomas (Goesta)

Traven, B. 1882(?)-1969 .... **CLC 8, 11**
See also CA 19-20; 25-28R; CAP 2; DLB
9, 56; EWL 3; MTCW 1; RGAL 4

Trediakovsky, Vasilii Kirillovich
1703-1769 .... **LC 68**
See also DLB 150

Treitel, Jonathan 1959- .... **CLC 70**
See also CA 210; DLB 267

Trelawny, Edward John
1792-1881 .... **NCLC 85**
See also DLB 110, 116, 144

Tremain, Rose 1943- .... **CLC 42**
See also CA 97-100; CANR 44, 95; CN 4,
5, 6, 7; DLB 14, 271; RGSF 2; RHW

Tremblay, Michel 1942- .... **CLC 29, 102, 225**
See also CA 116; 128; CCA 1; CWW 2;
DAC; DAM MST; DLB 60; EWL 3; GLL
1; MTCW 1, 2; MTFW 2005

Trevanian .... **CLC 29**
See Whitaker, Rod

Trevor, Glen
See Hilton, James

Trevor, William .. **CLC 7, 9, 14, 25, 71, 116;
SSC 21, 58**
See Cox, William Trevor
See also BRWS 4; CBD; CD 5, 6; CN 1, 2,
3, 4, 5, 6, 7; DLB 14, 139; EWL 3; LATS
1:2; RGEL 2; RGSF 2; SSFS 10; TCLE
1:2

Trifonov, Iurii (Valentinovich)
See Trifonov, Yuri (Valentinovich)
See also DLB 302; RGWL 2, 3

Trifonov, Yuri (Valentinovich)
1925-1981 .... **CLC 45**
See Trifonov, Iurii (Valentinovich); Tri-
fonov, Yury Valentinovich
See also CA 126; 103; MTCW 1

Trifonov, Yury Valentinovich
See Trifonov, Yuri (Valentinovich)
See also EWL 3

Trilling, Diana (Rubin) 1905-1996 . **CLC 129**
See also CA 5-8R; 154; CANR 10, 46; INT
CANR-10; MTCW 1, 2

Trilling, Lionel 1905-1975 ..... **CLC 9, 11, 24;
SSC 75**
See also AMWS 3; CA 9-12R; 61-64;
CANR 10, 105; CN 1, 2; DLB 28, 63;
EWL 3; INT CANR-10; MAL 5; MTCW
1, 2; RGAL 4; TUS

Trimball, W. H.
See Mencken, H(enry) L(ouis)

Tristan
See Gomez de la Serna, Ramon

Tristram
See Housman, A(lfred) E(dward)

Trogdon, William (Lewis) 1939-
See Heat-Moon, William Least
See also AAYA 66; CA 115; 119; CANR
47, 89; CPW; INT CA-119

Trollope, Anthony 1815-1882 .... **NCLC 6, 33,
101; SSC 28; WLC 6**
See also BRW 5; CDBLB 1832-1890; DA;
DA3; DAB; DAC; DAM MST, NOV;
DLB 21, 57, 159; RGEL 2; RGSF 2;
SATA 22

Trollope, Frances 1779-1863 .... **NCLC 30**
See also DLB 21, 166

Trollope, Joanna 1943- .... **CLC 186**
See also CA 101; CANR 58, 95, 149; CN
7; CPW; DLB 207; RHW

Trotsky, Leon 1879-1940 .... **TCLC 22**
See also CA 118; 167

Trotter (Cockburn), Catharine
1679-1749 .... **LC 8**
See also DLB 84, 252

Trotter, Wilfred 1872-1939 .... **TCLC 97**

Trout, Kilgore
See Farmer, Philip Jose

Trow, George W. S. 1943- .... **CLC 52**
See also CA 126; CANR 91

Troyat, Henri 1911- .... **CLC 23**
See also CA 45-48; CANR 2, 33, 67, 117;
GFL 1789 to the Present; MTCW 1

Trudeau, Garry B. .... **CLC 12**
See Trudeau, G.B.
See also AAYA 10; AITN 2

Trudeau, G.B. 1948-
See Trudeau, Garry B.
See also AAYA 60; CA 81-84; CANR 31;
SATA 35, 168

Truffaut, François 1932-1984 ... **CLC 20, 101**
See also CA 81-84; 113; CANR 34

Trumbo, Dalton 1905-1976 .... **CLC 19**
See also CA 21-24R; 69-72; CANR 10; CN
1, 2; DLB 26; IDFW 3, 4; YAW

Trumbull, John 1750-1831 .... **NCLC 30**
See also DLB 31; RGAL 4

Trundlett, Helen B.
See Eliot, T(homas) S(tearns)

Truth, Sojourner 1797(?)-1883 ...... **NCLC 94**
See also DLB 239; FW; LAIT 2

Tryon, Thomas 1926-1991 .... **CLC 3, 11**
See also AITN 1; BPFB 3; CA 29-32R; 135;
CANR 32, 77; CPW; DA3; DAM POP;
HGG; MTCW 1

Tryon, Tom
See Tryon, Thomas

Ts'ao Hsueh-ch'in 1715(?)-1763 .... **LC 1**

Tsurayuki Ed. fl. 10th cent. - .... **PC 73**

Tsushima, Shuji 1909-1948
See Dazai Osamu
See also CA 107

Tsvetaeva (Efron), Marina (Ivanovna)
1892-1941 .... **PC 14; TCLC 7, 35**
See also CA 104; 128; CANR 73; DLB 295;
EW 11; MTCW 1, 2; RGWL 2, 3

Tuck, Lily 1938- .... **CLC 70**
See also CA 139; CANR 90

Tu Fu 712-770 .... **PC 9**
See Du Fu
See also DAM MULT; TWA; WP

Tunis, John R(oberts) 1889-1975 ..... **CLC 12**
See also BYA 1; CA 61-64; CANR 62; DLB
22, 171; JRDA; MAICYA 1, 2; SATA 37;
SATA-Brief 30; YAW

Tuohy, Frank .... **CLC 37**
See Tuohy, John Francis
See also CN 1, 2, 3, 4, 5, 6, 7; DLB 14,
139

Tuohy, John Francis 1925-
See Tuohy, Frank
See also CA 5-8R; 178; CANR 3, 47

Turco, Lewis (Putnam) 1934- ..... **CLC 11, 63**
See also CA 13-16R; CAAS 22; CANR 24,
51; CP 1, 2, 3, 4, 5, 6, 7; DLBY 1984;
TCLE 1:2

Turgenev, Ivan (Sergeevich)
1818-1883 ..... **DC 7; NCLC 21, 37, 122;
SSC 7, 57; WLC 6**
See also AAYA 58; DA; DAB; DAC; DAM
MST, NOV; DFS 6; DLB 238, 284; EW
6; LATS 1:1; NFS 16; RGSF 2; RGWL 2,
3; TWA

Turgot, Anne-Robert-Jacques
1727-1781 .... **LC 26**
See also DLB 314

Turner, Frederick 1943- .... **CLC 48**
See also CA 73-76, 227; CAAE 227; CAAS
10; CANR 12, 30, 56; DLB 40, 282

Turton, James
See Crace, Jim

Tutu, Desmond M(pilo) 1931- .. **BLC 3; CLC
80**
See also BW 1, 3; CA 125; CANR 67, 81;
DAM MULT

Tutuola, Amos 1920-1997 ..... **BLC 3; CLC 5,
14, 29**
See also AFW; BW 2, 3; CA 9-12R; 159;
CANR 27, 66; CDWLB 3; CN 1, 2, 3, 4,
5, 6; DA3; DAM MULT; DLB 125; DNFS
2; EWL 3; MTCW 1, 2; MTFW 2005;
RGEL 2; WLIT 2

Twain, Mark .... **SSC 6, 26, 34, 87; TCLC 6,
12, 19, 36, 48, 59, 161; WLC 6**
See Clemens, Samuel Langhorne
See also AAYA 20; AMW; AMWC 1; BPFB
3; BYA 2, 3, 11, 14; CLR 58, 60, 66; DLB
11; EXPN; EXPS; FANT; LAIT 2; MAL
5; NCFS 4; NFS 1, 6; RGAL 4; RGSF 2;
SFW 4; SSFS 1, 7, 16, 21; SUFW; TUS;
WCH; WYA; YAW

Tyler, Anne 1941- . **CLC 7, 11, 18, 28, 44, 59,
103, 205**
See also AAYA 18, 60; AMWS 4; BEST
89:1; BPFB 3; BYA 12; CA 9-12R; CANR
11, 33, 53, 109, 132; CDALBS; CN 1, 2,
3, 4, 5, 6, 7; CPW; CSW; DAM NOV,
POP; DLB 6, 143; DLBY 1982; EWL 3;
EXPN; LATS 1:2; MAL 5; MBL; MTCW
1, 2; MTFW 2005; NFS 2, 7, 10; RGAL
4; SATA 7, 90, 173; SSFS 17; TCLE 1:2;
TUS; YAW

Tyler, Royall 1757-1826 .... **NCLC 3**
See also DLB 37; RGAL 4

Tynan, Katharine 1861-1931 .... **TCLC 3**
See also CA 104; 167; DLB 153, 240; FW

Tyndale, William c. 1484-1536 .... **LC 103**
See also DLB 132

Tyutchev, Fyodor 1803-1873 .... **NCLC 34**

Tzara, Tristan 1896-1963 .... **CLC 47; PC 27;
TCLC 168**
See also CA 153; 89-92; DAM POET; EWL
3; MTCW 2

Uchida, Yoshiko 1921-1992 .... **AAL**
See also AAYA 16; BYA 2, 3; CA 13-16R;
139; CANR 6, 22, 47, 61; CDALBS; CLR
6, 56; CWRI 5; DLB 312; JRDA; MAI-
CYA 1, 2; MTCW 1, 2; MTFW 2005;
SAAS 1; SATA 1, 53; SATA-Obit 72

Udall, Nicholas 1504-1556 .... **LC 84**
See also DLB 62; RGEL 2

Ueda Akinari 1734-1809 .... **NCLC 131**

Uhry, Alfred 1936- .... **CLC 55**
See also CA 127; 133; CAD; CANR 112;
CD 5, 6; CSW; DA3; DAM DRAM, POP;
DFS 11, 15; INT CA-133; MTFW 2005

Ulf, Haerved
See Strindberg, (Johan) August

Ulf, Harved
See Strindberg, (Johan) August

Ulibarri, Sabine R(eyes)
1919-2003 .... **CLC 83; HLCS 2**
See also CA 131; 214; CANR 81; DAM
MULT; DLB 82; HW 1, 2; RGSF 2

Unamuno (y Jugo), Miguel de
1864-1936 .. **HLC 2; SSC 11, 69; TCLC
2, 9, 148**
See also CA 104; 131; CANR 81; DAM
MULT, NOV; DLB 108, 322; EW 8; EWL
3; HW 1, 2; MTCW 1, 2; MTFW 2005;
RGSF 2; RGWL 2, 3; SSFS 20; TWA

Uncle Shelby
See Silverstein, Shel

Undercliffe, Errol
See Campbell, (John) Ramsey

Underwood, Miles
See Glassco, John

Undset, Sigrid 1882-1949 .. **TCLC 3; WLC 6**
See also CA 104; 129; DA; DA3; DAB;
DAC; DAM MST, NOV; DLB 293; EW
9; EWL 3; FW; MTCW 1, 2; MTFW
2005; RGWL 2, 3

Ungaretti, Giuseppe 1888-1970 ... **CLC 7, 11,
15; PC 57**
See also CA 19-20; 25-28R; CAP 2; DLB
114; EW 10; EWL 3; PFS 20; RGWL 2,
3; WLIT 7

Unger, Douglas 1952- .... **CLC 34**
See also CA 130; CANR 94, 155

Unsworth, Barry (Forster) 1930- .... **CLC 76,
127**
See also BRWS 7; CA 25-28R; CANR 30,
54, 125; CN 6, 7; DLB 194, 326

Updike, John 1932- . **CLC 1, 2, 3, 5, 7, 9, 13,
15, 23, 34, 43, 70, 139, 214; SSC 13, 27;
WLC 6**
See also AAYA 36; AMW; AMWC 1;
AMWR 1; BPFB 3; BYA 12; CA 1-4R;
CABS 1; CANR 4, 33, 51, 94, 133;
CDALB 1968-1988; CN 1, 2, 3, 4, 5, 6,
7; CP 1, 2, 3, 4, 5, 6, 7; CPW 1; DA;
DA3; DAB; DAC; DAM MST, NOV,
POET, POP; DLB 2, 5, 143, 218, 227;
DLBD 3; DLBY 1980, 1982, 1997; EWL
3; EXPP; HGG; MAL 5; MTCW 1, 2;
MTFW 2005; NFS 12, 24; RGAL 4;
RGSF 2; SSFS 3, 19; TUS

Updike, John Hoyer
See Updike, John

Upshaw, Margaret Mitchell
See Mitchell, Margaret (Munnerlyn)

Upton, Mark
See Sanders, Lawrence

Upward, Allen 1863-1926 .... **TCLC 85**
See also CA 117; 187; DLB 36

Voznesensky, Andrei (Andreievich)
1933- .... **CLC 1, 15, 57**
See Voznesensky, Andrey
See also CA 89-92; CANR 37; CWW 2;
DAM POET; MTCW 1

Voznesensky, Andrey
See Voznesensky, Andrei (Andreievich)
See also EWL 3

Wace, Robert c. 1100-c. 1175 .... **CMLC 55**
See also DLB 146

Waddington, Miriam 1917-2004 .... **CLC 28**
See also CA 21-24R; 225; CANR 12, 30;
CCA 1; CP 1, 2, 3, 4, 5, 6, 7; DLB 68

Wagman, Fredrica 1937- .... **CLC 7**
See also CA 97-100; INT CA-97-100

Wagner, Linda W.
See Wagner-Martin, Linda (C.)

Wagner, Linda Welshimer
See Wagner-Martin, Linda (C.)

Wagner, Richard 1813-1883 ..... **NCLC 9, 119**
See also DLB 129; EW 6

Wagner-Martin, Linda (C.) 1936- .... **CLC 50**
See also CA 159; CANR 135

Wagoner, David (Russell) 1926- .... **CLC 3, 5, 15; PC 33**
See also AMWS 9; CA 1-4R; CAAS 3;
CANR 2, 71; CN 1, 2, 3, 4, 5, 6, 7; CP 1,
2, 3, 4, 5, 6, 7; DLB 5, 256; SATA 14;
TCWW 1, 2

Wah, Fred(erick James) 1939- .... **CLC 44**
See also CA 107; 141; CP 1, 6, 7; DLB 60

Wahloo, Per 1926-1975 .... **CLC 7**
See also BPFB 3; CA 61-64; CANR 73;
CMW 4; MSW

Wahloo, Peter
See Wahloo, Per

Wain, John (Barrington) 1925-1994 . **CLC 2, 11, 15, 46**
See also CA 5-8R; 145; CAAS 4; CANR
23, 54; CDBLB 1960 to Present; CN 1, 2,
3, 4, 5; CP 1, 2, 3, 4, 5; DLB 15, 27, 139,
155; EWL 3; MTCW 1, 2; MTFW 2005

Wajda, Andrzej 1926- .... **CLC 16, 219**
See also CA 102

Wakefield, Dan 1932- .... **CLC 7**
See also CA 21-24R, 211; CAAE 211;
CAAS 7; CN 4, 5, 6, 7

Wakefield, Herbert Russell
1888-1965 .... **TCLC 120**
See also CA 5-8R; CANR 77; HGG; SUFW

Wakoski, Diane 1937- ...... **CLC 2, 4, 7, 9, 11, 40; PC 15**
See also CA 13-16R, 216; CAAE 216;
CAAS 1; CANR 9, 60, 106; CP 1, 2, 3, 4,
5, 6, 7; CWP; DAM POET; DLB 5; INT
CANR-9; MAL 5; MTCW 2; MTFW
2005

Wakoski-Sherbell, Diane
See Wakoski, Diane

Walcott, Derek 1930- ... **BLC 3; CLC 2, 4, 9, 14, 25, 42, 67, 76, 160; DC 7; PC 46**
See also BW 2; CA 89-92; CANR 26, 47,
75, 80, 130; CBD; CD 5, 6; CDWLB 3;
CP 1, 2, 3, 4, 5, 6, 7; DA3; DAB; DAC;
DAM MST, MULT, POET; DLB 117;
DLBY 1981; DNFS 1; EFS 1; EWL 3;
LMFS 2; MTCW 1, 2; MTFW 2005; PFS
6; RGEL 2; TWA; WWE 1

Waldman, Anne (Lesley) 1945- .... **CLC 7**
See also BG 1:3; CA 37-40R; CAAS 17;
CANR 34, 69, 116; CP 1, 2, 3, 4, 5, 6, 7;
CWP; DLB 16

Waldo, E. Hunter
See Sturgeon, Theodore (Hamilton)

Waldo, Edward Hamilton
See Sturgeon, Theodore (Hamilton)

Walker, Alice 1944- ...... **BLC 3; CLC 5, 6, 9, 19, 27, 46, 58, 103, 167; PC 30; SSC 5; WLCS**
See also AAYA 3, 33; AFAW 1, 2; AMWS
3; BEST 89:4; BPFB 3; BW 2, 3; CA 37-
40R; CANR 9, 27, 49, 66, 82, 131;
CDALB 1968-1988; CN 4, 5, 6, 7; CPW;
CSW; DA; DA3; DAB; DAC; DAM MST,
MULT, NOV, POET, POP; DLB 6, 33,
143; EWL 3; EXPN; EXPS; FL 1:6; FW;
INT CANR-27; LAIT 3; MAL 5; MBL;
MTCW 1, 2; MTFW 2005; NFS 5; RGAL
4; RGSF 2; SATA 31; SSFS 2, 11; TUS;
YAW

Walker, Alice Malsenior
See Walker, Alice

Walker, David Harry 1911-1992 ...... **CLC 14**
See also CA 1-4R; 137; CANR 1; CN 1, 2;
CWRI 5; SATA 8; SATA-Obit 71

Walker, Edward Joseph 1934-2004
See Walker, Ted
See also CA 21-24R; 226; CANR 12, 28,
53

Walker, George F(rederick) 1947- .. **CLC 44, 61**
See also CA 103; CANR 21, 43, 59; CD 5,
6; DAB; DAC; DAM MST; DLB 60

Walker, Joseph A. 1935-2003 .... **CLC 19**
See also BW 1, 3; CA 89-92; CAD; CANR
26, 143; CD 5, 6; DAM DRAM, MST;
DFS 12; DLB 38

Walker, Margaret 1915-1998 .. **BLC; CLC 1, 6; PC 20; TCLC 129**
See also AFAW 1, 2; BW 2, 3; CA 73-76;
172; CANR 26, 54, 76, 136; CN 1, 2, 3,
4, 5, 6; CP 1, 2, 3, 4, 5, 6; CSW; DAM
MULT; DLB 76, 152; EXPP; FW; MAL
5; MTCW 1, 2; MTFW 2005; RGAL 4;
RHW

Walker, Ted .... **CLC 13**
See Walker, Edward Joseph
See also CP 1, 2, 3, 4, 5, 6, 7; DLB 40 ·

Wallace, David Foster 1962- ... **CLC 50, 114; SSC 68**
See also AAYA 50; AMWS 10; CA 132;
CANR 59, 133; CN 7; DA3; MTCW 2;
MTFW 2005

Wallace, Dexter
See Masters, Edgar Lee

Wallace, (Richard Horatio) Edgar
1875-1932 .... **TCLC 57**
See also CA 115; 218; CMW 4; DLB 70;
MSW; RGEL 2

Wallace, Irving 1916-1990 .... **CLC 7, 13**
See also AITN 1; BPFB 3; CA 1-4R; 132;
CAAS 1; CANR 1, 27; CPW; DAM NOV,
POP; INT CANR-27; MTCW 1, 2

Wallant, Edward Lewis 1926-1962 ... **CLC 5, 10**
See also CA 1-4R; CANR 22; DLB 2, 28,
143, 299; EWL 3; MAL 5; MTCW 1, 2;
RGAL 4; RGHL

Wallas, Graham 1858-1932 .... **TCLC 91**

Waller, Edmund 1606-1687 .... **LC 86; PC 72**
See also BRW 2; DAM POET; DLB 126;
PAB; RGEL 2

Walley, Byron
See Card, Orson Scott

Walpole, Horace 1717-1797 .... **LC 2, 49**
See also BRW 3; DLB 39, 104, 213; GL 3;
HGG; LMFS 1; RGEL 2; SUFW 1; TEA

Walpole, Hugh (Seymour)
1884-1941 .... **TCLC 5**
See also CA 104; 165; DLB 34; HGG;
MTCW 2; RGEL 2; RHW

Walrond, Eric (Derwent) 1898-1966 . **HR 1:3**
See also BW 1; CA 125; DLB 51

Walser, Martin 1927- .... **CLC 27, 183**
See also CA 57-60; CANR 8, 46, 145;
CWW 2; DLB 75, 124; EWL 3

Walser, Robert 1878-1956 ..... **SSC 20; TCLC 18**
See also CA 118; 165; CANR 100; DLB
66; EWL 3

Walsh, Gillian Paton
See Paton Walsh, Gillian

Walsh, Jill Paton .... **CLC 35**
See Paton Walsh, Gillian
See also CLR 2, 65; WYA

Walter, Villiam Christian
See Andersen, Hans Christian

Walters, Anna L(ee) 1946- .... **NNAL**
See also CA 73-76

Walther von der Vogelweide c.
1170-1228 .... **CMLC 56**

Walton, Izaak 1593-1683 .... **LC 72**
See also BRW 2; CDBLB Before 1660;
DLB 151, 213; RGEL 2

Wambaugh, Joseph (Aloysius), Jr.
1937- .... **CLC 3, 18**
See also AITN 1; BEST 89:3; BPFB 3; CA
33-36R; CANR 42, 65, 115; CMW 4;
CPW 1; DA3; DAM NOV, POP; DLB 6;
DLBY 1983; MSW; MTCW 1, 2

Wang Wei 699(?)-761(?) .... **PC 18**
See also TWA

Warburton, William 1698-1779 .... **LC 97**
See also DLB 104

Ward, Arthur Henry Sarsfield 1883-1959
See Rohmer, Sax
See also CA 108; 173; CMW 4; HGG

Ward, Douglas Turner 1930- .... **CLC 19**
See also BW 1; CA 81-84; CAD; CANR
27; CD 5, 6; DLB 7, 38

Ward, E. D.
See Lucas, E(dward) V(errall)

Ward, Mrs. Humphry 1851-1920
See Ward, Mary Augusta
See also RGEL 2

Ward, Mary Augusta 1851-1920 ... **TCLC 55**
See Ward, Mrs. Humphry
See also DLB 18

Ward, Nathaniel 1578(?)-1652 .... **LC 114**
See also DLB 24

Ward, Peter
See Faust, Frederick (Schiller)

Warhol, Andy 1928(?)-1987 .... **CLC 20**
See also AAYA 12; BEST 89:4; CA 89-92;
121; CANR 34

Warner, Francis (Robert le Plastrier)
1937- .... **CLC 14**
See also CA 53-56; CANR 11; CP 1, 2, 3, 4

Warner, Marina 1946- .... **CLC 59, 231**
See also CA 65-68; CANR 21, 55, 118; CN
5, 6, 7; DLB 194; MTFW 2005

Warner, Rex (Ernest) 1905-1986 ...... **CLC 45**
See also CA 89-92; 119; CN 1, 2, 3, 4; CP
1, 2, 3, 4; DLB 15; RGEL 2; RHW

Warner, Susan (Bogert)
1819-1885 .... **NCLC 31, 146**
See also DLB 3, 42, 239, 250, 254

Warner, Sylvia (Constance) Ashton
See Ashton-Warner, Sylvia (Constance)

Warner, Sylvia Townsend
1893-1978 .. **CLC 7, 19; SSC 23; TCLC 131**
See also BRWS 7; CA 61-64; 77-80; CANR
16, 60, 104; CN 1, 2; DLB 34, 139; EWL
3; FANT; FW; MTCW 1, 2; RGEL 2;
RGSF 2; RHW

Warren, Mercy Otis 1728-1814 ..... **NCLC 13**
See also DLB 31, 200; RGAL 4; TUS

Warren, Robert Penn 1905-1989 .. **CLC 1, 4, 6, 8, 10, 13, 18, 39, 53, 59; PC 37; SSC 4, 58; WLC 6**
See also AITN 1; AMW; AMWC 2; BPFB
3; BYA 1; CA 13-16R; 129; CANR 10,
47; CDALB 1968-1988; CN 1, 2, 3, 4;
CP 1, 2, 3, 4; DA; DA3; DAB; DAC;

DAM MST, NOV; DLB 2, 102, 143;
DLBD 12; DLBY 1987, 2001; EWL 3;
EXPS; HGG; LAIT 3; MAL 5; MBL;
MTCW 1, 2; MTFW 2005; NFS 13, 15;
RGAL 4; RGSF 2; RHW; SSFS 2, 10;
TUS

Welty, Eudora Alice
See Welty, Eudora

Wen I-to 1899-1946 .... **TCLC 28**
See also EWL 3

Wentworth, Robert
See Hamilton, Edmond

Werfel, Franz (Viktor) 1890-1945 ... **TCLC 8**
See also CA 104; 161; DLB 81, 124; EWL
3; RGWL 2, 3

Wergeland, Henrik Arnold
1808-1845 .... **NCLC 5**

Wersba, Barbara 1932- .... **CLC 30**
See also AAYA 2, 30; BYA 6, 12, 13; CA
29-32R, 182; CAAE 182; CANR 16, 38;
CLR 3, 78; DLB 52; JRDA; MAICYA 1,
2; SAAS 2; SATA 1, 58; SATA-Essay 103;
WYA; YAW

Wertmueller, Lina 1928- .... **CLC 16**
See also CA 97-100; CANR 39, 78

Wescott, Glenway 1901-1987 .. **CLC 13; SSC
35**
See also CA 13-16R; 121; CANR 23, 70;
CN 1, 2, 3, 4; DLB 4, 9, 102; MAL 5;
RGAL 4

Wesker, Arnold 1932- .... **CLC 3, 5, 42**
See also CA 1-4R; CAAS 7; CANR 1, 33;
CBD; CD 5, 6; CDBLB 1960 to Present;
DAB; DAM DRAM; DLB 13, 310, 319;
EWL 3; MTCW 1; RGEL 2; TEA

Wesley, Charles 1707-1788 .... **LC 128**
See also DLB 95; RGEL 2

Wesley, John 1703-1791 .... **LC 88**
See also DLB 104

Wesley, Richard (Errol) 1945- .... **CLC 7**
See also BW 1; CA 57-60; CAD; CANR
27; CD 5, 6; DLB 38

Wessel, Johan Herman 1742-1785 .... **LC 7**
See also DLB 300

West, Anthony (Panther)
1914-1987 .... **CLC 50**
See also CA 45-48; 124; CANR 3, 19; CN
1, 2, 3, 4; DLB 15

West, C. P.
See Wodehouse, P(elham) G(renville)

West, Cornel (Ronald) 1953- .... **BLCS; CLC
134**
See also CA 144; CANR 91; DLB 246

West, Delno C(loyde), Jr. 1936- .... **CLC 70**
See also CA 57-60

West, Dorothy 1907-1998 ...... **HR 1:3; TCLC
108**
See also BW 2; CA 143; 169; DLB 76

West, (Mary) Jessamyn 1902-1984 ... **CLC 7,
17**
See also CA 9-12R; 112; CANR 27; CN 1,
2, 3; DLB 6; DLBY 1984; MTCW 1, 2;
RGAL 4; RHW; SATA-Obit 37; TCWW
2; TUS; YAW

West, Morris L(anglo) 1916-1999 ..... **CLC 6,
33**
See also BPFB 3; CA 5-8R; 187; CANR
24, 49, 64; CN 1, 2, 3, 4, 5, 6; CPW; DLB
289; MTCW 1, 2; MTFW 2005

West, Nathanael 1903-1940 .. **SSC 16; TCLC
1, 14, 44**
See also AMW; AMWR 2; BPFB 3; CA
104; 125; CDALB 1929-1941; DA3; DLB
4, 9, 28; EWL 3; MAL 5; MTCW 1, 2;
MTFW 2005; NFS 16; RGAL 4; TUS

West, Owen
See Koontz, Dean R.

West, Paul 1930- .... **CLC 7, 14, 96, 226**
See also CA 13-16R; CAAS 7; CANR 22,
53, 76, 89, 136; CN 1, 2, 3, 4, 5, 6, 7;
DLB 14; INT CANR-22; MTCW 2;
MTFW 2005

West, Rebecca 1892-1983 ... **CLC 7, 9, 31, 50**
See also BPFB 3; BRWS 3; CA 5-8R; 109;
CANR 19; CN 1, 2, 3; DLB 36; DLBY
1983; EWL 3; FW; MTCW 1, 2; MTFW
2005; NCFS 4; RGEL 2; TEA

Westall, Robert (Atkinson)
1929-1993 .... **CLC 17**
See also AAYA 12; BYA 2, 6, 7, 8, 9, 15;
CA 69-72; 141; CANR 18, 68; CLR 13;
FANT; JRDA; MAICYA 1, 2; MAICYAS
1; SAAS 2; SATA 23, 69; SATA-Obit 75;
WYA; YAW

Westermarck, Edward 1862-1939 . **TCLC 87**

Westlake, Donald E. 1933- .... **CLC 7, 33**
See also BPFB 3; CA 17-20R; CAAS 13;
CANR 16, 44, 65, 94, 137; CMW 4;
CPW; DAM POP; INT CANR-16; MSW;
MTCW 2; MTFW 2005

Westmacott, Mary
See Christie, Agatha (Mary Clarissa)

Weston, Allen
See Norton, Andre

Wetcheek, J. L.
See Feuchtwanger, Lion

Wetering, Janwillem van de
See van de Wetering, Janwillem

Wetherald, Agnes Ethelwyn
1857-1940 .... **TCLC 81**
See also CA 202; DLB 99

Wetherell, Elizabeth
See Warner, Susan (Bogert)

Whale, James 1889-1957 .... **TCLC 63**

Whalen, Philip (Glenn) 1923-2002 .... **CLC 6,
29**
See also BG 1:3; CA 9-12R; 209; CANR 5,
39; CP 1, 2, 3, 4, 5, 6, 7; DLB 16; WP

Wharton, Edith (Newbold Jones)
1862-1937 ... **SSC 6, 84; TCLC 3, 9, 27,
53, 129, 149; WLC 6**
See also AAYA 25; AMW; AMWC 2;
AMWR 1; BPFB 3; CA 104; 132; CDALB
1865-1917; DA; DA3; DAB; DAC; DAM
MST, NOV; DLB 4, 9, 12, 78, 189; DLBD
13; EWL 3; EXPS; FL 1:6; GL 3; HGG;
LAIT 2, 3; LATS 1:1; MAL 5; MBL;
MTCW 1, 2; MTFW 2005; NFS 5, 11,
15, 20; RGAL 4; RGSF 2; RHW; SSFS 6,
7; SUFW; TUS

Wharton, James
See Mencken, H(enry) L(ouis)

Wharton, William (a pseudonym)
1925- .... **CLC 18, 37**
See also CA 93-96; CN 4, 5, 6, 7; DLBY
1980; INT CA-93-96

Wheatley (Peters), Phillis
1753(?)-1784 ... **BLC 3; LC 3, 50; PC 3;
WLC 6**
See also AFAW 1, 2; CDALB 1640-1865;
DA; DA3; DAC; DAM MST, MULT,
POET; DLB 31, 50; EXPP; FL 1:1; PFS
13; RGAL 4

Wheelock, John Hall 1886-1978 .... **CLC 14**
See also CA 13-16R; 77-80; CANR 14; CP
1, 2; DLB 45; MAL 5

Whim-Wham
See Curnow, (Thomas) Allen (Monro)

Whitaker, Rod 1931-2005
See Trevanian
See also CA 29-32R; 246; CANR 45, 153;
CMW 4

White, Babington
See Braddon, Mary Elizabeth

White, E. B. 1899-1985 .... **CLC 10, 34, 39**
See also AAYA 62; AITN 2; AMWS 1; CA
13-16R; 116; CANR 16, 37; CDALBS;
CLR 1, 21, 107; CPW; DA3; DAM POP;
DLB 11, 22; EWL 3; FANT; MAICYA 1,
2; MAL 5; MTCW 1, 2; MTFW 2005;
NCFS 5; RGAL 4; SATA 2, 29, 100;
SATA-Obit 44; TUS

White, Edmund 1940- .... **CLC 27, 110**
See also AAYA 7; CA 45-48; CANR 3, 19,
36, 62, 107, 133; CN 5, 6, 7; DA3; DAM
POP; DLB 227; MTCW 1, 2; MTFW
2005

White, Elwyn Brooks
See White, E. B.

White, Hayden V. 1928- .... **CLC 148**
See also CA 128; CANR 135; DLB 246

White, Patrick (Victor Martindale)
1912-1990 ...... **CLC 3, 4, 5, 7, 9, 18, 65,
69; SSC 39; TCLC 176**
See also BRWS 1; CA 81-84; 132; CANR
43; CN 1, 2, 3, 4; DLB 260; EWL 3;
MTCW 1; RGEL 2; RGSF 2; RHW;
TWA; WWE 1

White, Phyllis Dorothy James 1920-
See James, P. D.
See also CA 21-24R; CANR 17, 43, 65,
112; CMW 4; CN 7; CPW; DA3; DAM
POP; MTCW 1, 2; MTFW 2005; TEA

White, T(erence) H(anbury)
1906-1964 .... **CLC 30**
See also AAYA 22; BPFB 3; BYA 4, 5; CA
73-76; CANR 37; DLB 160; FANT;
JRDA; LAIT 1; MAICYA 1, 2; RGEL 2;
SATA 12; SUFW 1; YAW

White, Terence de Vere 1912-1994 ... **CLC 49**
See also CA 49-52; 145; CANR 3

White, Walter
See White, Walter F(rancis)

White, Walter F(rancis) 1893-1955 ... **BLC 3;
HR 1:3; TCLC 15**
See also BW 1; CA 115; 124; DAM MULT;
DLB 51

White, William Hale 1831-1913
See Rutherford, Mark
See also CA 121; 189

Whitehead, Alfred North
1861-1947 .... **TCLC 97**
See also CA 117; 165; DLB 100, 262

Whitehead, E(dward) A(nthony)
1933- .... **CLC 5**
See Whitehead, Ted
See also CA 65-68; CANR 58, 118; CBD;
CD 5; DLB 310

Whitehead, Ted
See Whitehead, E(dward) A(nthony)
See also CD 6

Whiteman, Roberta J. Hill 1947- ...... **NNAL**
See also CA 146

Whitemore, Hugh (John) 1936- .... **CLC 37**
See also CA 132; CANR 77; CBD; CD 5,
6; INT CA-132

Whitman, Sarah Helen (Power)
1803-1878 .... **NCLC 19**
See also DLB 1, 243

Whitman, Walt(er) 1819-1892 .. **NCLC 4, 31,
81; PC 3; WLC 6**
See also AAYA 42; AMW; AMWR 1;
CDALB 1640-1865; DA; DA3; DAB;
DAC; DAM MST, POET; DLB 3, 64,
224, 250; EXPP; LAIT 2; LMFS 1; PAB;
PFS 2, 3, 13, 22; RGAL 4; SATA 20;
TUS; WP; WYAS 1

Whitney, Isabella fl. 1565-fl. 1575 ..... **LC 130**
See also DLB 136

Whitney, Phyllis A(yame) 1903- .... **CLC 42**
See also AAYA 36; AITN 2; BEST 90:3;
CA 1-4R; CANR 3, 25, 38, 60; CLR 59;

Wilmot, John 1647-1680 .... **LC 75; PC 66**
See Rochester
See also BRW 2; DLB 131; PAB

Wilson, A.N. 1950- .... **CLC 33**
See also BRWS 6; CA 112; 122; CANR
155; CN 4, 5, 6, 7; DLB 14, 155, 194;
MTCW 2

Wilson, Andrew Norman
See Wilson, A.N.

Wilson, Angus (Frank Johnstone)
1913-1991 . **CLC 2, 3, 5, 25, 34; SSC 21**
See also BRWS 1; CA 5-8R; 134; CANR
21; CN 1, 2, 3, 4; DLB 15, 139, 155;
EWL 3; MTCW 1, 2; MTFW 2005; RGEL
2; RGSF 2

Wilson, August 1945-2005 .. **BLC 3; CLC 39,
50, 63, 118, 222; DC 2; WLCS**
See also AAYA 16; AFAW 2; AMWS 8; BW
2, 3; CA 115; 122; 244; CAD; CANR 42,
54, 76, 128; CD 5, 6; DA; DA3; DAB;
DAC; DAM DRAM, MST, MULT; DFS
3, 7, 15, 17; DLB 228; EWL 3; LAIT 4;
LATS 1:2; MAL 5; MTCW 1, 2; MTFW
2005; RGAL 4

Wilson, Brian 1942- .... **CLC 12**

Wilson, Colin (Henry) 1931- .... **CLC 3, 14**
See also CA 1-4R; CAAS 5; CANR 1, 22,
33, 77; CMW 4; CN 1, 2, 3, 4, 5, 6; DLB
14, 194; HGG; MTCW 1; SFW 4

Wilson, Dirk
See Pohl, Frederik

Wilson, Edmund 1895-1972 .. **CLC 1, 2, 3, 8,
24**
See also AMW; CA 1-4R; 37-40R; CANR
1, 46, 110; CN 1; DLB 63; EWL 3; MAL
5; MTCW 1, 2; MTFW 2005; RGAL 4;
TUS

Wilson, Ethel Davis (Bryant)
1888(?)-1980 .... **CLC 13**
See also CA 102; CN 1, 2; DAC; DAM
POET; DLB 68; MTCW 1; RGEL 2

Wilson, Harriet
See Wilson, Harriet E. Adams
See also DLB 239

Wilson, Harriet E.
See Wilson, Harriet E. Adams
See also DLB 243

Wilson, Harriet E. Adams
1827(?)-1863(?) .... **BLC 3; NCLC 78**
See Wilson, Harriet; Wilson, Harriet E.
See also DAM MULT; DLB 50

Wilson, John 1785-1854 .... **NCLC 5**

Wilson, John (Anthony) Burgess 1917-1993
See Burgess, Anthony
See also CA 1-4R; 143; CANR 2, 46; DA3;
DAC; DAM NOV; MTCW 1, 2; MTFW
2005; NFS 15; TEA

Wilson, Lanford 1937- .. **CLC 7, 14, 36, 197;
DC 19**
See also CA 17-20R; CABS 3; CAD; CANR
45, 96; CD 5, 6; DAM DRAM; DFS 4, 9,
12, 16, 20; DLB 7; EWL 3; MAL 5; TUS

Wilson, Robert M. 1941- .... **CLC 7, 9**
See also CA 49-52; CAD; CANR 2, 41; CD
5, 6; MTCW 1

Wilson, Robert McLiam 1964- .... **CLC 59**
See also CA 132; DLB 267

Wilson, Sloan 1920-2003 .... **CLC 32**
See also CA 1-4R; 216; CANR 1, 44; CN
1, 2, 3, 4, 5, 6

Wilson, Snoo 1948- .... **CLC 33**
See also CA 69-72; CBD; CD 5, 6

Wilson, William S(mith) 1932- .... **CLC 49**
See also CA 81-84

Wilson, (Thomas) Woodrow
1856-1924 .... **TCLC 79**
See also CA 166; DLB 47

Wilson and Warnke eds. .... **CLC 65**

Winchilsea, Anne (Kingsmill) Finch
1661-1720
See Finch, Anne
See also RGEL 2

Winckelmann, Johann Joachim
1717-1768 .... **LC 129**
See also DLB 97

Windham, Basil
See Wodehouse, P(elham) G(renville)

Wingrove, David 1954- .... **CLC 68**
See also CA 133; SFW 4

Winnemucca, Sarah 1844-1891 .... **NCLC 79;
NNAL**
See also DAM MULT; DLB 175; RGAL 4

Winstanley, Gerrard 1609-1676 .... **LC 52**

Wintergreen, Jane
See Duncan, Sara Jeannette

Winters, Arthur Yvor
See Winters, Yvor

Winters, Janet Lewis .... **CLC 41**
See Lewis, Janet
See also DLBY 1987

Winters, Yvor 1900-1968 .... **CLC 4, 8, 32**
See also AMWS 2; CA 11-12; 25-28R; CAP
1; DLB 48; EWL 3; MAL 5; MTCW 1;
RGAL 4

Winterson, Jeanette 1959- .... **CLC 64, 158**
See also BRWS 4; CA 136; CANR 58, 116;
CN 5, 6, 7; CPW; DA3; DAM POP; DLB
207, 261; FANT; FW; GLL 1; MTCW 2;
MTFW 2005; RHW

Winthrop, John 1588-1649 .... **LC 31, 107**
See also DLB 24, 30

Wirth, Louis 1897-1952 .... **TCLC 92**
See also CA 210

Wiseman, Frederick 1930- .... **CLC 20**
See also CA 159

Wister, Owen 1860-1938 .... **TCLC 21**
See also BPFB 3; CA 108; 162; DLB 9, 78,
186; RGAL 4; SATA 62; TCWW 1, 2

Wither, George 1588-1667 .... **LC 96**
See also DLB 121; RGEL 2

Witkacy
See Witkiewicz, Stanislaw Ignacy

Witkiewicz, Stanislaw Ignacy
1885-1939 .... **TCLC 8**
See also CA 105; 162; CDWLB 4; DLB
215; EW 10; EWL 3; RGWL 2, 3; SFW 4

Wittgenstein, Ludwig (Josef Johann)
1889-1951 .... **TCLC 59**
See also CA 113; 164; DLB 262; MTCW 2

Wittig, Monique 1935-2003 .... **CLC 22**
See also CA 116; 135; 212; CANR 143;
CWW 2; DLB 83; EWL 3; FW; GLL 1

Wittlin, Jozef 1896-1976 .... **CLC 25**
See also CA 49-52; 65-68; CANR 3; EWL
3

Wodehouse, P(elham) G(renville)
1881-1975 . **CLC 1, 2, 5, 10, 22; SSC 2;
TCLC 108**
See also AAYA 65; AITN 2; BRWS 3; CA
45-48; 57-60; CANR 3, 33; CDBLB
1914-1945; CN 1, 2; CPW 1; DA3; DAB;
DAC; DAM NOV; DLB 34, 162; EWL 3;
MTCW 1, 2; MTFW 2005; RGEL 2;
RGSF 2; SATA 22; SSFS 10

Woiwode, L.
See Woiwode, Larry (Alfred)

Woiwode, Larry (Alfred) 1941- ... **CLC 6, 10**
See also CA 73-76; CANR 16, 94; CN 3, 4,
5, 6, 7; DLB 6; INT CANR-16

Wojciechowska, Maia (Teresa)
1927-2002 .... **CLC 26**
See also AAYA 8, 46; BYA 3; CA 9-12R,
183; 209; CAAE 183; CANR 4, 41; CLR
1; JRDA; MAICYA 1, 2; SAAS 1; SATA
1, 28, 83; SATA-Essay 104; SATA-Obit
134; YAW

Wojtyla, Karol (Josef)
See John Paul II, Pope

Wojtyla, Karol (Jozef)
See John Paul II, Pope

Wolf, Christa 1929- ...... **CLC 14, 29, 58, 150**
See also CA 85-88; CANR 45, 123; CD-
WLB 2; CWW 2; DLB 75; EWL 3; FW;
MTCW 1; RGWL 2, 3; SSFS 14

Wolf, Naomi 1962- .... **CLC 157**
See also CA 141; CANR 110; FW; MTFW
2005

Wolfe, Gene 1931- .... **CLC 25**
See also AAYA 35; CA 57-60; CAAS 9;
CANR 6, 32, 60, 152; CPW; DAM POP;
DLB 8; FANT; MTCW 2; MTFW 2005;
SATA 118, 165; SCFW 2; SFW 4; SUFW
2

Wolfe, Gene Rodman
See Wolfe, Gene

Wolfe, George C. 1954- .... **BLCS; CLC 49**
See also CA 149; CAD; CD 5, 6

Wolfe, Thomas (Clayton)
1900-1938 ...... **SSC 33; TCLC 4, 13, 29,
61; WLC 6**
See also AMW; BPFB 3; CA 104; 132;
CANR 102; CDALB 1929-1941; DA;
DA3; DAB; DAC; DAM MST, NOV;
DLB 9, 102, 229; DLBD 2, 16; DLBY
1985, 1997; EWL 3; MAL 5; MTCW 1,
2; NFS 18; RGAL 4; SSFS 18; TUS

Wolfe, Thomas Kennerly, Jr.
1931- .... **CLC 147**
See Wolfe, Tom
See also CA 13-16R; CANR 9, 33, 70, 104;
DA3; DAM POP; DLB 185; EWL 3; INT
CANR-9; MTCW 1, 2; MTFW 2005; TUS

Wolfe, Tom .... **CLC 1, 2, 9, 15, 35, 51**
See Wolfe, Thomas Kennerly, Jr.
See also AAYA 8, 67; AITN 2; AMWS 3;
BEST 89:1; BPFB 3; CN 5, 6, 7; CPW;
CSW; DLB 152; LAIT 5; RGAL 4

Wolff, Geoffrey 1937- .... **CLC 41**
See also CA 29-32R; CANR 29, 43, 78, 154

Wolff, Geoffrey Ansell
See Wolff, Geoffrey

Wolff, Sonia
See Levitin, Sonia (Wolff)

Wolff, Tobias 1945- .... **CLC 39, 64, 172; SSC
63**
See also AAYA 16; AMWS 7; BEST 90:2;
BYA 12; CA 114; 117; CAAS 22; CANR
54, 76, 96; CN 5, 6, 7; CSW; DA3; DLB
130; EWL 3; INT CA-117; MTCW 2;
MTFW 2005; RGAL 4; RGSF 2; SSFS 4,
11

Wolitzer, Hilma 1930- .... **CLC 17**
See also CA 65-68; CANR 18, 40; INT
CANR-18; SATA 31; YAW

Wollstonecraft, Mary 1759-1797 .... **LC 5, 50,
90**
See also BRWS 3; CDBLB 1789-1832;
DLB 39, 104, 158, 252; FL 1:1; FW;
LAIT 1; RGEL 2; TEA; WLIT 3

Wonder, Stevie 1950- .... **CLC 12**
See also CA 111

Wong, Jade Snow 1922-2006 .... **CLC 17**
See also CA 109; 249; CANR 91; SATA
112

Woodberry, George Edward
1855-1930 .... **TCLC 73**
See also CA 165; DLB 71, 103

Woodcott, Keith
See Brunner, John (Kilian Houston)

Woodruff, Robert W.
See Mencken, H(enry) L(ouis)

Young, Andrew (John) 1885-1971 ...... **CLC 5**
See also CA 5-8R; CANR 7, 29; CP 1;
RGEL 2
Young, Collier
See Bloch, Robert (Albert)
Young, Edward 1683-1765 .... **LC 3, 40**
See also DLB 95; RGEL 2
Young, Marguerite (Vivian)
1909-1995 .... **CLC 82**
See also CA 13-16; 150; CAP 1; CN 1, 2,
3, 4, 5, 6
Young, Neil 1945- .... **CLC 17**
See also CA 110; CCA 1
Young Bear, Ray A. 1950- ... **CLC 94; NNAL**
See also CA 146; DAM MULT; DLB 175;
MAL 5
Yourcenar, Marguerite 1903-1987 ... **CLC 19,
38, 50, 87**
See also BPFB 3; CA 69-72; CANR 23, 60,
93; DAM NOV; DLB 72; DLBY 1988;
EW 12; EWL 3; GFL 1789 to the Present;
GLL 1; MTCW 1, 2; MTFW 2005;
RGWL 2, 3
Yuan, Chu 340(?)B.C.-278(?)B.C. . **CMLC 36**
Yurick, Sol 1925- .... **CLC 6**
See also CA 13-16R; CANR 25; CN 1, 2,
3, 4, 5, 6, 7; MAL 5
Zabolotsky, Nikolai Alekseevich
1903-1958 .... **TCLC 52**
See Zabolotsky, Nikolay Alekseevich
See also CA 116; 164
Zabolotsky, Nikolay Alekseevich
See Zabolotsky, Nikolai Alekseevich
See also EWL 3
Zagajewski, Adam 1945- .... **PC 27**
See also CA 186; DLB 232; EWL 3
Zalygin, Sergei -2000 .... **CLC 59**
Zalygin, Sergei (Pavlovich)
1913-2000 .... **CLC 59**
See also DLB 302
Zamiatin, Evgenii
See Zamyatin, Evgeny Ivanovich
See also RGSF 2; RGWL 2, 3
Zamiatin, Evgenii Ivanovich
See Zamyatin, Evgeny Ivanovich
See also DLB 272
Zamiatin, Yevgenii
See Zamyatin, Evgeny Ivanovich
Zamora, Bernice (B. Ortiz) 1938- .. **CLC 89;
HLC 2**
See also CA 151; CANR 80; DAM MULT;
DLB 82; HW 1, 2

Zamyatin, Evgeny Ivanovich
1884-1937 .... **SSC 89; TCLC 8, 37**
See Zamiatin, Evgenii; Zamiatin, Evgenii
Ivanovich; Zamyatin, Yevgeny Ivanovich
See also CA 105; 166; SFW 4
Zamyatin, Yevgeny Ivanovich
See Zamyatin, Evgeny Ivanovich
See also EW 10; EWL 3
Zangwill, Israel 1864-1926 ... **SSC 44; TCLC
16**
See also CA 109; 167; CMW 4; DLB 10,
135, 197; RGEL 2
Zanzotto, Andrea 1921- .... **PC 65**
See also CA 208; CWW 2; DLB 128; EWL
3
Zappa, Francis Vincent, Jr. 1940-1993
See Zappa, Frank
See also CA 108; 143; CANR 57
Zappa, Frank .... **CLC 17**
See Zappa, Francis Vincent, Jr.
Zaturenska, Marya 1902-1982 ..... **CLC 6, 11**
See also CA 13-16R; 105; CANR 22; CP 1,
2, 3
Zayas y Sotomayor, Maria de 1590-c.
1661 .... **LC 102; SSC 94**
See also RGSF 2
Zeami 1363-1443 .... **DC 7; LC 86**
See also DLB 203; RGWL 2, 3
Zelazny, Roger 1937-1995 .... **CLC 21**
See also AAYA 7, 68; BPFB 3; CA 21-24R;
148; CANR 26, 60; CN 6; DLB 8; FANT;
MTCW 1, 2; MTFW 2005; SATA 57;
SATA-Brief 39; SCFW 1, 2; SFW 4;
SUFW 1, 2
Zhang Ailing
See Chang, Eileen
See also CWW 2; DLB 328; RGSF 2
Zhdanov, Andrei Alexandrovich
1896-1948 .... **TCLC 18**
See also CA 117; 167
Zhukovsky, Vasilii Andreevich
See Zhukovsky, Vasily (Andreevich)
See also DLB 205
Zhukovsky, Vasily (Andreevich)
1783-1852 .... **NCLC 35**
See Zhukovsky, Vasilii Andreevich
Ziegenhagen, Eric .... **CLC 55**
Zimmer, Jill Schary
See Robinson, Jill
Zimmerman, Robert
See Dylan, Bob
Zindel, Paul 1936-2003 ...... **CLC 6, 26; DC 5**
See also AAYA 2, 37; BYA 2, 3, 8, 11, 14;
CA 73-76; 213; CAD; CANR 31, 65, 108;

CD 5, 6; CDALBS; CLR 3, 45, 85; DA;
DA3; DAB; DAC; DAM DRAM, MST,
NOV; DFS 12; DLB 7, 52; JRDA; LAIT
5; MAICYA 1, 2; MTCW 1, 2; MTFW
2005; NFS 14; SATA 16, 58, 102; SATA-
Obit 142; WYA; YAW
Zinn, Howard 1922- .... **CLC 199**
See also CA 1-4R; CANR 2, 33, 90
Zinov'Ev, A.A.
See Zinoviev, Alexander
Zinov'ev, Aleksandr
See Zinoviev, Alexander
See also DLB 302
Zinoviev, Alexander 1922-2006 .... **CLC 19**
See Zinov'ev, Aleksandr
See also CA 116; 133; 250; CAAS 10
Zinoviev, Alexander Aleksandrovich
See Zinoviev, Alexander
Zizek, Slavoj 1949- .... **CLC 188**
See also CA 201; MTFW 2005
Zoilus
See Lovecraft, H. P.
Zola, Emile (Edouard Charles Antoine)
1840-1902 .. **TCLC 1, 6, 21, 41; WLC 6**
See also CA 104; 138; DA; DA3; DAB;
DAC; DAM MST, NOV; DLB 123; EW
7; GFL 1789 to the Present; IDTP; LMFS
1, 2; RGWL 2; TWA
Zoline, Pamela 1941- .... **CLC 62**
See also CA 161; SFW 4
Zoroaster 628(?)B.C.-551(?)B.C. ... **CMLC 40**
Zorrilla y Moral, Jose 1817-1893 .... **NCLC 6**
Zoshchenko, Mikhail (Mikhailovich)
1895-1958 .... **SSC 15; TCLC 15**
See also CA 115; 160; EWL 3; RGSF 2;
RGWL 3
Zuckmayer, Carl 1896-1977 .... **CLC 18**
See also CA 69-72; DLB 56, 124; EWL 3;
RGWL 2, 3
Zuk, Georges
See Skelton, Robin
See also CCA 1
Zukofsky, Louis 1904-1978 ... **CLC 1, 2, 4, 7,
11, 18; PC 11**
See also AMWS 3; CA 9-12R; 77-80;
CANR 39; CP 1, 2; DAM POET; DLB 5,
165; EWL 3; MAL 5; MTCW 1; RGAL 4
Zweig, Paul 1935-1984 .... **CLC 34, 42**
See also CA 85-88; 113
Zweig, Stefan 1881-1942 .... **TCLC 17**
See also CA 112; 170; DLB 81, 118; EWL
3; RGHL
Zwingli, Huldreich 1484-1531 .... **LC 37**
See also DLB 179

Literary Criticism Series
Cumulative Topic Index

This index lists all topic entries in Thompson Gale's *Children's Literature Review* (CLR), *Classical and Medieval Literature Criticism* (CMLC), *Contemporary Literary Criticism* (CLC), *Drama Criticism* (DC), *Literature Criticism from 1400 to 1800* (LC), *Nineteenth-Century Literature Criticism* (NCLC), *Short Story Criticism* (SSC), and *Twentieth-Century Literary Criticism* (TCLC). The index also lists topic entries in the Gale Critical Companion Collection, which includes the following publications: *The Beat Generation* (BG), *Feminism in Literature* (FL), *Gothic Literature* (GL), and *Harlem Renaissance* (HR).

Topic Index

CLC Cumulative Nationality Index

Nationality Index

Nationality Index

Nationality Index

CLC-230 Title Index